Lecture Notes in Computer Science
Edited by G. Goos, J. Hartmanis, and J. van Leeu

Springer
Berlin
Heidelberg
New York
Barcelona
Hong Kong
London
Milan
Paris
Tokyo

Naoki Kobayashi Benjamin C. Pierce (Eds.)

Theoretical Aspects of Computer Software

4th International Symposium, TACS 2001
Sendai, Japan, October 29-31, 2001
Proceedings

Springer

Series Editors

Gerhard Goos, Karlsruhe University, Germany
Juris Hartmanis, Cornell University, NY, USA
Jan van Leeuwen, Utrecht University, The Netherlands

Volume Editors

Naoki Kobayashi
Tokyo Institute of Technology
Graduate School of Information Science and Engineering
Department of Computer Science
2-12-1 Oo-okayama, Meguro-ku, Tokyo 152-8552, Japan
E-mail: kobayasi@cs.titech.ac.jp

Benjamin C. Pierce
University of Pennsylvania
Department of Computer and Information Science
200 S. 33rd St., Philadelphia, PA 19104, USA
E-mail: bcpierce@cis.upenn.edu

Cataloging-in-Publication Data applied for

Die Deutsche Bibliothek - CIP-Einheitsaufnahme

Theoretical aspects of computer software : 4th international symposium ; proceedings / TACS 2001, Sendai, Japan, October 29 - 31, 2001. Naoki Kobayashi ; Benjamin C. Pierce (ed.). - Berlin ; Heidelberg ; New York ; Barcelona ; Hong Kong ; London ; Milan ; Paris ; Tokyo : Springer, 2001
(Lecture notes in computer science ; Vol. 2215)
ISBN 3-540-42736-8

CR Subject Classification (1998): F.3, D.1-3, F.4.2-3

ISSN 0302-9743
ISBN 3-540-42736-8 Springer-Verlag Berlin Heidelberg New York

Springer-Verlag Berlin Heidelberg New York
a member of BertelsmannSpringer Science+Business Media GmbH

http://www.springer.de

© Springer-Verlag Berlin Heidelberg 2001
Printed in Germany

Typesetting: Camera-ready by author, data conversion by Steingräber Satztechnik GmbH, Heidelberg
Printed on acid-free paper SPIN: 10840868 06/3142 5 4 3 2 1 0

Foreword

This volume constitutes the proceedings of the Fourth International Symposium on Theoretical Aspects of Computer Software (TACS 2001) held at Tohoku University, Sendai, Japan in October 2001.

The TACS symposium focuses on the theoretical foundations of programming and their applications. As this volume shows, TACS is an international symposium, with participants from many different institutions and countries.

TACS 2001 was the fourth symposium in the TACS series, following TACS'91, TACS'94, and TACS'97, whose proceedings were published as Volumes 526, 789, and 1281, respectively, of Springer-Verlag's Lecture Notes in Computer Science series.

The TACS 2001 technical program consisted of invited talks and contributed talks. In conjunction with this program there was a special open lecture by Benjamin Pierce; this lecture was open to non-registrants.

TACS 2001 benefited from the efforts of many people; in particular, members of the Program Committee and the Organizing Committee. Our special thanks go to the Program Committee Co-chairs:

Naoki Kobayashi (Tokyo Institute of Technology)
Benjamin Pierce (University of Pennsylvania).

TACS 2001 gratefully acknowledges the generous support provided by Tohoku University and Sendai Tourism & Convention Bureau, and the cooperation of the following organizations:

Information Processing Society of Japan
Japan Society of Software Science and Technology
Association for Computing Machinery - SIGACT
Association for Symbolic Logic

Also, we thank Alfred Hofmann of Springer-Verlag for his assistance in the publication of the proceedings. Shinya Miyakawa, Nobuto Izumi, Takuya Ohishi, and Masahiko Ohtomo of Tohoku University lent their assistance in making local arrangements and in preparing the conference web pages. Finally, we would like to express our sincere thanks to all those who helped organize, and those who participated in, the TACS 2001 symposium for their invaluable contributions.

July 2001

Takayasu Ito
Symposium Chair

Preface

The program of TACS 2001 included the presentations of 21 contributed papers and 6 invited talks. The program committee, with help from additional referees, selected these papers from 59 submissions. The invited speakers – Luca Cardelli, Kazunori Ueda, Andrew M. Pitts, Christine Paulin-Mohring, Jon G. Riecke, and Daniel Jackson – were chosen by the program co-chairs in collaboration with the symposium chair.

We would like to thank the members of the program committee and the additional referees, who are listed below. Special thanks to Prof. Takayasu Ito and his staff for their advice and help.

July 2001

Naoki Kobayashi
Benjamin C. Pierce
Program Co-chairs

Program Committee

Zena Ariola	University of Oregon
Cédric Fournet	Microsoft Research
Jacques Garrigue	Kyoto University
Masami Hagiya	University of Tokyo
Robert Harper	Carnegie Mellon University
Masahito Hasegawa	Kyoto University
Nevin Heintze	Agere Systems
Martin Hofmann	Edinburgh University
Zhenjiang Hu	University of Tokyo
Naoki Kobayashi	Tokyo Institute of Technology
Martin Odersky	Ecole Polytechnique Fédérale de Lausanne
Catuscia Palamidessi	Pennsylvania State University
Benjamin Pierce	University of Pennsylvania
François Pottier	INRIA
Andre Scedrov	University of Pennsylvania
Natarajan Shankar	SRI International
Ian Stark	Edinburgh University
Makoto Tatsuta	National Institute of Informatics, Tokyo

Additional Referees

Luca Aceto
Nick Benton
Stefano Berardi
Michele Boreale
Julian Bradfield
Didier Buchs
Cristiano Calcagno
Luca Cardelli
Tom Chothia
Sylvain Conchon
Tristan Crolard
Dennis Dams
Steven Dawson
Pierpaolo Degano
Bruno Dutertre
Jérôme Feret
Marcelo Fiore
Harald Ganzinger
Paola Giannini
Jean Goubault-Larrecq
Robert Harper
Thomas Hildebrandt
Yoshihiko Kakutani
Dilsun Kırlı
Michal Konecny
Manolis Koubarakis
Antonín Kučera
Guy McCusker
Leonardo de Moura
Robert Muller
Keisuke Nakano
Kedar Namjoshi
Uwe Nestmann
Shin-ya Nishizaki
Doron Peled
Frank Pfenning
Lucia Pomello
John Power
Rosario Pugliese
Shaz Qadeer
Christine Roeckl
Harald Rueß
Takafumi Sakurai
Isao Sasano
Alan Schmitt
Peter Selinger
Peter Sestoft
Paula Severi
Peter Sewell
Maria Sorea
Christoph Sprenger
Rick Statman
Colin Stirling
Thomas Streicher
Koichi Takahashi
Makoto Tanabe
Francis Tang
Ashish Tiwari
Keith Wansbrough
Mitsuharu Yamamoto
Jianjun Zhao

Table of Contents

Invited Talk 3

Session 4

Invited Talk 4

Session 5

Session 6

Invited Talk 5

Session 7

Invited Talk 6

Session 8

TACS Open Lecture

A Spatial Logic for Concurrency
(Part I)

Luís Caires[1] and Luca Cardelli[2]

[1] Departamento de Informática FCT/UNL, Lisboa, Portugal
[2] Microsoft Research, Cambridge, UK

Abstract. We present a logic that can express properties of freshness, secrecy, structure, and behavior of concurrent systems. In addition to standard logical and temporal operators, our logic includes spatial operations corresponding to composition, local name restriction, and a primitive fresh name quantifier. Properties can also be defined by recursion; a central theme of this paper is then the combination of a logical notion of freshness with inductive and coinductive definitions of properties.

1 Introduction

We present a logic for describing the behavior and spatial structure of concurrent systems. Logics for concurrent systems are certainly not new [13, 9], but the intent to describe spatial properties seems to have arisen only recently. The spatial properties that we consider here are essentially of two kinds: whether a system is composed of two or more identifiable subsystems, and whether a system restricts the use of certain resources to certain subsystems. Previous work [5] has considered also whether a system is composed of named locations; in that case, the notion of spatial structure is particularly natural.

The initial motivation for studying these logics was to be able to specify systems that deal with fresh or secret resources such as keys, nonces, channels, and locations. In previous papers [5, 3], we have found that the spatial properties of process composition and of location structures are fairly manageable. Instead, the properties of restriction are much more challenging, and are closely related to the study of logical notions of freshness [11].

The main aim of this paper is to advance the study of restriction started in [6, 3] and to build a closer correspondence with treatments of freshness [11]. For simplicity, we use a basic process calculus (the asynchronous π-calculus) that includes composition and restriction. We omit locations in this paper because they are easy to add along the lines of [5], and are comparatively easier to handle than composition or restriction. It will become clear that our general approach is fairly insensitive to the details of specific process calculi, and is largely insensitive to the "dynamics" (reduction behavior) of specific calculi. Therefore, it can be easily adapted to other calculi, and perhaps even generalized to process frameworks [12].

A formula in our logic describes a property of a particular part of a concurrent system at a particular time; therefore it is modal in space as well as in time.

N. Kobayashi and B.C. Pierce (Eds.): TACS 2001, LNCS 2215, pp. 1–37, 2001.

This dual modality can be captured by standard box and diamond operators, reflecting reachability in space and in time [5, 3]. As a further contribution of this paper, though, we wish to investigate a more general framework akin to the μ-calculus [15], where formulas can be recursive and can subsume box and diamond operators. We can then define new and interesting modalities, such as "under an arbitrary number of restrictions". The most technically challenging part of the paper is then the interaction of recursive formulas, already present in [3, 4], with a logical notion of freshness, already present in [6].

We now give a brief overview of the constructs of the logic, before moving on to the formal treatment. Let $\mathcal{P}$ be the set of (asynchronous π-calculus) processes. A *property* is a set of processes; a subset of $\mathcal{P}$. A closed formula denotes a property, namely, it denotes the collection of processes satisfying that formula.

- The collection of all properties (which is not quite the powerset of $\mathcal{P}$, as we shall discuss) has the structure of a Boolean Algebra under set inclusion, so we naturally get boolean connectives in the logic (we take $\mathtt{F}$, $A \wedge B$ and $A \Rightarrow B$ as primitive).
- The above propositional fragment is extended to predicate logic via a universal quantifier $\forall x.A$. This quantifier has standard properties, but the bound variable x ranges always over the countable set of channel names of the process calculus.
- The collection of all properties has also the structure of a quantale, induced by the parallel composition operator over processes. In the logic, this is reflected by the operators $A|B$ (the tensor, or parallel composition, of two properties), $\mathbf{0}$ (the unit of the tensor, or collection of void processes), and $A \triangleright B$ (the linear implication associated with the tensor). This last operator corresponds to context-system specifications, which are the concurrency theory equivalent of pre/post conditions.
- In much the same way that parallel process composition induces the quantale structure, process restriction induces a pair of operators $n®A$ and $A\oslash n$, called revelation and hiding, that give us a basis for describing restricted processes at the logical level.
- The notion of "fresh name" is introduced by a quantifier $\text{И}x.A$; this means that x denotes a name that is fresh with respect to the names used either in A or in processes satisfying A. This quantifier allows us to then derive a hidden name quantifier [6, 3]. $\text{И}x.A$ is defined along the lines of the freshness quantifier of Gabbay-Pitts [11]: the connections will be discussed. A similar $\text{И}x.A$ quantifier is studied in [6] (in absence of recursion), but is handled as a meta-level construct, and not as a proper formula that can be mixed with recursion.
- A logical operator $n\langle m\rangle$ allows us to assert that a message m is present over channel n, giving us some minimal power to observe the behavior of processes.
- A "next step" temporal operator, $\diamondsuit A$, allows us to talk about the behavior of a process after a single (unspecified) reduction step.
- Finally, a maximal fixpoint operator $\boldsymbol{\nu} X.A$ (where A is monotonic in X) introduces recursive formulas and, together with the other constructs, has the ability to define standard modal operators for temporal and spatial modalities,

for instance $\Box A$ denoting that A holds anytime in the future, and $\maltese\, A$, meaning that A holds everywhere in space. A least fixpoint operator is definable.

The paper is organised as follows. We start with a concise review of the asynchronous π-calculus. In Section 3 we give a detailed presentation of the syntax of the spatial logic. In Section 4, we introduce the central notion of property set, we define satisfaction, and we proceed with the analysis of semantical aspects of the logic. In Section 5 we study an appropriate notion of logical validity. In Sections 6 and 7 we motivate and discuss fresh and hidden name quantification, and the recursive definition of properties.

2 Preliminaries on the Asynchronous π-Calculus

We review the syntax and operational semantics of the asynchronous π-calculus [1, 14], following the notations of [16]. We base our presentation on the use of transpositions (simple name replacements), which will become prominent later in the paper.

Definition 2.1 (Processes). *Given a countable set Λ of* names, *the set $\mathcal{P}$ of* processes *is given by the following abstract syntax*

$$
\begin{array}{lll}
m, n, p \in & & \Lambda \text{ (Names)} \\
 & & \\
P, Q, R ::= & & \\
 & \mathbf{0} & \text{(Void)} \\
 & P|Q & \text{(Par)} \\
 & (\boldsymbol{\nu} n)P & \text{(Restriction)} \\
 & m\langle n\rangle & \text{(Message)} \\
 & m(n).P & \text{(Input)} \\
 & !P & \text{(Replication)}
\end{array}
$$

We note by $na(P)$ the set of all names that textually occur in a process P (either bound or free).

Definition 2.2 (Free names in Processes). *For any process P, the set of* free names *of P, noted $fn(P)$, is inductively defined as follows.*

$$
\begin{array}{l}
fn(\mathbf{0}) \triangleq \mathbf{0} \\
fn(P|Q) \triangleq fn(P) \cup fn(Q) \\
fn(m\langle n\rangle) \triangleq \{m, n\} \\
fn((\boldsymbol{\nu} n)P) \triangleq fn(P) \setminus \{n\} \\
fn(m(n).P) \triangleq (fn(P) \setminus \{n\}) \cup \{m\} \\
fn(!P) \triangleq fn(P)
\end{array}
$$

In restriction $(\boldsymbol{\nu} n)P$ and input $m(n).P$, the distinguished occurrence of the name n is bound, with scope the process P. We will note by $bn(P)$ the set of names which occur bound in the process P, and by ©N the set $\{P \mid N \subseteq fn(P)\}$ of processes that contain all names in N free. If N is a finite set of names, and N'

is a any set of names, a substitution $\theta : N \to N'$ of *domain* N and *codomain* N' is a mapping assigning $\theta(n) \in N'$ to each $n \in N$, and n to each $n \notin N$. Thus, outside its domain, any substitution behaves like the identity. Given a substitution θ, we note by $\mathfrak{D}(\theta)$ its domain. The *image* of a substitution θ, noted $\mathfrak{I}(\theta)$, is the set $\{\theta(n) \mid n \in \mathfrak{D}(\theta)\}$. We will write $\{n\leftarrow m\}$ for the singleton substitution of domain $\{n\}$ that assigns m to n. If N is a set of names, we define $\theta(N) \triangleq \{\theta(n) \mid n \in N\}$.

Substitutions that just interchange a pair of names will play a special role in technical developments to follow. More precisely, the *transposition* of n and m, noted $\{n\leftrightarrow m\}$, denotes the substitution $\tau : \{m, n\} \to \{m, n\}$ such that $\tau(n) = m$ and $\tau(m) = n$. Note that $\{n\leftrightarrow m\} = \{m\leftrightarrow n\}$. Before defining safe substitution on processes, we first introduce transposition, and then define α-congruence in the style of [11].

Definition 2.3 (Transposition). *Given a process P and a transposition τ, we denote by $\tau{\cdot}P$ the process inductively defined as follows.*

$$\begin{array}{llll} \tau{\cdot}\mathbf{0} & \triangleq \mathbf{0} & \tau{\cdot}((\boldsymbol{\nu} n)P) & \triangleq (\boldsymbol{\nu}\tau(n))\tau{\cdot}P \\ \tau{\cdot}m\langle n\rangle & \triangleq \tau(m)\langle\tau(n)\rangle & \tau{\cdot}(p(n).P) & \triangleq \tau(p)(\tau(n)).(\tau{\cdot}P) \\ \tau{\cdot}(P|Q) & \triangleq (\tau{\cdot}P)|(\tau{\cdot}Q) & \tau{\cdot}(!P) & \triangleq\, !\tau{\cdot}P \end{array}$$

Proposition 2.4. *For all processes P and Q, and transpositions τ,*

1. $\tau{\cdot}\tau{\cdot}P = P$
2. $\{m\leftrightarrow n\}{\cdot}\tau{\cdot}P = \tau{\cdot}\{\tau(m)\leftrightarrow\tau(n)\}{\cdot}P$

Definition 2.5 (Congruence). *A binary relation $\cong$ on processes is a* congruence *whenever for all processes P, Q and R,*

$$\begin{array}{ll} P \cong P & \text{(Cong Refl)} \\ P \cong Q \Rightarrow Q \cong P & \text{(Cong Symm)} \\ P \cong Q, Q \cong R \Rightarrow P \cong R & \text{(Cong Trans)} \\ P \cong Q \Rightarrow P|R \cong Q|R & \text{(Cong Parl)} \\ P \cong Q \Rightarrow R|P \cong P|Q & \text{(Cong Parr)} \\ P \cong Q \Rightarrow (\boldsymbol{\nu} n)P \cong (\boldsymbol{\nu} n)Q & \text{(Cong Res)} \\ P \cong Q \Rightarrow m(n).P \cong m(n).Q & \text{(Cong In)} \\ P \cong Q \Rightarrow\, !P \cong\, !Q & \text{(Cong Repl)} \end{array}$$

In this paper we essentially make use of two congruences: α-congruence and structural congruence. As usual, *α-congruence* $\equiv_\alpha$ is the congruence that identifies processes up to the safe renaming of bound names.

Definition 2.6 (α-congruence). α-congruence, *noted $\equiv_\alpha$, is the least congruence on processes such that,*

$$\begin{array}{lll} (\boldsymbol{\nu} n)P \equiv_\alpha (\boldsymbol{\nu} p)\{n\leftrightarrow p\}{\cdot}P & \textit{where } p \notin na(P) & \text{(Alpha Res)} \\ m(n).P \equiv_\alpha m(p).\{n\leftrightarrow p\}{\cdot}P & \textit{where } p \notin na(P) & \text{(Alpha In)} \end{array}$$

Definition 2.7 (Safe substitution). *For any process P and substitution θ we denote by $\theta(P)$ the process inductively (and nondeterministically) defined as follows.*

$$\begin{array}{lll}
\theta(\mathbf{0}) & \triangleq \mathbf{0} & \\
\theta(m\langle n\rangle) & \triangleq \theta(m)\langle\theta(n)\rangle & \\
\theta(P|Q) & \triangleq \theta(P)|\theta(Q) & \\
\theta((\boldsymbol{\nu}n)P) & \triangleq (\boldsymbol{\nu}p)\theta(P\{n\leftrightarrow p\}) & \text{where } p \notin \mathfrak{D}(\theta) \cup \mathfrak{I}(\theta) \cup fn(P) \\
\theta(m(n).P) & \triangleq \theta(m)(p).\theta(P\{n\leftrightarrow p\}) & \text{where } p \notin \mathfrak{D}(\theta) \cup \mathfrak{I}(\theta) \cup fn(P) \\
\theta(!P) & \triangleq !\theta(P) &
\end{array}$$

We write $P\theta$ for $\theta(P)$ when θ has the form $\{n\leftarrow m\}$ or $\{n\leftrightarrow m\}$. We have

Lemma 2.8. *Let P be a process. Then*

1. $\tau{\cdot}P \equiv_\alpha \tau(P)$ *where τ is any transposition*
2. $P\{n\leftarrow p\} \equiv_\alpha \{n\leftrightarrow p\}{\cdot}P$ *where $p \notin fn(P)$*

From Lemma 2.8 the following alternative characterization of α-congruence immediately follows.

Proposition 2.9. *α-congruence is the least congruence on processes such that*

$$\begin{array}{ll}
(\boldsymbol{\nu}n)P \equiv_\alpha (\boldsymbol{\nu}p)P\{n\leftarrow p\} & \text{where } p \notin fn(P) \\
m(n).P \equiv_\alpha m(p).P\{n\leftarrow p\} & \text{where } p \notin fn(P)
\end{array}$$

As expected, safe substitution preserves α-congruence:

Proposition 2.10. *If $P \equiv_\alpha Q$ then $\theta(P) \equiv_\alpha \theta(Q)$.*

Definition 2.11 (Structural congruence). Structural congruence, *noted $\equiv$, is the least congruence on processes such that*

$$\begin{array}{ll}
P \equiv_\alpha Q \Rightarrow P \equiv Q & \text{(Struct Alpha)} \\
P|\mathbf{0} \equiv P & \text{(Struct Par Void)} \\
P|Q \equiv Q|P & \text{(Struct Par Comm)} \\
P|(Q|R) \equiv (P|Q)|R & \text{(Struct Par Assoc)} \\
n \notin fn(P) \Rightarrow P|(\boldsymbol{\nu}n)Q \equiv (\boldsymbol{\nu}n)(P|Q) & \text{(Struct Res Par)} \\
n \neq p, n \neq m \Rightarrow (\boldsymbol{\nu}n)p(m).P \equiv p(m).(\boldsymbol{\nu}n)P & \text{(Struct Res Inp)} \\
(\boldsymbol{\nu}n)\mathbf{0} \equiv \mathbf{0} & \text{(Struct Res Void)} \\
(\boldsymbol{\nu}n)(\boldsymbol{\nu}m)P \equiv (\boldsymbol{\nu}m)(\boldsymbol{\nu}n)P & \text{(Struct Res Comm)} \\
!\mathbf{0} \equiv \mathbf{0} & \text{(Struct Repl Void)} \\
!P \equiv !P|P & \text{(Struct Repl Copy)} \\
!(P|Q) \equiv !P|!Q & \text{(Struct Repl Par)} \\
!!P \equiv !P & \text{(Struct Repl Repl)}
\end{array}$$

Although the axiom (Struct Res Inp) is absent from standard presentations of π-calculi, the general consensus seems to be that such axiom is quite sensible as a structural congruence. (Struct Res Inp) is implicit in early work of Boudol on the chemical abstract machine, and is irrelevant as far as extensional properties of processes (eg. behavioral equivalence) are concerned. On the other hand, it has some convenient consequences in the setting of an intensional logic like ours. The axioms (Struct Repl Void/Par/Repl) were proposed by Engelfriet [10] in order to show the decidability of $\equiv$ in a version of the π-calculus.

Proposition 2.12 (Basic properties of $\equiv$). *For all processes P and Q,*

1. *If $P \equiv Q$ then $fn(P) = fn(Q)$.*
2. *If $n \notin fn(P)$ then $(\boldsymbol{\nu} n)P \equiv P$.*
3. *$P \equiv Q$ if and only if $\tau(P) \equiv \tau(Q)$.*
4. *For all substitutions θ, if $P \equiv Q$, then $\theta(P) \equiv \theta(Q)$.*

Proposition 2.13 (Inversion). *For all processes P and Q,*

1. *If $(\boldsymbol{\nu} n)P \equiv \mathbf{0}$ then $P \equiv \mathbf{0}$.*
2. *If $(\boldsymbol{\nu} n)P \equiv R|Q$ then there are R' and Q' such that either $R \equiv (\boldsymbol{\nu} n)R'$ and $Q \equiv Q'$ and $n \notin fn(Q)$, or $R \equiv R'$ and $Q \equiv (\boldsymbol{\nu} n)Q'$ and $n \notin fn(R)$.*
3. *If $(\boldsymbol{\nu} n)P \equiv (\boldsymbol{\nu} m)Q$ then either $P \equiv \{n \leftrightarrow m\} \cdot Q$ or there are P' and Q' such that $P \equiv (\boldsymbol{\nu} m)P'$, $Q \equiv (\boldsymbol{\nu} n)Q'$ and $P' \equiv Q'$.*

Versions of Proposition 2.13(1–2) for the Ambient Calculus have been proved in [8] and [7]. Proposition 2.13(3) has a simple proof based on results in [10], as suggested by J. Engelfriet.

The dynamics of processes is captured by reduction:

Definition 2.14 (Reduction). *Reduction is the least binary relation $\to$ on processes inductively defined as follows.*

$m\langle n\rangle \mid m(p).P \to P\{p \leftarrow n\}$	(Red React)
$Q \to Q' \Rightarrow P \mid Q \to P \mid Q'$	(Red Par)
$P \to Q \Rightarrow (\boldsymbol{\nu} n)P \to (\boldsymbol{\nu} n)Q$	(Red Res)
$P \equiv P', P' \to Q', Q' \equiv Q \Rightarrow P \to Q$	(Red Struct)

Proposition 2.15 (Basic properties of $\to$). *For all processes P and Q,*

1. *If $P \to Q$ then $fn(Q) \subseteq fn(P)$.*
2. *For all substitutions θ, if $P \to Q$, then $\theta(P) \to \theta(Q)$.*
3. *If $P \to Q$ and $Q \equiv (\boldsymbol{\nu} n)Q'$ for some Q', then there are P' and Q'' such that $P \equiv (\boldsymbol{\nu} n)P'$, $P' \to Q''$ and $Q'' \equiv Q'$.*

Proposition 2.15(3) is a consequence of Proposition 2.13(3) and does not hold for versions of π-calculi where $\equiv$ does not satisfy (Struct Res Inp).

Remark 2.16. Reduction as defined in Definition 2.14 is "almost the same" as the usual one in the following sense. Let $\equiv_c$ be the the standard structural congruence of [16] restricted to the asynchronous π-calculus. Thus $\equiv_c \subseteq \equiv$. Likewise, let $\to_c$ be the standard reduction of the asynchronous π-calculus. It is clear that $\to_c \subseteq \to$. We also have that for all processes P and Q, if $P \to Q$ then there is a process R such that $P \to_c R$ and $Q \equiv R$.

3 Syntax of the Spatial Logic

Basic constructs of the spatial logic include logical, spatial and temporal operations, and a greatest fixpoint combinator supporting recursive (inductive and coinductive) definition of properties.

$x, y, z \in \mathcal{V}$ (Name variables)
$X, Y, Z \in \mathcal{X}$ (Propositional variables)
$\eta \in \Lambda \cup \mathcal{V}$ (Names or name variables)

$A, B, C ::=$

$\mathtt{F}$	(False)
$A \wedge B$	(Conjunction)
$A \Rightarrow B$	(Implication)
$\mathbf{0}$	(Void)
$A \mid B$	(Composition)
$A \triangleright B$	(Guarantee)
$\eta ® A$	(Revelation)
$A \oslash \eta$	(Hiding)
$\eta\langle\eta'\rangle$	(Message)
$\forall x.A$	(Universal quantification)
$И\, x.A$	(Fresh name quantification)
$\Diamond A$	(Next step)
X	(Propositional variable)
$\nu X.A$	(Greatest fixpoint)

Fig. 1. Formulas.

Definition 3.1 (Formulas). *Given an infinite set $\mathcal{V}$ of name variables, and an infinite set $\mathcal{X}$ of propositional variables (mutually disjoint from Λ), formulas are defined as shown in Fig. 1.*

The meaning of these formulas was briefly discussed in the introduction; their semantics is given later in Definition 4.14. We highlight here some or the more unusual operators. The formula $\mathbf{0}$ is satisfied by any process in the structural congruence class of $\mathbf{0}$. The formula $A|B$ is satisfied by any process that can be decomposed into processes that satisfy respectively A and B. Guarantee is the logical adjunct of composition: $A \triangleright B$ is satisfied by those processes whose composition with any process satisfying A results in a process satisfying B. The formula $n®A$ is satisfied by all processes congruent with some process $(\boldsymbol{\nu} n)P$, where P satisfies A; hiding is the logical adjunct of revelation. Message $m\langle n\rangle$ holds of processes structurally congruent to a message $m\langle n\rangle$. The formula $Иx.A$ denotes fresh name quantification; a process satisfies $Иx.A$ if for (some/all) fresh names n (fresh in the process and in the formula), it satisfies $A\{x\leftarrow n\}$. This quantifier exhibits the universal/existential ambivalence typical of freshness: a

C	$fn(C)$	$fv(C)$	$fpv(C)$
$\mathbf{F}$ $\mathbf{0}$	$\emptyset$	$\emptyset$	$\emptyset$
$A \wedge B$ $A \Rightarrow B$ $A \mid B$ $A \triangleright B$	$fn(A) \cup fn(B)$	$fv(A) \cup fv(B)$	$fpv(A) \cup fpv(B)$
$\eta\langle\eta'\rangle$	$\{\eta, \eta'\} \cap \Lambda$	$\{\eta, \eta'\} \cap \mathcal{V}$	$\emptyset$
$\eta \circledR A$ $A \oslash \eta$	$fn(A) \cup (\{\eta\} \cap \Lambda)$	$fv(A) \cup (\{\eta\} \cap \mathcal{V})$	$fpv(A)$
$\forall x.A$ I $x.A$	$fn(A)$	$fv(A) \setminus \{x\}$	$fpv(A)$
$\Diamond A$	$fn(A)$	$fv(A)$	$fpv(A)$
X	$\emptyset$	$\emptyset$	$\{X\}$
$\boldsymbol{\nu} X.A$	$fn(A)$	$fv(A)$	$fpv(A) \setminus \{X\}$

Fig. 2. Free names in formulas.

property holding of some fresh names should also hold of any other fresh name. As we shall see, combining the fresh name quantifier with revelation will enable us to define a hidden name quantifier, that is a quantifier over names that are locally restricted in the process at hand.

In formulas of the form $\forall x.A$, И$x.A$ and $\boldsymbol{\nu} X.A$ the distinguished occurrences of x and X are binding, with scope the formula A. We define on formulas the relation $\equiv_\alpha$ of α-congruence in the standard way, that is, as the least congruence identifying formulas modulo safe renaming of bound (name and propositional) variables. We will consider formulas always modulo α-congruence.

Definition 3.2 (Free names and variables in formulas). *For any formula C, we introduce the following sets, inductively defined in Fig. 2.*

$fn(C)$	*free names in C*
$fv(C)$	*free name variables in C*
$fpv(C)$	*free propositional variables in C*

By $fnv(A)$ we mean the set $fv(A) \cup fn(A)$. A formula is *name-closed* if it has no free name variables, and *closed* if it has no free variables whatsoever.

Definition 3.3 (Negative and Positive Occurrences). *For any formula C, the set* Neg(C) *(resp.* Pos(C)*) of the variables which occur negatively (resp. positively) in C are inductively defined in Fig. 3.*

We say that a propositional variable X is *positive* (resp. *negative*) in A if $X \in$ Pos(A) (resp. $X \in$ Neg(A)). We also say that a formula A is *monotonic in X* (resp. *antimonotonic in X*) whenever $X \notin$ Neg(A) (resp. $X \notin$ Pos(A)). Note that a variable X can be both positive and negative in a formula A. Moreover, if X is either positive or negative in A then $X \in fpv(A)$.

C	$\mathrm{Neg}(C)$	$\mathrm{Pos}(C)$
$\mathbf{F}$ $\mathbf{0}$ $\eta\langle\eta'\rangle$	$\emptyset$	$\emptyset$
$A \wedge B$ $A \vert B$	$\mathrm{Neg}(A) \cup \mathrm{Neg}(B)$	$\mathrm{Pos}(A) \cup \mathrm{Pos}(B)$
$A \Rightarrow B$ $A \triangleright B$	$\mathrm{Pos}(A) \cup \mathrm{Neg}(B)$	$\mathrm{Neg}(A) \cup \mathrm{Pos}(B)$
$n®A$ $A \oslash n$ $\forall x.A$ $\text{И}\, x.A$ $\Diamond A$	$\mathrm{Neg}(A)$	$\mathrm{Pos}(A)$
X	$\emptyset$	$\{X\}$
$\boldsymbol{\nu} X.A$	$\mathrm{Neg}(A) \setminus \{X\}$	$\mathrm{Pos}(A) \setminus \{X\}$

Fig. 3. Negative and Positive occurrences.

A formula A is *well-formed* if for every sub-formula of A of the form $\boldsymbol{\nu} X.B$, B is well-formed and monotonic in X. In other words, if $\boldsymbol{\nu} X.B$ is well-formed, all free occurrences of X in B must occur just at positive positions. As usual, the well-formedness condition ensures monotonicity of the denotation mapping associated with fixpoint formulas. In what follows we will just consider well-formed formulas.

We extend the previously given notion of substitution to name variables and formulas as follows. When S is a finite set of either variables and names, and N is a set of names, $\theta : S \to N$ means that θ is a substitution assigning a name in N to each variable or name in S. If $\theta : S \to N$ is a substitution then θ_{-x} denotes the substitution of domain $S \setminus \{x\}$ and codomain N defined by $\theta_{-x}(y) = \theta(y)$, for all $y \in S \setminus \{x\}$.

Definition 3.4 (Safe substitution). *For any formula A and substitution θ we denote by $\theta(A)$ the formula inductively defined as follows.*

$$
\begin{array}{llll}
\theta(\mathbf{F}) & \triangleq \mathbf{F} & \theta(\eta ® A) & \triangleq \theta(\eta) ® \theta(A) \\
\theta(\mathbf{0}) & \triangleq \mathbf{0} & \theta(A \oslash \eta) & \triangleq \theta(A) \oslash \theta(\eta) \\
\theta(A \wedge B) & \triangleq \theta(A) \wedge \theta(B) & \theta(\text{И} x.A) & \triangleq \text{И} x.\theta_{-x}(A) \\
\theta(A \Rightarrow B) & \triangleq \theta(A) \Rightarrow \theta(B) & \theta(\forall x.A) & \triangleq \forall x.\theta_{-x}(A) \\
\theta(A|B) & \triangleq \theta(A)|\theta(B) & \theta(\Diamond A) & \triangleq \Diamond \theta(A) \\
\theta(A \triangleright B) & \triangleq \theta(A) \triangleright \theta(B) & \theta(X) & \triangleq X \\
\theta(m\langle n\rangle) & \triangleq \theta(m)\langle\theta(n)\rangle & \theta(\boldsymbol{\nu} X.A) & \triangleq \boldsymbol{\nu} X.\theta(A)
\end{array}
$$

When A and B are formulas, we denote by $A\{X \leftarrow B\}$ the capture avoiding substitution of all free occurrences of X in A by B, defined in the expected way. By $F\{-\}$ we denote a formula context with possibly multiple occurrences of the hole $-$. Then, whenever A is a formula, we denote by $F\{A\}$ the formula obtained by textually replacing every occurrence of the hole $-$ in the context $F\{-\}$ by A. Note that free (name or propositional) variables in A will be captured by binders present in $F\{-\}$; cf. the standard notion of context substitution.

4 Semantics

The semantics of formulas is defined by assigning to each formula A a set of processes $[\![A]\!]$, namely the set of all processes that satisfy the property denoted by A.

However, as we shall justify soon, not any set of processes can denote a property in a proper way. For instance, it is sensible to require $[\![A]\!]$ to be closed under structural congruence. That is, if a process P satisfy some property A, then any process Q such that $Q \equiv P$ must also satisfy A. Moreover, suppose we have $P \in [\![A]\!]$, $n \notin fn(A)$ but $n \in fn(P)$. Since $n \notin fn(A)$, the free occurrences of n in $fn(P)$ are *fresh* w.r.t. formula A. Now, the particular choice of the name n should not depend on A itself, since it is natural to consider that all fresh names w.r.t. A are to be treated uniformly (all alike). Therefore, it is natural to require that also $P\{n{\leftarrow}m\} \in [\![A]\!]$, where m is any other fresh name w.r.t. A and P, that is $m \notin fn(P) \cup fn(A)$.

Hence, we say that a set of processes Φ is supported by a set of names N if, for all m, n not in the support N, if P belongs to Φ then $P\{n{\leftrightarrow}m\}$ is also in Φ. We then take as properties only those sets of processes that have a finite support. Intuitively, the support of a property is the semantic counterpart of the set of free names of a formula; the least support of the denotation of a formula is included in the set of free names of the formula. Sets with infinite support could only correspond to formulas that have an infinite set of free names, and are therefore excluded.

Moreover, the notion of finite support seems crucial for the semantics of the fresh name quantifier, $\text{И}x.A$, and consequently for the semantics of the derived hidden name quantifier $\mathsf{H}x.A$. For example, the semantics of the spatial logics of [6, 5, 3] is given in terms of sets of processes that are closed only under structural congruence. If we try to extend that semantics to recursive formulas, we run into a problem: $\text{И}x.A$ is not a monotonic operator, and could not be used together with recursion. This discussion is continued in more detail in Section 4.3.

4.1 Property Sets

The above observations motivate the following notion of *property set*. A property set is a set of processes closed under structural congruence and finitely supported.

Definition 4.1 (Property Set). *Given a finite set of names N, a* property set *(Pset) supported by N is a set of processes Ψ such that*

1. *(closure under $\equiv$) If $P \in \Psi$ and $P \equiv Q$ then $Q \in \Psi$.*
2. *(finite support) For all $n, m \notin N$, if $P \in \Psi$ then $P\{n{\leftrightarrow}m\} \in \Psi$.*

In general, by "a Pset" we intend a Pset supported by some N; then, N is the support of the Pset. We use Ψ, Φ to range over property sets. The support N plays for some Pset Ψ a role similar to the one played by the set of free names of a given formula, and enables the definition of a notion of name freshness w.r.t. a possibly infinite set of processes. Given a finite set of names N, we will denote by $\mathbb{P}_N$ the set of all Psets supported by N, and by $\mathbb{P}_-$ the set of all Psets.

Lemma 4.2 (Operations on Psets). *For all finite $N \subseteq \Lambda$,*

1. *If $N \subseteq N'$ then $\mathbb{P}_N \subseteq \mathbb{P}_{N'}$.*
2. *(Bottom and Top) $\emptyset \in \mathbb{P}_N$ and $\mathcal{P} \in \mathbb{P}_N$.*
3. *(Meet and Join) If $S \subseteq \mathbb{P}_N$ then $\bigcap S \in \mathbb{P}_N$ and $\bigcup S \in \mathbb{P}_N$.*
4. *(Inverse) If $\Psi \in \mathbb{P}_N$ then $\overline{\Psi} = \mathcal{P} \setminus \Psi \in \mathbb{P}_N$.*

Note that Lemma 4.2(2-4) implies

Proposition 4.3 (Lattice). *For all finite $N \subseteq \Lambda$, we have*

1. *$\langle \mathbb{P}_N, \subseteq, \cup, \cap \rangle$ is a complete lattice.*
2. *$\langle \mathbb{P}_N, \cup, \cap, \overline{\cdot} \rangle$ is a Boolean algebra.*

Remark 4.4. Note that $\mathbb{P}_-$ is not closed under arbitrary unions. For instance, let $\langle m_1, m_2, \ldots \rangle$ be a linear ordering of Λ, let $P_0 \triangleq \mathbf{0}$ and for any $i > 0$, $P_i \triangleq m_i(n).P_{i-1}$. Then $\{P_i\}$ is finitely supported (with support $\{m_1, \ldots, m_i\}$) for any $i \geq 0$, but $\bigcup_{i \geq 0}\{P_i\}$ is not.

For any operator $f : \mathbb{P}_N \to \mathbb{P}_N$, we denote by $\mathsf{lfix}_{\mathbb{P}_N}(f)$ the least fixpoint of f and by $\mathsf{gfix}_{\mathbb{P}_N}(f)$ the greatest fixpoint of f.

Definition 4.5 (Tensor and Unit). *For every $\mathbb{P}_N$, define operations*

$$\otimes : \mathbb{P}_N \times \mathbb{P}_N \to \mathbb{P}_N \quad \mathbf{1} : \mathbb{P}_N$$

by letting, for all $\Psi, \Phi \in \mathbb{P}_N$

$$\Psi \otimes \Phi \triangleq \{P \mid \textit{there are } Q \textit{ and } R \textit{ st. } P \equiv Q|R \textit{ and } Q \in \Psi \textit{ and } R \in \Phi\}$$
$$\mathbf{1} \triangleq \{P \mid P \equiv \mathbf{0}\}$$

In [5] it is shown that the set of all $\equiv$-closed subsets of $\mathcal{P}$ gives rise to a commutative quantale. The same result still holds for domains of Psets.

Proposition 4.6 (Quantale). *For all finite $N \subseteq \Lambda$, $\langle \mathbb{P}_N, \subseteq, \bigcup, \otimes, \mathbf{1} \rangle$ is a commutative quantale, that is:*

1. *$\langle \mathbb{P}_N, \subseteq, \bigcup \rangle$ is a complete join semilattice.*
2. *$\langle \mathbb{P}_N, \otimes, \mathbf{1} \rangle$ is a commutative monoid.*
3. *$\Phi \otimes \bigcup S = \bigcup \{\Phi \otimes \Psi \mid \Psi \in S\}$, for all $\Phi \in \mathbb{P}_N$ and $S \subseteq \mathbb{P}_N$.*

We now extend the application of transpositions (not of arbitrary substitutions!) to Psets as follows: if τ is a transposition and Ψ is a Pset, define $\tau(\Psi) \triangleq \{\tau(P) \mid P \in \Psi\}$.

Lemma 4.7 (Transposing Psets). *We have*

1. *For any process P and Pset Ψ, $P \in \tau(\Psi)$ if and only if $\tau(P) \in \Psi$.*
2. *$\Psi \in \mathbb{P}_N$ if and only if $\tau(\Psi) \in \mathbb{P}_{\tau(N)}$.*
3. *If $m, n \notin N$ and $\Psi \in \mathbb{P}_N$ then $\{m \leftrightarrow n\}(\Psi) = \Psi$.*

We can verify that a Pset Ψ supported by N is finitely supported by N in the precise sense of [11].

Definition 4.8 (Support). *Let N be a set of names. A Pset Ψ is* supported *by N whenever every permutation that fixes N also fixes Ψ. Moreover Ψ is* finitely supported *by N if supported by N and N is finite.*

A name permutation π over Λ is an injective name substitution such that $\mathfrak{D}(\pi) = \mathfrak{I}(\pi)$. Let S_Λ be the group of all name permutations; recall that any permutation can be expressed as a composition of transpositions. For any Pset Ψ, $\pi(\Psi) \in \mathbb{P}_-$, by Lemma 4.7(2). Hence $\mathbb{P}_-$ is an S_Λ−set.

Now, let $\Psi \in \mathbb{P}_N$. Pick any $\pi \in S_\Lambda$ and assume that π is not the identity permutation. This implies that there is some permutation π', such that $\pi'(m) = \pi(m)$ for all $m \in \Lambda$ and $\pi'(m) \neq m$, for all $m \in \mathfrak{D}(\pi')$. Assume that for all $n \in N$, $\pi(n) = n$. Then, for all $n \in N$, $\pi'(n) = n$. We can see that N is disjoint from $\mathfrak{D}(\pi') = \mathfrak{I}(\pi')$. Hence, π' can be written as a composition of transpositions $\tau_1 \cdots \tau_k$ such that $\tau_i = \{p_i \leftrightarrow q_i\}$ and $p_i, q_i \notin N$, for all $i = 1, \cdots, k$. Therefore $\pi'(\Psi) = \pi(\Psi) = \Psi$. This means that N (finitely) supports Ψ. We conclude that $\mathbb{P}_-$ is a *perm*(Λ)-set with the finite support property.

We also have

Proposition 4.9 (Least Support). *Let $\Phi \in \mathbb{P}_N$. Then*

1. *There is a least set of names $supp(\Phi)$ such that $\Phi \in \mathbb{P}_{supp(\Phi)}$.*
2. *For any transposition τ, if $supp(\Phi) = M$ then $supp(\tau(\Phi)) = \tau(M)$.*

Intuitively, the set of names $supp(\Phi)$ represents the set of "free names" of the Pset Φ (in the sense of Lemma 4.7(3)), hence $supp(-)$ is the semantic counterpart of the set $fn(-)$ of free names of a formula.

If a Pset Ψ is supported by N and $N \subseteq M$, Ψ is also supported by M. On the other hand, for any finite set of names S, we can always find a minimal Pset Φ containing Ψ and supported by S, given by

Definition 4.10 (Closure). *Let $\Phi \in \mathbb{P}_M$ and let N be a finite set of names. The* closure *of Φ on N is given by*

$$Cl(\Phi, N) \triangleq \bigcup_{\pi \in \Pi_N} \pi(\Phi)$$

where by Π_N we denote the the set of all permutations that fix N.

For any finite set of names N, $Cl(-, N)$ is a closure operator. We also have

Lemma 4.11. *If $\Phi \in \mathbb{P}_M$ and N is a finite set of names, $Cl(\Phi, N) \in \mathbb{P}_N$.*

4.2 Satisfaction

We define the semantics of a formula A by a Pset $[\![A]\!] \in \mathbb{P}_{fn(A)}$. Since A may contain free occurrences of propositional variables, its denotation depends on the denotation of such variables, which is given by a valuation.

Definition 4.12 (Valuation). *A valuation v is a mapping from a finite subset of $\mathcal{X}$, assigning to each propositional variable X in its domain $\mathfrak{D}(v)$ a Pset Ψ. Given a formula A, a valuation for A is any valuation v such that $fpv(A) \subseteq \mathfrak{D}(v)$.*

Thus, the role of valuations is to interpret free propositional variables occurring in the formula A. When v is a valuation, we will write $v[X \leftarrow \Psi]$ to denote the valuation of domain $\mathfrak{D}(v) \cup \{X\}$ that assigns Ψ to X, and behaves like v w.r.t. any other propositional variable $Z \neq X$. For any valuation v, we let

$$fn(v) \triangleq \bigcup\{supp(v(X)) \mid X \in \mathfrak{D}(v)\}$$

Taking into account the extra information yielded by a valuation, we now give a more refined characterization of the free names in a formula A as follows

Definition 4.13 (Free names under a valuation). *If A is a formula and v a valuation for A, we define the set $fn^v(A)$ of free names of A under v by*

$$\begin{array}{ll}
fn^v(\mathbf{0}) = fn^v(\mathtt{F}) & \triangleq \emptyset \\
fn^v(A \wedge B) = fn^v(A|B) = & \\
\quad fn^v(A \triangleright B) = fn^v(A \Rightarrow B) & \triangleq fn^v(A) \cup fn^v(B) \\
fn^v(\eta \circledR A) = fn^v(A \oslash \eta) & \triangleq (\{\eta\} \cap \Lambda) \cup fn^v(A) \\
fn^v(\forall x.A) = fn^v(\text{И} x.A) = \Diamond A & \triangleq fn^v(A) \\
fn^v(\boldsymbol{\nu} X.A) & \triangleq fn^{v[X \leftarrow \emptyset]}(A) \\
fn^v(X) & \triangleq supp(v(X))
\end{array}$$

Note that the definition of $fn^v(A)$ mimics the one given for $fn(A)$ except in the clauses for fixpoint and propositional variable. The set $fn^v(A)$ is used in an essential way in the definition of the semantics of the fresh name quantifier, where the quantification witness is tested for freshness w.r.t. the property denoted by the formula A, which may contain free occurrences of propositional variables.

Definition 4.14 (Denotation and Satisfaction). *The* denotation map $[\![A]\!]_v$ *is the function that assigns a Pset to each name-closed formula A and valuation (for A) v. It is inductively defined in Fig 4. We write $P \models_v A$ whenever $P \in [\![A]\!]_v$: this means that P* satisfies *formula A under valuation v.*

We now show that the denotation map is well-defined. In particular, we show that $[\![A]\!]_v$ is indeed a Pset (actually, $[\![A]\!]_v \in \mathbb{P}_{fn^v(A)}$) and that the semantics of the fixpoint operation is the intended one (that is, $\boldsymbol{\nu} X.B$ indeed denotes the greatest fixpoint). A more natural formulation of $[\![\boldsymbol{\nu} X.A]\!]_v$ will be given and justified in Proposition 4.27.

Since we are considering formulas up to α-congruence, we start by verifying that the denotation map is well-defined on the corresponding equivalence classes.

$$
\begin{array}{ll}
[\![\mathbf{F}]\!]_v & \triangleq \emptyset \\
[\![A \wedge B]\!]_v & \triangleq [\![A]\!]_v \cap [\![B]\!]_v \\
[\![A \Rightarrow B]\!]_v & \triangleq \{Q \mid \textit{if } Q \in [\![A]\!]_v \textit{ then } Q \in [\![B]\!]_v\} \\
[\![\mathbf{0}]\!]_v & \triangleq \mathbf{1} \\
[\![A|B]\!]_v & \triangleq [\![A]\!]_v \otimes [\![B]\!]_v \\
[\![A \triangleright B]\!]_v & \triangleq \{Q \mid \textit{if } P \in [\![A]\!]_v \textit{ then } P|Q \in [\![B]\!]_v\} \\
[\![n \circledR A]\!]_v & \triangleq \{Q \mid Q \equiv (\boldsymbol{\nu} n)P \textit{ and } P \in [\![A]\!]_v\} \\
[\![A \oslash n]\!]_v & \triangleq \{Q \mid (\boldsymbol{\nu} n)Q \in [\![A]\!]_v\} \\
[\![m\langle n\rangle]\!]_v & \triangleq \{Q \mid Q \equiv m\langle n\rangle\} \\
[\![\forall x.A]\!]_v & \triangleq \bigcap_{n \in \Lambda} [\![A\{x \leftarrow n\}]\!]_v \\
[\![\text{И}\, x.A]\!]_v & \triangleq \bigcup_{n \notin fn^v(A)} ([\![A\{x \leftarrow n\}]\!]_v \setminus \copyright\{n\}) \\
[\![\Diamond A]\!]_v & \triangleq \{P \mid P \rightarrow Q \textit{ and } Q \in [\![A]\!]_v\} \\
[\![X]\!]_v & \triangleq v(X) \\
[\![\boldsymbol{\nu} X.A]\!]_v & \triangleq \bigcup\{\Psi \in \mathbb{P}_{fn^v(\boldsymbol{\nu} X.A)} \mid \Psi \subseteq [\![A]\!]_{v[X \leftarrow \Psi]}\}
\end{array}
$$

Fig. 4. Denotation of formulas.

Lemma 4.15. *For all formulas A, B and valuations v for A and B, if $A \equiv_\alpha B$, then $[\![A]\!]_v = [\![B]\!]_v$.*

Note that assignments to propositional variables which do not occur free in the interpreted formula do not affect its denotation. Therefore, valuations can always be weakened and thinned whenever appropriate.

Remark 4.16. For any formula A, Pset Φ and valuation v for A, if $X \notin fpv(A)$ then $[\![A]\!]_v = [\![A]\!]_{v[X \leftarrow \Phi]}$.

We now extend the application of transpositions to valuations, this is done in the expected way: when v is a valuation, let $\tau(v)$ be the valuation with same domain as v and defined by $\tau(v)(X) \triangleq \tau(v(X))$, for all $X \in \mathfrak{D}(v)$.

Lemma 4.17. *For any formula A, valuation v and transposition τ*

1. *If $\tau = \{m \leftrightarrow n\}$ and $m, n \notin fn(v)$ then $[\![A]\!]_v = [\![A]\!]_{\tau(v)}$.*
2. *$\tau(fn^v(A)) = fn^{\tau(v)}(\tau(A))$.*
3. *Let $fn^v(\boldsymbol{\nu} X.A) \subseteq M$. Then $fn^v(\boldsymbol{\nu} X.A) \subseteq fn^{v[X \leftarrow \Psi]}(A) \subseteq M$, for all $\Psi \in \mathbb{P}_M$.*

We conclude that if $N = fn^v(\boldsymbol{\nu} X.A)$ then $fn^{v[X \leftarrow \Psi]}(A) = N$, for all $\Psi \in \mathbb{P}_N$.

Fundamental properties of the denotation mapping are stated in the following main theorem, from which all correctness properties of the semantics follow.

Theorem 4.18. *For all formulas A, appropriate valuations v, and Psets Ψ, Φ*

1. *$[\![A]\!]_v \in \mathbb{P}_{fn^v(A)}$.*
2. *For all transpositions τ, $\tau([\![A]\!]_v) = [\![\tau(A)]\!]_{\tau(v)}$.*
3. *If $X \notin \mathrm{Neg}(A)$ and $\Psi \subseteq \Phi$ then $[\![A]\!]_{v[X \leftarrow \Psi]} \subseteq [\![A]\!]_{v[X \leftarrow \Phi]}$.*
4. *If $X \notin \mathrm{Pos}(A)$ and $\Psi \subseteq \Phi$ then $[\![A]\!]_{v[X \leftarrow \Phi]} \subseteq [\![A]\!]_{v[X \leftarrow \Psi]}$.*

Proof. See Appendix.

Lemma 4.19. *For any formula A and valuation v for A we have*

$$supp([\![A]\!]_v) \subseteq fn^v(A)$$

Proof. By Theorem 4.18(1) $[\![A]\!]_v \in \mathbb{P}_{fn^v(A)}$; hence by Proposition 4.9 there is a least set $N = supp([\![A]\!]_v)$ such that $[\![A]\!]_v \in \mathbb{P}_N$. So $supp([\![A]\!]_v) \subseteq fn^v(A)$.

Remark 4.20. By inspection of the proof of Theorem 4.18 we can verify

– Assume $[\![A]\!]_v \in \mathbb{P}_N$ and $[\![B]\!]_v \in \mathbb{P}_M$. Then

$$\begin{array}{lll} [\![\mathbf{F}]\!]_v \in \mathbb{P}_\emptyset & [\![A \Rightarrow B]\!]_v \in \mathbb{P}_{N\cup M} & [\![A \oslash n]\!]_v \in \mathbb{P}_{N\cup\{n\}} \\ [\![\mathbf{0}]\!]_v \in \mathbb{P}_\emptyset & [\![A|B]\!]_v \in \mathbb{P}_{N\cup M} & [\![\Diamond A]\!]_v \in \mathbb{P}_N \\ [\![p\langle q\rangle]\!]_v \in \mathbb{P}_{\{p,q\}} & [\![A \triangleright B]\!]_v \in \mathbb{P}_{N\cup M} & [\![X]\!]_v \in \mathbb{P}_{supp(v(X))} \\ [\![A \wedge B]\!]_v \in \mathbb{P}_{N\cup M} & [\![n \circledR A]\!]_v \in \mathbb{P}_{N\cup\{n\}} & \end{array}$$

– If $[\![A\{x\leftarrow n\}]\!]_v \in \mathbb{P}_{N\cup\{n\}}$ for all $n \in \Lambda$, then $[\![\forall x.A]\!]_v \in \mathbb{P}_N$
– If $[\![A\{x\leftarrow n\}]\!]_v \in \mathbb{P}_{N\cup\{n\}}$ for all $n \notin fn^v(A)$ then $[\![\text{И} x.A]\!]_v \in \mathbb{P}_N$
– If $\Psi \in \mathbb{P}_N$ and $[\![A]\!]_{v[X\leftarrow\Psi]} \in \mathbb{P}_N$ then $[\![\boldsymbol{\nu} X.A]\!]_v \in \mathbb{P}_N$

Lemma 4.21. *Let A be a formula monotonic in X, v a valuation for $\boldsymbol{\nu} X.A$, and $fn^v(\boldsymbol{\nu} X.A) \subseteq M$. Then the function*

$$\boldsymbol{\lambda}\Psi.[\![A]\!]_{v[X\leftarrow\Psi]} : \mathbb{P}_M \to \mathbb{P}_M$$

is a monotonic operator over the complete lattice $\mathbb{P}_M$.

Proof. Let $\Psi \in \mathbb{P}_M$. By Lemma 4.17(3), we have $fn^{v[X\leftarrow\Psi]}(A) \subseteq M$. By Theorem 4.18(1) and Proposition 4.3(1), we conclude $[\![A]\!]_{v[X\leftarrow\Psi]} \in \mathbb{P}_M$. Monotonicity then follows from Theorem 4.18(3).

Lemma 4.22. *Let A be a formula monotonic in X and v a valuation for $\boldsymbol{\nu} X.A$. Then*

$$[\![\boldsymbol{\nu} X.A]\!]_v = \mathsf{gfix}_{\mathbb{P}_{fn^v(\boldsymbol{\nu} X.A)}}(\boldsymbol{\lambda}\Psi.[\![A]\!]_{v[X\leftarrow\Psi]})$$

Proof. Let $N = fn^v(\boldsymbol{\nu} X.A)$. By Lemma 4.21, the function $\boldsymbol{\lambda}\Psi.[\![A]\!]_{v[X\leftarrow\Psi]} : \mathbb{P}_N \to \mathbb{P}_N$ is a monotonic operator in the complete lattice $\mathbb{P}_N$. We conclude by Knaster-Tarski Lemma.

Lemma 4.23. *Let A be any formula, $v[X\leftarrow\Psi]$ a valuation for A and B, and B any formula in which X does not occur free. Then*

$$[\![A\{X\leftarrow B\}]\!]_v = [\![A]\!]_{v[X\leftarrow[\![B]\!]_v]}$$

Note that Lemmas 4.23 and 4.22 imply $[\![\boldsymbol{\nu} X.A]\!]_v = [\![A\{X\leftarrow\boldsymbol{\nu} X.A\}]\!]_v$.

The next lemma clarifies the relationship between free names in formulas and the supports of their denotations in fixpoint formulas. It essentially says that any pre-fixpoint of the mapping $\boldsymbol{\lambda}\Psi.[\![A]\!]_{v[X\leftarrow\Psi]}$ is contained in a larger pre-fixpoint of the same mapping with a smaller support, which is bounded from below by the set of names $fn^v(\boldsymbol{\nu} X.A)$. A consequence is that the greatest fixpoint of such mapping inhabits $\mathbb{P}_{fn^v(\boldsymbol{\nu} X.A)}$, cf. Lemma 4.26 below.

Lemma 4.24. *Let A be a formula and $v[X \leftarrow \Phi]$ a valuation for A such that $fn^v(\boldsymbol{\nu} X.A) \subseteq N \subseteq M$, $\Phi \subseteq [\![A]\!]_{v[X \leftarrow \Phi]}$ and $\Phi \in \mathbb{P}_M$.*
Then $Cl(\Phi, N) \subseteq [\![A]\!]_{v[X \leftarrow Cl(\Phi,N)]}$.

Proof. See Appendix.

Relying on Lemma 4.24 we can now provide a crisper (after-the-fact) justification for the choice of the particular support N in the semantic clause for the fixpoint operator. Indeed,

Lemma 4.25. *Let M be a finite set of names such that $fn^v(\boldsymbol{\nu} X.A) \subseteq M$. Then*

$$\mathsf{gfix}_{\mathbb{P}_M}(\boldsymbol{\lambda}\Psi.[\![A]\!]_{v[X \leftarrow \Psi]}) \subseteq [\![\boldsymbol{\nu} X.A]\!]_v$$

Proof. Assume $M \supseteq fn^v(\boldsymbol{\nu} X.A) = N$. Pick $P \in \mathsf{gfix}_{\mathbb{P}_M}(\boldsymbol{\lambda}\Psi.[\![A]\!]_{v[X \leftarrow \Psi]})$. Then $P \in \Phi$ for some $\Phi \in \mathbb{P}_M$ such that $\Phi \subseteq [\![A]\!]_{v[X \leftarrow \Phi]}$. By Lemma 4.24, we have $Cl(\Phi, N) \subseteq [\![A]\!]_{v[X \leftarrow Cl(\Phi,N)]}$. Hence $Cl(\Phi, N) \subseteq [\![\boldsymbol{\nu} X.A]\!]_v$. Since $\Phi \subseteq Cl(\Phi, N)$, we conclude $P \in [\![\boldsymbol{\nu} X.A]\!]_v$.

Therefore, on the one hand the fixpoint must be taken in the lattice $\mathbb{P}_M$, where the set M must necessarily include $fn^v(\boldsymbol{\nu} X.A)$. In fact, it is not hard to find a formula A for which the induced operator fails to be closed on $\mathbb{P}_M$ if $fn^v(\boldsymbol{\nu} X.A) \not\subseteq M$ (eg. $M = \emptyset$ and $A = p\langle p \rangle$). On the other hand, Lemma 4.25 states that nothing is lost by picking the set N instead of any bigger support M. More precisely, we have

Lemma 4.26. *Let $\boldsymbol{\nu} X.A$ be a formula and v a valuation for $\boldsymbol{\nu} X.A$. Suppose there is a $\subseteq$-greatest Pset Φ such that $\Phi = [\![A]\!]_{v[X \leftarrow \Phi]}$. Then $\Phi = [\![\boldsymbol{\nu} X.A]\!]_v$.*

Proof. Since Φ is a Pset, then $\Phi \in \mathbb{P}_M$ for some M. By Proposition 4.2(1), $\Phi \in \mathbb{P}_{M'}$ where $M' = M \cup fn^v(\boldsymbol{\nu} X.A)$. By assumption and Lemma 4.25, we have $\Phi \subseteq \{\Phi \in \mathbb{P}_{M'} \mid \Phi \subseteq [\![A]\!]_{v[X \leftarrow \Phi]}\} = \mathsf{gfix}_{\mathbb{P}_{M'}}(\boldsymbol{\lambda}\Phi.[\![A]\!]_{v[X \leftarrow \Phi]}) \subseteq [\![\boldsymbol{\nu} X.A]\!]_v$. Now, $[\![\boldsymbol{\nu} X.A]\!]_v = [\![A]\!]_{v[X \leftarrow [\![\boldsymbol{\nu} X.A]\!]_v]}$. Hence, $[\![\boldsymbol{\nu} X.A]\!]_v \subseteq \Phi$ by assumption. We conclude $\Phi = [\![\boldsymbol{\nu} X.A]\!]_v$.

In fact, even though $\mathbb{P}_{-}$ is not a complete lattice, the uniformity across renamings out of $\boldsymbol{\nu} X.A$ that exists among the pre-fixpoints of the denotation mapping (cf. Lemma 4.24) implies the following characterisation for the semantics of greatest fixpoint formulas.

Proposition 4.27. *We have $[\![\boldsymbol{\nu} X.A]\!]_v = \{\Psi \in \mathbb{P}_{-} \mid \Psi \subseteq [\![A]\!]_{v[X \leftarrow \Psi]}\}$.*

Proof. (Right to left). If $P \in \{\Psi \in \mathbb{P}_{-} \mid \Psi \subseteq [\![A]\!]_{v[X \leftarrow \Psi]}\}$ then there is $\Phi \in \mathbb{P}_{-}$ such that $P \in \Phi$ and $\Phi \subseteq [\![A]\!]_{v[X \leftarrow \Phi]}$. But $\Phi \in \mathbb{P}_M$ for some finite set of names M. Let $M' = fn^v(\boldsymbol{\nu} X.A)$. Then $\Phi \in \mathbb{P}_{M' \cup M}$. By Lemma 4.24 we have $Cl(\Phi, M') \subseteq [\![A]\!]_{v[X \leftarrow Cl(\Phi,M')]}$. Since $P \in Cl(\Phi, M') \in \mathbb{P}_{M'}$, we conclude $P \in [\![\boldsymbol{\nu} X.A]\!]_v$. (Left to right) Immediate since $\mathbb{P}_{fn^v(\boldsymbol{\nu} X.A)} \subset \mathbb{P}_{-}$.

Another consequence of the closure property stated in Theorem 4.18(2) is that the relation of satisfaction between processes and formulas is closed under fresh name renaming, that is, properties depend on the distinctions between names and not on their particular identity (a property called *equivariance* in [11]).

Lemma 4.28 (Fresh renaming). *Let P be a process and A a closed formula such that $P \models A$. If $m \notin fn(A) \cup fn(P)$ then $P\{n{\leftarrow}m\} \models A\{n{\leftarrow}m\}$.*

Proof. Since $m \notin fn(P) \cup fn(A)$, by Lemma 2.8(2) we have $P\{n{\leftarrow}m\} \equiv P\{n{\leftrightarrow}m\}$, and $A\{n{\leftarrow}m\} = A\{n{\leftrightarrow}m\}$. We conclude by Theorem 4.18(2).

It should be stressed that the use of transpositions, as suggested to us by A. Pitts, together with the notion of support, yields for Lemma 4.28 a proof that is much simpler than direct ones (eg. [2, 5]).

Basic Derived Connectives Some derived connectives of basic interest are defined as shown next.

$\neg A$	$\triangleq A \Rightarrow \mathtt{F}$	(Negation)
$\mathtt{T}$	$\triangleq \neg\mathtt{F}$	(True)
$A \vee B$	$\triangleq \neg A \Rightarrow B$	(Disjunction)
$A \Vert B$	$\triangleq \neg(\neg A \vert \neg B)$	(Decomposition)
$\exists x.A$	$\triangleq \neg\forall x.\neg A$	(Existential quantification)
$©\eta$	$\triangleq \neg\eta®\mathtt{T}$	(Free name)
$\eta = \eta'$	$\triangleq \neg(©\eta \triangleright (©\eta \oslash \eta'))$	(Equality)
$\boxdot A$	$\triangleq \neg\Diamond\neg A$	(All next)

Standard operations of the classical predicate calculus, namely $\neg A$ (Negation), $\exists x.A$ (Existential quantification), $A \vee B$ (Disjunction) and $\mathtt{T}$ (True) are defined as expected. Another interesting connective is $A\Vert B$, the DeMorgan dual of composition $A|B$, which supports the definition of a form of spatial quantification. A process satisfies $A\Vert B$ if and only if every component of P w.r.t. composition, satisfies either A or B. We also have the modality $\boxdot$, which is the dual of $\Diamond$. A process satisfies $\boxdot A$ if and only if all processes to which it reduces in one step satisfy A. The free name predicate $©\eta$ holds of any process with a free occurrence of name η. Name equality is defined from general properties of restriction.

Proposition 4.29. *For every process P and names n, p we have*

1. *$P \in [\![©n]\!]_v$ if and only if $n \in fn(P)$.*
2. *$P \in [\![n = p]\!]_v$ if and only if $n = p$.*

Proof. 1. See [6]. 2. We verify that $P \in [\![©n \triangleright (©n \oslash p)]\!]_v$ if and only if $n \neq p$. Suppose $P \in [\![©n \triangleright (©n \oslash p)]\!]_v$. Then, for every Q such that $n \in fn(Q)$ we have $Q|P \in [\![©n \oslash p]\!]_v$. This implies $n \in fn((\boldsymbol{\nu}p)(Q|P))$, and thus $n \neq p$. Conversely, if $n \neq p$ and $n \in fn(Q)$ then $n \in fn((\boldsymbol{\nu}p)(Q|P))$ and $n \in fn(Q|P)$, for all P. Thus, for every Q such that $n \in fn(Q)$, we have $Q|P \in [\![©n \oslash p]\!]_v$ for all P.

4.3 Discussion

The semantics of the fresh quantifier $\text{И}x.A$ is based on finding fresh names outside of $fn^v(A) = fn^v(\text{И}x.A)$, and therefore outside the support of $[\![\text{И}x.A]\!]_v$ (by Lemma 4.19). The fact that names outside the support can be freely renamed (cf. Theorem 4.18(2) and Lemma 4.28) implies that any choice for a fresh name will work equally well.

It is instructive to see how freshness interacts with recursion. Consider the formula

$$\boldsymbol{\nu} Y.\text{И}x.n\langle x\rangle \triangleright \Diamond Y$$

By the fixpoint unfolding property, this formula must have the same meaning as

$$\text{И}x.n\langle x\rangle \triangleright \Diamond(\text{И}x'.n\langle x'\rangle \triangleright \Diamond \cdots)$$

Obviously, the $fn^-(-)$ of the original formula and of its expansion are the same. So, "at each iteration" we have to choose fresh names outside the same set of names, and there is an infinite supply of them. Moreover, at each iteration, the ©n part of the semantic definition of $\text{И}x.A$ subtracts those processes that use names that have been chosen in previous iterations. Further, since the fresh names used at each iteration can be freely renamed, they do not affect the support set, by Definition 4.1(2).

As already discussed, the notion of finite support and Pset seems crucial for the semantics of $\text{И}x.A$. In particular, without a notion of finite support (cf. Definition 4.1(2)), it seems natural to set $fn^v(X) \triangleq \{n \mid n \in fn(P) \text{ and } P \in v(X)\}$, since we must somehow take into account the names contributed by (a binding of) X. Then, consider the set $\Psi = \{p\langle p\rangle\}^{\equiv}$ (we note by $\{-\}^{\equiv}$ closure under structural congruence) and the formula $A = \text{И}x.(\neg x\langle x\rangle | X)$, with $fn^{[X\leftarrow\Psi]}(A) = \{p\}$. We can easily check that

$$q\langle q\rangle | p\langle p\rangle \in [\![A]\!]_{[X\leftarrow\Psi]} = \bigcup_{n \notin \{p\}} ([\![\neg n\langle n\rangle | X]\!]_{[X\leftarrow\Psi]} \setminus \copyright n)$$

Now consider $\Phi = \{r\langle r\rangle \mid r \in \Lambda\}^{\equiv}$ with $fn^{[X\leftarrow\Phi]}(A) = \Lambda$. So we have that $q\langle q\rangle | p\langle p\rangle \notin [\![A]\!]_{[X\leftarrow\Phi]} = \emptyset$. Hence, $\Psi \subseteq \Phi$, but $[\![A]\!]_{[X\leftarrow\Psi]} \not\subseteq [\![A]\!]_{[X\leftarrow\Phi]}$; a failure of monotonicity.

Instead, in our semantics $\text{И}x.A$ is a monotonic operator (cf. Theorem 4.18 (3,4)), the functional associated with a fixpoint formula $\boldsymbol{\nu} X.A$ is in fact a closed monotonic operator $\mathbb{P}_M \to \mathbb{P}_M$ (cf. Lemma 4.21). To take the fixpoint of the map $\boldsymbol{\lambda}\Phi.[\![A]\!]_{v[X\leftarrow\Phi]}$ we must pick a lattice $\mathbb{P}_M$ where M is some finite set of names. This is because the set of all Psets is not a complete lattice and we find it convenient to use the general result of Knaster-Tarski to solve the recursion. Then a question arises about what M should we pick.

Note that for each Pset Φ such that $\Phi \subseteq [\![A]\!]_{v[X\leftarrow\Phi]}$ there is a possibly different $supp([\![A]\!]_{v[X\leftarrow\Phi]})$, depending on $supp(\Phi)$. In principle, we could pick $M = supp([\![\boldsymbol{\nu} X.A]\!]_v)$, but $supp([\![\boldsymbol{\nu} X.A]\!]_v)$ is not known in advance. Now, by Lemma 4.19, $fn^v(\boldsymbol{\nu} X.A)$ always contains the support of $[\![\boldsymbol{\nu} X.A]\!]_v$, so $fn^v(\boldsymbol{\nu} X.A)$

can be used to approximate $supp([\![\boldsymbol{\nu}X.A]\!]_v)$. In fact, on the one hand we cannot pick M such that M does not contain $fn^v(\boldsymbol{\nu}X.A)$: as discussed above, there are formulas A for which $\boldsymbol{\lambda}\Phi.[\![A]\!]_{v[X\leftarrow\Phi]}$ is not a closed operator in $\mathbb{P}_M$. So M must contain $fn^v(\boldsymbol{\nu}X.A)$. On the other hand, Lemma 4.25 states that we can set exactly $M = fn^v(\boldsymbol{\nu}X.A)$.

Now, the uniform relation between the renamings out of M of the pre-fixpoints of $\boldsymbol{\lambda}\Phi.[\![A]\!]_{v[X\leftarrow\Phi]}$ made clear by Lemma 4.24 has as immediate consequence: although $\mathbb{P}_-$ is not closed under arbitrary unions, the union of all the pre-fixpoints of $\boldsymbol{\lambda}\Phi.[\![A]\!]_{v[X\leftarrow\Phi]}$ is indeed finitely supported (cf. Lemma 4.27). Hence, the semantic definition for $\boldsymbol{\nu}X.A$ in Fig. 4 just makes explicit that the support of the greatest fixpoint of the monotonic map $\boldsymbol{\lambda}\Phi.[\![A]\!]_{v[X\leftarrow\Phi]}$ is always to be found inside $fn^v(\boldsymbol{\nu}X.A)$.

5 Validity

We now introduce a notion of logical validity. A formula A is valid if all of its ground instances, under all valuations, is satisfied by all processes.

Definition 5.1 (Valid Formula). *A formula A is* valid *if for all substitutions θ with $fv(A) \subseteq \mathfrak{D}(\theta)$, for all valuations v such that $fpv(A) \subseteq \mathfrak{D}(v)$, we have $[\![\theta(A)]\!]_v = \mathcal{P}$.*

We will use the meta-level statement $valid(A)$ to assert validity of formula A. Logical validity satisfies the following general principles.

Proposition 5.2 (Instantiation). *Let $F\{-\}$ be any formula context. We have*

1. *For any η and formula A, $valid(A) \Rightarrow valid(A\{x\leftarrow\eta\})$.*
2. *For any formula A, $valid(F\{X\}) \Rightarrow valid(F\{A\})$*

Proof. 1. Assume $valid(A)$. Then for all substitutions θ where $fv(A) \subseteq \mathfrak{D}(\theta)$, for all valuations v such that $fpv(A) \subseteq \mathfrak{D}(v)$, we have $\mathcal{P} \subseteq [\![\theta(A)]\!]_v$. Let θ' be any substitution with $\mathfrak{D}(\theta') \subseteq fv(A\{x\leftarrow\eta\})$ and define $\sigma = \theta'_{-x} \circ \{x\leftarrow\theta'(\eta)\}$. Now, $\mathfrak{D}(\sigma) \subseteq fv(A)$. Thus $\mathcal{P} \subseteq [\![\sigma(A)]\!]_v$ for any appropriate valuation v. Since $\sigma(A) = \theta'(A\{x\leftarrow\eta\})$, we are done.

2. Similar to proof on Lemma 5.3 (induction in the size of $F\{-\}$).

Lemma 5.3 (Substitutivity). *Let $[\![\theta(A)]\!]_v = [\![\theta(B)]\!]_v$ for all substitutions θ and valuations v, and let $F\{-\}$ be a formula context. Then, for all substitutions σ and valuations w we have $[\![\sigma(F\{A\})]\!]_w = [\![\sigma(F\{B\})]\!]_w$.*

A direct consequence of substitutivity is

Proposition 5.4 (Replacement of equivalents). *Let $F\{-\}$ be any formula context. We have $valid(A \Leftrightarrow B) \Rightarrow valid(F\{A\} \Leftrightarrow F\{B\})$.*

Proof. Assume $valid(A \Leftrightarrow B)$. Then $[\![\theta(A)]\!]_v = [\![\theta(B)]\!]_v$ for any valuation v for $A \Leftrightarrow B$ and substitution θ. Let w be any valuation for $F\{A\} \Leftrightarrow F\{B\}$; we must show that $[\![\sigma(F\{A\})]\!]_w = [\![\sigma(F\{B\})]\!]_w$, for any substitution σ. But this follows directly from Lemma 5.3.

Proposition 5.5 (Coinduction). *Let the formula F be monotonic in X. For any formula A such that $X \notin fpv(A)$*

$$valid(A \Rightarrow F\{X\leftarrow A\}) \Rightarrow valid(A \Rightarrow \boldsymbol{\nu} X.F)$$

Proof. We assume $valid(A \Rightarrow F\{X\leftarrow A\})$, and prove $valid(A \Rightarrow \boldsymbol{\nu} X.F)$. To that end, we select any valuation v for $A \Rightarrow \boldsymbol{\nu} X.F$, any substitution θ and show $[\![\theta(A)]\!]_v \subseteq [\![\theta(\boldsymbol{\nu} X.F)]\!]_v$. We have

$$[\![\theta(A)]\!]_v \subseteq [\![\theta(F\{X\leftarrow A\}))]\!]_v = [\![\theta(F)\{X\leftarrow\theta(A)\}]\!]_v$$

By Lemma 4.23, $[\![\theta(F)\{X\leftarrow\theta(A)\}]\!]_v = [\![\theta(F)]\!]_{v[X\leftarrow[\![\theta(A)]\!]_v]}$.

Let $M = fn^v(\theta(F\{X\leftarrow A\})) \supseteq fn^v(\theta(\boldsymbol{\nu} X.F))$. By Lemma 4.21, the mapping

$$\mathfrak{G} \triangleq \boldsymbol{\lambda}\Psi.[\![\theta(F)]\!]_{v[X\leftarrow\Psi]} : \mathbb{P}_M \rightarrow \mathbb{P}_M$$

is a monotonic operator in the complete lattice $\mathbb{P}_M$. Moreover, we have $[\![\theta(A)]\!]_v \subseteq [\![\theta(F)]\!]_{v[X\leftarrow[\![\theta(A)]\!]_v]}$. Thus $[\![\theta(A)]\!]_v \subseteq \mathsf{gfix}_{\mathbb{P}_M}(\mathfrak{G})$. By Lemma 4.25, $\mathsf{gfix}_{\mathbb{P}_M}(\mathfrak{G}) \subseteq [\![\theta(\boldsymbol{\nu} X.F)]\!]_v$. Hence, $[\![\theta(A)]\!]_v \subseteq [\![\theta(\boldsymbol{\nu} X.F)]\!]_v$.

6 Fresh and Hidden Name Quantification

In this section the semantics of Section 4 is used to investigate basic properties of the fresh name quantifier and of the derived hidden name quantifier.

6.1 The Fresh Name Quantifier

As we have seen, freshness plays a central role in the spatial logic, but uses of the freshness quantifier $\text{И}x.A$ can be rather subtle. Consider, as an example, the formula $\text{И}x.x\langle m\rangle$, satisfied by any process P such that, for any n fresh in P and different from m, P satisfies $n\langle m\rangle$. But if P satisfies $n\langle m\rangle$, it must be congruent to $n\langle m\rangle$, and hence it must contain n. Therefore, n is not fresh in P, and the denotation of $\text{И}x.x\langle m\rangle$ is empty. This shows that many simple uses of И are trivial, when the fresh name maps directly to a free name of the process.

There are, however, two basic ways of making good use of the fresh quantifier. The first way is to use И in conjunction with ®, so that the fresh name is used to reveal a restricted name of the process (then the fresh name does not map to a free name of the original process). In this situation, we definitely do not want the name used to reveal a restricted name to clash with some other name of the process. This is one of the reasons that motivates the use of \©n in the semantics of $\text{И}x.A$ (Fig. 4), to eliminate such a possibility. The combination of И and ® is discussed further in Section 6.2.

The second way is to use И in conjunction with $\triangleright$, so that the fresh name maps to a free name of the context, but not of the process. For example, consider the formula

$$\text{И}x.\forall y.(x\langle y\rangle \triangleright \boxdot(x\langle y\rangle | \mathrm{T}))$$

This formula holds of all processes P that verify the following: if a message on a fresh channel x is composed in parallel with P, then no reduction from the resulting process consumes such a message.

Intuitively, we expect such a property to hold of every process. In fact, let P be any process, n some name not free in P, and m any name. Pick any process Q such that $Q \models_v n\langle m\rangle$. So, $Q \equiv n\langle m\rangle$. Now, we verify that if $Q|P \to R$, then $R \equiv n\langle m\rangle|P'$, where $P \to P'$, because $P \not\equiv n(q).R'|R''$. Thus $P \models_v n\langle m\rangle \triangleright \boxdot(n\langle m\rangle|\mathrm{T})$. Since m is arbitrary, $P \models_v \forall y.n\langle y\rangle \triangleright \boxdot(n\langle y\rangle|\mathrm{T})$. Since n is neither free in P nor belongs to $fn^v(\forall y.x\langle y\rangle \triangleright \boxdot(x\langle y\rangle|\mathrm{T}))$, we conclude $P \models_v И x.\forall y.x\langle y\rangle \triangleright \boxdot(x\langle y\rangle|\mathrm{T})$.

A fundamental consequence of closure of satisfaction under fresh renaming (Lemma 4.28) is the following characterisation of fresh name quantification, that makes clear the universal/existential ambivalence of freshness: if some property holds of a fresh name, it holds of all fresh names.

Proposition 6.1 (Gabbay-Pitts Property). *Let $И x.A$ be a name-closed formula, P a process, and v a valuation for $И x.A$. Then, the following statements are equivalent*

1. $P \models_v И x.A$.
2. *There is $n \notin fn(P) \cup fn^v(A)$ such that $P \models_v A\{x\leftarrow n\}$.*
3. *For all $n \notin fn(P) \cup fn^v(A)$ we have $P \models_v A\{x\leftarrow n\}$.*

Proof. ($1 \Rightarrow 2$) By definition. ($2 \Rightarrow 3$) By Remark 4.16, there is n such that $n \notin fn(P) \cup fn^{v_A}(A)$ and $P \models_{v_A} A\{x\leftarrow n\}$, where v_A is the restriction of v to the free propositional variables of A. Now, pick $m \notin fn(P) \cup fn^{v_A}(A)$, and let $\tau = \{m\leftrightarrow n\}$. By Theorem 4.18(2), we conclude $\tau(P) \models_{\tau(v_A)} \tau(A\{x\leftarrow n\})$, that is, $P \models_{\tau(v_A)} A\{x\leftarrow m\}$. Note that $m, n \notin fn(v_A)$; hence $P \models_{v_A} A\{x\leftarrow m\}$, by Lemma 4.17(1). Hence $P \models_v A\{x\leftarrow m\}$, by Remark 4.16. ($3 \Rightarrow 1$) Immediate.

A corollary of the previous proposition is

Proposition 6.2. *Let A be a name-closed formula and v a valuation for A and B. We have*

1. $[\![\forall x.A]\!]_v \subseteq [\![И x.A]\!]_v \subseteq [\![\exists x.A]\!]_v$
2. $[\![И x.(A \Rightarrow B)]\!]_v = [\![И x.A \Rightarrow И x.B]\!]_v$

Proof. 2. (Left to right) Assume $P \in [\![И x.(A \Rightarrow B)]\!]_v$ and $P \in [\![И x.A]\!]_v$. Then $P \in [\![A\{x\leftarrow n\}]\!]_v$ for some $n \notin fn(P) \cup fn^v(A)$, and $P \in [\![A\{x\leftarrow m\} \Rightarrow B\{x\leftarrow m\}]\!]_v$ for some $m \notin fn(P) \cup fn^v(A \Rightarrow B)$. By Proposition 6.1(3), for all $n \notin fn(P) \cup fn^v(A)$ we have $P \in [\![A\{x\leftarrow n\}]\!]_v$. In particular, $P \in [\![A\{x\leftarrow m\}]\!]_v$, thus $P \in [\![B\{x\leftarrow m\}]\!]_v$. We conclude $P \in [\![И x.B]\!]_v$. (Right to left) Assume $P \in [\![И x.A \Rightarrow И x.B]\!]_v$. Pick $m \notin fn(P) \cup fn^v(A \Rightarrow B)$ and assume $P \in [\![A\{x\leftarrow m\}]\!]_v$. Then $P \in [\![И x.A]\!]_v$, this implies $P \in [\![И x.B]\!]_v$. By Proposition 6.1(3), $P \in [\![B\{x\leftarrow m\}]\!]_v$. Hence $P \in [\![И x.(A \Rightarrow B)]\!]_v$.

We can verify that fresh quantification distributes over all boolean connectives, not only implication (cf. Proposition 6.2(2), it suffices to note that (trivially) $[\![И x.\mathrm{F}]\!]_v = [\![\mathrm{F}]\!]_v$). In the next lemma, we exemplify some other interesting properties of fresh name quantification.

Lemma 6.3 (Some properties of И). *We have*

1. $[\![\text{И}x.(A|B)]\!]_v = [\![\text{И}x.A|\text{И}x.B]\!]_v$
2. $[\![\text{И}x.\Diamond A]\!]_v = [\![\Diamond\text{И}x.A]\!]_v$

Proof. 1. (Right to left inclusion) Let $P \models_v \text{И}x.A|\text{И}x.B$. Then there are processes Q and R such that $P \equiv Q|R$ and $Q \models_v \text{И}x.A$ and $R \models_v \text{И}x.B$. Pick a name $n \notin fn(P) \cup fn^v(\text{И}x.(A|B))$. Then $n \notin fn(Q) \cup fn^v(\text{И}x.A)$ and $n \notin fn(R) \cup fn^v(\text{И}x.B)$. By Proposition 6.1(3) we have $Q \models_v A\{x\leftarrow n\}$ and $R \models_v B\{x\leftarrow n\}$. Then $P \models_v \text{И}x.(A|B)$ as claimed. (Left to right inclusion) Similar, use Proposition 6.1(2).

2. (Left to right inclusion) Let $P \models_v \text{И}x.\Diamond A$. Then there is a process Q, and a name n, fresh w.r.t. P and $fn^v(A)$ such that $P \to Q$ and $Q \models_v A\{x\leftarrow n\}$. But if n is fresh w.r.t P it is also fresh w.r.t. Q since $fn(Q) \subseteq fn(P)$. Hence $Q \models_v \text{И}x.A$ and $P \models_v \Diamond\text{И}x.A$. (Right to left inclusion) Let $P \models_v \Diamond\text{И}x.A$. Then there is Q and n fresh w.r.t. Q and $fn^v(A)$ such that $P \to Q$ and $Q \models_v A\{x\leftarrow n\}$. Pick any name m, fresh w.r.t. v and P (and thus fresh w.r.t. Q). Let $\tau = \{m\leftrightarrow n\}$, by Theorem 4.18(2) we have $Q \models_v A\{x\leftarrow m\}$, since $\tau(Q) = Q$, $\tau(v) = v$ and $\tau(A\{x\leftarrow n\}) = A\{x\leftarrow m\}$. Hence $P \models_v \Diamond A\{x\leftarrow m\}$, and then $P \models_v \text{И}x.\Diamond A$.

In [11] a И-quantifier for FM-set theory is defined, such that

$$\text{И}x.A \Leftrightarrow \{n \mid A\{x\leftarrow n\}\} \text{ is cofinite}$$

There is a quite close connection between this И-quantifier and ours, superficial differences being related to the fact that we are working in a modal logic. In our case, we have

Proposition 6.4. *$P \models_v \text{И}x.A$ if and only if $\{n \mid P \models_v A\{x\leftarrow n\}\}$ is cofinite.*

Proof. (Left to right) Pick $P \models_v \text{И}x.A$. Thus there is $n \notin fn^v(A) \cup fv(P)$ such that $P \models_v A\{x\leftarrow n\}$. By Gabbay-Pitts (Proposition 6.1(3)) we have that for all n if $n \notin fn^v(A) \cup fv(P)$ then $P \models_v A\{x\leftarrow n\}$. Hence $\{n \mid P \models_v A\{x\leftarrow n\}\}$ is cofinite. (Right to left) Assume $S = \{n \mid P \models_v A\{x\leftarrow n\}\}$ is cofinite. Then, there is a finite set $M(= \Lambda \setminus S)$ such that for all n, if $n \notin M$ then $P \models_v A\{x\leftarrow n\}$. Pick $m \notin fn^v(A) \cup fn(P) \cup M$. Then $P \models_v A\{x\leftarrow m\}$, hence $P \models_v \text{И}x.A$.

Now, let us define the following (meta-level) quantifier

$$\text{И}^*x.\mathcal{B} \triangleq \{n \in \Lambda \mid \mathcal{B}\{x\leftarrow n\}\} \text{ is cofinite}$$

where $\mathcal{B}$ is a meta-level statement of the (informal) theory of Psets of Section 4. Note that $\text{И}^*x.\mathcal{B}$ is defined exactly as the И-quantifier of Gabbay-Pitts. Then, we can read the statement of the previous proposition as:

$$P \in [\![\text{И}x.A]\!]_v \text{ if and only if } \text{И}^*n.P \in [\![A\{x\leftarrow n\}]\!]_v.$$

It is interesting to discuss alternative fresh quantifiers. Our semantics of $Иx.A$ is such that $P \models_v Иx.A$ holds if and only if there is a name n, fresh both in A and P, such that $P \models A\{x \leftarrow n\}$ (cf. Proposition 6.1). It is natural then to ask what happens if n only is required to be fresh in A. Let us define for this propose a different quantifier $\mathsf{F}x.A$ where

$$P \in [\![\mathsf{F}x.A]\!] \text{ if and only if } \exists n \notin fn(A) \text{ such that } P \in [\![A\{x \leftarrow n\}]\!]$$

One could then attempt to define $Иx.A$ as $\mathsf{F}x.(A \wedge \neg ©x)$. Although $[\![\mathsf{F}x.A]\!]$ is a Pset, the main problems with $\mathsf{F}x.A$, with respect to $Иx.A$, are a failure of monotonicity (Theorem 4.18 (3)), a failure of the substitutivity property (Lemma 5.3), and a failure of the Gabbay-Pitts property (Proposition 6.1) relating to a proper notion of "freshness".

For substitutivity, we have that $[\![n\langle n\rangle \vee \neg n\langle n\rangle]\!] = [\![\mathrm{T}]\!]$. So, we would expect that $[\![\mathsf{F}x.((n\langle n\rangle \vee \neg n\langle n\rangle) \wedge x\langle x\rangle)]\!] = [\![\mathsf{F}x.(\mathrm{T} \wedge x\langle x\rangle)]\!]$. But $n\langle n\rangle \in [\![\mathsf{F}x.(\mathrm{T} \wedge x\langle x\rangle)]\!]$, while $n\langle n\rangle \notin [\![\mathsf{F}x.((n\langle n\rangle \vee \neg n\langle n\rangle) \wedge x\langle x\rangle)]\!]$. So, $\mathsf{F}x.A$ is not a proper "compositional" logical operator. While, rather amazingly, $Иx.A$ is.

For monotonicity, consider

$$\psi = \{q\langle q\rangle\}^{\equiv} \subseteq \{p\langle p\rangle, q\langle q\rangle\}^{\equiv} = \phi$$

Note that $\psi, \phi \in \mathbb{P}_{\{p,q\}}$, $fn^{v[X \leftarrow \psi]}(X|x\langle x\rangle) = \{q\}$ and $fn^{v[X \leftarrow \phi]}(X|x\langle x\rangle) = \{p, q\}$. On the one hand, $q\langle q\rangle|p\langle p\rangle \in [\![\mathsf{F}x.X|x\langle x\rangle]\!]_{v[X \leftarrow \psi]}$, because there is $n \notin \{q\}$ (namely p) such that $q\langle q\rangle|p\langle p\rangle \in [\![X|n\langle n\rangle]\!]_{v[X \leftarrow \psi]}$. On the other hand, we have $q\langle q\rangle|p\langle p\rangle \notin [\![\mathsf{F}x.(X|x\langle x\rangle)]\!]_{v[X \leftarrow \Phi]}$, because there is no n out of $\{p, q\}$ such that $q\langle q\rangle|p\langle p\rangle \in [\![X|n\langle n\rangle]\!]_{v[X \leftarrow \Phi]}$. So $[\![\mathsf{F}x.(X|x\langle x\rangle)]\!]_{v[X \leftarrow \psi]} \not\subseteq [\![\mathsf{F}x.(X|x\langle x\rangle)]\!]_{v[X \leftarrow \phi]}$. We conclude that $\mathsf{F}x.A$ cannot be used with recursive formulas.

For the Gabbay-Pitts property, consider whether $p\langle p\rangle \in [\![\mathsf{F}x.\neg x\langle x\rangle]\!]$. This means, by definition: there is a name n such that $p\langle p\rangle \in [\![\neg n\langle n\rangle]\!]$. This is true, take any $n \neq p$. If we had a Gabbay-Pitts property for $\mathsf{F}x.A$ we would obtain that for all names n, $p\langle p\rangle \in [\![n\langle n\rangle]\!]$. But this is false: take $n = p$. So, by the interpretation of the Gabbay-Pitts property, the candidate $\mathsf{F}x.A$ is not a proper "freshness" quantifier.

We may also consider an apartness connective (not a quantifier) $\eta \# A$ with semantics given by

$$P \in [\![n\#A]\!]_v \text{ if and only if } n \notin fn^v(A)$$

and then attempt to define fresh name quantification from © and $\exists$. Indeed, we can verify that $[\![Иx.A]\!]_v = [\![\exists x.(\neg ©x \wedge x\#\exists x.A \wedge A)]\!]_v$. But substitutivity also fails for $x\#A$, eg. $\mathcal{P} = [\![n\#\mathrm{T}]\!]_v \neq [\![n\#(n\langle n\rangle \vee \neg n\langle n\rangle)]\!]_v = \emptyset$, hence it is not sensible to adopt $\eta\#A$ as a primitive formula.

6.2 The Hidden Name Quantifier

When combined with revelation, the fresh name quantifier gives rise to a natural operation of quantification over hidden (restricted) names in a process.

Intuitively, a name is revealed under a fresh identity, and then a property is asserted of the restricted process.

$$\mathsf{H}x.A \triangleq \mathsf{И}x.x\circledR A$$

A formula $\mathsf{H}x.A$ reads "there is a restricted name x such that A holds for the process under the restriction". From the above definition, we get the following direct semantic characterization of the name-closed formula $\mathsf{H}x.A$

$$[\![\mathsf{H}x.A]\!]_v = \{Q \mid Q \equiv (\boldsymbol{\nu}n)P \text{ and } n \notin fn(Q) \cup fn^v(A) \text{ and } P \in [\![A\{x\leftarrow n\}]\!]_v\}$$

The hidden name quantifier makes it possible to express properties of processes that depend on (or need to mention) some secret name. For a quite simple example, consider the closed formula $\exists y.\mathsf{H}x.(y\langle x\rangle|\mathsf{T})$.

This formula holds precisely of those processes which are ready to send a secret name over a public channel. As a further example, let A be some formula with a free occurrence of the name variable x, and consider

$$Keeps(A,x) \triangleq \mathsf{H}x.A \wedge (\mathsf{T} \triangleright \boxdot\mathsf{H}x.A|\mathsf{T})$$

A process that satisfies $Keeps(A,x)$ is always able to guarantee, until the next step, persistence of property A w.r.t. some secret x it owns, even when attacked by some other arbitrary process. Let K be the process

$$(\boldsymbol{\nu}m)(m\langle n\rangle|!a(p).m(q).m\langle p\rangle)$$

We have $fn(K) = \{a,n\}$. Now define $Msg(x,y) \triangleq (x\langle y\rangle|\mathsf{T})$. We can verify that K satisfies $Keeps(\exists y.Msg(x,y),x)$.

Lemma 6.5 (Some properties of H). *We have*

1. $[\![\mathsf{H}x.(A \wedge \neg\copyright x)]\!]_v = [\![\mathsf{И}x.A]\!]_v$
2. $[\![\mathsf{H}x.\Diamond A]\!]_v = [\![\Diamond\mathsf{H}x.A]\!]_v$

Proof. 1. (Left to right inclusion) Pick some process $P \in [\![\mathsf{H}x.(A \wedge \neg\copyright x)]\!]_v$. By the characterization given above, this means that $P \equiv (\boldsymbol{\nu}n)Q$ for some Q and n such that $n \notin fn(P) \cup fn^v(A)$ and $Q \in [\![A\{x\leftarrow n\} \wedge \copyright n]\!]_v$. But then, $n \notin fn(Q)$ and $Q \in [\![A\{x\leftarrow n\}]\!]_v$. We conclude $P \equiv (\boldsymbol{\nu}n)Q \equiv Q$, by Proposition 2.12(2). Therefore, $P \in [\![\mathsf{И}x.A]\!]_v$. In the other direction the proof is similar.

2. (Left to right inclusion) Pick some process $P \in [\![\mathsf{H}x.\Diamond A]\!]_v$. So, $P \equiv (\boldsymbol{\nu}n)Q$ for some Q and n such that $Q \to Q'$ and $Q' \in [\![A\{x\leftarrow n\}]\!]_v$, where n is fresh w.r.t. P and A. But then $P \to (\boldsymbol{\nu}n)Q'$. Since n is also fresh w.r.t. $(\boldsymbol{\nu}n)Q'$, we conclude $(\boldsymbol{\nu}n)Q' \in [\![\mathsf{H}x.A]\!]_v$. Hence $P \in [\![\Diamond\mathsf{H}x.A]\!]_v$. (Right to left inclusion) Take some process $P \in [\![\Diamond\mathsf{H}x.A]\!]_v$. Then there is Q such that $P \to Q$ and $Q \in [\![\mathsf{H}x.A]\!]_v$. Then $Q \equiv (\boldsymbol{\nu}n)R$ where $R \in [\![A\{x\leftarrow n\}]\!]_v$ and $n \notin fn(Q) \cup fn^v(A)$. Now, since $P \to Q$, by Proposition 2.15(3) there are P' and R' such that $P \equiv (\boldsymbol{\nu}n)P'$, $P' \to R'$ and $R' \equiv R$. This means that $P \in [\![\mathsf{H}x.\Diamond A]\!]$.

7 Recursive Definitions

The possibility of defining spatial, temporal and freshness properties by induction and coinduction is a major source of expressiveness of the spatial logic. For instance, by combining fixpoints formulas with hidden name quantification we can describe a "nonce generator", that is, a process that sends an unbounded number of fresh names on a channel:

$$\nu X.\mathsf{H}x.m\langle x\rangle|X$$

We can verify that $!(\nu n)m\langle n\rangle \models \nu X.\mathsf{H}x.m\langle x\rangle|X$. Let $\Phi = \{P \mid P \equiv\, !(\nu n)m\langle n\rangle\}$. We have that $\Phi \in \mathbb{P}_{\{m\}}$. It suffices to check that $\Phi \subseteq [\![\mathsf{H}x.m\langle x\rangle|X]\!]_{[X\leftarrow\Phi]}$. For this, take any $P \in \Phi$, so that we have $P \equiv\, !(\nu n)m\langle n\rangle \equiv (\nu n)m\langle n\rangle|!(\nu n)m\langle n\rangle$. The left subprocess is in $[\![\mathsf{H}x.m\langle x\rangle]\!]_{[X\leftarrow\Phi]}$, and the right one is in $\Phi = [\![X]\!]_{[X\leftarrow\Phi]}$. More generally, we can verify that $P \models A$ implies $!P \models \nu X.(A|X)$.

The least fixpoint operator is defined from the greatest fixpoint operator in the standard way. From these, the standard "always in the future" $\Box A$ and "eventually in the future" $\Diamond A$ modalities of (branching time) temporal logic are also defined.

$$\begin{array}{lll} \mu X.A \triangleq \neg\nu X.\neg A\{X\leftarrow\neg X\} & \text{(Least fixpoint)} \\ \Box A \quad\triangleq \nu X.(A \wedge \boxdot X) & \text{(Always)} \\ \Diamond A \quad\triangleq \mu X.(A \vee \diamond X) & \text{(Eventually)} \end{array}$$

Proposition 7.1. *We have*

1. $[\![\mu X.A]\!]_v = \mathsf{lfix}_{\mathbb{P}_N}(\lambda\Psi.[\![A]\!]_{v[X\leftarrow\Psi]})$ *where* $N = fn^v(\mu X.A)$
2. $P \in [\![\Box A]\!]_v$ *if and only if for all* Q *such that* $P \xrightarrow{*} Q$ *we have* $Q \in [\![A]\!]_v$
3. $P \in [\![\Diamond A]\!]_v$ *if and only if there is* Q *such that* $P \xrightarrow{*} Q$ *and* $Q \in [\![A]\!]_v$

Proposition 7.2 (Induction). *Let the formula* F *be monotonic in* X. *For any formula* A *such that* $X \notin fpv(A)$

$$valid(F\{X\leftarrow A\} \Rightarrow A) \Rightarrow valid(\mu X.F \Rightarrow A)$$

By combining fixpoints with spatial and temporal connectives one can define many other interesting properties. For instance, let

$$\begin{array}{lll} \textbf{\textit{group}}\ A & \triangleq \mu X.(\mathbf{0} \vee A|X) & \text{(Group)} \\ \textbf{\textit{inside}}^{\exists}\ A & \triangleq \mu X.(A \vee \mathsf{H}x.X) & \\ \textbf{\textit{inside}}^{\forall}\ A & \triangleq \neg\ \textbf{\textit{inside}}^{\exists}\ \neg A & \\ \diamond\!\!\!\!\diamond A & \triangleq \textbf{\textit{inside}}^{\exists}(A|\mathrm{T}) & \text{(Somewhere)} \\ \boxtimes A & \triangleq \textbf{\textit{inside}}^{\forall}(A\|\mathrm{F}) & \text{(Everywhere)} \end{array}$$

The formula ***group*** A holds of any process P such that $P \equiv Q_1|\ldots|Q_k$ for some processes $Q_1, \ldots, Q_k$, where each Q_i satisfies A. The formula ***inside*** $^{\exists}A$ holds of any process P such that $P \equiv (\nu n_1)\cdots(\nu n_k)Q$ for some fresh names $n_1, \ldots, n_k$ and process Q, where Q satisfies A.

Lemma 7.3. *We have*

$$[\![\mu X.(A \vee \mathsf{H}x.X)]\!]_v = \{(\nu n_1)\cdots(\nu n_k)Q \mid Q \in [\![A]\!]_v \textit{ and } n_i \notin fn^v(A)\}^{\equiv}$$

Proof. Let $\Psi \triangleq \{(\nu n_1)\cdots(\nu n_k)Q \mid Q \in [\![A]\!]_v$ and $n_i \notin fn^v(A)\}^{\equiv}$. Let $M = fn^v(A) = fn^v(\boldsymbol{inside}\ ^{\exists}A)$; it is easy to check that $\Psi \in \mathbb{P}_M$. Ψ is closed under structural congruence by construction. Also, pick any process $P \in \Psi$, names $p, q \notin M$ and let $\tau = \{p\leftrightarrow q\}$. Then $P \equiv (\nu n_1)\cdots(\nu n_k)Q$ where $Q \in [\![A]\!]_v$. Hence $\tau(P) = (\nu\tau(n_1))\cdots(\nu\tau(n_k))\tau(Q)$, and we have $\tau(Q) \in [\![A]\!]_v$. We want to show that $\Psi = [\![\mu X.(A \vee \mathsf{H}x.X)]\!]_v$.

We first prove $\Psi \subseteq [\![\mu X.(A \vee \mathsf{H}x.X)]\!]_v$. To that end, we take any $\Phi \in \mathbb{P}_M$ such that $[\![A \vee \mathsf{H}x.X]\!]_{v[X\leftarrow\Phi]} \subseteq \Phi$ and verify $\Psi \subseteq \Phi$.

Pick $P \in \Psi$. Then $P \equiv (\nu n_1)\cdots(\nu n_k)Q$ and $Q \in [\![A]\!]_v$, for some $k \geq 0$. We show by induction on k that $P \in \Phi$.

If $k = 0$, we have $P \equiv Q \in [\![A]\!]_v$, and thus $P \in [\![A \vee \mathsf{H}x.X]\!]_{v[X\leftarrow\Phi]}$ by Remark 4.16, since X is not free in A. Hence $P \in \Phi$. If $k > 0$ we have $P \equiv (\nu n_1)P'$ where $P' = (\nu n_2)\cdots(\nu n_k)Q \in \Psi$. By induction hypothesis, we have $P' \in \Phi$. Hence $P' \in [\![X]\!]_{v[X\leftarrow\Phi]}$. Thus $P \in [\![n_1 \circledR X]\!]_{v[X\leftarrow\Phi]}$. We have $n_1 \notin fn(P)$ and $n_1 \notin M = fn^{v[X\leftarrow\Phi]}(X) = fn^{v[X\leftarrow\Phi]}(\mathsf{И}x.x \circledR X)$. Then $P \in [\![\mathsf{H}x.X]\!]_{v[X\leftarrow\Phi]}$, and so $P \in [\![A \vee \mathsf{H}x.X]\!]_{v[X\leftarrow\Phi]}$. We conclude $P \in \Phi$, also in this case. Hence $\Psi \subseteq [\![\mu X.(A \vee \mathsf{H}x.X)]\!]_v$.

Finally, to show $[\![\mu X.(A \vee \mathsf{H}x.X)]\!]_v \subseteq \Psi$, it suffices to verify the inclusion $[\![A \vee \mathsf{H}x.X]\!]_{v[X\leftarrow\Psi]} \subseteq \Psi$. If $P \in [\![A \vee \mathsf{H}x.X]\!]_{v[X\leftarrow\Psi]}$ then either $P \in [\![A]\!]_v$ and thus $P \in \Psi$, or $P \equiv (\nu n)P'$ where $P' \in \Psi$ and $n \notin fn^v(A) \cup fn(P)$. In the last case, is also immediate that $P \in \Psi$. We conclude $\Psi = [\![\mu X.(A \vee \mathsf{H}x.X)]\!]_v$.

A process P satisfies $\diamondsuit A$ if somewhere inside P, possibly under some restricted names, there is a component satisfying A. In a similar way, a process satisfies $\boldsymbol{inside}^{\forall}$ A if and only if for all names $n_1, \ldots, n_k$ fresh w.r.t. A, and processes Q such that $P \equiv (\nu n_1)\cdots(\nu n_k)Q$, Q satisfies A. A process P satisfies $\boxtimes\, A$ if and only if all components of P, regardless of the local name context in which they are placed, satisfy A. For example, a process P satisfies the closed formula $\boxtimes \neg\exists x.\exists y.x\langle y\rangle$ if and only if it contains no unguarded messages. Thus the formula $\boxtimes \neg\exists x.\exists y.x\langle y\rangle \Rightarrow \boxdot\mathsf{F}$, asserting that every process without unguarded messages is bound to inactivity, is logically valid.

For an example of a property making use of several of the spatial and temporal modalities consider

$$\begin{array}{l} \mathit{Member}(x) \triangleq \copyright x \wedge \forall y.(y\langle x\rangle|\mathsf{T} \Rightarrow y = x) \\ \mathit{Group} \triangleq \Box\mathsf{H}x.(\boldsymbol{group}\ \mathit{Member}(x)) \end{array}$$

A process satisfies *Group* if all of its future states will always be composed by a group of processes sharing a secret x, and such that each member of the group is unable to send x on a public channel.

8 Conclusions

We have investigated the satisfaction relation for a logic of concurrent processes that includes spatial operators, freshness quantifiers, and recursive formulas. In particular, we have shown how coinductively defined logical properties including freshness quantification can be given a semantics in terms of maximal fixpoints in a complete lattice of finitely supported sets of processes.

The logical rules arising from such a satisfaction relation will be investigated in Part II of this paper. Several interesting logical properties have already been discussed with respect to this model.

Some properties of the logic are very sensitive to the formulation of structural congruence (in fact, Sangiorgi has shown that the process equivalence induced by a similar logic is essentially structural congruence [17]). There is always a tension between embedding an expected process equivalence into the definition of structural congruence, or leaving it as a derived behavioral equivalence. Some desired logical properties have provided new insights into this delicate balance.

The general structure of our definitions can be easily adapted to various process calculi, and is also largely independent from the details of the operational semantics. Although the semantics considered here is based on unlabeled transition systems, it could be extended in a natural way to labeled transition systems, motivating then the introduction of Hennessy-Milner-like "labeled" modalities into the spatial logic. Nevertheless, some basic features of what a formula denotes, namely closure under structural congruence and finite support, should be expected to hold in all variations.

In conclusion, the general term of "spatial logic" has a fairly well defined, though informal, meaning. A spatial logic is a very intensional logic, that talks about fine details of process structure. This is what is required if we want to meaningfully describe the distribution of processes and the use of resources over a network.

Acknowledgments Andy Gordon contributed to the early stages of this paper. Thanks also to Giorgio Ghelli and Philippa Gardner for related discussions. Caires acknowledges the support of Microsoft Research for a visit to the Cambridge Lab during the time we worked on this paper.

References

1. G. Boudol. Asynchrony and the π-calculus (note). Rapport de Recherche 1702, INRIA Sofia-Antipolis, May 1992.
2. L. Caires. *A Model for Declarative Programming and Specification with Concurrency and Mobility.* PhD thesis, Departamento de Informática, Faculdade de Ciências e Tecnologia, Universidade Nova de Lisboa, 1999.
3. L. Caires and L. Monteiro. Verifiable and Executable Specifications of Concurrent Objects in $\mathcal{L}_\pi$. In C. Hankin, editor, *Programming Languages and Systems: Proceedings of the 7th European Symposium on Programming (ESOP 1998)*, number 1381 in Lecture Notes in Computer Science, pages 42–56. Springer-Verlag, 1998.

4. L. Cardelli and G. Ghelli. A Query Language Based on the Ambient Logic. In David Sands, editor, *Programming Languages and Systems: Proceedings of the 10th European Symposium on Programming (ESOP 2001)*, volume 2028 of *Lecture Notes in Computer Science*, pages 1–22. Springer-Verlag, 2001.
5. L. Cardelli and A. D. Gordon. Anytime, Anywhere. Modal Logics for Mobile Ambients. In *27th ACM Symposium on Principles of Programming Languages*, pages 365–377. ACM, 2000.
6. L. Cardelli and A. D. Gordon. Logical Properties of Name Restriction. In S. Abramsky, editor, *Typed Lambda Calculi and Applications*, number 2044 in Lecture Notes in Computer Science. Springer-Verlag, 2001.
7. W. Charatonik and J.-M. Talbot. The decidability of model checking mobile ambients. In *Proceedings of the 15th Annual Conference of the European Association for Computer Science Logic*, Lecture Notes in Computer Science. Springer-Verlag, 2001. To appear.
8. S. Dal-Zilio. Spatial Congruence for Ambients is Decidable. In *Proceedings of ASIAN'00 — 6th Asian Computing Science Conference*, number 1961 in Lecture Notes in Computer Science, pages 365–377. Springer-Verlag, 2000.
9. M. Dam. Relevance Logic and Concurrent Composition. In *Proceedings, Third Annual Symposium on Logic in Computer Science*, pages 178–185, Edinburgh, Scotland, 5–8 July 1988. IEEE Computer Society.
10. J. Engelfriet and Tj. Gelsema. A Multiset Semantics for the π-calculus with Replication. *Theoretical Computer Science*, (152):311–337, 1999.
11. M. J. Gabbay and A. M. Pitts. A New Approach to Abstract Syntax Involving Binders. In *14th Annual Symposium on Logic in Computer Science*, pages 214–224. IEEE Computer Society Press, Washington, 1999.
12. P. Gardner. From Process Calculi to Process Frameworks. In Catuscia Palamidessi, editor, *CONCUR 2000: Concurrency Theory (11th International Conference, University Park, PA, USA)*, volume 1877 of *Lecture Notes in Computer Science*, pages 69–88. Springer, August 2000.
13. M. Hennessy and R. Milner. Algebraic laws for Nondeterminism and Concurrency. *JACM*, 32(1):137–161, 1985.
14. K. Honda and M. Tokoro. On Asynchronous Communication Semantics. In M. Tokoro, O. Nierstrasz, and P. Wegner, editors, *Object-Based Concurrent Computing 1991*, number 612 in Lecture Notes in Computer Science, pages 21–51. Springer-Verlag, 1992.
15. D. Kozen. Results on the Propositional μ-Calculus. *TCS*, 27(3):333–354, 1983.
16. R. Milner. *Communicating and Mobile Systems: the π-calculus.* Cambridge University Press, 1999.
17. D. Sangiorgi. Extensionality and Intensionality of the Ambient Logics. In *28th Annual Symposium on Principles of Programming Languages*, pages 4–13. ACM, 2001.

Appendix (Proofs)

Lemma 4.2 For all finite $N \subseteq \Lambda$,

1. If $N \subseteq N'$ then $\mathbb{P}_N \subseteq \mathbb{P}_{N'}$.
2. (Bottom and Top) $\emptyset \in \mathbb{P}_N$ and $\mathcal{P} \in \mathbb{P}_N$.
3. (Meet and Join) If $S \subseteq \mathbb{P}_N$ then $\bigcap S \in \mathbb{P}_N$ and $\bigcup S \in \mathbb{P}_N$.
4. (Inverse) If $\Psi \in \mathbb{P}_N$ then $\overline{\Psi} = \mathcal{P} \setminus \Psi \in \mathbb{P}_N$.

Proof. 1. Pick $\Psi \in \mathbb{P}_N$. Now, Ψ is closed under $\equiv$; we must just verify that Ψ is supported by N'. Pick $m, n \notin N'$. Since $N \subseteq N'$, we have $m, n \notin N$. Therefore, since $\Psi \in \mathbb{P}_N$, for all $P \in \Psi$, we have $P\{m\leftrightarrow n\} \in \Psi$. Thus $\Psi \in \mathbb{P}_{N'}$.

2. Immediate.
3. Let $S \subseteq \mathbb{P}_N$.
   (a) Pick $P \in \bigcap S$. Then, for all $\Psi \in S$, we have $P \in \Psi$ and $\Psi \in \mathbb{P}_N$. Now, if $Q \equiv P$, then $Q \in \Psi$, for all $\Psi \in S$. Thus $Q \in \bigcap S$. Now let $m, n \notin N$. We have $P\{m\leftrightarrow n\} \in \Psi$, for all $\Psi \in S$. Hence $P\{m\leftrightarrow n\} \in \bigcap S$. We conclude $\bigcap S \in \mathbb{P}_N$.
4. Pick $P \in \bigcup S$. Then, there is $\Psi \in S$ such that $P \in \Psi$ and $\Psi \in \mathbb{P}_N$. Thus, if $Q \equiv P$, then $Q \in \Psi \subseteq \bigcup S$. Now let $m, n \notin N$. Then, $P\{m\leftrightarrow n\} \in \Psi \subseteq \bigcup S$. Hence $\bigcup S \in \mathbb{P}_N$.
5. Assume $\Psi \in \mathbb{P}_N$. Pick $P \in \overline{\Psi}$. Let $Q \equiv P$ and suppose $Q \notin \overline{\Psi}$. Then $Q \in \Psi$ and $P \in \Psi$, contradiction. Hence $Q \in \overline{\Psi}$. Likewise, pick $m, n \notin N$ and suppose $P\{m\leftrightarrow n\} \notin \overline{\Psi}$. Then $P\{m\leftrightarrow n\} \in \Psi$, and this implies $P \in \Psi$, a contradiction. Hence we must have $P\{m\leftrightarrow n\} \in \overline{\Psi}$. We conclude $\overline{\Psi} \in \mathbb{P}_N$.

Lemma 4.7 We have

1. For any process P and Pset Ψ, $P \in \tau(\Psi)$ if and only if $\tau(P) \in \Psi$.
2. $\Psi \in \mathbb{P}_N$ if and only if $\tau(\Psi) \in \mathbb{P}_{\tau(N)}$.
3. If $m, n \notin N$ and $\Psi \in \mathbb{P}_N$ then $\{m\leftrightarrow n\}(\Psi) = \Psi$.

Proof. 1. Let $P \in \tau(\Psi)$. Then there is $Q \in \Psi$ with $\tau(Q) = P$. Thus $Q \equiv \tau(P)$. Since Ψ is closed under $\equiv$, $\tau(P) \in \Psi$.

2. Assume $\Psi \in \mathbb{P}_N$. Pick $P \in \tau(\Psi)$. We have $P = \tau(Q)$ for some $Q \in \Psi$. Pick $R \equiv P$. Hence we have $\tau(R) \equiv Q$, and thus $\tau(R) \in \Psi$, by closure under $\equiv$ of Ψ. Therefore $R \in \tau(\Psi)$, and we conclude that $\tau(\Psi)$ is closed under $\equiv$. Now, pick $m, n \notin \tau(N)$, and let $\tau' = \{m\leftrightarrow n\}$. We have $\tau(m), \tau(n) \notin N$. Thus $\{\tau(m)\leftrightarrow\tau(n)\}(Q) \in \Psi$. This implies $\tau(\{\tau(m)\leftrightarrow\tau(n)\}(Q)) \in \tau(\Psi)$. But $\tau(\{\tau(m)\leftrightarrow\tau(n)\}(Q)) \equiv \{m\leftrightarrow n\}(\tau(Q)) \equiv \tau'(P)$, by Proposition 2.4(2). Hence $\tau'(P) \in \tau(\Psi)$.
   We conclude $\tau(\Psi) \in \mathbb{P}_{\tau(N)}$.
3. Assume $P \in \Psi \in \mathbb{P}_N$. Then $\{m\leftrightarrow n\}(P) \in \Psi$, and thus $P \in \{m\leftrightarrow m\}(\Psi)$. On the other hand, if $P \in \{m\leftrightarrow m\}(\Psi)$ then there is $Q \in \Psi$ such that $P = \{m\leftrightarrow m\}(Q)$. But $\{m\leftrightarrow m\}(Q) \in \Psi$, so $P \in \Psi$.

Lemma 4.11 If $\Phi \in \mathbb{P}_M$ and N is a finite set of names, $Cl(\Phi, N) \in \mathbb{P}_N$.

Proof. If $Q \in Cl(\Phi, N)$ then $Q \in \pi(\Phi)$ for some $\pi \in \Pi_N$. By Lemma 4.7(2), $\pi(\Phi)$ is a Pset, hence closed under structural congruence. Moreover, if we pick $n, m \notin N$ and let $\tau = \{n\leftrightarrow m\}$, then $\tau(Q) \in \tau(\pi(\Phi)) \subseteq Cl(\Phi, N)$. Hence $Cl(\Phi, N) \in \mathbb{P}_N$.

Proposition 4.6 For all finite $N \subseteq \Lambda$, $(\mathbb{P}_N, \subseteq, \bigcup, \otimes, \mathbf{1})$ is a commutative quantale.

Proof. We first verify that $(\mathbb{P}_N, \otimes, \mathbf{1})$ is a commutative monoid.

First, note that $\mathbf{1}$ is closed under $\equiv$ by definition. Moreover, for any $P \in \mathbf{1}$ and transposition τ, we have $\tau(P) \equiv \tau(\mathbf{0}) \equiv \mathbf{0}$. Hence, $\tau(P) \in \mathbf{1}$, for any transposition τ. We conclude that $\mathbf{1} \in \mathbb{P}_N$.

To verify that $\otimes$ is a binary operation on $\mathbb{P}_N$, pick any Ψ and Φ in $\mathbb{P}_N$, and some $P \in \Psi \otimes \Phi$. If $P' \equiv P$ then $P' \equiv Q|R$ where $Q \in \Psi$ and $R \in \Psi$. Hence $P' \in \Psi \otimes \Phi$. Moreover, if $m, n \notin N$ and $\tau = \{m \leftrightarrow n\}$, then $\tau(P) \equiv \tau(Q|R) \equiv \tau(Q)|\tau(R)$. Since $\tau(Q) \in \Psi$ and $\tau(R) \in \Phi$, we conclude $\tau(P) \in \Psi \otimes \Phi$. Now, from simple properties of structural congruence it follows that $\otimes$ is commutative, associative, and has unit $\mathbf{1}$.

Since $(\mathbb{P}_N, \subseteq, \cup, \cap)$ is a complete lattice, and thus closed under arbitrary joins, it remains to verify that $\otimes$ distributes over arbitrary joins, that is $\Psi \otimes \bigcup S = \bigcup\{\Psi \otimes \Phi \mid \Phi \in S\}$, for any $S \subseteq \mathbb{P}_N$. But this is an immediate consequence of the definition of $\otimes$.

Proposition 4.9 Let $\Phi \in \mathbb{P}_N$ then

1. There is a least set of names $supp(\Phi)$ such that $\Phi \in \mathbb{P}_{supp(\Phi)}$.
2. For any transposition τ, if $supp(\Phi) = M$ then $supp(\tau(\Phi)) = \tau(M)$.

Proof. (1) See [11].

(2) Let τ be a transposition, Φ be a Pset and assume $supp(\Phi) = M$. This means that $\Phi \in \mathbb{P}_M$ and for all N such that $\Phi \in \mathbb{P}_N$ we have $M \subseteq N$. To verify that $supp(\tau(\Phi)) = \tau(M)$ we need to show $\tau(\Phi) \in \mathbb{P}_{\tau(M)}$ (which holds by Lemma 4.7(2)) and that for all finite M' such $\tau(\Phi) \in \mathbb{P}_{M'}$ we have $\tau(M) \subseteq M'$. So, take a finite set of names M' and assume $\tau(\Phi) \in \mathbb{P}_{M'}$. Thus $\Phi \in \mathbb{P}_{\tau(M')}$, by Lemma 4.7(2). By assumption, we conclude $M \subseteq \tau(M')$. But then $\tau(M) \subseteq M'$ (for τ is an bijective mapping $\wp_{fin}(\Lambda) \rightarrow \wp_{fin}(\Lambda)$), and we are done.

Lemma 4.17 For any formula A, valuation v and transposition τ

1. If $\tau = \{m \leftrightarrow n\}$ and $m, n \notin fn(v)$ then $[\![A]\!]_v = [\![A]\!]_{\tau(v)}$.
2. $\tau(fn^v(A)) = fn^{\tau(v)}(\tau(A))$.
3. Let $fn^v(\boldsymbol{\nu} X.A) \subseteq M$.
   Then $fn^v(\boldsymbol{\nu} X.A) \subseteq fn^{v[X \leftarrow \Psi]}(A) \subseteq M$, for all $\Psi \in \mathbb{P}_M$.

Proof. (1) For any $X \in \mathfrak{D}(v)$ we have $m, n \notin supp(v(X))$ and $v(X) \in \mathbb{P}_{supp(v(X))}$. Thus $\tau(supp(X)) = supp(X)$ by Lemma 4.7(3). Hence $\tau(v) = v$.

(2) By induction on the size of the formula A. If A is $\mathbf{0}$ or $\mathtt{F}$ the result is immediate. If A is $B \Box C$, for a binary connective $\Box$ (eg. $A \wedge B$, $A|B$) we have

$$\tau(fn^v(B \Box C)) = \tau(fn^v(B) \cup fn^v(C)) =$$
$$\tau(fn^v(B)) \cup \tau(fn^v(C)) = fn^{\tau(v)}(\tau(B)) \cup fn^{\tau(v)}(\tau(C)) = fn^{\tau(v)}(\tau(B \Box C))$$

where the second equality results from τ being a bijection, and the third from the induction hypothesis. The cases for unary connectives (eg. $\Diamond B$), indexed connectives ($n®B$ and $B \oslash n$) and quantifiers ($\forall x.B$, $\text{И}x.B$) are handled in a similar way. If A is a variable X then $\tau(\mathit{fn}^v(X)) = \tau(\mathit{supp}(v(X))) = \mathit{supp}(\tau(v(X))) = \mathit{fn}^{\tau(v)}(X) = \mathit{fn}^{\tau(v)}(\tau(X))$. If A is $\boldsymbol{\nu}X.B$ then

$$\tau(\mathit{fn}^v(\boldsymbol{\nu}X.B)) = \tau(\mathit{fn}^{v[X\leftarrow\emptyset]}(B)) = \mathit{fn}^{\tau(v)[X\leftarrow\emptyset]}(\tau(B)) = \mathit{fn}^{\tau(v)}(\tau(\boldsymbol{\nu}X.B))$$

(3) Let $N = \mathit{fn}^v(\boldsymbol{\nu}X.A) = \mathit{fn}^{v[X\leftarrow\emptyset]}(A) \subseteq M$. We have

$$\begin{aligned} N = \mathit{fn}(\boldsymbol{\nu}X.A) \cup \bigcup\{\mathit{supp}(v(Y)) \mid Y \in \mathit{fpv}(A)\} = \\ \mathit{fn}(A) \cup \bigcup\{\mathit{supp}(v(Y)) \mid Y \in \mathit{fpv}(A) \setminus \{X\}\} \end{aligned}$$

Now, for any $\Psi \in \mathbb{P}_M$ we have $\mathit{supp}(\Psi) \subseteq M$. Hence

$$\begin{aligned} &N \subseteq \mathit{fn}(A) \cup \bigcup\{\mathit{supp}(v(Y)) \mid Y \in \mathit{fpv}(A) \setminus \{X\}\} \cup \mathit{supp}(\Psi) = \\ &\mathit{fn}^{v[X\leftarrow\Psi]}(A) \subseteq N \cup M \subseteq M \end{aligned}$$

(since $N \subseteq M$).

Theorem 4.18 For any formula A and valuation v

1. $[\![A]\!]_v \in \mathbb{P}_{\mathit{fn}^v(A)}$.
2. For all transpositions τ, $\tau([\![A]\!]_v) = [\![\tau(A)]\!]_{\tau(v)}$.
3. If $X \notin \mathrm{Neg}(A)$ and $\Psi \subseteq \Phi$ then $[\![A]\!]_{v[X\leftarrow\Psi]} \subseteq [\![A]\!]_{v[X\leftarrow\Phi]}$.
4. If $X \notin \mathrm{Pos}(A)$ and $\Psi \subseteq \Phi$ then $[\![A]\!]_{v[X\leftarrow\Phi]} \subseteq [\![A]\!]_{v[X\leftarrow\Psi]}$.

Proof. The proof of (1—4) proceeds by mutual induction on the size of the formula A. Note that the size of a formula does not change when replacing names and variables for names. All induction hypotheses are interdependent in the cases for $\text{И}x.B$ and $\boldsymbol{\nu}X.B$. Instead of the equality presented in (2) we prove that $\tau([\![A]\!]_v) \subseteq [\![\tau(A)]\!]_{\tau(v)}$. From this fact, the equality immediately follows. Indeed, if $P \in [\![\tau(A)]\!]_{\tau(v)}$, we have $\tau(P) \in \tau([\![\tau(A)]\!]_{\tau(v)}) \subseteq [\![A]\!]_v$, and then $P \in \tau([\![A]\!]_v)$.

- Case $A = \mathbf{F}$
  (1) Clearly $[\![\mathbf{F}]\!]_v = \emptyset \in \mathcal{P}_{\mathit{fn}^v(\mathbf{F})}$.
  (2) Trivial, since $\tau([\![\mathbf{F}]\!]_v) = \tau(\emptyset) = \emptyset$.
  (3—4) Immediate.
- Case $A = B \wedge C$.
  (1) Then $[\![B \wedge C]\!]_v = [\![B]\!]_v \cap [\![C]\!]_v$.
  By induction hypothesis (1) and Lemma 4.2(1) both $[\![B]\!]_v$ and $[\![C]\!]_v$ belong to $\mathcal{P}_{\mathit{fn}^v(A)}$. We conclude by Lemma 4.2(3).
  (2) Let τ be a transposition. If $P \in \tau([\![A \wedge B]\!]_v)$ then there is P' such that $P = \tau(P')$ with $P' \in [\![A]\!]_v$ and $P' \in [\![B]\!]_v$. Then $P \in \tau([\![A]\!]_v)$ and $P \in \tau([\![B]\!]_v)$. By induction hypothesis (2), $P \in [\![\tau(A)]\!]_{\tau(v)}$ and $P \in [\![\tau(B)]\!]_{\tau(v)}$. Hence, $P \in [\![\tau(A \wedge B)]\!]_{\tau(v)}$.
  (3—4) Immediate.

- Case $A = B \Rightarrow C$.
  (1) Pick $P \in [\![B \Rightarrow C]\!]_v$. Therefore, if $P \in [\![B]\!]_v$ then $P \in [\![C]\!]_v$. By induction hypothesis (1), $[\![B]\!]_v \in \mathbb{P}_{fn^v(B)}$ and $[\![C]\!]_v \in \mathbb{P}_{fn^v(C)}$.
  Pick any $Q \equiv P$. Assume $Q \in [\![B]\!]_v$. Then $P \in [\![B]\!]_v$ and thus $P \in [\![C]\!]_v$. Hence $Q \in [\![C]\!]_v$, and we conclude $Q \in [\![B \Rightarrow C]\!]_v$.
  Now pick $m, n \notin fn^v(B \Rightarrow C)$ and let $\tau = \{m \leftrightarrow n\}$. We have, $m, n \notin fn^v(B)$ and $m, n \notin fn^v(C)$. Assume $\tau(P) \in [\![B]\!]_v$. Thus $P \in [\![B]\!]_v$ by induction hypothesis (1). Then $P \in [\![C]\!]_v$ and by induction hypothesis (1) again $\tau(P) \in [\![C]\!]_v$. Hence $\tau(P) \in [\![B \Rightarrow C]\!]_v$.
  (2) Let τ be a transposition. Pick $P \in \tau([\![B \Rightarrow C]\!]_v)$. Then, $\tau(P) \in [\![B]\!]_v$ implies $\tau(P) \in [\![C]\!]_v$. Assume $P \in [\![\tau(B)]\!]_{\tau(v)}$. By induction hypothesis (2), we conclude $\tau(P) \in [\![B]\!]_v$. Then, $\tau(P) \in [\![C]\!]_v$. By induction hypothesis (2) again, $P \in [\![\tau(C)]\!]_{\tau(v)}$. Therefore $P \in [\![\tau(B \Rightarrow C)]\!]_{\tau(v)}$.
  (3) Then $X \notin \mathrm{Neg}(C)$ and $X \notin \mathrm{Pos}(B)$. Assume $P \in [\![B \Rightarrow C]\!]_{v[X \leftarrow \Psi]}$. This implies that if $P \in [\![B]\!]_{v[X \leftarrow \Psi]}$ then $P \in [\![C]\!]_{v[X \leftarrow \Psi]}$. Assume $P \in [\![B]\!]_{v[X \leftarrow \Phi]}$. Since $X \notin \mathrm{Pos}(B)$, by induction hypothesis (4), $P \in [\![B]\!]_{v[X \leftarrow \Psi]}$. Then $P \in [\![C]\!]_{v[X \leftarrow \Psi]}$. By induction hypothesis (3), $P \in [\![C]\!]_{v[X \leftarrow \Phi]}$. Hence $P \in [\![B \Rightarrow C]\!]_{v[X \leftarrow \Phi]}$.
  (4) Symmetric to (3).
- Case $A = \mathbf{0}$.
  (1) $[\![\mathbf{0}]\!]_v = \mathbf{1} \in \mathbb{P}_{fn^v(\mathbf{0})} = \mathbb{P}_\emptyset$ by Proposition 4.6.
  (2) Let τ be a transposition. Pick $P \in \tau([\![\mathbf{0}]\!]_v)$. Then $\tau(P) \equiv \mathbf{0}$ and $P \equiv \mathbf{0}$. So $P \in [\![\tau(\mathbf{0})]\!]_{\tau(v)} = \mathbf{1}$.
  (3—4) Immediate.
- Case $A = B|C$.
  (1) By induction hypothesis (1) and Lemma 4.2(1) we have $[\![B]\!]_v \in \mathbb{P}_{fn^v(B)} \subseteq \mathbb{P}_{fn^v(B|C)}$. Likewise we conclude $[\![C]\!]_v \in \mathbb{P}_{fn^v(B|C)}$.
  By Proposition 4.6, $[\![B|C]\!]_v = [\![B]\!]_v \otimes [\![C]\!]_v \in \mathbb{P}_{fn^v(B|C)}$.
  (2) Let τ be a transposition. Pick $P \in \tau([\![B|C]\!]_v)$. Hence $\tau(P) \equiv Q'|Q''$ with $Q' \in [\![B]\!]_v$ and $Q'' \in [\![C]\!]_v$, for some Q' and Q''. Then $\tau(Q') \in \tau([\![B]\!]_v)$, and $\tau(Q') \in [\![\tau(B)]\!]_{\tau(v)}$, by induction hypothesis (2). Likewise, $\tau(Q'') \in [\![\tau(C)]\!]_{\tau(v)}$. Hence $\tau(Q'|Q'') \in [\![\tau(B|C)]\!]_{\tau(v)}$. To conclude, just note that $P \equiv \tau(Q'|Q'')$.
  (3—4) Like (Case $A = B \wedge C$) above.
- Case $A = B \triangleright C$.
  (1) Pick $P \in [\![B \triangleright C]\!]_v$. Then, for all $Q \in [\![B]\!]_v$, we have $Q|P \in [\![C]\!]_v$. Pick any $P' \equiv P$, and any $Q' \in [\![B]\!]_v$. We have $Q'|P' \equiv Q'|P$. By assumption, $Q'|P \in [\![C]\!]_v$, and, by induction hypothesis (1), $Q'|P' \in [\![C]\!]_v$. Hence $P' \in [\![B \triangleright C]\!]_v$.
  Pick $m, n \notin fn^v(B \triangleright C)$ and let $\tau = \{m \leftrightarrow n\}$. Then $m, n \notin fn^v(B)$ and $m, n \notin fn^v(C)$. Now, pick any Q' such that $Q' \in [\![B]\!]_v$. By induction hypothesis (1), $\tau(Q') \in [\![B]\!]_v$. Therefore $\tau(Q')|P \in [\![C]\!]_v$. By induction hypothesis (1) and Proposition 2.12(3), $\tau(\tau(Q')|P) \equiv Q'|\tau(P) \in [\![C]\!]_v$. Hence $\tau(P) \in [\![B \triangleright C]\!]_v$.
  (2) Let τ be a transposition. Pick $P \in \tau([\![B \triangleright C]\!]_v)$. Then there is $P' \equiv \tau(P)$ such that for all $Q \in [\![B]\!]_v$, we have $Q|P' \in [\![C]\!]_v$. Pick any $Q' \in [\![\tau(B)]\!]_{\tau(v)}$. Then $\tau(Q') \in \tau([\![\tau(B)]\!]_{\tau(v)})$. By induction hypothesis (2), $\tau(Q') \in [\![B]\!]_v$.

Then $\tau(Q')|\tau(P) \in [\![C]\!]_v$. So, $Q'|P \in \tau([\![C]\!]_v)$. By induction hypothesis (2), $Q'|P \in [\![\tau(C)]\!]_{\tau(v)}$. Hence $P \in [\![\tau(B \triangleright C)]\!]_{\tau(v)}$.
(3—4) Like (Case $A = B \Rightarrow C$) above.

- Case $A = q®B$.
(1) Pick any $P \in [\![q®B]\!]_v$. Then $P \equiv (\boldsymbol{\nu} q)Q$ and $Q \in [\![B]\!]_v$. Pick any $P' \equiv P$, we have $P' \equiv (\boldsymbol{\nu} q)Q$, and thus $P' \in [\![q®B]\!]_v$. Pick $m, n \notin fn^v(q®B)$ and let $\tau = \{m \leftrightarrow n\}$. Then $m, n \notin fn^v(B)$, $m \neq q$ and $n \neq q$. Hence $\tau(P) \equiv (\boldsymbol{\nu} q)\tau(Q)$, by Proposition 2.12(3). By induction hypothesis (1), we have $\tau(Q) \in [\![B]\!]_v$. So $\tau(P) \in [\![q®B]\!]_v$.
(2) Let τ be a transposition. Pick $P \in \tau([\![q®B]\!]_v)$. Then there is $P' = \tau(P)$ such that $P' \equiv (\boldsymbol{\nu} q)Q$ and $Q \in [\![B]\!]_v$. We have $\tau(P') \equiv (\boldsymbol{\nu}\tau(q))\tau(Q)$, by Lemma 2.8(1). By induction hypothesis (2), we have $\tau(Q) \in [\![\tau(B)]\!]_{\tau(v)}$. Hence $P = \tau(P') \in [\![\tau(q)®\tau(B)]\!]_{\tau(v)} = [\![\tau(q®B)]\!]_{\tau(v)}$.
(3) Then $X \notin \mathrm{Pos}(B)$. Assume $P \in [\![q®B]\!]_{v[X\leftarrow\Psi]}$. Then $P \equiv (\boldsymbol{\nu} q)Q$ and $Q \in [\![B]\!]_{v[X\leftarrow\Psi]}$. By induction hypothesis (3), $Q \in [\![B]\!]_{v[X\leftarrow\Phi]}$. Hence $P \in [\![q®B]\!]_{v[X\leftarrow\Phi]}$.
(4) Symmetrical.

- Case $A = B\oslash q$.
(1) Pick any $P \in [\![B\oslash q]\!]_v$. Then $(\boldsymbol{\nu} q)P \in [\![B]\!]_v$. Pick any $P' \equiv P$, we have $(\boldsymbol{\nu} q)P' \equiv (\boldsymbol{\nu} q)P$, and thus, by induction hypothesis (1), $(\boldsymbol{\nu} q)P' \in [\![B]\!]_v$. Therefore, $P' \in [\![B\oslash q]\!]_v$. Pick $m, n \notin fn^v(B\oslash q)$ and let $\tau = \{m \leftrightarrow n\}$. Then $m, n \notin fn^v(B)$, $m \neq q$ and $n \neq q$. By induction hypothesis (1), we have $\tau((\boldsymbol{\nu} q)P) \in [\![B]\!]_v$. Since $\tau((\boldsymbol{\nu} q)P) = (\boldsymbol{\nu} q)\tau(P)$, we have $\tau(P) \in [\![B\oslash q]\!]_v$.
(2) Let τ be a transposition. Pick $P \in \tau([\![B\oslash q]\!]_v)$. Then there is $P' = \tau(P)$ such that $(\boldsymbol{\nu} q)P' \in [\![B]\!]_v$. Then $\tau(P) \in [\![B\oslash q]\!]_v$, that is, $(\boldsymbol{\nu} q)\tau(P) \in [\![B]\!]_v$. Then $\tau((\boldsymbol{\nu} q)\tau(P) = (\boldsymbol{\nu}\tau(q))P \in \tau([\![B]\!]_v)$. By induction hypothesis (2), $(\boldsymbol{\nu}\tau(q))P \in [\![\tau(B)]\!]_{\tau(v)}$. Hence $P \in [\![\tau(B)\oslash\tau(q)]\!]_{\tau(v)} = [\![\tau(B\oslash q)]\!]_{\tau(v)}$.
(3—4) Like (Case $A = q®B$) above.

- Case $A = p\langle q\rangle$.
(1) We have $[\![p\langle q\rangle]\!]_v = \{P \mid P \equiv p\langle q\rangle\}$, which is closed under $\equiv$ by definition. Additionally, for all $m, n \notin \{p, q\}$, we have that $\{n \leftrightarrow m\}P \equiv p\langle q\rangle$ for all $P \equiv p\langle q\rangle$.
(2) Let $\tau = \{m \leftrightarrow n\}$. If $P \in \tau([\![p\langle q\rangle]\!]_v)$ then $\tau(P) \equiv p\langle q\rangle$, and $P \equiv \tau(p\langle q\rangle)$. It is clear that $P \in [\![\tau(p\langle q\rangle)]\!]_{\tau(v)}$.
(3—4) Immediate.

- Case $A = Ӏx.B$.
(1) Pick $P \in [\![Ӏx.B]\!]_v$. Then, there is q such that $q \notin fn^v(B) \cup fn(P)$ and $P \in [\![B\{x\leftarrow q\}]\!]_v$. Pick $Q \equiv P$, by induction hypothesis (1) also $Q \in [\![B\{x\leftarrow q\}]\!]_v$, and $q \notin fn(Q)$ by Proposition 2.12(1). Thus $Q \in [\![Ӏx.B]\!]_v$.
Now, pick $\tau = \{m \leftrightarrow n\}$ with $m, n \notin fn^v(Ӏx.B) = fn^v(B)$. Pick any $p \notin fn^v(B) \cup \{m, n, q\} \cup fn(P) \cup fn(\tau(P))$ and let $\tau' = \{q \leftrightarrow p\}$. By induction hypothesis (2), we have $\tau'(P) \in [\![\tau'(B\{x\leftarrow q\})]\!]_{\tau'(v)}$, that is $P \in [\![B\{x\leftarrow p\}]\!]_v$, by Lemma 4.7(3). By induction hypothesis (1), we conclude $\tau(P) \in [\![B\{x\leftarrow p\}]\!]_v$. Thus, $\tau(P) \in [\![Ӏx.B]\!]_v$, since $p \notin fn^v(B) \cup fn(\tau(P))$.
(2) Let $\tau = \{m \leftrightarrow n\}$. If $P \in \tau([\![Ӏx.B]\!]_v)$ then $\tau(P) \in [\![Ӏx.B]\!]_v$ and thus there is some $q \notin fn^v(B) \cup fn(\tau(P))$ such that $\tau(P) \in [\![B\{x\leftarrow q\}]\!]_v$.

Now, pick $p \notin \{m, n\} \cup fn(\tau(P)) \cup fn(P) \cup fn^v(B) \cup fn^{\tau(v)}(\tau(B))$ and let $\tau' = \{q \leftrightarrow p\}$. $\tau'(\tau(P)) = \tau(P) \in [\![\tau'(B\{x \leftarrow q\})]\!]_{\tau'(v)} = [\![B\{x \leftarrow p\}]\!]_{\tau'(v)}$.
By Remark 4.16 we have $[\![B\{x \leftarrow p\}]\!]_{\tau'(v)} = [\![B\{x \leftarrow p\}]\!]_{\tau'(w)}$, where w is the restriction of v to $fpv(B)$.
By Lemma 4.17(1) we have $[\![B\{x \leftarrow p\}]\!]_{\tau'(w)} = [\![B\{x \leftarrow p\}]\!]_w$, since $q, p \notin fn(w)$. So, $\tau(P) \in [\![B\{x \leftarrow p\}]\!]_w$.
By Remark 4.16, this implies $\tau(P) \in [\![B\{x \leftarrow p\}]\!]_v$.
But then $P \in [\![\tau(B)\{x \leftarrow p\}]\!]_{\tau(v)}$, by induction hypothesis (2). We conclude $P \in [\![\tau(\text{И}x.B)]\!]_{\tau(v)}$, since $p \notin fn^{\tau(v)}(\tau(B)) \cup fn(P)$.
(3) We have $X \notin \text{Neg}(B\{x \leftarrow n\})$, for all $n \in \Lambda$. Let $P \in [\![\text{И}x.B]\!]_{v[X \leftarrow \Psi]}$ and w be the restriction of v to the free propositional variables of $\text{И}x.B$ (we assume that $X \in fpv(A)$ otherwise the result is immediate).
By Remark 4.16, $P \in [\![\text{И}x.B]\!]_{w[X \leftarrow \Psi]}$. Then, there is q such that $q \notin fn^{w[X \leftarrow \Psi]}(B) \cup fn(P)$ and $P \in [\![B\{x \leftarrow q\}]\!]_{w[X \leftarrow \Psi]}$.
Now, pick $p \notin fn^{w[X \leftarrow \Psi]}(B) \cup fn(P) \cup fn^{w[X \leftarrow \Phi]}(B)$ and define $\tau = \{q \leftrightarrow p\}$. Note that $p, q \notin supp(\Psi) \cup fn(w)$. By induction hypothesis (2), we have $\tau(P) = P \in \tau([\![B\{x \leftarrow q\}]\!]_{w[X \leftarrow \Psi]}) \subseteq [\![B\{x \leftarrow p\}]\!]_{w[X \leftarrow \Psi]}$, since $\tau(\Psi) = \Psi$ and $\tau(w) = w$.
By induction hypothesis (3), $P \in [\![B\{x \leftarrow p\}]\!]_{w[X \leftarrow \Phi]}$.
But p was chosen such that $p \notin fn^{w[X \leftarrow \Phi]}(A)$, so $P \in [\![\text{И}x.B]\!]_{w[X \leftarrow \Phi]}$. This implies $P \in [\![\text{И}x.B]\!]_{v[X \leftarrow \Phi]}$, by Remark 4.16.
(4) Symmetrical.

– Case $A = \forall x.B$.
(1) Pick any $P \in [\![\forall x.B]\!]_v$. Then, for all $q \in \Lambda$, $P \in [\![B\{x \leftarrow q\}]\!]_v$.
Pick any $Q \equiv P$. For all $q \in \Lambda$, by induction hypothesis (1), $Q \in [\![B\{x \leftarrow q\}]\!]_v$. Therefore, $Q \in [\![\forall x.B]\!]_v$.
Pick $m, n \notin fn^v(\forall x.B) = fn^v(B)$ and let $\tau = \{m \leftrightarrow n\}$. We need to show that for all $q \in \Lambda$, $\tau(P) \in [\![B\{x \leftarrow q\}]\!]_v$.
For all $q \notin \{m, n\}$, by induction hypothesis (1) we have $\tau(P) \in [\![B\{x \leftarrow q\}]\!]_v$.
For $q = m$, we have $P \in [\![B\{x \leftarrow m\}]\!]_v$. Then $\tau(P) \in [\![B\{x \leftarrow n\}]\!]_{\tau(v)}$, by induction hypothesis (2).
Let w be the restriction of v to $fpv(B)$. Note that $m, n \notin fn(w)$, for if (say) $n \in fn(w)$, then $n \in supp(w(X))$ for some $X \in fpv(B)$, and we would have $n \in fn^w(B) = fn^v(B)$, a contradiction.
By Remark 4.16, $\tau(P) \in [\![B\{x \leftarrow n\}]\!]_{\tau(w)}$.
Since we have $m, n \notin fn(w)$, by Lemma 4.17(1) we conclude $[\![B\{x \leftarrow n\}]\!]_{\tau(w)} = [\![B\{x \leftarrow n\}]\!]_w$. By Remark 4.16, $[\![B\{x \leftarrow n\}]\!]_w = [\![B\{x \leftarrow n\}]\!]_v$ and then $\tau(P) \in [\![B\{x \leftarrow n\}]\!]_v$.
For $q = n$, we conclude $\tau(P) \in [\![B\{x \leftarrow m\}]\!]_v$ in a similar way.
Then $\tau(P) \in [\![B\{x \leftarrow q\}]\!]_v$, for all $q \in \Lambda$; this implies $\tau(P) \in [\![\forall x.B]\!]_v$.
(2) Let τ be a transposition. Pick $P \in \tau([\![\forall x.B]\!]_v)$. Then $\tau(P) \in [\![B\{x \leftarrow q\}]\!]_v$, for all $q \in \Lambda$.
By induction hypothesis (2), for all $q \in \Lambda$, $P \in [\![\tau(B)\{x \leftarrow \tau(q)\}]\!]_{\tau(v)}$. Then $P \in [\![\tau(B)\{x \leftarrow q\}]\!]_{\tau(v)}$, for all $q \in \Lambda$, since τ is a bijection $\Lambda \to \Lambda$. Therefore, $P \in [\![\tau(\forall x.B)]\!]_{\tau(v)}$.

(3) We have $X \notin \text{Neg}(B\{x \leftarrow n\})$, for all $n \in \Lambda$. Let $P \in [\![\forall x.B]\!]_{v[X \leftarrow \Psi]}$, that is, for all $n \in \Lambda$, $P \in [\![B\{x \leftarrow n\}]\!]_{v[X \leftarrow \Psi]}$. By induction hypothesis (3), for each $n \in \Lambda$, $P \in [\![B\{x \leftarrow n\}]\!]_{v[X \leftarrow \Phi]}$. Hence $P \in [\![\forall x.B]\!]_{v[X \leftarrow \Phi]}$.
(4) Symmetrical.

- Case $A = \Diamond B$.
(1) If $P \in [\![\Diamond B]\!]_v$ then there is R such that $P \to R$ and $R \in [\![B]\!]_v$. If $Q \equiv P$ then also $Q \to R$, so $Q \in [\![\Diamond B]\!]_v$. Now, pick $m, n \notin fn^v(\Diamond B) = fn^v(B)$, and let $\tau = \{m \leftrightarrow n\}$. By Proposition 2.15(2), $\tau(P) \to \tau(R)$. By induction hypothesis (1), $\tau(R) \in [\![B]\!]_v$. Hence $\tau(P) \in [\![\Diamond B]\!]_v$.
(2) Let τ be a transposition. If $P \in \tau([\![\Diamond B]\!]_v)$ then $\tau(P) \in [\![\Diamond B]\!]_v$. Thus there is Q such that $\tau(P) \to Q$ and $Q \in [\![B]\!]_v$. By Proposition 2.15(2), and induction hypothesis (2), $P \to \tau(Q)$ and $\tau(Q) \in [\![\tau(B)]\!]_{\tau(v)}$. Hence $P \in [\![\tau(\Diamond B)]\!]_{\tau(v)}$.
(3—4) Immediate, by the induction hypothesis.
- Case $A = Z$.
(1) We have $[\![Z]\!]_v = v(Z)$. Since $fn^v(Z) = supp(v(Z))$, we have that $[\![Z]\!]_v \in \mathbb{P}_{fn^v(Z)}$.
(2) Let τ be a transposition. If $P \in \tau([\![Z]\!]_v)$ then $\tau(P) \in v(Z)$. Therefore, $P \in \tau(v(Z)) = \tau(v)(Z) = [\![Z]\!]_{\tau(v)}$.
(3) The case $Z \neq X$ is trivial. If $Z = X$, the assumption yields $[\![X]\!]_{v[X \leftarrow \Psi]} = \Psi \subseteq \Phi = [\![X]\!]_{v[X \leftarrow \Phi]}$.
(4) $X \notin \text{Pos}(Z)$ implies $X \neq Z$, and we conclude.
- Case $A = \boldsymbol{\nu} Z.B$.
Let $M = fn^v(\boldsymbol{\nu} Z.B)$.
(1) We have $[\![\boldsymbol{\nu} Z.B]\!]_v = \bigcup\{\Psi \in \mathbb{P}_M \mid \Psi \subseteq [\![B]\!]_{v[Z \leftarrow \Psi]}\}$. Pick $\Psi \in \mathbb{P}_M$. Then $v[Z \leftarrow \Psi]$ is a valuation. By induction hypothesis (1), $[\![B]\!]_{v[Z \leftarrow \Psi]} \in \mathbb{P}_M$, since $fn^{v[Z \leftarrow \Psi]}(B) = M$ by Lemma 4.17(3). Hence

$$\mathfrak{G} \triangleq \boldsymbol{\lambda}\Psi.[\![B]\!]_{v[Z \leftarrow \Psi]}$$

is a mapping $\mathbb{P}_M \to \mathbb{P}_M$. By induction hypothesis (3), $\mathfrak{G}$ is monotonic. By Knaster-Tarski Lemma, it admits a greatest fixpoint $\mathcal{G} \in \mathbb{P}_M$ and $[\![\boldsymbol{\nu} Z.B]\!]_v = \mathcal{G}$.
(2) Let τ be a transposition.
We must show $\tau([\![\boldsymbol{\nu} Z.B]\!]_v) \subseteq [\![\boldsymbol{\nu} Z.\tau(B)]\!]_{\tau(v)}$. We claim that the right-hand side of this inclusion is the greatest fixpoint of the mapping

$$\mathfrak{T} \triangleq \boldsymbol{\lambda}\Phi.[\![\tau(B)]\!]_{\tau(v)[Z \leftarrow \Phi]}$$

To verify the claim, we start by showing that $\mathfrak{T}$ is a monotonic operator on $\mathbb{P}_{\tau(M)}$. Pick any $\Phi \in \mathbb{P}_{\tau(M)}$. By Lemma 4.7(2), we have $\tau(\Phi) \in \mathbb{P}_M$. As in subcase (1) above, we conclude that $v[Z \leftarrow \tau(\Phi)]$ is a valuation and that $[\![B]\!]_{v[Z \leftarrow \tau(\Phi)]} \in \mathbb{P}_M$. By induction hypothesis (2) $\tau([\![B]\!]_{v[Z \leftarrow \tau(\Phi)]}) \subseteq [\![\tau(B)]\!]_{\tau(v)[Z \leftarrow \Phi]}$, and $[\![\tau(B)]\!]_{\tau(v)[Z \leftarrow \Phi]} \in \mathbb{P}_{fn^{\tau(v)[Z \leftarrow \Phi]}(B)}$, by induction hypothesis (1). By Lemma 4.17(2—3), $fn^{\tau(v)[Z \leftarrow \Phi]}(\tau(B)) = \tau(M)$.

So $[\![\tau(B)]\!]_{\tau(v)[Z\leftarrow\Phi]} \in \mathbb{P}_{\tau(M)}$ and we conclude that $\mathfrak{T}$ is indeed a mapping $\mathbb{P}_{\tau(M)} \to \mathbb{P}_{\tau(M)}$. Moreover, such operator is monotonic by induction hypothesis (3). Thus, by Knaster-Tarski Lemma, it admits a greatest fixpoint $\mathcal{T} \in \mathbb{P}_{\tau(M)}$ where $\mathcal{T}$ coincides with $[\![\boldsymbol{\nu} Z.\tau(B)]\!]_{\tau(v)}$, since by Lemma 4.17(2) $\tau(M) = fn^{\tau(v)}(\boldsymbol{\nu} Z.\tau(B))$. We have thus proved the claim.
To conclude, it remains to show $\tau(\mathcal{G}) \subseteq \mathcal{T}$ (we now use $\mathcal{G}$ and $\mathfrak{G}$, defined in subcase (1) above). Pick any $Q \in \tau(\mathcal{G}) = \tau(\mathfrak{G}(\mathcal{G})) = \tau([\![B]\!]_{v[Z\leftarrow\mathcal{G}]})$. By induction hypothesis (2), $Q \in [\![\tau(B)]\!]_{\tau(v[Z\mapsto\mathcal{G}])} = [\![\tau(B)]\!]_{\tau(v)[Z\mapsto\tau(\mathcal{G})]} = \mathfrak{T}(\tau(\mathcal{G}))$.
Hence $\tau(\mathcal{G}) \subseteq \mathfrak{T}(\tau(\mathcal{G}))$, that is $\tau(\mathcal{G})$ is a pre-fixpoint of $\mathfrak{T}$. Therefore, we conclude $\tau(\mathcal{G}) \subseteq \mathcal{T}$, by Knaster-Tarski Lemma.
(3) We have $Z \notin \mathrm{Neg}(B)$. By Lemma 4.15, we may assume $Z \neq X$. We need to show (†)

$$\bigcup\{\varphi \in \mathbb{P}_M \mid \varphi \subseteq [\![B]\!]_{v[X\leftarrow\Psi][Z\leftarrow\varphi]}\} \subseteq$$

$$\bigcup\{\varphi \in \mathbb{P}_{M'} \mid \varphi \subseteq [\![B]\!]_{v[X\leftarrow\Phi][Z\leftarrow\varphi]}\}$$

where $M = fn^{v[X\leftarrow\Psi]}(\boldsymbol{\nu} Z.B)$ and $M' = fn^{v[X\leftarrow\Phi]}(\boldsymbol{\nu} Z.B)$. To that end, pick any process P in the left-hand side of the inclusion (†). Then, there is $\varphi \in \mathbb{P}_M$ such that $P \in \varphi$ and $\varphi \subseteq [\![B]\!]_{v[X\leftarrow\Psi][Z\leftarrow\varphi]}$.
Now, define $\varphi^* \triangleq Cl(\varphi, M')$. We have $\varphi^* \in \mathbb{P}_{M'}$ by Lemma 4.11; we also have $\varphi \subseteq \varphi^*$, hence $P \in \varphi^*$. By induction hypothesis (3) (twice), we have $\varphi \subseteq [\![B]\!]_{v[X\leftarrow\Phi][Z\leftarrow\varphi^*]}$, since $Z \notin \mathrm{Neg}(B)$.
It remains to show $\varphi^* \subseteq [\![B]\!]_{v[X\leftarrow\Phi][Z\leftarrow\varphi^*]}$. Let w be the restriction of v to the free propositional variables of B. Then $[\![B]\!]_{v[X\leftarrow\Phi][Z\leftarrow\varphi^*]} = [\![B]\!]_{w[X\leftarrow\Phi][Z\leftarrow\varphi^*]}$ by Remark 4.16(1) (we assume $X \in fpv(B)$, for otherwise the result would be immediate).
Pick $Q \in \varphi^*$. By Definition 4.10 $Q = \pi(Q')$ for some $Q' \in \varphi$ and $\pi \in \Pi_{M'}$. Thus $\pi(Q') \in \pi([\![B]\!]_{w[X\leftarrow\Phi][Z\leftarrow\varphi^*]})$. By induction hypothesis (2), we have $\pi(Q') = Q \in [\![B]\!]_{w[X\leftarrow\Phi][Z\leftarrow\varphi^*]}$, since $\pi(B) = B$, $\pi(w) = w$, $\pi(\Phi) = \Phi$ (because $M' = fn^{w[X\leftarrow\Phi]}(\nu Z.B)$), and also $\pi(\varphi^*) = \varphi^*$.
Since by Remark 4.16 $[\![B]\!]_{v[X\leftarrow\Phi][Z\leftarrow\varphi^*]} = [\![B]\!]_{w[X\leftarrow\Phi][Z\leftarrow\varphi^*]}$, we conclude $\varphi^* \subseteq [\![B]\!]_{v[X\leftarrow\Phi][Z\leftarrow\varphi^*]}$. Hence φ^* is included on the right-hand side of (†). So P belongs to the right-hand side of (†) and we are done.
(4) Symmetrical.

Lemma 4.24 Let A be a formula and $v[X\leftarrow\Phi]$ a valuation for A such that $fn^v(\boldsymbol{\nu} X.A) \subseteq N \subseteq M$, $\Phi \subseteq [\![A]\!]_{v[X\leftarrow\Phi]}$ and $\Phi \in \mathbb{P}_M$.
Then $Cl(\Phi, N) \subseteq [\![A]\!]_{v[X\leftarrow Cl(\Phi,N)]}$.

Proof. By definition, we have $Cl(\Phi, N) \triangleq \bigcup_{\pi\in\Pi_N} \pi(\Phi)$ where Π_N is the set of all permutations that fix N. Note that any permutation in Π_N can be written as a composition of a finite number of transpositions $\{p\leftrightarrow q\}$ such that $p, q \notin N$.

We have $\Phi \subseteq Cl(\Phi, N)$ and $Cl(\Phi, N) \in \mathbb{P}_N$. Therefore, by Theorem 4.18(3), $[\![A]\!]_{v[X\leftarrow\Phi]} \subseteq [\![A]\!]_{v[X\leftarrow Cl(\Phi,N)]}$. We now prove $Cl(\Phi, N) \subseteq [\![A]\!]_{v[X\leftarrow Cl(\Phi,N)]}$.

Pick $P \in Cl(\Phi, N)$. Then $P = \pi(P')$ for some $P' \in \Phi$ and $\pi \in \Pi_N$. Let w be the restriction of v to the free propositional variables of $\boldsymbol{\nu} X.A$. By Remark 4.16

we have $\Phi \subseteq [\![A]\!]_{w[X \leftarrow Cl(\Phi,N)]}$. Note that for all $\pi \in \Pi_N$ we have $\pi(w) = w$ (since $fn^w(\boldsymbol{\nu}X.A) \subseteq N$), $\pi(A) = A$, and $\pi(Cl(\Phi, N)) = Cl(\Phi, N)$. Hence $P' \in [\![A]\!]_{w[X \leftarrow Cl(\Phi,N)]}$. But then, by Theorem 4.18(2) and Remark 4.16

$$\pi(P') = P \in \pi([\![A]\!]_{w[X \leftarrow Cl(\Phi,N)]}) = \\ [\![A]\!]_{\pi(w)[X \leftarrow \pi(Cl(\Phi^N,N))]} = [\![A]\!]_{w[X \leftarrow Cl(\Phi,N)]} = [\![A]\!]_{v[X \leftarrow Cl(\Phi,N)]}$$

We conclude $Cl(\Phi, N) \subseteq [\![A]\!]_{v[X \leftarrow Cl(\Phi,N)]}$.

Lemma 5.3 Let $[\![\theta(A)]\!]_v = [\![\theta(B)]\!]_v$ for all substitutions θ and valuations v, and let $F\{-\}$ be a context. Then, for all substitutions σ and valuations w we have $[\![\sigma(F\{A\})]\!]_w = [\![\sigma(F\{B\})]\!]_w$.

Proof. By induction on the size of the context $F\{-\}$.

- Case $F\{-\} = G\{-\} \Rightarrow H\{-\}$.
  By definition, $[\![\sigma(F\{A\})]\!]_w$ is the set of all processes Q such that if $Q \in [\![\sigma(G\{A\})]\!]_w$ then $Q \in [\![\sigma(H\{A\})]\!]_w$. By induction hypothesis, $[\![\sigma(G\{A\})]\!]_w = [\![\sigma(G\{B\})]\!]_w$ and $[\![\sigma(H\{A\})]\!]_w = [\![\sigma(H\{B\})]\!]_w$.
  Hence $[\![\sigma(F\{A\})]\!]_v = [\![\sigma(F\{B\})]\!]_v$.
- Cases $F\{-\} = G\{-\} \wedge H\{-\}$, $F\{-\} = G\{-\}|H\{-\}$, $F\{-\} = G\{-\} \triangleright H\{-\}$, $F\{-\} = \boxdot G\{-\}$, $F\{-\} = n \circledR G\{-\}$, and $F\{-\} = n \oslash G\{-\}$. By induction hypothesis, as above.
- Case $F\{-\} = \forall x.G\{-\}$. Assume $x \notin \mathfrak{D}(\sigma)$.
  We have $[\![\sigma(F\{A\})]\!]_w = \bigcap_{n \in \Lambda} [\![\sigma(G\{A\})\{x \leftarrow n\}]\!]_w$. By induction hypothesis, $[\![\sigma(G\{A\})\{x \leftarrow n\}]\!]_w = [\![\sigma(G\{B\})\{x \leftarrow n\}]\!]_w$, for all n.
  Therefore $\bigcap_{n \in \Lambda} [\![\sigma(G\{A\})\{x \leftarrow n\}]\!]_w = \bigcap_{n \in \Lambda} [\![\sigma(G\{B\})\{x \leftarrow n\}]\!]_w$.
  But $\bigcap_{n \in \Lambda} [\![\sigma(G\{B\})\{x \leftarrow n\}]\!]_w = [\![\sigma(F\{B\})]\!]_w$.
- Case $F\{-\} = \text{И}x.G\{-\}$. Assume $x \notin \mathfrak{D}(\sigma)$.
  (Left to right inclusion) Pick $P \in [\![\sigma(\text{И}x.G\{A\})]\!]_w$. Then there is $n \notin fn^w(\sigma(G\{A\})) \cup fn(P)$ such that $P \in [\![\sigma(G\{A\})\{x \leftarrow n\}]\!]_w$.
  Let $m \notin fn^w(\sigma(G\{A\})) \cup fn^w(\sigma(G\{B\})) \cup fn(P)$, let $\tau = \{m \leftrightarrow n\}$. Let u be the restriction of w to the free propositional variables of $G\{A\}$, we have $[\![\sigma(G\{A\})\{x \leftarrow n\}]\!]_w = [\![\sigma(G\{A\})\{x \leftarrow n\}]\!]_u$. By Theorem 4.18(2), $\tau(P) = P \in \tau([\![\sigma(G\{A\})\{x \leftarrow n\}]\!]_u) = [\![\sigma(G\{A\})\{x \leftarrow m\}]\!]_u = [\![\sigma(G\{A\})\{x \leftarrow m\}]\!]_w$.
  By the induction hypothesis we conclude $P \in [\![\sigma(G\{B\})\{x \leftarrow m\}]\!]_w$.
  Since $m \notin fn^w(\sigma(G\{B\}))$, we obtain $P \in [\![\sigma(F\{B\})]\!]_w$.
  (Right to left inclusion) Symmetrical.
- Case $F\{-\} = X$. Then $F\{A\} = X = F\{B\}$ and we have $[\![\sigma(F\{A\})]\!]_w = [\![\sigma(X)]\!]_w = w(X) = [\![\sigma(X)]\!]_w = [\![\sigma(F\{B\})]\!]_w$.
- Case $F\{-\} = \boldsymbol{\nu}Z.G\{-\}$.
  (Left to right inclusion) Take $P \in [\![\sigma(\boldsymbol{\nu}Z.G\{A\})]\!]_w$. By definition, $P \in \Psi$ where $\Psi \in \mathbb{P}_{M_A}$, and $\Psi \subseteq [\![\sigma(G\{A\})]\!]_{w[Z \leftarrow \Psi]}$, and $M_A = fn^w(\sigma(\boldsymbol{\nu}Z.G\{A\}))$.
  Let $M_B = fn^w(\sigma(\boldsymbol{\nu}Z.G\{B\}))$. We have $\Psi \in \mathbb{P}_{M_A \cup M_B}$, by Lemma 4.2(1).
  By induction hypothesis, $\Psi \subseteq [\![\sigma(G\{B\})]\!]_{w[Z \leftarrow \Psi]}$. Then we conclude that $\Psi \subseteq [\![\sigma(G\{B\})]\!]_{w[Z \leftarrow \Psi]}$, so $\Psi \subseteq \mathsf{gfix}_{M_A \cup M_B}(\boldsymbol{\lambda}\Phi.[\![\sigma(G\{B\})]\!]_{w[Z \leftarrow \Phi]})$.
  Since $fn^w(\sigma(\boldsymbol{\nu}Z.G\{B\})) \subseteq M_A \cup M_B$, by Lemma 4.25, we conclude $\Psi \subseteq [\![\sigma(\boldsymbol{\nu}Z.G\{B\})]\!]_w$. Therefore $P \in [\![\sigma(\boldsymbol{\nu}Z.G\{B\})]\!]_w$.
  (Right to left inclusion) Handled symmetrically.

Boxed Ambients *

Michele Bugliesi[1], Giuseppe Castagna[2], and Silvia Crafa[1,2]

[1] Dipartimento di Informatica
Univ. "Ca' Foscari", Venezia, Italy

[2] Département d'Informatique
École Normale Supérieure, Paris, France

Abstract. *Boxed Ambients* are a variant of Mobile Ambients that result from (i) dropping the open capability and (ii) providing new primitives for ambient communication while retaining the constructs in and out for mobility. The new model of communication is faithful to the principles of distribution and location-awareness of Mobile Ambients, and complements the constructs for Mobile Ambient mobility with finer-grained mechanisms for ambient interaction.

1 Introduction

There is a general agreement that calculi and programming languages for wide-area computing and mobile-code environments should be designed according to appropriate principles, among which distribution and location awareness are the most fundamental.

Cardelli and Gordon's Mobile Ambients [CG98] are one of the first, and currently one of the most successful implementations of these principles into a formal calculus. Their design is centered around four basic notions: location, mobility, authorization to move (based on acquisition of names and capabilities), and communication by shared location.

Boxed Ambients[1] are a variant of Mobile Ambients, from which they inherit the primitives in and out for mobility, with the exact same semantics. On the other hand, Boxed Ambients rely on a completely different model of communication, which results from dropping the open capability. The new communication primitives fit nicely the design principles of Mobile Ambients, and complement the existing constructs for ambient mobility with finer-grained, and more effective, mechanisms for ambient interaction. As a result Boxed Ambients retain the computational flavor of the Ambient Calculus, as well as the elegance of its formal presentation. In addition, they enhance the flexibility of typed communications over Mobile Ambients, and provide new insight into the relationship between synchronous and asynchronous input-output.

1.1 Mobile Ambients

Ambients are named process of the form $a[\,P\,]$ where a is a name and P a process. Processes can be composed in parallel, as in $P \mid Q$, exercise a capability, as in $M.P$, declare local names as in $(\boldsymbol{\nu} x)P$, or simply do nothing as in $\mathbf{0}$. Ambients may be nested to form a tree structure that can be dynamically reconfigured by exercising the capabilities in, out and open. In addition, ambients and processes may communicate. Communication is anonymous, and happens inside ambients. The configuration $(\boldsymbol{x})P \mid \langle M \rangle$ represents the parallel composition of two processes, the output process $\langle M \rangle$ "dropping" the message M, and the input process $(\boldsymbol{x})P$ reading the message M and continuing as

* Work partially supported by MURST Project 9901403824_003, by CNRS Program *Telecommunications*: "Collaborative, distributed, and secure programming for Internet", and by Galileo Action n. 02841UD

[1] The name is inspired by Sewell and Vitek's *Boxed π-Calculus* [SV00].

N. Kobayashi and B.C. Pierce (Eds.): TACS 2001, LNCS 2215, pp. 38–63, 2001.

$P\{x := M\}$. The open capability has a fundamental interplay with communication: in fact, communication results from a combination of mobility and opening control. To exemplify, consider two ambients running in parallel as in the following configuration $a[\,(x)P \mid Q\,] \mid b[\,\langle M\rangle \mid R\,]$. The exchange of the value M from b to the process P enclosed in a happens as a result of, say, first b moving inside a, and then a opening b. Thus, if Q is the process open b, and R is in a, the exchange of M is the result of the following sequence of reductions:

$$
\begin{array}{rll}
a[\,(x)P \mid \mathsf{open}\ b\,] \mid b[\,\langle M\rangle \mid \mathsf{in}\ a\,] & \rightarrow a[\,(x)P \mid \mathsf{open}\ b \mid b[\,\langle M\rangle\,]\,] & \mathsf{in}\ a\text{: enter } a \\
& \rightarrow a[\,(x)P \mid \langle M\rangle\,] & \mathsf{open}\ b\text{: unleash } M \\
& \rightarrow a[\,P\{x := M\}\,] & \text{exchange } M
\end{array}
$$

A case against ambient opening. While fundamental to the Ambient Calculus for the reasons just illustrated, an unrestricted use of the open capability appears to bring about serious security concerns in wide-area distributed applications. Consider a scenario where a process P running on host h downloads an application program Q from some other host over the network. This situation can be modeled by the configuration $a[\,\mathsf{in}\ h.Q\,] \mid h[\,P\,]$, where Q is included in the transport ambient a which is routed to h in response to the download request from P. As a result of a exercising the capability in h, the system evolves into the new configuration $h[\,a[\,Q\,] \mid P\,]$, where the download is completed. The application program Q may be running and computing within a, but as long as it is encapsulated into a, there is no way that P and Q can effectively interact. To allow for interactions, P will need to dissolve the transport ambient a. Now, dissolving a produces the new configuration $h[\,P \mid Q\,]$ where now P and Q are granted free access to each other's resources: the problem, of course, is that there is no way to tell what Q may do with them. An alternative, but essentially equivalent, solution to the above scenario, is to treat a as a *sandbox* and take the Java approach to security: P clones itself and enters the sandbox to interact with Q. Again, however, the kind of interaction between P and Q is not fully satisfactory: either they interact freely within a, or are isolated from each other.

Static or dynamic analysis of incoming code are often advocated as solutions to the above problem: incoming code must be statically checked and certified prior to being granted access to resources and sensitive data. Various papers explore this possibility, proposing control-flow analyses [NNHJ99,NN00,DLB00] and type systems [CGG99,DCS00,BC01] for Mobile Ambients. The problem with these solutions is that they may not be always possible, or feasible, in practice. The source code of incoming software may be not available for analysis, or be otherwise inaccessible or too complex to ensure rigorous assessment of its behavior. This is not meant to dismiss the role of static analysis: on the contrary, it should be taken as a motivation to seek new design principles enabling static analysis to be used more effectively. One such principle for Mobile Ambients, which we advocate and investigate in this paper, is that ambient interaction should be controlled by finer-grained policies to prevent from unrestricted resource access while still providing effective communication primitives.

1.2 Boxed Ambients: Overview and Main Results

Boxed Ambients result from Cardelli and Gordon's Mobile Ambients essentially by dropping the open capability while retaining the in and out capabilities for mobility.

Disallowing open represents a rather drastic departure from the Ambient Calculus, and requires new primitives for process communication.

As in the Ambient Calculus, processes in the new calculus communicate via anonymous channels, inside ambients. This is a formal parsimony that simplifies the definition of the new calculus while not involving any loss of expressive power: in fact, named communication channels can be coded in faithful ways using the existing primitives. In addition, to compensate for the absence of open, Boxed Ambients are equipped with primitives for communication across ambient boundaries, between parent and children. Syntactically, this is obtained by means of tags specifying the *location* where the communication has to take place: for instance, $(x)^n P$ indicates an input from child ambient n, while $\langle M \rangle^\uparrow$ is an output to the parent ambient.

The choice of these primitives, and the resulting model of communication is inspired to Castagna and Vitek's *Seal Calculus* [VC99], from which Boxed Ambients also inherit the two principles of *mediation* and *locality*. Mediation implies that remote communication, i.e. between sibling ambients, is not possible: it either requires mobility, or intervention by the ambients' parent. Locality means that communication resources are *local* to ambients, and message exchanges result from explicit read and write requests on those resources. To exemplify, consider the following nested configuration:

$$n[\,(x)^p P \mid p[\,\langle M \rangle \mid (x)Q \mid q[\,\langle N \rangle^\uparrow\,]\,]\,]$$

Ambient n makes a downward request to read p's local value M, while ambient q makes an upward write request to communicate its value N to its parent. The downward input request $(x)^p P$ may only synchronize with the output $\langle M \rangle$ local to p. Instead, $(x)Q$ may non-deterministically synchronize with either output: of course, type safety requires that M and N be of the same type. Interestingly, however, exchanges of different types may take place within the same ambient without type confusion:

$$n[\,(x)^p P \mid (x)^q Q \mid p[\,\langle M \rangle\,] \mid q[\,\langle N \rangle\,]\,]$$

The two values M and N are local to p and q, respectively, and may very well have different types: there is no risk of type confusion, as $(x)^p P$ requests a read from p, while $(x)^q Q$ requests a read from q.

This flexibility of communication results from the combination of two design choices: directed input/output operations, and resource locality. In fact, these choices have other interesting consequences.

- They provide the calculus with fine-grained primitives for ambient interaction, and with clear notions of resource ownership and access request. Based on that, Boxed Ambients enable a rather direct formalization of classical security policies for resource protection and access control: this is not easy (if at all possible) with Mobile Ambients (see [BCC01]).
- They ease the design of type systems providing precise accounts of ambient behavior. As we show in § 4, a rather simple structure of types suffices for that purpose. Ambient and process types are defined simply as two-place constructors describing the types of exchanges that may take place locally, and with the enclosing context. Interestingly, this simple type structure is all that is needed to give a full account of

ambient interaction. This is a consequence of (i) there being no way for ambients to communicate directly across more than one boundary, and (ii) communication being the only means for ambient to interact. Based on that, the typing of Boxed Ambients provides for more flexibility of communication and mobility than existing type systems for Mobile Ambients (see § 5).

- Finally, resource locality and directed input/output provide new insight into the relation between the synchronous and asynchronous models of communication. Specifically, the classic π-calculus relations between synchronous and asynchronous output, as stated by Boudol in [Bou92], no longer hold as a result of combining remote communications, resource locality and mobility. More precisely asynchronous output may *no longer* be viewed as a special case of synchronous output with null continuation, neither can it be encoded by structural equivalence, by stipulating that $\langle M \rangle P \equiv \langle M \rangle \mid P$. As we show (see § 7) these two solutions, which are equivalent in the π-calculus, have rather different consequences in Boxed Ambients.

1.3 Plan of the Paper

§ 2 introduces Boxed Ambients. We first define the calculus in terms of synchronous output, and the subsequent four sections discuss various aspects of this formulation. In § 3 we give the encoding of different forms of channeled communications, based either on π-calculus' channels or on the Seal Calculus' *located* channels. In § 4, we introduce a type system, and in § 5 we compare the expressive power of typed Boxed Ambients and Mobile Ambients. In § 6 we give a different type system that further enhances typed communication and mobility. In § 7 we study an asynchronous variant of the calculus, and discuss the relationship between the two forms of communication and their impact on mobility. We conclude in § 8, with final remarks and comparisons with related work.

2 Boxed Ambients

Syntax. The syntax of the untyped calculus is defined by the following productions:

Expressions

$$\begin{array}{lcll} M & ::= & a, b, \ldots & \text{names} \\ & \mid & x, y, \ldots & \text{variables} \\ & \mid & \mathsf{in}\ M & \text{enter } M \\ & \mid & \mathsf{out}\ M & \text{exit } M \\ & \mid & (M_1, \ldots, M_k) & \text{tuple}, k \geqslant 0 \\ & \mid & M.M & \text{path} \end{array}$$

Processes

$$\begin{array}{lcll} P & ::= & \mathbf{0} & \text{stop} \\ & \mid & M.P & \text{action} \\ & \mid & (\nu x)P & \text{restriction} \\ & \mid & P \mid P & \text{composition} \\ & \mid & M[\![P]\!] & \text{ambient} \\ & \mid & !P & \text{replication} \\ & \mid & (\boldsymbol{x})^\eta P & \text{patterned input} \\ & \mid & \langle M \rangle^\eta P & \text{synchronous output} \end{array}$$

Locations

$$\begin{array}{lcll} \eta & ::= & M & \text{names and variables} \\ & \mid & \uparrow & \text{enclosing ambient} \\ & \mid & \star & \text{local} \end{array}$$

Patterns

$$\begin{array}{lcll} \boldsymbol{x} & ::= & x & \text{variable} \\ & \mid & \boldsymbol{x}_1, \ldots, \boldsymbol{x}_k & \text{tuple}, k \geqslant 0 \end{array}$$

Patterns and expressions are as in the polyadic Ambient Calculus, save that the capability open and the "empty path" ε are left out. As in the Ambient Calculus, the syntax allows the formation of meaningless process forms such as in $(\mathsf{out}\, m)$ or $(\mathsf{open}\, a)[P]$: these terms may arise as a result of reduction, in the untyped calculus, but are ruled out by the type system. We use a number of notational conventions. We reserve $a - -q$ for ambient names, and x, y, z for variables. As usual we omit trailing dead processes, writing M for $M.\mathbf{0}$, and $\langle M \rangle$ for $\langle M \rangle\mathbf{0}$. The empty tuple plays the role of synchronization messages. Finally, the superscript $\star$ denoting local communication, is omitted.

The operational semantics is defined in terms of reduction and structural congruence.

Structural Congruence. It is defined essentially as in the Ambient Calculus, as the least congruence relation that is a commutative monoid for $\mathbf{0}$ and $\mid$ and closed under the following rules ($fn(P)$, the set of free names of P, has the standard definition):

(Res Dead)	$(\nu x)\mathbf{0} \equiv \mathbf{0}$	(Res Res)	$(\nu x)(\nu y)P \equiv (\nu y)(\nu x)P$	$x \neq y$
(Path Assoc)	$(M.M').P \equiv M.(M'.P)$	(Res Par)	$(\nu x)(P \mid Q) \equiv P \mid (\nu x)Q$	$x \notin fn(P)$
(Repl)	$!P \equiv !P \mid P$	(Res Amb)	$(\nu x)y[P] \equiv y[(\nu x)P]$	$x \neq y$

As usual, structural congruence is used to rearrange the process so that they can reduce: $P' \equiv P,\ P \rightarrow Q,\ Q \equiv Q' \Rightarrow P' \rightarrow Q'$. Reduction is defined by the rules for mobility and communication given below plus the standard context reduction rules [CG98].

Mobility. Ambient mobility is governed by the following rules, inherited from Mobile Ambients:

(enter)	$a[\mathsf{in}\, b.P \mid Q] \mid b[R] \rightarrow b[a[P \mid Q] \mid R]$
(exit)	$a[b[\mathsf{out}\, a.P \mid Q] \mid R] \rightarrow b[P \mid Q] \mid a[R]$

Communication. Communication can be local, as in Mobile Ambients, or across ambient boundaries, between parent and child.

(local)	$(x)P \mid \langle M \rangle Q \rightarrow P\{x := M\} \mid Q$
(input n)	$(x)^n P \mid n[\langle M \rangle Q \mid R] \rightarrow P\{x := M\} \mid n[Q \mid R]$
(input $\uparrow$)	$\langle M \rangle P \mid n[(x)^{\uparrow} Q \mid R] \rightarrow P \mid n[Q\{x := M\} \mid R]$
(output n)	$\langle M \rangle^n P \mid n[(x)Q \mid R] \rightarrow P \mid n[Q\{x := M\} \mid R]$
(output $\uparrow$)	$(x)P \mid n[\langle M \rangle^{\uparrow} Q \mid R] \rightarrow P\{x := M\} \mid n[Q \mid R]$

Four different reduction rules for parent-child communication may be thought of as redundant, especially because there are only two reducts. Instead, introducing different *directions* for input/output is a key design choice that provides the calculus with precise notions of resource locality and resource access request. Directed (towards parent or child) output captures the notion of *write access* to a resource, by identifying the ambient towards which the request is directed. Dually, directed input captures the notion of *read access*.[2] Based on these intuitions, the definition of reduction enables the study of properties related to standard resource access control policies, even in the absence of channels (see § 5; for more details refer to [BCC01]). Channels, on the other hand, can be encoded elegantly, as we show in the next section.

[2] Other alternatives would be possible: we discuss them in § 8.

As we noted, in the present formulation output is synchronous. For the time being, asynchronous output can either be considered as the special case of synchronous communication with null continuation, or else be accounted for by introducing the following rule of structural equivalence inspired by [Bou92]: $\langle M \rangle^\eta P \equiv \langle M \rangle^\eta \mid P$. As we shall discuss later on, these interpretations are equivalent, and both type sound, with "simple" types, that is, up to § 5. Instead, with "moded types" we introduce in § 6 they are different, and neither one satisfactory, as the former is too restrictive while the latter is unsound.

3 Communication Channels

We first show how to define π-calculus channels: then we refine the encoding to account for parent-child channeled communications. Throughout this section, we use two extra congruence laws: $(\boldsymbol{\nu} x)x[\,\mathbf{0}\,] \equiv \mathbf{0}$ and $!P \equiv !P \mid !P$ to garbage collect inert ambients and useless replications, respectively. Neither of the two relations is derivable as a congruence law: on the other hand, they both would be derivable as observational equivalences for any reasonable notion of observable for the calculus.

3.1 π-Calculus Channels

We start with asynchronous output, and then use it to encode synchronous output.

Asynchronous output. Two π-calculus processes communicating over a channel, say c, have the form $c\langle y \rangle$ (output) and $c(x)P$ (input). With Boxed Ambients, a first way to implement the channel c is to use the ambient $c[\,!(x)\langle x \rangle\,]$ representing a buffer with an unbounded number of positions: the buffer simply waits for local input and, once received, releases local output. The output and input prefixes may then be represented, respectively, as the write request $\langle y \rangle^c$ and the read request $(x)^c$ on the buffer. We use a slightly different encoding based on an unbounded number of these buffers.

The following sequence of reductions shows that the encoding captures the intended behavior:

$$\begin{aligned} !c[\,!(x)\langle x \rangle\,] \mid \langle y \rangle^c \mid (x)^c P &\equiv\, !\,c[\,!(x)\langle x \rangle\,] \mid c[\,!(x)\langle x \rangle \mid (x)\langle x \rangle\,] \mid \langle y \rangle^c \mid (x)^c P \\ &\rightarrow\, !\,c[\,!(x)\langle x \rangle\,] \mid c[\,!(x)\langle x \rangle \mid \langle y \rangle\,] \mid (x)^c P \\ &\rightarrow\, !\,c[\,!(x)\langle x \rangle\,] \mid P\{x := y\} \end{aligned}$$

Based on these intuitions, we may define the encoding compositionally, as follows:

$$\begin{array}{lll} \langle\!\langle (\boldsymbol{\nu} x)P \rangle\!\rangle = (\boldsymbol{\nu} x)\langle\!\langle P \rangle\!\rangle & \langle\!\langle !P \rangle\!\rangle = !\langle\!\langle P \rangle\!\rangle & \langle\!\langle c\langle x \rangle \rangle\!\rangle = !c[\,!(x)\langle x \rangle\,] \mid \langle x \rangle^c \\ \langle\!\langle P \mid Q \rangle\!\rangle = \langle\!\langle P \rangle\!\rangle \mid \langle\!\langle Q \rangle\!\rangle & \langle\!\langle \mathbf{0} \rangle\!\rangle = \mathbf{0} & \langle\!\langle c(x)P \rangle\!\rangle = !c[\,!(x)\langle x \rangle\,] \mid (x)^c \langle\!\langle P \rangle\!\rangle \end{array}$$

An input and an output on the same channel, say c, generate multiple copies of the buffer $!c[\,!(x)\langle x \rangle\,]$: this is not a problem, however, since the multiple copies can be garbage collected by the congruence law $!P \mid !P \equiv !P$. Of course, there are other ways for structuring the encoding. For instance, one could create the buffer when the channel name is introduced by a restriction: this would avoid the proliferation of channels. A further alternative would be to collect free and bound names in the inductive cases of the translation, as in $\langle\!\langle (\boldsymbol{\nu} x)P \rangle\!\rangle_{\Delta} = (\boldsymbol{\nu} x) \langle\!\langle P \rangle\!\rangle_{\Delta\cup\{x\}}$, $\langle\!\langle c(x)P \rangle\!\rangle_{\Delta} = (x)^c \langle\!\langle P \rangle\!\rangle_{\Delta\cup\{c,x\}}$, and introduce them in the base cases[3]: $\langle\!\langle \mathbf{0} \rangle\!\rangle_{\{c_1,\ldots,c_n\}} = !c_1[\,!(x)\langle x\rangle\,] \mid \ldots \mid !c_n[\,!(x)\langle x\rangle\,]$.

However, none of the alternatives would scale to the case of communication with local channels of § 3.2: this justifies our choice of the encoding given above.

Synchronous output. Let now $cx.P$ and $\bar{c}x.P$ denote π-calculus *synchronous* input and output on channel c. Synchronous input-output can be encoded in the asynchronous polyadic π-calculus as follows: $\bar{c}x.P = (\boldsymbol{\nu} r)(c\langle x, r\rangle \mid r()P)$, $cy.P = c(y,r)(r\langle\rangle \mid P)$ where $r \notin fn(P)$. That is, the output process sends the intended message as well as a private channel r for the reader to acknowledge receipt of the message.

Based on this idea, a direct definition for the synchronous prefix forms can be given as follows:

$$\langle\!\langle \bar{c}x.P \rangle\!\rangle = !c[\,!(u,v)\langle u,v\rangle\,] \mid (\boldsymbol{\nu} r)(r[\,()\langle\rangle\,] \mid \langle x,r\rangle^c ()^r \langle\!\langle P \rangle\!\rangle)\quad r \notin fn(P)$$

$$\langle\!\langle cy.Q \rangle\!\rangle = !c[\,!(u,v)\langle u,v\rangle\,] \mid (y,s)^c \langle\rangle^s \langle\!\langle Q \rangle\!\rangle \quad s \notin fn(Q)$$

3.2 Parent-Child Channeled Communication à la Seal Calculus

Having looked at π-calculus channels, we now discuss an extension of the encoding that conforms with the notion of locality and directed input-output of the core calculus. The extension yields a notion of located channels and a set of communication protocols that are similar, in spirit, to those given as primitive in the Seal Calculus [VC99]. In the Seal Calculus, one can express output prefixes of the form $c^n\langle M\rangle$ requesting a write access on the channel c residing in ambient (or seal) n. Dually, the input prefix $c^{\uparrow}(x)$ denotes a read request on the channel c residing in the parent ambient. Upward output and downward input on local channels may be expressed in similar ways. All these communication protocols can be expressed in the core calculus: below, we only consider the asynchronous case and we give detailed descriptions of downward output and upward input.

The intended reduction of a downward output is:

$$c^n\langle M\rangle \mid n[\,c(x)P \mid Q\,] \rightarrow n[\,P\{x := M\} \mid Q\,].$$

The channel c is local to n, and the outer process requests a write access on c. There are several ways that the reduction can be captured with the existing constructs. Here, we describe an encoding that renders the locality of c. The channel c is represented as before as a buffer, and the input prefix $c(x)$ as read access request to c:

$$c(x)P \triangleq !c[\,!(x)\langle x\rangle\,] \mid (x)^c P$$

Now, however, the write access to c cannot be represented directly as we did above for the π-calculus channel, because c is located into n. To capture the desired behavior we can rely on mobility:

$$c^n\langle M\rangle \triangleq (\boldsymbol{\nu} p)p[\,\mathsf{in}\ n.\mathsf{in}\ c.\langle M\rangle^{\uparrow}\,]$$

The output M is encapsulated into a transport ambient p, which enters n and then c to deliver the message (the name of the transport ambient p must be fresh). Thus, the Seal Calculus process $c^n\langle M\rangle \mid n[\,c(x)P \mid Q\,]$ is encoded as follows:

[3] Of course, for parallel composition, one has to arbitrarily choose one subprocess; for example the left one: $\langle\!\langle P \mid Q \rangle\!\rangle_{\Delta} = \langle\!\langle P \rangle\!\rangle_{\Delta} \mid \langle\!\langle Q \rangle\!\rangle_{\emptyset}$

$$(\nu p)p[\,\mathsf{in}\ n.\mathsf{in}\ c.\langle M\rangle^{\uparrow}\,] \quad | \quad n[\,!c[\,!(x)\langle x\rangle\,] \mid (x)^{c}P \mid Q\,]$$

By a sequence of reductions, the process above evolves into

$$n[\,!c[\,!(x)\langle x\rangle\,] \mid c[\,!(x)\langle x\rangle \mid (\nu p)p[\,\mathbf{0}\,]\,] \mid P\{x := M\} \mid Q\,],$$

which is equivalent to $n[\,!c[\,!(x)\langle x\rangle\,] \mid P\{x := M\} \mid Q\,]$ by structural congruence.

Remote inputs are slightly more complex, since the transport ambient must fetch the output and bring it back. The intended reduction is

$$c\langle M\rangle \mid n[\,c^{\uparrow}(x)P \mid Q\,] \rightarrow n[\,P\{x := M\} \mid Q\,].$$

Upward input from within a seal n is simulated in Boxed Ambients as

$$c^{\uparrow}(x)P \triangleq (\nu p)p[\,\mathsf{out}\ n.\mathsf{in}\ c.(x)^{\uparrow}\mathsf{out}\ c.\mathsf{in}\ n.\langle x\rangle\,] \mid (x)^{p}P$$

Note that the definition depends on the name n of the enclosing ambient. For a formal definition, it is enough to keep track of this information, and extend the encoding of the asynchronous π calculus with the following clauses:

$$\begin{aligned}
\langle\!\langle c^{m}\langle x\rangle \rangle\!\rangle_{n} &= (\nu p)p[\,\mathsf{in}\ m.\mathsf{in}\ c.\langle x\rangle^{\uparrow}\,]\\
\langle\!\langle c^{\uparrow}\langle x\rangle \rangle\!\rangle_{n} &= (\nu p)p[\,\mathsf{out}\ n.\mathsf{in}\ c.\langle x\rangle^{\uparrow}\,]\\
\langle\!\langle c^{m}(x)P \rangle\!\rangle_{n} &= (\nu p)p[\,\mathsf{in}\ m.\mathsf{in}\ c.(x)^{\uparrow}\mathsf{out}\ c.\mathsf{out}\ m.\langle x\rangle\,] \mid (x)^{p}\langle\!\langle P \rangle\!\rangle_{n}\\
\langle\!\langle c^{\uparrow}(x)P \rangle\!\rangle_{n} &= (\nu p)p[\,\mathsf{out}\ n.\mathsf{in}\ c.(x)^{\uparrow}\mathsf{out}\ c.\mathsf{in}\ n.\langle x\rangle\,] \mid (x)^{p}\langle\!\langle P \rangle\!\rangle_{n}\\
\langle\!\langle a[\,P\,] \rangle\!\rangle_{n} &= a[\,\langle\!\langle P \rangle\!\rangle_{a}\,]
\end{aligned}$$

4 Typing Boxed Ambients

As we stated at the outset, one of the motivations for the design of Boxed Ambients was to enhance static reasoning on ambient and process behavior, by enabling focused and precise analyses while preserving the expressive power of the calculus. The definition of the type system, given in this section, proves that the design satisfies these requirements

A rather simple structure of types suffices to provide precise accounts of process behavior. Ambient and process types are defined simply as two-place constructors describing the types of the exchanges that may take place locally and with the enclosing context. Interestingly, this simple type structure is all that is needed to give a full account of ambient interaction. This is a consequence of (i) there being no way for ambients to communicate directly across more than one boundary, and (ii) communication being the only means for ambient to interact.

4.1 Types

The structure of types is defined by the following productions.

Expression Types			*Exchange Types*		
$W ::=$	$\mathsf{Amb}[E,F]$	ambient	$E,F ::=$	shh	no exchange
$\mid$	$\mathsf{Cap}[E]$	capability	$\mid$	W	exchange
$\mid$	$W_1 \times \cdots \times W_n$	tuple	*Process Types*		
			$T ::=$	$\mathsf{Pro}[E,F]$	composite exchange

The type structure is superficially similar to that of companion type systems for the Ambient Calculus [CG99,CGG99]. The interpretation, however, is different.

$\mathsf{Amb}[E,F]$ ambients that enclose processes of type $\mathsf{Pro}[E,F]$,
$\mathsf{Cap}[E]$ capabilities exercised within ambients with E upward exchanges,
$\mathsf{Pro}[E,F]$ processes with local and upward exchanges of types E and F, respectively.

Notice that capability types are defined as one-place constructors, and disregard the local exchanges of the ambients where they are exercised. This is because (i) exercising a capability within an ambient, say a, may only cause a to move, and (ii) the safety of ambient mobility may be established regardless of the ambient's local exchanges.

As for process types, a few examples should help explain the intuition about composite exchange. We use a "Church style" typed syntax, in which all inputs and restrictions specify the type of the bound variable: more precisely we use $(\boldsymbol{\nu} x : W)P$ and $(x : W)P$ instead of $(\boldsymbol{\nu} x)P$ and $(x)P$, respectively.

$(x{:}W)\langle x\rangle$: $\mathsf{Pro}[W,\mathsf{shh}]$. W is exchanged (read and written) locally, and there is no upward exchange.

$(x{:}W)^{\uparrow}\langle x\rangle^{n}$: $\mathsf{Pro}[\mathsf{shh},W]$. W is exchanged (i.e. read from) upwards, and then written to ambient n. There is no local exchange, hence the type shh as the first component of the process type. For the typing to be derivable, one needs n : $\mathsf{Amb}[W,E]$ for some exchange type E.

$(x{:}W)^{\uparrow}(y{:}W')(\langle x\rangle^{n} \mid \langle y\rangle)$: $\mathsf{Pro}[W',W]$. W is exchanged (read from) upwards, and then forwarded to ambient n, while W' is exchanged (read and written) locally. Again, for the typing to be derivable, one needs n : $\mathsf{Amb}[W,E]$ for some exchange type E.

$(x{:}W)\langle x\rangle^{\uparrow}$: $\mathsf{Pro}[W,W]$. W is read locally, and written upwards.

These simple examples give a flavor of the flexibility provided by the constructs for communication: like mobile ambients, boxed ambients are "places of conversation", but unlike ambients they allow more than just one "topic" of conversation. This is made possible by the local nature of (anonymous) channels, and the consequent "directed" forms of input/output. Specifically, every ambient may exchange values of different types with any of its children, as long as the exchange is directed from the ambient to the children. Instead, upward communication is more constrained: all the children must agree on the (unique) type of exchange they may direct to their parent.

4.2 Typing Rules

The judgments of the type system have two forms: $\Gamma \vdash M : W$, read "*expression M has type W*", and $\Gamma \vdash P : T$, read "*process P has type T*". Accordingly we have two sets of typing rules, one for names and capabilities, one for processes. In addition, we introduce a subsumption rule for process types, based on the following definition of subtyping.

Definition 1 (*Subtyping*). *We denote by $\leqslant$ the smallest reflexive and transitive relation over exchange types such that* shh $\leqslant E$ *for every exchange type E. Exchange subtyping is lifted to process types as follows:* $\mathsf{Pro}[\mathsf{shh},F] \leqslant \mathsf{Pro}[E,F]$.

Process subtyping is used in conjunction with subsumption, exchange subtyping is not. The intuition for exchange subtyping is that a (locally or upward) shh exchange is always type compatible with a situation in which some exchange is expected: this is useful in the typing of capabilities. As for process subtyping, it would be tempting to extend the subtyping relation so as to allow subtyping over upward exchanges, as well. However, as we explain later in this section, uses of this relation in conjunction with a subsumption rule for process types would not be sound. As a final remark, note that our notion of subtyping is quite shallow: it is "almost equality" as there is no *deep* subtyping. This holds true for the moded types of Section 6, as well.

Typing of Expressions

(PROJ)
$$\frac{\Gamma(n)=W}{\Gamma \vdash n : W}$$

(TUPLE)
$$\frac{\Gamma \vdash M_i{:}W_i \quad \forall i \in 1..k}{\Gamma \vdash (M_1, ..., M_k) : W_1 \times ... \times W_k}$$

(PATH)
$$\frac{\Gamma \vdash M_1{:}\mathsf{Cap}[F] \quad \Gamma \vdash M_2{:}\mathsf{Cap}[F]}{\Gamma \vdash M_1.M_2 : \mathsf{Cap}[F]}$$

(IN)
$$\frac{\Gamma \vdash M : \mathsf{Amb}[F, E] \quad F' \leqslant F}{\Gamma \vdash \mathsf{in}\ M : \mathsf{Cap}[F']}$$

(OUT)
$$\frac{\Gamma \vdash M : \mathsf{Amb}[E, F] \quad F' \leqslant F}{\Gamma \vdash \mathsf{out}\ M : \mathsf{Cap}[F']}$$

The (PROJECTION), (TUPLE), and (PATH) rule are standard. The rules (IN) and (OUT) define the constraints for safe ambient mobility, and explain why capability types are built around a single component. The intuition is as follows: take a capability, say in n with $n : \mathsf{Amb}[F, E]$, and suppose that this capability is exercised within ambient, say, m. If m has upward exchanges of type F', then in $n : \mathsf{Cap}[F']$. Now, for the move of m into n to be safe, one must ensure that the type F of the local exchanges of n be equal to the type F' of the upward exchanges of m. In fact, the typing can be slightly more flexible, for if m has no upward exchange, then $F' = \mathsf{shh} \leqslant F$, and m may safely move into n. Dual reasoning applies to the (OUT) rule: the upward exchanges of the exiting ambient must have type $\leqslant$-compatible with the type of the upward exchanges of the ambient being exited.

Typing of Processes

(DEAD)
$$\frac{}{\Gamma \vdash \mathbf{0} : T}$$

(NEW)
$$\frac{\Gamma, x : W \vdash P : T}{\Gamma \vdash (\nu x{:}W)P : T}$$

(PARALLEL)
$$\frac{\Gamma \vdash P : \mathsf{Pro}[E, F] \quad \Gamma \vdash Q : \mathsf{Pro}[E, F]}{\Gamma \vdash P \mid Q : \mathsf{Pro}[E, F]}$$

(PREFIX)
$$\frac{\Gamma \vdash M : \mathsf{Cap}[F] \quad \Gamma \vdash P : \mathsf{Pro}[E, F]}{\Gamma \vdash M.P : \mathsf{Pro}[E, F]}$$

(AMB)
$$\frac{\Gamma \vdash M : \mathsf{Amb}[E, F] \quad \Gamma \vdash P : \mathsf{Pro}[E, F]}{\Gamma \vdash M[\![P]\!] : \mathsf{Pro}[F, G]}$$

(SUBSUM PROC)
$$\frac{\Gamma \vdash P : T \quad T \leqslant T'}{\Gamma \vdash P : T'}$$

(REPLICATION)
$$\frac{\Gamma \vdash P : \mathsf{Pro}[E, F]}{\Gamma \vdash !P : \mathsf{Pro}[E, F]}$$

(DEAD), (NEW), (PARALLEL), (REPLICATION) and the subsumption rule are standard[4]. In the (PREFIX) rule, the typing of the capability M ensures, via the (IN), (OUT), and (PATH) rules introduced earlier, that each of the ambients being traversed as a result of exercising M have local exchanges of type compatible with the upward exchanges of the current ambient.

The rule (AMB) establishes the constraints that must be satisfied by P to be enclosed in M: specifically, the exchanges declared for M must have the same types E and F as the exchanges of P. In fact, P could be locally silent, and the typing of $M[\![P]\!]$ be derivable from $\Gamma \vdash P : \mathsf{Pro}[\mathsf{shh}, F]$ by subsumption. In addition, if $\Gamma \vdash M : \mathsf{Amb}[E, \mathsf{shh}]$, and $\Gamma \vdash P : \mathsf{Pro}[E, \mathsf{shh}]$, then by (AMB) and subsumption one derives $\Gamma \vdash M[\![P]\!] : \mathsf{Pro}[F, G]$ for any F and G, as the rule imposes no constraint on the upward exchanges of the process $M[\![P]\!]$.

(INPUT $\star$)
$$\frac{\Gamma, x{:}W \vdash P : \mathsf{Pro}[W, E]}{\Gamma \vdash (x{:}W)P : \mathsf{Pro}[W, E]}$$

(OUTPUT $\star$)
$$\frac{\Gamma \vdash M : W \quad \Gamma \vdash P : \mathsf{Pro}[W, E]}{\Gamma \vdash \langle M \rangle P : \mathsf{Pro}[W, E]}$$

(INPUT M)
$$\frac{\Gamma \vdash M : \mathsf{Amb}[W, E] \;\; \Gamma, x{:}W \vdash P : T}{\Gamma \vdash (x{:}W)^M P : T}$$

(OUTPUT M)
$$\frac{\Gamma \vdash M : \mathsf{Amb}[W, E] \;\; \Gamma \vdash N : W \;\; \Gamma \vdash P : T}{\Gamma \vdash \langle N \rangle^M P : T}$$

(INPUT $\uparrow$)
$$\frac{\Gamma, x{:}W \vdash P : \mathsf{Pro}[E, W]}{\Gamma \vdash (x{:}W)^\uparrow P : \mathsf{Pro}[E, W]}$$

(OUTPUT $\uparrow$)
$$\frac{\Gamma \vdash M : W \quad \Gamma \vdash P : \mathsf{Pro}[E, W]}{\Gamma \vdash \langle M \rangle^\uparrow P : \mathsf{Pro}[E, W]}$$

The rules for input/output are not surprising. In all cases, the type of the exchange must comply with the local exchange type of the target ambient, as expected. Also note that input/output exchanges with children, in the rules (INPUT M) and (OUTPUT M), do not impose any constraint on local and upward exchanges.

As we noted earlier, type soundness requires that subtyping between upward silent and upward non-silent processes be disallowed. To see why, consider for example allowing the relation $\mathsf{Pro}[E, \mathsf{shh}] \leqslant \mathsf{Pro}[E, F]$, implying that upward-silent processes may be subsumed to non-silent processes with any upward exchange type F. While this form of subsumption seems reasonable, it is unsound in the presence of parallel composition. Consider the ambient $a[\![\mathsf{in}\ b.\mathbf{0} \mid \langle M \rangle^\uparrow P]\!]$ with, say $M : W$ for some type W, and note that $\mathsf{in}\ b.\mathbf{0}$ can be typed as $\mathsf{Pro}[\mathsf{shh}, \mathsf{shh}]$ regardless of the type of b. If the suggested subtyping were available, then the parallel composition could be typed as $\mathsf{Pro}[\mathsf{shh}, W]$. However, if $b : \mathsf{Amb}[W', F]$ for some $W' \neq W$, the ambient a could move into b and have unsound upward exchanges after the move. By forbidding subtyping on the upper component of process types, instead, the types that can be deduced for the process in $b.\mathbf{0}$ above may only be $\mathsf{Pro}[E\,, W']$ or $\mathsf{Pro}[E, \mathsf{shh}]$ for some exchange E.

[4] The reason why in (PARALLEL) and (REPLICATION) we used $\mathsf{Pro}[E, F]$ rather than T will become clear in Section 6.

The type system rules ensures that communication inside and across ambients never leads to type mismatches. The latter result is a consequence of the subject reduction property stated next.

Theorem 1 (Subject Reduction). *If $\Gamma \vdash P : T$ and and $P \rightarrow Q$, then $\Gamma \vdash Q : T$.*

Proof. *By induction on the derivation of $P \rightarrow Q$, and appeal to standard lemmas of substitution and subject congruence.*

5 Mobile Ambients versus Boxed Ambients

We now look at the impact of typing on mobility and communication, and contrast it with mobility and communication of Mobile Ambients.

We already noted that type safety for ambient mobility can be established irrespective of local exchanges. On the other hand, upward communication does impose somewhat restrictive constraints over ambient mobility. Specifically, ambients with upward exchanges of type W may only traverse ambients whose local exchanges also have type W. However, when we compare the flexibility of mobility and communication in Boxed Ambients versus the corresponding constructs found in Mobile Ambients, we find that typed Mobile Ambients have, in fact, even more severe constraints.

To see that, it is instructive to note that the type system of the previous section can be specialized to only allow upward-silent ambient types in the form $\mathsf{Amb}[E, \mathsf{shh}]$. This effectively corresponds to inhibiting all forms of upward exchanges (this follows from the format of the (AMB) rule). On the other hand, it provides full flexibility for mobility while still allowing powerful forms of communication. We may note the following of the specialized type system.

Mobility for Boxed Ambients is as flexible as mobility for typed Mobile Ambients. This follows by the (IN) and (OUT) rules discussed in § 4.2. Capabilities exercised within upward silent ambients have type $\mathsf{Cap}[\mathsf{shh}]$, and $\mathsf{shh} \leqslant F$ for every F: consequently, upward silent ambients have full freedom of moving across ambient boundaries. Furthermore, since Boxed Ambients may not be opened, they may move regardless of the local exchanges of the ambients they traverse. As a consequence, with the specialized type system, an ambient can move independently of its type, and of the type of its (intermediate and final) destinations.

Communication is more flexible than in the Ambient Calculus, even in the absence of upward exchanges . "Upward silent" does not imply "non communicating": an upward-silent ambient may very well move to a target ambient a, and communication between a and the incoming ambient may rely on a accessing the incoming ambient by downward requests. Indeed, an ambient may access all of its children's anonymous channels as well as those of any incoming ambient: all these exchanges may be of different types. Besides, the ambient may hold local exchanges of yet a different type. The encoding of channels given § 3.1 can also be used for encoding local exchanges of different types: the ambient $c[\,!(x\!:\!W)\langle x\rangle\,]$ can be viewed as a local channel c of type W, whose input output operators are $(x\!:\!W)^c$ and $\langle M\rangle^c$: the type system allows (encoded) channels of different types to be used in the same ambient.

In the ambient calculus, instead, parent-child communication requires the parent to first open the child (or else a "messenger" ambient [CG98] exiting the child). As a consequence, either the parent, and all the children's exchanges have the same type, or there is no way that the parent may communicate with all of its children.

5.1 Security and Resource Access Control

The communication model underlying the calculus has other interesting payoffs when it comes to security and resource protection policies.

As we have argued, the primitives for communication have immediate and very natural interpretations as access requests: once again, the input prefix $(x)^n$ can be seen as a request to read from (the anonymous channel located into) child ambient n and, dually, $\langle M \rangle^{\uparrow}$ can be interpreted as write request to the parent ambient (equivalently, its local channel). Based on that, Boxed Ambients provide for a direct characterization of classical resource access control mechanisms, such as *Mandatory Access Control* or MAC policies. In addition, *multilevel security*, and the associated *Military* (no read-up, no write-down) and *Commercial* (no read-up, no write-up) security models may directly be accounted for by embedding security levels into types, and using typing rules to statically enforce the desired constraints on the access requests. For a thorough discussion of MAC multilevel security for Boxed Ambients the reader is referred to [BCC01]. What is interesting to note here, instead, is that the mechanisms for ambient interaction and communication fit nicely and complement the security model of Mobile Ambients, which predicates in/out access to ambients on possession of appropriate passwords or cryptokeys.

The download example, revisited. To exemplify, consider again the download example in § 1. With Mobile Ambients, security relies solely on authorization based on knowledge of names: the agent $a[\,Q\,]$ acquires authorization to enter the host h by knowing the name h and embedding it into the capability in b: the capability, or the name, may thus be seen as passwords that enable the access to h, as in $h[\,a[\,Q\,] \mid P\,]$. Once inside h, the ambient a (or a messenger ambient exiting a) is dissolved to enable interaction. As we argued, this may be upsetting to the host, as it grants Q (or the messenger inside a) indiscriminate access to whatever is inside h.

Instead, if a and h are Boxed Ambients, authorization by possession of capabilities can be complemented by finer-grained control over the access requests by Q to the contents of h. Assume, for the purpose of the example, that h encapsulates its resources in a set of subambients $r_1, \ldots, r_n$. Then P inside h could mediate the access requests by a to each of the r_i's by means of an interface process of the form $(x{:}W)^a \langle x \rangle^{r_i}$. In addition, the incoming agent can be forced to be upward silent to prevent it from interfering with the local exchanges held within h: this can be accomplished by imposing a suitable security policy, based on typing, as shown in [BCC01].

5.2 Discussion

Having argued in favor of the communication model of Boxed Ambients with the specialized type system, it is obvious that giving up upward exchanges is a problem: for instance, we would not be able to type-check "transport" ambients such as those used in the encoding of the Seal Calculus' channels of § 3.2, whose function is to silently carry a process to a certain destination where the process will eventually deliver its output to and/or receive input from its enclosing context. As we show next, it is actually possible to refine and extend the type system to support a smoother and type safe interaction of upward communication and mobility.

6 Moded Typing

The typing technique we develop in this section is based on a refinement of the observation we just made of the specialized type system, namely that ambients enclosing upward-silent processes may safely move across other ambients, regardless of the types of the latter. The new type system uses type modifiers to characterize the computation progress of processes, and in particular to identify the silent and non-silent phases in the computation of the processes enclosed within ambients: based on that, it enhances the typing of mobility during the ambients' silent phases.

6.1 Moded Types

The new type system is built around the extended classes of process and expression types defined below:

$$\textit{Process Types} \quad T ::= \mathsf{Pro}[E,F] \mid \mathsf{Pro}[E,{}^{\bullet}F] \mid \mathsf{Pro}[E,{}^{\circ}F] \mid \mathsf{Pro}[E,{}^{\vartriangle}F]$$

$$\textit{Expression Types} \; W ::= \mathsf{Amb}[E,F] \mid \mathsf{Amb}^{\circ}[E,F] \mid \mathsf{Cap}[E] \mid W_1 \times \cdots \times W_n$$

Ambient types of the form $\mathsf{Amb}[E,F]$ are exactly as in § 4, and their enclosed processes have "regular" process types $\mathsf{Pro}[E,F]$, deduced by the same rules. On the other hand, ambient types of the form $\mathsf{Amb}^{\circ}[E,F]$ are associated with "transport" (or moded) ambients, whose enclosed processes are assigned moded types, according to the following intuitions:

$\mathsf{Pro}[E,{}^{\bullet}W]$: upward silent processes with local exchanges of type E. The type W signals that processes with this type may be safely run in parallel with processes with upward exchanges of type W.

$\mathsf{Pro}[E,{}^{\circ}W]$: processes with local exchanges of type E and upward exchanges of type W. The upward exchanges are temporarily inactive since the process is moving.

$\mathsf{Pro}[E,{}^{\vartriangle}W]$: processes with local exchanges of type E and that after holding upward exchanges of type W, evolve into processes of type $\mathsf{Pro}[E,{}^{\circ}W]$ or $\mathsf{Pro}[E,{}^{\vartriangle}W]$.

The syntax allows the formation of process types of the form $\mathsf{Pro}[E,{}^{\bullet}\mathsf{shh}]$, $\mathsf{Pro}[E,{}^{\circ}\mathsf{shh}]$ and $\mathsf{Pro}[E,{}^{\vartriangle}\mathsf{shh}]$. These types are convenient in stating definitions and typing rules: to make sense of them, we stipulate that ${}^{\bullet}\mathsf{shh} = {}^{\circ}\mathsf{shh} = {}^{\vartriangle}\mathsf{shh} = \mathsf{shh}$. To exemplify moded types, consider the following process, where we assume $\Gamma \vdash M : W$.

$$(x{:}W')\langle x\rangle^{m} \mid \mathsf{in}\; n.\langle M\rangle^{\uparrow}.\mathsf{out}\; n : \mathsf{Pro}[W',{}^{\circ}W].$$

The left component of this process does not have upward exchanges, hence it can be assigned the type $\mathsf{Pro}[W',{}^{\bullet}W]$ provided, of course, that $m : \mathsf{Amb}[W',E]$ for some E. On the other hand, the right component does have upward exchanges, but is currently silent because the output prefix is blocked by the move: thus in $n.\langle M\rangle^{\uparrow}.\mathsf{out}\ n : \mathsf{Pro}[W', {}^{\circ}W]$, provided that $n : \mathsf{Amb}[W, W]$. The type $\mathsf{Pro}[W', {}^{\circ}W]$ can also be assigned to the parallel composition which is, in fact, currently silent. Interestingly, the type $\mathsf{Pro}[W', {}^{\circ}W]$ can *not* be assigned to the continuation process $\langle M\rangle^{\uparrow}.\mathsf{out}\ n$ (nor to the parallel composition $(x{:}W')\langle x\rangle^{m} \mid \langle M\rangle^{\uparrow}.\mathsf{out}\ n$), because, after consuming the capability in n, the upward exchanges of this process are active. At this stage, a legal type for the process is $\mathsf{Pro}[W', {}^{\vartriangle}W]$, signaling, that after the upward exchange, the process enters again an upward-silent phase.

As the example shows, processes that are subject to moded typing may have different types at different stages of their computation. This does not break subject reduction, as it would seem, as reductions involving the consumption of capabilities only involve the ambients enclosing the capabilities being consumed: as a consequence, while the process enclosed in an ambient changes its type according to the process' progress, the type of the ambient itself is invariant through reduction.

The reader may wonder whether the new class of "transport" ambients is really necessary, and why the same effect can not be obtained by solely relying on "regular" ambient types. The problem is that moded typing is not powerful enough to control mobility: in particular, moded types can not be employed to prevent non-silent ambients to exit their parent during the upward-silent phases of the latter. To see the problem, assume that ambient, say a, is currently silent and moving across ambients with local exchanges, say W. Also assume that a contains a non-silent ambient b with upward exchanges of type W' incompatible with W. As long as b is enclosed in a, its upward exchanges do not interfere with the local exchanges W of the ambients traversed by a. However, if b exits a, then its upward exchanges may indeed cause a type mismatch. In our system, the problem is solved by providing guarantees that transport ambients can only be exited by (regular or transport) ambients whose upward exchanges have type shh.[5]

6.2 Capabilities and Moded Judgments

The modes attached to process types also affect the typing of capabilities. This is accounted for by a new form of judgment, denoted by $\Gamma \vdash_{\circ} M : \mathsf{Cap}[E]$. This notation indicates a "silent mode" for typing the capability M, which is useful when typing capability paths: if typed in silent mode, every intermediate move on the path may safely disregard the type of the ambient traversed along the move.

6.3 Typing Rules

The new type system includes all the typing rules from § 4.2. In addition, we have a richer subtype structure for process types, and new rules for deriving silent typings of capabilities, and moded types for processes.

[5] A different solution would be possible by extending the calculus with co-capabilities à la *Safe Ambients* [LS00]. In that case, an ambient would be in a silent phase when its enclosed process does not perform upward exchanges and does not offer a *co-out* capability for nested ambients to exit.

Definition 2 (*Process Subtyping*).
Let $\leqslant$ *denote the same relation of exchange subtyping of Definition 1. Process subtyping is the smallest reflexive and transitive relation such that* $\mathsf{Pro}[\mathsf{shh}, {}^{*}F] \leqslant \mathsf{Pro}[E, {}^{*}F]$ *and in addition, satisfies the diagram on the right for all E and F.*

$$\begin{array}{ccccc} & & \mathsf{Pro}[E, {}^{\vartriangle}F] & & \\ & \nearrow & & \nwarrow & \\ \mathsf{Pro}[E, F] & & & & \mathsf{Pro}[E, {}^{\circ}F] \\ & \nwarrow & & \nearrow & \\ & & \mathsf{Pro}[E, {}^{\bullet}F] & & \end{array}$$

The intuition underlying process subtyping is as follows. The type $\mathsf{Pro}[\_, {}^{\bullet}E]$ identifies upward-silent processes that move their enclosing ambient only through locations with local exchanges of type E. Clearly, any such process can always be considered as a process of type $\mathsf{Pro}[\_, E]$ that is, as a process whose all upward exchanges are of type E and that is guaranteed to carry enclosing ambient only through locations with local exchanges of type E. In fact, it can also be considered as a process of type $\mathsf{Pro}[\_, {}^{\circ}E]$, that is as a temporarily upward-silent which becomes upward-active only when its enclosing ambients is in a context with local exchanges of type E. The two types $\mathsf{Pro}[\_, E]$ and $\mathsf{Pro}[\_, {}^{\circ}E]$ are incompatible, as processes of the first type may not be assumed to be (even temporarily) upward-silent, while processes of the second type may move across ambients regardless of the types of the latter and therefore across ambients whose local exchanges are of a type other than E. Nevertheless, the two types have a common supertype $\mathsf{Pro}[\_, {}^{\vartriangle}E]$, as this type identifies processes that may be currently upward-active, and whose enclosing ambients are guaranteed to reside in contexts with local exchanges of type E.

Typing for Expressions. We use the following notation and conventions: ${}^{*}W$ denotes any of the exchanges ${}^{\vartriangle}W, {}^{\bullet}W, {}^{\circ}W$, while ${}^{?}W$ denotes either ${}^{*}W$ or W; when occurring in definitions and typing rules, the notations ${}^{*}W$ and ${}^{?}W$ are intended to be used uniformly (i.e., all the occurrences of $*$ and ? in a rule or in the definition denote the same symbol, unless otherwise stated).

The key rules that characterize moded ambients are those that govern mobility into and out from a moded ambient:

$$\text{(OUT}\ \circ\text{)}\quad \frac{\Gamma \vdash M : \mathsf{Amb}^{\circ}[E, F]}{\Gamma \vdash \mathsf{out}\ M : \mathsf{Cap}[\mathsf{shh}]} \qquad \text{(IN}\ \circ\text{)}\quad \frac{\Gamma \vdash M : \mathsf{Amb}^{\circ}[F, E] \quad F' \leqslant F}{\Gamma \vdash \mathsf{in}\ M : \mathsf{Cap}[F']}$$

There is no constraint for entering a moded ambient —as the rule (IN $\circ$) imposes exactly the same restrictions as the rule (IN). Instead, the rule (OUT $\circ$) requires that if M is moded, then out M can only be exercised in ambients that are upward silent.
The next rules are those that relate and differentiate $\vdash\!\!\circ$ from $\vdash$.

$$\text{(POLYCAP)}\quad \frac{\Gamma \vdash M : \mathsf{Cap}[E]}{\Gamma \vdash\!\!\circ\, M : \mathsf{Cap}[E]} \qquad \text{(POLYPATH)}\quad \frac{\Gamma \vdash\!\!\circ\, M_1 : \mathsf{Cap}[E_1] \quad \Gamma \vdash\!\!\circ\, M_2 : \mathsf{Cap}[E_2]}{\Gamma \vdash\!\!\circ\, M_1.M_2 : \mathsf{Cap}[E_2]}$$

The rule *PolyCap* states that typing and moded-typing coincide for all capabilities. In addition, for capability paths —that is, for sequences of in and out moves— we have the special, and more flexible rule (POLYPATH) stating that we may disregard intermediate steps, as no communication takes place during those steps: we only need to trace precise information on the last move on the path. This effectively corresponds to interpreting $\mathsf{Cap}[E]$ as the type of capability paths whose *last* move requires upward exchanges of type E.

Moded typing of capabilities helps derive moded process types for prefixed processes as illustrated by the rules below[6].

Typing of Processes
As we said, the new type system includes all the typing rules for processes in § 4.2. In addition, we have the following rules. We start with the typing of prefixes.

(PREFIX ∘)
$$\frac{\Gamma \vdash_{\circ} M : \mathsf{Cap}[G] \quad \Gamma \vdash P : \mathsf{Pro}[E, {}^{\circ}F]}{\Gamma \vdash M.P : \mathsf{Pro}[E, {}^{\circ}F]}$$

(PREFIX △)
$$\frac{\Gamma \vdash_{\circ} M : \mathsf{Cap}[F] \quad \Gamma \vdash P : \mathsf{Pro}[E, {}^{\vartriangle}F]}{\Gamma \vdash M.P : \mathsf{Pro}[E, {}^{\circ}F]}$$

(PREFIX •)
$$\frac{\Gamma \vdash M : \mathsf{Cap}[F] \quad \Gamma \vdash P : \mathsf{Pro}[E, {}^{\bullet}F]}{\Gamma \vdash M.P : \mathsf{Pro}[E, {}^{\bullet}F]}$$

(PREFIX ∘) and (PREFIX △) state that prefixing a process P with a move capability always yields "moving" types, that is types with mode ∘. In particular, (PREFIX ∘) says that we may disregard the type of M (as long as M is a capability) if P is also a moving process [7]. This rule has the same rationale as the (POLYPATH) rule above: both rules are necessary for subject congruence: specifically, for the congruence rule $(M_1.M_2).P \equiv M_1.(M_2.P)$. On the other hand, by (PREFIX △), the upward exchanges of M and P must be consistent (equal) when P is not moving. In other words, the *last* move of the prefix must be compatible with the upward exchanges that the process will have right after. Notice, to this regard, that by subsumption, (PREFIX △) also accounts for the case of prefixing a process P of type $\mathsf{Pro}[E, F]$.

The rule (PREFIX •) types silent processes running in a context whose upward exchanges (if any) have type F. In this case, the type of the path M in the premise guarantees that P is type compatible with the local exchanges of the ambients hit on the move. Hence the typing of the capability must be "standard", as in the (PREFIX) rule from § 4.

The next two rules apply to parallel compositions.

(PARALLEL ∗ LEFT)
$$\frac{\Gamma \vdash P : \mathsf{Pro}[E, {}^{*}W] \quad \Gamma \vdash Q : \mathsf{Pro}[E, {}^{\bullet}W]}{\Gamma \vdash P \mid Q : \mathsf{Pro}[E, {}^{*}W]}$$

(PARALLEL ∗ RIGHT)
$$\frac{\Gamma \vdash P : \mathsf{Pro}[E, {}^{\bullet}W] \quad \Gamma \vdash Q : \mathsf{Pro}[E, {}^{*}W]}{\Gamma \vdash P \mid Q : \mathsf{Pro}[E, {}^{*}W]}$$

Two rules, and an appeal to subsumption, suffice to capture all cases. If P and Q are upward-silent (i.e. with upward exchanges ${}^{\bullet}W$), then $P \mid Q$ is also upward silent (with upward exchanges ${}^{\bullet}W$). $P \mid Q$ can be typed as moving (that is, with upward exchanges ${}^{\circ}W$), only when (i) either P or Q is moving and (ii) the other process is upward silent and type compatible with the exchanges of the moving process. The same reasoning

[6] The reader may wonder why we introduced a new turn-stile symbol rather then adding a mode to capabilities types, as in Cap°. In fact, the two choices are almost equivalent, in terms of expressive power, while the current is slightly less verbose.

[7] This characterization is possible because our syntax does not include the empty path.

applies when $P \mid Q : \mathsf{Pro}[E, {}^{\vartriangle}W]$, i.e. when $P \mid Q$ perform some upward exchange and then eventually move, hence the types $\mathsf{Pro}[E, {}^{\vartriangle}W]$ are derived with the same rules. We need two rules because we have to handle the two cases when the moving subprocess is P or Q.

The rules (DEAD) and (NEW) from § 4 handle also the cases for moded types (of course, save the fact that now T ranges over the extended class of process types). This is not true of the rule (REPL). In fact, if P and Q are both moving, then $P \mid Q$ may not be typed as moving, as either of the two could start its upward exchanges before the other. For this reason, there is no way to type a replicated process as a moving process: the only two possible types for a replicated process are a "regular" type (deduced by the rule REPL from § 4) or a silent type, as stated by the following new rule [8]:

(REPL •)

$$\frac{\Gamma \vdash P : \mathsf{Pro}[E, {}^{\bullet}F]}{\Gamma \vdash !P : \mathsf{Pro}[E, {}^{\bullet}F]}$$

For processes of the form $M[\![P]\!]$, we need new rules. The rule (AMB) from § 4 is modified so that it now deduces an upward-silent type, compatible with all the other modes. Two new rules handle the case when M is a transport ambient, distinguishing the cases when the enclosed process is moving or not.

(AMB)

$$\frac{\Gamma \vdash M : \mathsf{Amb}[E, F] \quad \Gamma \vdash P : \mathsf{Pro}[E, F]}{\Gamma \vdash M[\![P]\!] : \mathsf{Pro}[F, {}^{\bullet}H]}$$

(AMB △)

$$\frac{\Gamma \vdash M : \mathsf{Amb}^{\circ}[E, F] \quad \Gamma \vdash P : \mathsf{Pro}[E, {}^{\vartriangle}F]}{\Gamma \vdash M[\![P]\!] : \mathsf{Pro}[F, {}^{\bullet}H]}$$

(AMB ○)

$$\frac{\Gamma \vdash M : \mathsf{Amb}^{\circ}[E, F] \quad \Gamma \vdash P : \mathsf{Pro}[E, {}^{\circ}F]}{\Gamma \vdash M[\![P]\!] : \mathsf{Pro}[G, {}^{\bullet}H]}$$

In (AMB △) P is not moving, and the rule imposes type constraints equivalent to those imposed by the (AMB) rule: note, in fact, that the judgment $\Gamma \vdash P : \mathsf{Pro}[E, {}^{\vartriangle}F]$ could be derived by subsumption from $\Gamma \vdash P : \mathsf{Pro}[E, F]$. If, instead, P is moving, as in (AMB ○), its upward exchanges are blocked by the move, and we have freedom to chose the type of local exchanges of the process $M[\![P]\!]$. Once again, subject reduction does not break if exercising the capability in P activates upward exchanges: (AMB △) can be used to type the reductum.

We conclude with the rules for input-output.

(INPUT ⋆ ∗)

$$\frac{\Gamma, x{:}W \vdash P : \mathsf{Pro}[W, {}^{*}F]}{\Gamma \vdash (x{:}W)P : \mathsf{Pro}[W, {}^{*}F]}$$

(OUTPUT ⋆ ∗)

$$\frac{\Gamma \vdash M : W \quad \Gamma \vdash P : \mathsf{Pro}[W, {}^{*}F]}{\Gamma \vdash \langle M \rangle P : \mathsf{Pro}[W, {}^{*}F]}$$

[8] This is due to the particular semantics of replication we use, which yields to an unrestrained generation of copies. It is clear that the use of guarded replication or call by need would make replication compatible with moded types (see also next section).

(INPUT $\uparrow \vartriangle$)
$$\frac{\Gamma, x{:}W \vdash P : \mathsf{Pro}[F, {}^{\vartriangle}W]}{\Gamma \vdash (x{:}W)^{\uparrow} P : \mathsf{Pro}[F, {}^{\vartriangle}W]}$$

(OUTPUT $\uparrow \vartriangle$)
$$\frac{\Gamma \vdash M : W \quad \Gamma \vdash P : \mathsf{Pro}[F, {}^{\vartriangle}W]}{\Gamma \vdash \langle M \rangle^{\uparrow} P : \mathsf{Pro}[F, {}^{\vartriangle}W]}$$

Local communications are not affected by modes: it is the mode of the continuation process that determines the moded type of the input/output process itself.

Upward exchanges have only non-moving types, for obvious reasons. The particular type they have —that is, either $\mathsf{Pro}[F, {}^{\vartriangle}W]$ or the more informative $\mathsf{Pro}[F, W]$— depends on the type of their continuation. If their continuation is of type $\mathsf{Pro}[F, {}^{\bullet}W]$ or $\mathsf{Pro}[F, W]$, then the process —which is clearly not silent— can be typed as $\mathsf{Pro}[F, W]$. These cases are captured by the rule (INPUT/OUTPUT $\uparrow$) of § 4 (together with subsumption for the case $\mathsf{Pro}[F, {}^{\bullet}W]$). If instead the continuation has type $\mathsf{Pro}[F, {}^{\vartriangle}W]$ or $\mathsf{Pro}[F, {}^{\circ}W]$, as in (INPUT/OUTPUT $\uparrow \vartriangle$), we can just say that the process may eventually evolve into a moving process, hence the type $\mathsf{Pro}[F, {}^{\vartriangle}W]$ in the conclusion.

Finally, downward communications are not affected by whether the target ambient is moded or not. The rules from § 4 work just as well for the new system: two new rules, with the same format, handle the case when target ambient is moded (see Appendix A).

Note that in all output rules, the typing of the expression M being output is subject to "regular" typing. As a consequence, capability paths may be communicated only if well-typed under regular typing. This restriction could be lifted, had we employed moded capability types as suggested in § 6.3 (cf. footnote 6), but with no significant additional expressive power.

6.4 Subject Reduction

The results of § 4 hold for the new system as well. As a matter of fact, subject reduction for the type system of § 4 is a direct consequence of the subject reduction for moded typing. The theorem, and its proof are standard.

Lemma 1 (Substitution). *Let $\vdash^{?}$ denote either $\vdash$ or $\vdash_{\circ}$.*

- *Assume $\Gamma, x : W \vdash^{?} M : W'$ and $\Gamma \vdash N : W$. Then $\Gamma \vdash^{?} M\{x := N\} : W'$.*
- *Assume $\Gamma, x{:}W \vdash P : T$ and $\Gamma \vdash N : W$. Then $\Gamma \vdash P\{x := N\} : T$.*

Proof. *By induction on the derivations of the judgments $\Gamma, x : W \vdash^{?} M : W'$ and $\Gamma \vdash P : T$.*

Lemma 2 (Subject Congruence). *If $\Gamma \vdash P : T$ and $P \equiv Q$ then $\Gamma \vdash Q : T$.*

Proof. *By simultaneous induction on the derivations of $P \equiv Q$ and $Q \equiv P$.*

Theorem 2 (Subject Reduction). *If $\Gamma \vdash P : T$ and $P \rightarrow Q$ then $\Gamma \vdash Q : T$.*

Proof. *By induction on the derivation of $P \rightarrow Q$.*

We conclude this section with an example showing how moded typing help type-check the transport ambients used in § 3.2 to encode communication on named channels à la Seal Calculus. We give the case of downward input on a channel of type W, as in $c^{m}(x : W)P$, as representative.

In the typed encoding, the channel c is expressed by the ambient $c[\,!(x{:}W)\langle x \rangle\,]$, and the encoding of downward input is as follows:

$$\langle\!\langle c^m(x{:}W)P \rangle\!\rangle = (\boldsymbol{\nu} p{:}\mathsf{Amb}^{\circ}[W,W])p[\,\mathsf{in}\; m.\mathsf{in}\; c.(x{:}W)^{\uparrow}\mathsf{out}\; c.\mathsf{out}\; m.\langle x\rangle\,] \mid (x{:}W)^{p}\langle\!\langle P \rangle\!\rangle$$

We give a derivation under the most general assumptions $P{:}\mathsf{Pro}[E, {}^{?}F], m{:}\mathsf{Amb}^{?}[G, H]$ (where E, F, G, H can be any type), and $c{:}\mathsf{Amb}[W, \mathsf{shh}]$. The fact that the ambient p is typed as a transport ambient is essential for the typed encoding to type-check. This is shown by the following analysis that also illustrate the interplay between the modes $\circ$ and $\vartriangle$. Let $\varGamma$ be a type environment where $m{:}\mathsf{Amb}^{?}[G, H], c{:}\mathsf{Amb}[W, \mathsf{shh}]$ and $p{:}\mathsf{Amb}^{\circ}[W, W]$. First observe that, for the encoding to be typable we need

$$\varGamma \vdash p[\,\mathsf{in}\; m.\mathsf{in}\; c.(x{:}W)^{\uparrow}\mathsf{out}\; c.\mathsf{out}\; m.\langle x\rangle\,] \;:\; \mathsf{Pro}[E, {}^{\bullet}F]$$

This judgment may be derived by the rule (AMB $\circ$), provided that the process enclosed in p can be typed with mode $\circ$, that is, if

$$\varGamma \vdash \mathsf{in}\; m.\mathsf{in}\; c.(x{:}W)^{\uparrow}\mathsf{out}\; c.\mathsf{out}\; m.\langle x\rangle \;:\; \mathsf{Pro}[W, {}^{\circ}W].$$

This follows by (PREFIX $\circ$) from $\varGamma \vdash^{\circ} \mathsf{in}\; m{:}\mathsf{Cap}[G]$ and

$$\varGamma \vdash \mathsf{in}\; c.(x{:}W)^{\uparrow}\mathsf{out}\; c.\mathsf{out}\; m.\langle x\rangle \;:\; \mathsf{Pro}[W, {}^{\circ}W]$$

Here we use the flexibility of moded typing as no relation is required between G and W. The last judgment follows again by (PREFIX $\circ$) from $\varGamma \vdash^{\circ} \mathsf{in}\; c{:}\mathsf{Cap}[W]$ and from

$$\varGamma \vdash (x{:}W)^{\uparrow}\mathsf{out}\; c.\mathsf{out}\; m.\langle x\rangle \;:\; \mathsf{Pro}[W, {}^{\vartriangle}W],$$

This judgment can be derived by (INPUT $\uparrow$ $\vartriangle$) from

$$\varGamma, x{:}W \vdash \mathsf{out}\; c.\mathsf{out}\; m.\langle x\rangle{:}\mathsf{Pro}[W, {}^{\vartriangle}W].$$

Again, we rely on moded typing: the whole process type-checks since the move that precedes the upward output brings the ambient in an environment with the right exchange type. Deriving the last judgment is not difficult. From $\varGamma, x{:}W \vdash^{\circ} \mathsf{out}\; m{:}\mathsf{Cap}[H]$ and from $\varGamma, x{:}W \vdash \langle x\rangle{:}\mathsf{Pro}[W, {}^{\circ}W]$, we have $\varGamma, x{:}W \vdash \mathsf{out}\; m.\langle x\rangle : \mathsf{Pro}[W, {}^{\circ}W]$. Now, from the last judgment and from $\varGamma, x{:}W \vdash^{\circ} \mathsf{out}\; c{:}\mathsf{Cap}[\mathsf{shh}]$ an application of (PREFIX $\circ$) yields $\varGamma, x{:}W \vdash \mathsf{out}\; c.\mathsf{out}\; m.\langle x\rangle{:}\mathsf{Pro}[W, {}^{\circ}W]$ as desired. To conclude, we can apply subsumption, based on the subtyping $\mathsf{Pro}[W, {}^{\circ}W] \leqslant \mathsf{Pro}[W, {}^{\vartriangle}W]$, and then (INPUT $\uparrow$ $\vartriangle$) to obtain the desired typing.

7 Asynchronous Communications

As noted in [Car99], mobile and distributed computation can hardly rely on synchronous input-output as the only mechanism of communication. Also, experience with implementation of distributed calculi [BV02,FLA00] shows that the form of consensus required for synchronous communication is quite hard to implement in a distributed environment.

In § 2 we said that asynchronous communication can be recovered in our calculus in two ways: (i) either by coding it with synchronous output and null continuations, or (ii) by introducing the additional equivalence $\langle M\rangle^{\eta}P \equiv \langle M\rangle^{\eta} \mid P$. The first solution allows synchronous and asynchronous output to coexist: an asynchronous output-prefix $\langle M\rangle^{\eta}$ followed by a continuation P can be expressed in terms of synchronous output by the parallel composition $\langle M\rangle^\eta \mathbf{0} \mid P$. The second solution takes this idea to its extreme, by providing the exact same effect by structural congruence, and thus leads to a purely asynchronous calculus.

Neither alternative is fully satisfactory. One problem is that $\langle M\rangle^\eta P$ and $\langle M\rangle^\eta \mathbf{0} \mid P$ are only equivalent under the type system of § 4, not with moded types. In fact, for $\eta =\uparrow$, it is not difficult to find situations where $\langle M\rangle^\eta P$ is well-typed and $\langle M\rangle^\eta \mathbf{0} \mid P$ is not (with moded typing). An immediate consequence of this observation is that the congruence law $\langle M\rangle^\uparrow P \equiv \langle M\rangle^\uparrow \mid P$ is not preserved by moded typing.

A further reason for being unsatisfied with these solutions is that the use of null continuations to express asynchronous output has the effect of essentially defeating moded typing. Moded typing is possible, and effective, only along a single thread, while the coding of asynchronous output introduces parallel compositions and leaves no residual following an output. Notice, however, that the problem is not a consequence of moded typing and asynchrony being inherently incompatible. To see that, observe that in $\langle M\rangle^\uparrow P$ the continuation P could be typed with a mode independently of whether the prefix denotes synchronous or asynchronous output. All that matters for P to receive a (sound) "moving" type is that $\langle M\rangle$ gets delivered to the parent ambient before unleashing P: once delivered, whether or not $\langle M\rangle$ also synchronizes with local input is irrelevant.

Based on this observation, a smoother integration of asynchronous output and moded typing may be achieved by re-stating the congruence law as a reduction rule, and making it location-aware so that the output is delivered to the appropriate ambient.

Different formulations of the asynchronous version of the calculus are possible. A first solution, given below, is to replace the reductions (*output n*) and (*output* $\uparrow$) of § 2 with the reductions (*asynch output n*) and (*asynch output* $\uparrow$) below, and to introduce the new reduction (*asynch output* $\star$):

(*asynch output* $\star$)	$\langle M\rangle P \rightarrow \langle M\rangle \mid P$
(*asynch output n*)	$\langle M\rangle^n P \mid n[Q] \rightarrow P \mid n[\langle M\rangle \mid Q]$
(*asynch output* $\uparrow$)	$n[\langle M\rangle^\uparrow P \mid Q] \rightarrow \langle M\rangle \mid n[P \mid Q]$

With these reductions, the problem with moded types is solved: an upward output followed by a move, as in $\langle N\rangle^\uparrow M.P$ may safely be typed with mode $\vartriangle$ (based on the mode $\circ$ for $M.P$) irrespective of whether the output synchronizes or not. More generally, we may prove that subject reduction holds for this form of asynchronous reduction and the moded type system presented in the previous section: no further modification is needed.

A second possibility, is to combine synchrony and asynchrony. Cardelli [Car00], advocates that local exchanges can be synchronous, while remote communication ought to be asynchronous. This is a sound choice for our calculus: in fact, the reduction (*asynch output* $\star$) for local exchanges may be dispensed with, as local asynchronous output may be coded by $\langle M\rangle\mathbf{0} \mid P$ without affecting moded typing. Although this is sound, it would introduce some form of asymmetry in the implementation since non-local read accesses on local synchronous output would be synchronous with this solution.

A third possibility arises from the observation that the new output rules described for the first solution, together with the reduction rules for input prefixes of § 2 derive the following new set of reductions for input:

$$
\begin{array}{lr}
(\textit{asynch input} \star) & (x)P \mid \langle M \rangle \rightarrow P\{x := M\} \\
(\textit{asynch input } n) & (x)^n P \mid n[\,\langle M \rangle \mid Q\,] \rightarrow P\{x := M\} \mid n[\,Q\,] \\
(\textit{asynch input} \uparrow) & \langle M \rangle \mid n[\,(x)^{\uparrow} P \mid Q\,] \rightarrow n[\,P\{x := M\} \mid Q\,]
\end{array}
$$

One could then take the *asynch input* rules as primitive, and use them instead of the corresponding rules of § 2. In other words the third solution consists in replacing all the reduction rules of Section 2 by the six *asynch*-rules defined in this section. Although this solution is very close to the first one (but more "inefficient" since it adds new intermediate reduction steps), the result is rather interesting, as it suggests a novel interpretation of the process form $\langle M \rangle$ as a *memory cell*. Indeed, one may view $\langle M \rangle \mathbf{0}$ and $\langle M \rangle$ as denoting two very distinct processes, the former being a local output with a null continuation, the latter being a memory cell (more precisely a one-place buffer)[9]. Taking this view, every communication becomes a two-step protocol and the reductions have new interpretations. To exemplify, (*asynch output* $\star$) describes how a writer process $\langle M \rangle P$ writes a memory cell $\langle M \rangle$ and then continues as P; (*asynch input* $\star$) shows a reader that makes a destructive access to a memory cell $\langle M \rangle$. The same reasoning applies to downward and upward exchanges. As a result, memory cells, that is the output form $\langle M \rangle$, take the role of the resources of the calculus, which are bound to their location.

Whatever solution we choose in this section, they are all compatible with the moded typing of § 6 and, *a fortiori*, with the type system of § 4.

7.1 Synchrony versus Asynchrony: Security Trade-Offs

The choice of synchronous versus asynchronous communication has other consequences on the calculus, specifically, in terms of the security guarantees that can be made for it.

On one side, it is well known that synchronous communication generates hard-to-detect information flows based on synchronization. Our definition of synchronous input-output of § 2 also has this problem. For example, in the system $a[\,Q \mid b[\,\langle M \rangle P\,]\,]$, the sub-ambient b, gets to know exactly when (and if) Q makes a downward read access to its contents. Therefore one bit of information flowed by a read access from the reader to the writer. This makes non-interference [GM82,FG97] quite hard to satisfy.

On the other hand, by asynchronous communication we effectively give up *mediation* (see § 1.2), that is, control over interaction between sibling ambients. With synchronous input-output no ambient can be "spoiled" with unexpected (and possibly unwanted) output by its enclosing or enclosed ambients. As an example, consider the system $a[\,(x{:}W)^b P \mid b[\,c[\,\langle M \rangle^{\uparrow} \mid Q\,]\,]\,]$ which is typable in our system provided that $M{:}W$ and the b is declared of type $\mathsf{Amb}[W, F]$ for some F. With synchronous reductions there is no way for the upward output in c and the downward input in a to synchronize. Instead, in the asynchronous case, the initial configuration would evolve into $a[\,(x{:}W)^b P \mid b[\,\langle M \rangle \mid c[\,Q\,]\,]\,]$; by a further reduction step the ambient a gets hold of the message $\langle M \rangle$ without any mediation of b. Similarly, two siblings may establish a covert channel, as in the system $b[\,a[\,(x{:}W)^{\uparrow} P\,] \mid c[\,\langle M \rangle^{\uparrow} Q\,]\,]$ which reduces to $b[\,a[\,P\{x := M\}\,] \mid c[\,Q\,]\,]$ in two steps.

---

[9] To make it more explicit, for this last solution we could have used a different syntax for a memory cell containing M, say $\{\!\mid M \mid\!\}$, so that for example the local reduction rules would be written as $\langle M \rangle P \rightarrow \{\!\mid M \mid\!\} \mid P$ (output) and $(x)P \mid \{\!\mid M \mid\!\} \rightarrow P\{x := M\}$ (input).

These kind of covert channels are two examples of security breaches that cannot be prevented by the existing primitives of the calculus. A possible solution is to resort to further synchronization mechanisms, such as those offered by *portals* in the Seal calculus: this however, would essentially defeat asynchrony. A different, and more effective, way to avoid covert channels is by multilevel security, based on types, as we show in [BCC01].

8 Conclusion and Related Work

We have presented a variant of Mobile Ambients based on a different choice of communication primitives. The new calculus complements the constructs for mobility of Mobile Ambients with what we believe to be more effective mechanisms for resource protection and access control. In addition, it provides for more flexible typing of communications, and new insight into the relation between synchrony and asynchrony.

As we mentioned, other alternatives for parent-child communication would be possible. The anonymous referees suggested one alternative, based on the following reductions:

$$(x)^n P \mid n[\,\langle M\rangle^{\uparrow} Q \mid R\,] \rightarrow P\{x := M\} \mid n[\,Q \mid R\,]$$
$$\langle M\rangle^n P \mid n[\,(x)^{\uparrow} Q \mid R\,] \rightarrow P \mid n[\,Q\{x := M\} \mid R\,]$$

These reductions are similar in spirit to the corresponding reductions adopted in [CGZ01] for the Seal Calculus. We had considered this option for our Boxed Ambients, and initially dismissed it because it appeared to be enforcing an interpretation of channels as shared resources, thus undermining the notion of locality we wished to express. Looking at it retrospectively, it is now only fair to observe that the alternative reductions would still enable the view of an ambient as having two channels: a private channel which is only available for local exchanges, and an "upward channel" which the ambient offers to its enclosing context for read and write access.

In fact, a first analysis shows that there are trade-offs between our solution and the one given above. The latter has a number of security benefits, as it provides ambients with full control of the exchanges they may have with their children. Our solution, instead, enables communication protocols that would be difficult (if at all possible) to express with the above reductions. One example is the possibility for an ambient to "broadcast" a message to *any* entering ambient: $a[\,!\,\langle M\rangle\,]$. Here, a could be thought of as an "information site" which any ambient can enter to get a copy of M (reading it from upwards, after having entered a). The same protocol could hardly be expressed with the reductions given above, as they requires an ambient to know the names of its children in order to communicate with them. Nevertheless, a more in-depth analysis of the trade-offs between the two solutions deserves to be made, and is part of our plans of future work.

Besides Mobile Ambients and Seals, whose relationships with Boxed Ambients have been discussed all along, the new calculus shares the same motivations, and is superficially similar to Sewell and Vitek's Boxed-π [SV00]. The technical development, however, is entirely different. We do not provide direct mechanisms for constructing *wrappers*, rather we propose a new construct for ambient interaction in the attempt to provide easier-to-monitor communications. Also, our form of communication is anonymous, and based on a notion of locality which is absent in the Boxed-π Calculus. This latter choice has important consequences in the formalization of classic security models as we discuss in [BCC01]. Finally Boxed-π does not address mobility which is a fundamental component of our work.

Our type system is clearly also related to other typing systems developed for Mobile Ambients. In [CG99] types guarantees absence of type confusion for communications. The type systems of [CGG99] and [Zim00] provide control over ambients moves and opening. Furthermore, the introduction of *group* names [CGG00] and the possibility of creating fresh group names, give flexible ways to statically prevent unwanted propagation of names. The powerful type discipline for Safe Ambients, presented in [LS00], add a finer control over ambient interactions and remove all *grave interference*, i.e. all non-deterministic choice between logical incompatible interactions.

All those approaches are orthogonal to the particular communication primitives. We believe that similar typing disciplines as well as the use of group names and mobility types (without opening control, of course), can be adapted to Boxed Ambients to obtain similar strong results.

Finally, in [HR01,HR00] Hennessy and Riley discuss resource protection in $D\pi$-calculus, a distributed variant of π-calculus, where processes can migrate across locations. Although the design choices in the two calculi are different, and largely unrelated (different primitives, no location nesting,...) the ideas discussed in [HR01,HR00] were a source of inspiration for our work.

Acknowledgments. Thanks to Santiago Pericas for his comments of on earlier draft of the paper. Comments by the anonymous referees were very helpful to improve the presentation: we gratefully acknowledge their effort.

References

[BC01] M. Bugliesi and G. Castagna. Secure safe ambients. In *Proc. of the 28th ACM Symposium on Principles of Programming Languages*, pages 222–235, London, 2001. ACM Press.

[BCC01] M. Bugliesi, G. Castagna, and S. Crafa. Reasoning about security in mobile ambients. In *CONCUR 2001 (12th. International Conference on Concurrency Theory)*, Lecture Notes in Computer Science, Aahrus, Danemark, 2001. Springer. To appear.

[Bou92] G. Boudol. Asynchrony and the π-calculus. Research Report 1702, INRIA, http://www-sop.inria.fr/mimosa/personnel/Gerard.Boudol.html, 1992.

[BV02] C. Bryce and J. Vitek. The JavaSeal mobile agent kernel. *Autonomous Agents and Multi-Agent Systems*, 2002. To appear.

[Car99] L. Cardelli. *Abstractions for Mobile Computation*, volume 1603 of *Lecture Notes in Computer Science*, pages 51–94. Springer, 1999.

[Car00] L. Cardelli. Global computing. In *IST FET Global Computing Consultation Workshop*, 2000. Slides.

[CG98] L. Cardelli and A. Gordon. Mobile ambients. In *Proceedings of POPL '98*. ACM Press, 1998.

[CG99] L. Cardelli and A. Gordon. Types for mobile ambients. In *Proceedings of POPL '99*, pages 79–92. ACM Press, 1999.

[CGG99] L. Cardelli, G. Ghelli, and A. Gordon. Mobility types for mobile ambients. In *Proceedings of ICALP '99*, number 1644 in Lecture Notes in Computer Science, pages 230–239. Springer, 1999.

[CGG00] L. Cardelli, G. Ghelli, and A. D. Gordon. Ambient groups and mobility types. In *International Conference IFIP TCS*, number 1872 in Lecture Notes in Computer Science, pages 333–347. Springer, 2000.

[CGZ01] G. Castagna, G. Ghelli, and F. Zappa. Typing mobility in the Seal Calculus. In *CONCUR 2001 (12th. International Conference on Concurrency Theory)*, Lecture Notes in Computer Science, Aahrus, Danemark, 2001. Springer. To appear.

[DCS00] M. Dezani-Ciancaglini and I. Salvo. Security types for safe mobile ambients. In *Proceedings of ASIAN '00*, pages 215–236. Springer, 2000.

[DLB00] P. Degano, F. Levi, and C. Bodei. Safe ambients: Control flow analysis and security. In *Proceedins of ASIAN '00*, volume 1961 of *LNCS*, pages 199–214. Springer, 2000.

[FG97] R. Focardi and R. Gorrieri. Non interference: Past, present and future. In *Proceedings of DARPA Workshop on Foundations for Secure Mobile Code*, pages 26–28, march 1997.

[FLA00] C. Fournet, J-J. Levy, and Shmitt. A. An asynchronous, distributed implementation of mobile ambients. In *International Conference IFIP TCS*, number 1872 in Lecture Notes in Computer Science. Springer, 2000.

[GM82] J.A. Goguen and J. Meseguer. Security policy and security models. In *Proceedings of Symposium on Secrecy and Privacy*, pages 11–20. IEEE Computer Society, april 1982.

[HR00] M. Hennessy and J. Riely. Information flow vs. resource access in the asynchronous π-calculus (extended abstract). In *Automata, Languages and Programming, 27th International Colloquium*, volume 1853 of *LNCS*, pages 415–427. Springer, 2000.

[HR01] M. Hennessy and J. Riely. Resource access control in systems of mobile agents. *Information and Computation*, 2001. To appear.

[LS00] F. Levi and D. Sangiorgi. Controlling interference in Ambients. In *POPL '00*, pages 352–364. ACM Press, 2000.

[NN00] H. R. Nielson and F. Nielson. Shape analysis for mobile ambients. In *POPL '00*, pages 135–148. ACM Press, 2000.

[NNHJ99] F. Nielson, H. Riis Nielson, R. R. Hansen, and J. G. Jensen. Validating firewalls in mobile ambients. In *Proc. CONCUR '99*, number 1664 in LNCS, pages 463–477. Springer, 1999.

[SV00] P. Sewell and J. Vitek. Secure composition of untrusted code: Wrappers and causality types. In *13th IEEE Computer Security Foundations Workshop*, 2000.

[VC99] J. Vitek and G. Castagna. Seal: A framework for secure mobile computations. In *Internet Programming Languages*, number 1686 in LNCS. Springer, 1999.

[Zim00] P. Zimmer. Subtyping and typing algorithms for mobile ambients. In *Proceedins of FoSSaCS '99*, volume 1784 of *LNCS*, pages 375–390. Springer, 2000.

A Moded Typing: The Complete Type System

We use again the following shorthands: ${}^{*}W$ to denote any of the exchanges ${}^{\vartriangle}W, {}^{\bullet}W, {}^{\circ}W$, and use ${}^{?}W$ to denote either ${}^{*}W$ or W. Similarly we use $\mathsf{Amb}^{?}[E,F]$ to denote either $\mathsf{Amb}[E,F]$ or $\mathsf{Amb}^{\circ}[E,F]$. The use of such shorthands make it possible to express different rules of § 4 and 6 as instances of a same rule.

Expressions

(PROJECTION)
$$\frac{\Gamma(M) = W}{\Gamma \vdash M : W}$$

(IN)
$$\frac{\Gamma \vdash M : \mathsf{Amb}^{?}[F,E] \quad F' \leqslant F}{\Gamma \vdash \mathsf{in}\ M : \mathsf{Cap}[F']}$$

(OUT)
$$\frac{\Gamma \vdash M : \mathsf{Amb}[E,F] \quad F' \leqslant F}{\Gamma \vdash \mathsf{out}\ M : \mathsf{Cap}[F']}$$

(TUPLE)
$$\frac{\Gamma \vdash M_i : W_i \quad \forall i \in 1..k}{\Gamma \vdash (M_1, \ldots, M_k) : W_1 \times \cdots \times W_k}$$

(PATH)
$$\frac{\Gamma \vdash M_1 : \mathsf{Cap}[F]\ \Gamma \vdash M_2 : \mathsf{Cap}[F]}{\Gamma \vdash M_1.M_2 : \mathsf{Cap}[F]}$$

(OUT $\circ$)
$$\frac{\Gamma \vdash M : \mathsf{Amb}^{\circ}[E,F]}{\Gamma \vdash \mathsf{out}\ M : \mathsf{Cap}[\mathsf{shh}]}$$

(CAP $\circ$)
$$\frac{\Gamma \vdash M : \mathsf{Cap}[E]}{\Gamma \vdash_{\circ} M : \mathsf{Cap}[E]}$$

(POLYPATH)
$$\frac{\Gamma \vdash_{\circ} M_1 : \mathsf{Cap}[E_1] \quad \Gamma \vdash_{\circ} M_2 : \mathsf{Cap}[E_2]}{\Gamma \vdash_{\circ} M_1.M_2 : \mathsf{Cap}[E_2]}$$

Processes

(PREFIX ∘)
$$\frac{\Gamma \vdash_{\circ} M : \mathsf{Cap}[G] \quad \Gamma \vdash P : \mathsf{Pro}[E, {}^{\circ}F]}{\Gamma \vdash M.P : \mathsf{Pro}[E, {}^{\circ}F]}$$

(PREFIX △)
$$\frac{\Gamma \vdash_{\circ} M : \mathsf{Cap}[F] \quad \Gamma \vdash P : \mathsf{Pro}[E, {}^{\vartriangle}F]}{\Gamma \vdash M.P : \mathsf{Pro}[E, {}^{\circ}F]}$$

(PREFIX •)
$$\frac{\Gamma \vdash M : \mathsf{Cap}[F] \quad \Gamma \vdash P : \mathsf{Pro}[E, {}^{\bullet}F]}{\Gamma \vdash M.P : \mathsf{Pro}[E, {}^{\bullet}F]}$$

(PREFIX)
$$\frac{\Gamma \vdash M : \mathsf{Cap}[F] \quad \Gamma \vdash P : \mathsf{Pro}[E, F]}{\Gamma \vdash M.P : \mathsf{Pro}[E, F]}$$

(PAR)
$$\frac{\Gamma \vdash P : \mathsf{Pro}[E, F] \quad \Gamma \vdash Q : \mathsf{Pro}[E, F]}{\Gamma \vdash P \mid Q : \mathsf{Pro}[E, F]}$$

(PAR ∗)
$$\frac{\Gamma \vdash P : \mathsf{Pro}[E, {}^{*}W] \quad \Gamma \vdash Q : \mathsf{Pro}[E, {}^{\bullet}W]}{\Gamma \vdash P \mid Q,\ Q \mid P : \mathsf{Pro}[E, {}^{*}W]}$$

(DEAD)
$$\frac{}{\Gamma \vdash \mathbf{0} : T}$$

(NEW)
$$\frac{\Gamma, x : W \vdash P : T}{\Gamma \vdash (\boldsymbol{\nu} x{:}W)P : T}$$

(REPL)
$$\frac{\Gamma \vdash P : \mathsf{Pro}[E, F]}{\Gamma \vdash !P : \mathsf{Pro}[E, F]}$$

(REPL •)
$$\frac{\Gamma \vdash P : \mathsf{Pro}[E, {}^{\bullet}F]}{\Gamma \vdash !P : \mathsf{Pro}[E, {}^{\bullet}F]}$$

(AMB)
$$\frac{\Gamma \vdash M : \mathsf{Amb}[E, F] \quad \Gamma \vdash P : \mathsf{Pro}[E, F]}{\Gamma \vdash M[\![P]\!] : \mathsf{Pro}[F, {}^{\bullet}H]}$$

(AMB △)
$$\frac{\Gamma \vdash M : \mathsf{Amb}^{\circ}[E, F] \quad \Gamma \vdash P : \mathsf{Pro}[E, {}^{\vartriangle}F]}{\Gamma \vdash M[\![P]\!] : \mathsf{Pro}[F, {}^{\bullet}H]}$$

(AMB ∘)
$$\frac{\Gamma \vdash M : \mathsf{Amb}^{\circ}[E, F] \quad \Gamma \vdash P : \mathsf{Pro}[E, {}^{\circ}F]}{\Gamma \vdash M[\![P]\!] : \mathsf{Pro}[G, {}^{\bullet}H]}$$

(INPUT ⋆)
$$\frac{\Gamma, x{:}W \vdash P : \mathsf{Pro}[W, {}^{?}E]}{\Gamma \vdash (x{:}W)P : \mathsf{Pro}[W, {}^{?}E]}$$

(OUTPUT ⋆)
$$\frac{\Gamma \vdash M : W \quad \Gamma \vdash P : \mathsf{Pro}[W, {}^{?}E]}{\Gamma \vdash \langle M \rangle P : \mathsf{Pro}[W, {}^{?}E]}$$

(INPUT M)
$$\frac{\Gamma \vdash M : \mathsf{Amb}^{?}[W, E] \quad \Gamma, x{:}W \vdash P : T}{\Gamma \vdash (x{:}W)^{M} P : T}$$

(OUTPUT N)
$$\frac{\Gamma \vdash N : \mathsf{Amb}^{?}[W, E]\ \Gamma \vdash M : W\ \Gamma \vdash P : T}{\Gamma \vdash \langle M \rangle^{N} P : T}$$

(INPUT ↑)
$$\frac{\Gamma, x{:}W \vdash P : \mathsf{Pro}[E, W]}{\Gamma \vdash (x{:}W)^{\uparrow} P : \mathsf{Pro}[E, W]}$$

(OUTPUT ↑)
$$\frac{\Gamma \vdash M : W \quad \Gamma \vdash P : \mathsf{Pro}[E, W]}{\Gamma \vdash \langle M \rangle^{\uparrow} P : \mathsf{Pro}[E, W]}$$

(INPUT ↑ △)
$$\frac{\Gamma, x{:}\ W \vdash P : \mathsf{Pro}[F, {}^{\vartriangle}W]}{\Gamma \vdash (x{:}\ W)^{\uparrow} P : \mathsf{Pro}[F, {}^{\vartriangle}W]}$$

(OUTPUT ↑ △)
$$\frac{\Gamma \vdash M : W \quad \Gamma \vdash P : \mathsf{Pro}[F, {}^{\vartriangle}W]}{\Gamma \vdash \langle M \rangle^{\uparrow} P : \mathsf{Pro}[F, {}^{\vartriangle}W]}$$

In addition, we have a standard subsumption rule to deduce $\Gamma \vdash P : T'$ from $\Gamma \vdash P : T$ and $T \leqslant T'$.

A Typed Process Calculus for Fine-Grained Resource Access Control in Distributed Computation

Daisuke Hoshina[1], Eijiro Sumii[2], and Akinori Yonezawa[2]

[1] TOSHIBA Corporation, Japan,
hoshina@ivc.toshiba.co.jp
[2] Department of Computer Science,
Graduate School of Information Science and Engineering,
University of Tokyo, Japan,
{sumii,yonezawa}@yl.is.s.u-tokyo.ac.jp

Abstract. We propose the π^D*-calculus*, a process calculus that can flexibly model fine-grained control of resource access in distributed computation, with a type system that statically prevents access violations. Access control of resources is important in distributed computation, where resources themselves or their contents may be transmitted from one domain to another and thereby vital resources may be exposed to unauthorized processes. In π^D, a notion of hierarchical *domains* is introduced as an abstraction of protection domains, and considered as the unit of access control. Domains are treated as first-class values and can be created dynamically. In addition, the hierarchal structure of domains can be extended dynamically as well. These features are the source of the expressiveness of π^D. This paper presents the syntax, the operational semantics, and the type system of π^D, with examples to demonstrate its expressiveness.

1 Introduction

Background. Keeping access to resources under control is an issue of central importance in distributed computation: by definition, a distributed system consists of multiple computation domains, such as separate Java virtual machines [8] on different computers, where resources are transmitted from one domain to another; accordingly, a non-trivial amount of effort needs to be spent on ensuring that vital resources are protected from unauthorized access. Although several foundational calculi [3, 7, 10, 22] have been proposed for the purpose of studying distributed computation, few of them have notions of access rights and can guarantee properties about resource access—such as "this high-level integer is read only by high-level processes"—and none of them are flexible enough to allow various policies of access control.

The π^D*-Calculus.* To address the above issue, we propose the π^D*-calculus*, a typed process calculus that can flexibly model fine-grained resource access control in distributed computation, where the type system statically prevents access

N. Kobayashi and B.C. Pierce (Eds.): TACS 2001, LNCS 2215, pp. 64–81, 2001.

violations. π^D has a notion of *domains*, an abstraction of hierarchical protection domains as the unit of access control. For example, consider a situation where only high-level processes, such as a super user process, can access high-level resources, such as the file /etc/passwd. This situation can be modeled as a system with a communication channel *readPasswd* of type $\mathtt{chan}\langle high\_level, high\_level\rangle String$. Here, a channel type $\mathtt{chan}\langle i, o\rangle T$ means that channels of this type can be used for *receiving* a value of type T only by processes running in the domain i or a greater domain, and for *sending* a value of type T only by processes running in the domain o or a greater domain. Thus, the system $high\_level[readPasswd?(x).P]$, which represents a process running at the domain *high_level* and trying to read a value x from the channel *readPasswd*, is well-typed provided that P is well-typed at *high_level*, while the system $low\_level[readPasswd?(x).Q]$ is not.

The role of our domains is similar to that of Riely and Hennessy's *security levels* [11]. Unlike their security levels, however, *domains can be created dynamically and are treated as first-class values.* This feature is the source of the expressiveness of π^D, as demonstrated by the following examples.

Dynamic Creation of Domains. First, we give examples that take advantage of the dynamic creation of domains. Consider a situation where there are some CGI programs in a web server. The web server receives a request from a client and executes the corresponding CGI program in the domain *user*, so that the CGI program cannot access vital resources in the web server. This situation can be modeled as follows

$$server[*req_1?(x).\mathtt{spawn}@user.\mathbf{CGI_1} \mid *req_2?(x).\mathtt{spawn}@user.\mathbf{CGI_2} \mid \cdots]$$

where the process $\mathbf{CGI}_i$ represents each CGI program in the web server. The construct $\mathtt{spawn}@user.\mathbf{CGI}_i$ represents the spawning of the process $\mathbf{CGI}_i$ in the domain *user*. After receiving requests, the above process will evolve to a process like

$$\begin{array}{l} server[*req_1?(x).\mathtt{spawn}@user.\mathbf{CGI_1} \mid *req_2?(x).\mathtt{spawn}@user.\mathbf{CGI_2} \mid \cdots] \mid \\ user[\mathbf{CGI}'_1] \mid user[\mathbf{CGI}'_2] \mid \cdots \end{array}$$

where the process $\mathbf{CGI}'_i$ represents an instance of the CGI program $\mathbf{CGI}_i$. Suppose that $\mathbf{CGI}'_1$ has vital resources which *should not* be accessed by other CGI programs (or other instances of the same CGI program). Suppose furthermore that $\mathbf{CGI}'_2$ may be a malicious process trying to interfere with other processes through shared resources in the environment. Since $\mathbf{CGI}_2$ is a process running in the same domain *user* as $\mathbf{CGI}_1$ is running in, it *is* actually possible for $\mathbf{CGI}_2$ to access the vital resources of $\mathbf{CGI}_1$.

A naive solution to this problem would be to prepare another domain $user_2$, in which the web server executes $\mathbf{CGI}_2$. However, doing so means that if every $\mathbf{CGI}_i$ is malicious, we must prepare a distinct domain for each $\mathbf{CGI}_i$ *in advance.* Furthermore, even doing so does not protect different instances of the same CGI program from one another.

These problems can be solved by taking advantage of the *dynamic creation* of domains and rewriting the above process as follows.

$$\begin{array}{l} \mathit{server}[*\mathit{req}_1?(x).(\nu \mathit{user} : \mathtt{dom}\langle \mathit{server}/\bot\rangle)\mathtt{spawn}@\mathit{user}.\mathbf{CGI_1} \mid \\ \qquad *\mathit{req}_2?(x).(\nu \mathit{user} : \mathtt{dom}\langle \mathit{server}/\bot\rangle)\mathtt{spawn}@\mathit{user}.\mathbf{CGI_2} \mid \cdots] \end{array}$$

The construct $(\nu \mathit{user} : T)$ denotes the dynamic creation of the domain *user* of type T. The types of domains have the form $\mathtt{dom}\langle \tilde{m}/\tilde{n}\rangle$, which determines a hierarchical structure of domains: if a domain l has type $\mathtt{dom}\langle \tilde{m}/\tilde{n}\rangle$, then l is a child domain of each m_i in $\tilde{m}$ and a parent domain of each n_j in $\tilde{n}$; that is, l is less than each m_i and greater than each n_j. We assume that there exist the greatest domain $\top$ and the least domain $\bot$.

The above solution—that is, creating a fresh domain for each request and executing the requested CGI program in the fresh domain—amounts to *sandboxing* each instance of the CGI program within a separate domain. In practice, however, it is too restrictive to disallow CGI programs to share *any* resources. Let us consider a more flexible policy where there is some public resource—the standard Perl library, for example—which can be accessed by any CGI programs. This policy can be described as follows.

$$\begin{array}{l} (\nu \mathit{public} : \mathtt{dom}\langle \mathit{server}/\bot\rangle)(\nu \mathit{perl\_library} : \mathtt{chan}\langle \mathit{server}, \mathit{public}\rangle T) \\ \mathit{server}[\mathit{perl\_library}?(x).P \mid \\ \qquad *\mathit{req}_1?(x).(\nu \mathit{user} : \mathtt{dom}\langle \mathit{server}/\mathit{public}\rangle)\mathtt{spawn}@\mathit{user}.\mathbf{CGI}_1 \mid \\ \qquad *\mathit{req}_2?(x).(\nu \mathit{user} : \mathtt{dom}\langle \mathit{server}/\mathit{public}\rangle)\mathtt{spawn}@\mathit{user}.\mathbf{CGI}_2 \mid \cdots] \end{array}$$

Here, the channel *perl_library* is the resource which can be used by any CGI programs. Note that not only domains but also their hierarchical structure is created dynamically: each instance of *user* is declared to be less than *server* and greater than *public*.

Domains as First-Class Values. Now, we give an example where domains are treated as first-class values. Consider a situation where a server receives a request from a client and creates a library which is supposed to be used only by the client. This situation can be modeled as a system $\mathbf{Server} \mid \mathbf{Client}_1 \mid \mathbf{Client}_2 \mid \mathbf{Client}_3 \mid \cdots$, where

$$\begin{array}{l} \mathbf{Server} = \mathit{server}[*\mathit{req}?(x).(\nu \mathit{lib} : \mathtt{dom}\langle x, \mathit{server}/\bot\rangle)\mathtt{spawn}@\mathit{lib}.\mathbf{Lib} \mid \cdots] \\ \mathbf{Client}_i = \mathit{client}_i[\mathit{req}!\langle \mathit{client}_i\rangle \mid P_i] \end{array}$$

Here, the process **Lib** represents the library. The server first receives a domain client_i, creates a fresh child domain *lib*, and then runs the library in this domain. Thus, the above system evolves to

$$\mathbf{Server}|\mathit{client}_1[P_1]|\mathit{lib}_1[\mathbf{Lib}]|\mathit{client}_2[P_2]|\mathit{lib}_2[\mathbf{Lib}]|\mathit{client}_3[P_3]|\mathit{lib}_3[\mathbf{Lib}]|\cdots$$

where the domain lib_i is less than both *server* and client_i. The server does not know the domain client_i of each client in advance. A client, however, informs the server of the client's own domain client_i by sending it to the server through the channel *req*, so that the server can execute the library in the client's child domain lib_i.

Table 1. Meta-variables for names

$a - d \in \mathit{Chan}$	$l - n \in \mathit{Dom} \supset \{\top, \bot\}$	$u - w \in \mathit{Name} = \mathit{Chan} \cup \mathit{Dom}$

Outline of the Paper. The rest of this paper is organized as follows. Section 2 presents the syntax and the operational semantics of π^D. Then, Section 3 describes our type system for controlling access to resources in π^D, and Section 4 proves the type system sound with respect to the operational semantics. Furthermore, Section 5 extends π^D with subtyping. Finally, Section 6 discusses related work and Section 7 concludes with future work.

2 The Language

This section presents the syntax and the operational semantics of the π^D-calculus. It is an extension of the polyadic π-calculus [15] with hierarchical domains, the unit of access control. Although they are similar to security levels of Hennessy and Riely [11], our domains can be created dynamically and passed through communication channels. Every process is located in a domain, which determines which resources the process can access.

Domains are partially ordered. We assume that there exist the greatest domain $\top$ and the least domain $\bot$. Intuitively, processes in a domain which is greater with respect to the partial order can access more resources. We will come back to this point in Section 3.1.

2.1 Syntax

We assume that there are two disjoint countably infinite sets *Chan* of *channels* and *Dom* of *domains*. We also assume that the set *Dom* has two special elements $\top$ and $\bot$. Our meta-variable convention for elements of these sets is given in Table 1.

Types. We introduce three kinds of types: *channel types*, *domain types* and *dependent pair types*. They are given in Table 2.

Channel types: $\mathtt{chan}\langle m, n\rangle T$ is the type of a channel for communicating compound names of type T. The pair $\langle m, n\rangle$ means that this channel can be used for input (resp. output) only by processes located in the domain m (resp. n) or a greater domain. If m is $\top$, no process can use this channel for input and if m is $\bot$, any process can use this channel for input. The case for output is similar when n is either $\top$ or $\bot$. When a channel c has type $\mathtt{chan}\langle m, n\rangle T$, we say that c has the input level m and the output level n.

Domain types: If a domain l has type $\mathtt{dom}\langle \tilde{m}/\tilde{n}\rangle$, then l is a child domain of each m in $\tilde{m}$ and a parent domain of each n in $\tilde{n}$. That is, l is less than any of $\tilde{m}$ and greater than any of $\tilde{n}$.

Table 2. Types

(Type)		
$S, T ::=$	$\texttt{chan}\langle m, n\rangle T$	channel type
	$\texttt{dom}\langle \tilde{m}/\tilde{n}\rangle$	domain type
	$\Sigma u : S.T$	dependent pair type

Table 3. Threads and systems

(Threads)		
$P, Q, R ::=$	$P \mid Q$	parallel
	$c!\langle V\rangle$	output
	$c?(U : T).P$	input
	$*P$	replication
	$(\nu v : T)P$	name creation
	0	nil
	$\texttt{spawn@}m.P$	spawning
(Systems)		
$L, M, N ::=$	$M \mid N$	parallel
	$(\nu v : T)M$	name creation
	0	nil
	$m[P]$	located thread
(CompoundNames)		
$U - W ::=$	u	
	(u, U)	

Dependent pair types: If a name v has type S and another name v' has type $\{v/u\}T$, then the pair (v, v') has a dependent pair type $\Sigma u : S.T$. Note that if u does not appear free in T, this dependent pair type can actually be considered as an ordinary pair type $S \times T$.

Processes. The syntax of *threads* and *systems* is given in Table 3. Both threads and systems are called *processes*. Their intuitive meanings are as follows.

- An *output* $c!\langle V\rangle$ sends the compound name V on the channel c. An *input* $c?(U : T).P$ receives a compound name through the channel c, binds the compound name to U, and then executes P.
- A *name creation* $(\nu v : T)P$ or $(\nu v : T)M$ creates a fresh name, binds it to v, and then executes P or M. Note that not only channels but also domains can be created dynamically.
- A *spawning* $\texttt{spawn@}m.P$ spawns the process P in the domain m.
- A *located thread* $m[P]$ denotes the thread P running in the domain m.

We write $fn(T)$, $fn(U)$, $fn(P)$ and $fn(M)$ for the set of free names appearing in T, U, P and M, respectively. Their formal definition is omitted in this paper.

Table 4. Structural preorder

$m[P \mid Q] \preceq m[P] \mid m[Q]$		(SP-SPLIT)
$m[(\nu v : T)P] \preceq (\nu v : T)m[P]$	if $v \neq m$	(SP-NAME)
$m[0] \preceq 0$		(SP-ZERO)
$(\nu v : T)M \mid N \preceq (\nu v : T)(M \mid N)$	if $v \notin fn(N)$	(SP-EXTR)
$m[*P] \preceq m[P] \mid m[*P]$		(SP-REPL)
$(\nu v : T)(\nu w : S)M \preceq (\nu w : S)(\nu v : T)M$	if $v \notin fn(S) \wedge w \notin fn(T)$	(SP-EX)

2.2 Operational Semantics

We define the operational semantics of π^D by using two binary relations: the *structural relation* $\preceq$ and the *reduction relation* $\longrightarrow$.

Definition 1 (Structural Relation). *The structural relation $\preceq$ is the least reflexive and transitive relation over systems satisfying the rules in Table 4 and the monoid laws: $M \mid 0 \equiv M, M \mid N \equiv N \mid M$ and $(L \mid M) \mid N \equiv L \mid (M \mid N)$. Here, $P \equiv Q$ is defined as $P \preceq Q \wedge Q \preceq P$.*

The rule (SP-SPLIT) allows a thread $P \mid Q$ to split into two independent threads P and Q. (SP-EX) says that adjacent name bindings can be swapped. Note that the side-condition is necessary since we have dependent pair types [22].

Definition 2 (Reduction Relation). *The* reduction relation $\longrightarrow$ *over systems is the least relation satisfying the rules in Table 5. $M \longrightarrow M'$ means that M can evolve to M' by one-step communication or spawning. The relation $\longrightarrow^*$ is the reflexive and transitive closure of $\longrightarrow$.*

The rule (R-COMM) allows two processes running in parallel to exchange a compound name through a channel. Be aware that the communication can take place across domains. Thus, unlike in $D\pi$ [10], channel names are global in π^D. The rule (R-SPAWN) allows a process to spawn a thread in a domain. Obviously, it is dangerous if any process can spawn a new process in any domain by using the spawn statement. Our type system will guarantee that processes in a domain m can spawn new processes in another domain n only if m is greater than n. The other rules are standard in the π-calculus.

2.3 Example

Computation Server. We give an example to show how we protect channels from unauthorized access by assigning them suitable types. Consider a situation where a computation server receives a request from a client and creates a library which is supposed to be used only by the client, like the last example in Section 1. The library here is an integer successor function: it receives an integer i with a

Table 5. Reduction relation

$$m[c!\langle V\rangle] \mid m'[c?(U:T).P] \longrightarrow m'[\{V/U\}P] \quad \text{(R-COMM)}$$

$$m[\mathtt{spawn@}n.P] \longrightarrow n[P] \quad \text{(R-SPAWN)}$$

$$\frac{M \longrightarrow M'}{M \mid N \longrightarrow M' \mid N} \ \text{(R-PAR)} \qquad \frac{M \longrightarrow N}{(\nu v:T)M \longrightarrow (\nu v:T)N} \ \text{(R-NEW)}$$

$$\frac{M \preceq M' \quad M' \longrightarrow N' \quad N' \preceq N}{M \longrightarrow N} \ \text{(R-CONG)}$$

where the substitution $\{V/U\}$ of compound names is defined as follows:

$$\{V/U\} \stackrel{def}{=} \begin{cases} \{v/u\} & \text{if } V = v \text{ and } U = u \\ (\{v/u\} \bullet \{V'/U'\}) & \text{if } V = (v, V') \text{ and } U = (u, U') \end{cases}$$

$$\{v_1/u_1, \cdots, v_i/u_i\} \bullet \{v'_1/u'_1, \cdots, v'_j/u'_j\} \stackrel{def}{=} \{v_1/u_1, \cdots, v_i/u_i, v'_1/u'_1, \cdots, v'_j/u'_j\}$$

channel r, and sends $i+1$ back through r. Assuming arithmetic primitives for integer operation, this situation can be modeled as

$$(\nu Serv : \mathtt{dom}\langle\top/\bot\rangle)(\nu Client_1 : \mathtt{dom}\langle\top/\bot\rangle)(\nu Client_2 : \mathtt{dom}\langle\top/\bot\rangle)\cdots$$
$$(\nu serv : \mathbf{TServ})(\mathbf{Serv} \mid \mathbf{Client}_1 \mid \mathbf{Client}_2 \mid \cdots)$$

where

$$\begin{aligned}
\mathbf{Serv} &= Serv[*serv?(c, r : \mathbf{TServReq}). \\
&\qquad (\nu Succ : \mathtt{dom}\langle Serv/\bot\rangle)(\nu succ : \mathbf{TSucc}_{c,Succ}) \\
&\qquad (\mathtt{spawn@}Succ.\mathbf{Succ} \mid r!\langle Succ, succ\rangle)] \\
\mathbf{Succ} &= *succ?(x, y : \mathbf{TSuccReq}_{c,Succ}).y!\langle x+1\rangle \\
\mathbf{Client}_i &= Client_i[(\nu reply : \mathtt{chan}\langle Client_i, Serv\rangle\mathbf{TServAns}_{Client_i}) \\
&\qquad serv!\langle Client_i, reply\rangle \mid \\
&\qquad reply?(MySucc, mysucc : \mathbf{TServAns}_{Client_i}). \\
&\qquad \ldots \text{use } mysucc \text{ as a library} \ldots)]
\end{aligned}$$

$$\begin{aligned}
\mathbf{TServ} &= \mathtt{chan}\langle Serv, \bot\rangle\mathbf{TServReq} \\
\mathbf{TServReq} &= \Sigma x : \mathtt{dom}\langle\top/\bot\rangle.\mathtt{chan}\langle x, Serv\rangle\mathbf{TServAns}_x \\
\mathbf{TServAns}_m &= \Sigma y : \mathtt{dom}\langle Serv/\bot\rangle.\mathbf{TSucc}_{m,y} \\
\mathbf{TSucc}_{m,n} &= \mathtt{chan}\langle n, m\rangle\mathbf{TSuccReq}_{m,n} \\
\mathbf{TSuccReq}_{m,n} &= \mathsf{int} \times \mathbf{TSuccAns}_{m,n} \\
\mathbf{TSuccAns}_{m,n} &= \mathtt{chan}\langle m, n\rangle\mathsf{int}
\end{aligned}$$

Note that the computation server does not know in advance how many clients exist, and thus every client must send its own domain to the computation server.

Table 6. Type environments

$$\Gamma, \Delta ::= \bullet \mid \Gamma, u : T$$

This process evolves to:

$$\begin{aligned}
&(\nu Serv : \mathtt{dom}\langle\top/\bot\rangle)(\nu Client_1 : \mathtt{dom}\langle\top/\bot\rangle)(\nu Client_2 : \mathtt{dom}\langle\top/\bot\rangle)\cdots\\
&(\nu serv : \mathbf{TServ})(\mathbf{Serv}|\\
&\qquad (\nu Succ_1 : \mathtt{dom}\langle Serv/\bot\rangle)(\nu succ_1 : \mathbf{TSucc}_{Client_1, Succ_1})\\
&\qquad\quad (Client_1[\{Succ_1/MySucc, succ_1/mysucc\}\cdots] \mid Succ_1[\mathbf{Succ}])|\\
&\qquad (\nu Succ_2 : \mathtt{dom}\langle Serv/\bot\rangle)(\nu succ_2 : \mathbf{TSucc}_{Client_2, Succ_2})\\
&\qquad\quad (Client_2[\{Succ_2/MySucc, succ_2/mysucc\}\cdots] \mid Succ_2[\mathbf{Succ}]) \mid\\
&\qquad \cdots)
\end{aligned}$$

The type of the channel *reply* says that, for each i, the channel can be used only in $Client_i$ for input and only in *Serv* for output, so that the communication between $Client_i$ and *Serv* is never intercepted by other processes. The type of the channel *succ* says that, for each i, the channel can be used only in *Serv* for input and only in $Client_i$ for output, so that only processes in the domain $Client_i$ can invoke the successor function and only processes in the domain *Succ* can provide the successor function.

3 The Type System

The primary judgments of the type system are of the form $\Gamma \vdash P : Th[m]$ for threads and of the form $\Gamma \vdash M : Sys$ for systems, where Γ is a *type environment* defined as in Table 6. We write $\Gamma(u) = T$ to mean that Γ maps u to T, that is, there exist some Γ_1 and Γ_2 such that $\Gamma = \Gamma_1, u : T, \Gamma_2$. The domain of Γ, written $dom(\Gamma)$, is the set of names which Γ maps. We write $Dom(\Gamma)$ for the set of names having a domain type in Γ.

3.1 Environments and Partially Ordered Sets of Domains

Type environments determine a partial order among domains. We write $\leq^\Gamma$ for this partial order, whose formal definition is as follows.[1]

Definition 3 (Partial Order under Γ).

$$m \leq^\Gamma n \quad \stackrel{def}{=} \quad (m = \bot \ \vee \ n = \top \ \vee \ m \dot{\leq}^\Gamma n) \ \wedge \ \{m, n\} \subseteq Dom(\Gamma)$$

where

$$\dot{\leq}^\Gamma \stackrel{def}{=} \begin{cases} \emptyset & \text{if } \Gamma = \bullet \\ \dot{\leq}^{\Gamma'} & \text{if } \Gamma = \Gamma', c : \mathtt{chan}\langle m_1, m_2\rangle T \\ (\dot{\leq}^{\Gamma'} \cup \{(m, n_i), (n'_j, m) \mid n_i \in \{\tilde{n}\}, n'_j \in \{\tilde{n'}\}\})^* & \\ \qquad \text{if } \Gamma = \Gamma', m : \mathtt{dom}\langle \tilde{n}/\tilde{n'}\rangle & \end{cases}$$

[1] $\Re^*$ denotes the reflexive and transitive closure of the relation $\Re$.

Table 7. Good environments

$$\frac{}{\vdash \bullet\ ok}\text{(E-EMPTY)}$$

$$\frac{u \notin dom(\Gamma) \cup \{\top, \bot\} \quad \vdash \Gamma\ ok \quad \Gamma \models T \quad T \text{ is a channel type or a domain type}}{\vdash \Gamma, u : T\ ok}\text{(E-TYPE)}$$

$$\frac{\forall m'_i \in \{\tilde{m'}\}.\ \forall m_i \in \{\tilde{m}\}.\ m'_i \leq^{\Gamma} m_i \ \wedge\ m'_i \neq m_i \quad \{\tilde{m}\} \subseteq Dom(\Gamma) \cup \{\top\} \quad \{\tilde{m'}\} \subseteq Dom(\Gamma) \cup \{\bot\}}{\Gamma \models \mathtt{dom}\langle \tilde{m}/\tilde{m'} \rangle}\text{(T-DOM)}$$

$$\frac{m_1, m_2 \in Dom(\Gamma) \cup \{\top, \bot\} \quad \Gamma \models T}{\Gamma \models \mathtt{chan}\langle m_1, m_2 \rangle T}\text{(T-CHAN)}$$

$$\frac{\Gamma \models S \quad \Gamma, u : S \models T \quad u \notin dom(\Gamma) \cup \{\top, \bot\}}{\Gamma \models \Sigma u : S.T}\text{(T-DEP)}$$

For example, the type environment $m_1{:}\mathtt{dom}\langle \top/\bot \rangle, m_2{:}\mathtt{dom}\langle m_1/\bot \rangle, m_3{:}\mathtt{dom}\langle m_1/m_2 \rangle, m_4 : \mathtt{dom}\langle \top/m_3 \rangle$ defines the partially ordered set shown in Fig. 1. Note that $m_2 \leq^{\Gamma} m_4$ also holds by transitivity.

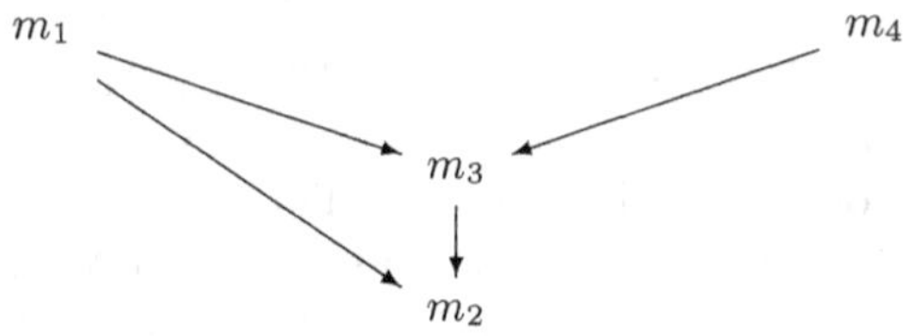

Fig. 1. Example of domain hierarchy. The domains $\top$ and $\bot$ are omitted.

The formation rules for environments, which are of the form $\vdash \Gamma\ ok$, are given in Table 7. They are defined by using the formation rules for channel types and domain types, which are of the form $\Gamma \models T$. The rule (T-DOM) deserves mention. The premise in the first line ensures that parents of a domain must always be greater than children of the domain. This condition is important for keeping $\leq^{\Gamma}$ a partial order. The premises in the second line ensure that $\top$ is always the greatest element and $\bot$ is always the least element. The rule (T-DEP) says that we must check T under Γ extended with $u{:}S$, since u may appear free in T.

The following proposition assures that if Γ is a good environment, $\leq^{\Gamma}$ is indeed a partial order.

Proposition 1. *If* $\vdash \Gamma$ *ok, then* $\leq^{\Gamma}$ *is a partial order over* $Dom(\Gamma) \cup \{\top, \bot\}$.

3.2 Typing Rules

Typing Rules for Threads. The typing rules for threads in π^D are given in Table 8. The judgment $\Gamma \vdash P : Th[l]$ indicates that the thread P is well-typed under the type environment Γ and can be located in the domain l. Intuitive explanation of key rules is as follows.

G-DEP This rule follows from the meaning of compound names of a dependent pair type.
TH-ZERO Since a null thread does nothing, it can be located in any domain which is present in the environment.
TH-OUT The first and third premises say that c is a channel with the output level m_2, and that the compound name V must have the type T of names communicated through the channel. The second premise ensures that c is used for output only by processes in the domain m_2 or a greater domain. The forth premise ensures that there is no process located in the domain $\top$.
TH-IN This rule is similar to (TH-OUT) except that we must check that the continuation process P is well-typed under Γ extended with $U : T$.
TH-SPAWN The second premise of this rule ensures that only a thread in a domain n greater than m can spawn a new thread in m.

Typing Rules for Systems. The judgment $\Gamma \vdash M : Sys$ indicates that the system M is well-typed under the type environment Γ. The typing rules for systems are also given in Table 8. The rules (SYS-ZERO), (SYS-NEW) and (SYS-PAR) are similar to those for threads. The rule (SYS-EX) allows adjacent elements of a type environment to be switched. This rule is necessary only for a technical reason, that is, for proving the case of (SP-EX) in Lemma 2 in Section 4. The rule (SYS-LOCATED) says that only threads of type $Th[m]$ can be located in the domain m.

Well-typedness of processes is obviously decidable since the typing rules are purely syntax-directed and the partial order among domains is finite.

4 Type Soundness

4.1 Subject Reduction

Our first main result is the subject reduction theorem. In order to prove that, we need the following lemmas:

Lemma 1 (Substitution).

– *If* $\Gamma, u : T, \Gamma' \vdash P : Th[n]$ *and* $\Gamma, \{v/u\}\Gamma' \vdash v : T$*, then* $\Gamma, \{v/u\}\Gamma' \vdash \{v/u\}P : \{v/u\}Th[n]$.

Table 8. Typing rules for threads and systems

$$\Gamma + U : T \stackrel{def}{=} \begin{cases} \Gamma + u : T & \text{if } U : T = u : T \\ (\Gamma, u : S) + U' : \{u/u'\}T' & \text{if } X : T = (u, U') : (\Sigma u' : S.T') \end{cases}$$

$$\frac{\vdash \Gamma\ ok \quad \Gamma(u) = T}{\Gamma \vdash u : T}\text{(G-NAME)} \qquad \frac{\Gamma \vdash v : S \quad \Gamma \vdash V : \{v/u\}T}{\Gamma \vdash (v, V) : (\Sigma u : S.T)}\text{(G-DEP)}$$

$$\frac{\Gamma \vdash c : \mathbf{chan}\langle m_1, m_2\rangle T \quad m_2 \leq^{\Gamma} l \quad \Gamma \vdash V : T \quad l \neq \top}{\Gamma \vdash c!\langle V\rangle : Th[l]}\text{(TH-OUT)}$$

$$\frac{\begin{array}{c}\Gamma \vdash c : \mathbf{chan}\langle m_1, m_2\rangle T \quad m_1 \leq^{\Gamma} l \quad l \notin fn(U) \\ \Gamma + U : T \vdash P : Th[l] \quad l \neq \top\end{array}}{\Gamma \vdash c?(U : T).P : Th[l]}\text{(TH-IN)}$$

$$\frac{\Gamma \vdash P : Th[m] \quad m \leq^{\Gamma} n}{\Gamma \vdash \mathbf{spawn}@m.P : Th[n]}\text{(TH-SPAWN)} \qquad \frac{\Gamma \vdash P : Th[l]}{\Gamma \vdash *P : Th[l]}\text{(TH-REP)}$$

$$\frac{\vdash \Gamma\ ok \quad l \in Dom(\Gamma)}{\Gamma \vdash 0 : Th[l]}\text{(TH-ZERO)} \qquad \frac{\Gamma, v : T \vdash P : Th[l] \quad v \neq l}{\Gamma \vdash (\nu v : T)P : Th[l]}\text{(TH-NEW)}$$

$$\frac{\Gamma \vdash P : Th[l] \quad \Gamma \vdash Q : Th[l]}{\Gamma \vdash P \mid Q : Th[l]}\text{(TH-PAR)}$$

$$\frac{\vdash \Gamma\ ok}{\Gamma \vdash 0 : Sys}\text{(SYS-ZERO)} \qquad \frac{\Gamma, v : T \vdash M : Sys}{\Gamma \vdash (\nu v : T)M : Sys}\text{(SYS-NEW)}$$

$$\frac{\Gamma \vdash P : Th[m]}{\Gamma \vdash m[P] : Sys}\text{(SYS-LOCATED)} \qquad \frac{\Gamma \vdash M : Sys \quad \Gamma \vdash N : Sys}{\Gamma \vdash M \mid N : Sys}\text{(SYS-PAR)}$$

$$\frac{\Gamma_1, u_1 : S, u_2 : T, \Gamma_2 \vdash M : Sys \quad u_1 \notin fn(T) \quad u_2 \notin fn(S)}{\Gamma_1, u_2 : T, u_1 : S, \Gamma_2 \vdash M : Sys}\text{(SYS-EX)}$$

– *If* $\Gamma + X : T \vdash P : Th[n]$ *and* $\Gamma \vdash V : T$, *then* $\Gamma \vdash \{V/X\}P : \{V/X\}Th[n]$.

Lemma 2 (Subject Preordering). *If* $\Gamma \vdash M : Sys$ *and* $M \preceq N$, *then* $\Gamma \vdash N : Sys$.

In π^D, domains appear free in types, so the substitution lemmas above are a little different from usual ones: the subjects of substitution are not only free names of P but also those of Γ' and $Th[n]$.

Theorem 1 (Subject Reduction). *If* $\Gamma \vdash M : Sys$ *and* $M \longrightarrow^* N$, *then* $\Gamma \vdash N : Sys$.

Proof. Follows from Lemma 1 and Lemma 2. See the full version [12] for details. □

Table 9. Tagged systems

(Tagged Systems)		
E, F, G	$::= \ldots$	
	$m[P]^{\tilde{n}}$	tagged located thread

This theorem says that well-typedness of processes is preserved throughout computation.

4.2 The Tagged Language and Type Safety

Roughly, our type safety theorem says that:

> A channel c of type $\mathtt{chan}\langle m_1, m_2\rangle T$ can be used for output only by processes which were located in m_2 or a greater domain *at the beginning of the computation.* (The case for input is similar and omitted.)

In order to state and prove this theorem, we introduce a tagged language. Each process of the tagged language carries its own tag, which records the history of domains it has moved across. Note that tags are introduced only for stating properties of processes and do not affect their execution.

The Tagged Language

Tagged Systems. The formal definition of tagged systems is given in Table 9. Systems in the tagged language are the same as in the original language except that located threads are tagged with a sequence of domains. The tag $\tilde{n}$ of a located thread P_1 represents the domain in which P_1 was spawned, the domain in which the parent thread P_2 which spawned P_1 was spawned, the domain in which the grand parent thread P_3 which spawned P_2 was spawned, and so forth. For example, a thread which is located in m_1 now, whose parent thread was located in m_2, and whose grand parent thread was located in m_3, is represented as $m_1[P]^{m_1,m_2,m_3}$.

Operational Semantics. The operational semantics of the tagged language is given in Table 10. The definition of the structural preorder is a straightforward extension of the original. We show only (TS-SPLIT) and (TS-NAME). As for the reduction relation, only (R-SPAWN) is changed so that when a new thread is spawned in a domain, it is recorded in the thread's tag.

Technical Properties of Tagged Language. We present two lemmas stating that the semantics of a program does not depend on whether it is written in the original language or in the tagged language.

For convenience, we define a function *Tag*, which maps terms of the original language to terms of the tagged language, and *Erase*, which is the inverse of *Tag*.

Table 10. Structural preorder and reduction relation

$m[P \mid Q]^{\tilde{n}} \preceq m[P]^{\tilde{n}} \mid m[Q]^{\tilde{n}}$	(TS-SPLIT)
$m[(\nu v : T)P]^{\tilde{n}} \preceq (\nu v : T)m[P]^{\tilde{n}}$ if $v \notin \{m, \tilde{n}\}$	(TS-NAME)
$m[\mathtt{spawn@}n.P]^{\tilde{n}'} \longrightarrow n[P]^{n,\tilde{n}'}$	(TR-SPAWN)

Definition 4 (Tagging)

$$\begin{array}{ll} Tag(M' \mid N') & = Tag(M') \mid Tag(N') \\ Tag((\nu v : T)M') & = (\nu v : T)\, Tag(M') \\ Tag(0) & = 0 \\ Tag(n[P]) & = n[P]^n \end{array}$$

Definition 5 (Erase). *Erase(_) is the function mapping tagged system expressions to ordinary system expressions by erasing tags.*

Lemma 3 (Correspondence w.r.t $\preceq$)

1. *If $E \preceq F$, then $Erase(E) \preceq Erase(F)$.*
2. *If $Erase(E) \preceq M$, then there is some F such that $E \preceq F$ and $M = Erase(F)$.*

Lemma 4 (Correspondence w.r.t $\longrightarrow$)

1. *If $E \longrightarrow F$, then $Erase(E) \longrightarrow Erase(F)$.*
2. *If $Erase(E) \longrightarrow M$, then there is some some E' such that $E \longrightarrow E'$ and $M = Erase(E')$.*

Type Safety. Before describing the formal definition of our type safety theorem, we make some preparations for proving it. First, we define the notion of *guarded* threads and *guarded tagged systems,* used in the lemma below.

Definition 6 (Guarded Threads and Guarded Tagged Systems). *A thread is guarded if it is an input, output, replication, spawning or null. A tagged system is guarded if it is a located thread or null.*

The following lemma says that each domain in the history of a well-typed system is less than the previous domain.

Lemma 5. *Suppose $\Gamma \vdash M : Sys$ and $E = Tag(M)$. If there is some F such that $E \longrightarrow^* F \preceq (\nu\Gamma')(F_1 \mid \cdots \mid F_q)$ where $F_1 \cdots F_q$ are guarded, then $m^i = m^i_1 \leq^{\Gamma,\Gamma'} \ldots \leq^{\Gamma,\Gamma'} m^i_{p^i}$ holds for every $F_i = m^i[P_i]^{m^i_1,\ldots,m^i_{p^i}}$.*

From the above lemma and the type system, the following lemma can be proved. This lemma guarantees that, for example, a channel having the output level n_2 is used for output only by processes whose history contains only domains greater than n_2.

Lemma 6. *Suppose $\Gamma \vdash M : Sys$ and $E = Tag(M)$. If there is some F such that $E \longrightarrow^* F \preceq (\nu\Gamma')(m'[c!\langle V\rangle]^{m'_1,\ldots,m'_i} \mid F')$ and $(\Gamma,\Gamma')(c) = \mathtt{chan}\langle n_1, n_2\rangle T$, then $n_2 \leq^{\Gamma,\Gamma'} m' = m'_1 \leq^{\Gamma,\Gamma'} \ldots \leq^{\Gamma,\Gamma'} m'_i$.*[2]

Furthermore, in order to prove the type safety theorem, we need the following lemma. This lemma says that, for example, if $m \leq^{\Gamma,l:\mathtt{dom}\langle n/m\rangle} n$, then $m \leq^{\Gamma} n$ even though $l : \mathtt{dom}\langle n/m\rangle$ is removed from $\Gamma, l : \mathtt{dom}\langle n/m\rangle$.

Lemma 7. *Suppose $\vdash \Gamma, \Gamma'$ ok and $m \leq^{\Gamma,\Gamma'} n$. If $m, n \in dom(\Gamma)$, then $m \leq^{\Gamma} n$.*

Finally, we prove the type safety theorem. Its formal statement is as follows.

Theorem 2 (Type Safety). *Suppose $\Gamma \vdash M : Sys$, $E = Tag(M)$ and $\Gamma, \Gamma' = \Delta, c\!:\!\mathtt{chan}\langle n_1, n_2\rangle T, \Delta'$. Suppose also $M \longrightarrow^* N \preceq (\nu\Gamma')(m'[c!\langle V\rangle] \mid N')$. Then, there exist some F, F', and $\tilde{m}'$ such that $E \longrightarrow^* F \preceq (\nu\Gamma')(m'[c!\langle V\rangle]^{m'_1,\ldots,m'_k} \mid F')$ and $N = Erase(F)$. Furthermore, $n_2 \leq^{\Gamma,\Gamma'} m' = m'_1 \leq^{\Gamma,\Gamma'} \ldots \leq^{\Gamma,\Gamma'} m'_k$ where $n_2 \leq^{\Delta} m'_j$ for every $m'_j \in dom(\Delta)$.*

Proof. Immediately follows from Lemma 4, Lemma 6 and Lemma 7. □

Intuitively, this statement means that if a process uses the channel c for output, then:

1. each domain in the history of the process (i.e., $m'_1, \cdots, m'_k$) must be greater than n_2, and
2. for each j, if m'_j was created before c (i.e., $m'_j \in dom(\Delta)$), then m'_j was *originally* greater than n_2.

In other words, processes which were not located in n_2 or a greater domain at the beginning of the execution of M can never use c for output throughout computation.

We give two examples to demonstrate how the typing rules in Section 3 prevents failure of type safety. Suppose $\Gamma = m : \mathtt{dom}\langle\top/\bot\rangle, n : \mathtt{dom}\langle m/\bot\rangle, c : \mathtt{chan}\langle\top, m\rangle\mathtt{int}$.

- First, consider a process $P \stackrel{def}{=} n[c!\langle 1\rangle]$ trying to use c, a channel with an output level m, for output within n. Since the tagged version of P is $n[c!\langle 1\rangle]^n$ and $m \not\leq^{\Gamma} n$, the first claim above of the theorem does not hold for P. By (TH-OUT), however, P cannot be well-typed, since m is not greater than or equal to n.
- Second, consider a more cunning process $Q \stackrel{def}{=} n[(\nu l\!:\!\mathtt{dom}\langle n/m\rangle)\mathtt{spawn}@l.c!\langle 1\rangle]$, which tries to create a new domain l as a *parent* of the domain m, and then

[2] $(\nu\Gamma)$ is an abbreviation of $(\nu u_1 : T_1) \cdots (\nu u_n : T_n)$ for $\Gamma = u_1 : T_1, \cdots, u_n : T_n$.

Table 11. Subtyping relation

$$\frac{\begin{array}{c} m \leq^{\Gamma} m' \quad m' \neq \top \Rightarrow \Gamma \vdash S \sqsubseteq T \\ n \leq n' \quad n' \neq \top \Rightarrow \Gamma \vdash T \sqsubseteq S \end{array}}{\Gamma \vdash \mathtt{chan}\langle m, n\rangle S \sqsubseteq \mathtt{chan}\langle m', n'\rangle T} \text{(SUB-CHAN)}$$

$$\frac{\{\tilde{m}'\} \subseteq \{\tilde{m}\} \subseteq Dom(\Gamma) \quad \{\tilde{n}'\} \subseteq \{\tilde{n}\} \subseteq Dom(\Gamma)}{\Gamma \vdash \mathtt{dom}\langle \tilde{m}/\tilde{n}\rangle \sqsubseteq \mathtt{dom}\langle \tilde{m}'/\tilde{n}'\rangle} \text{(SUB-DOM)}$$

$$\frac{\Gamma, u : S \vdash T \sqsubseteq T' \quad \Gamma \vdash S \sqsubseteq S' \quad u \text{ is fresh}}{\Gamma \vdash \Sigma u : S.T \sqsubseteq \Sigma u : S'.T'} \text{(SUB-DEP)}$$

spawn a process trying to use the channel c for output. Although the first claim of the theorem *does* hold for Q, the second does not for the following reason: the tagged version of P is $n[(\nu l : \mathtt{dom}\langle n/m\rangle)\mathtt{spawn@}l.c!\langle 1\rangle]^n$ which evolves to $(\nu l : \mathtt{dom}\langle n/m\rangle)l[c!\langle 1\rangle]^{l,n}$; indeed $m \leq^{\Gamma,l:\mathtt{dom}\langle n/m\rangle} l \leq^{\Gamma,l:\mathtt{dom}\langle n/m\rangle} n$ holds, but $m \leq^{\Gamma} n$ does not. By (T-DOM), however, Q cannot be well-typed either, since n is not greater than or equal to m.

5 Subtyping

The partial order among domains induces a subtyping relation on types. Intuitively, the subtyping relation $\Gamma \vdash S \sqsubseteq T$ says that a name of type S may be used as a name of type T. A possible definition of the subtyping relation is given in Table 11.

SUB-CHAN. The first premise follows from the intuition that a channel with input level m can be used by threads in a domain m' greater than or equal to m. The third premise is similar. The second and forth premises say that an input capability implies covariance of the channel type, whereas an output capability implies contravariance [16].

SUB-DOM. This rule follows from the intuition that a child (resp. parent) domain of both m and n can be used as a child (resp. parent) domain of only m.

SUB-DEP. This rule can be considered as an extension of the usual definition of subtyping relation for pair types. The difference is that we must check $T \sqsubseteq T'$ under Γ extended with $u : S$.

Furthermore, the typing rules for threads can be refined as in Table 12.

TH-OUT. The first, third, and fourth premises say that V must be of less restrictive type than the type T of names communicated through the channel.

TH-IN. The first, forth, and fifth premises say that compound names received through c can be regarded as names of more restrictive type than T.

Although the definitions in Table 11 and Table 12 seem reasonable, we have not yet proved soundness of the type system with this subtyping relation.

Table 12. Typing rules for threads with subtyping

$$\frac{\Gamma \vdash c : \mathbf{chan}\langle m_1, m_2\rangle T \quad m_2 \leq^{\Gamma} l \quad \Gamma \vdash T' \sqsubseteq T \quad \Gamma \vdash V : T' \quad l \neq \top}{\Gamma \vdash c!\langle V\rangle : Th[l]} \text{(TH-OUT)}$$

$$\frac{\Gamma \vdash c : \mathbf{chan}\langle m_1, m_2\rangle T \quad m_1 \leq^{\Gamma} l \quad l \notin fn(U) \quad \Gamma \vdash T \sqsubseteq T' \quad \Gamma + U : T' \vdash P : Th[l] \quad l \neq \top}{\Gamma \vdash c?(U : T').P : Th[l]} \text{(TH-IN)}$$

6 Related Work

We have already made reference to Riely and Hennessy's work [10, 11]. Besides it, several other foundational calculi have been proposed for access control in distributed computation.

- Yoshida and Hennessy [22] proposed a type system for access control in the higher-order π-calculus. Their type system can be used for controlling access to resources in higher-order code transmitted from one domain to another. Introducing our notion of domains into their calculus might enable finer-grained access control in the higher-order π-calculus.
- De Nicola, Ferrari and Pugliese [5] also studied access control in distributed computation. They dealt with a variant of Linda with multiple tuple spaces as a target language. Tuple spaces correspond to domains in π^D, and tuples (named data) correspond to resources. Since the type system in [5] controls access to tuple spaces rather than to specific tuples, it provides coarser-grained access control than [10] and π^D.
- Dezani-Ciancaglini and Salvo [6] introduced *security levels* [11] into the ambient calculus [3]. Their security levels are associated with ambients: it is guaranteed that an ambient at security level s can be traversed or opened only by ambients at security level s or greater. The role of security levels are similar to that of our domains. They, however, are not first-class values and cannot be created dynamically. Again, adapting our notion of domains for the ambient calculus might enable more flexible access control.
- Cardelli and Gordon [4] introduced *groups* into the π-calculus. The role of groups is similar to that of domains. Groups can be created dynamically, but are not first-class values.

Foundational calculi for studying various security issues have also been proposed by several authors [1, 2, 9, 21]. Abadi and Gordon [1] proposed the spi calculus, an extension of the π-calculus with cryptographic primitives. It allows programmers to describe and analyze security protocols. Bugliesi and Castagna [2] proposed a typed variant of safe ambient [14]. Their type system can capture not only explicit but also implicit behavior of processes and thereby detects security attacks such as Trojan horses. Heintze and Riecke [9] proposed an extension of the λ-calculus with a type system for preserving secrecy and integrity of resources. Vitek and Castagna [21] proposed a low level language, called the seal calculus, for writing secure distributed applications over a large-scale open network.

Our notion of domains is orthogonal to the notion of locations [7, 10, 20]: locations are targets of code movement, while domains are the unit of access control; it is possible to have different domains within a single location, or to have a single domain across multiple locations.

7 Future Work

Our type safety theorem holds if and only if all processes are well-typed. This assumption is quite restrictive since it is not realistic to verify open systems, such as the Internet, as a whole [19]. This limitation would be overcome by adapting type systems where a certain type safety theorem holds even if some of the processes are not well-typed [4, 19].

Types constrain the behavior of processes and their environments, and thereby allow a coarser notion of behavioral equivalence. Typed equivalence has already been investigated in various process calculi [13, 16, 17, 18]. It may be possible to develop a similar theory in π^D.

Acknowledgment

First and foremost, our work benefited greatly from Naoki Kobayashi's suggestive and insightful technical advise. The TACS reviewers also gave us helpful comments on an earlier version of the present paper. Finally, we would like to thank the current and former members of Yonezawa's group in the University of Tokyo, especially Hidehiko Masuhara and Atsushi Igarashi.

References

1. M. Abadi and A. D. Gordon. A calculus for cryptographic protocols: The spi calculus. In *Proceedings of the Fourth ACM Conference on Computer and Communications Security*. ACM Press, 1997.
2. M. Bugliesi and G. Castagna. Secure safe ambients. In *POPL'01*. ACM Press, 2001.
3. L. Cardelli and A. D. Gordon. Mobile ambients. In *FoSSaCS'98*. Springer-Verlag, 1998.
4. L. Cardelli and A. D. Gordon. Secrecy and group creation. In *CONCUR'2000*. Springer-Verlag, 2000.
5. R. De Nicola, G. Ferrari, and R. Pugliese. Klaim : a kernel language for agents interaction and mobility. *IEEE Trans. on Software Engineering*, 24(5), 1998.
6. M. Dezani-Ciancaglini and I. Salvo. Security types for mobile safe ambients. In *ASIAN'00*, 2000.
7. C. Fournet, G. Gonthier, J. J. Levy, L. Maranget, and D. Remy. A calculus of mobile agents. In *CONCUR'96*. Springer-Verlag, 1996.

8. J. Gosling, B. Joy, and G. Steele. *The Java language specification.* Addison-Wesley, 1996.
9. N. Heintze and J. G. Riecke. The SLam calculus: Programming with secrecy and integrity. In *POPL'98.* ACM Press, 1998.
10. M. Hennessy and J. Riely. Resource access control in systems of mobile agents. In *HLCL'98.* Elsevier, 1998.
11. M. Hennessy and J. Rily. Information flow vs. resource access in the asynchronous pi-calculus (extended abstract). In *ICALP'00*, January 2000.
12. D. Hoshina, E. Sumii, and A. Yonezawa. A typed process calculus for fine-grained resource access control in distributed computation (full version), 2001. Available from `http://www.yl.is.s.u-tokyo.ac.jp/~hoshina/papers/tacs01full.ps.gz`.
13. N. Kobayashi, B. Pierce, and D. Turner. Linearity and the pi-calculus. In *POPL'96.* ACM Press, 1996.
14. F. Levi and D. Sangiorgi. Controlling interference in ambients. In *POPL'00.* ACM Press, 2000.
15. R. Milner. The polyadic π-calculus: a tutorial. Technical Report ECS-LFCS-91-180, Laboratory for Foundations of Computer Science,Department of Computer Science, University of Edinburgh, Octorber 1991.
16. B. Pierce and D. Sangiorgi. Typing and subtyping for mobile processes. *Mathematical Structure in Computer Science*, 6(5):409–454, 1996.
17. B. Pierce and D. Sangiorgi. Behavioral equivalence in the polymorphic pi-calculus. In *POPL'97.* ACM Press, 1997.
18. J. Riely and M. Hennessy. A typed language for distributed mobile processes. In *POPL'98.* ACM Press, 1998.
19. J. Riely and M. Hennessy. Trust and partial typing in open systems of mobile agents. In *POPL'99.* ACM Press, 1999.
20. P. Sewell. Global/local subtyping and capability inference for a distributed π-calculus. In *ICALP'98.* Springer-Verlag, 1998. LNCS 1433.
21. J. Vitek and G. Castagna. Seal: A framework for secure mobile computations. In *Internet Programming Languages*, 1999. LNCS 1686.
22. N. Yoshida and M. Hennessy. Assigning types to processes. In *LICS'00.* IEEE, 2000.

Formal Eavesdropping and Its Computational Interpretation

Martín Abadi[1] and Jan Jürjens[2]

[1] InterTrust, Strategic Technologies and Architectural Research Laboratory*
[2] Computing Laboratory, University of Oxford

Abstract. We compare two views of symmetric cryptographic primitives in the context of the systems that use them. We express those systems in a simple programming language; each of the views yields a semantics for the language. One of the semantics treats cryptographic operations formally (that is, symbolically). The other semantics is more detailed and computational; it treats cryptographic operations as functions on bitstrings. Each semantics leads to a definition of equivalence of systems with respect to eavesdroppers. We establish the soundness of the formal definition with respect to the computational one. This result provides a precise computational justification for formal reasoning about security against eavesdroppers.

1 Introduction

This work is part of an effort to bridge the gap between the formal and the computational views of cryptography and cryptographic protocols. The formal view is based on ideas and methods from logic and programming languages (e.g., [1, 8, 16, 18, 22]). It has led, in particular, to techniques for high-level reasoning (even automated reasoning) about security protocols. The computational view relies on the vocabulary of complexity theory (e.g., [5, 7, 10, 12, 13, 26]). It has developed sophisticated foundations and proof techniques. Several recent projects have made progress in the direction of linking these two views [3, 17, 23, 24, 25]. These projects differ in their approaches and their technical details. Overall, however, they aim to refine and to provide foundations for formal treatments of cryptography, and to combine the benefits of both treatments for reasoning about systems that use cryptography.

More specifically, this work extends the recent work of Abadi and Rogaway [3], which compares a formal account of symmetric (shared-key) encryption [19] with a computational account. Both of these accounts are fairly standard in the respective communities. That work deals with expressions that represent pieces of data: booleans, pairs, randomly generated keys, and symmetric encryptions. Each expression induces an ensemble (that is, for each choice of a security parameter, a probability distribution over the bitstrings that the expression represents). The main result there is that if two expressions are equivalent

* This work was started while the author was at Bell Labs Research.

N. Kobayashi and B.C. Pierce (Eds.): TACS 2001, LNCS 2215, pp. 82–94, 2001.

in the formal model then the ensembles that they induce are computationally indistinguishable. The result means that formal reasoning about equivalence of expressions is sound with respect to the computational model. Furthermore, the hypotheses of the result indicate a few significant discrepancies between the two accounts (for example, in the treatment of encryption cycles).

Here we go further by considering systems that use symmetric encryption and decryption. The systems may in particular represent cryptographic protocols with several parties. We describe systems in a simple programming language, a small but expressive calculus of the kind common in the programming-language literature. We present the two models as two semantics for the language. Thus, we rely on basic concepts and techniques from programming-language theory [21]. In both the formal model and the computational model, systems generate traces, traces are sequences of tuples of values (one value for each communication channel at each time instant), and two systems are equivalent if an eavesdropping adversary cannot distinguish a trace generated by one from a trace generated by the other. In the formal model, a value is a formal expression; the adversary is allowed only simple symbolic computations over expressions. In the computational model, a value is a bitstring; the adversary is a resource-bounded Turing machine that computes over bitstrings.

We obtain a soundness result analogous to that of Abadi and Rogaway: if two systems are equivalent in the formal model then the probability ensembles that they induce are computationally indistinguishable. This means that formal reasoning about equivalence of systems is sound with respect to the computational model, and that computational eavesdroppers have no more power than the simpler formal eavesdroppers.

This study of eavesdroppers presents difficulties and offers some insights, beyond those encountered in previous work. In particular, we treat situations where exactly the same ciphertext appears twice in a piece of data, and the adversary can notice a repetition (cf. [3]). In addition, we analyze programs where the control flow depends on the properties of the underlying cryptosystem, for example a program that generates two keys, compares them, and branches on the result of the comparison. In such examples, the formal model and the computational model do not give rise to exactly corresponding traces, but we show that the differences are negligible. Finally, we consider a substantial difference between the formal and the computational accounts of decryption. Formal models that treat symmetric encryption commonly assume that decrypting a message with a key K succeeds only if the message was encrypted under K, and that the success or failure of a decryption is evident to whoever performs it. This property is convenient in both protocol design and analysis; one may even argue that "encryption without integrity checking is all but useless" [6]. The property can be implemented by means of checkable redundancy. Computational models typically do not build it in. One outcome of our work is a precise computational counterpart of this property.

The next section presents the programming language. Sections 3 and 4 give formal semantics and computational semantics of the language, respectively, each with a notion of equivalence. Section 5 establishes our main soundness result; for this purpose, it develops some hypotheses. Section 6 concludes. A longer version of this paper [2] contains proofs and secondary results.

While the present work focuses on eavesdroppers and symmetric cryptosystems, we hope that it will serve as a stepping stone toward treating active adversaries and other cryptographic primitives. In these respects, there might be an opportunity for some convergence with the work of Lincoln et al. [17], which develops a process calculus with some features of the computational approach, and with the recent work of Pfitzmann and Waidner [24, 25], which investigates the secure composition of reactive systems with a simulatability approach. However, those works—unlike ours—consider formal models with probabilistic aspects; we would prefer to avoid this interesting complication as long as possible. (We refer to previous papers [3, 24] for further discussion of background and other, less closely related work.)

2 The Language (Syntax and Informal Semantics)

This section defines the basic programming language that serves as setting for our work. We let **Bool** be $\{0,1\}$. We let **Keys**, **Coins**, and **Var** be fixed, infinite sets of symbols and **Channels** be a finite set of symbols (which may vary from system to system), all disjoint from **Bool** and each other. We partition **Channels** into $\mathbf{Channels}_i$ and $\mathbf{Channels}_e$, intuitively sets of internal (private) channels and external (public) channels.

A *system* is a collection of programs that communicate synchronously (in rounds) through channels, with the constraint that for each channel c the system contains exactly one program P_c that outputs on c. This program P_c may take input from any channels, including c. Intuitively, the program is a description of a value to be output on the channel c in round $n+1$, computed from values found on channels in round n. Local state can be maintained through the use of feedback channels, and used for iteration (for instance, for coding *while* loops).

More precisely, the set of *programs* is defined by the following grammar:

$P, Q ::=$	programs
ε	null value
K	key ($K \in \mathbf{Keys}$)
b	bit ($b \in \mathbf{Bool}$)
$\perp$	error
a	input on channel ($a \in \mathbf{Channels}$)
x	variable ($x \in \mathbf{Var}$)
(P, Q)	pair
$(\nu K)P$	"new" ($K \in \mathbf{Keys}$)
$(\nu r)\{P\}_Q^r$	shared-key encryption ($r \in \mathbf{Coins}$)
$\mathit{if}\ P = Q\ \mathit{then}\ P'\ \mathit{else}\ Q'$	conditional
$\mathit{case}\ P\ \mathit{of}\ (x, y)\ \mathit{do}\ Q\ \mathit{else}\ R$	case: pair ($x, y \in \mathbf{Var}$)
$\mathit{case}\ P\ \mathit{of}\ \{x\}_{P'}\ \mathit{do}\ Q\ \mathit{else}\ R$	case: encryption ($x \in \mathbf{Var}$)

In other words, the set of programs is defined inductively to contain a null value, keys, bits, pairs of programs, etc.; and we typically use letters like P and Q for programs. The expression ε represents the null value; it is the initial value on all channels. An occurrence of a channel name a refers to the value found on a at the previous instant. Variables are introduced in case constructs, which determine their values. The "new" construct (ν), borrowed from the pi calculus [20] (see also [1]), introduces a fresh key K; the symbol K is bound. The "new" notation also appears in $(\nu r)\{P\}_Q^r$, which represents the result of encrypting the value of P using the value of Q as key and randomizing the encryption with the fresh coins r. Informally, we may just write $\{P\}_Q$ instead of $(\nu r)\{P\}_Q^r$; this notation is unambiguous since each encryption operation uses fresh coins. The first case construct tests whether P is a pair, of the form (x, y); if so, Q is evaluated, using the actual values of (x, y); if not, R is evaluated. The second case construct tests whether P is a ciphertext under the key represented by P' with contents x; if so, Q is evaluated, using the actual value of x; if not, R is evaluated. This construct reflects the assumption (discussed in the introduction) that decrypting a message with a key succeeds only if the message was encrypted under the key, and that the success or failure of a decryption is evident. In the case constructs, x and y are bound variables. For example, suppose that $c_0, c_1 \in$ **Channels** and $K_0, K_1 \in$ **Keys**. Then the following is a program:

$$\textit{case } c_0 \textit{ of } \{x\}_{K_0} \textit{ do } (0, x) \textit{ else case } c_0 \textit{ of } \{x\}_{K_1} \textit{ do } (1, x) \textit{ else } \varepsilon$$

This program looks at the value in c_0. If it is a ciphertext with plaintext x under K_i then it outputs (i, x); otherwise, it outputs ε. We may form a system for example by letting this program output on c_1 and adding the trivial program $\{0\}_{K_1}$ to output on c_0. We may write the resulting system as:

$$\begin{aligned} &c_0 := \{0\}_{K_1} \\ &c_1 := \textit{case } c_0 \textit{ of } \{x\}_{K_0} \textit{ do } (0, x) \textit{ else case } c_0 \textit{ of } \{x\}_{K_1} \textit{ do } (1, x) \textit{ else } \varepsilon \end{aligned}$$

(See [14, 15] for further examples in a fragment of this calculus.)

Our choice of a synchronous model avoids consideration of scheduling, and the delicate mix of non-deterministic and probabilistic choices (cf. [17]). While scheduling issues are interesting, we believe that they are best addressed in the context of active adversaries.

Other aspects of the language are somewhat more arbitrary. Our main concern is to have a tractable language with which we can express examples (though not always in the most convenient way), identify problematic issues, and develop precise solutions. The exact details of the language are secondary.

3 Formal Model

This section gives the first precise semantics for programs, and a corresponding notion of equivalence between programs.

$$
\begin{array}{ll}
[\![\varepsilon]\!](\boldsymbol{M}) = \varepsilon & \\
[\![K]\!](\boldsymbol{M}) = K & (K \in \mathbf{Keys}) \\
[\![b]\!](\boldsymbol{M}) = b & (b \in \mathbf{Bool}) \\
[\![\bot]\!](\boldsymbol{M}) = \bot & \\
[\![u]\!](\boldsymbol{M}) = \boldsymbol{M}_u & (u \in \mathbf{Channels} \cup \mathbf{Var}) \\
[\![(P,Q)]\!](\boldsymbol{M}) = ([\![P]\!](\boldsymbol{M}), [\![Q]\!](\boldsymbol{M})) & \\
[\![(\nu v)P]\!](\boldsymbol{M}) = [\![P]\!](\boldsymbol{M}) & (v \in \mathbf{Keys} \cup \mathbf{Coins}) \\
[\![\{P\}_Q^r]\!](\boldsymbol{M}) = \{[\![P]\!](\boldsymbol{M})\}^r_{[\![Q]\!](\boldsymbol{M})} & \text{if } [\![P]\!](\boldsymbol{M}) \in \mathbf{Plain} \text{ and } [\![Q]\!](\boldsymbol{M}) \in \mathbf{Keys} \\
[\![\{P\}_Q^r]\!](\boldsymbol{M}) = \{0\}^r_{[\![Q]\!](\boldsymbol{M})} & \text{if } [\![P]\!](\boldsymbol{M}) \notin \mathbf{Plain} \text{ and } [\![Q]\!](\boldsymbol{M}) \in \mathbf{Keys} \\
[\![\{P\}_Q^r]\!](\boldsymbol{M}) = \bot & \text{if } [\![Q]\!](\boldsymbol{M}) \notin \mathbf{Keys} \\
[\![\mathit{if}\ P = Q\ \mathit{then}\ P'\ \mathit{else}\ Q']\!](\boldsymbol{M}) = [\![P']\!](\boldsymbol{M}) & \text{if } [\![P]\!](\boldsymbol{M}) = [\![Q]\!](\boldsymbol{M}) \\
[\![\mathit{if}\ P = Q\ \mathit{then}\ P'\ \mathit{else}\ Q']\!](\boldsymbol{M}) = [\![Q']\!](\boldsymbol{M}) & \text{if } [\![P]\!](\boldsymbol{M}) \neq [\![Q]\!](\boldsymbol{M}) \\
[\![\mathit{case}\ P\ \mathit{of}\ (x,y)\ \mathit{do}\ Q\ \mathit{else}\ R]\!](\boldsymbol{M}) = [\![Q]\!](\boldsymbol{M}[x \to M_1, y \to M_2]) & \\
 & \text{if } [\![P]\!](\boldsymbol{M}) = (M_1, M_2) \\
[\![\mathit{case}\ P\ \mathit{of}\ (x,y)\ \mathit{do}\ Q\ \mathit{else}\ R]\!](\boldsymbol{M}) = [\![R]\!](\boldsymbol{M}) & \text{if } [\![P]\!](\boldsymbol{M}) \text{ is not a pair} \\
[\![\mathit{case}\ P\ \mathit{of}\ \{x\}_{P'}\ \mathit{do}\ Q\ \mathit{else}\ R]\!](\boldsymbol{M}) = [\![Q]\!](\boldsymbol{M}[x \to M]) & \text{if } [\![P]\!](\boldsymbol{M}) = \{M\}^r_{[\![P']\!](\boldsymbol{M})} \\
\quad \text{for } M \in \mathbf{Plain} \text{ and } r \in \mathbf{Coins} \text{ and if } [\![P']\!](\boldsymbol{M}) \in \mathbf{Keys} & \\
[\![\mathit{case}\ P\ \mathit{of}\ \{x\}_{P'}\ \mathit{do}\ Q\ \mathit{else}\ R]\!](\boldsymbol{M}) = [\![R]\!](\boldsymbol{M}) & \text{otherwise}
\end{array}
$$

Fig. 1. Definition of $[\![P]\!](\boldsymbol{M})$ in the formal semantics.

Expressions. As indicated in the introduction, this semantics views the values communicated on channels as formal expressions. The set of *expressions* **Exp** is generated by the grammar:

$M, N ::=$	expressions
ε	null value
K	key ($K \in \mathbf{Keys}$)
b	bit ($b \in \mathbf{Bool}$)
$\bot$	error
(M, N)	pair
$\{M\}_K^r$	encryption ($K \in \mathbf{Keys}, r \in \mathbf{Coins}$)

We fix a set $\mathbf{Plain} \subseteq \mathbf{Exp} \setminus \{\bot\}$, which represents the set of plaintexts.

Generating traces. Without loss of generality, we assume that keys and coins are renamed so that in a system $\mathcal{P}$ each key or coin symbol is bound at most once, and any bound key does not also occur free. We write $\mathbf{new}(P)$ for the set of bound keys in a program P. We also fix injective functions $\psi_k : \mathbb{N} \times \mathbf{Keys} \to \mathbf{Keys}$ and $\psi_c : \mathbb{N} \times \mathbf{Coins} \to \mathbf{Coins}$, for renaming keys and coins.

For any program P and $\boldsymbol{M} : \mathbf{Channels} \cup \mathbf{Var} \to \mathbf{Exp}$, we define $[\![P]\!](\boldsymbol{M})$ in Figure 1, so that $[\![P]\!](\boldsymbol{M})$ is the expression that results from running P once, when the variables and channels have the initial values given in $\boldsymbol{M}$. In the definition, $\boldsymbol{M}[x \to M]$ is the function in $\mathbf{Channels} \cup \mathbf{Var} \to \mathbf{Exp}$ that coincides with $\boldsymbol{M}$ except on x, which it maps to M.

A *trace* is a sequence of mappings $\mathbf{Channels} \to \mathbf{Exp}$ (that is, a sequence of **Channels**-indexed tuples of expressions). Suppose that $\mathcal{P}$ is a system that consists of a program P_c for each channel c, all without free variables. We define the semantics $[\![\mathcal{P}]\!]$ of $\mathcal{P}$ as an infinite trace $([\![\mathcal{P}]\!]_n)_{n\in\mathbb{N}}$:

- $[\![\mathcal{P}]\!]_1(c) = \ulcorner[\![P_c]\!]\urcorner^1(\varepsilon,\ldots,\varepsilon)$
- $[\![\mathcal{P}]\!]_{n+1}(c) = \ulcorner[\![P_c]\!]\urcorner^{n+1}([\![\mathcal{P}]\!]_n)$

where $\ulcorner\ldots\urcorner^n$ substitutes any occurrence of a key $K \in \mathbf{new}(P_c)$ in P_c by $\psi_k(n,K)$, any occurrence of a key $K \notin \mathbf{new}(P_c)$ in P_c by $\psi_k(0,K)$, and any occurrence of a coin r in P_c by $\psi_c(n,r)$. The substitutions guarantee that all fresh keys and coins are represented with different symbols. Intuitively, the trace $[\![\mathcal{P}]\!]$ is the result of running $\mathcal{P}$ forever.

Equivalence. Abadi and Rogaway define an equivalence relation on formal expressions; it is intended to relate two expressions if they look the same to an adversary. We adapt and extend their definition.

First, we define an *entailment* relation $\mathcal{M} \vdash N$, where $\mathcal{M}$ is a set of expressions and N is an expression. Intuitively, $\mathcal{M} \vdash N$ means that the adversary can derive N from $\mathcal{M}$. Formally, we define the relation inductively, as the least relation with the following properties:

- $\mathcal{M} \vdash M$ for any $M \in \mathcal{M}$,
- if $\mathcal{M} \vdash (N_1, N_2)$ then $\mathcal{M} \vdash N_1$ and $\mathcal{M} \vdash N_2$,
- if $\mathcal{M} \vdash \{N\}_K^r$ (for any $r \in \mathbf{Coins}$) and $\mathcal{M} \vdash K$ then $\mathcal{M} \vdash N$.

Next, we introduce the box symbol $\Box$, which represents a ciphertext that an attacker cannot decrypt. Since the attacker can test bitwise equality of ciphertexts, we index boxes by coins: $\Box_r$ and $\Box_{r'}$ represent the same ciphertext if and only if $r = r'$ (basically, because we do not permit coin reuse in programs). The set **Pat** of *patterns* is generated by the grammar:

$M, N ::=$	patterns
ε	null value
K	key ($K \in \mathbf{Keys}$)
b	bit ($b \in \mathbf{Bool}$)
$\perp$	error
(M, N)	pair
$\{M\}_K^r$	encryption ($K \in \mathbf{Keys}, r \in \mathbf{Coins}$)
$\Box_r$	undecryptable ($r \in \mathbf{Coins}$)

We define a function that, given a set of keys T and an expression M, reduces M to a pattern. Intuitively, this is the pattern that an attacker can see in M if the attacker has the keys in T.

$$
\begin{aligned}
p(\varepsilon, T) &= \varepsilon \\
p(K, T) &= K \qquad\qquad (\text{for } K \in \mathbf{Keys}) \\
p(b, T) &= b \qquad\qquad (\text{for } b \in \mathbf{Bool}) \\
p(\perp, T) &= \perp \\
p((M, N), T) &= (p(M, T), p(N, T)) \\
p(\{M\}_K^r, T) &= \begin{cases} \{p(M, T)\}_K^r & \text{if } K \in T \\ \Box_r & \text{otherwise} \end{cases}
\end{aligned}
$$

For any trace $\boldsymbol{t}$ we define a corresponding sequence $pattern(\boldsymbol{t})$ of tuples of patterns, using the set of keys obtained from the trace itself and projecting out the internal channels:

$$\begin{aligned}(pattern(\boldsymbol{t})) &= p(\boldsymbol{t}\lfloor_{\mathbf{Channels}_e}, T)\\ &\text{where } T = \{K \in \mathbf{Keys} \mid \{\boldsymbol{t}_i(c) : 1 \leq i \leq |\boldsymbol{t}|, c \in \mathbf{Channels}_e\} \vdash K\}\end{aligned}$$

where $\boldsymbol{t}\lfloor_{\mathbf{Channels}_e}$ is the projection of $\boldsymbol{t}$ onto $\mathbf{Channels}_e$ and $|\boldsymbol{t}| \leq \infty$ the length of the sequence $\boldsymbol{t}$. Roughly, this is the pattern that an attacker can see in $\boldsymbol{t}$ using the set of keys obtained from $\boldsymbol{t}$. We say that two traces are *equivalent* ($\equiv$) if they yield the same pattern, and *equivalent up to renaming* ($\cong$) if they are equivalent modulo renaming of keys and coins:

$$\begin{aligned}\boldsymbol{t} \equiv \boldsymbol{s} &\text{ if and only if } pattern(\boldsymbol{t}) = pattern(\boldsymbol{s})\\ \boldsymbol{t} \cong \boldsymbol{s} &\text{ if and only if there exist bijections } \sigma \text{ on } \mathbf{Keys} \text{ and } \sigma' \text{ on } \mathbf{Coins}\\ &\qquad\text{such that } \boldsymbol{t} \equiv \boldsymbol{s}\sigma\sigma'\end{aligned}$$

where $\boldsymbol{s}\sigma\sigma'$ is the result of applying σ and σ' as substitutions to $\boldsymbol{s}$.

Suppose that two systems $\mathcal{P}$ and $\mathcal{Q}$ have the same set of external channels (so we can compare them). They are *equivalent* if they generate equivalent traces:

$$\mathcal{P} \cong \mathcal{Q} \text{ if and only if } [\![\mathcal{P}]\!] \cong [\![\mathcal{Q}]\!]$$

Our intent is that $\mathcal{P} \cong \mathcal{Q}$ holds when an eavesdropper cannot distinguish $\mathcal{P}$ and $\mathcal{Q}$ by observing the external channels, with no a priori knowledge.

In the following simple examples, we consider pairs of systems that consist each of only one program that outputs on an external channel, and we identify the systems with the corresponding programs.

- First, $\{0\}_K$ and $\{1\}_K$ differ only in the bit that they send encrypted under a key that the eavesdropper does not have. According to the definition of equivalence, we obtain $\{0\}_K \cong \{1\}_K$. Thus, in the formal model there is no need to consider the possibility that the eavesdropper can guess the key.
- We also obtain $(\mathit{if}\ (\nu K)K = K'\ \mathit{then}\ P\ \mathit{else}\ Q) \cong Q$. Thus, in the formal model there is no need to consider the possibility that the keys K and K' are equal "by chance".
- Finally, we also obtain $(\mathit{case}\ (\nu K)\{M\}_K\ \mathit{of}\ \{x\}_{K'}\ \mathit{do}\ Q\ \mathit{else}\ R) \cong R$. Thus, in the formal model there is no need to consider the possibility that a ciphertext under K can be decrypted with K'.

Such simplifications contribute greatly to the convenience and practicality of formal reasoning.

4 Computational Model

This section gives a second semantics for programs, with a corresponding notion of equivalence between programs. The semantics relies on bitstrings, rather than formal expressions. The limitations of the adversary are expressed in terms of computational complexities and probabilities.

Elements of encryption schemes and other basics. We let $\mathsf{String} = \{0,1\}^*$ be the set of all finite strings, let $|m|$ be the length of string m, and let Cipher and Key be non-empty sets of finite strings. $\mathsf{Coins} = \{0,1\}^\omega$, the set of infinite strings, is endowed with a probability distribution. The set of *security parameters* $\mathsf{Parameter}$ is 1^* (the set of finite strings of 1 bits). For each $\eta \in \mathsf{Parameter}$, we let the set of *plaintexts* Plain_η be a finite non-empty set of finite strings, with $\mathsf{Plain}_\eta \subseteq \mathsf{Plain}_{\eta 1}$ for each η, and we write $\mathsf{Plain} = \bigcup_\eta \mathsf{Plain}_\eta$. In allowing the set of plaintexts to depend on a security parameter we follow for example Goldwasser and Bellare [11, p.105]. We let $0, 1, \varepsilon$ be particular strings in Plain_0 and $\perp$ a particular string in $\mathsf{String} \setminus (\mathsf{Plain} \cup \mathsf{Cipher})$. We assume that, for all η, if $m \in \mathsf{Plain}_\eta$ and $|m| = |m'|$ then $m' \in \mathsf{Plain}_\eta$.

An *encryption scheme*, Π, is a triple of algorithms $(\mathcal{K}, \mathcal{E}, \mathcal{D})$, where

$$\begin{aligned}
\mathcal{K}&\colon \mathsf{Parameter} \times \mathsf{Coins} \to \mathsf{Key}\\
\mathcal{E}&\colon \mathsf{Key} \times \mathsf{String} \times \mathsf{Coins} \to \mathsf{Cipher}\\
\mathcal{D}&\colon \mathsf{Key} \times \mathsf{String} \to \mathsf{Plain} \cup \{\perp\}
\end{aligned}$$

and each algorithm is computable in time polynomial in the size of its input (but without consideration for the size of Coins input). Algorithm $\mathcal{K}$ is the *key-generation* algorithm, $\mathcal{E}$ is the *encryption* algorithm, and $\mathcal{D}$ is the *decryption* algorithm. We usually write the first argument to $\mathcal{E}$ or $\mathcal{D}$, the key, as a subscript, and the last argument to $\mathcal{E}$, the coin, as a superscript. When we omit the final argument to $\mathcal{K}$ or $\mathcal{E}$, this indicates the corresponding probability space, or the support set of this space. We require that for all $\eta \in \mathsf{Parameter}$, $k \in \mathcal{K}(\eta)$, and $r \in \mathsf{Coins}$, if $m \in \mathsf{Plain}_\eta$ then $\mathcal{D}_k(\mathcal{E}_k^r(m)) = m$, while if $m \notin \mathsf{Plain}_\eta$ then $\mathcal{E}_k^r(m) = \mathcal{E}_k^r(0)$. We insist that $|\mathcal{E}_k^r(m)|$ depends only on η and $|m|$ when $k \in \mathcal{K}(\eta)$.

A function $\epsilon : \mathbb{N} \to \mathbb{R}$ is *negligible* if for all $c > 0$ there exists N_c such that $\epsilon(\eta) \le \eta^{-c}$ for all $\eta \ge N_c$. A Parameter-indexed family $D = (D_\eta)$ of distributions on a set S is called an *ensemble* on S. We write $x \stackrel{R}{\leftarrow} D_\eta$ to indicate that x is sampled from D_η. Let $D = \{D_\eta\}$ and $D' = \{D'_\eta\}$ be ensembles on a set S. We say that D and D' are (computationally) *indistinguishable*, and write $D \approx D'$, if for every probabilistic polynomial-time adversary $A : \mathsf{Parameter} \times S \times \mathsf{Coins} \to \{0,1\}$, the following function ϵ is negligible:

$$\epsilon(\eta) \stackrel{\text{def}}{=} \Pr\left[x \stackrel{R}{\leftarrow} D_\eta : A(\eta, x) = 1\right] - \Pr\left[x \stackrel{R}{\leftarrow} D'_\eta : A(\eta, x) = 1\right]$$

Generating traces. Again we assume that keys and coins are renamed so that in a system $\mathcal{P}$ each key or coin symbol is bound at most once, and any bound key does not also occur free. We write $\mathbf{keys}(P)$ and $\mathbf{coins}(P)$ for the sets of all key symbols and coin symbols that occur in P.

A function $\tau : \mathbf{keys}(P) \cup \mathbf{coins}(P) \to \mathsf{Key} \cup \mathsf{Coins}$ mapping $\mathbf{keys}(P)$ to Key and $\mathbf{coins}(P)$ to Coins is called a *choice function*. For any program P, any $\boldsymbol{m} \in \mathbf{Channels} \cup \mathbf{Var} \to \mathsf{String}$, and any choice function τ, we define $[\![P]\!]^\tau(\boldsymbol{m})$ in Figure 2, so that $[\![P]\!]^\tau(\boldsymbol{m})$ is the bitstring that results from running P once, when the variables and channels have the initial values given in $\boldsymbol{m}$ and keys and coins are chosen according to τ. In the definition, we write $\langle a_1, \ldots, a_n \rangle$ for a

$$
\begin{array}{ll}
[\![\varepsilon]\!]^\tau(\boldsymbol{m}) = \langle\, \varepsilon, \text{“null”}\,\rangle & \\
[\![K]\!]^\tau(\boldsymbol{m}) = \langle\, \tau(K), \text{“key”}\,\rangle & (K \in \mathbf{Keys}) \\
[\![b]\!]^\tau(\boldsymbol{m}) = \langle\, b, \text{“bool”}\,\rangle & (b \in \mathbf{Bool}) \\
[\![\bot]\!]^\tau(\boldsymbol{m}) = \langle\, \bot, \text{“error”}\,\rangle & \\
[\![u]\!]^\tau(\boldsymbol{m}) = \boldsymbol{m}_u & (u \in \mathbf{Channels} \cup \mathbf{Var}) \\
[\![(P,Q)]\!]^\tau(\boldsymbol{m}) = \langle\, [\![P]\!]^\tau(\boldsymbol{m}), [\![Q]\!]^\tau(\boldsymbol{m}), \text{“pair”}\,\rangle & \\
[\![(\nu v)P]\!]^\tau(\boldsymbol{m}) = [\![P]\!]^\tau(\boldsymbol{m}) & (v \in \mathbf{Keys} \cup \mathbf{Coins}) \\
[\![\{P\}^r_Q]\!]^\tau(\boldsymbol{m}) = \langle\, \mathcal{E}^{\tau(r)}_{[\![Q]\!]^\tau(\boldsymbol{m})}([\![P]\!]^\tau(\boldsymbol{m})), \text{“ciphertext”}\,\rangle & \text{if } [\![Q]\!]^\tau(\boldsymbol{m}) \in \mathbf{Keys}\ (r \in \mathbf{Coins}) \\
[\![\{P\}^r_Q]\!]^\tau(\boldsymbol{m}) = \langle\, \bot, \text{“error”}\,\rangle & \text{otherwise } (r \in \mathbf{Coins}) \\
[\![\mathit{if}\ P = Q\ \mathit{then}\ P'\ \mathit{else}\ Q']\!]^\tau(\boldsymbol{m}) = [\![P']\!]^\tau(\boldsymbol{m}) & \text{if } [\![P]\!]^\tau(\boldsymbol{m}) = [\![Q]\!]^\tau(\boldsymbol{m}) \\
[\![\mathit{if}\ P = Q\ \mathit{then}\ P'\ \mathit{else}\ Q']\!]^\tau(\boldsymbol{m}) = [\![Q']\!]^\tau(\boldsymbol{m}) & \text{if } [\![P]\!]^\tau(\boldsymbol{m}) \neq [\![Q]\!]^\tau(\boldsymbol{m}) \\
[\![\mathit{case}\ P\ \mathit{of}\ (x,y)\ \mathit{do}\ Q\ \mathit{else}\ R]\!]^\tau(\boldsymbol{m}) = [\![Q]\!]^\tau(\boldsymbol{m}[x \to m_1, y \to m_2]) & \\
& \text{if } [\![P]\!]^\tau(\boldsymbol{m}) = \langle\, m_1, m_2, \text{“pair”}\,\rangle \\
[\![\mathit{case}\ P\ \mathit{of}\ (x,y)\ \mathit{do}\ Q\ \mathit{else}\ R]\!]^\tau(\boldsymbol{m}) = [\![R]\!]^\tau(\boldsymbol{m}) & \\
\qquad \text{if there are no } m_1, m_2 \text{ with } [\![P]\!]^\tau(\boldsymbol{m}) = \langle\, m_1, m_2, \text{“pair”}\,\rangle & \\
[\![\mathit{case}\ P\ \mathit{of}\ \{x\}_{P'}\ \mathit{do}\ Q\ \mathit{else}\ R]\!]^\tau(\boldsymbol{m}) = [\![Q]\!]^\tau(\boldsymbol{m}[x \to \mathcal{D}_k(m)]) & \\
\qquad \text{if } [\![P']\!]^\tau(\boldsymbol{m}) = \langle\, k, \text{“key”}\,\rangle \text{ and } [\![P]\!]^\tau(\boldsymbol{m}) = \langle\, m, \text{“ciphertext”}\,\rangle & \\
\qquad \text{with } k \in \mathsf{Key} \text{ and } \mathcal{D}_k(m) \neq \bot & \\
[\![\mathit{case}\ P\ \mathit{of}\ \{x\}_{P'}\ \mathit{do}\ Q\ \mathit{else}\ R]\!]^\tau(\boldsymbol{m}) = [\![R]\!]^\tau(\boldsymbol{m}) & \text{otherwise}
\end{array}
$$

Fig. 2. Definition of $[\![P]\!]^\tau(\boldsymbol{m})$ in the computational semantics.

bitstring representation of the tupling of $a_1, \ldots, a_n$. We assume that bitstring representations are such that, for each η, all and only expression plaintexts in **Plain** are mapped to bitstring plaintexts in Plain_η (up to negligible probability). We write $\boldsymbol{m}[x \to m]$ for the function in **Channels** $\cup$ **Var** $\to$ String that coincides with $\boldsymbol{m}$ except on x, which it maps to m.

Despite superficial similarities, the definitions $[\![P]\!](\boldsymbol{M})$ and $[\![P]\!]^\tau(\boldsymbol{m})$ can assign different behaviors to programs. For example, in the formal model we have $[\![\mathit{if}\ K = K'\ \mathit{then}\ 1\ \mathit{else}\ 0]\!](\boldsymbol{M}) = 0$, while in the computational model we have $[\![\mathit{if}\ K = K'\ \mathit{then}\ 1\ \mathit{else}\ 0]\!]^\tau(\boldsymbol{m}) = \langle\, 1, \text{“bool”}\,\rangle$ or $= \langle\, 0, \text{“bool”}\,\rangle$ depending on τ. Part of the proof of our main theorem consists in showing that these differences are negligible.

A *trace* is a sequence of mappings **Channels** $\to$ String (that is, a sequence of **Channels**-indexed tuples of bitstrings). Suppose that $\mathcal{P}$ is a system that consists of a program P_c for each channel c, all without free variables. For any sequence $\tau = (\tau_n)_{n \in \mathbb{N}}$ of choice functions that agree on the free keys in $\mathcal{P}$, we define the result of running $\mathcal{P}$ with τ, inductively:

- $[\![\mathcal{P}]\!]^\tau_1(c) = [\![P_c]\!]^{\tau_1}(\varepsilon, \ldots, \varepsilon)$
- $[\![\mathcal{P}]\!]^\tau_{n+1}(c) = [\![P_c]\!]^{\tau_{n+1}}([\![\mathcal{P}]\!]^\tau_n)$

where P_c is the unique program having c as its output channel.

Computational indistinguishability. Suppose $\mathcal{P}$ and $\mathcal{Q}$ are systems with the same external channels. We let:

$$\mathcal{P} \approx_\Pi \mathcal{Q} \text{ if and only if for all } n \in \mathbb{N},\ [\![\mathcal{P}]\!]^e_{\leq n} \approx [\![\mathcal{Q}]\!]^e_{\leq n}$$

where $[\![\mathcal{P}]\!]^e_{\leq n}$ is:

$$\{([\![\mathcal{P}]\!]^\tau_1, \ldots, [\![\mathcal{P}]\!]^\tau_n) \restriction_{\mathbf{Channels}_e} : \tau \leftarrow \textsc{Init}_{\eta,n}(\mathbf{coins}(\mathcal{P}), \mathbf{keys}(\mathcal{P}), \mathbf{new}(\mathcal{P}))\}$$

and $\textsc{Init}_{\eta,n}(\mathbf{coins}(\mathcal{P}), \mathbf{keys}(\mathcal{P}), \mathbf{new}(\mathcal{P}))$ chooses a sequence $\tau = (\tau_1, \ldots, \tau_n)$ of choice functions $\tau_i : \mathbf{keys}(\mathcal{P}) \cup \mathbf{coins}(\mathcal{P}) \rightarrow \mathsf{Key} \cup \mathsf{Coins}$ that agree on $\mathbf{keys}(\mathcal{P}) \setminus \mathbf{new}(\mathcal{P})$ (the set of free keys in $\mathcal{P}$), generating keys by $\mathcal{K}(\eta)$ and coins according to the distribution on Coins.

Again, our intent is that $\mathcal{P} \approx_\Pi \mathcal{Q}$ holds when an eavesdropper cannot distinguish $\mathcal{P}$ and $\mathcal{Q}$ by observing external channels. However, the definition of $\mathcal{P} \approx_\Pi \mathcal{Q}$ relies on a computational view of the semantics of systems and of the powers of the eavesdropper, quite different from the formal view of section 3. The next section relates these two views.

Note that this definition of $\mathcal{P} \approx_\Pi \mathcal{Q}$ includes a quantification over all lengths n. One might have expected some bound on n, perhaps as a function of the security parameter η. The quantification over all n yields a simpler relation. It may be rather strong; it is nevertheless useful for our purposes.

5 Soundness

While the semantics of Section 4 does not specify security assumptions on the underlying encryption scheme, such assumptions are necessary in order to relate the two semantics. We use *type-0 security* (a variant of the standard notion of semantic security [4, 12], defined and justified in [3]):

Definition 1 (Type-0 security). *Let $\Pi = (\mathcal{K}, \mathcal{E}, \mathcal{D})$ be an encryption scheme, let $\eta \in$ Parameter be a security parameter. An encryption scheme Π is* type-0 secure *if, for every probabilistic polynomial-time adversary $A^{-,-}$ with two oracles, the function*

$$\epsilon(\eta) \stackrel{\text{def}}{=} \Pr\left[k, k' \stackrel{R}{\leftarrow} \mathcal{K}(\eta) : A^{\mathcal{E}_k(\cdot),\, \mathcal{E}_{k'}(\cdot)}(\eta) = 1\right] - \Pr\left[k \stackrel{R}{\leftarrow} \mathcal{K}(\eta) : A^{\mathcal{E}_k(0),\, \mathcal{E}_k(0)}(\eta) = 1\right]$$

is negligible.

In addition, we need a computational counterpart to the assumption that decrypting a message with the "wrong" key is a noticeable error, as this assumption is built into the formal model. We use the following concept of *confusion-free* encryption:

Definition 2 (Confusion-free encryption scheme). *The encryption scheme $\Pi = (\mathcal{K}, \mathcal{E}, \mathcal{D})$ is* confusion-free *if for all $m \in$ String the probability $\Pr[k, k' \stackrel{R}{\leftarrow} \mathcal{K}(\eta), x \stackrel{R}{\leftarrow} \mathcal{E}_k(m) : \mathcal{D}_{k'}(x) \neq \perp]$ is negligible.*

M. Fischlin's related concept of committing encryption requires the encryption function to be essentially injective (to map different plaintexts to different ciphertexts) [9]. Confusion-freedom differs in that it allows some collisions and puts requirements on the decryption function. The long version of this paper [2] describes a construction of confusion-free encryption schemes.

Finally, we need to rule out encryption cycles (such as encrypting a key with itself), as in [3]. These cycles are not supported in standard computational definitions of security (such as semantic security), which for example allow $\{K\}_K^r$ to reveal K. These cycles may however be acceptable in the random-oracle model, and they are allowed (silently!) in formal methods. According to [3], K *encrypts* K' in the expression M if there exist N and r such that $\{N\}_K^r$ is a subexpression of M and K' occurs in N. Here we adopt the slightly more liberal definition that ignores occurrences of K' as a subscript (that is, as an encryption key). For each M, this defines a binary relation on keys. We say that M is *cyclic* if this relation is cyclic, and is *acyclic* otherwise. Similarly, we say that a trace is cyclic or acyclic. A system $\mathcal{P}$ does not generate encryption cycles if the formal trace $[\![\mathcal{P}]\!]$ is acyclic.

Our main theorem says that if two systems are equivalent with respect to formal eavesdroppers, then they are also equivalent with respect to computational eavesdroppers. Thus, computational eavesdroppers do not have essentially more power than formal eavesdroppers, so we may reason with the higher-level formal eavesdroppers without loss of generality. (We believe that a converse also holds; it is interesting but less important.)

Theorem 1. *Let $\mathcal{P}$ and $\mathcal{Q}$ be two systems that do not generate encryption cycles. Suppose Π is a type-0 secure and confusion-free encryption scheme. If $\mathcal{P} \cong \mathcal{Q}$ then $\mathcal{P} \approx_{\Pi} \mathcal{Q}$.*

The proof of this theorem has several components. One of them is analogous to the main proof in Abadi and Rogaway's paper [3], with a few twists and extensions (for example, dealing with repetitions). Others deal with concepts not present in Abadi and Rogaway's work, for instance the control flow of processes. (See [2] for details.)

6 Conclusion

This paper relates two views of symmetric cryptographic primitives, in the context of the systems that use them. We express the systems in a simple programming language. This language has two semantics. Each of the semantics leads to a notion of equivalence of systems; roughly, two systems are equivalent if an eavesdropper cannot tell them apart. In one of the semantics, cryptographic operations are interpreted symbolically. In the other, they are interpreted as operations on bitstrings; this more concrete interpretation leads to reasoning with probabilities and computational complexities. Therefore, the formal semantics may seem attractively simpler but also naive. Nevertheless, under suitable hypotheses, formal equivalence implies computational equivalence. This result provides a computational justification for high-level, formal reasoning about security against eavesdroppers, and another significant and promising link between the formal and the computational views of cryptography and cryptographic protocols.

Acknowledgements

Discussions with Phillip Rogaway and John Mitchell contributed to the writing of this paper. This work was partly done while the second author was visiting Bell Labs Research, Palo Alto, whose hospitality is gratefully acknowledged.

References

1. Martín Abadi and Andrew D. Gordon. A calculus for cryptographic protocols: The spi calculus. *Information and Computation*, 148(1):1–70, January 1999. An extended version appeared as Digital Equipment Corporation Systems Research Center report No. 149, January 1998.
2. Martín Abadi and Jan Jürjens. Formal eavesdropping and its computational interpretation, 2001. Longer version of this paper, available at http://www.jurjens.de/jan/lambdaweb.ps.
3. Martín Abadi and Phillip Rogaway. Reconciling two views of cryptography (The computational soundness of formal encryption). In *Proceedings of the First IFIP International Conference on Theoretical Computer Science*, volume 1872 of *Lecture Notes in Computer Science*, pages 3–22. Springer-Verlag, August 2000.
4. Mihir Bellare, Anand Desai, Eron Jokipii, and Phillip Rogaway. A concrete security treatment of symmetric encryption: analysis of the DES modes of operation. In *Proceedings of 38th Annual Symposium on Foundations of Computer Science (FOCS 97)*, pages 394–403, 1997.
5. Mihir Bellare and Phillip Rogaway. Entity authentication and key distribution. In *Advances in Cryptology—CRYPTO '94*, volume 773 of *Lecture Notes in Computer Science*, pages 232–249. Springer-Verlag, 1993.
6. Steven M. Bellovin. Problem areas for the IP security protocols. In *Proceedings of the Sixth Usenix Unix Security Symposium*, pages 1–16, July 1996.
7. Manuel Blum and Silvio Micali. How to generate cryptographically strong sequences of pseudo random bits. In *Proceedings of the 23rd Annual Symposium on Foundations of Computer Science (FOCS 82)*, pages 112–117, 1982.
8. Danny Dolev and Andrew C. Yao. On the security of public key protocols. *IEEE Transactions on Information Theory*, IT-29(12):198–208, March 1983.
9. Marc Fischlin. Pseudorandom function tribe ensembles based on one-way permutations: Improvements and applications. In *Advances in Cryptology—Eurocrypt '99*, volume 1592 of *Lecture Notes in Computer Science*, pages 429–444. Springer-Verlag, 1999.
10. Oded Goldreich, Silvio Micali, and Avi Wigderson. How to play any mental game. In *Proceedings of the Nineteenth Annual ACM Symposium on Theory of Computing*, pages 218–229, 1987.
11. S. Goldwasser and M. Bellare. Lecture notes on cryptography, 1999.
12. Shafi Goldwasser and Silvio Micali. Probabilistic encryption. *Journal of Computer and System Sciences*, 28:270–299, April 1984.
13. Shafi Goldwasser, Silvio Micali, and Ronald Rivest. A digital signature scheme secure against adaptive chosen-message attack. *SIAM Journal on Computing*, 17:281–308, 1988.
14. Jan Jürjens. Composability of secrecy. In *International Workshop on Mathematical Methods, Models and Architectures for Computer Networks Security (MMM 2001)*, volume 2052 of *Lecture Notes in Computer Science*, pages 28–38. Springer-Verlag, 2001.

15. Jan Jürjens. Secrecy-preserving refinement. In J. Fiadeiro and P. Zave, editors, *Formal Methods Europe*, volume 2021 of *Lecture Notes in Computer Science*, pages 135–152. Springer-Verlag, 2001.
16. R. Kemmerer, C. Meadows, and J. Millen. Three system for cryptographic protocol analysis. *Journal of Cryptology*, 7(2):79–130, Spring 1994.
17. P. Lincoln, J. Mitchell, M. Mitchell, and A. Scedrov. A probabilistic poly-time framework for protocol analysis. In *Proceedings of the Fifth ACM Conference on Computer and Communications Security*, pages 112–121, 1998.
18. Gavin Lowe. Breaking and fixing the Needham-Schroeder public-key protocol using FDR. In *Tools and Algorithms for the Construction and Analysis of Systems*, volume 1055 of *Lecture Notes in Computer Science*, pages 147–166. Springer-Verlag, 1996.
19. A. Menezes, P. van Oorschot, and S. Vanstone. *Handbook of Applied Cryptography*. CRC Press, 1996.
20. Robin Milner. *Communicating and Mobile Systems: the π-Calculus*. Cambridge University Press, 1999.
21. John C. Mitchell. *Foundations for Programming Languages*. MIT Press, 1996.
22. Lawrence C. Paulson. The inductive approach to verifying cryptographic protocols. *Journal of Computer Security*, 6(1–2):85–128, 1998.
23. Birgit Pfitzmann, Matthias Schunter, and Michael Waidner. Cryptographic security of reactive systems (extended abstract). *Electronic Notes in Theoretical Computer Science*, 32, April 2000.
24. Birgit Pfitzmann and Michael Waidner. Composition and integrity preservation of secure reactive systems. In *Proceedings of the 7th ACM Conference on Computer and Communications Security*, pages 245–254, November 2000.
25. Birgit Pfitzmann and Michael Waidner. A model for asynchronous reactive systems and its application to secure message transmission. In *Proceedings of the 2001 IEEE Symposium on Security and Privacy*, pages 184–200, May 2001.
26. Andrew C. Yao. Theory and applications of trapdoor functions. In *Proceedings of the 23rd Annual Symposium on Foundations of Computer Science (FOCS 82)*, pages 80–91, 1982.

Resource-Passing Concurrent Programming

Kazunori Ueda

Dept. of Information and Computer Science, Waseda University,
3-4-1, Okubo, Shinjuku-ku, Tokyo 169-8555, Japan,
ueda@ueda.info.waseda.ac.jp

Abstract. The use of types to deal with access capabilities of program entities is becoming increasingly popular.

In concurrent logic programming, the first attempt was made in Moded Flat GHC in 1990, which gave polarity structures (modes) to every variable occurrence and every predicate argument. Strong moding turned out to play fundamental rôles in programming, implementation and the in-depth understanding of constraint-based concurrent computation.

The moding principle guarantees that each variable is written only once and encourages capability-conscious programming. Furthermore, it gives less generic modes to programs that discard or duplicate data, thus providing the view of "data as resources." A simple linearity system built upon the mode system distinguishes variables read only once from those read possibly many times, enabling compile-time garbage collection. Compared to linear types studied in other programming paradigms, the primary issue in constraint-based concurrency has been to deal with logical variables and highly non-strict data structures they induce.

In this paper, we put our resource-consciousness one step forward and consider a class of 'ecological' programs which recycle or return all the resources given to them while allowing concurrent reading of data structures via controlled aliasing. This completely recyclic subset enforces us to think more about resources, but the resulting programs enjoy high symmetry which we believe has more than aesthetic implications to our programming practice in general.

The type system supporting recyclic concurrent programming gives a $[-1, +1]$ capability to each occurrence of variable and function symbols (constructors), where positive/negative values mean read/write capabilities, respectively, and fractions mean non-exclusive read/write paths. The capabilities are intended to be statically checked or reconstructed so that one can tell the polarity and exclusiveness of each piece of information handled by concurrent processes. The capability type system refines and integrates the mode system and the linearity system for Moded Flat GHC. Its arithmetic formulation contributes to the simplicity.

The execution of a recyclic program proceeds so that every variable has zero-sum capability and the resources (i.e., constructors weighted by their capabilities) a process absorbs match the resources it emits. Constructors accessed by a process with an exclusive read capability can be reused for other purposes.

The first half of this paper is devoted to a tutorial introduction to constraint-based concurrency in the hope that it will encourage cross-fertilization of different concurrency formalisms.

N. Kobayashi and B.C. Pierce (Eds.): TACS 2001, LNCS 2215, pp. 95–126, 2001.

1 Introduction – Constraint-Based Concurrency

The *raison d'être* and the challenge of symbolic languages are to construct highly sophisticated software which would be too complicated or unmanageable if written in other languages.

Concurrent logic programming was born in early 1980's from the process interpretation of logic programs [47] and forms one of many interesting subfields addressed by the logic programming paradigm [45].

The prominent feature of concurrent logic programming is that it exploits the power of logical, single-assignment variables and data structures – exactly those of first-order logic – to achieve various forms of communication.

Essentially, a logical variable is a communication channel that can be used for output at most once (hence single-assignment) and for non-destructive input zero or more times. The two well-established operations, unification and matching (also called one-way unification), are used for output and input. Thanks to the single-assignment property, the set of all unification operations that have been performed determines the current binding environment of the universe, which is called a (*monotonic*) *store* (of equality constraints) in concurrent constraint programming (CCP) [28] that generalizes concurrent logic programming. The store records what messages have been sent to what channels and what channels has been fused together.

In CCP, variable bindings are generalized to constraints, unification is generalized to the *tell* of a constraint to the store, and matching is generalized to the *ask* of a constraint from the store. The *ask* operation checks if the current store logically entails certain information on a variable.

Constraint-based communication embodied by concurrent logic programming languages has the following characteristics:

1. *Asynchronous.* In most concurrent logic languages, *tell* is an independent process that does not occur as a prefix of another process as in *ask*. This form of *tell* is sometimes called *eventual tell* and is a standard mechanism of information sending. (We do not discuss the other, prefixed form, *atomic tell*, in this paper.) Since *eventual tell* simply adds a new constraint to the store, the store can become inconsistent when an attempt is made to equate a variable to two different values. This can be avoided by using a non-standard type system, called a *mode system* [41], that controls the number of write capabilities of each variable in the system. The advocation of *eventual tell* apparently motivated Honda and Tokoro's asynchronous π-calculus [15].
2. *Polyadic.* Concurrent logic programming incorporated (rather than devised) well-understood built-in data structuring mechanisms and operations. Messages can be polyadic at no extra cost on the formalism; it does not bother us to encode numbers, tuples, lists, and so on, from scratch. The single-assignment property of logical variables does not allow one to use it for repetitive communication, but streams – which are just another name of lists in our setting – can readily be used for representing a sequence of messages incrementally sent from a process to another.

3. *Mobile.* A process[1] (say P) can dynamically create another process (say P') and a fresh logical variable (say v) with which to communicate with P'. Although process themselves are not first-class, logical variables are first-class and its occurrences (other than the one 'plugged' to P') can be freely passed from P to other processes using another channel. The logical variable connected to a process acts as an object identity (or more precisely, channel identity because a process can respond to more than one channel) and the language construct does not allow a third process to forge the identity.
   When P creates two occurrences of the variable v and sends one of them to another process (say Q), v becomes a private channel between P' and Q that cannot be monitored by any other process unless P' or Q passes it to somebody else. This corresponds to scope extrusion in the π-calculus.
   Another form of reconfiguration happens when a process fuses two logical variables connected to the outside. The fusion makes sense when one of the variables can be read (input capability) and the other can be written (output capability), in which case the effect of fusing is implicit delegation of messages. Again, the process that fused two logical variables loses access to them unless it retains a copy of them. As will be discussed later, our type systems have dealt with read/write capabilities of logical variables and the number of access paths (occurrences) of each variable.
   Although not as widely recognized as it used to be, Concurrent Prolog [30] designed in early 1980s was the first simple high-level language that featured channel mobility in the sense of the π-calculus. When the author proposed Guarded Horn Clauses (GHC) [36] [37] as a simplification of Concurrent Prolog and PARLOG [8], the principal design constraint was to retain channel mobility and evolving process structures [32], because GHC was supposed to be the basis of KL1 [39], a language in which to describe operating systems of the Parallel Inference Machines as well as various knowledge-based systems.
4. *Non-strict.* Logical variables provide us with the paradigm of *computing with partial information.* Interesting programming idioms including short-circuits, difference lists and messages with reply boxes, as well as channel mobility, all exploit the power of partially instantiated data structures.

Some historical remarks would be appropriate here.

Concurrent logic programming was a field of active research throughout the 1980's, when a number of concurrent logic languages were proposed and the language constructs were tested through a number of implementations and applications [31]. The synchronization primitive, now known as *ask* based on logical entailment, was inspired independently around 1984 by at least three research groups, which suggests the stability of the idea [32].

Although concurrent logic languages achieved their flexibility with an extremely small number of language constructs, the fact that they were targeted

[1] We regard a process as an entity that is implemented as a multiset S of goals and communicates with other processes by generating and observing constraints on variables not local to S.

to programming rather than reasoning about concurrent systems lead to little cross-fertilization with later research on mobile processes.

CCP was proposed in late 1980s as a unified theory underlying concurrent logic languages. It helped high-level understanding of constraint-based concurrency, but the study of constraint-based communication at a concrete level and the design of type systems and static analyses call for a fixed constraint system – most typically that of (concurrent) logic programming known as the Herbrand system – to work with.

2 The Essence of Constraint-Based Communication

2.1 The Language

To further investigate constraint-based communication, let us consider a concrete language, a subset of Flat GHC [38] whose syntax is given in Fig. 1.

(program) P	$::=$ set of R's	(1)
(program clause) R	$::=$ A `:-` `|` B	(2)
(body) B	$::=$ multiset of G's	(3)
(goal) G	$::=$ T_1 `=` T_2 $\mid$ A	(4)
(non-unification atom) A	$::=$ $p(T_1, \ldots, T_n)$, $p \neq$ '='	(5)
(term) T	$::=$ (as in first-order logic)	(6)
(goal clause) Q	$::=$ `:-` B	(7)
(program clause, alternative) R	$::=$ $!\forall(A\ .\ B)$	(2′)
(goal clause, alternative) Q	$::=$ B, P	(7′)

Fig. 1. The simplified syntax of Flat GHC

For simplicity, the syntax given in Fig. 1 omits guard goals from (2), which correspond to conditions in conditional rewrite rules. We use the traditional rule-based syntax rather than the expression-based one because it facilitates our analysis. The alternative syntax (2′) (7′) indicates that a program clause, namely a rewrite rule of goals, could be regarded as a replicated process that accepts a message A and spawns B, where the universal closure $\forall$ means that a variable either occurs in A and will be connected to the outside or occurs only in B as local channels. In this formulation, the program is made to reside in a goal clause.

2.2 Operational Semantics

The reduction semantics of GHC deals with the rewriting of goal clauses.

Let B be a multiset of goals, C a multiset of equations (denoting equality constraints) that represents the store or the binding environment of B, and V

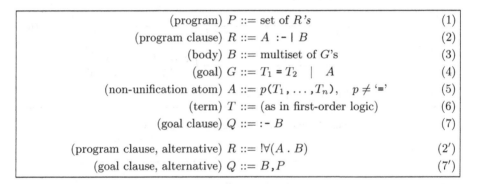

a set of variables. Let $\mathcal{V}_F$ denote the set of all variables occurring in a syntactic entity F. The current *configuration* is a triple, denoted $\langle B, C, V \rangle$, such that $\mathcal{V}_B \cup \mathcal{V}_C \subseteq V$. It records the goals to be reduced and the current store, as well as the variables already in use for the current computation. A computation under a program P starts with the initial configuration $\langle B_0, \emptyset, \mathcal{V}_{B_0} \rangle$, where B_0 is the body of the given goal clause.

We have three rules given in Fig. 2. In the rules, $F \models G$ means that G is a logical consequence of F. $\forall \mathcal{V}_F(F)$ and $\exists \mathcal{V}_F(F)$ are abbreviated to $\forall(F)$ and $\exists(F)$, respectively. $\mathcal{E}$ denotes so-called Clark's equality theory for finite terms as defined in Fig. 3. The second condition of Fig. 3, characterizing the finiteness of terms, is known as the *occur check*. Equality of atom(ic formula)s are understood to be handled by injecting predicate symbols to constructors as usual.

$$\frac{\mathcal{P} \vdash \langle B_1, C, V \rangle \longrightarrow \langle B_1', C', V' \rangle}{\mathcal{P} \vdash \langle B_1 \cup B_2, C, V \rangle \longrightarrow \langle B_1' \cup B_2, C', V' \rangle} \quad \text{(i)}$$

$$\frac{}{\mathcal{P} \vdash \langle \{t_1 = t_2\}, C, V \rangle \longrightarrow \langle \emptyset, C \cup \{t_1 = t_2\}, V \rangle} \quad \text{(ii)}$$

$$\frac{}{\begin{array}{l}\{h \mathtt{:-} B\} \cup \mathcal{P} \vdash \\ \quad \langle \{b\}, C, V \rangle \longrightarrow \langle B, C \cup \{b = h\}, (V \cup \mathcal{V}_{h\mathtt{:-|}B}) \rangle\end{array}} \left(\begin{array}{l} \mathcal{E} \models \forall\big(C \Rightarrow \exists \mathcal{V}_h(b = h)\big) \\ \text{and } \mathcal{V}_{h\mathtt{:-|}B} \cap V = \emptyset \end{array} \right) \quad \text{(iii)}$$

Fig. 2. The reduction semantics of GHC

1. $\forall\big(\neg(f(\mathtt{X}_1, \ldots, \mathtt{X}_m) = g(\mathtt{Y}_1, \ldots, \mathtt{Y}_n))\big)$, for all pairs f, g of distinct constructors (including constants)
2. $\forall\big(\neg(t = \mathtt{X})\big)$, for each term t other than and containing $\mathtt{X}$
3. $\forall\big(\mathtt{X} = \mathtt{X}\big)$
4. $\forall\big(f(\mathtt{X}_1, \ldots, \mathtt{X}_m) = f(\mathtt{Y}_1, \ldots, \mathtt{Y}_m) \Rightarrow \bigwedge_{i=1}^{m}(\mathtt{X}_i = \mathtt{Y}_i)\big)$, for each m-ary constructor f
5. $\forall\big(\bigwedge_{i=1}^{m}(\mathtt{X}_i = \mathtt{Y}_i) \Rightarrow f(\mathtt{X}_1, \ldots, \mathtt{X}_m) = f(\mathtt{Y}_1, \ldots, \mathtt{Y}_m)\big)$, for each m-ary constructor f
6. $\forall\big(\mathtt{X} = \mathtt{Y} \Rightarrow \mathtt{Y} = \mathtt{X}\big)$
7. $\forall\big(\mathtt{X} = \mathtt{Y} \land \mathtt{Y} = \mathtt{Z} \Rightarrow \mathtt{X} = \mathtt{Z}\big)$

Fig. 3. Clark's equality theory $\mathcal{E}$, in clausal form

In Fig. 2, Rule (i) expresses concurrent reduction of a multiset of goals. Rule (ii) says that a unification goal simply publishes (or posts) a constraint to the current store. Rule (iii) deals with the reduction of a non-unification goal b to B_i using a clause $h_i \mathtt{:-} \mid B_i$, which is enabled when the publication of $b = h_i$ will not constrain the variables in b. This means that the head unification is effectively restricted to matching. The second condition $\mathcal{V}_{h\mathtt{:-|}B} \cap V = \emptyset$ guarantees that the guarded clause has been renamed using fresh variables. An immediate consequence of Rules (i)–(iii) is that the store grows monotonically and the reduction of b using a clause h_i :- | B_i remains enabled once it becomes enabled.

Sometimes it's more convenient to treat reduction in a traditional way as rewriting of goal clauses. The goal clause corresponding to a configuration $\langle B, C, V\rangle$ is :- $B\theta$, where θ is the most general unifier (mgu) of the set C of constraints. This substitution-based formulation is closer to actual implementation, but an advantage of the constraint-based formulation is that it can represent inconsistent stores, while mgu's can represent consistent stores only.

Yet another formulation may omit the second component, C, of a configuration together with Rule (ii) that simply moves an unguarded unification goal to the separate store. In this case, the current store is understood to comprise all the unguarded unification goals in B. However, we think it makes sense to distinguish between the three entities, namely definitions (code), processes, and the store.

2.3 Relation to Name-Based Concurrency

How can the constraint-based concurrency defined above relates to name-based concurrency?

First of all, predicate names can be thought of as global channel names if we regard the reduction of a non-unification goal (predicate name followed by arguments) as message sending to predicate definition. However, we don't regard this as a crucially important observation. We would rather forget this correspondence and focus on other symbols, namely variables and constructors.

Variables are local names that can be used as communication channels. Instead of *sending* a message *along* a channel, the the message is written to the channel itself and the receiver can asynchronously read the channel's value. For instance, let `S` be shared by processes P and Q (but nobody else) and suppose P sends a message `S=[read(X)|S']`. The message sends two subchannels, one a reply box `X` for the request `read`, and the other a *continuation* for subsequent communication. Then the goal in Q that owns `S`, say `q(S)`, can read the message using a clause head `q([read(A)|B])`, identifying `A` with `X` and `B` with `S'` at the same time.[2] Alternatively, the identification of variables can be dispensed with by appropriately choosing an α-converted variant of the clause.

There is rather small difference between message passing of the asynchronous π-calculus and message passing by unification, as long as only one process holds a write capability *and* use it once. These conditions can be statically checked in well-moded concurrent logic programs [41] and in the π-calculus with a linear type system [19]. When two processes communicate repeatedly, constraint-based concurrency uses streams because one fresh logical variable must be prepared for each message passing, while in the linear π-calculus the same channel could be recycled as suggested in [19]. When two client processes communicate with a

[2] In the syntax advocated by CCP, one should first ask $\exists$`A,B(q(S) = q([read(A)|B]))` (or equivalently, $\exists$`A,B(S = [read(A)|B]))` first and then tell `q(S) = q([read(A)|B])`.

single server in constraint-based concurrency, an arbitration process should be explicitly created. A stream merger is a typical arbiter for repetitive multi-client communication:

```
merge([],Ys,Zs) :- | Zs=Ys.
merge(Xs,[],Zs) :- | Zs=Xs.
merge([A|Xs],Ys,Zs0) :- | Zs0=[A|Zs], merge(Xs,Ys,Zs).
merge(Xs,[A|Ys],Zs0) :- | Zs0=[A|Zs], merge(Xs,Ys,Zs).
```

In contrast, in name-based concurrency (without linearity), arbitration is built in the communication rule

$$a(y).Q \mid \overline{a}b \longrightarrow Q\{b/y\}$$

which chooses one of available outputs (forming a multiset of messages) on the channel a.

The difference in the semantics of input is much larger between the two formalisms. While *ask* is an non-destructive input, input in name-based concurrency destructively consumes a message, which is one of the sources of nondeterminism in the absence of choice operators. In constraint-based concurrency, non-destructiveness of *ask* is used to model one-way multicasting or data sharing naturally. At the same time, by using a linearity system, we can guarantee that only one process holds a read capability of a logical variable [46], in which case *ask* can destroy a message it has received, as will be discussed in detail in this paper.

One feature of constraint-based concurrency included into name-based concurrency only recently by the Fusion calculus [48] is that two channels can be fused into a single channel.

2.4 Locality in Global Store

The notion of shared, global store provided by CCP must be understood with care. Unlike conventional shared-memory multiprocessing, constraint store of CCP is highly structured and localized. All channels in constraint-based concurrency are created as local variables most of which are shared by two or a small community of processes, and a process can access them only when they are explicitly passed as (part of) messages or by fusing.

The only names understood globally are

1. predicate symbols used as the names of recursive programs, and
2. function symbols (constructors) for composing messages, streams, and data structures, and so on.

Although predicate symbols could be considered as channels, they are channels to classes rather than to objects. Constructors are best considered as non-channel names. They have various rôles as above, but cannot be used for sending messages through them. They can be examined by matching (*ask*) but cannot be equated with other constructors under strong moding.

3 I/O Mode Analysis

3.1 Motivation

By early 1990's, hundreds of thousands of lines of GHC/KL1 code were written inside and outside the Fifth Generation Computer Project [32]. The applications include an operating system for the Parallel Inference Machine (PIMOS) [6], a parallel theorem prover (MGTP) that discovered a new fact in finite algebra [10]. genetic information processing, and so on.

People found the communication and synchronization mechanisms of GHC/KL1 very natural. Bugs due to concurrency were rather infrequent[3] and people learned to model their problems in an object-based manner using concurrent processes and streams. At the same time, writing efficient *parallel* programs turned out to be a separate and much harder issue than writing correct *concurrent* programs.

By late 1980's, we had found that logical variables in concurrent logic languages were normally used for cooperative rather than competitive communication. Because the language and the model based on eventual *tell* provided no mechanism to cope with the inconsistency of a store (except for exception handers of KL1) and a inconsistent store allows any constraint to be read out, it was the responsibility of the programmers to keep the store consistent. Although shared logical variables were sometimes used for n-to-n signalling, in which two or more processes could write the same value to the same variable, for most applications it seemed desirable to provide syntactic control of interference so that the consistency of the store could be guaranteed statically. Obviously, a store remains consistent if only one process is allowed to have a write capability of each variable, as long as we ignore the *occur check* condition (Sect. 2.2).

The mode system[4] of Moded Flat GHC [41][43] was designed to establish this property while retaining the flexibility of constraint-based communication as much as possible. Furthermore, we can benefit very much from strong moding, as we do from strong typing in many other languages:

1. It helps programmers understand their programs better.
2. It detects a certain kind of program errors at compile-time. In fact, the Kima system we have developed [2][3] goes two steps forward: it *locates*, and then automatically *corrects*, simple program errors using constraint-based mode and type analyses. The technique used in Kima is very general and could be deployed in other typed languages as well.
3. It establishes some fundamental properties statically (Sect. 3.5):
   (a) well-moded programs do not collapse the store.
   (b) all variables are guaranteed to become *ground* terms upon termination.
4. It provides basic information for program optimization such as

[3] Most bugs were due to higher-level design problems that often arose in, for example, programs dealing with circular process structures concurrently.

[4] Modes have sometimes been called directional types. In any case modes are (non-standard) types that deal with read/write capabilities.

(a) elimination of various runtime checks,
(b) (much) simpler distributed unification, and
(c) message-oriented implementation [41][40].

3.2 The Mode System

The purpose of our mode system is to assign *polarity structures* (modes) to every predicate argument and (accordingly) every variable occurrence in a configuration, so that each part of data structures will be determined cooperatively, namely by *exactly one* process that owned a write capability. If more than one process owned a write capability to determine some part a structure, the communication would be competitive rather than cooperative. If no process owned a write capability, the communication would be neither cooperative or competitive, because the readers would never get a value.

Since variables may be bound to complex data structures in the course of computation whose exact shapes are not known beforehand, a polarity structure reconstructed by the mode system should tell the polarity structures of all possible data structures the program may create and read. To this end, a mode is defined as a function from the set of paths specifying positions in data structures occurring in goals, denoted P_{Atom}, to the set $\{in, out\}$. Paths here are strings of $\langle$*symbol*, *argument-position*$\rangle$ pairs in order to be able to specify positions in data structures that are yet to be formed.

Formally, the sets of paths for specifying positions in terms and atomic formulas are defined, respectively, using disjoint union as:

$$P_{Term} = (\sum_{f \in Fun} N_f)^* \ , \quad P_{Atom} = (\sum_{p \in Pred} N_p) \times P_{Term} \ ,$$

where *Fun* and *Pred* are the sets of constructors and predicate symbols, respectively, and N_f and N_p are the sets of positive integers up to and including the arities of f and p, respectively.

3.3 Mode Analysis

Mode analysis tries to find a mode $m : P_{Atom} \to \{in, out\}$ under which every piece of communication will be performed cooperatively. Such a mode is called a *well-moding*. A well-moding is computed by constraint solving. Constructors in a program/goal clause will impose constraints on the possible polarities of the paths at which they occur. Variable symbols may constrain the polarities not only of the paths at which they occur but of any positions below those paths. The set of all these mode constraints syntactically imposed by the symbols or the symbol occurrences in a program does not necessarily define a unique mode because the constraints are usually not strong enough to define one. Instead it defines a 'principal' mode that can best be expressed as a mode graph, as we will see in Section 3.6.

Mode constraints imposed by a clause h :- | B, where B are multisets of atomic formulae, are summarized in Fig. 4. Here, *Var* denotes the set of variable symbols, and $\widetilde{a}(p)$ denotes a symbol occurring at p in an atomic formula a. When p does not lead to a symbol in a, $\widetilde{a}(p)$ returns $\perp$. A *submode* of m at p, denoted m/p, is a function (from P_{Term} to $\{\mathit{in}, \mathit{out}\}$) such that $(m/p)(q) = m(pq)$. *IN* and *OUT* are constant submodes that always return *in* or *out*, respectively. An overline, "$-$", inverts the polarity of a mode, a submode, or a mode value.

(HF) $\forall p \in P_{\mathit{Atom}}\big(\widetilde{h}(p) \in \mathit{Fun} \Rightarrow m(p) = \mathit{in}\big)$
(if the symbol at p in h is a constructor, $m(p) = \mathit{in}$)

(HV) $\forall p \in P_{\mathit{Atom}}\big(\widetilde{h}(p) \in \mathit{Var} \wedge \exists p' \neq p\big(\widetilde{h}(p) = \widetilde{h}(p')\big) \Rightarrow m/p = \mathit{IN}\big)$
(if the symbol at p in h is a variable occurring elsewhere in h, then $m/p = \mathit{IN}$)

(BU) $\forall k > 0\, \forall t_1, t_2 \in \mathit{Term}\big((t_1 =_k t_2) \in B \Rightarrow m/\langle =_k, 1\rangle = \overline{m/\langle =_k, 2\rangle}\big)$
(the two arguments of a unification body goal have complementary submodes)

(BF) $\forall p \in P_{\mathit{Atom}} \forall a \in B\big(\widetilde{a}(p) \in \mathit{Fun} \Rightarrow m(p) = \mathit{in}\big)$
(if the symbol at p in a body goal is a constructor, $m(p) = \mathit{in}$)

(BV) Let $v \in \mathit{Var}$ occur $n\ (\geq 1)$ times in h and B at $p_1, \ldots, p_n$, of which the occurrences in h are at $p_1, \ldots, p_k$ $(k \geq 0)$. Then

$$\begin{cases} \mathcal{R}\big(\{m/p_1, \ldots, m/p_n\}\big), & k = 0; \\ \mathcal{R}\big(\{\overline{m/p_1}, m/p_{k+1}, \ldots, m/p_n\}\big), & k > 0; \end{cases}$$

where $\mathcal{R}$ is a 'cooperativeness' relation:

$$\mathcal{R}(S) \stackrel{\text{def}}{=} \forall q \in P_{\mathit{Term}}\, \exists s \in S\big(s(q) = \mathit{out} \wedge \forall s' \in S \backslash \{s\}\ \big(s'(q) = \mathit{in}\big)\big)$$

Fig. 4. Mode constraints imposed by a clause h :- | B

For goal clauses, Rules (BU), (BF) and (BV) are applicable.

Note that Rule (BV) ignores the second and the subsequent occurrences of v in h. The occurrences of v that are not ignored are called *channel occurrences.* Note also that s can depend on q in the definition of $\mathcal{R}$. Intuitively, Rule (BV) means that each constructor occurring in a possible instance of v will be determined by exactly one of the channel occurrences of v.

Unification body goals, dealt with by Rule (BU), are polymorphic in the sense that different goals are allowed to have different modes. To deal with polymorphism, we give each unification body goal a unique number. Polymorphism can be incorporated to other predicates as well [43], but we do not discuss it here.

3.4 Moding Principles

What are the principles behind these moding rules?

In concurrent logic programming, a process implemented by a multiset of goals can be considered an information processing device with inlets and outlets of constraints that we call *terminals*. A variable is a one-to-n ($n \geq 0$) communication channel connecting its occurrences, and each occurrence of a variable is considered to be plugged into one of the terminals of a goal.

We say that a variable is *linear* when it has exactly two occurrences in a goal clause. Similarly, a variable in a program clause is said to be *linear* when it has exactly two channel occurrences in the clause.

A variable occurring both in the head and in the body of a program clause is considered a channel that connects a goal (which the head matches) and its subgoals. A constructor is considered an unconnected plug that acts as the source or the absorber of atomic information, depending on whether it occurs in the body or the head. While channels and terminals of electric devices usually have array structures, those in our setting have nested structures. That is, a variable that connects the terminals at $p_1, \ldots, p_n$ also connects the terminals at $p_1q, \ldots, p_nq$, for all $q \in P_{Term}$. Linear variables are used as *cables* for one-to-one communication, while nonlinear variables are used as *hubs* for one-to-many communication.

A terminal of a goal always has its counterpart. The counterpart of a terminal at p on the caller side of a non-unification goal is the one at the same path on the callee side, and the counterpart of a terminal at $\langle =_k, 1\rangle q$ in the first argument of a unification goal is the one at $\langle =_k, 2\rangle q$ in the second argument. Reduction of a goal is considered the removal of the pairs of corresponding terminals whose connection has been established.

The mode constraints are concerned with the direction of information flow (1) in channels and (2) at terminals. The two underlying principles are:

1. When a channel connects n terminals of which at most one is in the head, exactly one of the terminals is the outlet of information and the others are inlets.
2. Of the two corresponding terminals of a goal, exactly one is the outlet of information and the other is an inlet.

Rule (BV) comes from Principle 1. An input (output) occurrence of a variable in the head of a clause is considered an outlet (inlet) of information from inside the clause, respectively, and this is why we invert the mode of the clause head in Rule (BV). Rule (BV) takes into account only one of the occurrences of v in the head. Multiple occurrences of the same variable in the head are for equality checking before reduction, and the only thing that matters after reduction is whether the variable occurs also in the body and conveys information to the body goals.

Rules (HF) and (HV) come from Principle 2. When some clause may examine the value of the path p in a non-unification goal, $m(p)$ should be constrained to *in* because the examination is done at the *outlet* of information on the *callee* side of a goal. The strong constraint imposed by Rule (HV) is due to the semantics of Flat GHC: when a variable occurs twice or more in a clause head, these occurrences must receive identical terms from the caller.

Rule (BU) is exactly the application of Principle 2 to unification body goals. Any value fed through some path $\langle =_k, i\rangle q$ in one of its arguments will come out through the corresponding path $\langle =_k, 3-i\rangle q$ in the other argument.

Rule (BF) also comes from Principle 2. A non-variable symbol on the caller side of a goal must appear only at the inlet of information, because the information will go out from the corresponding outlet.

The relation $\mathcal{R}$ enjoys the following properties:

$$\mathcal{R}(\{s\}) \Leftrightarrow s = \mathit{OUT} \tag{1}$$
$$\mathcal{R}(\{s_1, s_2\}) \Leftrightarrow s_1 = \overline{s_2} \tag{2}$$
$$\mathcal{R}(\{\mathit{IN}\} \cup S) \Leftrightarrow \mathcal{R}(S) \tag{3}$$
$$\mathcal{R}(\{\mathit{OUT}\} \cup S) \Leftrightarrow \forall s' \in S(s' = \mathit{IN}) \tag{4}$$
$$\mathcal{R}(\{s, s\} \cup S) \Leftrightarrow s = \mathit{IN} \wedge \mathcal{R}(S) \tag{5}$$
$$\mathcal{R}(\{\overline{s}, s\} \cup S) \Leftrightarrow \forall s' \in S(s' = \mathit{IN}) \tag{6}$$
$$\mathcal{R}(\{\overline{s}\} \cup S_1) \wedge \mathcal{R}(\{s\} \cup S_2) \Rightarrow \mathcal{R}(S_1 \cup S_2) \tag{7}$$
$$\mathcal{R}(\textstyle\bigcup_{1\le i\le n}\{s_i\}) \Rightarrow \mathcal{R}(\bigcup_{1\le i\le n}\{s_i/q\}), \quad q \in P_{\mathit{Term}} \tag{8}$$

Proofs are all straightforward. Property (7) is reminiscent of Robinson's resolution principle.

Properties (1) and (2) say that Rule (BV) becomes much simpler when the variable v has at most two channel occurrences. When it has exactly two channel occurrences at p_1 and p_2. Rule (BV) is equivalent to $m/p_1 = m/p_2$ or $m/p_1 = \overline{m/p_2}$, depending on whether one of the occurrences is in the head or the both occur in the body. When v has only one channel occurrence at p, Rule (BV) is equivalent to $m/p = \mathit{IN}$ or $m/p = \mathit{OUT}$, depending on whether the occurrence is in the head or the body.

3.5 Properties of Well-Moded Programs

The three important properties of well-moding are as follows:

1. Let m be a well-moding of a clause R, and let $t_1 =_k t_2$ be a unification (body) goal in R. Then there exists an i such that (i) $m(\langle =_k, i\rangle) = \mathit{out}$ and (ii) t_i is a variable.
   This means a unification body goal is effectively assignment to an variable with a write capability.
2. (*Subject Reduction*) Let m be a well-moding of a program P and a goal clause Q. Suppose Q is reduced by one step into a goal clause Q' (in the substitution-based formulation (Sect. 2.2)), where the reduced goal $g \in Q$ is *not* a unification goal that unifies a variable with itself or a term containing the variable. Then m is a well-moding of P and Q' as well.
   As a corollary, well-moded programs keep store consistent as long as the reductions obey the above condition on the reduced goal, which is called the *extended occur-check condition.*

3. (*Groundness*) Let m be a well-moding of a program P and a goal clause Q. Assume Q has been reduced to an empty multiset of goals under the extended occur-check condition. Then, in that execution, a unification goal of the form $v =_k t$ such that $m(\langle =_k, 1\rangle) = out$, or a unification goal of the form $t =_k v$ such that $m(\langle =_k, 2\rangle) = out$, must have been executed, for any variable v occurring in Q.
   As a corollary, the product of all substitutions generated by unification body goals maps all the variables in Q to ground (variable-free) terms.

3.6 Mode Graphs and Principal Modes

It turns out that most of the mode constraints are either of the six forms: (i) $m(p) = in$, (ii) $m(p) = out$, (iii) $m/p = IN$, (iv) $m/p = OUT$, (v) $m/p_1 = m/p_2$, or (vi) $m/p_1 = \overline{m/p_2}$. We call (i)–(iv) *unary* constraints and (v)–(vi) *binary* constraints.

A set of binary and unary mode constraints can be represented as a feature graph (feature structures with cycles), called a *mode graph*, in which

1. paths represent paths in P_{Atom},
2. nodes may have mode values determined by unary constraints,
3. arcs may have "negative signs" that invert the interpretation of the mode values beyond those arcs, and
4. binary constraints are represented by the sharing of nodes.

Figure 5 is the mode graph of the `merge` program. An arc of a mode graph represents the pair of a predicate/constructor (abbreviated to its initial in the figures) and an argument position. A dot "." stands for the list constructor. The pair exactly corresponds to a feature of a feature graph. A sequence of features forms a path both in the sense of our mode system and in the graph-theoretic sense.

A node is possibly labeled with a mode value (*in* shown as "↓", or *out* shown as "↑") to which any paths p_1, p_2, ... terminating with that node are constrained,

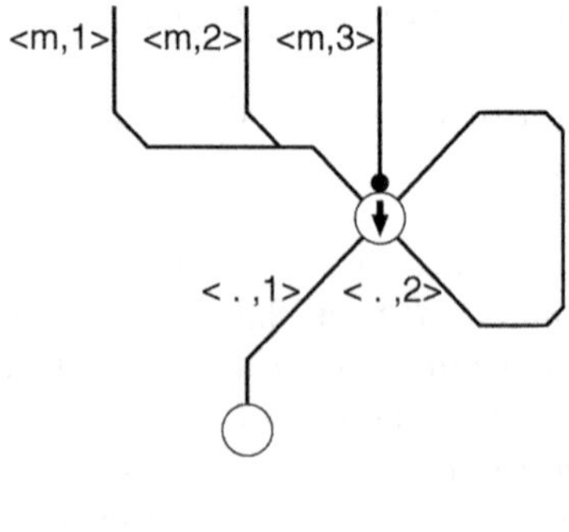

Fig. 5. Mode graph of the `merge` program

or with a constant submode (*IN* shown as "↓" with a grounding sign (as in Fig. 7), or *OUT*) to which the submodes m/p_1, m/p_2, ... are constrained.

An arc is either a negative arc (bulleted in the figures) or a positive arc. When a path passes an odd number of negative arcs, that path is said to be *inverted*, and the mode value of the path is understood to be inverted. Thus the number of bulleted arcs on a path determines the *polarity* of the path.

A binary constraint of the form $m/p_1 = m/p_2$ or $m/p_1 = \overline{m/p_2}$ is represented by a shared node with two (or more) incoming paths with possibly different polarities. When the polarities of the two incoming paths are different, the shared node stands for complementary submodes; otherwise the node stands for identical submodes.

Figure 5 has a node, under the arc labeled $\langle ., 1\rangle$, that expresses no constraints at all. It was created to express binary constraints, but all its parent nodes were later merged into a single node by other constraints.

All these ideas have been implemented in the mode analyzer for KL1 program, *klint v2* [44], which can output a text version of the mode graph as in Fig. 5.

As another example, consider a program that simply unifies its arguments:

```
p(X,Y) :- | X = Y.
```

The program forms a mode graph shown in Fig. 6. This graph can be viewed as the *principal mode* of the predicate p, which represents many possible particular modes satisfying the constraint $m/\langle \mathtt{p}, 1\rangle = \overline{m/\langle \mathtt{p}, 2\rangle}$. In general, the principal mode of a well-moded program, represented as a mode graph, is uniquely determined, as long as all the mode constraints imposed by the program are unary or binary.

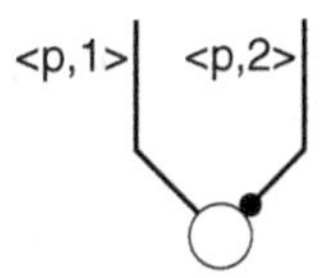

Fig. 6. Mode graph of the unify program

Constraints imposed by the rule (BV) may be non-binary. Non-binary constraints are imposed by nonlinear variables, and cannot be represented as mode graphs by themselves. However, by *delaying* them, most of them are reduced to unary/binary ones by other constraints. In this case they can be represented in mode graphs, and the programs that imposed them have unique principal modes (as long as they are well-moded). Theoretically, some non-binary constraints may remain unreduced, whose satisfiability must be checked eventually.

When some constraints remain non-binary after solving all unary or binary constraints, *klint v2* assumes that nonlinear variables involved are used for one-way multicasting rather than bidirectional communication. Thus, if a nonlinear variable occurs at p and $m(p)$ is known to be *in* or *out*, *klint v2* imposes a stronger constraint $m/p = IN$ or $m/p = OUT$, respectively. This means that a mode graph computed by *klint v2* is not always 'principal', but the strengthening of constraints reduces most non-binary constraints to unary ones. Our observation is that virtually all nonlinear variables have been used for one-way multicasting and the strengthening causes no problem in practice.

The union (i.e., conjunction) of two sets of constraints can be computed efficiently as unification over feature graphs. For instance, adding a new constraint $m/p_1 = m/p_2$ causes the subgraph rooted at p_1 and the subgraph rooted at p_2 to be unified. A good news is that an efficient unification algorithm for feature graphs has been established [1].

Figure 7 shows the mode graph of a quicksort program using difference lists. The second and the third clause of `part` checks the principal constructor of `A` and `X` using guard goals, so the moding rule of variables occurring in guard goals (not stated in this paper) constrains $m(\langle \texttt{part}, 1\rangle)$ and $m(\langle \texttt{part}, 2\rangle\langle ., 1\rangle)$ to *in*. The head and the tail of a difference list, namely the second and the third arguments of `qsort`, are constrained to have complementary submodes.

```
qsort([],      Ys0,Ys ) :- | Ys=Ys0.
qsort([X|Xs],Ys0,Ys3) :- |
    part(X,Xs,S,L), qsort(S,Ys0,[X|Ys2]), qsort(L,Ys2,Ys3).
part(_,[],      S, L ) :- | S=[], L=[].
part(A,[X|Xs],S0,L ) :- A>=X | S0=[X|S], part(A,Xs,S,L).
part(A,[X|Xs],S, L0) :- A< X | L0=[X|L], part(A,Xs,S,L).
```

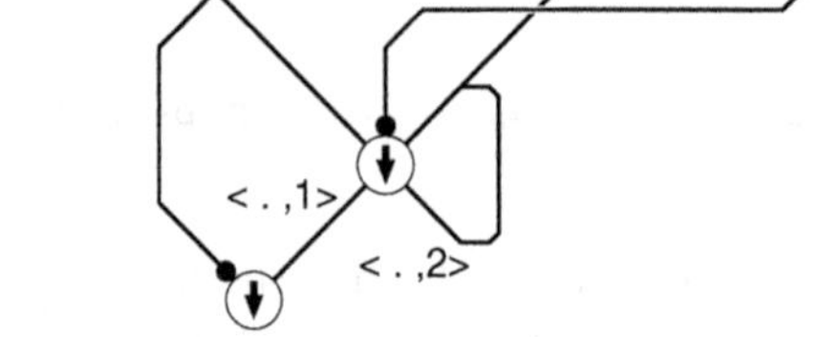

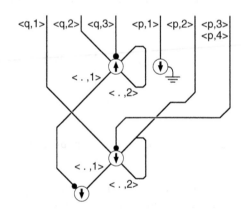

Fig. 7. A quicksort program and its mode graph

4 Linearity Analysis

4.1 Motivation and Observation

The mode system guarantees the uniqueness of *write* capability of each variable in a runtime configuration. Furthermore, although it does not impose any constraint on the number of read capabilities (occurrences), it imposes less generic, stronger mode constraints on programs that may discard or duplicate data. The modes of the paths where singleton variables (one-to-zero communication channels) may occur are constrained to *IN* or *OUT*, and paths of nonlinear variables (one-to-many communication channels) may very well be constrained to *IN* or *OUT*. Thus the mode system effectively prefers programs that do not discard or duplicate data by giving them weaker mode constraints, providing the view of "data as resources" to some extent.

Our experiences with Prolog and concurrent logic programming show that surprisingly many variables in Prolog and concurrent logic programs are *linear*. For instance, all the variables in the `merge` program (Fig. 5) are linear, and all but one of the variables in `qsort` (Fig. 7) are linear. This indicates that the majority of communication is one-to-one and deserves special attention.

As a non-toy example, we examined the mode constraint solver of *klint v2*, which comprised 190 KL1 clauses [43]. Those clauses imposed 1392 constraints by Rule (BV), one for each variable in the program, of which more than 90% were of the form $m/p_1 = m/p_2$ (1074) or $m/p_1 = \overline{m/p_2}$ (183). Thus we can say that the clauses are highly linear. Furthermore, all of the 42 non-binary constraints were reduced to unary or binary constraints using other unary or binary constraints. Actually they were reduced to 6 constraints of the form $m/p_1 = \overline{m/p_2}$ and 72 constraints of the form $m/p = IN$. This means that nonlinear variables were all used under simple, one-way communication protocols.

4.2 The Linearity System

The purpose of linearity analysis [46] is to statically analyze exactly *where* nonlinear variables and shared data structures may occur – in which predicates, in which arguments, and in which part of the data structures carried by those arguments. This complements mode analysis in the sense that it is concerned with the number of *read* capabilities.

To distinguish between non-shared and shared data structures in a reduction semantics without the notion of pointers, we consider giving a linearity annotation 1 or ω to every occurrence of a constructor f appearing in (initial or reduced) goal clauses and body goals in program clauses.[5] The annotations appear as f^1 or f^ω in the theoretical framework, though the purpose of linearity analysis is to reason about the annotations and compile them away so that the program can be executed without having to maintain linearity annotations at run time.

[5] The notation is after related work [19,35] on different computational models.

Intuitively, the principal constructor of a structure possibly referenced by more than one pointer must have the annotation ω, while a structure always pointed to by only one pointer in its lifetime can have the annotation 1. Another view of the annotation is that it models a one-bit reference counter that is not decremented once it reaches ω.

The annotations must observe the following closure condition: If the principal constructor of a term has the annotation ω, all constructors occurring in the term must have the annotation ω. In contrast, a term with the principal constructor annotated as 1 can contain a constructor with either annotation, which means that a subterm of a non-shared term may possibly be shared.

Given linearity annotations, the operational semantics is extended to handle them so that they may remain consistent with the above intuitive meaning.

1. The annotations of constructors in program clauses and *initial* goal clauses are given according to how the structures they represent are implemented. For instance, consider the following goal clause:

   ```
   :- p([1,2,3,4,5],X), q([1,2,3,4,5],X).
   ```

   If the implementation chooses to create a single instance of the list `[1,2,3,4,5]` and let the two goals share them, the constructors (there are 11 of them including `[]`) must be given ω. If two instances of the list are created and given to `p` and `q`, either annotation is compatible with the implementation.
2. Suppose a substitution $\theta = \{v_1 \leftarrow t_1, \ldots, v_n \leftarrow t_n\}$ is applied upon one-step reduction from Q to Q'.
   (a) When v_i is nonlinear, the substitution instantiates more than one occurrence of v_i to t_i and makes t_i shared. Accordingly, all subterms of t_i become shared as well. So, prior to rewriting the occurrences of v_i by t_i, we change all the annotations of the constructors constituting t_i to ω.
   (b) When v_i is linear, θ does not increase the number of references to t_i. So we rewrite v_i by t_i without changing the annotations in t_i.

As in mode analysis, the linearity of a (well-moded) program can be characterized using a linearity function, a mapping from P_{Atom} to the binary codomain $\{nonshared, shared\}$, which satisfies the closure condition

$$\forall p \in P_{Atom} \forall q \in P_{Term} \big(\lambda(p) = shared \Rightarrow \lambda(pq) = shared\big).$$

The purpose of linearity analysis is to reconstruct a linearity function (say λ) that satisfies all *linearity constraints* imposed by each program clause and a goal clause `:-` B, which are shown in Fig. 8. The *klint v2* system reconstructs linearity as well as mode information.

As expected, the linearity system enjoys the subject reduction theorem:

– Suppose λ satisfies the linearity constraints of a program P and a goal clause Q, and Q is reduced in one step to Q' under the extended occur-check condition. Then λ satisfies the linearity constraints of Q' as well.

(BF$_\lambda$) If a function symbol f^ω occurs at the path p in B, then $\lambda(p) = \mathit{shared}$.
(LV$_\lambda$) If a linear variable occurs both at p_1 and p_2, then
$\forall q \in P_{\mathit{Term}}\big(m(p_1q) = \mathit{in} \wedge \lambda(p_1q) = \mathit{shared} \Rightarrow \lambda(p_2q) = \mathit{shared}\big)$ (if p_1 is a head path);
$\forall q \in P_{\mathit{Term}}\big(m(p_1q) = \mathit{out} \wedge \lambda(p_1q) = \mathit{shared} \Rightarrow \lambda(p_2q) = \mathit{shared}\big)$ (if p_1 is a body path).
(NV$_\lambda$) If a nonlinear variable occurs at p, then
$\forall q \in P_{\mathit{Term}}\big(m(pq) = \mathit{out} \Rightarrow \lambda(pq) = \mathit{shared}\big)$ (if p is a head path);
$\forall q \in P_{\mathit{Term}}\big(m(pq) = \mathit{in} \Rightarrow \lambda(pq) = \mathit{shared}\big)$ (if p is a body path).
(BU$_\lambda$) For a unification body goal $=_k$, $\forall q \in P_{\mathit{Term}}\big(\lambda(\langle =_k, 1\rangle q) = \lambda(\langle =_k, 2\rangle q)\big)$.

Fig. 8. Linearity constraints imposed by a clause h :- | B

An immediate consequence of the subject reduction theorem is that a constructor with ω cannot appear at p such that $\lambda(p) = \mathit{nonshared}$. The (sole) reader of the data structure at a *nonshared* path can safely discard the top-level structure after accessing its elements. One feature of our linearity system is that it can appropriately handle data structures whose sharing properties change (from *nonshared* to *shared*) in their lifetime, allowing update-in-place of not yet shared data structures.

There is one subtle point in this optimization. The optimization is completely safe for built-in data types such as numeric or character arrays that allow only instantiated data to be stored. However, when a structure is implemented so that its field may itself represent an uninstantiated logical variable, the structure cannot be recycled until the variable is instantiated (through an *internal pointer* to the variable) and read. Most implementations of Prolog and concurrent logic languages (including KLIC [7]) represent structures this way for efficiency reasons, in which case local reuse requires strictness analysis, namely the analysis of instantiation states of variables, in addition to linearity analysis. The implementation of KL1 on the Parallel Inference Machine disallowed internal pointers to feature local reuse based on the 1-bit reference counting technique [5].

5 From Linearity to Strict Linearity

5.1 Polarizing Constructors

We already saw that most if not all variables in concurrent logic languages are linear variables. To start another observation, consider the following insertion sort program:

```
sort([],     S) :- | S=[].
sort([X|L0],S) :- | sort(L0,S0), insert(X,S0,S).
insert(X,[],     R) :-         | R=[X].
insert(X,[Y|L], R) :- X=<Y | R=[X,Y|L].
insert(X,[Y|L0],R) :- X>Y  | R=[Y|L], insert(X,L0,L).
```

Here again, all the variables are linear (we do not count the occurrences in guard goals when considering linearity). However, an even more striking fact is that, by slight modification, all constructors (including constants) can be made to occur exactly twice as well:

```
sort([],     S) :- | S=[].
sort([X|L0],S) :- | sort(L0,S0), insert([X|S0],S).
insert([X],       R) :-       | R=[X].
insert([X,Y|L], R) :- X=<Y | R=[X,Y|L].
insert([X,Y|L0],R) :- X>Y   | R=[Y|L], insert([X|L0],L).
```

This suggests that the notion of linearity could be extended to cover constructors as well. We call it *strict linearity.* A linear variable is a *dipole* with two occurrences with opposite polarities. Likewise, a linear constructor is a dipole with two occurrences with opposite polarities, one in the head and the other in the body of a clause. The two occurrences of a linear constructor can be regarded as two *polarized* instances of the same constructor.

If all the constructors are linear in program clauses as in the second version of `sort`, all deallocated cells can be reused locally to allocate new cells without accessing a non-local free list. That is, as long as the input list is not shared, the program can construct the final result by reorganizing input cells and without generating any garbage cells or allocating new cells from non-local storage.

5.2 Strict Linearity

We say that a program clause is *strictly linear* if all the variables have exactly two channel occurrences in the clause and all the constructors have exactly two occurrences, one in the head and the other in the body.

The above definition does not require that predicate symbols occur exactly twice. If this is enforced, all body goals can inherit its goal record (that records the argument of goals) from the parent and the program can run with a fixed space, but we must have a means to terminate tail recursion, as will be discussed in Sect. 5.3. Although strictly linear programs still require allocation and deallocation of goal records, goal records are inherently non-shared and much more manageable than heap-allocated data. So strict linearity is a significant step toward resource-conscious programming.

Let me give another example.

```
append([],    Y,Z ) :- | Z=Y.
append([A|X],Y,Z0) :- | Z0=[A|Z], append(X,Y,Z).
```

The base case receives an empty list but does not use it. A short value such as `[]` could be regarded as a zero-resource value, but we prefer to consider n-ary constructors to convey $n+1$ units in general, in which case the program recovers strict linearity using an extra argument:

```
append([],    Y,Z, U) :- | Z=Y, U=[].
append([A|X],Y,Z0,U) :- | Z0=[A|Z], append(X,Y,Z,U).
```

Note that the first version of append can be thought of as a *slice* of the second version.

5.3 Void: The Zero-Capability Symbol

All the examples above are transformational processes. It is much less clear how one can program reactive, server-type processes that respond to streams of requests in a strictly linear setting. Consider the following stack server:

```
stack([],          D     ) :- | true.
stack([push(X)|S],D      ) :- | stack(S,[X|D]).
stack([pop(X)|S], [Y|D]) :- | X=Y, stack(S,D).
```

One way to recover the strict linearity of this program is:

```
stack([](Z),                D) :- | Z=[](D).
stack([push([X|*],Y)|S],D) :- | Y=[push(*,*)|*], stack(S,[X|D]).
stack([pop(X)|S],      [Y|D]) :- | X=[pop([Y|*])|*], stack(S,D).
```

Note that an empty list, which can be regarded as an "end-of-transaction" message to a process, has been changed to a unary constructor conveying a reply box, through which the current "deposit" will be returned. The server responds to each message by returning the resource used by the client to send the message. In a physical mail metaphor, cons cells can be compared to envelopes and push and pop messages can be compared to cover letters, which real-world servers often fail to find a nice way of recycling.

Observe that we need to extend the language with a special symbol, *, to indicate void positions of structures. A void position will be given *zero capability* so that no read or write to the position will take place.

What is the resource aspect of variable occurrences and the void symbol? We assume that each variable occurrence uses one unit and one void symbol uses one unit. Furthermore, we assume that a non-variable term is always pointed to from a variable occurrence and an argument of a non-variable term or a goal always points to a variable occurrence. This canonical representation is not always space-optimal, but makes resource counting simple and uniform.

It is not difficult to see that the strictly linear versions of append and stack do not allocate or deallocate resources for variable occurrences and voids during tail-recursive iteration. Upon termination, append releases four of them and stack releases two of them.

An interesting aspect of the *void* construct is that it could be used to recover the linearity of *predicate* symbols by allowing multi-head clauses as in Constraint Handling Rules [12]. For instance, sort in Sect. 5.1 could be rewritten as

```
sort([],     S) :-                  | S=[], sort(*.*).
sort([X|L0],S), insert(*,*) :- | sort(L0,S0), insert([X|S0],S).
```

where the goals with void arguments could be considered as free, inactive goals waiting for habitants. The first clause makes the current goal inactive, while the second clause explicitly says that it requires one free `insert` goal for the reduction of `sort([X|L0],S)`. However, in this paper we assume that these free goals are implicit.

Some readers will enjoy the symmetry of the strictly linear version, while others may find it cumbersome and want compilers to reconstruct a strict linear version of their programs automatically. In any case, strictly linear programs are completely recyclic and are a step towards small-footprint symbolic computation with highly predictable behavior.

One natural question is how to write programs whose output size is essentially larger than the input size. An obvious solution is to require the initial process to pass a necessary number of cells obtained from the runtime library. This will work well as long as the output size is predictable. Some programs may have the output size that is essentially the same as the input size but may require more resource to represent intermediate results. We have two solutions to this. One is to let the initial process provide all necessary resource. The other is to require that the input size and the output size be balanced for each process spawned during computation, but allow a subprocess to use (and then return) more resource than that received from the parent process. The notion of strict linearity has to be relaxed somewhat to enable the latter alternative.

5.4 Constant-Time Property of Strictly Linear Programs

The cost of the primitive operations of strictly linear concurrent logic programs are highly predictable despite their non-strict data structures.

The primitive operations of concurrent logic programs are:

1. spawning of new non-unification goals (including tail-recursive ones),
2. termination of a non-unification goal (upon reduction with a base-case clause),
3. *ask* or term matching, which may involve
   (a) synchronization, namely suspension and resumption of the process, and
   (b) pointer dereferencing, and
4. *tell*, namely execution of a unification body goal, which may involve pointer dereferencing.

On a single-processor environment, spawning and termination of a goal involves (de)allocation of a fixed-size goal record and manipulation of a goal queue, which can both be regarded as constant-time operations.

Synchronization involves the hooking and unhooking of goals on an uninstantiated variable, but in a linear setting, the number of goals hooked on each variable is at most one.

The cost of dereferencing reflects the length of the chain of pointers formed by unification. Due to the flexibility logical variables bring in the way of data structure formation, even in sequential Prolog it is possible to create an arbitrarily long chain of pointers between variables.

In a linear setting, however, every uninstantiated variable has exactly two occurrences. We can represent it using two cells that form a size-two cycle by pointing to each other. Then the unification of two linear variables, say v_1 and v_2, which consumes one v_1 and one v_2 by the unification goal itself, can be implemented by letting the other occurrence of v_1 and the other occurrence of v_2 point to each other. This keeps the size-two property of uninstantiated linear variables unchanged. The writing to a linear variable v, which consumes one occurrence of v, dereferences the pointer to reach the other occurrence of v and instantiate it. The reader of v dereferences it exactly once to access its value.

6 Allowing Concurrent Access within Strict Linearity

Strict linearity can be checked by slightly extending the mode and linearity systems described earlier. However, rather than doing so, we consider extending the framework to allow concurrent access to shared resource. There are two reasonable ways of manipulating resource such as large arrays concurrently.

One is to give different processes exclusive (i.e., nonshared) read/write capabilities to *different* parts of a data structure. This is easily achieved by (i) splitting a non-shared structure, (ii) letting each process work on its own fragment and return results by update-in-place, and (iii) joining the results into one. For instance, parallel quicksort of an array has been implemented this way using optimized versions of KLIC's vectors [25]. This type of concurrent manipulation fits nicely within the present framework of mode and linearity systems because no part of an array becomes shared.

On the other hand, some applications require concurrent accesses with non-exclusive, read capability to the whole of a data structure to allow concurrent table lookup and so on. When the accesses can be sequentialized, the structure with an exclusive capability can be returned finally either

1. by letting each process receive and return an exclusive capability one after another or
2. by guaranteeing the sequentiality of accesses by other language constructs (`let`, guard, *etc.*) as in [49] and [18].

However, these solutions cannot be used when we need to run the readers concurrently or in parallel. Our goal is to allow some process (say P) to collect all released non-exclusive capabilities so that P may restore an *exclusive* capability and update it in place.

For this purpose, we refine the $\{in, out\}$ capability domain of the mode system to a continuous domain $[-1, +1]$. As in the mode system, the capability is attached to all paths. Let κ be the capability of the principal constructor of some occurrence of a variable in a configuration. Then

1. $\kappa = -1$ means 'exclusive write',
2. $-1 < \kappa < 0$ means 'non-exclusive write',
3. $\kappa = 0$ means no capability,
4. $0 < \kappa < 1$ means 'non-exclusive read', and
5. $\kappa = +1$ means 'exclusive read'.

This is a refinement of the mode system in the sense that *out* corresponds to -1 and *in* corresponds to $(0, +1]$. This is also a refinement of the linearity system in the sense that *nonshared* corresponds to ± 1 and *shared* corresponds to $(0, +1]$.

Then, what meaning should we give to the $(-1, 0]$ cases? Suppose a `read` process receives an exclusive read capability to access `X0` and split the capability to two non-exclusive capabilities using the following clause:

```
read(X0,X) :- | read1(X0,X1), read2(X0,X2), join(X1,X2,X).
```

The capability `X0` conveys can be written as a function $\mathbf{1}$, a constant function such that $\mathbf{1}(p) = +1$ for all $p \in P_{Atom}$. We don't care how much of the $\mathbf{1}$ capability goes to `read1` but just require that the capabilities of the two `X0`'s sum up to $\mathbf{1}$. Different paths in one of the split occurrences of `X0` may convey different capabilities. Also, we assume that the capabilities given to `read1` and `read2` are returned with the opposite polarity through `X1` and `X2`. Logically, `X1` and `X2` will become the same as `X0`. Then, `join` process defined as

```
join(A,A,B) :- | B = A.
```

checks if the first two arguments are indeed aliases and then returns it through the third argument. Note the interesting use of a nonlinear head. The capability constraint for the join program is that the capabilities of the three arguments must sum up to a constant function $\mathbf{0}$.

Now the `X` returned by `join` is guaranteed to convey the $\overline{\mathbf{1}}$ (exclusive write) capability that complements the capability received through `X0`.

7 Operational Semantics with Capability Counting

In the linearity analysis described earlier, the operational semantics was augmented with a linearity annotation 1 or ω given to every occurrence of a constructor f appearing in (initial or reduced) goal clauses. Here, we replace the annotation with a capability annotation κ $(0 < \kappa \leq 1)$. $\kappa = 1$ (exclusive) corresponds to the 1 annotation meaning 'non-shared', while $\kappa < 1$ (non-exclusive) refines (the reciprocal of) ω. Again, the annotations are to reason about capabilities statically and are to be compiled away.

The annotations must observe the following closure condition: If the principal constructor of a term has an non-exclusive capability, all constructors occurring in the term must have non-exclusive capabilities as well. In contrast, a term with an exclusive principal constructor can contain a constructor with any capability.

The operational semantics is extended to handle annotations so that they may remain consistent with the above intuitive meaning. However, before doing so, let us consider how we can start computation within a strictly linear framework. The goal clause

```
:- sort([3,1,4,1,5,9],X).
```

is not an ideal form to work with because variables and constructors are monopoles. Instead, we consider a strictly linear version of the goal clause

```
main([3,1,4,1,5,9],X) :- | sort([3,1,4,1,5,9],X).
```

in which the head complements the resources in the body. The head declares the resources necessary to initiate computation and the resources to be returned to the environment. The reduction semantics works on the body goal of as before, except that the unification goal to instantiate X remains intact. Then the above clause will be reduced to

```
main([3,1,4,1,5,9],X) :- | X = [1,1,3,4,5,9].
```

which can be thought of as a normal form in our polarized setting.

Hereafter, we assume that an initial goal clause is complemented by a head to make it strictly linear.

1. All the constructors in the body of an *initial* goal clause are given the annotation 1. This could be relaxed as we did in giving the linearity annotations (Sect. 4) to represent initially shared data, but without loss of generality we can assume that initial data are nonshared.
2. Suppose a substitution $\theta = \{v_1 \leftarrow t_1, \ldots, v_n \leftarrow t_n\}$ is applied upon one-step reduction from Q to Q'.
   (a) When v_i is nonlinear,[6] the substitution instantiates more than one occurrence of v_i to t_i and makes t_i shared. Accordingly, all the subterms of t_i become shared as well. So, prior to rewriting the occurrences of v_i by t_i, we change all the annotations of the constructors constituting t_i as follows: Let f^κ be a constructor in t_i and t_i is about to be copied to m places (this happens when v_i occurs $m+1$ times in the goal clause). Then κ is split into $\kappa_1, \ldots, \kappa_m$, where $\kappa_1 + \ldots + \kappa_m = \kappa$, $\kappa_j > 0$ $(1 \leq j \leq m)$, and the κ_j's are mutually different and not used previously as capabilities.
   (b) When v_i is linear, θ does not increase the number of references to t_i. So we rewrite v_i by t_i without changing the annotations in t_i.

Furthermore, to deal with capability polymorphism described later, we index the predicate symbols of the goals in an initial goal clause with 1, 2, and so on. The indices are in fact singleton sequences of natural numbers which will be extended in each reduction. That is, when reducing a non-unification goal b_s (s being the index) to spawn $b^1, \ldots, b^n$ using Rule (iii) of Fig. 2, the new goals are indexed as $b^1_{s.1}, \ldots, b^n_{s.n}$.

8 The Capability System

Our capability system generalizes the mode system. As suggested earlier, the capability type (say c) of a program or its fragment is a function

$$c : P_{Atom} \to [-1, +1].$$

[6] The term '*sublinear*' might be more appropriate than *nonlinear* here.

(BU$_c$) $\forall s \forall t_1, t_2 \in \mathit{Term}\big((t_1 =_s t_2) \in B \Rightarrow c/\langle =_s, 1\rangle + c/\langle =_s, 2\rangle = \mathbf{0}\big)$
(the arguments of a unification body goal have complementary capabilities)

(BV$_c$) Let $v \in \mathit{Var}$ occur $n\,(\geq 1)$ times in h and B at $p_1, \ldots, p_n$, of which the occurrences in h are at $p_1, \ldots, p_k$ $(k \geq 0)$. Then

1. $-c/p_1 - \ldots - c/p_k + c/p_{k+1} + \ldots + c/p_n = \mathbf{0}$ (*Kirchhoff's Current Law*)
2. if $k = 0$ and $n > 2$ then $\mathcal{R}\big(\{c/p_1, \ldots, c/p_n\}\big)$
3. if $k \geq 1$ and $n - k \geq 2$ then $\mathcal{R}\big(\{\overline{c/p_1}, c/p_{k+1}, \ldots, c/p_n\}\big)$

where $\mathcal{R}$ is a 'cooperativeness' relation:

$$\mathcal{R}(S) \stackrel{\text{def}}{=} \exists s \in S\big(s < \mathbf{0} \wedge \forall s' \in S\backslash\{s\}\,(s' > \mathbf{0})\big)$$

(HV$_c$) $\forall p \in P_{Atom}\big(\widetilde{h}(p) \in \mathit{Var} \wedge \exists p' \neq p\big(\widetilde{h}(p) = \widetilde{h}(p')\big) \Rightarrow c/p > \mathbf{0}\big)$
(if the symbol at p in h is a variable occurring elsewhere in h, then $c/p > \mathbf{0}$)

(HF$_c$) $\forall p \in P_{Atom}\big(\widetilde{h}(p) \in \mathit{Fun} \Rightarrow (c(p) > 0$
$\wedge\, \exists! q \in P_{Atom} \exists a \in B(\widetilde{a}(q) = \widetilde{h}(p) \wedge c(p) = c(q) \wedge (c(p) < 1 \Rightarrow c/p = c/q)))\big)$
(if the symbol at p in h is a constructor, $c(p) > 0$ and there's exactly one partner in B at q such that $c(p) = c(q)$ (and $c/p = c/q$ if non-exclusive))

(BF$_c$) $\forall p \in P_{Atom} \forall a \in B\big(\widetilde{a}(p) \in \mathit{Fun} \Rightarrow (c(p) > 0$
$\wedge\, \exists! q \in P_{Atom}(\widetilde{h}(q) = \widetilde{a}(p) \wedge c(p) = c(q) \wedge (c(p) < 1 \Rightarrow c/p = c/q)))\big)$
(if the symbol at p in B is a constructor, $c(p) > 0$ and there's exactly one partner at q in h such that $c(p) = c(q)$ (and $c/p = c/q$ if non-exclusive))

(Z$_c$) $\forall p \in P_{Atom} \forall a \in B\big((\widetilde{h}(p) = * \vee \widetilde{a}(p) = *) \Rightarrow c/p = \mathbf{0}\big)$
(a void path has a zero capability)

(NZ$_c$) $\forall p \in P_{Atom} \forall a \in B\big((\widetilde{h}(p) \in \mathit{Fun} \cup \mathit{Var} \vee \widetilde{a}(p) \in \mathit{Fun} \cup \mathit{Var}) \Rightarrow c(p) \neq 0\big)$
(a non-void path has a non-zero capability)

Fig. 9. Capability constraints imposed by a clause h :- | B

The framework is necessarily polymorphic with respect to non-exclusive capabilities because a non-exclusive capability may be split into two or more capabilities. This is why different goals created at runtime should be distinguished using indices.

The following closure conditions of a capability function represent the uniformity of non-exclusive capabilities:

1. $0 < c(p) < 1 \Rightarrow \forall q\big(0 < c(pq) < 1\big)$
2. $-1 < c(p) < 0 \Rightarrow \forall q\big(-1 < c(pq) < 0\big)$

Our capability constraints, shown in Fig. 9, generalizes mode constraints (Fig. 4) without complicating it. Here we have inherited all the notational conventions from the mode system (see Sect. 3.3) and modified them appropriately.

As an example, consider the following program.

$\mathtt{p}_s\mathtt{(X,Y,\ldots)}$:- | $\mathtt{r}_{s.1}\mathtt{(X,Y1,\ldots)}$, $\mathtt{p}_{s.2}\mathtt{(X,Y2,\ldots)}$, $\mathtt{join}_{s.3}\mathtt{(Y1,Y2,Y)}$.

```
p_s(X,Y,...) :- | X =_{s.1} Y.
join_s(A,A,B) :- | B =_{s.1} A.
```

Then the capability constraints they impose include:

1. From the first clause of p:
   (a) $-c/\langle \mathtt{p}_s, 1\rangle + c/\langle \mathtt{r}_{s.1}, 1\rangle + c/\langle \mathtt{p}_{s.2}, 1\rangle = \mathbf{0}$
   (b) $c/\langle \mathtt{r}_{s.1}, 2\rangle + c/\langle \mathtt{join}_{s.3}, 1\rangle = \mathbf{0}$
   (c) $c/\langle \mathtt{p}_{s.2}, 2\rangle + c/\langle \mathtt{join}_{s.3}, 2\rangle = \mathbf{0}$
   (d) $-c/\langle \mathtt{p}_s, 2\rangle + c/\langle \mathtt{join}_{s.3}, 3\rangle = \mathbf{0}$
2. From the second clause of p:
   (a) $-c/\langle \mathtt{p}_s, 1\rangle + c/\langle \mathtt{=}_s, 1\rangle = \mathbf{0}$
   (b) $-c/\langle \mathtt{p}_s, 2\rangle + c/\langle \mathtt{=}_s, 2\rangle = \mathbf{0}$
   (c) $c/\langle \mathtt{=}_s, 1\rangle + c/\langle \mathtt{=}_s, 2\rangle = \mathbf{0}$
3. From join:
   (a) $c/\langle \mathtt{join}_s, 1\rangle > \mathbf{0}$
   (b) $c/\langle \mathtt{join}_s, 2\rangle > \mathbf{0}$
   (c) $-c/\langle \mathtt{join}_s, 1\rangle - c/\langle \mathtt{join}_s, 2\rangle + c/\langle \mathtt{=}_s, 2\rangle = \mathbf{0}$
   (d) $-c/\langle \mathtt{join}_s, 3\rangle + c/\langle \mathtt{=}_s, 1\rangle = \mathbf{0}$
   (e) $c/\langle \mathtt{=}_s, 1\rangle + c/\langle \mathtt{=}_s, 2\rangle = \mathbf{0}$

In each constraint, the index s is universally quantified. These constraints are satisfiable if (and only if) $c/\langle \mathtt{r}_{s.1}, 1\rangle + c/\langle \mathtt{r}_{s.1}, 2\rangle = \mathbf{0}$. Suppose this can be derived from other constraints. Suppose also that $c/\langle p_{s_0}, 1\rangle = \mathbf{1}$ holds, that is, p is initially called with a non-shared, read-only first argument. Then the above set of constraints guarantees $c/\langle p_{s_0}, 2\rangle = \overline{\mathbf{1}}$, which means that the references to X distributed to the r's will be fully collected as long as all the r's return the references they have received.

Note that the above constraints (1(a) and several others) and Rule (NZ_c) entail $\mathbf{0} < c/\langle \mathtt{r}_{s.1}, 1\rangle < \mathbf{1}$ and $\mathbf{0} < c/\langle \mathtt{p}_{s.2}, 1\rangle < \mathbf{1}$. That is, these paths are constrained to be non-exclusive paths. It is easy to see that a set of constraints cannot entail a constraint of the form $\mathbf{0} < c/p < \mathbf{1}$ unless some variable is nonlinear.

We have not yet worked out on theoretical results, but conjecture that the following properties hold (possibly with minor modification):

1. The three properties shown in Sect. 3.5, namely (i) degeneration of unification to assignment, (ii) subject reduction, and (iii) groundness.
2. (*Conservation of Constructors*) A reduction does not gain or lose any constructor in the goal clause, with its capability taken into account as its weight.

The Rules (HF_c) and (BF_c) can be relaxed so that the name of the constructor examined in the head can be changed when it is recycled in the body, as long as the constructor comes with an exclusive capability and its arity does not change. When this modification is done, the Conservation of Constructors property should be modified accordingly to allow the changes of names.

This modification is important when computation involves a lot of constants such as numbers. Indeed, some relaxation will be necessary to accommodate arithmetics in our framework in a reasonable way. For instance, to perform local computation such as `Y:=X+2`, it would be unrealistic to obtain constructors `+` and 2 from the parent process and let them escape through `Y`. Rather, we want to allocate and garbage-collect them locally and let `Y` emit an integer constant.[7]

9 Related Work

Relating the family of π-calculi and the CCP formalism has been done as proposals of calculi such as the γ-calculus [33], the ρ-calculus [24] and the Fusion calculus [48], all of which incorporate constraints (or name equation) in some form. The γ-calculus is unique in that it uses procedures with encapsulated states to model concurrency and communication rather than the other way around. The ρ-calculus introduces constraints into name-based concurrency, while constraint-based concurrency aims to demonstrate that constraints alone are adequate for modeling and programming concurrency. The Fusion calculus simplifies the binding operators of the π-calculus using the unification of names. A lesson learned from Constraint Logic Programming [17] is that, even when general constraint satisfaction is not intended, formulation in terms of constraints can be more elegant and less error-prone. The simplicity of constraint-based concurrency and the existence of working implementations suggest that encoding all these calculi in constraint-based concurrency would be worthwhile.

In addition to ρ and Fusion, various calculi based on the π-calculus have been proposed, which include Lπ (Local π) [22], the Join calculus [11] and πI (Internal π) [26]. They are aimed at nicer semantical properties and/or better correspondence to programming constructs. Some of the motivations of these calculi are in common – at least at a conceptual level – with the design of constraint-based concurrency with strong moding. For instance, πI restricts communicated data to local names in order to control name scope, and Lπ restricts communicated data to those with output capabilities in order to allow names to act as object identities. Both objectives have been achieved in constraint-based concurrency. Lπ abolished name matching based on the observation that it would be too strong a capability. The counterpart of name matching in constraint-based concurrency is matching with a nonlinear head, which imposes a strong mode constraint that bans the comparison of channels used for bidirectional communication.

In concurrent, logic, and/or functional languages and calculi, a number of type systems to deal with polarities and linearities have been proposed.

In π-calculi and functional languages, Kobayashi proposes a linear type system for the π-calculus [19], which seems to make the calculus close to constraint-based concurrency with linear, moded variables because both linear channels and linear logic variables disallow more than one write access and more than one read access. Turner *et al.* introduce linearity annotation to a type system

[7] In actual implementations, `+` and 2 will be embedded in compiled code and can be considered zero-resource values.

for call-by-need lambda calculus [35]. All these pieces of work could be considered the application of ideas with similar motivations to different computational models. In concurrent logic programming, the difficulty lies in the treatment of arbitrarily complex information flow expressed using logical variables. Walker discusses types supporting more explicit memory management [50]. Session types [13] shares the same objective with our mode system.

Languages that feature linearity can be found in various programming paradigms. Linear Lisp [4] and Lilac [20] are two examples outside logic programming, while a survey of linear logic programming languages can be found in [23].

There is a lot of work on compile-time garbage collection other than that based on typing. In logic programming, most of the previous work is based on abstract interpretation [14]. Mercury [34] is a logic programming language known for its high-performance and enables compile-time garbage collection using mode and uniqueness declarations [21]. However, the key difference between Mercury and GHC is that the former does not allow non-strict data structures while the latter is highly non-strict.

Message-oriented implementation of Moded Flat GHC, which compiles stream communication into tight control flow between communicating processes, can be thought of as a form of compile-time garbage collection [41][40]. Another technique related to compile-time garbage collection is process fusion by unfold/fold transformation [38], which should have some relationship with deforestation of functional programs.

Janus [27] establishes the linearity property by allowing each variable to occur only twice. In Janus, a reserved unary constructor is used to give a variable occurrence an output capability. Our technique allows both linear and nonlinear variables and distinguishes between them by static analysis, and allows output capabilities to be inferred rather than specified.

Concurrent read accesses under linear typing was motivated by the study on parallel array processing in Moded Flat GHC [42] [25], which again has an independent counterpart in functional programming [29].

10 Conclusions and Future Work

This is the first report on the ongoing project on garbage-free symbolic computation based on constraint-based concurrency.

The sublanguage we propose, namely a strictly linear subset of Guarded Horn Clauses, retains most of the power of the cooperative use of logical variables, and also allows resource sharing without giving up the linguistic-level control over the resource handled by the program.

The capability type system integrates and generalizes the mode system and the linearity system developed and used for Flat GHC. Thanks to its arithmetic and constraint-based formulation, the type system is kept quite simple. We plan to build a constraint-based type reconstructor in the near future. A challenging issue from the theoretical point of view is the static analysis of the extended occur-check condition. However, we have already been successful in detecting the (useless) unification of identical nonlinear variable as erroneous; if `X` is unified with itself when it has the third occurrence elsewhere, the third occurrence is constrained to have zero capability, which contradicts Rule (NZ_c). Another important direction related to resource-consciousness is to deal with time as well as space bounds. We need to see how type systems developed in different settings to deal with resource bounds [16][9] can relate to our concurrent setting.

Undoubtedly, the primary concern is the ease of programming. Does resource-conscious programming help programmers write correct programs enjoying better properties, or is it simply burdensome? We believe the answer to the former is at least partly affirmative, but to a varying degree depending on the applications. One of the grand challenges of concurrent languages and their underlying theories is to provide a common platform for various forms of non-conventional computing including parallel computing, distributed/network computing, real-time computing, and mobile computing [45]. All these areas are strongly concerned with physical aspects and we hope that a flexible framework with the notion of resources will be a promising starting point towards a common platform.

Acknowledgments

Discussions with the members of the programming language research group at Waseda helped the development of the ideas described here. This work is partially supported by Grant-In-Aid ((C)(2)11680370) for Scientific Research, Ministry of Education.

References

1. Aït-Kaci, H. and Nasr, R., LOGIN: A Logic Programming Language with Built-In Inheritance. *J. Logic Programming*, Vol. 3, No. 3 (1986), pp. 185–215.
2. Ajiro, Y., Ueda, K. and Cho, K., Error-Correcting Source Code. In *Proc. Fourth Int. Conf. on Principles and Practice of Constraint Programming (CP'98)*, LNCS 1520, Springer-Verlag, 1998, pp. 40–54.
3. Ajiro, Y. and Ueda, K., Kima: an Automated Error Correction System for Concurrent Logic Programs. To appear in *Automated Software Engineering*, 2001.
4. Baker, H. G., Lively Linear Lisp—'Look Ma, No Garbage!' *Sigplan Notices*, Vol. 27, No. 8 (1992), pp. 89–98.
5. Chikayama, T. and Kimura, Y., Multiple Reference Management in Flat GHC. In *Logic Programming: Proc. of the Fourth Int. Conf. (ICLP'87)*, The MIT Press, 1987, pp. 276–293.
6. Chikayama, T., Operating System PIMOS and Kernel Language KL1. In *Proc. Int. Conf. on Fifth Generation Computer Systems 1992 (FGCS'92)*, Ohmsha and IOS Press, Tokyo, 1992, pp. 73–88.
7. Chikayama, T., Fujise, T. and Sekita, D., A Portable and Efficient Implementation of KL1. In *Proc. 6th Int. Symp. on Programming Language Implementation and Logic Programming (PLILP'94)*, LNCS 844, Springer-Verlag, 1994, pp. 25–39.
8. Clark, K. L. and Gregory, S., PARLOG: Parallel Programming in Logic. *ACM. Trans. Prog. Lang. Syst.*, Vol. 8, No. 1 (1986), pp. 1–49.

9. Crary, K. and Weirich, S., Resource Bound Certification. In *Proc. 27th ACM Symp. on Principles of Programming Languages (POPL'00)*, 2000, pp. 184–198.
10. Fujita, H. and Hasegawa, R., A Model Generation Theorem Prover in KL1 Using a Ramified-Stack Algorithm. In *Proc. Eighth Int. Conf. on Logic Programming (ICLP'91)*, The MIT Press, Cambridge, MA, 1991, pp. 535–548.
11. Fournet, C., Gonthier, G. Lévy, J.-J., Maranget, L. and Rémy, D., A Calculus of Mobile Agents. In *Proc. 7th Int. Conf. on Concurrency Theory (CONCUR'96)*, LNCS 1119, Springer-Verlag, 1996, pp. 406–421.
12. Frühwirth, T., Theory and Practice of Constraint Handling Rules. *J. Logic Programming*, Vol. 37, No. 1–3 (1998), pp. 95–138.
13. Gay, S. and Hole, M., Types and Subtypes for Client-Server Interactions. In *Proc. European Symp. on Programming (ESOP'99)*, LNCS 1576, Springer-Verlag, 1999, pp. 74–90.
14. Gudjonsson, G. and Winsborough, W. H., Compile-time Memory Reuse in Logic Programming Languages Through Update in Place. *ACM Trans. Prog. Lang. Syst*, Vol. 21, No. 3 (1999), pp. 430–501.
15. Honda, K. and Tokoro, M., An Object Calculus for Asynchronous Communication. In *Proc. Fifth Conf. on Object-Oriented Programming (ECOOP'91)*, LNCS 512, Springer-Verlag, 1991, pp. 133–147.
16. Hughes, J. and Pareto, L., Recursion and Dynamic Data-structures in Bounded Space: Towards Embedded ML Programming. In *Proc. Fourth ACM SIGPLAN Int. Conf. on Functional Programming (ICFP'99)*, 1999, pp. 70–81.
17. Jaffar, J. and Maher, M. J., Constraint Logic Programming: A Survey. *J. Logic Programming*, Vol. 19–20 (1994), pp. 503–582.
18. Kobayashi, N., Quasi-Linear Types In *Proc. 26th ACM Symp. on Principles of Programming Languages (POPL'99)*, ACM, 1999, pp. 29–42.
19. Kobayashi, N., Pierce, B. and Turner, D., Linearity and the Pi-Calculus. *ACM Trans. Prog. Lang. Syst.*, Vol. 21, No. 5 (1999), pp. 914–947.
20. Mackie, I., Lilac: A Functional Programming Language Based on Linear Logic. *J. Functional Programming*, Vol. 4, No. 4 (1994), pp. 1–39.
21. Mazur, N., Janssens, G. and Bruynooghe, M., A Module Based Analysis for Memory Reuse in Mercury. In *Proc. Int. Conf. on Computational Logic (CL2000)*, LNCS 1861, Springer-Verlag, 2000, pp. 1255–1269.
22. Merro, M., Locality in the π-calculus and Applications to Distributed Objects. PhD Thesis, Ecol des Mines de Paris, 2000.
23. Miller, D., A Survey on Linear Logic Programming. *The Newsletter of the European Network in Computational Logic*, Vol. 2, No. 2 (1995), pp.63–67.
24. Niehren, J. and Müller, M., Constraints for Free in Concurrent Computation. In *Proc. Asian Computing Science Conf. (ACSC'95)*, LNCS 1023, Springer-Verlag, 1995, pp. 171–186.
25. Sakamoto, K., Matsumiya, S. and Ueda, K., Optimizing Array Processing of Parallel KLIC. In *IPSJ Trans. on Programming*, Vol. 42, No. SIG 3(PRO 10) (2001), pp. 1–13 (in Japanese).
26. Sangiorgi, D., π-Calculus, Internal Mobility and Agent-Passing Calculi. *Theoretical Computer Science*, Vol. 167, No. 1–2 (1996), pp. 235–274.
27. Saraswat, V. A., Kahn, K. and Levy, J., Janus: A Step Towards Distributed Constraint Programming. In *Proc. 1990 North American Conf. on Logic Programming (NACLP'90)*, The MIT Press, Cambridge, MA, 1990, pp. 431–446.
28. Saraswat, V. A. and Rinard, M., Concurrent Constraint Programming (Extended Abstract). In *Proc. 17th Annual ACM Symp. on Principles of Programming Languages (POPL'90)*, ACM, 1990, pp. 232–245.

29. Sastry, A. V. S. and Clinger, W., Parallel Destructive Updating in Strict Functional Languages. In *Proc. 1994 ACM Conf. on LISP and Functional Programming*, 1994, pp. 263–272.
30. Shapiro, E. Y., Concurrent Prolog: A Progress Report. *IEEE Computer*, Vol. 19, No. 8 (1986), pp. 44–58.
31. Shapiro, E., The Family of Concurrent Logic Programming Languages. *ACM Computing Surveys*, Vol. 21, No. 3 (1989), pp. 413–510.
32. Shapiro, E. Y., Warren, D. H. D., Fuchi, K., Kowalski, R. A., Furukawa, K., Ueda, K., Kahn, K. M., Chikayama, T. and Tick, E., The Fifth Generation Project: Personal Perspectives. *Comm. ACM*, Vol. 36, No. 3 (1993), pp. 46–103.
33. Smolka, G., A Foundation for Higher-order Concurrent Constraint Programming. In *Proc. First Int. Conf. on Constraints in Computational Logics*, LNCS 845, Springer-Verlag, 1994, pp. 50–72.
34. Somogyi, Z., Henderson, F. and Conway, T., The Execution Algorithm of Mercury, An Efficient Purely Declarative Logic Programming Language. *J. Logic Programming*, Vol. 29, No. 1–3 (1996), pp. 17–64.
35. Turner, D. N., Wadler, P. and Mossin, C., Once Upon a Type. In *Proc. Seventh Int. Conf. on Functional Programming Languages and Computer Architecture (FPCA'95)*, ACM, 1995, pp. 1–11.
36. Ueda, K., Guarded Horn Clauses. ICOT Tech. Report TR-103, ICOT, Tokyo, 1985. Also in *Logic Programming '85*, Wada, E. (ed.), LNCS 221, Springer-Verlag, 1986, pp. 168–179.
37. Ueda, K., Guarded Horn Clauses. D. Eng. Thesis, Univ. of Tokyo, 1986.
38. Ueda, K. and Furukawa, K., Transformation Rules for GHC Programs. In *Proc. Int. Conf. on Fifth Generation Computer Systems 1988 (FGCS'88)*, ICOT, Tokyo, 1988, pp. 582–591.
39. Ueda, K. and Chikayama, T. Design of the Kernel Language for the Parallel Inference Machine. *The Computer Journal*, Vol. 33, No. 6 (1990), pp. 494–500.
40. Ueda, K. and Morita, M., Message-Oriented Parallel Implementation of Moded Flat GHC. *New Generation Computing*, Vol. 11, No. 3–4 (1993), pp. 323–341.
41. Ueda, K. and Morita, M., Moded Flat GHC and Its Message-Oriented Implementation Technique. *New Generation Computing*, Vol. 13, No. 1 (1994), pp. 3–43.
42. Ueda, K., Moded Flat GHC for Data-Parallel Programming. In *Proc. FGCS'94 Workshop on Parallel Logic Programming*, ICOT, Tokyo, 1994, pp. 27–35.
43. Ueda, K., Experiences with Strong Moding in Concurrent Logic/Constraint Programming. In *Proc. Int. Workshop on Parallel Symbolic Languages and Systems (PSLS'95)*, LNCS 1068, Springer-Verlag, 1996, pp. 134–153.
44. Ueda, K., *klint* — Static Analyzer for KL1 Programs. Available from `http://www.icot.or.jp/ARCHIVE/Museum/FUNDING/funding-98-E.html`, 1998.
45. Ueda, K., Concurrent Logic/Constraint Programming: The Next 10 Years. In *The Logic Programming Paradigm: A 25-Year Perspective*, Apt, K. R., Marek, V. W., Truszczynski M., and Warren D. S. (eds.), Springer-Verlag, 1999, pp. 53–71.
46. Ueda, K., Linearity Analysis of Concurrent Logic Programs. In *Proc. Int. Workshop on Parallel and Distributed Computing for Symbolic and Irregular Applications*, Ito, T. and Yuasa, T. (eds.), World Scientific, 2000, pp. 253–270.
47. van Emden, M. H. and de Lucena Filho, G. J., Predicate Logic as a Language for Parallel Programming. In *Logic Programming*, Clark, K. L. and Tärnlund, S. -Å. (eds.), Academic Press, London, 1982, pp. 189–198.
48. Victor, B., The Fusion Calculus: Expressiveness and Symmetry in Mobile Processes, PhD Thesis, Uppsala Univ., 1998.

49. Wadler, P., Linear Types Can Change the World! In *Prof. IFIP TC2 Working Conf. on Programming Concepts and Methods*, Broy, M. and Jones, C. (eds.), North-Holland, 1990, pp. 347–359.
50. Walker, D. P., Typed Memory Management. PhD thesis, Cornell Univ., 2001.

Solo Diagrams

Cosimo Laneve[1], Joachim Parrow[2], and Björn Victor[3]

[1] Dept. of Computer Science, University of Bologna, Italy.
laneve@CS.UniBO.IT
[2] Royal Institute of Technology, Kista, Sweden.
joachim@it.kth.se
[3] Dept. of Computer Systems, Uppsala University, Sweden.
victor@DoCS.UU.SE

Abstract. We address the problems of implementing the replication operator efficiently in the solos calculus – a calculus of mobile processes without prefix. This calculus is expressive enough to admit an encoding of the whole fusion calculus and thus the π-calculus. We show that nested occurrences of replication can be avoided, that the size of replicated terms can be limited to three particles, and that the usual unfolding semantics of replication can be replaced by three simple reduction rules. To illustrate the results and show how the calculus can be efficiently implemented we present a graphic representation of agents in the solos calculus, adapting ideas from interaction diagrams and pi-nets.

1 Introduction

The π-calculus [15] has proved remarkably successful in modelling diverse computational phenomena, and it is natural to ask how much of it is really necessary in order to attain the expressive power. This has led to several interesting and expressive subcalculi. For example, in the more easily implemented asynchronous subcalculus [2, 8] the output prefix $\overline{u}\,v\,.\,P$ is replaced by the output particle $\overline{u}\,v$. In the fusion calculus [19] the reduction of an input and output results in a *fusion* of names rather than a substitution. In that calculus both input and output prefix can be replaced by their corresponding particles, in other words, there is no need for explicit representation of temporal precedence. These particles are called *solos* and take the general forms $u\,\widetilde{x}$ for input and $\overline{u}\,\widetilde{x}$ for output, where $\widetilde{x}$ is a sequence of names. This *solos calculus* additionally includes only parallel composition $P \mid Q$, scoping $(x)P$ and replication $!\,P$, giving a very lean formalism. We refer the reader to [10] for further explanation of the expressive power of solos.

The replication operator $!\,P$ is often used in place of recursive definitions, since it has nice algebraic properties. For example, if the number of recursive definitions is finite, recursion can be coded in terms of replication [13]. Replication can be defined in terms of unguarded recursion: $!\,P \stackrel{def}{=} P \mid !\,P$. This definition is, however, hard to implement – when should the unfolding stop? How many (possibly nested) replications need be expanded in order to infer a

N. Kobayashi and B.C. Pierce (Eds.): TACS 2001, LNCS 2215, pp. 127–144, 2001.

reduction? For the π-calculus Sangiorgi has shown [21] that replication of general agents is not necessary, but it can be replaced by the guarded variant $!\,\alpha\,.\,P$. This corresponds to using guarded recursion ($!\,\alpha\,.\,P \stackrel{def}{=} \alpha\,.\,(P \mid !\,\alpha\,.\,P)$). In languages based on the asynchronous communication such as Pict [20] or Join [3], it is relatively easy to see that it suffices to have input-guarded replication of the form $!\,x(y)\,.\,P$.

These guarded variants of replication cannot be used in the solos calculus, where there are no prefix-guarded terms present, but only solos. However, we can replace the unguarded unfolding of $!\,P \stackrel{def}{=} P \mid !\,P$ with three reduction rules which pinpoint when a reduction involving a replicated agent can be inferred. We show that the new formulation of the semantics coincides with the standard one. This result rests on a flattening law, which allows us to remove nested replications.

Another problem with implementing replication is that the term being unfolded may be arbitrarily large, making interaction with a replicated term computationally expensive. We address this problem by presenting a decomposition law allowing us to limit the size of replicated terms to three solos.

The resulting formalism is thus very slender, and provides a simple canonical form for agents: $(\widetilde{x})(P \mid \prod_{i \in I} !\,(\widetilde{y_i})Q_i)$ where P and Q_i are compositions of solos, and $\widetilde{y_i}$ is a subset of the names in Q_i. We argue that this calculus can be easily and efficiently implemented, and illustrate both this fact and the general results using a new graphical formalism for the solos calculus, the *solo diagrams*.

The underlying idea is quite simple. To draw an agent, pick one node for each name, and label the node with the name. Outputs $\overline{u}\,\widetilde{x}$ become multiedges from the nodes labelled $\widetilde{x}$ to the node labelled u, and conversely for inputs. Parallel composition is just graph union and scope restriction erases the label of nodes. Reductions between inputs and outputs are possible when two types of edges meet at the same node, and results in the corresponding object nodes being fused or merged together, preserving any additional edges connecting them. As an example, Figure 1 shows a simple agent and reduction. Note that the two kinds of edges are distinguished by the shape of the arrow which has either a head or a tail.

In the first three figures, dotted lines indicate which solos correspond to which edges. These lines are not technically part of the diagrams.

As a further example, Figure 2 illustrates an agent with a nondeterministic behaviour: depending on which output solo is scheduled for the reduction, the agent produces two alternative graphs.

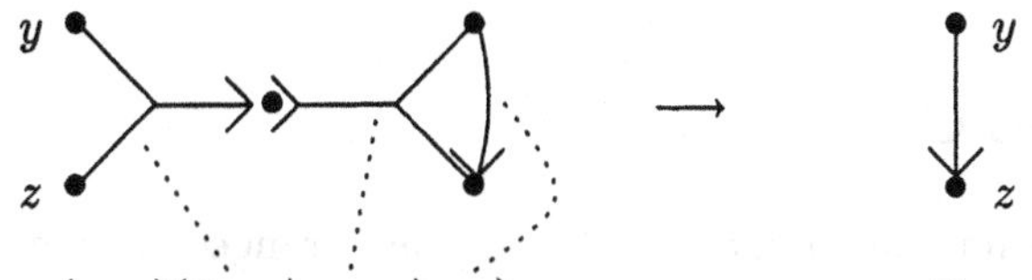

$$(xuv)(\overline{x}\,yz \mid x\,vu \mid u\,v) \quad \longrightarrow \quad \overline{z}\,y$$

Fig. 1. A simple diagram reduction and its correponding term reduction.

$$(xu)(\overline{x}\,y \mid \overline{x}\,z \mid x\,u \mid u\,ab)$$

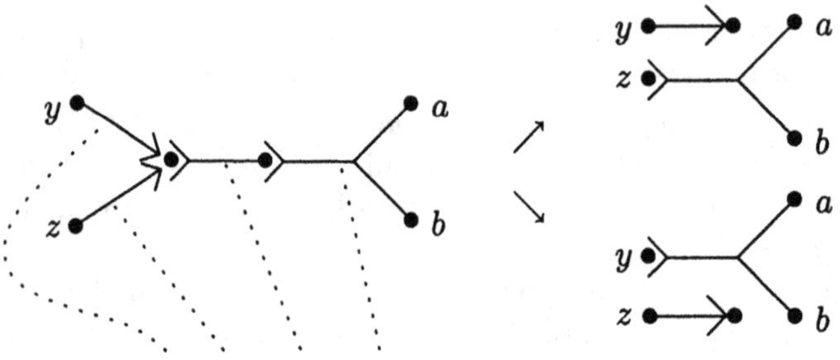

Fig. 2. The reductions of the diagram corresponding to $(xu)(\overline{x}\,y \mid \overline{x}\,z \mid x\,u \mid u\,ab)$

$!\,(yw)(\overline{y}\,w \mid \overline{x}\,yz) \mid (uv)(x\,uv \mid u\,v)$ $\longrightarrow$ $!\,(yw)(\overline{y}\,w \mid \overline{x}\,yz) \mid (uw')(u\,z \mid \overline{u}\,w')$

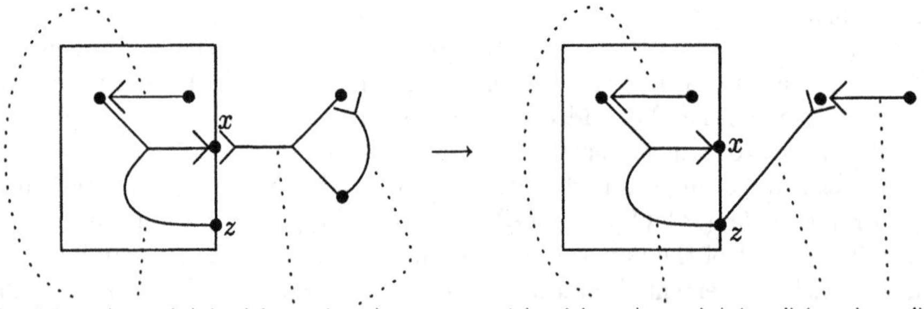

Fig. 3. The reduction of a diagram with a box, and its corresponding term reduction.)

Replication is modelled by boxes. These are drawn as rectangles surrounding the replicated graph, and are regarded as copying-machines for edges and nodes therein: when an edge of a box is involved in a reduction, all the content of the box is first copied. An example is shown in Figure 3. Here, the rightmost edge of the right-hand diagram is the remainder of the copy of the box after the reduction.

We continue by presenting the solos calculus; in Section 3 we introduce the graphical formalism. In Section 4 we formally relate this to the solos calculus; in particular, the usual structural congruence in the solos calculus is shown to coincide with diagram isomorphism, and the solo diagram reductions are shown to yield the same reductions as the standard unfolding approach. In Section 5 we consider a generalisation to graphs with multiply labelled nodes, giving a finer semantics. The paper concludes with a discussion of related work.

2   The Solos Calculus

Syntax. We assume an infinite set $\mathcal{N}$ of *names* ranged over by $u, v, x, z, \cdots$. Names represent communication channels, which are also the values transmitted. We write $\widetilde{x}$ for a (possibly empty) finite sequence $x_1 \cdots x_n$ of names.

The *solos* α are *inputs* $u\,\widetilde{x}$ and *outputs* $\overline{u}\,\widetilde{x}$. The names $\widetilde{x}$ are the *objects* of the solo, and the name u is the *subject.*

The *agents* $P, Q, R, \cdots$ are defined by

$$P ::= \underset{(\textit{Inaction})}{\mathbf{0}} \;\Big|\; \underset{(\textit{Solo})}{\alpha} \;\Big|\; \underset{(\textit{Composition})}{P \mid P} \;\Big|\; \underset{(\textit{Scope})}{(x)P} \;\Big|\; \underset{(\textit{Replication})}{!\,P}$$

The name x is said to be *bound* in $(x)P$. We write $(\widetilde{x})P$ for $(x_1)\cdots(x_n)P$, $n \geq 0$, and often $\prod_{i\in I} P_i$ for the composition of all P_i for $i \in I$, where I is a finite set. The *free names* in P, denoted $fn(P)$, are the names in P with a non-bound occurrence. The (choice-free) fusion calculus [19] consists of the above agents and those formed using the prefix operator, namely agents of the form $\alpha\,.\,P$.

Operational semantics. We begin by defining a structural congruence which equates all agents we will never want to distinguish for any semantic reason, and then use this when giving the operational semantics.

Definition 1. *The* structural congruence, $\equiv$, *between agents is the least congruence satisfying the abelian monoid laws for Composition, alpha-renaming, and the laws for scope and replication*

$$(x)\mathbf{0} \equiv \mathbf{0}, \quad (x)(y)P \equiv (y)(x)P,$$
$$P \mid (z)Q \equiv (z)(P \mid Q), \quad \textit{if } z \notin \textit{fn}(P)$$
$$!\,P \equiv P \mid !\,P$$

The reduction relation of the calculus of solos is the least relation satisfying the rules in Figure 4. Here and in the following σ will range over name substitutions, and we use $dom(\sigma) = \{u : \sigma(u) \neq u\}$ and $ran(\sigma) = \{\sigma(u) : \sigma(u) \neq u\}$. We write $\{\widetilde{x} = \widetilde{y}\}$ for the smallest total equivalence relation on $\mathcal{N}$ relating each x_i with y_i, and say that σ *agrees with* the equivalence φ if $\forall x, y : x\,\varphi\,y \Leftrightarrow \sigma(x) = \sigma(y)$. We say that two names are *fused* by a reduction if they are made equal by the resulting substitution. The side condition of Figure 4 bans reductions that fuse two different free names. For instance, the agent $\overline{x}\,y \mid x\,z$ is irreducible. See Section 5 and [19] for alternative semantics allowing such reductions.

Equivalence. To define an extensional semantics, we use the standard notion of *barbed bisimulation* developed in [16].

Definition 2. *The* observation relation *is the least relation satisfying the rules below.*

$$\begin{array}{lll} x\,\widetilde{y}\downarrow x & (P \mid Q)\downarrow x & \textit{if } P\downarrow x \textit{ or } Q\downarrow x \\ \overline{x}\,\widetilde{y}\downarrow x & (z)P\downarrow x & \textit{if } P\downarrow x \textit{ and } x \neq z \end{array}$$

Definition 3. *A* weak barbed bisimulation *is a symmetric binary relation S between agents such that $P\;S\;Q$ implies:*

1. *If $P \longrightarrow P'$ then $Q \longrightarrow^* Q'$ and $P'\;S\;Q'$.*
2. *If $P\downarrow x$ for some x, then $Q \longrightarrow^*\downarrow x$.*

$$(\widetilde{z})\Big(\overline{u}\,\widetilde{x} \mid u\,\widetilde{y} \mid P\Big) \longrightarrow P\sigma$$

$$\frac{P \longrightarrow P'}{P \mid Q \longrightarrow P' \mid Q} \qquad \frac{P \longrightarrow P'}{(x)P \longrightarrow (x)P'} \qquad \frac{P \equiv Q \quad Q \longrightarrow Q' \quad Q' \equiv P'}{P \longrightarrow P'}$$

Side conditions in the first rule:
$|\widetilde{x}| = |\widetilde{y}|$, σ agrees with $\{\widetilde{x} = \widetilde{y}\}$, $ran(\sigma) \cap \widetilde{z} = \emptyset$, and $dom(\sigma) = \widetilde{z}$.

Fig. 4. Reduction rules for the calculus of solos.

P is barbed bisimilar *to Q, written* $P \stackrel{\cdot}{\approx} Q$, *if* $P \; \mathcal{S} \; Q$ *for some weak barbed bisimulation* $\mathcal{S}$. *P is* barbed congruent *to Q, written* $P \approx Q$, *if for all contexts* $C[\cdot]$, $C[P] \stackrel{\cdot}{\approx} C[Q]$.

The solos calculus, although simple, is expressive enough. The next theorem recalls a result in [10].

Theorem 4. *There exists an encoding* $[\![\cdot]\!]$ *of the fusion calculus into the calculus of solos such that* $[\![P]\!] \approx [\![Q]\!]$ *implies* $P \approx Q$, *and* $P \stackrel{\cdot}{\approx} Q$ *implies* $[\![P]\!] \stackrel{\cdot}{\approx} [\![Q]\!]$.

This result only gives full abstraction up-to encoded contexts, i.e., $C[P] \stackrel{\cdot}{\approx} C[Q]$ iff $[\![C[P]]\!] \stackrel{\cdot}{\approx} [\![C[Q]]\!]$ for any fusion calculus context $C[\cdot]$.

2.1 The Implementation of the Replication Operator

Although the standard definition of the replication operator is algebraically elegant, an unconstrained implementation of the equality $!P \equiv P \mid !P$ would quickly give an "out-of-memory error". This problem is well-known in implementations of mobile calculi. In Pict, for instance, the authors implement the so-called *replicated input* [20]. We cannot use the same machinery because the solos calculus has no prefix operator. Instead, we use a definition of the replication operator which is closer to a realistic implementation.

We begin by showing that nested replication may be flattened into non-nested replications [11]:

Theorem 5 (Flattening).

$$!(\widetilde{x})(P \mid !Q) \quad \approx \quad (y)(!(\widetilde{x})(P \mid \overline{y}\,\widetilde{z}) \mid !(\widetilde{w})(y\,\widetilde{w} \mid Q\{\widetilde{w}/\widetilde{z}\}))$$

where $\widetilde{z} = fn(Q)$ *and* y *and* $\widetilde{w}$ *are fresh.*

Corollary 6. *For all P there exists a Q such that it does not contain nested replications, and* $P \approx Q$.

Proof. *By structural induction on P. The only interesting case is where P is on the form matching the left-hand side of the equality in Theorem 5.*

In view of this corollary there is no substantial loss of generality to only consider non-nested replication. Therefore we from now on adopt the restriction that in $!Q$, the agent Q may not contain replications. This has several advantages. For example there is an attractive kind of canonical form:

Proposition 7. *Every agent P is structurally equivalent to an agent of the form $(\widetilde{x})(Q \mid (\prod_{i\in I} !(\widetilde{x}_i)Q_i))$, where Q, Q_i are compositions of solos, $\widetilde{x}_i \subseteq fn(Q_i)$ and $\widetilde{x} \subseteq fn(Q \mid (\prod_{i\in I} !(\widetilde{x}_i)Q_i))$.*

Notwithstanding these simplifications, the implementation difficulties coming from the equality $!P \equiv P \mid !P$ are almost unchanged. Therefore we give an alternative semantics of the replication operator, which has the same formal power as the standard replication but is more easily implemented.

Let $\equiv_r$ be the structural congruence introduced earlier in this section, without the rule $!P \equiv P \mid !P$. Let $\longrightarrow_r$ be the $\longrightarrow$ reduction rule, where $\equiv_r$ replaces $\equiv$ in the last rule, and with the three rules in Figure 5. These reduction rules account for interactions between two solos when (1) exactly one is replicated, (2) both are under different replications, and (3) both are under the same replication. Note that the outermost sequence of scopes in the right-hand-side of the rules may contain redundant scopes; these can be removed by structural congruence. The scopes of $\widetilde{z}$ are removed since $ran(\sigma) \cap \widetilde{z} = \emptyset$ just like in Figure 4.

$$(\widetilde{z})\Big(P \mid \overline{u}\,\widetilde{y} \mid !(\widetilde{w})(u\,\widetilde{x} \mid Q)\Big) \longrightarrow_r (\widetilde{w})\Big(P \mid Q \mid !(\widetilde{w})(u\,\widetilde{x} \mid Q)\Big)\sigma$$

$$(\widetilde{z})\Big(P \mid !(\widetilde{v})(\overline{u}\,\widetilde{y} \mid Q) \mid !(\widetilde{w})(u\,\widetilde{x} \mid R)\Big)$$
$$\longrightarrow_r (\widetilde{v}\widetilde{w})\Big(P \mid Q \mid R \mid !(\widetilde{v})(\overline{u}\,\widetilde{y} \mid Q) \mid !(\widetilde{w})(u\,\widetilde{x} \mid R)\Big)\sigma$$

$$(\widetilde{z})\Big(P \mid !(\widetilde{w})(\overline{u}\,\widetilde{y} \mid u\,\widetilde{x} \mid Q)\Big) \longrightarrow_r (\widetilde{w})\Big(P \mid Q \mid !(\widetilde{w})(\overline{u}\,\widetilde{y} \mid u\,\widetilde{x} \mid Q)\Big)\sigma$$

Side conditions

In every rule: $|\widetilde{x}| = |\widetilde{y}|, \sigma$ agrees with $\{\widetilde{x} = \widetilde{y}\}$, and $dom(\sigma) \cap ran(\sigma) = \emptyset$

In the first rule: u and $\overline{u}$ may be interchanged, $u \notin \widetilde{w}, \widetilde{w} \cap fn(P) = \emptyset$, and $\widetilde{z} \subseteq dom(\sigma) \subseteq \widetilde{z} \cup \widetilde{w}$

In the second rule: $u \notin \widetilde{v} \cup \widetilde{w}, (\widetilde{v} \cup \widetilde{w}) \cap fn(P) = \widetilde{v} \cap fn(R) = \widetilde{w} \cap fn(Q) = \emptyset$, and $\widetilde{z} \subseteq dom(\sigma) \subseteq \widetilde{z} \cup \widetilde{v} \cup \widetilde{w}$

In the third rule: $\widetilde{z} \subseteq dom(\sigma) \subseteq \widetilde{z} \cup \widetilde{w}$

Fig. 5. Reduction rules for replication.

The rules in Figure 5 implement a lazy usage of replications: a replicated process is duplicated only if it is used in a reduction. Their correctness with respect to the standard replication operator strongly relies on considering non-nested replications:

Proposition 8. *If P has only non-nested replications, then $P \longrightarrow Q$ if and only if $P \longrightarrow_r R$ and $Q \equiv R$.*

This proposition states that if an agent moves according to $\longrightarrow$, possibly by unfolding replications, then it moves according to $\longrightarrow_r$ without any unfolding of replication at all (and the other way around). If the agent had a nested replication, for instance $!!P$, the correspondence between $\longrightarrow$ and $\longrightarrow_r$ fails, because $\longrightarrow_r$-reduction is only defined for non-nested replication. The correspondence between $\longrightarrow$ and $\longrightarrow_r$ is proved by induction on the depth of the proofs of $\longrightarrow$ and $\longrightarrow_r$. Each time a replica is used in $\longrightarrow$ then one of the reductions in Figure 5 may be used instead; and, *vice versa*, when one reduction of Figure 5 is used in $\longrightarrow_r$, then its effects may be simulated by means of the replication law and the basic reduction of $\longrightarrow$.

3 Solo Diagrams

We now introduce a graphical formalism for solos, the *solo diagrams*. Diagrams are built out of an infinite set $\mathcal{U}$ of *nodes*, ranged over by $a, b, \ldots$.

Definition 9. *An* edge *is a tuple in* $\mathcal{U}$. *There are two kinds of edges: input edges* $\langle a, a_1, \cdots, a_k\rangle_i$ *and output edges* $\langle a, a_1, \cdots, a_k\rangle_o$.

Indexes o, i are omitted when the kind of an edge is irrelevant. Given an edge $\langle a, a_1, \cdots, a_k\rangle$, k is its *arity*, a is the subject node, and a_i are the object nodes. Let *nodes*$[\cdot]$ be the function taking a multiset of edges and returning the set of nodes therein.

Graphically, we draw output and input edges as follows:

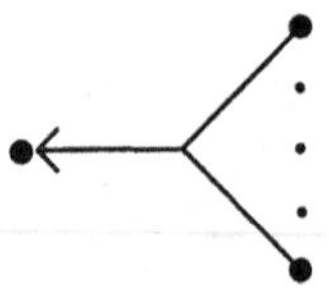

output edge $\langle a, a_1, \cdots, a_k\rangle_o$

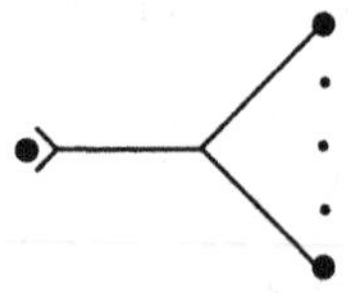

input edge $\langle a, a_1, \cdots, a_k\rangle_i$

We keep implicit the name of the nodes in the drawings: names are only used to identify or separate nodes. 0-arity edges are drawn as:

output and input edges with 0 arity

We also introduce boxes:

Definition 10. *A* box B *is a pair* $\langle \mathsf{G}, S\rangle$ *where* G *is a* graph *(a finite multiset of edges) and* $S \subseteq$ *nodes*$[\mathsf{G}]$. S *is called the* internal nodes *of* B *and nodes*$[\mathsf{G}] \setminus S$ *the* principal nodes *of* B.

Boxes are ranged over by $B, B', \ldots$, and M ranges over finite multisets of boxes. We extend *nodes*$[\cdot]$ to boxes by stating that *nodes*$[\langle \mathsf{G}, S\rangle] \stackrel{def}{=}$ *nodes*$[\mathsf{G}]$, and define

$\mathit{principals}[\langle \mathsf{G}, S\rangle] = \mathit{nodes}[\langle \mathsf{G}, S\rangle] \setminus S$. For multisets we extend these functions pointwise.

Boxes are drawn as rectangles where principal nodes are on the perimeter and internal nodes and all edges are inside. The intuition is that everything inside the box, i.e., all edges and internal nodes, can be replicated. Principal nodes cannot be replicated and can be thought of as the interface between the box and the rest of the diagram. As an example, we illustrate a box with two edges and three nodes. Two nodes are principal, one x-labelled and one unlabelled; the third node is internal.

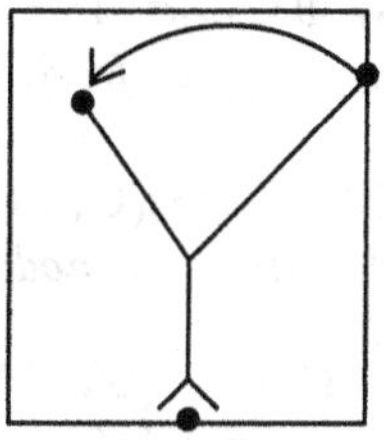

Definition 11. *A* solo diagram, *in brief SD, is a triple* $(\mathsf{G}, \mathsf{M}, \ell)$ *where* G *is a finite multiset of edges,* M *is a finite multiset of boxes, and* ℓ *is a partial injective function from* $\mathit{nodes}[\mathsf{G}] \cup \mathit{principals}[\mathsf{M}]$ *to* $\mathcal{N}$*, such that internal nodes of every box in* M *do not occur outside the box.*

The labelling ℓ is partially injective to enforce different nodes having different labels. Nodes in $\mathit{dom}(\ell)$ are *labelled nodes*, corresponding to free names; the others represent bound names. In the figures, labels will be explicitly written beside the node they mark. The condition in the definition of solo diagram says that internal nodes are not visible outside the box, i.e., they cannot occur in edges elsewhere. For instance, $(\{\langle a, a''\rangle_i\}, \{\langle\{\langle a, a'\rangle_i\}, \{a\}\rangle\}, \emptyset)$ is not an SD because the internal node a occurs outside the box. Note that internal nodes must also be unlabelled since the domain of ℓ only contains the principal nodes. Note also that an SD cannot contain isolated nodes.

In Definition 11, G represents the solos of an agent that are not replicated, while each box in M corresponds to one term under a replication operator. The edges within the box are the solos under that operator, the internal nodes of the box are the Scope operators under it. Principal nodes may be labelled or unlabelled; unlabelled principal nodes are under a Scope that does not sit under a replication. Both G and M are multisets rather than sets, in order to model agents such as $(x \mid x)$ or $!x \mid !x$. In the following, $\uplus$ denotes multiset union.

The SDs come with four rewriting rule, whose formal definition is the following, where we use σ as a substitution on nodes and $\mathsf{G}\sigma$ (and $\mathsf{M}\sigma$, respectively) to mean the graph obtained by replacing a by $\sigma(a)$ in all edges in G (and M, respectively).

Definition 12. *The reduction relation* $\longrightarrow$ *of SDs consists of the following schema, where* G_1 *and* G_2 *are arbitrary graphs,* M' *an arbitrary finite multiset of boxes. Let* $\alpha = \langle a, a'_1, \cdots, a'_k\rangle_o$, $\beta = \langle a, a_1, \cdots, a_k\rangle_i$ *or vice versa with reversed i/o polarity.*

1. *edge-edge reduction:* $(\mathsf{G} \uplus \{\alpha, \beta\}, \mathsf{M}, \ell) \longrightarrow (\mathsf{G}\sigma, \mathsf{M}\sigma, \ell')$.
2. *edge-box reduction:*
   Let $\mathsf{G} = \{\alpha\} \uplus \mathsf{G}_1$,
   $\mathsf{M} = \langle\{\beta\} \uplus \mathsf{G}_2, S\rangle \uplus \mathsf{M}'$,
   Then $(\mathsf{G}\,,\,\mathsf{M}\,,\,\ell) \longrightarrow ((\mathsf{G}_1 \uplus \mathsf{G}_2\rho)\sigma\,,\,\mathsf{M}\sigma\,,\,\ell')$
   where ρ *is a renaming of nodes in* S *into fresh nodes.*
3. *box-box reduction:*
   Let $B_1 = \langle\{\alpha\} \uplus \mathsf{G}_1, S_1\rangle$, $B_2 = \langle\{\beta\} \uplus \mathsf{G}_2, S_2\rangle$, *and* $\mathsf{M} = \{B_1, B_2\} \uplus \mathsf{M}'$
   Then $(\mathsf{G}\,,\,\mathsf{M}\,,\,\ell) \longrightarrow ((\mathsf{G} \uplus \mathsf{G}_1\rho \uplus \mathsf{G}_2\rho)\sigma\,,\,\mathsf{M}\sigma\,,\,\ell')$
   where ρ *is a renaming from* $S_1 \cup S_2$ *to fresh nodes.*
4. *internal box reduction:*
   Let $\mathsf{M} = \langle\{\alpha, \beta\} \uplus \mathsf{G}_1, S\rangle \uplus \mathsf{M}'$. *Then* $(\mathsf{G}\,,\,\mathsf{M}\,,\,\ell) \longrightarrow ((\mathsf{G} \uplus \mathsf{G}_1\rho)\sigma\,,\,\mathsf{M}\sigma\,,\,\ell')$
   where ρ *is a renaming from* S *into fresh nodes.*

where, for every reduction $(\mathsf{G}, \mathsf{M}, \ell) \longrightarrow (\mathsf{G}'\sigma, \mathsf{M}'\sigma, \ell')$, $ran(\sigma) \cap dom(\sigma) = \emptyset$, $dom(\sigma) \cap dom(\ell) = \emptyset$ *and* σ *agrees with* $\{a_i' = a_i : 1 \leq i \leq k\}$. *Moreover,* ℓ' *restricts* ℓ *to* $nodes[\mathsf{G}'\sigma] \cup nodes[\mathsf{M}'\sigma]$.

As in the solos calculus, the edge-edge reduction may fuse either two unlabelled nodes or one labelled node and an unlabelled one. This follows from the constraint that $dom(\sigma) \cap dom(\ell) = \emptyset$: a labelled node cannot be substituted. The edge-edge reduction is illustrated in Figure 1 for a simple agent.

Figures 6, 7 and 8 describe the reductions involving boxes. As said above we regard boxes as copying-machines for edges and internal nodes: when an interaction involves an edge of the box, all the contents of the box are instantiated at once. In particular, internal nodes are duplicated and renamed into fresh new nodes. Principal nodes, whether labelled or not, are not duplicated and will remain shared with the rest of the diagram. In Figure 6, we describe a box-instantiation due to the interaction on the principal node x. The overall effect is the appearance of the edge $\langle y, z\rangle_o$ on the right hand side, together with the box on the left hand side. Figure 7 shows a box-instantiation due to an interaction between edges in different boxes. This rule produces a copy of the contents of the two boxes, where the two interacting edges have been consumed. The rewriting in Figure 8 describes the box-instantiation due to a reduction internal to the box. The effect of this reduction is the fusion of two nodes, which turn out to be the arguments of an input on the principal node x. As a consequence, the instance of the box contents consists of the edge $\langle x, n, n\rangle_i$ only, where $n \in \mathcal{U}$ is fresh and unlabelled.

We conclude with few remarks about the SD reductions:

1. The definition of SD implicitly carries out a garbage collection of disconnected nodes.
2. The labelling function of an SD always decreases during the computation. In other words, no free name is ever created by internal reductions.
3. Very small parts of the graph are involved in the reduction. Apart from the removal of the interacting edges α and β, the residuals of the involved boxes

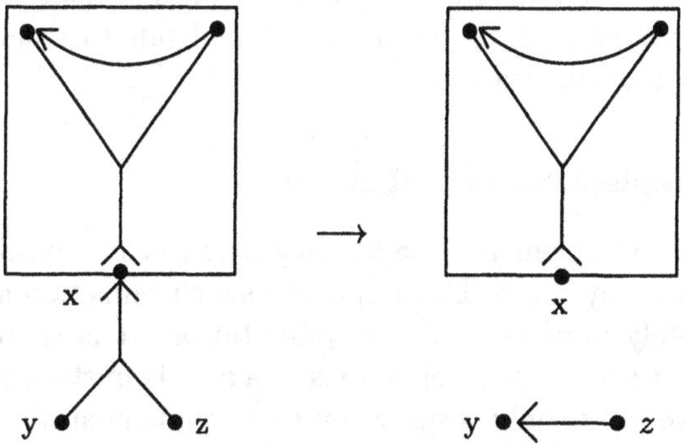

Fig. 6. The edge-box reduction $\overline{x}\,yz \mid !\,(uv)(x\,uv \mid \overline{u}\,v) \longrightarrow \overline{y}\,z \mid !\,(uv)(x\,uv \mid \overline{u}\,v)$

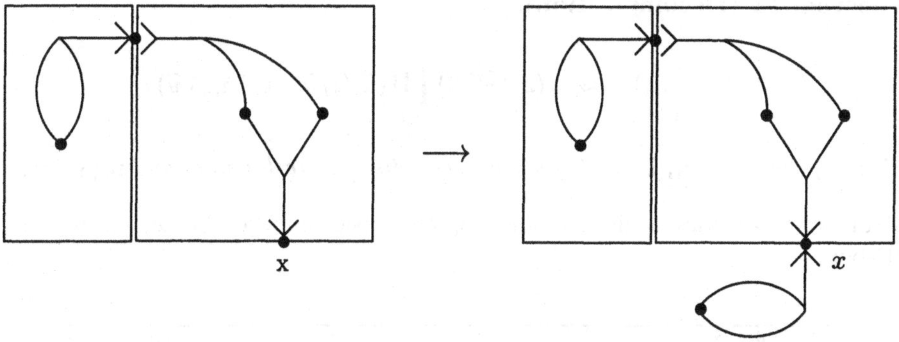

Fig. 7. The box-box reduction $(z)\big(!\,(u)\overline{z}\,uu \mid !\,(uv)(z\,uv \mid x\,uv)\big) \longrightarrow (z)\big(!\,(u)\overline{z}\,uu \mid !\,(uv)(z\,uv \mid x\,uv)\big) \mid (u)\overline{x}\,uu$

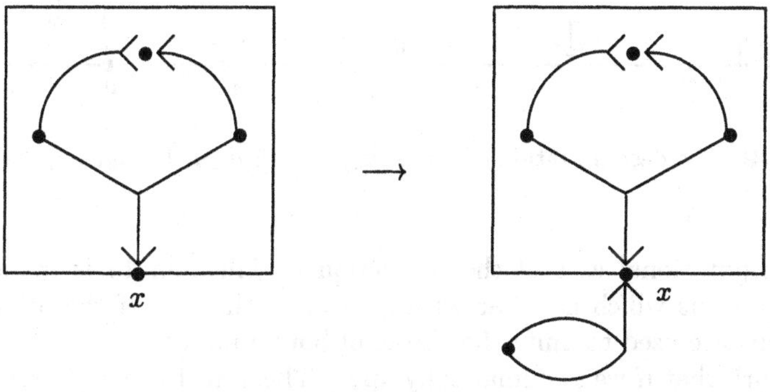

Fig. 8. The internal box reduction $!\,(uvw)(x\,uv \mid \overline{w}\,v \mid w\,u) \longrightarrow (v')x\,v'v' \mid !\,(uvw)(x\,uv \mid \overline{w}\,v \mid w\,u)$

are copied after renaming internal nodes, and in the next subsection we will see how this copying can be minimized. This lends to a simple and slender implementation of the graphs.

3.1 A Local Implementation of Boxes

Boxes are difficult to implement because they require code-duplication that may involve arbitrarily many edges. This imposes a synchronization among edges and hinders a completely local view of the computation. It is therefore interesting that we can restrict such code-duplications to a small constant number of edges. In this respect, we are mainly inspired by local implementations of linear logic boxes [7] and Parrow's trios [18].

In our solos calculus, boxes may be decomposed to boxes of three edges, without affecting the expressiveness:

Theorem 13 (Decomposition).

$$!\,(\widetilde{u})(\prod_{i=1}^{n} \alpha_i) \quad \approx \quad (z_i{}^{1\leq i\leq n}) \prod_{i=1}^{n} !\,(\widetilde{u})(z_i\,\widetilde{u} \mid \alpha_i \mid \overline{z_{i+1}}\,\widetilde{u})$$

where α_i are solos, z_i, $1 \leq i \leq n$ are pairwise distinct fresh names and $z_{n+1} = z_1$.

In Figure 9 we draw a diagram showing the basic units for implementing any SD-box.

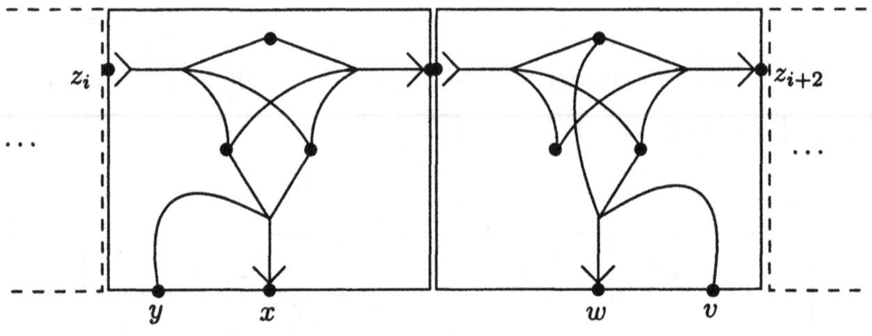

Fig. 9. The decomposition of $!\,(u_1u_2u_3)(\cdots \mid \overline{x}\,yu_1u_2 \mid \overline{w}\,u_3u_2v \mid \cdots)$.

The computational cost of the restriction in Theorem 13 is to perform a number of fusions which is linear with respect to the size of the original box. These fusions are used to unify the choice of bound names $\widetilde{u}$.

We remark that if we systematically apply Theorem 13 to all boxes containing at least 2 edges, then the last reduction rule in Definition 12 (internal box reduction) becomes redundant.

3.2 The Connection with Proof Nets

In this section we briefly discuss the connection between our SDs and linear logic proof nets [6] (this topic will be detailed in the full paper). The reader without some background in linear logic may safely skip this section.

We begin with Multiplicative Proof Nets, which are graphs with four kinds of edges: *axioms*, *cuts*, *par operators*, and *tensor operators*. This subset of Proof Nets may be put in correspondence with SDs without boxes: par and tensor operators correspond to input and output edges, respectively (or, equivalently, the other way around), axiom and cut edges are interpreted by fusing the nodes they connect. This interpretation lifts to the dynamics: cut-elimination is exactly the edge-edge reduction in SDs. Graphically, Proof Net cut-elimination is illustrated by the following reduction

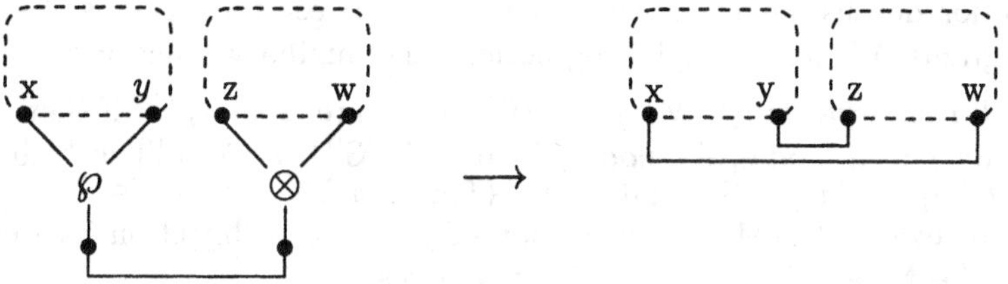

where, in the net on the left hand side, ℘ is the par operator, ⊗ is the tensor, and the edge in the bottom is the cut operator. We observe that this reduction is mimicked by the SD rewriting

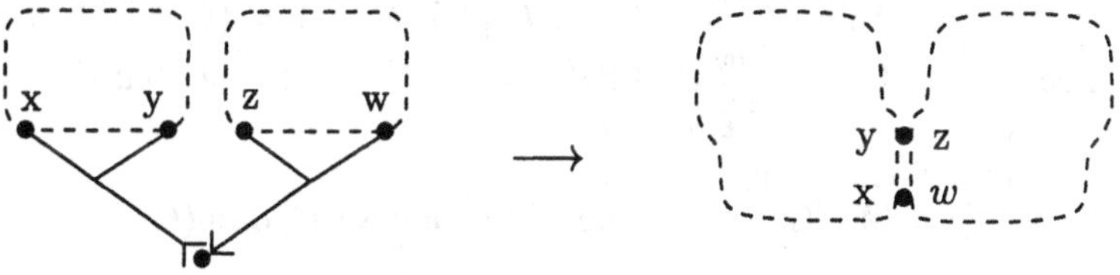

The converse connection is complicated because solo diagrams are more expressive than Proof Nets. Nevertheless, it is possible to show that well-sorted SDs (see [11]) with nodes occurring at most two times in the graph correspond to a superset of Proof Nets (the *proof structures* – a collection of nets that may possibly be unsound [6]).

When boxes come into the picture the above relationship is more tenuous. The reason is that boxes are used differently. In Proof Nets, boxes may be safely replaced by their content, thus disallowing the copying capability. This operation is reasonable in a functional language like Proof Nets, where resources, when plugged in some context agent, cannot be used by other agents. In a concurrent scenario, where systems are open, resources may be used by several agents who are not aware of each other. In such contexts an agent cannot erase resources just because it does not need them anymore. Resources may be garbage collected, provided they can never be accessed again, a property which usually follows by some equivalence (such as barbed congruence).

Another difference is that, in Proof Nets, a reduction inside a box does not create copies of its contents, but instead modifies the original box. This is plausible in Proof Nets, which are deterministic, and such simplifications may shorten computations. In contrast these simplifications are conceptually wrong in SDs because of the nondeterminism. Reductions inside a box can also be seen as infinitely many computation steps (affecting all future copies of the box contents), which from an operational viewpoint is unagreeable.

Notwithstanding these differences it may still be possible to relate the two systems. There are suitable evaluation strategies of proof nets that may be implemented in SDs, e.g. according to the techniques illustrated by Milner in [12].

4 Agents and Solo Diagrams

This section details the formal correspondence between the calculus of solos and solo diagrams. We use the following notions and auxiliary functions:

- *graph-isomorphism*: $(\mathsf{G}, \mathsf{M}, \ell)$ and $(\mathsf{G}', \mathsf{M}', \ell')$ are *isomorphic* if there is a bijection f from $nodes[\mathsf{G}] \cup nodes[\mathsf{M}]$ to $nodes[\mathsf{G}'] \cup nodes[\mathsf{M}']$ such that
  1. $\langle a, a_1, \cdots, a_k \rangle \in \mathsf{G}$ if and only if $\langle f(a), f(a_1), \cdots, f(a_k) \rangle \in \mathsf{G}'$;
  2. for every $B \in \mathsf{M}$, the restriction of f to B is a bijection into nodes of $B' \in \mathsf{M}'$ which preserves principal nodes;
  3. $\ell(a) = \ell'(f(a))$.

  In the following we shall never be interested in distinguishing isomorphic SDs.
- *graph-composition*: Let $(\mathsf{G}, \mathsf{M}, \ell)$ and $(\mathsf{G}', \mathsf{M}', \ell')$ be two SDs such that $\ell(a) = \ell'(a')$ if and only if $a = a'$. Then $(\mathsf{G}, \mathsf{M}, \ell) \mid (\mathsf{G}', \mathsf{M}', \ell') \stackrel{def}{=} (\mathsf{G} \uplus \mathsf{G}', \mathsf{M} \uplus \mathsf{M}', \ell \cup \ell')$.
- *graph-scope*: $(x)(\mathsf{G}, \mathsf{M}, \ell) \stackrel{def}{=} (\mathsf{G}, \mathsf{M}, \ell')$, where ℓ' is the function:
  $$\ell'(a) = \begin{cases} \ell(a) & \text{if } \ell(a) \neq x \\ \text{undefined} & \text{if } \ell(a) = x \end{cases}$$
- $\mathsf{box}[(\mathsf{G}, \emptyset, \ell)] = (\emptyset, \langle \mathsf{G}, S \rangle, \ell)$, where $S = nodes[\mathsf{G}] \setminus dom(\ell)$.

We remark that graph-composition is a partial function. In order to compose two arbitrary SDs, we consider diagrams isomorphic to them such that nodes are equal if and only if they have the same label ("$\ell(a) = \ell'(a')$ if and only if $a = a'$"). Scope is simply removing the node labelled x from the domain of the labelling function.

We can now define the function $graph[\cdot]$ from agents to SDs such that each solo corresponds to one edge.

Definition 14. *Let graph[·] be the function from agents to SDs, defined inductively as follows:*

$$\begin{aligned}
graph[\mathbf{0}] &= (\emptyset, \emptyset, \emptyset) \\
graph[x_0\, x_1 \cdots x_k] &= (\{\langle a_0, a_1, \cdots, a_k \rangle_i\}, \emptyset, [a_i \mapsto x_i]^{i \leq k}) \quad (x_i = x_j \textit{ iff } a_i = a_j) \\
graph[\overline{x_0}\, x_1 \cdots x_k] &= (\{\langle a_0, a_1, \cdots, a_k \rangle_o\}, \emptyset, [a_i \mapsto x_i]^{i \leq k}) \quad (x_i = x_j \textit{ iff } a_i = a_j) \\
graph[Q \mid R] &= graph[Q] \mid graph[R] \\
graph[(x)Q] &= (x) graph[Q] \\
graph[!\, Q] &= \mathsf{box}[graph[Q]]
\end{aligned}$$

Conversely, the function $term[\cdot]$ takes a graph and returns the corresponding canonical agent.

Definition 15. *Let* $term[\cdot]$ *be the function from SDs to agents defined as follows.*

$$term[(\mathsf{G},\mathsf{M},\ell)] = (\widetilde{z})\Big(\prod_{e\in\mathsf{G}} term[e,\rho] \mid \prod_{B\in\mathsf{M}} term[B,\rho]\Big)$$

$$term[\langle\mathsf{G},S\rangle,\rho] = !\,\big(\rho(S)\big)\Big(\prod_{e\in\mathsf{G}} term[e,\rho]\Big)$$

$$term[\langle a,a_1,\cdots,a_k\rangle_i,\rho] = (a\,a_1\cdots a_k)\rho$$

$$term[\langle a,a_1,\cdots,a_k\rangle_o,\rho] = (\overline{a}\,a_1\cdots a_k)\rho$$

where ρ *is a bijection from* $nodes[\mathsf{G}]\cup nodes[\mathsf{M}]$ *into names that extends* ℓ, *and* $\widetilde{z} = \big(\mathrm{ran}(\rho)\setminus \mathrm{ran}(\ell)\big)\setminus \bigcup_{\langle \mathsf{G},S\rangle\in\mathsf{M}}\rho(S)$.

It is easy to check that $graph[\cdot]$ and $term[\cdot]$ are well-defined functions. Moreover, they are in a precise sense the inverses of each other.

Proposition 16. *1.* $P \equiv_r term[graph[P]]$.
2. $(\mathsf{G},\mathsf{M},\ell)$ *and* $graph[term[(\mathsf{G},\mathsf{M},\ell)]]$ *are isomorphic.*

The graphical representation of agents identifies structurally congruent terms. This is proved with suitable isomorphisms for every structural law. The converse also holds: terms mapped onto isomorphic graphs are structurally congruent.

Proposition 17. $P \equiv_r Q$ *iff* $graph[P]$ *is isomorphic to* $graph[Q]$.

The correspondence between agents and SDs also lifts to the dynamics: two agents reduce provided the corresponding SDs reduce, and *vice versa*.

Theorem 18. *If* $P \longrightarrow_r Q$ *then* $graph[P] \longrightarrow graph[Q]$; *if* $(\mathsf{G},\mathsf{M},\ell)\longrightarrow(\mathsf{G}',\mathsf{M}',\ell')$ *then* $term[(\mathsf{G},\mathsf{M},\ell)] \longrightarrow_r term[(\mathsf{G}',\mathsf{M}',\ell')]$.

Proof. By induction on the depth of the proof of $P \longrightarrow_r Q$ and by properties of the mappings $term[\cdot]$ and $graph[\cdot]$.

5 Multi-labelled Solo Diagrams

The reduction relation of SDs so far corresponds exactly to the reduction relation of the calculus of solos. In turn, this latter reduction corresponds to the internal, unobservable transition of the fusion calculus, which in the labelled transition semantics is the $\xrightarrow{\mathbf{1}}$ relation, where $\mathbf{1}$ is the identity fusion [19].

It may be interesting to extend the reduction relation to include the general fusion actions of the labelled transition semantics, noted $\xrightarrow{\varphi}$, where φ is an equivalence relation on names such as $\{\widetilde{x}=\widetilde{y}\}$. Ignoring replication, the rules for fusion actions in the calculus of solos are defined in Figure 10, which relaxes the side conditions of the previous rules (Figure 4). We define $\varphi\backslash z$ to mean

$$\left(\overline{u}\widetilde{x} \mid u\widetilde{y} \mid P\right) \xrightarrow{\{\widetilde{x}=\widetilde{y}\}} P \qquad \frac{P \xrightarrow{\varphi} P'}{P \mid Q \xrightarrow{\varphi} P' \mid Q}$$

$$\frac{P \xrightarrow{\varphi} P',\ x \notin \mathrm{n}(\varphi)}{(x)P \xrightarrow{\varphi} (x)P'} \qquad \frac{P \xrightarrow{\varphi} P',\ z\,\varphi\,x,\ z \neq x}{(x)P \xrightarrow{\varphi \backslash x} P'\{z/x\}} \qquad \frac{P \equiv Q \quad Q \xrightarrow{\varphi} Q' \quad Q' \equiv P'}{P \xrightarrow{\varphi} P'}$$

Side condition in the first rule: $|\widetilde{x}| = |\widetilde{y}|$

Fig. 10. Fusion rules for the calculus of solos.

$\varphi \cap (\mathcal{N} - \{z\})^2 \cup \{(z,z)\}$, i.e., the equivalence relation φ with all references to z removed (except for the identity). For example, $\{x = z, z = y\}\backslash z = \{x = y\}$, and $\{x = y\}\backslash y = \mathbf{1}$. We write $n(\varphi)$ for the names in non-singular equivalence classes of φ.

The corresponding SDs are defined by changing the labelling function to be a total function $\mathcal{U} \to \mathcal{P}_f(\mathcal{N})$, where $\mathcal{P}_f(\mathcal{N})$ is the set of finite subsets of $\mathcal{N}$. Where ℓ previously was undefined, it now returns $\emptyset$; where it returned a single name, it now returns a singleton.

Definition 19. *A (basic)* Multi-labelled solo diagram, *in brief MSD, is a pair* (G, ℓ), *where* G *is a finite multiset of edges, and* ℓ, *the* labelling function, *is a function from* nodes$[\mathsf{G}]$ *to* $\mathcal{P}_f(\mathcal{N})$ *such that, for every* $a, a' \in dom(\ell)$, $a \neq a'$ *implies* $\ell(a) \cap \ell(a') = \emptyset$.

In MSDs, the labelling function has the constraint that sets in the range have empty intersection. Intuitively, these sets represent names that have been fused, and the condition guarantees that the same name cannot occur in different sets. This is a generalization of Definition 11 where the same name cannot mark two different nodes. It may thus be easier to think of a mapping from names to nodes: for each name the node (if any) is uniquely defined. This is true in SDs as well as MSDs; the extension to MSD means this mapping is not necessarily injective since different names can label the same node.

Definition 20. *The reduction relation* $\longrightarrow$ *of MSDs is defined by the following rule schema:*

- *edge-edge reduction:* $(\mathsf{G} \uplus \{\langle a, a_1, \cdots, a_k\rangle_o, \langle a, a'_1, \cdots, a'_k\rangle_i\}, \ell) \longrightarrow (\mathsf{G}\sigma, \ell')$ *where* σ *agrees with* $\{a_i = a'_i : 1 \leq i \leq k\}$, $ran(\sigma) \cap dom(\sigma) = \emptyset$ *and* $\forall a : \ell'(a) = \bigcup_{\sigma(a')=a} \ell(a')$

As an example of MSD reduction, in Figure 11 we illustrate the dynamics of an agent that is irreducible with the semantics of section 3.

As the reader may suspect, MSDs are strongly related to agents. Given an equivalence relation on names (representing the fusions that have occurred so far), we can define a mapping from agents to MSDs, and given the equivalence relation induced by ℓ, we can define a mapping from MSDs to agents. This relationship lifts to the dynamics: every reduction in MSD corresponds to a fusion action in the calculus of solos with the semantics of Figure 10, and *vice versa*. Finally, basic MSDs can be extended with boxes, in the style of section 3.

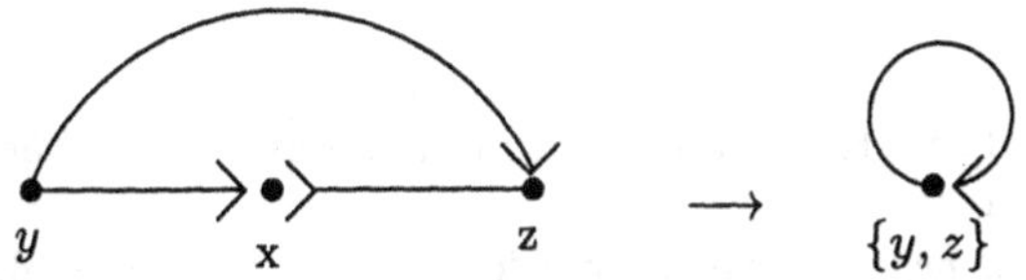

Fig. 11. The transition $(\overline{x}\,y \mid x\,z \mid \overline{z}\,y) \xrightarrow{\{y=z\}} \overline{z}\,y$.

6 Related Work

The direct ancestor of our solo diagrams are Parrow's Interaction Diagrams [17], which were presented as a graphical form of the π-calculus. Interaction Diagrams are more complex, due to the asymmetries of π-calculus. Three types of nodes are used, corresponding to parameters, input bound names, and other names, respectively. To encode input prefixing, Parrow uses a method similar to that of [10], increasing the polyadicity to express causal dependency. Parrow's replication box is considered as a regeneration mechanism that can generate an unbounded number of copies of itself. In this respect, it is a straight implementation of the law $!P \equiv P \mid !P$.

π-nets [14] were introduced by Milner as a graphical form of the action calculus PIC, where the π-calculus can be encoded. π-nets are also very similar to our solo diagrams, except for the treatment of boxes/replication, where an additional *link* arrow is introduced, and for prefixing, which uses a box inhibiting reductions inside the box until its box arc (representing the guard) has been consumed.

In retrospect it is interesting to see that the purely graphical parts of both Interaction Diagrams and π-nets have all the power of our solo diagrams, but Parrow and Milner, respectively, constrain how they may be constructed and thereby avoid constructing the solo diagrams and possibly the calculus of solos.

In [5], Fu investigated the communication mechanism of mobile calculi in terms of cut-elimination in multiplicative proof nets, and inspired by Interaction Diagrams introduced *reaction graphs* to this end. (This investigation led to the χ-calculus [4].) Reaction graphs have some elements in common with solo diagrams, e.g. symmetry of input and output edges. Only a limited form of guarded replication box is handled: no labelled nodes are allowed inside, neither reaction between boxes, nor nested boxes are treated. Fu only uses monadic edges, and thus cannot encode prefixing without these guarded boxes.

Bellin and Scott also give a detailed interpretation of proofs in terms of π-calculus processes [1]. Overall, their interpretations use prefixes. As a consequence, reductions that do not occur at the bottom of the proofs are not mirrored.

Yoshida in [22] discusses the relationship between processes and a general framework for proof nets, the so-called Interaction Nets [9]. The analogy mostly concerns the modes of connecting edges in the two systems (by using polarities and principal/auxiliary ports) and of defining interactions (as connections between principal ports). A behavioural analysis is missing.

References

[1] G. Bellin and P. Scott. On the π-calculus and linear logic. *Theoretical Computer Science*, 135:11–65, 1994.

[2] G. Boudol. Asynchrony and the π-calculus (note). Rapport de Recherche 1702, INRIA Sophia-Antipolis, May 1992.

[3] C. Fournet and G. Gonthier. The reflexive chemical abstract machine and the join-calculus. In *Proc. of POPL '96*, pages 372–385. ACM, Jan. 1996.

[4] Y. Fu. A proof-theoretical approach to communication. In P. Degano, R. Gorrieri, and A. Marchetti-Spaccamela, editors, *Proc. of ICALP '97*, volume 1256 of *LNCS*, pages 325–335. Springer, 1997.

[5] Y. Fu. Reaction graph. *Journal of Computer Science and Technology, Science Press, China*, 13(6):510–530, 1998.

[6] J.-Y. Girard. Linear logic. *Theoretical Computer Science*, 50, 1987.

[7] G. Gonthier, M. Abadi, and J.-J. Lévy. The geometry of optimal lambda reduction. In *Proc. of POPL '92*, pages 15–26. ACM Press, 1992.

[8] K. Honda and M. Tokoro. An object calculus for asynchronous communication. In P. America, editor, *Proc. of ECOOP '91*, volume 512 of *LNCS*, pages 133–147. Springer, July 1991.

[9] Y. Lafont. Interaction nets. In *Proc. of POPL '90*, pages 95–108. ACM Press, 1990.

[10] C. Laneve and B. Victor. Solos in concert. In J. Wiederman, P. van Emde Boas, and M. Nielsen, editors, *Proc. of ICALP '99*, volume 1644 of *LNCS*, pages 513–523. Springer, July 1999.

[11] C. Laneve and B. Victor. Solos in concert. Full version of [10], submitted for journal publication, February 2001.

[12] R. Milner. Functions as processes. *Journal of Mathematical Structures in Computer Science*, 2(2):119–141, 1992.

[13] R. Milner. The polyadic π-calculus: A tutorial. In F. L. Bauer, W. Brauer, and H. Schwichtenberg, editors, *Logic and Algebra of Specification*, volume 94 of *Series F*. NATO ASI, Springer, 1993.

[14] R. Milner. Pi-nets: A graphical form of π-calculus. In D. Sannella, editor, *Proc. of ESOP '94*, volume 788 of *LNCS*, pages 26–42. Springer, 1994.

[15] R. Milner, J. Parrow, and D. Walker. A calculus of mobile processes, part I/II. *Information and Computation*, 100:1–77, Sept. 1992.

[16] R. Milner and D. Sangiorgi. Barbed bisimulation. In W. Kuich, editor, *Proc. of ICALP '92*, volume 623 of *LNCS*, pages 685–695. Springer, 1992.

[17] J. Parrow. Interaction diagrams. *Nordic Journal of Computing*, 2:407–443, 1995.

[18] J. Parrow. Trios in concert. In G. Plotkin, C. Stirling, and M. Tofte, editors, *Proof, Language and Interaction: Essays in Honour of Robin Milner*, Foundations of Computing. MIT Press, May 2000.

[19] J. Parrow and B. Victor. The fusion calculus: Expressiveness and symmetry in mobile processes. In *Proc. of LICS '98*, pages 176–185. IEEE, Computer Society Press, July 1998.

[20] B. C. Pierce and D. N. Turner. Pict: A programming language based on the pi-calculus. In G. Plotkin, C. Stirling, and M. Tofte, editors, *Proof, Language and Interaction: Essays in Honour of Robin Milner*, Foundations of Computing. MIT Press, May 2000.

[21] D. Sangiorgi. On the bisimulation proof method. *Mathematical Structures in Computer Science*, 8(5):447–479, 1998.

[22] N. Yoshida. Graph notation for concurrent combinators. In T. Ito and A. Yonezawa, editors, *Proc. of TPPP '94*, volume 907 of *LNCS*, pages 393–412. Springer, 1995.

Observational Equivalence for Synchronized Graph Rewriting with Mobility*

Barbara König and Ugo Montanari

Dipartimento di Informatica, Università di Pisa, Italia
{koenigb,ugo}@di.unipi.it

Abstract. We introduce a notion of bisimulation for graph rewriting systems, allowing us to prove observational equivalence for dynamically evolving graphs and networks.
We use the framework of synchronized graph rewriting with mobility which we describe in two different, but operationally equivalent ways: on graphs defined as syntactic judgements and by using tile logic. One of the main results of the paper says that bisimilarity for synchronized graph rewriting is a congruence whenever the rewriting rules satisfy the basic source property. Furthermore we introduce an up-to technique simplifying bisimilarity proofs and use it in an example to show the equivalence of a communication network and its specification.

1 Introduction

Graph rewriting can be seen as a general framework in which to specify and reason about concurrent and distributed systems [8]. The topology and connection structure of these systems can often be naturally represented in terms of nodes and connecting edges, and their dynamic evolution can be expressed by graph rewriting rules. We are specifically interested in hypergraphs where an arbitrarily long sequence of nodes—instead of a pair of nodes—is assigned to every edge.

However, the theory of graph rewriting [24] lacks a concept of observational equivalence, relating graphs which behave the same in all possible context, which is quite surprising, since observational equivalences, such as bisimilarity or trace equivalence, are a standard tool in the theory of process calculi.

We are therefore looking for a semantics for (hyper-)graph rewriting systems that abstracts from the topology of a graph, and regards graphs as processes which are determined by their interaction with the environment, rather than by their internal structure. It is important for the observational equivalence to be a congruence, since this will enable compositional proofs of equivalence and assure substitutivity, i.e. that equivalent subcomponents of a system are exchangeable.

The applications we have in mind are the verification of evolving networks, consisting, e.g., of processes, messages and other components. A possible scenario

* Research partly supported by TMR Network GETGRATS, by Esprit WG APPLIGRAPH and by MURST project TOSCA.

N. Kobayashi and B.C. Pierce (Eds.): TACS 2001, LNCS 2215, pp. 145–164, 2001.

would be a user who has limited access to a dynamically changing network. We want to show that the network is transparent with respect to the location of resources, failure of components, etc. by showing that it is equivalent to a simpler specification. Such an equivalence of networks is treated in the example in Section 7.

One possible (and well-studied) candidate for an observational equivalence is bisimilarity. So the central aim of this paper is to introduce bisimilarity for graph rewriting—we will explain below why it is convenient to base this equivalence on the model of synchronized graph rewriting, as opposed to other models—and to introduce an up-to proof technique, simplifying actual proofs of bisimilarity.

When defining bisimulation and bisimilarity for graph rewriting systems, two possibilities come to mind: the first would be to use unlabelled context-sensitive rewrite rules as, for example, in the double-pushout approach [7]. The definition of an observational congruence in this context, however, ordinarily requires universal quantification over all possible contexts of an expression, which is difficult to handle in practice. This makes us choose the second possibility, which is closer to process algebras: we use synchronized graph rewriting, which allows only context-free rewrite rules whose expressive power is increased considerably by adding synchronization and mobility (i.e. communication of nodes), thus including a large class of rewriting systems. In this case we can define a simple syntactic condition (the basic source property) on the rewrite rules ensuring that bisimilarity is a congruence (compare with the de Simone format [5] and the `tyft/tyxt`-format [12]).

As synchronization mechanism we choose Hoare synchronization which means that all edges that synchronize via a specific node produce the same synchronization action. This is different from Milner synchronization (as in CCS [19]) where two synchronizing processes produce two different signals: an action a and a coaction $\bar{a}$.

We prefer Hoare synchronization since it makes it easier to handle the kind of multiple synchronization we have in mind: several edges connected to each other on a node must agree on an action a, which means that there is no clear distinction between action and coaction. This, in turn, causes other nodes connected to the same edges to perform a different action, and in this way synchronization is propagated by edges and spreads throughout an entire connected component. It is conceivable to implement different synchronization mechanisms as processes working as "connectors", thus modeling in this way a variety of coordination mechanisms.

Edges synchronizing with respect to an action a may, at the same time, agree to create new nodes which are then shared among the right-hand sides of the respective rewrite rules. (This form of mobility was first presented in [13] and is also extensively treated in [14].) From the outside it is not possible to determine whether newly created nodes are different or equal, it is only possible to observe the actions performed.

Apart from the obvious representation of graphs in terms of nodes and edges, there are several other approaches representing graphs by terms, which allow for a more compositional presentation of graphs and enable us, for example, to do induction on the graph structure. We will introduce two of these term representations: first graphs as syntactic judgements, where nodes are represented by names and we have operators such as parallel composition and name hiding at our disposal. This representation allows for a straightforward definition of graph rewriting with synchronization and mobility.

The second representation defines graphs in terms of arrows of a P-monoidal category [3]. This allows for an easy presentation of graph rewriting in tile logic, a rewriting framework which deals with the rewriting of open terms that can still be contextualized and instantiated and allows for different ways of composing partial rewrites. To show the compositionality of our semantics, we use a property of tile logic, i.e. the fact that if a tile system satisfies a so-called decomposition property, then bisimilarity defined on top of this tile system is a congruence (see also [1]).

Apart from the fact that we use tile logic as a tool to obtain the congruence result, we also show how mobility, and specifically the form of mobility used in synchronized graph rewriting, can be handled in the context of tile logic.

2 Synchronized Graph Rewriting with Mobility

We start by introducing a representation of (hyper-)graphs as syntactic judgements, where nodes in general correspond to names, external nodes to free names and (hyper-)edges to terms of the form $s(x_1, \ldots, x_n)$ where the x_i are arbitrary names.

Definition 1 (Graphs as Syntactic Judgements). *Let N be a fixed infinite set of names. A* syntactic judgement *is of the form $\Gamma \vdash G$ where $\Gamma \subseteq N$ is a set of names (the interface of the graph) and G is generated by the grammar*

$$G ::= nil \text{ (empty graph) } \mid G|G \text{ (parallel composition) } \mid$$
$$(\nu x)G \text{ (node hiding) } \mid s(x_1, \ldots, x_n) \text{ (edge)}$$

where $x \in N$ and $s(x_1, \ldots, x_n)$ with arbitrary $x_i \in N$ is called an edge of arity n labelled s. (Every label is associated with a fixed arity.)

Let $fn(G)$ denote the set of all free names of G, i.e. all names not bound by a ν-operator. We demand that $fn(G) \subseteq \Gamma$.

We assume that whenever we write Γ, x, then x is not an element of Γ.

We need to define a structural congruence on syntactic judgements in order to identify those terms that represent isomorphic graphs (up to isolated nodes) (see [15,16]).

Definition 2 (Structural Congruence). *Structural congruence $\equiv$ on syntactic judgements obeys the rules below and is closed under parallel composition $|$ and the hiding operator ν. (We abbreviate equations of the form $\Gamma \vdash G \equiv \Gamma \vdash G'$ by $G \equiv G'$.)*

$$\Gamma \vdash G \equiv \rho(\Gamma) \vdash \rho(G) \text{ where } \rho \text{ is an injective substitution}$$

$$(G_1|G_2)|G_3 \equiv G_1|(G_2|G_3) \qquad G_1|G_2 \equiv G_2|G_1 \qquad G|nil \equiv G$$

$$(\nu x)(\nu y)G \equiv (\nu y)(\nu x)G \qquad (\nu x)nil \equiv nil \qquad (\nu x)G \equiv (\nu y)G\{y/x\} \text{ if } y \notin fn(G)$$

$$(\nu x)(G|G') \equiv (\nu x)G|G' \text{ if } x \notin fn(G')$$

We sometimes abbreviate $(\nu x_1)\ldots(\nu x_n)G$ by $(\nu\{x_1,\ldots,x_n\})G$.

Example 1. We regard the syntactic judgement $y \vdash (\nu x)(\nu z)(P(x) \mid S(x,y,z) \mid P(z))$ which consists of two processes P which are connected to each other and the only external node y via a switch S. A graphical representation of this syntactic judgement can be found in Figure 2 (graph in the lower left corner).

In order to define rewriting on syntactic judgements we introduce the notion of rewriting rule. We use a set *Act* of arbitrary actions, which can be thought of as the set of signals which are allowed in a network.

Definition 3 (Rewriting Rules). *Let Act be a set of actions, containing also the idle action ε. Each action $a \in Act$ is associated with an arity $ar(a) \in \mathbb{N}$, the arity of ε is 0. (The arity indicates the number of nodes created by an action.)*

A rewriting rule is of the form

$$x_1,\ldots,x_n \vdash s(x_1,\ldots,x_n) \xrightarrow{\Lambda} x_1,\ldots,x_n,\Gamma_\Lambda \vdash G$$

where all x_i are distinct, $\Lambda \subseteq \{x_1,\ldots,x_n\} \times Act\backslash\{\varepsilon\} \times N^*$ such that Λ is a total function in its first argument, i.e. if $(x_i,a_i,\tilde{y}_i) \in \Lambda$ we write $\Lambda(x_i) = (a_i,\tilde{y}_i)$, respectively $act_\Lambda(x_i) = a_i$ and $n_\Lambda(x_i) = \tilde{y}_i$, and we demand that $ar(a_i) = |\tilde{y}_i|$.

Furthermore[1] $\Gamma_\Lambda = \bigcup_{x_i \in \Lambda} Set(n_\Lambda(x_i))$ *and we demand that* $\{x_1,\ldots,x_n\} \cap \Gamma_\Lambda = \emptyset$.

A rewriting rule of the form given above indicates that an edge $s(x_1,\ldots,x_n)$ is rewritten, synchronizing on each node x_i with an action a_i, and during this synchronization a string $\tilde{y}_i$ of new nodes is created. The set Γ_Λ contains all new nodes in the interface which are created by the rewriting step.

The following example will be used as a running example throughout the paper.

Example 2. We describe a network of processes P of arity 1 and processes Q of arity 2 connected to each other via switches S of arity 3.

We use three kinds of actions, apart from the idle action ε: τ and a (both of arity 0) and s (of arity 1) which is the action used for establishing a shared name. A process of our example network can perform the following rewriting steps:[2] P can either send a signal a, or it can extend the network by transforming itself into a switch with two processes connected to it, or it can perform an s action and fork a process Q whose second node is connected to a newly created, privately

[1] For any string $\tilde{s}$, we denote the set of its elements by $Set(\tilde{s})$.

[2] The empty sequence is denoted by $\langle\rangle$.

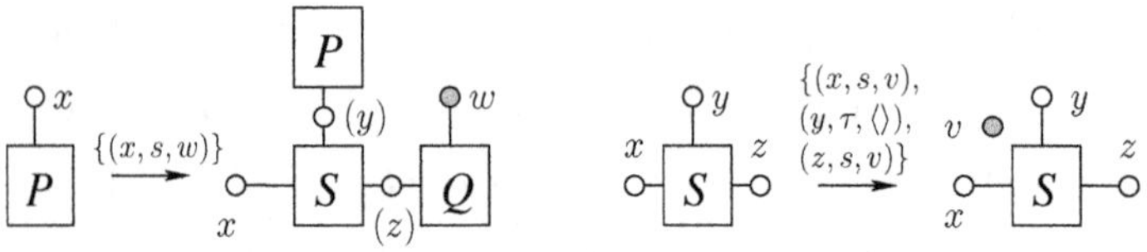

Fig. 1. Graphical representation of example rules

shared channel. The action τ is different from the idle action and is used in this example to represent internal activity.

$$x \vdash P(x) \xrightarrow{\{(x,a,\langle\rangle)\}} x \vdash P(x)$$
$$y \vdash P(y) \xrightarrow{\{(y,\tau,\langle\rangle)\}} y \vdash (\nu x)(\nu z)(P(x) \mid S(x,y,z) \mid P(z))$$
$$x \vdash P(x) \xrightarrow{\{(x,s,w)\}} x, w \vdash (\nu y)(\nu z)(S(x,y,z) \mid P(y) \mid Q(z,w)).$$

The process Q, on the other hand, can perform any combination of a and τ actions.

$$x, y \vdash Q(x,y) \xrightarrow{\{(x,a_1,\langle\rangle),(y,a_2,\langle\rangle)\}} x, y \vdash Q(x,y) \quad \text{where } a_1, a_2 \in \{a, \tau\}.$$

Switches have the task to route the signals and actions originating at the processes and in the case of an s action a new node v is created. In both rules we require that $\{x, y, z\} = \{x_1, x_2, x_3\}$:

$$x, y, z \vdash S(x,y,z) \xrightarrow{\{(x_1,a,\langle\rangle),(x_2,a,\langle\rangle),(x_3,\tau,\langle\rangle)\}} x, y, z \vdash S(x,y,z)$$
$$x, y, z \vdash S(x,y,z) \xrightarrow{\{(x_1,s,v),(x_2,s,v),(x_3,\tau,\langle\rangle)\}} x, y, z, v \vdash S(x,y,z)$$

A graphical representation of the third rule for P and the second rule for S (with $x_1 = x, x_2 = z, x_3 = y$) is depicted in Figure 1, where the bound names are indicated by their enclosure in round brackets.

In order to be able to define inference rules which describe how to derive more complex transitions from the basic rules, we first introduce the following notion of a most general unifier which transforms a relation Λ, which does not necessarily satisfy the conditions of definition 3, into a function.

Definition 4 (Most General Unifier). *Let $\sigma : N \to N$ be a name substitution. If $\Lambda = \{(x_i, a_i, \tilde{y}_i) \mid i \in \{1,\ldots,n\}\}$, then $\sigma(\Lambda) = \{(\sigma(x_i), a_i, \sigma^*(\tilde{y}_i)) \mid i \in \{1,\ldots,n\}\}$ where σ^* is the extension of σ to strings.*

For any $\Lambda = \{(x_i, a_i, \tilde{y}_i) \mid i \in \{1,\ldots,n\}\} \subseteq N \times Act \times N^*$ we call a substitution $\rho : N \to N$ a unifier *of Λ whenever $\rho(x_i) = x_i$ for $i \in \{1,\ldots,n\}$ and $x_i = x_j$ implies $a_i = a_j$ and $\rho^*(\tilde{y}_i) = \rho^*(\tilde{y}_j)$.*

The mapping ρ is called a most general unifier *whenever it is a unifier with a minimal degree of non-injectivity. Unifiers do not necessarily exist.*

Example 3. The substitution $\rho = \{u/v, u/r, u/s, u/w, u/t\}$ is a unifier for $\Lambda = \{(x, a, uuvw), (x, a, rsst)\}$ since $\rho(\Lambda) = \{(x, a, uuuu)\}$. A most general unifier is, for example, $\rho' = \{u/v, u/r, u/s, w/t\}$ where $\rho'(\Lambda) = \{(x, a, uuuw)\}$.

The set $\Lambda = \{(x, a, u), (x, b, v)\}$, where $a \neq b$, does not have a unifier.

Most general unifiers are needed in order to make sure that whenever two nodes are merged, the strings of nodes created by synchronizing on them, are also merged. Regard, for example, the rewriting rules

$$x \vdash s(x) \overset{\Lambda_1 = \{(x,a,y)\}}{\longrightarrow} x, y \vdash s'(x, y) \text{ and } x \vdash t(x) \overset{\Lambda_2 = \{(x,a,z)\}}{\longrightarrow} x, z \vdash t'(x, z).$$

Then—since the edges s and t should agree on a common new name—we expect that

$$x \vdash s(x) \mid t(x) \overset{\Lambda = \{(x,a,y)\}}{\longrightarrow} x, y \vdash s'(x, y) \mid t'(x, y)$$

where Λ can be obtained by applying the most general unifier to $\Lambda_1 \cup \Lambda_2$.

We introduce the following inference rules for transitions, which are similar to the rules given in [13,14].

Definition 5 (Inference Rules for Transitions). *All possible transitions $\Gamma \vdash G \overset{\Lambda}{\longrightarrow} \Gamma' \vdash G'$ between graphs are generated by a set R of rewriting rules and the inference rules given below and are closed under injective renaming of all names occurring in a transition.*

$$\textit{(ren)} \quad \frac{\Gamma \vdash G \overset{\Lambda}{\longrightarrow} \Gamma, \Gamma_\Lambda \vdash G'}{\rho(\Gamma) \vdash \rho(G) \overset{\rho'(\rho(\Lambda))}{\longrightarrow} \rho(\Gamma), \Gamma_{\rho'(\rho(\Lambda))} \vdash \rho'(\rho(G'))}$$

where $\rho : \Gamma \to \Gamma$ and ρ' is the most general unifier for $\rho(\Lambda)$.

$$\textit{(par)} \quad \frac{\Gamma \vdash G_1 \overset{\Lambda_1}{\longrightarrow} \Gamma, \Gamma_{\Lambda_1} \vdash G_1' \quad \Gamma \vdash G_2 \overset{\Lambda_2}{\longrightarrow} \Gamma, \Gamma_{\Lambda_2} \vdash G_2'}{\Gamma \vdash G_1 | G_2 \overset{\rho(\Lambda_1 \cup \Lambda_2)}{\longrightarrow} \Gamma, \Gamma_{\rho(\Lambda_1 \cup \Lambda_2)} \vdash \rho(G_1' | G_2')}$$

if $\Gamma_{\Lambda_1} \cap \Gamma_{\Lambda_2} = \emptyset$ and ρ is the most general unifier for $\Lambda_1 \cup \Lambda_2$.

$$\textit{(hide)} \quad \frac{\Gamma, x \vdash G \overset{\Lambda \uplus \{(x,a,\tilde{y})\}}{\longrightarrow} \Gamma, x, \Gamma_\Lambda, Y \vdash G'}{\Gamma \vdash (\nu x) G \overset{\Lambda}{\longrightarrow} \Gamma, \Gamma_\Lambda \vdash (\nu x)(\nu Y) G'} \quad \text{where } Y = Set(\tilde{y}) \backslash \Gamma_\Lambda.$$

$$\textit{(idle)} \quad \Gamma \vdash G \overset{\Lambda}{\longrightarrow} \Gamma \vdash G \quad \text{where}^3\ \Lambda(x) = (\varepsilon, \langle\rangle) \text{ for } x \in \Gamma.$$

$$\textit{(new)} \quad \frac{\Gamma \vdash G \overset{\Lambda}{\longrightarrow} \Gamma, \Gamma_\Lambda \vdash G'}{\Gamma, x \vdash G \overset{\Lambda \uplus \{(x,a,\tilde{y})\}}{\longrightarrow} \Gamma, x, \Gamma_\Lambda, \tilde{y} \vdash G'}$$

We also write $R \Vdash (\Gamma \vdash G \overset{\Lambda}{\longrightarrow} \Gamma' \vdash G')$ whenever this transition can be derived from a set R of rewriting rules.

In every transition Λ assigns to each free name the action it performs and the string of new nodes it creates. Rule *(ren)* deals with non-injective renaming

[3] The empty sequence is denoted by $\langle\rangle$.

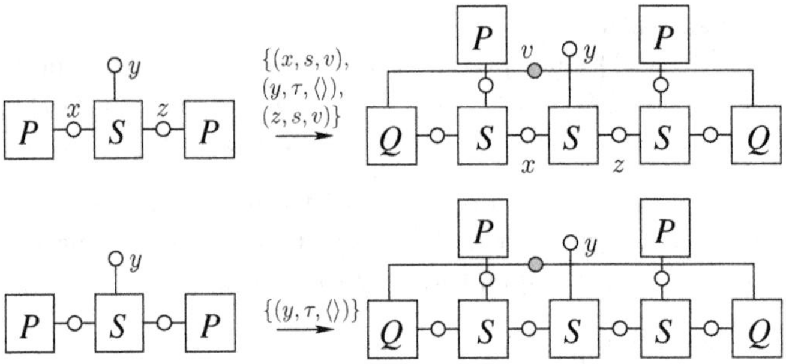

Fig. 2. Processes establishing a privately shared channel

of the nodes of a graph, which is necessary in order to handle edges of the form $s(\ldots, x, \ldots, x, \ldots)$, i.e. edges which are connected several times to the same node. Parallel composition of syntactic judgements is treated in rule *(par)* which makes sure that whenever a synchronization on a node creates a string $\tilde{y}_1$ in the rewriting of $\Gamma \vdash G_1$ and the synchronization on the same node creates a string $\tilde{y}_2$ in the rewriting of $\Gamma \vdash G_2$, then both strings are identified by ρ. In rule *(hide)*, which deals with hiding of names, we do not only have to hide the name itself, but all the names which have been created exclusively by interaction on this name, i.e. all names in the set Y. Furthermore every syntactic judgement can always make an explicit idle step by performing action ε on all its external nodes (rule *(idle)*) and we can add an additional name to the interface which performs arbitrary actions (rule *(new)*). This is due to Hoare synchronization which requires that any number of edges, and therefore also zero edges, can synchronize on a given node.

Example 4. One of the most interesting rewriting steps which can be derived from the rules of example 2 is the forking of two processes Q at the same time and the establishment of a privately shared channel between them. We intend to reduce the syntactic judgement $y \vdash (\nu x)(\nu z)(P(x) \mid S(x, y, z) \mid P(z))$ from example 1. The task of the switch S is to route the signal s on which both processes synchronize, and also to propagate the newly created name.

We first derive a transition for $x, y, z \vdash P(x) \mid S(x, y, z) \mid P(z)$ which is depicted in the upper half of Figure 2 and which can be obtained by composing the rewriting rules given in Figure 1 where the concept of the most general unifier forces $v = w$. Then in the next step we hide both names x and z which causes all names produced by interaction on x or z to be hidden as well, which means that v is removed from the interface (see the lower half of Figure 2).

We can also observe that when a process P creates a new node which is communicated to the environment, a form of name extrusion as in the π-calculus [21] is performed. In the extrusion rule of the labelled transition semantics of the π-calculus, a private, but extruded, name may also appear free in the right-hand side of the rule.

3 Representation of Graphs in a P-Monoidal Category

In order to be able to describe graph rewriting in tile logic, we will now describe a second possibility of graph representation, which abstracts from names, i.e. nodes are not addressed via their name, but via their position in the interface. In this way we identify all graphs which can be seen as isomorphic, i.e. which are equal up to the laws of structural congruence given in Definition 2.

We will introduce new operators, such as the duplicator ∇ and the coduplicator Δ (splitting respectively merging nodes), the permutation ρ, the discharger ! and the codischarger ? (hiding respectively creating nodes), which will be defined below (see also Figure 3). For the representation of rewriting steps as tiles, it is convenient to be able to describe these unary operators as graphs as well. In order to achieve this, we introduce an interface consisting of two sequences of nodes: root and variable nodes. Additionally we have two binary operators: composition ; and a monoidal operation $\otimes$.

We will now describe graphs as arrows of a P-monoidal (or Part-monoidal) category [3], which can be obtained from dgs-monoidal categories [10] by adding an axiom.

P-monoidal categories are an extension of gs-monoidal categories. These describe term graphs, i.e. terms minus copying and garbage collection. Intuitively P-monoidal categories do not only contain term graphs, but also term graphs turned "upside down" and all possible combinations of these graphs.

We first give a formal definition in terms of category theory and then informally describe the meaning of the constants and operations in our setting.

Definition 6 (P-monoidal category). *A* gs-monoidal category $\mathbf{G}$ *is a six-tuple* $(\mathbf{C}, \otimes, e, \rho, \nabla, !)$ *where* $(\mathbf{C}, \otimes, e, \rho)$ *is a symmetric strict monoidal category and* $! : Id \Rightarrow e : \mathbf{C} \to \mathbf{C}$, $\nabla : Id \Rightarrow \otimes \circ D : \mathbf{C} \to \mathbf{C}$ *are two transformations (D is the diagonal functor), such that* $!_e = \nabla_e = id_e$ *and the following* coherence axioms

$$\nabla_a; id_a \otimes \nabla_a = \nabla_a; \nabla_a \otimes id_a \qquad \nabla_a; id_a \otimes !_a = id_a \qquad \nabla_a; \rho_{a,a} = \nabla_a$$

and the monoidality axioms

$$\nabla_{a \otimes b}; id_a \otimes \rho_{b,a} \otimes id_b = \nabla_a \otimes \nabla_b \qquad !_a \otimes !_b = !_{a \otimes b}$$

are satisfied.

A P-monoidal category $\mathbf{D}$ *is an eight-tuple* $(\mathbf{C}, \otimes, e, \rho, \nabla, !, \Delta, ?)$ *such that both the six-tuples* $(\mathbf{C}, \otimes, e, \rho, \nabla, !)$ *and* $(\mathbf{C}^{op}, \otimes, e, \rho, \Delta, ?)$ *are gs-monoidal categories (where* $\mathbf{C}^{op}$ *is the dual category of* $\mathbf{C}$*) and satisfy*

$$\Delta_a; \nabla_a = id_a \otimes \nabla_a; \Delta_a \otimes id_a \qquad \nabla_a; \Delta_a = id_a \qquad ?_a; !_a = id_e$$

In order to model graphs we use a P-monoidal category where the objects are of the form $\underline{n}$, $n \in \mathbb{N}$, $e = \underline{0}$ *and* $\underline{n} \otimes \underline{m}$ *is defined as* $\underline{n+m}$. *If* Σ *is a set of symbols each associated with a sort* $\underline{n} \to \underline{0}$, *then* $\mathbf{PMon}(\Sigma)$ *is the P-monoidal category freely generated from the symbols in* Σ *which are interpreted as arrows.*

$id_{\underline{1}}$	$\rho_{\underline{1},\underline{1}}$	$\nabla_{\underline{1}}$	$\Delta_{\underline{1}}$	$!_{\underline{1}}$	$?_{\underline{1}}$	edge $s : \underline{n} \to \underline{0}$
1 ○ [1]	1 2 ○ ○ [2] [1]	1 ○ [1] [2]	1 2 ○ [1]	1 ○	○ [1]	1○ ⋯ ○n $\boxed{s}$

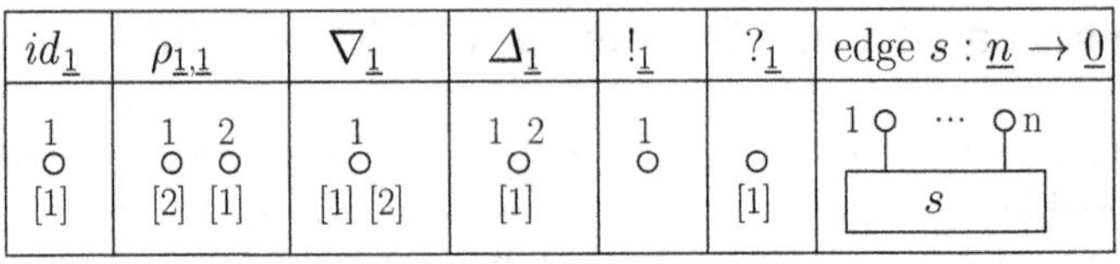

Fig. 3. P-monoidal operators

In order to save brackets we adopt the convention that the monoidal operation $\otimes$ takes precedence over ; (the composition operator of the category). Note that by omitting the last axiom $?_a; !_a = id_e$ we obtain exactly the definition of a dgs-monoidal category.

We depict an arrow $t : \underline{n} \to \underline{m}$ of $\mathbf{PMon}(\Sigma)$ by drawing a hypergraph with two sequences of external nodes: n root nodes and m variable nodes (see Figure 3). Root nodes are indicated by labels $1, 2, \ldots$, variable nodes by labels $[1], [2], \ldots$ The composition operator ; merges the variable nodes of its first argument with the root nodes of its second argument. The tensor product $\otimes$ takes the disjoint union of two graphs and concatenates the sequences of root respectively variable nodes of its two arguments. Note that the axiom $?_a; !_a = id_e$ has the intuitive meaning that isolated nodes are garbage-collected.

Similar to the case of syntactic judgements it can be shown that two terms of $\mathbf{PMon}(\Sigma)$ are equal if and only if the underlying hypergraphs are isomorphic (up to isolated nodes) [3].

There is a one-to-one correspondence between P-monoidal terms $w : \underline{m} \to \underline{n} \in \mathbf{PMon}(\emptyset)$ (corresponding to the set of all discrete graphs) and equivalence relations on the union of $\{r\} \times \{1, \ldots, m\}$ and $\{v\} \times \{1, \ldots, n\}$. We say that $(r, i) \equiv_w (r, j)$ whenever the i-th and the j-th root node of w are equal, additionally $(r, i) \equiv_w (v, j)$ whenever the i-th root node and the j-th variable node are equal and $(v, i) \equiv_w (v, j)$ whenever the i-th and the j-th variable node are equal. An equivalence relation on a set can also be seen as a partition of this set, which is the origin of the name P(art)-monoidal category.

Syntactic judgements can be encoded into P-monoidal terms. We introduce a mapping α assigning to each name its position in the sequence of external nodes. One name may appear in several positions.

Definition 7 (Encoding of Syntactic Judgements). *Let $\Gamma \vdash G$ be a syntactic judgement and let $\alpha : \{1, \ldots, n\} \to \Gamma$ be a surjective (but not necessarily injective) function, indicating which positions a name should occupy in the interface. We will also call α an n-ary interface mapping.*

Then $[\![\Gamma \vdash G]\!]_\alpha : \underline{n} \to \underline{0}$ is an arrow of $\mathbf{PMon}(\Sigma)$ where Σ contains $s : \underline{m} \to \underline{0}$ for every edge of the form $s(x_1, \ldots, x_m)$. The encoding is defined as follows:

$$[\![\Gamma \vdash G_1 | G_2]\!]_\alpha = \nabla_{\underline{n}}; [\![\Gamma \vdash G_1]\!]_\alpha \otimes [\![\Gamma \vdash G_2]\!]_\alpha$$
$$[\![\Gamma \vdash (\nu x) G]\!]_\alpha = id_{\underline{n}} \otimes ?_{\underline{1}}; [\![\Gamma, x \vdash G]\!]_{\alpha \cup \{n+1 \mapsto x\}} \text{ if } x \notin \Gamma$$
$$[\![\Gamma \vdash nil]\!]_\alpha = !_{\underline{n}}$$

$$[\![\Gamma \vdash s(x_1,\dots,x_m)]\!]_\alpha = w; s$$

where $w : \underline{n} \to \underline{m} \in$ **PMon**$(\emptyset)$ *(the "wiring") such that* $\equiv_w$ *is the smallest equivalence containing* $\{((r,i),(v,j)) \mid \alpha(i) = x_j\}$.

Note that if α is injective, all P-monoidal terms of the form $[\![\Gamma \vdash G]\!]_\alpha$ lie in a subcategory of **PMon**(Σ) which is generated by all symbols and constants apart from $\Delta_{\underline{n}}$, which means in practice that all root nodes in the interface of a graph are distinct.

Example 5. By encoding the syntactic judgement $\Gamma \vdash G = y \vdash (\nu x)(\nu z)(P(x) \mid S(x,y,z) \mid P(z))$ of Example 1 with the mapping $\alpha : \{1\} \to \{y\}$, $\alpha(1) = y$ we obtain the following P-monoidal term

$$id_{\underline{1}} \otimes ?_{\underline{1}}; id_{\underline{2}} \otimes ?_{\underline{1}}; \nabla_{\underline{3}}; (!_{\underline{1}} \otimes id_{\underline{1}} \otimes !_{\underline{1}}; P) \otimes (\nabla_{\underline{3}}; (\rho_{\underline{1},\underline{1}} \otimes id_{\underline{1}}; S) \otimes (!_{\underline{2}} \otimes id_{\underline{1}}; P)).$$

Proposition 1. *It holds that* $\Gamma \vdash G \equiv \Gamma' \vdash G'$ *if and only if there exist injective* α, α' *such that* $[\![\Gamma \vdash G]\!]_\alpha = [\![\Gamma' \vdash G']\!]_{\alpha'}$.

4 A Tile Logic Representation for Synchronized Graph Rewriting with Mobility

We now describe graph rewriting in the framework of tile logic, in which we consider rewrites of the form $s \xrightarrow[b]{a} t$ where s and t are configurations (i.e. hypergraphs) of a system and both may have root and variable nodes, their interface to the environment. The observation a describes the actions of s with respect to its root nodes, while b describes the interaction with respect to its variable nodes. The rules of tile logic describe how to derive partial rewrites and how to extend them whenever configurations are contextualized or instantiated, or—in this case—whenever two graphs are combined.

We first define the notion of a tile.

Definition 8. *Let* $\mathcal{H}$ *and* $\mathcal{V}$ *be two categories which coincide in their set of objects, which is* $\{\underline{n} \mid n \in \mathbb{N}\}$. *We call* $\mathcal{H}$ *the* horizontal category *and* $\mathcal{V}$ *the* vertical category. *The arrows of* $\mathcal{H}$ *are also called* configurations *and the arrows of* $\mathcal{V}$ *are called* observations.

A tile (compare [11]) is of the form $s \xrightarrow[b]{a} t$ *where* $s : \underline{n} \to \underline{m}, t : \underline{n'} \to \underline{m'}$ *are elements of* $\mathcal{H}$, *and* $a : \underline{n} \to \underline{n'}, b : \underline{m} \to \underline{m'}$ *are elements of* $\mathcal{V}$.

Tiles can be depicted as squares (see the leftmost square in Figure 4).

We can now define the more specific tiles of tile graph rewriting and the way in which they can be composed.

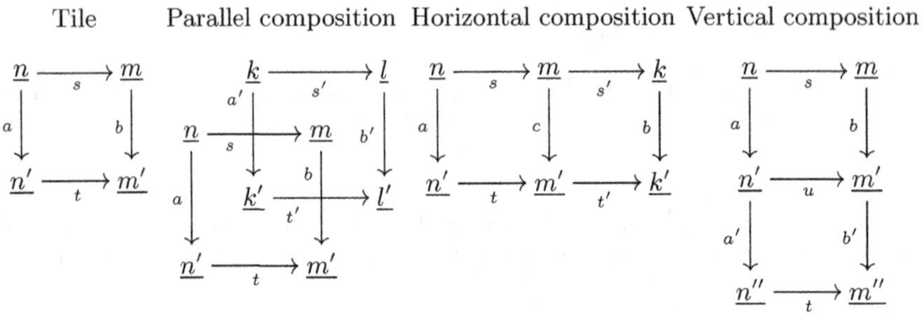

Fig. 4. Composing tiles

Definition 9 (Tile graph rewriting).

Let $\Sigma = \{s : \underline{n} \to \underline{0} \mid s$ is an edge of arity $n\}$ and let $\mathbf{PMon}(\Sigma)$ *be the horizontal category $\mathcal{H}$ whereas the vertical category $\mathcal{V}$ is the free monoidal category*[4] *generated by the arrows $a : \underline{1} \to \underline{1+n}$ for every $a \in Act\backslash\{\varepsilon\}$ with $ar(a) = n$. The idle action ε corresponds to the identity arrow $id_{\underline{1}}$.*

Tiles can be constructed in the following way: a tile is either taken from a fixed set $\mathcal{R}$ of generator tiles, *or it is a* reflexive tile *(h-refl) or (v-refl), or it is one of the auxiliary tiles (dupl), (codupl), (disch), (codisch) or (perm), or it is obtained by parallel composition (p-comp), horizontal composition (h-comp) or vertical composition (v-comp) (see also Figure 4).*

We write $\mathcal{R} \Vdash s \xrightarrow[b]{a} t$ whenever this tile can be derived from the generator tiles in $\mathcal{R}$.

$$\text{(h-refl)}\ \frac{s : \underline{n} \to \underline{m} \in \mathcal{H}}{s \xrightarrow[id_{\underline{m}}]{id_{\underline{n}}} s} \qquad \text{(v-refl)}\ \frac{a : \underline{n} \to \underline{m} \in \mathcal{V}}{id_{\underline{n}} \xrightarrow[a]{a} id_{\underline{m}}} \qquad \text{(dupl)}\ \frac{a : \underline{n} \to \underline{m} \in \mathcal{V}}{\nabla_{\underline{n}} \xrightarrow[a \otimes a]{a} \nabla_{\underline{m}}}$$

$$\text{(codupl)}\ \frac{a : \underline{n} \to \underline{m} \in \mathcal{V}}{\Delta_{\underline{n}} \xrightarrow[a]{a \otimes a} \Delta_{\underline{m}}} \qquad \text{(disch)}\ \frac{a : \underline{n} \to \underline{m} \in \mathcal{V}}{!_{\underline{n}} \xrightarrow[id_{\underline{0}}]{a} !_{\underline{m}}} \qquad \text{(codisch)}\ \frac{a : \underline{n} \to \underline{m} \in \mathcal{V}}{?_{\underline{n}} \xrightarrow[a]{id_{\underline{0}}} ?_{\underline{m}}}$$

$$\text{(perm)}\ \frac{a : \underline{n} \to \underline{m},\ b : \underline{n'} \to \underline{m'} \in \mathcal{V}}{\rho_{\underline{n},\underline{n'}} \xrightarrow[b \otimes a]{a \otimes b} \rho_{\underline{m},\underline{m'}}} \qquad \text{(p-comp)}\ \frac{s \xrightarrow[b]{a} t,\ s' \xrightarrow[b']{a'} t'}{s \otimes s' \xrightarrow[b \otimes b']{a \otimes a'} t \otimes t'}$$

$$\text{(h-comp)}\ \frac{s \xrightarrow[c]{a} t,\ s' \xrightarrow[b]{c} t'}{s; s' \xrightarrow[b]{a} t; t'} \qquad \text{(v-comp)}\ \frac{s \xrightarrow[b]{a} u,\ u \xrightarrow[b']{a'} t}{s \xrightarrow[b;b']{a;a'} t}$$

[4] Given a set A of arrows, the free monoidal category generated by A consists of all arrows which can be obtained from composing the arrows of A with the composition operator ; and the monoidal operator $\otimes$, observing the category axioms (; is associative and $\varepsilon = id_{\underline{1}}$ is its unit), the monoidality axioms ($\otimes$ is associative and $id_{\underline{0}}$ is its unit) and $a_1; a_1' \otimes a_2; a_2' = (a_1 \otimes a_2); (a_1' \otimes a_2')$.

We first show that if the generator tiles exhibit a certain well-formedness property, then we can construct every tile in the following way: first, we can use all rules apart from *(v-comp)* in order to construct several tiles which, finally, can be combined with rule *(v-comp)*. This says, basically, that it is sufficient to examine tiles which describe one single rewriting step.

Proposition 2. *We assume that the set $\mathcal{R}$ of generator tiles satisfies the following properties: let $s \xrightarrow[b]{a} t$ be a generator tile, then it holds that $s \in \Sigma$ and furthermore there are actions $a_1, \ldots, a_n \in Act \backslash \{\varepsilon\}$, such that $a = a_1 \otimes \ldots \otimes a_n$ and $b = id_{\underline{0}}$.*

Now let $\mathcal{R} \Vdash s \xrightarrow[b]{a} t$. Then it holds that there are configurations $s = s_0, s_1, \ldots, s_m = t$ and observations $a'_1, \ldots, a'_m, b'_1, \ldots, b'_m$ such that $\mathcal{R} \Vdash s_{i-1} \xrightarrow[b'_i]{a'_i} s_i$ for $i \in \{1, \ldots, n\}$ and the respective tiles can be derived without rule (v-comp). Furthermore $a = a'_1; \ldots; a'_m$ and $b = b'_1; \ldots; b'_m$.

We can now formulate one of the two main results of this paper: the operational correspondence between rewriting of syntactic judgements and of P-monoidal terms.

We first introduce the following notation: let $x_1 \ldots x_n$ be a string of names. By $\alpha = \langle x_1 \ldots x_n \rangle$ we denote the interface mapping $\alpha : \{1, \ldots, n\} \to \{x_1, \ldots, x_n\}$ where $\alpha(i) = x_i$.

Proposition 3 (Operational Correspondence). *Let R be a set of rewriting rules on syntactic judgements. We define a set $\mathcal{R}$ of generator tiles as follows:*

$$\mathcal{R} = \{s \xrightarrow[id_{\underline{0}}]{a_1 \otimes \ldots \otimes a_m} [\![\Gamma' \vdash G']\!]_{\langle x_1 \tilde{y}_1 \ldots x_m \tilde{y}_m \rangle} \mid$$
$$(x_1, \ldots, x_m \vdash s(x_1, \ldots, x_m) \xrightarrow{\Lambda} \Gamma' \vdash G') \in R,\ a_i = act_\Lambda(x_i), \tilde{y}_i = n_\Lambda(x_i)\}.$$

- *It holds that $R \Vdash (\Gamma \vdash G \xrightarrow{\Lambda} \Gamma' \vdash G')$ implies $\mathcal{R} \Vdash ([\![\Gamma \vdash G]\!]_\alpha \xrightarrow[id_{\underline{0}}]{a_1 \otimes \ldots \otimes a_m} [\![\Gamma' \vdash G']\!]_{\langle \alpha(1)\tilde{y}_1 \ldots \alpha(m)\tilde{y}_m \rangle})$ where $a_i = act_\Lambda(\alpha(i))$, $\tilde{y}_i = n_\Lambda(\alpha(i))$.*
- *And it holds that if $\mathcal{R} \Vdash ([\![\Gamma \vdash G]\!]_\alpha \xrightarrow[id_{\underline{0}}]{a_1 \otimes \ldots \otimes a_m} t)$ for some P-monoidal term t, then $R \Vdash (\Gamma \vdash G \xrightarrow{\Lambda} \Gamma' \vdash G')$ where $a_i = act_\Lambda(\alpha(i))$, $\tilde{y}_i = n_\Lambda(\alpha(i))$ and $[\![\Gamma' \vdash G']\!]_{\langle \alpha(1)\tilde{y}_1 \ldots \alpha(m)\tilde{y}_m \rangle} = t$.*

Proof (Sketch). The first half of the proposition can be shown by induction on the inference rules applied. The second half of the proposition is shown by induction on the syntactic structure of $\Gamma \vdash G$ and with the decomposition property (Proposition 4 which will be proved in Section 5 without referring back to this proposition). □

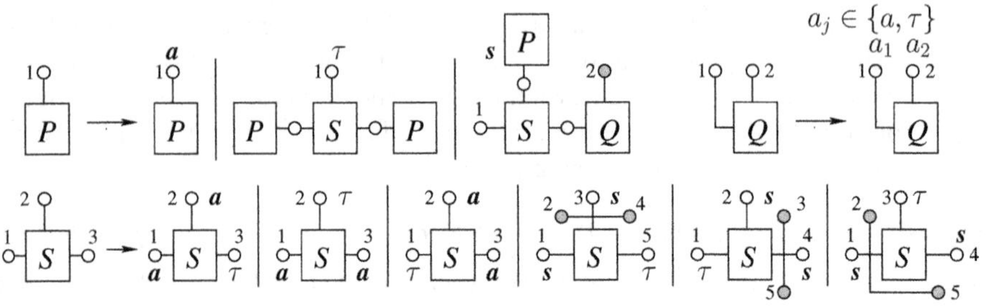

Fig. 5. Generator tiles

Example 6. Encoding the rewrite rules on syntactic judgements from Example 2 into generator tiles gives us the tiles depicted in Figure 5.

Here we represent a tile of the form $s \xrightarrow[id_{\underline{0}}]{a_1 \otimes \ldots \otimes a_n} t$ by drawing s and t as graphs and by labelling the free nodes of t by the actions $a_1, \ldots, a_n$. Specifically if $N_i = \sum_{j=1}^{i}(ar(a_j)+1)$, then the $N_{i-1}+1$-st free node of t is labelled a_i, while the next $ar(a_i) - 1$ nodes stay unlabelled (and are shaded grey in the graphical representation), indicating that these nodes are generated by the action a_i. Two nodes that are connected by a line represent one and the same node.

5 Bisimilarity Is a Congruence

Based on tiles we can now define the notions of bisimulation and bisimilarity and thus define a notion of an observable, compositional equivalence on graphs.

Definition 10 (Bisimulation on tiles). *Given a labelled transition system, a bisimulation is a symmetric, reflexive relation $\sim$ on the states of the transition system, such that if $s \sim t$ and $s \overset{a}{\to} s'$, then there exists a transition $t \overset{a}{\to} t'$ such that $s' \sim t'$. We say that two states s and t are bisimilar ($s \simeq t$) whenever there is a bisimulation $\sim$ such that $s \sim t$.*

In tile graph rewriting the tile $s \xrightarrow[b]{a} t$ is considered to be a transition with label (a, b). We say that two configuration s, t are bisimilar wrt. a set $\mathcal{R}$ of generator tiles (in symbols $s \simeq_{\mathcal{R}} t$) whenever s and t are bisimilar in the transition system generated by $\mathcal{R}$.

It is already known that bisimilarity is a congruence whenever the underlying tile system satisfies the following decomposition property.

Definition 11 (Decomposition Property). *A tile system satisfies the decomposition property if for all tiles $s \xrightarrow[b]{a} t$ entailed by the tile system, it holds that (1) if $s = s_1; s_2$ then there exist $c \in \mathcal{V}, t_1, t_2 \in \mathcal{H}$ such that $s_1 \xrightarrow[c]{a} t_1$, $t_1 \xrightarrow[b]{c} t_2$ and $t = t_1; t_2$ (2) if $s = s_1 \otimes s_2$ then there exist $a_1, a_2, b_1, b_2 \in$*

$\mathcal{V}, t_1, t_2 \in \mathcal{H}$ such that $s_1 \xrightarrow[b_1]{a_1} t_1$, $s_2 \xrightarrow[b_2]{a_2} t_2$, $a = a_1 \otimes a_2$, $b = b_1 \otimes b_2$ and $t = t_1 \otimes t_2$.

Proposition 4 (cf. [11]). *If a tile system satisfies the decomposition property, then bisimilarity defined on its transition system is a congruence.*

Similar to the case of de Simone [5] or `tyft/tyxt`-formats [12], there is a sufficient syntactical property ensuring that bisimilarity is indeed a congruence, which is stated in the second main result of this paper.

Proposition 5. *If, in tile graph rewriting, all generator tiles satisfy the basic source property, i.e. if for every generator tile $s \xrightarrow[b]{a} t$ it holds that $s \in \Sigma$, then the decomposition property holds. Thus bisimilarity is a congruence.*

Proof (Sketch). By induction on the derivation of a tile, following the lines of a similar proof in [2].

Corollary 1. *All the tile graph rewriting systems derived from rewriting rules on syntactic judgements satisfy the basic source property. Thus the decomposition property holds and bisimilarity is a congruence.*

Having established that bisimilarity is indeed a congruence in the case of tile graph rewriting we now transfer this result back to rewriting on syntactic judgements with the help of the operational correspondence (Proposition 3). First we have to define bisimulation on syntactic judgements. We use the following intuition: an observer from the outside has access to the external nodes of a graph, however he or she is not able to determine their names and he or she should also not be able to find out whether or not two nodes are equal. So, given two syntactic judgements, we add an interface mapping α which assigns numbers to names and in this way hides the internal details from an external observer.

For the next definition remember that the mapping $i \mapsto x_i$ is denoted by $\langle x_1 \ldots x_n \rangle$.

Definition 12 (Bisimulation on syntactic judgements). *Let $\Gamma \vdash G$ be a syntactic judgements. An n-ary interface for a syntactic judgement is a surjective mapping $\alpha : \{1, \ldots, n\} \to \Gamma$, as defined in Definition 7.*

A symmetric, reflexive relation $\sim$ on pairs consisting of syntactic judgements and their corresponding interfaces is called a bisimulation (wrt. a set R of rewriting rules) if whenever $(\Gamma_1 \vdash G_1, \alpha_1) \sim (\Gamma_2 \vdash G_2, \alpha_2)$, then

- *there is an $n \in \mathbb{N}$ such that α_1 and α_2 are both n-ary interfaces*
- *whenever $\Gamma_1 \vdash G_1 \xrightarrow{\Lambda_1} \Gamma_1' \vdash G_1'$ with $\Lambda_1(\alpha_1(i)) = (a_i, \tilde{y}_i)$, then it holds that $\Gamma_2 \vdash G_2 \xrightarrow{\Lambda_2} \Gamma_2' \vdash G_2'$ with $\Lambda_2(\alpha_2(i)) = (a_i, \tilde{z}_i)$ and*

$$(\Gamma_1' \vdash G_1', \langle \alpha_1(1)\tilde{y}_1 \ldots \alpha_1(n)\tilde{y}_n \rangle) \sim (\Gamma_2' \vdash G_2', \langle \alpha_2(1)\tilde{z}_1 \ldots \alpha_2(n)\tilde{z}_n \rangle).$$

We say that two pairs $(\Gamma_1 \vdash G_1, \alpha_1)$ and $(\Gamma_2 \vdash G_2, \alpha_2)$ are bisimilar (wrt. a set R of rewriting rules) whenever there is a bisimulation $\sim$ (wrt. a set R of rewriting rules) such that $(\Gamma_1 \vdash G_1, \alpha_1) \sim (\Gamma_2 \vdash G_2, \alpha_2)$. Bisimilarity on syntactic judgements is denoted by the symbol $\simeq_R$.

In order to show that bisimilarity on syntactic judgements is a congruence with respect to parallel composition and hiding, we need the following result on full abstraction.

Proposition 6 (Full abstraction). *The encoding $[\![\_]\!]_\alpha$ is fully abstract in the following sense: for any set R of rewriting rules it holds that*

$$(\Gamma_1 \vdash G_1, \alpha_1) \simeq_R (\Gamma_2 \vdash G_2, \alpha_2) \iff [\![\Gamma_1 \vdash G_1]\!]_{\alpha_1} \simeq_{\mathcal{R}} [\![\Gamma_2 \vdash G_2]\!]_{\alpha_2}$$

where $\mathcal{R}$ is defined as in Proposition 3.

Proof (Sketch). Straightforward by regarding the respective definitions of bisimilarity, from Proposition 2 and the operational correspondence result in Proposition 3. □

Now it is straightforward to show that bisimilarity on syntactic judgements is a congruence as well.

Proposition 7. *Let R be a set of rewriting rules and let $\mathcal{R}$ be the corresponding set of generator tiles defined as in Proposition 3.*

We assume that $(\Gamma_1, X_1 \vdash G_1, \alpha_1) \simeq_R (\Gamma_2, X_2 \vdash G_2, \alpha_2)$ such that $\alpha_i : \{1, \dots, n+m\} \to \Gamma_i \cup X_i$ and $\alpha_i^{-1}(X_i) = \{n+1, \dots, n+m\}$ for $i \in \{1,2\}$. Then it holds that $(\Gamma_1 \vdash (\nu X_1)G_1, \alpha_1|_{\{1,\dots,n\}}) \simeq_R (\Gamma_2 \vdash (\nu X_2)G_2, \alpha_2|_{\{1,\dots,n\}})$.

And if $(\Gamma_1 \vdash G_1, \alpha_1) \simeq_R (\Gamma_2 \vdash G_2, \alpha_2)$ and $(\Gamma_1 \vdash G_1', \alpha_1) \simeq_R (\Gamma_2 \vdash G_2', \alpha_2)$, then it follows that $(\Gamma_1 \vdash G_1 \mid G_1', \alpha_1) \simeq_R (\Gamma_2 \vdash G_2 \mid G_2', \alpha_2)$.

Proof (Sketch). Straightforward by using the full abstraction result from Proposition 6, by using that fact that bisimilarity on P-monoidal terms is a congruence (see Proposition 5) and by regarding the definition of the encoding $[\![\_]\!]_\alpha$ in Definition 7. □

6 Bisimulation Up-to Congruence

In order to show that two graphs are bisimilar in practice, we need a proof technique for bisimulation, a so-called bisimulation up-to congruence (for up-to techniques see also [18]).

Definition 13. *For a given relation B on P-monoidal terms, we denote by $\equiv_B$ the smallest congruence (with respect to the operators ; and $\otimes$) that contains B.*

A symmetric relation B is called a bisimulation up-to congruence whenever $(s,t) \in B$ and $s \xrightarrow[b]{a} s'$ imply $t \xrightarrow[b]{a} t'$ and $s' \equiv_B t'$.

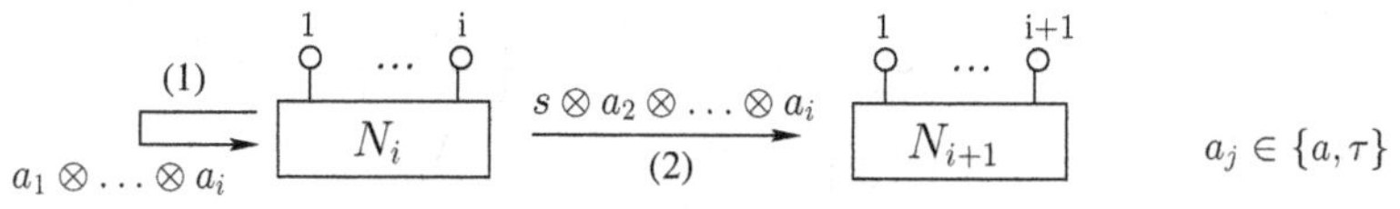

Fig. 6. Specification of the communication network

Proposition 8. *If the decomposition property holds for the respective tile logic and B is a bisimulation up-to congruence, then $\equiv_B$ is a bisimulation.*

It is typically easier to show that B is a bisimulation up-to congruence than to show that $\equiv_B$ is a bisimulation, mainly because B can be much smaller than $\equiv_B$ and so there are fewer cases to consider. It may even be the case that B is finite and $\equiv_B$ is infinite in size.

7 Example: Communication Network

We return to our running example and intend to investigate which steps a single process can perform, or rather which are the actions that are observable from the outside. To this aim we give a specification N_1 which models in a single edge the entire communication topology P may generate. Note that a process P may start with a single free node, but can create new free nodes by performing s actions. The specification has to take this into account and N_1 may therefore reduce to N_2, N_3 etc., where $N_i : \underline{i} \to \underline{0}$.

The generator tiles for the specification are depicted in Figure 6, where this time we put the observations on the arrows rather than on the free nodes of the right-hand side.

The edge N_i can either perform an arbitrary combination of a and τ actions and stay N_i or it can perform an s action on its first node and a's and τ's on the remaining nodes and become N_{i+1}.

In order to show that P and N_1 are indeed bisimilar we proceed as follows: We consider the tile system generated by both the tiles belonging to processes and switches and the tiles of the specification, and denote the combined set of generator tiles by $\mathcal{R}$. Since the set of edges involved in the first set of generator tiles is disjoint from that in the second set, the rules can not interfere with each other and P respectively N_1 can not perform more reductions with the additional tiles.

Proposition 9. *The symmetric closure of the relation B depicted in Figure 7 is a bisimulation up-to congruence. Since the basic source property and therefore the decomposition property hold, it follows that $\equiv_B$ is a bisimulation.*

And since $(P, N_1) \in B$, we conclude that $P \simeq_{\mathcal{R}} N_1$.

Proof (Sketch). From Proposition 2 it follows that it is sufficient to regard only tiles which can be composed without using rule *(v-comp)*.

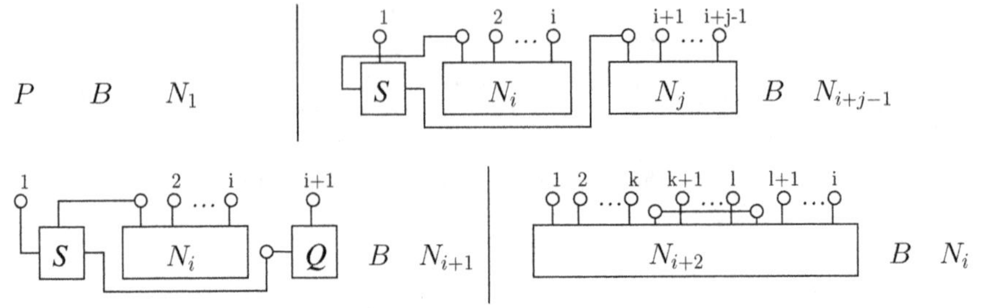

Fig. 7. Example of a bisimulation up-to congruence

We exemplarily treat the following case: let $(P, N_1) \in B$ and we assume that P performs a τ action and replaces itself with a switch and two processes, i.e. the second rewrite rule for P is applied. In this case $N_1 \xrightarrow[id_{\underline{0}}]{\tau} N_1$ and we have to show that the two resulting graphs are in the $\equiv_B$-relation:

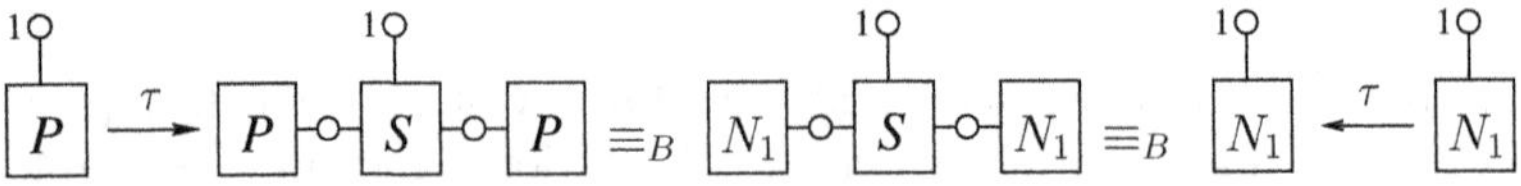

□

The scenario we have presented resembles the view of a user which starts with one single port of access to a network which may be huge. The user can request further connections into the network (with an s action) and he or she can send signals a which are received in the network. However, in whatever way the user interacts with the entire network, its topology will always be hidden, its expansion unobservable and it thus constitutes a black box. Internal communications, of which several may take place in parallel, are indistinguishable from τ-steps and thus completely hidden from the environment.

If, however, we start with a disconnected graph with i external nodes and compare it to an edge N_i, the two expressions are *not* bisimilar. Consider for example the two graphs $P \otimes P$ and N_2, both of arity 2. We observe that $P \otimes P \xrightarrow[id_{\underline{0}}]{a \otimes id_{\underline{1}}} P \otimes P$, whereas N_2 can not match this transition. If we assume that the first node of N_2 produces an action a, we either get a or τ as the action of the second node, but we never get $id_{\underline{1}}$. In general we can state that whenever we have a graph t consisting of processes and switches, we can determine its connected external nodes in the following way: a set of external nodes is connected if and only if there is a transition such that exactly the nodes of the set perform an action different from $id_{\underline{1}} = \varepsilon$, and that furthermore there is no proper subset with the same property.

Another scenario would be to start with a graph with several external nodes of which two or more are connected via switches. In this case an s action originating on one of the external nodes may be routed to a different external node, giving us two new nodes in the interface, which, however, must be equal.

8 Conclusion

We have presented synchronized graph rewriting with mobility for two forms of graph representation (syntactic judgements and arrows in a P-monoidal category) and we have shown that bisimilarity for synchronized graph rewriting is a congruence with respect to graph composition. A tile logic semantics for synchronized graph rewriting without mobility has already been defined in [23], whereas synchronized graph rewriting with mobility has so far only been considered for syntactic judgements [13,14], but not in the context of tile logics. Moreover no equivalence of graphs based on observations has been introduced there.

In [14] not only Hoare synchronization, but also Milner synchronization is treated and an encoding of the π-calculus into synchronized graph rewriting is given, using Milner synchronization.

An earlier form of synchronized graph rewriting has been treated in [6]. Furthermore, the mobility treated in this paper is reminiscent of the rendezvous mechanism presented in [4].

In general we know of little work concerning the definition of observational equivalences for graph rewriting. As already mentioned in the introduction there are basically two ways to go when one wants to introduce bisimilarity on graphs. The first alternative would be to base the theory on unlabelled production as in the double-pushout approach [7]. Without labels on the transitions it is necessary to define canonical forms of graphs, in order to be able to observe something. Work by Fernández and Mackie on interaction nets [9] and by Yoshida on process graphs [25] goes in that direction.

In π-calculus, for example, the canonical forms mentioned above are called "barbs" and a process has a barb for channel c whenever it is able to perform an input or output on c. The resulting bisimulation is therefore called barbed bisimulation [22], which ordinarily does not induce a congruence, and the definition of the smallest congruence containing barbed bisimilarity requires universal quantification over all possible contexts. This, however, makes actual proofs of bisimilarity complicated.

In this paper, however, we chose to use synchronized graph rewriting as a framework. We model transitions whose transition labels (observations) describe exactly the interaction of a single edge with its environment. This enables us to define a simple syntactic property on the rewriting rules which ensures that bisimilarity is a congruence. Existing work is mainly related to action calculi [20,17] which also have a graphical representation.

As we have seen in the example in Section 7, the bisimilarity defined in this paper is rather coarse-grained: it can determine whether a network is connected or disconnected, but we can, for example, not determine the degree of parallelism in a network. In order to be able to do this, it would be necessary to establish a concurrent semantics for synchronized graph rewriting. Another interesting extension would be to enrich the notion of observation: so far we are only able to observe the actions performed on external nodes, but we are not able to determine whether, for example, two nodes are connected by an edge. It seems therefore promising to extend the framework in such a way that we are allowed to observe occurrences of specific subgraphs.

Acknowledgements

We would like to thank Roberto Bruni and Dan Hirsch for their help.

References

1. R. Bruni, D. Frutos-Escrig, N. Martí-Oliet, and U. Montanari. Bisimilarity congruences for open terms and term graphs via tile logic. In *Proc. of CONCUR 2000*, pages 259–274. Springer-Verlag, 2000. LNCS 1877.
2. R. Bruni, D. Frutos-Escrig, N. Martí-Oliet, and U. Montanari. Tile bisimilarity congruences for open terms and term graphs. Technical Report TR-00-06, Dipartimento di Informatica, Università di Pisa, 2000.
3. Roberto Bruni, Fabio Gadducci, and Ugo Montanari. Normal forms for partitions and relations. In *Recents Trends in Algebraic Development Techniques, 12th International Workshop, WADT '98*, pages 31–47. Springer-Verlag, 1998. LNCS 1589, full version to appear in TCS.
4. Gnanamalar David, Frank Drewes, and Hans-Jörg Kreowski. Hyperedge replacement with rendezvous. In *Proc. of TAPSOFT (Theory and Practice of Software Development)*, pages 167–181. Springer-Verlag, 1993. LNCS 668.
5. Roberto de Simone. Higher level synchronizing devices in MEIJE-SCCS. *Theoretical Computer Science*, 37:245–267, 1985.
6. P. Degano and U. Montanari. A model of distributed systems based on graph rewriting. *Journal of the ACM*, 2(34):411–449, 1987.
7. H. Ehrig. Introduction to the algebraic theory of graphs. In *Proc. 1st International Workshop on Graph Grammars*, pages 1–69. Springer-Verlag, 1979. LNCS 73.
8. H. Ehrig, H.-J. Kreowski, U. Montanari, and G. Rozenberg, editors. *Handbook of Graph Grammars and Computing by Graph Transformation, Vol.3: Concurrency, Parallellism, and Distribution.* World Scientific, 1999.
9. Maribel Fernández and Ian Mackie. Coinductive techniques for operational equivalence of interaction nets. In *Proc. of LICS '98.* IEEE Computer Society Press, 1998.
10. F. Gadducci and R. Heckel. An inductive view of graph transformation. In *Recent Trends in Algebraic Development Techniques, 12th International Workshop, WADT '97*, pages 223–237. Springer-Verlag, 1997. LNCS 1376.
11. F. Gadducci and U. Montanari. The tile model. In Gordon Plotkin, Colin Stirling, and Mads Tofte, editors, *Proof, Language and Interaction: Essays in Honour of Robin Milner.* MIT Press, 1999.
12. J.F. Groote and F. Vaandrager. Structured operational semantics and bisimulation as a congruence. *Information and Computation*, 100:202–260, 1992.
13. Dan Hirsch, Paola Inverardi, and Ugo Montanari. Reconfiguration of software architecture styles with name mobility. In António Porto and Gruia-Catalin Roman, editors, *Proc. of COORDINATION 2000*, pages 148–163. Springer-Verlag, 2000. LNCS 1906.

14. Dan Hirsch and Ugo Montanari. Synchronized hyperedge replacement with name mobility (a graphical calculus for mobile systems). In *Proc. of CONCUR '01*. Springer-Verlag, 2001. to appear.
15. Barbara König. *Description and Verification of Mobile Processes with Graph Rewriting Techniques*. PhD thesis, Technische Universität München, 1999.
16. Barbara König. A graph rewriting semantics for the polyadic pi-calculus. In *Workshop on Graph Transformation and Visual Modeling Techniques (Geneva, Switzerland), ICALP Workshops '00*, pages 451–458. Carleton Scientific, 2000.
17. James J. Leifer and Robin Milner. Deriving bisimulation congruences for reactive systems. In *Proc. of CONCUR 2000*, 2000. LNCS 1877.
18. R. Milner and D. Sangiorgi. Techniques of weak bisimulation up-to. In *Proc. of CONCUR '92*. Springer-Verlag, 1992. LNCS 630.
19. Robin Milner. *A Calculus of Communicating Systems*. Springer-Verlag, 1980. LNCS 92.
20. Robin Milner. Calculi for interaction. *Acta Informatica*, 33(8):707–737, 1996.
21. Robin Milner. *Communicating and Mobile Systems: the π-Calculus*. Cambridge University Press, 1999.
22. Robin Milner and Davide Sangiorgi. Barbed bisimulation. In *Proc. of ICALP '92*. Springer-Verlag, 1992. LNCS 623.
23. U. Montanari and F. Rossi. Graph rewriting, constraint solving and tiles for coordinating distributed systems. *Applied Categorical Structures*, 7:333–370, 1999.
24. Grzegorz Rozenberg, editor. *Handbook of Graph Grammars and Computing by Graph Transformation, Vol.1: Foundations*, volume 1. World Scientific, 1997.
25. Nobuko Yoshida. Graph notation for concurrent combinators. In *Proc. of TPPP '94*. Springer-Verlag, 1994. LNCS 907.

Fixed-Point Logic with the Approximation Modality and Its Kripke Completeness

Hiroshi Nakano

Ryukoku University, Japan
nakano@math.ryukoku.ac.jp

Abstract. We present two modal typing systems with the approximation modality, which has been proposed by the author to capture self-references involved in computer programs and their specifications. The systems are based on the simple and the F-semantics of types, respectively, and correspond to the same modal logic, which is considered the intuitionistic version of the logic of provability. We also show Kripke completeness of the modal logic and its decidability, which implies the decidability of type inhabitance in the typing systems.

1 Introduction

Although recursion, or self-reference, plays an indispensable role in both programs and their specifications, it also introduces serious difficulties into their formal treatment. Consider, for example, objects which represent integers and have an accessor method to obtain its value, and methods for doing subtraction and finding the greatest common divisor provided another integer object. In Java, the *interface*, or the coarse specification, of such objects could be written as:

```
interface Int {
    int getValue();
    Int sub(Int peer);
    Int getGCD(Int peer);
}
```

and we could implement it as the following class `Int1`, which includes some excessive occurrences of "`this`" for readability.

```
class Int1 implements Int {
    private int value;
    Int1(int v) { value = v; }          // constructor
    public int getValue() { return value; } // accessor
    public Int sub(Int peer) {          // subtraction method
      return new Int1(this.getValue() - peer.getValue());
    }
    public Int getGCD(Int peer) {       // gcd method
      if (this.getValue() == peer.getValue())
```

N. Kobayashi and B.C. Pierce (Eds.): TACS 2001, LNCS 2215, pp. 165–182, 2001.

```
            return this;
        else if (this.getValue() > peer.getValue())
            return this.sub(peer).getGCD(peer);
        else
            return peer.getGCD(this);
    }
}
```

We could also consider another implementation, say `Int2`, which employs the following definition of `getGCD` method:

```
public Int getGCD(Int peer) {
  if (this.getValue() == peer.getValue())
      return this;
  else if (this.getValue() < peer.getValue())
      return peer.sub(this).getGCD(this);
  else
      return peer.getGCD(this);
}
```

These two class are quite symmetrical to each other, and either one works fine as long as we only use objects of the same kind. However, these two kinds of objects are not interchangeable; if we mix objects of the two classes, they run into an infinite loop whenever their `getGCD` methods are invoked with objects of the other class. If the specification being supposedly satisfied by the objects of these two classes were identical, we would be able to mix the objects without problems. So we realize that it is inevitable to give different, maybe slightly different, specifications to these two implementations of `Int` in order to obtain modularity of programs with respect to their termination, or convergence.

The approximation modality has been proposed by the author in order to incorporate general self-reference into formal specification of programs and their implementations without such loss of modularity, with which we can construct a wider range of programs, such as fixed point combinators and objects with so-called binary methods in object-oriented programming, through the proof-as-programs paradigm. We refer the reader to [1] for the motivation of the modality and examples of applications (see also [2] for proofs).

The original typing system, however, would be now considered as a specific example of a class of more general systems. In this paper, we present two basic typing systems with the modality, of which the original system can be considered an extension. One is based on the simple semantics of types, and the other is its variant based on the F-semantics of types (cf. [3,4]). We show that both the systems have desirable convergence properties and correspond to the same modal logic, which is Kripke complete with respect to intuitionistic, transitive and converse wellfounded frames. The completeness theorem implies its decidability, and also the decidability of type inhabitance in the typing systems. We also show that the modal logic is a conservative extension of the intuitionistic version of the logic of provability (cf. [5]).

2 The Typing Systems

We introduce two basic modal typing systems denoted by S-$\lambda\bullet\mu$ and F-$\lambda\bullet\mu$, respectively. As a preparation for defining the syntax of type expressions, we first give one of *pseudo type expressions* **PTExp**, which are obtained by adding a unary type constructor $\bullet$ to those of $\lambda\mu$, namely the simply typed λ-calculus extended with recursive types (cf. [6,7]). Let **TVar** be a countably infinite set of type variable symbols X, Y, Z, ... The syntax of **PTExp** is given by:

$$
\begin{array}{rcll}
\mathbf{PTExp} & ::= & \mathbf{TVar} & \text{(type variables)} \\
& | & \mathbf{PTExp} \to \mathbf{PTExp} & \text{(function types)} \\
& | & \bullet\,\mathbf{PTExp} & \text{(approximative types)} \\
& | & \mu\mathbf{TVar}.\,\mathbf{PTExp} & \text{(recursive types)}
\end{array}
$$

Type constants are omitted for simplicity. We assume that $\to$ associates to the right as usual, and each (pseudo) type constructor associates according to the following priority: (highest) $\bullet$, $\to$, $\mu X.$ (lowest). For example, $\bullet\,\mu X.\bullet X \to Y \to Z$ is the same as $\bullet(\mu X.((\bullet X) \to (Y \to Z)))$. We use $\top$ as an abbreviation for $\mu X.\bullet X$ and use $\bullet^n A$ to denote a (pseudo) type expression $\underbrace{\bullet \ldots \bullet}_{n \text{ times}} A$, where $n \geq 0$.

Definition 1. *A type expression A is* an F-$\top$-variant *if and only if $A = \bullet^{m_0}\mu X_1.\bullet^{m_1}\mu X_2.\bullet^{m_2}\ldots\mu X_n.\bullet^{m_n}X_i$ for some n, m_0, m_1, m_2, ..., m_n, X_1, X_2, ..., X_n and i such that $1 \leq i \leq n$ and $m_i + m_{i+1} + m_{i+2} + \ldots + m_n \geq 1$. A type expression A is* an S-$\top$-variant *if and only if $\overline{A}$ is an F-$\top$-variant, where $\overline{A}$ is defined as follows:*

$$\overline{X} = X, \quad \overline{A \to B} = \overline{B}, \quad \overline{\mu X.A} = \mu X.\overline{A}.$$

An F-$\top$-variant is also an S-$\top$-variant, and by definition it is decidable whether a type expression is an S(F)-$\top$-variant or not. S(F)-$\top$-variants correspond to the universe into which λ-terms are interpretated. Hence, every λ-term should have these types in S(F)-$\lambda\bullet\mu$, respectively.

Definition 2. *We say that a pseudo type expression A is* S-proper *(respectively* F-proper*) in X if and only if X occurs freely only (a) in scopes of the $\bullet$-operator in A, or (b) in a subexpression $B \to C$ of A with C being an S-$\top$-variant (F-$\top$-variant).*[1]

For example, $\bullet X$, $\bullet(X \to Y)$, $\mu Y.\bullet(X \to Y)$, and $X \to \top$ are S(F)-proper in X, and neither X, $X \to Y$ nor $\mu Y.\mu Z.X \to Y$ is S(F)-proper in X.

Definition 3. *A* type expression *of S-$\lambda\bullet\mu$ (respectively F-$\lambda\bullet\mu$) is a pseudo type expression such that A is S-proper (F-proper) in X for any of its subexpressions in the form of $\mu X.A$. We denote the set of type expressions by* **TExp**.

[1] The condition (b) is included so that the equivalence relation $\simeq$ on type expressions (cf. Definition 4) preserves properness.

For example, X, $X \to Y$, $\mu X.\bullet X \to Y$, $\mu X.X \to \top$ and $\mu X.\bullet\,\mu Y.X \to Z$ are type expressions, and neither $\mu X.X \to Y$ nor $\mu X.\mu Y.X \to Y$ is a type expression. We use $A, B, C, D, \ldots$ to denote type expressions of $\lambda\bullet\mu$'s, and denote the set of type variables occurring freely in A by $FTV(A)$ regarding a type variable X as bound in $\mu X.A$. We also regard α-convertible type expressions as identical, and use $A[B_1/X_1, \ldots, B_n/X_n]$ to denote the type expression obtained from A by substituting $B_1, \ldots, B_n$ for each free occurrence of $X_1, \ldots, X_n$, respectively.

Definition 4. *The equivalence relation $\simeq$ on type expressions is defined as the smallest binary relation that satisfies:*

($\simeq$-*reflex*)	$A \simeq A$.
($\simeq$-*symm*)	*If* $A \simeq B$, *then* $B \simeq A$.
($\simeq$-*trans*)	*If* $A \simeq B$ *and* $B \simeq C$, *then* $A \simeq C$.
($\simeq$-$\bullet$)	*If* $A \simeq B$, *then* $\bullet A \simeq \bullet B$.
($\simeq$-$\to$)	*If* $A \simeq C$ *and* $B \simeq D$, *then* $A \to B \simeq C \to D$.
($\simeq$-*fix*)	$\mu X.A \simeq A[\mu X.A/X]$.
($\simeq$-*uniq*)	*If* $A \simeq C[A/X]$ *and* C *is S(F)-proper in* X, *then* $A \simeq \mu X.C$.

All the condition above are common to S-$\lambda\bullet\mu$ and F-$\lambda\bullet\mu$, and the following ones are respectively satisfied:

S-$\lambda\bullet\mu$: ($\simeq$-$\to\top$) $A \to \top \simeq \top$.
F-$\lambda\bullet\mu$: ($\simeq$-$\to\top$) $A \to \top \simeq B \to \top$.

Intuitively, two type expressions are equivalent if their (possibly infinite) type expression obtained by unfolding recursive types occurring in them indefinitely are identical modulo the rule ($\simeq$-$\to\top$). This equality on type expressions is decidable. One can also observe that a type expression A is an S(F)-$\top$-variant if and only if $A \simeq \top$ in S(F)-$\lambda\bullet\mu$, respectively.

We now define a subtyping relation on type expressions, which is induced by the $\bullet$-modality, by a set of the subtyping rules (cf. [8]). A *subtyping assumption* is a finite set of pairs of type variables such that any type variable appears at most once in the set. We write $\{X_1 \preceq Y_1, X_2 \preceq Y_2, \ldots, X_n \preceq Y_n\}$ to denote the subtyping assumption $\{ \langle X_i, Y_i\rangle \mid i = 1, 2, \ldots, n \}$, and use γ, γ', γ_1, γ_2, ... to denote subtyping assumptions, and $FTV(\gamma)$ to denote the set of type variables occurring in γ.

Definition 5 ($\preceq$). *The derivability of* a subtyping judgment $\gamma \vdash A \preceq B$ *is defined by the following subtyping rules:*

$$\frac{}{\gamma \cup \{X \preceq Y\} \vdash X \preceq Y}\ (\preceq\text{-}assump) \qquad \frac{}{\gamma \vdash A \preceq \top}\ (\preceq\text{-}\top)$$

$$\frac{}{\gamma \vdash A \preceq \bullet A}\ (\preceq\text{-}approx) \qquad \frac{}{\gamma \vdash A \preceq A'}\ (\preceq\text{-}reflex)\quad (A \simeq A')$$

$$\frac{\gamma_1 \vdash A \preceq B \qquad \gamma_2 \vdash B \preceq C}{\gamma_1 \cup \gamma_2 \vdash A \preceq C}\ (\preceq\text{-}trans)$$

$$\frac{\gamma \vdash A \preceq B}{\gamma \vdash \bullet A \preceq \bullet B}\ (\preceq\text{-}\bullet) \qquad \frac{\gamma_1 \vdash A' \preceq A \quad \gamma_2 \vdash B \preceq B'}{\gamma_1 \cup \gamma_2 \vdash A \to B \preceq A' \to B'}\ (\preceq\text{-}\to)$$

$$\frac{\gamma \cup \{X \preceq Y\} \vdash A \preceq B}{\gamma \vdash \mu X.A \preceq \mu Y.B}\ (\preceq\text{-}\mu) \quad \left(\begin{array}{l} X \notin FTV(\gamma) \cup FTV(B),\ Y \notin FTV(\gamma) \cup \\ FTV(A),\ \text{and } A \text{ and } B \text{ are } S(F)\text{-proper} \\ \text{in } X \text{ and } Y, \text{ respectively} \end{array}\right)$$

Note that $\gamma \cup \{X \preceq Y\}$ and $\gamma_1 \cup \gamma_2$ in the rules above must be (valid) subtyping assumptions, i.e., any type variable must not have more than one occurrence in them. All the rules above are common to S-$\lambda\bullet\mu$ and F-$\lambda\bullet\mu$, and they respectively have another rule called $(\to\preceq\text{-}\to\bullet)$ as follows:

$$\text{S-}\lambda\bullet\mu : \frac{}{\gamma \vdash \bullet(A \to B) \preceq \bullet A \to \bullet B}\ (\preceq\text{-}\to\bullet)$$

$$\text{F-}\lambda\bullet\mu : \frac{}{\gamma \vdash A \to B \preceq \bullet A \to \bullet B}\ (\preceq\text{-}\to\bullet)$$

The binary relation $\preceq$ on type expressions is defined as: $A \preceq B$ if and only if $\{\} \vdash A \preceq B$ is derivable. It should be noted that if $A \preceq B$ in F-$\lambda\bullet\mu$, then it is also the case in S-$\lambda\bullet\mu$.

We now define the typing rules for S-$\lambda\bullet\mu$ and F-$\lambda\bullet\mu$. A *typing context* is a finite mapping that assigns a type expression to each individual variable of its domain. We use $\Gamma, \Gamma', \ldots$ to denote typing contexts, and $\{x_1 : A_1, \ldots, x_m : A_m\}$ to denote the typing context that assigns A_i to x_i for every i. We write $\Gamma' \preceq \Gamma$ if and only if $Dom(\Gamma'(x)) = Dom(\Gamma(x))$ and $\Gamma'(x) \preceq \Gamma(x)$ for every $x \in Dom(\Gamma)$.

Definition 6. *The typing systems S-$\lambda\bullet\mu$ and F-$\lambda\bullet\mu$ are defined by the following derivation rules:*

$$\frac{}{\Gamma \cup \{x : A\} \vdash x : A}\ (var) \qquad \frac{\Gamma \vdash M : A}{\bullet\Gamma \vdash M : \bullet A}\ (nec)$$

$$\frac{}{\Gamma \vdash M : \top}\ (\top) \qquad \frac{\Gamma \vdash M : A \quad \Gamma'(x) \preceq \Gamma(x) \quad A \preceq A'}{\Gamma' \vdash M : A'}\ (\preceq)$$

$$\frac{\Gamma \cup \{x : A\} \vdash M : B}{\Gamma \vdash \lambda x.\, M : A \to B}\ (\to I) \qquad \frac{\Gamma_1 \vdash M : \bullet^n(A \to B) \quad \Gamma_2 \vdash N : \bullet^n A}{\Gamma_1 \cup \Gamma_2 \vdash MN : \bullet^n B}\ (\to E)$$

where $Dom(\bullet\Gamma) = Dom(\Gamma)$ and $(\bullet\Gamma)(x) = \bullet\Gamma(x)$ for every $x \in Dom(\Gamma)$. Note that since S-$\lambda\bullet\mu$ has the subtyping rule $\bullet(A \to B) \preceq \bullet A \to \bullet B$, the $(\to$E)-rule for S-$\lambda\bullet\mu$ can be simplified to the following usual form:

$$\frac{\Gamma_1 \vdash M : A \to B \quad \Gamma_2 \vdash N : A}{\Gamma_1 \cup \Gamma_2 \vdash MN : B}\ (\to \mathrm{E})$$

Since $A \preceq B$ in F-$\lambda\bullet\mu$ implies the same in S-$\lambda\bullet\mu$, one can observe the following.

Proposition 1. *If $\Gamma \vdash M : A$ is derivable in F-$\lambda\bullet\mu$, then so is it in S-$\lambda\bullet\mu$.*

The most interesting thing about S(F)-$\lambda\bullet\mu$ is that one can derive $\vdash \mathbf{Y} : (\bullet A \to A) \to A$ for any A, where $\mathbf{Y} = \lambda f.\,(\lambda x.\,f(xx))\,(\lambda x.\,f(xx))$ (cf. [1]). The typing systems S-$\lambda\bullet\mu$ and F-$\lambda\bullet\mu$ also enjoy some basic properties such as subject reduction property.

Proposition 2. *(1) If $\Gamma \vdash M : A$ is derivable, then $FV(M) \subset Dom(\Gamma)$.*

(2) If $\Gamma \cup \{x : A\} \vdash M : B$ and $\Gamma \vdash N : A$ are derivable, then so is $\Gamma \vdash M[N/x] : B$.

(3) If $\Gamma \vdash M : A$ is derivable and $M \underset{\beta}{\to} M'$, then $\Gamma \vdash M' : A$ is derivable.

Proof. Straightforward induction on the derivations. In the proof of (3), we apply the following property of $\preceq$ to the case that the derivation ends with ($\to$E): if $A \to B \preceq \bullet^n(C \to D)$ and $D \not\preceq \top$, then $\bullet^l B \preceq C$ and $D \preceq \bullet^l A$ for some l. □

3 Semantics

In this section, we show revised results presented in Sections 4 and 5 of [1]. We give two kinds of realizability interpretations, the simple semantics and the F-semantics, over certain Kripke-frames to S-$\lambda\bullet\mu$ and F-$\lambda\bullet\mu$, respectively, and show soundness of each typing system with respect to the corresponding interpretation. We also show that the new systems preserve the convergence properties of well-typed λ-terms presented in [1].

We now consider the following class of Kripke-frames.

Definition 7. *A transitive and converse wellfounded frame is a pair $<\mathcal{W}, \to>$, which consists of a set $\mathcal{W}$ of* possible worlds *and* an accessibility relation $\to$ *on $\mathcal{W}$ such that:*

(1) The relation $\to$ is transitive.

(2) The relation $\to$ is converse wellfounded, i.e., there is no infinite sequence such that $p_0 \to p_1 \to p_2 \to p_3 \to \dots$.

Let $<\mathcal{V}, \cdot, [\![\ ]\!]>$ be a λ-model of untyped λ-calculus. The meaning of a λ-term M is denoted by $[\![M]\!]_\rho$, where ρ is *an individual environment* that assigns an element of $\mathcal{V}$ to each individual variable. Each type expression is interpreted as a mapping $\mathcal{I}$ from $\mathcal{W}$ to the power set $\mathcal{P}(\mathcal{V})$ of $\mathcal{V}$ such that:

$$p \to q \quad \text{implies} \quad \mathcal{I}(p) \subset \mathcal{I}(q)$$

A mapping that assigns such a monotone mapping to each type variable is called *a type environment.*

Definition 8 (Semantics of types). *Let $<\mathcal{W}, \to>$ be a transitive and converse wellfounded frame, and ξ a type environment. We define a mapping $\mathcal{I}_S(A)^\xi$ from $\mathcal{W}$ to $\mathcal{P}(\mathcal{V})$ for each type expression A by extending ξ as follows, where we* *prefer to write* $\mathcal{I}_S(A)^\xi_p$ *rather than* $\mathcal{I}_S(A)^\xi(p)$.

$$\mathcal{I}_S(X)^\xi_p = \xi(X)_p$$
$$\mathcal{I}_S(\bullet A)^\xi_p = \{\, u \mid u \in \mathcal{I}_S(A)^\xi_q \ \textit{for every}\ q \leftarrow p \,\}$$
$$\mathcal{I}_S(A \to B)^\xi_p = \left\{ u \;\middle|\; \begin{array}{l} \textit{If } B \textit{ is not an S-T-variant, then } u \cdot v \in \mathcal{I}_S(B)^\xi_q \\ \textit{for every } v \in \mathcal{I}_S(A)^\xi_q \textit{ whenever } q = p \textit{ or } q \leftarrow p. \end{array} \right\}$$
$$\mathcal{I}_S(\mu X.A)^\xi_p = \mathcal{I}_S(A[\mu X.A/X])^\xi_p$$

$\mathcal{I}_S$ is called *the simple semantics* of types. We similarly define $\mathcal{I}_F(A)^\xi$, *the F-semantics* of types, where the only difference is the definition of $\mathcal{I}_F(A \to B)^\xi$, which is defined as:

$$\mathcal{I}_F(A \to B)^\xi_p = \left\{ u \;\middle|\; \begin{array}{l} 1.\ \text{If } B \text{ is not an F-T-variant, then } u \cdot v \in \mathcal{I}_F(B)^\xi_q \\ \quad \text{for every } v \in \mathcal{I}_F(A)^\xi_q \text{ whenever } q = p \text{ or } q \leftarrow p, \\ \quad \text{and} \\ 2.\ u = [\![\lambda x.\, M]\!]_\rho \text{ for some } x,\ \rho \text{ and } M. \end{array} \right\}$$

In the squeal, we prefer to write $\mathcal{I}(A)^\xi$, or $\mathcal{I}(A)$, rather than $\mathcal{I}_S(A)^\xi$ or $\mathcal{I}_F(A)^\xi$ when it would cause no confusion in context. Note that the $\mathcal{I}(A)^\xi_p$ has been defined by induction on the lexicographic ordering of $<p, r(A)>$, where the non-negative integer $r(A)$ is defined as:

$$r(X) = r(\bullet A) = 0$$
$$r(A \to B) = \begin{cases} 0 & (B \text{ is an S(F)-T-variant}) \\ \max(r(A), r(B)) + 1 & (\text{otherwise}) \end{cases}$$
$$r(\mu X.A) = r(A) + 1$$

$\mathcal{I}(\mu X.A)^\xi_p$ is well defined since $r(A[B/X]) < r(\mu X.A)$ for any B whenever A is S(F)-proper in X. We can easily verify that $p \to q$ implies $\mathcal{I}(A)^\xi_p \subset \mathcal{I}(A)^\xi_q$.

Proposition 3. *The equivalence relation* $\simeq$ *and the subtyping relation* $\preceq$ *on type expressions well respect these semantics. That is:*

(1) If $A \simeq B$, *then* $\mathcal{I}(A)^\xi_p = \mathcal{I}(B)^\xi_p$ *for every* $p \in \mathcal{W}$.
(2) If $A \preceq B$, *then* $\mathcal{I}(A)^\xi_p \subset \mathcal{I}(B)^\xi_p$ *for every* $p \in \mathcal{W}$.

From these results, we can also show the soundness of S-$\lambda\bullet\mu$ and F-$\lambda\bullet\mu$ with respect to the semantics of types $\mathcal{I}_S$ and $\mathcal{I}_F$, respectively.

Theorem 1 (Soundness). *If* $\{x_1 : A_1, \ldots, x_n : A_n\} \vdash M : B$ *is derivable, then* $[\![M]\!]_\rho \in \mathcal{I}(B)^\xi_p$ *for every* p, ξ *and* ρ *whenever* $\rho(x_i) \in \mathcal{I}(A_i)^\xi_p$ *for every* i $(i = 1, 2, \ldots, n)$.

Proof. By induction on the derivation and by cases of the last rule used in the derivation. Most cases are straightforward. Use Proposition 3 for the case of ($\preceq$). Prove it by induction on p in the case of ($\to$I). □

One can observe that F-$\lambda\bullet\mu$ is also sound with respect to the simple semantics $\mathcal{I}_S$ by Proposition 1. If the transitive and converse wellfounded frame $<\mathcal{W}, \to>$ also satisfies the following extra condition:

> if $r \to p$, then $r \overset{*}{\to} q \to p$ for some q such that $q \to s$ implies $p \overset{*}{\to} s$ for any s, where $\overset{*}{\to}$ denotes the reflexive (and transitive) closure of $\to$,

then the rule below is also sound with respect to $\mathcal{I}_S$ (respectively $\mathcal{I}_F$), when added to S-$\lambda\bullet\mu$ (F-$\lambda\bullet\mu$).

$$\frac{}{\gamma \vdash \bullet A \to \bullet B \preceq \bullet(A \to B)} \ (\preceq\text{-}\bullet\to)$$

Similarly, if for every $p \in \mathcal{W}$ there exists some $q \in \mathcal{W}$ such that $q \to p$, then

$$\frac{\bullet\Gamma \vdash M : \bullet A}{\Gamma \vdash M : A} \ (\bullet)$$

is sound. For example, the set of non-negative integers, or limit ordinals, and the "greater than" relation $>$, where a smaller number is accessible from a larger one, constitute a frame satisfying the two conditions above. We call the extended systems with these two rules S-$\lambda\bullet\mu^+$ and F-$\lambda\bullet\mu^+$, respectively, where the ($\preceq$-$\bullet\to$) rule makes (nec) redundant. It should be noted that the two rules provide the converses of ($\preceq$-$\to\bullet$) and (nec), respectively. The original system given in [1] is equivalent to F-$\lambda\bullet\mu^+$. Although the base systems S-$\lambda\bullet\mu$ and F-$\lambda\bullet\mu$ are somewhat weaker than that, all the examples of programs presented in the paper still work in them.

Theorem 1 assures us that the modularity of programs is preserved even if we regard type expressions, or specifications, as asserting the convergence of programs. For example, if a type B comprises of certain canonical values, and we have a program M of a type $A \to B$, then we can expect that M terminates and returns such a canonical value when we provide a value of A. By a discussion on soundness with respect to an interpretation over the term model of untyped λ-calculus, we can obtain such convergence properties of well-typed λ-terms. The corresponding results for the original system F-$\lambda\bullet\mu^+$ was first presented in Section 5 of [1].

Definition 9. *A type expression A is* tail finite *if and only if $A \simeq \bullet^{m_1}(B_1 \to \bullet^{m_2}(B_2 \to \bullet^{m_3}(B_3 \to \ldots \to \bullet^{m_n}(B_n \to X)\ldots)))$ for some n, m_0, m_1, m_2, …, m_n, B_1, B_2, …, B_n and X.*

A type expression is tail finite if and only if it is not an S-T-variant.

Definition 10. *Let A be a type expression. Two sets $ETV^+(A)$ and $ETV^-(A)$ of type variables are defined as follows:*

$$ETV^+(X) = \{X\}, \quad ETV^-(X) = \{\},$$
$$ETV^\pm(\bullet A) = ETV^\pm(A),$$
$$ETV^\pm(A \to B) = \begin{cases} \{\} & (B \text{ is an S(F)-}\top\text{-variant}) \\ ETV^\mp(A) \cup ETV^\pm(B) & (\text{otherwise}) \end{cases}$$
$$ETV^\pm(\mu X.A) = \begin{cases} (ETV^\pm(A) \cup ETV^\mp(A)) - \{X\} & (X \in ETV^-(A)) \\ ETV^\pm(A) - \{X\} & (\text{otherwise}) \end{cases}$$

It should be noted that the set $ETV^+(A)$ ($ETV^-(A)$) consists of the type variables that have free positive (negative) occurrences in A, where we ignore any subexpression $B \to C$ of A whenever C is an S(F)-$\top$-variant. If $X \in ETV^\pm(A)$ in S-$\lambda\bullet\mu$, then so is in F-$\lambda\bullet\mu$.

Definition 11. *A type expression A is* positively (negatively) finite *if and only if C is tail finite whenever $A \simeq B[C/X]$ for some B and X such that $X \in ETV^+(B)$ ($X \in ETV^-(B)$) and $X \notin ETV^-(B)$ ($X \notin ETV^+(B)$).*

Every positively finite type expression is tail finite. If a type expression of F-$\lambda\bullet\mu$ is tail (positively, or negatively) finite, then so is as a type expression of S-$\lambda\bullet\mu$.

Theorem 2 (Convergence). *Let $\Gamma \vdash M : A$ be derivable in S-$\lambda\bullet\mu$, F-$\lambda\bullet\mu$, S-$\lambda\bullet\mu^+$ or F-$\lambda\bullet\mu^+$.*

(1) If A is tail finite, then M is head normalizable.
(2) If A is positively finite, and $\Gamma(x)$ is negatively finite for every $x \in Dom(\Gamma)$, then the Böhm tree of M has no occurrence of $\bot$, i.e., a λ-term not being head normalizable.

Proof. It suffices to prove the case of S-$\lambda\bullet\mu^+$. See Appendix. □

Moreover, if the typing judgement is derivable in F-$\lambda\bullet\mu$ or F-$\lambda\bullet\mu^+$ for some A not being an F-$\top$-variant, then M is weakly head normalizable, i.e., β-reduces to the form $\lambda x.\, N$ or $x\, N_1\, N_2 \ldots N_n$ $(n \geq 0)$ (cf. [1]).

4 The Modal Logic behind S-$\lambda\bullet\mu$ and F-$\lambda\bullet\mu$

In this section, we consider S-$\lambda\bullet\mu$ and F-$\lambda\bullet\mu$ as modal logics by ignoring left hand sides of ":" from typing judgments, and show that they precisely correspond to the same modal logic.

Definition 12 (Formal system $L\bullet\mu$). *We define a modal logic considering type expressions as logical formulae, where the equivalence relation $\simeq_L$ on formulae is defined as the smallest binary relation that satisfies the conditions listed* *in Definition 4 except ($\simeq$-uniq) and ($\simeq$-$\to\top$). Let $L\bullet\mu$ be the formal system defined by the following inference rules, where Γ denotes a finite set of formulae.*

$$\frac{}{\Gamma \cup \{A\} \vdash A}\ (assump) \qquad \frac{\Gamma \vdash A}{\bullet\Gamma \vdash \bullet A}\ (nec) \qquad \frac{\Gamma \vdash A}{\Gamma \vdash A'}\ (\simeq_L)\quad (A \simeq_L A')$$

$$\frac{}{\Gamma \vdash \bullet(A \to B) \to \bullet A \to \bullet B}\ (K) \qquad \frac{}{\Gamma \vdash A \to \bullet A}\ (approx)$$

$$\frac{\Gamma \cup \{A\} \vdash B}{\Gamma \vdash A \to B}\ (\to I) \qquad \frac{\Gamma_1 \vdash A \to B \quad \Gamma_2 \vdash A}{\Gamma_1 \cup \Gamma_2 \vdash B}\ (\to E)$$

Proposition 4. *If $\{A_1, \ldots, A_n\} \vdash B$ is derivable in $L\bullet\mu$, then $\{x_1 : A_1, \ldots, x_n : A_n\} \vdash M : B$ is derivable in F-$\lambda\bullet\mu$ for some λ-term M and distinct individual variables $x_1, \ldots, x_n$, such that $FV(M) \subset \{x_1, \ldots, x_n\}$.*

Proof. Straightforward. □

Definition 13. *A $\bullet\mu$-frame is a triple $<\mathcal{W}, \to, R>$, which consists of a set $\mathcal{W}$ of possible worlds and two accessibility relations $\to$ and R on $\mathcal{W}$ such that:*

(1) $<\mathcal{W}, R>$ is a transitive and converse wellfounded frame.
(2) $\to$ is a transitive relation on $\mathcal{W}$.
(3) $p \to q$ implies $p\ R\ q$.

It should be noted that $\to$ is also converse wellfounded by the condition (3); and hence $<\mathcal{W}, \to>$ is also a transitive and converse wellfounded frame.

Definition 14 (Semantics of $L\bullet\mu$). *Let $<\mathcal{W}, \to, R>$ be a $\bullet\mu$-frame. A mapping $\mathcal{I}$ from $\mathcal{W}$ to $\{\mathbf{t}, \mathbf{f}\}$ is* hereditary *if and only if:*

$$\text{if } p\ R\ q, \text{ then } \mathcal{I}(p) = \mathbf{t} \text{ implies } \mathcal{I}(q) = \mathbf{t}.$$

A mapping ξ that assigns a hereditary mapping to each propositional variable, i.e., type variable, is called a valuation. *We define a hereditary mapping $\mathcal{I}_L(A)^\xi$ from $\mathcal{W}$ to $\{\mathbf{t}, \mathbf{f}\}$ for each formula A by extending ξ as follows, where we write $\models_p^\xi A$ to denote $\mathcal{I}_L(A)^\xi(p) = \mathbf{t}$.*

$\models_p^\xi X$ *iff* $\xi(X)_p = \mathbf{t}$

$\models_p^\xi A \to B$ *iff* $\models_q^\xi A$ *implies* $\models_q^\xi B$ *for every q such that $q = p$ or $p\ R\ q$*

$\models_p^\xi \bullet A$ *iff* $\models_q^\xi A$ *for every q such that $p \to q$ or $p\ R\ r \to q$ for some r*

$\models_p^\xi \mu X.A$ *iff* $\models_p^\xi A[\mu X.A/X]$

Note that $\models_p^\xi A$ is again defined by induction on the lexicographic ordering of $<p, r(A)>$. We write $\Gamma \models_p^\xi A$ if and only if $\models_p^\xi A$ whenever $\models_p^\xi B$ for every $B \in \Gamma$. By a discussion similar to Theorem 1, one observes soundness of S-$\lambda\bullet\mu$ as a logic with respect to this semantics of formulae.

Proposition 5. *If* $A \preceq B$ *in* S-$\lambda\bullet\mu$, *then* $\{A\} \models_p^{\xi} B$.

Proposition 6. *Let* $<\mathcal{W}, \rightarrow, R>$ *be a* $\bullet\mu$*-frame, and* ξ *a valuation. If* $\{x_1 : A_1, \ldots, x_n : A_n\} \vdash M : B$ *is derivable in* S-$\lambda\bullet\mu$, *then* $\{A_1, \ldots, A_n\} \models_p^{\xi} B$ *for every* $p \in \mathcal{W}$.

The main results of the present paper can be summarized as the following theorem.

Theorem 3. *The following four conditions are equivalent.*

(1) $\{A_1, \ldots, A_n\} \vdash B$ *is derivable in* $L\bullet\mu$.
(2) $\{x_1 : A_1, \ldots, x_n : A_n\} \vdash M : B$ *is derivable in* F-$\lambda\bullet\mu$ *for some* M, x_1, $\ldots$, x_n.
(3) $\{x_1 : A_1, \ldots, x_n : A_n\} \vdash M : B$ *is derivable in* S-$\lambda\bullet\mu$ *for some* M, x_1, $\ldots$, x_n.
(4) $\{A_1, \ldots, A_n\} \models_p^{\xi} B$ *for every* $\bullet\mu$*-frame* $<\mathcal{W}, \rightarrow, R>$, *valuation* ξ, *and* $p \in \mathcal{W}$.

Proof. We get (1) ⇒ (2), (2) ⇒ (3), and (3) ⇒ (4) by Propositions 4, 1 and 6, respectively. Hence, it suffices to show that (4) ⇒ (1), which is given by the following completeness theorem. □

Theorem 4 (Completeness of $L\bullet\mu$). *If* $\{A_1, \ldots, A_n\} \vdash M : B$ *is not derivable in* $L\bullet\mu$, *then there exist some* $\bullet\mu$*-frame* $<\mathcal{W}_0, \rightarrow_0, R_0>$, *valuation* ξ_0, *and* $p_0 \in \mathcal{W}_0$ *such that* $\not\models_{p_0}^{\xi_0} B$ *while* $\models_{p_0}^{\xi_0} A_i$ *for every* i $(i = 1, 2, \ldots, n)$.

The rest of the present section is devoted to proving this theorem. Suppose that $\{A_1, \ldots, A_n\} \vdash M : B$ is not derivable.

Let C and D be formulae, i.e., type expressions. We call C a *component* of D, and write $C \leq D$, if and only if

$$E[C/X] \simeq_L D \quad \text{and} \quad X \in FTV(E)$$

for some type expression E and type variable X. We also define *Comp*(D) as:

$$Comp(D) = \{C \mid C \leq D\}.$$

Note that $Comp(D)/\!\simeq_L$ is a finite set (cf. e.g. [9,8]). Let

$$\mathcal{F} = \{\, C \mid C \in Comp(B) \text{ or } C \in Comp(A_i) \text{ for some } i \,\},$$

and define W_0 and p_0 as:

$$W_0 = \{\, p \subset \mathcal{F} \mid C \in p \text{ whenever } C \in \mathcal{F} \text{ and } p \vdash C \text{ is derivable}^2 \,\}$$
$$p_0 = \{\, C \in \mathcal{F} \mid \{A_1, \ldots, A_n\} \vdash C \text{ is derivable} \,\}$$

Note that $\mathcal{W}_0$ is a finite set since $Comp(D)/{\simeq_L}$ is finite and $L{\bullet}\mu$ has the $(\simeq_L)$ rule. Then, for each $p \in \mathcal{W}_0$, define $\tilde{p}$ as:

$$\tilde{p} = \{\, C \in \mathcal{F} \mid p \vdash \bullet C \text{ is derivable} \,\}$$

Observe that $p \in \mathcal{W}_0$ implies $\tilde{p} \in \mathcal{W}_0$, since if $\tilde{p} \vdash C$ is derivable for some $C \in \mathcal{F}$, then so is $\bullet\tilde{p} \vdash \bullet C$ by (nec); and therefore, $p \vdash \bullet C$ is also derivable, i.e., $C \in \tilde{p}$. Note also that $p \subset \tilde{p}$ holds because $L{\bullet}\mu$ has the (approx) rule. The accessibility relations $\rightarrow_0$ and R_0 are defined as follows:

$$\begin{aligned} p \rightarrow_0 q \quad &\text{iff} \quad \tilde{p} \subset q \text{ and } \tilde{q} \neq q. \\ p \, R_0 \, q \quad &\text{iff} \quad p \subset q \text{ and } p \neq q. \end{aligned}$$

We can easily verify that $\rightarrow_0$ and R_0 are transitive, and $p{\rightarrow_0}q$ implies $p \, R_0 \, q$. Since $\mathcal{W}_0$ is finite, R_0 is also converse wellfounded. We finally define the valuation ξ_0 as:

$$\xi_0(X)_p = \begin{cases} \mathbf{t} & (X \in p) \\ \mathbf{f} & (X \notin p) \end{cases}$$

Obviously, ξ_0 is hereditary by the definition of R_0. Since $B \notin p_0$ while $A_i \in p_0$ for every i, to finish the proof of the completeness theorem, it suffices to prove the following lemma.

Lemma 1. *Let $C \in \mathcal{F}$ and $p \in \mathcal{W}_0$. Then, $C \in p$ if and only if $\models_p^{\xi_0} C$.*

Proof. The proof proceeds by induction on the lexicographic ordering of $\langle p, r(C)\rangle$, and by cases of the form of C.

Case: $C = X$. Trivial from the definition of $\xi_0(X)$.

Case: $C = D \rightarrow E$. For the "only if" part, suppose that $D \rightarrow E \in p$, $\models_q^{\xi_0} D$, and $q = p$ or $p \, R_0 \, q$. We get $D \in q$ from $\models_q^{\xi_0} D$ by induction hypothesis, since p decreases to q or else $r(D) < r(D \rightarrow E)$, and $D \rightarrow E \in q$ from $p \subset q$. Therefore, $E \in q$, and by induction hypothesis again, $\models_q^{\xi_0} E$. Thus we get $\models_p^{\xi_0} D \rightarrow E$. As for "if" part, suppose that $\models_p^{\xi_0} D \rightarrow E$, i.e.,

$$\models_q^{\xi_0} D \text{ implies } \models_q^{\xi_0} E \text{ whenever } q = p \text{ or } p \, R_0 \, q \tag{1}$$

Let q as:

$$q = \{\, C' \in \mathcal{F} \mid p \cup \{D\} \vdash C' \text{ is derivable} \,\}.$$

Note that $q = p$ or $p \, R_0 \, q$. Since $D \in q$, we get $\models_q^{\xi_0} D$ by induction hypothesis, and then $\models_q^{\xi_0} E$ from (1). Hence, by induction hypothesis again, $E \in q$, i.e., $p \cup \{D\} \vdash E$ is derivable, and so is $p \vdash D \rightarrow E$.

[2] More precisely, $\Gamma' \vdash C$ derivable for some finite $\Gamma' \subset p$.

Case: $C = \bullet D$. For the "only if" part, suppose that $\bullet D \in p$. If $p \to q$ or $p\ R\ r \to q$ for some r, then since $\tilde{p} \subset q$ and $p \vdash \bullet D$ is derivable, we get $D \in q$. Hence, $\models_q^{\xi_0} D$ by induction hypothesis. We thus get $\models_p^{\xi_0} \bullet D$. For "if" part, suppose that $\models_p^{\xi_0} \bullet D$, i.e.,

$$\models_q^{\xi_0} D \text{ for any } q \text{ if } p \to q \text{ or } p\ R\ r \to q \text{ for some } r\ . \tag{2}$$

Let q as:

$$q = \{\, C' \in \mathcal{F} \mid \tilde{p} \cup \{\bullet D\} \vdash C' \text{ is derivable} \,\}.$$

If $p \to q$, then $\models_q^{\xi_0} D$ by (2); therefore, $D \in q$ by induction hypothesis. Otherwise, $\tilde{q} = q$, i.e., also $D \in q$. Hence, $\tilde{p} \cup \{\bullet D\} \vdash D$ is derivable. On the other hand, there is a derivation of $\vdash (\bullet D \to D) \to D$ corresponding to the **Y**-combinator. Therefore, $\tilde{p} \vdash D$ is also derivable, and so is $\bullet\tilde{p} \vdash \bullet D$ by (nec). That is, $p \vdash \bullet D$ is derivable; and therefore, $\bullet D \in p$.

Case: $C = \mu X.D$. For the "only if" part, suppose that $\mu X.D \in p$, i.e., also $D[\mu X.D/X] \in p$ by ($\simeq_L$) rule. We get $\models_p^{\xi_0} D[\mu X.D/X]$ by induction hypothesis, since $r(D[\mu X.D/X]) < r(\mu X.D)$; and therefore, $\models_p^{\xi_0} \mu X.D$ by definition. For "if" part, suppose that $\models_p^{\xi_0} \mu X.D$, i.e., $\models_p^{\xi_0} D[\mu X.D/X]$. We get $D[\mu X.D/X] \in p$ by induction hypothesis; and therefore, $\mu X.D \in p$ by the ($\simeq_L$) rule. □

This completes the proof of Theorems 4 and 3. Since the counter model constructed in the proof of Lemma 1 is based on a finite frame, the logic $L\bullet\mu$ has the finite model property, and we therefore get the following corollary.

Corollary 1. *The following problems are decidable.*

(1) Provability in $L\bullet\mu$.
(2) Type inhabitance in S-$\lambda\bullet\mu$.
(3) Type inhabitance in F-$\lambda\bullet\mu$.

5 Relationship to the Intuitionistic Logic of Provability

The logic $L\bullet\mu$ permits self-referential formulae. In this section, we show that if $L\bullet\mu$ is restricted to finite formulae, i.e., those without any occurrence of μ, then one gets the *intuitionistic* version of the logic of provability GL (cf. [5]), where "intuitionistic" means that the interpretation is monotonic with respect to the accessibility relation, and not provability in intuitionistic systems such as HA. GL is also denoted by G (for Gödel), L (for Löb), PrL, KW, or K4W, in the literature.

Definition 15 (Formal system iKW). *We define a modal logic iKW, which only allows finite formulae, by replacing the $\simeq_L$ rule of $L\bullet\mu$ by the following inference rule.*

$$\frac{}{\Gamma \vdash \bullet(\bullet A \to A) \to \bullet A}\ (W)$$

We observe that iKW is sound with respect to the Kripke semantics over $\bullet\mu$-frames, i.e., Definition 14, because the (W) rule is derivable in $L\bullet\mu$, by (approx) and (K), from the seemingly more general $(\bullet A \to A) \to A$, which is derivable by the **Y**-combinator. And conversely, the axiom schema $\mathrm{W} : \bullet(\bullet A \to A) \to \bullet A$ implies $(\bullet A \to A) \to A$ as follows:

$$
\dfrac{\dfrac{\dfrac{}{\{\bullet A \to A\} \vdash \bullet A \to A}\,\text{(assump)} \qquad \dfrac{\dfrac{\dfrac{}{\{\bullet A \to A\} \vdash \bullet A \to A}\,\text{(assump)}}{\{\bullet A \to A\} \vdash \bullet(\bullet A \to A)}\,\text{(approx), }(\to\text{E})}{\{\bullet A \to A\} \vdash \bullet A}\,\text{(W), }(\to\text{E})}{\{\bullet A \to A\} \vdash A}\,(\to\text{E})}{\{\} \vdash (\bullet A \to A) \to A}\,(\to\text{I})
$$

Then, since the only role of $(\simeq_L)$ for finite formulae in the proof of Lemma 1 is the derivability of $(\bullet D \to D) \to D$, which is used in the "if" part of the case $C = \bullet D$, we get the following.

Theorem 5 (Completeness of iKW). *The formal system iKW is also Kripke complete with respect to $\bullet\mu$-frames.*

And hence, by Theorem 3, $L\bullet\mu$ is a conservative extension of iKW.

6 Concluding Remarks

Two modal typing systems S-$\lambda\bullet\mu$ and F-$\lambda\bullet\mu$, which are respectively based on the simple and the F-semantics of types, and a formal system of the modal logic behind them have been presented. We have shown that the modal logic is Kripke complete with respect to intuitionistic, transitive and converse well-founded frames. The completeness also connects provability in the modal logic to type inhabitance in the two modal typing systems, and implies their decidability. We have also shown that the modal logic is a conservative extension of the intuitionistic version of the logic of provability. We have not, however, yet obtained corresponding results for the extended typing systems S-$\lambda\bullet\mu^+$ and F-$\lambda\bullet\mu^+$, which are also logically equivalent to each other, and completeness and decidability of typing and typability of λ-terms in all the typing systems presented in the present paper are also still open.

References

1. Nakano, H.: A modality for recursion. In: Proceedings of the 15th IEEE Symposium on Logic in Computer Science. IEEE Computer Society Press (2000) 255–266
2. Nakano, H.: A modality for recursion (technical report). Available as `http://www602.math.ryukoku.ac.jp/~nakano/papers/modality-tr01.ps` (2001)
3. Hindley, R.: The completeness theorem for typing λ-terms. Theoretical Computer Science **22** (1983) 1–17

4. Hindley, R.: Curry's type-rules are complete with respect to F-sematics too. Theoretical Computer Science **22** (1983) 127–133
5. Boolos, G.: The logic of provability. Cambridge University Press (1993)
6. Barendregt, H.P.: Lambda calculi with types. In Abramsky, S., Gabbay, D.M., Maibaum, T.S.E., eds.: Handbook of Logic in Computer Science. Volume 2. Oxford University Press (1992) 118–309
7. Cardone, F., Coppo, M.: Type inference with recursive types: syntax and semantics. Information and Computation **92** (1991) 48–80
8. Amadio, R.M., Cardelli, L.: Subtyping recursive types. ACM Transactions on Programming Languages and Systems **15** (1993) 575–631
9. Courcelle, B.: Fundamental properties of infinite trees. Theoretical Computer Science **25** (1983) 95–169

Appendix: Proof of Theorem 2

We first give alternative definitions of tail finiteness and positively (negatively) finiteness.

Definition 16. *Let V be a set of type variables. We define subsets $\mathbf{TF}^V$, $\mathbf{PF}$ and $\mathbf{NF}$ of $\mathbf{TExp}$ as follows:*

$$
\begin{array}{rcl}
\mathbf{TF}^V & ::= & X \quad (X \notin V) \\
& | & \bullet\mathbf{TF}^V \ \mid \ \mathbf{TExp} \to \mathbf{TF}^V \ \mid \ \mu Y.\mathbf{TF}^{V \cup \{Y\}} \\
\mathbf{PF} & ::= & \mathbf{TVar} \ \mid \ \bullet\mathbf{PF} \ \mid \ \mathbf{NF} \to \mathbf{PF} \\
& | & \mu Y.A \quad (A \in \mathbf{TF}^{\{Y\}} \cap \mathbf{PF}, \textit{ and } Y \in ETV^-(A) \textit{ implies } A \in \mathbf{NF}). \\
\mathbf{NF} & ::= & \mathbf{TVar} \ \mid \ \bullet\mathbf{NF} \ \mid \ \mathbf{PF} \to \mathbf{NF} \ \mid \ C \quad (C \textit{ is an } S\text{-}\top\textit{-variant}) \\
& | & \mu Y.A \quad (A \in \mathbf{NF}, \textit{ and } Y \in ETV^-(A) \textit{ implies } A \in \mathbf{TF}^{\{Y\}} \cap \mathbf{PF}).
\end{array}
$$

Proposition 7. *(1) A is tail finite if and only if $A \in \mathbf{TF}^{\{\}}$.*
(2) A is positively finite if and only if $A \in \mathbf{PF}$.
(3) A is negatively finite if and only if $A \in \mathbf{NF}$.

It follows that tail finiteness and positively (negatively) finiteness are decidable properties of type expressions. Through these alternative definitions, we get the following proposition.

Proposition 8. *Suppose that $A \preceq B$.*

(1) If B is tail finite, then so is A.
(2) If B is positively finite, then so is A.
(3) If A is negatively finite, then so is B.

Proof of the first claim of Theorem 2. Suppose that $\Gamma \vdash M : A$ is derivable in S-$\lambda\bullet\mu^+$. We consider the frame $<\mathcal{N}, >>$, which consists of the set of non-negative integers and the "greater than" relation on it, over the term model $<\mathcal{V}, \cdot, [\![\ ]\!]>$ of untyped λ-calculus. Define a subset $\mathcal{K}$ of $\mathcal{V}$ as:

$$\mathcal{K} = \left\{ [xN_1N_2 \dots N_n] \;\middle|\; \begin{array}{l} x \text{ is an individual variable, } n \geq 0, \text{ and} \\ N_i \in \mathcal{V} \text{ for every } i \ (i = 1, 2, \dots, n) \end{array} \right\}.$$

Taking ρ as $\rho(x) = [x]$ for any x, we get $[M] = [\![M]\!]_\rho \in \mathcal{I}_S(A)_p^\xi$ by Theorem 1 for S-$\lambda\bullet\mu^+$. Note also that $\mathcal{K} \subset \mathcal{I}_S(A)_p^\xi$ for any A and p by Definition 8.

Since ξ can be any type environment, it suffices to show that M has a head normal form whenever
(a) $A \in \mathbf{TF}^V$,
(b) $\xi(X)_p = \mathcal{K}$ for every p and $X \notin V$, and
(c) $[M] \in \mathcal{I}(A)_p^\xi$ for every p.
The proof proceeds by induction on the complexity of A, and by cases of the form of A. Suppose (a) through (c).

Case: $A = X$. In this case, $\mathcal{I}(A)_p^\xi = \xi(X)_p = \mathcal{K}$ by (a) and (b). Therefore, M obviously has a head normal form.

Case: $A = \bullet B$. In this case, $B \in \mathbf{TF}^V$ by (a). Therefore, M has a head normal form by the induction hypothesis. Note that (c) implies $[M] \in \mathcal{I}(B)_p^\xi$ for every p, because there exists some q such that $q \to p$.

Case: $A = B \to C$. In this case, $C \in \mathbf{TF}^V$ by (a). Let y be a fresh individual variable. Since $[M] \in \mathcal{I}(B \to C)_p^\xi$ and $[y] \in \mathcal{K} \subset \mathcal{I}(B)_p^\xi$ for every p, we get $[My] \in \mathcal{I}(C)_p^\xi$ for every p. Therefore, My has a head normal form, say L, by the induction hypothesis. There are two possible cases: for some K, (1) $M \xrightarrow[\beta]{*} K \in \mathcal{K}$ and $L = Ky \in \mathcal{K}$, or (2) $M \xrightarrow[\beta]{*} \lambda y.\, K$ and $K \xrightarrow[\beta]{*} L$. In either case, M has a head normal form.

Case: $A = \mu Y.B$. In this case, $B \in \mathbf{TF}^{V\cup\{Y\}}$ by (a). By Definition 8, we get $\mathcal{I}(\mu Y.B)_p^\xi = \mathcal{I}(B[\mu Y.B/Y])_p^\xi = \mathcal{I}(B)_p^{\xi'}$, where $\xi' = \xi[\mathcal{I}(\mu Y.B)_p^\xi/Y]$, since $\mathcal{I}(C[D/Y])_p^\xi = \mathcal{I}(C)_p^{\xi[\mathcal{I}(D)^\xi/Y]}$ holds for any C and D. Note that (a′) $B \in \mathbf{TF}^{V\cup\{Y\}}$, (b′) $\xi'(X)_p = \mathcal{K}$ for every p and $X \notin V \cup \{Y\}$, and (c′) $M \in \mathcal{I}(B)_p^{\xi'}$ for every p. Therefore, M has a head normal form by the induction hypothesis. □

As for the second claim of Theorem 2, we employ the following lemma.

Lemma 2. *Suppose that* $A \not\simeq \top$. *If* $\Gamma \vdash xN_1N_2 \dots N_n : A$ *is derivable in S-*$\lambda\bullet\mu^+$*, then* $\Gamma(x) \preceq \bullet^{m_1}(B_1 \to \bullet^{m_2}(B_2 \to \dots \to \bullet^{m_n}(B_n \to C)\dots))$ *for some* $m_1, m_2, \dots, m_n, B_1, B_2, \dots, B_n$ *and* C *such that*
1. $\bullet^{m_1+m_2+\dots+m_n}C \preceq A$, *and*
2. *for every* i $(0 \leq i \leq n)$, $\Gamma \vdash N_i\, \bullet^{m'_i} B_i$ *is derivable for some* m'_i.

Proof. By induction on n. If $n = 0$, then since $A \not\preceq \top$, the derivation ends with:

$$\dfrac{\dfrac{}{\Gamma' \vdash x : \Gamma'(x)}\ (\text{var})}{\dfrac{\vdots\ 0 \text{ or more } (\preceq)\text{'s}}{\Gamma \vdash x : A}}$$

Therefore, we get $C \preceq A$ by taking C as $C = \Gamma'(x)$. If $n > 0$, then for some m', D and E, the derivation ends with:

$$\dfrac{\dfrac{\begin{array}{c}\vdots \\ \Gamma' \vdash xN_1N_2\ldots N_{n-1} : \bullet^{m'}(D \to E)\end{array} \quad \begin{array}{c}\vdots \\ \Gamma' \vdash N_n : \bullet^{m'}D\end{array}}{\Gamma' \vdash xN_1N_2\ldots N_n : \bullet^{m'}E}\ (\to\text{E})}{\dfrac{\vdots\ 0 \text{ or more } (\preceq)\text{'s}}{\Gamma \vdash xN_1N_2\ldots N_n : A}}$$

Note that $\bullet^{m'}E \preceq A$, and $E \not\preceq \top$ since $A \not\preceq \top$. By induction hypothesis, $\Gamma'(x) \preceq \bullet^{m_1}(B_1 \to \bullet^{m_2}(B_2 \to \ldots \to \bullet^{m_{n-1}}(B_{n-1} \to C')\ldots))$ for some m_1, m_2, $\ldots$, m_{n-1}, B_1, B_2, $\ldots$, B_{n-1} and C' such that:
- $\bullet^{m_1+m_2+\ldots+m_{n-1}}C' \preceq \bullet^{m'}(D \to E)$, and
- for every i $(0 \le i \le n-1)$, $\Gamma \vdash N_i \bullet^{m'_i} B_i$ is derivable for some m'_i.

This implies that there exist some m'', j, k, l, B_n and C such that:
- $\bullet^{m_1+m_2+\ldots+m_{n-1}}C' \simeq \bullet^{m''}(B_n \to C)$,
- $m''-j \le m'-k$, and
- $\bullet^k D \preceq \bullet^{j+l}B_n$ and $\bullet^{j+l}C \preceq \bullet^k E$.

We then get $C' \preceq \bullet^{m_n}(B_n \to C)$, where $m_n = m''-m_1-m_2-\ldots-m_{n-1}$; and therefore, $\Gamma(x) \preceq \bullet^{m_1}(B_1 \to \bullet^{m_2}(B_2 \to \ldots \to \bullet^{m_{n-1}}(B_{n-1} \to \bullet^{m_n}(B_n \to C)\ldots))$. On the other hand, $\bullet^{m_1+m_2+\ldots+m_{n-1}+m_n}C = \bullet^{m''}C \preceq \bullet^{m'-k}C \preceq \bullet^{m'-k+j+l}C \preceq \bullet^{m'}E \preceq A$ and $\bullet^{m'}D \preceq \bullet^{m'-k+j+l}B_n$. We get the derivation of $\Gamma \vdash N_n : \bullet^{m'-k+j+l}B_n$ from the one of $\Gamma \vdash N_n : \bullet^{m'}D$ by $(\preceq)$. □

Proof of the second claim of Theorem 2. Suppose that $\Gamma \vdash M : A$ is derivable in S-$\lambda\bullet\mu^+$ for some A and Γ such that A is positively finite and $\Gamma(x)$ is negatively finite for every $x \in \mathit{Dom}(\Gamma)$. We show that for every n, every node of the Böhm-tree of M at the level n is head normalizable, by induction on n. Since A is positively finite, M is head normalizable by (1) of Theorem 2, that is

$$M \xrightarrow[\beta]{*} \lambda x_1.\,\lambda x_2.\,\ldots\lambda x_m.\,yN_1\,N_2\,\ldots\,N_l$$

for some x_1, x_2, $\ldots$, x_m, y, N_1, N_2, $\ldots$, N_l. By (3) of Proposition 2, $\Gamma \vdash \lambda x_1.\,\lambda x_2.\,\ldots\lambda x_m.\,yN_1\,N_2\,\ldots\,N_l : A$ is also derivable; and this implies that so is $\Gamma \cup \{x_1 : B_1, x_2 : B_2, \ldots, x_m : B_m\} \vdash yN_1\,N_2\,\ldots\,N_l : C$ for some B_1, B_2, $\ldots$, B_m and C such that:

$$B_1 \to B_2 \to \ldots \to B_m \to C \preceq A.$$

Since A is positively finite, so is C, i.e., $C \not\preceq \top$, and $B_1, B_2, \ldots, B_m$ are negatively finite by Proposition 8. Let $\Gamma' = \Gamma \cup \{x_1 : B_1, x_2 : B_2, \ldots, x_m : B_m\}$. Since $C \not\preceq \top$, by Lemma 2, $\Gamma'(y) \preceq \bullet^{k_1}(D_1 \to \bullet^{k_2}(D_2 \to \ldots \to \bullet^{k_l}(D_l \to E)\ldots))$ for some $k_1, k_2, \ldots, k_l, D_1, D_2, \ldots, D_l$ and E such that:

- $\bullet^{k_1+k_2+\ldots+k_l} E \preceq C$, and
- for every i $(0 \leq i \leq l)$, $\Gamma' \vdash N_i : \bullet^{k'_i} D_i$ is derivable for some k'_i.

Since C is positively finite, so is E, i.e., $E \not\preceq \top$; and therefore, D_i is positively finite for every i $(0 \leq i \leq l)$ because $\Gamma'(z)$ is negatively finite for every $z \in Dom(\Gamma')$. Therefore, by the induction hypothesis, for every i $(0 \leq i \leq l)$, every node of the Böhm-tree of N_i at a level less than n is head normalizable; that is, so is one of M at a level less than or equal to n. □

Termination Proofs and Complexity Certification

Daniel Leivant*

Computer Science Department, Indiana University, Bloomington, IN 47405.
leivant@cs.indiana.edu.

Abstract. We show that simple structural conditions on proofs of convergence of equational programs, in the intrinsic-theories verification framework of [16], correspond to resource bounds on program execution. These conditions may be construed as reflecting finitistic-predicative reasoning. The results provide a user-transparent method for certifying the computational complexity of functional programs. In particular, we define natural notions of data-positive formulas and of data-predicative derivations, and show that restricting induction to data-positive formulas captures precisely the primitive recursive functions, data-predicative derivations characterize the Kalmar-elementary functions, and the combination of both yields the poly-time functions.

1 Introduction

1.1 Main Results

In [16] we put forth, for each sorted inductive algebra $\mathbb{A}(C)$ over a set C of generators, a formalism $\mathbf{IT}(C)$ for reasoning about equational programs over $\mathbb{A}(C)$. We showed that the resulting formalisms have the same proof theoretic power as first order (Peano) arithmetic. Here we consider simple structural properties on formulas in derivations, which guarantee that a program proved terminating in fact runs within certain resource bounds.

We consider two forms of structural restrictions on natural deductions:

1. Induction is restricted to "data-positive" formulas; these are the formulas where data-predicates do not occur negatively, and they include the (interpretations of) $\boldsymbol{\Sigma}_1^0$ formulas of **PA**.
2. The main premise of induction never depends on data-positive working assumptions, i.e. assumptions that are closed in the derivation, and where data-predicates occur positively.

We show that programs whose termination is provable under these restrictions characterize exactly major complexity classes, as listed below: every provable program uses the indicated resources, and every function in the indicated complexity class is computable by some program provable with the indicated restrictions:

* Research partially supported by NSF grants DMS-9870320 and CS-0105651

N. Kobayashi and B.C. Pierce (Eds.): TACS 2001, LNCS 2215, pp. 183–200, 2001.

- Condition (1) yields exactly the primitive recursive functions (Theorem 4).
- (2) yields exactly the (Kalmar-) elementary functions (Theorem 5).
- (1) and (2) combined yield linear space for programs over $\mathbb{N}$, and poly-time for programs over symbolic data, e.g. $\{0,1\}^*$ (Theorem 6).

Restrictions (1) and (2) can be construed as reflecting a certain "finitistic-predicative" view of data. In broad strokes, the underlying views can be stated as follows. Take the position that an inductive data system, say the set $\mathbb{N}$ of natural numbers, comes into being through a process, but cannot be admitted as a completed totality. In particular, determining the elements of $\mathbb{N}$ should not depend on assuming that the full outcome of the generative process for $\mathbb{N}$ is already in hand. To constructively justify a proof by induction of a formula $\varphi[\mathbf{t}]$ one needs then to posit that the induction formula $\varphi[x]$ is well-defined for all values for x, and that the term $\mathbf{t}$ is well-defined. A formula in which $\mathbf{N}$ occurs only positively, say $\exists x\, \mathbf{N}(f(x))$, asserts that the process of generating $\mathbb{N}$ eventually yields an element in the range of f; no invocation of $\mathbb{N}$ as completed totality is used. This justifies induction for data-positive formulas.

Consider, in contrast, a a formula which not data-positive, say $\forall x\, \mathbf{N}(x) \rightarrow \mathbf{N}(\mathbf{f}(x))$, which classically is equivalent to $\forall x\, \neg\mathbf{N}(x) \vee \mathbf{N}(\mathbf{f}(x))$. The meaning of such a formula clearly depends on admitting $\mathbb{N}$ as a completed totality.

The consequence of the finitistic-predicative viewpoint is even more dramatic when it comes to the eigen-term $\mathbf{t}$ of induction (recall that in our framework $\mathbf{t}$ may contain arbitrary function identifiers). Consider a Data-Elimination (i.e. Induction) rule, say for $\mathbb{N}$,

$$\frac{\mathbf{N}(\mathbf{t}) \quad \varphi[\mathbf{0}] \quad \varphi[u] \rightarrow \varphi[\mathbf{s}u]}{\varphi[\mathbf{t}]}$$

If we assert the major premise, $\mathbf{N}(\mathbf{t}[x])$, on the basis of $\mathbf{N}(x)$ as assumption, and x is later quantified in the derivation, then we implicitly posit that the scope of $\mathbb{N}$ is well delineated.

1.2 Motivation and Benefits

The simple framework of [16] yields surprisingly rich benefits. Practically, it enables explicit reasoning about functional programs without recourse to numeric codes or a logic of partially-denoting terms. This includes programs whose termination cannot be proved within the formal theory used. Conceptually, the framework lends itself to a delineation of various forms of finitistic and predicative ontologies of data, and to proof theoretic characterizations of computational complexity classes, as we do here. Such formalisms are quite different from the well developed framework of Bounded Arithmetic, and offer an expressively rich and unobtrusive setting for formalizing Feasible Mathematics, e.g. Poly-time or Poly-space Mathematics.

1.3 Comparisons

Several connections have been discovered between proof complexity and the computational complexity of provably-terminating programs. Gödel's famed Dialectica translation [4] can already be seen as such a connection, showing that the provably recursive functions of first-order arithmetic are precisely the functions definable by primitive-recursion in all finite types.

More recent connections between the complexity of program-termination proofs and computational complexity have used a number of paradigms.

1. Restriction on induction formulas. Parson [18] showed that restricting induction to $\boldsymbol{\Sigma}^0_1$ formulas yields precisely the primitive recursive functions, a special case of our Theorem 4 below. Inspired by Cobham's characterization of poly-time by bounded recursion, induction on bounded formulas was studied by Buss and others, leading to characterizations of several classes, notable poly-time and poly-space [3].
2. Restricted set existence in second and higher order logic [12].
3. Data ramification. Data ramification for functional programming was introduced independently in [22, 2, 11], and was subsequently shown to yield functional languages that characterize precisely major computational complexity classes. First order theories based on ramification were introduced in [14].[1] The ramified theory with first order induction yields linear space for numeric data, and poly-space for symbolic data.

Like the ramified formalisms introduced in [14], the present results are for the framework of intrinsic theories for inductive data (see [16] for details). The salient aspects of this approach are (1) programs are referred to explicitly at the assertion level, not through coding or modal operations; and (2) there are explicit predicates to convey that terms denote data of particular sorts. However, contrary to (3), the restrictions on proofs considered here are articulated in terms of restrictions on formulas in crucial positions in a proof, rather than data-tiering.

2 The Methodology of Intrinsic Theories

2.1 Intrinsic Theories

Consider the simplest non-degenerated inductively generated algebra, i.e. the set $\mathbb{N}$ of natural numbers, generated from the constructors $\mathbf{0}$ and $\mathbf{s}$ (zero and successor). The intrinsic theory $\mathbf{IT}(\mathbb{N})$ is defined as the first order theory over the vocabulary consisting of $\mathbf{0}$, $\mathbf{s}$, and a unary relational identifier $\mathbf{N}$, with the following axioms.

1 *Generative axioms:* $\mathbf{N}(\mathbf{0})$ and $\forall x.\, \mathbf{N}(x) \rightarrow \mathbf{N}(\mathbf{s}x)$;
2 The axiom schema of *Induction*: $\varphi[\mathbf{0}] \wedge \forall x.\, (\varphi[x] \rightarrow \varphi[\mathbf{s}x]) \rightarrow \forall x.\, (\mathbf{N}(x) \rightarrow \varphi[x])$.

[1] A more complete account of this development is in [17].

We also consider an extension $\overline{\mathbf{IT}}(\mathbb{N})$ of $\mathbf{IT}(\mathbb{N})$, with separation axioms for the constructors of $\mathbb{N}$ (i.e. Peano's third and fourth axioms):

3 $\forall x.\, \neg\, \mathsf{s}(x) = \mathbf{0}$,
4 $\forall x, y.\ \mathsf{s}x = \mathsf{s}y \rightarrow x = y$.

We use Gentzen-style natural deduction calculi, with the usual inference rules for equality, and a rendition of the axioms by inference rules. For the data system $\mathbb{N}$ these are simply Peano's first and second axioms, and the schema of Induction:

Data-introduction

$$\frac{}{\mathsf{N}(\mathbf{0})} \qquad \text{and} \qquad \frac{\mathsf{N}(t)}{\mathsf{N}(\mathsf{s}t)}$$

Data-Elimination (i.e., induction)

$$\frac{\mathsf{N}(t) \quad \varphi[\mathbf{0}] \quad \varphi[u] \rightarrow \varphi[\mathsf{s}u]}{\varphi[t]}$$

with u not free in open assumptions. A degenerate form of data-elimination is

$$\frac{\mathsf{N}(t) \quad \varphi[\mathbf{0}] \quad \varphi[\mathsf{s}u]}{\varphi[t]}$$

that is, proof by cases on the main constructor.

Separation

$$\frac{\mathsf{s}t = t}{\perp} \qquad \text{and} \qquad \frac{\mathsf{s}t = \mathsf{s}t'}{t = t'}$$

We shall use freely common concepts and terminology for natural deduction calculi, as presented e.g. in [24].

2.2 Provable Functions

We refer to equational programs as defined in [16]. In particular, an r-ary function f over $\mathbb{N}$ is *provable* in $\mathbf{IT}(\mathbb{N})$ if there is an equational program $(P, \mathbf{f})$ that computes f, and for which

$$\mathsf{N}(\boldsymbol{x}) \vdash \mathsf{N}(\mathbf{f}(\boldsymbol{x}))$$

where $\mathsf{N}(\boldsymbol{x})$ abbreviates the conjunction $\mathsf{N}(x_1) \wedge \cdots \wedge \mathsf{N}(x_r)$, and provability is in $\mathbf{IT}(\mathbb{N}) + \bar{P}$, where $\bar{P}$ is the universal closure of the conjunction of the equations in P. Function provability in $\overline{\mathbf{IT}}(\mathbb{N})$ is defined similarly.

In [16] we showed that the functions provable in $\mathbf{IT}(\mathbb{N})$, as well as those provable in $\overline{\mathbf{IT}}(\mathbb{N})$, are precisely the provably recursive functions of Peano Arithmetic. The following observations clarify the notion of functional provability, and will serve us in the sequel.

PROPOSITION 1 *Let* $\mathbf{IT}$ *be either* $\mathbf{IT}(\mathbb{N})$ *or* $\overline{\mathbf{IT}}(\mathbb{N})$, *based on any logic containing minimal logic with equality. The set of provable functions of* $\mathbf{IT}$ *is then closed under composition and simultaneous recurrence. Consequently, all primitive recursive functions are provable.*

Proof. Closure under composition is immediate from the definition.

To prove closure under simultaneous recurrence, consider without loss of generality functions $f_0, f_1 : \mathbb{N}^{r+1} \to \mathbb{N}$, defined by simultaneous recurrence:

$$f_i(\mathbf{0}, \boldsymbol{x}) = g_i(\boldsymbol{x})$$
$$f_i(\mathsf{s}n, \boldsymbol{x}) = h_i(f_0(n, \boldsymbol{x}), f_1(n, \boldsymbol{x}), \boldsymbol{x})$$

By assumption, the functions g_0, g_1, h_0, h_1 are computed by programs (which we assume do not share program-functions), which are provable as prescribed. We augment these programs by the definition above for function identifiers $\mathbf{f}_0, \mathbf{f}_1$. Using the abbreviation,

$$\psi[z] \quad \equiv_{\mathrm{df}} \quad \mathsf{N}(\mathbf{f}_0(z, \boldsymbol{x})) \wedge \mathsf{N}(\mathbf{f}_1(z, \boldsymbol{x}))$$

the given proofs for g_0, g_1, h_0, h_1, together with the defining equations for $\mathbf{f}_0, \mathbf{f}_1$, yield derivations of $\psi[\mathbf{0}]$ and $\psi[z] \to \psi[\mathsf{s}z]$ from the assumptions $\mathsf{N}(\boldsymbol{x})$. Thus, assuming $\mathsf{N}(n)$ we obtain, by Induction, $\mathsf{N}(\boldsymbol{x}) \to \psi[n]$, completing the construction of a proof for $\mathbf{f}_0, \mathbf{f}_1$, and showing that the provable functions are closed under simultaneous recurrence.

Now, the initial primitive recursive functions, namely Zero, Successor, and the projections, are trivially provable. Although the recurrence schema shown here (and often dubbed "iteration with parameters") is formally weaker than usual primitive recursion, it nonetheless suffices, with composition, to generate from the initial functions all primitive recursive functions [20]. This completes the proof. ⊣

2.3 The Generic Setting

While our discussion focuses here on $\mathbb{N}$ for expository reasons, all notions and results lift verbatim to $\mathbb{A}(C)$ for arbitrary inductively generated algebras C. In particular, for each $\mathbb{A}(C)$ one defines a first order theory $\mathbf{IT}(C)$, and an extension $\overline{\mathbf{IT}}(C)$ of $\mathbf{IT}(C)$ with separation axioms. Rather than one relational identifier for inductively-generated data, such as N for $\mathbf{IT}(\mathbb{N})$, the theory $\mathbf{IT}(C)$ has a relational identifier for each sort. For single-sorted systems we shall write below D for that predicate. For further definitions, examples, and discussion, see [16].

3 Statement of the Results

3.1 Data-Positive Induction and Primitive Recursion

As usual, we say that an occurrence of D in a formula φ is *positive* (respectively, *negative*) if it is in the negative scope of an even (respectively, odd) number of implications and negations. We call a formula φ in the vocabulary of $\mathbf{IT}(C)$ *data-positive* if D has no negative occurrence in φ. We define $\mathbf{IT}^+(C)$ to be $\mathbf{IT}(C)$ with induction restricted to data-positive formulas. $\overline{\mathbf{IT}}^+(C)$ is defined analogously.

For example, formulas of the form $\exists x\,(\,\mathbf{N}(x) \wedge E\,)$, E an equation of primitive recursive arithmetic, are data-positive. These are precisely the interpretations in $\mathbf{IT}(\mathbb{N})$ of Σ^0_1 formulas. Similarly, all $\mathbf{N}$-free formulas of $\mathbf{IT}(\mathbb{N})$ are data-positive, as are all formulas of the form $\mathcal{Q}.\,(\,\alpha \to \mathbf{N}(t)\,)$ where $\mathcal{Q}$ is a block of quantifiers and α is $\mathbf{N}$-free; these formulas are not interpretations in $\mathbf{IT}(\mathbb{N})$ of formulas of first order arithmetic. The interpretation in $\mathbf{IT}(\mathbb{N})$ of a Π^0_1 formula $\forall x.\,E$, E an equation, is $\forall x.\,(\,\mathbf{N}(x) \to E\,)$, which is not data-positive. The interpretation of a Π^0_2-formula $\forall x\,\exists y\,E$ is $\forall x\,(\,\mathbf{N}(x) \to \exists y\;\mathbf{N}(y) \wedge E\,)$, which has both positive and negative occurrences of $\mathbb{N}$.

Our results for induction restricted to data-positive formulas are as follows. From the proof of Proposition 1 we immediately get:

PROPOSITION **2** *If a function over $\mathbb{A}(C)$ is definable by composition and simultaneous recurrence from the constructors of C, then it is provable in $\mathbf{IT}(C)$, based on minimal logic, and with induction restricted to conjunctions of atomic formulas. In particular, all primitive recursive functions are provable in $\mathbf{IT}(\mathbb{N})$, based on minimal logic, and with induction for such formulas.* ⊣

For the converse, we have:

PROPOSITION **3** *Every function provable in $\overline{\mathbf{IT}}(C)$, based on intuitionistic logic, and with induction restricted to data-positive formulas, is definable by simultaneous recurrence over $\mathbb{A}(C)$. In particular, every functions over $\mathbb{N}$ provable as above in $\overline{\mathbf{IT}}(\mathbb{N})$ is primitive recursive.*

This will follow from Propositions 19 and 20 below. ¿From Propositions 2 and 3 we deduce:

THEOREM **4** *A function is provable in $\mathbf{IT}(\mathbb{N})$ (or $\overline{\mathbf{IT}}(\mathbb{N})$), based on minimal or intuitionistic logic,[2] with induction restricted to data-positive formulas, iff it is primitive recursive.*

More generally, a function over $\mathbb{A}(C)$ is provable in $\mathbf{IT}(C)$ (or $\overline{\mathbf{IT}}(C)$) based on intuitionistic or minimal logic, with induction restricted to data-positive formulas, iff it is generated from the constructors of C by composition and simultaneous $\mathbb{A}(C)$-recurrence. (These are also the functions that are primitive recursive modulo a canonical coding of C in $\mathbb{N}$.)

3.2 Data-Predicative Derivations

Theorem 4 shows that the restriction of induction to data-positive formulas reduces the class of provable functions quite dramatically, from the provably

[2] The results remain true for classical logic, but we do not know if the methods presented here can be extended to apply to proofs in classical logic. A proof for the classical case, based on a somewhat complex proof theoretic analysis, is included in the full version of this paper.

recursive functions of first order arithmetic to the primitive recursive functions. However, from the viewpoint of feasible computation and computer science, the latter is still an extremely large class. In [14] we defined a ramified intrinsic theory of data, yielding provable functions that fall precisely into major complexity classes, notable the poly-time, linear space, and Kalmar-elementary functions, depending on allowable instances of induction and on the underlying data system. Here we use an alternative approach, where impredicative references to data in derivations are prohibited explicitly.

We call a natural deduction derivation $\mathcal{D}$ of $\mathbf{IT}(\mathbb{N})$ *data-predicative* if no major premise $\mathbf{N}(t)$ of non-degenerate data-elimination (i.e. induction) depends on a data-positive assumption closed in $\mathcal{D}$. The generic definition for $\mathbf{IT}(C)$ is similar. Examples of data-predicative derivations are displayed in Tables 2 and 3. An example of a derivation that fails to be data-predicative is in Table 1. An ontological justification of this definition was given in the introduction. Its technical interest resides in the following two theorems.

THEOREM **5** *A function over* $\mathbb{N}$ *is provable by a data-predicative derivation of* $\mathbf{IT}(\mathbb{N})$ *(or* $\overline{\mathbf{IT}}(\mathbb{N})$*), iff it is elementary.*

More generally, if C *is an inductive data-system, then a function over* $\mathbb{A}(C)$ *is provable by a data predicative derivation of* $\mathbf{IT}(C)$ *(or* $\overline{\mathbf{IT}}(C)$*) iff it is computable in elementary resources.*

These equivalences hold regardless of whether the logic is classical, intuitionistic, or minimal.

THEOREM **6** *If* C *is an inductive data-system, then a function over* $\mathbb{A}(C)$ *is provable by a data predicative derivation of* $\mathbf{IT}(C)$ *(or* $\overline{\mathbf{IT}}(C)$*), based on intuitionistic or minimal logic, and with induction restricted to data-positive formulas, iff it is computable in poly-time on a register machine over* $\mathbb{A}(C)$ *(as defined e.g. in [13]).*

In particular, a function over $\mathbb{N}$ *is provable in* $\mathbf{IT}(\mathbb{N})$ *by a data-positive derivation with data-positive induction, based on intuitionistic or minimal logic, iff it is computable in linear space. And for any word algebra* $\mathbb{A}(C)$*, such as* $\{0,1\}^*$*, a function over* $\mathbb{A}(C)$ *is provable in* $\mathbf{IT}(C)$ *by a derivation as above iff it is computable in polynomial time on a Turing machine.*

We prove Theorems 5 and 6 in the remaining of the paper. The forward direction is Proposition 12, and the backward direction is an immediate consequence of propositions 19 and 20.

Note the generic character of Theorem 6. Here we get different complexity classes (according to common separation conjectures) depending on the underlying data. This is because the coding of one algebra in another exceeds here the computational complexity under consideration, contrary to broader classes, such as the Kalmar-elementary functions.

Table 1. A derivation for Ackermann's Function

$$\mathsf{a}(\mathsf{0}, z) = \mathsf{s}z \qquad \mathsf{a}(\mathsf{s}x, \mathsf{0}) = 2 \qquad \mathsf{a}(\mathsf{s}x, \mathsf{s}y) = \mathsf{a}(x, \mathsf{a}(\mathsf{s}x, y))$$

$$\dfrac{\overset{(1)}{\mathsf{N}(x)} \quad \dfrac{\dfrac{\dfrac{\overset{(3)}{\mathsf{N}(y)}}{\mathsf{N}(\mathsf{s}y)}}{\mathsf{N}(\mathsf{a}(\mathsf{0},y))}\,\text{P}}{\forall y.\,(\mathsf{N}(y) \to \mathsf{N}(\mathsf{a}(\mathsf{0},y)))}\,(3) \quad \dfrac{\dfrac{\overset{(4)}{\mathsf{N}(y)} \quad \dfrac{\dfrac{}{\mathsf{N}(\mathsf{ss0})}}{\mathsf{N}(\mathsf{a}(\mathsf{s}z,\mathsf{0}))}\,\text{P} \quad \dfrac{\dfrac{\dfrac{\overset{(2)}{\forall y.\,(\mathsf{N}(y) \to \mathsf{N}(\mathsf{a}(z,y)))} \quad \overset{(5)}{\mathsf{N}(\mathsf{a}(\mathsf{s}z,u))}}{\mathsf{N}(\mathsf{a}(\mathsf{s}z,u)) \to \mathsf{N}(\mathsf{a}(z,\mathsf{a}(\mathsf{s}z,u)))}}{\mathsf{N}(\mathsf{a}(z,\mathsf{a}(\mathsf{s}z,u)))}}{\mathsf{N}(\mathsf{a}(\mathsf{s}z,\mathsf{s}u))}\,\text{P}}{\mathsf{N}(\mathsf{a}(\mathsf{s}z,y))}\,\text{Ind }(5)}{\forall y.\,(\mathsf{N}(y) \to \mathsf{N}(\mathsf{a}(\mathsf{s}z,y)))}\,(4)}{\dfrac{\forall y.\,(\mathsf{N}(y) \to \mathsf{N}(\mathsf{a}(x,y)))}{\forall x.\,\mathsf{N}(x) \to \forall y.\,(\mathsf{N}(y) \to \mathsf{N}(\mathsf{a}(x,y)))}\,(1)}\,\text{Ind }(2)$$

Double-bars stand for contracted steps in the proof. Note that induction is not predicative, because assumption (4) is the major premise of induction and is closed in the derivation. Also, the lowest instance of induction is for a formula which is not data-positive.

3.3 Classical vs. Constructive Logic

In [16] we proved that every function provable in **IT**(C) based on classical logic is provable already in **IT**(C) based on minimal logic. That proof does not carry over to our restricted formalisms, because a classical-logic proof that uses induction only for positive formulas is mapped to a minimal-logic proof that may use induction for formulas that are not positive.

Indeed, the relation between the constructive and classical versions of the results above are more complex than in unrestricted intrinsic theories. Below we present a direct proof of Proposition 3 for the constructive logic case. However, as of this writing we do not know whether this proof can be modified to apply also to classical logic.

The difference between the classical and constructive variants of the theories is manifest in weak forms of induction. On the one hand we have:

PROPOSITION **7** *Based on classical logic, data-positive induction is equivalent to its dual, i.e. induction for formulas without positive occurrences of data-predicates.*

The proof here is, for $\mathbb{N}$, similar to the proof that Π^0_1-induction is equivalent to Σ^0_1-induction (see e.g. [5] or [23]). A bit more work is needed for other data systems.

In contrast to Proposition 7 we have:

PROPOSITION **8** *Every function provable in* **IT**(C), *based on intuitionistic logic, and with induction restricted to formulas without positive occurrences of data-predicates, is explicitly definable from the constructors of* C.

This is a consequence of the proof of Theorem 18 below.

3.4 Relativized Results

All results above can be relativized, as follows. If $\mathbf{f}$ is an r-ary function-identifier, we write

$$\mathrm{Tot}[\mathbf{f}] \quad \equiv_{\mathrm{df}} \quad \forall x_1 \ldots x_r .\, \mathbf{D}(x_1) \wedge \cdots \mathbf{D}(x_r) \rightarrow \mathbf{D}(\mathbf{f}(\boldsymbol{x}))$$

Suppose $\mathbb{A}(C)$ is an inductive data-system. Let $g_1, g_2 \ldots\}$ be functions over $\mathbb{A}(C)$, and $\mathbf{g}_1, \mathbf{g}_2$ identifiers denoting these functions. The aforementioned results then hold with "primitive recursive" replaced by "primitive recursive in $g_1, \ldots$", and with "provable" replaced by "provable from $\mathrm{Tot}[\mathbf{g}_1]$, $\mathrm{Tot}[\mathbf{g}_2], \ldots$."

Relativization of the results is of interest when embedding traditional first order theories in intrinsic theories. For example, embedding Peano's Arithmetic in $\mathbf{IT}(\mathbb{N})$, as in [16], introduces into $\mathbf{IT}(\mathbb{N})$ addition and multiplication as new primitives. This augmentation is inconsequential in virtually any application, since addition and multiplication are trivially provable. However, not so in $\mathbf{IT}(\mathbb{N})$ with induction restricted to formulas without positive occurrences of data-predicates. The relativized analog of Proposition 8 is then worth independent consideration:

PROPOSITION **9** *The functions provable in* $\mathbf{IT}(C)$, *based on constructive logic, and with induction for formulas without positive occurrences of data-predicates, from the statements of totality of functions* $f_1 \ldots f_k$, *are precisely the functions explicitly definable from the constructors of* C *and* $f_1 \ldots f_k$.

In particular, the provably recursive functions of Heyting's Arithmetic with induction restricted to $\boldsymbol{\Pi}_1^0$ *formulas are precisely the functions explicitly definable from* $0, 1, +$ *and* $\times$.

The latter part of Proposition 9 improves one of the results of [25].[3]

Another illustration of the crucial difference between constructive and classical version of the theories, when induction formulas are structurally restricted, is this:

THEOREM **10** *The provable functions of constructive* $\mathbf{IT}(\mathbb{N})$ *with induction restricted to prenex formulas are (classically, whence constructively) provable using* $\boldsymbol{\Pi}_2$*-induction.*

[3] The latter states that the provably recursive functions of $\mathbf{HA}$ based on $\boldsymbol{\Pi}_1^0$-induction are bounded by polynomials, and are the same as the provably recursive functions of $\mathbf{HA}$ with induction for formulas in either one of the classes $\neg\boldsymbol{\Sigma}_1$, $\neg\neg\boldsymbol{\Sigma}_1$, $\neg\boldsymbol{\Pi}_1$, or $\neg\neg\boldsymbol{\Pi}_1$. It should be noted, though, that induction for formulas with no strictly-positive data information is useless only when it comes to proving program termination. Indeed, one can prove by induction on $\boldsymbol{\Pi}_1$-formulas, i.e. of the form $\forall x\, \mathbf{N}(x) \rightarrow \boldsymbol{\alpha}$, $\boldsymbol{\alpha}$ quantifier-free, that addition is commutative, a result which cannot be proved using only $\boldsymbol{\Sigma}_1$-induction, even though the latter theory is so much more powerful than the former with respect to proving program termination.

Table 2. Proofs for addition and multiplication

$$\dfrac{\mathsf{N}(y) \qquad \dfrac{\mathsf{N}(x)}{\mathsf{N}(x+\mathbf{0})} \qquad \dfrac{\dfrac{\mathsf{N}(x+z)}{\mathsf{N}(\mathsf{s}(x+z))}}{\mathsf{N}(x+\mathsf{s}z)}}{\mathsf{N}(x+y)}$$

$$\dfrac{\mathsf{N}(y) \qquad \dfrac{\mathsf{N}(\mathbf{0})}{\mathsf{N}(x\times\mathbf{0})} \qquad \dfrac{\begin{array}{c}\mathsf{N}(x) \qquad \mathsf{N}(x+z)\\ \cdots \\ \mathsf{N}((x\times z)+x))\end{array}}{\mathsf{N}(x\times(\mathsf{s}z))}}{\mathsf{N}(x\times y)}$$

It is easy to extract from Theorem 18 below a proof outline: prenex formulas are mapped to types of order 2, and functions definable by order-2 primitive recursion are well known to be the same as the functions provable by $\boldsymbol{\Pi}_2$-induction.[4]

4 From Computational Complexity to Provability

LEMMA **11** *Addition and multiplication are provable by data-predicative derivations based on minimal logic, with induction over atomic formulas. Exponentiation is provable by a data-predicative derivation in minimal logic.*

Proof. We use the following programs for addition, multiplication, and base-2 exponentiation:

$$\begin{array}{ll} x+\mathbf{0}=x & x\times\mathbf{0}=\mathbf{0} \\ x+\mathsf{s}y=\mathsf{s}(x+y) & x\times\mathsf{s}y=(x\times y)+x \end{array}$$

$$\begin{array}{l} \mathsf{e}(\mathbf{0},y)=\mathsf{s}y \\ \mathsf{e}(\mathsf{s}x,y)=\mathsf{e}(x,\mathsf{e}(x,y)) \end{array} \qquad \mathsf{exp}(x)=\mathsf{e}(x,\mathbf{0}).$$

The corresponding proofs are displayed in Tables 2 and 3, where for readability we omit uses of the programs' equations, and use instead double-bars to indicate such uses (via equational rules). ⊣

Building on the construction of Lemma 11, we can prove the forward direction of Theorems 5 and 6.

PROPOSITION **12** *Let f be a function over $\mathbb{A}(C)$, computable by a register machine M over $\mathbb{A}(C)$, and T a function that bounds the run-time of M, as a function of the height of the input.*

[4] This follows, e.g. from Gödel's "Dialectica" interpretation [4]. A consequence of Theorem 10 is that the functions provably-recursive in **HA** with prenex induction are provably-recursive in **HA** with $\boldsymbol{\Pi}_2$ induction, which is the main theorem of [25].

Table 3. A proof for exponentiation

$$
\dfrac{\dfrac{\mathsf{N}(x) \quad \dfrac{\dfrac{\dfrac{\mathsf{N}(y)}{\mathsf{N}(\mathsf{s}y)}}{\mathsf{N}(\mathsf{e}(\mathsf{0},y))}}{\forall y\,(\mathsf{N}(y)\to\mathsf{N}(\mathsf{e}(\mathsf{0},y)))} \quad \dfrac{\dfrac{\dfrac{\dfrac{\forall y\,(\mathsf{N}(y)\to\mathsf{N}(\mathsf{e}(u,y))}{\mathsf{N}(\mathsf{e}(u,y))\to\mathsf{N}(\mathsf{e}(u,\mathsf{e}(u,y)))} \quad \dfrac{\dfrac{\forall y\,(\mathsf{N}(y)\to\mathsf{N}(\mathsf{e}(u,y))}{\mathsf{N}(y)\to\mathsf{N}(\mathsf{e}(u,y))} \quad \mathsf{N}(y)}{\mathsf{N}(\mathsf{e}(u,y))}}{\mathsf{N}(\mathsf{e}(u,\mathsf{e}(u,y)))}}{\mathsf{N}(\mathsf{e}(\mathsf{s}u,y))}}{\forall y\,(\mathsf{N}(y)\to\mathsf{N}(\mathsf{e}(\mathsf{s}u,y)))}}{\forall y\,(\mathsf{N}(y)\to\mathsf{N}(\mathsf{e}(x,y))}}{\dfrac{\mathsf{N}(\mathsf{e}(x,\mathsf{0}))}{\mathsf{N}(\mathbf{exp}(x))}}
$$

Note that here the induction formula has **N** in both positive and negative positions.

1. *If T is elementary, then f is provable in* $\mathbf{IT}(C)$ *by a data-predicative derivation based on minimal logic.*
2. *If T is polynomial, then f is provable in* $\mathbf{IT}(C)$ *by a data-predicative derivation based on minimal logic, using induction for the conjunction of atomic formulas.*

Proof Outline. We follow the construction of [13, §3.3]. Register-machine configurations are coded by tuples of algebra-terms (numbers, in the case of $\mathbb{N}$). Given a deterministic m-register machine M over $\mathbb{A} \equiv \mathbb{A}(C)$, there are functions $\tau_0, \tau_1 \ldots, \tau_m : \mathbb{A}^{m+1} \to \mathbb{A}$ such that, if M has a transition rule for state s, then $(s, [u_1, \ldots, u_m]) \vdash_M (s', [u'_1, \ldots, u'_m])$ iff $\tau_i(\#s, u_1, \ldots, u_m) = u'_i$ for $i = 1 \ldots m$, and $\tau_0(\#s, u_1, \ldots, u_m) = \#s'$; and if M has no such transition, then $\tau_i(u_0 \ldots u_m) = u_i$. The transition functions τ_i are provable, in the strong sense that $\bigwedge_i \mathsf{D}(u_i) \to \mathsf{D}(\tau_i(\boldsymbol{u}))$ has a data-predicative derivation, that uses only degenerate instances of induction.[5]

As in the proof of [13, Lemma 3.4], for every elementary function $f(n)$ we consider the function $\tilde{f}(n, \boldsymbol{x})$ obtained by replacing $\mathbf{0}$in the definition of f by the initial configuration of M for the input $\boldsymbol{x}$, and replacing the successor function by the tuple $\langle \tau_0 \ldots \tau_m \rangle$. The provability properties in Lemma 11 are unaffected. Then $\tilde{f}(n, \boldsymbol{x})$ is the configuration of M after n execution steps, for input $\boldsymbol{x}$.

If M runs in time $T(n)$, then a projection of $\tilde{T}(n, \boldsymbol{x})$ to the output register is the output M for input $\boldsymbol{x}$. Since every polynomial is majorized by a composition of multiplications, and every elementary function by a composition of exponentiations, the Proposition follows from from Lemma 11. ⊣

5 From Provability to Computational Complexity

5.1 Typed Lambda Calculus with Recurrence

By the well known Curry-Howard morphisms, natural deductions can be viewed as λ-terms [21, 7]. In [9, 10] we presented a Curry-Howard style mapping which

[5] Note that unrestricted use of degenerate induction is crucial here.

yields directly an applicative program for a function f from a derivation for the provability of f in various formalisms. We summarize here a similar construction that maps natural deduction derivations of intrinsic theories to terms of an applied simply typed λ-calculus. To concentrate on the essentials, we restrict attention to **IT**(ℕ), but the method is generic (see [16]).

Let $\mathbf{1\lambda}$ be the simply typed lambda with pairing. The types are generated from a base type ι by $\rightarrow$ and $\times$. We let $\rightarrow$ associate to the right, and write $\rho_1, \ldots, \rho_r \rightarrow \tau$ for $\rho_1 \rightarrow \cdots \rightarrow \rho_r \rightarrow \tau$ as well as for $\rho_1 \times \cdots \times \rho_r \rightarrow \tau$. If all ρ_i's are the same type ρ, we write $\rho^r \rightarrow \tau$ for the above. Terms are generated by λ-abstraction and type-correct application, as well as by pairing and projection. We write $\langle t, t' \rangle$ for the pair consisting of t, t', and π_0, π_1 for the two projection functions. The computational rules are the usual *β-reduction,* contracting $(\lambda x.t)s$ to $\{s/x\}t$, and *pair-reduction,* contracting $\pi_i \langle t_0, t_1 \rangle$ to t_i $(i = 0, 1)$.

The extension $\mathbf{1\lambda}(\mathbb{N})$ of $\mathbf{1\lambda}$ is obtained by admitting the constructors $\mathbf{0}$ and s are constants, of types ι and $\sigma \rightarrow \iota$, respectively. $\mathbf{1\lambda}(\mathbb{N})$ also has, for each type τ, a constant R_τ of type $(\tau \rightarrow \tau) \rightarrow \tau \rightarrow\rightarrow \iota\tau$. Aside from β-reduction and pair-reduction, $\mathbf{1\lambda}(\mathbb{N})$ has rules of *recurrence unfolding (in type τ):*

$$\mathsf{R}_\tau M_1 M_0 \mathbf{0} \Rightarrow M_0$$
$$\mathsf{R}_\tau M_1 M_0 (\mathsf{s}K) \Rightarrow M_1 (\mathsf{R}_\tau M_1 M_0 (\mathsf{s}K))$$

A term is *normal* if no subterm can be reduced. By the Tait-Prawitz method (see [19, 24]), we have

LEMMA **13** *Every reduction sequence in* $\mathbf{1\lambda}(\mathbb{N})$ *terminates.* ⊣

Note that each element of ℕ is represented in $\mathbf{1\lambda}(\mathbb{N})$ by itself (modulo currying), and that every closed normal term of type ι is an element of $\mathbb{A}$. Thus, every expression of type $\iota^r \rightarrow \iota$ represents an r-ary function over $\mathbb{A}(C)$. Thus, the constant R_τ denotes the operation of *recurrence*, i.e. *iteration with parameters,* over type τ. It follows that the functions over ℕ represented in $\mathbf{1\lambda}(\mathbb{N})$ are precisely the functions generated by explicit definitions and recurrence in finite types, which by [4] are precisely the provably recursive functions of Peano Arithmetic.

5.2 Natural Deduction Derivations as Applicative Programs

In [10] we defined a mapping of derivations to terms that disregards the first order part of formulas, in a suitable sense. Here we define such a mapping, from natural deduction derivations of **IT**(ℕ), based on minimal logic, to terms of $\mathbf{1\lambda}(\mathbb{N})$, which is oblivious also to equality. No proper term will correspond to a derivation of an equation. To convey this, we use an auxiliary atomic type $\perp$ (for "undefined"), as well as an auxiliary atomic term $\emptyset$, of type $\perp$.

We first define recursively a mapping κ from formulas to types, as in Table 4. We then define, in Tables 5 and 6, a mapping from natural deduction derivations of **IT**(ℕ), based on minimal logic, to terms of $\mathbf{1\lambda}(\mathbb{N})$. Without danger of

Table 4. The mapping κ from formulas to types

- $$\kappa(\mathbf{D}(t)) =_{\mathrm{df}} \mathbf{D}$$
- $$\kappa(t = t') =_{\mathrm{df}} \bot$$
- $$\kappa(\psi \to \chi) =_{\mathrm{df}} \begin{cases} \kappa(\chi) & \text{if } \kappa(\psi) = \bot \\ \bot & \text{if } \kappa(\chi) = \bot \\ \kappa\psi \to \kappa\chi & \text{otherwise} \end{cases}$$
- $$\kappa(\psi \wedge \chi) =_{\mathrm{df}} \begin{cases} \kappa(\chi) & \text{if } \kappa(\psi) = \bot \\ \kappa(\psi) & \text{if } \kappa(\chi) = \bot \\ \kappa\psi \times \kappa\chi & \text{otherwise} \end{cases}$$
- $$\kappa(\forall x.\psi) =_{\mathrm{df}} \kappa\psi$$

ambiguity we write κ also for this mapping.[6] By a straightforward structural induction on derivations we verify:

LEMMA **14** *If $\mathcal{D}$ is a derivation of φ from labeled open assumptions $\psi_1^{j_1}, \ldots, \psi_m^{j_m}$, then $\kappa\mathcal{D}$ is a term of type $\kappa\varphi$, with free variables among $x_{j_1}, \ldots, x_{j_m}$ of types $\kappa\psi_1, \ldots \kappa\psi_m$, respectively.* ⊣

5.3 Function Provability and Recurrence in Higher Type

LEMMA **15** *For every $n \in \mathbb{N}$ there is a normal deduction $\mathcal{T}_n$ of $\mathbf{IT}(C)$ deriving $\mathbf{N}(n)$, such that $\kappa\mathcal{T}_n = n$.*

Proof. Trivial induction on n. ⊣

LEMMA **16** *If $\mathcal{D}$ reduces to $\mathcal{D}'$ in $\mathbf{IT}(C)$, then either $\kappa\mathcal{D} = \kappa\mathcal{D}'$, or $\kappa\mathcal{D}$ reduces to $\kappa\mathcal{D}'$ in $\mathbf{1\lambda}(\mathbb{N})$.*

Proof. Straightforward inspection of the reductions. Note that for the case of Replacement reductions for Induction it is important that we allow non-atomic eigen-formulas in instances of Replacement.[7]

---

[6] We posit a concrete syntax for natural deductions, which assigns a common numeric label to each assumption class, i.e. the open assumptions that are closed jointly by an inference. Distinct labels are assigned to different assumption classes.

[7] Without this stipulation $\kappa\mathcal{D}$ would not reduce to $\kappa\mathcal{D}'$, but to a term to which $\kappa\mathcal{D}'$ η-reduces. The gist of our results would be preserved, but in a less transparent setting. Moreover, we must refer to Replacement reduction over Induction (data elimination), so using Replacement reduction over logical elimination rules only enhances uniformity and symmetry.

Table 5. The mapping κ from derivations to λ-terms: the logical rules
If $\kappa\mathcal{D} = \emptyset$ then $\mathcal{D}$ is data-void.

If $\mathcal{D}$ is data-nonvoid:

form of $\mathcal{D}$	**the term $\kappa\mathcal{D}$**
labeled assumption $[\ell :]\psi$	$x_\ell^{\kappa\psi}$ (ℓ-th variable of type $\kappa\psi$)
$\dfrac{\begin{matrix}\mathcal{D}_0 & \mathcal{D}_1\\ \varphi_0 & \varphi_1\end{matrix}}{\varphi_0 \wedge \varphi_1}$	$\langle\kappa\mathcal{D}_0, \kappa\mathcal{D}_1\rangle$ if both $\mathcal{D}_0$ and $\mathcal{D}_1$ are data-nonvoid, $\kappa\mathcal{D}_i$ if only $\mathcal{D}_i$ is data-nonvoid
$\dfrac{\begin{matrix}\mathcal{D}'\\ \varphi_0 \wedge \varphi_1\end{matrix}}{\varphi_i}$	$\pi_i\kappa\mathcal{D}'$ if both φ_0 and φ_1 are data-nonvoid $\kappa\mathcal{D}'$ otherwise
$\dfrac{\begin{matrix}[\ell :]\ \psi\\ \mathcal{D}'\\ \varphi\end{matrix}}{\psi \rightarrow \varphi}\ \ell$	$\lambda x_\ell^{\kappa\psi}.\,\kappa\mathcal{D}'$ if ψ is data-nonvoid $\kappa\mathcal{D}'$ otherwise
$\dfrac{\begin{matrix}\mathcal{D}_0 & \mathcal{D}_1\\ \psi \rightarrow \varphi & \psi\end{matrix}}{\varphi}$	$(\kappa\mathcal{D}_0)(\kappa\mathcal{D}_1)$ if ψ is data-nonvoid $\kappa\mathcal{D}_0$ otherwise (Note: since $\mathcal{D}$ is data-nonvoid, so is $\mathcal{D}_0$.)
$\dfrac{\mathcal{D}'}{\varphi}$	$\kappa\mathcal{D}'$ if the main inference is $\forall$I, $\forall$E, or equational

Lemma 17 *Let P be an equational program. If $\mathcal{D}$ is a normal derivation of* $\mathbf{IT}(\mathbb{N})$, *deriving an atomic formula $\mathbf{D}_i(t)$ from $\bar{P}$, where t is closed, then $\kappa\mathcal{D}$ is a numeral, and $t = \kappa\mathcal{D}$ is derived from P in equational logic.*

Proof. By basic properties of normal derivations $\mathcal{D}$ is without induction, and so every formula in $\mathcal{D}$ is atomic, or of the form $\forall \boldsymbol{x}.\, t = t'$ for some equation $t = t'$ in P.

We proceed to prove the Lemma by structural induction on $\mathcal{D}$. If $\mathcal{D}$ is a singleton derivation, then it must be $\mathbf{D}_i(\mathbf{0})$. The Lemma holds trivially.

If $\mathcal{D}$ is

$$\dfrac{\begin{matrix}\mathcal{D}_0 & \mathcal{D}_1\\ \mathbf{N}(t') & t' = t\end{matrix}}{\mathbf{N}(t)}$$

then $\kappa\mathcal{D} = \kappa\mathcal{D}_0$, where by IH $\kappa\mathcal{D}_0$ is a numeral, with $P \vdash^{=} t' = \kappa\mathcal{D}_0$. Also, $P \vdash^{=} t' = t$. Thus, $\kappa\mathcal{D}$ is a numeral, and $P \vdash^{=} t = \kappa\mathcal{D}$.

Table 6. The mapping κ from derivations to λ-terms: the data rules

form of $\mathcal{D}$	the term $\kappa\mathcal{D}$
$\mathsf{N}(\mathbf{0})$	$\mathbf{0}$
$\dfrac{\overset{\mathcal{D}'}{\mathsf{N}(t)}}{\mathsf{N}(\mathbf{s}t)}$	$\mathbf{s}(\kappa\mathcal{D}')$
$\dfrac{\overset{\mathcal{N}}{\mathsf{N}(t)} \quad \overset{\mathcal{D}_0}{\varphi[\mathbf{0}]} \quad \overset{\mathcal{D}_s}{\varphi[u] \to \varphi[\mathbf{s}u]}}{\varphi[t]}$	$\mathbf{R}_{\kappa\varphi}(\kappa\mathcal{D}_s)(\kappa\mathcal{D}_0)(\kappa\mathcal{N})$

Since φ is assumed data-nonvoid, all sub-derivations are data nonvoid

Finally, if $\mathcal{D}$ is

$$\dfrac{\overset{\mathcal{T}}{\mathsf{N}(t)}}{\mathsf{N}(\mathbf{s}t)}$$

then $\kappa\mathcal{D} = \mathbf{s}(\kappa\mathcal{T})$. By IH $\kappa\mathcal{T}$ is a numeral, where $P \vdash^{=} t = \kappa\mathcal{T}$. Therefore $\kappa\mathcal{D} = \mathbf{s}(\kappa\mathcal{T})$ is a numeral, and $P \vdash^{=} \mathbf{s}(t) = \kappa\mathcal{D}$. ⊣

THEOREM **18** [Representation] *Let $(P, \mathbf{f})$ be a program computing a function f over $\mathbb{N}$. If $\mathcal{D}$ is a deduction of* $\mathbf{IT}(\mathbb{N})$ *deriving $\mathsf{N}(x) \to \mathsf{N}(\mathbf{f}(x))$ from $\bar{P}$, then $\kappa\mathcal{D}$ represents f in $\mathbf{1\lambda}(\mathbb{N})$.*

Proof. Without loss of generality, let f be unary. Given $n \in \mathbb{N}$ let $\mathcal{D}_n$ be the result of substituting n for free occurrences of x in $\mathcal{D}$. We have $\kappa\mathcal{D}_n = \kappa\mathcal{D}$ trivially from the definition of κ. Let $\mathcal{T}_n$ be the straightforward derivation of $\mathsf{N}(n)$, using the data introduction rules. Then, for

$$\mathcal{D}_{fn} \;=_{\mathrm{df}}\; \dfrac{\overset{\mathcal{D}_n}{\mathsf{N}(n) \to \mathsf{N}(\mathbf{f}(n))} \quad \overset{\mathcal{T}_n}{\mathsf{N}(n)}}{\mathsf{N}(\mathbf{f}n)}$$

we have $\kappa(\mathcal{D}_{fn}) = (\kappa\mathcal{D}_n)(\kappa\mathcal{T}_n)$. By Lemma 13 $\mathcal{D}_{fn}$ reduces to a normal derivation $\mathcal{D}'_{fn}$, and by Lemma 17 $\kappa(\mathcal{D}'_{fn})$ is a numeral. We thus have

$$\begin{aligned}(\kappa\mathcal{D})(n) &= (\kappa\mathcal{D}_n)(\kappa\mathcal{T}_n) && \text{by Lemma 15}\\ &= \kappa\mathcal{D}_{fn} \\ &= \kappa\mathcal{D}'_{fn} && \text{by Lemma 16}\\ &= f(n)\end{aligned}$$

Thus $\kappa\mathcal{D}$ represents f. ⊣

5.4 Complexity from Provability

We can now use Theorem 18 to derive the backward direction of Theorems 4, 5 and 6, for intrinsic theories based on minimal logic. We state and prove these here for $\mathbb{N}$, but the proof is generic to all inductive data-systems.

PROPOSITION **19** *The following refer to provability based on minimal logic. Let f be a function over $\mathbb{N}$. Let* **IT** *be either* $\mathbf{IT}(\mathbb{N})$ *or* $\overline{\mathbf{IT}}(\mathbb{N})$.

1. *If f is provable in* **IT** *with induction restricted to data-positive formulas then f is primitive recursive.*
2. *If f is provable in* **IT** *by a data-predicative derivation then f is elementary.*
3. *If f is provable in* **IT** *by a data-predicative derivation with induction restricted to data-positive formulas then f is linear space.*

Proof. By Theorem 18, if a function f is provable in $\mathbf{IT}(\mathbb{N})$ by a derivation $\mathcal{D}$, then the λ-term $F \equiv \kappa\mathcal{D}$ represents f in $\mathbf{1\lambda}(\mathbb{N})$. Moreover, immediately from the definition of κ we have

1. If $\mathcal{D}$ uses induction only for data-positive formulas, then F refers to recurrence operators R_τ only for types τ of the form $\mathbf{N}^k$ ($k \geqslant 1$). Thus F defines a primitive recursive function.
2. If $\mathcal{D}$ is data-predicative, then in F every term of the form $\mathsf{R}_\tau M_s M_0 N$ has no variable free in N which is closed by a λ-abstraction in F. By [1], such terms define elementary functions (see also [15]).
3. If $\mathcal{D}$ is data predicative and uses induction only for data-positive induction, then F has both properties above. By [15] (which is akin also to [8]), such terms define poly-time functions.

□

As mentioned above, the Curry-Howard morphism κ above can be defined for any inductively generated algebra, with analogous results. To complete the proofs of theorems 4, 5 and 6, it remains to verify that logics other than minimal can be used as prescribed:

PROPOSITION **20** *1. If a function over $\mathbb{A}(C)$ is provable in $\mathbf{IT}(C)$ based on classical logic, by a data-predicative derivation, then it is provable in $\mathbf{IT}(C)$ based on minimal logic, by a data-predicative derivation.*

2. If a function over $\mathbb{A}(C)$ is provable in $\mathbf{IT}(C)$ based on intuitionistic logic, using induction only for data-positive formulas, then it is provable in $\mathbf{IT}(C)$ based on minimal logic, also using induction only for data-positive formulas. Moreover, if the former derivation is data-predicative, then so is the latter.

Proof. The proof of (1) is the same as [16, Proposition 8]. To prove (2) interpret $\bot$ as $\forall x, y.\, x = y$. Under this interpretation the intuitionistic $\bot$-rule is provable in minimal logic (with equality): every equation is trivially deduced from $\forall x, y. x =$

y, and every atomic formula $\mathbf{N}(t)$ is derived from $\mathbf{N}(\mathbf{0})$ and $\forall xy\, x = y$.[8] ¿From the intuitionistic $\perp$-rule for atomic formulas the general $\perp$-rule easily follows [19]. ⊣

References

1. Arnold Beckmann and Andreas Weiermann. Characterizing the elementary recursive functions by a fragment of Gödel's system **t**. *Archive of Math. Logic*, 39:475–491, 2000.
2. Stephen Bellantoni and Stephen Cook. A new recursion-theoretic characterization of the poly-time functions. *Computational Complexity*, 1992.
3. Samuel Buss. *Bounded Arithmetic.* Bibliopolis, Naples, 1986.
4. Kurt Gödel. Über eine bisher noch nicht benutzte erweiterung des finiten standpunktes. *Dialectica*, 12:280–287, 1958.
5. Petr Hájek and Pavel Pudlák. *Metamathematics of First-Order Arithmetic.* Springer, Berlin, 1993.
6. J.van Heijenoort. *From Frege to Gödel, A Source Book in Mathematical Logic, 1879–1931.* Harvard University Press, Cambridge, MA, 1967.
7. W. A. Howard. The formulae-as-types notion of construction. In J. P. Seldin and J. R. Hindley, editors, *To H. B. Curry: Essays on Combinatory Logic, Lambda Calculus and Formalism*, pages 479–490. Academic Press, New York, 1980. Preliminary manuscript: 1969.
8. N. Jones. *Computability and Complexity from a Programming Perspective.* MIT Press, Cambridge, MA, 1997.
9. Daniel Leivant. Reasoning about functional programs and complexity classes associated with type disciplines. In *Proceedings of the Twenty Fourth Annual Symposium on the Foundations of Computer Science*, pages 460–469, Washington, 1983. IEEE Computer Society.
10. Daniel Leivant. Contracting proofs to programs. In P. Odifreddi, editor, *Logic and Computer Science*, pages 279–327. Academic Press, London, 1990.
11. Daniel Leivant. Subrecursion and lambda representation over free algebras. In Samuel Buss and Philip Scott, editors, *Feasible Mathematics*, Perspectives in Computer Science, pages 281–291. Birkhauser-Boston, New York, 1990.
12. Daniel Leivant. A foundational delineation of poly-time. *Information and Computation*, 110:391–420, 1994. (Special issue of selected papers from LICS'91, edited by G. Kahn). Preminary report: A foundational delineation of computational feasibility, in Proceedings of the Sixth IEEE Conference on Logic in Computer Science, IEEE Computer Society Press, 1991.
13. Daniel Leivant. Ramified recurrence and computational complexity I: Word recurrence and poly-time. In Peter Clote and Jeffrey Remmel, editors, *Feasible Mathematics II*, Perspectives in Computer Science, pages 320–343. Birkhauser-Boston, New York, 1994. www.cs.indiana.edu/~leivant/papers.
14. Daniel Leivant. Intrinsic theories and computational complexity. In D. Leivant, editor, *Logic and Computational Complexity*, LNCS, pages 177–194, Berlin, 1995. Springer-Verlag.

[8] In generic inductive data system each non-empty sort has a constructor as element, so every atomic formula $\mathbf{D}(t)$ is derived from $\forall xy\, x = y$.

15. Daniel Leivant. Applicative control and computational complexity. In J. Flum and M. Rodriguez-Artalejo, editors, *Computer Science Logic (Proceedings of the Thirteenth CSL Conference*, pages 82–95, Berlin, 1999. Springer Verlag (LNCS 1683). www.cs.indiana.edu/~leivant/papers.
16. Daniel Leivant. Intrinsic reasoning about functional programs I: first order theories. *Annals of Pure and Applied Logic*, 2001. www.cs.indiana.edu/~leivant/papers.
17. Daniel Leivant. Substructural proofs and feasibility. www.cs.indiana.edu/~leivant/papers, 2001.
18. Charles Parsons. On a number-theoretic choice schema and its relation to induction. In A. Kino, J. Myhill, and R. Vesley, editors, *Intuitionism and Proof Theory*, pages 459–473. North-Holland, Amsterdam, 1970.
19. D. Prawitz. *Natural Deduction.* Almqvist and Wiksell, Uppsala, 1965.
20. H.E. Rose. *Subrecursion.* Clarendon Press (Oxford University Press), Oxford, 1984.
21. M. Schönfinkel. Über die Bausteine der mathematischen Logik. *Mathematische Annalen*, 92:305–316, 1924. English translation: On the building blocks of mathematical logic, in [6], 355-366.
22. Harold Simmons. The realm of primitive recursion. *Archive for Mathematical Logic*, 27:177–188, 1988.
23. S. Simpson. *Subsystems of Second-Order Arithmetic.* Springer-Verlag, Berlin, 1999.
24. A.S. Troelstra and H. Schwichtenberg. *Basic Proof Theory.* Cambridge University Press, Cambridge, 1996, 2000.
25. Kai F. Wehmeier. Fragments of HA based on Σ_1-induction. *Archive for Mathematical Logic*, 37:37–49, 1997.

A Renee Equation for Algorithmic Complexity

Keye Martin

Oxford University Computing Laboratory,
Wolfson Building, Parks Road, Oxford OX1 3QD,
kmartin@comlab.ox.ac.uk
http://web.comlab.ox.ac.uk/oucl/work/keye.martin

Abstract. We introduce a notion of complexity for the renee equation and use it to develop a method for analyzing search algorithms which enables a uniform treatment of techniques that manipulate *discrete* data, like linear and binary search of lists, as well as those which manipulate *continuous* data, like methods for zero finding in numerical analysis.

1 Introduction

The renee equation $\varphi = \delta + \varphi \circ r$ was introduced in [3] to give both an intuitive and formal characterization of the notion algorithm. There it was shown that the class of partial recursive functions can be captured in a natural way, by using the renee equation, instead of minimization, as the preferred method of iteration. In this paper, we begin by considering two questions about algorithms $\varphi = \delta + \varphi \circ r$.

The first concerns how one can prove that φ has property P for a certain class of inputs I. This is the problem of *verification.* We establish necessary and sufficient conditions that $(\forall x \in I)\, \varphi(x) \in P$ hold. But once we know how to verify that a process has a certain property, we usually want to compare it to other processes with the same property, as a means of determining which is more efficient.

This is the second problem we consider: Analyzing the *complexity* of φ. The idea considered is that the complexity $c_\varphi(x)$ of calculating φ on input x is determined by the cost of calculating $\delta(x)$, $r(x)$, $\varphi(rx)$ and $\delta(x) + \varphi(rx)$. This leads to a new renee equation, $c_\varphi = c_\delta + c_r + c_+(\delta, \varphi \circ r) + c_\varphi(r)$, whose solution c_φ gives the complexity of φ.

The structure of this paper is as follows. After reviewing the formal definition of a renee equation, the existence and uniqueness theorem, which asserts that renee equations have unique solutions, and the results mentioned earlier on the recursive functions, we consider the verification issue and then the complexity equation above. We close with an application that involves a definition of *search method* based on the aforementioned work, and then results which show how to calculate the complexity of such methods. Among the processes included in the definition of search method are linear search, binary search, the bisection method and the golden section search. The highlight of this application is the ability to analyze processes without regard to whether or not the data they manipulate is continuous or discrete.

N. Kobayashi and B.C. Pierce (Eds.): TACS 2001, LNCS 2215, pp. 201–218, 2001.

2 Background

2.1 Domain Theory

Let $(P, \sqsubseteq)$ be a partially ordered set or *poset* [1]. A nonempty subset $S \subseteq P$ is *directed* if $(\forall x, y \in S)(\exists z \in S)\, x, y \sqsubseteq z$. The *supremum* $\bigsqcup S$ of $S \subseteq P$ is the least of its upper bounds when it exists. A *dcpo* is a poset in which every directed set has a supremum.

For elements x, y of a dcpo D, we write $x \ll y$ iff for every directed subset S with $y \sqsubseteq \bigsqcup S$, we have $x \sqsubseteq s$, for some $s \in S$. In the special case that this occurs for $x = y$, we call x *compact.*

Definition 1. Let $(D, \sqsubseteq)$ be a dcpo. We set

- $\twoheaddownarrow x := \{y \in D : y \ll x\}$ and $\twoheaduparrow x := \{y \in D : x \ll y\}$
- $\downarrow x := \{y \in D : y \sqsubseteq x\}$ and $\uparrow x := \{y \in D : x \sqsubseteq y\}$

and say D is *continuous* if $\twoheaddownarrow x$ is directed with supremum x for each $x \in D$. A *domain* is a continuous dcpo.

The *Scott topology* on a domain D has as a basis all sets of the form $\twoheaduparrow x$ for $x \in D$. A function $f : D \to E$ between domains is *Scott continuous* if it reflects Scott open sets. This is equivalent to saying that f is *monotone,*

$$(\forall x, y \in D)\, x \sqsubseteq y \Rightarrow f(x) \sqsubseteq f(y),$$

and that it *preserves directed suprema:*

$$f(\bigsqcup S) = \bigsqcup f(S),$$

for all directed $S \subseteq D$.

Definition 2. A subset B of a dcpo D is a *basis* for D if $B \cap \twoheaddownarrow x$ contains a directed subset with supremum x, for each $x \in D$. A dcpo is *algebraic* if its compact elements form a basis. A dcpo is *ω-continuous* if it has a countable basis.

2.2 Examples of Domains

In this section, we give examples of domains that we will use in this paper.

Example 1. Orders on the naturals.

(i) The naturals $\mathbb{N}^\infty = \mathbb{N} \cup \{\infty\}$ in their usual order with a top element ∞:

$$(\forall x, y \in \mathbb{N}^\infty)\, x \sqsubseteq y \Leftrightarrow (x \leq y \;\&\; x, y \in \mathbb{N}) \text{ or } y = \infty.$$

(ii) The naturals $\mathbb{N}^* = \mathbb{N}$ in their dual order: $x \sqsubseteq y \Leftrightarrow y \leq x$.
(iii) The naturals $\mathbb{N}^\flat = \mathbb{N}$ ordered flatly: $x \sqsubseteq y \Leftrightarrow x = y$.

Example 2. The *interval domain* is the collection of compact intervals of the real line

$$\mathbf{I}\mathbb{R} = \{[a,b] : a,b \in \mathbb{R} \ \&\ a \leq b\}$$

ordered under reverse inclusion

$$[a,b] \sqsubseteq [c,d] \Leftrightarrow [c,d] \subseteq [a,b]$$

is an ω-continuous dcpo. The supremum of a directed set $S \subseteq \mathbf{I}\mathbb{R}$ is $\bigcap S$, while the approximation relation is characterized by $I \ll J \Leftrightarrow J \subseteq \text{int}(I)$. A countable basis for $\mathbf{I}\mathbb{R}$ is given by $\{[p,q] : p,q \in \mathbb{Q} \ \&\ p \leq q\}$.

Our final example is the domain $[S]$ of finite lists over a poset $(S, \leq)$.

Definition 3. A *list* over S is a function $x : \{1,...,n\} \to S$, for $n \geq 0$. The *length* of a list x is $|\text{dom}\, x|$. The set of all (finite) lists over S is $[S]$. A list x is *sorted* if x is monotone as a map between posets.

A list x can be written as $[x(1),...,x(n)]$, where the *empty list* (the list of length 0) is written $[\,]$. We also write lists as $a :: x$, where $a \in S$ is the *first element* of the list $a :: x$, and $x \in [S]$ is the *rest* of the list $a :: x$. For example, the list $[1,2,3]$ is written $1 :: [2,3]$.

Definition 4. A set $K \subseteq \mathbb{N}$ is *convex* if $a,b \in K \ \&\ a \leq x \leq b \Rightarrow x \in K$. Given a finite convex set $K \subseteq \mathbb{N}$, the map $\text{scale}(K) : \{1,...,|K|\} \to K$ given by

$$\text{scale}(K)(i) = \min K + i - 1$$

relabels the elements of K so that they begin with one.

Definition 5. For $x,y \in [S]$, x is a *sublist* of y iff there is a convex subset $K \subseteq \{1,\ldots,\text{length}\ y\}$ such that $y \circ \text{scale}\ K = x$.

Example 3. If $L = [1,2,3,4,5,6]$, then $[1,2,3], [4,5,6], [3,4,5], [2,3,4], [3,4], [5]$ and $[\,]$ are all sublists of L. However, $[1,4,5,6], [1,3]$ and $[2,4]$ are *not* sublists of L.

Lemma 1 (Martin [3]). *The finite lists $[S]$ over a set S, ordered under reverse convex containment,*

$$x \sqsubseteq y \Leftrightarrow y \textit{ is a sublist of } x,$$

form an algebraic dcpo with $[S] = K([S])$. Thus, $[S]$ is ω-continuous iff S is countable.

The order on $[S]$ is based on computational progress: Intuitively, it is easier to solve a problem on input $[\,]$ than for any other input x, hence $x \sqsubseteq [\,]$.

2.3 The μ Topology

It is during the study of measurement [3] that one encounters for the first time the μ topology on a domain. Let $[0,\infty)^*$ denote the domain of nonnegative reals in the order opposite to their natural one.

Definition 6. A Scott continuous map $\mu : D \to [0,\infty)^*$ on a domain *measures* the elements in a set $X \subseteq D$ when for all $x \in X$, if (x_n) is a sequence with $x_n \ll x$ then

$$\lim_{n\to\infty} \mu x_n = \mu x \Rightarrow \bigsqcup_{n\in\mathbb{N}} x_n = x,$$

and this supremum is directed. We write this as $\mu \to \sigma_X$.

The terminology used in [3] and [5] is different, but the ideas are identical.

Definition 7. A *measurement* is a map $\mu : D \to [0,\infty)^*$ which measures the set $\ker\mu := \{x \in D : \mu x = 0\}$.

If x is an approximation of r, that is, $x \ll r$, then $|\mu x - \mu r|$ is a measure of how closely x approximates r, while μx is a measure of the uncertainty in x. If we obtain an improved approximation y of r, $x \sqsubseteq y \ll r$, then y should be more certain than x. Hence $\mu x \geq \mu y$.

Definition 8. The *μ topology* on a continuous dcpo D has as a basis all sets of the form $\twoheaduparrow x \cap \downarrow y$ where $x, y \in D$.

To clarify the relation between the two ideas, given a measurement $\mu \to \sigma_D$, consider the elements ε-close to $x \in D$, for $\varepsilon > 0$, given by

$$\mu_\varepsilon(x) := \{y \in D : y \sqsubseteq x \;\&\; |\mu x - \mu y| < \varepsilon\}.$$

Regardless of the measurement we use, these sets are *always* a basis for the μ topology.

Theorem 1 (Martin [3]). *For a Scott continuous mapping $\mu : D \to [0,\infty)^*$, $\mu \to \sigma_D$ iff $\{\mu_\varepsilon(x) : x \in D \;\&\; \varepsilon > 0\}$ is a basis for the μ topology on D.*

The μ topology on a continuous dcpo is *Hausdorff*: For each pair of distinct points x and y, there are disjoint open sets U and V with $x \in U$ and $y \in V$. This is one simple illustration of the sharp difference between the μ and the Scott topology on a domain.

Another is the computational relevance of their respective notion of limits. Ideally, one would hope that any sequence with a limit in the Scott topology had a supremum. But this is far from true. For instance, on a continuous dcpo with least element $\bot$, all sequences converge to $\bot$. As the following result reveals, μ limits are the Scott limits with computational significance.

Lemma 2 (Martin [3]). *Let D be a continuous dcpo. Then*

(i) *A sequence* (x_n) *converges to a point* x *in the* μ *topology iff it converges to* x *in the Scott topology and* $(\exists n)\, x_k \sqsubseteq x$, *for all* $k \geq n$.
(ii) *If* $x_n \to x$ *in the* μ *topology, then there is a least integer* n *such that*

$$\bigsqcup_{k \geq n} x_k = x.$$

(iii) *If* (x_n) *is a sequence with* $x_n \sqsubseteq x$, *then* $x_n \to x$ *in the* μ *topology iff* $x_n \to x$ *in the Scott topology.*

The relation between these two notions of limits also has an interesting consequence at the level of morphisms. A map between domains is μ *continuous* if it reflects μ open sets.

Proposition 1. *A monotone map* $f : D \to E$ *between continuous dcpo's is* μ *continuous iff it is Scott continuous.*

Thus, we can quite well think of a μ continuous map as a "Scott continuous map that is not necessarily monotone." Of course, a better model for such maps is provided by the class of functions which are μ-σ continuous. This is discussed in the third chapter of [3].

2.4 The Renee Equation

The applicability of measurement([4],[5],[6]) also extends to its abstract interpretation, the μ topology, the essential concept in formulating the renee equation – a mechanism for justifying recursive definitions at the level of base types. It is worth pointing out the difference between this idea with classical domain theory, which employs the least fixed point operator for defining recursion, and in doing so, requires one to reason about more complex objects, like function spaces between base types.

Definition 9. Let $(X, +)$ be a Hausdorff space with a binary operation that is associative. If (x_n) is a sequence in X, then its *infinite sum* is

$$\sum_{n \geq 1} x_n := \lim_{n \to \infty} (x_1 + \cdots + x_n)$$

provided that the limit of the partial sums on the right exists.

Definition 10. Let $+ : D^2 \to D$ be a binary operation on a domain. A point $x \in D$ is *idle* if there is a μ open set $\sigma(x)$ around x such that

(i) $(\sigma(x), +)$ is a semigroup, and
(ii) If (x_n) is any sequence in $\sigma(x)$ which converges to x in the μ topology, then

$$\sum_{n \geq 1} x_n \text{ exists and } \lim_{n \to \infty} \sum_{k \geq n} x_k = \lim_{n \to \infty} x_n.$$

The operation $+$ is said to be *idle* at x.

An idle point is one where the "unwinding" of a recursive definition stops. For example, $0 \in \mathbb{N}$, or the empty list.

Definition 11. Let D be a continuous dcpo. A binary operation $+ : D^2 \to D$ is *iterative* if it is μ continuous and has at least one idle point.

Example 4. Data types with iterative operations.

(i) $([S], \cdot)$ concatenation of lists. The idle points are $\{[\,]\}$.
(ii) $(\mathbb{N}^*, +)$ addition of natural numbers. The idle points are $\{0\}$.
(iii) $(\mathbb{N}^*, \times)$ multiplication of natural numbers. The idle points are $\{0, 1\}$.
(iv) $(\{\bot, \top\}, \vee)$ Boolean 'or.' The idle points are $\{\bot, \top\}$.
(v) $(\{\bot, \top\}, \wedge)$ Boolean 'and.' The idle points are $\{\bot, \top\}$.

The μ topology in each case above is discrete.

Definition 12. A *splitting* on a poset P is a function $s : P \to P$ with $x \sqsubseteq s(x)$ for all $x \in P$.

The *fixed points* of a function $f : P \to P$ are $\text{fix}(f) = \{x \in P : f(x) = x\}$.

Definition 13. A splitting $r : D \to D$ on a dcpo D is *inductive* if for all $x \in D$, $\bigsqcup r^n x \in \text{fix}(r)$.

Definition 14. Let D be a dcpo and $(E, +)$ be a domain with an iterative operation. A function $\delta : D \to E$ *varies* with an inductive map $r : D \to D$ provided that

(i) For all $x \in \text{fix}(r)$, $\delta(x)$ is idle in E, and
(ii) For all $x \in D$, $\delta(r^n x) \to \delta(\bigsqcup r^n x)$ in the μ topology on E.

A simple example of δ varying with r is when r and δ are μ continuous and δ maps the fixed points of r to idle points of $+$. The intuition underlying the idea is as follows: The simple step δ interprets the recursive part r of an algorithm in the domain $(E, +)$; a fixed point of r is mapped to an idle point in E – a point where recursion stops.

Definition 15. Let D be a dcpo and $(E, +)$ be a domain with an iterative operation. A *renee equation* on $D \to E$ is one of the form

$$\varphi = \delta + \varphi \circ r$$

where $\delta : D \to E$ varies with an inductive map $r : D \to D$.

The following is proven in [3].

Theorem 2 (Canonicity). *The renee equation*

$$\varphi = \delta + \varphi \circ r$$

has a solution which varies with r and agrees with δ on fix(r). *Further, it has only one solution with both of these properties.*

Here is a simple example of a renee equation.

Example 5. The length of a list

$$\text{len} : [S] \to \mathbb{N}$$

is given by

$$\begin{aligned} \text{len}\,[\,] &= 0 \\ \text{len}\, a :: x &= 1 + \text{len}\, x. \end{aligned}$$

Let $D = [S]$ and $E = (\mathbb{N}^*, +)$. Define $\delta : D \to E$ by

$$\delta(x) = \begin{cases} 0 \text{ if } x = [\,], \\ 1 \text{ otherwise.} \end{cases}$$

and rest : $D \to D$ by rest$(a :: x) = x$ and rest$([\,]) = [\,]$. The unique solution of

$$\varphi = \delta + \varphi \circ \text{rest}$$

which satisfies $\varphi([\,]) = 0$ is the length function.

It is shown in chapter four of [3] that the partial and primitive recursive functions may be captured using the renee equation. The highlight of the aforementioned results is the fundamental dependence displayed by notions of computability on order. We briefly review these results in the next section.

2.5 The Recursive Functions

Let D be a domain which as a set satisfies $\mathbb{N} \subseteq D \subseteq \mathbb{N} \cup \{\infty\}$. Three examples of such a domain are $\mathbb{N}^\infty, \mathbb{N}^*$, and $\mathbb{N}^\flat$. We first extend a few simple initial functions to D.

Definition 16. The initial functions.

(i) Addition of naturals $+ : D^2 \to D$ given by

$$(x, y) \mapsto \begin{cases} x + y \text{ if } x, y \in \mathbb{N}; \\ \infty \qquad \text{otherwise.} \end{cases}$$

(ii) Multiplication of naturals $\times : D^2 \to D$ given by

$$(x, y) \mapsto \begin{cases} x \times y \text{ if } x, y \in \mathbb{N}; \\ \infty \qquad \text{otherwise.} \end{cases}$$

(iii) The predicate $\leq: D^2 \to D$ given by

$$(x, y) \mapsto \begin{cases} x \leq y \text{ if } x, y \in \mathbb{N}; \\ \infty \quad \text{otherwise.} \end{cases}$$

(iv) The projections $\pi_i^n : D^n \to D$, for $n \geq 1$ and $1 \leq i \leq n$, given by

$$(x_1, \cdots, x_n) \mapsto \begin{cases} x_i \text{ if } (x_1, \cdots, x_n) \in \mathbb{N}^n; \\ \infty \text{ otherwise.} \end{cases}$$

A map $r : D^n \to D^n$ may be written in terms of its *coordinates* $r_i : D^n \to D$, for $1 \leq i \leq n$, as $r = (r_1, \cdots, r_n)$.

Definition 17. Let $\mathcal{C}(D)$ be the smallest class of functions $f : D^n \to D$ with the following properties:

(i) $\mathcal{C}(D)$ contains $+$, $\times$, $\leq$, and π_i^n, for $n \geq 1$ and $1 \leq i \leq n$,
(ii) $\mathcal{C}(D)$ is closed under substitution: If $f : D^n \to D$ is in $\mathcal{C}(D)$ and $g_i : D^k \to D$ is in $\mathcal{C}(D)$, for $1 \leq i \leq n$, then

$$f(g_1, \cdots, g_n) : D^k \to D \text{ is in } \mathcal{C}(D),$$

and
(iii) $\mathcal{C}(D)$ is closed under iteration: If $\delta : D^n \to D$ and $+ : D^2 \to D$ are in $\mathcal{C}(D)$, and $r : D^n \to D^n$ is a map whose coordinates are in $\mathcal{C}(D)$, then

$$\varphi = \delta + \varphi \circ r \in \mathcal{C}(D)$$

whenever this is a renee equation on $D^n \to D$.

$\mathcal{C}(D)$ contains maps of type $D^n \to D$. To obtain functions on the naturals, we simply restrict them to $\mathbb{N}^n$. In general, we obtain partial maps on the naturals, depending on whether or not D contains ∞.

Definition 18. The restriction of a mapping $f : D^n \to D$ to $\mathbb{N}^n$ is

$$|f| : \mathbb{N}^n \to \mathbb{N}_\perp$$

$$|f|(x) = \begin{cases} f(x) \text{ if } f(x) \in \mathbb{N}; \\ \perp \quad \text{otherwise.} \end{cases}$$

The information order on a domain determines a notion of computability *because* it determines our ability to iterate.

Theorem 3 (Martin [3]).

(i) $|\mathcal{C}(\mathbb{N}^\infty)|$ *is the class of partial recursive functions.*
(ii) $|\mathcal{C}(\mathbb{N}^*)|$ *is the class of primitive recursive functions.*
(iii) $|\mathcal{C}(\mathbb{N}^\flat)|$ *is the smallest class of functions containing the initial functions which is closed under substitution.*

The proof of the last result takes a while to write down, but can be found in [3], for those interested.

3 Verification

The importance of φ varying with r is that it enables a verification principle for the renee equation.

Proposition 2 (Correctness). *Let $\varphi = \delta + \varphi \circ r$ be the unique solution of a renee equation on $D \to E$. If P is any subset of E, then the following are equivalent:*

(i) $(\forall x)\, \varphi(x) \in P$.
(ii) *For every μ open set U containing P,*
 (a) $(\forall x \in \text{fix}(r))\, \delta(x) \in U$, *and*
 (b) $(\forall x)\, \varphi(rx) \in U \Rightarrow \varphi(x) \in U$.

Proof. (ii) $\Rightarrow$ (i): Let U be any μ open subset of E containing P. If $x \in D$ and $\varphi(x) \in E \setminus U$, then by repeatedly applying (b),

$$(\forall n)\, \varphi(r^n x) \in E \setminus U.$$

The set $E \setminus U$ is μ closed and $\varphi r^n x \to \varphi(\bigsqcup r^n x)$ hence $\varphi(\bigsqcup r^n x) \in E \setminus U$. But $\bigsqcup r^n x$ is a fixed point of the inductive map r and $\varphi = \delta$ on fix(r), so $\delta(\bigsqcup r^n x) \in E \setminus U$, which contradicts (a). Then $\varphi(x) \in U$ for all $x \in D$. But the μ topology on E is Hausdorff so P is the intersection of all open sets containing it. □

The last proposition tells us that, in order to prove a solution φ has property P for all inputs, we may verify the induction axioms (a) and (b) for all open sets containing the property P. However, very often we want to prove φ has property P for only a subset I of all possible inputs D. The next proposition is useful in that regard.

Proposition 3. *Let $\varphi = \delta + \varphi \circ r$ be the unique solution of a renee equation on $D \to E$. If $I \subseteq D$ is a set closed under directed suprema with $r(I) \subseteq I$, then the unique solution of*

$$\lambda = \delta|_I + \lambda \circ r|_I$$

is simply $\varphi|_I$.

Proof. The restriction of r to I yields an inductive map on I. Similarly, restricting δ to I yields a map which varies with $r|_I$. The solution of the new equation $\lambda = \delta|_I + \lambda \circ r|_I$ must be $\varphi|_I$ by uniqueness. □

Before proceeding, we need a result about iterative operations.

Lemma 3 (Martin [3]). *If $U \subseteq D$ is a Scott open subset of a domain D, then $+_U : D^2 \to D$ given by*

$$x +_U y = \begin{cases} x \text{ if } x \in U; \\ y \text{ otherwise,} \end{cases}$$

is iterative. It is idle at all points.

In the next example, $[0,\infty)^*$ is the domain of nonnegative reals ordered by $x \sqsubseteq y \Leftrightarrow y \leq x$, where $\leq$ is the usual order.

Example 6. Let $f : \mathbb{R} \to \mathbb{R}$ be a continuous map on the real line $\mathbb{R}$ and

$$C(f) := \{\ [a,b] \in \mathbf{I}\mathbb{R} : f(a) \cdot f(b) \leq 0\ \}.$$

The bisection algorithm,

$$\text{bisect} : \mathbf{I}\mathbb{R} \to \mathbf{I}\mathbb{R},$$

for $\varepsilon > 0$ fixed, is given by

$$\begin{array}{lll} \text{bisect}\,[a,b] = [a,b] & \text{if } \mu[a,b] < \varepsilon; \\ \text{bisect}\,[a,b] = \text{bisect left}[a,b] & \text{if left}[a,b] \in C(f); \\ \text{bisect}\,[a,b] = \text{bisect right}[a,b] & \text{otherwise.} \end{array}$$

Define an iterative operation $+_\varepsilon$ on $\mathbf{I}\mathbb{R}$ by

$$x +_\varepsilon y = \begin{cases} x \text{ if } \mu x < \varepsilon; \\ y \text{ otherwise,} \end{cases}$$

using Lemma 3 and the Scott continuous map $\mu : \mathbf{I}\mathbb{R} \to [0,\infty)^*$, $\mu[a,b] = b - a$. Let $D = \mathbf{I}\mathbb{R}$ and $E = (\mathbf{I}\mathbb{R}, +_\varepsilon)$. Finally, define $\delta : D \to E$ to be the identity map and $\text{split}_f : D \to D$ by

$$\text{split}_f[a,b] = \begin{cases} \text{left}[a,b] & \text{if left}[a,b] \in C(f); \\ \text{right}[a,b] & \text{otherwise.} \end{cases}$$

The unique solution of

$$\varphi = \delta +_\varepsilon \varphi \circ \text{split}_f$$

which satisfies $\varphi[r] = [r]$ for every r is bisect.

Now what we want to prove about φ is that

$$(\forall x \in C(f))\ \varphi(x) \in C(f)\ \&\ \mu\varphi(x) < \varepsilon.$$

Then we should let $I = C(f)$ and $P = C(f) \cap \mu^{-1}[0,\varepsilon)$. Since $\text{split}_f(I) \subseteq I$, we can apply Proposition 2 to $\varphi|_I$. If $U \subseteq \mathbf{I}\mathbb{R}$ is a μ open set containing the property P, then

(i) $(\forall x \in I \cap \text{fix}(\text{split}_f))\ \varphi(x) = \delta(x) = x \in P \subseteq U$, and
(ii) $(\forall x \in I)\ \varphi(\text{split}_f x) \in U \Rightarrow \varphi(x) \in U$,

where we note that (i) holds because the fixed points of split_f all have measure zero, while (ii) holds using the fact that

$$\varphi(x) = \begin{cases} x & \text{if } \mu x < \varepsilon; \\ \varphi(\text{split}_f x) & \text{otherwise.} \end{cases}$$

By Proposition 2, $\varphi|_I(x) \in P$, for all $x \in I$.

In the last example, we chose to have the operation $+_\varepsilon$ provide the test for termination. Another possibility is to use the $\sqcup$ operation and modify split_f so that it maps intervals of length less than ε to themselves [3].

4 Complexity

If we have an algorithm $\varphi = \delta + \varphi \circ r$, then in order to calculate $\varphi(x)$, we must calculate $\delta(x)$, $r(x)$, $\varphi(rx)$ and $\delta(x) + \varphi(rx)$. Thus, the *cost* $c_\varphi(x)$ of calculating $\varphi(x)$ is the sum of the four costs associated with computing $\delta(x)$, $r(x)$, $\varphi(rx)$ and $\delta(x) + \varphi(rx)$. In symbols,

$$c_\varphi(x) = c_\delta(x) + c_r(x) + c_\varphi(rx) + c_+(\delta(x), \varphi(rx)).$$

When the functions (c_δ, c_+, c_r) actually describe the complexity of an algorithm, the equation above can be solved uniquely for c_φ.

Proposition 4. *Let $\varphi = \delta + \varphi \circ r$ be a renee equation on $D \to E$. If $c_\delta : D \to \mathbb{N}^*$, $c_r : D \to \mathbb{N}^*$ and $c_+ : E^2 \to \mathbb{N}^*$ are functions such that for all $x \in D$,*

$$\lim_{n\to\infty} c_\delta(r^n x) = \lim_{n\to\infty} c_r(r^n x) = \lim_{n\to\infty} c_+(\delta(r^n x), \varphi r(r^n x)) = 0,$$

then

$$c_\varphi = c_\delta + c_r + c_+(\delta, \varphi \circ r) + c_\varphi(r)$$

is a renee equation on $D \to (\mathbb{N}^*, +)$.

Proof. The operation of addition $+ : \mathbb{N}^* \times \mathbb{N}^* \to \mathbb{N}^*$ is iterative: Its only idle point is 0. Thus, we need only check that c_δ, c_r and $c_+(\delta, \varphi \circ r)$ vary with r. We consider the case of c_+. For the fixed point $r^\infty = \bigsqcup r^n x$,

$$\lim_{n\to\infty} c_+(\delta(r^\infty), \varphi r(r^\infty)) = 0 = c_+(\delta(r^\infty), \varphi r(r^\infty)),$$

and so for any $x \in D$, we have

$$\lim_{n\to\infty} c_+(\delta(r^n x), \varphi r(r^n x)) = 0 = c_+(\delta(r^\infty), \varphi r(r^\infty)),$$

where we note that $c_+(\delta, \varphi \circ r)$ maps fix(r) to the idle point of $+$. The proofs for the cases c_δ and c_r are even simpler. This shows that we have a renee equation on $D \to (\mathbb{N}^*, +.)$ □

Thus, one renee equation describing an algorithm leads to another describing its complexity. We now apply this idea to calculate the complexity of a sorting algorithm. To do so, we need the merge operation on lists of integers,

$$\text{merge} : [\text{int}] \times [\text{int}] \to [\text{int}],$$

given by the following ML code

```
fun merge( [ ], ys )          = ys : int list
  | merge( xs, [ ] )          = xs
  | merge( x :: xs, y :: ys ) = if x <= y then
                                   x :: merge( xs, y :: ys )
                                else
                                   y :: merge( x :: xs, ys );
```

It is not difficult to show that this is really a renee equation, but this aspect does not concern us presently. What does concern us, however, is that merge is an iterative operation idle at [ ].

Example 7. The prototypical bubblesort of a list of integers

$$\text{sort} : [\text{int}] \to [\text{int}]$$

is given by

$$\begin{aligned} \text{sort}\ [\,] &= [\,] \\ \text{sort}\ x &= \text{merge}(\ [\text{first}\ x],\ \text{sort rest}\ x\ ) \end{aligned}$$

Let $D = [\text{int}]$ and $E = ([\text{int}], +)$ where

$$+ : [\text{int}]^2 \to [\text{int}]$$

$$(x, y) \mapsto \text{merge}(x, y)$$

is the merge operation mentioned above. Define $\delta : D \to E$ by

$$\delta(x) = \begin{cases} [\,] & \text{if } x = [\,] \\ [\text{first}\ x] & \text{otherwise} \end{cases}$$

and let $r : D \to D$ be the splitting $rx = \text{rest}\, x$. The unique solution of

$$\varphi = \delta + \varphi \circ r$$

satisfying $\varphi[\,] = [\,]$ is sort.

For the worst case analysis of sort $= \delta + \text{sort} \circ r$ the number of comparisons performed by r and δ on input x is zero. Hence,

$$c_r(x) = c_\delta(x) = 0,$$

while the cost of merging two lists x and y can be as great as $\mu x + \mu y$, so

$$c_+(x, y) = \mu x + \mu y.$$

By Prop. 4, we have a renee equation

$$c_{\text{sort}} = c_+(\delta, \text{sort} \circ r) + c_{\text{sort}}(r)$$

which *should* measure the complexity of bubblesort. But does it? By Theorem 2,

$$c_{\text{sort}}[\,] = 0,$$

while for any other list x, we have

$$\begin{aligned} c_{\text{sort}}(x) &= c_+(\delta(x), \text{sort}(rx)) + c_{\text{sort}}(rx) \\ &= \mu\, \delta(x) + \mu\, \text{sort}(rx) + c_{\text{sort}}(rx) \\ &= 1 + (\mu x - 1) + c_{\text{sort}}(rx) \\ &= \mu x + c_{\text{sort}}(rx). \end{aligned}$$

However, the function $f(x) = [\mu x(\mu x + 1)]/2$ varies with r, agrees with δ on $\text{fix}(r)$, and satisfies the equation above, so by the uniqueness in Theorem 2, we have

$$c_{\text{sort}}(x) = \frac{\mu x(\mu x + 1)}{2},$$

for all x.

5 An Analysis of Search Methods

In this section, we fix a domain with a measurement (D, μ), a second domain E, and a subset $I \subseteq D$ closed under directed suprema, the latter being the domain of an algorithm which is a partial map of type $D \rightharpoonup E$.

Definition 19. A *search method* (φ, ε) of uncertainty $\varepsilon > 0$ is a renee equation $\varphi = \delta + \varphi \circ r$ on $I \to E$ such that

(i) $(\forall x)\, \mu r^n(x) \to 0$,
(ii) $(\forall x)\, \delta x + \delta(rx) = \delta x$ provided $\mu x < \varepsilon$,

and whose complexity maps (c_δ, c_+, c_r) satisfy $c_+ = 0$ and

$$(c_\delta + c_r)x = \begin{cases} 0 \text{ if } \mu x < \varepsilon; \\ 1 \text{ otherwise.} \end{cases}$$

We begin by describing how a search method (φ, ε) works. On input x, δ checks part of x for a certain object, r then removes the part searched, and returns the remainder to δ, where a new fragment of x is checked. This interaction continues until the observable entirety of x has been searched. But how much of x can a search method examine?

Axiom (i) says that r can *theoretically* reduce x as much as possible, so that δ can, in theory, search all of x. However, in reality, this is not always possible. For example, on a machine, we cannot compute intervals of arbitrarily small length. Axiom (ii) acknowledges this physical aspect by specifying that we cannot search objects x with $\mu x < \varepsilon$: If δ looks at an x with $\mu x < \varepsilon$, then examining rx no longer yields a more informative observation since $\delta x + \delta(rx) = \delta x$.

Now what about the complexity c_φ of a search method (φ, ε)? It counts the number of times that φ *accesses* the object x. Because of the interaction between δ and r described above, we regard δx and rx as a single access, since they both work with the same part of x: δ examines this part, while r removes it afterward. Hence, $c_\delta(x) + c_r(x) = 1$. That $c_+ = 0$ simply reflects the fact that $+$ adds together data recorded by δ which are only known *after* the search is complete.

Proposition 5. *If (φ, ε) is a search method, then its complexity is*

$$c_\varphi(x) = \min\{n : \mu r^n x < \varepsilon\}.$$

In addition, for any x, the output of φ has a finite description, given by

$$\varphi x = \delta x + (\delta r x + (\cdots + (\delta r^n x) \cdots)),$$

for $n = c_\varphi(x)$.

Proof. By Prop. 4, we have a renee equation describing c_φ as

$$c_\varphi = c_\delta + c_r + c_\varphi(r).$$

Let $\lambda(x) = \min\{n : \mu r^n x < \varepsilon\}$. This map is well defined since $\mu r^n(x) \to 0$, for all x. The strategy of the proof is to exploit the uniqueness in Theorem 2.

First, λ agrees with $c_\delta + c_r$ on $\mathrm{fix}(r)$. If $x \in \mathrm{fix}(r)$, then $\mu x = 0$ since $\mu r^n(x) \to 0$. But then

$$\lambda(x) = 0 = c_\delta(x) + c_r(x),$$

where the first equality follows from the convention that $r^0(x) = x$, and the second is a consequence of the fact that $c_\delta(x) + c_r(x) = 0$ for $\mu x < \varepsilon$.

Next, λ varies with r. For any x, we have

$$\lim_{k\to\infty} \lambda r^k(x) = 0 = \lambda(\bigsqcup r^n x),$$

where the first equality holds because $\mu r^n x \to 0$ for all x, and the second follows from the fact that $\bigsqcup r^n x \in \mathrm{fix}(r)$.

Finally, λ solves the same equation as c_φ. For this we must consider the cases $\mu x < \varepsilon$ and $\mu x \geq \varepsilon$ separately. In the first case, when $\mu x < \varepsilon$, we have

$$0 = \lambda(x) = \lambda(rx) = c_\delta(x) + c_r(x) + \lambda(rx),$$

while for the case $\mu x \geq \varepsilon$, we have

$$\lambda(x) = 1 + \min\{n : \mu r^n(rx) < \varepsilon\} = 1 + \lambda(rx) = c_\delta(x) + c_r(x) + \lambda(rx).$$

Thus, $\lambda = c_\delta + c_r + \lambda(r)$ varies with r and agrees with $c_\delta + c_r$ on $\mathrm{fix}(r)$, so the uniqueness in Theorem 2 gives $c_\varphi = \lambda$.

The claim about φ is proven using the same exact technique, where one repeatedly exploits axiom (ii) in the definition of (φ, ε). □

The complexity c_φ supports the idea that objects with $\mu x < \varepsilon$ cannot be searched. Interestingly, it also says we can examine objects with $\mu x = \varepsilon$ once and only once: Looking at x forces it to evolve to rx, which is unobservable since $\mu rx < \varepsilon$.

Corollary 1. *If (φ, ε) is a search method, then*

$$c_\varphi(x) = \begin{cases} 0 \text{ if } \mu x < \varepsilon; \\ 1 \text{ if } \mu x = \varepsilon. \end{cases}$$

Here is a useful technique for bounding the complexity of a search method.

Proposition 6. *If (φ, ε) is a search method and there is a constant $0 < c < 1$ with $\mu r \leq c\mu$, then*

$$c_\varphi(x) \leq \left\lceil \frac{\log(\varepsilon/\mu x)}{\log c} \right\rceil + 1,$$

for any x with $\mu x \geq \varepsilon$.

Proof. By induction, $\mu r^n(x) \leq c^n \mu x$, for all $n \geq 0$ and all x. If we have an integer $n \geq 0$ with

$$n \geq \left\lceil \frac{\log(\varepsilon/\mu x)}{\log c} \right\rceil + 1 > \frac{\log(\varepsilon/\mu x)}{\log c},$$

then $\mu r^n x < \varepsilon$. Thus, $c_\varphi(x) \leq n$, by Prop. 5. □

In the next example, $[S] \times S^\flat$ is the product of two domains, the domain of lists over a set S, and the set S ordered discretely (or flatly). A measurement $\mu : [S] \times S^\flat \to \mathbb{N}^*$ is given by

$$\mu(x, k) = \mu x = \text{length}\, x,$$

for all $(x, k) \in [S] \times S^\flat$.

Example 8. The linear search of a list x for a key k

$$\text{search} : [S] \times S \to \{\bot, \top\}$$

is given by

$$\begin{aligned} \text{search}([\,], k) &= \bot \\ \text{search}(x, k) &= \top & \text{if first } x = k, \\ \text{search}(x, k) &= \text{search}(\text{rest } x, k) & \text{otherwise.} \end{aligned}$$

Let $D = [S] \times S^\flat$ and $E = (\{\bot, \top\}^\flat, \vee)$. Define $\delta : D \to E$ by

$$\delta(x, k) = \begin{cases} \bot \text{ if } x = [\,], \\ \top \text{ if first } x = k, \\ \bot \text{ otherwise.} \end{cases}$$

and $r : D \to D$ by $r(x, k) = (\text{rest } x, k)$. The unique solution of

$$\varphi = \delta \vee \varphi \circ r$$

which satisfies $\varphi([\,], k) = \bot$ for all k is search.

We regard φ as a search method of uncertainty $\varepsilon = 1$. For its worst case complexity, we set $c_r = c_+ = 0$. This uniquely determines c_δ and c_{search}, the latter of which is given by Prop. 5 as

$$c_{\text{search}}(x, k) = \min\{n : \mu r^n(x, k) < 1\} = \min\{n : \mu\, \text{rest}^n x < 1\} = \mu x,$$

for all $(x, k) \in [S] \times S^\flat$.

With search algorithms on lists we count the number of elements that *must* be considered while searching x for k in the worst case. The last example says that for linear search we may have to consider them all. Now we consider another algorithm on lists over a linearly ordered set S, binary search.

To do so, we need three list functions,

$$\text{mid} : [S] \rightharpoonup S :: x \mapsto x(\mu x/2),$$

a partial map defined for nonempty lists which gives the *middle* element of the list x,

$$\text{left} : [S] \to [S] :: x \mapsto [x(1), \cdots, x(\mu x/2 - 1)],$$

which returns the left half of x, that is, all elements from first x to the one before mid x, with the convention that one and zero element lists both map to [ ], and finally,

$$\text{right} : [S] \to [S] :: x \mapsto [x(\mu x/2 + 1), \cdots, x(\mu x)],$$

which returns the right half of x, sending one and zero element lists to [ ]. In each definition, notice that we are using *integer arithmetic*, in particular, integer division.

Example 9. The binary search of a sorted list x for a key k

$$\text{bin} : [S] \times S \to \{\bot, \top\}$$

is given by

$$\begin{array}{lll} \text{bin}([\,], k) & = \bot & \\ \text{bin}(x, k) & = \top & \text{if mid}\, x = k, \\ \text{bin}(x, k) & = \text{bin}(\text{left}\, x, k) & \text{if mid}\, x > k, \\ \text{bin}(x, k) & = \text{bin}(\text{right}\, x, k) & \text{otherwise.} \end{array}$$

Let $D = [S] \times S^\flat$ and $E = (\{\bot, \top\}^\flat, \vee)$. Define $\delta : D \to E$ by

$$\delta(x, k) = \begin{cases} \bot \text{ if } x = [\,], \\ \top \text{ if mid } x = k, \\ \bot \text{ otherwise.} \end{cases}$$

and $r : D \to D$ by

$$r(x, k) = \begin{cases} (\text{left}\, x, k) & \text{if mid}\, x > k; \\ (\text{right}\, x, k) & \text{otherwise.} \end{cases}$$

The unique solution of

$$\varphi = \delta \vee \varphi \circ r$$

which satisfies $\varphi([\,], k) = \bot$ for all k is bin.

We regard bin as a search method of uncertainty $\varepsilon = 1$. To measure its worst case complexity, we again set $c_r = c_+ = 0$, as in the last example. However, instead of applying Prop. 5 to calculate c_φ, it is easier to first notice that

$$\mu r(x, k) \leq \mu(x, k)/2,$$

for all $(x, k) \in D$, and then appeal to Prop. 6, which asserts that the number of accesses made to a nonempty x while looking for k is bounded by

$$c_\varphi(x, k) \leq \left\lceil \frac{\log(1/\mu x)}{\log(1/2)} \right\rceil + 1 = \lceil \log_2 \mu x \rceil + 1.$$

For a list with one element, this bound is actually achieved, so it cannot be improved.

Now what is interesting is that certain numerical processes can also be regarded as search methods. For instance, we can regard the bisection method as a process which searches an interval for a zero of a continuous map on the real line. In this case, the uncertainty $\varepsilon > 0$ can be taken as one imposed by the machine, as noted earlier, or instead interpreted as an *accuracy* that we are interested in computing with. We adopt the latter point of view.

Example 10. Let $f : \mathbb{R} \to \mathbb{R}$ be a continuous map on the real line $\mathbb{R}$ and

$$C(f) := \{\ [a,b] \in \mathbf{I}\mathbb{R} : f(a) \cdot f(b) \leq 0\ \}.$$

Let $I = C(f)$ and $E = (\mathbf{I}\mathbb{R}, +_\varepsilon)$ for $\varepsilon > 0$. As shown in Example 6, the solution of

$$\varphi = 1 +_\varepsilon \varphi \circ \mathrm{split}_f$$

on $I \to E$ is a map which, given $x \in C(f)$, uses the bisection method to calculate $\varphi(x) \in C(f)$ with $\mu\varphi(x) < \varepsilon$. That is, given $x \in C(f)$, φx is an ε-approximation of a zero in $x \in C(f)$.

So how many iterations are required to achieve ε-accuracy? Because (φ, ε) is a search method and $\mathrm{split}_f : I \to I$ satisfies

$$\mu \mathrm{split}_f \leq \mu/2,$$

where $\mu : \mathbf{I}\mathbb{R} \to [0,\infty)^* :: [a,b] \mapsto b - a$ is the usual measurement, Prop. 6 guarantees that

$$c_\varphi(x) \leq \left\lceil \frac{\log(\mu x/\varepsilon)}{\log 2} \right\rceil + 1,$$

for $\mu x \geq \varepsilon$. This is the best bound possible. In addition, multiplying this bound by two gives an upper bound on the *number of evaluations of* f required to calculate φx.

To avoid becoming redundant, we close by pointing out that the *golden section search*, for maximizing unimodal functions on the real line, contractions on complete metric spaces, and a few other processes given in [3], can also be shown to be instances of search methods.

6 Conclusion

We have used a formal method, the renee equation $\varphi = \delta + \varphi \circ r$, not only to provide a reasonable mathematical definition of "search method," but have also demonstrated the ability of this formal method to be useful for obtaining a uniform view of the complexity of such methods. In particular, it suggests to us the true nature of a search method independent of whether the data searched is continuous or discrete. To understand, for example, the sense in which the binary search and the bisection method are exactly the same is interesting. It is also nice to see that both an algorithm and its complexity can be dealt with using one theoretical device: The renee equation.

There are few things worth pointing out about all this. First, the view of algorithm offered in this paper has nothing to do with domain theory; none of the functions in a renee equation need be monotone. But more is true: It is fundamental that mappings in this view not be monotone, or else only a very small fraction of computable mappings are describable. What we focus on is *not* the manner in which algorithms are defined, but rather what it is that an algorithm is made of. We are (perhaps) overly concerned with the exact process of computation.

This desire for precision has a major positive aspect as well as a major negative. The positive is that we are able to make precise quantitative statements about things like search methods in an intuitive and elementary manner – consider trying to use higher order operators to do what we have done here! But there is a negative too: Currently, to be blunt, the definition of the renee equation looks too complicated in the author's opinion. In actuality, less mathematics is needed to capture, say, the recursive functions on $\mathbb{N}^\infty$. We have merely given the renee equation in its full generality to maximize the potential applicability of the results in this paper.

References

1. S. Abramsky and A. Jung. *Domain Theory.* In S. Abramsky, D. M. Gabbay, T. S. E. Maibaum, editors, Handbook of Logic in Computer Science, vol. III. Oxford University Press, 1994
2. Neil Jones. *Computability and complexity: from a programming perspective.* MIT Press, 1997.
3. K. Martin. *A foundation for computation.* Ph.D. thesis, Department of Mathematics, Tulane University, 2000.
4. K. Martin. *A principle of induction.* Proceedings of the European Association for Computer Science Logic, Lecture Notes in Computer Science, Springer-Verlag, 2001, to appear.
5. K. Martin. *The measurement process in domain theory.* Proceedings of the 27th International Colloquium on Automata, Languages and Programming (ICALP), Lecture Notes in Computer Science, vol. 1853, Springer-Verlag, 2000.
6. K. Martin. *Unique fixed points in domain theory.* Proceedings of MFPS XVII, Electronic Notes in Theoretical Computer Science, vol. 45, 2001.

Nominal Logic: A First Order Theory of Names and Binding*

Andrew M. Pitts

University of Cambridge, Computer Laboratory, Cambridge CB3 0FD, UK,
Andrew.Pitts@cl.cam.ac.uk

Abstract. This paper formalises within first-order logic some common practices in computer science to do with representing and reasoning about syntactical structures involving named bound variables (as opposed to nameless terms, explicit substitutions, or higher order abstract syntax). It introduces *Nominal Logic*, a version of first-order many-sorted logic with equality containing primitives for renaming via name-swapping and for freshness of names, from which a notion of binding can be derived. Its axioms express key properties of these primitives, which are satisfied by the *FM-sets* model of syntax introduced in [11]. Nominal Logic serves as a vehicle for making two general points. Firstly, name-swapping has much nicer logical properties than more general forms of renaming while at the same time providing a sufficient foundation for a theory of structural induction/recursion for syntax modulo α-conversion. Secondly, it is useful for the practice of operational semantics to make explicit the *equivariance property* of assertions about syntax – namely that their validity is invariant under name-swapping.

1 Introduction

It is commonplace, when using formal languages in computer science or mathematical logic, to abstract away from details of concrete syntax in terms of strings of symbols and instead work solely with parse trees – the 'abstract syntax' of a language. Doing so gives one access to two extremely useful and inter-related tools: definition by recursion on the structure of parse trees and proof by induction on that structure. However, conventional abstract syntax is not abstract enough if the formal language involves variable-binding constructs. In this situation the common practice of human (as opposed to computer) provers is to say one thing and do another. We say that we will quotient the collection of parse trees by a suitable equivalence relation of α-conversion, identifying trees up to renaming of bound variables; but then we try to make the use of α-equivalence classes as implicit as possible by dealing with them via suitably chosen representatives. How to make such suitable choices of representatives is well understood, so much so that is has a name – the 'Barendregt Variable Convention': choose a representative parse tree whose bound variables are *fresh*, i.e. mutually distinct and distinct from any (free) variables in the current context. This informal

* Research funded by UK EPSRC grant GR/R07615.

N. Kobayashi and B.C. Pierce (Eds.): TACS 2001, LNCS 2215, pp. 219–242, 2001.

practice of confusing an α-equivalence class with a member of the class with sufficiently fresh bound variables has to be accompanied by a certain amount of hygiene on the part of human provers: our constructions and proofs have to be independent of which particular fresh names we choose for bound variables. Nearly always, the verification of such independence properties is omitted, because it is tedious and detracts from more interesting business at hand. Of course this introduces a certain amount of informality into 'pencil-and-paper' proofs that cannot be ignored if one is in the business of producing fully formalised, machine-checked proofs. But even if you are not in that business and are content with your pencil and paper, I think there is a good reason to examine this informal use of 'sufficiently fresh names' and put it on a more precise, mathematical footing.

The reason I have in mind has to do with those intuitive and useful tools mentioned above: structural recursion for defining functions on parse trees and structural induction for proving properties of them. Although it is often said that the Barendregt Variable Convention allows one to work with α-equivalence classes of parse trees as though they were just parse trees, this is not literally the case when it comes to structural recursion/induction. For example, when dealing with an induction step for a variable-binding construct, it often happens that the step can be proved if the bound variable is chosen sufficiently fresh, but not for an arbitrary bound variable as the induction principle demands. The Barendregt Variable Convention papers over the crack in the proof at this point (by preventing one considering the case of an arbitrary bound variable rather than a fresh one), but the crack is still there. Although one can easily side-step the problem by using a suitable size function on parse trees to replace structural induction with mathematical induction, this is not a very satisfying solution. The size function will be defined by structural recursion and the crucial fact that α-equivalent parse trees have the same size will be proved by structural induction, so we are using structural recursion/induction anyway, but somehow not in the direct way we would like. We can do better than this.

Indeed, the work reported in [10, 11, 24] does so, by providing a mathematical notion of 'sufficiently fresh name' that remains very close to the informal practice described above while enabling α-equivalence classes of parse trees to gain useful inductive/recursive properties. The theory stems from the somewhat surprising observation that all of the concepts we need (α-conversion, freshness, variable-binding, ...) can be defined purely in terms of the operation of *swapping* pairs of names. In particular, the freshness of a name for an object is expressed in terms of the name not being in some finite set of names that *supports* the object – in the sense that swapping any pair of names not in that finite set leaves the object unchanged. This notion of support is weak second order, since it involves an existential quantification over finite sets of names. However, much of the development in [11] only makes use of certain first-order properties of the freshness (i.e. 'not-in-the-support-of') predicate in combination with the swapping operation. This paper presents this first-order theory of names, swapping and freshness, called *Nominal Logic*.

2 Equivariant Predicates

The fundamental assumption underlying Nominal Logic is that *the only predicates we ever deal with* (when describing properties of syntax) *are equivariant ones, in the sense that their validity is invariant under swapping* (i.e. transposing, or interchanging) *names.*

Names of what? Names of entities that may be subject to binding by some of the syntactical constructions under consideration. In Nominal Logic these sorts of names, the ones that may be subjected to swapping, will be called *atoms* – the terminology refers back to the origins of the theory in the Fraenkel-Mostowski permutation model of set theory. Atoms turn out to have quite different logical properties from *constants* (in the usual sense of first-order logic) which, being constant, are not subjected to swapping. Note that this distinction between atom and constant has to do with the issue of binding, rather than substitution. A syntactic category of *variables*, by which is usually meant entities that may be subject to substitution, might be represented in Nominal Logic by atoms or by constants, depending upon circumstances: constants will do if we are in a situation where variables are never bound, but can be substituted; otherwise we should use atoms. The interesting point is that we can make this (useful!) distinction between 'bindable' names and names of constants entirely in terms of properties of swapping names, prior to any discussion of substitution and its properties.

Why the emphasis on *swapping* two names, rather than on the apparently more primitive notion of *renaming* one name by another? The answer has to do with the fact that swapping is an idempotent operation: a swap followed by the same swap is equivalent to doing nothing. This means that the class of equivariant predicates, i.e. those whose validity is invariant under name-swapping, has excellent logical properties; it contains the equality predicate and is closed under negation, conjunction, disjunction, existential and universal quantification, formation of least and greatest fixed points of monotone operators, etc., etc. The same is not true for renaming. (For example, the validity of a negated equality between atoms is not necessarily preserved under renaming.)

That we should take equivariance into account when we reason about syntactical structures is one of the main messages of this paper. Even if you do not care about the details of Nominal Logic to be given below, it is worth taking note of the fact that *name swapping and the equivariance property provide a simple and useful foundation for discussing properties of names and binding in syntax.* Here is a simple example to illustrate this point, taken from type theory.

Example 2.1. McKinna and Pollack [19] note that in the naïve approach to named bound variables, there is a difficulty with proving the weakening property of type systems by rule induction. For example, consider the usual typing relation assigning simple types to terms of the untyped λ-calculus. We take the latter to mean α-equivalence classes $[t]_\alpha$ of parse trees t given by the grammar

$$t ::= a \mid \lambda a.t \mid t\,t \tag{1}$$

where a ranges over an infinite set of variables. The typing relation takes the form $\Gamma \vdash [t]_\alpha : \tau$ where types τ are given by the grammar $\tau ::= X \mid \tau \to \tau$ (with X ranging over an infinite collection of type variables) and the typing context Γ is a finite partial function from variables to types. The typing relation is inductively generated by axioms and rules following the structure of the parse tree t. (If the reader is not familiar with these rules, see [13, Chapter 2], for example; but note that as mentioned in the Introduction, the literature usually does not bother to make a notational distinction between t and $[t]_\alpha$.)

When trying to prove the weakening property of the typing relation

$$(\forall \Gamma)(\forall t)(\forall \tau)\ \Gamma \vdash [t]_\alpha : \tau \ \Rightarrow\ (\forall \tau')(\forall a' \notin \mathrm{dom}(\Gamma))\ \Gamma, a' : \tau' \vdash [t]_\alpha : \tau \tag{2}$$

it is natural to try to proceed by 'rule induction' and show that the predicate $\varphi(\Gamma, [t]_\alpha, \tau)$ given by

$$(\forall \tau')(\forall a' \notin \mathrm{dom}(\Gamma))\ \Gamma, a' : \tau' \vdash [t]_\alpha : \tau$$

defines a relation that is closed under the axioms and rules inductively defining the typing relation and hence contains that relation. But the induction step for the rule for typing λ-abstractions

$$\frac{\begin{array}{l}\Gamma, a : \tau_1 \vdash [t]_\alpha : \tau_2 \\ a \notin \mathrm{dom}(\Gamma)\end{array}}{\Gamma \vdash [\lambda a.t]_\alpha : \tau_1 \to \tau_2} \tag{3}$$

is problematic: we have to prove

$$\varphi(\Gamma, a : \tau_1,\ [t]_\alpha,\ \tau_2) \wedge a \notin \mathrm{dom}(\Gamma) \ \Rightarrow\ \varphi(\Gamma,\ [\lambda a.t]_\alpha,\ \tau_1 \to \tau_2);$$

i.e. given

$$\varphi(\Gamma, a : \tau_1,\ [t]_\alpha,\ \tau_2) \tag{4}$$

and

$$a \notin \mathrm{dom}(\Gamma), \tag{5}$$

we have to prove that

$$\Gamma, a' : \tau' \vdash [\lambda a.t]_\alpha : \tau_1 \to \tau_2 \tag{6}$$

holds for *all* $a' \notin \mathrm{dom}(\Gamma)$ (and all τ') – and there is a problem with doing this for the case $a' = a$.

But this difficulty with the induction step is easily circumvented if we take equivariance into account. The axioms and rules defining typing are closed under the operations of swapping pairs of variables (and also under swapping pairs of type variables, but we do not need to use that here). For example, if we have an instance of rule (3) and we swap any pair of variables throughout both the hypotheses and the conclusion, we get another valid instance of this rule. It follows from this swapping property of the axioms and rules that the typing relation, being the least relation closed under the axioms and rules, is also closed under the swapping operations. Therefore any assertion about typing that we make by combining the typing relation with other such equivariant predicates (such as '$a \in \mathrm{dom}(\Gamma)$') using the usual logical connectives and quantifiers will be equivariant. In particular the predicate φ defined above is equivariant. Thus if we know that (4) holds, then so does $\varphi(\Gamma, a'' : \tau_1, [(a''\, a) \cdot t]_\alpha, \tau_2)$ for any *fresh* variable a''. (Here $(a''\, a) \cdot t$ indicates the parse tree resulting from swapping a'' and a throughout t.) So by definition of φ, since $a' \notin \mathrm{dom}(\Gamma, a'' : \tau_1)$, we have $(\Gamma, a'' : \tau_1), a' : \tau' \vdash [(a''\, a) \cdot t]_\alpha : \tau_2$. Since $(\Gamma, a'' : \tau_1), a' : \tau' = (\Gamma, a' : \tau'), a'' : \tau_1$ (we are using partial functions for typing contexts) and $a'' \notin \mathrm{dom}(\Gamma, a' : \tau')$ (by choice of a''), we can apply typing rule (3) to conclude that $\Gamma, a' : \tau' \vdash [\lambda a''.((a''\, a) \cdot t)]_\alpha : \tau_1 \to \tau_2$. But $\lambda a''.((a''\, a) \cdot t)$ and $\lambda a.t$ are α-equivalent parse trees, so $\Gamma, a' : \tau' \vdash [\lambda a.t]_\alpha : \tau_1 \to \tau_2$ holds. Thus if (4) and (5) hold, so does $\varphi(\Gamma, [\lambda a.t]_\alpha, \tau_1 \to \tau_2)$ and we have completed the induction step. □

From the considerations of this section we abstract the following ingredients for a language to describe syntax involving names and binding: the language should contain a notion of atom together with operations for swapping atoms in expressions (in general we may need several different sorts of atoms – for example, atoms for variables and atoms for type variables in Example 2.1); and the formulas of the language should all be equivariant with respect to these swapping operations. Atoms and swapping are two of the three novelties of Nominal Logic. The third has to do with the crucial step in the proof in Example 2.1 when we chose a *fresh* variable a'': we need to give a freshness relation between atoms and expressions with sufficient properties to make such arguments go through.

3 Nominal Logic: Syntax and Semantics

The syntax of Nominal Logic is that of many-sorted first-order logic with equality, augmented by the following extra features.

- The collection of sorts S is partitioned into two kinds

$$
\begin{array}{lll}
S ::= & A & \textit{sorts of atoms} \\
 & D & \textit{sorts of data.}
\end{array}
$$

- For each sort of atoms A and each sort S there is a distinguished function symbol of arity $A, A, S \longrightarrow S$ whose effect on terms $a : A$, $a' : A$ and $s : S$ we write as the term $(a\, a') \cdot s$ and pronounce '*swap a and a' in s*'.
- For each sort of atoms A and each sort S there is a distinguished relation symbol of arity A, S whose effect on terms $a : A$ and $s : S$ we write as the formula $a \,\#\, s$ and pronounce '*a is fresh for s*'.

Just as for ordinary first-order logic, a *theory* in Nominal Logic is specified by a *signature* of sort, function and relation symbols, together with a collection of (non-logical) *axioms*, which are first-order formulas involving equality, swapping, freshness and symbols from the signature.

Example 3.1 (λ-Terms mod α-equivalence, version 1). Here is an example of a theory in Nominal Logic to which we will return to throughout the paper.

Sort of atoms: *Var*
Sort of data: *Term*
Function symbols:

$$\begin{aligned} var &: Var \longrightarrow Term \\ app &: Term, Term \longrightarrow Term \\ lam &: Var, Term \longrightarrow Term \\ subst &: Term, Var, Term \longrightarrow Term \end{aligned}$$

Axioms:

$$(\forall a : Var)(\forall t, t' : Term)\ \neg\, var(a) = app(t, t') \tag{7}$$

$$(\forall a, a' : Var)(\forall t : Term)\ \neg\, var(a) = lam(a', t) \tag{8}$$

$$(\forall a : Var)(\forall t, t', t'' : Term)\ \neg\, lam(a, t) = app(t', t'') \tag{9}$$

$$\begin{aligned}(\forall t : Term)\ &(\exists a : Var)\ t = var(a) \\ &\lor (\exists t', t'' : Term)\ t = app(t', t'') \\ &\lor (\exists a' : Var)(\exists t' : Term)\ t = lam(a', t')\end{aligned} \tag{10}$$

$$(\forall a, a' : Var)\ var(a) = var(a') \Rightarrow a = a' \tag{11}$$

$$(\forall t, t', t'', t''' : Term)\ app(t, t') = app(t'', t''') \Rightarrow t = t'' \land t' = t''' \tag{12}$$

$$\begin{aligned}(\forall a, a' : Var)\,(\forall t, t' : Term)\ & lam(a, t) = lam(a', t') \Leftrightarrow \\ & (a = a' \land t = t') \lor (a' \mathrel{\mathrm{B}} t \ \land\ t' = (a\,a') \cdot t)\end{aligned} \tag{13}$$

$$\begin{aligned}(\forall \vec{x} : \vec{S})\ &(\forall a : Var)\ \varphi(var(a), \vec{x}) \\ &\land (\forall t, t' : Term)\ \varphi(t, \vec{x}) \land \varphi(t', \vec{x}) \Rightarrow \varphi(app(t, t'), \vec{x}) \\ &\land (\exists a : Var)\ a \mathrel{\mathrm{B}} \vec{x} \land (\forall t : Term)\ \varphi(t, \vec{x}) \Rightarrow \varphi(lam(a, t), \vec{x}) \\ &\Rightarrow (\forall t : Term)\ \varphi(t, \vec{x})\end{aligned} \tag{14}$$

where the free variables of φ are in $t, \vec{x}$

$$(\forall t : Term)(\forall a : Var)\ subst(t, a, var(a)) = t \tag{15}$$

$$(\forall t : Term)(\forall a, a' : Var)\ \neg\, a = a' \Rightarrow subst(t, a, var(a')) = var(a') \tag{16}$$

$$\begin{aligned}(\forall t, t', t'' : Term)\,(\forall a : Var)\ & subst(t, a, app(t', t'')) = \\ & app(subst(t, a, t'), subst(t, a, t''))\end{aligned} \tag{17}$$

$$\begin{aligned}(\forall t, t' : Term)\,(\forall a, a' : Var)\ & \neg\, a' = a \land a' \mathrel{\mathrm{B}} t \Rightarrow \\ & subst(t, a, lam(a', t')) = lam(a', subst(t, a, t'))\end{aligned} \tag{18}$$

Axioms (7)–(10) say that *var*, *app* and *lam* have disjoint images that cover *Term*. Axioms (11)–(13) give the injectivity properties of these three constructors. In particular axiom (13) reflects the fact that equality of terms of sort *Term* should correspond to equality of α-equivalence classes of parse trees for the grammar in (1); and freshness $a \mathrel{\mathrm{B}} t$ to the fact that a variable does not occur freely in a parse tree. Axiom (14) formalises a structural induction principle for such α-equivalence classes (cf. [11, Theorem 6.8]). Finally, axioms (15)–(18) amount to a structurally recursive definition of capture-avoiding substitution for λ-terms (cf. [11, Example 6.9]).

This particular theory has a concrete model given by α-equivalence classes of parse trees for the grammar in (1). However, as explained in [11], in general the

Nominal Logic notions of atom, swapping and freshness can be given a meaning independent of any particular object-level syntax using *FM-sets* – the Fraenkel-Mostowski permutation model of set theory. The following definitions give a simplified, but essentially equivalent, presentation of FM-sets that emphasises swapping over more general permutations of atoms. At the same time we use a mild generalisation of [11] (mentioned in [10, Sect. 7]) in which the set of atoms is partitioned into countably many different kinds (and we only swap atoms of the same kind).

Definition 3.2 (Nominal sets). Fix a countably infinite family $(\mathbb{A}_n \mid n \in \mathbb{N})$ of pairwise disjoint, countably infinite sets. We write $\mathbb{A}$ for the union of all the $\mathbb{A}_n$ and call its elements *atoms*. A *nominal set* X is a set $|X|$ equipped with a well-behaved notion of swapping atoms in elements of the set. By definition this means that for each element $x \in |X|$ and each pair of atoms a, a' of the same kind (i.e. $a, a' \in \mathbb{A}_n$ for some $n \in \mathbb{N}$), we are given an element $(a\,a') \cdot_X x$ of X, called the result of swapping a and a' in x. These swapping operations are required to have the following properties:

(i) **Equational properties of swapping:** for each $x \in |X|$ and all pairs of atoms of equal sort, $a, a' \in \mathbb{A}_m$ and $b, b' \in \mathbb{A}_n$ (any $m, n \in \mathbb{N}$)

$$(a\,a) \cdot_X x = x \tag{19}$$

$$(a\,a') \cdot_X (a\,a') \cdot_X x = x \tag{20}$$

$$(a\,a') \cdot_X (b\,b') \cdot_X x = ((a\,a')b\ \ (a\,a')b'\ ) \cdot_X (a\,a') \cdot_X x \tag{21}$$

where

$$(a\,a')b \triangleq \begin{cases} a & \text{if } b = a' \\ a' & \text{if } b = a \\ b & \text{otherwise} \end{cases} \tag{22}$$

and similarly for $(a\,a')b'$.

(ii) **Finite support property:** we require that each $x \in |X|$ only involve finitely many atoms, in the sense that given x, there exists a finite subset $w \subseteq \mathbb{A}$ with the property that $(a\,a') \cdot_X x = x$ holds for all $a, a' \in \mathbb{A}_n - w$ (any $n \in \mathbb{N}$). It follows that

$$\mathit{supp}_X(x) \triangleq \bigcup_{n \in \mathbb{N}} \{a \in \mathbb{A}_n \mid \{a' \in \mathbb{A}_n \mid (a\,a') \cdot_X x \neq x\} \text{ is not finite}\} \tag{23}$$

is a finite set of atoms (see the proof of [11, Proposition 3.4]), which we call the *support* of x in X.

A *morphism of nominal sets*, $f : X \longrightarrow Y$, is by definition a function from the set $|X|$ to the set $|Y|$ that respects the swapping operations in the sense that

$$f((a\,a') \cdot_X x) = (a\,a') \cdot_Y f(x) \tag{24}$$

holds for all $x \in |X|$ and all atoms a, a' (of the same kind). Clearly the composition of two such functions is another such; and identity functions are morphisms.

Therefore nominal sets and morphisms form a category, which we denote by $\mathcal{N}om$.

Remark 3.3 (From swapping to permutations). The following remarks are for readers familiar with the mathematical theory of groups and group actions. It is a standard result of that theory that the group of all permutations of the n-element set $\{1, \ldots, n\}$ is isomorphic to the group freely generated by $n-1$ symbols g_i $(i = 1, \ldots, n-1)$, subject to the identities

$$\begin{aligned} (g_i)^2 &= id && (i < n) \\ (g_i\, g_{i+1})^3 &= id && (i < n-1) \\ (g_i\, g_j)^2 &= id && (j < i-1) \end{aligned}$$

with the generator g_i corresponding to the permutation transposing i and $i+1$. (See for example [16, Beispiel 19.7].) From this fact one can easily deduce that the group of all (kind-respecting) finite permutations of the set of atoms $\mathbb{A}$ is freely generated by the transpositions $(a\,a')$ (with $a, a' \in \mathbb{A}_n$ for some $n \in \mathbb{N}$), subject to the identities

$$\begin{aligned} (a\,a)(a\,a) &= id \\ (a\,a')(a\,a') &= id \\ (a\,a')(b\,b') &= ((a\,a')b\ \ (a\,a')b'\ )(a\,a') \end{aligned}$$

where the atoms $(a\,a')b$ and $(a\,a')b'$ are defined as in equation (22). It follows that if $|X|$ is a set equipped with swapping operations satisfying equations (19)–(21), then these operations extend uniquely to an action of all finite permutations on elements of $|X|$. If $|X|$ also satisfies property (ii) of Definition 3.2, then this action extends uniquely to all (kind-respecting) permutations, finite or not; and the elements of $|X|$ have the finite support property for this action in the sense of [11, Definition 3.3]. These observations form the basis of a proof that *the category $\mathcal{N}om$ of Definition 3.2 is equivalent to the Schanuel topos* [11, Sect. 7], which underlies the universe of FM-sets used in [11].

It is not hard to see that products $X \times Y$ in the category $\mathcal{N}om$ are given simply by taking the cartesian product $\{(x, y) \mid x \in |X| \wedge y \in |Y|\}$ of underlying sets and defining the swapping operations componentwise:

$$(a\,a') \cdot_{X \times Y} (x, y) \triangleq ((a\,a') \cdot_X x, (a\,a') \cdot_Y y).$$

(Clearly (x, y) has the finiteness property in $X \times Y$ required by Definition 3.2(ii), because x has it in X and y has it in Y.) Similarly, the terminal object 1 in $\mathcal{N}om$ has a one-element underlying set and (necessarily) trivial swapping operations.

So we can interpret many-sorted first-order signatures in the category $\mathcal{N}om$: sorts S are interpreted as objects $[\![S]\!]$; function symbols f, of arity $S_1, \ldots, S_n \longrightarrow S$ say, as morphisms $[\![f]\!] : [\![S_1]\!] \times \cdots \times [\![S_n]\!] \longrightarrow [\![S]\!]$; and relation symbols R, of arity $S_1, \ldots, S_n$ say, as subobjects of $[\![S_1]\!] \times \cdots \times [\![S_n]\!]$. Indeed, $\mathcal{N}om$ has sufficient properties to soundly interpret classical first-order logic with equality [1] using the

[1] And much more besides, since it is equivalent to the Schanuel topos, but that will not concern us here.

usual techniques of categorical logic – see [18], or [23, Sect. 5] for a brief overview. In fact, readers unfamiliar with such techniques need not become so just to understand the interpretation of first-order logic in the category of nominal sets, since it is just like the usual Tarskian semantics of first-order logic in the category of sets (at the same time remaining within the world of equivariant properties). For it is not hard to see that the subobjects of an object X in the category $\mathcal{N}om$ are in bijection with the subsets $A \subseteq |X|$ of the underlying set that are equivariant, in the sense that $(a\,a') \cdot_X x \in A$ whenever $x \in A$, for any atoms a, a' (of the same kind). As we mentioned in Sect. 2, the collection of equivariant subsets is closed under all the usual operations of first-order logic and contains equality. So it just remains to explain the interpretation in $\mathcal{N}om$ of the distinctive syntax of Nominal Logic – atoms, swapping and freshness.

Definition 3.4. Here is the intended interpretation of atoms, swapping and freshness in the category of nominal sets of Definition 3.2.

Atoms. A sort of atoms in a Nominal Logic signature will be interpreted by a *nominal set of atoms* A_n (for some $n \in \mathbb{N}$), which by definition has underlying set $|A_n| = \mathbb{A}_n$ and is equipped with the swapping operations given by

$$(a\,a') \cdot b \triangleq \begin{cases} a & \text{if } b = a' \\ a' & \text{if } b = a \\ b & \text{otherwise} \end{cases}$$

(where $b \in \mathbb{A}_n$ and $a, a' \in \mathbb{A}_m$ for any $m \in \mathbb{N}$). We always assume that distinct sorts of atoms are interpreted by distinct kinds of atoms. (So we are implicitly assuming that signatures contain at most countably many such sorts.)

Swapping. Note that by virtue of equation (21), the function $a, a', x \mapsto (a\,a') \cdot_X x$ determines a morphism $A_n \times A_n \times X \longrightarrow X$ in the category $\mathcal{N}om$. This morphism is used to interpret the distinguished function symbol $A, A, S \longrightarrow S$ for swapping, assuming the nominal set of atoms A_n is the interpretation of the sort of atoms A and that X is the interpretation of S. Thus

$$[\![(a\,a') \cdot s]\!] = ([\![a]\!]\,[\![a']\!]) \cdot_X [\![s]\!] \quad \text{when } s : S \text{ and } [\![S]\!] = X.$$

Freshness. The distinguished relation symbol $\mathtt{B}$ of arity A, S for freshness is interpreted as the 'not in the support of' relation $(-) \notin supp_X(-)$ between atoms and elements of nominal sets. Thus if the nominal set of atoms A_n is the interpretation of the sort of atoms A and X is the interpretation of the sort S, then for terms $a : A, s : S$, the formula $a \mathrel{\mathtt{B}} s$ is satisfied by the interpretation if and only if $[\![a]\!] \notin supp_X([\![s]\!])$, where $supp_X$ is as in equation (23). (It is not hard to see that this is an equivariant subset of $\mathbb{A}_n \times |X|$ and hence determines a subobject of $[\![A]\!] \times [\![S]\!]$ in $\mathcal{N}om$.)

4 Nominal Logic Axioms

For simplicity, we will use a Hilbert-style presentation of Nominal Logic: a single rule of Modus Ponens, the usual axiom schemes of first-order logic with equality, plus the axiom schemes for swapping and freshness given in Fig. 1.

Properties of swapping

S1 $(\forall a : A)(\forall x : S)\ (a\,a) \cdot x = x$
S2 $(\forall a, a' : A)(\forall x : S)\ (a\,a') \cdot (a\,a') \cdot x = x$
S3 $(\forall a, a' : A)\ (a\,a') \cdot a = a'$

Equivariance

E1 $(\forall a, a' : A)(\forall b, b' : A')(\forall x : S)\ (a\,a') \cdot (b\,b') \cdot x = ((a\,a') \cdot b\ (a\,a') \cdot b') \cdot (a\,a') \cdot x$
E2 $(\forall a, a' : A)(\forall b : A')(\forall x : S)\ b \mathrel{\#} x \Rightarrow (a\,a') \cdot b \mathrel{\#} (a\,a') \cdot x$
E3 $(\forall a, a' : A)(\forall \vec{x} : \vec{S})\ (a\,a') \cdot f(\vec{x}) = f((a\,a') \cdot \vec{x})$
where f is a function symbol of arity $\vec{S} \longrightarrow S$
E4 $(\forall a, a' : A)(\forall \vec{x} : \vec{S})\ R(\vec{x}) \Rightarrow R((a\,a') \cdot \vec{x})$
where R is a relation symbol of arity $\vec{S}$

Properties of freshness

F1 $(\forall a, a' : A)(\forall x : S)\ a \mathrel{\#} x \wedge a' \mathrel{\#} x \Rightarrow (a\,a') \cdot x = x$
F2 $(\forall a, a' : A)\ a \mathrel{\#} a' \Leftrightarrow \neg a = a'$
F3 $(\forall a : A)(\forall a' : A')\ a \mathrel{\#} a'$
where $A \neq A'$
F4 $(\forall \vec{x} : \vec{S})(\exists a : A)\ a \mathrel{\#} \vec{x}$

Notes

1. A, A' range over sorts of atoms, S ranges over sorts and $\vec{S}$ over finite lists of sorts.
2. In axiom **E3** and **E4**, $(a\,a') \cdot \vec{x}$ indicates the finite list of arguments given by $(a\,a') \cdot x_i$ as x_i ranges over $\vec{x}$.
3. In axiom **F4**, $a \mathrel{\#} \vec{x}$ indicates the finite conjunction of the formulas $a \mathrel{\#} x_i$ as x_i ranges over the list $\vec{x}$.

Fig. 1. The axiom schemes of Nominal Logic for freshness and swapping

The following result shows that the axioms in Fig. 1 validate the fundamental assumption mentioned at the start of Sect. 2, namely that all properties expressible in Nominal Logic are invariant under swapping atoms.

Proposition 4.1 (Equivariance). *For each term t and formula φ, with free variables amongst $\vec{x} : \vec{S}$ say, we have*

$$(\forall a, a' : A)(\forall \vec{x} : \vec{S})\ (a\,a') \cdot t(\vec{x}) = t((a\,a') \cdot \vec{x}) \tag{25}$$

$$(\forall a, a' : A)(\forall \vec{x} : \vec{S})\ \varphi(\vec{x}) \Leftrightarrow \varphi((a\,a') \cdot \vec{x}) \tag{26}$$

where $t((a\,a')\cdot\vec{x})$ *denotes the result of simultaneously substituting* $(a\,a')\cdot x_i$ *for* x_i *in* t *(as* x_i *ranges over* $\vec{x}$*) and similarly for* $\varphi((a\,a')\cdot\vec{x})$.

Proof. Property (25) follows from axioms **E1** and **E3**, by induction on the structure of the term t. For (26) we proceed by induction on the structure of the formula φ, using standard properties of first-order logic for the induction steps for connectives and quantifiers. Note that by virtue of axiom **S2**, equation (26) holds if and only if

$$(\forall a, a' : A)(\forall \vec{x} : \vec{S})\ \varphi(\vec{x}) \Rightarrow \varphi((a\,a')\cdot\vec{x}) \tag{27}$$

does. So the base case when φ is equality follows from the usual axioms for equality, the base case for the freshness predicate B follows from axiom **E2**, and that for relation symbols from axiom **E4** (using (25) in each case). □

Proposition 4.2 (Soundness). *The axioms in Fig. 1 are all satisfied by the nominal sets interpretation of atoms, swapping and freshness given in Sect. 3.*

Proof. Satisfaction of axioms **S1**–**S3** and **E1** is guaranteed by part (i) of Definition 3.2 (since the swapping action for a nominal set of atoms is given by equation (22)). Satisfaction of axioms **E2** and **F1**–**F3** is a simple consequence of the definition of support in equation (23). Axioms **E3** and **E4** are satisfied because function and relation symbols are interpreted by morphisms and subobjects in the category of nominal sets, which have these equivariance properties. Finally, axiom **F4** is satisfied because the support of an element of a nominal set is a finite subset of the fixed, countably infinite set $\mathbb{A}$ of all atoms. □

Did we forget any axioms? In other words are the axiom schemes in Fig. 1 complete for the intended interpretation in the category of nominal sets? Axiom **F4** says that there is an inexhaustible supply of atoms that are fresh, i.e. not in the support of elements in the current context. This is certainly a consequence of property (ii) of Definition 3.2, which guarantees that elements of nominal sets have finite support. However, that property is ostensibly a statement of weak second order logic, since it quantifies over finite sets of atoms. So we should not expect the first-order theory of Nominal Logic to completely axiomatise the notion of finite support. Example 4.5 confirms this expectation. Before giving it we state a useful property of freshness in Nominal Logic that we need below.

Proposition 4.3. *For any term* t*, with free variables amongst* $\vec{x} : \vec{S}$ *say, we have*

$$(\forall a : A)(\forall \vec{x} : \vec{S})\ a \,\mathrm{B}\, \vec{x} \Rightarrow a \,\mathrm{B}\, t(\vec{x}) \tag{28}$$

(Recall that $a \,\mathrm{B}\, \vec{x}$ *stands for the finite conjunction of the formulas* $a \,\mathrm{B}\, x_i$ *as* x_i *ranges over* $\vec{x}$*.)*

Proof. Given any $a : A$ and $\vec{x} : \vec{S}$, by axiom **F4** there is some $a' : A$ with $a' \,\mathrm{B}\, \vec{x}$ and $a' \,\mathrm{B}\, t(\vec{x})$. So if $a \,\mathrm{B}\, \vec{x}$, then by axiom **F1** $(a\,a')\cdot x_i = x_i$ holds for each x_i.

So since $a' \mathrel{\text{B}} t(\vec{x})$ by choice of a', we have

$$\begin{aligned} a &= (a\,a') \cdot a' && \text{by axioms } \mathbf{S2} \text{ and } \mathbf{S3} \\ &\mathrel{\text{B}} (a\,a') \cdot t(\vec{x}) && \text{by axiom } \mathbf{E2} \\ &= t((a\,a') \cdot \vec{x}) && \text{by (25)} \\ &= t(\vec{x}) && \text{by axiom } \mathbf{F1} \end{aligned}$$

as required. □

Corollary 4.4. *If a Nominal Logic theory contains a closed term $t : A$ with A a sort of atoms, then it is an inconsistent theory.*

Proof. Suppose that A is a sort of atoms and that $t : A$ is a term with no free variables. By the above proposition we have $(\forall a : A)\ a \mathrel{\text{B}} t$. Thus $t \mathrel{\text{B}} t$ and by axiom **F2** this means $\neg\, t = t$, contradiction. □

Example 4.5 (Incompleteness). Consider the following Nominal Logic theory.

Sort of atoms: A
Sorts of data: D, N
Function symbols: $o : N$
$s : N \longrightarrow N$
$f : D, N \longrightarrow A$
Axioms:

$$(\forall x : N)\ \neg\, o = s(x)$$
$$(\forall x, x' : N)\ s(x) = s(x') \Rightarrow x = x'$$

Claim: any model of this theory in the category of nominal sets satisfies the formula

$$(\forall y : D)(\exists x, x' : N)\ \neg\, x = x' \wedge f(y, x) = f(y, x') \tag{29}$$

but that formula cannot be proved in Nominal Logic from the axioms of the theory.

Proof of Claim. Note that in any model of this theory in the category $\mathcal{N}om$, the interpretation of the closed terms $n_k : N$ $(k \in \mathbb{N})$ defined by

$$\begin{cases} n_0 & \triangleq o \\ n_{k+1} & \triangleq s(n_k) \end{cases}$$

are distinct elements $[\![n_k]\!] \in |[\![N]\!]|$ of the nominal set $[\![N]\!]$. Therefore, to see that (29) is satisfied by the model it suffices to show for each $d \in |[\![D]\!]|$ that $[\![f]\!]([\![n_{k_1}]\!], d) = [\![f]\!]([\![n_{k_2}]\!], d) \in |[\![A]\!]|$ holds for some $k_1 \neq k_2 \in \mathbb{N}$. Note that $[\![A]\!]$ is a nominal set of atoms, $\mathbb{A}_n$ say. Suppose to the contrary that all the $[\![f]\!]([\![n_k]\!], d)$

are distinct atoms in $\mathbb{A}_n$. Then since the support $supp_{[\![D]\!]}(d)$ of $d \in |[\![D]\!]|$ is a finite subset of $\mathbb{A}$, we can find $k_1 \neq k_2 \in \mathbb{N}$ so that

$$a_1 \triangleq [\![f]\!]([\![n_{k_1}]\!], d) \quad \text{and} \quad a_2 \triangleq [\![f]\!]([\![n_{k_2}]\!], d)$$

satisfy $a_1, a_2 \notin supp_{[\![D]\!]}(d)$. We also have $a_1, a_2 \notin supp_{[\![N]\!]}(n_k)$ for all k (using (28) and the fact that the terms n_k have no free variables). Hence $a_1, a_2 \notin supp_{\mathbb{A}_n}([\![f]\!]([\![n_k]\!]), d)$ and thus $(a_1\, a_2) \cdot_{\mathbb{A}_n} [\![f]\!]([\![n_k]\!], d) = [\![f]\!]([\![n_k]\!], d)$, for all $k \in \mathbb{N}$. Taking $k = k_1$ and recalling the definition of a_1 and a_2, we conclude that

$$[\![f]\!]([\![n_{k_2}]\!], d) = a_2 = (a_1\, a_2) \cdot_{\mathbb{A}_n} a_1 = (a_1\, a_2) \cdot_{\mathbb{A}_n} [\![f]\!]([\![n_{k_1}]\!], d) = [\![f]\!]([\![n_{k_1}]\!], d)$$

with $k_1 \neq k_2$, contradicting our assumption that all the $[\![f]\!]([\![n_k]\!], d)$ are distinct.

To see that (29) is not provable in Nominal Logic it suffices to find a model in the usual sense of first-order logic for the axioms of this theory and the axioms in Fig. 1 which does not satisfy (29). We can get such a model by modifying Definition 3.2 by using an *uncountable* set of atoms and sets equipped with swapping actions all of whose elements have *countable* support. More concretely, we get a model M by taking $[\![A]\!]_M$ to be an uncountable set, the set $\mathbb{R}$ of real numbers say; taking $[\![N]\!]_M$ to be a countable subset of this set, the set $\mathbb{N}$ of natural numbers say; and taking $[\![D]\!]_M$ to be the set $\mathbb{R}^{\mathbb{N}}$ of all functions from $\mathbb{N}$ to $\mathbb{R}$ (all such functions are countably supported). The interpretation of the function symbols o, s and f are respectively zero, successor ($n \mapsto n + 1$) and the evaluation function $\mathbb{R}^{\mathbb{N}} \times \mathbb{N} \longrightarrow \mathbb{R}$ ($d, n \mapsto d(n)$). The interpretation of the swapping operation for sort A is as in equation (22) (i.e. $(r\, r') \cdot_{\mathbb{R}} r'' = (r\, r')r''$ for all $r, r', r'' \in \mathbb{R}$); for sort N, swapping is trivial (i.e. $(r\, r') \cdot_{\mathbb{N}} n = n$ for all $r, r' \in \mathbb{R}$ and $n \in \mathbb{N}$); and for sort D, it is given by $(r\, r') \cdot_{\mathbb{R}^{\mathbb{N}}} d = \lambda n \in \mathbb{N}.(r\, r') \cdot_{\mathbb{R}} d(n)$. The interpretation of the freshness predicate for sort A is $\neq$; for sort N, it is trivial (i.e. $r \,\#\, n$ holds for all $r \in \mathbb{R}$ and $n \in \mathbb{N}$); and for sort D, $r \,\#\, d$ holds if and only if $r \neq d(n)$ for all $n \in \mathbb{N}$. With these definitions one can check that all the axioms are satisfied. However (29) is not satisfied, because the inclusion of $\mathbb{N}$ into $\mathbb{R}$ gives an element $d \in \mathbb{R}^{\mathbb{N}} = [\![D]\!]_M$ for which $n \mapsto [\![f]\!]_M(d, n)$ is injective. □

Even though there is this incompleteness, it appears that the axioms of Nominal Logic are sufficient for a useful theory of names and name-binding along the lines of [11, 9]. The following sections give some evidence for this claim.

5 The Freshness Quantifier

We begin by proving within Nominal Logic the characteristic 'some/any' property of fresh atoms (cf. [11, Proposition 4.10]).

Proposition 5.1. *Suppose φ is a formula with free variables amongst $a : A, \vec{x} : \vec{S}$ (with A a sort of atoms). Then*

$$(\exists a : A)\, a \,\#\, \vec{x} \wedge \varphi(a, \vec{x}) \;\Leftrightarrow\; (\forall a : A)\, a \,\#\, \vec{x} \Rightarrow \varphi(a, \vec{x}) \tag{30}$$

is provable in Nominal Logic.

Proof. If $\varphi(a, \vec{x})$ holds, then by Proposition 4.1 and axiom **S3** we also have $\varphi(a', (a\, a') \cdot \vec{x})$; so if $a \mathrel{\#} \vec{x}$ and $a' \mathrel{\#} \vec{x}$, then axiom **F1** gives $\varphi(a', \vec{x})$. Thus we have the left-to-right implication in (30).

Conversely suppose $(\forall a : A)\ a \mathrel{\#} \vec{x} \Rightarrow \varphi(a, \vec{x})$ holds. For any $\vec{x} : \vec{S}$, using axiom **F4** we can find $a : A$ such that $a \mathrel{\#} \vec{x}$ and hence also satisfying $\varphi(a, \vec{x})$. □

This property of freshness crops up frequently in proofs about syntax with named bound variables (see [19] for example): we choose *some* fresh name with a certain property and later on, in a wider context, we have to revise the choice to accommodate finitely many more constraints and so need to know that we could have chosen *any* fresh name with that property. For this reason it is convenient to introduce a notation that tells us we have this 'some/any' property without mentioning the context of free variables $\vec{x}$ explicitly. (Note that (30) holds for any list $\vec{x}$ so long as it contains the free variables of φ other than the atom a being quantified over.

Definition 5.2 (И-quantifier). For each formula φ and each variable $a : A$ (with A a sort of atoms), define

$$(\text{И}a : A)\ \varphi \triangleq (\exists a : A)\ a \mathrel{\#} \vec{x} \wedge \varphi(a, \vec{x}) \tag{31}$$

where $\vec{x}$ is the list of free variables of φ not equal to the variable a. (There is no requirement that a actually occur free in φ.)

We could have formulated Nominal Logic with the И-quantifier as a primitive and the freshness predicate defined from it, since it is not hard to prove from the above definition and the axioms of Nominal Logic that

$$a \mathrel{\#} x \Leftrightarrow (\text{И}a' : A)\ (a\, a') \cdot x = x \tag{32}$$

holds. When taken as primitive, the axioms for И can be derived from the proof rules mentioned in [10, Remark 3.6]. Here we have chosen the presentation with # as primitive to emphasise that Nominal Logic is just a theory within usual first-order logic.

Further evidence of the naturalness of the И-quantifier is the fact that, in the semantics given in Sect. 3, it coincides with a cofiniteness quantifier: $(\text{И}a : A)\ \varphi$ *holds in the nominal sets interpretation if and only if* $\varphi(a)$ *holds for all but finitely many atoms* a. See [9] for the development of the properties and applications of the И-quantifier within the setting of FM-set theory.

Example 5.3 (λ-Terms mod α-equivalence, version 2). We can simplify some of the axioms of the theory in Example 3.1 using the И-quantifier. Specifically, axiom (13) explaining equality of λ-abstractions is equivalent to

$$\begin{aligned}(\forall a, a' : \mathit{Var})\ (\forall t, t' : \mathit{Term})\ \mathit{lam}(a, t) = \mathit{lam}(a', t') \Leftrightarrow \\ (\text{И}a'' : \mathit{Var})\ (a''\, a) \cdot t = (a''\, a') \cdot t'\end{aligned} \tag{33}$$

(cf. [11, Lemma 5.1]); axiom (14), which is the structural induction principle for α-equivalence classes of λ-terms, can be reformulated as follows (with the extra free variables in φ now implicit):

$$\begin{aligned}&(\forall a : \mathit{Var})\ \varphi(\mathit{var}(a))\\ &\wedge (\forall t, t' : \mathit{Term})\ \varphi(t) \wedge \varphi(t') \Rightarrow \varphi(\mathit{app}(t, t'))\\ &\wedge (\text{И} a : \mathit{Var})(\forall t : \mathit{Term})\ \varphi(t) \Rightarrow \varphi(\mathit{lam}(a, t))\\ &\Rightarrow (\forall t : \mathit{Term})\ \varphi(t)\end{aligned} \tag{34}$$

Finally axiom (18), which is the clause for λ-abstractions in the structurally recursive definition of capture-avoiding substitution, can be replaced by

$$\begin{aligned}&(\forall t : \mathit{Term})(\forall a : \mathit{Var})\,(\text{И} a' : \mathit{Var})(\forall t' : \mathit{Term})\\ &\qquad \mathit{subst}(t, a, \mathit{lam}(a', t')) = \mathit{lam}(a', \mathit{subst}(t, a, t')).\end{aligned} \tag{35}$$

The following result is the Nominal Logic version of [11, Lemma 6.3], which is used in that paper to introduce notation for 'locally fresh atoms' in FM-set theory. (We discuss extending the term language of Nominal Logic in Sect. 7.)

Proposition 5.4. *Suppose that t is a term of sort S with free variables amongst $a : A, \vec{x} : \vec{S}$ (with A a sort of atoms). Then the following is a theorem of Nominal Logic:*

$$\begin{aligned}&(\forall \vec{x} : \vec{S})\ ((\text{И} a : A)\ a \mathrel{\#} t(a, \vec{x}))\ \Rightarrow\\ &\qquad (\exists! x : S)(\forall a' : A)\ a' \mathrel{\#} \vec{x} \Rightarrow x = t(a', \vec{x})\end{aligned} \tag{36}$$

(where $\exists!$ means 'there exists a unique ...' and has the usual encoding in first-order logic).

Proof. Suppose $(\text{И} a : A)\ a \mathrel{\#} t(a, \vec{x})$. So there is some $a : A$ with $a \mathrel{\#} \vec{x}$ and $a \mathrel{\#} t(a, \vec{x})$. Put $x = t(a, \vec{x})$. Clearly, if x has the property $(\forall a' : A)\ a' \mathrel{\#} \vec{x} \Rightarrow x = t(a', \vec{x})$, it is the unique such (since by axiom **F4** there is some a' with $a' \mathrel{\#} \vec{x}$). To see that it does have this property, suppose $a' : A$ satisfies $a' \mathrel{\#} \vec{x}$. Since we want to show that $x = t(a', \vec{x})$, if $a' = a$ then we are done. So suppose $\neg\, a' = a$; thus $a' \mathrel{\#} a$ (by axiom **F2**) and hence $a' \mathrel{\#} t(a, \vec{x})$ by Proposition 4.3. Since $a \mathrel{\#} t(a, \vec{x})$, we have

$$\begin{aligned}x \triangleq t(a, \vec{x}) &= (a\, a') \cdot t(a, \vec{x}) && \text{by axiom } \mathbf{F1}\\ &= t((a\, a') \cdot a, (a\, a') \cdot \vec{x}) && \text{by Proposition 4.1}\\ &= t(a', \vec{x}) && \text{by axioms } \mathbf{S3} \text{ and } \mathbf{F1}\end{aligned}$$

as required. □

6 Binding

In Example 5.3, the fact that *lam* is a variable-binding operation is reflected in axiom (33), which explains equality of terms of the form $\mathit{lam}(a, t)$ via a swapping formulation of α-conversion (cf. [11, Sect. 2]). Instead of axiomatising binders on a case-by-case basis, we can make a definitional extension of Nominal Logic with a new sort-forming operation for *atom-abstraction* whose intended interpretation is the following construction on nominal sets.

Definition 6.1 (Nominal set of atom-abstractions). Given a nominal set X and a nominal set of atoms A_n (cf. Definition 3.4), the *nominal set of atom-abstractions* $[A_n]X$ is defined as follows.

Underlying set $|[A_n]X|$ is the set of equivalence classes for the equivalence relation on $\mathbb{A}_n \times |X|$ that relates (a, x) and (a', x') if and only if $(a''\,a) \cdot_X x = (a''\,a') \cdot_X x'$ for some (or indeed any) $a'' \in \mathbb{A}_n$ such that $a'' \notin supp_X(x) \cup supp_X(x') \cup \{a, a'\}$. We write $a.x$ for the equivalence class of the pair (a, x).
Swapping action is inherited from that for the product $A_n \times X$:

$$(b\,b') \cdot_{[A_n]X} (a.x) \triangleq a'.x' \quad \text{where } a' = (b\,b')a \text{ and } x' = (b\,b') \cdot_X x.$$

With these definitions one can check that the requirements of Definition 3.2 are satisfied (in particular the support of $a.x$ turns out to be the finite set $supp_X(x) - \{a\}$; cf. Proposition 6.2).

See [11, 9] for the use of this notion of atom-abstraction to treat syntax modulo α-equivalence as inductively defined sets (with useful associated structural induction/recursion principles) within the Fraenkel-Mostowski permutation model of set theory. Here we observe that the notion is definable within Nominal Logic. The situation is analogous to the fact that cartesian products are definable within ordinary first-order logic: given sorts S_1, S_2 and S, there is a first-order theory in all of whose models the interpretation of S is isomorphic to the cartesian product of the interpretations of S_1 and S_2. Indeed there are several such theories; for example, take a function symbol $pair : S_1, S_2 \longrightarrow S$ and axioms

$$(\forall x_1, x_1' : S_1)\,(\forall x_2, x_2' : S_2)\; pair(x_1, x_2) = pair(x_1', x_2') \Rightarrow (x_1 = x_1') \wedge (x_2 = x_2') \tag{37}$$

$$(\forall x : S)(\exists x_1 : S_1)(\exists x_2 : S_2)\; x = pair(x_1, x_2). \tag{38}$$

Within Nominal Logic there is a similar definability result for atom-abstraction sets. Given sorts A, S and S' (with A a sort of atoms), and a function symbol $abs : A, S \longrightarrow S'$, the axioms

$$(\forall a, a' : A)\,(\forall x, x' : S)\; abs(a, x) = abs(a', x') \Leftrightarrow (\text{И} a'' : A)\; (a''\,a) \cdot x = (a''\,a') \cdot x' \tag{39}$$

$$(\forall x' : S')(\exists a : A)(\exists x : S)\; x' = abs(a, x) \tag{40}$$

ensure that in the semantics of Sect. 3, the interpretation of S' is isomorphic to $[A_n]X$, where A_n and X are the nominal sets interpreting A and S respectively.

Figure 2 gives an extension of Nominal Logic with atom-abstractions. Axiom **E5** ensures that we still have the crucial equivariance properties of Proposition 4.1 for the extended syntax (and hence also the freshness property of Proposition 4.3). For axiom **A1** we have chosen an equivalent formulation of (39) avoiding the use of the freshness quantifier; as we noted above, this together with axiom **A2** determine the meaning of $[A]S$ and $a.s$ in the category

Add to the syntax of Nominal Logic as follows.

- For each sort of atoms A and each sort S, there is a sort of data $[A]S$, called the *sort of A-atom-abstractions of S*.
- For each sort of atoms A and each sort S there is a distinguished function symbol of arity $A, S \longrightarrow [A]S$ whose effect on terms $a : A$, and $s : S$ we write as the term $a.s$ and pronounce '*abstract a in s*'.

Add to the axioms of Nominal Logic the following.

E5 $(\forall b, b' : A')(\forall a : A)(\forall x : S)\ (b\,b') \cdot (a.x) = ((b\,b') \cdot a).((b\,b') \cdot x)$
A1 $(\forall a, a' : A)(\forall x, x' : S)\ a.x = a'.x' \Leftrightarrow (a = a' \wedge x = x') \vee (a' \mathrel{\mathrm{B}} x \ \wedge\ x' = (a\,a') \cdot x)$
A2 $(\forall y : [A]S)(\exists a : A)(\exists x : S)\ y = a.x$

Fig. 2. Nominal Logic with atom-abstractions

$\mathcal{N}om$ up to isomorphism. For this reason, the following characterisation of freshness for atom-abstractions is a theorem of the extended Nominal Logic, rather than one of its axioms.

Proposition 6.2. *If A and A' are distinct sorts of atoms and S is any sort, then the following formulas are provable in Nominal Logic extended as in Fig. 2.*

$$(\forall a, a' : A)(\forall x : S)\ a' \mathrel{\mathrm{B}} a.x \Leftrightarrow a' = a \ \vee\ a' \mathrel{\mathrm{B}} x \tag{41}$$
$$(\forall a : A)(\forall a' : A')(\forall x : S)\ a' \mathrel{\mathrm{B}} a.x \Leftrightarrow a' \mathrel{\mathrm{B}} x \tag{42}$$

Proof. In view of axioms **F2** and **F3**, it suffices to prove

$$(\forall a : A)(\forall x : S)\ a \mathrel{\mathrm{B}} a.x \tag{43}$$
$$(\forall a : A)(\forall a' : A')(\forall x : S)\ a' \mathrel{\mathrm{B}} x \Rightarrow a' \mathrel{\mathrm{B}} a.x \tag{44}$$
$$(\forall a : A)(\forall a' : A')(\forall x : S)\ a' \mathrel{\mathrm{B}} a \ \wedge\ a' \mathrel{\mathrm{B}} a.x \Rightarrow a' \mathrel{\mathrm{B}} x \tag{45}$$

for all sorts of atoms A and A' (possibly equal).

For (43), given $a : A$ and $x : S$, by axiom **F4** we can find $a' : A$ with $a' \mathrel{\mathrm{B}} a.x$ and hence

$$\begin{aligned} a &= (a\,a') \cdot a' && \text{by axioms } \mathbf{S2} \text{ and } \mathbf{S3} \\ &\mathrel{\mathrm{B}} (a\,a') \cdot (a.x) && \text{by axiom } \mathbf{E2} \text{ on } a' \mathrel{\mathrm{B}} a.x \\ &= a'.((a\,a') \cdot x) && \text{by axioms } \mathbf{E5} \text{ and } \mathbf{S3} \\ &= a.x && \text{by axiom } \mathbf{A1}. \end{aligned}$$

For (44), given $a : A$, $a' : A'$ and $x : S$ with $a' \mathrel{\mathrm{B}} x$, we argue by cases according to whether A and A' are the same and whether $a' = a$ or not. If the sorts are the same and $a' = a$, then we have $a' \mathrel{\mathrm{B}} a.x$ by (43); in the other three cases we always have $a' \mathrel{\mathrm{B}} a$ (using axioms **F2** and **F3**); so since $a' \mathrel{\mathrm{B}} a$

and $a' \mathrel{\mathrm{B}} x$, we have $a' \mathrel{\mathrm{B}} a.x$ by Proposition 4.3 (which holds for the extended syntax by virtue of axiom **E5**).

For (45), given $a : A$, $a' : A'$ and $x : S$ with $a' \mathrel{\mathrm{B}} a$ and $a' \mathrel{\mathrm{B}} a.x$, by axiom **F4** we can find $a'' : A'$ with $a'' \mathrel{\mathrm{B}} a$, $a'' \mathrel{\mathrm{B}} x$ and $a'' \mathrel{\mathrm{B}} a.x$. Then

$$\begin{aligned} a.x &= (a'\,a'') \cdot a.x && \text{by axiom } \mathbf{F1} \\ &= ((a'\,a'') \cdot a).(a'\,a'') \cdot x) && \text{by axiom } \mathbf{E5} \\ &= a.((a'\,a'') \cdot x) && \text{by axiom } \mathbf{F1} \end{aligned}$$

and hence $x = (a'\,a'') \cdot x$ by axiom **A1**. Since $a'' \mathrel{\mathrm{B}} x$, we get $a' = (a'\,a'') \cdot a'' \mathrel{\mathrm{B}} (a'\,a'') \cdot x = x$, as required. □

Example 6.3 (λ-Terms mod α-equivalence, version 3). We can reformulate Example 5.3 to use atom-abstractions by changing the arity of *lam* to be $[\mathit{Var}]\mathit{Term} \longrightarrow \mathit{Term}$. At the same time, axiom (33) is replaced by a simple injectivity requirement like axioms (11) and (12):

$$(\forall y, y' : [\mathit{Var}]\mathit{Term})\ \mathit{lam}(y) = \mathit{lam}(y') \Rightarrow y = y'. \tag{46}$$

Similarly the disjointness axioms (8) and (9) are replaced by

$$(\forall a : \mathit{Var})(\forall y : [\mathit{Var}]\mathit{Term})\ \neg\, \mathit{var}(a) = \mathit{lam}(y) \tag{47}$$

$$(\forall y : [\mathit{Var}]\mathit{Term})(\forall t, t' : \mathit{Term})\ \neg\, \mathit{lam}(y) = \mathit{app}(t, t') \tag{48}$$

and the exhaustion axiom (10) by

$$\begin{aligned} (\forall t : \mathit{Term})\ & (\exists a : \mathit{Var})\ t = \mathit{var}(a) \\ & \vee (\exists t', t'' : \mathit{Term})\ t = \mathit{app}(t', t'') \\ & \vee (\exists y : [\mathit{Var}]\mathit{Term})\ t = \mathit{lam}(y). \end{aligned} \tag{49}$$

The other axioms alter in straightforward ways to take account of the new arity of *lam*.

The following result is needed in the next section. It shows that atom-abstraction sorts $[A]X$ have a dual nature: their elements $a.x$ embody not only the notion of abstraction as a '(bound variable, body)-pair modulo renaming the bound variable', but also the notion of abstraction as a function (albeit a partial one) from atoms to individuals.

Proposition 6.4. *The following formula is provable in Nominal Logic extended as in Fig. 2.*

$$(\forall y : [A]S)(\forall a : A)\ a \mathrel{\mathrm{B}} y \Rightarrow (\exists! x : S)\ y = a.x \tag{50}$$

(where ∃! means 'there exists a unique ... ' and has the usual encoding in first-order logic).

Proof. The uniqueness part of (50) follows from

$$(\forall a : A)(\forall x, x' : S)\ a.x = a.x' \Rightarrow x = x'$$

which is a corollary of axioms **A1** and **S1**. For the existence part of (50), note that by Proposition 5.1

$$(\forall y : [A]S)(\forall a : A)\ a \mathrel{\text{B}} y \Rightarrow (\exists x : S)\ y = a.x$$

holds if and only if

$$(\forall y : [A]S)(\exists a : A)\ a \mathrel{\text{B}} y \wedge (\exists x : S)\ y = a.x$$

and the latter follows from axiom **A2** and Proposition 6.2 (specifically, property (43)). □

7 Choice

In informal arguments about syntax one often says things like '*choose* a fresh name such that ...'. Axiom **F4** in Fig. 1 ensures that we can comply with such directives for Nominal Logic's formalisation of freshness. But it is important to note that *in nominal Logic such choices cannot be made uniformly in the parameters*: it is in general inconsistent with the other axioms to Skolemize **F4** by adding function symbols $\mathit{fresh} : \vec{S} \longrightarrow A$ satisfying $(\forall \vec{x} : \vec{S})\ \mathit{fresh}(\vec{x}) \mathrel{\text{B}} \vec{x}$. Here is the simplest possible example of this phenomenon.

Proposition 7.1. *Suppose A is a sort of atoms. The formula*

$$(\forall a : A)(\exists a' : A)\ \neg\, a = a' \tag{51}$$

is a theorem of Nominal Logic. However, it is inconsistent to assume there is a function that, for each atom, picks out an atom different from it; in other words the Nominal Logic theory with a function symbol $f : A \longrightarrow A$ and the axiom

$$(\forall a : A)\ \neg\, a = f(a) \tag{52}$$

is inconsistent.

Proof. The formula (51) is an immediate consequence of axioms **F2** and **F4**. For the second part we show that $(\exists a : A)\ a = f(a)$ is a theorem. First note that by axiom **F4** (with the empty list of parameters $\vec{x}$), there is an atom a of sort A.[2] We show that $a = f(a)$. For any $a' : A$, by Proposition 4.3 we have $a' \mathrel{\text{B}} a \Rightarrow a' \mathrel{\text{B}} f(a)$, i.e. (by axiom **F2**) $\neg\, a' = a \Rightarrow \neg\, a' = f(a)$, i.e. $a' = f(a) \Rightarrow a' = a$. Taking a' to be $f(a)$, we get $f(a) = a$. □

This phenomenon is a reflection of the fact that the category $\mathcal{N}om$ of nominal sets fails to satisfy the Axiom of Choice (see [8] for a categorical treatment of choice), which in turn reflects the fact that, by design, the Axiom of Choice

[2] The reader can deduce at this point that the author, being of a category-theoretic bent, is not assuming a formulation of first-order logic that entails that all sorts are non-empty. Possibly empty sorts, like the empty set, have their uses!

fails to hold in the Fraenkel-Mostowski permutation model of set theory [17]. However, there is no problem with principles of *unique* choice. For example, if a Nominal Logic theory has a model in $\mathcal{N}om$ satisfying the sentence

$$(\forall \vec{x} : \vec{S})(\exists! x' : S')\ \varphi(\vec{x}, x') \tag{53}$$

then the theory extended by a function symbol $f : \vec{S} \longrightarrow S'$ and axiom

$$(\forall \vec{x} : \vec{S})\ \varphi(\vec{x}, f(\vec{x})) \tag{54}$$

can also be modelled in $\mathcal{N}om$ (simply because in a cartesian category any sub-object satisfying the properties of a single-valued and total relation is the graph of some morphism). Unfortunately a far more common situation than (53) is to have 'conditional unique existence':

$$(\forall \vec{x} : \vec{S})\ \delta(\vec{x}) \Rightarrow (\exists! x' : S')\ \varphi(\vec{x}, x') \tag{55}$$

so that $\varphi(\vec{x}, x')$ is the graph of a *partial* function with domain of definition given by $\delta(\vec{x})$ – we have already seen two examples of this, in Propositions 5.4 and 6.4. If the formula (55) is a theorem of a Nominal Logic theory, adding a function symbol $f : \vec{S} \longrightarrow S'$ and axiom

$$(\forall \vec{x} : \vec{S})\ \delta(\vec{x}) \Rightarrow \varphi(\vec{x}, f(\vec{x})) \tag{56}$$

can result in an inconsistent theory. This is because f represents a *total* function from $\vec{S}$ to S'. Given terms $\vec{s} : \vec{S}$, even if $\delta(\vec{s})$ does not hold and so (56) cannot be used to deduce properties of the term $f(\vec{s}) : S'$, nevertheless one may be able to use results such as Proposition 4.3 to deduce properties of $f(\vec{s}) : S'$ that lead to inconsistency, especially if S' happens to be a sort of atoms. The simplest possible example of this phenomenon is when $\vec{S}$ is the empty list of sorts and δ is *false*. In this case formula (55) is trivially a theorem; the Skolemizing function f is a constant of sort S', so if that is a sort of atoms we get inconsistency by Corollary 4.4.

This difficulty with introducing notations for possibly partially defined expressions is masked in [10] by the untyped nature of FM-set theory.[3] That work introduces term-formers for *locally fresh atoms* and for *concretion* of atom-abstractions at atoms, Skolemizing the conditional unique existence formulas of Propositions 5.4 and 6.4. These new forms of term only have a definite meaning when certain preconditions are met. Nevertheless they can be given a semantics as total elements of the universe of FM-sets simply by taking their meaning when the preconditions are not met to be some default element with empty support (the empty set, say). Such a 'hack' is available to us in classical logic when there are enough terms of empty support. One such term is enough in an untyped

[3] It is also masked in the programming language FreshML sketched in [24], which has a richer term language than does Nominal Logic; this is because FreshML features unrestricted fixed point recursion in order to be Turing powerful, and hence naturally contains partially defined expressions.

setting such as FM-set theory. In a many-sorted Nominal Logic theory there is nothing to guarantee that a sort S possesses a term $s : S$ of empty support (i.e. satisfying $(\forall a : A)\ a \mathrel{\#} s$ for all sorts of atoms A); indeed Corollary 4.4 shows that sorts of atoms do not possess such terms in a consistent theory. Therefore, to provide Nominal Logic with a richer term language, incorporating such things as terms with locally fresh atoms, concretions of atom-abstractions at atoms and maybe more besides, it seems that one should merge Nominal Logic's novel treatment of atoms and freshness with some conventional treatment of the logic of partial expressions (such as [1, Sect. VI.1] or [26]).

8 Related Work

One can classify work on fully formal treatments of names and binding according to the mathematical construct used to model the notion of an abstraction over names:

Abstractions as (name, term)-pairs. Here one tries to work directly with parse trees quotiented by alpha conversion; [19] and [27] are examples of this approach. Its drawback is not so much that many tedious details left implicit by informal practice become explicit, but rather that many of these details have to be revisited on a case-by-case basis for each object language. The use of parse trees containing de Bruijn indices [5] is more elegant; but this has its own complications and also side-steps the issue of formalising informal practice to do with named bound variables.

Abstractions as functions from terms to terms. The desire to take care of the tedious details of α-conversion and substitution once and for all at the meta-level leads naturally to encodings of object-level syntax in a typed λ-calculus. This is the approach of *higher-order abstract syntax* [22] and it is well-supported by existing systems for machine-assisted reasoning based on typed λ-calculus. It does not lend itself to principles of structural recursion and induction for the encoded object-language that are particularly straightforward, but such principles have been developed: see [6, 25].

Abstractions as functions from names to terms. The *Theory of Contexts* [15] reconciles the elegance of higher-order abstract syntax with the desire to deal with names at the object-level and have relatively simple forms of structural recursion/induction. It does so by axiomatizing a suitable type of names within classical higher order logic. The Theory of Contexts involves a 'non-occurrence' predicate and axioms quite similar to those for freshness in FM-set theory [11] and Nominal Logic. However, 'non-occurrence' in [15] is dependent upon the object language, whereas our notion of freshness is a purely logical property, independent of any particular object syntax. (The same remark applies to the axiomatization of α-conversion of λ-terms in higher order logic in [12]; and to the extension of first-order logic with binders studied in [7].) Furthermore, the use of total functions on names to model abstraction means that the Theory of Contexts is incompatible with the Axiom of Unique Choice (cf. Sect. 7), forcing the theory to have a relational rather than functional feel: see [20]. On the other hand, the Theory of

Contexts is able to take advantage of existing machine-assisted infrastructure (namely Coq [4]) quite easily, whereas Gabbay had to work hard to adapt the Isabelle [21] set theory package to produce his Isabelle/FM-sets package [9, Chapter III].

The notion of abstraction that is definable within Nominal Logic (see Sect. 6) captures something of the first and third approaches mentioned above: atom-abstractions are defined to be pairs in which the name-component has been made anonymous via swapping; but we saw in Proposition 6.4 that atom-abstractions also behave like functions, albeit partial ones. Whatever the pros and cons of the various views of name abstraction, at least one can say that, being first-order, Nominal Logic gives a more elementary explanation of names and binding than the work mentioned above; and a more general one, I would claim, because of the independence of the notions of atoms, swapping, freshness and atom-abstraction from any particular object-level syntax.

Nominal Logic gives a first-order axiomatisation of some of the key concepts of FM-set theory – atoms, swapping and freshness – which were used in [11] to model syntax modulo α-conversion with inductively defined sets whose structural induction/recursion properties remain close to informal practice. We have seen that, being first-order, Nominal Logic does not give a complete axiomatisation of the notion of *finite support* that underlies the notion of freshness in FM-sets. Nevertheless, the first-order properties of the freshness predicate $(-)\ \mathtt{B}\ (-)$ seem sufficient to develop a useful theory. Indeed, many of the axioms in Fig. 1 arose naturally in Gabbay's implementation of FM-set theory in the Isabelle system [9, Chapter III] as the practically useful properties of finite support. Nominal Logic is just a vehicle for exhibiting those properties clearly. If one wants a single, expressive meta-logic in which to develop the mathematics of syntax, one can use FM-set theory (and its automated support within Isabelle); it is certainly also worth considering developing a version of classical higher order logic incorporating Nominal Logic.

Finally, even if one does not care about the details of Nominal Logic, I think that two simple, but important ideas underlying it are worth taking on board for the practice of operational semantics (be it with pencil-and-paper, or with machine assistance):

- *Name-swapping* $(a\,a')\cdot(-)$ *has much nicer logical properties than renaming* $[a/a'](-)$.
- *The only assertions about syntax we should deal with are ones whose validity is invariant under swapping bindable names.*

Even if one only takes the naïve view of abstractions as (name, term)-pairs, it seems useful to define α-conversion and capture-avoiding substitution in terms of name-swapping and to take account of equivariance in inductive arguments. We gave a small illustration of this in Example 2.1. A further example is provided by the work of Caires and Cardelli on modal logic for the spatial structure of concurrent systems [2]; this and the related work [3] make use of the freshness quantifier of Sect. 5. See also [14] for the use of permutative renaming to treat naming aspects of process calculi.

Acknowledgements

The work described here draws upon joint work with Gabbay described in [10, 24, 11]. I also gratefully acknowledge conversations about FM-sets with members of the Cambridge *Logic and Semantics Group*, particularly Mark Shinwell and Michael Norrish; and thanks to Keith Wansbrough for designing the freshness relation (B) and quantifier (A) symbols in METAFONT.

References

[1] M. J. Beeson. *Foundations of Constructive Mathematics*. Ergebnisse der Mathematik und ihrer Grenzgebeite. Springer-Verlag, Berlin, 1985.
[2] L. Caires and L. Cardelli. A spatial logic for concurrency. Draft of 11 April, 2001.
[3] L. Cardelli and A. D. Gordon. Logical properties of name restriction. In S. Abramsky, editor, *Typed Lambda Calculus and Applications, 5th International Conference*, volume 2044 of *Lecture Notes in Computer Science*. Springer-Verlag, Berlin, 2001.
[4] The Coq proof assistant. Institut National de Recherche en Informatique et en Automatique, France. `http://coq.inria.fr/`
[5] N. G. de Bruijn. Lambda calculus notation with nameless dummies, a tool for automatic formula manipulation, with application to the Church-Rosser theorem. *Indag. Math.*, 34:381–392, 1972.
[6] J. Despeyroux, F. Pfenning, and C. Schürmann. Primitive recursion for higher-order abstract syntax. In *Typed Lambda Calculus and Applications, 3rd International Conference*, volume 1210 of *Lecture Notes in Computer Science*, pages 147–163. Springer-Verlag, Berlin, 1997.
[7] G. Dowek, T. Hardin, and C. Kirchner. A completeness theorem for an extension of first-order logic with binders. In S. Ambler, R. Crole, and A. Momigliano, editors, *Mechanized Reasoning about Languages with Variable Binding (MERLIN 20001)*, Proceedings of a Workshop held in conjunction with the *International Joint Conference on Automated Reasoning, IJCAR 2001, Siena, June 2001*, Department of Computer Science Technical Report 2001/26, pages 49–63. University of Leicester, 2001.
[8] P. J. Freyd. The axiom of choice. *Journal of Pure and Applied Algebra*, 19:103–125, 1980.
[9] M. J. Gabbay. *A Theory of Inductive Definitions with α-Equivalence: Semantics, Implementation, Programming Language*. PhD thesis, Cambridge University, 2000.
[10] M. J. Gabbay and A. M. Pitts. A new approach to abstract syntax involving binders. In *14th Annual Symposium on Logic in Computer Science*, pages 214–224. IEEE Computer Society Press, Washington, 1999.
[11] M. J. Gabbay and A. M. Pitts. A new approach to abstract syntax with variable binding. *Formal Aspects of Computing*, 2001. Special issue in honour of Rod Burstall. To appear.
[12] A. D. Gordon and T. Melham. Five axioms of alpha-conversion. In *Theorem Proving in Higher Order Logics: 9th Interational Conference, TPHOLs'96*, volume 1125 of *Lecture Notes in Computer Science*, pages 173–191. Springer-Verlag, Berlin, 1996.

[13] C. A. Gunter. *Semantics of Programming Languages: Structures and Techniques.* Foundations of Computing. MIT Press, 1992.
[14] K. Honda. Elementary structures in process theory (1): Sets with renaming. *Mathematical Structures in Computer Science*, 10:617–663, 2000.
[15] F. Honsell, M. Miculan, and I. Scagnetto. An axiomatic approach to metareasoning on systems in higher-order abstract syntax. In *Twenty-Eighth International Colloquium on Automata, Languages and Programming, ICALP 2001, Crete, Greece, July 2001, Proceedings*, Lecture Notes in Computer Science. Springer-Verlag, Heidelberg, 2001.
[16] B. Huppert. *Endliche Gruppen I*, volume 134 of *Grundlehren Math. Wiss.* Springer, Berlin, 1967.
[17] T. J. Jech. About the axiom of choice. In J. Barwise, editor, *Handbook of Mathematical Logic*, pages 345–370. North-Holland, 1977.
[18] M. Makkai and G. E. Reyes. *First Order Categorical Logic*, volume 611 of *Lecture Notes in Mathematics.* Springer-Verlag, Berlin, 1977.
[19] J. McKinna and R. Pollack. Some type theory and lambda calculus formalised. To appear in *Journal of Automated Reasoning*, Special Issue on Formalised Mathematical Theories (F. Pfenning, Ed.), 1998.
[20] M. Miculan. Developing (meta)theory of lambda-calculus in the theory of contexts. In S. Ambler, R. Crole, and A. Momigliano, editors, *Mechanized Reasoning about Languages with Variable Binding (MERLIN 20001)*, Proceedings of a Workshop held in conjunction with the *International Joint Conference on Automated Reasoning, IJCAR 2001, Siena, June 2001*, Department of Computer Science Technical Report 2001/26, pages 65–81. University of Leicester, 2001.
[21] L. C. Paulson. *Isabelle: A Generic Theorem Prover*, volume 828 of *Lecture Notes in Computer Science.* Springer-Verlag, Berlin, 1994.
[22] F. Pfenning and C. Elliott. Higher-order abstract syntax. In *Proc. ACM-SIGPLAN Conference on Programming Language Design and Implementation*, pages 199–208. ACM Press, 1988.
[23] A. M. Pitts. Categorical logic. In S. Abramsky, D. M. Gabbay, and T. S. E. Maibaum, editors, *Handbook of Logic in Computer Science, Volume 5. Algebraic and Logical Structures*, chapter 2. Oxford University Press, 2000.
[24] A. M. Pitts and M. J. Gabbay. A metalanguage for programming with bound names modulo renaming. In R. Backhouse and J. N. Oliveira, editors, *Mathematics of Program Construction. 5th International Conference, MPC2000, Ponte de Lima, Portugal, July 2000. Proceedings*, volume 1837 of *Lecture Notes in Computer Science*, pages 230–255. Springer-Verlag, Heidelberg, 2000.
[25] C. Schürmann. *Automating the Meta-Theory of Deductive Systems.* PhD thesis, Carnegie-Mellon University, 2000.
[26] D. S. Scott. Identity and existence in intuitionistic logic. In M. P. Fourman, C. J. Mulvey, and D. S. Scott, editors, *Applications of Sheaves, Proceedings, Durham 1977*, volume 753 of *Lecture Notes in Mathematics*, pages 660–696. Springer-Verlag, Berlin, 1979.
[27] R. Vestergaard and J. Brotherson. A formalised first-order confluence proof for the λ-calculus using one-sorted variable names. In A. Middeldorp, editor, *Rewriting Techniques and Applications, 12th International Conference, RTA 2001, Utrecht, The Netherlands, May 2001, Proceedings*, volume 2051 of *Lecture Notes in Computer Science*, pages 306–321. Springer-Verlag, Heidelberg, 2001.

A Logic Programming Language Based on Binding Algebras

Makoto Hamana

Department of Computer Science, University of Gunma,
hamana@cs.gunma-u.ac.jp

Abstract. We give a logic programming language based on Fiore, Plotkin and Turi's binding algebras. In this language, we can use not only first-order terms but also terms involving variable binding. The aim of this language is similar to Nadathur and Miller's λProlog, which can also deal with binding structure by introducing λ-terms in higher-order logic. But the notion of binding used here is finer in a sense than the usual λ-binding. We explicitly manage names used for binding and treat α-conversion with respect to them. Also an important difference is the form of application related to β-conversion, i.e. we only allow the form (M x), where x is a (object) variable, instead of usual application (M N). This notion of binding comes from the semantics of binding by the category of presheaves. We firstly give a type theory which reflects this categorical semantics. Then we proceed along the line of first-order logic programming language, namely, we give a logic of this language, an operational semantics by SLD-resolution and unification algorithm for binding terms.

1 Introduction

The notion of variable binding appears often in many formal systems, programming languages and logics. The three papers on abstract syntax with variable binding by Gabbay-Pitts, Fiore-Plotkin-Turi and Hofmann in LICS'99 gave clear mathematical semantics of binding [GP99,FPT99,Hof99]. In this paper we follow the approach by Fiore-Plotkin-Turi and proceed to go further; we give a type theory based on their semantics and apply it to a logic programming language which can treat terms involving variable binding.

We will briefly illustrate our binding logic programming language. As an example, consider symbolic differentiation defined by the predicate diff:

$$\mathsf{diff}([b]\mathsf{var}(a), [b]0)$$
$$\mathsf{diff}([b]\mathsf{var}(b), [b]1)$$
$$\forall f, f'.\ \mathsf{diff}([b]\mathsf{sin}(f), [b](\mathsf{cos}(f) \times f')) \Leftarrow \mathsf{diff}([b]f, [b]f')$$

The predicate $\mathsf{diff}([b]f, [b]g)$ expresses that the differentiation of the function $[b]f$ is $[b]g$, where b is a parameter (bound variable). For this program, we can ask

N. Kobayashi and B.C. Pierce (Eds.): TACS 2001, LNCS 2215, pp. 243–262, 2001.

queries involving (existentially quantified) variables to obtain values for them, e.g.

$$? - \mathsf{diff}([d]\mathsf{var}(c), z)$$

which asks the differentiation of the function $[d]\mathsf{var}(c)$ (a constant function returning the free variable c) for the result of an existentially quantified variable z. Then, the system will return an answer substitution $z \mapsto [d]0$.

This is just a result of an application of the first clause of the program, but notice that α-renaming of bound variables to unify the query and program clause is automatically done. Another example is

$$? - \mathsf{diff}([b]\mathsf{sin}(x), [b](\mathsf{cos}(x) \times z))$$
$$x \mapsto \mathsf{var}(b),\ z \mapsto 1 \quad ; \quad x \mapsto \mathsf{var}(a),\ z \mapsto 0$$

which has two different answers. Note also that by applying the first answer substitution $x \mapsto \mathsf{var}(b)$ to the query, the variable b becomes bound; the system does not do implicit α-renaming for avoiding capture of bound variables by substitution. More involved query is

$$? - \mathsf{diff}([d]([b]\mathsf{sin}(x)) @ c,\ [b](\mathsf{cos}(y) \times z))$$

and then there are three answers: $x \mapsto \mathsf{var}(d), y \mapsto \mathsf{var}(c), z \mapsto 0$; $x \mapsto \mathsf{var}(c), y \mapsto \mathsf{var}(c), z \mapsto 0$; $x \mapsto \mathsf{var}(b), y \mapsto \mathsf{var}(b), z \mapsto 1$. Here β-reduction is automatically performed during unification, while it cannot be used in case of first-order logic programming language. Although our binding logic programming language is a typed language, we omitted the type information in this example. A complete program will be given in Section 9.

This paper is organized into two parts. The first part Section 2-7 deals with a type theory for terms involving variable binding. The second part Section 8 and 9 gives a logic programming language based on the type theory defined in the first part. In Section 10, we give a comparison to related work.

2 Terms

We will give the definition of the language for our binding logic programs, which includes terms, type system and operations on the language. First, we define terms.

Variables and object variables. There are two kinds of variables in our language; usual variables $(x, y, \ldots)$ (as in first-order language) and *object variables* $(a, b, \ldots)$. Object variables are used for the names of bindings. The set of all object variables is denoted by OV. A *world* C is a sequence of object variables having no duplication of the same things.

Types. Types are defined by

$$\tau ::= \iota \mid \delta\tau$$

where ι is a base type and $\delta\tau$ is a higher type abstracted by an object variable (semantically $\delta\tau \cong (\mathsf{OV} \Rightarrow \tau)$ [FPT99]). The set of all types is denoted by Ty.

Signature. A signature Σ is a set of function symbols together with an arity function assigning to each function symbol f, a finite sequence of types as the source type and the type ι as the target type. This is denoted by $f : \tau_1, \ldots, \tau_n \to \iota$. In case of $n = 0$, the function symbol $f : \iota$ is regarded as a constant. Note that there are no higher type constants.

Terms. Terms are defined by

$$t ::= f(t_1, \ldots, t_n) \mid t@a \mid [a]t \mid \xi x \mid \mathsf{var}(a)$$
$$\xi ::= [a_1 := a'_1, \ldots, a_n := a'_n]$$

where $f \in \Sigma$ is a function symbol, a's are object variables. A term $t@a$ denotes an application, $[a]t$ an abstraction, $\mathsf{var}(a)$ an object variable, and ξx a variable where ξ is called an *(syntactic) object variable substitution.* Intuitive meaning of ξx is the following: a variable having suspended substitution for object variables and if x is substituted by some term, its suspension is released and the object variable substitution is applied. We may omit the identity assignment $a_i := a_i$ in this bracket, and the order of the assignment is not important. We often use the shorthand notation $[\boldsymbol{a} := \boldsymbol{a}']$. In case of $\xi = []$, we just write x. A type judgment is of the form

$$\Gamma \vdash_C t : \sigma : A$$

where
- a *context* Γ is a set of variable declarations $\{x_1 : \tau_1 : A_1, \ldots, x_n : \tau_n : A_n\}$,
- a *world* C is a sequence of object variables,
- a *type* σ,
- a *stage* A is a set of object variables.

Moreover, it must satisfy the condition $\bigcup_i A_i \cup A \cup \mathsf{FOV}(t) \cup \mathsf{GBOV}(t) \subseteq \widetilde{C}$ where FOV and GBOV are defined below, and $\widetilde{C}$ is a set of object variables occurring in C. Namely, the world C is considered as a pool of all possible object variables used (in future) in the judgment. We will see that in the type system the order of bound variables in t respects the order of object variables in C.

Some operations on terms. Let t be a term. Then $\mathsf{FOV}(t)$ denotes a set of all *free object variables*, $\mathsf{GBOV}(t)$ denotes a set of all *globally bound object variables*, i.e. object variables occurring in []-binders, and $\mathsf{OBV}(t)$ denotes a set of all *outermost bound variables*. These are defined as follows:

$$\mathsf{GBOV}([\boldsymbol{a} := \boldsymbol{b}]x) = \{\boldsymbol{a}\},\ \mathsf{GBOV}(t@a) = \mathsf{GBOV}(t),\ \mathsf{GBOV}([a]t) = \mathsf{GBOV}(t) \cup \{a\},$$
$$\mathsf{GBOV}(F(t_1, \ldots, t_n)) = \mathsf{GBOV}(t_1) \cup \ldots \cup \mathsf{GBOV}(t_n);$$
$$\mathsf{FOV}([\boldsymbol{a} := \boldsymbol{b}]x) = \{\boldsymbol{b}\}, \quad \mathsf{FOV}(t@a) = \{a\}, \quad \mathsf{FOV}([a]t) = \mathsf{FOV}(t) - \{a\},$$
$$\mathsf{FOV}(F(t_1, \ldots, t_n)) = \mathsf{FOV}(t_1) \cup \ldots \cup \mathsf{FOV}(t_n);$$
$$\mathsf{OBV}([\boldsymbol{a} := \boldsymbol{b}]x) = \varnothing, \quad \mathsf{OBV}([a]t) = \mathsf{OBV}(t) \cup \{a\},$$
$$\mathsf{OBV}(F(t_1, \ldots, t_n)) = \mathsf{OBV}(t_1) \cup \ldots \cup \mathsf{OBV}(t_n),$$
$$\mathsf{OBV}(((\ldots(([a_1] \ldots [a_n]t)@b_1)@\ldots)@b_n) = \mathsf{OBV}(t).$$

In the definition of $\mathsf{OBV}(([a_1]\dots[a_n]t)@b_1@\dots@b_n)$, the term t may have more binders on the top, and since we do not have constants of higher types in this system, an application can always be expressed as this form. These functions are obviously extended to a function on sets and sequences of terms.

3 Object Variable Substitutions

The important idea of our language involving binding is the distinction between object variables and usual variables. This idea actually comes from Fiore-Plotkin-Turi's semantics of abstract syntax with binding in the category $Set^{\mathbb{F}}$, where $\mathbb{F}$ is a category of (abstract) object variables and substitutions (the precise definition below). So we need the notion of object variable substitutions in syntax and semantic levels. In this section, we define these matters. We start with some preliminary definition on categories required in semantics.

The category of presheaves [FPT99]. Let $\mathbb{F}$ be the category which has finite cardinals $n = \{1, \dots, n\}$ (n is possibly 0) as objects, and all functions between them as arrows $m \to n$. We may also call $n \in \mathbb{F}$ a stage. The category $\mathbb{F}$ is also considered as the free cocartesian category on one object, generated from an initial object 1 by an operation $(\_) + 1$. From this viewpoint, we assume the following chosen coproduct structure

$$n \xrightarrow{\mathsf{old}_n} n+1 \xleftarrow{\mathsf{new}_n} 1$$

with $\mathsf{old}_n(i) = i$ $(1 \le i \le n)$ and $\mathsf{new}_n(*) = n+1$.

Let $\hat{\mathbb{F}}$ be the functor category $Set^{\mathbb{F}}$. The category $\hat{\mathbb{F}}$ is complete, cocomplete and cartesian closed. The functor (for stage extension) $\delta : \hat{\mathbb{F}} \to \hat{\mathbb{F}}$ is defined as follows: for $L \in \hat{\mathbb{F}}, n \in \mathbb{F}, \rho \in \operatorname{arr} \mathbb{F}$,

$$(\delta L)(n) = L(n+1); \quad (\delta L)(\rho) = A(\rho + \mathrm{id}_1)$$

and, for $f : L \to M \in \hat{\mathbb{F}}$, the map $\delta f : \delta L \to \delta M$ is given by

$$(\delta f)_n = f_{n+1} : L(n+1) \to M(n+1) \ (n \in \mathbb{F}).$$

Operations on sequences. We fix the notations for sequences: the bracket $\langle\dots\rangle$ is used for a sequence, $+\!\!+$ is the concatenation, ϵ is the empty sequence. Let B be a sequence of object variables. Then $\widetilde{B}$ denotes the set of object variables occurring in B. We write $B \trianglelefteq B'$ when B is a subsequence of B'. More precisely, let $(\widetilde{B}, \le_B)$ and $(\widetilde{B'}, \le_{B'})$ be the posets whose orders respect the orders of elements in B and B'. Then $B \trianglelefteq B'$ if and only if $\forall a_1, a_2 \in \widetilde{B}\,.\, a_1 \le_B a_2 \;\Rightarrow\; a_1 \le_{B'} a_2$. Let A be a set of object variables. A *sequentialization* of A with respect to a world C, denoted by $\overline{A}_C$, or simply $\overline{A}$ if C is clear from the context, is a sequence such that $\overline{A} \trianglelefteq C$ and $\widetilde{\overline{A}} = A$. The notation $|\_|$ is used for the number of object variables occurring in a set or sequence. Note that $|A| = |\overline{A}|$.

Object variable substitutions. Let $A = \langle a_1, \ldots, a_m \rangle$ and $B = \langle b_1, \ldots, b_n \rangle$ be sequences of object variables (which need not to be subsequences of a given world). A *(semantic) object variable substitution* $\rho : A \to B$ is a triple $(|\rho|, A, B)$ where $|\rho| : |A| \to |B|$ is an arrow in $\mathbb{F}$. Then we can define a function $\widetilde{\rho} : \widetilde{A} \to \widetilde{B}$ such that

$$\widetilde{\rho}(a_i) \triangleq b_{|\rho|(i)} \text{ for each } i \in \{1, \ldots, m\}.$$

By abuse of notation, we often write $\rho(a)$ as the value of $\widetilde{\rho}(a)$. The ρ gives rise the natural transformation $\hat{\rho} : \delta^{|A|} \dot{\to} \delta^{|B|} \in \text{arr } [\hat{\mathbb{F}}, \hat{\mathbb{F}}]$ whose component $\hat{\rho}_L : \delta^{|A|}L \dot{\to} \delta^{|B|}L \in \text{arr } \hat{\mathbb{F}}$ is defined by $\hat{\rho}_{L,k} \triangleq L(\text{id}_k + \rho) : L(k + |A|) \to L(k + |B|) \in \text{arr } \mathcal{S}et$ where $L \in \hat{\mathbb{F}}, k \in \mathbb{F}$. For arbitrary object variables a and b, the unique object variable substitution from $\langle a \rangle$ to $\langle b \rangle$ is denoted by $[a \mapsto b]$.

For a variable $\xi x : B$, where $\xi = [\boldsymbol{a} := \boldsymbol{b}], \{\boldsymbol{b}\} \subseteq B,\ A \triangleq \{\boldsymbol{a}\}$, a semantic object variable substitution $\xi^\circ : \overline{A} \to \overline{B}$ is defined to be $(|\xi^\circ|, \overline{A}, \overline{B})$, $|\xi^\circ|(i) = j$ if $((\overline{A})_i := (\overline{B})_j)$ is contained in ξ. Notice that the notation $[\boldsymbol{a} := \boldsymbol{b}]$ is a part of syntax which always occurs with a variable as $[\boldsymbol{a} := \boldsymbol{b}]x$ in the language, while $[a \mapsto b]$ is a meta-level operation for substituting object variables.

Sequences of object variables taken from OV and object variable substitutions form a category **OVS**. A composition $\phi \circ \rho : A \to D$ of two object variable substitutions $\rho : A \to B$ and $\phi : B \to D$ is given by $(|\phi| \circ |\rho|, A, D)$. It is clear that the category $\mathbb{F}$ and **OVS** are equivalent where $|\_| : \mathbf{OVS} \to \mathbb{F}$ is the equivalence, and **OVS** is considered as a named version of $\mathbb{F}$.

4 Type System and Its Interpretation

In this section, we give a type system of terms and its interpretation. A binding algebra is used for a model of the type theory (see [FPT99] for more detailed analysis on binding algebras).

Binding algebras. To a signature Σ, we associate the functor $\Sigma : \hat{\mathbb{F}} \to \hat{\mathbb{F}}$ given by $\Sigma(X) \triangleq \coprod_{f:n_1,\ldots,n_k \to \iota \in \Sigma} \prod_{1 \le i \le k} \delta^{n_i}(X)$. A *binding algebra* or simply Σ-*algebra* is a pair (L, α) with L a presheaf and $\alpha : \Sigma L \to L \in \hat{\mathbb{F}}$. We define the category of binding algebras associated to the signature Σ as the category Σ-**Alg**, with objects given by maps $f : (L, \alpha) \to (L', \alpha')$ that are *homomorphic* in the sense that $f \circ \alpha = \alpha' \circ \Sigma(f)$. The presheaf (of abstract object variables) $V \in \hat{\mathbb{F}}$ is defined by

$$V(n) = n \ (n \in \text{obj } \mathbb{F}); \quad V(\rho) = \rho \ (\rho \in \text{arr } \mathbb{F}).$$

A *model* for the language on the signature Σ is a (V+Σ)-algebra $\mathbb{M} = (M, [\gamma, \{\tau^{(f)}\}_{f \in \Sigma}])$ where M is a presheaf, $\gamma : V \to M$ and $\tau^{(f)} : \prod_{1 \le i \le k} \delta^{n_i} M \to M$ for $f : n_1, \ldots, n_k \to \iota$. The interpretation functions ($\mathbb{M}[\![-]\!]_0 : \mathsf{Ty} \to \text{obj } \hat{\mathbb{F}}$, $\mathbb{M}[\![-]\!]_1 : \Sigma \to \text{arr } \hat{\mathbb{F}}$)) are defined by

$$\mathbb{M}[\![\iota]\!]_0 \triangleq M, \quad \mathbb{M}[\![\delta\sigma]\!]_0 \triangleq \delta[\![\sigma]\!], \quad \mathbb{M}[\![f]\!]_1 \triangleq \tau^{(f)}.$$

As usual, given a context $\Gamma = \langle x_1 : \alpha_1, \ldots, x_n : \alpha_n \rangle$, we set $\mathbb{M}[\![\Gamma]\!] \triangleq \mathbb{M}[\![\alpha_1]\!]_0 \times \ldots \times \mathbb{M}[\![\alpha_n]\!]_0$. We omit the subscripts of $\mathbb{M}[\![\_]\!]_0$ and $\mathbb{M}[\![\_]\!]_1$ hereafter, and write just $[\![\_]\!]$ in the case of $\mathbb{M}$.

Type system and interpretation. We give the typing rules and simultaneously the interpretation of terms by an arbitrary model $\mathbb{M}$ in the category $\hat{\mathbb{F}}$ in Fig. 1. This definition is read as if the upper terms of a typing rule are interpreted as the arrows in the right-hand side of the definition, the interpretation of the lower term is given by the composition of these in $\mathbb{M}$ described in the lower part of the right-hand side.

Let the set St_C be $\wp\widetilde{C}$, which is the set of stages under a given world C. We use a $\mathsf{Ty}, \mathsf{St}_C$-indexed set for variable and term sets. A $\mathsf{Ty}, \mathsf{St}_C$-indexed set L is a disjoint union of its components: $L = \Sigma_{\tau \in \mathsf{Ty}, A \in \mathsf{St}_C} L_{\tau,A}$. We write $l : \tau : A \in L$ for $l \in L_{\tau,A}$. We often use the letter X or Γ (typing context) for denoting $\mathsf{Ty}, \mathsf{St}_C$-indexed set of *variables*. A $\mathsf{Ty}, \mathsf{St}_C$-indexed set $T(C,\Gamma)$ denotes terms under a signature Σ and a world C and a typing context Γ, which is defined as $T(C,\Gamma) = \Sigma_{\tau \in \mathsf{Ty}, A \in \mathsf{St}_C} T(\Gamma)_{\tau,A}$ where $T(\Gamma)_{\tau,A} = \{t \mid \Gamma \vdash_C t : \tau : A\}$.

Example 1.
We will show an example of typing derivation and interpretation. Assume a signature Σ for untyped lambda terms: $\mathsf{lam} : \delta\iota \to \iota$ and $\mathsf{app} : \iota, \iota \to \iota$. An example of typing for a term $\mathsf{lam}([a]\mathsf{var}(b))$ (intended meaning is a λ-term $\lambda a.b$) is

$$\frac{\dfrac{\vdash_{a,b} \mathsf{var}(b) : \iota : a, b}{\vdash_{a,b} [a]\mathsf{var}(b) : \delta\iota : b}}{\vdash_{a,b} \mathsf{lam}([a]\mathsf{var}(b)) : \iota : b.}$$

Let us interpret this term in a *syntactic algebra* [FPT99]: let Λ be the presheaf defined by $\Lambda(n) = \{t \mid n \vdash t\}$ $(n \in \mathbb{F})$ where

$$\frac{1 \le i \le n}{n \vdash \mathsf{VAR}(i)} \quad \frac{n+1 \vdash t}{n \vdash \mathsf{LAM}((n+1).t)} \quad \frac{n \vdash t_1 \quad n \vdash t_2}{n \vdash \mathsf{APP}(t_1, t_2).}$$

Define $[\![\iota]\!] = \Lambda$ and $(V + \Sigma)$-algebra Λ with an algebra structure

$$[\gamma, [\![\mathsf{lam}]\!], [\![\mathsf{app}]\!]] : V + \delta\Lambda + \Lambda \times \Lambda \to \Lambda$$

defined as follows: for $n \in \mathbb{F}$,

$$\begin{aligned} \gamma_n : n \to \Lambda(n), &\qquad \gamma_n(i) = \mathsf{VAR}(i), \\ [\![\mathsf{lam}]\!]_n : \Lambda(n+1) \to \Lambda(n), &\qquad [\![\mathsf{lam}]\!]_n(t) = \mathsf{LAM}((n+1).t), \\ [\![\mathsf{app}]\!]_n : \Lambda(n) \times \Lambda(n) \to \Lambda(n), &\qquad [\![\mathsf{app}]\!]_n(t_1, t_2) = \mathsf{APP}(t_1, t_2). \end{aligned}$$

The interpretation of a term $\vdash_{a,b} \mathsf{lam}([a]\mathsf{var}(b)) : \iota : b$ is the arrow

$$\mathbf{1} \xrightarrow{\gamma^*} \delta\Lambda \xrightarrow{\widehat{2}_\Lambda} \delta^2\Lambda \xrightarrow{\widehat{\rho}_\Lambda} \delta^2\Lambda \xrightarrow{\delta[\![\mathsf{lam}]\!]} \delta\Lambda \in \hat{\mathbb{F}}$$

whose component for $n \in \mathbb{F}$ is the function

$$\begin{array}{ccccccccc} 1 & \xrightarrow{\gamma_n^*} & \Lambda(n+1) & \xrightarrow{\widehat{2}_{\Lambda,n}} & \Lambda(n+2) & \xrightarrow{\widehat{\rho}_{\Lambda,n}} & \Lambda(n+2) & \xrightarrow{[\![\mathsf{lam}]\!]_{n+1}} & \Lambda(n+1) \in Set \\ * & \longmapsto & \mathsf{VAR}(n+1) & \longmapsto & \mathsf{VAR}(n+2) & \longmapsto & \mathsf{VAR}(n+1) & \longmapsto & \mathsf{LAM}((n+2).\mathsf{VAR}(n+1)) \end{array}$$

Variables

$$\frac{}{\Gamma_1, x:\sigma:A, \Gamma_2 \vdash_C [\boldsymbol{a} := \boldsymbol{b}]x:\sigma:B} \qquad \frac{}{\pi; \widehat{[\boldsymbol{a} := \boldsymbol{b}]^{\diamond}}_{[\![\sigma]\!]}}$$

where $A = \{\boldsymbol{a}\}$ and $B \supseteq \{\boldsymbol{b}\}$, $\pi : [\![\Gamma_1]\!] \times \delta^{|A|}[\![\sigma]\!] \times [\![\Gamma_2]\!] \to \delta^{|A|}[\![\sigma]\!]$ is a projection in $\hat{\mathbb{F}}$ (the operation "$\diamond$" is defined in Section 3).

Object variables

$$\frac{}{\Gamma \vdash_C \mathsf{var}(a) : \iota : A}\; a \in A \qquad \frac{}{!_{[\![\Gamma]\!]}; \gamma^*; \widehat{\mathsf{k}}_{[\![\iota]\!]} : [\![\Gamma]\!] \to \delta^{|A|}[\![\iota]\!]}$$

where k is the position of the object a occurring in $\overline{A}$, a map $|\mathsf{k}| : 1 \to |A| \in \mathbb{F}$ is defined by $|\mathsf{k}|(1) = k$, and $\gamma^* : \mathbf{1} \to \delta[\![\iota]\!]$ is the adjoint mate of $\gamma : V \to [\![\iota]\!]$ by the natural bijection $\hat{\mathbb{F}}(\mathbf{1}, \delta[\![\iota]\!]) \cong \hat{\mathbb{F}}(V, [\![\iota]\!])$ [FPT99].

Constants

$$\frac{}{\Gamma \vdash_C F:\sigma:A} \qquad \frac{}{!_{[\![\Gamma]\!]}; [\![F]\!]; \widehat{!}_{[\![\sigma]\!]} : [\![\Gamma]\!] \to \delta^{|A|}[\![\sigma]\!]}$$

where $F : \sigma \in \Sigma$, $!_{[\![\Gamma]\!]} : [\![\Gamma]\!] \to \mathbf{1} \in \hat{\mathbb{F}}$ and $! : 0 \to |A| \in \mathbb{F}$.

Function terms

$$\frac{\Gamma \vdash_C t_1 : \sigma_1 : A, \ldots, \Gamma \vdash_C t_n : \sigma_n : A}{\Gamma \vdash_C F(t_1, \ldots, t_n) : \sigma : A} \qquad \frac{f_1 \quad \ldots \quad f_n : [\![\Gamma]\!] \to \delta^{|A|}[\![\sigma_n]\!]}{\langle f_1, \ldots, f_n \rangle; \cong; \delta^{|A|}[\![F]\!]}$$

where $F : \sigma_1, \ldots, \sigma_n \to \sigma \in \Sigma$ and $\cong: \delta^{|A|}[\![\sigma_1]\!] \times \ldots \times \delta^{|A|}[\![\sigma_n]\!] \to \delta^{|A|}([\![\sigma_1]\!] \times \ldots \times [\![\sigma_n]\!])$.

Abstractions

$$\frac{\Gamma \vdash_C t : \sigma : A}{\Gamma \vdash_C [a]t : \delta\sigma : A - \{a\}}\; a \in A \text{ and } \langle a \rangle +\!\!+ \overline{\mathsf{OBV}(t)} \trianglelefteq C \qquad \frac{f : [\![\Gamma]\!] \to \delta^{|A|}[\![\sigma]\!]}{f; \widehat{\rho}_{[\![\sigma]\!]} : [\![\Gamma]\!] \to \delta^{|A|}[\![\sigma]\!]}$$

where $\rho : \overline{A} \to \overline{A - \{a\}} +\!\!+ \langle a \rangle$ is a permutation map defined by $|\rho|(i) = j$ where $(\overline{A})_i = (\overline{A - \{a\}} +\!\!+ \langle a \rangle)_j$.

Applications

$$\frac{\Gamma \vdash_C t : \delta\sigma : A}{\Gamma \vdash_C t@a : \sigma : A \cup \{a\}}\; a \trianglelefteq C \qquad \frac{g : [\![\Gamma]\!] \to \delta^{|A|+1}[\![\sigma]\!]}{g; \widehat{\rho}_{[\![\sigma]\!]} : [\![\Gamma]\!] \to \delta^{|A \cup \{a\}|}[\![\sigma]\!]}$$

where $\rho : \overline{A} +\!\!+ \langle a \rangle \to \overline{A \cup \{a\}}$ is a map defined by $|\rho|(i) = j$ where $(\overline{A} +\!\!+ \langle a \rangle)_i = (\overline{A \cup \{a\}})_j$. Notice that A may contain a, i.e. applying the same object variable more than twice is possible.

Fig. 1. Type system and interpretation

where $|\rho| : 2 \to 2$ is a swapping map. The presheaf of untyped lambda terms Λ can be shown to be an initial V+Σ-algebra [FPT99].

5 Free Object Variable Substitutions

In this section, we define how object variable substitutions defined in Section 3 are applied to terms. We need a notion of *free* object variable substitutions. The reason we consider free one is motivated by the following examples: Consider an object variable substitution $\rho : \langle a, b\rangle \to \langle a\rangle$ defined by $\widetilde{\rho}(a) = a$ and $\widetilde{\rho}(b) = a$ and apply it to a term $[a][b]F(\mathsf{var}(a), \mathsf{var}(b))$, we have an ill-typed term

$$[a][a]F(\mathsf{var}(a), \mathsf{var}(a)).$$

This violates the condition on a world consisting of the sequence of object variables having *no* duplication because in this case the world must contain the sequence $\langle a, a\rangle$. The order of binding is reflected from the order of object variables in a world (see the typing rule of abstractions). We must also avoid capturing of bound object variables. So we need the following definition.

A *free object variable substitution* $\rho : C \to C'$ *for a term* $t : \iota : A$ is an object variable substitution which satisfies

$$\widetilde{\rho}_{\restriction \mathsf{GBOV}(t)} \text{ is 1-1, and } \rho(a) \notin \mathsf{GBOV}(t) \text{ for } a \in A.$$

The substitution ρ is also obviously extended to functions on sequences, sets of object variables (written as ρA), and on typing contexts:

$$\rho(x_1 : \sigma_1 : A_1, \ldots, x_n : \sigma_n : A_n) = x_1 : \sigma_1 : \rho A_1, \ldots, x_n : \sigma_n : \rho A_n.$$

Also this ρ is extended to functions on terms in two ways $\rho^\sharp$ and $\rho^\natural$ from $T(C, \Gamma)$ to $T(C', \Gamma)$ defined as follows:

$$\rho^\sharp([\boldsymbol{a} := \boldsymbol{b}]x) = [\boldsymbol{a} := \boldsymbol{\rho(b)}]x, \quad \rho^\sharp(F(t_1, \ldots, t_n)) = F(\rho^\sharp(t_1), \ldots, \rho^\sharp(t_n)),$$
$$\rho^\sharp([a]t) = [a]\rho^\sharp_a(t), \quad \rho^\sharp(t@a) = \rho^\sharp(t)@\rho(a), \quad \rho^\sharp(\mathsf{var}(a)) = \mathsf{var}(\rho(a));$$
$$\rho^\natural([\boldsymbol{a} := \boldsymbol{b}]x) = [\boldsymbol{\rho(a)} := \boldsymbol{\rho(b)}]x, \quad \rho^\natural([a]t) = [\rho(a)]\rho^\natural(t),$$

and other cases for $\rho^\natural$ are the same as $\rho^\sharp$. Here ρ_a is the map defined by $\rho_a(a) = a, \rho_a(b) = \rho(b)$ if $b \neq a$.

Lemma 1.
Let $\rho : C \to C'$ be a free object variable substitution for a term t. Then the term t substituted by ρ is well-typed:

$$\frac{\boldsymbol{x} : \boldsymbol{\sigma} : \boldsymbol{A} \vdash_C t : \sigma : A}{\boldsymbol{x} : \boldsymbol{\sigma} : \boldsymbol{A} \vdash_{C'} \rho^\sharp t : \sigma : \rho A} \qquad \frac{\boldsymbol{x} : \boldsymbol{\sigma} : \boldsymbol{A} \vdash_C t : \sigma : A}{\boldsymbol{x} : \boldsymbol{\sigma} : \boldsymbol{\rho A} \vdash_{C'} \rho^\natural t : \sigma : \rho A}.$$

and the following diagrams commute in $\hat{\mathbb{F}}$:

$$\begin{array}{ccc} \Pi_i \delta^{|A_i|}[\![\sigma_i]\!] & \xrightarrow{[\![t]\!]} & \delta^{|A|}[\![\sigma]\!] \\ {\scriptstyle \Pi_i id}\downarrow & & \downarrow{\scriptstyle \hat{\rho}_{0\,[\![\sigma]\!]}} \\ \Pi_i \delta^{|A_i|}[\![\sigma_i]\!] & \xrightarrow{[\![\rho^\sharp t]\!]} & \delta^{|\rho A|}[\![\sigma]\!] \end{array} \qquad \begin{array}{ccc} \Pi_i \delta^{|A_i|}[\![\sigma_i]\!] & \xrightarrow{[\![t]\!]} & \delta^{|A|}[\![\sigma]\!] \\ {\scriptstyle \Pi_i \hat{\rho}_{i\,[\![\sigma_i]\!]}}\downarrow & & \downarrow{\scriptstyle \hat{\rho}_{0\,[\![\sigma]\!]}} \\ \Pi_i \delta^{|\rho A_i|}[\![\sigma_i]\!] & \xrightarrow{[\![\rho^\natural t]\!]} & \delta^{|\rho A|}[\![\sigma]\!] \end{array}$$

where $\rho_i : \overline{A_i} \to \overline{\rho A_i}$ *and* $\rho_0 : \overline{A} \to \overline{\rho A}$ *are defined by the restricted functions* $(\widetilde{\rho})_{\restriction A_i} : A_i \to \rho A_i$ *and* $(\widetilde{\rho})_{\restriction A} : A \to \rho A$ *respectively.*

Proof. By induction on the derivation of the judgment $\Gamma \vdash_C t : \sigma : A$. □

Note that this lemma also gives well-typedness of terms by weakening and strengthening of a world using suitable ρ. From these typing, the mnemonic for these two ways of extension is that $\rho^{\natural}$ is "naturally applied" because the stages in typing context and term equally are applied, and $\rho^{\sharp}$ is "half applied" because only the term part is applied.

6 Substitutions on Terms

In this section, we define substitution on terms. A *substitution* (not an object variable substitution) θ is a $\mathsf{Ty}, \mathsf{St}_C$-indexed function from Γ to $T(C, \Gamma')$, which gives mappings:

$$x : \tau : A \mapsto \Gamma' \vdash_C t : \tau : A$$

for each $x \in \Gamma$, and we use the shorthand notation $[\boldsymbol{x} \mapsto \boldsymbol{t}]$ for this. The identity substitution $[\boldsymbol{x} \mapsto \boldsymbol{x}]$ is also written as ϵ. The substitution θ is extended to a $\mathsf{Ty}, \mathsf{St}_C$-indexed function θ^* from $T(C, \Gamma)$ to $T(C, \Gamma')$ defined by

$$\theta^*(\xi x) = \xi^{\circ\sharp} \circ \theta(x) \ \ (x{:}\tau{:}A \in \Gamma), \quad \theta^*(F(t_1, \ldots, t_n)) = F(\theta^*(t_1), \ldots, \theta^*(t_n))$$
$$\theta^*([a]t) = [a]\theta^*_a(t), \quad \theta^*(t@a) = \theta^*(t)@a, \quad \theta^*(\mathsf{var}(a)) = \mathsf{var}(a)$$

where for $x : \sigma : A \in \Gamma$

$$\theta_a(x) = \theta(x) \text{ if } a \in A, \quad \theta_a(x) = \textit{undefined} \text{ if } a \notin A.$$

A composition $\theta_2 \circ \theta_1$ of two substitutions θ_2 and θ_1 is given by $\theta_2^* \circ \theta_1$. We omit the superscript $*$ from substitutions hereafter.

We say a term t_1 is an *instance* of t_2, written as $t_1 \succcurlyeq t_2$, if there exist a 1-1 free object variable substitution ρ and a substitution θ such that $t_1 = \theta\rho^{\sharp}t_2$. We say a substitution $\theta_2 : X \to \mathrm{T}(C, Y)$ is more *general* than $\theta_1 : X \to T(C, Y)$, written as $\theta_1 \succcurlyeq \theta_2$, if for all $x \in X$, $\theta_1(x) \succcurlyeq \theta_2(x)$. The relation $\preccurlyeq$ is the inverse of $\succcurlyeq$. Namely the notion of generality of substitution is defined modulo renaming of object variables, which is the different point from the usual notion of generality in first-order languages.

Also substitution can be given by a derived rule "cut".

Lemma 2.
Let $\theta : \Gamma \to T(C, \Gamma')$ *be a substitution and* $x \in \Gamma$. *Define the restricted substitution* $\theta' : \{x : \sigma : A\} \to T(C, \Gamma')$ *defined by* $\theta'(x) = \theta(x)$. *Then the "cut" rule is derivable.*

$$\frac{\Gamma' \vdash_C t : \sigma : A \quad x : \sigma : A, \Gamma'' \vdash_C s : \tau : B}{\Gamma', \Gamma'' \vdash_C \theta'(s) : \tau : B}$$

Example 2.
The substitution defined here also allows *captured* substitution which does not occur in case of ordinary systems having binding, e.g.

$$\frac{\vdash_a \mathsf{var}(a) : \iota : a \quad x : \iota : a \vdash_a [a]x : \iota : \varnothing}{\vdash_a [a]\mathsf{var}(a) : \iota : \varnothing}$$

where the object variable a is captured by the binder $[a]$. So, this $[\_]$-binder can be considered as a *hole of context* appeared in several context calculi [Oho96], [SSK01] rather than an ordinary binder. However this is because the stages of $\mathsf{var}(a)$ and x match in the substitution process and if these does not match, "capture avoiding" like substitution can also be simulated, e.g.

$$\frac{\vdash_a \mathsf{var}(a) : \iota : a \quad x : \iota : \underline{\varnothing} \vdash_a [a]x : \iota : \varnothing}{\textit{not substituted}}.$$

Generally, when all variables occurring in a binding term $[a]t$ have a stage not containing the bound variable a in the typing context, the binder $[a]$ can be considered as a usual (λ-like) binder.

7 Equational Logic

The final section of the type theory of our language is on equational logic. In a binding logic programming language, terms equated by the equational logic are implicitly identified. So, later we consider unification of terms, which is necessary in operational semantics, *modulo this equality*. This is similar in case of λProlog, where higher-order unification that is a unification modulo $\beta\eta$-equality is used.

The equational logic given in Fig. 2 is basically similar to the equational logic for the λ-calculus, but an important difference is the β-axiom which is restricted only for application of an object variable, not an arbitrary term.

Note that in these axioms, both sides of equations must be well-typed terms. So they satisfy some conditions to be well-typed, e.g. $a' \in A$ and $a' \in \mathsf{OBV}(t)$ in the axiom (α).

The reason why we use $\sharp$ for the extension of object variable substitution here is the both sides of terms of equations are in the same context. We call a term which matches the left-hand side of $\beta_0(\eta)$-axiom a $\beta_0(\eta)$-redex.

Example 3.
An example of an equation is

$$x : \iota : a \vdash_{a,b} ([a]x)@b = [a := b]x : \iota : b$$

where the first x in the equation is regarded as $[a := a]x$. This example shows why the syntactic object variable substitution part in variables is necessary, namely, it is needed to state (α) and (β_0)-axioms for terms involving usual variables. For an open term, application of a semantic object variable substitution (e.g. $[a \mapsto b]$) to the term results a corresponding syntactic object variable substitution (e.g. $[a := b]$) with the variable.

Axioms

$$(\alpha)\ \Gamma \vdash_C [a]t = [a'][a \mapsto a']^{\sharp}t : \delta\sigma : A$$
$$(\beta_0)\ \Gamma \vdash_C ([a]t)@b = [a \mapsto b]^{\sharp}t : \sigma : A$$
$$(\eta)\ \Gamma \vdash_C [a](t@a) = t : \delta\sigma : A$$

Inference rules

$$(\text{Congr-}F)\frac{\Gamma \vdash_C s_1 = t_1 : \sigma_1 : A, \ldots, \Gamma \vdash_C s_n = t_n : \sigma_n : A}{\Gamma \vdash_C F(s_1, \ldots, s_n) = F(t_1, \ldots, t_n) : \sigma : A}\ F : \sigma_1, \ldots, \sigma_n \to \sigma$$

$$(\text{Congr-}[])\frac{\Gamma \vdash_C s = t : \sigma : A}{\Gamma \vdash_C [a]s = [a]t : \delta\sigma : A - \{a\}}\ a \in A,\ \langle a\rangle +\!\!+ \overline{\mathsf{OBV}(s)} \trianglelefteq C,\ \langle a\rangle +\!\!+ \overline{\mathsf{OBV}(t)} \trianglelefteq C$$

$$(\text{Congr-}@)\frac{\Gamma \vdash_C s = t : \delta\sigma : A}{\Gamma \vdash_C s@a = t@a : \sigma : A \cup \{a\}}\ a \trianglelefteq C \quad (\text{Ref})\frac{\Gamma \vdash_C t : \sigma : A}{\Gamma \vdash_C t = t : \sigma : A}$$

$$(\text{Subst})\frac{\Gamma, x : \sigma : A \vdash_C t = t' : \sigma : A}{\Gamma \vdash_C [x \mapsto s]t = [x \mapsto s]t' : \sigma : A} \quad (\text{Sym})\frac{\Gamma \vdash_C s = t : \sigma : A}{\Gamma \vdash_C t = s : \sigma : A}$$

$$(\text{Tr})\frac{\Gamma \vdash_C s = t : \sigma : A \quad \Gamma \vdash_C t = u : \sigma : A}{\Gamma \vdash_C s = u : \sigma : A}$$

Fig. 2. Equational logic

Theorem 1.
The equational logic is sound and complete for the categorical semantics described in Section 4, i.e.

$$\Gamma \vdash_C s = t : \sigma : A \ \Leftrightarrow\ \forall \mathbb{M}\,.\,\mathbb{M}[\![\Gamma \vdash_C s : \sigma : A]\!] = \mathbb{M}[\![\Gamma \vdash_C t : \sigma : A]\!].$$

Proof. *Soundness is proved by checking each rules are sound and completeness is by ordinary way of constructing a term model.* □

8 Unification

Unification is a fundamental operation in the operational semantics of binding logic programming language by SLD-resolution. In this section, we give an unification algorithm for binding terms.

A *unification problem* is a pair $(\Gamma \vdash_C t : \tau : A, \Gamma' \vdash_{C'} t' : \tau : A')$ of terms. A *unifier* to the unification problem is a pair (θ, ρ) satisfying

$$\Gamma'' \vdash_{C'} \theta\rho^{\natural}t = \theta t' : A'$$

where

- $\theta : \rho\Gamma \cup \Gamma' \to T(C', \Gamma'')$ is a substitution,
- $\rho : C \to C'$ is an object variable substitution such that $\widetilde{\rho}_{\restriction A} : A \to A'$ is a 1-1 free object variable substitution (so $|A| \le |A'|$. If not, swap the order of the pair).

This means that ρ is a renaming to standardize the world C of the left-hand side of the unification problem to C', and then θ is a unifier (in usual first-order sense) of two terms.

A *standardized unification problem* is a unification problem satisfying the following properties:

(i) C and C' are mutually disjoint.
(ii) Γ and Γ' are mutually disjoint.
(iii) $|A| = |A'|$.
(iv) t and t' has no β_0, η-redexes.
(v) The bound variables in t and t' are numbered by the method of de Bruijn level. So C and C' contain some segments of natural numbers $\mathbb{N}$.
(vi) The types of all variables are ι.

Proposition 1.
If a unification problem $(\Gamma \vdash_C t : \tau : A, \Gamma' \vdash_{C'} t' : \tau : A')$ has a unifier $(\theta, \rho{:}C \to C')$, then it can be translated to the standardized unification problem

$$(\Gamma_0 \vdash_{C_0} \phi t : \tau : A_0, \Gamma'_0 \vdash_{C'_0} \phi' t' : \tau : A'_0)$$

having the "essentially same" unifier $(\theta', \rho'{:}C_0 \to C'_0)$ by the pair $(\phi{:}C \to C_0, \phi'{:}C' \to C'_0)$ of 1-1 object variable substitutions such that $\phi' \circ \rho = \rho_0 \circ \phi$. This "essentially same" means that each assignment

$$x : \delta^n \iota \mapsto [k] \dots [k+n] s \ \in \theta$$

1-1 corresponds to an assignment

$$x_0 : \iota \mapsto s_0 \ \in \theta'$$

and $\phi' s \equiv s_0$.

Proof. (sketch) The conditions for standardized unification problem can be satisfied by the following way:

(i) By suitably renaming object variables.
(ii) By suitably renaming variables.
(iii) By suitably weakening and strengthing of stages by using derived rules.
(iv) By β_0, η_0-rewriting using the equational axioms from left to right.
(v) By standard way.
(vi) For each variable $\xi f : \delta^n \iota : A$ occurring in t and t', replace it with

$$[k] \dots [k+n] \xi f_0 \text{ where } f_0 : \iota : A \cup \{k, \dots, k+n\}$$

where k is determined from the context which fits with the method of de Bruijn level [dB72,FPT99]. Since we do not have constants of higher-order types $(\delta^m \iota)$ all variables are represented by this form.

Also the object variables in the stages of the judgment were accordingly replaced by the above replacement including numbering by de Bruijn level. □

From this proposition, we see that it is sufficient to consider a unification algorithm for standardized unification problem, and any unification problem can be standardized. We can easily recover a unifier of original problem from the unifier of standardized one.

The unification problem is extended to a pair of sequences of terms and a unifier is similarly defined. For a unification problem, a *system* is of the form

$$t_1{:}A_1 =^? t'_1{:}A'_1, \ldots, t_n{:}A_n =^? t'_n{:}A'_n.$$

The substitution θ and object variable substitution ρ are extended to functions on systems defined by $\theta(t_i{:}A_i =^? t'_i{:}A'_i)_{i=1,\ldots,n} \stackrel{def}{=} (\theta t_i{:}A_i =^? \theta t'_i{:}A'_i)_{i=1,\ldots,n}$ and $\rho(t_i{:}A_i =^? t'_i{:}A'_i)_{i=1,\ldots,n} \stackrel{def}{=} (\rho^\sharp t_i{:}A_i =^? \rho^\sharp t'_i{:}A'_i)_{i=1,\ldots,n}$.

Unification algorithm BUA. The unification algorithm BUA for binding terms is given by the set of transformation rules on systems given in Fig. 3. This is based on Martelli and Montanari's unification algorithm for first-order terms by the set of transformations [MM82].

$$(F\text{-elim})\frac{G_1, F(s_1,\ldots,s_n) : A =^? F(t_1,\ldots,t_n) : B, G_2}{G_1, s_1 : A =^? t_1 : B, \ldots, s_n : A =^? t_n : B, G_2}$$

$$(\text{triv})\frac{G_1, \xi x : A =^? \xi x : A, G_2}{G_1, G_2} \qquad ([]\text{-elim})\frac{G_1, [k]s : A =^? [k]t : B, G_2}{G_1, s : A \cup \{k\} =^? t : B \cup \{k\}, G_2}$$

$$(\text{ov-elim})\frac{G_1, \mathsf{var}(a) : A =^? \mathsf{var}(b) : B, G_2}{\rho(G_1, s : A =^? t : B, G_2)} \qquad (@\text{-elim})\frac{G_1, s@a : A =^? t@b : B, G_2}{\rho(G_1, s : A =^? t : B, G_2)}$$

$$(\text{v-elim1})\frac{G_1, \xi x : B =^? t : A, G_2}{\theta\rho(G_1, G_2)} \qquad (\text{v-elim2})\frac{G_1, t : A =^? \xi x : B, G_2}{\theta\rho(G_1, G_2)}$$

In (v-elim1) and (v-elim2), $x \notin \mathsf{VAR}(t)$.

Fig. 3. Unification algorithm BUA

Side conditions in BUA: in (ov-elim) and (@-elim), $a, b \notin \mathbb{N}, \rho = [a \mapsto b], |\rho A| = |\rho B|$ (a is possibly b). In (v-elim1) (and (v-elim2)), the following data is used:

- $x : \tau : D \in \Gamma$ ($\in \Gamma'$ in (v-elim2)),
- an isomorphic object variable substitution $\rho : \overline{B} \to \overline{A}$, where $\overline{A} = \langle a_1, \ldots, a_n \rangle$, $\overline{B} = \langle b_1, \ldots, b_n \rangle$, is defined by $\overline{\rho}(i) \triangleq i$.
- an object variable substitution $\xi^\diamond : \overline{D} \to \overline{B}$,
- a substitution θ is arbitrarily taken from the set $\Theta = \{[x{:}\tau{:}D \mapsto s{:}\tau{:}D] \mid \langle s, E\rangle \in S,\ E \subseteq D\}$ (i.e. there are $\#\Theta$-different θ's) where

$$S \triangleq \{\langle t[p_1 := \xi'_1 \circ \rho^{-1}(t_{\restriction p_1}), \ldots, p_n := \xi'_n \circ \rho^{-1}(t_{\restriction p_n})], \bigcup_i \xi'_i B\rangle$$

$$\mid \{p_1, \ldots, p_n\} = \mathsf{OVPOS}(t) \text{ and } p_1 \neq \ldots \neq p_n,$$

$$\xi'_1, \ldots, \xi'_n \in \{\xi' : \overline{B} \to \overline{D} \mid \xi^\diamond \circ \xi' = \mathsf{id}_B\} \cup \{\epsilon\}\}.$$

Note that $\mathsf{OVPOS}(t)$ denotes the set of all positions of free object variables occurring in t, $t[p := s]$ is a replacement of a term t at the position p with the term s, and $t_{\restriction p}$ denotes a subterm of t at the position p. Also (v-elim1) and (v-elim2) produce $\#\Theta$-different branches of derivation.

Let G and G' be systems. We write $G \overset{\mathsf{BUA}}{\rightsquigarrow}_{\theta,\rho} G'$ for a one-step transformation with a computed substitution θ and ρ (in (@-elim), (v-elim1) and (v-elim2), these are obtained, otherwise they are ϵ). We write $G \overset{\mathsf{BUA}}{\rightsquigarrow}{}^{*}_{\theta,\rho} G'$ if there exists a sequence of transformation

$$G \equiv G_1 \overset{\mathsf{BUA}}{\rightsquigarrow}_{\theta_1,\rho_1} G_2 \overset{\mathsf{BUA}}{\rightsquigarrow}_{\theta_2,\rho_2} \cdots \overset{\mathsf{BUA}}{\rightsquigarrow}_{\theta_n,\rho_n} G_n \equiv G'$$

such that $\theta = \theta_{n-1} \circ \cdots \circ \theta_2 \circ \theta_1$ and $\rho = \rho_{n-1} \circ \cdots \circ \rho_2 \circ \rho_1$, where we suitably extend codomains and domains of object variable and usual substitutions to make them composable by adding identity assignments. If $n = 1$ then $\theta = \epsilon$ and $\rho = \epsilon$. We use $\square$ for the empty system. When $G \overset{\mathsf{BUA}}{\rightsquigarrow}{}^{*}_{\theta,\rho} \square$, we say that θ is a *computed unifier*.

Properties of BUA. As in the case of higher-order unification, a unification for binding terms also may not have most general unifiers. For example, a unification problem

$$(x{:}\iota{:}a, b \vdash_{a,b} ([a]x)@b,\ \vdash_{a,b} F(\mathsf{var}(b), \mathsf{var}(b)))$$

has the four unifiers

$$x \mapsto F(\mathsf{var}(a), \mathsf{var}(a)), \qquad x \mapsto F(\mathsf{var}(a), \mathsf{var}(b))$$
$$x \mapsto F(\mathsf{var}(b), \mathsf{var}(a)), \qquad x \mapsto F(\mathsf{var}(b), \mathsf{var}(b)).$$

The last two unifiers can be obtained from the first two. And there is no unifier more general than these first two unifiers (see the definition of generality in Section 6, where only a 1-1 free object variables substitution is allowed to get an instance). So instead of most general unifier, we will just compute unifiers that are more general than unifiers of a given unification problem (completeness).

The computed unifiers has the following desired properties: let $(\Gamma \vdash_C t{:}\tau{:}A, \Gamma' \vdash_{C'} t'{:}\tau{:}A')$ be a *standardized* unification problem.

- Soundness: if $t{:}A =^? t'{:}A' \overset{\mathsf{BUA}}{\rightsquigarrow}_{\theta,\rho} \square$, then (θ, ρ) is a unifier of the unification problem.
- Completeness: if (θ, ρ) is a unifier of the unification problem, then $\exists \theta' \preccurlyeq \theta$. $t{:}A =^? t'{:}A' \overset{\mathsf{BUA}}{\rightsquigarrow}_{\theta',\rho} \square$.
- Decidability: there are no infinite transformation sequence by BUA.
- Normalizedness: computed answer unifiers are β_0, η-normalized.
- An answer object variables substitution $\rho : A_1 \to A_1'$ in a computed unifier is free and 1-1 where $A_1 \trianglelefteq A$ and $A_1' \trianglelefteq A'$. This can be extended to a 1-1 object variable substitution $\rho_1 : C \to C'$ required in the definition of unifier.

These can be shown by a similar way to the first-order case. Note that in higher-order unification, a set of sound and complete idempotent unifiers is called a *complete set of unifiers* and is not decidable in general, but our BUA is decidable.

Example 4.
We will give an example of unification by BUA. Consider a unification problem

$$(\vdash_{a,b,c} [a][b]F(c,a,b) : c,\ x{:}\iota{:}a,b,c \vdash_{a,b,c} [b][c]x : a).$$

This problem is translated to a standardized unification problem

$$(\vdash_{1,2,c} [1][2]F(c,1,2) : c,\ x{:}\iota{:}a,1,2 \vdash_{a,1,2} [1][2]x : a).$$

The computed unifiers is $(x \mapsto F(a,1,2),\ c \mapsto a)$ and the corresponding unifier to the original problem is $(x \mapsto F(a',a,b),\ c \mapsto a')$ which is obtained by recovering names from de Bruijn numbers and putting dash to object variables in the right-hand side to make the worlds in both sides of the original unification problem disjoint.

Predicate terms:

$$\frac{\Gamma \vdash_C t_1 : \sigma_1 : A \quad \ldots \quad \Gamma \vdash_C t_n : \sigma_n : A}{\Gamma \vdash_C p(t_1,\ldots,t_n) : A} \quad p : \sigma_1, \ldots \sigma_n$$

Note that no types are given in predicate terms.

Definite Horn clauses:

$$\frac{\Gamma \vdash_C p(\boldsymbol{t}) : A \quad \Gamma \vdash_C p_1(\boldsymbol{t_1}) : A_1 \quad \ldots \quad \Gamma \vdash_C p_n(\boldsymbol{t_n}) : A_n}{\vdash_C \forall\Gamma\,.\,p(\boldsymbol{t}) : A \Leftarrow p_1(\boldsymbol{t_1}) : A_1, \ldots, p_n(\boldsymbol{t_n}) : A_n}$$

If n is 0, the symbol "$\Leftarrow$" is omitted.

Queries:

$$\frac{\Gamma \vdash_C p(\boldsymbol{t}) : A \quad \Gamma \vdash_C p_1(\boldsymbol{t_1}) : A_1 \quad \ldots \quad \Gamma \vdash_C p_n(\boldsymbol{t_n}) : A_n}{\vdash_C \exists\Gamma\,.\,p_1(t_1) : A_1, \ldots, p_n(t_n) : A_n}$$

Fig. 4. Typing rules for formulas

---

9 Binding Logic Programming

In this section, we describe a binding logic programming language.

9.1 Logic

We need formulas for logic programming. We assume the signature Σ is the disjoint union of Σ_F for function symbols and $\Sigma_P = \{p : \sigma_1, \ldots \sigma_n,\ \ldots\}$ for predicate symbols. The typing rules of formulas are given in Fig. 4.

Next we describe the logic of our logic programming language. A *program* P is a set of definite Horn clauses. Note that here a definite Horn clause includes

$$(\text{Axiom})\frac{P \rhd_C \forall\Gamma' . \theta(p_1(\boldsymbol{t_1})) : A_1 \quad \ldots \quad P \rhd_C \forall\Gamma' . \theta(p_n(\boldsymbol{t_n})) : A_n}{P \rhd_C \forall\Gamma' . \theta(p(\boldsymbol{t})) : A}$$

where
- $\vdash_C \forall\Gamma . p(\boldsymbol{t}) : A \Leftarrow p_1(\boldsymbol{t_1}) : A_1, \ldots, p_n(\boldsymbol{t_n}) : A_n \ \in P$
- a substitution $\theta : \Gamma \to T(C, \Gamma')$

$$(\exists\text{-intro})\frac{P \rhd_C \forall\Gamma' . p_1(\theta\boldsymbol{t_1}) : A_1 \quad \ldots \quad P \rhd_C \forall\Gamma' . p_n(\theta\boldsymbol{t_n}) : A_n}{P \rhd_C \exists\Gamma . p_1(\boldsymbol{t_1}) : A_1, \ldots, p_n(\boldsymbol{t_n}) : A_n}\ \theta : \Gamma \to T(C, \Gamma')$$

$$(\text{Inst})\frac{P \rhd_C \forall\Gamma . p(\boldsymbol{t}) : A}{P \rhd_C \forall\Gamma' . \theta(p(\boldsymbol{t})) : A}\ \theta : \Gamma \to T(C, \Gamma') \quad (\text{Wld-St})\frac{P \rhd_C \forall\Gamma . p(\boldsymbol{t}) : A}{P \rhd_{C'} \forall\Gamma . p(\boldsymbol{t}) : A}$$

$$(\text{Repl})\frac{P \rhd_C \forall\Gamma . p(\boldsymbol{t}) : A \quad \Gamma \vdash_C t_1 = t_1' : A \ldots \Gamma \vdash_C t_n = t_n' : A}{P \rhd_C \forall\Gamma . p(\boldsymbol{t'}) : A}$$

$$(\text{St-w})\frac{P \rhd_C \forall\Gamma . p(\boldsymbol{t}) : A}{P \rhd_C \forall\Gamma . p(\boldsymbol{t}) : A \cup \{a\}}\ a \notin \mathsf{OBV}(t) \quad (\text{St-s})\frac{P \rhd_C \forall\Gamma . p(\boldsymbol{t}) : A \cup \{a\}}{P \rhd_C \forall\Gamma . p(\boldsymbol{t}) : A}\ a \notin \mathsf{FOV}(t)$$

$$(\text{Rename})\frac{P \rhd_C \forall\Gamma . p(\boldsymbol{t}) : A}{P \rhd_{C'} \forall\rho\Gamma . p(\rho^\natural \boldsymbol{t}) : A} \quad (\text{Open } \alpha)\frac{P \rhd_C \forall\Gamma . p(\boldsymbol{t}) : A}{P \rhd_C \forall\Gamma . p(\rho^\sharp \boldsymbol{t}) : A}$$

In (Rename), $\rho : C \to C'$ is 1-1. In (Open α), $\rho : C \to C$ is 1-1. In (World-st), C' is obtained from C by deleting object variables not occurring in $\forall\Gamma . p(\boldsymbol{t}) : A$.

Fig. 5. Inference rules of the logic

the part $\vdash_C$ on the top, so in a program, each clause may have different world C. A *sequent* within this logic is of the form

$$P \rhd_C Q$$

where Q is a well-typed formula by $\vdash_C Q$. Note that we use the symbol $\vdash$ for the well-typed terms and formulas, and $\rhd$ for the sequent.

The inference rules of this logic is given in Fig. 5. The substitution θ in ($\exists$-intro) is called *witness* of this existentially quantified formula. Weakening of a world can be performed by (Rename) rule using suitable ρ.

The reason why we only let ρ be 1-1 for substituting object variables in the above rules comes from Hofmann's observation on the denotation on decidable equality in the presheaf category $\hat{\mathbb{F}}$ [Hof99]. Let us rephrase his observation in our system: consider a program for inequality of object variables by the predicate ineq and the following sequent:

$$\{\vdash_{a,b} \mathsf{ineq}(\mathsf{var}(a), \mathsf{var}(b)) : a, b\} \rhd_{a,b} \mathsf{ineq}(\mathsf{var}(a), \mathsf{var}(b)) : a, b.$$

Then, if we apply a surjective object variable substitution $\rho : \langle a, b\rangle \to \langle a\rangle$, we can derive the following

$$\{\vdash_{a,b} \mathsf{ineq}(\mathsf{var}(a), \mathsf{var}(b)) : a, b\} \rhd_{a} \mathsf{ineq}(\mathsf{var}(a), \mathsf{var}(a)) : a.$$

This says $\mathsf{var}(a)$ and $\mathsf{var}(a)$ are inequal, but clearly this cannot be considered as correct use of the predicate ineq. Same things will happen in any predicate having more than two object variables, so we restrict ρ to 1-1.

Example 5.
We describe a program for syntactic differentiation given in introduction more precisely in our typed language:

$$P = \left\{ \begin{array}{l} \vdash_{a,b} \mathsf{diff}([b]\mathsf{var}(a), [b]0) : a, \\ \vdash_{a,b} \mathsf{diff}([b]\mathsf{var}(b), [b]1) : \varnothing, \\ \vdash_{a,b} \forall f{:}\iota{:}b, f'{:}\iota{:}b \,.\, \mathsf{diff}([b]\mathsf{sin}(f), [b](\mathsf{cos}(f) \times f')) : \varnothing \Leftarrow \mathsf{diff}([b]f, [b]f') : \varnothing. \end{array} \right\}$$

A query under P is stated as the sequent

$$P \rhd_{d,c} \exists z{:}\delta\iota{:}\varnothing \,.\, \mathsf{diff}([d]\mathsf{var}(c), z) : c,$$

and an answer substitution for this is $\theta : \{z{:}\delta\iota{:}\varnothing\} \to T(\langle d\rangle, \varnothing)$ given by $z \mapsto [d]0$.

Example 6.
We also give a program for capture-avoiding substitution of λ-terms defined in Example 1. The predicate $\mathsf{sub}([a]s, t, u)$ means that u is a term obtained from the term s by replacing all a with t.

$$P = \left\{ \begin{array}{l} \vdash_{a} \ \forall y{:}\varnothing \,.\, \mathsf{sub}([a]\mathsf{var}(a), y, y) : \varnothing \\ \vdash_{a,b} \forall y{:}\varnothing \,.\, \mathsf{sub}([a]\mathsf{var}(b), y, \mathsf{var}(b)) : b \\ \vdash_{a} \ \forall e_1, e_2{:}a, z_1, z_2{:}\varnothing, y{:}\varnothing \,.\, \mathsf{sub}([a]\mathsf{app}(e_1, e_2), y, \mathsf{app}(z_1, z_2)) : \varnothing \\ \qquad \Leftarrow \mathsf{sub}([a]e_1, y, z_1) : \varnothing,\ \mathsf{sub}([a]e_2, y, z_2) : \varnothing \\ \vdash_{a,b} \forall x{:}a, b, y{:}\varnothing, z{:}b \,.\, \mathsf{sub}([a]\mathsf{lam}([b]x), y, \mathsf{lam}([b]z)){:}\varnothing \\ \qquad \Leftarrow \mathsf{sub}([a]x, y, z) : b \end{array} \right\}$$

9.2 Operational Semantics

As in ordinary logic programming language, we consider an existentially quantified formula as a *query* and witnesses as answer substitutions for the query. We will give a version of SLD-resolution which treats binding terms for a proof method of existentially quantified formulas with witnesses. Let us prove the following sequent

$$P \rhd_D \exists\Delta \,.\, p_1(\boldsymbol{s_1}) : A_1, \ldots, p_n(\boldsymbol{s_n}) : A_n$$

by getting witnesses. For this sequent, a *goal* is of the form

$$D, \Delta;\, p_1(\boldsymbol{s_1}){:}A_1, \ldots, p_n(\boldsymbol{s_n}){:}A_n.$$

We define SLD-resolution as a transformation rule on goals. Let G_1, G_2, G_3 be sequences of predicate terms.

SLD-resolution. Define a one-step SLD-resolution

$$D, \Delta;\, G_1,\, p(\boldsymbol{s}){:}B,\, G_2 \ \leadsto_{\underline{\theta},\rho}\ C_0, \Delta'; \theta_0(\rho G_1, \phi' G_3, \rho G_2)$$

where $\vdash_C \forall\Gamma \,.\, p(\boldsymbol{t}) : A \Leftarrow G_3\ \in P$,

$$\theta = \underline{\theta_0} \circ \phi_1 : \Delta \to T(C_0, \Delta'), \quad \rho = \rho_0 \circ \phi : D \to C_0,$$

and $\phi_1 : \Delta \to \rho_0\Delta_0 \cup \Gamma_0$ is defined by $x : \sigma : A \mapsto x : \sigma : \rho_0\phi A$. Here let (θ, ρ) be a computed unifier by BUA for the unification problem

$$(\Delta \vdash_D p(\boldsymbol{s}) : B,\ \Gamma \vdash_C p(\boldsymbol{t}) : A),$$

between the goal and the head of the Horn clause and (θ_0, ρ_0) a "essentially same" unifier for the standardized problem. Then $\underline{\theta_0}$ is obtained by recovering original variables from the substitution θ_0.

We write $H \rightsquigarrow^*_{\theta,\rho} H'$ if there exits a sequence of transformation

$$H \equiv H_1 \rightsquigarrow_{\theta_1,\rho_1} H_2 \rightsquigarrow_{\theta_2,\rho_2} \cdots \rightsquigarrow_{\theta_n,\rho_n} H_n \equiv H'$$

such that $\theta = \theta_{n-1} \circ \cdots \circ \theta_2 \circ \theta_1$ and $\rho = \rho_{n-1} \circ \cdots \circ \rho_2 \circ \rho_1$. If $n = 1$ then $\theta = \epsilon$ and $\rho = \epsilon$. We use $\Box$ for the empty goal. When $H \rightsquigarrow^*_{\theta,\rho} \Box$, this is a *successful* SLD-resolution, otherwise, it is fail.

Theorem 2.
The SLD-resolution is sound for the logic given in Section 9.1, i.e.

$$D, \Delta; G \rightsquigarrow_{\theta,\rho} \Box \quad \Rightarrow \quad P \rhd_{C_0} \forall\Delta_1.\theta G$$

where $\theta : \Delta \to T(C_0, \Delta_1)$ and $\rho : D \to C_0$.

Also, the SLD-resolution is complete, i.e. if $P \rhd_D \exists\Delta.G$ is provable and its previous sequent in the proof is $P \rhd_D \forall\Delta_1.\theta G$, then

$$D, \Delta; G \rightsquigarrow_{\theta',\rho} \Box$$

such that $\theta' \preccurlyeq \rho_1 \circ \theta$, where $\theta : \Delta \to T(D, \Delta_1)$, $\theta' : \Delta \to T(C_0, \Delta_2)$, $\rho : D \to C_0$, and $\rho_1 : \Delta_1 \to \Delta_2$ is defined by $x : \sigma : A \mapsto x : \sigma : \rho A$.

10 Related Work

Nadathur and Miller's λProlog [NM88] is one of the most famous language treating variable binding in logic programming. This language deals with higher-order hereditary Harrop formulas instead of first-order Horn clauses in case of Prolog. The unification is extended to that for simply typed λ-terms modulo α,β,η-conversion, called higher-order unification. A problem is that higher-order unification is undecidable in general and quite complex. This point is different from ours, our binding logic programming language uses simple decidable unification. But the class of formulas of λProlog is wider than ours, higher-order hereditary Harrop formulas can contain $\forall, \Rightarrow$ in the body of clauses.

Later, Miller proposed succeeding language L_λ [Mil91], which is a subset of λProlog where β-equality is restricted to β_0-equality defined by $(\lambda x.M)x = M$. Miller observed that "when examining typical λProlog programs, it is clear that most instances of β-conversion performed by the interpreter are, in fact, instances of β_0-conversion" [Mil00]. As a result, the unification modulo α,β_0,η becomes very simple and decidable, and also resemble first-order unification.

Our β_0-axiom is (essentially) same as Miller's β_0-axiom, but the motivation of this axiom comes from a different reason, i.e. initial algebra semantics of binding by presheaves [FPT99]. The recent consideration of semantics of abstract syntax with variable binding including Fiore-Plotkin-Turi's has a common principle, where they prohibit general function types in signature, such as $\mathsf{lam} : (term \Rightarrow term) \rightarrow term$, and instead, use restricted function types only from (object) variables, such as $\mathsf{lam} : (var \Rightarrow term) \rightarrow term$. The reason for this restriction is to get structural recursion (or induction) on data defined by this kind of signature [FPT99,Hof99,GP99,DFH95]. So, now Miller's practical observation on the restriction of β-equality in λProlog and the restriction of function types in semantical studies on variable binding coincide. Hence our type theory involving the β_0-axiom can be considered as reasonable.

So L_λ is similar to our language but again the class of formulas in L_λ (hereditary Harrop formulas) is wider than ours (Horn clauses). It is not currently clear whether all L_λ programs can be (easily) translated to our binding logic programs. Due to β_0's restriction, unification in L_λ becomes *pattern unification*, which is a higher-order unification only for particular class of λ-terms called higher-order patterns. A λ-term is a higher-order pattern if every free variable occurrence is applied to at most distinct bound variables. So, for example, $\lambda x.Fxx =^? \lambda y.gy$ (F is a free variable) is *not* a pattern unification problem, hence L_λ cannot solve it. But our BUA algorithm can solve it, this point is an advantage of our language on L_λ.

Pitts and Gabbay's FreshML [PG00] is a functional programming language based on their semantics of binding – FM-set theory [GP99]. FreshML is quite similar to ours, they use the notion of stage too (called support), but they attached object variables *not contained* by its stage as a type information of terms. They in particular payed attention to freshness of object variables in terms, which is not considered in this paper. In FM-set theory, a permutation group is used to formalize renaming and binding of object variables, where only injective variable substitutions are used. This affects to syntax, for example, an application of the same object variables twice, such as a term $t@a@a$, is impossible in their type system. But in our case, since the category $\mathbb{F}$ has all functions between (abstract) object variables, our type system allow such terms. Another difference is that FreshML does not use η-axiom.

Acknowledgments

I am grateful to Gordon Plotkin for motivating this work and designing the basis of the type theory in this paper. I also thank Daniele Turi for discussions on this work, Martin Hofmann, Hirofumi Yokouchi and the anonymous referees for helpful comments. This work was done while I was visiting LFCS, University of Edinburgh where I have been supported by JSPS Research Fellowships for Young Scientists.

References

[dB72] N. de Bruijn. Lambda clculus notation with nameless dummies, a tool for automatic formula manipulation, whith application to the church-rosser theorem. *Indagationes Mathematicae*, 34:381–391, 1972.

[DFH95] J. Despeyroux, A. Felty, and A. Hirschowitz. Higher-order abstract syntax in Coq. In M. Dezani and G. Plotkin, editors, *Typed Lambda Clculi and Apllications, LNCS 902*, pages 124–138, 1995.

[FPT99] M. Fiore, G. Plotkin, and D. Turi. Abstrat syntax and variable binding. In *14th Annual Symposium on Logic in Computer Science*, pages 193–202, Washington, 1999. IEEE Computer Society Press.

[GP99] M.J. Gabbay and A.M. Pitts. A new approach to abstract syntax involving binders. In *14th Annual Symposium on Logic in Computer Science*, pages 214–224, Washington, 1999. IEEE Computer Society Press.

[Hof99] M. Hofmann. Semantical analysis of higher-order abstract syntax. In *14th Annual Symposium on Logic in Computer Science*, pages 204–213, Washington, 1999. IEEE Computer Society Press.

[Mil91] D. Miller. A logic programming language with lambda-abstraction, function variables, and simple unification,. *Journal of Logic and Computation*, 1(4):497–536, 1991.

[Mil00] D. Miller. Abstract syntax for variable binders: An overview. In John Lloyd, et. al., editor, *Proceedings of Computation Logic 2000, LNAI 1861*, 2000.

[MM82] A. Martelli and U. Montanari. An efficient unification algorithm. *ACM Transactions of Programming Languages*, 4(2):258–282, 1982.

[NM88] G. Nadathur and D. Miller. An overview of λProlog. In *Fifth International Logic Programming Conference*, pages 810–827. MIT Press, 1988.

[Oho96] A. Ohori. A typed context calculus. In *Preprint RIMS-1098*. Research Institute for Mathematical Sciences, Kyoto University, 1996.

[PG00] A. M. Pitts and M. J. Gabbay. A metalanguage for programming with bound names modulo renaming. In R. Backhouse and J. N. Oliveira, editors, *Mathematics of Program Construction, MPC2000, Proceedings, Ponte de Lima, Portugal, July 2000*, volume 1837 of *Lecture Notes in Computer Science*, pages 230–255. Springer-Verlag, Heidelberg, 2000.

[SSK01] M. Sato, T. Sakurai, and Y. Kameyama. A simply typed context calculu with first-class environments. In *5th International Symposium on Functional and Logic Programming*, volume LNCS 2024, pages 359–374, 2001.

Proof-Search and Countermodel Generation in Propositional BI Logic
Extended Abstract

Didier Galmiche and Daniel Méry

LORIA – Université Henri Poincaré, Campus Scientifique,
BP 239, 54506 Vandœuvre-lès-Nancy, France,
galmiche{dmery}@loria.fr

Abstract. In this paper, we study proof-search in the propositional BI logic that can be viewed as a merging of intuitionistic logic and multiplicative intuitionistic linear logic. With its underlying sharing interpretation, BI has been recently used for logic programming or reasoning about mutable data structures. We propose a labelled tableau calculus for BI, the use of labels making it possible to generate countermodels. We show that, from a given formula A, a non-redundant tableau construction procedure terminates and yields either a tableau proof of A or a countermodel of A in terms of the Kripke resource monoid semantics. Moreover, we show the finite model property for BI with respect to this semantics.

1 Introduction

The logic of bunched implications, **BI**, freely combines a multiplicative (or linear) and an additive (or intuitionistic) implication in the same logic [12] and its propositional fragment can be viewed as a merging of intuitionistic logic (IL) and multiplicative intuitionistic linear logic (MILL) with well-defined proof-theoretic and semantic foundations [11,13]. The semantics of **BI** is motivated by modelling the notion of *resource*. With its underlying sharing interpretation, it has been recently used for logic programming [1] or reasoning about mutable data structures [8]. Our aim is to propose useful and efficient proof-search procedures for such a mixed logic. Because of the cohabitation of linear and intuitionistic connectives in a same logic and even if **BI** includes IL and MILL as subsystems, we cannot directly extend proof-search (sequent, tableau, or connection) calculi defined for each of them [2,4,5,14] to **BI**. Moreover we aim to design a **BI** prover that builds proofs but also generates countermodels for non-theorems. Such systems exist for IL [5] and MILL [14] and the tableau method directly provides countermodel generation for a wide range of logics, including IL, but not for substructural logics like linear logic (LL) [9,10]. An appropriate solution consists in designing calculi with labels which make it possible to generate countermodels in terms of a given semantics. Our approach is based on the Kripke resource semantics of **BI** where the possible worlds are justified in terms of pieces of information [15]

N. Kobayashi and B.C. Pierce (Eds.): TACS 2001, LNCS 2215, pp. 263–282, 2001.

and also on the methodology of LDS for analytic deduction [3] that has been recently used for MILL with a simple semantics [14].
In this paper, we define a labelled tableau calculus **TBI** for propositional **BI** with constraints (assertions and obligations). The provability is related to the search of a closed tableau in which the set of obligations can be verified from the assertions, following some specific conditions. We show that, for a given formula A, there exists a nonredundant tableau construction procedure for **TBI** that terminates and yields either a tableau proof or a countermodel for A. We prove the completeness of the calculus for **BI** (without $\perp$) with respect to the Kripke resource semantics and also the finite model property.
¿From these results, we will study some algorithmic aspects of proof-search and countermodel generation with this labelled calculus using appropriate structures (dependency graphs) dedicated to constraints solving. We will define a derived calculus with free variables in labels and moreover design a similar calculus with countermodel generation in **BI** (with $\perp$) starting from Grothendieck sheaf-theoretic models [12].

2 The Logic of Bunched Implications (BI)

In this section, we remind the essential features of the propositional logic of Bunched Implications (BI) [13], in which additive (intuitionistic) and multiplicative (linear) connectives cohabit.

2.1 Syntax and Proof-Theory of BI

The propositional language of **BI** consists of a multiplicative unit I, the multiplicative connectives $*$, $-\!\!*$, the additive units $\top$, $\perp$, the additive connectives $\wedge$, $\rightarrow$, $\vee$, a countable set $\mathrm{P} = A, B, \ldots$ of propositional variables. Propositions over P, referred to as $\mathcal{P}$, are inductively defined as follows:

$$\mathcal{P} ::= \mathrm{P} \mid \mathcal{I} \mid \mathcal{P} * \mathcal{P} \mid \mathcal{P} -\!\!* \mathcal{P} \mid \top \mid \mathcal{P} \wedge \mathcal{P} \mid \mathcal{P} \rightarrow \mathcal{P} \mid \perp \mid \mathcal{P} \vee \mathcal{P}$$

The additive connectives correspond to those of intuitionistic logic (IL) and the multiplicative connectives to those of multiplicative intuitionistic linear logic (MILL). The antecedents of logical consequences are not as lists but rather as bunches, in which there are two ways to combine operations that respectively display additive and multiplicative behavior.

Definition 1 (Bunches). *Bunches are inductively defined as follows:*

$$\Gamma ::= \mathcal{P} \mid \emptyset_{\Updownarrow} \mid -,- \mid \emptyset_{\dashv} \mid -;-$$

We write $\Gamma(\Delta)$ to represent a bunch in which Δ is a subtree. We consider "bunches" up to a structural equivalence ($\equiv$) defined as the least equivalence on "bunches" satisfying: a) commutative monoid equations for $\emptyset_a$ and ";", b) commutative monoid equations for $\emptyset_m$ and "," and c) congruence: $\Delta \equiv \Delta'$

– Identity and structures

$$\frac{}{A \vdash A}\,ax \qquad \frac{\Gamma \vdash A}{\Delta \vdash A}\,\Delta \equiv \Gamma \qquad \frac{\Gamma(\Delta) \vdash A}{\Gamma(\Delta;\Delta') \vdash A}\,w \qquad \frac{\Gamma(\Delta;\Delta) \vdash A}{\Gamma(\Delta) \vdash A}\,c$$

– Unities

$$\frac{}{\bot \vdash A}\,\bot_L \qquad \frac{\Gamma(\emptyset_m) \vdash A}{\Gamma(I) \vdash A}\,I_L \qquad \frac{}{\emptyset_m \vdash I}\,I_R \qquad \frac{\Gamma(\emptyset_a) \vdash A}{\Gamma(\top) \vdash A}\,\top_L \qquad \frac{}{\emptyset_a \vdash \top}\,\top_R$$

– Multiplicatives

$$\frac{\Gamma(A,B) \vdash C}{\Gamma(A * B) \vdash C}\,*_L \qquad \frac{\Gamma \vdash A \quad \Delta \vdash B}{\Gamma,\Delta \vdash A * B}\,*_R \qquad \frac{\Gamma \vdash A \quad \Delta(\Delta',B) \vdash C}{\Delta(\Delta',\Gamma,A \mathrel{-\!\!*} B) \vdash C}\,-\!\!*_L \qquad \frac{\Gamma, A \vdash B}{\Gamma \vdash A \mathrel{-\!\!*} B}\,-\!\!*_R$$

– Additives

$$\frac{\Gamma(A;B) \vdash C}{\Gamma(A \wedge B) \vdash C}\,\wedge_L \qquad \frac{\Gamma \vdash A \quad \Delta \vdash B}{\Gamma;\Delta \vdash A \wedge B}\,\wedge_R \qquad \frac{\Gamma \vdash A \quad \Delta(\Delta';B) \vdash C}{\Delta(\Delta';\Gamma;A \to B) \vdash C}\,\to_L$$

$$\frac{\Gamma; A \vdash B}{\Gamma \vdash A \to B}\,\to_R \qquad \frac{\Gamma(A) \vdash C \quad \Delta(B) \vdash C}{\Gamma(A \vee B);\Delta(A \vee B) \vdash C}\,\vee_L \qquad \frac{\Gamma \vdash A_{i\,(i=1,2)}}{\Gamma \vdash A_1 \vee A_2}\,\vee_R$$

Fig. 1. The **LBI** sequent calculus

implies $\Gamma(\Delta) \equiv \Gamma(\Delta')$. Let us note that ";" and "," do not distribute over one another.

The judgements are expressions of the form $\Gamma \vdash A$, where Γ is a "bunch" and A is a proposition. The **LBI** sequent calculus, given in figure 1, has the cut-elimination property and is equivalent to a sequent calculus with the following additive rules

$$\frac{}{\Gamma; A \vdash A}\,ax \qquad \frac{\Gamma \vdash A \quad \Gamma \vdash B}{\Gamma \vdash A \wedge B}\,\wedge_R \qquad \frac{\Gamma \vdash A \quad \Delta(\Gamma;B) \vdash C}{\Delta(\Gamma;A \to B) \vdash C}\,\to_L \qquad \frac{\Gamma(A) \vdash C \quad \Gamma(B) \vdash C}{\Gamma(A \vee B) \vdash C}\,\vee_L$$

that are derivable in the **LBI** calculus. Let us now show that the sequent $A * (B \wedge C) \vdash (A * B) \wedge (A * C)$ is provable in the additive version of **LBI**:

$$\dfrac{\dfrac{\dfrac{}{A \vdash A} \quad \dfrac{\dfrac{}{B;C \vdash B}}{B \wedge C \vdash B}\,\wedge_L}{A * (B \wedge C) \vdash A * B}\,*_R \qquad \dfrac{\dfrac{}{A \vdash A} \quad \dfrac{\dfrac{}{B;C \vdash C}}{B \wedge C \vdash C}\,\wedge_L}{A * (B \wedge C) \vdash A * C}\,*_R}{A * (B \wedge C) \vdash (A * B) \wedge (A * C)}\,\wedge_R$$

A proposition A is a theorem if either $\emptyset_a \vdash A$, or $\emptyset_m \vdash A$ is provable in **LBI**. Moreover we have the following results

Theorem 1. *$\Gamma(\emptyset_a) \vdash A$ (resp. $\Gamma(\emptyset_m) \vdash A$) is provable in* **LBI** *iff $\Gamma(\top) \vdash A$ (resp. $\Gamma(I) \vdash A$) is provable in* **LBI**.

Corollary 1. *A proposition A is a theorem iff $\emptyset_m \vdash A$ is provable in* **LBI**.

As **BI** contains IL and MILL as subsystems it is important to remind that **BI** is conservative over both logics. All these results are detailed in [12].

2.2 Kripke Resource Semantics

BI has two natural semantics: a categorical semantics of the proof theory (interpretation of proofs) using a doubly closed category (two monoidal closed structures) that has all the structure to model both IL and MILL and a Kripke-style semantics (interpretation of formulae) which combines the Kripke semantics of IL and Urquhart's semantics of MILL [12]. This one uses possible worlds, arranged as a commutative monoid and justified in terms of "pieces of information" [15]. In this paper we consider the second one that provides a way to read the formulae as propositions that are true or false relative to a given world. Let us summarize the main points about this semantics that is based on the notion of *resource*.

Definition 2. *A* Kripke resource monoid *(***Krm***) $\mathcal{M} = \langle M, \bullet, e, \sqsubseteq \rangle$ is a pre-ordered monoid in which $\bullet$ is order preserving, i.e., $m \sqsubseteq n$ and $m' \sqsubseteq n'$ implies $m \bullet m' \sqsubseteq n \bullet n'$. Let $\mathcal{M} = \langle M, \bullet, e, \sqsubseteq \rangle$ be a* **Krm***, a* forcing on $\mathcal{M}$ *is a binary relation $\models$ on $M \times$ P satisfying the Kripke monotonicity property, i.e., $m \models A$ and $m \sqsubseteq n$ implies $n \models A$.*

The relation $\models$ can be extended to the set $\mathcal{P}$ of propositions with the following inductive definition[1]:

- $m \models \top$ always
- $m \models A \wedge B$ iff $m \models A$ and $m \models B$
- $m \models \bot$ never
- $m \models A \vee B$ iff $m \models A$ or $m \models B$
- $m \models A \to B$ iff $(\forall n \in M \;/\; m \sqsubseteq n)(n \models A \text{ implies } n \models B)$
- $m \models I$ iff $e \sqsubseteq m$
- $m \models A * B$ iff $(\exists n, n' \in M \;/\; n \bullet n' \sqsubseteq m)(n \models A \text{ and } n' \models B)$
- $m \models A \mathrel{-\!\!*} B$ iff $(\forall n \in M)(n \models A \text{ implies } m \bullet n \models B)$

The monotonicity property extends to $\mathcal{P}$. Moreover these clauses can be read in terms of resources. For instance, one says that a world forces $A * B$ if and only if there is a partition of that world into components which force A and B. Moreover, one can understand the formula $A \mathrel{-\!\!*} B$ as follows: if m is the cost of the function and n is the cost of any argument then the cost of obtaining the application of the function to the argument is $m \bullet n$. Then, the multiplicatives depend on the internal structure of worlds and the additives should be understood in terms of conservation [12].

[1] Compared to the original definition we use the reverse order ($m \sqsubseteq n$ instead of $n \sqsubseteq m$) for presentation convenience

Definition 3. *A* Kripke resource interpretation *(***Kri***)* $\mathcal{I} = \langle M, \bullet, e, \sqsubseteq, \models \rangle$ *is a* **Krm** $\mathcal{M} = \langle M, \bullet, e, \sqsubseteq \rangle$ *together with a forcing* $\models$ *on* $\mathcal{M}$.

Let $\mathcal{I} = \langle M, \bullet, e, \sqsubseteq, \models \rangle$ be a **Kri** and Γ be a "bunch", we write $m \models \Gamma$ if and only if $m \models A_\Gamma$, where A_Γ is the formula obtained from Γ by replacing each ";" by $\wedge$ and each "," by $*$ with association respecting the tree structure of Γ.

Definition 4. *The sequent* $\Gamma \vdash A$ *is said to be* valid in $\mathcal{I} = \langle M, \bullet, e, \sqsubseteq, \models \rangle$ *(notation:* $\Gamma \models_{\mathcal{I}} A$*), if and only if for any world* $m \in M$*, we have that* $m \models \Gamma$ *implies* $m \models A$*. The sequent* $\Gamma \vdash A$ *is said to be* valid *(notation:* $\Gamma \models A$*), if and only if for all* $\mathcal{I}$*, we have* $\Gamma \models_{\mathcal{I}} A$.

Let us remind that the completeness result w.r.t. this semantics only holds for **BI** without the unit $\perp$, denoted $\mathbf{BI}^{\perp}$[12].

Theorem 2. *1. if* $\Gamma \vdash A$ *is provable in* **LBI***, then* $\Gamma \models A$ *(soundness).*
2. if $\Gamma \models A$ *in* $\mathbf{BI}^{\perp}$ *then* $\Gamma \vdash A$ *is provable in* $\mathbf{LBI}^{\perp}$ *(completeness).*

Corollary 2. *Let* A *be a formula of* $\mathbf{BI}^{\perp}$*, then* A *is valid if and only for any* $\langle M, \bullet, e, \sqsubseteq, \models \rangle$ *we have* $e \models A$.

Topological Kripke models have been proposed as a solution to have completeness for **BI** (with $\perp$) but it is out of the scope of this paper in which we focus on the Kripke resource semantics and the fragment $\mathbf{BI}^{\perp}$.

2.3 Resources and Sharing Interpretation

We have previously mentioned a resource-based interpretation of **BI** but it is important to notice that **BI** is different from Linear Logic (LL) and does not admit the standard number-of-uses reading of linear logic [7]. For instance, $A \mathrel{-\!\!*} B \nvdash A \to B$ holds in **BI**, whereas $A \multimap B \vdash A \to B$ in LL, with $A \to B$ defined as $!A \multimap B$. On the other hand, $\vdash A \mathrel{-\!\!*} (A \to A \to B) \to B$ is a judgement that holds in **BI** but not in LL because it does not respect the number-of-uses reading. **BI** offers a particular resource-based interpretation called the *sharing interpretation* and has promising results about logic programming [1], interference in imperative programs [11] and reasoning about mutable data structures like pointers [8]. For instance, the problem that arises when dealing with pointers is that you can have several pointers referencing the same cell in the computer store. This situation, called *aliasing*, is typically a problem of resource sharing once one has defined the resources as being "heaps" or, in other words, "portions of the computer store". The computer store is made of cons cells having basic data (integers, for example), or pointers to other cons cells in their components. The model proposed in [8] deals with atomic propositions are of the form $(x \mapsto E, F)$ which means that x is a location pointing to a cons cell with first and second components respectively containing E and F as values. An interesting example, which shows that $\mathrel{-\!\!*}$ is about describing fresh heaps is given by the formula $(x \mapsto 3, 5) * ((x \mapsto 7, 5) \mathrel{-\!\!*} P)$. This formula can only be satisfied by heaps which contain a location x pointing to a cons cell the content of which is 3, 5, and such that, when updating the cons cell to 7, 5, the resulting heap satisfy P. It corresponds to a description of the update operation in terms of deletion followed by extension. Similar ideas have been successfully applied to write pre and post-conditions, using **BI** as an assertion language, for operations such as assignment, allocation and deallocation of a cons cell [8]. In order to prove such formulae, assertions or properties expressed in **BI** it seems important to study proof-search methods for this logic that build proofs but also generate countermodels.

3 A Labelled Tableaux Calculus for $\mathbf{BI}^{\perp}$

Because of the cohabitation of linear and intuitionistic connectives in **BI** and even if it includes IL and MILL as subsystems, we cannot directly extend to **BI** the proof-search (sequent, tableau, or connection) calculi defined for both [2,4,5,14]. Here, we apply the methodology of Labelled Deductive Systems (LDS) [3] to the tableau method in order to propose a labelled tableau calculus **TBI** for propositional $\mathbf{BI}^{\perp}$, the use of labels making it possible to generate countermodels.

3.1 A Labelling Algebra

We define a set of labels and constraints and a corresponding labelling algebra, that is a partially ordered algebraic system whose elements are denoted by labels.

Definition 5. *A* labelling language L *contains the following symbols: a unit symbol* 1*, a binary function symbol* $\circ$*, a binary relation symbol* $\leq$*, a countable set of constants* $c_1, c_2, \ldots, c_n$*.*

Definition 6. *The* labels *on* L*, the set of which is denoted* $\mathcal{L}_{\mathrm{L}}$ *(or* $\mathcal{L}$*), are inductively defined from the unit* 1*, constants, and expressions of the form* $x \circ y$ *in which* x *and* y *are labels having no common constants.*
Atomic labels *are labels which do not contain any* $\circ$*, as opposed to* compound labels *which contain at least one* $\circ$*.*
Label constraints *on* L*, which we note* $\mathcal{K}_{\mathrm{L}}$ *(or* $\mathcal{K}$*), are expressions of the form* $x \leq y$*, where* x *and* y *are labels. The set* $\mathcal{L}_{\mathrm{L}} \cup \mathcal{K}_{\mathrm{L}}$ *is denoted* $\mathcal{LK}_{\mathrm{L}}$*.*
x *is a* sublabel *of* y *(notation:* $x \preceq y$*), if there exists a label* z *such that* $y = x \circ z$*. We note* $x \prec y$ *if* $x \preceq y$ *and* $x \neq y$*.* $\mathcal{P}(x)$ *denotes the set of the sublabels of* x*.*

Definition 7. *The labels and constraints are interpreted onto a* labelling algebra *in the following way:*

1. $\leq$ *is a preordering*
2. $\circ$ *is a binary operation on* L *satisfying:*
   - *associativity:* $(x \circ y) \circ z \leq x \circ (y \circ z)$ *and* $x \circ (y \circ z) \leq (x \circ y) \circ z$
   - *identity:* $x \circ 1 \leq 1 \circ x \leq 1$ *and* $1 \leq 1 \circ x \leq x \circ 1$
   - *commutativity:* $x \circ y \leq y \circ x$ *and* $y \circ x \leq x \circ y$

– *compatibility:* $x \leq y$ *and* $x' \leq y'$ *implies* $x \circ x' \leq y \circ y'$

Let us define a particular closure operator $\overline{(L, K)}$ on pairs (L, K) of sets of labels and constraints.

Definition 8. *The* closure $\overline{(L, K)}$ *is* $(\overline{L}, \overline{K})$ *that is defined as follows:*
1. $L \subset \overline{L}$ *and* $K \subset \overline{K}$
2. $x \in \overline{L}$ *implies* $\mathcal{P}(x) \subset \overline{L}$
3. $x \leq y \in \overline{K}$ *implies* $x, y \in \overline{L}$
4. $x \in \overline{L}$ *implies* $x \leq x \in \overline{K}$ *(reflexivity)*
5. $x \leq y \in \overline{K}$ *and* $y \leq z \in \overline{K}$ *implies* $x \leq z \in \overline{K}$ *(transitivity)*
6. $x \leq y \in \overline{K}$ *and* $x \circ z \in \overline{L}$ *implies* $x \circ z \leq y \circ z \in \overline{K}$ *(compatibility)*
7. $x \leq y \in \overline{K}$ *and* $y \circ z \in \overline{L}$ *implies* $x \circ z \leq y \circ z \in \overline{K}$ *(compatibility)*

3.2 Labelled Formulae and Configurations

In the LDS approach the basic units of a deductive process are *labelled formulae* with labels in a given labelling algebra [3]. The derivation rules act on the labels as well as on the formulae according to fixed rules of propagation. Let us consider such an approach for the **BI** logic.

Definition 9. *A* (labelled) signed formula *is a triple* $\langle Sg, A, l \rangle$, *denoted* $Sg\ A : l$, Sg *(*$\in \{F, T\}$*) being the sign of the formula* A *(*$\in \mathcal{P}$*) and* l *(*$\in \mathcal{L}$*) its label.*

Definition 10. *An* expansion set Es *is* $\langle Lf(Es), C(Es), Ass(Es), Req(Es) \rangle$ *where* $Lf(Es)$ *is a set of signed formulae built upon a set* $C(Es)$ *of constants,* $Lab(Es)$ *is the set of all labels in* $Lf(Es)$. $Ass(Es)$ *and* $Req(Es)$ *are constraints (on labels) built on* $C(Es)$ *which are respectively called* assertions *and* obligations *of* Es. *A* configuration t *is a set of expansion sets.*

We have distinguished two kinds of constraints. The assertions behave as known facts (or hypothesis) while the obligations express goals that must be satisfied (using assertions if necessary). Now, we define a set of expansion rules for a configuration. For a given configuration t_i, we choose an expansion set on which we apply the corresponding expansion rule and then obtain a new configuration t_{i+1}. For instance for the $(T\ A * B : l)$ signed formula we have the following rule

$$\frac{\langle Lf(T\ A * B : l), C, As, Rq \rangle \qquad c_i, c_j \notin C}{\langle Lf \cup \{T\ A : c_i, T\ B : c_j\}, C \cup \{c_i, c_j\}, As \cup \{c_i \circ c_j \leq l\}, Rq \rangle} *_T$$

that we can simply present as follows (with c_i and c_j being new constants):

$$T\ A * B : x$$

$$\boxed{as : c_i \circ c_j \leq x}$$

$$\begin{array}{c} | \\ T\ A : c_i \\ T\ B : c_j \end{array}$$

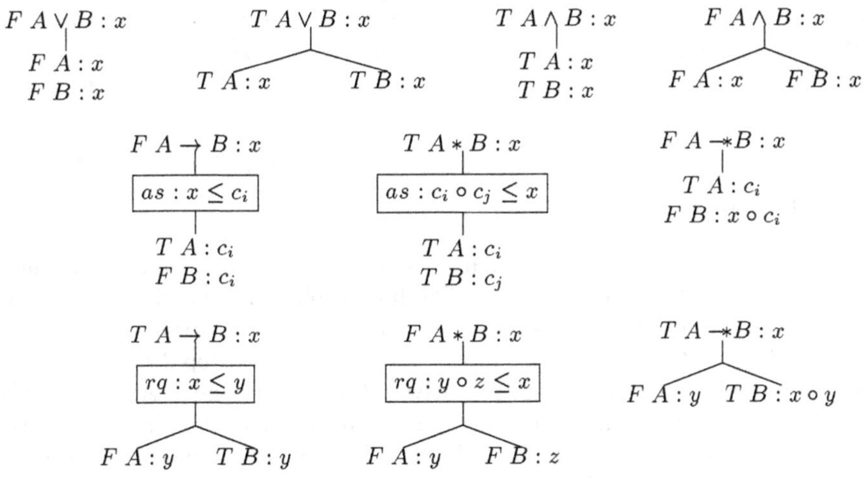

Fig. 2. Tableau Expansion Rules

A **TBI** tableau is in fact a rooted tree with nodes labelled with a signed formula and built according to the expansion rules of figure 2. A tableau is what we have initially called a configuration and a branch of a tableau is an expansion set of this configuration. Let us comment the rules of figure 2. The rules of the first line are the classical α and β rules. The rules of the second line (called $\pi\alpha$ rules) are such that the constants c_i and c_j are new constants and the constraints on labels are *assertions*. The rules of the third line (called $\pi\beta$ rules) are such that the labels y and z only contain existing constants (at the moment of expansion) and the constraints are *obligations*.

Definition 11. *Let A be a proposition of* $\mathbf{BI}^{\perp}$, *a* tableau sequence for A *is a sequence of tableaux (or configurations) $t_1, t_2, \ldots$ for which the initial one is $t_1 = \{\langle \{F\ A : 1\}, \emptyset, \emptyset, \emptyset \rangle\}$ and t_{i+1} is obtained from t_i by application of an expansion rule of figure 2 (on branch of t_i).*

Let us remind that we first expand the $\pi\alpha$ formulae that introduce new constants c_i and c_j and then $\pi\beta$ formulae[2] using such existing constants.

Definition 12. *Let Es be an expansion set, two signed formulae $T\ A : x$, $F\ A : y$ of $Lf(Es)$ are* complementary *in Es if and only if $x \leq y \in \overline{Ass}(Es)$, i.e., if the constraint $x \leq y$ belongs to the reflexive, transitive and compatible closure of the assertion set of Es.*

Definition 13. *A tableau (or configuration) t is* closed *if, for all its branches (or expansion sets) Es,*
1) there are two formulae $T\ A : x$ and $F\ A : y$ that are complementary in Es or

[2] The $\pi\alpha$ (resp. $\pi\beta$) formulae are the initial formulae of the $\pi\alpha$ (resp. $\pi\beta$) rules.

there is $F\ \top : x$ *in* Es *or* $F\ I : x$ *in* Es *with* $1 \leq x \in \overline{Ass}(Es)$ *or* $T\ I : x$ *in* Es *with* $1 \leq x \notin \overline{Ass}(Es)$*; 2)* $\forall x \leq y \in Req(Es)$, $x \leq y \in \overline{Ass}(Es)$.
A tableau sequence $\mathcal{T} = \sqcup_\infty, \sqcup_\in, \ldots$ *is* closed *if it contains at least one closed tableau.*

3.3 An Example

Let us now present the construction of a non-closed tableau for the formula $((A * B) \wedge (A * C)) \mathrel{-\!\!*} (A * (B \wedge C))$. The final tableau is given in figure 3. We begin the expansion with the initial multiplicative $\mathrel{-\!\!*}$, that produces two new formulae $T\ (A * B) \wedge (A * C) : c_1$ and $F\ A * (B \wedge C) : c_1$. Step 2 deals with the additive $\wedge$, and results in two multiplicatives: $T\ A * B : c_1$ and $T\ A * C : c_1$. The expansion of the first $*$ in step 3 introduces two new constants c_2, c_3 and the assertion $as_1 : c_2 \circ c_3 \leq c_1$. The second $*$ is handled in step 4 and introduces two new constants c_4, c_5 together with the assertion $as_2 : c_4 \circ c_5 \leq c_1$.
We are now left with the remaining $\pi\beta$ formula. To expand it, we must match an obligation and find a compound label $y \circ z$ such that $y \circ z \leq c_1$. From the assertions in the branch, we deduce that two instantiations are possible: either $y = c_2$ and $z = c_3$, or $y = c_4$ and $z = c_5$. Both instantiations must be used for the tableau expansion. Step 5 goes on with the first one, namely, $rq_1 : c_2 \circ c_3 \leq c_1$, and splits the tableau into two new branches. The first branch is immediately closed since it contains both $T\ A : c_2$ and $F\ A : c_2$ and one obviously has $c_2 \leq c_2$. The second branch yields a $\wedge$ connective which is immediately expanded in step 6 (remind that α and $\pi\alpha$ formulae have higher precedence than β and $\pi\beta$ formulae) and we obtain two new branches. Once again, the first branch is closed since it contains $\langle T\ B : c_3, F\ B : c_3 \rangle$. The second branch contains a potential connection $\langle T\ C : c_5, F\ C : c_3 \rangle$ but there is no way to prove $c_5 \leq c_3$ from the closure of the assertions that are in the branch. After step 6, there are no more α or $\pi\alpha$ formulae to expand. However, the tableau is not yet completely analyzed because we have not tested the second possibility for the $\pi\beta$ formula, that is $y = c_4$ and $z = c_5$. Therefore, step 7 expands the remaining unclosed branch with this second instantiation and yields a subtree which is similar to the one developed at step 5, except that c_2 and c_3 are respectively replaced by c_4 and c_5. We obtain two closed branches, one with $\langle T\ A : c_4, F\ A : c_4 \rangle$ and another one with $\langle T\ C : c_5, F\ C : c_5 \rangle$. Thus, all formulae have been treated and the fourth branch of the tree is not closed. Indeed, we have two potential connections $\langle T\ B : c_3, F\ B : c_5 \rangle$ and $\langle T\ C : c_5, F\ C : c_3 \rangle$, but neither $c_3 \leq c_5$, nor $c_5 \leq c_3$ can be deduced from the closure of the assertions that are in the branch.

4 Properties of the TBI Calculus

In this section we prove the soundness and completeness of the **TBI** calculus w.r.t. the Kripke resource semantics. It provides not only a procedure for proof construction but also for countermodel generation.

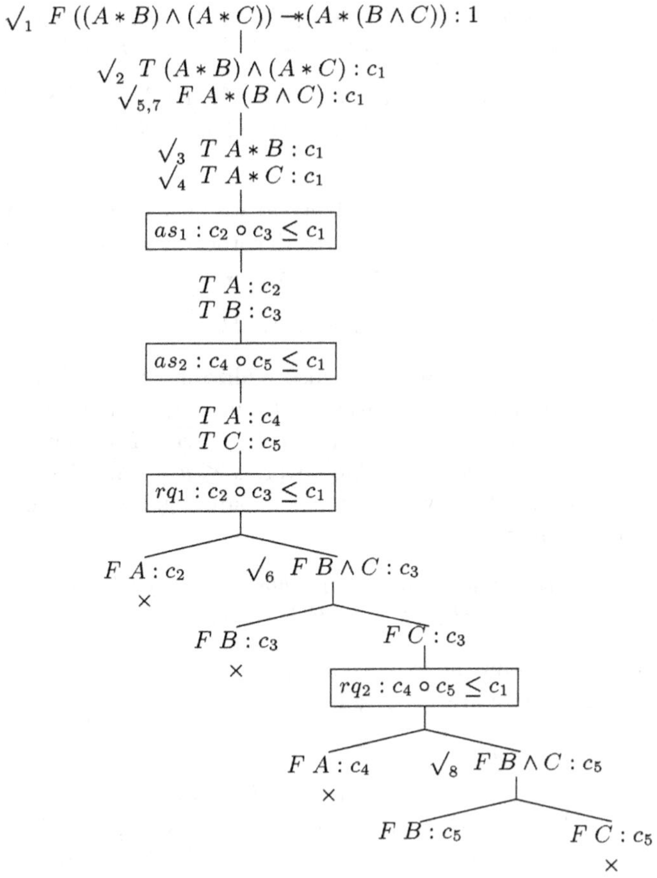

Fig. 3. Tableau for $((A * B) \wedge (A * C)) \mathrel{-\!\!*} (A * (B \wedge C))$

4.1 Soundness

Definition 14. *Let* $\mathcal{I} = \langle M, \bullet, e, \sqsubseteq, \models \rangle$ *be a* **Kri** *and* Es *be an expansion set, an* interpretation of Es in $\mathcal{I}$ *is an application* $\|\_\| : C(Es) \to M$.
An interpretation $\|\_\|$ *can straightforwardly be extended to labels and constraints as follows:* $\|1\| = e$, $\|x \circ y\| = \|x\| \bullet \|y\|$ *and* $\|x \leq y\| = \|x\| \sqsubseteq \|y\|$.
We say that an interpretation $\|\_\|$ *is a* realization of Es in $\mathcal{I}$, *or equivalently, that* $\|\_\|$ realizes Es *in* $\mathcal{I}$, *if:*
a) for any signed formula $T\ A : x$ *in* $Lf(Es)$ $\|x\| \models A$,
b) for any signed formula $F\ A : x$ *in* $Lf(Es)$ $\|x\| \not\models A$,
c) for any $x \leq y$ *in* $Ass(Es)$ $\|x\| \sqsubseteq \|y\|$.

Definition 15. *A branch* Es *is* realizable *if there exists* $\mathcal{I}=\langle M, \bullet, e, \sqsubseteq, \models\rangle$ *and a realization of* Es *in* $\mathcal{I}$. *A tableau* t *is* realizable *if it contains a realizable branch.*

Lemma 1. *Let* t *be a tableau and* Es *a branch of* t, *let* $\mathcal{I} = \langle M, \bullet, e, \sqsubseteq, \models\rangle$ *be a* **Kri** *and* $\|\_\|$ *be a realization of* Es *in* $\mathcal{I}$, *then for all* $x \leq y \in \overline{Ass}(Es)$ *we have* $\|x\| \sqsubseteq \|y\|$.

Proof. By definition, for all $x \leq y$ *in* $Ass(Es)$ we have $\|x\| \sqsubseteq \|y\|$. We have to show that the operation of closure preserves the ordering and it is straightforward because $\sqsubseteq$ is a preorder that is compatible with $\bullet$.

Theorem 3. *A closed tableau cannot be realizable.*

Proof. Let t be a closed tableau that is also realizable. Then, there are $Es \in t$, $\mathcal{I} = \langle M, \bullet, e, \sqsubseteq, \models\rangle$ and $\|\_\|$ a realization of Es in $\mathcal{I}$. By definition of closure on Es we have $T\ A : x$ and $F\ A : y$ such that $x \leq y \in \overline{Ass}(Es)$. Since $\|\_\|$ realizes t we have $\|x\| \models A$ and $\|y\| \not\models A$. Moreover, $x \leq y \in \overline{Ass}(Es)$ implies that $\|x\| \sqsubseteq \|y\|$ by lemma 1. Then, we obtain a contradiction because we should have $\|y\| \models A$ by monotonicity.

Theorem 4. *Let* t *be a tableau and* t' *a tableau obtained from* t *by application an expansion rule, if* t *is realizable then* t' *is realizable .*

Proof. By case analysis on the expansion rule.
Since t is realizable, there are $Es \in t$, $\mathcal{I} = \langle M, \bullet, e, \sqsubseteq, \models\rangle$ and $\|\_\|$ a realization of Es in $\mathcal{I}$.
- Case $T\ A * B : z \in Lf(Es)$;
Es is replaced in t' by a new expansion set Es' such that $Lf(Es') := Lf(Es) \cup \{T\ A : c_i, T\ B : c_j\}$, $Ass(Es') := Ass(Es) \cup \{c_i \circ c_j \leq z\}$, c_i and c_j being new constants. Since $\|\_\|$ realizes Es, we have $\|z\| \models A * B$. Therefore, there are $m, n \in M$ such that $m \bullet n \sqsubseteq \|z\|$ and $m \models A$ and $n \models B$. We extend $\|\_\|$ with $\|c_i\| = m$ and $\|c_j\| = n$. Thus, we obtain $\|c_i\| \models A$ and $\|c_j\| \models B$. Since $\|c_i\| \bullet \|c_j\| \sqsubseteq \|z\|$ is obtained from $\|c_i \circ c_j \leq z\|$, we have that Es' is realizable and, consequently, t' is realizable.
- Case $F\ A * B : z \in Lf(Es)$;
Es is replaced in t' by two new expansion sets Es' and Es'' such that $Lf(Es') := Lf(Es) \cup \{F\ A : x\}$, $Lf(Es'') := Lf(Es) \cup \{F\ B : y\}$ and $Req(Es') = Req(Es'') := Req(Es) \cup \{x \circ y \leq z\}$. A valid application of the $F*$ expansion rule requires that the obligation $x \circ y \leq z$ should be derivable from the closure of the assertions of Es. Thus, $x \circ y \leq z \in \overline{Ass}(Es)$ and lemma 1 imply $\|x\| \bullet \|y\| \sqsubseteq \|z\|$. Since $\|\_\|$ realizes Es, we have $\|z\| \not\models A * B$. Therefore, for all $m, n \in M$ such that $m \bullet n \sqsubseteq \|z\|$, either $m \not\models A$, or $n \not\models B$ which implies that either $\|x\| \not\models A$ or $\|y\| \not\models B$. Then, either Es', or Es'' is realized by $\|\_\|$ and we can conclude that t' is realizable.
- The other cases are similar.

Corollary 3. *Let* $\mathcal{T} = \sqcup_\infty, \sqcup_\in, \ldots, \sqcup_\backslash$ *be a tableau sequence, if* t_i *is realizable then, for* $j > i$, t_j *is realizable.*

Theorem 5 (soundness). *Let A a formula of* $\mathbf{BI}^{\perp}$ *if there exists a closed tableau $\mathcal{T}$ for A, then A is valid in Kripke resource semantics.*

Proof. Let $\mathcal{T} = \sqcup_{\infty}, \sqcup_{\in}, \ldots, \sqcup_{\setminus}$ be a closed tableau sequence. Let us suppose that A does not hold in Kripke resource semantics. Then, by corollary 2, there exists a **Kri** $\mathcal{I} = \langle M, \bullet, e, \sqsubseteq, \models \rangle$ such that $e \not\models A$.
Then, the configuration $t_1 = \{ \langle \{ F\ A : 1 \}, \emptyset, \emptyset, \emptyset \rangle \}$ is realizable. But theorem 4 implies that all t_i, for $i > 1$, are also realizable. It follows from theorem 3 that none of the t_i can be closed and consequently $\mathcal{T}$ cannot be closed.

4.2 A Tableau Construction Procedure

We introduce the notion of *completed* branch [3] for the **TBI** calculus. Moreover, we define what a *redundant* branch is and propose a procedure that builds a non-redundant tableau for a given formula A in a finite number of steps.

Definition 16. *Let Es be a tableau branch,*
a signed formula $F\ X : x$ is fulfilled *(or* completely analyzed*) in Es if*

1. *$X \equiv A \wedge B$ and either $F\ A : x \in Es$, or $F\ B : x \in Es$*
2. *$X \equiv A \vee B$ and both $F\ A : x \in Es$ and $F\ B : x \in Es$*
3. *$X \equiv A \to B$ and there exists y such that $x \leq y \in \overline{Ass}(Es)$ and both $T\ A : y \in Es$ and $F\ B : y \in Es$*
4. *$X \equiv A * B$ and for all y, z such that $y \circ z \leq x \in \overline{Ass}(Es)$ either $F\ A : y \in Es$, or $F\ B : z \in Es$*
5. *$X \equiv A \mathrel{-\!\!*} B$ and there exists y such that $x \circ y \in \overline{Lab}(Es)$ and both $T\ A : y \in Es$ and $F\ B : x \circ y \in Es$*

and a signed formula $T\ X : x$ is fulfilled *in Es if*

1. *$X \equiv A \wedge B$ and both $T\ A : x \in Es$ and $T\ B : x \in Es$*
2. *$X \equiv A \vee B$ and either $T\ A : x \in Es$, or $T\ B : x \in Es$*
3. *$X \equiv A \to B$ and for all y such that $x \leq y \in \overline{Ass}(Es)$ either $F\ A : y \in Es$, or $T\ B : y \in Es$*
4. *$X \equiv A * B$ and there exists y, z such that $y \circ z \leq x \in \overline{Ass}(Es)$ and both $T\ A : y \in Es$ and $T\ B : z \in Es$*
5. *$X \equiv A \mathrel{-\!\!*} B$ and for all y such that $x \circ y \in \overline{Lab}(Es)$ either $F\ A : y \in Es$, or $T\ B : x \circ y \in Es$*

Definition 17. *A tableau branch Es is* completed *if every labelled signed formula $Sg\ A : x$ in Es is fulfilled. A tableau is* completed *if it has a branch that is completed. A tableau branch Es is a* H-branch *if it is open and completed.*

Definition 18. *A tableau branch Es is* redundant *if it contains a signed formula $T\ C \mathrel{-\!\!*} D : x$ which has been expanded with a label $y \circ c_i$, where the constant c_i has been introduced by a signed formula $F\ A \mathrel{-\!\!*} B : x \circ y$ which derives from a previous expansion of $T\ C \mathrel{-\!\!*} D : x$ with the label y. Such a signed formula $T\ C \mathrel{-\!\!*} D : x$ that has been redundantly expanded in the branch Es is called a* redundant $T \mathrel{-\!\!*}$ formula.

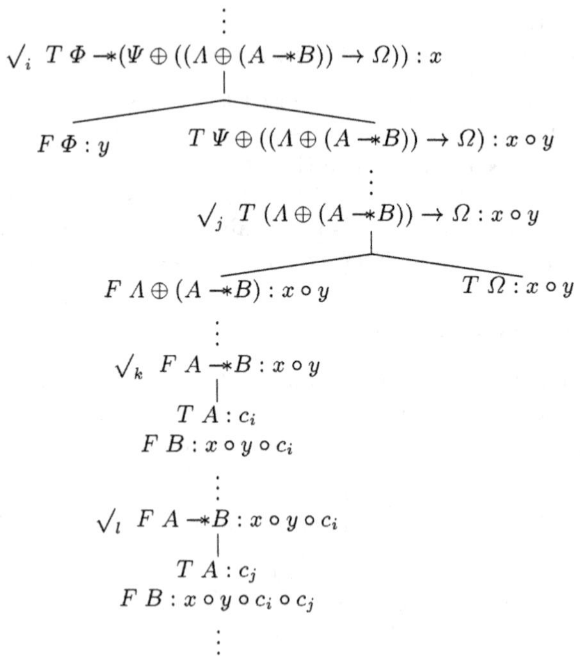

Fig. 4. Schema of a redundant branch

The notion of redundancy is illustrated in figure 4 that presents the general situation in which a branch can grow infinitely. The symbol $\oplus$ represents an additive conjunction or disjunction. Similarly, Ψ and Λ are formulae whose outermost connectives are either additive conjunction or disjunction. In the tableau, we can see that the step i expands a formula of type $T \mathrel{-\!\!*}$ with a label y to achieve fulfillment of the formula. Then, step k expands a formula of type $F \mathrel{-\!\!*}$ which derives from the preceding expansion (after a given number of successive expansions), introducing, by the way, a new constant c_i and new label $x \circ y \circ c_i$. Therefore, to retain fulfillment for the root formula, we are obliged to apply an expansion step with label $y \circ c_i$. It results in a redundant tableau since we already have expanded the tableau with label y and c_i has been introduced by the formula $F\ A \mathrel{-\!\!*} B : x \circ y$ which is derived from $T\ \Phi \mathrel{-\!\!*}(\Psi \oplus ((\Lambda \oplus (A \mathrel{-\!\!*} B)) \rightarrow \Omega)) : x$. If such a redundant expansion is performed then we obtain an infinite branch with the creation of new constants $c_j, c_k, \ldots$ and new labels $x \circ y \circ c_j$, $x \circ y \circ c_j \circ c_k, \ldots$. In the rest of the section, we will respectively note $c_{i1}, c_{i2}, \ldots, c_{ij}$ the copies of the initial constant c_i that are introduced by redundant expansion steps.

Definition 19. *A tableau sequence $\mathcal{T}$ is* redundant *if it contains a tableau that has at least one redundant branch. Otherwise, it is said* non-redundant.

A tableau construction procedure is an algorithm which, given a formula A, builds a tableau sequence $t_1, t_2, \ldots, t_n$ until there exists a tableau t_i that is either closed or with a H-branch. Otherwise it does not terminate.

Let us give a procedure that builds a tableau sequence $\mathcal{T}$ including a non-redundant tableau.

The initial signed formula is $F\ A : 1$.
Repeat until $\mathcal{T}$ is closed or completed

- choose an open branch Es
- **if** there is a unfulfilled α or $\pi\alpha$ formula $(Sg\ A : x)$ in Es
  then apply the corresponding expansion rule to it
  else if there is an unfulfilled β or $\pi\beta$ formula $(Sg\ A : x)$ in Es, on which one can apply an expansion rule without building a redundant tableau,
  then apply the corresponding expansion rule, with all labels for which the formula is not fulfilled.

Theorem 6. *This procedure that builds a non-redundant tableau terminates (in finitely many steps).*

Proof. To prove the termination, we must show that any expansion step performed by the procedure provides a closed tableau, or a completed tableau, or a redundant tableau. For that, we show that if a branch is open then it cannot be expanded without reaching a step where it is completed or redundant. We can define a measure of complexity of a branch as the sum of the complexities of all its signed formulae and the complexity of a signed formula is defined from the syntactic complexity of the formula and the number of labels for which it is unfulfilled. Another way to achieve termination could be to use liberalized versions of the $\pi\alpha$ rules, as explained in [3]. The $\pi\alpha$ rules require new constants and liberalized rules allow us, under given conditions, to reuse constants which have previously been introduced. Thus, they provide a way to control the syntactic complexity of the labels. For example, when expanding $F\ A \to B : x$, one can simply infer $F\ B : x$, instead of introducing a new constant c such that $x \leq c$, if there already exists $T\ A : y$ with $y \leq x$ in the branch. Similar considerations can be applied to the other $\pi\alpha$ rules.

4.3 Countermodel Construction

In this subsection, we describe how to construct a countermodel of A from a H-branch in a tableau for A.

Definition 20. *Let Es be a H-branch, the structure $\mathcal{M}(Es)$ associated to Es is defined by $\mathcal{M}(Es) = \langle M, \bullet, 1, \sqsubseteq \rangle$ where*
i) M is the set $\overline{Lab}(Es)$ extended with a particular element denoted by π.
ii) $\bullet$ is a composition law defined by

$$\begin{cases} x \bullet 1 = 1 \bullet x = x & \\ x \bullet y = y \bullet x = x \circ y & \text{if } x \circ y \in \overline{Lab}(Es) \\ x \bullet y = y \bullet x = \pi & \text{otherwise} \end{cases}$$

iii) the relation $\sqsubseteq$ between elements of M is defined by

$$x \sqsubseteq y \text{ if and only if } x = y = \pi \text{ or } x \leq y \in \overline{Ass}(Es)$$

Lemma 2. *Let Es be a H-branch and $\mathcal{M}(Es) = \langle M, \bullet, 1, \sqsubseteq \rangle$ the M-structure associated to Es, then $\mathcal{M}(Es)$ is a Kripke resource monoid.*

Proof. It is straightforward to show that $\bullet$ is a monoidal law on M. $\sqsubseteq$ is a preordering because of the reflexivity and transitivity of the set of assertions and it is compatible with the monoidal law $\bullet$ because of the closure operations performed on the assertion set.

Definition 21. *Let Es be a H-branch and $\mathcal{M}(Es) = \langle M, \bullet, 1, \sqsubseteq \rangle$ be the* **Krm** *built from Es, a forcing relation $\models_{Es}$ on $M \times \mathcal{A}$, where $\mathcal{A}$ is the set of atomic propositions that occur in Es, is defined as follows: 1) $\pi \models A$, 2) if $T\ A : x \in Es$ then $x \models A$ and 3) if $y \models A$ and $y \leq x \in \overline{Ass}(Es)$ then $x \models A$.*

Lemma 3. *Let Es be a H-branch, $\mathcal{M}(Es) = \langle M, \bullet, 1, \sqsubseteq \rangle$ be the* **Krm** *built from Es and the forcing relation $\models_{Es}$, the following properties hold:*
i) for any formula A, we have $\pi \models A$.
ii) $\langle M, \bullet, 1, \sqsubseteq, \models_{Es} \rangle$ is a model of Es, i.e., $T\ A : x \in Es$ implies $x \models A$ and $F\ A : x \in Es$ implies $x \not\models A$.

Proof. see in appendix A.

Theorem 7. *If Es is a H-branch then it has a Kripke resource model.*

Proof. Let us consider the previous intermediate lemmas. Lemma 2 shows how to build a Kripke resource monoid from the information that is in the set $\overline{Ass}(Es)$ of a H-branch. Lemma 3 allows to define a forcing relation on such a monoid to obtain a model of each labelled formula in the H-branch. The final result can be directly deduced.

4.4 Completeness and Finite Model Property

Theorem 8 (completeness). *If A is a proposition of* $\mathbf{BI}^{\perp}$ *which is valid in Kripke resource semantics, then there exists a closed tableau for A.*

Proof. Let us suppose that there is no closed tableau for A. Then, there exists a tableau for A which contains a H-branch from which we can build a model in which A is not satisfied.

In order to analyze the finite model property, we observe that we have the following result for a redundant H-branch Es.

Theorem 9. *If Es is a redundant H-branch then it has a finite Kripke resource model.*

Proof. see in appendix B.

Theorem 10. *If there is a tableau for A which contains a H-branch, then there is a model in which A is not satisfied. Moreover if the branch is finite then the model is finite.*

Proof. From a H-branch Es, redundant or not, we can build a model (see previous results). It is obvious by the construction that the model is finite if Es is finite.

Let us suppose there is no closed tableau for A. The procedure of construction of a non-redundant tableau yields a tableau for A which contains a finite H-branch (cf. termination result) from which we can construct a finite model in which A is not satisfied. Then, for a given A as input, the procedure yields either a closed tableau for A or a tableau for A which contains a H-branch, from which we can build a finite countermodel of A. Then we have the following result: $\mathbf{BI}^{\perp}$ has the finite model property with respect to Kripke resource semantics.

4.5 Extraction of a Countermodel

Let us consider the formula $((A*B)\wedge(A*C)) \multimap\!\!* (A*(B\wedge C))$ and its complete tableau expansion given in figure 3. It contains an open branch, which means that the formula is not provable. Since all formulae in the open branch are fulfilled, we have a finite H-branch Es. We can therefore extract the corresponding countermodel following the steps of the completeness proof.
First, we associate a Kripke resource monoid structure to $\overline{Ass}(Es)$ and add a particular element π. The monoidal law $\bullet$ is given by the following table:

$\bullet$	1	c_1	c_2	c_3	c_4	c_5	$c_2 \circ c_3$	$c_4 \circ c_5$	π
1	1	c_1	c_2	c_3	c_4	c_5	$c_2 \circ c_3$	$c_4 \circ c_5$	π
c_1	c_1	π	π	π	π	π	π	π	π
c_2	c_2	π	π	$c_2 \circ c_3$	π	π	π	π	π
c_3	c_3	π	$c_2 \circ c_3$	π	π	π	π	π	π
c_4	c_4	π	π	π	π	$c_4 \circ c_5$	π	π	π
c_5	c_5	π	π	π	$c_4 \circ c_5$	π	π	π	π
$c_2 \circ c_3$	$c_2 \circ c_3$	π	π	π	π	π	π	π	π
$c_4 \circ c_5$	$c_4 \circ c_5$	π	π	π	π	π	π	π	π
π	π	π	π	π	π	π	π	π	π

The preordering relation $\sqsubseteq$ is simply embodied by the relation $\leq$ in $\overline{Ass}(Es)$ and the atomic forcing relation $\models$ is defined as follows:

1	c_1	c_2	c_3	c_4	c_5	$c_2 \circ c_3$	$c_4 \circ c_5$	π
–	–	A	B	A	C	–	–	A, B, C

Now, we observe that $c_1 \models (A*B)\wedge(A*C)$. Indeed, from $c_2 \models A$ and $c_3 \models B$, we deduce $c_2 \bullet c_3 \models A*B$ and since $c_1 \sqsubseteq c_2 \bullet c_3$ we have by Kripke monotonicity, $c_1 \models A*B$. A similar analysis on c_4 and c_5 yields the second component of $\wedge$, namely, $c_1 \models A*C$. But, we have $c_1 \not\models A*(B\wedge C)$ because $B\wedge C$ is not forced by any world, other than π, and no world in relation with c_1 can be obtained from a composition involving π. Therefore, we have a countermodel of $((A*B)\wedge(A*C)) \multimap\!\!* (A*(B\wedge C))$.

5 Conclusion

In this paper we have designed a labelled tableau calculus for the propositional **BI** logic. This new logic has been recently studied as an assertion language for reasoning about mutable data structures [8]. It could be seen as a logical foundation for new specification logics, in order to specify and prove particular properties of programs or systems. Our labelled calculus for **BI** yields not only proofs for theorems but also countermodels for non-theorems. The resulting countermodels are finite and thus, in addition to the completeness of the calculus, we have proved the finite model property for **BI** with respect to the Kripke resource semantics. Our approach is based on this semantics and on the methodology of LDS for analytic deduction [3], that has been recently used for MILL and a simple semantics [14]. Labels and constraints are appropriate for proof-search in such a mixed logic, as observed in previous work in Mixed Linear Logic [6], in order to take into account the interaction between both kinds of connectives. In further work we will study the representation and resolution of constraints during the tableau construction and also the extraction of countermodels. We will define another labelled calculus with free variables in labels and also a related connection-based characterization of provability in **BI**. The restriction of our calculus to IL and MILL will provide new proof-search procedures for both logics that we will study. Finally, we will develop a similar method with countermodel generation in **BI** (with $\perp$) but starting from Grothendieck sheaf-theoretic models [12].

References

1. P.A. Armelin and D. Pym. Bunched logic programming (extended abstract). In *First International Joint Conference on Automated Reasoning, IJCAR 2001, LNCS 2083*, pages 289–304, Siena, Italy, 2001.
2. V. Balat and D. Galmiche. *Labelled Deduction*, volume 17 of *Applied Logic Series*, chapter Labelled Proof Systems for Intuitionistic Provability. Kluwer Academic Publishers, 2000.
3. M. D'Agostino and D.M. Gabbay. A Generalization of Analytic Deduction via Labelled Deductive Systems. Part I: Basic substructural logics. *Journal of Automated Reasoning*, 13:243–281, 1994.
4. D. Galmiche. Connection Methods in Linear Logic and Proof nets Construction. *Theoretical Computer Science*, 232(1-2):231–272, 2000.
5. D. Galmiche and D. Larchey-Wendling. Structural sharing and efficient proof-search in propositional intuitionistic logic. In *Asian Computing Science Conference, ASIAN'99, LNCS 1742*, pages 101–112, Phuket, Thailand, December 1999.
6. D. Galmiche and J.M. Notin. Proof-search and proof nets in mixed linear logic. *Electronic Notes in Theoretical Computer Science*, 37, 2000.
7. J.Y. Girard. Linear logic: its syntax and semantics. In J.Y. Girard, Y. Lafont, and L. Regnier, editors, *Advances in Linear Logic*, pages 1–42. Cambridge University Press, 1995.
8. S. Ishtiaq and P. O'Hearn. Bi as an assertion language for mutable data structures. In *28th ACM Symposium on Principles of Programming Languages, POPL 2001*, pages 14–26, London, UK, 2001.

9. H. Mantel and J. Otten. linTAP : A tableau prover for linear logic. In *Int. Conference TABLEAUX'99, LNCS 1617*, pages 216–231, Saratoga Springs, NY, USA, 1999.
10. R.K. Meyer, M.A. McRobbie, and N. Belnap. Linear analytic tableaux. In *Theorem proving with analytic tableaux and related methods, TABLEAUX'95, LNCS 918*, pages 278–293, St Goar am Rhein, Germany, 1995.
11. P. O'Hearn. Resource interpretations, bunched implications and the $\alpha\lambda$-calculus. In *Typed Lambda Calculi and Applications, TLCA'99, LNCS 581*, pages 258–279, L'Aquila, Italy, 1999.
12. P.W. O'Hearn and D. Pym. The logic of bunched implications. *Bulletin of Symbolic Logic*, 5(2):215–244, 1999.
13. D. Pym. On bunched predicate logic. In *14h Symposium on Logic in Computer Science*, pages 183–192, Trento, Italy, July 1999. IEEE Computer Society Press.
14. K. Terui. Labelled tableau calculi generating simple models for substructural logics. Technical report, ILLC publications, University of Amsterdam, 1999.
15. A. Urquhart. Semantics for relevant logic. *Journal of Symbolic Logic*, 37:159–169, 1972.

A Proof of Lemma 3

Lemma 3.
Let Es be a H-branch, $\mathcal{M}(Es) = \langle M, \bullet, 1, \sqsubseteq \rangle$ be the **Krm** *built from Es and the forcing relation $\models_{Es}$, the following properties hold:*
i) for any formula A, we have $\pi \models A$.
ii) $\langle M, \bullet, 1, \sqsubseteq, \models_{Es} \rangle$ is a model of Es.

Proof. We prove i) by induction on the degree of A.

- if A is atomic then, by definition, $\pi \models A$
- if $A \equiv B \wedge C$ then, by induction hypothesis, we have $\pi \models B$ and $\pi \models C$, and therefore, $\pi \models B \wedge C$.
- if $A \equiv B \vee C$ then, by induction hypothesis, we have $\pi \models B$ and therefore, $\pi \models B \vee C$.
- if $A \equiv B \to C$ then, by induction hypothesis, we have $\pi \models C$. Since no x in M other than π verifies $\pi \leq x$, we have $\pi \models B \to C$.
- if $A \equiv B \mathrel{-\!\!*} C$, then by induction hypothesis, we have $\pi \models C$. Since $\pi \bullet x = \pi$ whatever x in M, we have $\pi \models B \mathrel{-\!\!*} C$.
- if $A \equiv B * C$, then by induction hypothesis, we have $\pi \models B$ and $\pi \models C$. Since $\pi \bullet \pi = \pi$, we have $\pi \models B * C$.

We prove ii) by induction on the degree of the formula $Sg\ A : x$ in Es.

- if $T\ A : x \in Es$ and A is atomic then, by definition, $x \models A$.
- if $F\ A : x \in Es$ and A is atomic then, since Es is an H-branch, it cannot contain an occurrence of $T\ A : x$ at the same time. Moreover, since x cannot be π, we have $x \not\models A$.
- if $T\ B \wedge C : x \in Es$ then, since Es is a H-branch, both $T\ B : x \in Es$ and $T\ C : x \in Es$. By induction hypothesis, it follows that $x \models B$ and $x \models C$. Thus, $x \models B \wedge C$.

- if $F\ B \wedge C : x \in Es$ then, since Es is a H-branch, either $F\ B : x \in Es$, or $F\ C : x \in Es$. By induction hypothesis, it follows that either $x \not\models B$, or $x \not\models C$. Thus, $x \not\models B \wedge C$.
- case $T\ B \vee C : x \in Es$ is similar to case $F\ B \wedge C : x \in Es$
- case $F\ B \vee C : x \in Es$ is similar to case $T\ B \wedge C : x \in Es$
- if $T\ B \rightarrow C : x \in Es$ then, since Es is a H-branch, for all y in $\overline{Lab}(Es)$ such that $x \leq y \in \overline{Ass}(Es)$ we have either $F\ B : y \in Es$ or $T\ C : y \in Es$. Since $x \leq y$ implies $x \sqsubseteq y$, it follows from induction hypothesis that for all $y \in M$ such that $x \sqsubseteq y$, either $y \not\models B$ or $y \models C$. Thus, $x \models B \rightarrow C$.
- if $F\ B \rightarrow C : x \in Es$, then since Es is a H-branch, there exists y in $\overline{Ass}(Es)$ such that $x \leq y \in \overline{Ass}(Es)$ and both $F\ B : y \in Es$ and $T\ C : y \in Es$. It follows from induction hypothesis that there exists $y \in M$ such that $x \leq y$ and both $y \models B$ and $y \not\models C$. Thus, $x \not\models B \rightarrow C$.
- if $T\ B \mathrel{-\!\!*} C : x \in Es$, let $y \in M$. Suppose $x \circ y \in \overline{Ass}(Es)$ then $x \bullet y = x \circ y$ and since Es is a H-branch, we have that, for all y in $\overline{Ass}(Es)$ such that $x \circ y \in \overline{Ass}(Es)$, either $F\ B : y \in Es$ or $T\ C : x \circ y \in Es$. By induction hypothesis, it follows that either $y \not\models B$, or $x \bullet y \models C$. Suppose $x \circ y \notin \overline{Ass}(Es)$, then $x \bullet y = \pi$. By property i), we can conclude that $\pi \models C$. Therefore, we have shown that for all $y \in M$, either $y \not\models B$ or $x \bullet y \models C$, that is, $x \models B \mathrel{-\!\!*} C$.
- if $F\ B \mathrel{-\!\!*} C : x \in Es$ then, since Es is a H-branch, there exists y in $\overline{Ass}(Es)$ such that $x \circ y$ is in $\overline{Ass}(Es)$ and both $T\ B : y \in Es$ and $F\ C : x \circ y \in Es$. By induction hypothesis, it follows that $y \models B$ and $x \circ y \not\models C$. As $x \circ y \in \overline{Ass}(Es)$ implies $x \bullet y = x \circ y$, we have $x \bullet y \not\models C$, and thus $x \not\models B \mathrel{-\!\!*} C$.
- case $T\ B * C : x \in Es$ is similar to case $F\ B \rightarrow C : x \in Es$
- case $F\ B * C : x \in Es$ is similar to case $T\ B \rightarrow C : x \in Es$

B Proof of Theorem 9

Theorem 9.
A redundant H-branch Es has a finite Kripke resource model.

Proof. The proof is by induction on the number of redundant $T \mathrel{-\!\!*}$ formulae in the H-branch. Such formulae require an infinite number of elements of the monoid to be satisfied.
Base case: if there is no redundant formula, then Es is a finite H-branch and by theorem 7 we have a finite Kripke resource model of the H-branch.
Induction case: we assume that the proposition holds for any redundant H-branch with less than n redundant $T \mathrel{-\!\!*}$ formulae. Let us select a redundant $T \mathrel{-\!\!*}$ formula in the H-branch. Since the H-branch is redundant, it has the form given in figure 4 and is infinite. In this case, theorem 7 provides an infinite Kripke resource model $\mathcal{M}(Es)$ for the H-branch. The situation in $\mathcal{M}(Es)$ is the following:

$\boxed{x \circ y}$ $\quad$ $\boxed{x \circ y \circ c_i}\ F\ B$ $\quad$ $\boxed{x \circ y \circ c_i \circ c_{i1}}\ F\ B$ $\quad$ $\boxed{x \circ y \circ c_i \circ c_{i1} \circ c_{i2}}\ F\ B$

$\boxed{c_i}\ T\ A$ $\quad$ $\boxed{c_{i1}}\ T\ A$ $\quad$ $\boxed{c_{i2}}\ T\ A$ $\quad \cdots$

The infinite regression uses an infinity of copies of c_i to satisfy the $T \twoheadrightarrow$ formula. Let us now explain how to transform $\mathcal{M}(Es)$ into a Kripke resource model $\mathcal{M}'(Es)$ in which only a finite number of copies of c_i are used while preserving the property of being a model of the H-branch Es.
We define the composition $\times$ on $\mathcal{M}'(Es)$ as follows: $a \times b = x \circ y \circ c_i$ if $a \bullet b = x \circ y \circ c_i \circ c_{i1}$ and $a \bullet b$ otherwise. In fact, we have replaced each occurrence of $x \circ y \circ c_i \circ c_{i1}$ in the table of $\bullet$ by $x \circ y \circ c_i$. The fact that $\mathcal{M}(Es)$ is a monoid and that we have replaced all occurrences at the same time is enough to ensure that $\mathcal{M}'(Es)$ remains a monoid. But, since the element $x \circ y \circ c_i \circ c_{i1}$ can no longer be obtained in $\mathcal{M}'(Es)$, we can remove it from the monoid and also all the elements that depend on it, that is, all subsequent copies c_{i2},c_{i3},....
The situation in $\mathcal{M}'(Es)$ then becomes the following:

$$\boxed{x \circ y} \qquad \boxed{x \circ y \circ c_i}\, F\ B$$

$$\boxed{c_i}\, T\ A \qquad \boxed{c_{i1}}\, T\ A$$

We only keep one copy c_{i1} of c_i, meaning that all other copies are equivalent to the original one. It remains to show that $\mathcal{M}'(Es)$ is a Kripke resource model of the $\pi\beta$ formulae of Es. Since we only change the monoidal law, the only formulae that may be affected are the ones that involve the composition of the resources, that are the ones of type $T \twoheadrightarrow$ and $F*$.
Let us consider the formulae $F\ A * B : z$, knowing that the other case is similar. If z does not contain c_i or copies c_{ij} then the result is immediate because $\times$ behaves like $\bullet$ and $z \not\models A * B$ in $\mathcal{M}(Es)$. Otherwise, z contains c_i and copies of c_i. All these copies reduce to c_{i1} in $\mathcal{M}'(Es)$. Moreover, since z contains c_i, all copies are absorbed by c_i as prescribed in the definition of $\times$. Thus, we need to show that $x \circ y \circ c_i \not\models A * B$ in $\mathcal{M}'(Es)$. Compared with what happens in $\mathcal{M}(Es)$, the difference is that $x \circ y \circ c_i$ can also be obtained from compositions $u \times v$ such that u and v possibly contain copies of c_i. But, we necessarily have either $u \not\models A$ or $v \not\models B$, otherwise we would have $u \bullet v \models A * B$ in $\mathcal{M}(Es)$, which is impossible because $\mathcal{M}(Es)$ is a Kripke resource model. Thus, we have a H-branch Es which contains one less $T \twoheadrightarrow$ redundant formula that requires an infinite set of elements to be satisfied. The induction hypothesis can therefore be applied and we conclude that Es has a model.

Generation of a Linear Time Query Processing Algorithm Based on Well-Quasi-Orders

Mizuhito Ogawa

Japan Science and Technology Corporation, PRESTO, and
NTT Communication Science Laboratories,
3-1 Morinosato-Wakamiya Atsugi Kanagawa, 243-0198 Japan,
mizuhito@theory.brl.ntt.co.jp
http://www.brl.ntt.co.jp/people/mizuhito/

Abstract. This paper demonstrates the generation of a linear time query processing algorithm based on the constructive proof of Higman's lemma described by Murthy-Russell (IEEE LICS 1990). A linear time evaluation of a fixed disjunctive monadic query in an indefinite database on a linearly ordered domain, first posed by Van der Meyden (ACM PODS 1992), is used as an example. Van der Meyden showed the existence of a linear time algorithm, but an actual construction has, until now, not been published elsewhere.

1 Introduction

Temporal databases, which are the databases of events on the linearly ordered domain, have attracted attention from early 90's, and the complexity of evaluating various queries has been analyzed [1,8]. One of important issues is a query on indefinite database, i.e., processing a query whether all possible models of incomplete (partial) information hold it. Van der Meyden showed that the complexity of evaluating a conjunctive (n-ary) query containing inequalities is Π_2^p-complete [18], solving an open problem.

He also investigated tractable subclasses; for instance, a fixed monadic query can be evaluated in linear time (to the size of a database)[1]. However, for a fixed monadic disjunctive query, he only showed the existence of a linear time query processing algorithm, and an actual construction was not given. His (non-constructive) proof of the existence is based on Higman's lemma, which states that the embedding relation on finite words is a Well-Quasi-Order (WQO). Under a WQO, minimal elements of any set are guaranteed to be finitely many, and the linear time algorithm is constructed as to the comparison with these finitely many minimal elements (called *minors*).

This situation frequently appears in the upper bound complexity estimation based on WQO techniques. For instance, the Graph Minor Theorem states that the embedding relation on finite graphs is a WQO [14], and this implies the existence of square time algorithms for a wide range of graph problems [3,15,12].

[1] Either fixing a query or restricting to a monadic query remains in co-NP.

N. Kobayashi and B.C. Pierce (Eds.): TACS 2001, LNCS 2215, pp. 283–297, 2001.

Difficulty is; one could compute minors by brute force manner, but how one could know whether all have been found. Fortunately, we know constructive proofs of Higman's lemma [9,13,2], and what we expect is how to apply them.

In this paper, we describe the generation of a linear time query processing algorithm of a fixed disjunctive monadic query in an indefinite database over a linearly ordered domain. This problem is first posed by Van der Meyden in [18], and has, until now, not been published elsewhere. Our method will effectively compute minors for a given disjunctive monadic query, using the regular expression techniques appeared in Murthy-Russell's constructive proof of Higman's lemma [9], and thus will lead a linear time query processing algorithm.

This paper is organized as follows: Section 2 briefly outlines the problem. Section 3 reviews the results of query processing in an indefinite database [18]. Section 4 gives the constructive proof of Higman's lemma [9] and its extension. Section 5 proposes linear time algorithm generation for fixed disjunctive monadic query processing in an indefinite database. Section 6 concludes the paper.

2 A Tour

In this section, to get a basic feeling for our method, we introduce a simpler version of the target example. A complete description is included in Section 3.

Let x and y be lists, and let $sublst(x, y)$ be a predicate which returns *true* if x is a sublist of y. It returns *false* otherwise. More rigorously, we can write in Haskell as:

```
sublst :: [a] -> [a] -> Bool
sublst    []      ys   = true
sublst  x:xs      []   = false
sublst (x:xs) (y:ys)   = if x == y then sublst xs ys
                                   else sublst (x:xs) ys
```

Let us consider an easy problem. Fix a list x.

- **Input**: A finite set of lists $\bar{y} = \{y_1, \cdots, y_t\}$.
- **Output**: A decision as to whether $sublst(x, z)$ holds for each list z with $\wedge_{j=1}^{t} sublst(y_j, z)$.

This problem can be regarded a query as follows: we know partial information on events (which exclusively occur), and this partial information is represented as a set of lists y_j's. Then, *can we decide whether there exists an event sequence represented as x?*

This problem is simply solved by computing $sublst(x, y_j)$ for each y_j, and if some $sublst(x, y_j)$ returns *true* then it holds; otherwise it does not hold.

Now we consider two extensions: (simplified versions of) conjunctive query and disjunctive query. The conjunctive query is as follows: fix finite number of lists, $x_1, \cdots, x_s$.

- **Input**: A finite set of lists $\bar{y} = \{y_1, \cdots, y_t\}$.

- **Output**: A decision as to whether $\wedge_{i=1}^{s} sublst(x_i, z)$ holds for each list z with $\wedge_{j=1}^{t} sublst(y_j, z)$.

This is still easy; this problem is decomposed into the check on each x_i, i.e., whether for each x_i, $sublst(x_i, y_j)$ for some y_j holds [18].

However, the disjunctive query is much harder. The disjunctive query is formalized as follows: fix finite number of lists, $x_1, \cdots, x_s$.

- **Input**: A finite set of lists $\bar{y} = \{y_1, \cdots, y_t\}$.
- **Output**: A decision as to whether $\vee_{i=1}^{s} sublst(x_i, z)$ holds for each list z with $\wedge_{j=1}^{t} sublst(y_j, z)$.

Finding an efficient solution (a linear time algorithm) for this problem is not as easy as it appears. To illustrate, consider $x_1 = [P, Q, R]$, $x_2 = [Q, R, P]$, and $x_3 = [R, P, Q]$. This holds for $y_1 = [P, Q]$, $y_2 = [Q, R]$, and $y_3 = [R, P]$, even though none of x_i's and y_j's hold $sublst(x_i, y_j)$.

Of course, if one computes every possible combination of z, a decision is possible, but this requires an exponentially greater amount of time. For instance, for lists $y_1, \cdots, y_t$ of lengths $n_1, \cdots, n_s$, the number of combinations is $(n_1 + \cdots + n_t)!/(n_1! \times \cdots \times n_t!)$, which grows exponentially.

The aim of the paper is to generate the linear time algorithm for a given disjunctive query. In our method, a suitable finite set $\mathcal{M}$ of finite set of lists, called *minors* is generated corresponding to given x_i's. Namely, for the example $x_1 = [P, Q, R]$, $x_2 = [Q, R, P]$, and $x_3 = [R, P, Q]$ above,

$$\mathcal{M} = \left\{ \begin{array}{l} \{[P,Q],[Q,R],[R,P]\}, \{[P,Q,R]\}, \{[Q,R,P]\}, \{[R,P,Q]\}, \\ \{[P,Q,P],[Q,R]\}, \{[Q,R,Q],[R,P]\}, \{[R,P,R],[P,Q]\}, \\ \{[P,R,P],[Q,R]\}, \{[Q,P,Q],[R,P]\}, \{[R,Q,R],[P,Q]\} \end{array} \right\}$$

Then the disjunctive query for input $\bar{y} = \{y_1, \cdots, y_t\}$ is reduced as to whether there exists a minor $\bar{m}$ in $\mathcal{M}$ such that for each $m \in \bar{m}$ there exists y_j satisfying $sublst(m, y_j)$.

By Higman's lemma, minors are guaranteed to be finitely many. When generating minors, the most difficult aspect is knowing whether all have been found. To do this, we apply the regular expression techniques, called *sequential r.e.'s*, used in Murthy-Russell's constructive proof of Higman's lemma [9]. Then along generating minors, we explicitly estimate the remaining possibility of minors, that is represented by finite sets of sequential r.e.'s. Then, we will eventually find that the remaining possibility is empty. This means that all minors have been found.

3 Disjunctive Monadic Query on Indefinite Database

As a target example, we used the linear time fixed disjunctive monadic query processing of indefinite database, proposed by Van der Meyden [18]. He posed the following unsolved problem:

In a fixed disjunctive monadic query, there is an algorithm answering the query, which is linear wrt the size of the indefinite database on a linearly ordered domain. What is an actual algorithm ?

In this section, we briefly review his results. For details, please refer to [18].

Proper atoms are of the form $P(a)$, where P is a predicate symbol, and a is a tuple of constants or variables. *Order atoms* are of the form $u < v$, where u and v are order constants or variables. An *indefinite database* D is a set of ground atoms. The atoms are either proper atoms or order atoms. A model $\mathcal{D}$ of D is a linearly ordered domain (such as time) satisfying D. D is a collection of partial facts on a linearly ordered domain, and thus is called indefinite.

We concentrate on *monadic query processing*, (i.e., database and queries contain only monadic predicate symbols except for $<$). A predicate symbol is *monadic* if its arity is less than or equal to one. The class of monadic queries is restrictive, but contains nontrivial problems, such as a comparison between two gene alignments (regarding C, G, A, T as monadic predicates).

For linearly ordered domains $\mathcal{D}$ and $\mathcal{D}'$, a map $f : \mathcal{D} \to \mathcal{D}'$ is order-preserving if any constants $t, t' \in \mathcal{D}$ with $t < t'$ holds $f(t) < f(t')$, and predicate-preserving if a proper atom $P(t) \in \mathcal{D}$ implies $P(f(t)) \in \mathcal{D}'$ and vice versa. An embedding e is an order-preserving, predicate-preserving one-to-one map, and a projection p is an order-preserving, predicate-preserving onto map. A model $\mathcal{D}$ is embedded to a model $\mathcal{D}'$ if there is an embedding e from $\mathcal{D}$ to $\mathcal{D}'$, and A model $\mathcal{D}'$ is projected to a model $\mathcal{D}$ if there is a projection p from $\mathcal{D}'$ to $\mathcal{D}$.

A *disjunctive query* (or, simply a *query*) is a positive existential first-order clause constructed from proper and order atoms using only $\exists$, $\wedge$, and $\vee$. A *conjunctive query* is a first-order clause constructed from proper atoms and order atoms using only $\exists$ and $\wedge$. For simplicity, queries are expressed in disjunctive normal forms, i.e., disjunctions of conjunctive queries. Each conjunctive query in a disjunctive normal form is called a *conjunctive component.*

For an indefinite database D and a query φ, we define $D \models \varphi$ if φ is valid in any model of D. For instance, let $D = \{P(a), Q(b), a < b, Q(c), R(d), c < d, R(e), P(f), e < f\}$, and let $\varphi = \psi_1 \vee \psi_2 \vee \psi_3$ where

$$\begin{cases} \psi_1 = \exists xyz[P(x) \wedge Q(y) \wedge R(z) \wedge \ x < y < z], \\ \psi_2 = \exists xyz[Q(x) \wedge R(y) \wedge P(z) \wedge \ x < y < z], \text{ and} \\ \psi_3 = \exists xyz[R(x) \wedge P(y) \wedge Q(z) \wedge \ x < y < z]. \end{cases}$$

As a result, $D \models \varphi$. Note that neither $D \models \psi_1$, $D \models \psi_2$, nor $D \models \psi_3$.

Definition 1. A conjunctive query is *sequential* if its form is

$$\exists t_1 t_2 \cdots t_n \ [P_1(t_1) \wedge \cdots \wedge P_n(t_n) \wedge \ t_1 < t_2 < \cdots < t_n],$$

Let *Pred* be a set of monadic predicates, and let $\Sigma = \mathcal{P}(Pred)$ be the power set of *Pred*. Σ^* is the set of all the finite words of the symbols in Σ. Without losing generality, we can assume that a monadic query does not contain constants, i.e., if the query φ contains the constant u, we can eliminate u by adding $P_u(u)$

to a database and replacing φ with $\exists x\ [P_u(x) \wedge \varphi]$ for a new predicate P_u. Thus, up to variable-renaming, sequential monadic queries correspond one-to-one with words in Σ^*. For instance, $\exists t_1 t_2 t_3\ [P(t_1) \wedge Q(t_1) \wedge P(t_2) \wedge R(t_3) \wedge\ t_1 < t_2 < t_3]$ corresponds to $\{P,Q\}\{P\}\{R\}$. This correspondence is naturally extended to conjunctive queries, i.e., correspondence from a conjunctive query to a finite set of words in $\mathcal{F}(\Sigma^*)$. For instance, $\exists t_1 t_2 t_3\ [P(t_1) \wedge Q(t_1) \wedge P(t_2) \wedge R(t_3) \wedge\ t_1 < t_2 < t_3] \ \wedge\ \exists t_1 t_2 t_4\ [P(t_1) \wedge Q(t_1) \wedge P(t_2) \wedge S(t_4) \wedge\ t_1 < t_2 < t_4]$ corresponds to $\{\ \{P,Q\}\{P\}\{R\},\ \{P,Q\}\{P\}\{S\}\ \}$. If ψ is a conjunctive monadic query, a *path* in ψ is a maximal (wrt implication) sequential subquery of ψ. We use the expression $Paths(\psi)$ for the subset of Σ^* corresponding to paths of ψ, and $length(\psi)$ for the sum of the lengths of all the paths.

Lemma 1. Let D be a monadic database and ψ be a conjunctive monadic query. Then, $D \models \psi$ if and only if $D \models p$ for every path $p \in Paths(\psi)$.

Let $P_1, P_2, \cdots, P_n$ be either proper or order atoms. By regarding the indefinite database $D = \{P_1, P_2, \cdots, P_n\}$ as a conjunctive monadic formula $P_1 \wedge P_2 \wedge \cdots \wedge P_n$, the paths of the database are similarly defined. We denote the set of paths as $Paths(D)$. Note that the paths in an indefinite database can be computed in linear time wrt the size of the database.

Lemma 2. Let ψ be a sequential query, and let $\preceq$ be a subword relation on Σ^* constructed from $\subseteq$ on Σ (i.e., $u \preceq v$ if there is an order preserving injection f from u to v s.t. $u_i \subseteq v_{f(i)}$ for each i). Then $D \models \psi$ if, and only if, there is a path $\psi' \in Paths(D)$ s.t. $\psi \preceq \psi'$.

For a disjunctive query φ, $D \models \varphi$ may be *true* even if $D \models \psi$ does not for each conjunctive component ψ of φ. This makes it difficult to judge whether $D \models \varphi$. For the indefinite databases, D_1 and D_2, $D_1 \sqsubseteq D_2$ if $Paths(D_1) \leq_m Paths(D_2)$, where $U \leq_m V$ if $\forall u \in U \exists v \in V$ s.t. $u \preceq v$. We frequently identify an indefinite database D and the set of its paths $Paths(D)$, and also identify $\sqsubseteq$ and $\leq_m$.

Theorem 1. For any disjunctive monadic query φ, if $D_1 \models \varphi$ and $D_1 \sqsubseteq D_2$, then $D_2 \models \varphi$.

At the end of this section, we remark on the existence of the linear time algorithm to decide whether $D \models \varphi$ for a fixed disjunctive query φ. A *quasi order* (QO) $(\Sigma, \leq)$ is a reflexive and transitive binary relation on Σ

Definition 2. For a QO $(\Sigma, \leq)$, a sequence $x_1, x_2, x_3, \cdots$ (either finite or infinite) is *bad* if $x_i \not\leq x_j$ for all i, j with $i < j$. A $(\Sigma, \leq)$ is a WQO if any infinite sequence $x_1, x_2, x_3, \cdots$ in Σ is not bad (i.e., there exist i and j such that $i < j$ and $x_i \leq x_j$). When Σ is clear from the context, we simply denote as $\leq$.

Elements in *Pred* of interest is elements in the monadic queries. Thus, without loss of generality, we can assume that *Pred* is finite, and the set inclusion $\subseteq$ in $\Sigma = \mathcal{P}(Pred)$ is a WQO. Then, according to Higman's lemma, $(\Sigma^*, \preceq)$ and $(\mathcal{F}(\Sigma^*), \leq_m)$ are WQOs, where Σ^* is the set of finite words of Σ and $\mathcal{F}(\Sigma^*)$ is the set of finite sets of Σ^*. Based on Theorem 1, the set of indefinite databases which hold a fixed disjunctive query φ is upward closed wrt $\sqsubseteq$. Thus the problems of judging whether $D \models \varphi$ is reduced to a comparison of D with minimal (wrt $\sqsubseteq$) indefinite databases $\{D_i\}$ with $D_i \models \varphi$. The judgment can be made in linear in the size of D. From this observation, the next theorem follows.

Theorem 2. Let us fix a disjunctive monadic query φ. Then, there exists a linear time algorithm to decide $D \models \varphi$ for a monadic database D.

Note that if a disjunctive monadic query varies, the complexity becomes co-NP. This theorem only says the existence of a linear time algorithm, and the construction, which is reduced to the generation of all the minimal indefinite databases wrt $\sqsubseteq$, will be shown in Section 5.

4 Higman's Lemma and the Constructive Proof

In this section, we will briefly explain the constructive proof of Higman's lemma. Higman's lemma states that any bad sequence has finite length, and the constructive proof of Higman's lemma is presented by constructing the effective well-founded-order (WFO) among bad sequences.

The basic idea is as follows: for a bad sequence, we first assign a union of special regular expressions which approximate possible choice of the next element to enlarge a bad sequence. Next, we construct an WFO on sets of special regular expressions such that for each bad sequence the regular expression associated to the bad sequence strictly decreases when it is enlarged. Thus, this means that any extension of bad sequences eventually terminates. For details, please refer [9]. We also show an extension of the proof.

4.1 Constructive Proof by Murthy-Russell

Lemma 3 (Higman's lemma). [7] If $(\Sigma, \leq)$ is a WQO, then $(\Sigma^*, \preceq)$ is a WQO, where $\preceq$ is a subword relation constructed based on $\leq$ (i.e., $u \preceq v$ if there is an order preserving injection f from u to v s.t. $u_i \leq v_{f(i)}$ for each i).

The standard proof by Nash-Williams [10] is non-constructive, especially, the reasoning called *minimal bad sequence*, in which (1) the proof proceeds based on contradictions, (2) the existence of a minimal bad sequence is a result of Zorn's lemma, and (3) the arguments on a minimal bad sequence are heavily impredicative. An example is universal quantification over all bad sequences. A minimal bad sequence is a bad sequence which is minimal wrt the lexicographical order of sizes.

Murthy-Russell, Richman-Stolzenberg, and Coquand-Fridlender independently gave constructive proofs for Higman's lemma [9,13,2][2]. For a constructive proof, we must make the following assumptions.

[2] Similar idea to [13] is also found in [16].

1. Let A and B be bad sequences of Σ, and let $A \sqsubset_{seq} B$ if, and only if, A is a proper extension of B. $\sqsubset_{seq}$ is well founded and equipped with a well founded induction scheme.
2. The WQO $\leq$ on Σ is decidable.

Classically, the first assumption is obviously based on the WQO property of $\leq$, but constructively it is not. The WQO that satisfies the assumptions above is called a *constructive well-quasi-order* (*CWQO*) [16].

We will briefly review the techniques used in [9]. We will refer to an empty word as ϵ and an upward closure of words which contains w (i.e., $\{x \in \Sigma^* \mid w \preceq x\}$) as w°.

As a convention, we will refer to the symbols in Σ as $a, b, c, \cdots$, the words in Σ^* as $u, v, w, \cdots$, the finite sequences in Σ as $A, B, \cdots$, the finite sequences in Σ^* as $V, W, \cdots$, the subsets of Σ^* as $L, L', \cdots$, the finite subsets of Σ^* as $\alpha, \beta, \cdots$, the subsets of finite subsets of Σ^* as $\mathcal{L}, \mathcal{L}', \cdots$, the special periodic expressions called *sequential regular expressions* as $\sigma, \theta, \cdots$, the finite sets of sequential regular expressions as $\Theta, \Theta_1, \Theta_2, \cdots$, the special power set expressions called *base expressions* as $\bar{\sigma}, \bar{\theta}, \cdots$, and the finite sets of base expressions as $\Phi, \Phi_1, \Phi_2, \cdots$.

Definition 3. Let $b \in \Sigma$, and let $A = a_1, a_2, \cdots, a_k$ be a bad sequence in Σ. The constant expression $(b - A)$ denotes a subset of Σ defined by

$$\{x \in \Sigma \mid b \leq x \ \wedge \ a_i \not\leq x \text{ for each } \ i \leq k\},$$

and the starred expression $(\Sigma - A)^*$ denotes a subset of Σ^* defined by

$$\{w = c_1 c_2 \cdots c_n \in \Sigma^* \mid a_j \not\leq c_i \text{ for each } i \leq n, j \leq k\}.$$

The concatenation of A and $a \in \Sigma$ is $A|a$.

A *sequential regular expression* (sequential r.e.) σ is a (possibly empty) concatenation of either *constant* or *starred expressions.* The size $size(\sigma)$ of σ is the number of the concatenation. For a finite set Θ of sequential expressions, we define $L(\Theta) = \cup_{\sigma \in \Theta} \sigma$.

Let $w_1, w_2, w_3, \cdots$ be a bad sequence of elements in Σ^*. We will explicitly construct a finite set Θ_k of sequential r.e.'s for $w_1, w_2, \cdots, w_k$ such that $\Sigma^* \setminus (w_1^\circ \cup \cdots \cup w_k^\circ) \subseteq L(\Theta_k)$. For describing Θ_k, we define $\Theta(\sigma, w)$. The basic idea of $\Theta(\sigma, w)$ is, for a word not to be a superword of w, it can only contain a proper subword of w. So what we do is write down the sequential r.e.'s which accept classes of words containing different proper subwords of w.

Definition 4. For sequential r.e.'s $\sigma_1, \cdots, \sigma_n$, we define their concatenation $\sigma_1 \cdots \sigma_n$ as $\{w_1 \cdots w_n \mid w_i \in \sigma_i \text{ for } i \leq n\}$, and denote $+$ for the union operation. Let σ be a sequential r.e. and let $w \in \sigma$. We will define $\Theta(\sigma, w)$ as follows.

1. When σ is a constant expression $(b - A)$[3], we can identify w as a single symbol in Σ because $\sigma \subseteq \Sigma$. Then $\Theta(\sigma, w) = (b - A|w) + \epsilon$.

[3] Ref. [9] has a flaw that $\Theta(\sigma, w)$ is simply defined as $(b - A|w)$.

2. When σ is a starred expression $(\Sigma - A)^{*4}$, let $w = c_1c_2\cdots c_l$ with $c_j \in \Sigma$ for each j. Then $\Theta(\sigma, w)$ is

$$\cup_{j=1}^{l}\left\{\begin{array}{l}(\Sigma{-}A|c_1)^*((c_1{-}A){+}\epsilon)\cdots(\Sigma{-}A|c_{j-1})^*((c_{j-1}{-}A){+}\epsilon)\\ (\Sigma{-}A|c_j)^*((c_{j+1}{-}A){+}\epsilon)(\Sigma{-}A|c_{j+1})^*\cdots((c_l{-}A){+}\epsilon)(\Sigma{-}A|c_l)^*\end{array}\right\}$$

3. When $\sigma = \sigma_1\sigma_2\cdots\sigma_n$, where σ_i is either a constant or starred expression, we fix a decomposition of w into σ_is (i.e., $w = w_1w_2\cdots w_n$) with $w_i \in \sigma_i$ for each $i \leq n$. Then

$$\Theta(\sigma, w) = \cup_{i=1}^{n}\{\sigma_1\cdots\sigma_{i-1}\theta\sigma_{i+1}\cdots\sigma_n \mid \theta \in \Theta(\sigma_i, w_i)\}.$$

Let Θ be a finite set of sequential r.e.'s. The following lemma shows that if we remove the sequential r.e. σ from Θ, and replace it with the set $\Theta(\sigma, w)$ with $w \in \sigma$, the resulting (finite) set of sequential r.e.'s includes all the finite words in $L(\Theta)$ not containing w.

Lemma 4. Let $L \subseteq \Sigma^*$. Assume that there is a finite set Θ of sequential r.e.'s such that $L \subseteq L(\Theta)$. For any $w \in L$, $\sigma \in \Theta$ with $w \in \sigma$,

$$L \setminus w^\circ \subseteq L((\Theta \setminus \{\sigma\}) \cup \Theta(\sigma, w)).$$

Thus, for a bad sequence $w_1, w_2, \cdots$, we can construct Θ_k by starting from Σ^* and repeating the applications of Lemma 4. If this process terminates, Θ_k eventually empties. This means that $\preceq$ is a WQO. For termination, we construct a well-founded order $\sqsubset_{setexp}$ which strictly decreases when Lemma 4 is applied. This gives a constructive proof of Higman's lemma.

Definition 5. For the finite sequences A, B in Σ, $A \sqsubset_{seq} B$ if B is a proper prefix of A. For any pair of constant expressions $(a{-}A)$ and $(b{-}B)$, $(a{-}A) \sqsubset_{const} (b-B)$ if $a = b \wedge A \sqsubset_{seq} B$. For any pair of starred expressions $(\Sigma - A)^*$ and $(\Sigma - B)^*$, $(\Sigma - A)^* \sqsubset_* (\Sigma - B)^*$ if $A \sqsubset_{seq} B$. Let $\sqsubset_{exp} = \sqsubset_{const} \cup \sqsubset_* \cup \{(a - A)\} \times \{(\Sigma - B)\}$ (i.e., all the constant expressions are below the starred expressions). Let $\sqsubset_{setexp}$ be a multiset extension [11] of $\sqsubset_{exp}$.

We define an ordering $\sqsubset_{re}$ of sequential r.e.'s by $\sigma \sqsubset_{re} \theta \Leftrightarrow \uplus_{i=1}^{k}\{\sigma_i\} \sqsubset_{setexp} \uplus_{j=1}^{l}\{\theta_j\}$, for $\sigma = \sigma_1\cdots\sigma_k$ and $\theta = \theta_1\cdots\theta_l$, where the σ_is and θ_js are either constant or starred expressions. We also denote a multiset extension of $\sqsubset_{re}$ with $\sqsubset_{setre}$.

Theorem 3. Let $W = w_1, w_2, \cdots, w_k$ be a finite bad sequence in Σ^*. One can effectively compute a finite set Θ_i of sequential r.e.'s for $i \leq k$ such that

$$\Sigma^* \setminus (w_1^\circ \cup w_2^\circ \cup \cdots \cup w_i^\circ) \subseteq L(\Theta_i)$$

and $\Theta_{i+1} \sqsubset_{setre} \Theta_i$ for $i < k$.

4 Ref. [9] has a flaw that $\Theta(\sigma, w)$ is simply defined as $(\Sigma - A|c_1)^*(c_1 + \epsilon)\cdots(c_{l-1} + \epsilon)(\Sigma - A|c_l)^*$.

Corollary 1. If $(\Sigma, \leq)$ is a CWQO, then $(\Sigma^*, \preceq)$ is a CWQO.

Example 1. Let $\Sigma = \{a, b\}$. Consider the bad sequence $ab, bbaa, ba, bb, a, b$ wrt $\preceq$.

$$\begin{aligned}
\Theta_0 &= (\Sigma - \epsilon)^* \\
\Theta_1 &= (\Sigma - a)^*(b+\epsilon)(\Sigma - b)^* \cup (\Sigma - a)^*(a+\epsilon)(\Sigma - b)^* \\
&= \{b^*a^*\} \\
\Theta_2 &= (b+\epsilon)(\Sigma - b) \cup (\Sigma - a)(a+\epsilon) \\
&= \{ba^*, b^*a\} \\
\Theta_3 &= (\Sigma - b) \cup (b+\epsilon) \cup (a) \cup (\Sigma - a) \\
&= \{a^*, b^*\} \\
\Theta_4 &= (\Sigma - b) \cup (b+\epsilon) \\
&= \{a^*, b\} \\
\Theta_5 &= \{\epsilon, b\} \\
\Theta_6 &= \{\epsilon\}
\end{aligned}$$

4.2 An Extension

For our purposes, we need further extension to the sets of finite sets of finite words (which is not included in [9]). Let $\mathcal{F}(\Sigma^*)$ be the set of all finite sets of Σ^*. Assume that $(\Sigma, \leq)$ satisfies the CWQO assumptions. Note that an embedding $(\Sigma^*, \preceq)$ satisfies them as well. We define $\alpha \leq_m \beta$ for $\alpha, \beta \in \mathcal{F}(\Sigma^*)$ if, for each $x \in \alpha$, there exists $y \in \beta$ such that $x \leq y$. We also denote the upward closure of α in $\mathcal{F}(\Sigma^*)$ (i.e., $\{\gamma \in \mathcal{F}(\Sigma^*) \mid \alpha \leq_m \gamma\}$) with α°.

Definition 6. Let $W = w_1, w_2, \cdots, w_k$ be a finite bad sequence in Σ^*. The *base expression* is

$$(\Sigma^* \ominus W) = \mathcal{F}(\{u \in \Sigma^* \mid w_i \not\preceq u \text{ for each } i \leq k\})$$

We define $\Sigma^* \ominus V \sqsubset_{base} \Sigma^* \ominus W$ if $V \sqsubset_{seq} W$. For a finite set Φ of base expressions, we define $\mathcal{L}(\Phi) = \cup_{\bar{\sigma} \in \Phi} \bar{\sigma}$.

Let $\alpha_1, \alpha_2, \cdots$ be a bad sequence of elements in $\mathcal{F}(\Sigma^*)$. We will explicitly construct a finite set Φ_k of base expressions for $\alpha_1, \cdots, \alpha_k$ such that $\mathcal{F}(\Sigma^*) \setminus (\alpha_1^\circ \cup \cdots \cup \alpha_k^\circ) \subseteq \mathcal{L}(\Phi_i)$. For describing Φ_k, we define $\Phi(\Sigma^* \ominus V, \alpha)$. The basic idea of $\Phi(\Sigma^* \ominus V, \alpha)$ is, for a finite set not to be a superset of α, it must not contain at least one of the elements in α. What we do is write down base expressions which accept finite sets not containing some element of α.

Definition 7. Let $(\Sigma^* \ominus V)$ be the base expression for a finite bad sequence V in Σ^*, and let $\alpha \in (\Sigma^* \ominus V)$. We then define $\Phi(\Sigma^* \ominus V, \alpha) = \{\Sigma^* \ominus V|v \mid v \in \alpha \wedge v_i \not\preceq v \text{ for each } v_i \in V\}$.

Lemma 5. Let $\mathcal{L} \subseteq \mathcal{F}(\Sigma^*)$. Assume that there is a finite set Φ of base expressions such that $\mathcal{L} \subseteq \cup_{\bar{\sigma} \in \Phi} \bar{\sigma}$. For any $\alpha \in L$ and $\bar{\sigma} \in \Phi$ with $\alpha \in \bar{\sigma}$,

$$\mathcal{L} \setminus \alpha^\circ \subseteq \mathcal{L}((\Phi \setminus \{\bar{\sigma}\}) \cup \Phi(\bar{\sigma}, \alpha)).$$

Let $\sqsubset_{base}$ be the multiset extension of $\sqsubset_{seq}$. Since $\preceq$ is a WQO on Σ^*, $\sqsubset_{seq}$ is well founded, and so is $\sqsubset_{base}$. Thus, by using a constructive proof similar to Higman's lemma, we obtain the next theorem.

Theorem 4. Let $\mathcal{A} = \alpha_1, \alpha_2, \cdots, \alpha_k$ be a finite bad sequence in $\mathcal{F}(\Sigma^*)$. Then one can effectively compute a finite set Φ_i of base expressions for $i \leq k$ such that

$$\mathcal{F}(\Sigma^*) \setminus (\alpha_1^\circ \cup \alpha_2^\circ \cup \cdots \cup \alpha_i^\circ) \subseteq \mathcal{L}(\Phi_i)$$

and $\Phi_{i+1} \sqsubset_{base} \Phi_i$ for $i < k$.

Corollary 2. If $(\Sigma^*, \leq)$ is a CWQO, then $(\mathcal{F}(\Sigma^*), \leq_m)$ is a CWQO.

Example 2. Let $\Sigma = \{a, b\}$. Consider the bad sequence $\{ab, bbaa\}, \{ba, bb\}, \{a, b\}$ wrt $\leq_m$.

$$\begin{aligned}
\Phi_0 &= \{(\Sigma^* \ominus \epsilon)\} \\
\Phi_1 &= \{(\Sigma^* \ominus (ab)),\ (\Sigma^* \ominus (bbaa))\} \\
&= \{\mathcal{F}(\{b^*a^*\}),\ \mathcal{F}(\{a^*(b+\epsilon)a^*b^*(a+\epsilon)b^*\})\} \\
\Phi_2 &= \{(\Sigma^* \ominus (ab, ba)),\ (\Sigma^* \ominus (ab, bb)), \\
&\qquad (\Sigma^* \ominus (bbaa, ab)),\ (\Sigma^* \ominus (bbaa, bb))\} \\
&= \{\mathcal{F}(\{a^*, b^*\}),\ \mathcal{F}(\{(b+\epsilon)a^*, b^*(a+\epsilon)\}), \\
&\qquad \mathcal{F}(\{a^*(b+\epsilon)a^*\})\} \\
\Phi_3 &= \{(\Sigma^* \ominus (ab, ba, a)),\ (\Sigma^* \ominus (ab, ba, b)), \\
&\qquad (\Sigma^* \ominus (ab, bb, a)),\ (\Sigma^* \ominus (ab, bb, b)), \\
&\qquad (\Sigma^* \ominus (bbaa, ab, a)),\ (\Sigma^* \ominus (bbaa, ab, b)), \\
&\qquad (\Sigma^* \ominus (bbaa, bb, a)),\ (\Sigma^* \ominus (bbaa, bb, b))\} \\
&= \{\mathcal{F}(\{a^*\}),\ \mathcal{F}(\{b^*\})\}
\end{aligned}$$

5 Algorithm Generation Based on WQO Techniques

Throughout the section, we use the symbol D for an indefinite database, and we fix a disjunctive monadic query $\varphi = \psi_1 \vee \psi_2 \vee \cdots \vee \psi_m$, where the ψ_i's are conjunctive components (i.e., conjunctive monadic queries). In our situation, combining Theorem 3 and 4 shows that $\Sigma^* \ominus W$ is approximated with a finite set of sequential r.e.'s. More precisely,

$$(\Sigma^* \ominus W) \subseteq \mathcal{F}(\Theta(\cdots \Theta(\Theta(\Sigma^*, w_1), w_2), \cdots, w_k)$$

for a finite bad sequence $W = w_1, w_2, \cdots, w_k$ in Σ^*, and

$$\Phi(\Sigma^* \ominus W, \alpha) = \{\mathcal{F}(\Theta(\Theta \cdots \Theta(\Sigma^*, w_1), \cdots, w_k), v) \mid v \in \alpha \ \wedge\ w_i \not\preceq v\}.$$

From now on, we use a finite set of finite sets of sequential r.e.'s as a substitute for a base expression Φ.

```
1:    begin
2:       M:={ };
3:       L:={{Σ*}};
4:       n=0;
5:       begin
6:          while ExistsMinor(L) do
7:             begin
8:                NotFound:= true;
9:                while NotFound do
10:               begin
11:                  if QueryTest(Enumerate(n)) and In(Enumerate(n),L) then
12:                     begin
13:                        add Enumerate(n) to M;
14:                        L:= Exclude(L,Enumerate(n));
15:                        NotFound:= false;
16:                     end
17:                  n:= n+1;
18:               end
19:            end;
20:         M:= Minimize(M);
21:         return M;
22:      end
23:   end
```

Fig. 1. The algorithm to detect minors $\mathcal{M}_\varphi$

5.1   Design of Disjunctive Query Processing Algorithm

We say *minors* for minimal indefinite databases wrt $\sqsubseteq$ that are valid for φ, and a set of all minors is denoted by $\mathcal{M}_\varphi$. From the observation in Section 3, we know that the essence of linear time algorithm generation for deciding $D \models \varphi$ is reduced to generating $\mathcal{M}_\varphi$. Thus, our aim is to generate $\mathcal{M}_\varphi$.

Let *Pred* be the set of monadic predicate symbols appearing in φ, and let $\Sigma = \mathcal{P}(Pred)$. Σ is a lattice wrt set inclusion $\subseteq$, and $\subseteq$ is a WQO because *Pred* is finite. Thus, from Corollary 1 and 2, $\leq_m$ on $\mathcal{F}(\Sigma^*)$ is a WQO. Then the algorithm to generate minors is presented in Figure 1 with the following predicates and functions.

- Enumerate : $\mathbf{N} \to \mathcal{F}(\Sigma^*)$, that enumerates $\mathcal{F}(\Sigma^*)$.
- Exclude(Φ, α). For a finite set Φ of finite sets of sequential r.e.'s and $\alpha \in \mathcal{F}(\Sigma^*)$, construct a finite set Φ' of finite sets of sequential r.e.'s such that $\cup_{\Theta \in \Phi} L(\mathcal{F}(\Theta)) \setminus \alpha^\circ \subseteq \cup_{\Theta' \in \Phi'} L(\mathcal{F}(\Theta'))$ and $\Phi >_m \Phi'$.
- QueryTest(α). For $\alpha \in \mathcal{F}(\Sigma^*)$, decide whether $D \models \alpha$ implies $D \models \varphi$.
- ExistsMinor(Φ). For a finite set Φ of finite sets of sequential r.e.'s, decide whether there exists $\alpha \in \cup_{\Theta \in \Phi} \mathcal{F}(L(\Theta))$ satisfying QueryTest(α).
- Minimize(M). For a finite subset M of $\mathcal{F}(\Sigma^*)$, minimize M wrt $\leq_m$.

Their implementation is as follows: QueryTest(α) is decidable, because this is specified in the monadic second order logic S1S [17]. To illustrate, let $\varphi =$

$\psi_1 \vee \psi_2 \vee \psi_3$, where

$$\begin{cases} \psi_1 = \exists xyz[P(x) \wedge Q(y) \wedge R(z) \wedge\ x < y < z], \\ \psi_2 = \exists xyz[Q(x) \wedge R(y) \wedge P(z) \wedge\ x < y < z], \text{ and} \\ \psi_3 = \exists xyz[R(x) \wedge P(y) \wedge Q(z) \wedge\ x < y < z]. \end{cases}$$

and let $\alpha = \{PQ, QR, RP\}$. `QueryTest`(α) is represented in S1S as

$$\begin{array}{l} (\exists xyzuvw.\ P(x) \wedge Q(y) \wedge x < y\ \wedge Q(z) \wedge R(u) \wedge z < u\ \wedge R(v) \wedge P(w) \wedge v < w \\ \qquad \wedge\, x \neq y\ \wedge\ x \neq z\ \wedge\ x \neq u\ \wedge\ x \neq v\ \wedge\ x \neq w \\ \qquad \wedge\, y \neq z\ \wedge\ y \neq u\ \wedge\ y \neq v\ \wedge\ y \neq w\ \wedge\ z \neq u \\ \qquad \wedge\, z \neq v\ \wedge\ z \neq w\ \wedge\ u \neq v\ \wedge\ u \neq w\ \wedge\ v \neq w) \\ \quad \rightarrow (\psi_1 \vee \psi_2 \vee \psi_3) \end{array}$$

This is valid and `QueryTest`(α) is *true.*

`Exclude` is constructed by repeating the applications of Theorem 3 and Theorem 4. `Minimize` is easily computed by using $\leq_m$. Note that if `ExistsMinor(L)` then eventually `QueryTest(Enumerate(n)) and In(Enumerate(n),L)` becomes *true.* Thus, the test of `ExistsMinor(L)` ensures termination of the algorithm, and difficulties remain associated with `ExistsMinor(L)`.

5.2 Construction of `ExistsMinor(L)`

We will construct the *upper bound* of indefinite database for `ExistsMinor(L)`. The basic idea is to construct database $D_{\theta,n}$ for a sequential r.e. θ such that

$$\begin{aligned} Paths(D_{\theta,n}) &= \psi(\sigma_1)^{n_1} \times \cdots \times \psi(\sigma_l)^{n_l} \\ &= \{P_{1,1} \cdots P_{1,n_1} \cdots P_{l,n_l} \mid P_{i,j} \in \psi(\sigma_i) \text{ for } 1 \leq i \leq l, 1 \leq j \leq n_i\} \end{aligned}$$

where $n_i = 1$ if σ_i is a constant expression, and $n_i = n$ otherwise. Then we will show that $D_{\theta,n} \models \varphi$ and $D_{\theta,n'} \models \varphi$ are equivalent for sufficiently large n, n'.

Definition 8. Let A be a bad sequence $a_1, a_2, \cdots, a_k$ in Σ and $b \in \Sigma$. For the constant expression $(b - A)$ and the starred expression $(\Sigma - A)^*$, we define $\psi((b - A))$ as the set of the maximum elements in $(b - A)$ and $\psi((\Sigma - A)^*)$ as the set of the maximum elements in $\Sigma \setminus (a_1^\circ \cup a_2^\circ \cup \cdots a_k^\circ)$.

For the sequential r.e. $\theta = \sigma_1 \cdots \sigma_l$, we define an indefinite database $D_{\theta,n}$ by

$$\wedge_{P_{i,j} \in \psi(\sigma_i), 1 \leq j \leq n_i} \exists x_{1,1} \cdots x_{l,n_l}[P_{1,1}(x_{1,1}) \wedge \cdots \wedge P_{l,n_l}(x_{l,n_l}) \wedge x_{1,1} < \cdots < x_{l,n_l}]$$

where $n_i = 1$ if σ_i is a constant expression, and $n_i = n$ otherwise.

Definition 9. Let Θ be a finite set of sequential r.e.'s $\theta_1, \cdots, \theta_s$. Let $\varphi = \psi_1 \vee \psi_2 \vee \cdots \vee \psi_m$ where $\psi_1, \cdots, \psi_t$ are conjunctive components. Then $l(\varphi) = max\{length(\psi_i) \mid 1 \leq i \leq t\}$.

Lemma 6. Let Θ be a finite set of sequential r.e.'s $\theta_1, \cdots, \theta_s$. For each $n \geq l(\varphi)$, $\cup_{1\leq k\leq s} D_{\theta_k,n} \models \varphi$ if, and only if, $\cup_{1\leq k\leq s} D_{\theta_k,l(\varphi)} \models \varphi$.

Sketch of proof We show that if $\mathcal{D}_n \models \varphi$ for a model $\mathcal{D}_n$ of $\cup_{1\leq j\leq s} D_{\theta_j,n}$ then there exists a projection p from $\mathcal{D}_n$ to a model of $\cup_{1\leq k\leq s} D_{\theta_k,l(\varphi)}$ with $\mathcal{D}_{l(\varphi)} \models \varphi$.

For a model $\mathcal{D}_n$ of $\cup_{1\leq j\leq s} D_{\theta_j,n}$ let $t^k_{i,j}$ be a constant in $\mathcal{D}_n$ that corresponds to each bound variable $x_{i,j}$ in $D_{\theta_k,n}$. If $\mathcal{D}_n \models \varphi$, there is an embedding e from some conjunctive component ψ of φ (regarding ψ as a linearly ordered domain) to $\mathcal{D}_n$. Since the number of the bound variables in ψ is at most $l(\varphi)$, we can construct a projection p from $\{t^k_{i,j} \mid 1 \leq j \leq n\}$ to $\{t^k_{i,j} \mid 1 \leq j \leq l(\varphi)\}$ without degenerating the codomain of e. Then p is naturally extended from $\mathcal{D}_n$ to $\mathcal{D}_{l(\varphi)}$, and $e' = p \cdot e$ is an embedding from ψ to $\mathcal{D}_{l(\varphi)}$. Thus we conclude $\mathcal{D}_{l(\varphi)} \models \varphi$. ∎

Theorem 5. Let Φ be a finite set of finite sets of sequential r.e.'s. Then,

$$\texttt{ExistsMinor}(\Phi) = \vee_{\Theta\in\Phi}\ \texttt{QueryTest}(\cup_{\theta\in\Theta} D_{\theta,l(\varphi)}).$$

Theorem 6. The algorithm (in Figure 1) to detect a set of minors $\mathcal{M}_\varphi$ terminates.

Proof From Theorem 4, for each iteration of `while ExistsMinor(L)`, `L` strictly decreases wrt $\leq_m$, and $\leq_m$ is an WFO. ∎

Thus, we can effectively compute a set of minors $\mathcal{M}_\varphi$, and we can give a simple algorithm to decide $D \models \varphi$.

Corollary 3. For a fixed disjunctive monadic query φ, a linear time algorithm to decide whether $D \models \varphi$ for an indefinite database D is as follows:

```
begin
  Flag:= false;
  for each m in M_φ do Flag:= Flag or [m ≤_m D];
  return flag;
end
```

6 Concluding Remarks

This paper described a generation of a linear time query-processing algorithm for a fixed disjunctive monadic query in an indefinite database on a linearly ordered domain. This problem was first posed by Van der Meyden [18] and had, until now, not been published elsewhere. There are several future directions:

1. Our method is based on the regular expression techniques appeared in Murthy-Russell's constructive proof of Higman's lemma [9]. Among its known constructive proofs [9,13,2] (or intuitionistic proofs [5,4]), [2] would be one of the most simple and is implemented on Coq prover[5]. This could be applied to the simpler method to algorithm generation.

[5] See `http://coq.inria.fr/contribs/logic-eng.html`.

2. We are designing an automatic generator based on MONA (available at `http://www.brics.dk/mona`). MONA, which runs on Linux, efficiently decides the satisfiability of formulae in monadic second order logic S1S/S2S. Based on initial experiments, we expect reasonably fast calculations.
3. The next extension may be to use the constructive proof of Kruskal's theorem [10]. Gupta demonstrated the constructive proof of the weaker form [6], and recently Veldman presented an intuitionistic proof of Kruskal's theorem [19]. These would correspond to, for instance, query-processing in an indefinite database over partial ordered domains (i.e., events on branching time).
4. As the example of the disjunctive query in Section 2 suggests, the number of minors easily explode. To make it practical linear time, we expect that program transformational approach, such as stratification by folding, would be useful to reduce the number of the comparison with minors. For instance, the example of the disjunctive query in Section 2 needs the comparison with minors

$$\begin{array}{l}\{[P,Q],[Q,R],[R,P]\},\{[P,Q,R]\},\{[Q,R,P]\},\{[R,P,Q]\},\\ \{[P,Q,P],[Q,R]\},\{[Q,R,Q],[R,P]\},\{[R,P,R],[P,Q]\},\\ \{[P,R,P],[Q,R]\},\{[Q,P,Q],[R,P]\},\{[R,Q,R],[P,Q]\}\end{array}$$

and the number of the tests will be reduced (from 10 times to at most 6 times) if the comparison is stratified as below.

$$\begin{array}{lcl} query & & \\ \downarrow ? & & \\ \{[P,Q],[Q,R]\} & \xrightarrow{yes} & \left\{\begin{array}{l}\{[P,Q],[Q,R],[R,P]\},\ \{[P,Q,R]\},\\ \{[P,Q,P],[Q,R]\},\ \{[R,Q,R],[P,Q]\},\end{array}\right. \\ \downarrow No & & \\ \{[Q,R],[R,P]\} & \xrightarrow{yes} & \left\{\begin{array}{l}\{[Q,R,P]\},\\ \{[Q,R,Q],[R,P]\},\ \{[P,R,P],[Q,R]\},\end{array}\right. \\ \downarrow No & & \\ \{[R,P],[P,Q]\} & \xrightarrow{yes} & \left\{\begin{array}{l}\{[R,P,Q]\},\\ \{[R,P,R],[P,Q]\},\ \{[Q,P,Q],[R,P]\}.\end{array}\right. \end{array}$$

Acknowledgments

The author thanks Ronald van der Meyden for his private lectures on indefinite database theory during his stay at NTT. He would also like to thank the members of the Tokyo CACA seminar for their guidance.

References

1. J. Chomicki. Temporal query languages: a survey. In D.M. Gabbay and H.J. Ohlbach, editors, *Temporal Logic: (ICTL'94)*, pages 506–534, 1994. Lecture Notes in Artificial Intelligence, Vol.827, Springer-Verlag.

2. T. Coquand and D. Fridlender. A proof of Higman's lemma by structural induction, November 1993. available at `http://www.md.chalmers.se/~coquand/intuitionism.html`.
3. R.M. Fellows and M.A. Langston. Nonconstructive tools for proving polynomial-time decidability. *Journal of the ACM*, 35(3):727–739, 1988.
4. D. Fridlender. Higman's lemma in type theory. In E. Gimnez and C. P.-Mohring, editors, *Types for Proofs and Programs, TYPES'96*, pages 112–133, 1996. Lecture Notes in Computer Science, Vol. 1512, Springer-Verlag.
5. A. Geser. A proof of Higman's lemma by open induction. Technical Report MIP-9606, Passau University, April 1996.
6. A. Gupta. A constructive proof that tree are well-quasi-ordered under minors. In A. Nerode and M. Taitslin, editors, *Logical foundations of computer science - Tver'92*, pages 174–185, 1992. Lecture Notes in Computer Science, Vol. 620, Springer-Verlag.
7. G. Higman. Ordering by divisibility in abstract algebras. *Proc. London Mathematical Society*, 2:326–336, 1952.
8. M. Koubarakis. The complexity of query evaluation in indefinite temporal constraint databases. *Theoretical Computer Science*, 171:25–60, 1997.
9. C.R. Murthy and J.R. Russell. A constructive proof of Higman's lemma. In *Proc. 5th IEEE sympo. on Logic in Computer Science*, pages 257–267, 1990.
10. C.ST.J.A. Nash-Williams. On well-quasi-ordering finite trees. *Proc. Cambridge Phil. Soc.*, 59:833–835, 1963.
11. N.Dershowitz and Z.Manna. Proving termination with multiset orderings. *Communications of the ACM*, 22(8):465–476, 1979.
12. L. Perković and B. Reed. An improved algorithm for finding tree decompositions of small width. In et.al. Widmayer, editor, *WG'99*, pages 148–154, 1999. Lecture Notes in Computer Science, Vol. 1665, Springer-Verlag.
13. F. Richman and G. Stolzenberg. Well quasi-ordered sets. *Advances in Mathematics*, 97:145–153, 1993.
14. N. Robertson and P.D. Seymour. Graph minors XX. Wagner's conjecture, 1988. Manuscript.
15. N. Robertson and P.D. Seymour. Graph minors XIII. the disjoint path problem. *Journal of Combinatorial Theory Series B*, 63:65–110, 1995.
16. S.G. Simpson. Ordinal numbers and the Hilbert basis theorem. *Journal of Symbolic Logic*, 53(3):961–974, 1988.
17. W. Thomas. Automata on infinite objects. In J. van Leeuwen, editor, *Handbook of Theoretical Computer Science*, volume B, chapter 4, pages 133–192. Elsevier Science Publishers, 1990.
18. R. van der Meyden. The complexity of querying indefinite data about linearly ordered domains. *Journal of Computer and System Science*, 54(1):113–135, 1997. Previously presented at 11th ACM sympo. on Principles of Database Systems, pp.331–345, 1992.
19. W. Veldman. An intuitionistic proof of Kruskal's theorem. Technical Report 17, Department of Mathematics, University of Nijmegen, April 2000.

Modelisation of Timed Automata in Coq

Christine Paulin-Mohring

Université Paris-Sud, Laboratoire de Recherche en Informatique,
UMR 8623 CNRS, Bâtiment 490, F-91405 Orsay Cedex, France,
paulin@lri.fr, http://www.lri.fr/~paulin

Abstract. This paper presents the modelisation of a special class of timed automata, named p-automata in the proof assistant Coq. This work was performed in the framework of the CALIFE project[1] which aims to build a general platform for specification, validation and test of critical algorithms involved in telecommunications. This paper does not contain new theoretical results but explains how to combine and adapt known techniques in order to build an environment dedicated to a class of problems. It emphasizes the specific features of Coq which have been used, in particular dependent types and tactics based on computational reflection.

1 Introduction

An important research area is the design of methods and tools for simplifying the design of zero-default programs. Formal methods are mainly used in the context of specific algorithms involved in critical systems. The behavior of the program and its expected specification are represented in a mathematical model and then a proof of correctness has to be produced. This task represents often a lot of work but it cannot be avoided in order to gain a high-level of confidence in the appropriate behavior of the program. Formal models are indeed required for getting the highest level of certification for systems manipulating critical informations like smart-cards. The generalization of formal methods requires to provide appropriate computer tools and specialized libraries for simplifying the task of development of new algorithms.

1.1 Theorem Proving vs Model-Checking

Theorem proving and model-checking are two different formal methods for the validation of critical systems. Model-checking tries to automatically prove properties of programs represented as labelled transition systems. A specification on transition systems is often expressed as a temporal logic formula that is checked using exploration techniques on the graph representing the transition system. There are well-known problems when using model-checking: the model of the program has to be simplified in order to be treated automatically, then it becomes more difficult or impossible to insure that what is proven corresponds

[1] http://www.loria.fr/Calife

N. Kobayashi and B.C. Pierce (Eds.): TACS 2001, LNCS 2215, pp. 298–315, 2001.

to the real world. Because they are complex programs, model-checker are not bug-free. Model-checkers are appropriate tools for the automatic detection of errors. On the other hand, if the program correctness property is expressed as a mathematical statement, it is possible to handle it using general tools for theorem proving. The interest of this method is to be able to represent complicated systems involving non-finite or non specified data or continuous time. However, for such theories, the complete automation of proofs is hopeless and then the work has to performed by hand.

During the last years, there has been several attempts to combine these two methods. One possibility is to use a theorem prover to reduce an abstract problem into one that can be handle by a model-checker used as an external tool. It is possible to trust the model-checker like in the system PVS [19] or to be more suspicious and keep a trace of theorems which depend on properties justified by a non-certified procedure like in HOL [13]. Another attempt is to integrate model-checkers to theorem provers in a certified way [24,26,22] but it raises the problem of efficiency. Theorem proving can also be used in order to prove that a property is an invariant of the labelled transition system which models the system [12]. Interactive theorem prover based on higher-order logic are also appropriate tools for mechanizing meta-reasoning on the sophisticated formalisms involved in the modelisation of concurrent systems like the π-calculus [15,16].

1.2 Studying a Conformance Protocol

In this paper, we are considering the interaction between theorem proving and automatic proof-procedures in the context of the study of a conformance protocol (named ABR) normalized by France Telecom R& D to be used in ATM networks. This example has been widely studied since it was introduced as an industrial challenge for formal methods. Proofs of this protocol have been both done using theorem provers and automatic tools. A recent synthetic presentation of these experiments can be found in [4].

The purpose of the conformance algorithm is to control the bit rate available to the users in an ATM network. The system receives information from the network on the maximum rate available at time t, it also receives the data from the user and checks that the actually used rate does not exceed the available rate. But there are delays in the transmission, such that the information sent by the network at time t will only be known to the user after time $t+\tau_3$ and no later than $t+\tau_2$. The general principle is that the user is always allowed to choose the best rate available to him or her. Assume a maximum rate R_1 arrives at time t_1, the user should wait until $t_1+\tau_3$ to take this rate into account. Assume R_1 is less than the rate available before arrival of R_1, the user may wait until $t_1+\tau_2$ to conform to the R_1 rate. If a new better rate $R_2 > R_1$ arrive at time t_2 such that $t_2+\tau_3 < t_1+\tau_2$, the user will be allowed to ignore R_1 and adopt the rate R_2 already at time $t_2+\tau_3$. The algorithm has to program a schedule of maximum available rates. But because it has only a small amount of memory, the algorithm only computes an approximation of the schedule: it stores the currently available rate and at most two other rates with the corresponding time. The verification consists in proving that the algorithm favors the user, namely the computed rate is greater than the theoretical available rate.

This protocol involves generic time parameters τ_2 and τ_3, it was consequently first considered as more suited for interactive tools of theorem proving rather than automatic tools of model-checking. The first proofs were done by J.-F. Monin using Coq [17,18], a modelisation and proof was also developed by D. Rouillard using the CClair library [8] developed in HOL/Isabelle to reason on transitions systems. However, because the operations involved are of a simple shape, it appeared that it was possible to prove the algorithm using automatic tools like the model-checker for timed automata Hytech [14,3], the system of constraint logic programming Datalog [20,11] or the rewriting system ELAN [2].

When trying to modelise the problem in the theorem prover Spike, F. Klay introduced a generalized version of the protocol which uses a memory of arbitrary size. This general protocol has been studied in PVS [21] and in Coq [10].

A byproduct of the study of this example was the definition of a special class of timed automata called p-automata (for parameterized automata) introduced in [3]. We shall now describe how to represent this class of automata in Coq.

1.3 Outline of the Paper

The rest of the paper is organized as follows. In section 2, we briefly present the main features of the system Coq used in this paper. In section 3, we overview the model of timed automata which has been chosen. In section 4, we show the general principles for encoding automata in Coq. Finally in section 5, we discuss a method to automate the proofs of correctness of properties of automata.

2 Description of Coq

In this section, we give a quick overview of the system Coq and introduce the notations used in the rest of the paper.

2.1 What Is Coq?

Coq is a proof assistant based on Type Theory. It is an environment for the edition and verification of mathematical theories expressed in higher-order logic. Coq provides a language, called the Calculus of Inductive Constructions, to represent objects and properties. The main ingredient of this calculus is an higher-order typed lambda-calculus: functions, types or propositions are first-class objects and it is consequently allowed to quantify over functions, types or propositions variables.

It is well-known that the higher-order universal quantification over all propositions is sufficient together with implication to represent usual logical connectives such as conjunction, disjunction.

Example. We illustrate this fact on the definition of the conjunction $A \wedge B$ of two propositions A and B.

The three following properties that can be introduced as axioms for $A \wedge B$ in a first-order framework are easily derivable when $A \wedge B$ is defined as an abbreviation for $\forall X.(A \Rightarrow B \Rightarrow X) \Rightarrow X$.

$$A \Rightarrow B \Rightarrow A \wedge B \qquad A \wedge B \Rightarrow A \qquad A \wedge B \Rightarrow B$$

2.2 Particularities of Coq

Coq shares many similarities with other proof assistants based on higher-order logic such as systems in the HOL family (including Isabelle/HOL) and PVS. However Coq differs from these systems on some specific points that we shall explain.

Intuitionistic logic. Coq is based on an intuitionistic logic, which means that the principle of excluded middle which states that for any proposition A, we have $A \vee \neg A$ is not taken for granted. At first sight, this may seem to be a limitation. However, the classically equivalent property $\neg(\neg A \wedge \neg\neg A)$ is indeed intuitionistically provable. The intuitionistic aspect of the logic can be understood as a strong interpretation of the disjunction operator. In order to be able to prove $A \vee \neg A$, we should be able to provide a way to decide which one from A or $\neg A$ actually holds. On the same spirit, in order to prove the property $\exists x.P(x)$ we should be able to provide a witness a such that $P(a)$ holds.

Intensional functions. A function can be seen intensionally as an algorithm to transform an input into an output. Another point of view is to consider a function extensionally as an input-output relation. The type of functions from τ to σ in Coq represents the type of algorithm (described by λ-terms) taking inputs in the type τ and computing outputs in the type σ. This intensional point of view gives the possibility to the system to automatically compute with functions. An extensional function can also be represented by a binary relation in Coq but in that case, some deduction as to be performed in order to justify that some value is actually the output value of a function for some input.

To illustrate this point, we take the example of the div2 function on natural numbers. In an extensional framework, it is enough to specify relation $\texttt{div2}(x) = y$ as the property $x = 2 \times y \vee x = 2 \times y + 1$ while in an intensional framework, a method of computation has to be given in some kind of algorithmic language, for instance:

$$\texttt{div2}(x) \equiv \textsf{if } x = 0 \texttt{ or } x = 1 \textsf{ then } 0 \textsf{ else } \texttt{div2}(x-2)+1$$

Obviously different algorithms can be given for the same extensional function. If a function h is given as an algorithm, then it can easily be translated into a binary relation $H(x, y) \equiv h(x) = y$, the opposite is obviously not true: some functional relations do not correspond to recursive functions and consequently cannot be represented as algorithms. This is the case for instance for a function ϕ that takes a function f from natural numbers to boolean values as an argument and try to answer whether we have $f(x) = \texttt{true}$ for all integers x. ϕ cannot be represented in Coq as a function of type $(\texttt{nat} \rightarrow \texttt{bool}) \rightarrow \texttt{bool}$ and should instead be introduced as a binary relation:

$$\phi(f, b) \equiv \forall x. f(x) = \texttt{true}$$

The class of functions that can be represented as an algorithm in Coq is a subset of the class of recursive functions. For functions from natural numbers to natural numbers, it contains at least all recursive functions provably total in Higher-Order Logic.

The main interest to use intuitionistic logic and intensional functions is to reflect inside the logical system, informations related to the computational aspects of objects.

Dependent types In Coq, any object is given a type. The fact that an object inhabits a certain type can be verified automatically. A type is associated to an arbitrary expression representing a computation but it reflects actually a property of the value which is the result of the computation. It is important for the type system to be general enough to accept a large class of programs and allow their use in many different contexts. The type of inputs of a program should be as general as possible, and the type system should accept polymorphic programs. On the other side, the type of the output of the program should be as precise as possible depending on the inputs.

The Coq type system allows arbitrary polymorphism in the type of objects. For instance, assume that we have defined the type $\texttt{list}_\alpha$ of lists of elements of type α one may define a function of type:

$$\forall \alpha. \forall \beta. (\alpha \rightarrow \beta) \rightarrow \texttt{list}_\alpha \rightarrow \texttt{list}_\beta$$

This kind of polymorphism is usual in functional programming languages of the ML family. But it is also possible to build more complicated types, like for instance the type LIST of lists on an arbitrary type. An element in this type will be a pair built from a type τ and a list of type $\texttt{list}_\tau$. This kind of structure plays sometimes the role of module specification in programming languages and consequently is useful for building generic libraries. For instance, the type of automata will be, as in mathematics, a structure containing the type of labels and locations.

A type may depend not only on another type parameter like in the case of $\texttt{list}_\alpha$ but also on other objects. We may define for instance the type of lists of length n or of sorted lists or of lists which are a permutation of a given list or lists with elements satisfying a predicate P ...

We shall use this possibility in section 2 in order to define the synchronization of an arbitrary family of automata and to get a compact representation of state variables.

Explicit proof objects In Type Theory, terms are not only used for representing objects of the logic but also for representing proofs. A property P of the logic is represented as a type of the language, P is true when it is possible to exhibit a term p with type P which represents a proof of P. The correctness of the proof system consequently relies on the correctness of the type-checking algorithm. A proof-term can be built using arbitrary programs (called tactics) but it is eventually typechecked by the kernel of the Coq system.

In order to use a complicated decision procedure in a safe way in Coq it is necessary for this decision procedure not only to answer "yes" or "no" but in the case of a positive answer, it should compute a term with the appropriate type. However, because of the expressiveness of the language, there are many possible choices for this term. We shall come back to this matter in section 5.

2.3 Notations

We shall not enter into the details of the Coq syntax which are precisely described in the Reference Manual [23]. In the rest of the paper, we shall use a few constructions that we explain now.

Sets. Data-types are represented by objects with type a special constant named `Set`. For instance, the type `nat` of natural numbers is itself an object of type `Set`.

If T and U are objects of type `Set`, then $T \rightarrow U$ is a new object of type `Set` which represents the type of functions from T to U. New types may be introduced by inductive declarations:

Inductive *name* : Set := $c_1 : T_1 \mid \ldots \mid c_n : T_n$

This command adds a new concrete type *name* in the environment, as well as the constructors of this type named $c_1, \ldots, c_n$. Each c_i has type T_i. A constant constructor will be declared as c : *name*, a unary constructor expecting an argument of type α will be declared as $c : \alpha \rightarrow$ *name*. The constructor can accept recursive arguments of type *name*. For instance the definition of lists of type α is defined as:

Inductive $\texttt{list}_\alpha$: Set := $\texttt{nil} : \texttt{list}_\alpha \mid \texttt{cons} : \alpha \rightarrow \texttt{list}_\alpha \rightarrow \texttt{list}_\alpha$.

If t is an object in an inductive type T, it is possible to build an object by pattern-matching over the structure of the values in the type T. When T is inductively defined, it is possible to define a recursive function depending on x of type T as soon as the recursive calls in the definition of x are done on objects structurally smaller than x.

Propositions. Logical propositions are represented by objects with type a special constant named `Prop`. If T and U are objects of type `Prop`, then $T \rightarrow U$ (also written $T \Rightarrow U$ in this paper) is a new object of type `Prop` which represents the property "T implies U". The prelude of Coq contains the definition of usual logical connectives such as conjunction, disjunction or equality. The universal quantification of a property P depending on a variable x of type A is written $(x : A)P$.

Abstraction and application. A type or object t can be freely abstracted with respect to a type or object variable x of type τ. The abstracted term is written $[x : \tau]t$ or simply $[x]t$ when τ can be deduced from the context. A term t representing a functional construction can be applied to a term u of the appropriate type, the application is written $(t\ u)$.

Predicates. A predicate P over a type α is a term of type $\alpha \to$ `Prop`, ie a function which given an element a of type α produces a property $(P\ a)$ of type `Prop`.

It is possible to define a proposition either as a function defined by case and recursion over an inductively defined parameter or inductively. An inductively defined predicate looks like the definition of a Prolog program with clauses.

For instance, given a binary relation R of type $\alpha \to \alpha \to$ `Prop` and a predicate P of type $\alpha \to$ `Prop`, it is possible to define inductively the predicate `Pstar` which is true for any y of type α such that there exists a path from x which satisfied P to y with two consecutive elements satisfying R. The definition is as follows:

Inductive Pstar : $\alpha \to$`Prop`
  `init` : (x:α)(P x) $\to$ (Pstar x)
  | `add` : (x,y:α)(Pstar x) $\to$ (R x y) $\to$ (Pstar y)

Declarations. Declarations of the form:

Definition *name* := t.

are used to introduce *name* as an abreviation for the term t.

3 Description of p-Automata

Timed automata introduced by Alur and Dill [1] are widely used for the modelisation of real-time systems. In order to represent the ABR conformance algorithm, a generalization of timed automata called p-automata was introduced in [3]. In classical timed automata, states represent the current value of a finite set of clocks which can be reseted during a transition. In p-automata, there is a distinction between a universal clock which is never reseted and variables which are updated during transitions. The update of a variable may be non-deterministic (for instance we may assign to a variable an arbitrary value greater than 3, which is useful to model the behavior of the environment) and the update of one variable x may also depend on the value of another variable y in a linear way (for instance $x := y + 3$). The constraints used in location invariants may also involve a comparison between the values of two different variables (for instance $x \leq y + 3$).

In [6,7] this class of automata is precisely studied. In particular it is shown that deciding the emptiness of the language accepted by the automata is not decidable in general. One need to restrict either the class of constraints used as invariants or the class of updates. Decidability of emptiness is guaranteed when constraints are diagonal free (ie they only compare a variable to a constant and not another variable) or when the updates are of a simple shape: assigning a constant, another variable or an arbitrary value less than a constant.

If we plan to manipulate p-automata into a general proof assistant, it is not necessary to restrict the class of variables, formula and updates. The general p-automata are specified by a set of locations with an invariant associated to each location and transitions given by two locations (the source and the target) the name of the action labelling the transition and a relation between the value of the variables before and after the transition.

4 Encoding p-Automata in Coq

4.1 Deep versus Shallow Embeddings

When encoding a theory inside a proof assistant there is always a choice between what is called a *deep embedding* and a *shallow embedding*. A deep embedding introduces the (abstract) syntax of the theory as a concrete type of the proof assistant. A shallow embedding uses the objects of the logic (data types or proposition) to represent a model of the theory.

For instance, assume we want to manipulate arithmetic formulas built on 0, 1, variables, the binary addition + and the equality relation. A deep embedding will introduce a data type for representing arithmetic expression with two constants for representing 0 and 1, an unary operation `var` to represent variables (indexed for instance by some given set I) and a binary operation to represent addition. An equation can be represented as a pair of arithmetic terms (t_1, t_2) of type `expr * expr`.

```
Inductive expr : Set :=
  Zero : expr | One : expr | Var : I → expr | Plus : expr → expr → expr.
Definition equation := expr * expr.
```

In a shallow embedding, the Coq type of natural numbers can be used directly for interpreting arithmetic expressions. The variables of the object theory can be identified with Coq variables and the equality between terms can be represented using Coq equality.

It is not difficult to define a function going from the deep representation into the shallow one assuming we provide an interpretation of:

```
Fixpoint interp [i:I→nat; e:expr] : nat :=
  Cases e of Zero → O | One → (S O) | (Var x) → (i x)
         | (Plus e1 e2) → (plus (interp i e1) (interp i e2))
  end.
Definition interp_eq [i:I→nat] : equation → Prop :=
  [e]let (e1,e2) = e in (interp i e1)=(interp i e2).
```

It is also possible to go from a tCoq erm in the type `nat` or `Prop` to the concrete representation of type `expr` or `equation`. But these operations can only be done at the meta-level, and it is in general only a partial operation. The idea is to do an analysis on the syntax of a Coq expression t of type `nat` and try to find an interpretation i and an expression e such that the expression t is convertible with the expressions (`interp` i e). Any term t can be interpreted in a trivial way as a variable (`Var` x) and the interpretation i such that $(i\ x) = t$. But it is obviously not the case for equations, only terms of type `Prop` which are convertible to $t_1 = t_2$ with t_1, t_2 : `nat` can be transformed. This meta transformation can be done in Coq in a simple way using the new mechanism of `Tactic Definition` designed by D. Delahaye [9] which allows to define these transformations directly inside the Coq toplevel.

There are many possibilities to combine the two approaches, for instance it may be convenient, instead of specific constants for zero and one to introduce a general unary `Const` constructor which takes a natural number as an argument. Then the natural numbers at the meta-level are directly injected into the object-level arithmetic expressions.

4.2 The Type of p-Automata

As we explained earlier, the syntactic restriction on the shape of formulas is strongly related to the possibility to design decision procedures. This is not the major problem in an interactive proof assistant, so we prefer to define p-automata at a less syntactic level: invariants and transitions will be described using Coq predicates following a shallow embedding.

Before defining timed automata, we need a definition of time. We have chosen to introduce a type `Time` as a parameter and assume some properties. The type `Time` contains two constant elements 0 and 1; the available operations are the addition and the opposite. The relations are $<$, $\leq$ and $=$ with $x \leq y$ defined as $x < y \vee x = y$. The order is assumed to be total in a computational way. A model of this axiomatization can be built in Coq using either integers or rationals, in particular this axiomatization is consistent.

For building a p-automata, we need a type for the variables V, a type for locations L, a type for transition labels A. An invariant is given for each location, it depends on variables and the universal clock. An invariant is consequently an object of type $L \to \texttt{Time} \to V \to \texttt{Prop}$.

A transition takes place at some instant s, it is labeled by an action a, it goes from a location l to a location l' and transforms a variable v into a variable v'. The set of such transitions (a, s, l, v, l', v') is represented in Coq as a relation of type $A \to \texttt{Time} \to L \to V \to L \to V \to \texttt{Prop}$.

We may first introduce the type of automata built on the set of variable V, of locations L and actions A as a pair containing the invariant and the transition relations. It is also possible to see an automata as a package

$$\begin{aligned}\texttt{pAuto} \equiv <\ & V, L, A : \texttt{Set};\\ & \texttt{Inv} : L \to \texttt{Time} \to V \to \texttt{Prop};\\ & \texttt{Trans} : A \to \texttt{Time} \to L \to V \to L \to V \to \texttt{Prop}\ >\end{aligned}$$

containing the three types and both the invariant and the transition relations. Given an automata, it is possible to do a projection over each component. For instance one defines projections `V`, `L` and `A` from `pAuto` to `Set` which associates to each p-automata p respectively the type of its variables, locations and actions. There is also a projection `Inv` corresponding to the invariant which has type

$$\texttt{Inv} : (p : \texttt{pAuto})(\texttt{L}\ p) \to \texttt{Time} \to (\texttt{V}\ p) \to \texttt{Prop}$$

This is only possible because of the powerful type system of the Calculus of Inductive Constructions. It will give us the possibility to talk of an arbitrary family of automata, each one being built on its own types for variables, locations or actions.

4.3 Semantics

It is easy to associate to a p-automata a labeled transition system. The states are of the form (l, s, v) built from a location l, the time value s and the value of the variable v.

However there are a few choices to be made. There are at least two different ways to build the labeled transition system, the first one is to distinguish two kind of actions, the discrete ones labeled by the actions of the p-automata and the temporal ones parameterized by the time. Another possibility is to combine a temporal and a discrete transition into one transition parameterized by the action of the p-automata. This is possible because two consecutive temporal transitions of delay t and t' are always equivalent to one with delay $t + t'$. It is easy to define both interpretations.

Another subtle point is the role of invariants properties. A first point of view is to consider that transitions can only be done between states (called admissible) which satisfy the invariant property. However this invariant property is mainly used to restrict the amount of time spent in a location before taking a discrete transitions. The practical tools based on timed-automata have a restricted form of transitions, in order to be able to perform complicated operations on variables, it is necessary to introduce several successive transitions, the intermediate locations are called urgent because one does not want temporal transitions to take place in such places. Such urgent transitions or locations did not appear very natural in the model of p-automata, it was consequently decided to not consider this feature as a primitive one, but to encode it using invariants.

If we require discrete transitions to take place between admissible states then an urgent location should be such that the invariant is true exactly when we reach the state and becomes false immediately after. This can be achieved with an extra variable that we call `asap`. An urgent location will be such that the update $\texttt{asap} := s$ is added on each transition arriving on this place and the invariant of the location is $\texttt{asap} = s$. Another possibility which requires less encoding is to put on urgent location an invariant which is always false and to relax the condition on admissibility of states for discrete transitions. It leads to the following definition of transitions:

A discrete transition can take place between (l, s, v) and (l', s', v') if and only if $s = s'$ and there is a transition (a, s, l, v, l', v') in the p-automata.
A temporal transition can take place between (l, s, v) and (l', s', v') if and only if $l = l'$, $v = v'$ and $s \leq s'$ with the invariant of the p-automata satisfied for all states (l, t, v) with $s < t \leq s'$. We believe this second method will be easier to use in practice.

4.4 Synchronization

An important operation on automata is synchronization. With our modelisation, it was easy to define a very general synchronization mechanism.

We can start from a family of p-automata indexed by an arbitrary set I. It is represented in Coq as an object `PFam` of type $I \rightarrow$ `pAuto`.

It remains to understand what we expect as variables, transitions and actions for the synchronised automata. The easy case is locations. A location in the synchronised automata is just the product of the locations of each automata. This is expressed in Coq as:

Definition LocS := (i:I)(`L` (`PFam` i)).

A location l in type `LocS` is written in mathematical notations as $(l_i)_{(i:I)}$.

For the actions, we could do the same, however, it may be the case that we only want to synchronise a subset of the family of automata. It can easily be done by introducing a special action ϵ which corresponds to an identical transition $(\epsilon, s, l, v, l, v)$. If we name (**Eps** α) the type α extended with this extra element, the type of synchronised actions will be defined as:

Definition ActS := (i:I)(**Eps** (`A` (`PFam` i))).

For the variables, there is no canonical choice. Defining a variable of the synchronised automata as the product of the variables of the different systems corresponds to consider variables as local to each automata, this is not really convenient because variables are a mean to share information between automata. Another possibility would be to consider that variables are global. In that case, the complete family of p-automata should share the same set of variables that will also be the variable of the synchronised automata. Such a choice goes again modularity. For instance it will not be easy to introduce one automata and then to use the same automata up to the renaming of variables. For these reasons, it was decided, when designing the model of p-automata in the CALIFE project, to define a general notion of synchronisation, parameterised by a new set of variables V. What is only required is that one can define a family of projection functions $\texttt{proj}_i$ from V to each individual type of variable (`V` (`PFam` i)) and that this projections are injective. Namely if for all i, we have $(\texttt{proj}_i\ v) = (\texttt{proj}_i\ v')$ then $v = v'$. It is indeed the case for operations corresponding to global variables, local variables or renamings.

It remains to define the invariant `InvS` and the transition `TransS` of the synchronized automata. We define:

Definition $\texttt{InvS} : \texttt{LocS} \to \texttt{Time} \to \text{V} \to \texttt{Prop}$
$:= [l, s, v](i : I)(\texttt{Inv}\ (\texttt{PFam}\ i)\ (l\ i)\ s\ (\texttt{proj}_i\ v))$
Definition $\texttt{TransS} : \texttt{ActS} \to \texttt{Time} \to \texttt{LocS} \to \text{V} \to \texttt{LocS} \to \text{V} \to \texttt{Prop}$
$:= [a, s, l, v, l', v']$
$(i : I)$**if** $(a\ i) = \epsilon$
then$(l\ i) = (l'\ i) \wedge (\texttt{proj}_i\ v) = (\texttt{proj}_i\ v')$
else$(\texttt{Trans}\ (\texttt{PFam}\ i)\ (a\ i)\ s\ (l\ i)\ (\texttt{proj}_i\ v)\ (l'\ i)\ (\texttt{proj}_i\ v'))$

These transitions are restricted to a subset of synchronised actions.

4.5 Representing a Specific Automata

The development we made is appropriate for studying the meta properties of p-automata, like establishing a correspondence between the transition system of the synchronized automata and synchronization of transition systems associated to each automata.

But the goal is to use also this modelisation for verifying practical instances of p-automata like the ABR conformance protocol we started with.

When we study a particular example, we usually draw a picture with names for locations, variables, actions and formulas for invariants, and transitions. It remains to do the link between this concrete presentation and the abstract model we have presented.

We propose to do it in a systematic way. Names for locations, variables and actions are introduced as enumerated sets (a particular class of inductive definition with only constant constructors). For locations and actions, it gives us the type L and A used in the model. For variables, we need more. Assume N is the type of names of variables $N = \{n_1, \ldots, n_p\}$. To each element n of N is associated a type T_n. We may build a family T of type $N \to \texttt{Set}$ such that $(T\ n)$ is defined to be T_n. This can easily be done by case analysis on n or using the combinator *N_rect* automatically defined by Coq after the inductive definition is declared. Now we define the type V of variables as $(n : N)(T\ n)$. Assume that v_n is a value of type T_n for each variable of name n, a value of type v is simply built as the Coq expression $(N\_rec\ T\ v_{n_1}\ \ldots\ v_{n_p})$. The projection of a variable v onto the component of name n is easily obtained by the expression $(v\ n)$. With this representation, it is easy to define a generic notion of updates. Assume N is a set with a decidable equality, a family $T : N \to \texttt{Set}$ and V defined to be $(n : N)(T\ n)$. The update relation can be defined as:

Definition update : $V \to (n_0 : N)(T\ n_0) \to V$
$:= [v, n_0, v_0, n]\text{if } n = n_0 \text{ then } v_0 \text{ else } (v\ n)$

In order for this expression to be well-typed, we need to transform the value v_0 of type $(T\ n_0)$ into a value of type $(T\ n)$ using the proof of $n = n_0$, this is a well-known difficulty when dealing with dependent types, but it can be handle with a little care.

An alternative possibility would be to define the type V as a record (an inductive definition with only one constructor with p arguments corresponding to the p variables). But this representation with record does not allow for generic operations.

The invariant is defined by a case analysis on the location. If $\texttt{Inv}_l$ is the formula representing the invariant at location l and if the finite set of location is $\{l_1, \ldots, l_k\}$, then the Coq invariant will be defined as:

Definition `Inv` :L →`Time` →V →`Prop`
:= [l,s,v]**Cases** l **of**
$l_1 \Rightarrow \texttt{Inv}_{l_1}[n \leftarrow (v\ n)]_{n:N}$
$\vdots$
$\mid l_k \Rightarrow \texttt{Inv}_{l_k}[n \leftarrow (v\ n)]_{n:N}$
end

For each concrete formula $\texttt{Inv}_l$, we only have to perform the substitution of the symbolic name n of the variable by the corresponding value $(v\ n)$ of the variable v. We have denoted this operation by $\texttt{Inv}_l[n \leftarrow (v\ n)]_{n:N}$.

For the transition relation, one possibility would be to a double case analysis on the location l and l'. However, this leads to consider k^2 different cases, many of them being irrelevant. So it is better to define the transition relation as the disjunction of the transitions given in the concrete representation. Assume we are given formulas $\texttt{Trans}_{l,l',a}$ for describing the transition between l and l' labelled by a, this formula uses variables names n and n' to denote the value of n after the transition. The definition of the abstract transition relation will have the following form, with one clause in the inductive definition for each transition identified in the concrete representation:

Inductive `Trans` [s:`Time`,v,v':V] :A →L →L →`Prop` :=
...
$\mid t_i : \texttt{Trans}_{l,l',a}[n \leftarrow (v\ n), n' \leftarrow (v'\ n)]_{n:N} \rightarrow$(`Trans` s v v' a l l')
...

The only requirement is that the expressions $\texttt{Inv}_{l_1}[n \leftarrow (v\ n)]_{n:N}$ and $\texttt{Trans}_{l,l',a}[n \leftarrow (v\ n), n' \leftarrow (v'\ n)]_{n:N}$ which are obtained by syntactic manipulations correspond to well-formed Coq propositions.

Graphical interface. In the CALIFE project, a graphical interface is currently designed by B. Tavernier from CRIL Technology for editing p-automata and do an automatic translation towards the verification tools.

5 Automation of Proofs

It is interesting to have the full power of the Coq specification language and the interactive proof system. However it will be useless if we could not provide help for automation of the proof.

For doing proofs without too much human interaction, there are at least two different approaches. The first one is to develop the problem and try to solve it by computation. The second one is to abstract the problem and find a general theorem which can be applied.

What is interesting in Coq is the possibility to combine both approaches. For instance, abstract theorems can be used for establishing general properties of p-automata. For instance, it is easy to define a notion of bisimulation on labelled transitions systems, the use of primitive coinductive definitions of Coq is especially convenient for that.

Now it is possible to describe sufficient conditions on a relation on variables and time of a p-automata in order to build a bisimulation on the underlying transition system.

The first attempt to prove automatically the ABR conformance protocol was done by L. Fribourg using the Datalog system. The idea is to represent transitions using what is called gap-configurations. These configurations are disjunctions and conjunctions of atomic formulas of the form $x \leq y + k$ with x and y integer variables and c an integer constant. These configurations can be represented as directed graphs, the vertexes are the variables and the edges are labeled by the constants. The graph corresponds to a satisfiable formula if and only if there is no cycle in the graph with negative weight. In order to prove an arithmetic formula, it is enough to prove that the graph corresponding to the negation of the formula has a negative cycle. J. Goubault designed a Coq package for representing efficiently finite sets using a map structure indexed by addresses represented as binary integers. This structure has been used for certifying a BDD package [25] and building a symbolic model-checker on top of it. In his early development of map, J. Goubault developed a certified version of the algorithm to decide arithmetic formulas based on gap-configurations. This development is part of the Coq contribution library.

It uses the principle of computational reflection which was first introduced in Coq by S. Boutin [5]. The idea is to build a concrete type `Form` of arithmetic formula which contains variables indexed by addresses of type `adr`. A decision procedure `dec` of type `Form` $\rightarrow$ `bool` is constructed in Coq which translate the formula into a gap-configuration representing its negation and then try to find a negative cycle. An interpretation function `interp` of type (`adr` $\rightarrow$ `Z`) $\rightarrow$ `Form` $\rightarrow$ `Prop` is also defined. Given an interpretation of variables as integer values, and a formula, it builds its interpretation as a Coq proposition. This approach is a generalization of what we presented in the section 4.1. Now the key of the approach is to derive a proof of correctness of the decision procedure, namely a lemma proving:

Lemma `correct` : (f : `Form`)(`dec` f) = `true` $\rightarrow$ (r : `adr` $\rightarrow$ `Z`)(`interp` r f)

Now in order to prove an arithmetic goal G, it is enough to find a concrete formula f and an interpretation r such that (`interp` r f) is convertible to the goal G to be proven and to apply the lemma `correct`. Then one is left with the goal (`dec` f) = `true`. Because (`dec` f) is a closed term of type `bool` it reduces by computation to a value of type `bool`, namely `true` or `false`. If the property is true then (`dec` f) reduces to `true` and because Coq identifies terms up to computation, the trivial proof of `true` = `true` is also a proof (`dec` f) =

`true`. This method is a special case of combination of computation and abstract theorem. An important effort has to be done for the justification of the procedure, but the use of this method in particular cases relies only on computation done automatically by the system.

The Revesz procedure applies the method of gap-configurations for the computation of the transitive closure of a relation R. Assume the initial set P of states and the relation R are described by gap-formula and that we want to prove that a property Q is an invariant of the system. The main problem is usually to find an inductive invariant. We may define the `Pstar` formula inductively as it was done in section 2.3 on page 304. Given two predicates P and P' we write $P \subseteq P'$ to denote the fact that for all x, we have $(P\ x) \Rightarrow (P'\ x)$. Assume we want to prove that $\texttt{Pstar} \subseteq Q$. One may define for each natural number i the predicate P_i of objects that can be reached from P with at most i steps. It is easy to see that

$$(P_0\ x) \Leftrightarrow (P\ x) \qquad (P_{i+1}\ x) \Leftrightarrow ((P_i\ x) \vee \exists y.(P\ y) \wedge (R\ y\ x))$$

If P and R are represented by gap-configurations then P_i is also represented by a gap-configuration. In order to build this new gap-configuration, we need to formally program and justify the short-cut operation which implements the existential quantification.

If we can find i such that $P_{i+1} \subseteq P_i$ then it is easy to show that $\texttt{Pstar} \subseteq P_i$. Then we have a gap-configuration for representing `Pstar` and we can automatically check $\texttt{Pstar} \subset Q$.

An important problem is to ensure that the process which iteratively computes P_i will effectively reach a fixpoint. But this problem does not have to be formalized in Coq. In Coq, one proves a general theorem:

Lemma `fix` : $(i : \texttt{nat})(P_{i+1} \subseteq P_i) \to (P_i \subseteq Q) \to \texttt{Pstar} \subseteq Q$

It is enough to find with an external procedure an integer i, and to check in Coq (using for instance the gap procedure) the special instances $P_{i+1} \subseteq P_i$ and $P_i \subseteq Q$ in order to insure that Q is an inductive property of the transition system.

The main problem with this approach is the efficiency. Work is currently undertaken in order to compute with Coq term as efficiently as with functional programming languages like CAML. But the problem comes also from the efficiency of the procedures that are formalised, it is important to separate between what has to be done inside the proof assistant and what can be reused for the state-of-the-art automatic dedicated proof tools that are developed in the world.

6 Conclusion

In this paper, we have presented the main principles of a project to build on top of the Coq system a environment for the specification and proof of real-time systems represented by timed automata. We emphasized the features of Coq that makes it a good candidate among proof assistants to undertake this work.

This project shows a natural evolution of the proof assistant tools. Until now, doing proofs with these systems required to be able to translate a practical problem in the specific language of the proof-assistant. In this project, we use the full power of the language in order to design the general libraries and proof procedures. However, the end-user should mainly be involved with the specialized language of timed automata adapted to the class of problem (s)he is interested in. Coq becomes an environment for implementing dedicated tools for specification and verification. We can make an analogy with programs like the TEX word-processing tool or the emacs editor. Both of them provide a powerful meta-language, which is mainly used by a few experts; but the use of specialized TEX styles or emacs modes only requires ordinary skills. Like TEX or emacs, Coq is an open system, you can buy libraries or tactics designed by many different people without compromising the correctness of your own development. However, the adequation of this approach to industrial needs remains to be validated.

Acknowledgements

Many points presented in this paper were discussed during meeting of the CALIFE project. Emmanuel Freund participated to an early development of the library on p-automata in Coq.

References

1. R. Alur and D. Dill. A theory of timed automata. *Theoretical Computer Science*, 1994.
2. E. Beffara, O. Bournez, H. Kacem, and C. Kirchner. Verification of timed automata using rewrite rules and strategies. http://www.loria.fr/~kacem/AT/timed_automata.ps.gz, 2001.
3. B. Bérard and L. Fribourg. Automated verification of a parametric real-time program: the abr conformance protocol. In *11th Int. Conf. Computer Aided Verification (CAV'99)*, number 1633 in Lecture Notes in Computer Science, pages 96–107. Springer-Verlag, 1999.
4. B. Bérard, L. Fribourg, F. Klay, and J.-F. Monin. A compared study of two correctness proofs for the standardized algorithm of abr conformance. *Formal Methods in System Design*, 2001. To appear.
5. Samuel Boutin. Using reflection to build efficient and certified decision procedures. In Takahashi Ito and Martin Abadi, editors, *TACS'97*, volume 1281. LNCS, Springer-Verlag, 1997.
6. P. Bouyer, C. Dufourd, E. Fleury, and A. Petit. Are timed automata updatable? In *12th Int. Conf. Computer Aided Verification (CAV'2000)*, volume 1855 of *Lecture Notes in Computer Science*, pages 464–479, Chicago, IL, USA, July 2000. Springer-Verlag.
7. P. Bouyer, C. Dufourd, E. Fleury, and A. Petit. Expressiveness of updatable timed automata. In *25th Int. Symp. Math. Found. Comp. Sci. (MFCS'2000)*, volume 1893 of *Lecture Notes in Computer Science*, pages 232–242, Bratislava, Slovakia, August 2000. Springer-Verlag.
8. P. Castéran and D. Rouillard. Reasoning about parametrized automata. In *8th International Conference on Real-Time System*, 2000.

9. David Delahaye. A Tactic Language for the System coq. In *Logic for Programming and Automated Reasoning (LPAR' 00)*, volume 1955 of *Lecture Notes in Computer Science*, pages 85–95, Reunion Island, November 2000. Springer-Verlag.
10. C. Paulin & E. Freund. Timed automata and the generalised abr protocol. Contribution to the Coq system, 2000. http://coq.inria.fr.
11. L. Fribourg. A closed-form evaluation for extended timed automata. Research Report LSV-98-2, Lab. Specification and Verification, ENS de Cachan, Cachan, France, March 1998.
12. S. Graf and H. Saidi. Verifying invariants using theorem proving. In *8th Conf on Computer-Aided Verification (CAV'96)*, volume 1102 of *Lecture Notes in Computer Science*, New Brunswick, NJ, USA, July 1996. Springer-Verlag.
13. E. L. Gunter. Adding external decision procedures to hol90 securely. In Jim Grundy and Malcolm Newey, editors, *Theorem Proving in Higher Order Logics 11th International Conference (TPHOLs '98)*, volume 1479 of *Lecture Notes in Computer Science.* Canberra, Australia, Springer-Verlag, September 1998.
14. T. Henzinger, P.-F. Ho, and H. Wong-Toi. A user guide to HYTECH. In *TACAS'95*, volume 1019 of *Lecture Notes in Computer Science*, pages 41–71, 1995.
15. D. Hirschkoff. A full formalisation of the π-calculus theory in the Calculus of Constructions. In E. Gunter and A. Felty, editors, *Theorem Proving in Higher-Order Logics*, volume 1275 of *Lecture Notes in Computer Science.* Springer-Verlag, 1997.
16. F. Honsell, M. Miculan, and I. Scagnetto. Pi calculus in (co)inductive type theories. Technical report, Dipartimento di Matematica e Informatica, Universita‘ di Udine, 1998.
17. J.-F. Monin. Proving a real time algorithm for ATM in Coq. In *Types for Proofs and Programs (TYPES'96)*, volume 1512 of *Lecture Notes in Computer Science*, pages 277–293. Springer-Verlag, 1998.
18. J.-F. Monin and F. Klay. Correctness proof of the standardized algorithm for ABR conformance. In *Formal Methods'99*, volume 1708 of *Lecture Notes in Computer Science*, pages 662–681. Springer-Verlag, 1999.
19. S. Owre, S. Rajan, J.M. Rushby, N. Shankar, and M.K. Srivas. PVS: Combining specification, proof checking, and model checking. In Rajeev Alur and Thomas A. Henzinger, editors, *Computer-Aided Verification, CAV '96*, volume 1102 of *Lecture Notes in Computer Science*, pages 411–414, New Brunswick, NJ, July/August 1996. Springer-Verlag.
20. P. Z. Revesz. A closed-form evaluation for datalog queries with integer (gap)-order constraints. *Theoretical Computer Science*, 116:117–149, 1993.
21. M. Rusinowitch, S. Stratulat, and F. Klay. Mechanical verification of a generic incremental ABR conformance algorithm. In *12th Int. Conf. Computer Aided Verification (CAV'00)*, volume 1855 of *Lecture Notes in Computer Science*, Chicago, IL, USA, July 2000. Springer-Verlag.
22. C. Sprenger. A verified model-checker for the modal μ-calculus in Coq. In *TACAS'98*, volume 1384 of *Lecture Notes in Computer Science*, Lisbon, Portugal, 1998. Springer-Verlag.
23. The Coq Development Team. *The Coq Proof Assistant Reference Manual – Version V7.0*, April 2001. http://coq.inria.fr.
24. K. N. Verma. Reflecting symbolic model checking in coq. Mémoire de dea, DEA Programmation, September 2000. http://www.lsv.ens-cachan.fr/Publis/PAPERS/Ver-dea2000.ps.

25. K. N. Verma, J. Goubault-Larrecq, S. Prasad, and S. Arun-Kumar. Reflecting bdds in coq. In *6th Asian Computing Science Conference (ASIAN'2000)*, volume 1961 of *Lecture Notes in Computer Science*, pages 162–181. Springer-Verlag, November 2000.
26. S. Yu and Z. Luo. Implementing a model-checker for LEGO. In J. Fitzgerald, C. B. Jones, and P. Lucas, editors, *FME'97*, volume 1313 of *Lecture Notes in Computer Science*, pages 442–458, September 1997.

Model-Checking LTL with Regular Valuations for Pushdown Systems*

Javier Esparza[1], Antonín Kučera**[2], and Stefan Schwoon[1]

[1] Institute for Informatics TUM, Arcisstr. 21, 80290 Munich, Germany,
{esparza,schwoon}@in.tum.de
[2] Faculty of Informatics MU, Botanická 68a, 60200 Brno, Czech Republic,
tony@fi.muni.cz

Abstract. Recent works have proposed pushdown systems as a tool for analyzing programs with (recursive) procedures. In particular, the model-checking problem for LTL has been studied. In this paper we examine an extension of this, namely model-checking with regular valuations. The problem is solved via two different techniques, with an eye on efficiency – both techniques can be shown to be essentially optimal. Our methods are applicable to problems in different areas, e.g., data-flow analysis, analysis of systems with checkpoints, etc., and provide a general, unifying and efficient framework for solving these problems.

1 Introduction

Pushdown systems can be seen as a natural abstraction of programs written in procedural, sequential languages such as C. They generate infinite-state transition systems whose states are pairs consisting of a control location (which stores global information about the program) and stack content (which keeps the track of activation records, i.e., previously called procedures and their local variables).

Previous research has established applications of pushdown systems for the analysis of Boolean Programs [1,8] and certain data-flow analysis problems [7]. The model-checking problem has been considered for various logics, and quite efficient algorithms have emerged for linear time logics [2,6,9].

In this paper we revisit the model-checking problem for LTL and pushdown systems. Generally speaking, the problem is undecidable for arbitrary valuations, i.e., the functions that map the atomic propositions of a formula to the respective sets of pushdown configurations that satisfy them. However, it remains decidable for some restricted classes of valuations. In [2,6,9] valuations were completely determined by the control location and/or the topmost stack symbol (we call these

* This work was partially supported by the project "Advanced Validation Techniques for Telecommunication Protocols" of the Information Societies Technology Programme of the European Union.

** On leave at the Institute for Informatics, TU Munich. Supported by a Research Fellowship granted by the Alexander von Humboldt Foundation and by a grant GA ČR No. 201/00/1023.

N. Kobayashi and B.C. Pierce (Eds.): TACS 2001, LNCS 2215, pp. 316–339, 2001.

valuations 'simple' in the following). Here we propose (and solve) the problem for valuations depending on regular predicates over the complete stack content. We argue that this solution provides a general, efficient, and unifying framework for problems from different areas (e.g., data-flow analysis, analysis of systems with checkpoints, etc.)

We proceed as follows: Section 2 contains basic definitions. Most technical content is in Section 3 where we formally define simple and regular valuations and propose our solutions to the model-checking problem with regular valuations, based on a reduction to the case of simple valuations. We can thus re-use most of the theory from [6]. While the reduction itself is based on a standard method, we pay special attention to ensure its efficiency, modifying the algorithm of [6] to take advantage of specific properties of our constructions. We propose two different techniques – one for regular valuations in general and another for a restricted subclass – both of which increase the complexity by only a linear factor (in the size of an automaton for the atomic regular predicates). By contrast, a blunt reduction and analysis would yield up to a quadric ('n^4') blowup. Even though one technique is more powerful than the other at the same asymptotic complexity, we present them both since it is not clear how they might perform in practice.

In Section 4 we consider applicability of our abstract results. The first area (Section 4.1) are problems of interprocedural data-flow analysis. Here, regular valuations can be used to 'gather' pieces of information which dynamically depend on the history of procedure calls. LTL can express quite complex relationships among those dynamic properties and allows to solve relatively complicated problems using our model-checking algorithm. To give a concrete example, we indicate how to decide whether a given variable Y is dead at a given point of a recursive program with dynamic scoping. Another application (Section 4.2) is connected to systems with checkpoints. First, we introduce a formal model for such systems, called *pushdown systems with checkpoints*. The idea is that the computation is interrupted at certain points and some property of the stack content is checked. Further computational steps depend on the result of this inspection. This part of our work is motivated by the advent of programming languages which can enforce security requirements. Newer versions of Java, for instance, enable programs to perform local security checks in which the methods on the stack are checked for correct permissions. Jensen et al [10] first proposed a formal framework for such systems. With their techniques one can prove the validity of control flow based global security properties as well as to detect (and remove) redundant checkpoints. Our methods are more general, however; for instance, we are not restricted to safety properties, and our model can represent data-flow as well. Properties of pushdown systems with checkpoints can be expressed in LTL for which we provide an efficient model-checking algorithm. In Section 4.3 we present and analyze a model-checking algorithm for CTL*. In the context of finite-state systems it is well-known that model-checking the more powerful logic CTL* can be reduced to checking LTL [5]. This technique can be transferred to pushdown systems using model-checking with regular valuations.

The complexity of all of the previously developed algorithms is measured in certain parameters of the problem which are usually small, and our complexity bounds are polynomials in those parameters. In general, those parameters can be *exponential* in the size of a problem instance. Therefore, it is natural to ask whether it is possible to solve some of the studied problems more efficiently by other (possibly quite different) techniques. This question is answered (negatively) in Section 5 where we establish **EXPTIME** lower bounds for those problems (even for rather restricted forms of them). Hence, all of our algorithms are essentially optimal. Complexity measures are discussed in more detail in Remark 1 and in Section 5. We draw our conclusions in Section 6.

2 Preliminaries

2.1 Transition Systems

A *transition system* is a triple $\mathcal{T} = (S, \rightarrow, r)$ where S is a set of *states*, $\rightarrow \subseteq S \times S$ is a *transition relation*, and $r \in S$ is a distinguished state called *root*.

As usual, we write $s \rightarrow t$ instead of $(s,t) \in \rightarrow$. The reflexive and transitive closure of $\rightarrow$ is denoted by $\rightarrow^*$. We say that a state t is *reachable from a state* s if $s \rightarrow^* t$. A state t is *reachable* if it is reachable from the root.

A *run* of $\mathcal{T}$ is an infinite sequence of states $w = s_0 s_1 s_2 \ldots$ such that $s_i \rightarrow s_{i+1}$ for each $i \geq 0$. Observe that an arbitrary suffix of a run is again a run – for every $i \in \mathbb{N}_0$ we define the ith suffix of w, denoted $w(i)$, to be the run $s_i s_{i+1} s_{i+2} \ldots$

2.2 The Logic LTL

Let $At = \{A, B, C, \ldots\}$ be a (countable) set of *atomic propositions*. LTL formulae are built according to the following abstract syntax equation (where A ranges over At):

$$\varphi ::= \mathtt{tt} \mid A \mid \neg\varphi \mid \varphi_1 \wedge \varphi_2 \mid \mathcal{X}\varphi \mid \varphi_1 \,\mathcal{U}\, \varphi_2$$

Let $\mathcal{T} = (S, \rightarrow, r)$ be a transition system. A *valuation* of atomic propositions is a function $\nu\colon At \rightarrow 2^S$. The *validity* of an LTL formula φ for a run $w = s_0 v$ w.r.t. a valuation ν, denoted $w \models^\nu \varphi$, is defined inductively on the structure of φ as follows:

- $w \models^\nu \mathtt{tt}$
- $w \models^\nu A \iff s_0 \in \nu(A)$
- $w \models^\nu \neg\varphi \iff w \not\models^\nu \varphi$
- $w \models^\nu \varphi_1 \wedge \varphi_2 \iff w \models^\nu \varphi_1$ and $w \models^\nu \varphi_2$
- $w \models^\nu \mathcal{X}\varphi \iff w(1) \models^\nu \varphi$
- $w \models^\nu \varphi_1 \,\mathcal{U}\, \varphi_2 \iff \exists i\colon (w(i) \models^\nu \varphi_2) \wedge (\forall j < i\colon w(j) \models^\nu \varphi_1)$

We also define $\Diamond\varphi \equiv \mathtt{tt}\,\mathcal{U}\,\varphi$ and $\Box\varphi \equiv \neg(\Diamond\neg\varphi)$. An LTL formula φ is valid in a state s w.r.t. ν, written $s \models^\nu \varphi$, iff $w \models^\nu \varphi$ for each run w which starts in the state s.

2.3 Pushdown Systems

A *pushdown system* is a tuple $\mathcal{P} = (P, \Gamma, \Delta, q_0, \omega)$ where P is a finite set of *control locations*, Γ is a finite *stack alphabet*, $\Delta \subseteq (P \times \Gamma) \times (P \times \Gamma^*)$ is a finite set of *transition rules*, $q_0 \in P$ is an *initial control location*, and $\omega \in \Gamma$ is a *bottom stack symbol*.

We use Greek letters $\alpha, \beta, \ldots$ to denote elements of Γ, and small letters $v, w, \ldots$ from the end of the alphabet to denote elements of Γ^*. We also adopt a more intuitive notation for transition rules, writing $\langle p, \alpha \rangle \hookrightarrow \langle q, w \rangle$ instead of $((p, \alpha), (q, w)) \in \Delta$.

A *configuration* of $\mathcal{P}$ is an element of $P \times \Gamma^*$. To $\mathcal{P}$ we associate a unique transition system $\mathcal{T}_\mathcal{P}$ whose states are configurations of $\mathcal{P}$, the root is $\langle q_0, \omega \rangle$, and the transition relation is the least relation $\rightarrow$ satisfying the following:

$$\langle p, \alpha \rangle \hookrightarrow \langle q, v \rangle \implies \langle p, \alpha w \rangle \rightarrow \langle q, vw \rangle \text{ for every } w \in \Gamma^*$$

Without loss of generality we require that ω is never removed from the stack, i.e., whenever $\langle p, \omega \rangle \hookrightarrow \langle q, w \rangle$ then w is of the form $v\omega$.

Pushdown systems can be conveniently used as a model of recursive sequential programs. In this setting, the (abstracted) stack of activation records increases if a new procedure is invoked, and decreases if the current procedure terminates. In particular, it means that the height of the stack can increase at most by one in a single transition. Therefore, from now on we assume that all pushdown systems we work with have this property. This assumption does not influence the expressive power of pushdown systems, but it has some impact on the complexity analysis carried out in Section 3.1.

3 LTL on Pushdown Systems

Let $\mathcal{P} = (P, \Gamma, \Delta, q_0, \omega)$ be a pushdown system, φ an LTL formula, and $\nu \colon At \rightarrow 2^{P \times \Gamma^*}$ a valuation. We deal with the following variants of the *model checking problem*:

(I) The model checking problem for the initial configuration: does $\langle q_0, \omega \rangle \models^\nu \varphi$?

(II) The global model checking problem: compute (a finite description of) the set of all configurations, reachable or not, that violate φ.

(III) The global model checking problem for reachable configurations: compute (a finite description of) the set of all reachable configurations that violate φ.

In this paper we use so-called $\mathcal{P}$-*automata* to encode infinite sets of configurations of a pushdown system $\mathcal{P}$. As we shall see, in some cases we can solve the problems (II) and (III) by computing $\mathcal{P}$-automata recognizing the above defined sets of configurations.

Definition 1. *Let $\mathcal{P} = (P, \Gamma, \Delta, q_0, \omega)$ be a pushdown system. A $\mathcal{P}$-automaton is a tuple $\mathcal{A} = (Q, \Gamma, \delta, P, F)$ where Q is a finite set of* states, *Γ (i.e., the stack* *alphabet of* $\mathcal{P}$*) is the* input alphabet, $\delta: Q \times \Gamma \to 2^Q$ *is the* transition function, P *(i.e., the set of control locations of* $\mathcal{P}$*) is the set of* initial states, *and* $F \subseteq Q$ *is a finite set of* accepting states. *We extend* δ *to elements of* $Q \times \Gamma^*$ *in the standard way. A configuration* $\langle p, w \rangle$ *of* $\mathcal{P}$ *is* recognized *by* $\mathcal{A}$ *iff* $\delta(p, w) \cap F \neq \emptyset$.

In general, all of the above mentioned variants of the model checking problem are undecidable – if there are no 'effectivity assumptions' about valuations (i.e., if a valuation is an *arbitrary* function $\nu: At \to 2^{P \times \Gamma^*}$), one can easily express undecidable properties of pushdown configurations just by atomic propositions. Therefore, we search for 'reasonable' restrictions which do not limit the expressive power too much but allow to construct efficient model-checking algorithms at the same time. For example, we can restrict ourselves to those valuations which are completely determined by associating atomic propositions with subsets of $P \times \Gamma$ (see, e.g., [2,6]).

Definition 2. *Let* $\mathcal{P} = (P, \Gamma, \Delta)$ *be a pushdown system,* $f: (At \times P) \to 2^\Gamma$ *a function. A* simple valuation $\nu: At \to 2^{P \times \Gamma^*}$ *(specified by* f*) is defined as follows:* $\nu(A) = \{\langle p, \alpha w \rangle \mid \alpha \in f(A, p), w \in \Gamma^*\}$.

In other words, (in)validity of an atomic proposition in a given configuration depends only on its control location and the topmost stack symbol (in our framework, we are mainly interested in reachable configurations where the stack is always nonempty). Consequently, if we are given a pushdown system $\mathcal{P}$, an LTL formula φ, and a simple valuation ν, we can easily synchronize $\mathcal{P}$ with a Büchi automaton which recognizes exactly the models of $\neg\varphi$, reducing the model-checking problem to the problem whether a given Büchi pushdown system has an accepting run [2,6]. Here, it is crucial that atomic propositions are evaluated in a completely 'static' way because otherwise we could not perform the aforementioned synchronization.

In our paper, we propose a more general kind of valuations which are encoded by finite-state automata. We advocate this approach in the next sections by providing several examples of its applicability to practical problems; moreover, we show that this technique often results in rather efficient (or, at least, essentially optimal) algorithms by presenting relevant complexity results.

Definition 3. *Let* $\mathcal{P} = (P, \Gamma, \Delta, q_0, \omega)$ *be a pushdown system,* f *a function which assigns to each pair* (A, p) *of* $At \times P$ *a deterministic finite-state automaton* $\mathcal{M}_A^p$ *over the alphabet* Γ *with a total transition function; we also assume that the initial state of* $\mathcal{M}_A^p$ *is not accepting. A* regular valuation $\nu: At \to 2^{P \times \Gamma^*}$ *(specified by* f*) is defined as follows:* $\nu(A) = \{\langle p, w \rangle \mid w^R \in L(\mathcal{M}_A^p)\}$ *where* w^R *denotes the reverse of* w.

Hence, an atomic proposition A is valid in a configuration $\langle p, w \rangle$ iff the automaton $\mathcal{M}_A^p$ enters a final state after reading the stack contents bottom-up. As we shall see, the requirement that $\mathcal{M}_A^p$ is deterministic is rather natural and has an important impact on complexity analysis. The assumption that the initial state of $\mathcal{M}_A^p$ is not accepting simplifies our next constructions – as we already mentioned, we are only interested in reachable configurations where it is impossible to empty the stack. Hence, this assumption does not bring any 'real' restrictions from a practical point of view.

3.1 Model-Checking with Regular Valuations

The variants of the model checking problem defined in the previous section have been considered in [6] for simple valuations. The following theorems are taken from there:

Theorem 1. *Let $\mathcal{P} = (P, \Gamma, \Delta, q_0, \omega)$ be a pushdown system, φ an LTL formula, and ν a simple valuation. Let $\mathcal{B}$ be a Büchi automaton for $\neg\varphi$. Then one can compute*

- *a $\mathcal{P}$-automaton $\mathcal{R}$ with $\mathcal{O}(|P| + |\Delta|)$ states and $\mathcal{O}(|P| \cdot |\Delta| \cdot (|P| + |\Delta|))$ transitions in $\mathcal{O}(|P| \cdot |\Delta| \cdot (|P| + |\Delta|))$ time and space such that $\mathcal{R}$ recognizes exactly the reachable configurations of $\mathcal{P}$;*
- *a $\mathcal{P}$-automaton $\mathcal{A}$ of size $\mathcal{O}(|P| \cdot |\Delta| \cdot |\mathcal{B}|^2)$ in $\mathcal{O}(|P|^2 \cdot |\Delta| \cdot |\mathcal{B}|^3)$ time using $\mathcal{O}(|P| \cdot |\Delta| \cdot |\mathcal{B}|^2)$ space such that $\mathcal{A}$ recognizes exactly those configurations $\langle p, w \rangle$ of $\mathcal{P}$ (reachable or not) such that $\langle p, w \rangle \not\models^{\nu} \varphi$;*
- *a $\mathcal{P}$-automaton $\mathcal{A}'$ of size $\mathcal{O}(|P| \cdot |\Delta| \cdot (|P| + |\Delta|)^2 \cdot |\mathcal{B}|^2)$ in $\mathcal{O}(|P| \cdot |\Delta| \cdot (|P| + |\Delta|)^2 \cdot |\mathcal{B}|^3)$ time using $\mathcal{O}(|P| \cdot |\Delta| \cdot (|P| + |\Delta|)^2 \cdot |\mathcal{B}|^2)$ space such that $\mathcal{A}'$ recognizes exactly those reachable configurations $\langle p, w \rangle$ of $\mathcal{P}$ such that $\langle p, w \rangle \not\models^{\nu} \varphi$.*

Theorem 2. *Let $\mathcal{P} = (P, \Gamma, \Delta, q_0, \omega)$ be a pushdown system, φ an LTL formula, and ν a simple valuation. Let $\mathcal{B}$ be a Büchi automaton which corresponds to $\neg\varphi$.*

- *Problems (I) and (II) can be solved in $\mathcal{O}(|P|^2 \cdot |\Delta| \cdot |\mathcal{B}|^3)$ time and $\mathcal{O}(|P| \cdot |\Delta| \cdot |\mathcal{B}|^2)$ space.*
- *Problem (III) can be solved in either $\mathcal{O}(|P| \cdot |\Delta| \cdot (|P| + |\Delta|)^2 \cdot |\mathcal{B}|^3)$ time and $\mathcal{O}(|P| \cdot |\Delta| \cdot (|P| + |\Delta|)^2 \cdot |\mathcal{B}|^2)$ space, or $\mathcal{O}(|P|^3 \cdot |\Delta| \cdot (|P| + |\Delta|) \cdot |\mathcal{B}|^3)$ time and $\mathcal{O}(|P|^3 \cdot |\Delta| \cdot (|P| + |\Delta|) \cdot |\mathcal{B}|^2)$ space.*

Our aim here is to design efficient model checking algorithms for regular valuations. We show that one can actually build on top of Theorem 1.

For the rest of this section we fix a pushdown system $\mathcal{P} = (P, \Gamma, \Delta, q_0, \omega)$, an LTL formula φ, and a regular valuation ν. The Büchi automaton which corresponds to $\neg\varphi$ is denoted by $\mathcal{B} = (R, 2^{At}, \eta, r_0, G)$. Let $\{A_1, \ldots, A_n\}$ be the subset of atomic propositions which appear in φ, and let $\mathcal{M}^p_{A_i} = (Q^p_i, \Gamma, \varrho^p_i, s^p_i, F^p_i)$ be the deterministic finite-state automaton associated to (A_i, p) for all $p \in P$ and $1 \leq i \leq n$. Observe that we do *not* require the $\mathcal{M}^p_{A_i}$ automata to be pairwise different; as we shall see in Section 4.2, there are several 'safety' problems which can be reduced to the model-checking problem for pushdown systems and the LTL logic with regular valuations. In this case, many of the $\mathcal{M}^p_{A_i}$ automata are identical and this fact substantially influences the complexity. For simplicity, we assume that whenever $i \neq j$ or $p \neq q$, then the $\mathcal{M}^p_{A_i}$ and $\mathcal{M}^q_{A_j}$ automata are either identical or have disjoint sets of states. Let $\{\mathcal{M}_1, \ldots, \mathcal{M}_m\}$ be the *set* of all $\mathcal{M}^p_{A_i}$ automata where $1 \leq i \leq n$ and $p \in P$, and let Q_j be the set of states of $\mathcal{M}_j$ for each $1 \leq j \leq m$. The Cartesian product $\prod_{1 \leq j \leq m} Q_j$ is denoted by *States*. For given $\boldsymbol{r} \in \mathit{States}$, $p \in P$, and $1 \leq i \leq n$, we denote by $\boldsymbol{r}^p_i$ the element of Q^p_i which appears in $\boldsymbol{r}$ (observe that we can have $\boldsymbol{r}^p_i = \boldsymbol{r}^q_j$ even if $i \neq j$ or $p \neq q$). The vector of initial states (i.e., the only element of *States* where each component is an initial state of some $\mathcal{M}^p_{A_i}$) is denoted by $\boldsymbol{s}$. Furthermore, we write $\boldsymbol{t} = \boldsymbol{\varrho}(\boldsymbol{r}, \alpha)$ if $\boldsymbol{t}^p_i = \varrho^p_i(\boldsymbol{r}^p_i, \alpha)$ for all $1 \leq i \leq n$, $p \in P$. Now we present and evaluate two techniques for solving the model checking problems with $\mathcal{P}$, φ, and ν.

Remark 1 (On the complexity measures). The size of an instance of the model-checking problem for pushdown systems and LTL with regular valuations is given by $|\mathcal{P}| + |\nu| + |\varphi|$, where $|\nu|$ is the total size of all employed automata. However, in practice we usually work with small formulae and a small number of rather simple automata (see Section 4); therefore, we measure the complexity of our algorithms in $|\mathcal{B}|$ and $|\mathit{States}|$ rather than in $|\varphi|$ and $|\nu|$ (in general, $\mathcal{B}$ and *States* can be *exponentially* larger than φ and ν). This allows for a detailed complexity analysis whose results better match the reality because $|\mathcal{B}|$ and $|\mathit{States}|$ stay usually 'small'. This issue is discussed in greater detail in Section 5 where we provide some lower bounds showing that all algorithms developed in this paper are also essentially optimal from the point of view of worst-case analysis.

Technique 1 – extending the finite control

The idea behind this technique is to evaluate the atomic propositions $A_1, \ldots, A_n$ 'on the fly' by storing the (product of) $\mathcal{M}^p_{A_i}$ automata in the finite control of $\mathcal{P}$ and updating the vector of states after each transition according to the (local) change of stack contents. Note that here we conveniently use the assumptions that the $\mathcal{M}^p_{A_i}$ automata are deterministic, have total transition functions, and read the stack bottom-up. However, we also need one *additional* assumption to make this construction work:

> Each automaton $\mathcal{M}^p_{A_i}$ is also *backward deterministic*, i.e., for every $u \in Q^p_i$ and $\alpha \in \Gamma$ there is at most one state $t \in Q^p_i$ such that $\varrho^p_i(t, \alpha) = u$.

Note that this assumption is truly restrictive – there are quite simple regular languages which cannot be recognized by finite-state automata which are both deterministic and backward deterministic (as an example we can take the language $\{a^i \mid i > 0\}$).

We define a pushdown system $\mathcal{P}' = (P', \Gamma, \Delta', q'_0, \omega)$ where $P' = P \times \mathit{States}$, $q'_0 = (q_0, \boldsymbol{\varrho}(\boldsymbol{s}, \omega))$, and the transition rules Δ' are determined as follows: $\langle (p, \boldsymbol{r}), \alpha \rangle \hookrightarrow' \langle (q, \boldsymbol{u}), w \rangle$ iff the following conditions hold:

- $\langle p, \alpha \rangle \hookrightarrow \langle q, w \rangle$,
- there is $\boldsymbol{t} \in \mathit{States}$ such that $\boldsymbol{\varrho}(\boldsymbol{t}, \alpha) = \boldsymbol{r}$ and $\boldsymbol{\varrho}(\boldsymbol{t}, w^R) = \boldsymbol{u}$.

Observe that due to the backward determinism of $\mathcal{M}^p_{A_i}$ there is at most one $\boldsymbol{t}$ with the above stated properties; and thanks to determinism of $\mathcal{M}^p_{A_i}$ we further obtain that for given $\langle p, \alpha\rangle \hookrightarrow \langle q, w\rangle$ and $\boldsymbol{r} \in States$ there is at most one $\boldsymbol{u} \in States$ such that $\langle (p, \boldsymbol{r}), \alpha\rangle \hookrightarrow' \langle (q, \boldsymbol{u}), w\rangle$. From this it follows that $|\Delta'| = |\Delta| \cdot |States|$.

A configuration $\langle (q, \boldsymbol{r}), w\rangle$ of $\mathcal{P}'$ is *consistent* iff $\boldsymbol{r} = \varrho(\boldsymbol{s}, w^R)$ (remember that $\boldsymbol{s}$ is the vector of initial states of $\mathcal{M}^p_{A_i}$ automata). In other words, $\langle (q, \boldsymbol{r}), w\rangle$ is consistent iff $\boldsymbol{r}$ 'reflects' the stack contents w. Let $\langle p, w\rangle$ be a configuration of $\mathcal{P}$ and $\langle (p, \boldsymbol{r}), w\rangle$ be the (unique) associated consistent configuration of $\mathcal{P}'$. Now we can readily confirm that

(A) if $\langle p, w\rangle \rightarrow \langle q, v\rangle$, then $\langle (p, \boldsymbol{r}), w\rangle \rightarrow \langle (q, \boldsymbol{u}), v\rangle$ where $\langle (q, \boldsymbol{u}), v\rangle$ is consistent;
(B) if $\langle (p, \boldsymbol{r}), w\rangle \rightarrow \langle (q, \boldsymbol{u}), v\rangle$, then $\langle (q, \boldsymbol{u}), v\rangle$ is consistent and $\langle p, w\rangle \rightarrow \langle q, v\rangle$ is a transition of $\mathcal{T}_\mathcal{P}$.

As the initial configuration of $\mathcal{P}'$ is consistent, we see (due to (B)) that each reachable configuration of $\mathcal{P}'$ is consistent (but not each consistent configuration is necessarily reachable). Furthermore, due to (A) and (B) we also have the following:

(C) let $\langle p, w\rangle$ be a configuration of $\mathcal{P}$ (not necessarily reachable) and let $\langle (p, \boldsymbol{r}), w\rangle$ be its associated consistent configuration of $\mathcal{P}'$. Then the parts of $\mathcal{T}_\mathcal{P}$ and $\mathcal{T}_{\mathcal{P}'}$ which are reachable from $\langle p, w\rangle$ and $\langle (p, \boldsymbol{r}), w\rangle$, respectively, are isomorphic.

The underlying function f of the simple valuation ν' is defined by

$$f(A_i, (p, \boldsymbol{r})) = \begin{cases} \Gamma & \text{if } \boldsymbol{r}^p_i \in F^p_i \\ \emptyset & \text{otherwise} \end{cases}$$

for all $1 \le i \le n$, $(p, \boldsymbol{r}) \in P'$. Now it is easy to see (due to (C)) that for all $p \in P$ and $w \in \Gamma^*$ we have

$$\langle p, w\rangle \models^{\nu} \varphi \iff \langle (p, \boldsymbol{r}), w\rangle \models^{\nu'} \varphi \text{ where } \boldsymbol{r} = \varrho(\boldsymbol{s}, w^R) \quad (1)$$

During the construction of $\mathcal{P}'$ we observed that $|P'| = |P| \cdot |States|$ and $|\Delta'| = |\Delta| \cdot |States|$. Applying Theorem 2 naïvely, we obtain that using Technique 1, the model-checking problems (I) and (II) can be solved in cubic time and quadratic space (w.r.t. $|States|$), and that model-checking problem (III) takes even quadric time and space. However, closer analysis reveals that we can do *much* better.

Theorem 3. *Technique 1 (extending the finite control) gives us the following bounds on the model checking problems with regular valuations:*

1. *Problems (I) and (II) can be solved in* $\mathcal{O}(|P|^2 \cdot |\Delta| \cdot |States| \cdot |\mathcal{B}|^3)$ *time and* $\mathcal{O}(|P| \cdot |\Delta| \cdot |States| \cdot |\mathcal{B}|^2)$ *space.*
2. *Problem (III) can be solved in either* $\mathcal{O}(|P| \cdot |\Delta| \cdot (|P| + |\Delta|)^2 \cdot |States| \cdot |\mathcal{B}|^3)$ *time and* $\mathcal{O}(|P| \cdot |\Delta| \cdot (|P| + |\Delta|)^2 \cdot |States| \cdot |\mathcal{B}|^2)$ *space, or* $\mathcal{O}(|P|^3 \cdot |\Delta| \cdot (|P| + |\Delta|) \cdot |States| \cdot |\mathcal{B}|^3)$ *time and* $\mathcal{O}(|P|^3 \cdot |\Delta| \cdot (|P| + |\Delta|) \cdot |States| \cdot |\mathcal{B}|^2)$ *space.*

In other words, all problems take only *linear (!)* time and space in $|States|$.

Proof. We say that a $\mathcal{P}'$-automaton is *well-formed* iff its set of states is of the form $Q \times \mathit{States}$ where Q is a set such that $P \subseteq Q$. A transition $((p, \boldsymbol{t}), \alpha, (p', \boldsymbol{u}))$ of a well-formed $\mathcal{P}'$-automaton is *consistent* (w.r.t. ϱ) iff $\varrho(\boldsymbol{u}, \alpha) = \boldsymbol{t}$. A $\mathcal{P}'$-automaton is consistent iff it is well-formed and contains only consistent transitions.

For the proof we revisit the algorithms presented in [6]. Algorithm 1 shows the computation of *pre** from [6], restated for the special case of consistent $\mathcal{P}'$-automata.

Algorithm 1
Input: a pushdown system $\mathcal{P}' = (P \times \mathit{States}, \Gamma, \Delta', q_0, \omega)$;
a consistent $\mathcal{P}'$-automaton $\mathcal{A} = (Q \times \mathit{States}, \Gamma, \delta, P \times \mathit{States}, F)$
Output: the set of transitions of $\mathcal{A}_{pre^*}$

$\mathit{rel} \leftarrow \emptyset$; $\mathit{trans} \leftarrow \delta$; $\Delta'' \leftarrow \emptyset$;
for all $\langle (p, \boldsymbol{u}), \alpha\rangle \hookrightarrow \langle (p', \boldsymbol{u}'), \varepsilon\rangle \in \Delta'$ **do** $\mathit{trans} \leftarrow \mathit{trans} \cup \{((p, \boldsymbol{u}), \alpha, (p', \boldsymbol{u}'))\}$;
while $\mathit{trans} \neq \emptyset$ **do**
  pop $t = ((q, \boldsymbol{u}), \alpha, (q', \boldsymbol{u}'))$ from *trans*;
  if $t \notin \mathit{rel}$ **then**
    $\mathit{rel} \leftarrow \mathit{rel} \cup \{t\}$;
    for all $\langle (p_1, \boldsymbol{u}_1), \alpha_1\rangle \hookrightarrow \langle (q, \boldsymbol{u}), \alpha\rangle \in (\Delta' \cup \Delta'')$ **do**
      $\mathit{trans} \leftarrow \mathit{trans} \cup \{((p_1, \boldsymbol{u}_1), \alpha_1, (q', \boldsymbol{u}'))\}$;
    for all $\langle (p_1, \boldsymbol{u}_1), \alpha_1\rangle \hookrightarrow \langle (q, \boldsymbol{u}), \alpha\alpha_2\rangle \in \Delta'$ **do**
      $\Delta'' \leftarrow \Delta'' \cup \{\langle (p_1, \boldsymbol{u}_1), \alpha_1\rangle \hookrightarrow \langle (q', \boldsymbol{u}'), \alpha_2\rangle\}$;
      for all $((q', \boldsymbol{u}'), \alpha_2, (q'', \boldsymbol{u}'')) \in \mathit{rel}$ **do**
        $\mathit{trans} \leftarrow \mathit{trans} \cup \{((p_1, \boldsymbol{u}_1), \alpha_1, (q'', \boldsymbol{u}''))\}$;
return *rel*

We first show that computation of *pre** upholds the consistency of a $\mathcal{P}'$-automaton.

Lemma 1. *When receiving a consistent $\mathcal{P}'$-automaton as input, Algorithm 1 will output a consistent $\mathcal{P}'$-automaton.*

Proof. Recall that Algorithm 1 implements the saturation procedure of [2], i.e., all additions to the automaton correspond to the following situation:

> If $\langle (p, \boldsymbol{u}), \alpha\rangle \hookrightarrow \langle (p', \boldsymbol{u}'), w\rangle$ in Δ' and $(p', \boldsymbol{u}') \xrightarrow{w} (q, \boldsymbol{u}'')$ in the current automaton, then add a transition $((p, \boldsymbol{u}), \alpha, (q, \boldsymbol{u}''))$.

From the existence of the transition rule in Δ' we know that there exists $\boldsymbol{t} \in \mathit{States}$ such that $\varrho(\boldsymbol{t}, \alpha) = \boldsymbol{u}$ and $\varrho(\boldsymbol{t}, w^R) = \boldsymbol{u}'$. Provided that the automaton is consistent, we know that $\varrho(\boldsymbol{u}'', w^R) = \boldsymbol{u}'$. Exploiting the backward determinism we get $\boldsymbol{t} = \boldsymbol{u}''$, and hence the added transition is consistent. ◇

The fact that the algorithm only has to deal with consistent transitions influences the complexity analysis:

Lemma 2. *Given a consistent $\mathcal{P}'$-automaton $\mathcal{A}=(Q\times States, \Gamma, \delta, P\times States, F)$, we can compute $pre^*(L(\mathcal{A}))$ in $\mathcal{O}(|Q|^2\cdot|\Delta|\cdot|States|)$ time and $\mathcal{O}(|Q|\cdot|\Delta|\cdot|States|+|\delta|)$ space.*

Proof. A complete proof for the general case, discussing data structures and other details is given in [6]. Here we just point out the important differences for the special case of consistent automata.

- Line 10 will be executed once for every combination of a rule $\langle(p_1, \boldsymbol{u}_1), \alpha_1\rangle \hookrightarrow \langle(q, \boldsymbol{u}), \alpha\alpha_2\rangle$ and a (consistent) transition $((q, \boldsymbol{u}), \alpha, (q', \boldsymbol{u}'))$. Since $\boldsymbol{u}'$ is the single state for which $\varrho(\boldsymbol{u}', \alpha) = \boldsymbol{u}$ holds, there are $\mathcal{O}(|\Delta'|\cdot|Q|) = \mathcal{O}(|Q|\cdot|\Delta|\cdot|States|)$ such combinations. Thus, the size of Δ'' is also $\mathcal{O}(|Q|\cdot|\Delta|\cdot|States|)$.
- For the loop starting at line 11, $(q', \boldsymbol{u}')$ and α_2 (and hence $\boldsymbol{u}''$) are fixed, so line 12 is executed $\mathcal{O}(|Q|^2 \cdot |\Delta| \cdot |States|)$ times.
- Line 8 is executed once for every combination of rules $\langle(p_1, \boldsymbol{u}_1), \alpha_1\rangle \hookrightarrow \langle(q, \boldsymbol{u}), \alpha\rangle$ in $\Delta' \cup \Delta''$ and transitions $((q, \boldsymbol{u}), \alpha, (q', \boldsymbol{u}'))$. Since the size of Δ'' is $\mathcal{O}(|Q| \cdot |\Delta| \cdot |States|)$ and $\boldsymbol{u}'$ is unique, we have $\mathcal{O}(|Q|^2 \cdot |\Delta| \cdot |States|)$ such combinations. ◇

Lemma 3. *The repeating heads of the product of $\mathcal{P}'$ and $\mathcal{B}$ can be computed in $\mathcal{O}(|P|^2 \cdot |\Delta| \cdot |States| \cdot |\mathcal{B}|^3)$ time and $\mathcal{O}(|P| \cdot |\Delta| \cdot |States| \cdot |\mathcal{B}|^2)$ space.*

Proof. (analogous to [6]) The algorithm first computes the set $pre^*(\{\langle p', \varepsilon\rangle \mid p' \in P' \times R\})$. Since this set can be represented by a consistent automaton with $|P| \times |R| \times |States|$ many states and no transitions, this step is bounded by the aforementioned limitations on time and space. From the results a head reachability graph of size $\mathcal{O}(|P| \cdot |\Delta| \cdot |States| \cdot |\mathcal{B}|^2)$ is constructed. To find the repeating heads, we identify the strongly connected components of that graph which takes time linear in its size. ◇

We can now conclude the proof of Theorem 3. The steps required to solve the model-checking problems are as follows:

- Compute the set of repeating heads RH of the product of $\mathcal{P}'$ and $\mathcal{B}$. According to Lemma 3, this takes $\mathcal{O}(|P|^2 \cdot |\Delta| \cdot |States| \cdot |\mathcal{B}|^3)$ time and $\mathcal{O}(|P| \cdot |\Delta| \cdot |States| \cdot |\mathcal{B}|^2)$ space, and we have $|RH| = \mathcal{O}(|\Delta| \cdot |States| \cdot |\mathcal{B}|)$.
- Construct an automaton $\mathcal{A}$ accepting exactly the consistent subset of $RH\Gamma^*$. Take $\mathcal{A} = (((P\times R)\cup\{s\})\times States, \Gamma, \delta, P\times\{r_0\}\times States, \{(s, \boldsymbol{s})\})$. For every repeating head $\langle(p, r, \boldsymbol{u}), \alpha\rangle$, add to δ the unique transition $((p, r, \boldsymbol{u}), \alpha, (s, \boldsymbol{u}'))$ with $\varrho(\boldsymbol{u}', \alpha) = \boldsymbol{u}$. For every triple $(\boldsymbol{u}, \alpha, \boldsymbol{u}')$ such that $\varrho(\boldsymbol{u}', \alpha) = \boldsymbol{u}$ add to δ the transition $((s, \boldsymbol{u}), \alpha, (s, \boldsymbol{u}'))$. There are at most $\mathcal{O}(|States| \cdot |\Gamma|) \subseteq \mathcal{O}(|\Delta| \cdot |States|)$ such triples. This automaton is consistent and has $\mathcal{O}(|P| \cdot |States| \cdot |\mathcal{B}|)$ states and $\mathcal{O}(|\Delta| \cdot |States| \cdot |\mathcal{B}|)$ transitions.
- Compute the automaton $\mathcal{A}' = (((P \times R) \cup \{s\}) \times States, \Gamma, \delta', P \times \{r_0\} \times States, \{(s, \boldsymbol{s})\})$ corresponding to $pre^*(L(\mathcal{A}))$. According to Lemma 2, this takes $\mathcal{O}(|P|^2 \cdot |\Delta| \cdot |States| \cdot |\mathcal{B}|^3)$ time and $\mathcal{O}(|P| \cdot |\Delta| \cdot |States| \cdot |\mathcal{B}|^2)$ space. (Recall that the size of $\mathcal{B}$ is also a factor in the size of the product transition rules.)

- Due to Lemma 1, $\mathcal{A}'$ is consistent and accepts only consistent configurations. According to Proposition 3.1 in [6] we have $c \not\models^{\nu'} \varphi$ for every configuration in $L(\mathcal{A}')$. According to (1), we then have $\langle p, w\rangle \not\models^{\nu'} \varphi$ for every $c = \langle (p, \boldsymbol{u}), w\rangle$ in $L(\mathcal{A}')$. Hence, we can solve the problem (II) by modifying $\mathcal{A}'$ slightly; let $\mathcal{A}''$ be the automaton $\mathcal{A}'' = (((P \times R) \cup \{s\}) \times \mathit{States} \cup P, \Gamma, \delta'', P, \{(s, \boldsymbol{s})\})$ where $\delta'' = \delta' \cup \{\, (p, \alpha, q) \mid ((p, r, \boldsymbol{u}), \alpha, q) \in \delta' \,\}$. Problem (I) is solved by checking whether $\langle q_0, \omega\rangle \in L(\mathcal{A}'')$. Since none of the steps required to compute $\mathcal{A}''$ takes more than $\mathcal{O}(|P|^2 \cdot |\Delta| \cdot |\mathit{States}| \cdot |\mathcal{B}|^3)$ time and $\mathcal{O}(|P| \cdot |\Delta| \cdot |\mathit{States}| \cdot |\mathcal{B}|^2)$ space, the first part of our theorem is proven.
- To prove the second part we simply need to synchronise $\mathcal{A}''$ with the automaton $\mathcal{R}$ which recognizes all reachable configurations. Computing $\mathcal{R}$ takes $\mathcal{O}(|P| \cdot |\Delta| \cdot (|P| + |\Delta|))$ time and space according to Theorem 1. The synchronization is performed as follows: For all transitions (p, α, p') of $\mathcal{A}''$ and (q, α, q') of $\mathcal{R}$ we add a transition $((p, q), \alpha, (p', q'))$ to the product. A straightforward procedure however would give us a higher result than necessary. We can do better by employing the following trick from [6]: first all transitions (q, α, q') of $\mathcal{R}$ are sorted into buckets labelled by α. Then each transition of $\mathcal{A}''$ is multiplied with the transitions in the respective bucket. As $\mathcal{R}$ has $\mathcal{O}(|P| + |\Delta|)$ states, each bucket contains $\mathcal{O}((|P| + |\Delta|)^2)$ items. Hence, the product can be computed in $\mathcal{O}(|P| \cdot |\Delta| \cdot (|P| + |\Delta|)^2 \cdot |\mathit{States}| \cdot |\mathcal{B}|^2)$ time and space. Alternatively, we can sort the transitions of $\mathcal{A}''$ into buckets of size $\mathcal{O}(|P|^2 \cdot |\mathcal{B}|^2 \cdot |\mathit{States}|)$ (exploiting the consistency of $|\mathcal{A}''|$) and construct the product in $\mathcal{O}(|P|^3 \cdot |\Delta| \cdot (|P| + |\Delta|) \cdot |\mathit{States}| \cdot |\mathcal{B}|^2)$ time and space. If we add the time and space which is needed to construct $\mathcal{A}''$ and $\mathcal{R}$, we get the results stated in the second part of Theorem 3. □

Technique 2 – extending the stack

An alternative approach to model-checking with regular valuations is to store the vectors of *States* in the stack of $\mathcal{P}$. This technique works without any additional limitations, i.e., we do *not* need the assumption of backward determinism of $\mathcal{M}^p_{A_i}$ automata.

We define a pushdown system $\mathcal{P}' = (P, \Gamma', \Delta', q_0, \omega')$ where $\Gamma' = \Gamma \times \mathit{States}$, $\omega' = (\omega, \boldsymbol{s})$ where $\boldsymbol{s}$ is the vector of initial states of $\mathcal{M}^p_{A_i}$ automata, and the set of transition rules Δ' is determined as follows:

- $\langle p, (\alpha, \boldsymbol{r})\rangle \hookrightarrow' \langle q, \varepsilon\rangle \iff \langle p, \alpha\rangle \hookrightarrow \langle q, \varepsilon\rangle$
- $\langle p, (\alpha, \boldsymbol{r})\rangle \hookrightarrow' \langle q, (\beta, \boldsymbol{r})\rangle \iff \langle p, \alpha\rangle \hookrightarrow \langle q, \beta\rangle$
- $\langle p, (\alpha, \boldsymbol{r})\rangle \hookrightarrow' \langle q, (\beta, \boldsymbol{u})(\gamma, \boldsymbol{r})\rangle \iff \langle p, \alpha\rangle \hookrightarrow \langle q, \beta\gamma\rangle \wedge \boldsymbol{u} = \boldsymbol{\varrho}(\boldsymbol{r}, \gamma)$

Intuitively, the reason why we do not need the assumption of backward determinism in our second approach is that the stack carries complete information about the computational history of the $\mathcal{M}^p_{A_i}$ automata.

A configuration $\langle q, (\alpha_k, \boldsymbol{r}(\boldsymbol{k})) \cdots (\alpha_1, \boldsymbol{r}(\boldsymbol{1}))\rangle$ is called *consistent* iff $\boldsymbol{r}(\boldsymbol{1}) = \boldsymbol{s}$ and $\boldsymbol{r}(\boldsymbol{j+1}) = \boldsymbol{\varrho}(\boldsymbol{r}(\boldsymbol{j}), \alpha_j)$ for all $1 \le j < k$.

The underlying function f of the simple valuation ν' is defined by

$$f(A_i, p) = \{(\alpha, \boldsymbol{r}) \mid \alpha \in \Gamma, \varrho^p_i(\boldsymbol{r}^p_i, \alpha) \in F^p_i\}$$

It is easy to show that $\langle q, \alpha_k \cdots \alpha_1 \rangle \models^\nu \varphi \iff \langle q, (\alpha_k, \boldsymbol{r(k)}) \cdots (\alpha_1, \boldsymbol{r(1)}) \rangle \models^{\nu'} \varphi$ where $\langle q, (\alpha_k, \boldsymbol{r(k)}) \cdots (\alpha_1, \boldsymbol{r(1)}) \rangle$ is consistent.

Theorem 4. *Technique 2 (extending the stack) gives us the same bounds on the model checking problems with regular valuations as Technique 1, i.e.:*

1. *Problems (I) and (II) can be solved in* $\mathcal{O}(|P|^2 \cdot |\Delta| \cdot |States| \cdot |\mathcal{B}|^3)$ *time and* $\mathcal{O}(|P| \cdot |\Delta| \cdot |States| \cdot |\mathcal{B}|^2)$ *space.*
2. *Problem (III) can be solved in either* $\mathcal{O}(|P| \cdot |\Delta| \cdot (|P| + |\Delta|)^2 \cdot |States| \cdot |\mathcal{B}|^3)$ *time and* $\mathcal{O}(|P| \cdot |\Delta| \cdot (|P| + |\Delta|)^2 \cdot |States| \cdot |\mathcal{B}|^2)$ *space, or* $\mathcal{O}(|P|^3 \cdot |\Delta| \cdot (|P| + |\Delta|) \cdot |States| \cdot |\mathcal{B}|^3)$ *time and* $\mathcal{O}(|P|^3 \cdot |\Delta| \cdot (|P| + |\Delta|) \cdot |States| \cdot |\mathcal{B}|^2)$ *space.*

Proof. Since $|\Delta'| = |\Delta| \cdot |States|$ (here we use the fact that each $\mathcal{M}^p_{A_i}$ is deterministic), we can compute a $\mathcal{P}$-automaton $\mathcal{D} = (D, \Gamma', \gamma, P, G)$ of size $\mathcal{O}(|P| \cdot |\Delta| \cdot |States| \cdot |\mathcal{B}|^2)$ in $\mathcal{O}(|P|^2 \cdot |\Delta| \cdot |States| \cdot |\mathcal{B}|^3)$ time and $\mathcal{O}(|P| \cdot |\Delta| \cdot |States| \cdot |\mathcal{B}|^2)$ space such that $\mathcal{D}$ recognizes all configurations of $\mathcal{P}'$ which violate φ (see Theorem 1); then, to solve problem (I), we just look if $\mathcal{D}$ accepts $\langle q_0, \omega' \rangle$.

The problem with $\mathcal{D}$ is that it can also accept inconsistent configurations of $\mathcal{P}'$. Fortunately, it is possible to perform a kind of 'synchronization' with the reversed $\mathcal{M}^p_{A_i}$ automata. We define $\mathcal{A} = (Q, \Gamma, \delta, P, F)$ where $Q = (D \times States) \cup P$, $F = G \times \{\boldsymbol{s}\}$, and δ is defined as follows:

- if $g \xrightarrow{(\alpha, \boldsymbol{r})} h$ is a transition of γ, then δ contains a transition $(g, \boldsymbol{t}) \xrightarrow{\alpha} (h, \boldsymbol{r})$ where $\boldsymbol{t} = \varrho(\boldsymbol{r}, \alpha)$;
- if $(p, \boldsymbol{r}) \xrightarrow{\alpha} (g, \boldsymbol{t})$, $p \in P$, is a transition of δ, then $p \xrightarrow{\alpha} (g, \boldsymbol{t})$ is also a transition of δ.

Notice that $\mathcal{A}$ is the same size as $\mathcal{D}$ since in every transition $\boldsymbol{t}$ is uniquely determined by $\boldsymbol{r}$ and α. Now, for every configuration $\langle p, (\alpha_k, \boldsymbol{r(k)}) \cdots (\alpha_1, \boldsymbol{r(1)}) \rangle$, one can easily prove (by induction on k) that

$$\gamma(p, (\alpha_k, \boldsymbol{r(k)}) \cdots (\alpha_1, \boldsymbol{r(1)})) = q \text{ where } \boldsymbol{r(j{+}1)} = \varrho(\boldsymbol{r(j)}, \alpha_j) \text{ for all } 1 \leq j < k$$

iff

$$\delta((p, \boldsymbol{r}), \alpha_k \cdots \alpha_1) = (q, \boldsymbol{r(1)}) \text{ where } \boldsymbol{r} = \varrho(\boldsymbol{r(k)}, \alpha_k).$$

From this we immediately obtain that $\mathcal{A}$ indeed accepts exactly those configurations of $\mathcal{P}$ which violate φ. Moreover, the size of $\mathcal{A}$ and the time and space bounds to compute it are the same as for $\mathcal{D}$ which proves the first part of the theorem.

To solve problem (III), one can try out the same strategies as in Theorem 3. Again, it turns out that the most efficient way is to synchronize $\mathcal{A}$ with the $\mathcal{P}$-automaton $\mathcal{R}$ which recognizes all reachable configurations of $\mathcal{P}$. Employing the same trick as in Theorem 3 (i.e., sorting transitions of $\mathcal{R}$ into buckets according to their labels), we obtain that the size of $\mathcal{A}'$ is $\mathcal{O}(|P| \cdot |\Delta| \cdot (|P| + |\Delta|)^2 \cdot |States| \cdot |\mathcal{B}|^2)$ and it can be computed in $\mathcal{O}(|P| \cdot |\Delta| \cdot (|P| + |\Delta|)^2 \cdot |States| \cdot |\mathcal{B}|^3)$ time using $\mathcal{O}(|P| \cdot |\Delta| \cdot (|P| + |\Delta|)^2 \cdot |States| \cdot |\mathcal{B}|^2)$ space. Using the alternative method (sorting transitions of $\mathcal{A}$ into buckets instead and exploiting determinism) we get an automaton of size $\mathcal{O}(|P|^3 \cdot |\Delta| \cdot (|P| + |\Delta|) \cdot |States| \cdot |\mathcal{B}|^2)$ in $\mathcal{O}(|P|^3 \cdot |\Delta| \cdot (|P| + |\Delta|) \cdot |States| \cdot |\mathcal{B}|^3)$ in time and $\mathcal{O}(|P|^3 \cdot |\Delta| \cdot (|P| + |\Delta|) \cdot |States| \cdot |\mathcal{B}|^2)$ space. □

4 Applications

4.1 Interprocedural Data-Flow Analysis

Pushdown systems provide a very natural formal model for programs with recursive procedures. Hence, it should not be surprising that efficient analysis techniques for pushdown automata can be applied to some problems of interprocedural data-flow analysis (see, e.g., [7,11]). Here we briefly discuss the convenience of regular valuations in this application area. We do not present any detailed results about the complexity of concrete problems, because this would necessarily lead to a quite complicated and lengthy development which is beyond the scope of our work (though the associated questions are very interesting on their own). Our aim is just to provide convincing arguments demonstrating the importance of the technical results achieved in Section 3.

A standard way of abstracting recursive programs for purposes of interprocedural data-flow analysis it to represent each procedure P by its associated *flow graph*. Intuitively, the flow graph of P is a labelled binary graph whose nodes correspond to 'program points', and an arc $n \xrightarrow{c} n'$ indicates that the control flow is shifted from the point n to n' by performing the instruction c. The entry and exit points of P are modeled by distinguished nodes. To avoid undecidabilities, the `if-then-else` command (and related instructions) are modeled by nondeterminism, i.e., there can be several arcs from the same node. Moreover, there are special arcs with labels of the form *call* $Q(args)$ which model procedure calls (where *args* is a vector of terms which are passed as parameters). Flow graphs can be easily translated to pushdown systems; as transitions of pushdown systems are not labelled, we first perform a 'technical' modification of the flow graph, replacing each arc $n \xrightarrow{c} n'$ where n is a nondeterministic node (i.e., a node with more than one successor) by two arcs $n \xrightarrow{\varepsilon} n'' \xrightarrow{c} n'$ where n'' is a new node and ε is a 'dummy' instruction without any effect. This allows to associate the instruction of each arc $n \xrightarrow{c} n'$ directly to n (some nodes are associated to the dummy instruction). Now suppose there is a recursive system of procedures $P_1, \ldots, P_n, S$, where S is a distinguished starting procedure which cannot be called recursively. Their associated flow graphs can be translated to a pushdown automaton in the following way:

- for each node n of each flowgraph we introduce a fresh stack symbol X_n;
- for each arc of the form $n \xrightarrow{c} n'$ we add a rule $\langle \cdot, X_n \rangle \hookrightarrow \langle \cdot, X_{n'} \rangle$, where $\cdot$ is the (only) control location;
- for each arc of the form $n \xrightarrow{call\ Q(args)} n'$ we add the rule $\langle \cdot, X_n \rangle \hookrightarrow \langle \cdot, Q_{entry} X_{n'} \rangle$ where Q_{entry} is the stack symbol for the entry node of (the flow graph of) Q. Observe that one can also push special symbols corresponding to arguments if needed;

- for each procedure P different from S we add the rule $\langle \cdot, P_{exit} \rangle \hookrightarrow \langle \cdot, \varepsilon \rangle$, where P_{exit} corresponds to the exit node of P. For the starting procedure S we add the rule $\langle \cdot, S_{exit} \rangle \hookrightarrow \langle \cdot, S_{exit} \rangle$.

In other words, the top stack symbol corresponds to the current program point (and to the instruction which is to be executed), and the stack carries the information about the history of activation calls. Now, many of the well-known properties of data-flow analysis (e.g., liveness, reachability, very business, availability) can be expressed in LTL and verified by a model-checking algorithm (in some cases the above presented construction of a pushdown automaton must be modified so that all necessary information is properly reflected – but the principle is still the same). For example, if we want to check that a given variable Y is *dead* at a given program point n (i.e., whenever the program point n is executed, in each possible continuation we have that Y is either not used or it is redefined before it is used), we can model-check the formula

$$\Box(top_n \implies ((\neg used_Y \,\mathcal{U}\, def_Y) \;\vee\; (\Box \neg used_Y)))$$

in the configuration $\langle \cdot, S_{entry} \rangle$, where $used_Y$, $used_Y$, and def_Y are atomic propositions which are valid in exactly those configurations where the topmost stack symbol corresponds to the program point n, to an instruction which uses the variable Y, or to an instruction which defines Y, respectively. Even in this simple example, we can see that regular valuations are indeed useful – if we have a language with dynamic scoping (e.g., LISP), we *cannot* resolve to which Y the instruction $Y := 3$ at a program point n refers to without examining the stack of activation records (the Y refers to a local variable Y of the topmost procedure in the stack of activation records which declares it). So, $used_Y$ and def_Y would be interpreted by regular valuations in this case.

The example above is quite simple. The 'real' power of regular valuations would become apparent in a context of more complicated problems where we need to examine complex relationships among dynamically gathered pieces of information. This is one of the subjects of intended future work.

4.2 Pushdown Systems with Checkpoints

Another area where the results of Section 3.1 find a natural application is the analysis of recursive computations with local security checks. Modern programming languages contain methods for performing run-time inspections of the stack of activation records, and processes can thus take dynamic decisions based on the gathered information. An example is the class `AccessController` implemented in Java Development Kit 1.2 offering the method `checkPermission` which checks whether all methods stored in the stack are granted a given permission. If not, the method rises an exception.

We propose a (rather general) formal model of such systems called *pushdown system with checkpoints*. Our work was inspired by the paper [10] which deals with the same problem. Our model is more general, however. The model of [10] is suitable only for checking safety properties, does not model data-flow, and forbids mutually recursive procedure calls whereas our model has none of these restrictions. Properties of pushdown systems with checkpoints can be expressed in LTL and we provide an efficient model-checking algorithm for LTL with regular valuations.

Definition 4. *A* pushdown system with checkpoints *is a triple* $\mathcal{C} = (\mathcal{P}, \xi, \eta)$ *where*

- $\mathcal{P} = (P, \Gamma, \Delta, q_0, \omega)$ *is a pushdown system,*
- ξ *is a function with domain* $\mathcal{D} \subseteq P \times \Gamma$ *which assigns to each pair* $(p, \alpha) \in \mathcal{D}$ *a deterministic finite-state automaton* $\mathcal{M}^p_\alpha = (Q^p_\alpha, \Gamma, \delta^p_\alpha, s^p_\alpha, F^p_\alpha)$*. For technical convenience, we assume that* δ^p_α *is total,* $s^p_\alpha \notin F^p_\alpha$*, and* $L(\mathcal{M}^p_\alpha) \subseteq \{w\alpha \mid w \in \Gamma^*\}$*. Elements of* $\mathcal{D}$ *are called* checkpoints.
- $\eta\colon \Delta \to \{+, -, 0\}$ *is a function which partitions the set of transition rules into* positive, negative, *and* independent *ones. We require that if* (p, α) *is* not *a checkpoint, then all rules of the form* $\langle p, \alpha\rangle \hookrightarrow \langle q, v\rangle$ *are independent.*

The function η determines whether a rule can be applied when an inspection of the stack at a checkpoint yields a positive or negative result, or whether it is independent of such tests. Using positive and negative rules, we can model systems which perform `if-then-else` commands where the condition is based on dynamic checks; hence, these checks can be nested to an arbitrary level. The fact that a rule $\langle p, \alpha\rangle \hookrightarrow \langle q, v\rangle$ is positive, negative, or independent is denoted by $\langle p, \alpha\rangle \hookrightarrow^+ \langle q, v\rangle$, $\langle p, \alpha\rangle \hookrightarrow^- \langle q, v\rangle$, or $\langle p, \alpha\rangle \hookrightarrow^0 \langle q, v\rangle$, respectively.

To $\mathcal{C}$ we associate a unique transition system $\mathcal{T}_\mathcal{C}$ where the set of states is the set of all configurations of $\mathcal{P}$, $\langle q_0, \omega\rangle$ is the root, and the transition relation is the least relation $\to$ satisfying the following:

- if $\langle p, \alpha\rangle \hookrightarrow^+ \langle q, v\rangle$, then $\langle p, \alpha w\rangle \to \langle q, vw\rangle$ for all $w \in \Gamma^*$ s.t. $w^R\alpha \in L(\mathcal{M}^p_\alpha)$;
- if $\langle p, \alpha\rangle \hookrightarrow^- \langle q, v\rangle$, then $\langle p, \alpha w\rangle \to \langle q, vw\rangle$ for all $w \in \Gamma^*$ s.t. $w^R\alpha \notin L(\mathcal{M}^p_\alpha)$;
- if $\langle p, \alpha\rangle \hookrightarrow^0 \langle q, v\rangle$, then $\langle p, \alpha w\rangle \to \langle q, vw\rangle$ for all $w \in \Gamma^*$.

Some natural problems for pushdown processes with checkpoints are listed below.

- The reachability problem: given a pushdown system with checkpoints, is a given configuration reachable?
- The checkpoint-redundancy problem: given a pushdown system with checkpoints and a checkpoint (p, α), is there a reachable configuration where the checkpoint (p, α) is (or is not) satisfied?
  This problem is important because redundant checkpoints can be safely removed together with all negative (or positive) rules, declaring all remaining rules as independent. Thus, one can decrease the runtime overhead.
- The global safety problem: given a pushdown system with checkpoints and a formula φ of LTL, do all reachable configurations satisfy φ?
  An efficient solution to this problem allows to make 'experiments' with checkpoints with the aim of finding a solution with a minimal runtime overhead.

Actually, it is quite easy to see that all these problems (and many others) can be encoded by LTL formulae and regular valuations. For example, to solve the reachability problem, we take a predicate A which is satisfied only by the configuration $\langle p, w\rangle$ whose reachability is in question (the associated automaton $\mathcal{M}_A^p$ has *length*(w) states) and then we check the formula $\Box(\neg A)$. Observe that this formula in fact says that $\langle p, w\rangle$ is *unreachable*; the reachability itself is not directly expressible in LTL (we can only say that $\langle p, w\rangle$ is reachable in *every run*). However, it does not matter because we can simply negate the answer of the model-checking algorithm.

Model-Checking LTL for Pushdown Systems with Checkpoints. Let $\mathcal{C} = (\mathcal{P}, \xi, \eta)$ be a pushdown system with checkpoints, where $\mathcal{P} = (P, \Gamma, \Delta, q_0, \omega)$. We define a pushdown system $\mathcal{P}' = (P \times \{+, -, 0\}, \Gamma, \Delta', (q_0, 0), \omega)$ where Δ' is the least set of rules satisfying the following (for each $x \in \{+, -, 0\}$);

- if $\langle p, \alpha\rangle \hookrightarrow^{+} \langle q, v\rangle \in \Delta$, then $\langle (p, x), \alpha\rangle \hookrightarrow \langle (q, +), v\rangle \in \Delta'$;
- if $\langle p, \alpha\rangle \hookrightarrow^{-} \langle q, v\rangle \in \Delta$, then $\langle (p, x), \alpha\rangle \hookrightarrow \langle (q, -), v\rangle \in \Delta'$;
- if $\langle p, \alpha\rangle \hookrightarrow^{0} \langle q, v\rangle \in \Delta$, then $\langle (p, x), \alpha\rangle \hookrightarrow \langle (q, 0), v\rangle \in \Delta'$.

Intuitively, $\mathcal{P}'$ behaves in the same way as the underlying pushdown system $\mathcal{P}$ of $\mathcal{C}$, but it also 'remembers' what kind of rule (positive, negative, independent) was used to enter the current configuration.

Let ν be a regular valuation for configurations of $\mathcal{C}$ with an underlying function f (see Definition 3), and let φ be an LTL formula. Let *Check*, *Neg*, and *Pos* be fresh atomic propositions which do not appear in φ. We define a function f', which is the underlying function for a regular valuation ν' for configurations of $\mathcal{P}'$, as follows:

- if $A \in At \setminus \{\mathit{Check}, \mathit{Neg}, \mathit{Pos}\}$, then $f'(A, (p, x)) = f(A, p)$ for $x \in \{+, -, 0\}$
- $f'(\mathit{Check}, (p, x)) = \mathcal{M}$ for $x \in \{+, -, 0\}$, where $\mathcal{M}$ is the product automaton accepting $\bigcup_{\alpha \in \mathcal{S}} L(\mathcal{M}_\alpha^p)$ where $\mathcal{S} = \{\alpha \mid (p, \alpha) \text{ is a checkpoint}\}$
- $f'(\mathit{Neg}, (p, -)) = f'(\mathit{Pos}, (p, +)) = \mathcal{M}$, where $\mathcal{M}$ is a one-state automaton accepting Γ^*.
- $f'(\mathit{Neg}, (p, 0)) = f'(\mathit{Neg}, (p, +)) = f'(\mathit{Pos}, (p, -)) = f'(\mathit{Pos}, (p, 0)) = \mathcal{M}$, where $\mathcal{M}$ is a one-state automaton accepting $\emptyset$.

Now we can readily confirm the following:

Theorem 5. *Let $\langle p, w\rangle$ be a configuration of $\mathcal{C}$. We have that*

$$\langle p, w\rangle \models^{\nu} \varphi \iff \langle (p, 0), w\rangle \models^{\nu'} \psi \Longrightarrow \varphi$$

where $\psi \equiv \Box((\mathit{Check} \Longrightarrow \mathcal{X}(\neg \mathit{Neg})) \wedge (\neg \mathit{Check} \Longrightarrow \mathcal{X}(\neg \mathit{Pos})))$.

Proof. It suffices to realize that

$$\langle p, w\rangle \equiv \langle p_0, w_0\rangle \to \langle p_1, w_1\rangle \to \langle p_2, w_2\rangle \to \langle p_3, w_3\rangle \to \cdots$$

is an infinite path in $\mathcal{T}_{\mathcal{C}}$ iff

$$\langle (p,0), w\rangle \equiv \langle (p_0,x_0), w_0\rangle \to \langle (p_1,x_1), w_1\rangle \to \langle (p_2,x_2), w_2\rangle \to \cdots$$

is an infinite path in $\mathcal{T}_{\mathcal{P}'}$ satisfying ψ (where each x_i for $i > 0$ is either $+$, $-$, or 0; realize that all x_i are determined uniquely). Indeed, ψ ensures that all transitions in the latter path are 'consistent' with possible checkpoints in the former path. As all atomic propositions which appear in φ are evaluated identically for pairs $\langle p_i, w_i\rangle$, $\langle (p_i,x_i), w_i\rangle$ (see the definition of f' above), we can conclude that both paths either satisfy or do not satisfy φ. □

The previous theorem in fact says that the model-checking problem for LTL and pushdown systems with check-points can be reduced to the model-checking problem for LTL and 'ordinary' pushdown systems. As the formula ψ is fixed and the atomic propositions *Check*, *Neg*, and *Pos* are regular, we can evaluate the complexity bounds for the resulting model-checking algorithm using the results of Section 3.1. Let $\{A_1,\ldots,A_n\}$ be the set of all atomic propositions which appear in φ, and let $\mathcal{N} = \{\mathcal{M}_1,\ldots,\mathcal{M}_m\}$ be the set of all $\mathcal{M}^p_{A_i}$ automata. Let *States* be the Cartesian product of the sets of states of all $\mathcal{M}^p_\alpha$ automata and the automata of $\mathcal{N}$. Let $\mathcal{B}$ be a Büchi automaton which corresponds to $\neg\varphi$. Now we can state our theorem (remember that P is the set of control states and Δ the set of rules of the underlying pushdown system $\mathcal{P}$ of $\mathcal{C}$).

Theorem 6. *We have the following bounds on the model checking problems for LTL with regular valuations and pushdown systems with checkpoints:*

1. *Problems (I) and (II) can be solved in* $\mathcal{O}(|P|^2 \cdot |\Delta| \cdot |\mathit{States}| \cdot |\mathcal{B}|^3)$ *time and* $\mathcal{O}(|P| \cdot |\Delta| \cdot |\mathit{States}| \cdot |\mathcal{B}|^2)$ *space.*
2. *Problem (III) can be solved in either* $\mathcal{O}(|P| \cdot |\Delta| \cdot (|P| + |\Delta|)^2 \cdot |\mathit{States}| \cdot |\mathcal{B}|^3)$ *time and* $\mathcal{O}(|P| \cdot |\Delta| \cdot (|P| + |\Delta|)^2 \cdot |\mathit{States}| \cdot |\mathcal{B}|^2)$ *space, or* $\mathcal{O}(|P|^3 \cdot |\Delta| \cdot (|P| + |\Delta|) \cdot |\mathit{States}| \cdot |\mathcal{B}|^3)$ *time and* $\mathcal{O}(|P|^3 \cdot |\Delta| \cdot (|P| + |\Delta|) \cdot |\mathit{States}| \cdot |\mathcal{B}|^2)$ *space.*

Proof. We apply Theorem 5, which says that we can equivalently consider the model-checking problem for the pushdown system $\mathcal{P}'$, formula $\psi \Longrightarrow \varphi$, and valuation ν'. First, let us realize that the Büchi automaton which corresponds to $\neg(\psi \Longrightarrow \varphi)$ can be actually obtained by 'synchronizing' $\mathcal{B}$ with the Büchi automaton for ψ, because $\neg(\psi \Longrightarrow \varphi) \equiv \psi \wedge \neg\varphi$. As the formula ψ is *fixed*, the synchronization increases the size of $\mathcal{B}$ just by a constant factor. Hence, the automaton for $\neg(\psi \Longrightarrow \varphi)$ is asymptotically of the same size of $\mathcal{B}$. The same can be said about the sizes of P' and P, and about the sizes of Δ' and Δ. Moreover, if we collect all automata in the range of f' (see above) and consider the state space of their product, we see that it has *exactly* the size of *States* because the automata associated to *Pos* and *Neg* have only one state. □

4.3 Model-Checking CTL*

In this section, we apply the model-checking algorithm to the logic CTL* which extends LTL with existential path quantification [4]. More precisely, CTL* formulae are built according to the following abstract syntax equation:

$$\varphi ::= \mathtt{tt} \mid A \mid \neg\varphi \mid \varphi_1 \wedge \varphi_2 \mid \mathcal{E}\varphi \mid \mathcal{X}\varphi \mid \varphi_1 \,\mathcal{U}\, \varphi_2$$

where A ranges over the atomic propositions (interpreted, say, by a regular valuation represented by a finite automaton of size $|States|$).

For finite-state systems, model-checking CTL* can be reduced to checking LTL as follows [5]: For a CTL* formula φ, call the *path depth* of φ the maximal nesting depth of existential path quantifiers within φ. Subformulae of φ can be checked in ascending order of path depth; subformulae of the form $\mathcal{E}\,\varphi'$ where φ' is $\mathcal{E}$-free are checked with an LTL algorithm which returns the set of states $S_{\varphi'}$ satisfying φ'. Then $\mathcal{E}\,\varphi'$ is replaced by a fresh atomic proposition whose valuation yields true exactly on $S_{\varphi'}$, and the procedure is repeated for subformulae of higher path depth. The method can be transferred to the case of pushdown systems; running the LTL algorithm on $\mathcal{E}\,\varphi'$ returns an automaton $\mathcal{M}_{\varphi'}$. We can then replace $\mathcal{E}\,\varphi'$ by a fresh atomic proposition whose valuation is given by $\mathcal{M}_{\varphi'}$. This method was already proposed in [9], but without any complexity analysis.

Let us review the complexity of this procedure. For the rest of this subsection fix a pushdown system $\mathcal{P} = (P, \Gamma, \Delta, q_0, \omega)$. Given an $\mathcal{E}$-free formula φ, let $\mathcal{B} = (R, 2^{At}, \eta, r_0, G)$ be a Büchi automaton corresponding to φ, and let $|States|$ be the size of the $\mathcal{M}^p_{A_i}$ automata encoding the regular valuations of propositions in At.

The algorithms from section 3.1 (in general we can only use Technique 2) yield an automaton $\mathcal{M}_\varphi$ which accepts exactly the configurations satisfying $\mathcal{E}\,\varphi$. Observe that $\mathcal{M}_\varphi$ is non-deterministic, reads the stack top-down, and has $\mathcal{O}(|P| \cdot |\mathcal{B}| \cdot |States|)$ states. We need to modify the automaton before we can use it as an encoding for the regular valuation of $\mathcal{E}\,\varphi$. More precisely, we need to reverse the automaton (i.e. make it read the stack bottom-up) and then determinise it. Reversal does not increase the size, and due to the determinism of $\mathcal{M}^p_{A_i}$ (in bottom-up direction) the determinisation explodes only the '$P \times R$ part' of the states, i.e. we get an automaton $\mathcal{M}'_\varphi$ of size $O(|States| \cdot 2^{|P| \cdot |R|})$.

To check subformulae of higher path depth we replace $\mathcal{E}\,\varphi$ by a fresh atomic proposition A_φ. With (A_φ, p) we associate the automaton $\mathcal{M}^p_{A_\varphi}$ which is a copy of $\mathcal{M}'_\varphi$ where the set F^p_φ of accepting states is taken as $\{\, (q, s) \mid q \in 2^{P \times R}, q \ni (p, r_0), s \in States \,\}$. The cross product of these new automata with the 'old' $\mathcal{M}^p_{A_i}$ automata takes only $O(|States| \cdot 2^{|P| \cdot |R|})$ states again; we need just one copy of the new automaton, and all reachable states are of the form $((q, s), s)$ where $q \in 2^{P \times R}$ and $s \in States$.

As we go up in path depth, we can repeat this procedure: First we produce a deterministic valuation automaton by taking the cross product of the automata corresponding the atomic propositions and those derived from model-checking formulae of lower path depth. Then we model-check the subformula currently under consideration, and reverse and determinise the resulting automaton. By the previous arguments, each determinisation only blows up the non-deterministic part of the automaton, i.e. after each stage the size of the valuation automaton increases by a factor of $2^{|P| \cdot |\mathcal{B}_i|}$ where $\mathcal{B}_i$ is a Büchi automaton for the subformula currently under consideration.

With this in mind, we can compute the complexity for formulae of arbitrary path depth. Let $\mathcal{B}_1, \ldots, \mathcal{B}_n$ be the Büchi automata corresponding to the individual subformulae of a formula φ. Adding the times for checking the subformulas and using Theorem 4 we get that the model-checking procedure takes at most

$$\mathcal{O}\Big(|P|^2 \cdot |\Delta| \cdot |States| \cdot 2^{|P| \cdot \Sigma_{i=1}^n |\mathcal{B}_i|} \cdot \sum_{i=1}^{n} |\mathcal{B}_i|^3\Big)$$

time and

$$\mathcal{O}\Big(|P| \cdot |\Delta| \cdot |States| \cdot 2^{|P| \cdot \Sigma_{i=1}^n |\mathcal{B}_i|} \cdot \sum_{i=1}^{n} |\mathcal{B}_i|^2\Big)$$

space. The algorithm hence remains linear in both $|\Delta|$ and $|States|$. The algorithm of Burkart and Steffen [3], applied to CTL* formulae which are in the second level of the alternation hierarchy, would yield an algorithm which is cubic in $|\Delta|$. On the other hand, the performance of our algorithm in terms of the formula is less clear. In practice, it would depend strongly on the size of the Büchi automata for the subformulae, and on the result of the determinisation procedures.

5 Lower Bounds

In previous sections we established reasonably-looking upper bounds for the model-checking problem for pushdown systems (first without and then also with checkpoints) and LTL with regular valuations. However, the algorithms are polynomial in $|\mathcal{P}| + |States| + |\mathcal{B}|$, and not in the size of *problem instance* which is (as we already mentioned in Remark 1) $|\mathcal{P}| + |\nu| + |\varphi|$. In Remark 1 we also explained *why* we use these parameters – it has been argued that typical formulae (and their associated Büchi automata) are small, hence the size of $\mathcal{B}$ is actually more relevant (a model-checking algorithm whose complexity is exponential *just* due to the blowup caused by the transformation of φ into $\mathcal{B}$ is usually efficient in practice). The same can be actually said about $|States|$ – in Section 4 we have seen that there are interesting practical problems where the size of $|States|$ does not explode. Nevertheless, from the point of view of worst-case analysis (where we measure the complexity in the size of problem instance) our algorithms are *exponential.* A natural question is whether this exponential blowup is *indeed necessary*, i.e., whether we could (in principle) solve the model-checking problems more efficiently by some 'better' technique. In this section we show it is *not* the case, because all of the considered problems are **EXPTIME**-hard (even in rather restricted forms).

We start with the natural problems for pushdown systems with checkpoints mentioned in the previous section (the reachability problem, the checkpoint redundancy problem, etc.) All of them can be (polynomially) reduced to the model-checking problem for pushdown systems with checkpoints and LTL with regular valuations and therefore are solvable in **EXPTIME**. The next theorem says that this strategy is essentially optimal, because even the reachability problem provably requires exponential time.

Theorem 7. *The reachability problem for pushdown systems with checkpoints (even for those with just three control states and no negative rules) is* ***EXPTIME****-complete.*

Proof. The membership to **EXPTIME** follows from Theorem 6. We show **EXPTIME**-hardness by reduction from the acceptance problem for alternating LBA (which is known to be **EXPTIME**-complete). An *alternating LBA* is a tuple $\mathcal{M} = (Q, \Sigma, \delta, q_0, \vdash, \dashv, p)$ where $Q, \Sigma, \delta, q_0, \vdash$, and $\dashv$ are defined as for ordinary non-deterministic LBA ($\vdash$ and $\dashv$ are the left-end and right-end markers, resp.), and $p: Q \to \{\forall, \exists, acc, rej\}$ is a function which partitions the states of Q into *universal*, *existential*, *accepting*, and *rejecting*, respectively. We assume (w.l.o.g.) that δ is defined so that 'terminated' configurations (i.e., the ones from which there are no further computational steps) are exactly accepting and rejecting configurations. Moreover, we also assume that $\mathcal{M}$ always halts and that its branching degree is 2 (i.e., each configuration has at most two immediate successors). A *computational tree* for $\mathcal{M}$ on a word $w \in \Sigma^*$ is any (finite) tree T satisfying the following: the root of T is (labeled by) the initial configuration $q_0{\vdash}w{\dashv}$ of $\mathcal{M}$, and if N is a node of $\mathcal{M}$ labelled by a configuration uqv where $u, v \in \Sigma^*$ and $q \in Q$, then the following holds:

- if q is accepting or rejecting, then N is a leaf;
- if q is existential, then N has one successor whose label is some configuration which can be reached from uqv in one computational step (according to δ);
- if q is universal, then N has m successors where $m \leq 2$ is the number of configurations which can be reached from uqv in one step; those configurations are used as labels of the successors in one-to-one fashion.

$\mathcal{M}$ *accepts* w iff there is a computational tree T such that all leaves of T are accepting configurations.

Now we describe a polynomial algorithm which for a given alternating LBA $\mathcal{M} = (Q, \Sigma, \delta, q_0, \vdash, \dashv, p)$ and a word $w \in \Sigma^*$ of length n constructs a pushdown system with checkpoints $\mathcal{C} = (\mathcal{P}, \xi, \eta)$ and its configuration $\langle a, \omega \rangle$ such that $\langle a, \omega \rangle$ is reachable from the initial configuration of $\mathcal{C}$ iff $\mathcal{M}$ accepts w. Intuitively, the underlying system $\mathcal{P}$ of $\mathcal{C}$ simulates the execution of $\mathcal{M}$ and checkpoints are used to verify that there is no cheating during the process. We start with the definition of $\mathcal{P}$, putting $\mathcal{P} = (\{g, a, r\}, \Gamma, \Delta, g, \omega)$ where

- $\Gamma = \Sigma \times (Q \cup \{-\}) \cup \{\beta_1, \cdots, \beta_{n+3}\} \cup \{\gamma_1, \cdots, \gamma_n\} \cup \{\#_1^e, \#_2^e, \#_1^u, \#_2^u, A, R, \omega\}$
- Δ contains the following (families of) rules:
  1. $\langle g, \omega \rangle \hookrightarrow \langle g, \beta_1 \omega \rangle$
  2. $\langle g, \beta_i \rangle \hookrightarrow \langle g, \beta_{i+1} \varrho \rangle$ for all $1 \leq i \leq n+2$ and $\varrho \in \Sigma \times (Q \cup \{-\})$
  3. $\langle g, \beta_{n+3} \rangle \hookrightarrow \langle g, \gamma_1 \varrho \rangle$ for every $\varrho \in \{\#_1^e, \#_1^u, A, R\}$
  4. $\langle g, \gamma_i \rangle \hookrightarrow \langle g, \gamma_{i+1} \rangle$ for every $1 \leq i \leq n-1$
  5. $\langle g, \gamma_n \rangle \hookrightarrow \langle g, \varepsilon \rangle$
  6. $\langle g, A \rangle \hookrightarrow \langle a, \varepsilon \rangle$, $\langle g, R \rangle \hookrightarrow \langle r, \varepsilon \rangle$, $\langle g, \#_1^e \rangle \hookrightarrow \langle g, \beta_1 \#_1^e \rangle$, $\langle g, \#_1^u \rangle \hookrightarrow \langle g, \beta_1 \#_1^u \rangle$
  7. $\langle a, \varrho \rangle \hookrightarrow \langle a, \varepsilon \rangle$ for every $\varrho \in \Sigma \times (Q \cup \{-\})$
  8. $\langle a, \#_1^u \rangle \hookrightarrow \langle g, \beta_1 \#_2^u \rangle$, $\langle a, \#_2^u \rangle \hookrightarrow \langle a, \varepsilon \rangle$, $\langle a, \#_1^e \rangle \hookrightarrow \langle a, \varepsilon \rangle$, $\langle a, \#_2^e \rangle \hookrightarrow \langle a, \varepsilon \rangle$

9. $\langle r, \varrho\rangle \hookrightarrow \langle r, \varepsilon\rangle$ for every $\varrho \in \Sigma \times (Q \cup \{-\})$
10. $\langle r, \#_1^e\rangle \hookrightarrow \langle g, \beta_1 \#_2^e\rangle$, $\langle r, \#_2^e\rangle \hookrightarrow \langle r, \varepsilon\rangle$, $\langle r, \#_1^u\rangle \hookrightarrow \langle r, \varepsilon\rangle$, $\langle r, \#_2^u\rangle \hookrightarrow \langle r, \varepsilon\rangle$

Intuitively, the execution of $\mathcal{P}$ starts by entering the state $\langle g, \beta_1\omega\rangle$ (rule 1). Then, exactly $n+2$ symbols of $\Sigma \times (Q \cup \{-\})$ are pushed to the stack; the compound symbol $(X, t) \in \Sigma \times (Q \cup \{-\})$ indicates that the tape contains the symbol X and, if $t \in Q$, that the head is at this position and the control state of $\mathcal{M}$ is t; if $t = -$ it means that the head is elsewhere. During this process, the family of β_i symbols is used as a 'counter' (rules 2). Realize that the word w of length n is surrounded by the '$\vdash$' and '$\dashv$' markers, so the total length of the configuration is $n+2$. The last symbol β_{n+3} is then rewritten to $\gamma_1\varrho$, where ϱ is one of $\#_1^e, \#_1^u, A, R$ (rules 3). The purpose of ϱ is to keep information about the just stored configuration (whether it is existential, universal, accepting, or rejecting) and the index of a rule which is to be used to obtain the next configuration (always the first one; remember that accepting and rejecting configurations are terminal). After that, γ_1 is successively rewritten to all of the γ_i symbols and disappears (rules 4,5). Their only purpose is to invoke several consistency checks – as we shall see, each pair (g, γ_i) is a checkpoint and all rules of 4,5 are positive. Depending on the previously stored ϱ (i.e., on the type of the just pushed configuration), we either continue with guessing the next one, or change the control state to a or r (if the configuration is accepting or rejecting, resp.) Hence, the guessing goes on until we end up with an accepting or rejecting configuration. This must happen eventually, because $\mathcal{M}$ always halts. If we find an accepting configuration, we successively remove all existential configurations and those universal configuration for which we have already checked both successors. If we find a universal configuration with only one successor checked – it is recognized by the '$\#_1^u$' symbol – we change '$\#_1^u$' to '$\beta_1\#_2^u$' and check the other successor (rules 7 and 8). Similar things are done when a rejecting configuration is found. The control state is switched to r and then we remove all configurations until we (possibly) find an existential configuration for which we can try out the other successor (rules 9 and 10). We see that w is accepted by $\mathcal{M}$ iff we eventually pop the initial configuration when the control state is 'a', i.e., iff the state $\langle a, \omega\rangle$ is reachable.

To make all that work we must ensure that $\mathcal{P}$ cannot gain anything by 'cheating', i.e., by pushing inconsistent sequences of symbols which do *not* model a computation of $\mathcal{M}$ in the described way. This is achieved by declaring all pairs (g, γ_i) for $1 \leq i \leq n+1$ as checkpoints. The automaton $\mathcal{M}_{\gamma_i}^g$ for $1 \leq i \leq n$ accepts those words of the form $\omega v_1 \varrho_1 v_2 \varrho_2 \cdots v_m \varrho_m \gamma_i$, where $\mathit{length}(v_j) = n+2$, $\varrho_j \in \#_1^e, \#_2^e, \#_1^u, \#_2^u, A, R$ for every $1 \leq j \leq m$, such that the triples of symbols at positions $i, i+1, i+2$ in each pair of successive substrings v_k, v_{k+1} are consistent with the symbol ϱ_k w.r.t. the transition function δ of $\mathcal{M}$ (if some configuration has only one immediate successor, then $\mathcal{M}_{\gamma_i}^g$ 'ignores' the rule index stored in ϱ_k). Furthermore, the first configuration must be the initial one, and the last configuration v_m must be consistent with ϱ_m. Observe that $\mathcal{M}_{\gamma_i}^g$ needs just $\mathcal{O}(|\mathcal{M}|^6)$ states to store the two triples (after checking subwords v_k, ϱ_k, v_{k+1}, the triple of v_k is 'forgotten') the initial configuration, a 'counter' of capacity $n+2$, and some auxiliary information. Moreover, $\mathcal{M}_{\gamma_i}^g$ is deterministic and we can also assume that its transition function is total. As all rules associated with checkpoints are positive, any cheating move eventually results in entering a configuration where the system 'gets stuck', i.e., cheating cannot help to reach the configuration $\langle a, \omega \rangle$. □

From the (technical) proof of Theorem 7 we can easily deduce the following:

Theorem 8. *The model-checking problem (I) for pushdown systems with checkpoints (even for those with just three control states and no negative rules) is* ***EXPTIME****-complete even for a fixed LTL formula* $\Box(\neg \mathit{fin})$ *where* fin *is an atomic predicate interpreted by a* simple *valuation* ν.

Proof. Let us consider the pushdown system with checkpoints $\mathcal{C} = (\mathcal{P}, \xi, \eta)$ constructed in the proof of Theorem 7. To ensure that each finite path in $\mathcal{T}_\mathcal{C}$ is a prefix of some run, we extend the set of transition rules of Δ by a family of independent rules of the form $\langle s, \alpha \rangle \hookrightarrow \langle s, \alpha \rangle$ for each control state s and each stack symbol α. Now it suffices to realize that the initial configuration $\langle g, \omega \rangle$ cannot reach the state $\langle a, \omega \rangle$ iff it cannot reach *any* state of the form $\langle a, \omega v \rangle$ (where $v \in \Gamma^*$) iff $\langle g, \omega \rangle \models^\nu \Box(\neg \mathit{fin})$ where ν is a simple valuation with the underlying function f such that $f(\mathit{fin}) = \{(a, \omega)\}$. □

Hence, model-checking LTL for pushdown systems with checkpoints is **EXPTIME**-complete even for *simple* valuations.

Now we analyze the complexity of model-checking with (ordinary) pushdown systems and LTL formulae with regular valuations. First, realize that if we take any fixed formula and a subclass of pushdown systems where the number of control states is bounded by some constant, the model-checking problem is decidable in *polynomial* time. Now we prove that if the number of control states is not bounded, the model-checking problem becomes **EXPTIME**-complete even for a fixed formula. At this point, one is tempted to apply Theorem 5 to the formula $\Box(\neg \mathit{fin})$ of Theorem 8. Indeed, it allows to reduce the model-checking problem for pushdown systems with checkpoints and $\Box(\neg \mathit{fin})$ to the model-checking problem for ordinary pushdown systems and another fixed formula $\psi \Longrightarrow \Box(\neg \mathit{fin})$. Unfortunately, this reduction is *not* polynomial because the atomic proposition *Check* occurring in ψ is interpreted with the help of several *product* automata constructed out of the original automata which implement checkpoints (see the previous section). Therefore we need one more technical proof.

Theorem 9. *The model-checking problem (I) for pushdown systems and LTL formulae with regular valuations is* ***EXPTIME****-complete even for a fixed formula* $(\Box \mathit{correct}) \Longrightarrow (\Box \neg \mathit{fin})$.

Proof. This proof is similar to the proof of Theorem 7. Again, we construct a pushdown system $\mathcal{P}$ which simulates the execution of an alternating LBA $\mathcal{M} = (Q, \Sigma, \delta, q_0, \vdash, \dashv, p)$ on an input word $w \in \Sigma^*$ of length n. The difference is that, since there are no checkpoints, we must find a new way of 'cheating-detection', i.e., we must be able to recognize situations when the next configuration of $\mathcal{M}$ has not been guessed correctly. It is achieved by adding a family of control states $c_1, \ldots, c_n$; after guessing a new configuration, $\mathcal{P}$ successively switches its control state to $c_1, \ldots, c_n$ without modifying its stack. The underlying function f of the constructed regular valuation assigns to each pair $(\mathit{correct}, c_i)$ a deterministic automaton $\mathcal{M}^{c_i}_{\mathit{correct}}$ which checks that the triples of symbols at positions $i, i+1, i+2$ in each pair of successive configurations previously pushed to the stack are 'consistent' ($\mathcal{M}^{c_i}_{\mathit{correct}}$ is almost the same automaton as the $\mathcal{M}^{g}_{\gamma_i}$ of the proof of Theorem 7). All other pairs of the form $(\mathit{correct}, p)$ are assigned an automaton accepting Γ^*. The $\mathcal{P}$ is formally defined as follows: $\mathcal{P} = (\{g, a, r, c_1, \ldots, c_n\}, \Gamma, \Delta, g, \omega)$ where

- $\Gamma = \Sigma \times (Q \cup \{-\}) \cup \{\beta_1, \cdots, \beta_{n+3}\} \cup \{\#^e_1, \#^e_2, \#^u_1, \#^u_2, A, R, \omega\}$
- Δ contains the following (families of) rules:
  1. $\langle g, \omega\rangle \hookrightarrow \langle g, \beta_1\omega\rangle$
  2. $\langle g, \beta_i\rangle \hookrightarrow \langle g, \beta_{i+1}\varrho\rangle$ for all $1 \le i \le n+2$ and $\varrho \in \Sigma \times (Q \cup \{-\})$
  3. $\langle g, \beta_{n+3}\rangle \hookrightarrow \langle c_1, \varrho\rangle$ for every $\varrho \in \{\#^e_1, \#^u_1, A, R\}$
  4. $\langle c_i, \varrho\rangle \hookrightarrow \langle c_{i+1}, \varrho\rangle$ for every $1 \le i \le n-1$ and $\varrho \in \{\#^e_1, \#^u_1, A, R\}$
  5. $\langle c_n, \varrho\rangle \hookrightarrow \langle g, \varrho\rangle$ for every $\varrho \in \{\#^e_1, \#^u_1, A, R\}$
  6. $\langle g, A\rangle \hookrightarrow \langle a, \varepsilon\rangle$, $\langle g, R\rangle \hookrightarrow \langle r, \varepsilon\rangle$, $\langle g, \#^e_1\rangle \hookrightarrow \langle g, \beta_1\#^e_1\rangle$, $\langle g, \#^u_1\rangle \hookrightarrow \langle g, \beta_1\#^u_1\rangle$
  7. $\langle a, \varrho\rangle \hookrightarrow \langle a, \varepsilon\rangle$ for every $\varrho \in \Sigma \times (Q \cup \{-\})$
  8. $\langle a, \#^u_1\rangle \hookrightarrow \langle g, \beta_1\#^u_2\rangle$, $\langle a, \#^u_2\rangle \hookrightarrow \langle a, \varepsilon\rangle$, $\langle a, \#^e_1\rangle \hookrightarrow \langle a, \varepsilon\rangle$, $\langle a, \#^e_2\rangle \hookrightarrow \langle a, \varepsilon\rangle$
  9. $\langle r, \varrho\rangle \hookrightarrow \langle r, \varepsilon\rangle$ for every $\varrho \in \Sigma \times (Q \cup \{-\})$
  10. $\langle r, \#^e_1\rangle \hookrightarrow \langle g, \beta_1\#^e_2\rangle$, $\langle r, \#^e_2\rangle \hookrightarrow \langle r, \varepsilon\rangle$, $\langle r, \#^u_1\rangle \hookrightarrow \langle r, \varepsilon\rangle$, $\langle r, \#^u_2\rangle \hookrightarrow \langle r, \varepsilon\rangle$
  11. $\langle x, \varrho\rangle \hookrightarrow \langle x, \varrho\rangle$ for every control state x and every $\varrho \in \Gamma$.

Hence, the rules are almost the same as in the proof of Theorem 7, except for some changes in 3.,4.,5., and 11. The underlying function f of the constructed regular valuation assigns to (fin, a) an automaton recognizing all strings of Γ^* where the last symbol is ω, and to all other pairs of the form (fin, p) an automaton recognizing the empty language. We see that $\mathcal{M}$ accepts w iff there is an infinite path from the state $\langle g, \omega\rangle$ such that *correct* holds in all states of the path and *fin* holds in at least one state iff $\langle g, \omega\rangle \not\models^{\nu} (\Box \mathit{correct}) \Longrightarrow (\Box \neg \mathit{fin})$ where ν is the constructed regular valuation. □

Observe that model-checking with pushdown systems and any fixed LTL formula whose predicates are interpreted by a *simple* valuation is already *polynomial* (see Theorem 1).

6 Conclusion

We have presented two different techniques for checking LTL with regular valuations on pushdown systems. Both techniques rely on a reduction to (and slight modification of) the problem for simple valuations discussed in [6]. Both techniques take linear time and space in $|\mathit{States}|$ where *States* is the set of states of an automaton representing the regular predicates used in the formula. Since both take the same asymptotic time it would be interesting to compare their efficiency in practice (for cases where both techniques can be used).

The solution can be seamlessly combined with the concept of symbolic pushdown systems in [8]. These are used to achieve a succinct representation of Boolean Programs, i.e., programs with (recursive) procedures in which all variables are boolean.

The ability to represent data is a distinct advantage over the approaches hitherto made in our areas of application, namely data-flow analysis [7] and security properties [10]. For the latter, we have indicated that our model is more general. Our approach provides a unifying framework for these applications without losing efficiency. Both techniques take linear time in $|States|$ whereas the methods used in [7] were cubic (though erroneously reported as linear there, too). In [10] no complexity analysis was conducted.

References

1. T. Ball and S.K. Rajamani. Bebop: A symbolic model checker for boolean programs. In *SPIN 00: SPIN Workshop*, volume 1885 of *LNCS*, pages 113–130. Springer, 2000.
2. A. Bouajjani, J. Esparza, and O. Maler. Reachability analysis of pushdown automata: Application to model checking. In *Proc. CONCUR'97*, LNCS 1243, pages 135–150.
3. O. Burkart and B. Steffen. Model checking the full modal mu-calculus for infinite sequential processes. In *Proc. ICALP'97*, volume 1256 of *LNCS*, pages 419–429. Springer, 1997.
4. E.A. Emerson. Temporal and modal logic. *Handbook of Theoretical Comp. Sci.*, B, 1991.
5. E.A. Emerson and C. Lei. Modalities for model checking: Branching time logic strikes back. *Science of Computer Programming*, 8(3):275–306, 1987.
6. J. Esparza, D. Hansel, P. Rossmanith, and S. Schwoon. Efficient algorithms for model checking pushdown systems. In *Proc. CAV'00*, LNCS 1855, pages 232–247. Springer, 2000.
7. J. Esparza and J. Knoop. An automata-theoretic approach to interprocedural data-flow analysis. In *Proceedings of FoSSaCS'99*, volume 1578 of *LNCS*, pages 14–30. Springer, 1999.
8. J. Esparza and S. Schwoon. A BDD-based model checker for recursive programs. In *Proc. CAV'01*, LNCS 2102, pages 324–336. Springer, 2001.
9. A. Finkel, B. Willems, and P. Wolper. A direct symbolic approach to model checking pushdown systems. *Electronic Notes in Theoretical Computer Science*, 9, 1997.
10. T. Jensen, D. Le Métayer, and T. Thorn. Verification of control flow based security properties. In *IEEE Symposium on Security and Privacy*, pages 89–103, 1999.
11. B. Steffen, A. Claßen, M. Klein, J. Knoop, and T. Margaria. The fixpoint-analysis machine. In *Proceedings of CONCUR'95*, volume 962 of *LNCS*, pages 72–87. Springer, 1995.

What Will Be Eventually True of Polynomial Hybrid Automata?*

Martin Fränzle

Department of Computer Science, Carl-von-Ossietzky Universität Oldenburg,
P.O. Box 2503, D-26111 Oldenburg, Germany,
Martin.Fraenzle@Informatik.Uni-Oldenburg.De,
Phone/Fax: +49-441-798-3046/2145

Abstract. Hybrid automata have been introduced in both control engineering and computer science as a formal model for the dynamics of hybrid discrete-continuous systems. While computability issues concerning safety properties have been extensively studied, liveness properties have remained largely uninvestigated. In this article, we investigate decidability of state recurrence and of progress properties.

First, we show that state recurrence and progress are in general undecidable for polynomial hybrid automata. Then, we demonstrate that they are closely related for hybrid automata subject to a simple model of noise, even though these automata are infinite-state systems. Based on this, we augment a semi-decision procedure for recurrence with a semi-decision method for length-boundedness of paths in such a way that we obtain an automatic verification method for progress properties of linear and polynomial hybrid automata that may only fail on pathological, practically uninteresting cases. These cases are such that satisfaction of the desired progress property crucially depends on the complete absence of noise, a situation unlikely to occur in real hybrid systems.

Keywords: Hybrid systems; State recurrence; Progress properties; Decidability; Verification procedures

1 Introduction

Embedded digital systems have become ubiquitous in everyday life. Many such systems, and in particular many of the safety-critical ones, operate within or even comprise tightly coupled networks of both discrete-state and continuous-state components. The behaviour of such *hybrid discrete-continuous systems* cannot be fully understood without explicitly modelling the tight interaction of discrete and continuous dynamics. Tools for building such models and for simulating their dynamics are commercially available, e.g. Simulink with the Stateflow ex-

* This article reflects work that has been partially funded by the Deutsche Forschungsgemeinschaft under contract DFG Da 206/5-2.

N. Kobayashi and B.C. Pierce (Eds.): TACS 2001, LNCS 2215, pp. 340–359, 2001.

tension[1], Matrix$_X$[2], or Statemate MAGNUM[3]. Simulation is, however, inherently incomplete and has to be complemented by *verification*, which amounts to showing that the coupled dynamics of the embedded system and its environment is well-behaved, regardless of the actual disturbance. Basic notions of being well-behaved demand that the system under investigation may never reach an undesirable state (often called *safety*) or that it will eventually reach a desirable state (*progress*).

Verification of hybrid systems calls for integration of discrete and continuous reasoning within a single formal model. The hope is that such combined formalisms, e.g. those proposed in [GNRR93,AKNS95,AHS96], may ultimately help in developing real embedded systems. Among such formalisms, the automata-based ones provide the most immediate prospect for mechanization. Roughly, hybrid automata can be characterized as a *combination of finite automata* whose transitions are triggered by predicates on the continuous plant state *with a description of the evolution of the continuous plant.* The latter consists of a set of real-valued variables that are governed by sets of syntactically restricted differential (in-)equations from which a currently active set is selected depending on the current automaton state. Hybrid automata lend themselves to analysis by state-space exploration methods. The state of the art with respect to state-exploratory *automatic* verification methods for hybrid systems is marked by semi-decision procedure for state reachability, as available in e.g. the HyTech tool [HHWT95]. These can — at least in principle, if complexity does not become prohibitive — be used for effectively *falsifying* safety properties of hybrid system. However, as state reachability has been shown to be undecidable even for very simple hybrid systems [HKPV95], the complementary problem, i.e. *verifying* that no undesirable state may ever be reached, cannot always be done effectively.

However, a closer look at the proof technique used in [HKPV95] for showing undecidability of state reachability in linear hybrid automata reveals that the relevance of these undecidability results to hybrid control is questionable. The proofs use a representation of two-counter machines by hybrid systems which relies on encoding infinite information, namely the set of natural numbers, within a compact interval of continuous states, whereas the ubiquity of noise limits the information content encodable by any bounded continuous variable encountered in real hybrid systems to a finite value. Hence, on simple information-theoretic grounds, the undecidability results thus obtained can be said to be artefacts of an overly idealized formalization. They will not necessarily carry over to operationally more adequate models of hybrid dynamics.

While this implies that the particular proof pattern sketched above lacks physical interpretation, it does not yield any insight as to whether the state reachability problem for hybrid systems featuring noise is decidable or not. Yet, taking noise into account at least simplifies the verification problem, as the

[1] `http://www.mathworks.com/products/simulink/` and `http://www.mathworks.com/products/stateflow/`

[2] `http://www.windriver.com/products/html/matrixx_ds.html`

[3] `http://www.ilogix.com/products/magnum/statemate_magnum.pdf`

author has shown in a companion paper to the current: using a very simple model of noise, in [Frä99] the author devised an automatic verification method for *safety* of hybrid automata that can both falsify and verify automata and that may only fail on pathological, practically uninteresting, cases. It is able to decide safety for all hybrid automata where safety does not depend on the complete absence of noise, i.e. which, if not unsafe, can tolerate some amount of noise without becoming unsafe. In the present paper, we establish similar results for *progress* properties.

Outline. We start our investigation with a definition of polynomial hybrid automata, a generalization of the more frequently analyzed class of linear hybrid automata. The definitions as well as semi-decision procedures for safety and for state recurrence are exposed in the next section; furthermore, undecidability results for state reachability, for state recurrence, and for progress are given. In Section 3 we expand on progress properties. We expose a simple model of noisy automata which allows continuous evolutions to reach a neighborhood of the target state. Given that, we show that state recurrence and progress are closely related for hybrid automata subject to noise, even though these automata are infinite-state systems. Section 4 combines these results with a semi-decision method for length-boundedness of paths, yielding an almost complete automatic verification method for progress properties of polynomial hybrid automata. A sufficient semantic criterion for success of the verification method is also given. Section 5 discusses properties of that criterion, while Section 6 concludes with a review of related work.

2 Hybrid Automata

We start our investigation by providing a formalization of hybrid automata. The class of hybrid automata we will deal with goes beyond linear hybrid automata in that we will allow polynomial (instead of only linear) activities and polynomial (instead of linear) predicates for state invariants, transition guards, and transition effects. The reasons for adopting a more general class than usual are twofold. First, all our results can be shown for this more general class without any extra effort. Second, all definitions, statements, and proofs concerning this class of hybrid automata are more compact as no need to keep state invariants separate from activity predicates and transition guards separate from transition effects arises. Instead, every state and transition can be described by just one polynomial predicate, formalised through the first-order logic over the real-closed field, denoted $\mathrm{FOL}(\mathbb{R}, +, \cdot)$ in the remainder.

Therefore, within this article, a *(polynomial) hybrid automaton of dimensionality d* ($d \in \mathbb{N}$) is a five-tuple

$$(\Sigma, \mathbf{x}, (act_\sigma)_{\sigma\in\Sigma}, (trans_{\sigma\to\sigma'})_{\sigma,\sigma'\in\Sigma}, (initial_\sigma)_{\sigma\in\Sigma}) \ ,$$

where Σ is a finite set, representing the discrete states, and $\mathbf{x} = (x_1, \ldots, x_d)$ is a vector of length d of variable names, the continuous variables of the hybrid system.[4] $(act_\sigma)_{\sigma\in\Sigma}$ is a Σ-indexed family of formulae from FOL($\mathbb{R}, +, \cdot$) representing the continuous activities and corresponding state constraints, and $(trans_{\sigma\to\sigma'})_{\sigma,\sigma'\in\Sigma}$ is a doubly Σ-indexed family of formulae from FOL($\mathbb{R}, +, \cdot$) representing the discrete transitions and their guarding conditions. Finally, the initial states of the automaton are given by the Σ-indexed family $(initial_\sigma)_{\sigma\in\Sigma}$ of formulae from FOL($\mathbb{R}, +, \cdot$). The free variables of the $initial_\sigma$ predicates are from $\mathbf{x}$, while the free variables of the act_σ and the $trans_{\sigma\to\sigma'}$ predicates are from $\overleftharpoon{\mathbf{x}}$ and $\mathbf{x}$, as these predicates relate pre-states, which are denoted by the hooked variables $\overleftharpoon{\mathbf{x}}$, to post-states, which are denoted by undecorated variables $\mathbf{x}$.

The interpretation is as follows:

- An *activity predicate* act_σ defines the possible evolution of the continuous state while the system is in discrete state σ. Hooked variable names in the predicate refer to the values of the corresponding real-valued system variables before the activity, while undecorated variable names refer to the values thereafter. A satisfying valuation $I_{\overleftharpoon{\mathbf{x}},\mathbf{x}}$ of its free variables $\overleftharpoon{\mathbf{x}}, \mathbf{x}$ is interpreted as: if the system is in state σ and its continuous variables have values $I_{\overleftharpoon{\mathbf{x}}}$ then the continuous variables may evolve to $I_{\mathbf{x}}$ while staying in state σ. Note that this single predicate thus generalizes both the state invariants and the activity functions of classical hybrid automata. E.g. the activity predicate

$$\exists \Delta t.\ \overleftharpoon{x} + 3\cdot\Delta t \le x \wedge x < \overleftharpoon{x} + 5\cdot\Delta t \wedge 4 < x \wedge x \le 10$$

  encodes both the linear activity $\dot{x} \in [3, 5)$, where $\dot{x}$ denotes the first derivative of x over time, and the state invariant $x \in (4, 10]$.
- A *transition predicate* $trans_{\sigma\to\sigma'}$ defines when the system may evolve from state σ to state σ' by a discrete transition (i.e., it specifies the transition guard) and what the effect of that transition on the continuous variables is. A satisfying valuation $I_{\overleftharpoon{\mathbf{x}},\mathbf{x}}$ of its free variables $\overleftharpoon{\mathbf{x}}, \mathbf{x}$ is interpreted as: if the system is in state σ and its continuous variables have values $I_{\overleftharpoon{\mathbf{x}}}$ then the system may evolve to state σ' with its continuous variables taking the new values $I_{\mathbf{x}}$.
  Assignments as present in hybrid automata are simple to represent in this framework: e.g. for a hybrid system with continuous variables $(x_1, \ldots, x_8)$ the assignment $x_7 := 5$ (where all other continuous variables are left unchanged) is encoded by the predicate $x_7 = 5 \wedge \bigwedge_{i\in\{1,\ldots,6,8\}} x_i = \overleftharpoon{x_i}$. Accordingly, guards are simply encoded through predicates over the hooked variables: e.g. the guard $x_3 > 11$ is represented by $\overleftharpoon{x_3} > 11$. A transition with guard $x_3 > 11$ and assignment $x_7 := 5$ is thus encoded by the predicate

$$\overleftharpoon{x_3} > 11 \wedge x_7 = 5 \wedge \bigwedge_{i\in\{1,\ldots,6,8\}} x_i = \overleftharpoon{x_i} \quad .$$

[4] Here and in the following, we use the convention to print vectors of variables or values in boldface. All these vectors have length d.

Multiple different transitions between the same state pair can be represented by disjunction of their encodings.

It should be noted that there is no strict need to distinguish between activities and transitions in FOL($\mathbb{R}, +, \cdot$). However, we do not want to deviate too much from standard expositions of hybrid automata. Furthermore, this distinction turns out to be convenient in the further development, as activities and transitions are dissimilar in our model of noise.

We call a hybrid automaton *deadlock-free* iff any state that is reachable through a transition has an activity-successor and, vice versa, any state that is reachable through an activity has a transition-successor, i.e. iff

$$\bigwedge_{\sigma,\sigma' \in \Sigma} \forall \overleftarrow{\mathbf{x}}, \mathbf{x}\,.\, \left(trans_{\sigma \to \sigma'} \Rightarrow \exists \mathbf{x}'\,.\, \left(act_{\sigma'}[\mathbf{x}/\overleftarrow{\mathbf{x}}, \mathbf{x}'/\mathbf{x}] \right) \right)$$

and

$$\bigwedge_{\sigma \in \Sigma} \forall \overleftarrow{\mathbf{x}}, \mathbf{x}\,.\, \left(act_{\sigma} \Rightarrow \bigvee_{\sigma' \in \Sigma} \exists \mathbf{x}'\,.\, \left(trans_{\sigma \to \sigma'}[\mathbf{x}/\overleftarrow{\mathbf{x}}, \mathbf{x}'/\mathbf{x}] \right) \right) \quad ,$$

where $[y/x]$ denotes substitution of x by y, are tautologies.

Dynamic behaviour. During execution, hybrid automata engage in an alternating sequence of discrete transitions and evolution phases, where the continuous variables evolve according to an activity. Hence a (partial) execution containing $n \in \mathbb{N}$ transitions comprises n transitions interspersed between $n+1$ evolution phases, where the final states (wrt. both discrete and continuous state components) of the evolution phases meet the initial states of the following transition and vice versa the final states of the transitions meet the initial states of the following evolution phase. A (finite or infinite) *path* thus is a sequence $\langle(\sigma_0, \mathbf{y}_0), (\sigma_1, \mathbf{y}_1), \ldots\rangle \in (\Sigma \times \mathbb{R}^d)^\star$ or $\in (\Sigma \times \mathbb{R}^d)^\omega$, resp., such that $\sigma_i = \sigma_{i+1}$ for even i, and

$$I_{\mathbf{x}:=\mathbf{y}_0} \models initial_{\sigma_0} \quad ,$$

$$I_{\overleftarrow{\mathbf{x}}:=\mathbf{y}_i, \mathbf{x}:=\mathbf{y}_{i+1}} \models \begin{cases} act_{\sigma_i} \quad , & \text{if } i \text{ is even,} \\ trans_{\sigma_i \to \sigma_{i+1}} \quad , & \text{if } i \text{ is odd} \end{cases}$$

for each i less than the length of the path. Here, $I_{\mathbf{x}:=\mathbf{y}}$ denotes the valuation

$$I_{\mathbf{x}:=\mathbf{y}}(v) = \begin{cases} P_i(\mathbf{y}), & \text{if } v = x_i \text{ for some } i \in \{1, \ldots, d\}, \\ & \text{where } P_i \text{ denotes projection to the } i\text{-th component,} \\ I(v), & \text{otherwise.} \end{cases}$$

Note that the choice of I does not matter in above applications, as only variables in $\mathbf{x}$ occur free in $initial_{\sigma_0}$ and only variables in $\overleftarrow{\mathbf{x}}$ or $\mathbf{x}$ occur free in act_{σ_i} and $trans_{\sigma_i \to \sigma_{i+1}}$.

In accordance to the definition of paths, reachability of a discrete state σ' and a continuous state $I_{\mathbf{x}}$ from an discrete start state σ and a continuous start state

$I_{\overleftarrow{\mathbf{x}}}$ through an execution (i.e., a path segment that need not start in an initial state) of length n can be formalised through the inductively defined predicate $\phi^n_{\sigma\to\sigma'}$, where

$$\phi^0_{\sigma\to\sigma'} = \begin{cases} \texttt{false}, & \text{if } \sigma \neq \sigma' , \\ act_\sigma , & \text{if } \sigma = \sigma' , \end{cases}$$

$$\phi^{n+1}_{\sigma\to\sigma'} = \begin{cases} \bigvee_{\tilde{\sigma}\in\Sigma} \exists \tilde{\mathbf{x}} . \begin{pmatrix} \phi^n_{\sigma\to\tilde{\sigma}}[\tilde{\mathbf{x}}/\mathbf{x}] \wedge \\ trans_{\tilde{\sigma}\to\sigma'}[\tilde{\mathbf{x}}/\overleftarrow{\mathbf{x}}] \end{pmatrix} , & \text{if } n \text{ is even,} \\ \exists \tilde{\mathbf{x}} . \begin{pmatrix} \phi^n_{\sigma\to\sigma'}[\tilde{\mathbf{x}}/\mathbf{x}] \wedge \\ act_{\sigma'}[\tilde{\mathbf{x}}/\overleftarrow{\mathbf{x}}] \end{pmatrix} , & \text{if } n \text{ is odd.} \end{cases}$$

Accordingly,

$$Reach^{\leq n}_{\sigma'} \stackrel{\text{def}}{=} \bigvee_{i\in\mathbb{N}_{\leq n}} \bigvee_{\sigma\in\Sigma} initial_\sigma[\overleftarrow{\mathbf{x}}/\mathbf{x}] \wedge \phi^i_{\sigma\to\sigma'} \tag{1}$$

characterizes the continuous states reachable on a path of length at most n that ends in discrete state σ'. Consequently, state σ' is reachable iff there is some $n \in \mathbb{N}$ for which $Reach^{\leq n}_{\sigma'}$ is satisfiable.

Note that $Reach^{\leq n}_{\sigma'}$ is a formula of $\mathrm{FOL}(\mathbb{R}, +, \cdot)$ such that reachability of σ' within at most n steps is decidable due to the decidability of $\mathrm{FOL}(\mathbb{R}, +, \cdot)$ [Tar48]. By successively testing increasing n, this does immediately yield a (well-known) semi-decision procedure for state reachability:

Lemma 1 (Semi-decidability of reachability). *It is semi-decidable whether a given state in a polynomial hybrid automaton is reachable.* □

Now it is straightforward to derive from the definition of $Reach^{\leq n}_{\sigma'}$ a predicate

$$Recurr^{\leq n} \stackrel{\text{def}}{=} \bigvee_{i\in\mathbb{N}_{\leq n}} \bigvee_{\sigma\in\Sigma} \bigvee_{\sigma'\in\Sigma} \bigvee_{1\leq j\leq n-i} \begin{pmatrix} initial_\sigma[\overleftarrow{\mathbf{x}}/\mathbf{x}] \wedge \\ \phi^{2i+1}_{\sigma\to\sigma'} \wedge \\ \phi^{2j-1}_{\sigma'\to\sigma'}[\mathbf{x}/\overleftarrow{\mathbf{x}}] \end{pmatrix} \tag{2}$$

that formalizes whether a state recurrence is encountered within the first $n+1$ transitions, i.e. on a path of length at most $2n+1$. This predicate again being in $\mathrm{FOL}(\mathbb{R}, +, \cdot)$, we obtain a semi-decision procedure for state recurrence:

Lemma 2 (Semi-decidability of recurrence). *It is semi-decidable whether a given polynomial hybrid automaton has a recurrent state.* □

However, these semi-decision procedures do not generalize to decision procedures: state reachability is known to be undecidable even for hybrid automata featuring just two clocks and a single stop-watch and which are, furthermore, confined to a bounded state space [HKPV95]. Here, a clock is a continuous variable having constant slope 1 within any activity, and a stop-watch is a continuous variable alternating between slopes 0 and 1 only. Thus, undecidability applies already to hybrid automata with just three continuous variables x_1, x_2, x_3, and activity predicates of only the two forms $\exists\, \Delta t\,.\, (x_1 = \overleftarrow{x_1}) \wedge \bigwedge_{i=\{2,3\}} (x_i = \overleftarrow{x_i} + \Delta t)$ and $\exists\, \Delta t\,.\, \bigwedge_{i=\{1,2,3\}} (x_i = \overleftarrow{x_i} + \Delta t)$. In the sequel, we will pursue a construction that utilizes an even more restricted subclass of polynomial hybrid automata, namely that of parametric timed automata [AHV93], and that — beyond undecidability of state reachability — proves undecidability of state recurrence and of progress also. In parametric timed automata, the continuous variables are either clocks, i.e. have slope 1 in every state and may only be checked and/or reset to 0 in transitions, or parameters. Parameters have slope 0 throughout and may not be affected by transitions, thus remaining constant throughout.

Theorem 1 (Undecidability of dynamic properties). *It is in general undecidable whether a given polynomial hybrid automaton*

1. *can reach a given state (on* some *path),*
2. *has a recurrent state,*
3. *will* on all *its paths eventually (i.e., after a finite number of steps) reach a given state.*

Property 3 is not even semi-decidable.
All these properties do still apply if we restrict attention to parametric timed automata with bounded range of the clock and parameter values instead of general polynomial hybrid automata.

Proof. We reduce the halting problem or — for property 3 of the theorem — boundedness problem of two-counter machines to the problem of testing whether some effectively constructed hybrid automaton (1) can reach a given state, (2) has a recurrent state, or (3) will on all its paths eventually reach a given state. The hybrid automaton A_M that we associate to a two-counter machine M uses four continuous variables x, y, h, and p which take values in the range $[0, 1]$, i.e. remain bounded along each run. x, y, and h are clocks in the sense of Alur and Dill [AD94], i.e. $\dot{x} = \dot{y} = \dot{h} = 1$ holds in all states. The remaining variable p is a parameter, i.e. is held constant. Hence, A_M is in fact a parametric timed automaton [AHV93] with three clocks x, y, h and one parameter p. Furthermore, A_M confines its variables to bounded range.

The encoding we use is that the two counter values n and m of a two-counter machine M are represented by the continuous variables x and y of A_M through the encoding $x = n(1-p)$ and $y = m(1-p)$. As the counter values n and m are in general unbounded, this would of course imply unbounded range of x and y. We confine x and y to bounded range by clipping their values to the interval $[0, p)$. Therefore, we will not perform increments if the resulting values of x or y would reach or exceed p, but send A_M to a special sink state *overflow* instead. During short transients, x and y may reach larger values, however, but even then their values will never exceed 1. Fig. 1 shows the details of the encoding.

Clipping the values of x and y to the $[0, 1)$ confines the representable integer range to $\left\{0, \ldots, \left\lceil \frac{p}{1-p} \right\rceil - 1\right\}$. But as parameter $p \in (\frac{1}{2}, 1)$ is chosen arbitrarily, every bounded run of M is accurately simulated by some run of A_M, namely one

Initialization: l_0 is the start location of M.

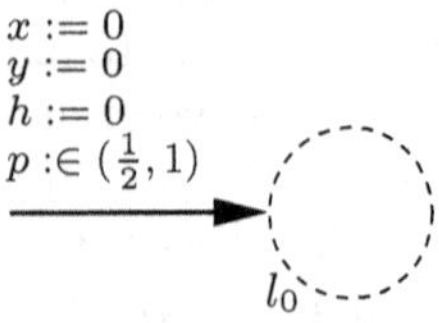

Increment: l_i : `increment`(y); `goto` l_j

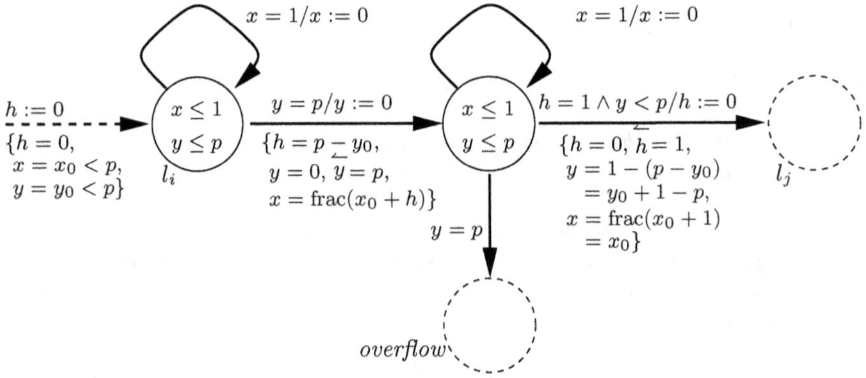

Test and decrement: l_i : `if` $y = 0$ `then goto` l_j `else decrement`(y); `goto` l_k

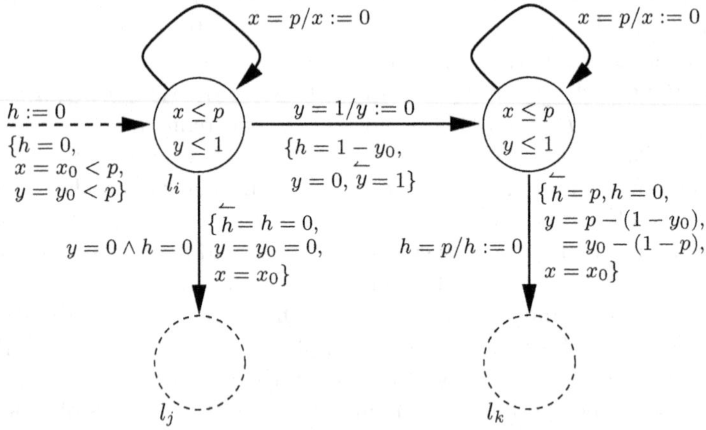

Fig. 1. Encoding the instructions of two-counter machines by parameterized timed automata. All variables except p are clocks, i.e. $\dot{x} = \dot{y} = \dot{h} = 1$ holds in all states (and has thus been omitted from the graphics). p is a parameter that is initially chosen and henceforth kept constant, i.e. $\dot{p} = 0$ holds everywhere. Annotations in curly brackets state key invariants that hold whenever the corresponding transitions are taken.

with p close enough to 1. On the other hand, runs that start with inadequate choice of p will inevitably end in the *overflow* state.

Using this encoding, location l_i of A_M is reachable iff M's computation reaches l_i. In particular, A_M's encoding of M's final location l_{stop} will be reachable in A_M iff M halts. As the halting problem for two-counter machines is undecidable, this implies undecidability of state reachability for bounded parametric timed automata. This proves undecidabililty of property (1) of the theorem.

Using a straightforward reduction of halting to state recurrence, this undecidability result can be generalized to recurrence properties, thus showing undecidability of (2). The essential steps are to make the terminal state l_{stop} of M recurrent and to ensure that all other states are non-recurrent. The latter can be done through the standard trick of adding a step counter to the two-counter machine that is simulated, thus — by counting up until the terminal state is reached — obtaining non-recurrence in the case of non-termination.

To deal with property (3) we observe that A_M will eventually reach state *overflow* on all its paths — i.e., independently of the particular choice of p — iff M's computation is unbounded. Hence, due to undecidability of boundedness of two-counter machines, it is in general undecidable whether some A_M will eventually reach state *overflow*. Consequently, it is undecidable whether a bounded parametric timed automaton will eventually reach a given state. I.e. property (3) is undecidable. Furthermore, this construction would yield a semi-decision method for unboundedness of two-counter machines if there were a semi-decision procedure for property (3). Thus, property (3) is not even semi-decidable. □

Note that Theorem 1 generalizes the undecidability result of Alur, Henzinger, and Vardi for parametric timed automata [AHV93] in two directions: first, it shows that undecidability of state reachability applies even when parameters and clocks are confined to bounded range, a case left open in [AHV93] where only the unbounded case was investigated. Second, we show that undecidability also holds for state recurrence and for progress of parametric timed automata.

3 Progress Properties and State Recurrence

According to Theorem 1, all interesting dynamic properties of hybrid automata are undecidable. Nevertheless, some prospects for mechanized analysis of hybrid automata remain, as state reachability and state recurrence are semi-decidable (Lemmata 1 and 2). However, at least to the practitioner, existence of recurrent states is hardly an interesting property in itself. It merely is a workhorse in the verification of finite-state systems, as there it is closely related to satisfaction of progress properties: for such systems, it can be used for disproving that on all possible computation paths, eventually something good will happen. For infinite-state systems, e.g. hybrid automata, there is no immediate correspondence between existence of infinite paths with (un-)desirable properties and existence of recurrent states with (un-)desirable properties, as with an infinity of states, infinite paths need not have recurrent states. Hence, the connection between state recurrence and progress properties for hybrid automata needs extra investigation, which is the theme of the current section. We start by formally defining satisfaction of a progress property by a hybrid automaton.

Definition 1 (Satisfaction of $\Diamond\phi$). *Let A be a deadlock-free polynomial hybrid automaton with $A = (\Sigma, \mathbf{x}, (act_\sigma)_{\sigma\in\Sigma}, (trans_{\sigma\to\sigma'})_{\sigma,\sigma'\in\Sigma}, (initial_\sigma)_{\sigma\in\Sigma})$, and let ϕ be an* FOL($\mathbb{R}, +, \cdot$)*-predicate with* free(ϕ) $\subseteq \mathbf{x}$. *We say that A* satisfies "eventually ϕ" (denoted $A \models \Diamond\phi$) *iff $A_{\neg\phi}$ has no infinite path, where $A_{\neg\phi}$ denotes A confined to the portion of the state space satisfying $\neg\phi$.*
Formally, given an arbitrary FOL($\mathbb{R}, +, \cdot$)*-predicate ψ with* free(ψ) $\subseteq \mathbf{x}$, *we define $A_\psi \stackrel{\text{def}}{=} (\Sigma, \mathbf{x}, (\widetilde{act}_\sigma)_{\sigma\in\Sigma}, (\widetilde{trans}_{\sigma\to\sigma'})_{\sigma,\sigma'\in\Sigma}, (\widetilde{initial}_\sigma)_{\sigma\in\Sigma})$, where $\widetilde{act}_\sigma \stackrel{\text{def}}{=} act_\sigma \wedge \psi$, $\widetilde{trans}_{\sigma\to\sigma'} \stackrel{\text{def}}{=} trans_{\sigma\to\sigma'} \wedge \psi$, and $\widetilde{initial}_\sigma \stackrel{\text{def}}{=} initial_\sigma \wedge \psi$ for each $\sigma, \sigma' \in \Sigma$.*

Remark 1. Note that the restriction to deadlock-free automata is essential: a non-deadlock-free automaton A with a single state and no transitions would, along the lines of Definition 1, satisfy any progress property $\Diamond\phi$, because A and thus also $A_{\neg\phi}$ do not have paths longer than 2.

Yet, while the restriction to deadlock-free automata circumvents such pathologies, there remain subtle effects that are debatable. These have to do with the pragmatics of using hybrid automata as a model of real-time systems. Models of real-time systems are subject to peculiar effects like Zeno behaviour or indefinite idling in a state. Individual expectations on the impact of these peculiarities on satisfaction of progress properties may vary, and thus may or may not coincide with our definition.

While polynomial hybrid automata have no built-in model of time, there is a standard way of representing time, namely through representing the timed behaviour of a differential inequation $\dot{x} = 3$ by an activity $\exists\, \Delta t\, .\, \overleftarrow{x} + 3 \cdot \Delta t = x$. Consequently, the entity Δt occurring in activity predicates corresponds to the time spent in that activity. Given such an encoding, we will observe that Zeno behaviour can block progress according to Definition 1, as an automaton like that of Fig. 2 will violate a progress property even though it could spend only finite time in a Zeno behaviour before progress occurs.

A dual situation occurs when a discrete state of the hybrid automaton may be held indefinitely long without a transition being enforced within finite time, as in automaton B of Fig. 3. Deadlock-freedom ensures that there always remains some transition that will eventually be enabled, and one may adopt or refute the fairness assumption that under these circumstances, some transition will indeed eventually be taken. If the fairness assumption is adopted, B satisfies $\Diamond x \neq 0$, which is the view taken by Definition 1. The opposite view would be that B may stay in state σ forever, thus violating $\Diamond x \neq 0$. The later view differs from Definition 1 and would call for either a change of the definition or a transformation on the hybrid automaton under investigation to accommodate that view. The latter is, however, simple as any automaton that can stay indefinitely long in some state may be augmented with extra transitions that may be taken during such idling phases. The standard way is to add transitions that become ripe periodically, thus not introducing Zenoness (which might prohibit other transitions

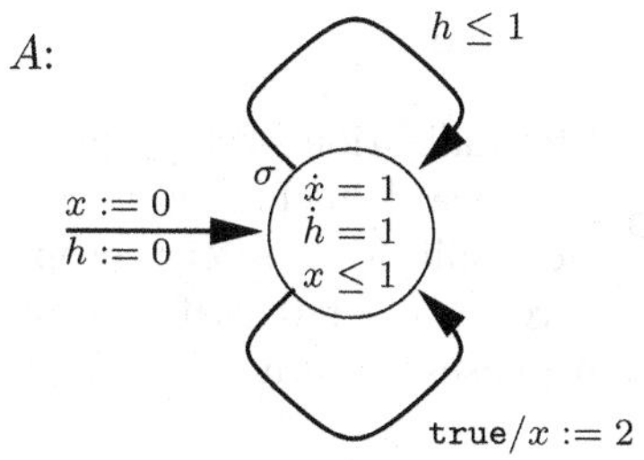

Fig. 2. Zeno behaviour may block progress: A, if formalized by the predicates $initial_\sigma = (x = 0 \wedge h = 0)$, $act_\sigma = (\exists \Delta t\,.\ \overleftarrow{x} + 1 \cdot \Delta t = x \wedge \overleftarrow{h} + 1 \cdot \Delta t = h \wedge x \leq 1)$, and $trans_{\sigma \to \sigma} = (\overleftarrow{h} \leq 1 \wedge \overleftarrow{h} = h \wedge \overleftarrow{x} = x \vee x = 2 \wedge \overleftarrow{h} = h)$, does not satisfy $\Diamond x = 2$.

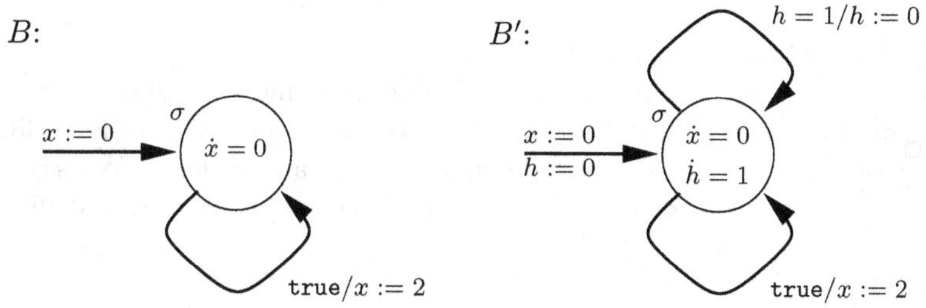

Fig. 3. Weak fairness implied by Definition 1: Automaton B — formally denoting $act_\sigma = (\exists \Delta t\,.\ \overleftarrow{x} + 0 \cdot \Delta t = x)$, $trans_{\sigma \to \sigma} = (x = 2)$, and $initial_\sigma = (x = 0)$ — satisfies $\Diamond x \neq 0$. I.e., it is assumed to eventually take a transition. If such fairness is not desired then its implications can be masked by adding clocks and transitions which become ripe periodically, as in automaton B'. B' violates $\Diamond x \neq 0$.

from contributing to progress), yet satisfying the implied fairness. An example of this transformation can be found in automaton B' of Fig. 3. •

According to Definition 1, verifying a progress property of the form $\Diamond \phi$ amounts to proving non-existence of an infinite path in $A_{\neg\phi}$, i.e. non-existence of an infinite path invariantly satisfying $\neg\phi$. In finite-state systems, this reduces to showing that there is no recurrent state on a $\neg\phi$-path. However, in infinite-state systems, infinite paths need not be recurrent. Thus, the semi-decision method of Lemma 2 does not even yield a semi-decision method for falsifying $\Diamond\phi$.

Nevertheless, there is a close relationship between state recurrence and progress if we deal with hybrid automata that are subject to disturbances due to noise. To demonstrate this, we will adopt the model of noise introduced in [Frä99]. However, this very simple notion — to be repeated in the next section — merely serves as a vehicle for illustration. We conjecture that the remainder of the theory holds true for a broader range of reasonable models of noise.

3.1 A Simple Model of Noise

We begin by repeating the formalization of a simple model of noise in hybrid automata that was first put forward in [Frä99], where it was analyzed for its impact on decidability of reachability (i.e., safety) properties. Within this model we assume that noise will leave the discrete state set and transitions unaffected, but will make the evolution phases more nondeterministic. I.e., given a hybrid automaton

$$A = (\Sigma, \mathbf{x}, (act_\sigma)_{\sigma\in\Sigma}, (trans_{\sigma\to\sigma'})_{\sigma,\sigma'\in\Sigma}, (initial_\sigma)_{\sigma\in\Sigma}) \ ,$$

a *disturbed variant* of A is any hybrid automaton

$$\tilde{A} = (\Sigma, \mathbf{x}, (\widetilde{act}_\sigma)_{\sigma\in\Sigma}, (trans_{\sigma\to\sigma'})_{\sigma,\sigma'\in\Sigma}, (initial_\sigma)_{\sigma\in\Sigma})$$

with $act_\sigma \Rightarrow \widetilde{act}_\sigma$ for each $\sigma \in \Sigma$.

Now assume that the continuous state space comes equipped with a first-order definable metrics *dist*, with $dist(\mathbf{x}, \mathbf{y})$ being its definition in FOL($\mathbb{R}, +, \cdot$). Furthermore, let ε be a first-order definable constant in $\mathbb{R}_{>0}$. We say that a disturbance $\tilde{A}$ of A is a *disturbance of noise level* ε *or more* wrt. *dist* iff

$$\exists \mathbf{y} \,.\, \big(act_\sigma[\mathbf{y}/\mathbf{x}] \wedge dist(\mathbf{x}, \mathbf{y}) < \varepsilon\big) \Rightarrow \widetilde{act}_\sigma \tag{3}$$

for each $\sigma \in \Sigma$. Thus, evolution phases can drift away within at least an open ball of radius ε under such disturbances, as depicted in Fig. 4. It seems reasonable to assume that within any realistic noise field such disturbances exist for some sufficiently small ε.[5]

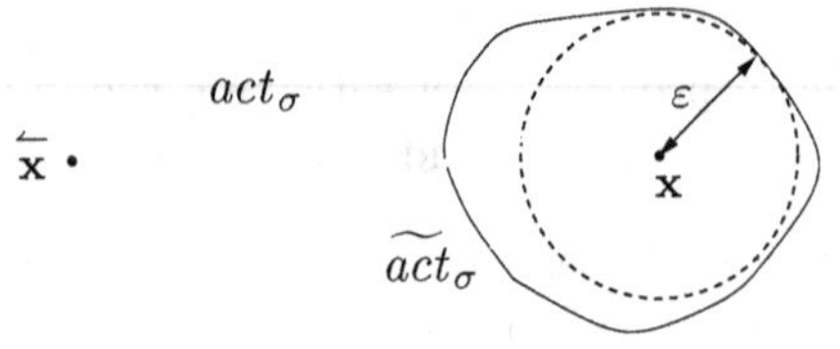

Fig. 4. Noise of level ε or more: if $\mathbf{x}$ is reachable from $\overleftarrow{\mathbf{x}}$ under some activity act_σ, then the corresponding disturbed activity $\widetilde{act}_\sigma$ can reach a superset of the open ball of radius ε around x.

---

[5] Concerning the range of applicability of the model, it is worth noting that for the theory exposed in the remainder, the fact that *every* activity is subject to drift of at least ε for some $\varepsilon > 0$ is not essential. While we have chosen such a model in order to simplify exposition, the theory itself can be easily extended to the more general situation that only every cycle in the discrete state space of the hybrid automaton (i.e. every alternating sequence of activities and transitions going from some discrete state σ via other discrete states back to σ) contains at least one activity with drift of at least ε.

Obviously, a disturbance will yield additional possible behaviours, possibly leading to otherwise unreachable states. It turns out that in case of existence of infinite paths, some of these noisily reachable states are always recurrent.

3.2 Infinite Paths and Noisy State Recurrence

We will in the remainder concentrate on progress properties of the form $\Diamond\neg\phi$ with ϕ being a bounded property, where an FOL($\mathbb{R}, +, \cdot$)-predicate ϕ with free(ϕ) $\subseteq \mathbf{x}$ is called *bounded* iff $\{\mathbf{y} \in \mathbb{R}^d \mid I_{\mathbf{x}:=\mathbf{y}} \models \phi\}$ is bounded.[6] I.e., the requirements formulae we want to verify demand that all possible trajectories of the hybrid automaton will eventually leave some bounded region. Note that the restriction to bounded properties actually poses no restriction in the quite common case that the reachable state space of the hybrid automaton is itself bounded.

Lemma 3. *Let ϕ be a bounded property and A a polynomial hybrid automaton. If A does not satisfy $\Diamond\neg\phi$ — i.e., if A_ϕ has an infinite path — then for any disturbance $\tilde{A}$ of positive noise level, $\tilde{A}_\phi$ has a recurrent state.*

Proof. Assume that A violates $\Diamond\neg\phi$ and that $\pi = \langle(\sigma_0, \mathbf{y}_0), (\sigma_1, \mathbf{y}_1), \ldots\rangle$ is a witness path for violation of $\Diamond\neg\phi$, i.e. an infinite path of A_ϕ. Let $\sigma \in \Sigma$ be a discrete state that is visited infinitely often in π and let $\pi_\sigma \stackrel{\text{def}}{=} \{\mathbf{y}_i \mid \sigma_i = \sigma,\ i \text{ is odd}\}$.

If π_σ is finite then π itself revisits some hybrid state infinitely often, which then also is a recurrent state of any disturbance $\tilde{A}$. Otherwise, as ϕ is bounded, the Bolzano-Weierstrass theorem, generalized to $\mathbb{R}^d$, implies that π_σ has an accumulation point $\mathbf{y} \in \mathbb{R}^d$. Consequently, for arbitrary $\varepsilon > 0$ there are infinitely many points $(\sigma_j, \mathbf{y}_j)$ in the witness path π such that j is odd and $\sigma_j = \sigma$ and $dist(\mathbf{y}_j, \mathbf{y}) < \frac{\varepsilon}{2}$. Any such point is recurrent in any disturbance of noise level ε or more, as for each such j there is an odd $k > j$ with $\sigma_k = \sigma$ and $dist(\mathbf{y}_k, \mathbf{y}) < \frac{\varepsilon}{2}$, which implies that $(\sigma_j, \mathbf{y}_j)$ is a direct successor state of $(\sigma_{k-1}, \mathbf{y}_{k-1})$ in a disturbance $\tilde{A}_\phi$ of noise level ε or more, because $dist(\mathbf{y}_j, \mathbf{y}_k) \leq dist(\mathbf{y}_j, \mathbf{y}) + dist(\mathbf{y}_k, \mathbf{y}) < \varepsilon$. □

Lemma 3 shows that existence of an infinite path in A_ϕ implies existence of a recurrent state in any disturbance of positive noise level. The converse implication holds if we add some constraint on the viable paths in a disturbed automaton. Up to now, we have defined disturbance in terms of hybrid automata, i.e. infinite-state transition systems without acceptance conditions. We may, however, add certain acceptance conditions in order to rule out certain undesirable limit behaviours. E.g., for a given polynomial hybrid automaton $A = (\Sigma, \mathbf{x}, (act_\sigma)_{\sigma\in\Sigma}, (trans_{\sigma\to\sigma'})_{\sigma,\sigma'\in\Sigma}), (initial_\sigma)_{\sigma\in\Sigma})$ and given $\varepsilon > 0$ consider its ε-disturbance $A^\varepsilon \stackrel{\text{def}}{=} (\Sigma, \mathbf{x}, (\widetilde{act}_\sigma)_{\sigma\in\Sigma}, (trans_{\sigma\to\sigma'})_{\sigma,\sigma'\in\Sigma}), (initial_\sigma)_{\sigma\in\Sigma})$ with $\widetilde{act}_\sigma \stackrel{\text{def}}{=} \exists\, \mathbf{y}\,.\, act_\sigma[\mathbf{y}/\mathbf{x}] \wedge dist(\mathbf{x}, \mathbf{y}) < \varepsilon$: here, all disturbances occurring along a path are *strictly less* than ε; yet, the supremum of disturbances may well equal

[6] Note that the choice of I does not matter in $\{\mathbf{y} \in \mathbb{R}^d \mid I_{\mathbf{x}:=\mathbf{y}} \models \phi\}$, as free($\phi$) $\subseteq \mathbf{x}$.

ε. We may avoid this by adding a further constraint on the viable paths, stating that a path is considered non-viable iff the supremum of the disturbances along the path equals ε. I.e., an infinite path $\langle(\sigma_0, \mathbf{y}_0), (\sigma_1, \mathbf{y}_1), \ldots\rangle$ of A^ε is *viable* iff there is $\delta < \varepsilon$ such that

$$I_{\overleftarrow{\mathbf{x}}:=\mathbf{y}_i, \mathbf{x}:=\mathbf{y}_{i+1}} \models \exists \mathbf{y} \,.\, act_{\sigma_i}[\mathbf{y}/\mathbf{x}] \wedge dist(\mathbf{x}, \mathbf{y}) \leq \delta$$

for each even i. In the remainder, we will denote A^ε restricted to its viable paths, i.e. augmented with above path-acceptance condition, by $A^{\sup<\varepsilon}$. From the definition it is obvious that $Paths(A^{\sup<\varepsilon}) = \bigcup_{\delta<\varepsilon} Paths(A^\delta)$, where $Paths(\cdot)$ denotes the set of possible paths of the respective automaton.

Lemma 4 (Progress vs. recurrence). *Let A be a polynomial hybrid automaton, ϕ bounded, and $\varepsilon > 0$. Then $A_\phi^{\sup<\varepsilon}$ has an infinite path iff $A_\phi^{\sup<\varepsilon}$ has a recurrent state, i.e. recurrence and existence of infinite paths are related in exactly the same way as for finite automata.*

Proof. Existence of a recurrent state trivially implies existence of an infinite path. For the converse inclusion note that $Paths(A_\phi^{\sup<\varepsilon}) = \bigcup_{\delta<\varepsilon} Paths(A_\phi^\delta)$. Hence, $A_\phi^{\sup<\varepsilon}$ has an infinite path iff some A_ϕ^δ for some $\delta < \varepsilon$ has. But then, according to Lemma 3, $A_\phi^{\frac{\delta+\varepsilon}{2}}$ has a recurrent path. Consequently, as $\frac{\delta+\varepsilon}{2} < \varepsilon$, $A_\phi^{\sup<\varepsilon}$ has a recurrent path. □

4 An Automatic Verification Procedure for Progress

While Lemmata 3 and 4 provide a connection between state recurrence and progress, they are not of much help for effectively falsifying $\Diamond\neg\phi$, as they relate progress to existence of recurrent states within *arbitrary* disturbances of strictly positive noise level — an infinite set of disturbances that could not be probed in finite time. Fortunately, Lemma 3 can be strengthened:

Lemma 5 (Recurrence vs. path boundedness). *Let ϕ be a bounded property and A a polynomial hybrid automaton. If A_ϕ has paths of arbitrary length — i.e., if there is no* finite *bound on path length in A_ϕ — then for any disturbance $\tilde{A}$ of positive noise level, $\tilde{A}_\phi$ has a recurrent state.*

Proof. The proof closely resembles that of Lemma 3. Instead of the infinite witness path π we just have to take, for given $\varepsilon > 0$, a sufficiently long path π of A_ϕ such that π contains two distinct odd indices k and j that satisfy $\sigma_k = \sigma_j$ and $dist(y_j, y_k) < \varepsilon$. Such a path exists due to unboundedness of path length in A_ϕ and boundedness of ϕ. □

Note that Lemma 5 is stronger than Lemma 3, as non-existence of a finite bound on path length does *not* imply existence of an infinite path in an infinite-state system.

Lemma 5 is a valuable stepping stone towards a semi-decision procedure due to the fact that its premise (that A_ϕ has paths of arbitrary finite length) is co-semidecidable:

Lemma 6 (Semi-decidability of path-boundedness). *It is semi-decidable whether a polynomial hybrid automaton has a finite bound on its path length.*

Proof. For arbitrary $n \in \mathbb{N}$, the FOL($\mathbb{R}, +, \cdot$) formula

$$Path^n \stackrel{\text{def}}{=} \bigvee_{\sigma \in \Sigma} \bigvee_{\sigma' \in \Sigma} initial_\sigma[\overleftarrow{\mathbf{x}} / \mathbf{x}] \wedge \phi^n_{\sigma \to \sigma'}$$

is satisfiable iff the automaton under investigation has a path of length n. Using a decision method for FOL($\mathbb{R}, +, \cdot$) we can check satisfiability of $Path^n$ for successively larger n until $Path^n$ is found to be unsatisfiable. If this ever happens then we can terminate the semi-decision method, having found a witness for A having finitely bounded path length. □

Now, Lemma 5 shows that Lemmata 2 and 6 are "almost complementary" in the sense that cases where none of the two semi-decision procedures matches are isolated: they are "borderline" in the sense that they do not feature recurrent ϕ-paths, yet any disturbance of *arbitrarily small* positive noise level has recurrent ϕ-paths, as the next theorem shows. Above notion of "borderline" is captured by the following definition:

Definition 2 (Fragility and robustness). *We say that A is* fragile wrt. recurrence of ϕ-states *iff A_ϕ has no recurrent state, yet for any disturbance $\tilde{A}$ of positive noise level, $\tilde{A}_\phi$ has a recurrent state.*

If A is not fragile wrt. recurrence of ϕ-states, i.e. if it either has recurrent ϕ-states itself or has disturbances without recurrent ϕ-states, then A is called robust wrt. recurrence of ϕ-states.

Using this definition and the semi-decision procedures of Lemmata 2 and 6, it is straightforward to show our main theorem:

Theorem 2 (Robustness implies decidability). *Let A be a polynomial hybrid automaton and ϕ a bounded property. If A is robust wrt. recurrence of ϕ-states then it is decidable whether $A \models \Diamond\neg\phi$.*

Proof. As A is robust wrt. recurrence of ϕ-states, there are two cases: either A_ϕ has a recurrent state — which is semi-decidable according to Lemma 2 — or there is $\delta > 0$ such that $(A^\varepsilon)_\phi$ has no recurrent state for each $\varepsilon < \delta$. In the latter case, A_ϕ has finitely bounded path length according to Lemma 5, which is semi-decidable due to Lemma 6. Consequently, we may start the semi-decision procedures of Lemmata 2 and 6 in parallel and can be sure that at least one of the two semi-decision procedures terminates on A_ϕ.

If the procedure of Lemma 2 terminates then A_ϕ has a recurrent state, which implies $A \not\models \Diamond\neg\phi$. Vice versa, if the procedure of Lemma 6 terminates then A_ϕ has finitely bounded path length, which is equivalent to $A \models \Diamond\neg\phi$ according to Definition 1. Hence, the parallel execution of the semi-decision procedures of Lemmata 2 and 6 decides satisfaction of progress properties for robust automata. □

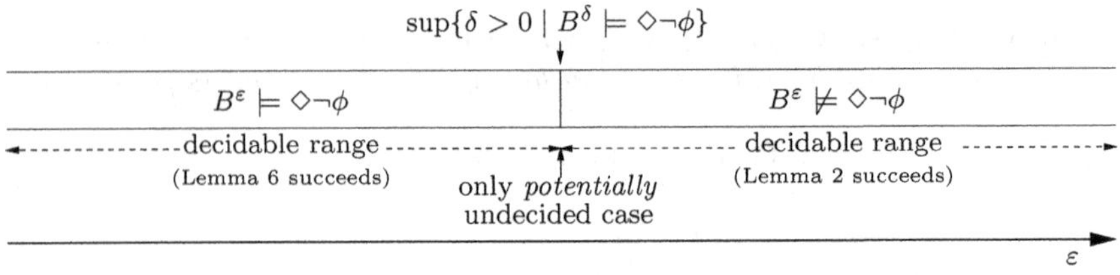

Fig. 5. The semi-decision procedure of Cor. 1 may only fail on a single noise level

Now, even though it is intuitively clear that fragility with respect to recurrence of ϕ-states is a rare borderline case, as for a fragile automaton even the slightest disturbance causes a drastic change in the recurrence pattern, it might still seem a dirty trick to have a verification method for progress with a premise concerning recurrence. However, we can replace this premise by a premise mentioning not being borderline with respect to progress instead, provided that the automaton A is itself a disturbed variant B^ε of another polynomial hybrid automaton B:

Corollary 1. *If $A = B^\varepsilon$ for some polynomial hybrid automaton B and some noise level $\varepsilon > 0$, and if ϕ is bounded then $A \models \Diamond\neg\phi$ is decidable unless $\varepsilon = \sup\{\delta > 0 \mid B^\delta \models \Diamond\neg\phi\}$, i.e. unless the noise level of A exactly matches the borderline between satisfaction and violation of $\Diamond\neg\phi$. This fact is illustrated in Figure 5.*

Proof. If $\varepsilon > \sup\{\delta > 0 \mid B^\delta \models \Diamond\neg\phi\}$ then $A_\phi = (B^\varepsilon)_\phi$ has a recurrent state due to Lemma 3 and thus A is robust wrt. recurrence of ϕ-states. If, on the other hand, $\varepsilon < \sup\{\delta > 0 \mid B^\delta \models \Diamond\neg\phi\}$ then — by Definition of $B^\delta \models \Diamond\neg\phi$ — all $(A^\gamma)_\phi$ in the range $\varepsilon \leq \gamma < \sup\{\delta > 0 \mid B^\delta \models \Diamond\neg\phi\}$ do not have recurrent states, and consequently, A is robust wrt. recurrence of ϕ-states. Hence, A is robust wrt. recurrence of ϕ-states whenever $\varepsilon \neq \sup\{\delta > 0 \mid B^\delta \models \Diamond\neg\phi\}$. Thus, the result follows from Theorem 2. □

Corollary 1 provides an almost complete automatic verification method for progress properties of noisy hybrid automata (i.e., automata of the form $A = B^\varepsilon$ for some polynomial hybrid automaton B and some $\varepsilon > 0$) which may only fail if we happen to test *exactly* the borderline case (i.e., $\varepsilon = \sup\{\delta > 0 \mid B^\delta \models \Diamond\neg\phi\}$).

By Lemma 4 and semi-decidability of state recurrence (Lemma 2), the result becomes even a little bit stronger if we restrict interest to viable paths of B^ε only, i.e. if we take $A = B^{\mathrm{sup}<\varepsilon}$:

Corollary 2. *If $A = B^{\mathrm{sup}<\varepsilon}$ for some polynomial hybrid automaton B and some $\varepsilon > 0$, and if ϕ is bounded then*

1. *$A \not\models \Diamond\neg\phi$ is semi-decidable, and*
2. *$A \models \Diamond\neg\phi$ is semi-decidable unless $\varepsilon = \sup\{\delta > 0 \mid B^\delta \models \Diamond\neg\phi\}$.*

Proof. If $A \not\models \Diamond\neg\phi$ then $A_\phi = B_\phi^{\sup<\varepsilon}$ has a recurrent state according to Lemma 4. Thus, $A \not\models \Diamond\neg\phi$ is semi-decidable by the procedure of Lemma 2.

$A \models \Diamond\neg\phi$, on the other hand, can be checked by the same technique as in the previous corollary. Thus, $A \models \Diamond\neg\phi$ is semi-decidable unless $\varepsilon = \sup\{\delta > 0 \mid B^\delta \models \Diamond\neg\phi\}$. □

I.e., if $A = B^{\sup<\varepsilon}$ for some noise level $\varepsilon > 0$ then falsification of $\Diamond\neg\phi$ always succeeds (if applicable) and it is only verification that may fail if we happen to test *exactly* the borderline case.

5 Decidability of Robustness

Given the fact that *robust* systems can be automatically verified, it remains the question whether robustness can be automatically detected.

Corollary 3 (Undecidability of robustness). *It is in general undecidable whether a hybrid automaton is robust or fragile wrt. recurrence of ϕ-states for a given bounded predicate ϕ. Robustness is, however, semi-decidable.*

Proof. All fragile systems do not have recurrent ϕ-states due to Definition 2. Hence, existence of recurrent ϕ-states of a hybrid automaton is trivially decidable once it is known to be fragile. For robust automata, on the other hand, existence of recurrent ϕ-states is decidable, as they either have recurrent ϕ-states (which is semi-decidable due to Lemma 2) or they have finitely bounded path length according to Lemma 5 (which is semi-decidable due to Lemma 6). Consequently, decidability of being robust would imply decidability of state recurrence for polynomial hybrid automata with bounded reachable state space (to see this, just take as ϕ an arbitrary bounded over-approximation of the reachable state space). However, state recurrence is undecidable even for parametric timed automata with finitely bounded state space (cf. Theorem 1), and therefore robustness wrt. recurrence of ϕ-states is undecidable.

However, robustness of A wrt. recurrence of ϕ-states is semi-decidable, as A is robust iff either A_ϕ has a recurrent state, which can be detected by the semi-decision procedure of Lemma 2, or has disturbances of strictly positive noise level without recurrent ϕ-states. According to Lemma 5, the latter implies existence of a disturbance $\tilde{A}$ of strictly positive noise level with finitely bounded path length. But then, for some sufficiently large $n \in \mathbb{N}$, $A^{\frac{1}{n}}$ will also have finitely bounded path length. We can search for such n using the semi-decision method for finitely bounded path length of Lemma 6. □

The undecidability result, while disappointing, should nevertheless be no serious obstacle in practice. It is good engineering practice to make systems tolerant against noise. Thus, any well-engineered system should be robust s.t. the decision procedure of Theorem 2 comes to an answer. In particular, no need for checking robustness should arise in practice.

It should furthermore be noted that the *known* undecidable cases are "ideal" hybrid automata A in the sense that A itself is not a disturbance of positive noise level of any other hybrid automaton, but follows ideal trajectories instead. It is currently unknown whether the verification method of Corollaries 1 and 2 may indeed fail on some automata $A = B^{\varepsilon}$ (or $A = B^{\sup<\varepsilon}$, resp.) with $\varepsilon > 0$, or whether it will in fact always succeed on such "noisy" automata.

6 Discussion

We have been able to show that progress properties $\Diamond\neg\phi$ of linear and polynomial hybrid automata can be decided algorithmically in most practically interesting cases. The remaining cases are such that non-existence of recurrent states satisfying ϕ depends on the *complete* absence of noise.

We have called such systems, where the recurrence pattern of ϕ-states does not change abruptly when an infinitesimally small amount of noise is added, *robust with respect to recurrence of ϕ-states.* It should be noted that our notion of robustness mentions ϕ and thus is with respect to the particular progress property under investigation. This distinguishes our approach from the closely related approaches to robust satisfaction of properties by Puri [Pur98] and Asarin & Bouajjani [AB01], which furthermore are currently confined to state reachability (i.e., safety), while our approach is available for both safety properties [Frä99] and progress properties (this paper).

The advantage of defining robustness relative to the property under investigation is that this yields a notion of robustness which in contrast to the other notion applies to some hybrid automata with non-recursive reachability relation, hence broadening the range of applicability of the method, which is guaranteed to succeed on *every* robust automaton (see Theorem 2 and, for safety properties, [Frä99, Theorem 1]). In detail, the different notions of robustness in the approaches [Frä99] and [AB01] dealing with safety of hybrid automata are as follows: Asarin and Bouajjani [AB01] define that a system is robust iff its undisturbed reachability relation equals the intersection of all perturbed reachability relations arising from disturbance levels $\varepsilon > 0$. I.e., they consider an automaton A to be robust iff the reachable state space of A's ε-disturbances in the limit for ε tending to 0 exactly equals A's reachable state space. This tight approximation of A's reach set by its disturbances implies that A's reach set is recursive according to [AB01, Corollary 8], i.e. recursiveness of the reach set is a necessary condition of robustness. In contrast, we define robustness in [Frä99] with respect to the safety property $\Box\phi$ to be verified: there, an automaton A is considered to be robust iff either it is unsafe (i.e., $A \not\models \Box\phi$) or it has disturbances of positive noise level which are safe (i.e., $A \models \Box\phi$ for some $\varepsilon > 0$). Clearly, this notion does not have recursiveness of the reach set as a necessary condition. It should, however, be noted that the notion of robustness of [Frä99] is not strictly weaker than that of [AB01]; the two notions are in general incomparable.

As noise is a general phenomenon in continuous systems, the effect of noise on the computational power of different kinds of analog computation has been extensively studied, e.g. by Maass and Sontag in [MS97] and by Moore in [Moo98].

Their findings are not directly comparable to ours because of the quite simplistic, qualitative model of noise used in our approach and the probabilistic models used there. We do agree that a realistic model of noise should better be quantitative, representing noise as a probabilistic process. Within this article we have deliberately refrained from this, as such a model would hardly yield any practical verification procedure due to the large computational overhead caused by calculating the density function when iterating the probabilistic transition and evolution steps. Yet, the results obtained in [MS97] with respect to noise of a wide support, meaning that the system may be driven to arbitrary continuous state with some low probability, indicate that the question posed in the end of Section 5, namely whether undecidability may still prevail if the automaton A is of the form $A = B^{\varepsilon}$ or $A = B^{\mathrm{sup}<\varepsilon}$, is a viable one.

Finally, it should be noted that a fundamentally different approach to modeling noisy behaviour of timed or hybrid automata has been proposed by Gupta, Henzinger, and Jagadeesan [GHJ97]. In that line of work, the idealized behavioural model of timed automata is essentially kept and only filtered a posteriori by removing accepted and adding rejected trajectories that are isolated with respect to some topology on trajectories. However, it seems that this model has less favorable consequences with respect to decidability issues than the model of Puri [Pur98], which is more akin to our approach in that it models the impact of noise (i.e. clock drift, as only timed automata are dealt with) as a widening of the transition relation and defines the reachable states as those that are reachable under arbitrarily small positive noise.

Acknowledgements

Eugene Asarin and Ahmed Bouajjanni deserve special thanks for their kind hospitality which I enjoyed during a visit to Grenoble this spring. The many fruitful discussions we had helped in clarifying the relation between our different notions of robustness. Furthermore, I would like to thank the anonymous referees for their exceptionally detailed comments.

References

[AB01] Eugene Asarin and Ahmed Bouajjani. Perturbed turing machines and hybrid systems. In *Proceedings of the Sixteenth Annual IEEE Symposium on Logic in Computer Science (LICS 2001)*. IEEE, 2001.

[AD94] Rajeev Alur and David L. Dill. A theory of timed automata. *Theoretical Computer Science*, 126(2):183–235, 1994.

[AHS96] Rajeev Alur, Thomas A. Henzinger, and Eduardo D. Sontag, editors. *Hybrid Systems III — Verification and Control*, volume 1066 of *Lecture Notes in Computer Science*. Springer-Verlag, 1996.

[AHV93] Rajeev Alur, Thomas A. Henzinger, and Moshe Y. Vardi. Parametric real-time reasoning. In *Proceedings of the 25th Annual ACM Symposium on Theory of Computing*, pages 592–601, 1993.

[AKNS95] P. Antsaklis, W. Kohn, A. Nerode, and S. Sastry, editors. *Hybrid Systems II*, volume 999 of *Lecture Notes in Computer Science*. Springer-Verlag, 1995.

[Frä99] Martin Fränzle. Analysis of hybrid systems: An ounce of realism can save an infinity of states. In Jörg Flum and Mario Rodríguez-Artalejo, editors, *Computer Science Logic (CSL'99)*, volume 1683 of *Lecture Notes in Computer Science*, pages 126–140. Springer-Verlag, 1999.

[GHJ97] Vineet Gupta, Thomas A. Henzinger, and Radha Jagadeesan. Robust timed automata. In Oded Maler, editor, *Proceedings of the First International Workshop on Hybrid and Real-Time Systems (HART 97)*, volume 1201 of *Lecture Notes in Computer Science*, pages 331–345. Springer-Verlag, 1997.

[GNRR93] Robert L. Grossman, Anil Nerode, Anders P. Ravn, and Hans Rischel, editors. *Hybrid Systems*, volume 736 of *Lecture Notes in Computer Science*. Springer-Verlag, 1993.

[HHWT95] Thomas A. Henzinger, Pei-Hsin Ho, and Howard Wong-Toi. HyTech: The next generation. In *16th Annual IEEE Real-time Systems Symposium (RTSS 1995)*, pages 56–65. IEEE Computer Society Press, 1995.

[HKPV95] Thomas A. Henzinger, Peter W. Kopke, Anuj Puri, and Pravin Varaiya. What's decidable about hybrid automata. In *Proceedings of the Twenty-Seventh Annual ACM Symposium on the Theory of Computing*, pages 373–382. ACM, 1995.

[Moo98] Chris Moore. Finite-dimensional analog computers: Flows, maps, and recurrent neural networks. In C.S. Calude, J. Casti, and M.J. Dinneen, editors, *1st International Conference on Unconventional Models of Computation*. Springer-Verlag, 1998.

[MS97] Wolfgang Maass and Eduardo D. Sontag. Analog neural nets with Gaussian or other common noise distributions cannot recognize arbitrary regular languages. In *Electronic Colloquium on Computational Complexity, technical reports*. 1997.

[Pur98] Anuj Puri. Dynamical properties of timed automata. In A. P. Ravn and H. Rischel, editors, *Formal Techniques in Real-Time and Fault-Tolerant Systems (FTRTFT'98)*, volume 1486 of *Lecture Notes in Computer Science*, pages 210–227. Springer-Verlag, 1998.

[Tar48] Alfred Tarski. A decision method for elementary algebra and geometry. RAND Corporation, Santa Monica, Calif., 1948.

Non-structural Subtype Entailment in Automata Theory

Joachim Niehren and Tim Priesnitz

Programming Systems Lab, Universität des Saarlandes, Saarbrücken, Germany
www.ps.uni-sb.de/~{niehren,tim}

Abstract. Decidability of non-structural subtype entailment is a long standing open problem in programming language theory. In this paper, we apply automata theoretic methods to characterize the problem equivalently by using regular expressions and word equations. This characterization induces new results on non-structural subtype entailment, constitutes a promising starting point for further investigations on decidability, and explains for the first time why the problem is so difficult. The difficulty is caused by implicit word equations that we make explicit.

1 Introduction

Subtyping is a common concept of many programming languages (including C++ and Java). A subtype relation $\tau' \leq \tau$ means that all functions in a program that expect an argument of type τ are sufficiently polymorphic so that they can also be applied to values of the subtype τ'. Thus, one can safely replace values of a type τ by values of subtype τ'.

Subtype constraints are systems of inequations $t \leq t'$ that talk about the subtype relation. Terms t and t' in subtype constraints are built from type variables and type constructors. Two logical operations on subtype constraints were investigated: satisfiability and entailment [6, 12, 1, 4, 18, 20]. *Subtype satisfiability* can be checked in cubic time for many type languages [9, 16]. A quadratic time algorithm for the variable free case is presented in [10].

Interest in *subtype entailment* was first raised by practical questions on type inference engines with subtyping [5, 21, 19]. The efficiency of such systems relies on the existence of powerful simplification algorithms for typings. Such operations can be formulated on the basis of algorithms for subtype entailment.

It then turned out that subtype entailment is a quite complex problem, even for unexpressive type languages where types are ordinary trees. Rehof and Henglein [22] clarified the situation for structural subtyping. This is a tree ordering that relates trees of the same shape only. It is induced by lifting an ordering on constants. If trees are built over the signature $\{int, real, \times, \rightarrow\}$, for instance, then structural subtyping is induced by the usual axiom $int \leq real$ which says that every integer is a real number. Rehof and Henglein showed that structural subtype entailment is coNP-complete [7] for finite trees (simple types) and PSPACE-complete [8] for possibly infinite trees (recursive types).

N. Kobayashi and B.C. Pierce (Eds.): TACS 2001, LNCS 2215, pp. 360–384, 2001.

Subtyping becomes *non-structural* if the constants $\bot$ and $\top$ are admitted that stand for the least and greatest type. Now, trees of different shapes can be related since all trees τ satisfy $\bot \leq \tau \leq \top$. Several cases are to be distinguished: one can consider only *finite* trees or admit *infinite* trees, or one may assume that all function symbols are *co-variant* (such as $\times$) or that some are *contra-variant* (as the function type constructor $\rightarrow$ in its first argument). One can also vary the number of type constructors of each *arity*.

Decidability of non-structural subtype entailment (NSSE) is a prominent open problem in programming language theory. Only a PSPACE lower bound is known which holds in both cases, for finite trees and for infinite trees [8]. The signature $\{\bot, f, \top\}$ is enough to prove PSPACE hardness if f is a type constructor of arity at least 2. But this result does not explain why finding a decision procedure for NSSE is so difficult. On the other hand, only a fragment of NSSE could be proved decidable [15] (and PSPACE-complete).

The idea behind the approach of this paper is to first reformulate Rehof and Henglein's approach for structural subtype entailment in automata theory and second to lift it to the non-structural case. We have carried out both steps successfully but report only on the second step.

A similar automata theoretic approach is already known for satisfiablity but not for entailment [9, 16]. Our extension to entailment yields a new characterization of NSSE that uses regular expressions and word equations [11, 17]. Word equations raise the real difficulty behind NSSE since they spoil the usual pumping arguments from automata theory. They also clarify why NSSE differs so significantly from seemingly similar entailment problems [13, 14].

2 Characterization

We now formulate the main result of this paper and discuss its relevance (Theorem 1). This is a new characterization of NSSE which is based on a new class of extended regular expressions: *cap set expressions* that we introduce first.

A *word* over an alphabet $\mathbf{A}$ is a finite sequence of letters in $\mathbf{A}$. We denote words by π, μ, or ν and the set of words over $\mathbf{A}$ with $\mathbf{A}^*$. The *empty word* is written as ε and the free-monoid *concatenation* of words π and μ by juxtaposition $\pi\mu$, with the property that $\varepsilon\pi = \pi\varepsilon = \pi$. A *prefix* of a word π is a word μ for which there exists a word ν such that $\pi = \mu\nu$. If μ is a prefix of π then we write $\mu \leq \pi$ and if μ is a proper prefix of π then we write $\mu < \pi$. We define *regular expressions* R over alphabet $\mathbf{A}$ as usual:

$$R := a \mid \varepsilon \mid R_1 R_2 \mid R^* \mid R_1 \cup R_2 \mid \emptyset \qquad \text{where } a \in \mathbf{A}$$

Every regular expression R defines a regular language of words $\mathcal{L}(R) \subseteq \mathbf{A}^*$. We next introduce *cap set expressions* E over $\mathbf{A}$. (Their name will be explained in Sec. 5.)

$$E ::= R_1 R_2^\circ \mid E_1 \cup E_2$$

Cap set expressions E denote sets of words $\mathcal{L}(E) \subseteq \mathbf{A}^*$ that we call *cap sets*. We have to define the *cap set operator* $^\circ$ on sets of words, i.e we must define the set $S^\circ \subseteq \mathbf{A}^*$ for all sets $S \subseteq \mathbf{A}^*$. Let pr be the prefix operator lifted to sets of words. We set:

$$S^\circ = \{\pi \mid \pi \in pr(\mu^*),\ \mu \in S\}$$

A word π belongs to S° if π is a prefix of a power $\mu \dots \mu$ of some word $\mu \in S$. Note that cap set expressions subsume regular expressions: indeed, $\mathcal{L}(R) = \mathcal{L}(R\,\varepsilon^\circ)$ for all R. But the cap operator adds new expressiveness when applied to an infinite set: there exist regular expression R such that the language of the cap set expression R° is neither regular nor context free. Consider for instance $(21^*)^\circ$ which denotes the set of all prefixes of words $21^n\,21^n \dots 21^n$ where $n \geq 0$. Clearly this set is not context-free.

We will derive appropriate *restrictions* on cap set expressions (Def. 27) such that following theorem becomes true.

Theorem 1 (Characterization). *The decidability of NSSE for a signature* $\{\bot, f, \top\}$ *with a single function symbol of arity* $n \geq 1$ *is equivalent to the decidability of the universality problem for the class of restricted cap set expressions over the alphabet* $\{1, \dots, n\}$. *This result holds equally for finite and for possibly infinite trees.*

The theorem allows to derive the following robustness result of NSSE against variations from automata transformations (Sec. 12).

Corollary 2. *All variants of NSSE with signature* $\{\bot, f, \top\}$ *where the arity of* f *at least* $n \geq 2$ *are equivalent. It does not even matter whether finite or infinite trees are considered.*

Theorem 1 can also be used to relate NSSE to word equations. The idea is to express membership in cap sets in the positive existential fragment of word equations with regular constraints [23]. The reduction can easily be based on the following lemma that is well known in the field of string unification.

Lemma 3. *For all words* $\pi \in \mathbf{A}^*$ *and nonempty words* $\mu \in \mathbf{A}^+$ *it holds that* $\pi \in pr(\mu^*)$ *if and only if* $\pi \in pr(\mu\pi)$. *Thus, all sets* $S \subseteq \mathbf{A}^+$ *of nonempty words satisfy:*

$$\pi \in S^\circ \leftrightarrow \exists\mu\exists\nu\ (\mu \in S \wedge \pi\nu = \mu\pi)$$

We can thus express the universality problem of cap set expressions E in the positive $\forall\exists^*$ fragment of the first-order theory of word equations with regular constraints.

Corollary 4. *NSSE with a single function symbol of arity* $n \geq 1$ *can be expressed in the positive* $\forall\exists^*$ *fragment of the first-order theory of word equations with regular constraints over the alphabet* $\{1, \dots, n\}$.

Unfortunately, even the positive $\forall\exists^3$ fragment of a single word equation is undecidable [3] except if the alphabet is infinite [2] or a singleton [24]. Therefore, it remains open whether NSSE is decidable or not. But it becomes clear that the difficulty is raised by word equations hidden behind cap set expressions R°, i.e. the equation $\pi\nu = \mu\pi$ in Lemma 3.

Theorem 1 constitutes a promising starting point to further investigate decidability of NSSE. For instance, we can infer a new decidability result for the monadic case directly from Corollary 4.

Corollary 5. *NSSE is decidable for the signature* $\{\bot, f, \top\}$ *if* f *is unary.*

Plan of the Paper. We first recall the precise definition of NSSE (Sec. 3) and then prove Theorem 1 in 5 subsequent steps. This covers most of the paper (Sec. 4 – 11).

First, we express NSSE by a so called *safety* property for sets of words (Sec. 4). Second, we introduce *cap-automata* – a restricted version of P-automata as introduced [15] – which can recognize exactly the same languages as cap set expressions (Sec. 5). Third, we show how to construct cap automata corresponding to entailment judgments. This construction encodes NSSE into universality of cap automata (Sec. 6). We prove the soundness (Sec. 7) and completeness (Sec. 8) of our construction. Fourth, we infer restrictions that are satisfied by all constructed cap automata and define corresponding restrictions for cap set expressions (Sec. 9 and 10). Fifth, we give a back translation (Sec. 11) that reduces universality of restricted cap automata into NSSE.

Finally, we present transformations on restricted cap automata that allow us to derive Corollary 2 from Theorem 1 (Sec. 12), and conclude.

3 Non-structural Subtype Constraints

In this paper we investigate non-structural subtype constraints over signatures of function symbols $\Sigma = \{\bot, f, \top\}$ with a single non-constant function symbol f that is co-variant. We write ar_g for the *arity* of a function symbol $g \in \Sigma$, i.e $\mathsf{ar}_\bot = \mathsf{ar}_\top = 0$ and $\mathsf{ar}_f \geq 1$.

The choice of such signatures imposes two restrictions: first, we do not allow for contravariant type constructors. These could be covered in our framework even though this is not fully obvious. Second, we do not treat larger signature with more than one non-constant function symbol. This is a true restriction that cannot be circumvented easily.

3.1 Non-structural Subtyping

We next define finite and infinite trees over Σ. We consider trees as partial functions $\tau : \mathbb{N}^* \rightsquigarrow \Sigma$ which map words over natural numbers to function symbols. A tree τ is *finite* if its domain D_τ is finite and otherwise *infinite*. The words in $D_\tau \subseteq \mathbb{N}^*$ are called the *nodes* or *paths* of the tree. The idea is to identify a node with the path that addresses it relative to the root. We require that every tree has a root $\varepsilon \in D_\tau$ and that tree domains D_τ are always prefix closed and arity-consistent. The latter means for all trees τ, nodes $\pi \in D_\tau$, and naturals $i \in \mathbb{N}$ that $\pi i \in D_\tau$ if and only if $1 \leq i \leq \mathsf{ar}_{\tau(\pi)}$.

We will freely interpret function symbols in Σ as tree constructors. To make clear distinctions, we will write $=_\Sigma$ for equality of symbols in Σ and $=$ for equality of trees over Σ. Given $g \in \Sigma$ and trees $\tau_1, \ldots, \tau_{\mathsf{ar}_g}$ we define $\tau = g(\tau_1, \ldots, \tau_{\mathsf{ar}_g})$ by $\tau(\varepsilon) =_\Sigma g$ and $\tau(i\pi) =_\Sigma \tau_i(\pi)$ for all $\pi \in D_{\tau_i}$ and $1 \leq i \leq \mathsf{ar}_g$. We thus consider ground terms over Σ as (finite) trees, for instance $f(\bot, \top)$ or $\bot$. Thereby, we have overloaded our notation since a constant $a \in \Sigma$ can also be seen as tree $\varepsilon \mapsto a$. But this should never lead to confusion.

Let $<_\Sigma$ be the irreflexive partial order on Σ that satisfies $\bot \ <_\Sigma \ f \ <_\Sigma \ \top$ and $\leq_\Sigma$ its reflexive counterpart. We define *non-structural subtyping* to be the unique partial order on trees which satisfies for all trees τ_1, τ_2 over Σ:

$$\tau_1 {\leq} \tau_2 \quad \text{iff} \quad \tau_1(\pi) \leq_\Sigma \tau_2(\pi) \text{ for all } \pi \in D_{\tau_1} \cap D_{\tau_2}$$

3.2 Constraint Language

We assume an infinite set of tree valued variables that we denote by x, y, z, u, v, w. A *subtype constraint* φ is a conjunction of literals with the following abstract syntax:

$$\varphi, \varphi' ::= x{\leq}f(y_1, \ldots, y_n) \mid f(y_1, \ldots, y_n){\leq}x \mid x{=}\bot \mid x{=}\top \mid \varphi \wedge \varphi'$$

where $n = \mathsf{ar}_f$. We interpret constraints φ in the structure of trees over Σ with non-structural subtyping. We distinguish two cases, the structure of finite trees or else of possibly infinite trees. We interpret function symbols in both cases as tree constructors and the predicate symbol $\leq$ by the non-structural subtype relation. Again, this overloads notation: we use the same symbol $\leq$ for the subtype relation on trees and the predicate symbol denoting the subtype relation in constraints. Again, this should not raise confusion.

Note that we do not allow for formulas $x{\leq}y$ in our constraint language. This choice will help us to simplify our presentation essentially. It is, however, irrelevant from the point of view of expressiveness. We can still express $x{\leq}y$ by using existential quantifiers:

$$x{\leq}y \leftrightarrow \exists z \exists u \ (f(x, u, \ldots, u){\leq}z \wedge z{\leq}f(y, u, \ldots, u))$$

As in this equivalence, we will sometimes use first-order formulas Φ built from constraints and the usual first-order connectives. We will write V_Φ for the set of free variables occurring in Φ. A solution of Φ is a variable assignment α into the set of finite (resp. possibly infinite) trees which satisfies the required subtype relations; we write $\alpha \models \Phi$ if α solves Φ and say that Φ is *satisfiable.*

Example 6. The constraint $x{\leq}f(x)$ is satisfiable, even when interpreted over finite trees. We can solve it by mapping x to $\bot$. In contrast, the equality constraint $x{\leq}f(x) \wedge f(x){\leq}x$ is unsatisfiable over finite trees. It can however be solved by mapping x to the infinite tree $f(f(f(\ldots)))$.

A formula Φ_1 *entails* Φ_2 (we write $\Phi_1 \models \Phi_2$) if all solutions $\alpha \models \Phi_1$ satisfy $\alpha \models \Phi_2$. We will consider entailment judgments that are triples of the form

(φ, x, y) that we write as $\varphi \models^? x{\leq}y$. *Non-structural subtype entailment* (NSSE) for Σ is the problem to check whether entailment $\varphi \models x{\leq}y$ holds for a given entailment judgment $\varphi \models^? x{\leq}y$.

Note that entailment judgments of the simple form $\varphi \models^? x{\leq}y$ can express general entailment judgments, where both sides are conjunctions of inequations $t_1{\leq}t_2$ between nested terms or variables (i.e. $t ::= x \mid f(t_1, \ldots, t_n) \mid \bot \mid \top$). The main trick is to replace a judgment $\varphi \models^? t_1{\leq}t_2$ with terms t_1 and t_2 by $\varphi \wedge x{=}t_1 \wedge y{=}t_2 \models^? x{\leq}y$ where x and y are fresh variables. Note also that the omission of formulas $u{\leq}v$ on the left hand side does not restrict the problem. (Existential quantifier on the left hand side of an entailment judgment can be removed.)

Example 7. The prototypical example where NSSE holds somehow surprisingly is:

$$x{\leq}f(y) \wedge f(x){\leq}y \models^? x{\leq}y \qquad \text{(yes)}$$

To see this, note that all finite trees in the unary case are of the form $f \ldots f(\bot)$ or $f \ldots f(\top)$. Thus, $x{\leq}y \vee y{<}x$ is valid in this case. Next let us contradict the assumption that there is a solution $\alpha \models y{<}x \wedge x{\leq}f(y) \wedge f(x){\leq}y$. Transitivity yields $\alpha(y){\leq}f(\alpha(y))$ and then also $f(\alpha(x)){\leq}f(\alpha(y))$. Hence $\alpha(x){\leq}\alpha(y)$ which contradicts $\alpha(y){<}\alpha(x)$.

4 Entailment via Safety

We now characterize NSSE by properties of sets of words that we call safety properties. Appropriate safety properties can be verified by P-automata as we will show in Section 6.

We use terms $x(\pi)$ to denote the node label of the value of x at path π. Whenever we use this term, we presuppose the existence of π in the tree domain of the value of x. For instance, the formula $x(12) \leq_\Sigma \top$ is satisfied by a variable assignment if and only if the tree assigned to x contains the node 12.

We next recall the notion of safety from [15]. Let $\varphi \models^? x{\leq}y$ be an entailment judgment and π a word in $\{1, \ldots, \mathsf{ar}_f\}^*$. We call π *safe* for $\varphi \models^? x{\leq}y$ if entailment cannot be contradicted at π, i.e. if $\varphi \wedge y(\pi) <_\Sigma x(\pi)$ is unsatisfiable. Clearly entailment $\varphi \models x{\leq}y$ is equivalent to that all paths are safe for $\varphi \models^? x{\leq}y$.

For a restricted class of entailment judgments it is shown in [15] that the above notion of safety can be checked by testing universality of P-automata. Unfortunately, it is unclear how to lift this result to the general case. To work around, we refine the notion of safety into two dual notions: *left (l) safety* and *right (r) safety*.

$$\pi \text{ is } \textit{l-safe} \text{ for } \varphi \models^? x{\leq}y \;\text{ iff }\; \varphi \models \begin{cases} \qquad\quad x(\pi) =_\Sigma f \\ \vee \bigvee_{\pi' \leq \pi} x(\pi') =_\Sigma \bot \\ \vee \bigvee_{\pi' \leq \pi} y(\pi') =_\Sigma \top \end{cases}$$

This means that $\varphi \models^? x{\leq}y$ cannot be contradicted by a solution α of φ that maps the left hand side x at node π to $\top$, i.e. where $\alpha(x)(\pi) = \top$. The notion of r-safety is analogous, expect that one tries to contradict at the right hand side with $\bot$.

$$\pi \text{ is } r\text{-}safe \text{ for } \varphi \models^? x{\leq}y \text{ iff } \varphi \models \begin{cases} y(\pi) =_\Sigma f \\ \vee \bigvee_{\pi' \leq \pi} x(\pi') =_\Sigma \bot \\ \vee \bigvee_{\pi' \leq \pi} y(\pi') =_\Sigma \top \end{cases}$$

We define a variable assignment α to be l-safe or r-safe for $\alpha \models^? x{\leq}y$ by replacing φ literally with α in the above definitions.

We first illustrate these concepts by a judgment with a unary function symbol:

$$z{=}\top \wedge f(z){\leq}y \models^? x{\leq}y \qquad \text{(no)}$$

Here, ε is r-safe but not l-safe. All other paths $\pi \in 1^+$ are both l-safe and r-safe. There is a variable assignment α which contradicts entailment: $\alpha(x) = \top$, $\alpha(z) = \top, \alpha(y) = f(\top)$. This shows that ε is indeed not l-safe for $\alpha \models^? x{\leq}y$.

Proposition 8. *Entailment $\varphi{\models}x{\leq}y$ holds if and only if all words $\pi{\in}\{1,\ldots,\mathsf{ar}_f\}^*$ are l-safe and r-safe for $\varphi \models^? x{\leq}y$.*

Proof. We first assume that entailment does not hold and show that either l-safety or r-safety can be contradicted for some path. As argued above, there exists an unsafe path π such that $\varphi \wedge y(\pi) <_\Sigma x(\pi)$ is satisfiable. Let α be a solution of this formula.

1. If $\alpha(y)(\pi) =_\Sigma \bot$ then $\alpha(x)(\pi) \in \{f, \top\}$ and π fails to be r-safe.
2. Otherwise $\alpha(y)(\pi) =_\Sigma f$. Thus $\alpha(x)(\pi) =_\Sigma \top$ which contradicts that π is l-safe.

For the converse, we assume entailment $\varphi \models x{\leq}y$ and show that all paths are l-safe and r-safe for $\varphi \models^? x{\leq}y$. We fix a path π and solution α of φ, and show that π is l-safe and r-safe for $\alpha \models^? x{\leq}y$. Let π' be the longest prefix of π which belongs to $D_{\alpha(x)} \cap D_{\alpha(y)}$.

1. If $\alpha(x)(\pi') =_\Sigma \bot$ then π satisfies the second condition of both l-safety and r-safety for $\alpha \models^? x{\leq}y$.
2. Suppose $\alpha(x)(\pi') =_\Sigma \top$. Since $\alpha \models \varphi$ and $\varphi \models x{\leq}y$, we know that $\alpha \models x{\leq}y$. Since π' is a node of both trees it follows that $\alpha(x)(\pi') \leq_\Sigma \alpha(y)(\pi')$ and thus $\alpha(y)(\pi') =_\Sigma \top$. Thus, π satisfies the third condition of l-safety and r-safety for $\alpha \models^? x{\leq}y$.
3. The last possibility is $\alpha(x)(\pi') =_\Sigma f$. We can infer from entailment that $\alpha(y)(\pi') \in \{f, \top\}$. If $\alpha(y)(\pi') =_\Sigma \top$ we are done as before. Otherwise, $\alpha(y)(\pi') =_\Sigma \alpha(x)(\pi') =_\Sigma f$ such that the maximality of π' and $\mathsf{ar}_f \geq 1$ yields $\pi = \pi'$. Now, π satisfies the first conditions of l-safety and r-safety for $\alpha \models^? x{\leq}y$.

Example 9. The surprising effect of Example 7 seems to go away if one replaces the unary function symbol there by a binary function symbol:

$$x \le f(y,y) \wedge f(x,x) \le y \models^? x \le y \qquad \text{(no)}$$

Now, all words in $1^* \cup 2^*$ are l-safe and r-safe, but 12 is neither. Entailment can be contradicted by variable assignments mapping x to $f(f(\bot,\top),\bot)$ and y to $f(f(\top,\bot),\top)$.

Example 10. This example is a little more complicated. Its purpose is to show that entailment in the binary case can also be raised by a similar effect as in Example 7. How to understand this effect in general will be explained in Section 6.

$$x \le f(y,y) \wedge f(z,z) \le y \wedge f(u,u) \le z \wedge u = \top \models^? x \le y \qquad \text{(yes)}$$

5 Cap Automata and Cap Sets

We now restrict the class of P-automata introduced in [15] to the class of so called *cap automata*[1]. We then show that the class of languages recognized by cap automata is precisely the class of cap sets, i.e. those sets of words described by cap set expressions.

A *finite automaton* $\mathcal{A}$ over alphabet $\mathbf{A}$ consists of a set Q of *states*, a set $I \subseteq Q$ of *initial* states, a set $F \subseteq Q$ of *final* states, and a set $\Delta \subseteq Q \times (\mathbf{A} \cup \{\varepsilon\}) \times Q$ of *transitions*. Note that Δ permits ε transitions and single letter transitions. We will write $\mathcal{A} \vdash q$ if $q \in Q$ is a state of $\mathcal{A}$, $\mathcal{A} \vdash \underline{\underline{q}}$ if $q \in F$ is a final state of $\mathcal{A}$, and $\mathcal{A} \vdash {>}q$ if $q \in I$ is an initial state of $\mathcal{A}$. The statement $\mathcal{A} \vdash q \xrightarrow{\pi} q'$ says that $\mathcal{A}$ started at q permits a sequence of transitions consuming π and ending in q'. Note that $\mathcal{A} \vdash q \xrightarrow{\varepsilon} q$ holds for all states $q \in Q$. We call $\mathcal{A}$ complete if for every word $\pi \in \mathbf{A}^*$ there exists states q_0 and q_1 such that $\mathcal{A} \vdash {>}q_0 \xrightarrow{\pi} q_1$.

Definition 11. *A* cap automaton $\mathcal{P}$ *over alphabet* $\mathbf{A}$ *consists of a finite automaton* $\mathcal{A}$ *over* $\mathbf{A}$ *and a set of* P-edges $P \subseteq Q \times Q$. *We write* $\mathcal{P} \vdash q \dashrightarrow q'$ *if* $\mathcal{P}$ *has a P-edge* $(q,q') \in P$. *A cap automaton* $\mathcal{P}$ *over* $\mathbf{A}$ *recognizes the following language* $\mathcal{L}(\mathcal{P}) \subseteq \mathbf{A}^*$*:*

$$\mathcal{L}(\mathcal{P}) = \{\pi \mid \mathcal{P} \vdash {>}q_0 \xrightarrow{\pi} \underline{\underline{q_1}}\} \cup \{\pi\mu' \mid \mu' \in \mathrm{pr}(\mu^*), \mathcal{P} \vdash {>}q_0 \xrightarrow{\pi} \underline{\underline{q_1}} \xrightarrow{\mu} q_2 \dashrightarrow \underline{\underline{q_1}}\}$$

The first set is the language of the finite automaton underlying $\mathcal{P}$. The second set add the contribution of P-edges: if a cap automaton traverses a P-edge $\mathcal{P} \vdash$

[1] Cap automata are the same objects as P-automata, i.e. finite automata with a set of P-edges. The difference between both concepts concerns the corresponding language definitions only. Both definitions coincide for those automata $\mathcal{P}$ that satisfy the following condition (the proof is straightforward): if $\mathcal{P} \vdash q_1 \xrightarrow{\pi} q_2 \xrightarrow{\mu} q_3 \dashrightarrow q_1$ then q_2 is a final state in $\mathcal{P}$. This condition can be assumed w.l.o.g for all cap automata, since it is satisfied by all those constructed in the proof of Proposition 12. Thus, cap automata are indeed properly subsumed by the P-automata.

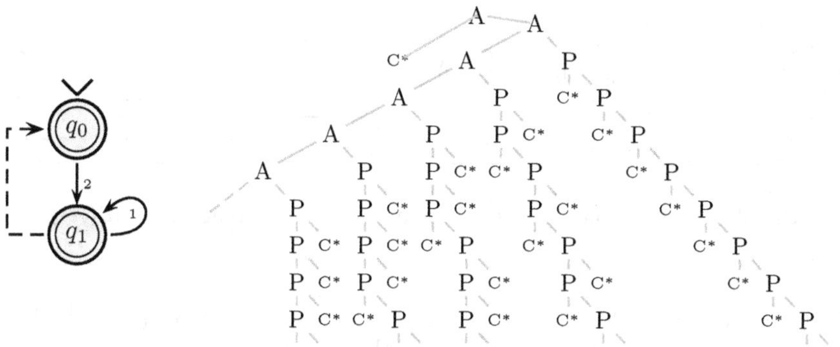

Fig. 1. A cap automaton with a non context-free language $(21^*)^\circ$.

$q_2 \dashrightarrow q_1$ then it must have reached q_2 from q_2 of some word μ, i.e. $\mathcal{P} \vdash q_1 \xrightarrow{\mu} q_2 \dashrightarrow q_1$; in the sequel the automaton can loop through μ^* and quit the loop at any time.

Fig. 1 contains a cap automaton over the alphabet $\{1, 2\}$ that recognizes the non-context free cap set from the introduction, i.e. described by the cap set expression $(21^*)^\circ$. We generally draw cap automata as one draws finite automata but with additional dashed arrows to indicate P-edges.

The tree on the right in Fig. 1 represents the language recognized by this cap automaton. The language of a cap automaton $\mathcal{P}$ with alphabet $\{1, \ldots, n\}$ is drawn as a n-ary class tree. This is a complete infinite n-ary tree whose nodes are labeled by classes A, P, and C. Each node of the class tree is a word in $\{1, \ldots, n\}^*$ that is labeled by the class that $\mathcal{P}$ adjoins to it. We assign the class C to all words in the complement of $\mathcal{L}(\mathcal{P})$ of a cap automaton $\mathcal{P}$. The words with class A are recognized by the finite automaton underlying $\mathcal{P}$. All remaining words belong to class P. These are accepted by $\mathcal{P}$ but not by the underlying finite automaton.

We now explain the name *cap*: it is an abbreviation for the regular expression $(\,\mathrm{C} \cup \mathrm{A}^+\mathrm{P}^*\,)^*$. Branches in class trees of cap automata always satisfy that expression. This means that all nodes of class P in a class tree have a mother node in either of the classes A or P. To see this, note first that root nodes of class trees can never belong to class P Thus, all P nodes must have a mother. Furthermore, the mother of a P node cannot belong to the C class due to the cap property.

Proposition 12. *Cap set expressions and cap automata recognize precisely the same class of languages. Universality of cap set expressions and cap automata are equivalent modulo deterministic polynomial time transformations.*

Proof. For the one direction, let R_{q_1,q_2} be a regular expression for the set $\{\pi \mid \mathcal{P} \vdash q_1 \xrightarrow{\pi} q_2\}$ then the language of a cap automaton is equal to the union of

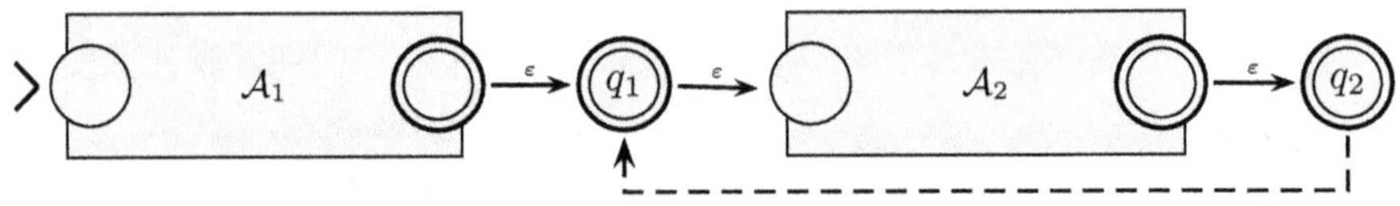

Fig. 2. Construction of a cap automaton for the language $\mathcal{L}(\mathcal{A}_1)\mathcal{L}(\mathcal{A}_2)^\circ$.

$\cup_{\mathcal{P}\vdash >q_0} \cup_{\mathcal{P}\vdash \underline{\underline{q_1}}} R_{q_0,q_1}$ and $\cup_{\mathcal{P}\vdash >q_0} \cup_{\mathcal{P}\vdash \underline{\underline{q_1}}} \cup_{\mathcal{P}\vdash q_2 \dashrightarrow q_1} R_{q_0,q_1}(R_{q_1,q_2})^\circ$. The needed regular expressions can be computed in polynomial time

For the converse, we first note that the class of languages recognized by cap automata is closed under union since cap automata may have several initial states. There thus only remains to built cap automata for expressions $R_1 R_2^\circ$. Let $\mathcal{A}_1$ and $\mathcal{A}_2$ be finite automata that recognize R_1 respectively R_2. W.l.o.g. we can assume that both automata have a unique initial and a unique final state. Multiple initial or final states of finite automata (but not of cap automata) can be eliminated by introducing new ε-transitions. We now compose $\mathcal{A}_1$ and $\mathcal{A}_2$ into a new cap automaton that recognizes the language of $R_1 R_2^\circ$ as illustrated in Fig. 2: we add two fresh final states q_1 and q_2 and link $\mathcal{A}_1$ and $\mathcal{A}_2$ over these states. This requires 3 new ε-edges and a new P-edge from q_2 to q_1. To account for the prefix closure within the $^\circ$ operator, we finally turn all states of $\mathcal{A}_2$ into additional final states.

6 Automata Construction

We now construct cap automata that test l-safety and r-safety of entailment judgments. The same construction applies for finite trees and possibly infinite trees. The only difference between both cases is hidden in different application conditions required for completeness. The appropriate conditions for both cases can be ensured by different preprocessing steps and satisfiability tests (as Prop. 21 will explain).

The automata construction is given in Table 1. For each entailment judgment $\varphi \models^? x \leq y$ we construct a left automaton $\mathcal{P}_l(\varphi \models^? x \leq y)$ and a right automaton $\mathcal{P}_r(\varphi \models^? x \leq y)$. The left automaton is supposed to accept all l-safe paths for $\varphi \models^? x \leq y$, and the right automaton all r-safe paths (up to appropriate assumptions). Entailment then holds if and only if the languages of both cap automata are universal. Note that it remains open whether the set of simultaneously l-safe and r-safe paths can be recognized by a single cap automaton. The problem is that cap automata are not closed under intersection (proof omitted).

The left and right automaton always have the same states, transitions, and initial states. When testing for $\varphi \models^? x \leq y$ the only **initial state** is (x, y). A state (u, s) of the left automaton is made **final** if there is an upper bound $u \leq f(u_1, \ldots, u_n)$ in φ, which proves that the actual path is l-safe. The **descend**

Table 1. Construction of the cap automata $\mathcal{P}_\theta = \mathcal{P}_\theta(\varphi \models^? x \leq y)$ for both sides $\theta \in \{l, r\}$.

alphabet	$A_\Sigma = \{1, \ldots, \mathsf{ar}_f\}$	
states	$\mathcal{P}_\theta \vdash (s, s')$	if $s, s' \in V_\varphi \cup \{x, y, \_\}$
	$\mathcal{P}_\theta \vdash \underline{\underline{\text{all}}}$	
initial state	$\mathcal{P}_\theta \vdash\ >(x, y)$	
final states	$\mathcal{P}_l \vdash \underline{\underline{(u, s)}}$	if $u \leq f(u_1, \ldots, u_n)$ *in* φ
	$\mathcal{P}_r \vdash \underline{\underline{(s, v)}}$	if $f(v_1, \ldots, v_n) \leq v$ *in* φ
descend	$\mathcal{P}_\theta \vdash (u, s) \xrightarrow{i} (u_i, \_)$	if $u \leq f(u_1, \ldots, u_n)$ *in* φ, $i \in A_\Sigma$
	$\mathcal{P}_\theta \vdash (s, v) \xrightarrow{i} (\_, v_i)$	if $f(v_1, \ldots, v_n) \leq v$ *in* φ, $i \in A_\Sigma$
	$\mathcal{P}_\theta \vdash (u, v) \xrightarrow{i} (u_i, v_i)$	if $\begin{cases} u \leq f(u_1, \ldots, u_n) \textit{ in } \varphi, \\ f(v_1, \ldots, v_n) \leq v \textit{ in } \varphi,\ i \in A_\Sigma \end{cases}$
bot	$\mathcal{P}_\theta \vdash \underline{\underline{(u, s)}} \xrightarrow{i} \underline{\underline{\text{all}}}$	if $u = \bot$ *in* φ, $i \in A_\Sigma$
top	$\mathcal{P}_\theta \vdash \underline{\underline{(s, v)}} \xrightarrow{i} \underline{\underline{\text{all}}}$	if $v = \top$ *in* φ, $i \in A_\Sigma$
reflexivity	$\mathcal{P}_\theta \vdash \underline{\underline{(u, u)}} \xrightarrow{i} \underline{\underline{\text{all}}}$	if $u \in V_\varphi \cup \{x, y\}, i \in A_\Sigma$
all	$\mathcal{P}_\theta \vdash \underline{\underline{\text{all}}} \xrightarrow{i} \underline{\underline{\text{all}}}$	if $i \in A_\Sigma$
P−edges	$\mathcal{P}_l \vdash (u, s) \dashrightarrow (v, u)$	
	$\mathcal{P}_r \vdash (s, v) \dashrightarrow (v, u)$	

rule can also be applied in that case. The safety check then continues in some state (u_i, s') and extends the actual path by i. It can chose $s' = \_$ while ignoring the right hand side, or if s is also a variable descend simultaneously on the right hand side. There are three rules that prove that the actual path and **all** its extensions are l-safe: **bot**, **top**, and **reflexivity**. Finally there is a single rule that adds **P-edges** to the left automaton. The rules for the right automaton are symmetric.

When drawing the constructed left and right automata (Fig. 3 and 4), we always share the states and transitions for reasons of economy. Different elements of the two automata carry extra annotations. Final states of the left (right) automaton are put into a left (right) double circle. If a state is final for both automata then it is drawn within a complete double circle. We annotate P-edges of the left automaton by l and of the right automaton with r.

We first illustrate the automata construction for the unary Example 7, recalled in Fig. 3. The alphabet of both automata is the singleton $\{1\}$. The relevant states are $\{(x, y), (y, x)\}$; all others are either unreachable or do not lead to a final state. The constraints $x \leq f(y)$ and $f(x) \leq y$ let both cap automata **descend** simultaneously by the transition $(x, y) \xrightarrow{1} (y, x)$ and turn (x, y) into a **final state** of both automata. There are **P-edges** $(y, x) \dashrightarrow (x, y)$ for both cap automata. Note that we ignore the symmetric P-edges $(x, y) \dashrightarrow (y, x)$ in the picture since they don't contribute to the respective languages.

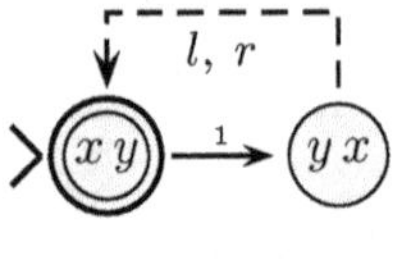

$x \leq f(y) \wedge f(x) \leq y \models^? x \leq y$

Fig. 3. Automata construction for Example 7. Entailment holds.

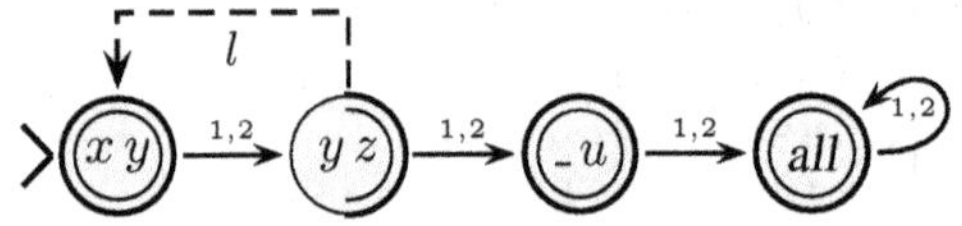

$x \leq f(y, y) \wedge f(z, z) \leq y \wedge f(u, u) \leq z \wedge u = \top \models^? x \leq y$

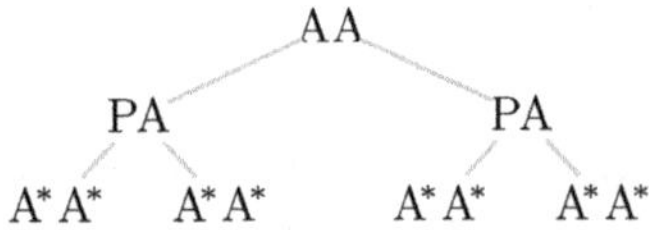

Fig. 4. Automata construction for Example 10. Entailment holds.

Fig. 3 also contains the class trees for both cap automata but in an overlaid fashion. The languages of both cap automata are universal due to their P-edges. Given that our construction is sound (see Sec. 7) this proves entailment.

We now consider the more complex binary Example 10 in Fig. 4 where the alphabet is $\{1, 2\}$. The constraint $f(u, u) \leq z$ permits to **descend** from (y, z) while ignoring the variable y on the left hand side; this justifies the transition $(y, z) \xrightarrow{1,2} (_, u)$. Since the left hand side is ignored, the state (y, z) is only put to the **final states** of the right automaton. The **top** rule can be applied to $u = \top$; hence there are transitions $(_, u) \xrightarrow{1,2}$ *all* where $(_, u)$ and *all* are universal states according to the **all** rule. Finally, there is a **P-edge** $(y, z) \dashrightarrow (x, y)$ for the left cap automaton. We again ignore the symmetric **P-edge** $(x, y) \dashrightarrow (y, z)$ since it does not contribute to the language. The languages of both automata are again universal, in case of the left automaton because of a P-edge.

Theorem 13 (Reduction). *NSSE for a signature* $\{\bot, f, \top\}$ *can be reduced in polynomial time to the universality problem of cap automata over the alphabet* $\{1, \ldots, ar_f\}$. *This holds equally for finite or possibly infinite trees.*

The automata construction is proven sound in Sec. 7 and complete in Sec. 8.

7 Soundness

In this section, we prove the soundness of the automata construction. The proof is non-trivial and requires a new argument compared to [15]. This argument (see the proof of Proposition 20) is based on Lemma 3 from the introductory Sec. 2.

Proposition 14 (Soundness). *For all φ, variables x, y, and sides $\theta \in \{l, r\}$ it holds that all paths accepted by $\mathcal{P}_\theta(\varphi \models^? x \leq y)$ are θ-safe for $\varphi \models^? x \leq y$.*

We only consider the left side $\theta = l$. We proceed in two steps: we first treat accepted words in class A (Proposition 17) and second in class P (Proposition 20). For both steps, we have to give meaning to the transitions of the constructed finite automata. For variables x, and paths $\pi \in \{1, \ldots, \mathsf{ar}_f\}^*$, we define *path terms* $\pi(x)$ recursively such that we can interpret *path constraints* of the form $x \leq \pi(y)$ and $\pi(y) \leq x$.

$$\varepsilon(x) =_{\mathrm{def}} x \qquad \text{and} \qquad i\pi(x) =_{\mathrm{def}} f(\top, \ldots, \underbrace{\pi(x)}_{i\text{-th position}}, \ldots, \top)$$

Lemma 15 (Semantics of transitions). *For all constraints φ, variables x, y, u, v, tokens $s, s' \in V_\varphi \cup \{x, y, \_\}$, and words $\pi \in \{1, \ldots, \mathsf{ar}_f\}^*$:*

$$\textit{if} \;\; \mathcal{P}_l(\varphi \models^? x \leq y) \vdash (u, s) \xrightarrow{\pi} (v, s') \;\; \textit{then} \;\; \varphi \models u \leq \pi(v).$$

Proof. This can be shown by induction on paths π. Note that the considered transitions are built by the **descend** rule exclusively.

Lemma 16 (Path constraints and safety). *If $\alpha \models x \leq \pi(u)$ then all proper prefixes of π are l-safe for $\alpha \models^? x \leq y$.*

Proof. Let π' be a proper prefix of π. Every solution $\alpha \models x \leq \pi(u)$ satisfies either $\alpha(x)(\pi') =_\Sigma f$ or there exists a path $\nu < \pi'$ with $\alpha(x)(\nu) =_\Sigma \perp$; thus all π' are l-safe for $\alpha \models^? x \leq y$.

Proposition 17 (Soundness for class A). *For all φ, variables x, y it holds that all paths π with class A accepted by $\mathcal{P}_l(\varphi \models^? x \leq y)$ are l-safe for $\varphi \models^? x \leq y$.*

Proof. We have to consider all recognizing transitions of the constructed finite automaton. For illustration, we treat the case where π is accepted in a state to which the **final states** rule applies, i.e. π is recognized by a transition of the following form:

$$\mathcal{P}_l(\varphi \models^? x \leq y) \vdash \;>(x, y) \xrightarrow{\pi} \underline{\underline{(u, s)}} \xrightarrow{i} (u', s').$$

Lemma 15 yields $\varphi \models x \leq \pi i(u')$. Thus π is l-safe for $\varphi \models^? x \leq y$ by Lemma 16.

We now approach the soundness of P-edges. It mainly relies on Lemma 18 in combination with Lemma 3 from the introduction.

Lemma 18 (Safety and word equations). *Let $\pi \neq \varepsilon$ be a path, u, v variables, and $\alpha \models u \leq \pi(v)$. All words π' with $\pi' \in \mathrm{pr}(\pi\pi')$ are l-safe for $\alpha \models^? u \leq v$.*

Proof. We distinguish two cases depending on whether π' belongs to $D_{\alpha(v)}$ or not.

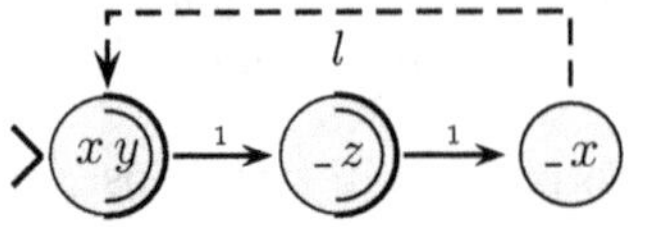

$f(x) \leq z \wedge z \leq f(z) \wedge f(z) \leq y \models^? x \leq y$

Fig. 5. Entailment holds even though the language of the left cap automaton is empty.

a. Case $\pi' \in D_{\alpha(v)}$. It follows in this case from $\alpha \models u \leq \pi(v)$, that $\alpha \models \exists v'(u \leq \pi\pi'(v'))$. By Lemma 16 all proper prefixes of $\pi\pi'$ are l-safe for $\alpha \models^? u \leq v$. Thus π' has this property since π' is a prefix of $\pi\pi'$ and $\pi \neq \varepsilon$ by assumption.
b. Case $\pi' \notin D_{\alpha(v)}$. Let π'' be the maximal prefix of π' in $D_{\alpha(v)}$. Hence, $\alpha(v)(\pi'') \in \{\bot, \top\}$. First we assume the case $\alpha(v)(\pi'') =_\Sigma \top$ which implies that all paths σ with $\pi'' \leq \sigma$, in particular π', are l-safe. Second we assume the left case $\alpha(v)(\pi'') =_\Sigma \bot$. Since $\alpha \models u \leq \pi(v)$, there exists a path π''' with $\pi''' \leq \pi\pi'$ such that $\alpha(u)(\pi''') =_\Sigma \bot$. Both together, $\pi''' \leq \pi\pi'$ and the assumption $\pi' \leq \pi\pi'$ show that the paths π''' and π' are comparable: if $\pi' \geq \pi'''$ then π' is l-safe according to the definition of l-safe. Otherwise, $\pi' < \pi'''$ holds and $\alpha(u)(\pi') =_\Sigma f$ implies π' to be l-safe.

Lemma 19 (Composing safety). *If $\alpha \models x \leq \pi(u)$, $\alpha \models \pi(v) \leq y$, and π' is l-safe for $\alpha \models^? u \leq v$ then $\pi\pi'$ is l-safe for $\alpha \models^? x \leq y$.*

Proposition 20 (Soundness for class P). *For all φ and variables x, y, all paths of class P accepted by $\mathcal{P}_l(\varphi \models^? x \leq y)$ are l-safe for $\varphi \models^? x \leq y$.*

Proof. A path ν of class P can only be recognized by using a P-edge. Thus, there exists words μ, μ', π such that $\nu = \pi\mu'$, $\mu' \in pr(\mu^*)$ and for some $u, v \in V_\varphi \cup \{x, y\}$ and $s \in V_\varphi \cup \{x, y, _\}$:

$$\mathcal{P}_l(\varphi \models^? x \leq y) \vdash (x, y) \xrightarrow{\pi} \underline{\underline{(u, v)}} \xrightarrow{\mu} (v, s) \dashrightarrow \underline{\underline{(u, v)}}$$

Lemma 15 yields $\varphi \models x \leq \pi(u)$, $\varphi \models \pi(v) \leq y$, and $\varphi \models u \leq \mu(v)$. We fix an arbitrary solution $\alpha \models \varphi$ and show that ν is l-safe for $\alpha \models x \leq y$. Note that $\mu \neq \varepsilon$ since ν would belong to class A otherwise. We can thus apply **Lemma 3 on word equations** to our assumption $\mu' \in pr(\mu^*)$ to derive $\mu' \in pr(\mu\mu')$. This verifies the assumptions of Lemma 18 which shows that μ' is l-safe for $\alpha \models^? u \leq v$. Finally, the composition Lemma 19 show that $\pi\mu'$ is l-safe for $\alpha \models^? x \leq y$ as required.

Table 2. Syntactic support.

reflexivity	$\varphi \vdash x \leq x$	if $x \in V_\varphi$
transitivity	$\varphi \vdash x \leq z$	if $\varphi \vdash x \leq y$ and $\varphi \vdash y \leq z$
decomp.	$\varphi \vdash x_i \leq y_i$	if $1 \leq i \leq n,\ \varphi \vdash x \leq y,\ f(x_1, \ldots, x_n) \leq x \wedge y \leq f(y_1, \ldots, y_n)$ *in* φ

Table 3. Closure rules.

closure 1a	$f(x_1, \ldots x_n) \leq y$ *in* φ	if $f(x_1, \ldots x_n) \leq x$ *in* φ and $\varphi \vdash x \leq y$
closure 1b	$y \leq f(x_1, \ldots x_n)$ *in* φ	if $x \leq f(x_1, \ldots x_n)$ *in* φ and $\varphi \vdash y \leq x$
closure 2a	$f(y_1, \ldots y_n) \leq x$ *in* φ	if $f(x_1, \ldots x_n) \leq x$ *in* φ and for all $1 \leq i \leq n : \varphi \vdash y_i \leq x_i$
closure 2b	$x \leq f(y_1, \ldots y_n)$ *in* φ	if $x \leq f(x_1, \ldots x_n)$ *in* φ and for all $1 \leq i \leq n : \varphi \vdash x_i \leq y_i$

8 Completeness

In this section, we state the completeness of the automata construction. Its proof is non-trivial but can be obtained as a straightforward extension of the completeness proof in [15].

We first note that completeness depends on additional assumptions. For instance, entailment holds in Fig. 5 even though the corresponding left cap automaton does not accept any word. The problem is that the constraint on the left $f(x) \leq z \wedge z \leq f(z)$ entails $x \leq z$ which has to be derived by decomposition at before hand. Otherwise, it will not be taken into account by the automaton construction. The closure under these rules can also be used for satisfiability checking and can be imposed in polynomial time w.l.o.g.

We define the notion of syntactic support $\varphi \vdash x \leq y$ in Table 2 (rather than admitting inequations $x \leq y$ on the left hand side of entailment judgments). The definition is based on three standard rules expressing **reflexivity**, **transitivity**, and the **decomposition** property. We then call a constraint φ *closed* if it satisfies all **closure** rules in Table 3. The constraint in Fig. 5 is not closed. Its closure contains $x \leq f(z)$ in addition.

Proposition 21 (Completeness). *Let φ be a closed constraint, x, y variables and $\theta \in \{l, r\}$ a side. If $\varphi \wedge x \leq y$ is satisfiable for finite (resp. infinite) trees. Then $\mathcal{P}_\theta(\varphi \models^? x \leq y)$ accepts all paths that are θ-safe for $\varphi \models^? x \leq y$.*

The proof of Proposition 21 covers the rest of this section. By symmetry, it is sufficient to treat the case $\theta = l$. We prove it by contradiction. Let φ be closed constraint with $x, y \in V_\varphi$ such that $\varphi \wedge x \leq y$ is satisfiable, and ν a minimal path in $\mathbf{A}^*_\Sigma \setminus \mathcal{P}_\theta(\varphi \models^? x \leq y)$. We prove that ν is not l-safe, i.e. there exists a variable assignment α satisfying:

$$\alpha \quad \models \quad \varphi \wedge x(\nu) \neq_\Sigma f \wedge \bigwedge_{\nu' \leq \nu} x(\nu') \neq_\Sigma \bot \wedge \bigwedge_{\nu' \leq \nu} y(\nu') \neq_\Sigma \top.$$

Table 4. Additional Syntactic Support.

$\varphi \vdash x \leq \varepsilon(y)$	if $\varphi \vdash x \leq y$
$\varphi \vdash \varepsilon(y) \leq y$	if $\varphi \vdash x \leq y$
$\varphi \vdash x \leq \pi i(y)$	if $\varphi \vdash x \leq \pi(z),\ z \leq f(z_1, \ldots z_i \ldots, z_n)\ in\ \varphi,\ \varphi \vdash z_i \leq y$
$\varphi \vdash \pi i(x) \leq y$	if $\varphi \vdash \pi(z) \leq y,\ f(z_1, \ldots z_i \ldots, z_n) \leq z\ in\ \varphi,\ \varphi \vdash x \leq z_i$

Table 5. Saturation $sat(\varphi, \nu)$ of a constraint φ at path ν.

a. φ *in* $\mathsf{sat}(\varphi, \nu)$
b. for all $q^z_\pi \in W(\varphi, \nu) : q^z_\pi \leq f(q^z_{\pi 1}, \ldots, q^z_{\pi n}) \wedge f(q^z_{\pi 1}, \ldots, q^z_{\pi n}) \leq q^z_\pi$ *in* $\mathsf{sat}(\varphi, \nu)$ if $\pi < \nu$
c. $q^y_\nu \leq f(q^y_{\nu 1}, \ldots, q^y_{\nu n}) \wedge f(q^y_{\nu 1}, \ldots, q^y_{\nu n}) \leq q^y_\nu$ *in* $\mathsf{sat}(\varphi, \nu)$
d. $q^x_\nu = \top$ *in* $\mathsf{sat}(\varphi, \nu)$
e. for all $q^z_\pi \in W(\varphi, \nu), u \in V_\varphi, i \in \mathbf{A}_\Sigma :\ q^z_\pi \leq i[\,u\,]$ *in* $\mathsf{sat}(\varphi, \nu)$ if $\varphi \vdash z \leq \pi i(u)$
f. for all $q^z_\pi \in W(\varphi, \nu), u \in V_\varphi, i \in \mathbf{A}_\Sigma :\ i[\,q^z_\pi\,] \leq u$ *in* $\mathsf{sat}(\varphi, \nu)$ if $\varphi \vdash z \leq i\pi(u)$
g. for all $q^z_{o\pi}, q^{z'}_{o'\pi} \in W(\varphi,\nu), i \in A_\Sigma : q^z_{o\pi} \leq i[q^{z'}_{o'\pi}]$ *in sat* (φ,ν) if $\exists v. \varphi \vdash z \leq o(v), \varphi \vdash o' i(v) \leq z'$

Every solution of $\varphi \wedge x(\nu) =_\Sigma \top \wedge y(\nu) =_\Sigma f$ has this property. It remains to show that such a solution exists. We will define a constraint $sat(\varphi, \nu)$ in Definition 23 that is satisfaction equivalent to $\varphi \wedge x(\nu) =_\Sigma \top \wedge y(\nu) =_\Sigma f$ and prove that it is satisfiable.

The definition of $sat(\varphi, \nu)$ requires an additional notion of *syntactic support* given in Table 4. Furthermore, we write $x \leq i[\,y\,]$ as a shortcut for $x \leq f(y_1, \ldots, y_n)$ where $y_1, \ldots, y_n$ are fresh variables except for $y_i = y$.

Definition 22. *We call a set $D \subseteq \{1, ..., n\}^*$* domain closed *if D is prefixed-closed and satisfies the following property for all $\pi \in \{1, ..., n\}^*$: if $i, j \in \{1, ..., n\}$ and $\pi i \in D$ then $\pi j \in D$. The* domain closure $dc(D)$ *is the least domain closed set containing D.*

Definition 23 (Saturation). *Let φ be a constraint over $\Sigma = \{\bot, f, \top\}$ which contains variables x, y. Let $\nu \in \mathbf{A}^*_\Sigma$ where $\mathbf{A}_\Sigma = \{1, \ldots, \mathsf{ar}_f\}$.*

For every $z \in \{x, y\}$ and $\pi \in dc(\{\nu 1, \ldots, \nu n\})$ let q^z_π be a fresh variable and $W(\varphi, \nu)$ the collection of these fresh variables. The saturation $\mathsf{sat}(\varphi, \nu)$ of φ at path ν is the constraint of minimal size satisfying properties **a.**–**g.** *of Table 5.*

Lemma 24. *If φ is closed, $\varphi \wedge x \leq y$ is satisfiable (over finite resp. possible infinite trees), and ν is the minimal word in $\mathbf{A}^*_\Sigma \setminus \mathcal{L}(\mathcal{P}_l(\varphi \models^? x \leq y))$ then the saturation $\mathsf{sat}(\varphi, \nu)$ is satisfiable.*

Proof. We have to prove that the saturation $sat(\varphi, \nu)$ satisfiable. First note that $sat(\varphi, \nu)$ is closed. We omit the proof for lack of space. We will exploit the fact that a closed constraint is satisfiable if and only if it does not contain any clash according to Table 6. Beside of the usual label clashes, there is a cycle clash expressing the finiteness of trees, which has to be removed in the case of infinite trees.

Table 6. Clashes: the **cycle clash** has to be omitted in the case of infinite trees

label clash 1	$x{=}\top \wedge y{=}\bot$ *in* φ and $\varphi \vdash x{\leq}y$
label clash 2	$x{=}\top \wedge x{\leq}f(x_1, \ldots, x_n)$ *in* φ
label clash 3	$x{=}\bot \wedge f(x_1, \ldots, x_n){\leq}x$ *in* φ
cycle clash	$x_1{=}x_{n+1}$ and forall $i \leq n : x_i{\leq}f(\ldots,x_{i+1},\ldots) \wedge f(\ldots,x_{i+1},\ldots){\leq}x_i$ *in* φ

For illustration, we elaborate one of the more interesting cases of the proof of clash-freeness. Assume that there were a **label clash** containing $q^x_\nu{=}\top$ that was introduced by saturation (rule **d.** of Table 5). Such a clash must of the form **label clash1** or **label clash2**. We treat the second case only. There exist $w, w_1, \ldots, w_n \in V_{sat(\varphi,\nu)}$ such that: $q^x_\nu{=}\top$ and $q^x_\nu{\leq}f(w_1, \ldots, w_n)$ *in* $sat(\varphi, \nu)$.

We have to distinguish all possible rules of Definition 23 which may have added $q^x_\nu{\leq}f(w_1, \ldots, w_n)$ to $sat(\varphi, \nu)$; the candidates are **b**, **e**, and **g**. Rule **b** cannot be applied since it requires $\pi < \nu$. Rule **e** imposes $\varphi \vdash x{\leq}\nu i(w_i)$; thus π is l-safe which a contradiction to our assumption $\nu \notin \mathcal{L}(\mathcal{P}_l(\varphi \models^? x{\leq}y))$. Finally consider rule **g**. This rule requires that there is a variable v in V_φ with: $\varphi \vdash x{\leq}o(v)$ and $\varphi \vdash o'i(v){\leq}z'$.

- **Case** $z' = y$ **and** $o = o'i$**:** We have $\varphi \vdash x{\leq}o(v)$ and $\varphi \vdash o(v){\leq}y$. The **reflexivity** rule in the automaton construction yields $o \in \mathcal{L}(\mathcal{P}_l)$ and thus $\nu \in \mathcal{L}(\mathcal{P}_l)$ - a contradiction.
- **Case** $z' = y$ **and** $o = o'i\sigma$ **where** $\sigma \neq \varepsilon$**:** We have $\varphi \vdash x{\leq}o'i\sigma(v)$ and $\varphi \vdash o'i(v){\leq}y$. We can identify a transition $\mathcal{P}_l \vdash (x, y) \xrightarrow{o'i} (s, v) \xrightarrow{\sigma} (v, t)$, where s and t are arbitrary tokens. According to the automaton construction there is a left P-edge which validates all paths $o'i\,\sigma'$ with $o'i\,\sigma' < o'i\,\sigma\sigma'$ to be in $\mathcal{L}(\mathcal{P}_l)$. Since $o'i{\leq}\nu$ and $o'i\sigma{\leq}\nu$ it holds $\nu \in \mathcal{L}(\mathcal{P}_l)$ - a contradiction.
- The remaining cases where $z' = x$ or $o \neq o'i\pi$ are analogous.

9 Restrictions of Constructed Automata

Constructed cap automata satisfy restrictions that we need to translate back (Sec 11).

Definition 25. *We call a cap automaton $\mathcal{P}$ over* **A** restricted *if it is strictly epsilon free, gap universal, strictly cap, and shuffled.*

strictly epsilon free: *$\mathcal{P}$ has a unique initial state and no ε-transition.*

gap universal: *For all transitions $\mathcal{P} \vdash q_1 \xrightarrow{i} \underline{\underline{q_2}}$, $i \in \mathbf{A}$ from a non-final state q_1 it holds that q_2 is universal: for all $\pi \in \mathbf{A}^*$ there is q_3 with $\mathcal{P} \vdash \underline{\underline{q_2}} \xrightarrow{\pi} \underline{\underline{q_3}}$.*

strictly cap: *If $\mathcal{P} \vdash q_2 \xrightarrow{\pi} q_3 \dashrightarrow q_1$ with $\pi \neq \varepsilon$ then q_2 is a final state.*

shuffled: *If there are transitions $\mathcal{P} \vdash q \xleftarrow{\pi} q_0 \xrightarrow{\pi} q' \dashrightarrow q$ where $\mathcal{P} \vdash\ >q_0$ is the initial state and $q \neq q'$ then the language $\{\pi' \mid \pi\pi' \in \mathcal{L}(\mathcal{P})\}$ is universal.*

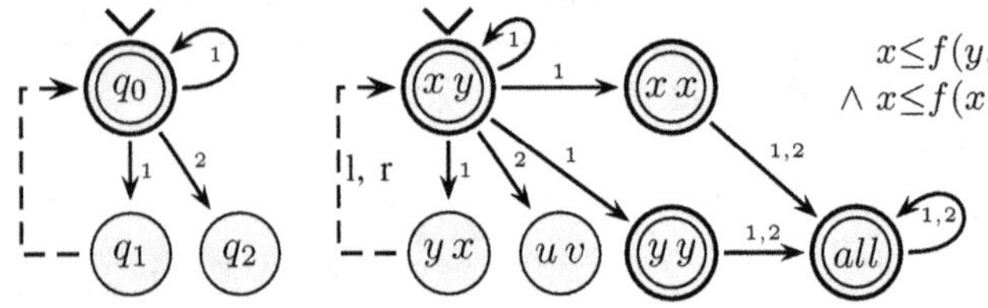

$$\left.\begin{array}{r} x{\leq}f(y,u) \wedge f(x,v){\leq}y \\ \wedge\, x{\leq}f(x,u) \wedge f(y,v){\leq}y \end{array}\right\} \models^? x{\leq}y$$

Fig. 6. An unshuffled cap automaton (on the left) and a shuffled extension (in the middle).

We conjecture that these restrictions don't truly restrict the universality problem of cap automata but cannot prove this so far. Indeed, every cap automaton that is built on top of a deterministic finite automaton can be made restricted. Again, this is not obvious. The proof exploits that "deterministic" cap automata are always shuffled. But unfortunately, the usual determination procedure fails for cap automata.

A cap automaton where the word 1 violates the shuffle condition is given on the left-hand of Table 6. A shuffled extension of this automaton is displayed in the middle of Table 6. This automaton is constructed from an entailment judgment displayed to the right. This example illustrates that shuffling simulates the interaction between multiple lower and upper bounds in constraints.

Proposition 26. *Constructed cap automata $\mathcal{P}_\theta(\varphi \models^? x{\leq}y)$ are restricted.*

Proof. Let $\mathcal{P}_l = \mathcal{P}_l(\varphi \models^? x{\leq}y)$ be a constructed cap automaton for the left side. $\mathcal{P}_l$ is clearly strictly epsilon free, as it has a unique initial state (x, y) and no ε-transitions. To see that it is gap universal, suppose that there is a transition from a non-final to a final state in $\mathcal{P}_l$. The second form of the **descend** rule is the only rule which may licence such a transition. It thus has the form $\mathcal{P}_l \vdash (s, u) \xrightarrow{i} (\_, v)$ for some $u, v \in V_\varphi$, and $s \in V_\varphi \cup \{\_\}$. The only rule which can turn $(\_, v)$ into a final state is the **top** rule, but this rule turns $(\_, v)$ directly into a universal state. (The **final states** rule does not apply because of the underscore on the left.)

To prove that $\mathcal{P}_l$ is shuffled, we assume a path π and two different states q and q' with $\mathcal{P}_l \vdash q \xleftarrow{\pi} q_0 \xrightarrow{\pi} q' \dashrightarrow q$. We unify the states q_0, q, q' with the rules of Table 1 and get $\mathcal{P}_l \vdash (v, u) \xleftarrow{\pi} (x, y) \xrightarrow{\pi} (u, s) \dashrightarrow (v, u)$ for some $u, v \in V_\varphi \cup \{x, y\}$ and $s \in V_\varphi \cup \{x, y, \_\}$. By construction of the automaton (Table 1), $\mathcal{P}_l \vdash (x, y) \xrightarrow{\pi} (u, u)$ must also hold. By **reflexivity** and **all**, the language $\{\pi' \mid \pi\pi' \in \mathcal{L}(\mathcal{P}_l)\}$ is universal.

We finally prove the strict cap property. All P-edges of $\mathcal{P}_l$ are of the form $\mathcal{P} \vdash (u, s) \dashrightarrow q$ for some state q. The last transition in all transition sequences reaching (u, s) must be licenced by the **descend** rule, and thus is of the form $\mathcal{P} \vdash (v, s_0) \xrightarrow{i} (u, s)$. Now, the **final states** rule applies to (v, s_0). Repeating this argument inductively shows that all states leading to (v, s_0) are final too.

10 Restricted Cap Set Expressions

We now formulate corresponding restrictions for cap set expressions. Thereby, we obtain the restrictions needed for Theorem 1 to hold.

Definition 27. *We call a cap set expression over alphabet* $\mathbf{A}$ restricted *if it is a shuffled expression generated by the following grammar, where* R_1, R_2, R *range over regular expressions over* $\mathbf{A}$*:*

$$F ::= pr(R_1 R_2^\circ) \mid R\mathbf{A}^* \mid F_1 \cup F_2$$

A cap set expression of sort F *is called* shuffled *if all its components of the form* $pr(R_1 R_2^\circ)$ *satisfy:*

shuffle: *for all word* $\pi \in \mathcal{L}(R_1) \cap \mathcal{L}(R_1 R_2)$ *it holds that* $\pi \mathbf{A}^* \subseteq \mathcal{L}(R_1)$.

Proposition 28. *Universality of restricted cap set expressions and restricted cap automata are equivalent modulo deterministic polynomial time transformations.*

Proof. It is easy to see that the cap automata that are constructed for restricted cap expressions (proof or Proposition 12) are gap-universal, strictly cap, and shuffled. They can be made strictly ε-free by a post-processing step (Lemma 30).

Conversely, given a restricted cap automaton $\mathcal{P}$, we can express the regular part of $\mathcal{P}$ by a restricted cap set expression $pr(R_1\varepsilon^\circ) \cup R_2\mathbf{A}^*$, because of $\mathcal{P}$ is gap universal. The cap automaton $\mathcal{P}$ is also strictly cap, so we can translate every P-edge of $\mathcal{P}$ in a restricted cap set expression $pr(R_1 R_2^\circ)$. All build restricted cap set expressions are shuffled since $\mathcal{P}$ is shuffled.

Our next goal is to make cap automata strictly ε-free. We call a state q of a cap automaton $\mathcal{P}$ *normalized* if q has no in-going transitions and no out-going P-edges.

Lemma 29. *If a cap automaton* $\mathcal{P}$ *has a unique initial state, then this state can be normalized (while preserving the language gap-universality, strict cap, and shuffle).*

Proof. Let $\mathcal{P}$ be a cap automaton with one initial state q_0. We construct a new automaton $\mathcal{P}'$ by adding a state q_0' to $\mathcal{P}$ which inherits all out-going Δ-transitions and in-going P-edges from q_0. We let q_0' be the unique initial state of $\mathcal{P}'$. This state is normalized.

Lemma 30. *Every cap automaton can be made strictly* ε*-free in polynomial time, while preserving the language and the properties: gap-universal, strictly cap, and shuffle.*

Proof. First, we eliminate ε-edges in the underlying finite automaton. This yields a cap automaton which may have more than one initial states. W.l.o.g. we assume

Table 7. Back translation: the constraint $\varphi_\mathcal{P}$ of a restricted cap automaton $\mathcal{P}$.

left	$l(q) \leq f(l(q_1), \ldots, l(q_n))$ *in* $\varphi_\mathcal{P}$	if $\mathcal{P} \vdash \underline{\underline{q}} \xrightarrow{i} q_i$ for all $1 \leq i \leq n$.
right	$f(r(q_1), \ldots, r(q_n)) \leq r(q)$ *in* $\varphi_\mathcal{P}$	if $\mathcal{P} \vdash q \xrightarrow{i} q_i$ for all $1 \leq i \leq n$
top	$r(q') = \top$ *in* $\varphi_\mathcal{P}$	if $\mathcal{P} \vdash q \xrightarrow{i} \underline{\underline{q'}}$, q not final
P-edges	$l(q) \leq i[\,r(q_2)\,]$ *in* $\varphi_\mathcal{P}$	if $\mathcal{P} \vdash \underline{\underline{q}} \xrightarrow{i} q_1 \dashrightarrow q_2$, $q_1 \neq q_2$

$x \leq f(y) \models^? x \leq y$

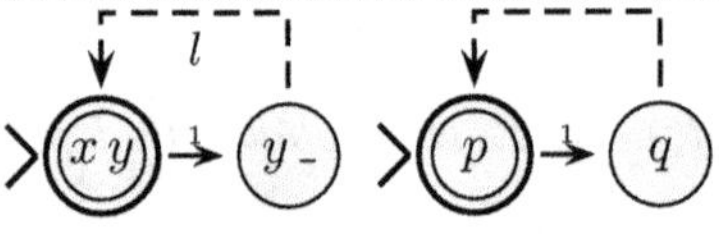

$$\left.\begin{array}{l} l(p) \leq f(l(q)) \\ \wedge\ f(r(q)) \leq r(p) \\ \wedge\ l(p) \leq f(r(p)) \end{array}\right\} \models^? l(p) \leq r(p)$$

Fig. 7. A judgment, its pair of cap automata, and the back translation of the left cap automaton.

w.l.o.g that this automaton consists of n independent parts where each part has exactly one initial state. Second, we normalize all n initial states according to Lemma 29.

Third, we unify all n initial states into a single initial state. The unified initial state inherits all P- and Δ-edges of the unified initial states. It is final if and only if one of the previous initial states was. Since all initial states are normalized this step does neither change the language of $\mathcal{P}$, nor gap-universal, the strict cap nor the shuffle property.

11 Back Translation for Restricted Cap Automata

We now encode universality of restricted cap automata over alphabet $\{1, \ldots, n\}$ back to NSSE over the signature $\{\bot, f, \top\}$ where $\mathsf{ar}_f = n$. Again, our construction applies to both finite and possibly infinite trees.

Definition 31. *Given a restricted cap automaton we assume two fresh variables $l(q)$ and $r(q)$ for each state $\mathcal{P} \vdash q$. The judgment $J(\mathcal{P})$ of a restricted cap automaton $\mathcal{P}$ with initial state $\mathcal{P} \vdash {>}q_0$ is $\varphi_\mathcal{P} \models^? l(q_0) \leq r(q_0)$ where $\varphi_\mathcal{P}$ is the least constraint with the properties in Table 7.*

The judgment $J(\mathcal{P})$ is defined such that $\mathcal{P}$ recognizes exactly the set of l-safe words for $J(\mathcal{P})$ whereas the set of r-safe words for $J(\mathcal{P})$ is $\mathbf{A}^*$.

Proposition 32 (Correctness). *Every complete and restricted cap automaton $\mathcal{P}$ with initial state $\mathcal{P} \vdash {>}q_0$ over alphabet $\mathbf{A}$ satisfies:*

$$\mathcal{L}(\mathcal{P}) \;=\; \mathcal{L}(\mathcal{P}_l(J(\mathcal{P}))) \quad and \quad \mathbf{A}^* \;=\; \mathcal{L}(\mathcal{P}_r(J(\mathcal{P}))).$$

Proof. 1. The language $\mathcal{L}(\mathcal{P}_r(J(\mathcal{P})))$ is universal: Since $\mathcal{P}$ is complete such that the **right** rule implies for all words $\pi \in \mathbf{A}^*$ that there exists a state $\mathcal{P} \vdash q$ satisfying $\varphi_{\mathcal{P}} \models \pi(r(q)) \leq r(q_0)$. Thus, $\mathcal{P}_r(J(\mathcal{P})) \vdash \underline{\underline{(l(q_0), r(q_0))}} \xrightarrow{\pi} \underline{\underline{(\_, l(q))}}$ by the second case of the **descend** rule, i.e. π is accepted by $\mathcal{P}_r(J(\mathcal{P}))$.

2. We omit the proof for $\mathcal{L}(\mathcal{P}) \subseteq \mathcal{L}(\mathcal{P}_l(J(\mathcal{P})))$ which only requires the completeness of $\mathcal{P}$ and the strictly cap property.
3. The remaining inclusion $\mathcal{L}(\mathcal{P}_l(J(\mathcal{P}))) \subseteq \mathcal{L}(\mathcal{P})$ is most interesting. We start with an auxiliary **claim**: If $\mathcal{P}$ provides transitions

$$\mathcal{P}_l(J(\mathcal{P}) \vdash (l(q_0), s_0) \xrightarrow{\pi} (l(q_n), s_n) \xrightarrow{i} (l(q), s)$$

then there exist transitions $\mathcal{P} \vdash \underline{\underline{q_0}} \xrightarrow{\pi} \underline{\underline{q_n}}$. This claim can be proved as follows: All transitions must be licensed by a constraint in $\varphi_{\mathcal{P}}$ which is of the form $l(q_i) \leq f(\ldots, l(q_{i+1}), \ldots)$ where $1 \leq i \leq n$. Such constraints can only be created by the **left** rule. There thus exist transitions $\mathcal{P} \vdash \underline{\underline{q_0}} \xrightarrow{\pi} q_n$ such $\mathcal{P} \vdash \underline{\underline{q_i}}$ for all $0 \leq i < n$. We can infer $\mathcal{P} \vdash \underline{\underline{q_n}}$ as required.

We now come back to the main proof. Suppose $\pi \in \mathcal{L}(\mathcal{P}_l(J(\mathcal{P})))$. There are three kinds of transitions by which π can be recognized.

(a) We first consider transitions using the **reflexivity** rule to recognize π. These contain a transition sequence of the following form for some prefix $\pi' \leq \pi$:

$$\mathcal{P}_l(J(\mathcal{P})) \vdash (l(q_0), r(q_0)) \xrightarrow{\pi'} \underline{\underline{(r(q_n), r(q_n))}}$$

Either $\pi' = \pi$ or this sequence can be continued to recognize π in the state $\underline{\underline{all}}$. The first continuation step is by the **reflexivity** rule itself and all subsequent steps are due to the **all** rule.

Note that $n \geq 1$. We first consider the descendants on the left hand side, which starts from state $l(r_0)$ and continues over $l(l_{n-1})$ to $r(q_m)$. The last step must be induced by a constraint in $\varphi_{\mathcal{P}}$ that is contributed by the **P-edges** rule. This and the preceding claim yield the existence of the following transitions for some state $q \neq q_n$:

$$\mathcal{P} \vdash q_0 \xrightarrow{\pi'} q \dashrightarrow q_n$$

We next consider the descendants on the right hand side. They must be induced by constraints in $\varphi_{\mathcal{P}}$ that are inherited form the following transition sequence:

$$\mathcal{P} \vdash q_0 \xrightarrow{\pi'} q_n$$

Now we can apply that $\mathcal{P}$ is shuffled which shows that the language $\{\pi'' \mid \pi'\pi'' \in \mathcal{L}(\mathcal{P})\}$ is universal (since $q \neq q_n$)). Thus, $\pi \in \mathcal{L}(\mathcal{P})$ as required.

(b) Second, we consider transitions using the **top** rule. These contain a part of the following form for some prefix $\pi' \leq \pi$ and such that $r(q_n) = \top$ in $\varphi_{\mathcal{P}}$.

$$\mathcal{P}_l(J(\mathcal{P})) \vdash (l(q_0), r(q_0)) \xrightarrow{\pi'} \underline{\underline{(s_n, r(q_n))}}$$

Again, either $\pi' = \pi$ or this sequence can be continued to recognize π in the state $\underline{\underline{\mathit{all}}}$. The first continuation step is by the **top** rule itself and all subsequent steps are due to the **all** rule.
The above transitions of $\mathcal{P}_l(J(\mathcal{P}))$ are induced by the following transition sequence in $\mathcal{P}$ where q_{n-1} is not final:

$$\mathcal{P} \vdash q_0 \xrightarrow{\pi'} \underline{\underline{q_n}}$$

The gap universal property which holds for $\mathcal{P}$ by assumption yields that $\{\pi'' \mid \mathcal{P} \vdash q_n \xrightarrow{\pi''} \underline{\underline{q_n}}\}$ is universal. Thus, $\pi \in \mathcal{L}(\mathcal{P})$.

(c) Third, we consider the last case where the class of π is A in $\mathcal{P}_l(J(\mathcal{P}))$. The recognizing transition has to apply the rule for **final states**:

$$\mathcal{P}_l(J(\mathcal{P})) \vdash \underline{\underline{(l(q_0), r(q_0))}} \xrightarrow{\pi} \underline{\underline{(l(q_n), s_n))}} \xrightarrow{i} (\theta(q), p(\pi))$$

All transitions except the last one must be contributed by the **left** rule. The **P-edges** can only apply at the end. In this case however, we can freely exchange the last transition by another using the **left** rule as well. Given this, we can apply our initial claim which yields:

$$\mathcal{P} \vdash \underline{\underline{q_0}} \xrightarrow{\pi} \underline{\underline{q_n}}$$

Thus, we have shown that $\pi \in \mathcal{L}(\mathcal{P})$ for this case too.

(d) Finally, we have to consider transitions that recognize π through P-edges of $\mathcal{P}_l(J(\mathcal{P}))$. Here we have transitions where π is a prefix of $\pi_1\pi_2^k$ for some $k \geq 0$:

$$\mathcal{P}_l(J(\mathcal{P})) \vdash (l(q_0), r(q_0)) \xrightarrow{\pi_1} (l(q_i), r(q_i)) \xrightarrow{\pi_2} (r(q_n), s_n) \dashrightarrow (l(q_i), r(q_i))$$

The **P-edges** rule in the construction of $\mathcal{P}_l$ requires $q_n = q_i$. The automaton $\mathcal{P}$ thus has the following transitions for some state q:

$$\mathcal{P} \vdash q_0 \xrightarrow{\pi_1} q_i \xrightarrow{\pi_2} q \dashrightarrow q_i$$

This transition and the strictly cap property allows $\mathcal{P}$ to recognize all prefixes of $\pi_1\pi_2^k$ for all $k \geq 0$, i.e. $\pi \in \mathcal{L}(\mathcal{P})$.

For illustration, we reconstruct an entailment judgment for the cap automaton $\mathcal{P}_l(x \leq f(y) \models^? x \leq y)$ given in Table 7. Before we start we rename the states of $\mathcal{P}_l(x \leq f(y) \models^? x \leq y)$ to p and q. We translate the edge $\underline{\underline{p}} \xrightarrow{1} q$ to the constraint $l(p) \leq f(l(q)) \wedge f(r(q)) \leq r(p)$ (rule **left** and **right** of Table 7). The rule **P-edges** maps the P-edge $q \dashrightarrow p$ to the constraint $l(p) \leq f(r(p))$. If we now construct the left automaton of the computed constraint, we get the original automaton back.

Lemma 33. *Let $\mathcal{P}$ be a restricted cap automaton with initial state $\mathcal{P} \vdash\ >q$. The constructed constraint $\varphi_{\mathcal{P}}$ is then closed and $\varphi_{\mathcal{P}} \wedge l(q) \leq r(q)$ is satisfiable over finite and infinite trees.*

Theorem 34 (Back translation). *Universality of restricted cap automata over the alphabet* $\{1, \ldots, ar_f\}$ *can be reduced in polynomial time to NSSE with signature* $\{\bot, f, \top\}$ *(both over finite or possibly infinite trees).*

Proof. Let $\mathcal{P}$ be complete and restricted cap automaton. Universality of $\mathcal{L}(\mathcal{P})$ is equivalent to universality of both languages: $\mathcal{L}(\mathcal{P}_l(J(\mathcal{P})))$ and $\mathcal{L}(\mathcal{P}_r(J(\mathcal{P})))$ (Proposition 32). Since $\varphi_{\mathcal{P}}$ is closed and clash-free (Lemma 33), the latter is equivalent to that NSSE holds for the judgment $J(\mathcal{P})$ (Theorem 13).

12 Equivalence of Variants of NSSE

We prove Corollary 2 which states that all variants of NSSE over the signature $\{\bot, f, \top\}$ are equivalent if the arity of f is at least 2. Given the characterization of NSSE in Theorem 1 it remains to prove a corresponding result for restricted cap automata:

Proposition 35. *The universality problems of restricted cap automata over the alphabet* $\{1, \ldots, n\}$ *are equivalent for all* $n \geq 2$ *modulo polynomial time transformations.*

Proof. We first show how to extend to alphabet. Consider a restricted cap automaton $\mathcal{P}$ and an alphabet $A = \{1, \ldots, n{-}1\}$. We construct another restricted cap automaton $\mathcal{P}'$ with an alphabet $A' = \{1, \ldots, n\}$ in linear time. The cap automaton $\mathcal{P}'$ is identical to $\mathcal{P}$ up to the addition

$$\mathcal{P}' \vdash q_0 \xrightarrow{1,\ldots,n} q_1 \xrightarrow{1,\ldots,n} q_1 \xrightarrow{n} \underline{\underline{q_2}} \xrightarrow{1,\ldots,n} \underline{\underline{q_2}}$$

where q_0 is the initial state of $\mathcal{P}$ and $\mathcal{P}'$ and q_1, q_2 are two fresh states. This construction imposes:

$$\mathcal{L}(\mathcal{P}') = \{\ \pi\sigma \mid \pi \in \mathcal{L}(\mathcal{P}), \ \text{ and } \sigma \in n(1, \ldots, n)^*\ \}.$$

We now consider alphabet restriction. Let $\mathcal{P}$ be a restricted cap automaton with alphabet $A = \{1, \ldots, n^2\}$ where $n^2 \geq 3$. We can assume w.l.o.g that A is of that form. Otherwise we can increase A by the previous construction until this form is reached.

We next construct a restricted cap automaton $\mathcal{P}'$ with alphabet $A' = \{1, \ldots, n\}$ in polynomial time such that $\mathcal{L}(\mathcal{P})$ is universal iff $\mathcal{L}(\mathcal{P}')$ is universal. We encode a letter of A in two letters of A' to the base n via the standard encoding $d : A \to A' \times A'$:

$$d(i) = (\, d_1(i)\, ,\, d_2(i)\,) = \left(\left\lfloor \frac{i}{n} \right\rfloor \, , \, i \, mod \, n \right).$$

The cap automaton $\mathcal{P}'$ has two states q and q' for every state q of $\mathcal{P}$. The states q and q' are final in $\mathcal{P}'$ if q is final in $\mathcal{P}$, i.e.

$$\mathcal{P}' \vdash \underline{\underline{q_1}} \text{ and } \mathcal{P}' \vdash \underline{\underline{q_1'}} \quad \text{if} \quad \mathcal{P}' \vdash \underline{\underline{q_1}}.$$

The cap automaton $\mathcal{P}$ and $\mathcal{P}'$ share the same initial state and the same P-edges. We define the transitions of $\mathcal{P}'$ by

$$\mathcal{P}' \vdash q_1 \xrightarrow{d_1(i)} q_1' \xrightarrow{d_2(i)} q_2 \quad \text{if} \quad \mathcal{P} \vdash q_1 \xrightarrow{i} q_2.$$

We can show by induction that the word $i_1 \ldots i_m$ is in $\mathcal{L}(\mathcal{P})$ iff the words $d_1(1)\, d_2(1) \ldots d_1(m-1)\, d_2(m-1)\, d_1(m)$ and $d_1(1)\, d_2(1) \ldots d_1(m)\, d_2(m)$ are in $\mathcal{L}(\mathcal{P}')$.

Conclusion and Future Work

We have characterized NSSE equivalently by using regular expressions and word equations. This explains why NSSE is so difficult to solve and links NSSE to the area of string unification where powerful proof methods are available. Given that NSSE is equivalent to universality of restricted cap set expressions, one cannot expect to solve NSSE without treating word equations.

We have also shown that all variants of NSSE with a single non-constant function symbol are equivalent modulo polynomial time transformations. One might also want to extend the presented characterization to richer signatures. For instance, it should be possible to treat NSSE with a contra-variant function symbol. But how to deal with more than one non-constant function symbol is much less obvious. We finally note that cap automata seem to be related to tree automata with equality tests (tuple reduction automata).

Acknowledgements

We would like to thank Zhendong Su, Klaus Schulz, Jean-Marc Talbot, Sophie Tison, and Ralf Treinen for discussions and comments on early versions.

References

1. R. M. Amadio and L. Cardelli. Subtyping recursive types. *ACM Transactions on Programming Languages and Systems*, 15(4):575–631, September 1993.
2. F. Baader and K. Schulz. Unification in the union of disjoint equational theories: Combining decision procedures. In *Journal of Symbolic Computation*, volume 21, pages 211–243, 1996.
3. V. Durnev. Unsolvability of positive $\forall\exists^3$-theory of free groups. In *Sibirsky mathematichesky jurnal*, volume 36(5), pages 1067–1080, 1995. In Russian, also exists in English translation.
4. J. Eifrig, S. Smith, and V. Trifonow. Sound polymorphic type inference for objects. In *ACM Conference on Object-Oriented Programming: Systems, Languages, and Applications*, 1995.
5. J. Eifrig, S. Smith, and V. Trifonow. Type inference for recursively constrained types and its application to object-oriented programming. *Elec. Notes in Theor. Comp. Science*, 1, 1995.

6. Y. Fuh and P. Mishra. Type inference with subtypes. *Theo. Comp. Science*, 73, 1990.
7. F. Henglein and J. Rehof. The complexity of subtype entailment for simple types. In *Proceedings of the 12th IEEE Symposium on Logic in Computer Science*, pages 362–372, 1997.
8. F. Henglein and J. Rehof. Constraint automata and the complexity of recursive subtype entailment. In *25th Int. Conf. on Automata, Languages, & Programming*, LNCS, 1998.
9. D. Kozen, J. Palsberg, and M. I. Schwartzbach. Efficient inference of partial types. *Journal of Computer and System Sciences*, 49(2):306–324, 1994.
10. D. Kozen, J. Palsberg, and M. I. Schwartzbach. Efficient recursive subtyping. *Mathematical Structures in Computer Science*, 5:1–13, 1995.
11. G. Makanin. The problem of solvability of equations in a free semigroup. *Math. USSR Sbornik*, 32, 1977. (English translation).
12. J. C. Mitchell. Type inference with simple subtypes. *The Journal of Functional Programming*, 1(3):245–285, July 1991.
13. M. Müller, J. Niehren, and R. Treinen. The first-order theory of ordering constraints over feature trees. In *IEEE Symposium on Logic in Computer Science*, pages 432–443, 1998.
14. J. Niehren, M. Müller, and J.-M. Talbot. Entailment of atomic set constraints is PSPACE-complete. In *14th IEEE Symposium on Logic in Computer Sience*, pages 285–294, 1999.
15. J. Niehren and T. Priesnitz. Entailment of non-structural subtype constraints. In *Asian Computing Science Conference*, LNCS, pages 251–265. Springer-Verlag, Berlin, 1999.
16. J. Palsberg, M. Wand, and P. O'Keefe. Type Inference with Non-structural Subtyping. *Formal Aspects of Computing*, 9:49–67, 1997.
17. W. Plandowski. Satisfiability of word equations with constants is in PSPACE. In *Proc. of the 40th IEEE Symp. on Found. of Comp. Science*, pages 495–500, 1999.
18. F. Pottier. Simplifying subtyping constraints. In *Proceedings of the ACM SIGPLAN International Conference on Functional Programming*, pages 122–133, 1996.
19. F. Pottier. A framework for type inference with subtyping. In *Proc. of the third ACM SIGPLAN International Conference on Functional Programming*, pages 228–238, 1998.
20. F. Pottier. *Type inference in the presence of subtyping: from theory to practice.* PhD thesis, Institut de Recherche d'Informatique et d'Automatique, 1998.
21. J. Rehof. Minimal typings in atomic subtyping. In *ACM Symposium on Principles of Programming Languages*. ACM Press, 1997.
22. J. Rehof. *The Complexity of Simple Subtyping Systems.* PhD thesis, DIKU, Copenh., 1998.
23. K. U. Schulz. Makanin's algorithm for word equations – two improvements and a generalization. In *Word Equations and Related Topics*, LNCS 572, pages 85–150, 1991.
24. Y. Vazhenin and B. Rozenblat. Decidability of the positive theory of a free countably generated semigroup. In *Math. USSR Sbornik*, volume 44, pages 109–116, 1983.

Bisimulation and Other Undecidable Equivalences for Lossy Channel Systems

Ph. Schnoebelen

Lab. Spécification & Vérification, ENS de Cachan & CNRS UMR 8643,
61, av. Pdt. Wilson, 94235 Cachan Cedex France,
phs@lsv.ens-cachan.fr

Abstract. Lossy channel systems are systems of finite state automata that communicate via unreliable unbounded fifo channels. Today the main open question in the theory of lossy channel systems is whether bisimulation is decidable.
We show that bisimulation, simulation, and in fact all relations between bisimulation and trace inclusion are undecidable for lossy channel systems (and for lossy vector addition systems).

1 Introduction

Channel Systems, also called *Finite State Communicating Machines*, are systems of finite state automata that communicate via asynchronous unbounded fifo channels. Fig. 1 displays an example. Channel systems are a natural model for asynchronous communication protocols and constitute the semantical basis for ISO protocol specification languages such as SDL and Estelle.

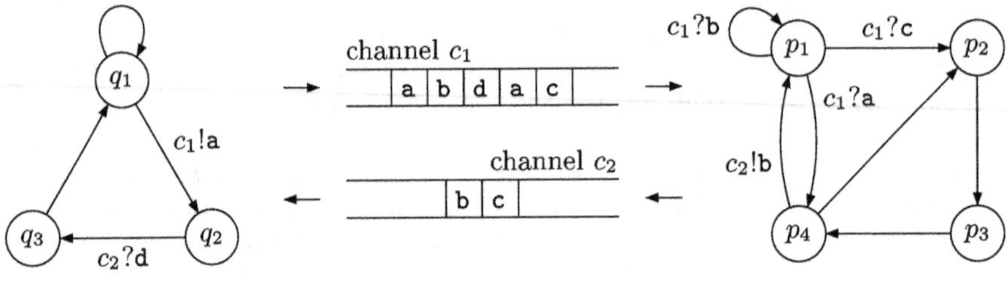

Fig. 1. A channel system with two automata and two channels

Automated verification of channel systems. Formal verification methods for channel systems are important since even the simplest communication protocols can have tricky behaviors and hard-to-find bugs. But channel systems are Turing powerful, and no verification method for them can be general and fully algorithmic. For example, existing methods only check sufficient but not necessary conditions for correctness (e.g. [JJ93]), or only terminate in some cases (e.g. [PP91]), or only deal with channel systems of a certain type (e.g. [CF97]).

N. Kobayashi and B.C. Pierce (Eds.): TACS 2001, LNCS 2215, pp. 385–399, 2001.

Lossy channels. A few years ago, Finkel, Abdulla and Jonsson independently identified *lossy channel systems* as a very promising class of channel systems. With lossy systems, one assumes that messages can be lost while they are in transit, without any notification. Protocol designers know that unreliable channels are very real but, because they know how to cope with unreliability (e.g. with the alternating bit protocol), the classical model assumed perfect channels [Boc78, BZ81]. Therefore it is really ironic, and somewhat paradoxical, that lossy channels are "easier to analyze than perfect ones!", quoting [CFP95].

Finkel showed that termination is decidable for lossy systems [Fin94]. Abdulla and Jonsson showed the decidability of reachability, safety properties over traces, and eventuality properties over states [AJ96b]. These are fundamental results, with many practical applications in automated protocol verification.

One should not believe that lossy channel systems are trivial models where everything is decidable. First the main decidable problems do not have primitive recursive complexity [Sch01], and secondly many problems are undecidable: Abdulla and Jonsson proved that recurrent reachability properties are undecidable, so that model-checking problems for (branching-time or linear-time) temporal logic is undecidable for lossy channel systems [AJ96a], and Mayr showed that boundedness is undecidable [May00]. Also, systems where the channels are unreliable but fair (do not lose all messages all the time) cannot be analyzed [AJ96a], and one cannot say whether systems are correct with probability 1 when messages are lost with low (less than $\frac{1}{2}$) probability [ABPJ00]. Hence lossy channel systems are an example of a *partially analyzable* infinite-state system model (along with Petri nets, pushdown systems, ...) that has important practical applications [AKP97, ABJ98, AAB99].

Equivalence checking. Behavioral equivalences are a special class of verification problems where one asks whether a system S is "equivalent" to another system S' (or if two configurations of a single system are equivalent), that is whether they have the "same behavior". For such questions the first system, S, is usually a model of an implementation, while S' is a specification or a more abstract model of the same implementation. There exist several behavioral equivalences (and, more generally, implementation preorders), and one uses this or that notion depending on the situation at hand and the semantic properties of the chosen equivalence (e.g. the equivalence is a congruence). It is widely admitted that all interesting behavioral equivalences sit in van Glabbeek's *branching time – linear time spectrum* [Gla01], with bisimulation as the strongest equivalence, and trace equivalence as the weakest. For partially analyzable infinite-state systems, bisimulation is sometimes decidable [HJ99, Jan00] and sometimes not [Jan95], and other equivalences are usually at least as hard as bisimulation. Surveys can be found in [Mol96, JM99, BCMS01].

Bisimulation between lossy channel systems. Today, the main open question in the theory of lossy channel systems is the decidability of bisimulation, and other equivalences. In this direction, almost nothing is known[1]. Abdulla and

[1] Note that undecidability of trace equivalence can be derived easily from the undecidability of boundedness, but we are not aware of any paper making this observation.

Kindahl [AK95] studied equivalence problems between a lossy channel system and a finite state system, but such problems are less general than checking equivalence between two infinite systems [JKM01] and the decidability results of [AK95] cannot be used for the general case.

Our contribution. In this paper we show that all equivalences in the branching time – linear time spectrum are undecidable between two lossy channel systems. Our construction is inspired by Jančar's breakthrough result[2] and extends it. The same undecidability proof applies to bisimulation, simulation, trace inclusion, all the standard equivalences (like ready-simulation and failure equivalence), all the exotic equivalences (like 2-nested simulation and possible futures equivalences), and any equivalence or preorder (in fact, any relation) not yet invented as long as it is more discriminating than trace inclusion and less than bisimulation. The proof even shows undecidability for lossy vector addition systems, a weaker model that one uses when channels are not fifo [BM99].

Plan of the paper. Section 2 recalls basic notions (words, transition systems, behavioral equivalences). We define channel systems (extended, standard, and lossy) in section 3. The main results, given in section 4, are stated in terms of so called "front-lossy" systems, and section 5 considers the situation with "classic-lossy" systems.

2 Basic Notions

2.1 Words and the Subword Relation

Given a finite alphabet $\Sigma = \{a, b, \ldots\}$, we let $\Sigma^* = \{u, v, \ldots\}$ denote the set of all finite words over Σ. For $u, v \in \Sigma^*$, we write $u.v$ (also uv) for the *concatenation* of u and v. We write ε for the empty word and Σ^+ for $\Sigma^* \setminus \{\varepsilon\}$. The length of $u \in \Sigma^*$ is denoted $|u|$.

The *subword relation*, denoted $u \sqsubseteq v$, relates any two words u and v s.t. u can be obtained by erasing some (possibly zero) letters from v, i.e. when u is some $a_1 \ldots a_n$, v is some $b_1 \ldots b_m$ and there are indexes $1 \leq k_1 < k_2 < \cdots < k_n \leq m$ s.t. $a_i = b_{k_i}$ for all $i = 1, \ldots, n$. For example $\mathtt{abba} \sqsubseteq \underline{\mathtt{ab}}\mathtt{racada}\underline{\mathtt{b}}\mathtt{r}\underline{\mathtt{a}}$, as we explain by underlining the b_{k_i}s. The subword relation is a partial ordering, with ε as least element, and compatible with concatenation: $u \sqsubseteq v$ and $u' \sqsubseteq v'$ entail $uu' \sqsubseteq vv'$. We write $u \sqsubset v$ when $u \sqsubseteq v$ and $v \not\sqsubseteq u$, that is when $u \sqsubseteq v$ and $|u| < |v|$.

When C is a finite index set, $\Sigma^{*C} = \{U, V, \ldots\}$ is the set of mappings from C to Σ^*, i.e. the set of C-indexed tuples of words. Subword ordering, concatenation and size extend to tuples from Σ^{*C} in the obvious way:

$$U \sqsubseteq V \overset{\text{def}}{\Leftrightarrow} \forall c \in C : U(c) \sqsubseteq V(c), \qquad (U.V)(c) \overset{\text{def}}{=} U(c).V(c) \text{ for any } c \in C,$$

$$U \sqsubset V \overset{\text{def}}{\Leftrightarrow} U \sqsubseteq V \text{ and } V \not\sqsubseteq U, \qquad |U| \overset{\text{def}}{=} \sum_{c \in C} |U(c)|.$$

[2] The proof that all behavioral equivalences are undecidable for P/T nets [Jan95]. Proving undecidability of (bi)simulation can be difficult, and all the non-trivial cases we know of are inspired by Jančar's method.

We abuse notation and write ε for any tuple of empty words.

For finite sets X (like Σ and C) we write $|X|$ to denote the cardinal of X.

2.2 Labeled Transition Systems and Behavioral Equivalences

A *labeled transition system* (a LTS) is a triple $\langle Conf, \Gamma, \rightarrow\rangle$ where $Conf = \{s, t, \ldots\}$ is a set of *configurations* (or states), $\Gamma = \{\alpha, \beta, \ldots\}$ is a set of *labels* and $\rightarrow \subseteq Conf \times \Gamma \times Conf$ is a set of *labeled transitions*. LTSs are used as models for the behavior of systems and usually *Conf* (and sometimes Γ) are infinite.

We write $s \xrightarrow{\alpha} s'$ for $(s, \alpha, s') \in \rightarrow$. As is usual with LTSs, we rely on a lot of special notations for sequences of transitions:

- For $\sigma \in \Gamma^*$, $s \xrightarrow{\sigma} s'$ iff $\sigma = \varepsilon$ and $s = s'$ or $\sigma = \alpha\sigma'$ and there is a s'' s.t. $s \xrightarrow{\alpha} s'' \xrightarrow{\sigma'} s'$.
- $s \xrightarrow{*} s'$ (resp. $\xrightarrow{+}$) $\stackrel{\text{def}}{\Leftrightarrow}$ $s \xrightarrow{\sigma} s'$ for some $\sigma \in \Gamma^*$ (resp. $\sigma \in \Gamma^+$).

We write $s \xrightarrow{\sigma}$ when $s \xrightarrow{\sigma} s'$ for some s' and say σ is a *trace* (sometimes called "prefix trace" to distinguish from maximal traces) of s.

For our purpose we only need define bisimulation and trace equivalence (and inclusion). We refer to [Gla01] for more definitions and motivations of the behavioral equivalences.

Trace equivalence: We write $s \subseteq_{\mathrm{Tr}} t$ when all traces of s are traces of t, i.e. when $s \xrightarrow{\sigma}$ implies $t \xrightarrow{\sigma}$ for all $\sigma \in \Gamma^*$. We write $s =_{\mathrm{Tr}} t$ when $s \subseteq_{\mathrm{Tr}} t \subseteq_{\mathrm{Tr}} s$ and say s and t are *trace-equivalent.*

Bisimulation: A relation $R \subseteq Conf \times Conf$ between the configurations of some LTS is a *simulation* if it has the *transfer property*, i.e. if for any pair $(s, t) \in R$ and any step $s \xrightarrow{\alpha} s'$, there is a $t \xrightarrow{\alpha} t'$ s.t. $(s', t') \in R$. R is a *bisimulation* if it has the transfer property both ways, i.e. if R and R^{-1} are simulations. Two configurations s and t are *bisimilar*, written $s \sim t$, if $(s, t) \in R$ for some bisimulation R.

3 Channel Systems

A channel system combines several finite automata but here we restrict to *one single* automaton[3]. However, we introduce *extended* channel systems, which are channel systems extended with the possibility of testing a channel for emptiness (a test standard channel systems cannot do).

[3] This is no loss of generality since one can always safely replace several automata by a single product automaton, perhaps at the cost of an exponential blowup but this paper is only concerned with (un)decidability issues. Replacing several communicating automata with one single global automaton also has the consequence that the global automaton ends up sending messages to itself, in which case it is more natural to think in term of fifo *buffers* rather than channels.

Definition 3.1 (Extended channel system). *An* extended channel system *is a tuple* $S = \langle Q, \Sigma, C, \Gamma, \Delta, \Theta \rangle$ *where*
- $Q = \{q, p, \ldots\}$ *is a finite set of* control states,
- $\Sigma = \{a, b, \ldots\}$ *is a finite alphabet of* messages,
- $C = \{c_1, \ldots, c_m\}$ *is a finite set of* channels,
- $\Gamma = \{\alpha, \beta, \ldots\}$ *is a finite alphabet of* labels,
- $\Delta \subseteq Q \times \Sigma^{*C} \times \Gamma \times Q \times \Sigma^{*C}$ *is a finite set of* standard rules, *and*
- $\Theta \subseteq Q \times C \times \Gamma \times Q$ *is a finite set of* extended rules.

A *configuration* of S is a pair $(q, W) \in Q \times \Sigma^{*C}$ where q is the current control state of the system, and W is the current content of the channels: $W(c) = u$ means that c contains u.

A standard rule of the form $\langle q, U, \alpha, q', V \rangle$, written $\langle q, ?U, \alpha, q', !V \rangle$ for clarity, means that S can move from q to q' by reading U from the front of its channels, and then writing V to their tails. For a rule $\langle q, ?U, \alpha, q', !V \rangle$, we may omit writing $?U$ (resp. $!V$) when $U = \varepsilon$ (resp. $V = \varepsilon$).

An extended rule of the form $\langle q, c, \alpha, q' \rangle$, written $\langle q, c = \varepsilon?, \alpha, q' \rangle$ for clarity, means that S can move from q to q' if c is empty.

The corresponding steps give rise to visible label α. This is formalized by associating a labeled transition system with S:

Definition 3.2 (Behavior of channel systems). *For a channel system* $S = \langle Q, \Sigma, C, \Gamma, \Delta, \Theta \rangle$, *the labeled transition system* $\mathcal{S}_S = \langle Conf_S, \Gamma, \rightarrow \rangle$ *associated with* S *is defined by*
- $Conf_S = Q \times \Sigma^{*C}$, *and*
- $(q, W) \xrightarrow{\alpha} (q', W')$ *iff (1) there exists a standard rule* $\langle q, ?U, \alpha, q', !V \rangle \in \Delta$ *and some* $W'' \in \Sigma^{*C}$ *s.t.* $W = U.W''$ *and* $W' = W''.V$, *or (2)* $W' = W$ *and there exists an extended rule* $\langle q, c = \varepsilon?, \alpha, q' \rangle \in \Theta$ *s.t.* $W(c) = \varepsilon$.

3.1 Standard Channel Systems and Other Restrictions

We say S is a *standard channel system* when Θ is empty (no emptiness tests) and then simply write $S = \langle Q, \Sigma, C, \Gamma, \Delta \rangle$.

We say S is a *counter machine* (also a Minsky machine) when Σ contains one single message (say, $\Sigma = \{1\}$). Then the channels are called counters since they behave like registers containing numbers. For a counter machine, we may replace words $u, v \in \{1\}^*$ by numbers and write e.g. $W(c) = 3$ and $c = 0?$ for $W(c) = 1^3$ and $c = \varepsilon?$.

We say S is a *vector addition systems with states* (a VASS) when it is both a counter machine and a standard channel system, i.e. a counter machine without zero-test. VASSes (and counter machines) can be used to model channel systems where the channels are not fifo, i.e. where messages can be read in any order.

We say S is an *m-channel(s) system* if C has m elements. For a 1-channel system, we may omit the name of the single channel and write standard rules as $\langle q, ?u, \alpha, q', !v \rangle$ (where $u, v \in \Sigma^*$). Note that a 0-channel system S is just a classical FSA, and is its own $\mathcal{S}_S$!

We say S is *unlabeled* when $|\Gamma| = 1$. For an unlabeled S, we sometimes omit writing Γ in S and α in the rules.

3.2 Undecidability of Reachability

Extended channel systems have undecidable reachability problems for two reasons: (1) standard rules can be used to simulate the tape of a Turing machine on a single fifo channel as soon as $|\Sigma| \geq 2$ [BZ81, p. 31], and (2) extended rules allow one to simulate a Turing machine on a 2-counters machine [SS63].

For our purposes we introduce the following problem, a variant of the halting problem that makes the reduction in section 4 smoother:
Non-empty Reachability.
Instance: An extended channel system S with two designated states $q, q' \in Q$,
Question: Is there some $W \in \Sigma^{*C}$ such that $W \neq \varepsilon$ and $(q, \varepsilon) \xrightarrow{*} (q', W)$?

Theorem 3.3 ([BZ81, SS63]). *Non-empty reachability is undecidable even if we restrict to one of the following two cases:*

1. *S is a standard 1-channel system,*
2. *S is a 2-counters machine.*

3.3 Lossy Channel Systems

We now define the behavior of lossy channel systems. Note that only *standard* channel systems are considered under a lossy point of view. One could investigate lossy extended channel systems, for which reachability can be proven decidable along the lines of [May98, BM99, May00], but this is not our purpose here.

Modeling lossy channels can be done in several ways. The early way was to model a non-ideal channel by inserting an additional automaton that corrupts messages passing through it [ZWR+80]. This led Finkel to his definition of *completely specified protocols*, where lossiness is modeled by adding to Δ all rules of the form $\langle q, c?a, q\rangle$ for all $q \in Q$, $c \in C$ and $a \in \Sigma$ [Fin94].

Following Abdulla and Jonsson [AJ96b, AJ96a], we prefer to see lossy systems as systems with an altered semantics (rather than altering Δ). It turns out there are several natural possibilities:

Classic Lossiness: one assumes that any number of messages from anywhere in the channels can be lost at any time.
Front Lossiness: one assumes that messages are lost at the front of the channels (or, equivalently, while the system attempts to read them).

These are the two main proposals one finds in the literature (but each of them comes in several variants). The relative merits of these several semantics have never been discussed in the literature (even in [CFP95] where both Front Lossiness and Classic Lossiness are considered). It is not clear which proposal better fits the real world. Certainly, the Classic Lossiness semantics is mathematically more elegant, and the Front Lossiness semantics mimics Finkel's completely specified protocols.

In fact, for all practical purposes, these semantics and their variants are equivalent in the sense that a lossy channel system terminates (or is bounded, or has a given trace set, or recurrently visits a given control state) under one semantics iff it does under the other. Informally, the reason is that if a message is lost and you cannot help it, nor know it, then when and where that happens makes no difference.

Unfortunately, this sensible line of reasoning does not extend to branching-time notions of behavior, where the timing of non-deterministic choices is important. The consequence is that two configurations can be bisimilar under one lossy semantics and not under the other [GV93]. Because of this, we consider both semantics and prove undecidability of bisimulation under each one.

Definition 3.4 (Two Lossy Semantics). *With a channel system* $S = \langle Q, \Sigma, C, \Gamma, \Delta\rangle$ *we associate two labeled transition systems* $\mathcal{L}_S = \langle Conf_S, \Gamma, \rightarrow_{\mathrm{l}}\rangle$ *(Classic Lossy),* $\mathcal{FL}_S = \langle Conf_S, \Gamma, \rightarrow_{\mathrm{f}}\rangle$ *(Front Lossy) that only differ from* $\mathcal{S}_S$ *by the labeled transitions:*
– $(q, W) \xrightarrow{\alpha}_{\mathrm{l}} (q', W')$ *iff there are some* $V, V' \in \Sigma^{*C}$ *s.t.* $V \sqsubseteq W$, $W' \sqsubseteq V'$*, and* $(q, V) \xrightarrow{\alpha} (q', V')$ *is a step in* $\mathcal{S}_S$*.*
– $(q, W) \xrightarrow{\alpha}_{\mathrm{f}} (q', W')$ *iff there exists a rule* $\langle q, ?U, \alpha, q', !V\rangle \in \Delta$ *and some* $U', W'' \in \Sigma^{*C}$ *s.t.* $U \sqsubseteq U'$, $W = U'.W''$ *and* $W' = W''.V$*.*

Observe that $\rightarrow \subseteq \rightarrow_{\mathrm{f}} \subseteq \rightarrow_{\mathrm{l}}$ and that the inclusions are strict in general.

4 Reducing from Perfect to Lossy Systems

Our undecidability proof reduces the non-empty reachability problem for an extended channel system S to the behavioral equivalence of twin configurations in some standard channel system S' obtained from S.

Let $S = \langle Q, \Sigma, C, \Delta, \Theta, q_f\rangle$ be an arbitrary unlabeled extended channel system with a designated state $q_f \in Q$. From S we build a standard system $S' = \langle Q', \Sigma, C, \Gamma', \Delta'\rangle$ where

- Q' contains two copies of the states in Q. Formally $Q' \stackrel{\text{def}}{=} Q \times \{+, -\}$. Given $x \in \{+, -\}$, we shortly write q^x for (q, x), Q^x for $Q \times \{x\}$. For $q^x \in Q'$, the value of x is called the *polarity* of q^x.
- $\Gamma' \stackrel{\text{def}}{=} \Delta \cup \Theta \cup \{\#\}$ has one label for every rule in S, plus an extra label #.

There remains to define Δ', the rules of S'. These rules are all rules of one of the following type:

type 0: For any U s.t. $|U| = 1$, Δ' has a rule $\langle q_f^+, ?U, \#, q_f^+, !\varepsilon\rangle$.
type 1a: If $r = \langle q, ?U, p, !V\rangle \in \Delta$ and $x \in \{+, -\}$, then Δ' has a rule $\langle q^x, ?U, r, p^x, !V\rangle$.
type 1b: If $r = \langle q, c = \varepsilon?, p\rangle \in \Theta$ and $x \in \{+, -\}$, then Δ' has a rule $\langle q^x, ?\varepsilon, r, p^x, !\varepsilon\rangle$.

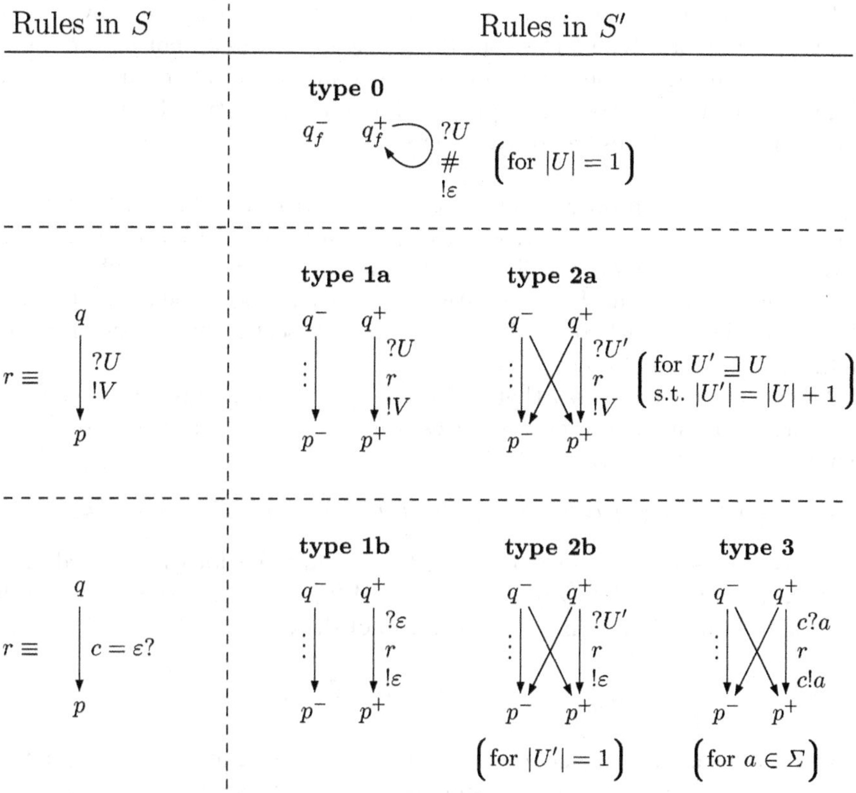

Fig. 2. Lossy system S' associated with perfect system S

type 2a: If $r = \langle q, ?U, p, !V\rangle \in \Delta$, $x, y \in \{+, -\}$ and U' is any vector s.t. $U \sqsubseteq U'$ and $|U'| = |U| + 1$, then Δ' has a rule $\langle q^x, ?U', r, p^y, !V\rangle$.

type 2b: If $r = \langle q, c = \varepsilon?, p\rangle \in \Theta$, $x, y \in \{+, -\}$ and U' is any vector s.t. $|U'| = 1$, then Δ' has a rule $\langle q^x, ?U', r, p^y, !\varepsilon\rangle$.

type 3: If $r = \langle q, c = \varepsilon?, p\rangle \in \Theta$, $x, y \in \{+, -\}$, and $a \in \Sigma$, then Δ' has a rule $\langle q^x, c?a, r, p^y, c!a\rangle$.

A type 1 rule is type 1+ (resp. 1−) if $x = +$ (resp. $x = -$).

The construction is illustrated on Fig. 2. The intuition behind the rules of S' is the following: the behavior of S from some (q, W) can be imitated perfectly by S' from (q^+, W) and from (q^-, W) with the type 1 rules. Note that S' does not have extended rules, but this does not forbid imitating S.

Imitating from (q^+, W) only uses control states from Q^+, and imitating from (q^-, W) only uses Q^-. States from Q^+ and Q^- can be distinguished in q_f where type 0 rules exist for q_f^+ only : these rules consume from the channels, emitting one $\#$ per message, and allow to count how many messages were in the channels.

It is possible to "cross" (to move from Q^+ to Q^-, or the other way around) by a type 2 rule or a type 3 rule, but these crossing moves do not imitate moves of S. Indeed, using a type 2 rule consumes one more message from the channel (compared to the corresponding type 1 rule) and using a type 3 rule assumes c is not empty when S tests c for emptiness.

Some behavioral properties of S, seen as an error-free channel system, can be expressed as properties of S', seen as a lossy system: say that a configuration (q, W) is *bad* if it allows reaching q_f on non-empty channels, i.e. if $(q, W) \xrightarrow{*} (q_f, W')$ in $\mathcal{S}_S$ for some $W' \neq \varepsilon$. We say (q, W) is *good* when it is not bad. The predecessors of a bad configuration are bad, so the successors of a good configuration are good.

The next two lemmas say that bad configurations in $\mathcal{S}_S$ give rise in $\mathcal{FL}_{S'}$ to twin configurations with different traces, while good configurations give rise to bisimilar twin configurations.

Lemma 4.1. *If (q, W) is bad in $\mathcal{S}_S$, then $(q^+, W) \not\subseteq_{\mathrm{Tr}} (q^-, W)$ in $\mathcal{FL}_{S'}$.*

Proof. We just sketch the idea and refer to appendix A.1 for the detailed proof.

If $\mathcal{S}_S$ has a run $(q, W) \xrightarrow{*} (q_f, W')$ where $|W'| = k > 0$ and the run uses rules $r_1 \dots r_m$ in that order, then $\mathcal{FL}_{S'}$ has a run of the form:

$$(q_0^+, W_0) \xrightarrow{r_1 \dots r_m} (q_f^+, W') \xrightarrow{\#^k} (q_f^+, \varepsilon) \tag{1}$$

Now (q^-, W) can only display the same trace by crossing at some time (only q_f^+ can issue #) and this requires consuming one more message than in (1). Thus $(q^-, W) \xrightarrow{r_1 \dots r_m} (q_f^+, W'')$ implies $|W''| < k$ and $r_1 \dots r_m \#^k$ is not a trace of (q^-, W). □

Lemma 4.2. *Assume S is a standard channel system, or a counter machine. Let $R = \{(q^+, W), (q^-, W) \mid (q, W) \text{ good in } \mathcal{S}_S\}$. Then $R \cup Id_{Conf}$ is a bisimulation for $\mathcal{FL}_{S'}$.*

Proof. We just sketch the idea and refer to appendix A.2 for the detailed proof.

When the attacker plays in $\mathcal{FL}_{S'}$ a move $(q_1^x, W_1) \xrightarrow{r} (q_2^x, W_2)$ that exists in $\mathcal{S}_S$, the defender plays the corresponding move from (q_1^{-x}, W_1) and is safe since the game remains in good configurations where one cannot use the type 0 rule. If the attacker plays a move that does not exist in $\mathcal{S}_S$ (e.g. because some messages are lost, or because a type 2 or 3 rule is used) then the defender can cross and reach the attacker's configuration (perhaps using a different rule and losing messages). □

Corollary 4.3. *When S is a standard channel system or a counter machine, For any configuration (q, W), the following are equivalent:*

1. *(q, W) is a good configuration of $\mathcal{S}_S$,*

2. (q^+, W) *and* (q^-, W) *are bisimilar configurations of* $\mathcal{FL}_{S'}$,
3. $(q^+, W) \subseteq_{\mathrm{Tr}} (q^-, W)$ *in* $\mathcal{FL}_{S'}$.

Proof. *(3.)* implies *(1.)* (Lemma 4.1) and *(1.)* implies *(2.)* (Lemma 4.2). *(2.)* implies *(3.)* since bisimilarity entails trace equivalence. □

Let now ρ be any relation between configurations of labeled transition systems, that sits between bisimulation and trace inclusion. Corollary 4.3 yields:

Lemma 4.4. *Let* S *be a standard channel system or a counter machine with a designated* q_f, *let* (q, W) *be any configuration of* S. *Then* (q, W) *is good in* $\mathcal{S}_S$ *iff* $(q^+, W)\rho(q^-, W)$ *in* $\mathcal{FL}_{S'}$.

We can now state our main result with the following two theorems:

Theorem 4.5 (Undecidability for front-lossy systems). *Any relation* ρ *in the branching time – linear time spectrum is undecidable between configurations of front-lossy channel systems, even if we restrict to* 1*-channel systems, or to VASSes.*

Proof. Combine Theorem 3.3 and Lemma 4.4. □

Theorem 4.6 (Undecidability for classic-lossy systems). *Any relation* ρ *in the branching time – linear time spectrum is undecidable between configurations of classic-lossy channel systems, even if we restrict to VASSes.*

Proof (Idea). We would like to say that $\mathcal{L}_S$ and $\mathcal{FL}_S$ coincide (i.e., $\rightarrow_{\mathrm{l}}=\rightarrow_{\mathrm{f}}$) when S is a VASS, so that Theorem 4.6 is a consequence of Theorem 4.5. But this is not exactly true since front-lossy systems cannot lose what a rule just wrote into the channel. So we have to show that Lemmas 4.1 and 4.2 still hold for classic-lossy systems: the proof stays unchanged for Lemma 4.1 and only needs minor changes for Lemma 4.2. □

5 Classic-Lossy Systems with One Channel

Our proof does not apply to classic-lossy systems with one channel: the difficulty is that a losing move in some $(q^?, W)$ cannot be punished by a crossing move in the twin configuration since rules for crossing moves can only consume from the head of the channels.

The decidability of bisimulation for these systems is the main remaining open problem. We have no strong argument that would favor a conjecture of decidability or of undecidability.

Of course, for equivalences that are weaker than bisimulation, undecidability is easy to prove, and we can state the following two results:

Theorem 5.1. *Any relation* ρ *between trace inclusion and* simulation *equivalence is undecidable between configurations of classic-lossy single-channel systems.*

Proof (Idea). This uses a slight modification of our construction. When a step from (q^x, W) loses message(s), the twin configuration follows by not losing (unless this is necessary for firing the same transition). In effect, this relies on the idea that postponing losses allows more behaviors, and is compatible with the simulation preorder.

Theorem 5.2. *Any relation ρ between τ-trace inclusion and τ-bisimulation (a.k.a. observational equivalence) is undecidable between configurations of classic-lossy single-channel systems.*

Proof (Idea). This uses another slight modification of our construction. Here, when (q^x, W) loses some message(s), the twin configuration can use τ-steps to rotate the buffer, putting the lost message at the head of the buffer, then consuming it by a crossing rule, and rotating the buffer back in place.

6 Conclusion

We showed undecidability of all behavioral relations over lossy channel systems, where a behavioral relation is any relation that sits between bisimulation and trace inclusion (the two endpoints of van Glabbeek's branching time – linear time spectrum [Gla01]).

The proof also applies to lossy vector addition systems. It can deal with the front-lossy semantics (as soon as we have one channel or two counters) and the classic-lossy semantics (as soon as we have two counters). Note that with only one counter, bisimulation is decidable even for perfect systems [Jan00].

The proof *does not apply* to systems with one single channel under the classic-lossy semantics, and this is the main direction we see for future work. Another case where the proof does not apply is when we restrict to systems where the rules $\langle q, ?U, q', !V\rangle$ satisfy $|UV| \leq 1$ (at most one message is consumed/produced at a time).

A Technical Appendix

A.1 Proof of Lemma 4.1

Assume (q, W) is bad, i.e. $\mathcal{S}_S$ has a run of the form $(q, W) \xrightarrow{*} (q_f, W')$ where $|W'|$ is some $k > 0$. Assume this run has length m and uses rules $r_1 \dots r_m$ in that order.

S' can mimic this run. Formally, S' has a run (of length $m+k$) of the following form:

$$(q_0^+, W_0) \xrightarrow{r_1} (q_1^+, W_1) \xrightarrow{r_2} \cdots \xrightarrow{r_m} (q_m^+, W_m) \xrightarrow{\#} \dots \xrightarrow{\#} (q_{m+k}^+, \varepsilon) \qquad (2)$$

where $(q_0^+, W_0) = (q^+, W)$, $(q_m^+, W_m) = (q_f^+, W')$ and $q_{m+j}^+ = q_f^+$ for all $j = 0, \dots, k$. Run (2) first uses type 1+ rules (m times), then type 0 rules (k times). Since no message is lost, this is at the same time a run of $\mathcal{S}_{S'}$, a run of $\mathcal{FL}_{S'}$, and a run of $\mathcal{L}_{S'}$.

Write σ for $r_1 \ldots r_m.\#^k$. Run (2) proves that σ is a trace of (q^+, W) in $\mathcal{FL}_{S'}$. We show σ is not a trace of (q^-, W): for this we assume, by way of contradiction, that $\mathcal{FL}_{S'}$ has a run

$$(p_0, V_0) \xrightarrow{r_1}_{\mathrm{f}} (p_1, V_1) \xrightarrow{r_2}_{\mathrm{f}} \cdots \xrightarrow{r_m}_{\mathrm{f}} (p_m, V_m) \xrightarrow{\#}_{\mathrm{f}} (p_{m+1}, V_{m+1}) \ldots \xrightarrow{\#}_{\mathrm{f}} (p_{m+k}, V_{m+k}) \quad (3)$$

with $(p_0, V_0) = (q^-, W)$. We derive a contradiction in a few easy lemmas.

Lemma A.1. *If* $0 \leq i \leq m$ *then* $p_i = q_i^+$ *or* $p_i = q_i^-$. *If* $m \leq i \leq m+k$ *then* $p_i = q_f^+$.

Proof. Obvious since the label (r_i or $\#$) of the step taken in (p_i, V_i) uniquely determines what are the possible values for p_i (here we rely on $k > 0$). □

One can relate the i-th step $(q_{i-1}^+, W_{i-1}) \to (q_i^+, W_i)$ of run (2) and the i-th step $(p_{i-1}, V_{i-1}) \to_{\mathrm{f}} (p_i, V_i)$ of run (3) by the following:

Lemma A.2. *For all* $1 \leq i \leq m$ *and all* $c \in C$

$$|W_i(c)| \geq |V_i(c)|, \quad (4)$$
$$|W_i(c)| - |W_{i-1}(c)| \geq |V_i(c)| - |V_{i-1}(c)|. \quad (5)$$

Furthermore, if p_i *and* p_{i-1} *have different polarities, then*

$$|W_i| - |W_{i-1}| > |V_i| - |V_{i-1}|. \quad (6)$$

Proof. The proof is by induction over i.

We first prove (5) and (6) assuming (4) holds for $i-1$ (note that (4) holds for $i = 0$ since $W_0 = W = V_0$).

The i-th step of run (2) uses the type 1+ rule associated with $r_i \in \Delta \cup \Theta$. We have two subcases:

- If r_i is a standard rule $\langle q_{i-1}, ?U, q_i, !V\rangle$, then $|W_i(c)| = |W_{i-1}(c)| - |U(c)| + |V(c)|$ for any c (since this run is not lossy).
  Now the i-th step of run (3) may use the corresponding type 1a– rule, so that in general $|V_i(c)| \leq |V_{i-1}(c)| - |U(c)| + |V(c)|$ (since this step can be lossy) and we get (5). This step may also use a type 2a rule where one more message is consumed (notwithstanding possible losses), in which case we have both (5) and (6).
- If r_i is an extended rule $\langle q_{i-1}, c = \varepsilon?, q_i\rangle$, then $W_i = W_{i-1}$ and $W_{i-1}(c) = \varepsilon$. We deduce $V_{i-1}(c) = \varepsilon$ by ind. hyp., using (4), so that the i-th step of run (3) cannot use a type 3 rule.
  Thus that step uses a type 1b rule (and then we get $|V_i(c)| \leq |V_{i-1}(c)|$ because losses are possible, so that (5) holds), or a type 2b rule, where we further have (6) since one message must be consumed.

Note that a polarity change *requires* a type 2 rule, so that (6) holds in these cases. Once (5) is proven for i, we get (4) for i by adding (4) for $i-1$ to (5). □

Lemma A.3. *For $i = 0, \ldots, m$, let n_i be the number of polarity changes in the first i steps of run (3). Then $n_i \leq |W_i| - |V_i|$.*

Proof. Easy induction over i. The base case uses $V_0 = W = W_0$ and $n_0 = 0$. The inductive step is given by Lemma A.2. □

Now we have our contradiction : since $p_0 = q^-$ and $p_m = q_f^+$ do not have the same polarity, we have $n_m > 0$, and hence $|V_m| < |W_m| = k$ by Lemma A.3. But if $|V_m| < k$, we cannot have $(p_m, V_m) \xrightarrow{\#^k}_{\mathrm{f}}$ since type 0 rules consume messages.

Thus our assumption is contradictory. There is no run of the form (3) and σ is not a trace of (q^-, W) in $\mathcal{FL}_{S'}$. Q.E.D.

A.2 Proof of Lemma 4.2

We show $R \cup Id_{Conf}$ has the transfer property in both directions. It is enough to consider a pair $(q^+, W) R (q^-, W)$ where (q, W) is a good configuration.

We first deal with the left-to-right transfer: Assume $(q^+, W) \xrightarrow{\alpha}_{\mathrm{f}} (p^x, W')$. We proceed by case analysis and consider what rule was used by that step:

a type 0 rule: This implies $q = q_f$, $W \neq \varepsilon$, and contradicts the assumption that (q, W) is good.

a type 2 or a type 3 rule: These rules allow crossing, $(q^-, W) \xrightarrow{\alpha}_{\mathrm{f}} (p^x, W')$ is possible and we are connected in Id_{Conf}.

a type 1a+ rule and the step loses no message: Then $x = +$ and $(q, W) \xrightarrow{\alpha} (p, W')$ is a step in $\mathcal{S}_S$, so that (p, W') is good. We have $(q^-, W) \xrightarrow{\alpha}_{\mathrm{f}} (p^-, W')$ using a type 1a– rule, $(p^+, W') R (p^-, W')$ and we are connected in R.

a type 1a+ rule and the step loses some message(s): Then $(q^-, W) \xrightarrow{\alpha}_{\mathrm{f}} (p^x, W')$ can be obtained with a type 2a rule (one picks the rule where U' accounts for both what the type 1a+ rule consumes and one of the lost messages) and we are connected in Id_{Conf}.

a type 1b+ rule and $W(c)=\varepsilon$ and the step loses no message: Then $x=+$ and, since c is empty, $(q, W) \xrightarrow{\alpha} (p, W')$ is a step in $\mathcal{S}_S$, so that (p, W') is good. We have $(q^-, W) \xrightarrow{\alpha}_{\mathrm{f}} (p^-, W')$ using a type 1b– rule, $(p^+, W') R (p^-, W')$ and we are connected in R.

a type 1b+ rule and the step loses some message(s): Then $(q^-, W) \xrightarrow{\alpha}_{\mathrm{f}} (p^x, W')$ can be obtained with a type 2b rule.

a type 1b+ rule and $W(c) \neq \varepsilon$ and the step loses no message: Then $(q^-, W) \xrightarrow{\alpha}_{\mathrm{f}} (p^x, W')$ can be obtained with a type 3 rule. This rule consumes some message a at the front of c and inserts it at the back, but Lemma 4.2 only applies to counter machines or standard systems, and the use of a type 1b rule implies S' is a VASS.

The right-to-left part of the transfer property is similar.

References

[AAB99] P.A. Abdulla, A. Annichini, and A. Bouajjani. Symbolic verification of lossy channel systems: Application to the bounded retransmission protocol. In *Proc. 5th Int. Conf. Tools and Algorithms for the Construction and Analysis of Systems (TACAS'99), Amsterdam, The Netherlands, March 1999*, volume 1579 of *Lecture Notes in Computer Science*, pages 208–222. Springer, 1999.

[ABJ98] P.A. Abdulla, A. Bouajjani, and B. Jonsson. On-the-fly analysis of systems with unbounded, lossy FIFO channels. In *Proc. 10th Int. Conf. Computer Aided Verification (CAV'98), Vancouver, BC, Canada, June-July 1998*, volume 1427 of *Lecture Notes in Computer Science*, pages 305–318. Springer, 1998.

[ABPJ00] P.A. Abdulla, C. Baier, S. Purushothaman Iyer, and B. Jonsson. Reasoning about probabilistic lossy channel systems. In *Proc. 11th Int. Conf. Concurrency Theory (CONCUR'2000), University Park, PA, USA, Aug. 2000*, volume 1877 of *Lecture Notes in Computer Science*, pages 320–333. Springer, 2000.

[AJ96a] P.A. Abdulla and B. Jonsson. Undecidable verification problems for programs with unreliable channels. *Information and Computation*, 130(1):71–90, 1996.

[AJ96b] P.A. Abdulla and B. Jonsson. Verifying programs with unreliable channels. *Information and Computation*, 127(2):91–101, 1996.

[AK95] P.A. Abdulla and M. Kindahl. Decidability of simulation and bisimulation between lossy channel systems and finite state systems. In *Proc. 6th Int. Conf. Theory of Concurrency (CONCUR'95), Philadelphia, PA, USA, Aug. 1995*, volume 962 of *Lecture Notes in Computer Science*, pages 333–347. Springer, 1995. Long version available at `http://www.docs.uu.se/docs/avds/`.

[AKP97] P.A. Abdulla, M. Kindahl, and D. Peled. An improved search strategy for lossy channel systems. In *Proc. Joint Int. Conf. Formal Description Techniques and Protocol Specification, Testing, and Verification (FORTE/PSTV'97), Osaka, Japan, Nov. 1997*, pages 251–264. Chapman & Hall, 1997.

[BCMS01] O. Bukart, D. Caucal, F. Moller, and B. Steffen. Verification on infinite structures. In J.A. Bergstra, A. Ponse, and S.A. Smolka, editors, *Handbook of Process Algebra*, chapter 9, pages 545–623. Elsevier Science, 2001.

[BM99] A. Bouajjani and R. Mayr. Model checking lossy vector addition systems. In *Proc. 16th Ann. Symp. Theoretical Aspects of Computer Science (STACS'99), Trier, Germany, Mar. 1999*, volume 1563 of *Lecture Notes in Computer Science*, pages 323–333. Springer, 1999.

[Boc78] G. von Bochmann. Finite state description of communication protocols. *Computer Networks and ISDN Systems*, 2:361–372, 1978.

[BZ81] D. Brand and P. Zafiropulo. On communicating finite-state machines. Research Report RZ 1053, IBM Zurich Research Lab., June 1981. A short version appears in J.ACM 30(2):323–342, 1983.

[CF97] G. Cécé and A. Finkel. Programs with quasi-stable channels are effectively recognizable. In *Proc. 9th Int. Conf. Computer Aided Verification (CAV'97), Haifa, Israel, June 1997*, volume 1254 of *Lecture Notes in Computer Science*, pages 304–315. Springer, 1997.

[CFP95] G. Cécé, A. Finkel, and S. Purushothaman Iyer. Unreliable channels are easier to verify than perfect channels. *Information and Computation*, 124(1):20–31, 1995.

[Fin94] A. Finkel. Decidability of the termination problem for completely specificied protocols. *Distributed Computing*, 7(3):129–135, 1994.

[Gla01] R.J. van Glabbeek. The linear time – branching time spectrum I. In J.A. Bergstra, A. Ponse, and S.A. Smolka, editors, *Handbook of Process Algebra*, chapter 1, pages 3–99. Elsevier Science, 2001.

[GV93] R.J. van Glabbeek and F.W. Vaandrager. Modular specification of process algebras. *Theoretical Computer Science*, 113(2):293–348, 1993.

[HJ99] Y. Hirshfeld and M. Jerrum. Bisimulation equivalence is decidable for normed process algebra. In *Proc. 26th Int. Coll. Automata, Languages, and Programming (ICALP'99), Prague, Czech Republic, July 1999*, volume 1644 of *Lecture Notes in Computer Science*, pages 412–421. Springer, 1999.

[Jan95] P. Jančar. Undecidability of bisimilarity for Petri nets and some related problems. *Theoretical Computer Science*, 148(2):281–301, 1995.

[Jan00] P. Jančar. Decidability of bisimilarity for one-counter processes. *Information and Computation*, 158(1):1–17, 2000.

[JJ93] T. Jéron and C. Jard. Testing for unboundedness of fifo channels. *Theoretical Computer Science*, 113(1):93–117, 1993.

[JKM01] P. Jančar, A. Kučera, and R. Mayr. Deciding bisimulation-like equivalences with finite-state processes. *Theoretical Computer Science*, 258(1–2):409–433, 2001.

[JM99] P. Jančar and F. Moller. Techniques for decidability and undecidability of bisimilarity. In *Proc. 10th Int. Conf. Concurrency Theory (CONCUR'99), Eindhoven, The Netherlands, Aug. 1999*, volume 1664 of *Lecture Notes in Computer Science*, pages 30–45. Springer, 1999.

[May98] R. Mayr. Lossy counter machines. Tech. Report TUM-I9830, Institut für Informatik, TUM, Munich, Germany, October 1998.

[May00] R. Mayr. Undecidable problems in unreliable computations. In *Proc. 4th Latin American Symposium on Theoretical Informatics (LATIN'2000), Punta del Este, Uruguay, Apr. 2000*, volume 1776 of *Lecture Notes in Computer Science*, pages 377–386. Springer, 2000.

[Mol96] F. Moller. Infinite results. In *Proc. 7th Int. Conf. Concurrency Theory (CONCUR'96), Pisa, Italy, Aug. 1996*, volume 1119 of *Lecture Notes in Computer Science*, pages 195–216. Springer, 1996.

[PP91] Wuxu Peng and S. Purushothaman Iyer. Data flow analysis of communicating finite state machines. *ACM Transactions on Programming Languages and Systems*, 13(3):399–442, 1991.

[Sch01] Ph. Schnoebelen. Verifying lossy channel systems has nonprimitive recursive complexity. In preparation, 2001.

[SS63] J.C. Shepherdson and H.E. Sturgis. Computability of recursive functions. *Journal of the ACM*, 10(2):217–255, 1963.

[ZWR+80] P. Zafiropulo, C. West, H. Rudin, D. Cowan, and D. Brand. Towards analysing and synthesizing protocols. *IEEE Transactions on Communication*, 28(4):651–661, 1980.

Weakest Congruence Results Concerning "Any-Lock"

Antti Puhakka

Tampere University of Technology, Software Systems Laboratory,
PO Box 553, FIN-33101 Tampere, Finland,
anpu@cs.tut.fi

Abstract. In process algebras the weakest congruences that preserve interesting properties of systems are of theoretical and practical importance. A system can stop executing visible actions in two ways: by deadlocking or livelocking. The weakest deadlock-preserving congruence was published in [20]. The weakest livelock-preserving congruence and the weakest congruence that preserves all traces of visible actions leading to a livelock were published in [17]. In this paper we will equate deadlock and livelock. We introduce the weakest congruence that preserves the predicate "any-lock" which distinguishes those systems that can stop executing visible actions from those that cannot. We also present the weakest congruence that preserves all traces after which the system can stop executing visible actions. Finally, we give two simple weakest-congruence characterisations for the CSP failures-divergences equivalence, one of which is a minimal characterisation in a well-defined sense. However, we also show that there is no minimum (least) characterisation.

1 Introduction

Process algebras are one important approach for the specification and verification of concurrent systems. In a process algebra processes are constructed from other processes by using *operators.* A semantic *equivalence* tells whether the behaviour of two processes is the same with respect to the properties we are interested in. Such properties can be, for example, the presence of deadlocks or livelocks in the process. However, an equivalence is usually only deemed useful if it is a *congruence.* This means that when two equivalent processes, $P \simeq Q$, are placed in any process context $C[\cdot]$ constructed from operators and processes, the results have to be equivalent: $C[P] \simeq C[Q]$. Whether or not an equivalence is a congruence may thus depend on the set of operators we are allowed to use. An equivalence "$\simeq_1$" is *weaker* (coarser) than another equivalence "$\simeq_2$" if and only if $P \simeq_2 Q$ implies $P \simeq_1 Q$.

The weakest congruences that preserve certain interesting properties are of both theoretical and practical interest. These are the equivalences that contain just enough information, and nothing more, that is needed to deduce the given property of any system that can be constructed using our operators. For practical verification, congruences are important because they can be used in

N. Kobayashi and B.C. Pierce (Eds.): TACS 2001, LNCS 2215, pp. 400–419, 2001.

compositional construction of LTSs (labelled transition systems). This means that a reduction algorithm which preserves the equivalence is applied to an LTS before using the LTS as a component in a larger system. The congruence property then guarantees that the resulting overall system is equivalent to the system without the reduction. That the equivalence is as weak as possible, on the other hand, means that it makes least distinctions between processes, thus giving us most opportunities for reducing processes.

A process communicates with its environment by executing visible actions, and it can stop executing visible actions in two ways. It can either *deadlock*, meaning that it cannot execute any actions, or *livelock*, meaning that it executes infinitely many internal actions. The weakest congruence that distinguishes deadlocking and non-deadlocking systems was identified in [20]. The weakest congruence that distinguishes livelocking and non-livelocking systems was found in [17]. Also, [17] presented the (strictly stronger than the former) weakest congruence that preserves all *traces* of visible actions leading to a livelock.

Based on these results on deadlock and livelock we know the weakest congruences that preserve both of these properties individually. However, sometimes the most important thing to know is whether or not the system can stop executing visible actions, not whether this happens through deadlock or livelock. In a typical situation, we want to make sure that our system has neither deadlocks nor livelocks.

In this paper we determine the weakest congruence that distinguishes systems that can stop executing visible actions from those that cannot, that is, preserves the predicate "deadlock-or-livelock". This turns out to be strictly weaker than the congruence needed for preserving both of the above predicates. Also, in [17] it was conjectured that for finitely nondeterministic systems such a congruence would be strictly weaker than Hoare's well-known CSP failures-divergences equivalence [19]. Here we prove that this is indeed the case. We also present the weakest congruence that preserves all traces of visible actions after which the system can stop executing further visible actions, i.e., deadlock or livelock. Finally, we give two simple models for which CSP-equivalence is the weakest preserving congruence. One of these is an optimal or, *minimal*, characterisation in an intuitively defined sense. However, we also show that there is no unique *minimum* characterisation.

In the next section we define our framework which is a CSP-like process algebra with LTSs as processes. The weakest any-lock-preserving congruence is given in Section 3, and the corresponding weakest congruence for any-lock-traces in Section 4. In Section 5 the CSP failures-divergences-equivalence is given the above-mentioned characterisations. In Section 6 we describe related work, and in Section 7 we present some conclusions.

2 Background

Let A^* denote the set of finite and A^ω infinite strings of elements of a set A. The empty string is denoted with ε, and it is an element of A^*, but not of A^ω.

That a (finite) string σ is a prefix of a (finite or infinite) string ρ is denoted with $\sigma \leq \rho$, and $\sigma < \rho$ means that $\sigma \leq \rho \wedge \sigma \neq \rho$.

The behaviour of a process consists of executing *actions*. There are two kinds of actions: *visible* and *invisible*. The invisible actions are denoted with a special symbol τ. Here the behaviour of a process is represented as a *labelled transition system*. It is a directed graph whose edges are labelled with action names, with one state distinguished as the initial state of the process.

Definition 1. *A* labelled transition system, *abbreviated* LTS, *is a four-tuple* $(S, \Sigma, \Delta, \hat{s})$, *where*

- S *is the set of* states,
- Σ, *the* alphabet, *is the set of the* visible actions *of the process; we assume that* $\tau \notin \Sigma$,
- $\Delta \subseteq S \times (\Sigma \cup \{\tau\}) \times S$ *is the set of* transitions, *and*
- $\hat{s} \in S$ *is the* initial state.

Definition 2. *An LTS* $(S, \Sigma, \Delta, \hat{s})$ *is* finitely nondeterministic *(finitely branching), if and only if for each* $s \in S$ *and* $a \in \Sigma \cup \{\tau\}$, *the set* $\{\, s' \mid (s, a, s') \in \Delta \,\}$ *is finite. An LTS* $(S, \Sigma, \Delta, \hat{s})$ *is* finite *if and only if* S *and* Σ *are finite.*

We use $s -a\rightarrow s'$ as an abbreviation for $(s, a, s') \in \Delta$, and this is extended in the obvious way to $s -\sigma\rightarrow s'$ and $s -\xi\rightarrow$, where σ is a finite and ξ a finite or infinite sequence of actions. Let $restr(\sigma, A)$ denote the result of removal of all actions from σ that are not in A. We write $s =\rho\Rightarrow s'$ iff there is σ such that $s -\sigma\rightarrow s'$ and $\rho = restr(\sigma, \Sigma)$. $s =\rho\Rightarrow$ is defined similarly.

The semantic equivalences that we will discuss will use the following abstract sets extracted from an LTS. The *traces* of an LTS are the sequences of visible actions generated by any finite execution that starts in the initial state. An infinite execution that starts in the initial state generates either an *infinite trace* or a *divergence trace*, depending on whether the number of visible actions in the execution is infinite. The *stable failures* describe the ability of the LTS to refuse actions after executing a particular trace.

Definition 3. *Let* $L = (S, \Sigma, \Delta, \hat{s})$ *be an LTS.*

- $Tr(L) = \{\, \sigma \in \Sigma^* \mid \hat{s} =\sigma\Rightarrow \,\}$ *is the set of the* traces *of* L.
- $Inftr(L) = \{\, \xi \in \Sigma^\omega \mid \hat{s} =\xi\Rightarrow \,\}$ *is the set of the* infinite traces *of* L.
- $Divtr(L) = \{\, \sigma \in \Sigma^* \mid \exists s : \hat{s} =\sigma\Rightarrow s \wedge s -\tau^\omega\rightarrow \,\}$, *where* τ^ω *denotes an infinite sequence of* τ*-actions, is the set of the* divergence traces *of* L.
- $Sfail(L) = \{\, (\sigma, A) \in \Sigma^* \times 2^\Sigma \mid \exists s \in S : \hat{s} =\sigma\Rightarrow s \wedge \forall a \in A \cup \{\tau\} : \neg s -a\rightarrow \,\}$ *is the set of the* stable failures *of* L.

It is obvious that $Divtr(L) \subseteq Tr(L)$ and, furthermore, if $\xi \in Inftr(L)$ and $\sigma < \xi$, then $\sigma \in Tr(L)$. If an LTS (or just its set of states) is finite, then its infinite traces are determined by its ordinary traces, as was shown in [23].

Proposition 1. *Let* $L = (S, \Sigma, \Delta, \hat{s})$ *be an LTS. If* S *is finite, then*
$Inftr(L) = \{\, \xi \in \Sigma^\omega \mid \forall \sigma < \xi : \sigma \in Tr(L) \,\}$.

It is also easy to show that $Tr(L)$ can be determined if $Divtr(L)$ and $Sfail(L)$ are known:

Proposition 2. *Let* $(S, \Sigma, \Delta, \hat{s})$ *be an LTS. Then*
$Tr(L) = Divtr(L) \cup \{ \sigma \in \Sigma^* \mid (\sigma, \emptyset) \in Sfail(L) \}$.

We will later define some additional abstract sets. Tr, $Divtr$, $Inftr$ and $Sfail$ are actually functions that take an LTS as input. Any collection of such functions can be used to define a semantic model of, and an equivalence between, LTSs as is shown below. Please notice that we will talk about an equivalence between two LTSs only if the LTSs have the same alphabet.

Definition 4. *Let* $f_1, f_2, \ldots, f_k$ *be any unary functions that take an LTS as their arguments.*

- *The* semantic model *of an LTS L* induced by $f_1, f_2, \ldots, f_k$ *is the k-tuple* $(f_1(L), f_2(L), \ldots, f_k(L))$.
- *Assume that the LTSs L and L′ have the same alphabet. The* equivalence induced by $f_1, f_2, \ldots, f_k$ *is the equivalence "$\simeq$" defined as* $L \simeq L' \iff f_1(L) = f_1(L') \wedge f_2(L) = f_2(L') \wedge \cdots \wedge f_k(L) = f_k(L')$. *We will call it the* f_1-f_2-...-f_k-equivalence.

Almost every process algebra contains some *parallel composition operator*. In this article we use the version which forces precisely those component processes to participate in the execution of a visible action that have that action in their alphabets. The invisible action is always executed by exactly one component process at a time. We first define the product of LTSs as the LTS that satisfies the above description and has the Cartesian product of component state sets as its set of states, and then define parallel composition by picking the part of the product that is reachable from the initial state of the product.

Definition 5. *Let* $L_1 = (S_1, \Sigma_1, \Delta_1, \hat{s}_1)$ *and* $L_2 = (S_2, \Sigma_2, \Delta_2, \hat{s}_2)$ *be LTSs. Their* product *is the LTS* $(S', \Sigma, \Delta', \hat{s})$ *such that the following hold:*

- $S' = S_1 \times S_2$
- $\Sigma = \Sigma_1 \cup \Sigma_2$
- $((s_1, s_2), a, (s_1', s_2')) \in \Delta'$ *if and only if either*
  - $a \in (\Sigma_1 \cup \{\tau\}) \setminus \Sigma_2$ *and* $(s_1, a, s_1') \in \Delta_1 \wedge s_2' = s_2$, *or*
  - $a \in (\Sigma_2 \cup \{\tau\}) \setminus \Sigma_1$ *and* $(s_2, a, s_2') \in \Delta_2 \wedge s_1' = s_1$, *or*
  - $a \in \Sigma_1 \cap \Sigma_2$ *and* $(s_1, a, s_1') \in \Delta_1$ *and* $(s_2, a, s_2') \in \Delta_2$.
- $\hat{s} = (\hat{s}_1, \hat{s}_2)$

The parallel composition $L_1 || L_2$ *is the LTS* $(S, \Sigma, \Delta, \hat{s})$ *such that*

- $S = \{ s \in S' \mid \exists \sigma \in \Sigma^* : \hat{s} =\sigma\Rightarrow s \}$
- $\Delta = \Delta' \cap (S \times (\Sigma \cup \{\tau\}) \times S)$

The following formulae describe the traces, etc. of a parallel composition as functions of the traces, etc. of its component processes. Their proofs are omitted because they basically consist of tedious systematic checking against the definitions given above. Similar formulae can be found in the literature, for instance in [23].

Proposition 3. *Let* $L_1 = (S_1, \Sigma_1, \Delta_1, \hat{s}_1)$ *and* $L_2 = (S_2, \Sigma_2, \Delta_2, \hat{s}_2)$ *be LTSs.*

- $\mathit{Tr}(L_1||L_2) =$
  $\{ \sigma \in (\Sigma_1 \cup \Sigma_2)^* \mid \mathit{restr}(\sigma, \Sigma_1) \in \mathit{Tr}(L_1) \wedge \mathit{restr}(\sigma, \Sigma_2) \in \mathit{Tr}(L_2) \}$
- $\mathit{Divtr}(L_1||L_2) =$
  $\{ \sigma \in \mathit{Tr}(L_1||L_2) \mid \mathit{restr}(\sigma, \Sigma_1) \in \mathit{Divtr}(L_1) \vee \mathit{restr}(\sigma, \Sigma_2) \in \mathit{Divtr}(L_2) \}$
- $\mathit{Inftr}(L_1||L_2) = \{ \xi \in (\Sigma_1 \cup \Sigma_2)^\omega \mid$
  $[\mathit{restr}(\xi, \Sigma_1) \in \mathit{Inftr}(L_1) \wedge \mathit{restr}(\xi, \Sigma_2) \in \mathit{Inftr}(L_2)] \vee$
  $[\mathit{restr}(\xi, \Sigma_1) \in \mathit{Inftr}(L_1) \wedge \mathit{restr}(\xi, \Sigma_2) \in \mathit{Tr}(L_2)] \vee$
  $[\mathit{restr}(\xi, \Sigma_1) \in \mathit{Tr}(L_1) \wedge \mathit{restr}(\xi, \Sigma_2) \in \mathit{Inftr}(L_2)] \}$
- $\mathit{Sfail}(L_1||L_2) = \{ (\sigma, A) \in (\Sigma_1 \cup \Sigma_2)^* \times 2^{\Sigma_1 \cup \Sigma_2} \mid \exists (\rho_1, B_1) \in \mathit{Sfail}(L_1), (\rho_2, B_2) \in \mathit{Sfail}(L_2) : \mathit{restr}(\sigma, \Sigma_1) = \rho_1 \wedge \mathit{restr}(\sigma, \Sigma_2) = \rho_2 \wedge A = B_1 \cup B_2 \}$

Another operator that is almost invariably found in process algebras in one form or another is *hiding*, which converts visible actions into τ-actions and removes them from the alphabet.

Definition 6. *Let* $L = (S, \Sigma, \Delta, \hat{s})$ *be an LTS, and* A *any set of action names. Then* **hide** A **in** L *is the LTS* $(S, \Sigma', \Delta', \hat{s})$ *such that the following hold:*

- $\Sigma' = \Sigma \setminus A$
- $(s, a, s') \in \Delta'$ *if and only if*
  $a = \tau \wedge \exists b \in A : (s, b, s') \in \Delta$, *or* $a \notin A \wedge (s, a, s') \in \Delta$.

The traces, etc. of also **hide** A **in** L are functions of the traces, etc. of L.

Proposition 4. *Let* $L = (S, \Sigma, \Delta, \hat{s})$ *be an LTS, and let* Σ' *be the alphabet of* **hide** A **in** L.

- $\mathit{Tr}(\textbf{hide}\ A\ \textbf{in}\ L) = \{ \sigma \in \Sigma'^* \mid \exists \rho \in \mathit{Tr}(L) : \sigma = \mathit{restr}(\rho, \Sigma') \}$
- $\mathit{Divtr}(\textbf{hide}\,A\,\textbf{in}\,L) = \{ \sigma \in \Sigma'^* \mid \exists \zeta \in \mathit{Divtr}(L) \cup \mathit{Inftr}(L) : \sigma = \mathit{restr}(\zeta, \Sigma') \}$
- $\mathit{Inftr}(\textbf{hide}\ A\ \textbf{in}\ L) = \{ \xi \in \Sigma'^\omega \mid \exists \zeta \in \mathit{Inftr}(L) : \xi = \mathit{restr}(\zeta, \Sigma') \}$
- $\mathit{Sfail}(\textbf{hide}\ A\ \textbf{in}\ L) = \{ (\sigma, B) \in \Sigma'^* \times 2^{\Sigma'} \mid \exists (\rho, C) \in \mathit{Sfail}(L) : \sigma = \mathit{restr}(\rho, \Sigma') \wedge C = B \cup A \}$

An equivalence "$\simeq$" *preserves* $f_1, \ldots, f_k$ if and only if "$L \simeq L'$" implies $f_1(L) = f_1(L') \wedge \cdots \wedge f_k(L) = f_k(L')$, that is, iff "$\simeq$" is stronger than the f_1-…-f_k-equivalence.

An equivalence "$\simeq$" is a *congruence* with respect to a process operator $\mathit{op}(L_1, \ldots, L_n)$ if and only if $L_1 \simeq L'_1 \wedge \cdots \wedge L_n \simeq L'_n$ implies $\mathit{op}(L_1, \ldots, L_n) \simeq \mathit{op}(L'_1, \ldots, L'_n)$. As a simple example, we can reason from the above formulae that the Tr-equivalence is a congruence with respect to "$||$" and "**hide**". Namely, if $\mathit{Tr}(L) = \mathit{Tr}(L')$, then because $\mathit{Tr}(\textbf{hide}\,A\,\textbf{in}\,L)$ is a function of A and $\mathit{Tr}(L)$ only, then necessarily also $\mathit{Tr}(\textbf{hide}\,A\,\textbf{in}\,L) = \mathit{Tr}(\textbf{hide}\,A\,\textbf{in}\,L')$. The same reasoning shows that $\mathit{Tr}(L_1||L_2) = \mathit{Tr}(L'_1||L'_2)$ given that $\mathit{Tr}(L_1) = \mathit{Tr}(L'_1)$, $\mathit{Tr}(L_2) = \mathit{Tr}(L'_2)$.

In general, if $f_1(\mathit{op}(L_1, \ldots, L_n)), \ldots, f_k(\mathit{op}(L_1, \ldots, L_n))$ can be represented as functions of $f_1(L_1), \ldots, f_k(L_1), \ldots, f_1(L_n), \ldots, f_k(L_n)$, then the equivalence induced by $f_1, \ldots, f_k$ is a congruence with respect to op.

3 The Weakest Any-Lock-Preserving Congruence

There are two ways in which a process can stop executing visible actions: it can either deadlock or livelock. A deadlock means that the system is in a state where no actions are possible. For dealing with deadlocks we need the notion of stable failures. As a remainder, the set *Sfail*(L) contains the pair (σ, A) exactly when L can execute the trace σ and end up in a state that has neither invisible actions (the state is thus *stable*) nor any actions from the subset A of the alphabet as outgoing actions.

Deadlock traces are the traces of visible actions after which the system can deadlock.

Definition 7. *Let* $L = (S, \Sigma, \Delta, \hat{s})$ *be an LTS. The set of the* deadlock traces *of* L *is* $\mathit{Dltr}(L) = \{\, \sigma \in \Sigma^* \mid (\sigma, \Sigma) \in \mathit{Sfail}(L) \,\}$

The following predicate tells whether or not there are any deadlocks in L:

Definition 8. *Let* L *be an LTS. Then*
$\mathit{deadlock}(L) :\Longleftrightarrow \mathit{Dltr}(L) \neq \emptyset$.

In [20] it was shown that the *Sfail*-equivalence is the weakest equivalence that preserves *deadlock* and is a congruence with respect to "||" and "**hide**". Since the *Sfail*-equivalence preserves *Dltr*, this means that it is also the weakest congruence that preserves all deadlock traces.

A livelock/divergence means that the system can execute infinitely many invisible τ-actions, i.e., engage in an endless internal computation. For describing divergences we use the notion of divergence traces, defined in the previous section. The following predicate tells whether or not L can diverge:

Definition 9. *Let* L *be an LTS. Then*
$\mathit{diverge}(L) :\Longleftrightarrow \mathit{Divtr}(L) \neq \emptyset$.

For dealing with divergences, three new semantic sets were defined in [17]: the traces and infinite traces that do not have divergence traces as their prefixes, and the divergence traces that do not have divergence traces as their proper prefixes. These sets are defined formally as follows:

Definition 10. *Let* L *be an LTS and* Σ *its alphabet.*

- *If* $X \subseteq \Sigma^*$, *then* $\mathit{minimals}(X) = \{\, \sigma \in X \mid \forall \rho \in X : \rho \not< \sigma) \,\}$
- *The set of the* minimal divergence traces *of* L *is* $\mathit{Mindiv}(L) = \mathit{minimals}(\mathit{Divtr}(L))$
- *The set of the* extended divergence traces *of* L *is* $\mathit{Divext}(L) = \{\, \zeta \in \Sigma^* \cup \Sigma^\omega \mid \exists \rho \in \mathit{Mindiv}(L) : \rho \leq \zeta \,\}$
- *The set of the* nondivergent traces *of* L *is* $\mathit{Ndtr}(L) = \mathit{Tr}(L) \setminus \mathit{Divext}(L)$
- *The set of the* nondivergent infinite traces *of* L *is* $\mathit{Ndinftr}(L) = \mathit{Inftr}(L) \setminus \mathit{Divext}(L)$

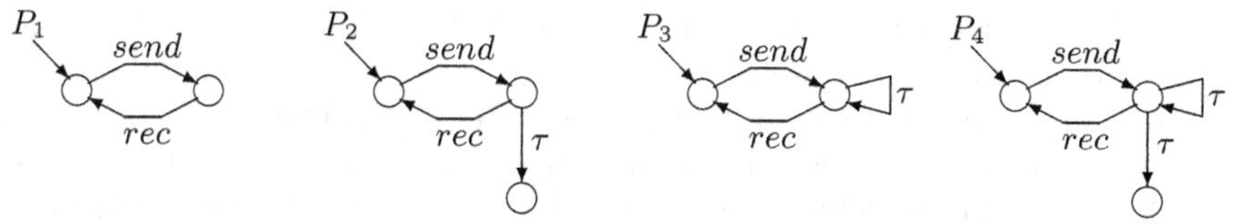

Fig. 1. Four example processes

In [17] it was shown that the *Ndtr-Mindiv-Ndinftr*-equivalence is the weakest congruence with respect to "||" and "**hide**" that preserves the existence of divergences, that is, preserves the predicate *diverge*.

In this article we will consider the combined effect of deadlocks and livelocks. It is easy to see that $Ndtr(L) = \{\, \sigma \in \Sigma^* \mid (\sigma, \emptyset) \in Sfail(L) \,\} \setminus Divext(L)$, so the set $Ndtr(L)$ can be determined from $Sfail(L)$ and $Mindiv(L)$ and becomes redundant in the presence of these two sets. Combined with the above-mentioned result for the *Sfail*-equivalence this means that the *Mindiv-Ndinftr-Sfail*-equivalence is the weakest congruence with respect to "||" and "**hide**" that preserves both the *deadlock*- and *diverge*-predicates.

However, in some cases we only need to know whether or not the system can stop executing visible actions, not whether this happens by deadlocking or livelocking. Typically, we want to make sure that our system has neither deadlocks nor divergences. In such a situation the above requirement of preserving both predicates is unnecessarily strong. Instead, we would like to know the weakest congruence that preserves the information as to whether there are deadlocks *or* divergences in the system, i.e., the weakest congruence that distinguishes systems that can stop executing visible actions from those that cannot. Determining this equivalence is our goal in this section.

Definition 11. *Let L be an LTS. Then*
$anylock(L) :\Longleftrightarrow deadlock(L) \vee diverge(L)$.

Example 1. To illustrate the difference between the predicates, let us consider the simple example shown in Figure 1. Process P_1 could be, for example, the behaviour of a simple communication protocol. The other P_i differ from P_1 by having deadlocks and/or divergences. It holds that $deadlock(P_1) = deadlock(P_3) = False$, but $deadlock(P_2) = deadlock(P_4) = True$. On the other hand, $diverge(P_1) = diverge(P_2) = False$, $diverge(P_3) = diverge(P_4) = True$. However, only $anylock(P_1) = False$, and $anylock(P_2) = anylock(P_3) = anylock(P_4) = True$. (Note, however, that the congruence developed below will need to distinguish all these LTSs except P_3 and P_4.)

It turns out, unsurprisingly, that we do not have to preserve all of *Sfail* to preserve *anylock*. Let us define the following subset of *Sfail*:

Definition 12. *Let* $L = (S, \Sigma, \Delta, \hat{s})$ *be an LTS. The set of the* divergence-free failures *of L is* $Dffail(L) = \{\, (\sigma, A) \in Sfail(L) \mid \forall a \in A : \sigma a \notin Mindiv(L) \,\} \setminus Divext(L) \times 2^{\Sigma}$.

Perhaps the most interesting point about this definition is that we not only reject those pairs where a prefix of σ is a divergence trace, but we also do not include in A actions that lead to a divergence after σ. Intuitively, the idea is that if the environment offers such an action, this automatically creates a divergence. Therefore, because we make no distinction between deadlock and divergence, it does not matter if refusing the action also creates a deadlock.

We next present the functions that give the resulting *Dffail*-set as a function of *Mindiv* and the *Dffail* sets of the parameters of the "||" and "**hide**" operators. The functions that give the *Mindiv*, *Ndtr* and *Ndinftr* sets as functions of the corresponding sets of the parameters have been presented in [17].

Proposition 5. *Let* L_1 *and* L_2 *be LTSs with alphabets* Σ_1 *and* Σ_2. *Then* $\mathit{Dffail}(L_1||L_2) = \{ (\sigma, A) \in (\Sigma_1 \cup \Sigma_2)^* \times 2^{\Sigma_1 \cup \Sigma_2} \mid \exists (\rho_1, B_1) \in \mathit{Dffail}(L_1), (\rho_2, B_2) \in \mathit{Dffail}(L_2) : \mathit{restr}(\sigma, \Sigma_1) = \rho_1 \wedge \mathit{restr}(\sigma, \Sigma_2) = \rho_2 \wedge A = B_1 \cup B_2 \wedge \forall a \in A : \sigma a \notin \mathit{Mindiv}(L_1||L_2) \} \setminus \mathit{Divext}(L_1||L_2) \times 2^{\Sigma_1 \cup \Sigma_2}$.

Proof. Assume $(\sigma, A) \in \mathit{Dffail}(L_1||L_2) \subseteq \mathit{Sfail}(L_1||L_2)$. By Proposition 3 there are $(\rho_1, C_1) \in \mathit{Sfail}(L_1)$ and $(\rho_2, C_2) \in \mathit{Sfail}(L_2)$ such that $\mathit{restr}(\sigma, \Sigma_1) = \rho_1$, $\mathit{restr}(\sigma, \Sigma_2) = \rho_2$ and $A = C_1 \cup C_2$. Next we will divide each of the refusal sets C_1, C_2 into two disjoint parts. Namely, let $C_1^\dagger = \{ a \in C_1 \mid \rho_1 a \in \mathit{Mindiv}(L_1) \}$ and $C_2^\dagger$ similarly, and let $C_1' = C_1 \setminus C_1^\dagger$ and $C_2' = C_2 \setminus C_2^\dagger$. Firstly, if a prefix of ρ_1 were in $\mathit{Divtr}(L_1)$, then because $\rho_2 \in \mathit{Tr}(L_2)$, we see by Proposition 3 that a prefix of σ would be in $\mathit{Divtr}(L_1||L_2)$, which contradicts the assumption that $(\sigma, A) \in \mathit{Dffail}(L_1||L_2)$. Then, by the definition of C_1', we can conclude that $(\rho_1, C_1') \in \mathit{Dffail}(L_1)$. By symmetry, $(\rho_2, C_2') \in \mathit{Dffail}(L_2)$. Secondly, we will show that for all $a \in C_1^\dagger$ (in process L_1) it holds that $a \in \Sigma_2$ but $\rho_2 a \notin \mathit{Tr}(L_2)$ (in process L_2). If this were not true, then either $a \notin \Sigma_2$ or $\rho_2 a \in \mathit{Tr}(L_2)$. By definition, $\rho_1 a \in \mathit{Mindiv}(L_1)$, so in both cases it would hold that $\sigma a \in \mathit{Divtr}(L_1||L_2)$, which contradicts the original assumption. Thus, the claim has to hold, and L_2 can refuse a in every stable state reachable with ρ_2. Because furthermore $\rho_2 a \notin \mathit{Mindiv}(L_2)$ (which is a subset of $\mathit{Tr}(L_2)$), we can conclude that $(\rho_2, C_2' \cup C_1^\dagger) \in \mathit{Dffail}(L_2)$. By symmetry, $(\rho_1, C_1' \cup C_2^\dagger) \in \mathit{Dffail}(L_1)$. We can now use $(C_1' \cup C_2^\dagger)$ and $(C_2' \cup C_1^\dagger)$ as the sets B_1 and B_2 in the above formula, because $(C_1' \cup C_2^\dagger) \cup (C_2' \cup C_1^\dagger) = (C_1' \cup C_1^\dagger) \cup (C_2' \cup C_2^\dagger) = C_1 \cup C_2 = A$. The other direction of the proof is a straightforward consequence of Proposition 3 and the definition of *Dffail*. □

Proposition 6. *Let* L *be an LTS, and* $\Sigma' = \Sigma \setminus A$. *Then* $\mathit{Dffail}(\textbf{hide}\ A\ \textbf{in}\ L) = \{ (\sigma, B) \in \Sigma'^* \times 2^{\Sigma'} \mid \exists (\rho, C) \in \mathit{Dffail}(L) : \mathit{restr}(\rho, \Sigma') = \sigma \wedge C = B \cup A \wedge \forall a \in B : \sigma a \notin \mathit{Mindiv}(\textbf{hide}\ A\ \textbf{in}\ L) \} \setminus \mathit{Divext}(\textbf{hide}\ A\ \textbf{in}\ L)$.

Proof. By Proposition 4 and the definition of *Dffail*, the above formula is clearly correct when "*Dffail*(L)" on the right hand side of the equation is replaced by "*Sfail*(L)". It then remains to show that the set $\mathit{Sfail}(L) \setminus \mathit{Dffail}(L)$ contributes nothing to the result. For each pair (ρ, C) in this set, a prefix of ρ or ρa, for some $a \in C$, is in $\mathit{Mindiv}(L)$. It follows that a prefix of σ or σa is in

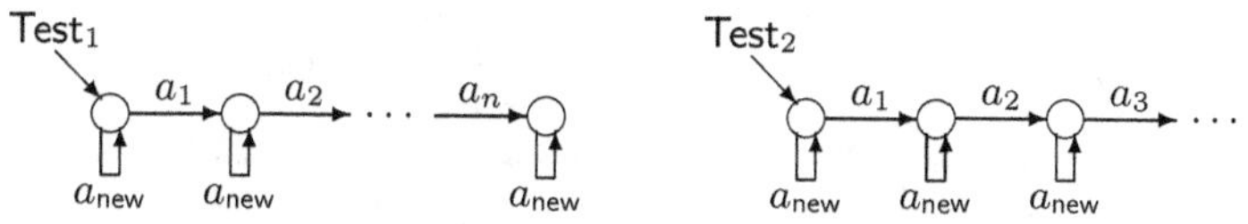

Fig. 2. Two LTSs used in *anylock*-proofs

Mindiv(**hide** A **in** L). In the former case, the pair is removed by "$\backslash Divext(\ldots)$". In the latter case, $a \notin A$ and because $C = B \cup A$, $a \in B$ and the pair is removed by the condition "$\forall a \in B : \sigma a \notin Mindiv(\ldots)$". □

The following propositions show that the congruence requirement forces us to preserve each of the sets *Mindiv*, *Ndinftr*, *Dffail*. The technique we use is to devise contexts in which processes which differ with respect to any of the above sets would result in *anylock*-different results.

Proposition 7. *Let "$\simeq$" be a congruence with respect to "$||$" such that $L \simeq L'$ implies $anylock(L) = anylock(L')$. Then $L \simeq L'$ implies $Mindiv(L) = Mindiv(L')$.*

Proof. Let $L \simeq L'$ and let Σ be the common alphabet of L and L'. Assume $\sigma \in Mindiv(L)$, where $\sigma = a_1 a_2 \cdots a_n$. Let a_{new} be a novel action not in Σ and let Test_1 be the LTS with alphabet $\Sigma \cup \{a_{\mathsf{new}}\}$ and with other components as shown in Figure 2. Then $\sigma \in Divtr(L||\mathsf{Test}_1)$, so $anylock(L||\mathsf{Test}_1) = True$ and, by the congruence requirement, $anylock(L'||\mathsf{Test}_1) = True$. Because of the a_{new}-loops it clearly holds that $deadlock(L'||\mathsf{Test}_1) = False$, so there is a divergence in $L'||\mathsf{Test}_1$. Thus, some prefix ρ of σ is in $Mindiv(L')$. By repeating the argument with the roles of L and L' reversed we see that ρ has a prefix σ' such that $\sigma' \in Mindiv(L)$. Due to the definition of *Mindiv* we have $\sigma' = \sigma$, so $\rho = \sigma$ and we get $Mindiv(L) \subseteq Mindiv(L')$. The other direction follows from symmetry. □

Proposition 8. *Let "$\simeq$" be a congruence with respect to "$||$" and "**hide**" such that $L \simeq L'$ implies $anylock(L) = anylock(L')$. Then $L \simeq L'$ implies $Ndinftr(L) = Ndinftr(L')$.*

Proof. Let $L \simeq L'$ and let Σ be the common alphabet of L and L'. Assume $\xi = a_1 a_2 a_3 \cdots \in Ndinftr(L)$. Let a_{new} be a novel action not in Σ, and let Test_2 be the LTS with alphabet $\Sigma \cup \{a_{\mathsf{new}}\}$ in Figure 2. Clearly **hide** Σ **in** $(L||\mathsf{Test}_2)$ diverges, so *anylock*(**hide** Σ **in** $(L||\mathsf{Test}_2)$) $= True$ and, by the congruence requirement, *anylock*(**hide** Σ **in** $(L'||\mathsf{Test}_2)$) $= True$. Because of the a_{new}-loops there can be no deadlock in $L'||\mathsf{Test}_2$, so there is none in **hide** Σ **in** $(L'||\mathsf{Test}_2)$ either. Thus, there is a divergence. Because Test_2 (with alphabet $\Sigma \cup \{a_{\mathsf{new}}\}$) allows only those executions of L' whose visible traces are prefixes of ξ, the divergence can only exist if either some prefix of ξ is a divergence trace of L', or $\xi \in Ndinftr(L')$. However, the previous proposition and the definition of $Ndinftr(L)$ rule out the former possibility. The other direction follows again from symmetry. □

Proposition 9. *Let "$\simeq$" be a congruence with respect to "$||$" such that $L \simeq L'$ implies $anylock(L) = anylock(L')$. Then $L \simeq L'$ implies $Dffail(L) = Dffail(L')$.*

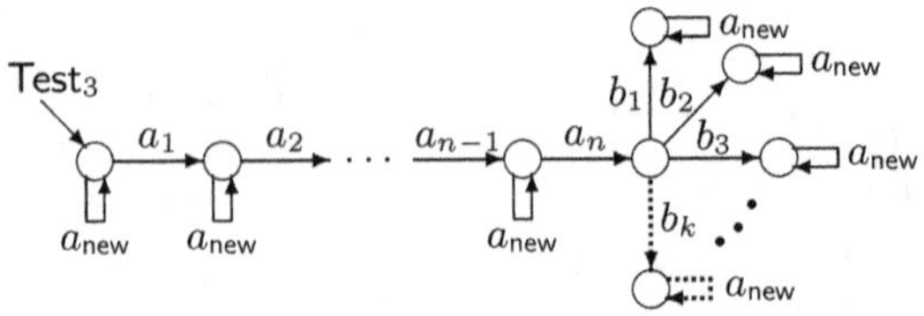

Fig. 3. An LTS for testing failures

Proof. Let Σ and a_{new} be as in the previous proofs. Assume $(\sigma, A) \in \mathit{Dffail}(L)$, where $\sigma = a_1 a_2 \ldots a_n$ and $A = \{b_1, b_2, \ldots [, b_k]\}$ is finite or infinite. Let Test_3 be the LTS with alphabet $\Sigma \cup \{a_{\mathsf{new}}\}$ in Figure 3. Clearly, $\sigma \in \mathit{Dltr}(L||\mathsf{Test}_3)$. Thus, $\mathit{anylock}(L||\mathsf{Test}_3) = \mathit{True}$, so $\mathit{anylock}(L'||\mathsf{Test}_3) = \mathit{True}$. Because of Proposition 7 and the definition of *Dffail*, no prefix of σ or σb_i, where $b_i \in A$, can be a divergence trace of L or L'. It follows that there are no divergences in $L'||\mathsf{Test}_3$, so there has to be a deadlock. Because of the a_{new}-loops there can be no deadlock trace other than σ, so $\sigma \in \mathit{Dltr}(L'||\mathsf{Test}_3)$. Because of the structure of Test_3, we see that $(\sigma, A) \in \mathit{Sfail}(L')$, and then by the above observations, $(\sigma, A) \in \mathit{Dffail}(L')$. The reverse follows again from symmetry. □

The following straightforward result shows that $\mathit{anylock}(L)$ can be determined from $\mathit{Mindiv}(L)$ and $\mathit{Dffail}(L)$.

Proposition 10. $\mathit{anylock}(L) \iff \mathit{Mindiv}(L) \neq \emptyset \vee \mathit{Dffail}(L) \cap (\Sigma^* \times \{\Sigma\}) \neq \emptyset$

We are now in a position to state the weakest-congruence result we were after:

Theorem 1. *The weakest congruence with respect to "||" and "**hide**" that preserves anylock (i.e. distinguishes processes that can stop executing visible actions from those that cannot) is the Mindiv-Ndinftr-Dffail-equivalence.*

Proof. As mentioned above, the functions that give the *Mindiv*, *Ndtr* and *Ndinftr* sets as functions of the sets of the parameters of "||" and "**hide**" can be found in [17]. Propositions 5 and 6 give the required additional functions for *Dffail*. $\mathit{Ndtr}(L) = \{\, \sigma \in \Sigma^* \mid (\sigma, \emptyset) \in \mathit{Dffail}(L) \,\}$, so the *Ndtr* component is redundant. These results show that the equivalence is a congruence, and Proposition 10 shows that it preserves *anylock*. Propositions 7, 8 and 9 show that any congruence that preserves *anylock* implies the *Mindiv-Ndinftr-Dffail*-equivalence. □

After dealing with the general case of all LTSs, we next consider two special cases, namely the subsets of finitely nondeterministic and finite LTSs. The following result for the *Ndtr* and *Ndinftr* sets of a finitely nondeterministic LTS has been shown in [17]; essentially the same result, although in a different form, can also be found as Theorem 7.4.2 in [19]. It should be noted that the corresponding result for *Tr* and *Inftr*, Proposition 1, holds only for finite LTSs but not for all finitely nondeterministic LTSs.

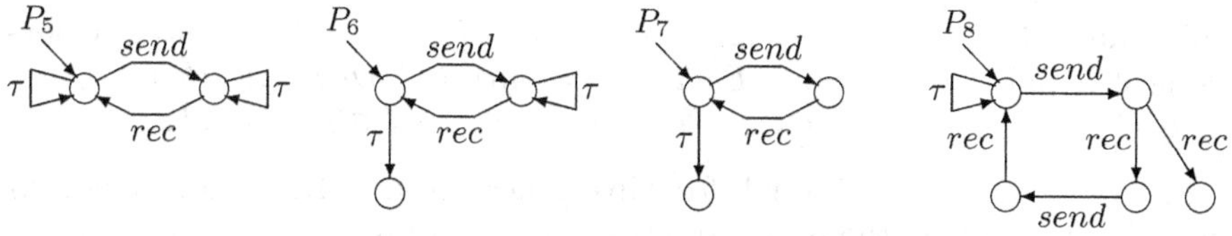

Fig. 4. Four new example processes

Proposition 11. *If L is a finitely nondeterministic LTS, then*
$Ndinftr(L) = \{\, \xi \in \Sigma^\omega \mid \forall \rho < \xi : \rho \in Ndtr(L) \,\}$.

This shows that in the class of finitely nondeterministic (or finite) LTSs, *Ndinftr* becomes redundant and the *Mindiv-Ndinftr-Dffail*-equivalence collapses to the *Mindiv-Dffail*-equivalence.

Theorem 2. *The weakest congruence between finitely nondeterministic / finite LTSs with respect to "||" and "**hide**" that preserves anylock is the Mindiv-Dffail-equivalence. The claim remains valid if the part 'and "**hide**"' is removed.*

Proof. Proposition 7, which uses a finite LTS, shows that every congruence with respect to "||" preserves *Mindiv*. As for Proposition 9, process Test_3 in Figure 3 is always finitely nondeterministic (each b_i occurs only once). If the LTSs are finite, then Σ is finite, and therefore A and Test_3 are also finite. Thus, in both cases the proof of the proposition remains valid, and the equivalence has to preserve *Dffail*. We have already shown that the *Mindiv-Ndinftr-Dffail*-equivalence is a congruence with respect to both "||" and "**hide**", and this equivalence is now the same as the *Mindiv-Dffail*-equivalence. □

4 The Weakest Any-Lock-Trace-Preserving Congruence

After presenting the weakest *anylock*-preserving congruence, we will complete the spectrum of deadlock and/or livelock -preserving congruences by looking into the weakest congruence that preserves all traces of visible actions that lead either to a deadlock or a livelock. In other words, we want to preserve precisely the traces after which the system can stop executing visible actions.

Definition 13. *Let L be an LTS. The set of the* any-lock-traces *of L is*
$Anylocktr(L) = Dltr(L) \cup Divtr(L)$.

Example 2. For process P_5 in Figure 4 it holds that $anylock(P_5) = True$, like it did for the processes P_2, P_3 and P_4 in Figure 1. However, in terms of *Anylocktr*, P_5 is different from every process in Figure 1. On the other hand, P_5 is *Anylocktr*-equivalent to P_6, because $Anylocktr(P_5) = Anylocktr(P_6) = (send\,rec)^* \cup (send\,rec)^* send$. Furthermore, P_7 is *Anylocktr*-different from $P_1, \ldots, P_6$, but $Anylocktr(P_7) = Anylocktr(P_8) = (send\,rec)^*$.

For preserving all of *Anylocktr* we will need the following semantic set, which was defined in [17]:

Definition 14. *Let $L = (S, \Sigma, \Delta, \hat{s})$ be an LTS. The set of the* eventually non-divergent infinite traces *of L is $\mathit{Enditr}(L) = \mathit{Inftr}(L) \setminus \mathit{Divcl}(L)$, where*
$\mathit{Divcl}(L) = \{\, \xi \in \Sigma^\omega \mid \forall \sigma < \xi : \exists \sigma' : \sigma \leq \sigma' < \xi \wedge \sigma' \in \mathit{Divtr}(L) \,\}$.

The abbreviation *Divcl* stands for "divergence closure". Eventually nondivergent infinite traces are those infinite traces, of whose prefixes only finitely many are divergence traces. In [17] it was shown that the *Tr-Divtr-Enditr*-equivalence is the weakest congruence with respect to "||" and "**hide**" that preserves all divergence traces.

We also need a new failure-set definition. It turns out that we need to preserve precisely those stable failures for which the trace part is not a divergence trace. This semantic set is taken from [10], where it was used as part of the weakest "LTL_{-X}"-preserving congruence.

Definition 15. *Let $L = (S, \Sigma, \Delta, \hat{s})$ be an LTS. The set of the* nondivergent failures *of L is $\mathit{Ndfail}(L) = \mathit{Sfail}(L) \setminus \mathit{Divtr}(L) \times 2^\Sigma$.*

The following properties of *Ndfail* are easy to establish:

Proposition 12. *Let $L = (S, \Sigma, \Delta, \hat{s})$ be an LTS. Then*

- $\mathit{Tr}(L) = \mathit{Divtr}(L) \cup \{\, \sigma \in \Sigma^* \mid (\sigma, \emptyset) \in \mathit{Ndfail}(L) \,\}$*, and*
- $\mathit{Anylocktr}(L) = \mathit{Divtr}(L) \cup \{\, \sigma \in \Sigma^* \mid (\sigma, \Sigma) \in \mathit{Ndfail}(L) \,\}$.

The functions which relate the *Ndfail* set resulting from "||" or "**hide**" with the *Ndfail* sets of the parameter processes and the *Divtr* set of the result can be obtained from [23]. The functions for *Tr*, *Divtr* and *Enditr* can be found in [17]. Furthermore, the above proposition shows that *Tr* becomes redundant if *Divtr* and *Ndfail* are both included in the semantic model. Thus, we can conclude that the *Divtr-Enditr-Ndfail*-equivalence is a congruence with respect to "||" and "**hide**". Proposition 12 also shows that this equivalence preserves *Anylocktr*. It then only remains to prove minimality.

Proposition 13. *Let "$\simeq$" be a congruence with respect to "||" such that $L \simeq L'$ implies $\mathit{Anylocktr}(L) = \mathit{Anylocktr}(L')$. Then $L \simeq L'$ implies $\mathit{Divtr}(L) = \mathit{Divtr}(L')$.*

Proof. Let $L \simeq L'$ and let Test_1 be similar as in the proof of Proposition 7. Then $\sigma \in \mathit{Divtr}(L) \iff \sigma \in \mathit{Divtr}(L||\mathsf{Test}_1) \iff \sigma \in \mathit{Anylocktr}(L||\mathsf{Test}_1) \iff \sigma \in \mathit{Anylocktr}(L'||\mathsf{Test}_1) \iff \sigma \in \mathit{Divtr}(L'||\mathsf{Test}_1) \iff \sigma \in \mathit{Divtr}(L')$. The second and penultimate logical equivalences follow from the fact that, because of the structure of Test_1, σ cannot lead to a deadlock in $L||\mathsf{Test}_1$ or $L'||\mathsf{Test}_1$. □

Proposition 14. *Let "$\simeq$" be a congruence with respect to "||" and "**hide**" such that $L \simeq L'$ implies $\mathit{Anylocktr}(L) = \mathit{Anylocktr}(L')$. Then $L \simeq L'$ implies $\mathit{Enditr}(L) = \mathit{Enditr}(L')$.*

Proof. Let $L \simeq L'$ and let Σ be the common alphabet of L and L'. Assume $\xi = a_1 a_2 a_3 \cdots \in \mathit{Enditr}(L)$. By definition, ξ has a prefix $a_1 a_2 \cdots a_n$ such that there

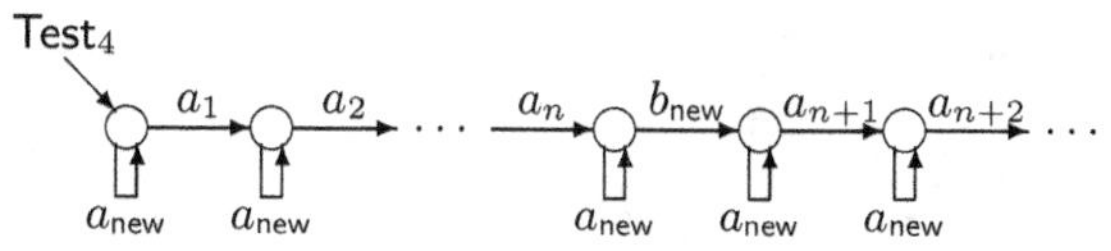

Fig. 5. An LTS used in proofs

is no $\sigma \in \mathit{Divtr}(L)$ with $a_1 a_2 \cdots a_n \leq \sigma < \xi$. Let a_{new}, b_{new} be two novel actions not in Σ, and let Test_4 be the LTS with alphabet $\Sigma \cup \{a_{\mathsf{new}}, b_{\mathsf{new}}\}$ in Figure 5. We see that $b_{\mathsf{new}} \in \mathit{Divtr}(\textbf{hide}\, \Sigma\, \textbf{in}\, (L || \mathsf{Test}_4)) \subseteq \mathit{Anylocktr}(\textbf{hide}\, \Sigma\, \textbf{in}(L || \mathsf{Test}_4))$, so by the congruence requirement $b_{\mathsf{new}} \in \mathit{Anylocktr}(\textbf{hide}\, \Sigma\, \textbf{in}\, (L' || \mathsf{Test}_4))$. Because of the a_{new}-loops in Test_4 there can be no deadlocks in $L' || \mathsf{Test}_4$, so there are none in $\textbf{hide}\, \Sigma\, \textbf{in}\, (L' || \mathsf{Test}_4)$ either. Thus, $b_{\mathsf{new}} \in \mathit{Divtr}(\textbf{hide}\, \Sigma\, \textbf{in}\, (L' || \mathsf{Test}_4))$. From this we can conclude that either $\xi \in \mathit{Inftr}(L')$, or $\mathit{Divtr}(L')$ contains some σ such that $a_1 a_2 \cdots a_n \leq \sigma < \xi$. The latter is a contradiction, because by the previous proposition $\mathit{Divtr}(L) = \mathit{Divtr}(L')$. The same argument also rules out the possibility that $\xi \in \mathit{Divcl}(L')$, so we can conclude that $\xi \in \mathit{Enditr}(L')$. The other direction follows from symmetry. □

The following result can be shown similarly as the earlier results by using Test_3 from Figure 3:

Proposition 15. *Let "$\simeq$" be a congruence with respect to "$||$" such that $L \simeq L'$ implies $\mathit{Anylocktr}(L) = \mathit{Anylocktr}(L')$. Then $L \simeq L'$ implies $\mathit{Ndfail}(L) = \mathit{Ndfail}(L')$.*

Theorem 3. *The weakest congruence with respect to "$||$" and "**hide**" that preserves Anylocktr (the traces after which a process can stop executing visible actions) is the Divtr-Enditr-Ndfail-equivalence.*

We now again consider the special cases of finitely nondeterministic and finite systems. The processes used in Propositions 13 to 15 are finitely nondeterministic. Thus, the claim in Theorem 3 holds also among finitely nondeterministic systems.

For *finite* systems we can show by using Proposition 1 and the definition of *Enditr* the following:

Proposition 16. *If $L = (S, \Sigma, \Delta, \hat{s})$ is a finite LTS, then*
$\mathit{Enditr}(L) = \{\, \xi \in \Sigma^\omega \mid \forall \sigma < \xi : \sigma \in \mathit{Tr}(L) \,\} \setminus \mathit{Divcl}(L)$.

Thus, in the class of finite systems the *Divtr-Enditr-Ndfail*-equivalence collapses to the *Divtr-Ndfail*-equivalence. The processes used in Propositions 13 and 15 are finite when Σ is finite. Therefore we can conclude:

Theorem 4. *The weakest congruence with respect to "$||$" [and "**hide**"] between finite systems that preserves Anylocktr is the Divtr-Ndfail-equivalence.*

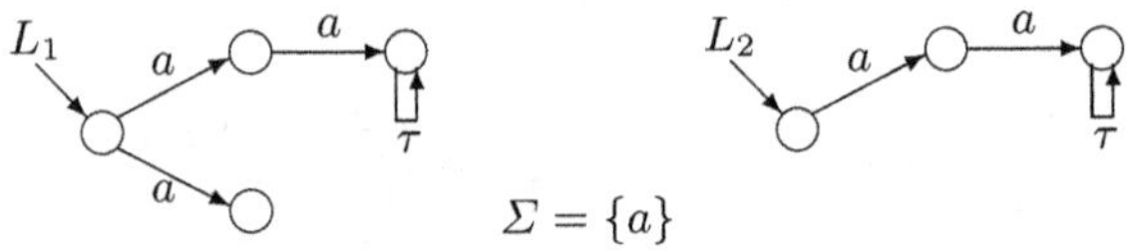

Fig. 6. Two *Mindiv-Dffail*-equivalent but not CSP-equivalent LTSs

5 Weakest Congruence Characterisation of CSP-Equivalence

Readers who are familiar with the CSP theory have probably noticed a close resemblance between the *Mindiv(-Ndinftr)-Dffail*-equivalence of Section 3 and the CSP failures-divergences equivalence of [5,9,19]. As the latter is a very well-known and important equivalence, we would now like to make this connection explicit.

Because the CSP failures-divergences equivalence (or CSP-equivalence for short) is only a congruence among finitely nondeterministic systems ([19] p. 200), we will in this section consider only finitely nondeterministic LTSs. As shown in Section 3, in this class of systems the *Mindiv-Ndinftr-Dffail*-equivalence reduces to the *Mindiv-Dffail*-equivalence, and it is the weakest congruence among these systems that preserves *anylock*.

CSP-equivalence can be defined in the LTS framework as follows ([19] p. 191).

Definition 16. *Let* $L = (S, \Sigma, \Delta, \hat{s})$ *be a finitely nondeterministic LTS.*

- $\mathit{CSPdivtr}(L) = \{ \sigma \in \Sigma^* \mid \exists \rho \leq \sigma : \rho \in \mathit{Divtr}(L) \}$
- $\mathit{CSPfail}(L) = \mathit{Sfail}(L) \cup (\mathit{CSPdivtr}(L) \times 2^{\Sigma})$
- CSP-equivalence *is the CSPfail-CSPdivtr-equivalence.*

The following proposition shows that CSP-equivalence implies the *Mindiv-Dffail*-equivalence.

Proposition 17. *Let L be a finitely nondeterministic LTS. Then*

- $\mathit{Mindiv}(L) = \mathit{minimals}(\mathit{CSPdivtr}(L))$, *and*
- $\mathit{Dffail}(L) = \{ (\sigma, A) \in \mathit{CSPfail}(L) \mid \forall a \in A : \sigma a \notin \mathit{CSPdivtr}(L) \} \setminus \mathit{CSPdivtr}(L) \times 2^{\Sigma}$.

In the opposite direction, clearly $\mathit{CSPdivtr}(L) = \{ \sigma \in \Sigma^* \mid \exists \rho \leq \sigma : \rho \in \mathit{Mindiv}(L) \}$. However, $\mathit{CSPfail}(L)$ cannot be obtained from $\mathit{Mindiv}(L)$ and $\mathit{Dffail}(L)$. Indeed, CSP-equivalence is strictly stronger than the *Mindiv-Dffail*-equivalence. This is shown by the processes in Figure 6, which are *Mindiv-Dffail*-equivalent but not CSP-equivalent: $(a, \{a\}) \in \mathit{CSPfail}(L_1)$, but $(a, \{a\}) \notin \mathit{Dffail}(L_1)$, because "$aa$" leads to a divergence.

These results mean that CSP-equivalence preserves *anylock* but is not the weakest congruence that preserves this predicate. This raises the question as to whether there is some similar characterisation for which CSP-equivalence is the weakest preserving congruence. Of course, we could trivially characterise CSP-equivalence as the weakest congruence that preserves *CSPfail* and *CSPdivtr*, but this is obviously not very useful. Rather, we would like to find a characterisation that is as weak (and, hopefully, simple) as possible while still requiring all the information preserved by CSP-equivalence to be a congruence.

The corrected form of Theorem 9.3.1 (iii) in [19] (see the errata on the www-page of the book *http://www.comlab.ox.ac.uk/oucl/publications/books/concurrency*) characterises CSP-equivalence as the weakest "immediate-any-lock"-preserving congruence, that is, as the weakest congruence that distinguishes systems that can deadlock or diverge *before executing any visible actions* from those that cannot. However, this result depends crucially on the use of a multiple (double) renaming operator that can convert a transition into two transitions with different labels.

To illustrate the idea, we can again consider the CSP-different processes L_1 and L_2 in Figure 6. To show that they have to be differentiated, we should find a context $C[\cdot]$ such that $C[L_1]$ and $C[L_2]$ are different in terms of "immediate-any-lock". L_1 has the failure $(a, \{a\})$, i.e. deadlock, that L_2 does not have (if the failure were something less than a deadlock, we could make it one by using parallel composition with a tester process similar to the one in Figure 3). We can make this an *immediate* deadlock by hiding a. However, the problem is that this also hides the second a-action, so that the divergence can be reached with τ-actions. Thus, both systems become immediately divergent, which nullifies the effect of the immediate deadlock.

With a clever technique based on double renaming it is possible to hide the actions in the trace under investigation (the first a in the example) without hiding the actions after the trace that correspond to the failure set (the second a in the example), and therefore the proof of the above-mentioned theorem can nevertheless be carried through (see the above www-page for details).

However, we conjecture that the proof *cannot* be carried through without the double renaming operator, meaning that the weakest congruence with respect to "$||$" and "**hide**" (and ordinary renaming) that preserves "immediate-any-lock" is strictly weaker than CSP-equivalence. It would therefore be interesting to find a characterisation for CSP-equivalence that does not depend on the multiple renaming operator, namely, for which the more common "$||$" and "**hide**" would suffice.

In the following we define the set of deadlock traces that do not have divergence traces as prefixes. These are the sequences of visible actions after which the system can terminate without having had a chance to diverge earlier.

Definition 17. *Let* $L = (S, \Sigma, \Delta, \hat{s})$ *be an LTS. Then the set of the* divergence-free deadlock traces *of* L *is* $Dfdltr(L) = Dltr(L) \setminus Divext(L)$.

Starting from this definition it is straightforward to show that $Dfdltr(L) = \{\, \sigma \mid (\sigma, \Sigma) \in CSPfail(L) \,\} \setminus CSPdivtr(L)$. Thus, CSP-equivalence preserves *Dfdltr*. CSP-equivalence is well known to be a congruence among finitely nondeterministic systems [19]. The following two propositions then show that it is the weakest congruence with respect to "$||$" and "**hide**" that preserves *Dfdltr*.

Proposition 18. *Let "$\simeq$" be a congruence with respect to "$||$" and "**hide**" such that $L \simeq L'$ implies $Dfdltr(L) = Dfdltr(L')$. Then $L \simeq L'$ implies $CSPdivtr(L) = CSPdivtr(L')$.*

Proof. Let $L \simeq L'$ and let Σ be the common alphabet of L and L'. Let Test_5 be an LTS with alphabet Σ that is like Test_1 in Figure 2 but without the a_{new}-loops. Assume $\sigma \in CSPdivtr(L)$. Then some prefix ρ of σ is a divergence trace of L, and $\rho \in Divtr(L||\mathsf{Test}_5)$. Thus, $\varepsilon \in Divtr(\textbf{hide } \Sigma \textbf{ in } (L||\mathsf{Test}_5))$ and therefore $Dfdltr(\textbf{hide } \Sigma \textbf{ in } (L||\mathsf{Test}_5)) = \emptyset$, so $Dfdltr(\textbf{hide } \Sigma \textbf{ in } (L'||\mathsf{Test}_5)) = \emptyset$. Now some prefix of σ has to be a divergence trace of L', implying $\sigma \in CSPdivtr(L')$. Namely, if no prefix were a divergence trace, then $L'||\mathsf{Test}_5$ would have to deadlock after some prefix of σ, because Test_5 only allows executions whose visible traces are prefixes of σ. This would create a divergence-free deadlock in $\textbf{hide } \Sigma \textbf{ in } (L'||\mathsf{Test}_5)$, which is a contradiction. □

Proposition 19. *Let "$\simeq$" be a congruence with respect to "$||$" such that $L \simeq L'$ implies $Dfdltr(L) = Dfdltr(L')$. Then $L \simeq L'$ implies $CSPfail(L) = CSPfail(L')$.*

Proof. Let Σ, σ, A, a_{new} and Test_3 be as in the proof of Proposition 9, and let $(\sigma, A) \in CSPfail(L)$. Then either some prefix ρ of σ is a divergence trace of L, or no prefix is a divergence trace and $(\sigma, A) \in Sfail(L)$. In the former case, $\rho \in CSPdivtr(L)$, so by the previous proposition, $\rho \in CSPdivtr(L')$, whereby $(\sigma, A) \in CSPfail(L')$. In the latter case, clearly $\sigma \in Dltr(L||\mathsf{Test}_3)$ and, furthermore, no prefix of σ is a divergence trace of $L||\mathsf{Test}_3$. Thus, $\sigma \in Dfdltr(L||\mathsf{Test}_3)$, and by the congruence requirement, $\sigma \in Dfdltr(L'||\mathsf{Test}_3) \subseteq Dltr(L'||\mathsf{Test}_3)$. From the structure of Test_3 we see that $(\sigma, A) \in Sfail(L') \subseteq CSPfail(L')$. □

We have shown that *Dfdltr* is a weakest congruence characterisation for CSP-equivalence. However, as mentioned above, we would like to find a characterisation that is as weak as possible, and it quickly turns out that *Dfdltr* is not a weakest possible characterisation. Let us define a predicate that tells whether or not there are any divergence-free deadlocks in L:

Definition 18. *Let L be an LTS. Then $dfdl(L) :\Longleftrightarrow Dfdltr(L) \neq \emptyset$.*

Since *dfdl* is (strictly) weaker than *Dfdltr*, CSP-equivalence preserves this predicate. We can then show with a straightforward modification of the above two proofs that CSP-equivalence is the weakest congruence that preserves *dfdl*. Thus, *dfdl* is also a characterisation of CSP-equivalence.

Furthermore, it is easy to see that *dfdl* is a *minimal* characterisation in the sense that no strictly weaker equivalence is a characterisation of CSP-equivalence. Namely, *dfdl* is a predicate, so as an equivalence it has only two equivalence classes (those processes for which it holds and those for which it does not). Therefore, the only strictly weaker equivalence is the trivial one which equates all processes, for which CSP-equivalence is clearly not the weakest preserving congruence (since it is itself a congruence).

However, *dfdl* is not *the weakest* characterisation in the sense that every other characterisation would imply it. As a trivial counterexample, we can define the predicate *non-ε-dfdl* which states that there are divergence-free deadlock traces *other than* ε. This is also weaker than *Dfdltr*, so CSP-equivalence preserves it, and we can again modify the earlier proofs (namely, by suitable b_{new}-actions) to show that CSP-equivalence is the weakest preserving congruence. So, as it is a predicate, *non-ε-dfdl* is also a minimal characterisation of CSP-equivalence. Thus, there is no *minimum* characterisation.

6 Related Work

Robin Milner's remark on p. 206 of [13] can be said to be one of the origins of the research on weakest congruences: "Hoare's failures equivalence ... is important, because it appears to be the weakest equivalence which never equates a deadlocking agent with one which does not deadlock." Milner no doubt also required that the equivalence must be a congruence, because otherwise the weakest equivalence would be the trivial one that has precisely two equivalence classes: the processes (that is, Milner's agents) that deadlock, and those that do not. In [20] it was proven that Milner's guess was not precisely correct. The weakest deadlock-preserving congruence depends on the set of allowed process composition operators. Furthermore, assuming a reasonable choice of operators, it is the same as Hoare's failures equivalence only in the absence of divergence.

Vogler [24] identified the weakest congruence with respect to parallel composition of Petri Nets that preserves a predicate comprising deadlock and nonexitable divergence, as well as the weakest congruence that preserves the visible traces of all maximal occurrence sequences.

As already mentioned, the weakest congruence that preserves the traces leading to a livelock and the weakest congruence that preserves the existence of livelocks were identified in [17].

In [10] the so-called *nondivergent failures divergences equivalence* (*NDFD-equivalence*) was shown to be the weakest congruence that preserves the validity of formulae written in classic Manna-Pnueli linear time temporal logic [12] from which the "next state" operator "$\bigcirc$" has been removed. This logic is extremely important in verification of concurrent systems. Furthermore, if the congruence has to preserve also deadlocks, then the weakest congruence is the *Chaos-free failures divergences* (*CFFD*) *equivalence.* A formulation that is perhaps more relevant for practical verification can be found in [21] and in ([22] pp. 498–499).

Some researchers have tried to find the weakest congruence that preserves the results of certain kinds of *tests* on processes, an approach introduced by De Nicola and Hennessy [6,8]. The solution with a fair way of testing was given by Brinksma, Rensink and Vogler in [4], and Leduc came to the conclusion that with another view to testing, the NDFD-equivalence is the solution [11]. Some equivalences investigated in weakest congruence research have their origin in [1].

Boreale, De Nicola and Pugliese [3] give the must-testing [6] and fair testing [4] equivalences new characterisations as the weakest congruences that preserve certain simple predicates in a CCS-like language. It is also shown in [3] (where only finitely nondeterministic systems are considered) that essentially the same equivalence that in [17] was shown to be the weakest congruence among finitely nondeterministic systems that preserves the existence of divergences, is the weakest congruence that preserves *immediate* divergence/convergence. Indeed, it is possible to construct contexts which demonstrate that the weakest congruence preserving immediate and non-immediate divergence has to be the same (this is not, however, the case for "any-lock"; see the discussion in Section 5).

Furthermore, [3] proposes a new testing framework, which differs from must-testing in that the observed process is not allowed to diverge at the point of success. Interestingly, the resulting equivalence (preorder) resembles closely the finitely nondeterministic case for the "any-lock"-predicate at the end of Section 3 of this paper. This is because the above requirement forces one to consider also divergence after the refused/accepted actions. On the other hand, [3] shows that this is the weakest congruence that preserves a predicate which is very different from "any-lock": it considers for each visible action ℓ the ability to diverge before or after the first ℓ, as well as the reachability ("guarantee") of ℓ from every state reachable from the initial state with invisible actions.

It is also interesting to compare Theorem 4.11 from [3], dealing with must-testing, and the proof discussed in Section 5 concerning CSP-equivalence and "immediate-any-lock". The proof of the former theorem does not require multiple renaming, which is apparently because of the difference in the given predicate: instead of deadlock it considers the "guarantee" for each visible action. An interesting question is also whether the latter proof could be adapted to CCS. This does not appear to be the case, because in CCS communications turn immediately into invisible actions.

In [15] strong bisimulation [13] is characterised as the weakest congruence that preserves a *barbed bisimulation*, which observes invisible actions and at each step preserves the possibility to perform (any) visible actions. In [7] a corresponding result for the weak case is shown to hold in the asynchronous name-passing π-calculus [14].

7 Conclusions

We proved that the weakest congruence that distinguishes systems that can stop executing visible actions from those that cannot (i.e., preserves "any-lock") is the *Mindiv-Ndinftr-Dffail*-equivalence. We also proved that the weakest congruence that preserves all traces after which the system can stop executing visible actions is the *Divtr-Enditr-Ndfail*-equivalence.

Hoare's well-known CSP-equivalence was shown to be strictly (albeit only slightly) stronger than the *Mindiv*(*-Ndinftr*)*-Dffail*-equivalence. Finally, we gave CSP-equivalence two weakest congruence characterisations, *Dfdltr* and *dfdl*, the latter of which is a minimal characterisation.

Although we have omitted the less important operators in this article, the weakest-congruence results in Sections 3 and 4 hold also for larger sets of operators that include ordinary and multiple renaming as well as *action prefix* and *sequential composition* (which requires a special termination action). This can be shown by giving the appropriate semantic functions for these operators. However, if we include a *choice* operator, defined as in e.g. LOTOS [2], we have to strengthen those equivalences by one bit of information, namely by the *initial stability* bit that tells whether or not there are τ-actions from the initial state of the process. This is a well-known phenomenon for failure-based congruences (CSP, however, uses a different kind of choice operator). A similar observation holds for the *interrupt* operator of LOTOS.

As for Section 5, a characterisation (e.g. with respect to parallel composition and hiding) is also a characterisation with any larger set of operators for which the given congruence retains its congruence property. Therefore, the given characterisations of CSP-equivalence hold also with any larger set of operators for which CSP-equivalence is a congruence (including multiple renaming).

This and other work on weakest congruences can be said to advocate one particular approach for defining process equivalences: we first define a property of systems we are interested in, and then identify a congruence, preferably the weakest one, that preserves this property with respect to our process operators. It is clear that no single equivalence can be universally better than all others. Preserving information that is not needed for the case at hand can sometimes be harmful. Also, the state-explosion problem may limit the amount of information that we are able to preserve. Therefore, it is useful if our verification system supports a hierarchy of equivalences with different strengths.

One interesting research direction are congruences that preserve information related to different notions of *fairness* (e.g. weak and strong fairness). As pointed out in [18], most present equivalences either do not preserve enough of this type of information, or are too strong because they do not allow us to abstract away invisible actions. Such congruences have already been developed in [16], although for communicating imperative programs rather than "classical" process algebra.

Acknowledgements

The author wishes to thank Antti Valmari for useful comments on this paper. This work has been supported by the Academy of Finland, project "Unifying Action-Based and State-Based Verification Techniques", and the TISE Graduate School.

References

1. Bergstra, J. A., Klop, J. W. & Olderog, E.-R.: "Failures without Chaos: A New Process Semantics for Fair Abstraction". *Formal Description of Programming Concepts III*, North-Holland 1987, pp. 77–103.
2. Bolognesi, T. & Brinksma, E.: "Introduction to the ISO Specification Language LOTOS". Computer Networks and ISDN Systems 14, 1987, pp. 25-59.
3. Boreale, M., De Nicola, R. & Pugliese, R.: "Basic Observables for Processes". *Information and Computation* 149 (1999), pp. 77–98.
4. Brinksma, E., Rensink, A. & Vogler, W.: "Fair Testing". *Proc. CONCUR '95, 6th International Conference on Concurrency Theory*, Lecture Notes in Computer Science 962, Springer-Verlag 1995, pp. 313–327.

5. Brookes, S. D. & Roscoe, A. W.: "An Improved Failures Model for Communicating Sequential Processes". *Proc. NSF-SERC Seminar on Concurrency*, Lecture Notes in Computer Science 197, Springer-Verlag 1985, pp. 281–305.
6. De Nicola, R. & Hennessy, M.: "Testing Equivalences for Processes". *Theoretical Computer Science* 34 (1984), pp. 83–133.
7. Fournet, C. & Gonthier, G.: "A Hierarchy of Equivalences for Asynchronous Calculi". *Proc. ICALP'98, 25th International Colloquium on Automata, Languages and Programming*, Lecture Notes in Computer Science 1443, Springer-Verlag 1998, pp. 844–855.
8. Hennessy, M.: "Synchronous and Asynchronous Experiments on processes". *Information and Control* 59 (1983), pp. 36–83.
9. Hoare, C. A. R.: *Communicating Sequential Processes.* Prentice-Hall 1985, 256 p.
10. Kaivola, R. & Valmari, A.: "The Weakest Compositional Semantic Equivalence Preserving Nexttime-less Linear Temporal Logic". *Proc. CONCUR '92, Third International Conference on Concurrency Theory*, Lecture Notes in Computer Science 630, Springer-Verlag 1992, pp. 207–221.
11. Leduc, G.: "Failure-based Congruences, Unfair Divergences and New Testing Theory". *Proc. Protocol Specification, Testing and Verification*, XIV, Chapman & Hall, London (1995), pp. 252–267.
12. Manna, Z. & Pnueli, A.: *The Temporal Logic of Reactive and Concurrent Systems, Volume I: Specification.* Springer-Verlag 1992, 427 p.
13. Milner, R.: *Communication and Concurrency.* Prentice-Hall 1989, 260 p.
14. Milner, R.: "The polyadic π-calculus: a tutorial". In Bauer, F. L., Brauer, W. & Schwichtenberg, H. (editors), *Logic and Algebra of Specification*, Springer-Verlag 1993, pp. 203–246.
15. Milner, R. & Sangiorgi, D.: "Barbed Bisimulation". *Proc. ICALP92, 19th International Colloquium on Automata, Languages and Programming*, Lecture Notes in Computer Science 623, Springer-Verlag 1992, pp. 685–695.
16. Older, S.: "Strong Fairness and Full Abstraction for Communicating Processes". *Information and Computation* 163 (2000), pp. 471–509.
17. Puhakka, A. & Valmari, A.: "Weakest-Congruence Results for Livelock-Preserving Equivalences". *Proc. CONCUR'99, 10th International Conference on Concurrency Theory*, Lecture Notes in Computer Science 1664, Springer-Verlag 1999, pp. 510–524.
18. Puhakka, A. & Valmari, A.: "Liveness and Fairness in Process-Algebraic Verification". To appear in *Proc. CONCUR'01, 12th International Conference on Concurrency Theory*, Lecture Notes in Computer Science, Springer-Verlag.
19. Roscoe, A. W.: *The Theory and Practice of Concurrency.* Prentice-Hall 1998, 565 p.
20. Valmari, A.: "The Weakest Deadlock-Preserving Congruence". *Information Processing Letters* 53 (1995), pp. 341–346.
21. Valmari, A.: "Failure-based Equivalences Are Faster Than Many Believe". *Proc. Structures in Concurrency Theory 1995*, Springer-Verlag "Workshops in Computing" series, 1995, pp. 326–340.
22. Valmari, A.: "The State Explosion Problem". *Lectures on Petri Nets I: Basic Models*, Lecture Notes in Computer Science 1491, Springer-Verlag 1998, pp. 429–528.
23. Valmari, A. & Tienari, M.: "Compositional Failure-Based Semantic Models for Basic LOTOS". *Formal Aspects of Computing* 7 (1995), pp. 440–468.
24. Vogler, W.: "Failures Semantics and Deadlocking of Modular Petri Nets". *Acta Informatica* 26 (1989), pp. 333–348.

Design and Correctness of Program Transformations Based on Control-Flow Analysis

Anindya Banerjee[1], Nevin Heintze[2], and Jon G. Riecke[3]

[1] Kansas State University, Manhattan, KS 66506, USA,
banerjee@cis.ksu.edu
[2] Agere Systems, Murray Hill, NJ 07974, USA,
nch@agere.com
[3] Aleri, Inc., New York, NY 10011, USA,
Jon.Riecke@aleri.com

Abstract. We show how control-flow-based program transformations in functional languages can be proven correct. The method relies upon "defunctionalization," a mapping from a higher-order language to a first-order language. We first show that defunctionalization is correct; using this proof and common semantic techniques, we then show how two program transformations – flow-based inlining and lightweight defunctionalization – can be proven correct.

1 Introduction

Control-flow analysis (CFA) [20,37,38] is a program analysis that computes an approximation to the set of functions or methods that may be called at a call site. CFA's usefulness stems from the style of programming in functional and object-oriented languages. Typically, programs in such languages have small basic blocks and use recursive functions for loops. These factors limit the applicability of standard intraprocedural optimizations [2,25], and increase the importance of interprocedural optimizations. CFA enables interprocedural optimizations, and so is used frequently [7,9,10,17,19,38,41,46].

The correctness of CFA itself has been widely studied [15,18,19,20,28,29,30], [37,38], but little is known about how to prove the correctness of CFA-based *transformations*. An analogous situation for dataflow analysis and dataflow-analysis-based transformations was recognized and addressed in the 1980s [27]. The correctness proofs that we know of, notably those of Wand and his coauthors [39,42,43], are based on special-purpose operational semantics, and prove only one direction of correctness: if the source program evaluates to a final answer, then so does the transformed program (this is often called soundness). In this paper we give alternative and more general methods for proving the correctness of CFA-based transformations, based on a simple denotational semantics and principles from data abstraction.

We begin by describing a simply typed, call-by-value functional language that has control-flow information incorporated into types (Section 2). The type system is essentially the same as Heintze's [15]. We then show how to translate that

N. Kobayashi and B.C. Pierce (Eds.): TACS 2001, LNCS 2215, pp. 420–447, 2001.

language, in a type-directed way, into a first-order programming language (Sections 3 and 4). We call this translation *CFA-based defunctionalization* [7,41]; it refines Reynolds's defunctionalization method for turning higher-order programs into first-order programs [32,34,35]. The first-order target language is Pascal-like and includes rudimentary support for abstract data types as well as support for nested function definitions. The main results of the paper are the following:

- We prove CFA-based defunctionalization correct using a denotational semantics for the target language (Section 4). That is, we prove that a source program evaluates to a final answer iff the defunctionalized program evaluates to the same final answer.
- Using the semantics of the target, we prove the correctness of flow-based inlining (Section 5), a source-to-source transformation.
- We augment the CFA-based type system and give a new, type-based specification of "lightweight defunctionalization" (Section 6), the analog of "lightweight closure conversion" [39]. We also show how to transform new type system into the first-order target language, and prove correctness using principles from data abstraction.

The second and third results both use the first result, albeit in different ways. We expect that other correctness results can reuse the correctness theorem for CFA-based defunctionalization.

To illustrate how correctness proofs go, consider the following example of flow-based inlining. This example is adapted from Shivers's thesis [38], and is written in ML-style syntax.

```
let fun g x = x in
let fun f h y =
    (if (y=0) then (h 1)
    else f h (h y)) in
f g 2
```

Source program

```
let fun g x = x in
let fun f h y =
    (if (y=0) then (g 1)
     else f g (g y)) in
f g 2
```

Transformed program

CFA predicts that the only function that can flow to `h` is `g`, and thus `h` can be replaced by `g`. (A separate transformation, useless variable elimination [22,38,44], could be used to remove `h` from `f`.) One might expect that β-reduction or β-equality could be used to prove that the source and transformed programs are the same. However, the source and transformed programs are *not* equivalent via β-reduction or β-equality, because of the recursive definition of `f`. In Section 5, we shall prove the two programs equivalent by showing that their defunctionalized versions are equivalent. The correctness then follows from the correctness of defunctionalization (Section 4).

2 The Source Language

The source language, PCFA, is a version of PCF [31,36] with control-flow types [15]. Each function definition in a program has a unique label; we use ℓ to range over these labels. Each call site has a set of labels representing the functions that may flow to that site; we use L to range over finite sets of labels. Function types include these label sets, and the type system ensures that the functions that reach call sites have labels in the label set associated with the call site.

More specifically, the types and terms of the language are given by following grammar, where `op` abbreviates either the `succ` or the `pred` operations.

$$\begin{aligned} s &::= \texttt{int} \mid (s \to s, L) \\ D &::= (\texttt{fun}^{\ell}\ f\ (x : s) = e) \\ e &::= n \mid x \mid (e_1 \mathbin{@_L} e_2) \mid (\texttt{let}\ D\ \texttt{in}\ e) \mid (\texttt{let val}\ x = e\ \texttt{in}\ e) \\ &\quad \mid (\texttt{op}\ e) \mid (\texttt{if0}\ e\ \texttt{then}\ e_1\ \texttt{else}\ e_2) \end{aligned}$$

The symbols x, f range over ordinary variables, n over integers, s, t over types, and e over terms. A recursive function f with argument x is defined using the construct $(\texttt{fun}^{\ell}\, f\, (x : s) = e)$, where e is the body of the recursive definition. Following standard conventions [5], we identify terms up to renaming of bound variables and use the notation $e[x := e']$ for the capture-free substitution of e' for x in e. Finally, we often omit types when they can be reconstructed.

The type rules for PCFA appear in Table 1, and include five forms of judgement. The rules use two different contexts, one denoted ψ and the other denoted Γ. The context ψ is a label context: it maps a function label ℓ to a triple (Γ, s, t), where Γ is the type context in which the function labelled ℓ is defined, and s and t are respectively the argument and return types of the function. The second form of context, Γ, is a list of assignments of types to variables. We will use the notation $x_1 : s_1, \ldots, x_n : s_n$ to denote such type contexts. Standard presentations of type-based CFA [15] use only the type context Γ. As the analysis is a whole-program analysis, the label context ψ can be used to provide information about which functions can be legally used at a program point.

For example, consider the rule for recursive function declaration. The label ℓ occurs in the label context ψ. The type context, Γ, used to define the recursive function makes sense because it is exactly the definition type context of the recursive function stipulated in the side condition $\psi(\ell) = (\Gamma, s, t)$.

The operational semantics of PCFA appears in Table 2 using a natural semantics [21]. The form of the judgement is $(e, \gamma) \Downarrow v$, where γ is a finite function from variables to values, v ranges over values, and the set of values includes the numerals n and closures of the form $\langle \texttt{fun}^{\ell}\ f\ (x : s) = e, \gamma \rangle$. In the rules, $\dot{-}$ denotes the operation that subtracts one unless its argument is 0, in which case it returns 0. Most of the rules are self-explanatory. One can prove the following theorem:

Theorem 1 (Subject Reduction). *Suppose* $\Psi \mid \emptyset \vdash e : s$ *and* $(e, \emptyset) \Downarrow v$. *Then* $\Psi \mid \emptyset \vdash v : s$ *is derivable.*

This theorem encompasses the usual correctness criterion for control-flow analysis: a function labelled ℓ called at an application site labelled L is such that $\ell \in L$.

Table 1. Typing rules for the source language.

Well-formed types $\boxed{\psi \vdash s}$

$$\psi \vdash \texttt{int} \qquad \frac{\psi \vdash s \quad \psi \vdash t \quad L \subseteq dom(\psi)}{\psi \vdash (s \to t, L)}$$

Subtyping $\boxed{\psi \vdash s \leq t}$

$$\frac{\psi \vdash s}{\psi \vdash s \leq s} \qquad \frac{\psi \vdash s_1' \leq s_1 \quad \psi \vdash s_2 \leq s_2' \quad L \subseteq L' \subseteq dom(\psi)}{\psi \vdash (s_1 \to s_2, L) \leq (s_1' \to s_2', L')}$$

Well-formed contexts $\boxed{\psi \mid \Gamma \vdash \diamond}$

$$\frac{\forall \ell \text{ such that } \psi(\ell) = ((x_1{:}s_1, \ldots, x_n{:}s_n), s_{n+1}, s_{n+2}). \psi \vdash s_i}{\psi \mid \emptyset \vdash \diamond} \qquad \frac{\psi \mid \Gamma \vdash \diamond \quad x \notin \Gamma \quad \psi \vdash s}{\psi \mid \Gamma, x : s \vdash \diamond}$$

Well-formed declarations $\boxed{\psi \mid \Gamma \vdash D \rhd \Gamma'}$

$$\frac{\psi \mid \Gamma_i, f : (s_i \to t_i, \{\ell_i\}), x : s_i \vdash e : t_i \quad f, x \notin \Gamma_i}{\psi \mid \Gamma_i \vdash (\texttt{fun}^{\ell_i}\ f\ (x : s_i) = e) \rhd (f : (s_i \to t_i, \{\ell_i\}))} \quad \psi(\ell_i) = (\Gamma_i, s_i, t_i)$$

Well-formed expressions $\boxed{\psi \mid \Gamma \vdash e : s}$

$$\frac{\psi \mid \Gamma \vdash e : s \quad \psi \vdash s \leq s'}{\psi \mid \Gamma \vdash e : s'} \qquad \frac{\psi \mid \Gamma \vdash e : \texttt{int} \quad \psi \mid \Gamma \vdash e_i : s}{\psi \mid \Gamma \vdash (\texttt{if0}\ e\ \texttt{then}\ e_1\ \texttt{else}\ e_2) : s}$$

$$\frac{\psi \mid \Gamma, x : s, \Gamma' \vdash \diamond}{\psi \mid \Gamma, x : s, \Gamma' \vdash x : s} \qquad \frac{\psi \mid \Gamma \vdash D \rhd \Gamma' \quad \psi \mid \Gamma, \Gamma' \vdash e : s}{\psi \mid \Gamma \vdash \texttt{let}\ D\ \texttt{in}\ e : s}$$

$$\frac{\psi \mid \Gamma \vdash \diamond}{\psi \mid \Gamma \vdash n : \texttt{int}} \qquad \frac{\psi \mid \Gamma \vdash e' : t \quad \psi \mid \Gamma, x : t \vdash e : s \quad x \notin \Gamma}{\psi \mid \Gamma \vdash \texttt{let val}\ x = e'\ \texttt{in}\ e : s}$$

$$\frac{\psi \mid \Gamma \vdash e : \texttt{int}}{\psi \mid \Gamma \vdash (\texttt{op}\ e) : \texttt{int}} \qquad \frac{\psi \mid \Gamma \vdash e_1 : (s \to t, L) \quad \psi \mid \Gamma \vdash e_2 : s}{\psi \mid \Gamma \vdash e_1\ @_L\ e_2 : t} \quad L \subseteq dom(\psi)$$

3 The Target Language

The target language of defunctionalization is a first-order language with rudimentary datatype support. The syntax of the target language is given by the following grammar.

Table 2. Operational semantics for the source language.

$$(n,\gamma) \Downarrow n \qquad\qquad (x,\gamma) \Downarrow \gamma(x)$$

$$\frac{(e,\gamma) \Downarrow n}{(\texttt{succ}\ e,\gamma) \Downarrow (n+1)} \qquad\qquad \frac{(e,\gamma) \Downarrow n}{(\texttt{pred}\ e,\gamma) \Downarrow (n-1)}$$

$$\frac{(e,\gamma) \Downarrow 0 \qquad (e_1,\gamma) \Downarrow v}{(\texttt{if0}\ e\ \texttt{then}\ e_1\ \texttt{else}\ e_2,\gamma) \Downarrow v} \qquad\qquad \frac{(e,\gamma) \Downarrow (n+1) \qquad (e_2,\gamma) \Downarrow v}{(\texttt{if0}\ e\ \texttt{then}\ e_1\ \texttt{else}\ e_2,\gamma) \Downarrow v}$$

$$\frac{(e',\gamma[f \mapsto \langle \texttt{fun}^\ell\ f\ (x:s) = e,\gamma\rangle]) \Downarrow v}{(\texttt{let fun}^\ell\ f\ (x:s) = e\ \texttt{in}\ e',\gamma) \Downarrow v} \qquad\qquad \frac{(e,\gamma) \Downarrow v' \qquad (e',\gamma[x \mapsto v']) \Downarrow v}{(\texttt{let val}\ x = e\ \texttt{in}\ e',\gamma) \Downarrow v}$$

$$\frac{(e,\gamma) \Downarrow \langle \texttt{fun}^\ell\ f\ (x:s) = e'',\gamma'\rangle = v_0 \quad (e',\gamma) \Downarrow v' \quad (e'',\gamma'[f \mapsto v_0, x \mapsto v']) \Downarrow v}{((e\ @_L\ e'),\gamma) \Downarrow v}\ \ell \in L$$

$$\begin{aligned}
s &::= \texttt{unit} \mid \texttt{int} \mid (s \times s) \mid (\alpha_1 \cup \ldots \cup \alpha_n) \\
D &::= \texttt{tagtype}\ \alpha \ = \ C\ \texttt{of}\ s \mid \texttt{fun}\ f\ (x:s) = e \\
e &::= x \mid n \mid (\texttt{op}\ e) \mid (\texttt{if0}\ e\ \texttt{then}\ e_1\ \texttt{else}\ e_2) \mid \langle\rangle \mid \langle e_1, e_2\rangle \\
&\quad \mid (\texttt{proj}_1\ e) \mid (\texttt{proj}_2\ e) \mid f(e) \mid C(e) \\
&\quad \mid (\texttt{case}\ e\ \texttt{of}\ C_1(x) \Rightarrow e_1 \mid \ldots \mid C_n(x) \Rightarrow e_n) \\
&\quad \mid (\texttt{let}\ D\ \ldots\ D\ \texttt{in}\ e) \mid (\texttt{let val}\ x = e\ \texttt{in}\ e)
\end{aligned}$$

The symbols α, β range over type variables and C over constructors. Types in the target language include product types and union types but not function types. As in Pascal, there is a means of declaring functions inside other functions; we will use this feature in our translation of lightweight defunctionalization in Section 6.

To make programs in the target simpler to read, we adopt a few notational conventions. Terms are identified up to renaming of bound variables; note that the expression ($\texttt{tagtype}\ \alpha\ =\ C\ \texttt{of}\ s$) binds both α and C. Product types are extended to $(s_1 \times \ldots \times s_n)$, with the convention that such types associate to the right; we also use the notation ($\texttt{proj}_i\ e$) for projections from these expanded types, with tuples extended correspondingly, and use pattern-matching syntax in function declarations instead of projections. Union types that are the same except for the order are regarded as equal types.

The type rules for the target language appear in Tables 3 and 4. In these rules, type contexts Δ are lists of type variables and bindings of constructors and ordinary variables to "extended types" σ, which are ordinary types s or function types $(s \to t)$. Note that the extended function types are "second-class": functions with such types can not accept functions as arguments and return functions as results. Also, note that in the rule for `let`, the declarations $D_1, \ldots, D_n$ are possibly mutually recursive. This explains the use of type contexts $\Delta_1, \ldots, \Delta_n$ in the antecedent of the rule for `let`.

The operational semantics of the target language appears in Table 5. We use the same style as the operational semantics for PCFA, i.e., a natural semantics,

Table 3. Typing rules for the target language.

Well-formed types $\boxed{\Delta \vdash s}$

$$\frac{\Delta \vdash \diamond}{\Delta \vdash \texttt{int}} \qquad \frac{\Delta \vdash \diamond}{\Delta \vdash \texttt{unit}} \qquad \frac{\Delta \vdash \diamond \qquad \alpha_i \in \Delta}{\Delta \vdash \alpha_1 \cup \ldots \cup \alpha_n} \qquad \frac{\Delta \vdash s \qquad \Delta \vdash t}{\Delta \vdash (s \times t)}$$

Subtyping $\boxed{\Delta \vdash s \leq t}$

$$\frac{\Delta \vdash s}{\Delta \vdash s \leq s} \qquad \frac{\Delta \vdash (\alpha_1 \cup \ldots \cup \alpha_n) \quad \{j_1, \ldots, j_k\} \subseteq \{1, \ldots, n\}}{\Delta \vdash (\alpha_{j_1} \cup \ldots \cup \alpha_{j_k}) \leq (\alpha_1 \cup \ldots \cup \alpha_n)}$$

$$\frac{\Delta \vdash s \leq s' \qquad \Delta \vdash s' \leq s''}{\Delta \vdash s \leq s''} \qquad \frac{\Delta \vdash s_i \leq s_i'}{\Delta \vdash (s_1 \times \ldots \times s_n) \leq (s_1' \times \ldots \times s_n')}$$

Well-formed contexts $\boxed{\Delta \vdash \diamond}$

$$\emptyset \vdash \diamond \qquad \frac{\Delta \vdash \diamond \qquad \alpha \notin \Delta}{\Delta, \alpha \vdash \diamond} \qquad \frac{\Delta \vdash \diamond \qquad \Delta \vdash s \qquad x \notin \Delta}{\Delta, x : s \vdash \diamond}$$

$$\frac{\Delta \vdash \alpha \qquad \Delta \vdash s \qquad C \notin \Delta}{\Delta, C : s \to \alpha \vdash \diamond} \qquad \frac{\Delta \vdash \diamond \qquad \Delta \vdash s \qquad \Delta \vdash t \qquad f \notin \Delta}{\Delta, f : s \to t \vdash \diamond}$$

Well-formed declarations $\boxed{\Delta \vdash D \rhd \Delta'}$

$$\frac{\Delta, \alpha, C : s \to \alpha, \Delta' \vdash \diamond}{\Delta, \alpha, C : s \to \alpha, \Delta' \vdash (\texttt{tagtype}\ \alpha \ = \ C\ \texttt{of}\ s) \rhd (\alpha, C : (s \to \alpha))}$$

$$\frac{\Delta, f : (s \to t), \Delta', x : s \vdash e : t \qquad f, x \notin \Delta, \Delta'}{\Delta, f : (s \to t), \Delta' \vdash (\texttt{fun}\ f\ (x : s) = e) \rhd (f : s \to t)}$$

and write $(e, \delta) \Downarrow v$ when the term e, in environment δ, returns the final value v of the form n, $\langle\rangle$, $\langle v_1, v_2\rangle$, or $C(v)$. It is straightforward to prove the following theorem:

Theorem 2 (Subject Reduction). *Suppose* $\emptyset \vdash e : s$ *and* $(e, \emptyset) \Downarrow v$. *Then* $\emptyset \vdash v : s$ *is derivable.*

In addition to the operational semantics, we also define a denotational semantics of the target. The denotational semantics – with its emphasis on extensional functions and interpretation of recursion as least-fixed-point – simplifies some of the proofs, especially those involving data abstraction. The denotational se-

Table 4. Typing rules for the target language, continued.

Well-formed expressions $\boxed{\Delta \vdash e : s}$

$$\frac{\Delta, x : s, \Delta' \vdash \diamond}{\Delta, x : s, \Delta' \vdash x : s} \qquad \frac{\Delta \vdash \diamond}{\Delta \vdash n : \mathtt{int}}$$

$$\frac{\Delta \vdash e : \mathtt{int}}{\Delta \vdash (\mathtt{op}\ e) : \mathtt{int}} \qquad \frac{\Delta \vdash e : \mathtt{int} \quad \Delta \vdash e_i : s}{\Delta \vdash (\mathtt{if0}\ e\ \mathtt{then}\ e_1\ \mathtt{else}\ e_2) : s}$$

$$\frac{\Delta \vdash \diamond}{\Delta \vdash \langle\rangle : \mathtt{unit}} \qquad \frac{\Delta, f : (s \to t), \Delta' \vdash e : s}{\Delta, f : (s \to t), \Delta' \vdash f(e) : t}$$

$$\frac{\Delta \vdash e_i : s_i}{\Delta \vdash \langle e_1, e_2\rangle : (s_1 \times s_2)} \qquad \frac{\Delta \vdash e : (s_1 \times s_2)}{\Delta \vdash (\mathtt{proj}_i\ e) : s_i}$$

$$\frac{\Delta, \alpha, C : (s \to \alpha), \Delta' \vdash e : s}{\Delta, \alpha, C : (s \to \alpha), \Delta' \vdash C(e) : \alpha} \qquad \frac{\Delta \vdash e : s \quad \Delta \vdash s \leq s'}{\Delta \vdash e : s'}$$

$$\frac{\Delta \vdash e : (\alpha_1 \cup \ldots \cup \alpha_n) \quad \Delta, x : s_i \vdash e_i : s \quad \Delta(C_i) = (s_i \to \alpha_i)}{\Delta \vdash (\mathtt{case}\ e\ \mathtt{of}\ C_1(x) \Rightarrow e_1 \mid \ldots \mid C_n(x) \Rightarrow e_n) : s}$$

$$\frac{\Delta, \Delta_1, \ldots, \Delta_n \vdash D_i \rhd \Delta_i, \text{ for all } i \quad \Delta, \Delta_1, \ldots, \Delta_n \vdash e : s}{\Delta \vdash (\mathtt{let}\ D_1 \ldots\ D_n\ \mathtt{in}\ e) : s}$$

$$\frac{\Delta \vdash e' : t \quad \Delta, x : t \vdash e : s \quad x \notin \Delta}{\Delta \vdash (\mathtt{let\ val}\ x = e'\ \mathtt{in}\ e) : s}$$

mantics of the target language is set-theoretic: no domain theory or posets are needed due to the lack of higher-order functions. It is given in two parts: a meaning function for types and a meaning function for terms. Since types involve type variables, the meaning function for types requires a notion of type environment. Suppose $\Delta \vdash \diamond$ and η is a finite partial function from type variables to sets. We say η is **type environment for Δ** if

- For any $\alpha \in \Delta$, $\alpha \in dom(\eta)$, and
- If $\alpha_0 \neq \alpha_1$ with $\eta(\alpha_i)$ defined, then $\eta(\alpha_0)$ and $\eta(\alpha_1)$ are disjoint sets.

Note that

Proposition 1. *For any $\Delta \vdash \diamond$, there is a canonical type environment η for Δ.*

The proof uses standard set-theoretic techniques. For example, if

$$\Delta = \alpha, C : (\mathtt{int} \times \alpha) \cup \mathtt{unit} \to \alpha,$$

Table 5. Operational semantics for the target language.

$$(n, \delta) \Downarrow n \qquad (\langle\rangle, \delta) \Downarrow \langle\rangle$$

$$\frac{(e, \delta) \Downarrow n}{(\texttt{succ}\ e, \delta) \Downarrow (n+1)} \qquad \frac{(e, \delta) \Downarrow n}{(\texttt{pred}\ e, \delta) \Downarrow (n-1)}$$

$$\frac{(e, \delta) \Downarrow 0 \quad (e_1, \delta) \Downarrow v}{(\texttt{if0}\ e\ \texttt{then}\ e_1\ \texttt{else}\ e_2, \delta) \Downarrow v} \qquad \frac{(e, \delta) \Downarrow (n+1) \quad (e_2, \delta) \Downarrow v}{(\texttt{if0}\ e\ \texttt{then}\ e_1\ \texttt{else}\ e_2, \delta) \Downarrow v}$$

$$\frac{(e_i, \delta) \Downarrow v_i}{(\langle e_1, e_2\rangle, \delta) \Downarrow \langle v_1, v_2\rangle} \qquad \frac{(e, \delta) \Downarrow \langle v_1, v_2\rangle}{(\texttt{proj}_i\ e, \delta) \Downarrow v_i}$$

$$\frac{(e, \delta) \Downarrow C_i(v') \quad (e_i, \delta[x \mapsto v']) \Downarrow v}{(\texttt{case}\ e\ \texttt{of}\ C_1(x) \Rightarrow e_1 \mid \ldots \mid C_n(x) \Rightarrow e_n, \delta) \Downarrow v} \qquad \frac{(e, \delta) \Downarrow v}{(C(e), \delta) \Downarrow C(v)}$$

$$(x, \delta) \Downarrow \delta(x) \qquad \frac{(e, \delta) \Downarrow v}{(\texttt{let}\ \ \texttt{in}\ e, \delta) \Downarrow v}$$

$$\frac{(\texttt{let}\ D_1 \ldots D_n\ \texttt{in}\ e, \delta) \Downarrow v}{(\texttt{let}\ \texttt{tagtype}\ \alpha_1 \ = \ C_1\ \texttt{of}\ s_1\ D_1 \ldots D_n\ \texttt{in}\ e, \delta) \Downarrow v}$$

$$\frac{(\texttt{let}\ D_1 \ldots D_n\ \texttt{in}\ e, \delta[f \mapsto \texttt{fun}\ f\ (x : s) = e']) \Downarrow v}{(\texttt{let}\ \texttt{fun}\ f\ (x : s) = e'\ D_1 \ldots D_n\ \texttt{in}\ e, \delta) \Downarrow v}$$

$$\frac{\delta(f) = (\texttt{fun}\ f\ (x : s) = e') \quad (e, \delta) \Downarrow v' \quad (e', \delta[x \mapsto v']) \Downarrow v}{(f(e), \delta) \Downarrow v}$$

$$\frac{(e', \delta) \Downarrow v' \quad (e, \delta[x \mapsto v']) \Downarrow v}{(\texttt{let}\ \texttt{val}\ x = e'\ \texttt{in}\ e, \delta) \Downarrow v}$$

the canonical η assigns α to finite lists of integers. For a type environment η, and a type s, we define $[\![\Delta \vdash s]\!]\eta$ as follows:

$$\begin{aligned}
[\![\Delta \vdash \texttt{unit}]\!]\eta &= \{\langle\rangle\} \\
[\![\Delta \vdash \texttt{int}]\!]\eta &= \mathbf{N} \\
[\![\Delta \vdash \alpha_1 \cup \ldots \cup \alpha_n]\!]\eta &= \eta(\alpha_1) \cup \ldots \cup \eta(\alpha_n) \\
[\![\Delta \vdash s \times s']\!]\eta &= [\![\Delta \vdash s]\!]\eta \times [\![\Delta \vdash s']\!]\eta
\end{aligned}$$

Since terms involve variables too, the meaning of terms also requires a notion of environment. An (ordinary) **environment** ρ is a finite partial function from variables to elements of sets or to partial functions. Just like type environments, there are some well-formedness conditions on environments. Suppose ρ is an environment, and η is a type environment compatible with Δ. We say that ρ is **compatible with** η, Δ if for any $x \in dom(\Delta)$,

- If $x : s \in \Delta$, then $\rho(x) \in [\![\Delta \vdash s]\!]\eta$;
- If $(f : s \to t) \in \Delta$, then $\rho(f)$ is a partial function from $[\![\Delta \vdash s]\!]\eta$ to $[\![\Delta \vdash t]\!]\eta$; and
- If $(C : s \to \alpha) \in \Delta$, then $\rho(C)$ is an isomorphism from $[\![\Delta \vdash s]\!]\eta$ to $\eta(\alpha)$.

Suppose ρ is compatible with η, Δ. The meaning of a judgement $\Delta \vdash e : s$ in the target language can be defined by induction on the typing derivation. The semantics of terms is standard (see *e.g.*, Gunter's text [13] or Mitchell's text [24]). For space reasons, we omit most of the clauses and concentrate on the meaning of `let`. Suppose the term is $e = (\texttt{let}\ D_1 \ldots D_n\ \texttt{in}\ e')$, and we want to interpret it in the type environment η and ordinary environment ρ. Let $E_1, \ldots, E_m$ be the type declarations (each of the form $(\texttt{tagtype}\ \alpha_i\ =\ C_i\ \texttt{of}\ s_i)$) and let $F_1, \ldots, F_k$ be the function declarations (each of the form $(\texttt{fun}\ f_i\ (x : s_i) = e_i)$). Let η' be the canonical extension of η compatible with

$$\Delta' = \Delta, \alpha_1, C_1 : s_1 \to \alpha_1, \ldots, \alpha_m, C_m : s_m \to \alpha_m, f_1 : s_1 \to t_1, \ldots, f_k : s_k \to t_k$$

(which must exist by the Proposition above). Let h_i be the isomorphism from $[\![\Delta \vdash s_i]\!]\eta$ to $\eta(\alpha_i)$, and let $g_1, \ldots, g_n$ be the least partial functions such that for all i and any $d \in [\![\Delta' \vdash s_i]\!]\eta'$,

$$g_i(d) = [\![\Delta', x : s_i \vdash e_i : s_i']\!]\eta'\ \rho'[x \mapsto d]$$

where

$$\rho' = \rho[C_1 \mapsto h_1, \ldots, C_m \mapsto h_m, f_1 \mapsto g_1, \ldots, f_n \mapsto g_n]$$

Then define

$$[\![\Delta \vdash e : s]\!]\eta\rho \simeq [\![\Delta' \vdash e' : s]\!]\eta'\ \rho'$$

where $\simeq$ means that the left side is defined and equal to the right side iff the right side is defined.

The following theorem shows that we may use the denotational semantics to reason safely about programs:

Theorem 3 (Adequacy). *Suppose* $\emptyset \vdash e : \mathit{int}$. *Then* $[\![\emptyset \vdash e : \mathit{int}]\!]\emptyset\emptyset = n$ *iff* $(e, \emptyset) \Downarrow n$.

Proof. (Sketch) The ($\Leftarrow$) direction relies on an induction on the proof of $(e, \emptyset) \Downarrow n$. The ($\Rightarrow$) direction, on the other hand, relies on a lexicographic induction on (k, e), where k denotes a finite number of unwindings of recursive function definitions.

4 Defunctionalization

We next show how to translate the source language to the target, and prove that the translation is correct.

The translation is a modified version of Reynolds's defunctionalization [32,34] that takes advantage of control-flow information. In defunctionalization, functions in the source are represented in the target as tagged tuples, where the tag indicates the code of the closure, and the tuple represents the values of the free variables of the closure. Function application in the source must therefore be made explicit in the target via an *apply* function. Specifically, if f_t is the representation in the target of a source function f_s, and a_t is the representation in the target of an argument a_s of f_s, then the result of $apply(f_t, a_t)$ will be the representation in the target of the result of $f_s(a_s)$ [32,34].

Before giving the details of the translation, we give an example to show how all of the elements of the target language are used in the translation. Consider the following implementation of sets-as-characteristic functions in ML:

```
let fun empty x = false in
let fun insert x s =
    let fun test(y) = (x=y) || (s y) in test in
let fun member x s = s x in
...
```

When rendered in a simple extension of PCFA with booleans, the above code becomes

```
let fun^ℓ1 empty (x:int) = false in
let fun^ℓ2 insert(x:int) =
  (let fun^ℓ3 check(s:u) =
   let fun^ℓ4 test(y:int) = (x = y) || (s @_{ℓ1,ℓ4} y) in test
   in check) in
let fun^ℓ5 member(x:int) =
  (let fun^ℓ6 check'(s:u) = s @_{ℓ1,ℓ4} x in check') in
...
```

where u is the type $(\texttt{int}\rightarrow\texttt{bool},\{\ell_1,\ell_4\})$.

The representation of functions in the target language is based on abstract types and constructor functions. We translate each function label into an abstract type declaration, where the concrete representation type reflects the types of the free variables. For the functions `empty`, `insert` and `member`, we set

$$\begin{aligned}
&\texttt{tagtype}\ \alpha_1 = \mathrm{C}_1\ \texttt{of unit}\\
&\texttt{tagtype}\ \alpha_2 = \mathrm{C}_2\ \texttt{of}\ \alpha_1\\
&\texttt{tagtype}\ \alpha_5 = \mathrm{C}_5\ \texttt{of}\ \alpha_1 \times \alpha_2
\end{aligned}$$

since `insert` lies in the scope of `empty` and `member` lies in the scope of `empty` and `insert`. (A less simplistic defunctionalization would take into account only free variables.) Likewise, the corresponding types for the functions `check`, `test`, and `check'` are

$$\begin{aligned}
&\texttt{tagtype}\ \alpha_3 = \mathrm{C}_3\ \texttt{of}\ \alpha_1 \times \alpha_2 \times \texttt{int}\\
&\texttt{tagtype}\ \alpha_4 = \mathrm{C}_4\ \texttt{of}\ \alpha_1 \times \alpha_2 \times \texttt{int} \times \alpha_3 \times (\alpha_1 \cup \alpha_4)\\
&\texttt{tagtype}\ \alpha_6 = \mathrm{C}_6\ \texttt{of}\ \alpha_1 \times \alpha_2 \times \alpha_5 \times \texttt{int}
\end{aligned}$$

Note that the definition of α_4 is recursive: since `s` is a free variable of `test`, and since the type of `s` in the source is $(\texttt{int} \rightarrow \texttt{int}, \{\ell_1, \ell_4\})$, the type translation of `s` in the target is the disjoint union type $\alpha_1 \cup \alpha_4$, making α_4's definition recursive.

Function application in the source is defined via *apply* functions in the target. A standard defunctionalization would yield the following monolithic version of *apply*.

```
fun apply⟨F,a⟩ =
  case F of
    (empty as C1⟨⟩) => false
  | (insert as C2⟨d⟩) =>
    let val check = C3⟨d,insert,a⟩ in check
  | (check as C3⟨d,e,x⟩) =>
    let val test  = C4⟨d,e,x,check,a⟩ in test
  | (test as C4⟨d,e,x,v,s⟩) =>
    (x = a) || apply(s,a)
  | (member as C5⟨d,e⟩) =>
    let val check'= C6⟨d,e,member,a⟩ in check'
  | (check' as C6⟨d,e,v,x⟩) => apply(a,x)
```

Using the control-flow types, we can split the monolithic *apply* function into multiple (possibly mutually recursive) application functions, one for each function label [7,41]. Thus, the above monolithic `apply` function can be split as

```
fun apply1(empty as C1⟨⟩, a)  = false
fun apply2(insert as C2⟨d⟩,a) =
  let val check = C3⟨d,insert,a⟩ in check
fun apply3(check as C3⟨d,e,x⟩,a)=
  let val test = C4⟨d,e,x,check,a⟩ in test
fun apply4(test as C4⟨d,e,x,v,s⟩,a)=
  (x = a) || (case s of
                 (empty as C1⟨⟩) => apply1(empty,a)
               | (test  as C4⟨d,e,x,v,s⟩) => apply4(test,a))
  ...
```

Note how the case analysis occurs only at the application points. Also, note that while the *source program has no recursive functions, the target program has a recursive function*, namely, $\texttt{apply}_4$. This is one source of complication in proving the correctness of defunctionalization.

To treat the representation of function types more abstractly, it is helpful to use functions to construct values:

```
fun make1()       = C1⟨⟩         fun make4(d,e,x,v,a)= C4⟨d,e,x,v,a⟩
fun make2(d)      = C2⟨d⟩        fun make5(d,e)      = C5⟨d,e⟩
fun make3(d,e,x)= C3⟨d,e,x⟩  fun make6(d,e,v,x)  = C6⟨d,e,v,x⟩
```

This is a key idea: the `make` functions for different program transformations, *e.g.*, lightweight defunctionalization (Section 6), will use different concrete representations of functions in the source program. The complete translation of the example appears in Figure 1.

The algorithm for defunctionalization works by recursion on the typing derivation of the source program. A typing derivation for the judgement $\psi \mid \Gamma \vdash e : s$ in the source language is translated into the target language derivation of $\psi^*, \Gamma^* \vdash e^* : s^*\ ;\ D$, where

– For types, $\texttt{int}^* = \texttt{int}$ and $(s \to t, \{\ell_1, \ldots, \ell_k\})^* = \alpha_1 \cup \ldots \cup \alpha_k$.

```
let tagtype α1 = C1 of unit
    tagtype α2 = C2 of α1
    tagtype α3 = C3 of α1 × α2×int
    tagtype α4 = C4 of α1 × α2×int×α3 × (α1 ∪ α4)
    tagtype α5 = C5 of α1 × α2
    tagtype α6 = C6 of α1 × α2 × α5×int
    fun make1()            = C1⟨⟩
    fun make2(d)           = C2⟨d⟩
    fun make3(d,e,x)       = C3⟨d,e,x⟩
    fun make4(d,e,x,v,a)   = C4⟨d,e,x,v,a⟩
    fun make5(d,e)         = C5⟨d,e⟩
    fun make6(d,e,v,x)     = C6⟨d,e,v,x⟩
    fun apply1(empty as C1⟨⟩, a)   = false
    fun apply2(insert as C2⟨d⟩,a) =
      let val check = make3(d,insert,a) in check
    fun apply3(check as C3⟨d,e,x⟩,a)=
      let val test = make4(d,e,x,check,a) in test
    fun apply4(test as C4⟨d,e,x,v,s⟩,a)=
      (x = a) || (case s of
                   (empty as C1⟨⟩) => apply1(empty,a)
                 | (test  as C4⟨d,e,x,v,s⟩) => apply4(test,a))
      ...
 in let val empty  = make1() in
    let val insert = make2(empty) in
    let val member = make5(empty,insert) in
 ...
```

Fig. 1. Defunctionalization of sets-as-functions example.

– For label contexts,

$$(\ell_1 \mapsto (\Gamma_1, s_1, t_1), \ldots)^* = (\alpha_1, \ldots, C_1 : \Gamma_1^\dagger \to \alpha_1, \ldots, \mathit{make}_1 : \Gamma_1^\dagger \to \alpha_1, \ldots, \\ \mathit{apply}_1 : \alpha_1 \times s_1^* \to t_1^*, \ldots)$$

where $(x_1 : s_1, \ldots, x_k : s_k)^\dagger = (s_1^* \times \ldots \times s_k^*)$. The ψ^* thus provide the specifications for the abstract types, application functions and creation functions (*i.e.*, the *make*'s) for every function label defined in the program. In an actual implementation, one might want to have *apply* functions defined for sets of labels that label the application sites in a program. However, for technical simplicity, we do not pursue this direction in this paper.
– For type contexts, $(x_1 : s_1, \ldots, x_k : s_k)^* = (x_1 : s_1^*, \ldots, x_k : s_k^*)$.
– For terms, e^* is a term in the target and D is a collection of declarations in the target. The declarations in the target provide implementations of the abstract types, application functions, and creation functions specified in ψ^*.

The complete specification appears in Table 6. Consider, for instance, the translation rule for applications. The algorithm uses the information encoded in ψ as

Table 6. Defunctionalization as a type-directed translation.

Declarations $\boxed{(\psi \mid \Gamma \vdash D \rhd \Gamma') \Rightarrow (\psi^*, \Gamma^* \vdash D^* : \alpha; D')}$

$$\frac{\psi \mid \Gamma, f : (s \to t, \{\ell\}), x : s \vdash e : t \quad f, x \notin \Gamma}{\psi \mid \Gamma \vdash (\mathtt{fun}^{\ell}\, f\,(x : s) = e) \rhd (f : s \to t, \{\ell\})} \Rightarrow \frac{\psi^*, \Gamma^*, f : \alpha, x : s^* \vdash e^* : t^* \;;\; D}{\psi^*, \Gamma^* \vdash \mathit{make}\langle x_1, \ldots, x_n\rangle : \alpha \;;\; D \cup D'}$$

$$\text{where} \begin{cases} \psi(\ell) = (\Gamma, s, t) \\ \Gamma = \langle x_1 : u_1, \ldots, x_n : u_n\rangle \\ D' = \{\, \mathtt{tagtype}\ \alpha \ = \ C \ \mathtt{of}\ \Gamma^*, \\ \qquad \mathtt{fun}\ \mathit{make}\,(\langle x_1, \ldots, x_n\rangle) = C\langle x_1, \ldots, x_n\rangle, \\ \qquad \mathtt{fun}\ \mathit{apply}\,(f\ \mathtt{as}\ C\langle x_1, \ldots, x_n\rangle, x) = e^*\} \end{cases}$$

Expressions $\boxed{(\psi \mid \Gamma \vdash e : s) \Rightarrow (\psi^*, \Gamma^* \vdash e^* : s^*; D)}$

$$\frac{\psi \mid \Gamma, x : s, \Gamma' \vdash \diamond}{\psi \mid \Gamma, x : s, \Gamma' \vdash x : s} \Rightarrow \frac{\psi^*, \Gamma^*, x : s^*, (\Gamma')^* \vdash \diamond}{\psi^*, \Gamma^*, x : s^*, (\Gamma')^* \vdash x : s^* \;;\; \emptyset}$$

$$\frac{\psi \mid \Gamma \vdash \diamond}{\psi \mid \Gamma \vdash n : \mathtt{int}} \Rightarrow \frac{\psi^*, \Gamma^* \vdash \diamond}{\psi^*, \Gamma^* \vdash n : \mathtt{int} \;;\; \emptyset}$$

$$\frac{\psi \mid \Gamma \vdash e : \mathtt{int}}{\psi \mid \Gamma \vdash (\mathtt{op}\ e) : \mathtt{int}} \Rightarrow \frac{\psi^*, \Gamma^* \vdash e^* : \mathtt{int} \;;\; D}{\psi^*, \Gamma^* \vdash (\mathtt{op}\ e^*) : \mathtt{int} \;;\; D}$$

$$\frac{\psi \mid \Gamma \vdash e : \mathtt{int} \qquad \psi \mid \Gamma \vdash e_i : s}{\psi \mid \Gamma \vdash (\mathtt{if0}\ e\ \mathtt{then}\ e_1\ \mathtt{else}\ e_2) : s} \Rightarrow \frac{\psi^*, \Gamma^* \vdash e^* : \mathtt{int} \;;\; D \qquad \psi^*, \Gamma^* \vdash e_i^* : s^* \;;\; D_i}{\psi^*, \Gamma^* \vdash (\mathtt{if0}\ e^*\ \mathtt{then}\ e_1^*\ \mathtt{else}\ e_2^*) : s^*; D \cup D_i}$$

$$\frac{\psi \mid \Gamma \vdash e' : t \ \psi \mid \Gamma, x : t \vdash e : s \ x \notin \Gamma}{\psi \mid \Gamma \vdash \mathtt{let\ val}\ x = e'\ \mathtt{in}\ e : s} \Rightarrow \frac{\psi^*, \Gamma^* \vdash (e')^* : t^*; D_1 \ \psi^*, \Gamma^*, x : t^* \vdash e^* : s^*; D_2}{\psi^*, \Gamma^* \vdash \mathtt{let\ val}\ x = (e')^*\ \mathtt{in}\ e^* : s^* \;;\; D_1 \cup D_2}$$

$$\frac{\psi \mid \Gamma \vdash e : s \quad \psi \mid \Gamma \vdash s \le t}{\psi \mid \Gamma \vdash e : t} \Rightarrow \frac{\psi^*, \Gamma^* \vdash e^* : s^*; D \quad \psi^*, \Gamma^* \vdash s^* \le t^*}{\psi^*, \Gamma^* \vdash e^* : t^*; D}$$

$$\frac{\psi \mid \Gamma \vdash D \rhd \Gamma' \quad \psi \mid \Gamma, \Gamma' \vdash e : s}{\psi \mid \Gamma \vdash \mathtt{let}\ D\ \mathtt{in}\ e : s} \Rightarrow \frac{\psi^*, \Gamma^* \vdash D^* : \alpha_i; D_1 \ \psi^*, \Gamma^*, (\Gamma')^* \vdash e^* : s^*; D_2}{\psi^*, \Gamma^* \vdash \mathtt{let\ val}\ f = D^*\ \mathtt{in}\ e^* : s^*; D_1 \cup D_2}$$

where $D = (\mathtt{fun}^{\ell_i}\, f\,(x : s_i) = e')$

$$\frac{\psi \mid \Gamma \vdash e_1 : (s \to t, L) \quad \psi \mid \Gamma \vdash e_2 : s}{\psi \mid \Gamma \vdash e_1 \mathbin{@_L} e_2 : t} \Rightarrow \frac{\psi^*, \Gamma^* \vdash e_1^* : \alpha_{i_1} \cup \ldots; D_1 \quad \psi^*, \Gamma^* \vdash e_2^* : s^*; D_2}{\psi^*, \Gamma^* \vdash e : t^*; D_1 \cup D_2}$$

$$\text{where} \begin{cases} L = \{\ell_{i_1}, \ldots, \ell_{i_k}\} \\ e = \mathtt{case}\ e_1^*\ \mathtt{of} \\ \quad (f_{i_1}\ \mathtt{as}\ C_{i_1}(x)) \Rightarrow \mathit{apply}_{i_1}(f_{i_1}, e_2^*) \\ \quad | \ldots \\ \quad | \ (f_{i_k}\ \mathtt{as}\ C_{i_k}(x)) \Rightarrow \mathit{apply}_{i_k}(f_{i_k}, e_2^*) \end{cases}$$

well as in the context Γ. Note that $apply_1, \ldots, apply_k$ are all specified in ψ^* and defined in D_1 since $L \subseteq dom(\psi)$.

The translation seems straightforward, but it must be proven correct; that is, if we translate a source program, the source and target programs agree on the answers they produce. Correctness is particularly crucial here, since the proof of correctness of various transformations relies on the proof of correctness of defunctionalization. There are two parts to correctness. First, one must establish that the translation produces well-formed programs.

Lemma 1. *If $\psi \mid \Gamma \vdash e : s$ is provable in PCFA and $(\psi \mid \Gamma \vdash e : s) \Rightarrow (\psi^*, \Gamma^* \vdash e^* : s^*\ ;\ D)$ then $\psi^*, \Gamma^* \vdash e^* : s^*$ is provable in the target language.*

A similar property holds for every declaration $d \in D$.

Theorem 4. *If $\psi \mid \emptyset \vdash e : \mathtt{int}$ is provable in PCFA and $(\psi \mid \emptyset \vdash e : \mathtt{int}) \Rightarrow (\psi^* \vdash e^* : \mathtt{int}\ ;\ D)$ then $\emptyset \vdash \mathtt{let}\ D\ \mathtt{in}\ e^* : \mathtt{int}$ is provable in the target language.*

The proofs go by induction on the typing derivation in the source language.

A more difficult property to establish is correctness of the translation, which relates the final answers produced by a program and its translation.

Theorem 5 (Correctness). *If $\psi \mid \emptyset \vdash e : \mathtt{int}$ is provable in PCFA and $(\psi \mid \emptyset \vdash e : \mathtt{int}) \Rightarrow (\psi^* \vdash e^* : \mathtt{int}\ ;\ D)$ then $(e, \emptyset) \Downarrow n$ in PCFA iff $(\mathtt{let}\ D\ \mathtt{in}\ e^*, \emptyset) \Downarrow n$ in the target language.*

Proof. (Sketch) Using the Adequacy Theorem 3, it is enough to show $(e, \emptyset) \Downarrow n$ iff $[\![\emptyset \vdash \mathtt{let}\ D\ \mathtt{in}\ e^* : \mathtt{int}]\!]\emptyset\emptyset = n$. Again, we use induction for the $(\Leftarrow)$ direction and lexicographic induction for the $(\Rightarrow)$ direction.

The reason for the lexicographic induction in the $(\Rightarrow)$ direction is due to recursion. Indeed, we know of no other proofs of correctness (that is, both directions) for ordinary or CFA-based defunctionalization in the presence of recursion.

5 Flow-Based Inlining

The first example, flow-based inlining or what Shivers calls "super β-reduction", is best described by way of the example from the introduction. We want to show that

```
let fun^ℓ1 g x = x in
let fun^ℓ2 f h =
  (let fun^ℓ3 u y =
   if0 y then (h @{ℓ1} 1) else f @{ℓ2} h @{ℓ3} (h @{ℓ1} y)
   in u) in
f @{ℓ2} g @{ℓ3} 2
```

is the same as

```
let fun^{ℓ1} g x = x in
let fun^{ℓ2} f h =
  (let fun^{ℓ3} u y =
    if0 y then (g @_{ℓ1} 1) else f @_{ℓ2} g @_{ℓ3} (g @_{ℓ1} y)
    in u) in
f @_{ℓ2} g @_{ℓ3} 2
```

where the example is slightly reformulated to take into account that recursive functions in PCFA take one argument. Our method of proof is to prove that the defunctionalized versions of these two programs are equivalent in the denotational model of the target. By the Adequacy Theorem 3, the programs in the target will return the same results operationally; thus, by the Correctness Theorem 5, the original programs in PCFA will return the same results operationally.

```
let tagtype a1 = C1 of unit
    fun make1 <> = C1<>
    fun apply1 (g as C1<>, x) = x
    tagtype a2 = C2 of a1
    fun make2 (g) = C2<g>
    fun apply2 (f as C2<g>, h) = let val u = make3(h, f, g) in u
    tagtype a3 = C3 of a1 x a2 x a1
    fun make3 (<h, f, g>) = C3 <h, f, g>
    fun apply3 (u as C3<h, f, g>, y) =
      if0 y then apply1 (h,1)
             else apply3 (apply2(f,h),apply1(h,y))
in let val g = make1 <> in
   let val f = make2 (g) in
   apply3 (apply2(f,g), 2)

let tagtype a1 = C1 of unit
    fun make1 <> = C1<>
    fun apply1 (g as C1<>, x) = x
    tagtype a2 = C2 of a1
    fun make2 (g) = C2<g>
    fun apply2 (f as C2<g>, h) = let val u = make3(h, f, g) in u
    tagtype a3 = C3 of a1 x a2 x a1
    fun make3 (<h, f, g>) = C3 <h, f, g>
    fun apply3 (u as C3<h, f, g>, y) =
      if0 y then apply1 (g,1)
             else apply3 (apply2(f,g),apply1(g,y))
in  let val g = make1 <> in
    let val f = make2 (g) in
    apply3 (apply2(f,g), 2)
```

Fig. 2. Translation of flow-based inlining examples.

The translation of the original and alternative programs appears in Figure 2. The proof of equivalence of the above two pieces of code uses least fixpoint reasoning and beta reduction. For the first piece of code, we can β-reduce it to

```
apply3 (apply2(f,g), 2)
  = apply3 (make3 (g,f,g), 2)
  = apply3 (C3 <g,f,g>, 2)
  = if0 2 then apply1 (g, 1)
    else apply3 (apply2(f,g), apply1(g,2))
  = if0 2 then apply1 (g, 1)
    else apply3 (make3 (g,f,g), apply1(g,2))
```

and for the second piece of code, we can β-reduce it to

```
apply3 (apply2(f,g), 2)
  = apply3 (make3 (g,f,g), 2)
  = apply3 (C3 <g,f,g>, 2)
  = if0 2 then apply1 (g, 1)
    else apply3 (apply2(f,g), apply1(g,2))
  = if0 2 then apply1 (g, 1)
    else apply3 (make3 (g,f,g), apply1(g,2))
```

Now a simple fixpoint induction on `apply3` suffices to prove the equivalence.

We can use our methods to prove general theorems about flow-based inlining. For example,

Theorem 6. *Suppose* $\psi \mid \emptyset \vdash e : \mathit{int}$, *where* e *is the term*

$$\mathtt{let}\ \mathtt{fun}^{\ell}\ f\ (x : s) = e_0\ \mathtt{in}\ K[y\ @_{\{\ell\}}\ e_1],$$

and K *is a context (a term with a hole) that does not bind* f. *Let* e' *be the term*

$$\mathtt{let}\ \mathtt{fun}^{\ell}\ f\ (x : s) = e_0\ \mathtt{in}\ K[f\ @_{\{\ell\}}\ e_1].$$

Then $(e, \emptyset) \Downarrow n$ *iff* $(e', \emptyset) \Downarrow n$.

6 Lightweight Defunctionalization

Section 4 describes a relatively naive version of defunctionalization in which a function f in a source program is represented as a tagged tuple in the target. The tuple contains the values of all the free variables of the function. It is possible to be more clever. Among the set of free variables of a function f, if there is a subset S that is guaranteed to be in scope whenever f is applied, then S can be safely excluded from the tuple, provided for each $x \in S$, both f and x do not escape their respective scopes of definition.

The goal of this section is to develop this optimization, called "lightweight defunctionalization" in analogy with lightweight closure conversion [14,39]. As with flow-based inlining, we prove the correctness of it using the correctness of ordinary defunctionalization. In contrast to flow-based inlining, the translation is *not* a source-to-source transformation; it is rather a source-to-target transformation, with a slightly modified type system for the source.

The possibilities for lightweight defunctionalization are best demonstrated by two examples. Example 1 shows when such an optimization is possible:

```
let val x = 1 in
let fun^ℓ1 g (y:int) = succ x in
g @_{ℓ1} 2
```

In this example, the naive representation of function g is the tagged tuple $C_1\langle \mathrm{x}\rangle$, since x is free in the body of g. Notice, though, that at the only application site for g, the variable x is always in scope. Therefore, it is not necessary to include it in the tagged tuple $C_1\langle \mathrm{x}\rangle$; the representation of g can just be $C_1\langle\rangle$.

Example 2 shows some of the subtlety in making such an optimization:

```
let fun^ℓ1 g(x:int) =
  let fun^ℓ2 u(y:(int→int,{ℓ3,ℓ4})) =
    let w = y @_{ℓ3,ℓ4} 3 in let fun^ℓ3 v(z:int) = x+w in v in u in
g @_{ℓ1} 0 @_{ℓ2} (g @_{ℓ1} 1 @_{ℓ2} (let fun^ℓ4 h(p:int) = 2 in h))
```

Here, the function g is first called with argument 1, and the function u is called with argument ℓ_4. The result of the application is the function ℓ_3, which is then fed back via a call to g that binds x to 0 and y to ℓ_3. Thus simultaneous bindings of x, one to 1 and the other to 0 are alive during the computation. Since the function ℓ_3 is one of the functions called at the application site (y $@_{\{\ell_3,\ell_4\}}$ 3), one might think that x need not be in the representation of ℓ_3, since x is always in scope. This is, however, wrong: the function ℓ_3 escapes the scope of its definition and gets bound to y with a different binding for its free variable x.

These examples give us clues regarding the specification of lightweight defunctionalization. It is helpful to think how we might translate a source term into the target language. Suppose a subexpression e in the source has type t in environment Γ. Suppose also that among the function labels occurring in e, there is a subset L that occurs neither in e's result type t nor in the environment Γ. Then we can conclude that these functions will not escape from e, will not be used any further in the computation, and are hence *local* to e. Therefore, in e's translation, we should make sure that the corresponding *make* and *apply* functions for each label in L are also local, since these *make*'s and *apply*'s will never be used in the rest of the computation. This notion of locality is similar to locality in the region calculus [40].

With this intuition, one can think of the *make* and *apply* functions as capabilities that are currently available for use by e. When we make some of them local, the rest of the program cannot use these capabilities any more. This change of perspective dictates a small change in the reading of typing judgements in PCFA. Before, we used the context ψ in $\psi \mid \Gamma \vdash e : s$ to determine the labels of functions, and their attendant types, when typechecking e. Now, we will use ψ like a typing context, and remove capabilities from it when we wish to make functions local to a particular scope.

Table 7. Modified type rules for LPCFA.

Well-formed declarations $\boxed{\psi \mid \Gamma \vdash D \rhd \Gamma'}$

$$\frac{\psi \mid \Gamma, f : (s \to t, \{\ell\}), x : s \vdash e : t \quad \psi(\ell) = (\Delta, \Pi, s, t) \quad (\Delta, \Pi) = \Gamma}{\psi \mid \Gamma \vdash (\mathtt{fun}^{\ell}\, f\,(x : s) = e) \rhd (f : s \to t, \{\ell\})}$$

Well-formed expressions $\boxed{\psi \mid \Gamma \vdash e : s}$

$$\frac{\psi, \ell_1 : (\Gamma, \Pi_1, t_1, t_1') \ldots \ell_k : (\Gamma, \Pi_k, t_k, t_k') \mid \Gamma \vdash e : s}{\psi \mid \Gamma \vdash e : s}$$

$$\text{where} \begin{cases} \ell_1 \ldots \ell_k \text{ occurs in } e \\ \ell_1 \ldots \ell_k \text{ does not occur in } \mathit{Labels}(s, \Gamma) \\ \ell_1 \ldots \ell_k \notin \mathit{dom}(\psi) \end{cases}$$

The changes to the type system for PCFA appropriate for lightweight defunctionalization appear in Table 7; we call the new language LPCFA. One rule is modified, namely the rule for function declarations, and one rule is added. The function declaration rule makes clear that ψ is now slightly different: it maps a label ℓ to a quadruple (Δ, Π, s, t). In the quadruple, Δ is the global environment, *i.e.*, free variables in ℓ that are always in scope and which therefore need not appear in the representation of the function, and Π is the local environment of free variables that may escape their scopes of definition and which therefore must appear in the representation of the function in the target. Algorithmically, the split between global and local variables would have to be determined; in the type system, the "guess" of the split is merely checked.

We reconsider the examples in turn. In Example 1, the type of x is `int`, the type of g is $(\mathtt{int} \to \mathtt{int}, \{\ell_1\})$ and the type of the whole program is `int`. Whenever g is applied, the variable x is in its scope. The typing derivation uses the new rules to make this locality explicit. First, when typechecking the bindings of the inner `let`, we need an appropriate ψ to check

$$J_1 = \psi \mid x : \mathtt{int} \vdash \mathtt{fun}^{\ell_1}\, g\,(y : \mathtt{int}) = \mathtt{succ}\ x \ \rhd (g : \mathtt{int} \to \mathtt{int}, \{\ell_1\})$$

To make x global, we choose

$$\psi = [\ell_1 \mapsto (\{x : \mathtt{int}\}, \emptyset, \mathtt{int}, \mathtt{int})]$$

It is then evident that the judgement J_1 is provable, and from that it is easy to see that

$$\psi \mid x : \mathtt{int} \vdash\ (\mathtt{let\ fun}^{\ell_1}\, g\,(y : \mathtt{int}) = \mathtt{succ}\ x\ \mathtt{in}\ g\ @_{\{\ell_1\}}\ 2) : \mathtt{int}$$

is provable. Now we can make g local, since ℓ_1 does not appear either in the result type int, or in the type context $x : \mathtt{int}$. Thus,

$$\emptyset \mid x : \mathtt{int} \vdash (\mathtt{let\ fun}^{\ell_1}\ g\,(y : \mathtt{int}) = \mathtt{succ}\ x\ \mathtt{in}\ g\ @_{\{\ell_1\}}\ 2) : \mathtt{int}$$

is provable.

Table 8. Modified rules for lightweight defunctionalization of LPCFA.

$$\frac{\psi \mid \Gamma, f : (s \to t, \{\ell\}), x : s \vdash e : t \quad \psi(\ell) = (\Delta, \Pi, s, t) \quad (\Delta, \Pi) = \Gamma}{\psi \mid \Gamma \vdash (\mathtt{fun}^{\ell}\ f\,(x : s) = e) \rhd (f : s \to t, \{\ell\})} \quad \Rightarrow$$

$$\frac{\psi^*, \Gamma^*, f : \alpha, x : s^* \vdash e^* : t^*\ ;\ D}{\psi^*, \Gamma^* \vdash \mathit{make}\langle y_1, \ldots, y_m\rangle : \alpha\ ;\ D \cup D'}$$

$$\text{where} \begin{cases} \Pi = \langle y_1 : u_1, \ldots, y_m : u_m\rangle \\ D' = \{\mathtt{tagtype}\ \alpha\ =\ C\ \mathtt{of}\ \Pi^*, \\ \qquad \mathtt{fun}\ \mathit{make}\ (\langle y_1, \ldots, y_m\rangle) = C\langle y_1, \ldots, y_m\rangle, \\ \qquad \mathtt{fun}\ \mathit{apply}\ (f\ \mathtt{as}\ C\langle y_1, \ldots, y_m\rangle, x) = e^*\} \end{cases}$$

$$\frac{\psi, \ell_1 : (\Gamma, \Pi_1, t_1, t_1') \ldots \ell_k : (\Gamma, \Pi_k, t_k, t_k') \mid \Gamma \vdash e : s}{\psi \mid \Gamma \vdash e : s} \quad \Rightarrow$$

$$\frac{\psi^*, \alpha_j,\ C_j,\ \mathit{make}_j,\ \mathit{apply}_j,\ \Gamma^* \vdash e^* : s^*\ ;\ D \quad j = 1 \ldots k}{\begin{array}{l}\psi^*, \Gamma^* \vdash \mathtt{let\ tagtype}\ \alpha_j\ =\ C_j\ \mathtt{of}\ \Pi_j^* \\ \qquad \mathtt{fun}\ \mathit{make}_j\ (\langle z_{1j}, \ldots, z_{p_j}\rangle) = C_j\langle z_{1j}, \ldots, z_{p_j}\rangle \\ \qquad \mathtt{fun}\ \mathit{apply}_j\ (f_j\ \mathtt{as}\ C_j\langle z_{1j}, \ldots, z_{p_j}\rangle, u : t_j^*) = e_j^* \\ \quad \mathtt{in}\ e^* : s^*\ ;\ D - D'\end{array}}$$

$$\text{where} \begin{cases} \ell_1 \ldots \ell_k \text{ occurs in } e \\ \ell_1 \ldots \ell_k \notin \mathit{Labels}(s, \Gamma) \\ \ell_1 \ldots \ell_k \notin \mathit{dom}(\psi) \\ \Pi_j = z_{1j} : s_{1j}, \ldots, z_{p_j} : s_{p_j} \\ C_j : \Pi_j^* \to \alpha_j,\ \mathit{make}_j : \Pi_j^* \to \alpha_j,\ \mathit{apply}_j : \alpha_j \times t_j^* \to (t_j')^* \\ D' = \{\ \mathtt{tagtype}\ \alpha_j\ =\ C_j\ \mathtt{of}\ \Pi_j^* \\ \qquad \mathtt{fun}\ \mathit{make}_j(\ldots) = \ldots, \\ \qquad \mathtt{fun}\ \mathit{apply}_j(\ldots) = \ldots \mid j = 1 \ldots k\} \end{cases}$$

The use of the new rule for locality is invisible: it does not have a syntactic marker in the source language. Nevertheless, it is crucial in the translation to the target. The modifications to the translation appear in Table 8, where the translation of label contexts is now determined by

$$\begin{array}{l}(\ell_1 \mapsto (\Delta_1, \Pi_1, s_1, t_1), \ldots, \ell_n \mapsto (\Delta_n, \Pi_n, s_n, t_n))^* = \\ \quad \alpha_1, C_1 : \Pi_1^\dagger \to \alpha_1, \ldots, \alpha_n, C_n : \Pi_n^\dagger \to \alpha_n, \ldots, \\ \quad \mathit{make}_1 : \Pi_1^\dagger \to \alpha_1, \mathit{apply}_1 : \alpha_1 \times s_1^* \to t_1^*, \ldots, \\ \quad \mathit{make}_n : \Pi_n^\dagger \to \alpha_n, \mathit{apply}_n : \alpha_n \times s_n^* \to t_n^*\end{array}$$

The rest of the translation follows *mutatis mutandis*. Note how the type of $make_i$ is $\Pi_i^\dagger \to \alpha_i$, and that Π_i does not necessarily include *all* of the free variables of the recursive function. This fact is used in the translation of the new rule. In this case, we know that $\ell_1, \ldots, \ell_k$ are all the function labels that can be made local in the source term e. Accordingly, in the translation, the definitions of the tagged types $\alpha_1, \ldots, \alpha_k$, and the functions $make_1, \ldots, make_k$ and $apply_1, \ldots, apply_k$ are made local to e^*. Moreover, these local definitions are subtracted from D.

It is helpful to go back to Example 1 to see how the translation works. Note first that

$$\psi^* = \alpha_1, C_1 : \texttt{unit} \to \alpha_1, make_1 : \texttt{unit} \to \alpha_1,\ apply_1 : \alpha_1 \times \texttt{int} \to \texttt{int}.$$

The translation of the judgement J_1 is then

$$\begin{array}{l} \psi^*, x : \texttt{int} \vdash \texttt{let val } g = make_1\langle\rangle \texttt{ in} \\ \qquad\qquad \texttt{case } g \texttt{ of } (g \texttt{ as } C_1\ \langle\rangle)\ \Rightarrow\ apply_1(g, 2) : \texttt{int}\ ;\ D \end{array}$$

where

$$\begin{array}{l} D = \{\texttt{tagtype } \alpha_1 \ = \ C_1 \texttt{ of unit},\ \texttt{fun } make_1\ (\langle\rangle) = C_1\langle\rangle, \\ \qquad \texttt{fun } apply_1\ (g \texttt{ as } C_1\langle\rangle,\ y) = \texttt{succ } x\}. \end{array}$$

An application of the translation rules yields the following program (call it P):

$$\begin{array}{l} \emptyset \vdash \texttt{let val } x = 1 \texttt{ in} \\ \quad \texttt{let tagtype } \alpha_1 \ = \ C_1 \texttt{ of unit} \\ \qquad \texttt{fun } make_1\ (\langle\rangle) = C_1\langle\rangle \\ \qquad \texttt{fun } apply_1\ (g \texttt{ as } C_1\langle\rangle,\ y) = \texttt{succ } x \texttt{ in} \\ \quad \texttt{let val } g = make_1\langle\rangle \texttt{ in} \\ \quad \texttt{case } g \texttt{ of } (g \texttt{ as } C_1\ \langle\rangle)\ \Rightarrow\ apply_1(g, 2) : \texttt{int}\ ;\ \emptyset \end{array}$$

which is the translation of Example 1.

In Example 2, we need an appropriate ψ to check

$$J_2 = \psi \mid \emptyset \vdash \texttt{fun}^{\ell_1}\, g\, (x : \texttt{int}) = \ldots \rhd (g : s)$$

where $s = (\texttt{int} \to ((\texttt{int} \to \texttt{int}, \{\ell_3, \ell_4\}) \to (\texttt{int} \to \texttt{int}, \{\ell_3\})), \{\ell_2\})$. Then we can show

$$J_3 = \psi \mid g : s \vdash g\ @_{\{\ell_1\}}\ 0\ @_{\{\ell_2\}}\ (g\ @_{\{\ell_1\}}\ 1\ @_{\{\ell_2\}}\ e) : t$$

where $t = (\texttt{int} \to \texttt{int}, \{\ell_3\})$ and $e = (\texttt{let fun}^{\ell_4}\, h\, (p : \texttt{int}) = 2 \texttt{ in } h)$. But what can ψ contain? Clearly, from J_3 it must contain bindings for ℓ_1, ℓ_2 and ℓ_4, otherwise the applications cannot take place. Moreover, to typecheck g's body, we need to typecheck the judgement

$$J_4 = \psi \mid g : s, x : \texttt{int}, u : r \vdash (\texttt{let } w = y\ @_{\{\ell_3, \ell_4\}}\ 3 \texttt{ in } e') : p$$

where $r = ((\texttt{int} \to \texttt{int}, \{\ell_3, \ell_4\}) \to (\texttt{int} \to \texttt{int}, \{\ell_3, \ell_4\}), \{\ell_2\})$ and $p = (\texttt{int} \to \texttt{int}, \{\ell_3\})$ and $e' = (\texttt{let fun}^{\ell_3}\, v\, (z : \texttt{int}) = x + w \texttt{ in } v)$. To typecheck the application in J_4, ψ must contain a binding for ℓ_3. Finally, note that the return type p

indicates that ℓ_3 escapes the scope of its definition. So ℓ_3 cannot be made local. The defunctionalized version of Example 2 and its lightweight defunctionalized version are exactly the same and is shown below. Note how the *make* and *apply* functions for each of the labels are available globally.

```
let tagtype α1 = C1 of unit
    tagtype α2 = C2 of α1×int
    tagtype α3 = C3 of α1×int×α2 × (α1 ∪ α3)×int
    tagtype α4 = C4 of α1
    fun make1() = C1⟨⟩
    fun make2(d,x) = C2⟨d,x⟩
    fun make3(d,x,e,v,w) = C3⟨d,x,e,v,w⟩
    fun make4(d) = C4⟨d⟩
    fun apply1(g as C1⟨⟩, x:int) = let val u = make2(g,x) in u
    fun apply2(u as C2⟨d,x⟩, y) =
      let val w =
        (case y of (v as C3⟨d',x',e',v',w'⟩) => apply3(v,3)
                 | (h as C4⟨d⟩) => apply4(h,3)) in
      let val v = make3(x,w) in v
    fun apply3(v as C3⟨d,x,e,v,w⟩,z) = x + w
    fun apply4(h as C4⟨d⟩,p) = 2
in  let val g = make1⟨⟩ in
    apply2(apply1(g,0),apply2(apply1(g,1),
           let val h = make4(g) in h))
```

We use principles from the theory of data abstraction to show that the program produces the same output as the original defunctionalized program. Our strategy is to produce an intermediate transformation of the program, where the transformation is essentially defunctionalization, but takes into account the new rule. This allows us to use the Fundamental Theorem of Logical Relations [24,33] to relate two programs with similar scoping structure. Finally, we can show that the program produced by the intermediate transformation and the original defunctionalized program are β-convertible.

Consider the use of ordinary defunctionalization on Example 1, yielding:

$$
\begin{array}{l}
\emptyset \vdash \texttt{let tagtype}\ \alpha_1 \ = \ C_1\ \texttt{of int} \\
\qquad\qquad \texttt{fun}\ make_1\ (x) = C_1\langle x\rangle \\
\qquad\qquad \texttt{fun}\ apply_1\ (g\ \texttt{as}\ C_1\langle x\rangle,\ y) = \texttt{succ}\ x\ \texttt{in} \\
\qquad \texttt{let val}\ x = 1\ \texttt{in} \\
\qquad \texttt{let val}\ g = make_1(x)\ \texttt{in} \\
\qquad \texttt{case}\ g\ \texttt{of}\ (g\ \texttt{as}\ C_1\ \langle x\rangle)\ \Rightarrow\ apply_1(g,2) : \texttt{int}\ ;\ D.
\end{array}
$$

We can also choose to defunctionalize by taking advantage of the new locality rule, but without reducing the size of the environments, *i.e.*, C_1 still carries an int. Under this version, the translated program is

$$\begin{array}{l}\emptyset \vdash \texttt{let val } x = 1 \texttt{ in} \\ \quad \texttt{let tagtype } \alpha_1 \;=\; C_1 \texttt{ of int} \\ \qquad \texttt{fun } \mathit{make}_1\ (\langle\rangle) = C_1\langle x\rangle \\ \qquad \texttt{fun } \mathit{apply}_1\ (g \texttt{ as } C_1\langle x\rangle,\ y) = \texttt{succ } x \texttt{ in} \\ \quad \texttt{let val } g = \mathit{make}_1\langle\rangle \texttt{ in} \\ \quad \texttt{case } g \texttt{ of } (g \texttt{ as } C_1\langle x\rangle) \Rightarrow \mathit{apply}_1(g, 2) : \texttt{int} \ ; \ \emptyset\end{array}$$

It is simple to prove that these two programs are the same, using β-conversion, which is valid in the target language. To show that this last version is equivalent to the result of lightweight defunctionalization, (*i.e.*, program P), we use the Fundamental Theorem of Logical Relations, appropriately extended to the target language. We build a relation between the representations of the abstract type α_1, namely $R_{\alpha_1} = \{\langle C_1\langle\rangle, C_1(1)\rangle\}$. We then show that the implementations of make_1 and apply_1 are related in the scope where x is bound to 1, and thus the bodies of the two implementations are related. Since the relation at base type int is the equality relation, both programs produce the same final answers.

More formally, we can prove:

Theorem 7 (Correctness). *If $\psi \mid \emptyset \vdash e : \textbf{\textit{int}}$ is provable in LPCFA and $(\psi \mid \emptyset \vdash e : \textbf{\textit{int}}) \Rightarrow (\psi^* \vdash e^* : \textbf{\textit{int}}\ ;\ D)$ via lightweight defunctionalization, then $(e, \emptyset) \Downarrow n$ in LPCFA iff $(\textbf{\textit{let}}\ D\ \textbf{\textit{in}}\ e^*, \emptyset) \Downarrow n$ in the target language.*

7 Discussion

We have shown how to prove the correctness of ordinary CFA-based defunctionalization using denotational methods, and how to prove the correctness of two CFA-based transformations using this result. Our methods seem to be more modular and reusable than previous correctness proofs. Nevertheless, the proof methods developed here are not a silver bullet: although the proof of correctness for defunctionalization can serve as a building block, the proofs of correctness for the transformations must be carried out afresh.

Defunctionalization, first formulated by Reynolds, in his celebrated paper on definitional interpreters [32], is an important program transformation technique that has surfaced in several contexts. Reynolds developed defunctionalization as an aid to understanding meta-circular interpreters for higher-order applicative languages since such interpreters do not "shed much light on the nature of higher-order functions"; an interpreter for a higher-order applicative language must thus be written in a *first-order* metalanguage. Defunctionalization is proposed as a way of systematically eliminating higher-order functions by representing them using records containing the free variables of these functions: these records are essentially closures. More recently, CFA-based defunctionalization has been used in whole-program compilers for ML [7,41] for efficient code generation. In a recent dissertation, Boquist shows how to transform Haskell programs into efficient, first-order programs [6]. His method uses (essentially) a form of CFA to reduce the complexity of the defunctionalized program. However, no formal proofs of correctness for the transformations or of defunctionalization are provided. Finally, Wang and Appel in their work on type-safe garbage collection [45] assume whole-program compilation and CPS convert and defunctionalize source programs before performing garbage collection.

Defunctionalization plays two distinct roles in this paper: as a basis for proofs of correctness, and as a basis for program transformations. The two roles come together here in the proof of correctness of lightweight defunctionalization.

We have sketched, but not reported here, a CFA-based defunctionalization for two other versions of PCFA, one untyped and one with recursive types. Interestingly, neither change in the source seems to require additional features in the target. In the Appendix we sketch an extension of PCFA with imperative features, namely, references, assignment and dereference. For this language, CFA also calculates, in addition to the possible set of functions, the possible set of references that may be the result of evaluation at a program point. In this case, however, the target language needs to be augmented with imperative features. To make references local, a rule similar to the "locality" rule in LPCFA may be employed. Going further, one might consider a source language with simple concurrency primitives. We conjecture that this would not add higher-order features to the target language, and thus avoid powerdomains in the denotational semantics of the target.

A fundamental intuition in this paper is that control-flow analysis allows one to choose different concrete representations of data (*e.g.*, functions, references, *etc.*) This is why it can be used as the basis of program transformations. The choice is made explicit in the translation of *e.g.*, a function type (or a reference type) in the source into an *abstract type* in the target. Then, creation of a function and application of a function become operations on the abstract type. Different program transformations can choose to implement a function differently by choosing different concrete representations for it. This view allows one to use common semantic techniques (*e.g.*, principles of data abstraction) to prove correctness of the transformations. The intuition of using CFA to choose representations does not seem to be explicit in Steckler and Wand's treatment of lightweight closure conversion [39].

Defunctionalization, as reported in this paper, is a whole-program transformation. It crucially depends on results of a whole-program CFA. But what happens if we want to compile separate program modules independently? We are currently developing an approach based on the restricted introduction of variables ξ ranging over sets of labels. Corresponding to these variables, we introduce a new class of types $(s \to s, \xi)$. These types are used to describe a module's imported functions. In the defunctionalization of a module, an imported function f maps into a representation of f and any apply functions necessary to apply f and its "residuals". For example, if f has type $((\mathtt{int} \to \mathtt{int}, \xi) \to \mathtt{int}, \xi')$, we need apply functions $apply_{\xi}$ and $apply_{\xi'}$.

To formalize these notions we need a concrete model of linking. Since the essence of defunctionalization is the transformation of higher-order programs to first-order ones, we want a linking model where linked programs are first-order programs. One immediate complication is that non-recursive modules map to recursive modules under defunctionalization. To see this, suppose that module M imports a function f from module M_f. Now, suppose that (in M_f) the definition of f takes a function as argument and applies this function within its body (i.e. this application occurs in M_f). Also, suppose that in M, the function f is applied to a locally defined function h. Then we have (a) M must import a representation of f and "$apply_f$" from M_f, and (b) M_f must import "$apply_h$" from M since h is applied within M_f. We remark that the type system must be restricted in a number of ways to ensure that the linking can be done statically. We are working on a system based on existential and universal types to capture this recursive linking process.

Another potential example for using defunctionalization is useless variable elimination [38,44], although in this case Kobayashi [22] has already given an elegant operational proof of correctness. We also conjecture that our earlier work on dependency analyses [1] can be extended to handle useless variable elimination. One might apply our techniques to study access-control security, as in the SLam calculus [16], whose type-based specification is closely related to CFA.

Acknowledgements

Anindya Banerjee is a member of the Church Project, and was supported in part by NSF grant EIA-9806835.

References

1. M. Abadi, A. Banerjee, N. Heintze, and J. G. Riecke. A core calculus of dependency. In *POPL'99*, ACM Press.
2. A. Aho, R. Sethi, and J. Ullman. *Compilers: Principles, Techniques, and Tools.* Addison-Wesley Publishing Co., 1986.
3. A. W. Appel. *Compiling with Continuations.* Cambridge University Press, 1992.
4. A. Banerjee. A modular, polyvariant and type-based closure analysis. In *ICFP'97*, ACM Press.
5. H. P. Barendregt. *The Lambda Calculus: Its Syntax and Semantics*, volume 103 of *Studies in Logic.* North-Holland, 1981. Revised Edition, 1984.
6. U. Boquist. *Code Optimisation Techniques for Lazy Functional Languages.* PhD thesis, Chalmers University of Technology, Göteborg University, 1999.
7. H. Cejtin, S. Jagannathan, and S. Weeks. Flow-directed closure conversion for typed languages. In *ESOP 2000*, number 1782 in Lect. Notes in Computer Sci. Springer-Verlag.
8. H. Cejtin, S. Jagannathan, and S. Weeks. Flow-directed closure conversion for typed languages (Extended Summary). Available from URL:http://www.neci.nj.nec.com/homepages/jagannathan/publications.html, 2000.
9. J. Dean, G. DeFouw, D. Grove, and C. Chambers. Vortex: An Optimizing Compiler for Object-Oriented Languages. In *OOPSLA'96*, ACM Press.

10. A. Dimock, R. Muller, F. Turbak, and J. B. Wells. Strongly typed flow-directed representation transformations. In *ICFP'97*, ACM Press.
11. M. Fähndrich and A. Aiken. Making set-constraint based program analyses scale. Technical Report 96-917, University of California, Berkeley, Computer Science Division, 1996.
12. C. Flanagan and M. Felleisen. Componential set-based analysis. In *ACM Trans. on Programming Languages and Systems*, 21(2):370-416, March 1999.
13. C. A. Gunter. *Semantics of Programming Languages.* MIT Press, 1992.
14. J. Hannan. Type systems for closure conversion. In H. R. Nielson and K. L. Solberg, editors, *Proceedings of the Workshop on Types in Program Analysis.* Technical Report PB-493, University of Aarhus, 1995.
15. N. Heintze. Control-flow analysis and type systems. In *SAS'95*, number 983 in Lect. Notes in Computer Sci. Springer-Verlag.
16. N. Heintze and J. G. Riecke. The SLam calculus: programming with secrecy and integrity. In *POPL'98*, ACM Press.
17. U. Hölzle and O. Agesen. Dynamic vs. static optimization techniques for object-oriented languages. *Theory and Practice of Object Systems*, 1(3), 1996.
18. S. Jagannathan and S. Weeks. A unified treatment of flow analysis in higher-order languages. In *POPL'95*, ACM Press.
19. S. Jagannathan and A. Wright. Effective flow analysis for avoiding runtime checks. In *SAS'95*, number 983 in Lect. Notes in Computer Sci. Springer-Verlag.
20. N. D. Jones. Flow analysis of lambda expressions (preliminary version). In S. Even and O. Kariv, editors, *Automata, Languages and Programming: Eighth Colloquium*, volume 115 of *Lect. Notes in Computer Sci.*, pages 114–128. Springer-Verlag, July 1981.
21. G. Kahn. Natural semantics. In *Proceedings Symposium on Theoretical Aspects of Computer Science*, volume 247 of *Lect. Notes in Computer Sci.*, New York, 1987. Springer-Verlag.
22. N. Kobayashi. Type-based useless variable elimination. In *ACM SIGPLAN Workshop on Partial Evaluation and Semantics-based Program Manipulation*, pages 84–93, ACM, 2000.
23. Y. Minamide, G. Morrisett and R. Harper. Typed Closure Conversion. In *POPL'96*, ACM Press.
24. J. C. Mitchell. *Foundations for Programming Languages.* MIT Press, 1996.
25. S. S. Muchnick. *Advanced Compiler Design and Implementation.* Morgan Kaufmann, 1997.
26. L. R. Nielsen. A Denotational Investigation of Defunctionalization. *Progress Report, BRICS Ph.D. School*, June 1998.
27. F. Nielson. Program transformations in a denotational setting. *ACM Trans. on Programming Languages and Systems*, 7(3):359–379, 1985.
28. F. Nielson and H. R. Nielson. Infinitary control flow analysis: a collecting semantics for closure analysis. In *POPL'97*, ACM Press.
29. F. Nielson, H. R. Nielson and C. Hankin. *Principles of Program Analysis.* Springer-Verlag, 1999.
30. J. Palsberg. Closure analysis in constraint form. *ACM Trans. on Programming Languages and Systems*, 17(1):47-62, 1995.
31. G. D. Plotkin. LCF considered as a programming language. *Theoretical Computer Sci.*, 5:223–257, 1977.
32. J. C. Reynolds. Definitional interpreters for higher-order programming languages. In *Proceedings of the ACM National Meeting (Boston, 1972)*, pages 717–740, 1972.

33. J. C. Reynolds. Types, abstraction and parametric polymorphism. In R. E. A. Mason, editor, *Information Processing 83*, pages 513–523. North Holland, Amsterdam, 1983.
34. J. C. Reynolds. Definitional interpreters for higher-order programming languages. *Higher-Order and Symbolic Computation*, 11(4):363–397, December 1998.
35. J. C. Reynolds. Definitional interpreters revisited. *Higher-Order and Symbolic Computation*, 11(4):355–361, December 1998.
36. D. Scott. A type theoretical alternative to CUCH, ISWIM, OWHY. *Theoretical Computer Science*, 121:411–440. Published version of unpublished manuscript, Oxford University, 1969.
37. P. Sestoft. Replacing function parameters by global variables. Master's thesis, DIKU, University of Copenhagen, Denmark, October 1988.
38. O. Shivers. *Control-flow analysis of higher-order languages.* PhD thesis, School of Computer Science, Carnegie Mellon University, 1991. Available as Technical Report CMU-CS-91-145.
39. P. A. Steckler and M. Wand. Lightweight closure conversion. *ACM Trans. Programming Languages and Systems*, 19(1):48–86, January 1997.
40. M. Tofte and J.-P. Talpin. Region-based memory management. *Information and Computation*, 132(2):109–176, 1997.
41. A. Tolmach and D. P. Oliva. From ML to Ada: Strongly-typed language interoperability via source translation. *Journal of Functional Programming*, 8(4):367–412, July 1998.
42. M. Wand. Specifying the Correctness of Binding-Time Analysis. In *Journal of Functional Programming*, 3(3):365–387, July 1993.
43. M. Wand and W. Clinger. Set Constraints for Destructive Array Update Optimization. In *Journal of Functional Programming*, 2000, to appear.
44. M. Wand and I. Siveroni. Constraint systems for useless variable elimination. In *POPL'99*, ACM Press.
45. D. Wang and A. Appel. Type-preserving garbage collectors. In *POPL'01*, ACM Press.
46. K. Yi. An abstract interpretation for estimating uncaught exceptions in Standard ML programs. In *Science of Computer Programming*, 31(1):147-173, 1998.

A Imperative Features

In this section we sketch how to extend the source language with imperative features: creation of reference cells, assignment, dereference. Control-flow analysis, in addition to calculating the set of possible function labels that can arise as a result of evaluation at a program point, also calculates the set of possible reference cells that can be the result of evaluation at a program point.

A.1 The Source Language

We show the extension of PCFA with imperative features below. Reference cells are annotated by the label of the cell. Dereference and assignments are labeled by the set of possible reference cells that maybe dereferenced or assigned at the particular program point. Finally, similar to function types in PCFA types of reference cells are also labelled.

$$s ::= \ldots \mid (\texttt{ref}\ s, L)$$
$$e ::= \ldots \mid \texttt{ref}^{\ell}\ e \mid \texttt{deref}_L\ e \mid \texttt{assign}_L\ e_1\, e_2$$

The type rules below provide a specification for CFA in the presence of references. The label context ψ now also contains labels of reference cells in its domain. Let ℓ be the label of a reference cell that can store a value of type s. Then $\psi(\ell) = s$.

$$\frac{\psi \mid \Gamma \vdash e : s}{\psi \mid \Gamma \vdash \texttt{ref}^{\ell}\ e : (\texttt{ref}\ s, \{\ell\})}\ \psi(\ell) = s$$

$$\frac{\psi \mid \Gamma \vdash e : (\texttt{ref}\ s, L)}{\psi \mid \Gamma \vdash \texttt{deref}_L\ e : s}\ L \subseteq dom(\psi)$$

$$\frac{\psi \mid \Gamma \vdash e_1 : (\texttt{ref}\ s, L) \quad \psi \mid \Gamma \vdash e_2 : s}{\psi \mid \Gamma \vdash \texttt{assign}_L\ e_1\, e_2 : s}\ L \subseteq dom(\psi)$$

Note how for the dereference and assignment rules, we have a similar side condition as for the application rule: a reference cell can be dereferenced or assigned to only if it is currently available in ψ.

A.2 The Target Language

The target language needs to be extended with imperative features also. The extension is standard: reference cells, dereference and assignment are added without any labels. Type rules are as follows.

$$[Ref]\ \frac{\Delta \vdash e : s}{\Delta \vdash \texttt{ref}\ e : \texttt{ref}\ s} \qquad [Deref]\ \frac{\Delta \vdash e : \texttt{ref}\ s}{\Delta \vdash \texttt{deref}\ e : s}$$

$$[Assign]\ \frac{\Delta \vdash e_1 : \texttt{ref}\ s \quad \Delta \vdash e_2 : s}{\Delta \vdash \texttt{assign}\ e_1\ e_2 : s}$$

Denotational Semantics The only addition is the meaning of the reference type. Let $Loc = \mathbf{N}$. For a type environment η, we define

$$[\![\Delta \vdash \texttt{ref}\ s]\!]\eta \ = \ Loc.$$

A *state* over η is a function $(\mathbf{N} \to Storable_\eta) \times \mathbf{N}$, where

$$Storable_\eta \ = \ \{\langle\rangle\} + \mathbf{N} + Loc + \bigcup_{\alpha \in dom(\eta)} \eta(\alpha) + (Storable_\eta \times Storable_\eta)$$

Meanings of terms are now defined over an environment ρ and a state σ. For example

$$[\![\Delta \vdash \texttt{ref}\ e : \texttt{ref}\ s]\!]\eta\rho\sigma \ = \ (v, \sigma')$$

where

$$\begin{array}{ll} (v, \sigma_1) & = [\![\Delta \vdash e : s]\!]\eta\rho\sigma \\ \sigma_1 & = (f, n) \\ f'(x) & = \begin{cases} v, & \text{if } x = n+1 \\ f(x) & \text{otherwise} \end{cases} \\ \sigma' & = (f', n+1) \end{array}$$

A.3 Translation into Target

- Type translation is extended as follows: Let L=$(\ell_1, \ldots, \ell_k)$. Then $(\texttt{ref}\ s, L)^*$= $\alpha_1 \cup \ldots \cup \alpha_k$.
- Label context translation is extended as follows:

$$(\ell \mapsto s, \ldots)^* = (\alpha_\ell, C_\ell : (\texttt{ref}\ s^*) \to \alpha_\ell,\ \mathit{makeref}_\ell : s^* \to \alpha_\ell,\\ \mathit{deref}_\ell : \alpha_\ell \to s^*\ \ \mathit{assign}_\ell : \alpha_\ell \times s^* \to s^*, \ldots)$$

We now show how judgements in the extended PCFA can be translated into the extended target:

$$\frac{\psi \mid \Gamma, e : s}{\psi \mid \Gamma \vdash \texttt{ref}^\ell\ e : (\texttt{ref}\ s, \{\ell\})}\ \psi(\ell) = s \qquad \Rightarrow$$

$$\frac{\psi^*, \Gamma^* \vdash e^* : s^*\ ;\ D}{\psi^*, \Gamma^* \vdash \mathit{makeref}_\ell e^* : \alpha_\ell ; D \cup D'} \quad \begin{cases} D' = \{\ \texttt{tagtype}\ \alpha_\ell\ =\ C_\ell\ \texttt{of}\ (\texttt{ref}\ s^*), \\ \quad \texttt{fun}\ \mathit{makeref}_\ell\ (x) = C_\ell(\texttt{ref}\ x) \\ \quad \texttt{fun}\ \mathit{deref}_\ell\ (C_\ell(x)) = \texttt{deref}(x) \\ \quad \texttt{fun}\ \mathit{assign}_\ell\ (C_\ell(x), y) = \texttt{assign}\ x\ y\} \end{cases}$$

$$\frac{\psi \mid \Gamma \vdash e : (\texttt{ref}\ s, L)}{\psi \mid \Gamma \vdash \texttt{deref}_L\ e : s}\ \ L = \{\ell_1, \ldots, \ell_k\} \subseteq \mathit{dom}(\psi) \qquad \Rightarrow$$

$$\frac{\psi^*, \Gamma^* \vdash e^* : \alpha_1 \cup \ldots \cup \alpha_k\ ;\ D}{\psi^*, \Gamma^* \vdash \texttt{case}\ e^*\ \texttt{of}\ C_1(r) \Rightarrow \mathit{deref}_{\ell_1}(r) \mid \ldots \mid C_k(r) \Rightarrow \mathit{deref}_{\ell_k}(r) : s^*\ ;\ D}$$

$$\frac{\psi \mid \Gamma \vdash e_1 : (\texttt{ref}\ s, L) \quad \psi \mid \Gamma \vdash e_2 : s}{\psi \mid \Gamma \vdash \texttt{assign}_L\ e_1\ e_2 : s}\ \ L = \{\ell_1, \ldots, \ell_k\} \subseteq \mathit{dom}(\psi) \Rightarrow$$

$$\frac{\psi^*, \Gamma^* \vdash e_1^* : \alpha_1 \cup \ldots \cup \alpha_k\ ;\ D_1 \quad \psi^*, \Gamma^* \vdash e_2^* : s^*\ ;\ D_2}{\Psi^*, \Gamma^* \vdash \texttt{case} e_1^* \texttt{of} C_1(r) \Rightarrow \mathit{assign}_{\ell_1}(C_1(r), e_2^*) | \ldots | C_k(r) \Rightarrow \mathit{assign}_{\ell_k}(C_k(r), e_2^* {:} s^* ; D_1 \cup D_2}$$

Infinite Intersection and Union Types for the Lazy Lambda Calculus

Marcello M. Bonsangue and Joost N. Kok

Leiden Institute of Advanced Computer Science,
Leiden University, Leiden, The Netherlands,
marcello@liacs.nl and joost@liacs.nl

Abstract. A type theory with *infinitary* intersection and union types for the lazy λ-calculus is introduced. Types are viewed as upper closed subsets of a Scott domain. Intersection and union type constructors are interpreted as the set-theoretic intersection and union, respectively, even when they are not finite. The assignment of types to λ-terms extends naturally the basic type assignment system. We prove soundness and completeness using a generalization of Abramsky's finitary domain logic for applicative transition systems.

1 Introduction

Intersection types were introduced in [10] as an extension of Curry's simply typed λ-calculus. A remarkable property of intersection types is their ability to express computational information of λ-terms, such as termination properties (e.g. strong normalization [16] and weak head normalization [1]) and reduction properties (e.g. reduction to a closed term [11]). In [6], an intersection type system was proved to be sound and complete with respect to Scott's set-theoretic semantics for simple types.

Since then, several variations of the original intersection type discipline have been explored, including enrichment with new type constructors like union of types [15, 3, 4], conservative extensions like infinite intersection types [14, 3], and modifications inducing more computationally adequate models, like the lazy λ-calculus [1].

Leivant showed in [14] that considering infinite intersection types has several advantages over the ordinary intersection type discipline. Firstly, infinite intersection types form a framework in which several typing mechanisms, such as parametric polymorphism, stratified parametric polymorphism, and recursive types can be interpreted. Secondly, there is a relationship between the size of the types allowed and the computational nature of the functions representable by finite λ-terms. And finally, infinite intersection types allow for typing in a uniform way a number of interesting classes of λ-terms, like those representing the Berarducci numerals (a result independently obtained also in [3]).

Although infinite intersection types conceptually express better the idea of multiple typing, not much work has been done in generalizing the filter model

N. Kobayashi and B.C. Pierce (Eds.): TACS 2001, LNCS 2215, pp. 448–458, 2001.

of [6] towards a complete set-theoretical model for infinite intersection types. The reason is maybe due to the fact that a study of infinite intersection types cannot be carried out easily without considering infinite union types. As a consequence, a set theoretic-model has to be a completely distributive lattice, in contrast to the fact that canonical models for λ-calculi, like some Scott domains, induce topologies that do not satisfy the complete distributivity laws.

In this paper we solve this open problem by proving soundness and completeness of a type system for the lazy λ-calculus, in which arbitrary intersection and union types are allowed. Types are interpreted as upper closed subsets of a Scott domain, the so-called saturated sets. The meaning of the intersection and union type constructors is the set-theoretic intersection and union, respectively, even when they are not finite. Types are assigned to λ-terms in a such way that the interpretation of a λ-term belongs to the interpretation of all types it is assigned to. The completeness result for our infinitary type system is based on the connection between Abramsky's domain logic for applicative transition systems and the Scott compact opens of a suitable domain [1].

We have chosen to focus on the lazy λ-calculus, but similar results hold also for the λ-calculus. The reason of our choice is simplicity. In fact, to obtain a non-trivial model for the λ-calculus one needs to consider a fixed collection of basic types. To fall into the scope of the general theory developed by Abramsky, a logical presentation of the associated Scott domains from scratch would use lifting to get off the ground. However the resulting type expression would be rather complicated.

This work fits into our studies towards an infinitary logic of domains. In [8, 9] we focussed on an infinitary logical form for Plotkin's powerdomain construction, while in this paper we concentrate on the function space construction. The key ingredients are a Stone-like duality for $\mathcal{T}_0$ topological spaces [7] and a characterization of sober spaces in terms of their completely distributive lattice of saturated sets (i.e. upper closed sets with respect to the specialization preorder induced by the opens) [9]. These results allow us to freely extend Abramsky's finitary logic of compact opens [2] to the infinitary logic of the saturated sets.

The paper is organized as follows. In the next section we introduce the lazy λ-calculus, its syntax, and its domain theoretical model. In Section 3 we present our infinitary type theory and prove soundness and completeness. Then, in Section 4 we give similar results for a type assignment system. We conclude in Section 5 with some final remarks.

Acknowledgments We are thankful to M. Dezani-Ciancaglini, M. Coppo and J. Rutten for pointing out infinite intersection types as a possible application of our results towards an infinitary logic of domains [9]. We are also grateful to S. Abramsky and D. Scott for discussions on this topic.

2 The Lazy Lambda Calculus

In this section we recall some basic definitions of the lazy λ-calculus. Its syntax coincides with that of the λ-calculus.

Definition 1. *The set Λ of λ-term is defined by the following grammar*

$$M ::= x \mid \lambda x.M \mid MM,$$

where x is a variable from a fixed set Var.

The definitions of free variables, substitution and closed terms are standard [5]. As usual, the set of closed λ-terms is denoted by Λ^o.

The operational model of the lazy λ-calculus is described by a convergence relation.

Definition 2. *The convergence to principal weak head normal form $\Downarrow$ on closed λ-terms is defined inductively by*

1. $\lambda x.M \Downarrow \lambda x.M$,
2. *if* $M \Downarrow \lambda x.P$ *and* $P[N/x] \Downarrow Q$ *then* $MN \Downarrow Q$.

Informally, $M \Downarrow \lambda x.P$ means that given a term M, the environment sees whether it converges to some function $\lambda x.P$. If this is the case, then it can continue by providing another term N and applying it to $\lambda x.P$. As for ordinary transition systems in concurrency theory, the above convergence relation can be used to identify λ-terms with the same observable behavior. A natural observational equivalence is applicative bisimulation.

Definition 3. *A binary relation R on closed λ-terms is called an* applicative bisimulation *whenever, if $\langle M, N\rangle \in R$ then*

- $M \Downarrow \lambda x.M_1$ *implies there exists N_1 such that* $N \Downarrow \lambda x.N_1$ *and* $\langle M_1[P/x], N_1[P/x]\rangle \in R$ *for all closed λ-terms P.*

We write $M \lesssim^B N$ if there exists an applicative bisimulation R with $\langle M, N\rangle \in R$.

Applicative bisimulation as an observational equivalence for the lazy λ-calculus coincides with the contextual congruence $\lesssim^C$ defined on closed λ-terms by $M \lesssim^C N$ if and only if for every closed context $C[\cdot]$, whenever $C[M] \Downarrow M_1$ for some closed term M_1, also $C[N] \Downarrow N_1$ for some closed term N_1 [1].

Abramsky [1] gives a domain theoretical model of the lazy λ-calculus. Let **SDom** be the category with Scott domains as objects and Scott continuous function as morphisms. Define $\mathcal{D}$ to be the Scott domain obtained as the canonical solution in the category **SDom** of the recursive domain equation

$$X \cong (X \to X)_\perp$$

where $(-)_\perp$ is the lifting construction, and $- \to -$ is the set of all Scott continuous functions endowed with the pointwise order. Furthermore, let *unfold* be the isomorphism mapping $\mathcal{D} \to (\mathcal{D} \to \mathcal{D})_\perp$, and *fold* be its inverse. The meaning of a λ-term at an environment $\rho: Var \to \mathcal{D}$ is defined by induction on its structure as follows:

$$\begin{aligned}
[\![x]\!]_\rho &= \rho(x)\\
[\![MN]\!]_\rho &= \mathit{lift}(Ap)(\mathit{unfold}([\![M]\!]_\rho))([\![N]\!]_\rho)\\
[\![\lambda x.M]\!]_\rho &= \mathit{fold}(\mathit{up}(\lambda d \in \mathcal{D}.[\![M]\!]_{\rho[d/x]}))
\end{aligned}$$

where $Ap:(\mathcal{D} \to \mathcal{D}) \to \mathcal{D} \to \mathcal{D}$ is the standard (continuous) application function, $lift(Ap)$ is the lifting of Ap to the strict function space $(\mathcal{D} \to \mathcal{D})_\perp \to_\perp \mathcal{D} \to \mathcal{D}$, and $up(d)$ is the lifting of $d \in \mathcal{D}$ to the correspondent element in the domain $(\mathcal{D})_\perp$.

The above semantics when restricted to closed terms is fully abstract with respect to applicative bisimulation, meaning that for all closed terms M and N, $M \lesssim^B N$ if and only if $[\![M]\!] \sqsubseteq [\![N]\!]$, where $\sqsubseteq$ is the partial order of the domain $\mathcal{D}$ [1].

3 An Infinitary Type Theory

Types are syntactical entities built by means of the function type constructor '$\to$', lifting '$(\cdot)_\perp$', an infinitary intersection type constructor '$\bigwedge$' and an infinitary union type constructor '$\bigvee$'.

Definition 4. *The class* $(\phi \in)\mathbf{T}$ *is defined inductively by the following grammar:*

$$\phi ::= \bigvee_{i\in I} \phi_i \mid \bigwedge_{i\in I} \phi_i \mid (\psi)_\perp$$

$$\psi ::= \bigvee_{i\in I} \psi_i \mid \bigwedge_{i\in I} \psi_i \mid \phi_1 \to \phi_2,$$

where I is an arbitrary index set. If $I = \emptyset$ then we write tt for $\bigwedge_{i\in I} \phi_i$ and $\bigwedge_{i\in I} \psi_i$, and we write ff for $\bigvee_{i\in I} \phi_i$ and $\bigvee_{i\in I} \psi_i$.

We denote by $\mathbf{T}_\omega$ the sub-language of $\mathbf{T}$ obtained by restricting to finite intersection type and finite union type constructors. Semantics of types in $\mathbf{T}$ is given in terms of the Scott domain $\mathcal{D}$. It is defined inductively as follows:

$$\begin{array}{lcl} d \models \bigvee_{i\in I} \phi_i & \iff & \exists i \in I.\ d \models \phi_i \\ d \models \bigwedge_{i\in I} \phi_i & \iff & \forall i \in I.\ d \models \phi_i \\ d \models (\psi)_\perp & \iff & unfold(d) = f \neq \perp \text{ and } f \models \psi \end{array}$$

$$\begin{array}{lcl} f \models \bigvee_{i\in I} \psi_i & \iff & \exists i \in I.\ f \models \psi_i \\ f \models \bigwedge_{i\in I} \psi_i & \iff & \forall i \in I.\ f \models \psi_i \\ f \models \phi_1 \to \phi_2 & \iff & \forall d \in \mathcal{D}.\ d \models \phi_1 \text{ implies } f(d) \models \phi_2. \end{array}$$

As usual, for $d \in \mathcal{D}$, we write $\mathbf{T}(d)$ for the set $\{\phi \in \mathbf{T} \mid d \models \phi\}$. Next we present a formal proof system for deriving *assertions* over $\mathbf{T}$ of the form $\phi_1 \leq \phi_2$ and $\phi_1 = \phi_2$. Their semantics is defined by

$$\begin{array}{lcl} \models \phi_1 \leq \phi_2 & \iff & \forall d \in \mathcal{D}.\ d \models \phi_1 \text{ implies } d \models \phi_2 \\ \models \phi_1 = \phi_2 & \iff & \models \phi_1 \leq \phi_2 \text{ and } \models \phi_2 \leq \phi_1 . \end{array}$$

Our goal is to define a complete theory in the sense that $\phi_1 \leq \phi_2$ is provable in the theory if and only $\models \phi_1 \leq \phi_2$.

For a complete axiomatization of the above assertions we will need an auxiliary *coprimeness predicate* $\mathsf{C}(\phi)$ on types ϕ of $\mathbf{T}$. Types for which the coprimeness predicate holds will play a role in validating the axiom about the distribution of union types over the $\rightarrow$ constructor when appearing at its right-hand side. Clearly such an axiom is not valid in general. The following table presents a formal system for the *coprimeness judgment.*

- $\mathsf{C}(tt)$

- $$\frac{\mathsf{C}(\phi_1) \text{ and } \phi_1 = \phi_2}{\mathsf{C}(\phi_2)}$$

- $$\frac{\{\mathsf{C}(\phi_i)\}_{i\in I} \text{ and } \{\mathsf{C}(\phi'_i)\}_{i\in I} \quad (\forall J \subseteq I.\ \bigwedge_{j\in J}\phi'_j = \mathit{ff} \Longrightarrow \bigwedge_{j\in J}\phi_j = \mathit{ff})}{\mathsf{C}(\bigwedge_{i\in I}(\phi_i \rightarrow \phi'_i)_\perp)}\ I \text{ finite}$$

The last rule bears great resemblance to the definition of the finite elements of the function space between two Scott domains, the so-called step functions [18]. Indeed, types for which the coprimeness predicate holds are precisely the upper closure of finite elements of the Scott domain $\mathcal{D}$ [2].

Note that $\mathsf{C}(\phi)$ implies that no disjunctions (up-to $=$) occur in ϕ, whereas the type theory Π given in [4] uses a predicate $\mathbf{P}(\phi)$ which essentially allows for disjunctions only if they occur on the left-hand side of the $\rightarrow$ constructors.

The following *logical axioms and rules* give to $\mathbf{T}$ the structure of a large completely distributive lattice.

- $\phi \le \phi$

- $$\frac{\phi_1 \le \phi_2 \text{ and } \phi_2 \le \phi_3}{\phi_1 \le \phi_3}$$

- $$\frac{\phi_1 \le \phi_2 \text{ and } \phi_2 \le \phi_1}{\phi_1 = \phi_2}$$

- $$\frac{\phi_1 = \phi_2}{\phi_1 \le \phi_2 \text{ and } \phi_2 \le \phi_1}$$

- $$\frac{\{\phi \le \phi_i\}_{i\in I}}{\phi \le \bigwedge_{i\in I}\phi_i}$$

- $$\frac{k \in I}{\bigwedge_{i\in I}\phi_i \le \phi_k}$$

- $$\frac{\{\phi_i \le \phi\}_{i\in I}}{\bigvee_{i\in I}\phi_i \le \phi}$$

- $$\frac{k \in I}{\phi_k \le \bigvee_{i\in I}\phi_i}$$

- $\bigwedge_{i\in I}\bigvee_{j\in J_i}\phi_{i,j} = \bigvee_{f\in\Phi(\{J_i \mid i\in I\})}\bigwedge_{i\in I}\phi_{i,f(i)}$

The last axiom is about complete distributivity (its dual can be derived [17]). We use $\Phi(\mathcal{S})$, for a set of sets $\mathcal{S}$, to denote the set of all functions choosing an element from their input, that is, all functions $f\colon \mathcal{S} \rightarrow \bigcup \mathcal{S}$ such that $f(S) \in S$ for all $S \in \mathcal{S}$. Because of the presence of arbitrary choice functions, proofs involving the axiom of complete distributivity require the axiom of choice.

Finally, we give *structural axioms and rules* that relate the atomic formulas to the logical structure.

- $$\frac{\phi_2 \leq \phi_1 \text{ and } \phi_3 \leq \phi_4}{\phi_1 \to \phi_3 \leq \phi_2 \to \phi_4}$$
- $$\frac{\psi_1 \leq \psi_2}{(\psi_1)_\perp \leq (\psi_2)_\perp}$$
- $$\frac{I \neq \emptyset}{(\bigwedge_{i\in I} \psi_i)_\perp = \bigwedge_{i\in I}(\psi_i)_\perp}$$
- $(\bigvee_{i\in I} \psi_i)_\perp = \bigvee_{i\in I}(\psi_i)_\perp$
- $\bigwedge_{i\in I}(\phi \to \phi_i) \leq \phi \to \bigwedge_{i\in I} \phi_i$
- $\bigwedge_{i\in I}(\phi_i \to \phi) \leq \bigvee_{i\in I} \phi_i \to \phi$
- $$\frac{\mathsf{C}(\phi) \text{ and } I \text{ finite}}{\phi \to \bigvee_{i\in I} \phi_i \leq \bigvee_{i\in I}(\phi \to \phi_i)}$$
- $$\frac{\{\phi_i \in \mathbf{T}_\omega\}_{i\in I} \text{ and } \{\phi_j \in \mathbf{T}_\omega\}_{j\in J}}{\bigwedge_{i\in I} \phi_i \to \bigvee_{j\in J} \phi_j \leq \bigvee_{H\in Fin(I)} \bigvee_{K\in Fin(J)}(\bigwedge_{h\in H} \phi_h \to \bigvee_{k\in K} \phi_k)}$$

In the last rule we use $Fin(S)$, for a set S, to denote the set of all finite subsets of S. As usual, we write $\vdash A$ if the assertion A of $\mathbf{T}$ is derivable from the above axioms and rules. If we restrict our proof system to the finitary language $\mathbf{T}_\omega$ then it coincides with Abramsky's domain logic $\mathcal{L}(\sigma)$, for the type expression $\sigma \equiv \mathbf{rec}\, t.(t \to t)_\perp$ [2]. The last axiom scheme is new, and makes sense only in a language with arbitrary disjunctions and conjunctions. It is a statement of continuity of the '$\to$' type constructor, both on its left- and right-hand side. Note that because '$\to$' is contravariant on its left argument, filtered intersections are transformed into directed unions.

The next proposition shows that coprimeness judgment is essentially defined for the finitary sub-language $\mathbf{T}_\omega$. Indeed, it extends only to those infinitary types in $\mathbf{T}$ which are provably equivalent to finitary types in $\mathbf{T}_\omega$ for which the predicate C holds.

Proposition 1. *For each infinitary type $\phi \in \mathbf{T}$, if $\mathsf{C}(\phi)$ holds then there exists a finitary type $\phi' \in \mathbf{T}_\omega$ such that $\vdash \phi = \phi'$.*

Proof. By induction on the lenght of the derivation of $\mathsf{C}(\phi)$. □

As an immediate consequence we have that the restriction of the index set I to be finite in the rule

$$\frac{\mathsf{C}(\phi) \text{ and } I \text{ finite}}{\phi \to \bigvee_{i\in I} \phi_i \leq \bigvee_{i\in I}(\phi \to \phi_i)}$$

can be omitted. To prove this, we can use the above propositon to substitute a finitary type $\phi' \in \mathbf{T}_\omega$ for the type ϕ; then apply the last structural rule for moving outside the $\rightarrow$ constructor the infinite unions at its right; distribute the remaining finite unions at the right of the $\rightarrow$ constructor using the above proof rule, and finally substituting again ϕ for ϕ'.

The last structural rule can also be understood as an expression of compactness and finite approximability (as it will become clear by reading the sketch of the proof following Theorem 1). Logically, it allows for rewriting an arbitrary infinitary type in $\mathbf{T}$ as intersections of unions of finitary types in $\mathbf{T}_\omega$. This fact will be essential in the proof of the completeness result.

Lemma 1. *(Normal form) For each infinitary type $\phi \in \mathbf{T}$ there exist finitary types $\phi_{i,j} \in \mathbf{T}_\omega$, $i \in I$ and $j \in J$, such that $\vdash \ \phi = \bigwedge_{i\in I} \bigvee_{j\in J} \phi_{i,j}$.*

Proof. The proof proceed by induction on the structure of ϕ. We only treat the case $\phi \equiv \phi^l \rightarrow \phi^r$. By induction hypothesis we have that, for some types $\phi^l_{i,j}$'s and $\phi^r_{h,k}$'s in $\mathbf{T}_\omega$, the assertions $\phi^l = \bigwedge_{i\in I} \bigvee_{j\in J} \phi^l_{i,j}$ and $\phi^r = \bigwedge_{h\in H} \bigvee_{k\in K} \phi^r_{h,k}$ are both derivable in $\mathbf{T}$. Thus we have

$$
\begin{aligned}
&\phi^l \rightarrow \phi^r \\
&= \textstyle\bigwedge_{i\in I} \bigvee_{j\in J} \phi^l_{i,j} \rightarrow \bigwedge_{h\in H} \bigvee_{k\in K} \phi^r_{h,k} \quad \text{[induction hypothesis]} \\
&= \textstyle\bigvee_{m\in M} \bigwedge_{i\in I} \phi^l_{i,m} \rightarrow \bigwedge_{h\in H} \bigvee_{k\in K} \phi^r_{h,k} \quad \text{[complete distribuitivity, for some } M\text{]} \\
&= \textstyle\bigwedge_{h\in H} (\bigvee_{m\in M} \bigwedge_{i\in I} \phi^l_{i,m} \rightarrow \bigvee_{k\in K} \phi^r_{h,k}) \quad [\bigwedge \text{ distributes over} \rightarrow \text{at the right}] \\
&= \textstyle\bigwedge_{h\in H} \bigwedge_{m\in M} (\bigwedge_{i\in I} \phi^l_{i,m} \rightarrow \bigvee_{k\in K} \phi^r_{h,k}) \quad [\bigvee \text{ distributes over} \rightarrow \text{at the left}] \\
&= \textstyle\bigwedge_{h\in H} \bigwedge_{m\in M} \bigvee_{I'\in Fin(I)} \bigvee_{K'\in Fin(K)} (\bigwedge_{i\in I'} \phi^l_{i,m} \rightarrow \bigvee_{k\in K'} \phi^r_{h,k}),
\end{aligned}
$$

where in the last equality we used the axiom about distribution of infinite intersections and infinite unions over $\rightarrow$. Clearly, $\bigwedge_{i\in I'} \phi^l_{m,i} \rightarrow \bigvee_{k\in K'} \phi^r_{h,k}$ is a type in $\mathbf{T}_\omega$. Therefore $\phi^l \rightarrow \phi^r$ is provably equivalent in $\mathbf{T}$ to the intersection of unions of types in $\mathbf{T}_\omega$. □

Next we come to the soundness and completeness of the above system. Both results rely on the duality between the Scott domain $\mathcal{D}$ and the Lindenbaum algebra of $\mathbf{T}_\omega$. The following proposition is due to Abramsky [1].

Proposition 2. *Let $\mathcal{KO}(\mathcal{D})$ be the distributive lattice of Scott compact open sets of $\mathcal{D}$ ordered by subset inclusion. There is a well-defined order isomorphism between $\mathcal{KO}(\mathcal{D})$ and the Lindenbaum algebra $(\mathbf{T}_\omega/ =, \leq / =)$ which restricts to an isomorphism between the coprime elements of $\mathcal{KO}(\mathcal{D})$ and (equivalence classes of) types ϕ in $\mathbf{T}_\omega$ for which $\mathsf{C}(\phi)$ is provable.*

In other words, we can identify the finitary types in $\mathbf{T}_\omega$ with Scott compact open subsets of $\mathcal{D}$. This fact is used in the following soundness theorem.

Theorem 1. *(Soundness) Let ϕ_1 and ϕ_2 be two infinitary types in $\mathbf{T}$. If $\vdash \phi_1 \leq \phi_2$ then $\models \phi_1 \leq \phi_2$.*

The proof of the above theorem follows easily from the soundness proof given in [2], except for the soundness of the last structural rule. To validate it, we proceed as follows. First we apply the Scott open filter theorem by Hofmann and Mislove [12] to prove that for all Scott continuous functions $f:\mathcal{D} \to \mathcal{D}$, filtered collections of Scott compact saturated subsets $\{k_i\}_I$ of $\mathcal{D}$, and Scott open subsets u of $\mathcal{D}$, if $f(\bigcap_{i\in I} k_i) \subseteq u$ then there exists $i \in I$ such that $f(k_i) \subseteq u$. Secondly, we use compactness to prove that for all compact saturated subsets k of $\mathcal{D}$ and directed collection of open subsets $\{u_i\}_I$ of $\mathcal{D}$, if $f(k) \subseteq \bigcup_{i\in I} u_i$ then there exists $i \in I$ such that $f(k) \subseteq u_i$.

For proving the completeness of the infinitary type system $\mathbf{T}$ we need the following characterization of sober topological spaces [8, 9].

Proposition 3. *A T_0-space X is sober if and only if the completely distributive lattice of saturated sets $\mathcal{Q}(X)$ (ordered by subset inclusion) is free over the frame of open sets $\mathcal{O}(X)$ (ordered by subset inclusion).*

The collection of Scott compact open subsets of a Scott domain X is closed under finite intersection and it forms a basis for its Scott topology. More abstractly, the frame of Scott open sets $\mathcal{O}(X)$ (ordered by subset inclusion) is free over the distributive lattice of Scott compact opens $\mathcal{KO}(X)$ (ordered by subset inclusion) [13]. Applying this result to the Scott domain $\mathcal{D}$ and combining it with the previous proposition (since a Scott domain together with its Scott topology forms a sober space) we obtain that the completely distributive lattice of saturated sets $\mathcal{Q}(\mathcal{D})$ is free over the distributive lattice of Scott compact opens $\mathcal{KO}(\mathcal{D})$.

Using the normal form Lemma 1 we obtain a more syntactic description of the free completely distributive lattice over $\mathcal{KO}(\mathcal{D})$.

Lemma 2. *The Lindenbaum algebra $(\mathbf{T}/=, \leq/=)$ forms a completely distributive lattice which is free over the distributive lattice $(\mathbf{T}_\omega/=, \leq/=)$.*

Combining the above lemma with Proposition 3, and using the fact that free constructions are unique up-to isomorphism, we can now lift the isomorphism of Proposition 2 to an isomorphism between infinitary types and saturated sets of the Scott topology of $\mathcal{D}$.

Theorem 2. *The order isomorphism of Proposition 2 extends uniquely to a well-defined order isomorphism between the completely distributive lattice $\mathcal{Q}(\mathcal{D})$ of saturated sets of the Scott topology of $\mathcal{D}$ ordered by subset inclusion and the Lindenbaum algebra $(\mathbf{T}/=, \leq/=)$.*

Strong completeness of $\mathbf{T}$ now follows easily.

Corollary 1. *(Completeness) For ϕ_1 and ϕ_2 in $\mathbf{T}$, we have $\models \phi_1 \leq \phi_2$ if and only if $\vdash \phi_1 \leq \phi_2$.*

Another consequence of the above order isomorphism is that the order of $\mathcal{D}$ coincides with the preorder induced by $\mathbf{T}$ on $\mathcal{D}$: For every $d_1, d_2 \in \mathcal{D}$, $d_1 \sqsubseteq d_2$ if and only if $\mathbf{T}(d_1) \subseteq \mathbf{T}(d_2)$. From the discussion at the end of the previous section, we can conclude that the infinitary type theory $\mathbf{T}$ characterizes applicative bisimulation in terms of the types of the closed terms: $M \lesssim^B N$ if and only if $\mathbf{T}([\![M]\!]) \subseteq \mathbf{T}([\![N]\!])$.

Furthermore, $\mathcal{D}$ is a good model for $\mathbf{T}$ in the sense that continuous functions preserve logical properties, that is, for every $d \in \mathcal{D}$, if $unfold(d) = f \neq \bot$ then $\mathbf{T}(d_1) \subseteq \mathbf{T}(d_2)$ implies $\mathbf{T}(f(d_1)) \subseteq \mathbf{T}(f(d_2))$.

4 The Type Assignment System

In this section we define a type assignment system relative to the infinitary type theory $\mathbf{T}$. Judgments have the form $\Gamma \vdash M{:}\phi$, where the *subject* M is an untyped λ-term, the *predicate* ϕ is a type in $\mathbf{T}$, and the *assumption* Γ is a set consisting of pairs $x{:}\phi_x$ for x a variable in Var and ϕ_x a type in $\mathbf{T}$. We assume that each variable in Γ appears at most once, and that all free variables of M are declared in Γ. Furthermore we denote by $\Delta \leq \Gamma$ the fact that Δ and Γ are both assumptions about the same variables, and $\vdash \phi_x \leq \phi'_x$ for all $x{:}\phi_x \in \Delta$ and $x{:}\phi'_x \in \Gamma$.

Validity of the typing judgments is defined in terms of the meaning of λ-terms as elements of $\mathcal{D}$ defined previously:

$$\Gamma \models M{:}\phi \iff \forall \rho{:}Var \to \mathcal{D}.\, \forall x{:}\phi_x \in \Gamma. \quad \rho(x) \models \phi_x \text{ implies } [\![M]\!]_\rho \models \phi.$$

The following system gives an axiomatization of the type judgments.

- $$\frac{\Gamma \leq \Delta \text{ and } \Delta \vdash M{:}\phi_1 \text{ and } \phi_1 \leq \phi_2}{\Gamma \vdash M{:}\phi_2}$$
- $$\frac{\{\Gamma \vdash M{:}\phi_i\}_{i \in I}}{\Gamma \vdash M{:} \bigwedge_{i \in I} \phi_i}$$
- $$\frac{\{\Gamma, x{:}\phi_i \vdash M{:}\phi\}_{i \in I}}{\Gamma, x{:} \bigvee_{i \in I} \phi_i \vdash M{:}\phi}$$
- $$\frac{\Gamma \vdash M{:}(\phi_1 \to \phi_2)_\bot \text{ and } \Gamma \vdash N{:}\phi_1}{\Gamma \vdash MN{:}\phi_2}$$
- $$\frac{\Gamma, x{:}\phi_1 \vdash M{:}\phi_2}{\Gamma \vdash \lambda x.M{:}(\phi_1 \to \phi_2)_\bot}$$
- $$\frac{x{:}\phi \in \Gamma}{\Gamma \vdash x{:}\phi}$$

The above type judgment is standard. Basically, it is Abramsky's endogenous logic $\Lambda(\sigma)$ for the type expression $\sigma \equiv \mathbf{rec}\,t.(t \to t)_\bot$ [2] augmented to allow for infinite meets and joins. Its presentation is rather intuitive, and differs from the standard intersection type assignment system because abstractions receive a type that is build by means of the type constructors '$\to$' and '$(\cdot)_\bot$'.

Soundness is proved by induction on the lengh of the proofs.

Theorem 3. *For all assumptions Γ, λ-terms M, and types $\phi \in T$,*

$\Gamma \vdash M{:}\phi$ *implies* $\Gamma \models M{:}\phi$.

To get completeness we proceed as before. First we consider the finitary restriction of the above type judgment and apply Abramsky's completeness theorem for the endogenous logic $\Lambda(\sigma)$ [2].

Proposition 4. *For all λ-terms M, finitary types $\phi \in \mathbf{T}_\omega$, and assumptions Γ such that $\phi_x \in \mathbf{T}_\omega$ for every $x{:}\phi_x \in \Gamma$,*

$\Gamma \models M{:}\phi$ *implies* $\Gamma \vdash M{:}\phi$.

Using now Lemma 1 we can finally state the following completeness theorem.

Theorem 4. *(Completeness) For all assumptions Γ, λ-terms M, and types $\phi \in T$,*

$\Gamma \models M{:}\phi$ *if and only if* $\Gamma \vdash M{:}\phi$.

5 Conclusion

We have presented a complete infinitary intersection type system with respect to the ordinary set-theoretic semantics. Although we have defined it only for the lazy λ-calculus, our result is general enough to be applied to other λ-calculi based on other domain theoretical function spaces (e.g. the Scott function space, the strict function space, and the Landin-Plotkin function space [1]). Also extensions with basic types can be considered by associating each basic type to a fixed Scott domain, and extending coprimeness, entailment, and typing judgements by taking into account upper-closed subsets of these domains as formulae.

Our type system includes union types, and inherits from [2] the need of a 'coprimeness predicate' for proving completeness. This implies that it is not clear how to interpret our type system, maintaining completeness, to applicative transition systems rather than to a single Scott domain. One possibility could be to restrict the syntax of the types, for example by not allowing for (infinite) union types to occur at the right-hand side of the $\rightarrow$ constructor. Another possibility would be to define a type interpretation directly connected to the usual one for intersection types only, as in [4].

The types we consider in this paper are infinite. However there are interesting fragments that have a finite and transparent representation [14]. The size of the types can be limited without losing completeness. Since $\mathcal{D}$ is an ω-algebraic cpo, its cardinality is at most $2^{\aleph_0}$, while that of the collection of its saturated sets is at most $2^{|\mathcal{D}|} = 2^{2^{\aleph_0}}$. By Theorem 2 types in $\mathbf{T}$ are identified (up-to logical equivalence) with saturated sets of $\mathcal{D}$. Thus we can constrain the size of the index set of the intersection and union type constructors by any cardinal greater than $2^{2^{\aleph_0}}$, that is, under the Generalized Continuum Hypothesis, the infinite cardinal $\aleph_2$.

References

1. S. Abramsky. The lazy lambda calculus. In *Research Topics in Functional Programming*, pp. 65–117, Addison Wesley, 1990.
2. S. Abramsky. Domain theory in logical form. *Annals of Pure and Applied Logic*, 51(1):1–77, 1991.
3. F. Barbanera and M. Dezani-Ciancaglini. Intersection and union types. In *Proceedings of TACS'91*, vol. 526 of *Lecture Notes in Computer Science*, pp. 651–674. Springer-Verlag, 1991.
4. F. Barbanera, M. Dezani-Ciancaglini, and U. dé Liguoro. Intersection and union types: syntax and semantics. *Information and Computation*, 119:202–230, 1995.
5. H. Barendregt. *The Lambda Calculus: Its Syntax and Semantics.* North Holland, 1984.
6. H. Barendregt, M. Coppo, and M. Dezani-Ciancaglini. A filter lambda model and the completeness of type assignment. *Journal of Symbolic Logic* 48(4):931–940, 1983.
7. M.M. Bonsangue, B. Jacobs, and J.N. Kok. Duality beyond sober spaces: topological spaces and observation frames. *Theoretical Computer Science*, 151(1):79–124, 1995.
8. M.M. Bonsangue. *Topological Dualities in Semantics.* Vol. 8 of *Electronic Notes in Theoretical Computer Science.* Elsevier Science, 1997.
9. M.M. Bonsangue and J.N. Kok. Towards an infinitary logic of domains: Abramsky logic for transition systems. *Information and Computation*, 155:170–201, 1999.
10. M. Coppo and M. Dezani-Ciancaglini. A new type-assignment for λ-term. In *Archiv. Math. Logik*, 19:139–156, 1978.
11. M. Dezani-Ciancaglini, F. Honsell and Y. Motohama. Compositional characterizations of λ-terms using intersection types. In *Proceedings of MFCS 2000*, vol. 1893 of *Lecture Notes in Computer Science*, pp. 304–313. Springer-Verlag, 2000.
12. K.H. Hofmann and M.W. Mislove. Local compactness and continuous lattices. In *Continuous lattices - Proceedings Bremen 1979*, vol. 871 of *Lecture Notes in Mathematics*, pp. 209–248. Springer-Verlag, 1981.
13. P.T. Johnstone. *Stone Spaces.* Cambridge University Press, 1982.
14. D. Leivant. Discrete polymorphism. In *Proceedings of 1990 ACM Conference of LISP and Functional Programming*, pp. 288–297.
15. B.C. Pierce. Programming with intersection types, union types, and polymorphism. Technical Report CMU-CS-91-106, Carnegie Mellon University, 1991.
16. G. Pottinger. A type assignment for the strongly normalizable λ-term. In *To H.B. Curry: Essays on Combinatory Logic, Lambda Calculus, and Formalism*, pp. 561-577. Academic Press, 1980.
17. G. Raney. Completely distributive complete lattices. In *Proceedings of the American Mathematical Society* vol. 3(4), pp. 677–680, 1952.
18. D.S. Scott Domains for denotational semantics. In M. Nielson and E.M. Schmidt (eds.), *International Colloquioum on Automata, Languages, and Programs*, volume 140 of *Lecture Notes in Computer Science*, pp 577-613, Springer-Verlag, 1982.

Strong Normalization of Second Order Symmetric Lambda-mu Calculus

Yoriyuki Yamagata

Department of Mathematical Science, University of Tokyo,
yoriyuki@ms.u-tokyo.ac.jp

Abstract. Parigot suggested symmetric structural reduction rules for application to μ-abstraction in [9] to ensure unique representation of data type. We prove strong normalization of second order $\lambda\mu$-calculus with these rules.

1 Introduction

Originally, $\lambda\mu$-calculus was defined to clarify correspondence between classical logic and control operators in functional programming languages. In this respect, $\lambda\mu$-calculus seems quite successful [5] [6] [7] [12]. In fact, $\lambda\mu$-calculus can be seen as an extension of λ-calculus equipped with variables, binding construct and application for continuation [12]. This makes $\lambda\mu$-calculus suitable for the study of programming languages.

In addition, Parigot was also motivated in [8] by possibility of witness extraction from classical proofs of Σ_1^0-sentences. Unfortunately, reduction rules of $\lambda\mu$-calculus seems not sufficient for this purpose. For example, let $A(x)$ be an atomic formula of arithmetic and $A'(x)$ be its code in second order predicate logic. We represent $\exists x.A(x)$ as $\forall X.\forall x(A(x) \to X) \to X$ in second order language, where X is a variable over propositions. We expect that a closed normal deduction of $\exists x.A'(x)$ somehow contains a unique first order term t such that $A(t)$ holds. However, consider the following situation. Suppose that $A(t)$ holds but $A(u)$ does not hold. Let M be a deduction of $A'(t)$ represented as $\lambda\mu$-terms. $\Lambda X.\lambda\alpha.\mu\beta.[\beta]\alpha u(\mu\gamma.[\beta]\alpha t M)$ is a closed and normal deduction of $\exists x A'(x)$ but apparently contains two terms t, u. Moreover, u is not a witness of $\exists x A(x)$. This suggests that we need additional reduction to extract the witness. In fact, Parigot proposed addition of new reduction rules (symmetric structural reduction) $M(\mu\alpha.N) \Rightarrow \mu\beta.N[M^*/\alpha]$ to solve similar problem on normal forms of the natural number type. $N[M^*/\alpha]$ is defined by inductively replacing all occurrence of $[\alpha]L$ in N to $[\alpha]M(L[M^*/\alpha])$. We will present a new calculus from which rules above can be derivable, and prove that it suffices to ensure that a closed normal term of type $\exists x A(x)$ for an atomic $A(x)$ contains one and only one first order term t and $A(t)$ holds. While numerous works on computational interpretation of classical proof are done, properties of normal form does not seem so well understood. Barbanera and Berardi shows that in symmetric lambda calculus for first order Peano arithmetic, closed normal forms of this calculus consist of introduction rules alone [3]. In addition to this work, we have to mention Parigot's

N. Kobayashi and B.C. Pierce (Eds.): TACS 2001, LNCS 2215, pp. 459–467, 2001.

work on output operators, which extract church numeral from classical proof of inhabitance of natural number type [9]. Danos et al. applied this technique to second order sequent calculus and show that it can be used for witness extraction from proofs of Σ^0_1-formulae [4]. Our work could be seen a sequel to these studies.

Obviously, to use such calculus for witness extraction, we need normalization property of it. In addition, if we expect that reduction rules fully specify extraction algorithm of witness, strong normalization is desirable. However, symmetric nature of reduction of application to μ-abstraction seems to prevent direct adaption of the proof of strong normalization of original $\lambda\mu$-calculus [10]. Luke Ong and Charles Stewart addressed strong normalization of a calculus with call-by-value restriction of symmetric structural reduction rules [7]. Their calculus $\lambda\mu_v$ is confluent, hence useful as a programming language, in contrast to our calculus. However, imposing reduction strategy seems to be an alien idea in a logical calculus. Non-confluency is come from unrestricted use of symmetric structural rules, hence essential feature of such calculus.

Barbanera and Berardi proved strong normalization of a non-deterministic calculus for propositional classical logic using fixed point construction for reducibility candidates [2]. We will prove strong normalization of second order $\lambda\mu$-calculus with the rules above based on this method.

2 Symmetric $\lambda\mu$-calculus

Our formalization is a second order extension of symmetric $\lambda\mu$-calculus in [11]. Usually, a term of $\lambda\mu$-calculus is understood as a proof with multiple conclusions. On the contrary, we consider a $\lambda\mu$-term as a proof with a single conclusion but two kinds of hypothesis, ordinary hypothesis and denials of propositions, which correspond conclusions other than a principal formula in usual $\lambda\mu$-calculus. Moreover, we do not distinguish λ-variables and μ-variables. $x, y, x_1, \cdots$ and $t, u, t_1, \cdots$ stand for first order variables and terms. X^n, Y^n, X^n_i and denotes n-ary predicate variables.

Definition 1. *The set of* first order term *consists of a constant* 0, *unary function* S, *and function symbols* f *for all primitive recursive function on natural numbers. A* proposition *is that of second order predicate logic built up by equality* $=$, *predicate variables* X^n_i *and logical connectives* $\rightarrow$, $\forall$. *Formally,*

$$A ::= t_1 = t_2 \mid X^n_i t_1 \cdots t_n \mid A \rightarrow A \mid \forall x_i A \mid \forall X^n_i A.$$

A formula *is a proposition* A *or a denial* $\bullet A$ *of proposition or contradiction* $\perp$. *Note that* $\perp$ *is not counted as a proposition. Other connectives are defined by using second order construct. For example,* $\exists x.A(x)$ *is defined as* $\forall X^0.\forall x(A(x) \rightarrow X^0) \rightarrow X^0$ *and* $A \wedge B$ *as* $\forall X^0.(A \rightarrow B \rightarrow X) \rightarrow X$.

Definition 2. *An* abstraction term T *is a form* $\lambda x_1 \cdots x_n.A$ *for a proposition* A. *Substitution* $B[T/X^n]$ *of* T *for a predicate variable* X^n *in* B *is defined by* *replacing each occurrences of $X^n t_1 \cdots t_n$ whose X^n is a free variable in B, to $A[t_1, \cdots, t_n/x_1, \cdots, x_n]$.*

Definition 3. *The set of* axioms *consists of equality axioms, defining axioms for primitive recursive functions and the proposition $S0 = 0 \to \forall X.X$. We note that equality axioms and defining axioms can be formulated as atomic rules, that is the set of formulae of forms $A_1 \to A_2 \to \cdots \to A_n$ with atomic formula A_i. This constraint is relevant to the fact that a closed term of type of atomic formula without μ consists of axiom alone.*

Definition 4. $\lambda\mu$-terms of type A *are given by followings rules. (In the figure, $t : A$ means t have the type A.) For each formula A,* $\lambda\mu$-terms of type A *are defined inductively as follows. We denote variable by Greek letters $\alpha, \beta, \cdots$.*

$$\frac{}{\text{axiom}_i : A} \qquad \frac{[\alpha^C]}{\alpha : C}$$

$$\frac{M : \bullet A \quad N : A}{[M]N : \bot}\,[] \qquad \frac{\begin{matrix}[\alpha^A] \\ \vdots \\ M : \bot\end{matrix}}{\mu\alpha.M : \bullet A}\,\mu \qquad \frac{\begin{matrix}[\alpha^{\bullet A}] \\ \vdots \\ M : \bot\end{matrix}}{\mu\alpha.M : A}\,\mu$$

$$\frac{M : A \to B \quad N : A}{MN : B}\,\text{app.} \qquad \frac{\begin{matrix}[\alpha^A] \\ \vdots \\ M : B\end{matrix}}{\lambda\alpha.M : A \to B}\,\lambda$$

$$\frac{M : \forall x A}{Mt : A[t/x]}\,app.^1 \qquad \frac{M : A}{\lambda x.M : \forall x A}\,\lambda^1$$

$$\frac{M : \forall X A}{MT : A[T/X]}\,app.^2 \qquad \frac{M : A}{\lambda X.M : \forall x A}\,\lambda^2$$

In the above rules λ^1, λ^2, the derivation of M does not contains x or X as free variables.

Remark 1. Well typed terms of Parigot's $\lambda\mu$-calculus can be translated to the calculus above, by replacing μ-variables of type A to variables of type $\bullet A$.

Remark 2. The reason of "Church style formulation", that is, incorporating typing information as a part of term, is that in the proof of strong normalization, we seems to need the fact that each term has a unique type.

Definition 5. Reduction rules *are the followings. Let β, γ, δ be fresh variables.*

$$
\begin{array}{llll}
(\lambda_1) & (\lambda\alpha.M)N & \Rightarrow M[N/\alpha] & \\
(\lambda_2) & (\lambda x.M)t & \Rightarrow M[t/x] & \\
(\lambda_3) & (\lambda X^n.M)T & \Rightarrow M[T/X^n] & \\
(\mu) & [M]\mu\alpha.N & \Rightarrow N[M/\alpha] & [\mu\alpha.M]N \Rightarrow M[N/\alpha] \\
(\zeta_1) & (\mu\alpha.M)N & \Rightarrow \mu\beta.M[\mu\gamma.[\beta](\gamma N)/\alpha] & M(\mu\alpha.N) \Rightarrow \mu\beta.N[\mu\gamma.[\beta](M\gamma)/\alpha] \\
(\zeta_2) & (\mu\alpha.M)t & \Rightarrow \mu\beta.M[\mu\gamma.[\beta](\gamma t)/\alpha] & \\
(\zeta_3) & (\mu\alpha.M)T & \Rightarrow \mu\beta.M[\mu\gamma.[\beta](\gamma T)/\alpha] &
\end{array}
$$

As usual, compatible closure of the rules above is called *one-step reduction relation* (denoted $\Rightarrow_1$) and reflexive and transitive closure of one-step reduction is called *reduction relation* (denoted $\Rightarrow$). $w(M)$ is the maximal length of sequences $M \Rightarrow_1 M_1 \cdots \Rightarrow_1 M_n$ if the maximum exists. Otherwise $w(M)$ is undefined. M is *strongly normalizable* if and only if $w(M)$ is defined.

Using μ and ζ-rules, Parigot's structural reduction [8] and symmetric one [9] mentioned in Section 1 can be derived.

$$(\mu\alpha. \ldots[\alpha]N\ldots)L \Rightarrow_\zeta \mu\beta. \ldots[\mu\gamma.[\beta](\gamma L)]N\ldots \Rightarrow_\mu \mu\beta. \ldots[\beta](NL)\ldots$$

$$N(\mu\alpha. \ldots[\alpha]L\ldots) \Rightarrow_\zeta \mu\beta. \ldots[\mu\gamma.[\beta](N\gamma)]L\ldots \Rightarrow_\mu \mu\beta. \ldots[\beta](NL)\ldots$$

If we understand $\bullet$ as the usual negation symbol, our ζ-rules resemble to Andou's reduction for $\bot_c$ [1].

3 Extraction of Witnesses from Σ_1^0-formulae

Let $N(x)$ be the formula $\forall X^1.X^1 0 \to \forall x(X^1 x \to X^1 Sx) \to X^1 x$. It is well known that we can encode the second order Peano arithmetic into second order predicate logic as presented above. Σ_1^0-sentences are represented as $\exists x N(x) \wedge A(x)$. Since $\exists x A(x)$ is derivable from such formula, we extract a witness from the proof of the formula $\exists x A(x)$.

Definition 6. *I-context $E_I[]$ is a context defined by the following grammar.*

$$I[] ::= \lambda\alpha.E_I[] \mid \lambda x.E_I[] \mid \lambda X.E_I[]$$

$$E_I[] ::= [] \mid I[] \mid \mu\alpha.[\beta]I[]$$

Definition 7. *For a proposition A, $\alpha(A)$, $\beta(A)$ and $\gamma(A)$ are defined as follows. $\alpha(A)$ is the set of formulae $\{A\}$ for atomic A and $\{A\} \cup \alpha(A_2)$ for the case $A \equiv A_1 \to A_2, \forall x A_2, \forall X A_2$. $\beta(A)$ is the set of formulae $\{\bullet A\}$ for atomic A, $\{\bullet A\} \cup \beta(A_1)$ for $A \equiv \forall x A_1, \forall X A_1$ and $\{A_1\} \cup \{\bullet A\} \cup \beta(A_2)$ for $A \equiv A_1 \to A_2$. $\gamma(A)$ is the set of variables $\emptyset$ for atomic A, $\{x\} \cup \gamma(A_1)$ for $A \equiv \forall x A_1$, $\{X\} \cup \gamma(A_1)$ for $A \equiv \forall X A_1$, $\gamma(A_2)$ for $A \equiv A_1 \to A_2$. For a set S of formulae, $\alpha(S) = \bigcup_{A \in S} \alpha(A)$. $\beta(S), \gamma(S)$ are defined similarly. Note that $S \subset \alpha(S)$ and if $B \in \alpha(A)$ then $\alpha(B) \subset \alpha(A)$.*

Lemma 1. *Let $E_I[M]$ be a term of type A with free variables of type $A_1, \cdots, A_m$ (usual propositions) and $\bullet B_1, \cdots, \bullet B_n$ (denials). Then, the type of M is an element of $\alpha(\{A, B_1, \cdots, B_n\})$, types of free variables are contained in the set $\{A_1, \cdots, A_m\} \cup \beta(\{A, B_1, \cdots, B_n\})$. Free first order and predicate variable contained in M are those of $E_I[M]$ or elements of $\gamma(A)$.*

Proof. By induction on construction of $E_I[M]$.

Lemma 2. *All normal forms of $\lambda\mu$-term have forms $E_I[\alpha M_1 \cdots M_n]$.*

Proof. By induction on construction of a term.

Proposition 1. *Let $A(x)$ be an atomic formula and M be a normal closed term of type $\exists x A(x)$. M contains one and only one first order term t and $A(t)$ holds.*

Proof. By Lemma 2 and considering $\beta(\exists x A(x))$, together with consistency of the calculus, we see that M has a form $E_I[\alpha t K]$ where α has type $\forall x(A(x) \to X)$, t is a first order term and K is a term of type $A(t)$. Since K can not begin with μ, and whose type is atomic, $K \equiv K_1 K_2 \cdots K_m$. K_1 is either a variable of type $\forall x(A(x) \to X)$ or axioms, but $\forall x(A(x) \to X)$ is impossible since $A(x)$ does not contain X as a free variable. Hence K_1 is an axiom and types of all of $K_2, \cdots, K_m$ are atomic. By similar argument to K, $K_2, \cdots, K_m$ have a form of application to axioms. Repeatedly applying this argument, we can conclude that K consists of axioms alone.

4 Strong Normalization

This section is devoted to the proof of strong normalization theorem.

Definition 8. *First we prepare several notations.*

1. *A term beginning with μ is called a μ-form.*
2. *For a set S of terms of type C, $Cl(S)$ is defined as the smallest set which satisfies clauses*
   (a) *$S \subset Cl(S)$ and contains all variables of type C.*
   (b) *$MN \in Cl(S)$ if $L \in Cl(S)$ for all L such that $MN \Rightarrow_1 L$.*
   (c) *$Mt \in Cl(S)$ if $L \in Cl(S)$ for all L such that $Mt \Rightarrow_1 L$ for a first order term t.*
   (d) *$MT \in Cl(S)$ if $L \in Cl(S)$ for all L such that $MT \Rightarrow_1 L$ for an abstraction term T.*
3. *The set of strongly normalizable terms of type $\bot$ is also denoted $\bot$.*
4. *For a set S of terms of type $C \neq \bot$,*

$$\bullet S := \{\mu\alpha.M | \forall N \in S, M[N/\alpha] \in \bot\}$$

where α is a variable of type C and M has a type $\bot$.

5. *the operator $D(\mathcal{X})$ is defined as $Cl(\mathcal{X} \cup \bullet\bullet\mathcal{X})$. Note that $\bullet\bullet$ and hence D are monotone operators. For ordinal κ,*

$$D^{\kappa}(\mathcal{X}) := D(\bigcup_{\tau<\kappa} D^{\tau}(\mathcal{X})).$$

Definition 9 (Reducibility candidates). *Let ω_1 be the first uncountable ordinal and A be a proposition. Let S be a set of strongly normalizable terms of type A. Suppose S does not contain a μ-form and S is closed under reduction relation. Then, a set $D^{\omega_1}(S)$ is called a* reducibility candidate *of the proposition A. Note that from monotonicity of D, a reducibility candidate is a fixed point of D. The set of candidates of the proposition A is denoted by $\mathbf{R}_A$. $\mathbf{R}$ is the union of all $\mathbf{R}_A$.*

Lemma 3. *Let $\mathcal{R}$ be a reducibility candidate. Then the followings hold.*

1. *All terms in $\mathcal{R}$ are strongly normalizable.*
2. *$\mathcal{R} = Cl(S \cup \bullet\bullet\mathcal{R})$.*
3. *For $M \in \bullet\mathcal{R}$ and $N \in \mathcal{R}$, $[M]N \in \bot$*

Proof. The clause 1 follows from induction on ω_1.

Since $\mathcal{R}$ is a fixed point of D, we have $\mathcal{R} = Cl(\mathcal{R} \cup \bullet\bullet\mathcal{R}) \supset Cl(S \cup \bullet\bullet\mathcal{R})$, while $D^{\kappa}(S) \subset Cl(S \cup \bullet\bullet\mathcal{R})$. We have the clause 2.

To prove the clause 3, it suffices to prove that all L such that $[M]N \Rightarrow_1 L$ are strongly normalizable. The proof is induction on $w(M)+w(N)$. We consider each possibility of the reduction of $[M]N$.

The case where L has the form $[M']N'$ and $M \Rightarrow M'$ and $N \Rightarrow N'$. The thesis follows from induction hypothesis on $w(M) + w(N)$.

The case where $M \equiv \mu\alpha.M_1$ and $L \equiv M_1[N/\alpha]$. By the hypothesis $M \in \bullet\mathcal{R}$.

The case where $N \equiv \mu\alpha.N_1$ and $L \equiv N_1[M/\alpha]$. By Lemma 3, N should be an element of $\bullet\bullet\mathcal{R}$. We have the thesis.

Definition 10. *Let $\mathcal{A} \in \mathbf{R}_A$ and $\mathcal{B} \in \mathbf{R}_B$. Assume that $(t_i)_{i\in I}$ is a non-empty family of first order terms and $(T_j)_{j\in J}$ is a non-empty family of abstraction terms. Further, $\mathcal{A}_i$ is a candidate of the proposition $A[t_i/x]$ for each $i \in I$ and $\mathcal{A}_j$ is a candidate of the proposition $A[T_j/X]$ for each $j \in J$. Candidates $\mathcal{A} \to \mathcal{B}$ $\bigwedge^1_{i\in I} \mathcal{A}_i$, $\bigwedge^2_{j\in J} \mathcal{A}_j$ are defined by the following steps.*

$$L(\mathcal{A},\mathcal{B}) := \{\lambda\alpha^A.M | \forall N \in \mathcal{A}, M[N/\alpha^A] \in \mathcal{B}\} \tag{1}$$

$$\Pi^1_{i\in I}\mathcal{A}_i := \{\lambda x.M | \forall i \in I, M[t_i/x] \in \mathcal{A}_i\} \tag{2}$$

$$\Pi^2_{j\in J}\mathcal{A}_j := \{\lambda X.M | \forall j \in J, M[T_j/X] \in \mathcal{A}_j\} \tag{3}$$

$$\mathcal{A} \to \mathcal{B} := D^{\omega_1}(L(\mathcal{A},\mathcal{B})) \tag{4}$$

$$\bigwedge^1_{i\in I} \mathcal{A}_i := D^{\omega_1}(\Pi^1_{i\in I}\mathcal{A}_i) \tag{5}$$

$$\bigwedge^2_{j\in J} \mathcal{A}_i := D^{\omega_1}(\Pi^2_{j\in J}\mathcal{A}_i) \tag{6}$$

Lemma 4. *Let $\mathcal{A} \in \mathbf{R}_A$ and $\mathcal{B} \in \mathbf{R}_B$. If $M \in \mathcal{A} \to \mathcal{B}$ and $N \in \mathcal{A}$, $MN \in \mathcal{B}$.*

Proof. Let $\mathcal{A} = D^{\omega_1}(S)$. Assume that κ is the least ordinal such that $M \in D^{\kappa}(L(\mathcal{A}, \mathcal{B}))$ and τ is the least ordinal such that $N \in D^{\tau}(S)$. By induction on the natural sum $\kappa \oplus \tau$ and $w(M) + w(N)$, we will prove that if $MN \Rightarrow_1 L$, $L \in \mathcal{B}$, which is the exact condition of $MN \in \mathcal{B}$.

The case $L \equiv M'N'$ and either $M \Rightarrow_1 M'$ and $N \equiv N'$ or $M \equiv M'$ and $N \Rightarrow_1 N'$. The thesis follows from induction hypothesis on $w(M) + w(N)$.

The case $M \equiv \lambda\alpha.M_1$ and $L \equiv M_1[N/\alpha]$. Since $M \in L(\mathcal{A}, \mathcal{B})$, we have the thesis.

The case where M has a form $\mu\alpha.M_1$ and L is obtained from reduction of the outermost redex. Then, L has a form $\mu\beta.M_1[\mu\gamma.[\beta](\gamma N)/\alpha]$. Let $J \in \bullet\mathcal{B}$, $K \in D^{\kappa_1}(L(\mathcal{A}, \mathcal{B}))$ for $\kappa_1 < \kappa$. We can assume that $kappa_1$ is smallest one such that $D^{\kappa_1}(L(\mathcal{A}, \mathcal{B}))$ contains K. By induction hypothesis on κ_1, we have $KN \in \mathcal{B}$. It follows $[J](KN) \in \bot$. From arbitrariness of K and κ_1, $\mu\gamma.[J](\gamma N) \in \bullet\bigcup_{\kappa_1<\kappa} D^{\kappa_1}(L(\mathcal{A}, \mathcal{B}))$ follows. Since M is a μ-form, $M \in \bullet\bullet\bigcup_{\kappa_1<\kappa} D^{\kappa_1}(L(\mathcal{A}, \mathcal{B}))$. We can infer $M_1[\mu\gamma.[J](\gamma N)/\alpha] \in \bot$. Since $J \in \bullet\mathcal{B}$, we have $L \in \bullet\bullet\mathcal{B}$. Now, from $\bullet\bullet\mathcal{B} \subset \mathcal{B}$, the thesis follows.

The case where N has a form $\mu\alpha.N_1$ and L is obtained from reduction of the outermost redex. L has a form $\mu\beta.N_1[\mu\gamma.[\beta](M\gamma)/\alpha]$. Let $J \in \mathcal{B}$ and $K \in D^{\tau_1}(S)$ for $\tau_1 < \tau$. (as the above, we chose the smallest one.) From induction hypothesis on τ_1, we have $MK \in \mathcal{B}$. Similarly as above, it follows $\mu\gamma.[J](M\gamma) \in \bullet\bigcup_{\tau_1<\tau} D^{\tau_1}(S)$. Since N has a μ-form, $N \in \bullet\bullet\bigcup_{\tau_1<\tau} D^{\tau_1}(S)$. We have $N_1[\mu\gamma.[\beta](M\gamma)/\alpha] \in \bot$ and hence, $L \in \mathcal{B}$.

Lemma 5. *Assume that $(t_i)_{i\in I}, (\mathcal{A}_i)_{i\in I}$ is defined as Definition 10. If $M \in \bigwedge^1_{i\in I} \mathcal{A}_i$, $Mt_i \in \mathcal{A}_i$. Similarly, for $(T_j)_{j\in J}$ and $(\mathcal{A}_j)_{j\in J}$ defined as Definition 10, if $M \in \bigwedge^2_{j\in J} \mathcal{A}_j$, $MT_j \in \mathcal{A}_j$.*

Proof. The proof goes on the same line of that of Lemma 4. We concentrate the second order case. Let $D^{\omega_1}(S) = \bigwedge_{i\in I} \mathcal{A}_i$. Assume that κ is the least ordinal such that $t \in D^{\kappa}(S)$. We will prove that for all L such that $MT_j \Rightarrow_1 L$, $L \in \mathcal{A}_j$ holds, by induction on κ and $w(M)$.

The case where $L \equiv M'T_j$ and $M \Rightarrow_1 M'$. From induction hypothesis of $w(M')$, the thesis follows.

The case where $M \equiv \lambda X.M_1$ and $L \equiv M_1[T_j/X]$. Since $M \in \Pi^2_{j\in J}\mathcal{A}_j$, we have the thesis.

The case where $M \equiv \mu\alpha.M_1$ and $L \equiv \mu\beta.M_1[\mu\gamma.[\beta](\gamma T_i)/\alpha]$. Let $J \in \bullet\mathcal{A}_i$ and $K \in D^{\kappa_1}(S)$. (as Lemma 4, we choose the smallest one.) By induction hypothesis on κ_1, we have $KT_i \in \mathcal{A}_i$. From arbitrariness of K and κ_1, it follows

$$\mu\gamma.[J](\gamma T_i) \in \bullet \bigcup_{\kappa_1<\kappa} D^{\kappa_1}(S).$$

Since M has a μ-form, $M \in \bullet\bullet\bigcup_{\kappa_1<\kappa} D^{\kappa_1}(S)$. We can infer $M_1[\mu\gamma.[J](\gamma T_i)/\alpha] \in \bot$. Hence we have $L \in \bullet\bullet\mathcal{A}_i$.

The rest of the proof runs similarly to the usual method of reducibility candidates. Let $\mathcal{T}$ be the set of all first order terms. $\mathcal{F}^n$ denotes the set of all functions from $\mathcal{T}^n$ to $\mathbf{R}$. Suppose that ξ is a map sending first order variables to first order terms, a predicate variable X^n to n-ary function from the set of first order terms to $\mathbf{R}$. We extend ξ to be a map on the whole types using $\xi(\bot) = \bot$ and the following clauses.

$$\xi(\bullet A) = \bullet\xi(A) \tag{7}$$

$$\xi(A \to B) = \xi(A) \to \xi(B) \tag{8}$$

$$\xi(\forall x A) = \bigwedge_{t \in \mathcal{T}}^{1} \xi[t/x](A) \tag{9}$$

$$\xi(\forall X^n A) = \bigwedge_{f \in \mathcal{F}^n}^{2} \xi[f/X^n](A) \tag{10}$$

where $\xi[a/b]$ is defined as a map $\xi[a/b](b) = a$ and for $c \neq b$, $\xi[a/b](c) = \xi(c)$.

Proposition 2. *Let M be a term of type A. Assume that free first order variables of M are $x_1, \cdots, x_m$, free predicate variables of M are $X_1, \cdots, X_n$ and free variables of M are $\alpha_1^{A_1}, \cdots, \alpha_l^{A_l}$. Suppose that ξ is a map sending first order variables to first order terms, a predicate variable X^k to k-ary function from the set of first order terms to $\mathbf{R}$. For each $1 \leq i \leq n$ and $t_1, \cdots, t_k \in \mathcal{T}$ (k is the arity of $\xi(X_i)$) $\xi(X_i)t_1 \cdots t_n \in \mathbf{R}_{B_i[t_1/x_1, \cdots, t_n/x_k]}$. Let $N_j \in \xi(A_j)$ for $1 \leq j \leq l$. We define $\tilde{M}$ by simultaneous substitution $\xi(x_1), \cdots, \xi(x_m)$ into $x_1, \cdots, x_m$, $B_1, \cdots, B_n$ into $X_1, \cdots, X_n$, $N_1, \cdots, N_l$ into $\alpha_1, \cdots, \alpha_l$ on M. Then we have $\tilde{M} \in \xi(A)$.*

Proof. By induction on the construction of M.

As a special case, $t \in \xi(A)$ holds. From Lemma 3, we have the following theorem.

Theorem 1. *All terms are strongly normalizable.*

Acknowledgement. I am grateful to Ken-etsu Fujita, Ryu Hasegawa and Charles Stewart for their helpful comments and discussion.

References

1. Yuuki Andou. A normalization-procedure for the first order classical natural deduction with full symbols. *Tsukuba Journal of Mathematics*, 19(1):153–162, 1995.
2. F. Barbanera and S. Berardi. A strong normalization result for classical logic. *Ann. Pure Appl. Logic*, 76:99–116, 1995.
3. F. Barbanera and S. Berardi. A symmetric lambda calculus for "classical" program extraction. *Inf. Comput.*, 125(2):103–117, 1996.

4. V. Danos, J. B. Joinet, and H. Schellinx. A new deconstructive logic:linear logic. *J. Symb. Log.*, 62(3):755–807, 1997.
5. Ph. de Groote. A cps-translation of the $\lambda\mu$-calculus. In *Trees in algebra and programming, CAAP '94*, number 787 in Lect. Notes Comput. Sci, pages 85–99. Springer-Verlag, 1994.
6. Ph. de Groote. On the relation between $\lambda\mu$-calculus and the syntactic theory of sequential control. In *Logic programming and automated reasoning*, volume 822 of *Lect. Notes Comput. Sci*, pages 31–43. Springer-Verlag, 1994.
7. C.-H. L. Ong and C. A. Stewart. A curry-howard foundation for functional computation with control. In *Proceedings of the 24th Annual ACM SIGPLAN-SIGACT Symposium on Principles of Programming Languages*. ACM press, January 1997.
8. M. Parigot. $\lambda\mu$-calculus: an algorithmic interpretation of classical natural deduction. In A. Voronkov, editor, *Logic Programming and Automated Reasoning*, volume 624 of *Lecture Notes in Artificial Intelligence*, pages 190–201. Springer-Verlag, 1992.
9. M. Parigot. Classical proofs as programs. In *Computational logic and proof theory*, volume 713 of *Lect. Notes Comput. Sci*, pages 263–276. Springer-Verlag, 1993.
10. M. Parigot. Strong normalization for second order classical natural deduction. *J. Symb. Log.*, 62(4):1461–1479, 1997.
11. M. Parigot. On the computational interpretation of negation. In P. Clote and H. Schwichtenberg, editors, *Computer Science Logic*, volume 1862 of *Lect. Notes Comput. Sci*, pages 472–484. Springer-Verlag, 2000.
12. Th. Streicher and B. Reus. Classical logic, continuation semantics and abstract machines. *Journal of Functional Programming*, 8(6):543–572, 1998.

The Girard-Reynolds Isomorphism

Philip Wadler

Avaya Labs, wadler@avaya.com

Abstract. The second-order polymorphic lambda calculus, F2, was independently discovered by Girard and Reynolds. Girard additionally proved a *representation theorem*: every function on natural numbers that can be proved total in second-order intuitionistic propositional logic, P2, can be represented in F2. Reynolds additionally proved an *abstraction theorem*: for a suitable notion of logical relation, every term in F2 takes related arguments into related results. We observe that the essence of Girard's result is a projection from P2 into F2, and that the essence of Reynolds's result is an embedding of F2 into P2, and that the Reynolds embedding followed by the Girard projection is the identity. The Girard projection discards all first-order quantifiers, so it seems unreasonable to expect that the Girard projection followed by the Reynolds embedding should also be the identity. However, we show that in the presence of Reynolds's *parametricity* property that this is indeed the case, for propositions corresponding to inductive definitions of naturals, products, sums, and fixpoint types.

1 Introduction

Double-barreled names in science may be special for two reasons: some belong to ideas so subtle that they required two collaborators to develop; and some belong to ideas so sublime that they possess two independent discoverers. The Curry-Howard isomorphism is an idea of the first sort that guarantees the existence of ideas of the second sort, such as the Hindley-Milner type system and the Girard-Reynolds polymorphic lambda calculus.

The Curry-Howard isomorphism consists of a correspondence between a logical calculus and a computational calculus. Each logical formula corresponds to a computational type, each logical proof corresponds to a computational term, and reduction of proofs corresponds to reductions of terms. This last point means that it is not just formulas and proofs that are preserved by the correspondence, but the structure between them as well; hence we have no mere bijection but a true isomorphism.

Curry formulated this principle for combinatory logic and combinator terms [CF58]. Howard observed that it also applies to intuitionistic propositional logic and simply-typed lambda terms [How80]. The same idea extends to a correspondence between first-order intuitionistic logic with propositional variables and simply-typed lambda calculus with type variables, which explains why the logician Hindley and the computer scientist Milner independently discovered the Hindley-Milner type system [Hin69,Mil78,DM82]. It also extends to a

N. Kobayashi and B.C. Pierce (Eds.): TACS 2001, LNCS 2215, pp. 468–491, 2001.

correspondence between second-order intuitionistic logic with quantifiers over proposition variables and second-order typed lambda calculus with quantifiers over type variables, which explains why the logician Girard and the computer scientist Reynolds independently discovered the polymorphic lambda calculus [Gir72,Rey74].

Girard and Reynolds each made additional discoveries about the calculus that bears their name, henceforth referred to as F2. Girard proved a *representation theorem*: every function on natural numbers that can be proved total in second-order predicate calculus P2 (with both first- and second-order quantifiers) can be represented in F2 (using second-order quantifiers only). Reynolds proved an *abstraction theorem*: for a suitable notion of logical relation, every term in F2 takes related arguments into related results [Rey83].

The calculus P2 is larger than the image under the Curry-Howard isomorphism of F2: the former has first-order terms (we will take these to be terms of untyped lambda calculus) and both first- and second-order quantifiers, while the latter has second-order quantifiers only. Nonetheless, the essence of Girard's result is a projection from P2 onto F2 that is similar to the Curry-Howard isomorphism, in that it takes formulas to types and proofs to terms, but differs in that it erases all information about first-order terms and first-order quantifiers. This mapping also preserves reductions, so it is no mere surjection but a true homomorphism.

Reynolds's result traditionally concerns binary relations, but it extends to other notions of relation, including a degenerate unary case. In the unary version, the essence of Reynolds's result is an embedding from F2 into P2 that is similar to the Curry-Howard isomorphism, in that it takes types to formulas and proofs to terms, but differs in that it adds information about first-order quantifiers and first-order terms. This mapping also preserves reductions, so it is no mere injection but a true homomorphism. Furthermore, the result on binary relations can be recovered from the result on unary relations by a doubling operation, an embedding from P2 into P2 that takes formulas into formulas, proofs into proofs, and preserves reductions.

Strachey distinguished two types of polymorphism, where the meaning of a term depends upon a type [Str67]. In *parametric* polymorphism, the meaning of the term varies uniformly with the type (an example is the length function), while in *ad hoc* polymorphism, the meaning of the term at different types may not be related (an example is plus, which may have quite different meanings on integers, floats, and strings). Reynolds introduced a *parametricity* condition to capture a semantic notion corresponding to Strachey's parametric polymorphism. One consequence of the parametricity condition is the Identity Extension Lemma, which asserts that the relation corresponding to a type is the identity relation, so long as the relation corresponding to any free type variable is also taken to be the identity relation.

The Reynolds embedding followed by the Girard projection is the identity. Remarkably, I can find no place in the literature where this is remarked! While reading between the lines suggests that some researchers have intuitively grasped this duality, its precise description seems to have been more elusive.

Going the other way, it seems unreasonable to expect that the Girard projection followed by the Reynolds embedding should also yield the identity, because the projection discards all information about first-order terms. For instance, here is the standard inductive definition of natural numbers in P2.

$$\mathsf{Nat} \;\equiv\; \{\, n \,|\, \forall Z.\, (\forall m.\, m \in Z \to \mathsf{succ}\, m \in Z) \to \mathsf{zero} \in Z \to n \in Z \,\}$$

Here succ and zero are the usual successor and zero operations on Church numerals in untyped lambda calculus. Applying the Girard projection yields $\mathbf{Nat} \equiv \mathsf{Nat}^{\circ}$, the type of the Church numerals in F2.

$$\mathbf{Nat} \;\equiv\; \forall Z.\, (Z \to Z) \to (Z \to Z)$$

Then applying the Reynolds embedding in turn yields the following predicate, back in P2.

$$\mathbf{Nat}^{*} \;\equiv\; \{\, n \,|\, \forall Z. \forall s.\, (\forall m.\, m \in Z \to s\, m \in Z) \to \forall z.\, z \in Z \to n\, s\, z \in Z \,\}$$

This predicate does not look much like Nat — it makes no mention of succ or zero. However we will see that if we assume that the type **Nat** satisfies an analogue of Reynolds's *parametricity* condition, then Nat and $\mathbf{Nat}^{*}$ are equivalent, in that one can prove that any term satisfying the first predicate also satisfies the second, and conversely.

Hence, in the presence of parametricity, not only does the Girard projection take Nat to **Nat**, but also the Reynolds embedding takes **Nat** to Nat, and so in this important case one has not merely an embedding-projection pair but a true isomorphism.

We will show that similar results hold for all algebraic types, those types built from products, sums, and fixpoints. An alternative characterization of algebraic types is given by Böhm and Berarducci, where they are shown to be equivalent to the types of rank two with all quantifiers on the outside [BB85].

This paper contains a version of Reynold's Abstraction Theorem, but only hints at Girard's Representation Theorem. For a complete exposition of the latter, consult the excellent tutorials by Girard, Taylor, and Lafont [GLT89] or by Leivant [Lei90].

Both Girard's and Reynold's results have spawned large bodies of related work. The representation of algebraic data types in polymorphic lambda calculus was proposed by Böhm and Berarducci [BB85]. Girard's representation theorem is has been further explored by Leivant [Lei83,Lei90] and by Krivine and Parigot [KP90], among others. Reynolds's parametricity has been further explored by Reynolds [Rey84,Rey90,MR91], Reynolds and Plotkin [RP90], Bainbridge, Freyd, Scedrov and Scott [BFSS90], Hasegawa [Has94], Pitts [Pit87,Pit89,Pit98], and Wadler [Wad89,Wad91], among others. Formulations of the abstraction theorem in terms of logics have been examined by Mairson [Mai91], in various combinations by Abadi, Cardelli, Curien, and Plotkin [ACC93,PA93,PAC94], and by Takeuti [Tak98]. Many of these works observe some connection between parametricity and algebraic types [RP90,Has94,BFSS90,ACC93,PA93,PAC94,Tak98]. Breazu-Tannen and Coquand [BC88], building on work of Moggi [Mog86], show how to turn any model of untyped lambda calculus into a model of polymorphic lambda calculus that satisfies a parametricity condition at all algebraic types.

The results here are not so much new proofs as old proofs clarified. In particular, we set Girard's and Reynolds's proofs in a common framework, highlighting the relationship between them. Unlike some previous work, no complex semantic formalism or specialized logic is required; all is formulated within the well-known system of second-order predicate logic. And teasing apart the relation between parametric and extensive types appears to be new.

Particularly strong influences on this work have been: the original work of Girard and Reynolds; Leivant [Lei90], who presents Girard's result as a projection from P2 to F2; Mairson [Mai91], who presents Reynolds's result as an embedding of F2 in P2; Plotkin and Abadi [PA93] and Takeuti [Tak98], who present typed analogues of the untyped logic used here; Krivine and Parigot [KP90], who use a logic over untyped lambda terms similar to P2.

Treating Girard's representation theorem requires use of a logic with untyped terms, since the whole point of the theorem is to demonstrate that functions defined without reference to types may be represented in a typed calculus. However, use of an untyped calculus does severely restrict the available models. A typed calculus, such as that considered by Plotkin and Abadi [PA93] or Takeuti [Tak98], allows a fuller range of models.

Mairson [Mai91] appears to have grasped the inverse relation between the Reynolds embedding and the Girard projection, though he does not quite manage to state it. However, Mairson does seem to have missed the power of parametricity. He mislabels as "parametricity" the analogue of Reynolds's Abstraction Theorem, and he never states an analogue of Reynolds's parametricity condition or the Identity Extension Lemma. Thus when he writes "proofs of these equivalences still seem to require structural induction, as well as stronger assumptions than parametricity" [Mai91], I believe this is misleading: the equivalences he refers to cannot be proved using the Abstraction Theorem alone, but can indeed be proved in the presence of parametricity.

The Curry-Howard isomorphism has informed the development of powerful lambda calculi with dependent types, such as de Bruijn's Automath [deB70], Martin-Löf's type theory [Mar82], Constable's Nuprl [Con86], Coquand and Huet's calculus of constructions [CH88], and Barendregt's lambda cube [Bar91]. Each of these calculi introduces dependent types (types that depend upon values) to map first-order quantifiers into the type system. In contrast, the Girard projection discards all first-order information. To quote Leivant [Lei90],

> we pursue a dual approach: rather than enriching the type systems to match logic, we impoverish logic to match the type structure.

What is remarkable is that even after this impoverishment enough power remains to capture much of what matters in computing: the algebraic types, such as naturals, products, sums, and fixpoints.

The remainder of this paper is organized as follows. Section 2 introduces the second-order lambda calculus F2 and the second-order logic P2. Section 3 describes the Reynolds embedding and the Girard projection, and observes that the embedding followed by the projection is the identity. Section 4 explains doubling and parametricity. Section 5 shows that the two definitions of the naturals are equivalent under the parametricity postulate, and similarly for other algebraic types, and hence that there is a sense in which the Girard projection followed by the Reynolds embedding is also the identity.

2 Second-Order Lambda Calculus and Logic

The second-order lambda calculus F2 is summarized in Figure 1, and second-order intuitionistic logic P2 is summarized in Figure 2. For each calculus we list the syntactic categories, the proof rules, and the reductions that act upon proofs. We deliberately use x, y, z to range over individual variables in both calculi, and use X, Y, Z to range over type variables in F2 and predicate variables in P2. We write $\equiv$ for syntactic equivalence of terms, formulas, or proofs.

Judgements in F2 have the form $\Gamma \vdash t : A$, expressing that term t has type A in context Γ, where a context consists of pairs $x : A$ associating individual variables with types. Types are formed from type variables X, functions $A \rightarrow B$, and quantification over types $\forall X.\, B$. Terms are formed from individual variables x, abstraction $\lambda x : A.\, u$, application $s\, t$, type abstraction $\Lambda X.\, u$, and type application $s\, A$. A proof δ uniquely determines its concluding judgement $\Gamma \vdash t : A$, and conversely, δ is uniquely determined by Γ and t. A proof reduces when an introducer is followed by the corresponding eliminator. We write $\delta[x := \epsilon]$ for the proof that results by substituting proof ϵ for each use of (Id) on x in the proof δ.

Judgements in P2 have the form $\Theta \vdash \phi$, expressing that the formula list Θ has the formula ϕ as a consequence. An atomic formula has the form $M \in X$, where M is a term and X is a predicate variable. Fomulas are formed from atomic formulas, implication $\phi \rightarrow \psi$, quantification over individual variables $\forall x.\, \psi$, and quantification over predicate variables $\forall X.\, \psi$.

A term is an untyped lambda term. We write $M =_\beta N$ if M and N can be shown equivalent by β reduction.

Predicate variables X range over properties of terms. Notationally, we treat these as sets. Thus we write $M \in X$ to mean that term M satisfies predicate X. The comprehension notation $\{\, x \mid \phi \,\}$ denotes the predicate of x that is satisfied when the formula ϕ over x holds; so x is free in ϕ but bound in $\{\, x \mid \phi \,\}$. We write $\psi[X := \{\, x \mid \phi \,\}]$ for the formula that results by replacing each occurrence of an atomic formula $M \in X$ in ψ by the formula $\phi[x := M]$. (Some formulations write $X(M)$ or $X\, M$ instead of $M \in X$, and $(x)\phi$ or $x.\phi$ instead of $\{\, x \mid \phi \,\}$.)

It will prove convenient to have a notation for arbitrary predicates. We let P and Q range over comprehensions of the form $\{\, x \mid \phi \,\}$, and write $M \in P$ as shorthand for $\phi[x := M]$, when P is $\{\, x \mid \phi \,\}$.

Syntax

Type variables	X, Y, Z	
Individual variables	x, y, z	
Types	A, B	$::= X \mid A \to B \mid \forall X.\, B$
Typed terms	s, t, u	$::= x \mid \lambda x{:}A.\, u \mid s\, t \mid \Lambda X.\, u \mid s\, A$
Contexts	Γ	$::= x_1 : A_1, \ldots, x_n : A_n$

Rules

$$\frac{}{x_1 : A_1, \ldots, x_n : A_n \vdash x_i : A_i}\ \text{Id}$$

$$\frac{\Gamma, x : A \vdash u : B}{\Gamma \vdash \lambda x{:}A.\, u : A \to B}\ \to\text{-I} \qquad \frac{\Gamma \vdash s : A \to B \qquad \Gamma \vdash t : A}{\Gamma \vdash s\, t : B}\ \to\text{-E}$$

$$\frac{\Gamma \vdash u : B}{\Gamma \vdash \Lambda X.\, u : \forall X.\, B}\ \forall^2\text{-I} \quad \text{when } X \text{ not free in } \Gamma \qquad \frac{\Gamma \vdash s : \forall X.\, B}{\Gamma \vdash s\, A : B[X := A]}\ \forall^2\text{-E}$$

Reductions

$$\frac{\dfrac{\begin{array}{c}\vdots\,\delta\\ \Gamma, x : A \vdash u : B\end{array}}{\Gamma \vdash \lambda x{:}A.\, u : A \to B}\ \to\text{-I} \qquad \begin{array}{c}\vdots\,\epsilon\\ \Gamma \vdash t : A\end{array}}{\Gamma \vdash (\lambda x{:}A.\, u)\, t : B}\ \to\text{-E} \quad \Rightarrow \quad \begin{array}{c}\vdots\,\delta[x := \epsilon]\\ \Gamma \vdash u[x := t] : B\end{array}$$

$$\frac{\dfrac{\begin{array}{c}\vdots\,\delta\\ \Gamma \vdash u : B\end{array}}{\Gamma \vdash \Lambda X.\, u : \forall X.\, B}\ \forall^2\text{-I}}{\Gamma \vdash (\Lambda X.\, u)\, A : B[X := A]}\ \forall^2\text{-E} \quad \Rightarrow \quad \begin{array}{c}\vdots\,\delta[X := A]\\ \Gamma \vdash u[X := A] : B[X := A]\end{array}$$

Fig. 1. Second-order lambda calculus (F2)

A proof reduces when an introducer is followed by the corresponding eliminator. We write $\pi[\phi := \rho]$ for the proof that results by substituting ρ for each use of (Id) on ϕ in the proof of π.

In addition to the listed reductions, we also have a number of commuting conversions for (β). Here is the commuting conversion to pass (β) down through ($\to$-E), on the assumption that $M = N$ is a substitution instance of an equation in β.

Syntax

Predicate variables	X, Y, Z
Individual variables	x, y, z
Terms	$L, M, N ::= x \mid \lambda x.\, M \mid M\, N$
Formulas	$\phi, \psi \quad ::= M \in X \mid \phi \to \psi \mid \forall x.\, \psi \mid \forall X.\, \psi$
Contexts	$\Theta \quad ::= \phi_1, \ldots, \phi_n$

Rules

$$\frac{}{\phi_1, \ldots, \phi_n \vdash \phi_i}\,\text{Id}$$

$$\frac{\Theta, \phi \vdash \psi}{\Theta \vdash \phi \to \psi}\,{\to}\text{-I} \qquad \frac{\Theta \vdash \phi \to \psi \qquad \Theta \vdash \phi}{\Theta \vdash \psi}\,{\to}\text{-E}$$

$$\frac{\Theta \vdash \psi}{\Theta \vdash \forall x.\, \psi}\,\forall^1\text{-I} \quad \text{when } x \text{ not free in } \Theta \qquad \frac{\Theta \vdash \forall x.\, \psi}{\Theta \vdash \psi[x := M]}\,\forall^1\text{-E}$$

$$\frac{\Theta \vdash \psi}{\Theta \vdash \forall X.\, \psi}\,\forall^2\text{-I} \quad \text{when } X \text{ not free in } \Theta \qquad \frac{\Theta \vdash \forall X.\, \psi}{\Theta \vdash \psi[X := \{\, x \mid \phi \,\}]}\,\forall^2\text{-E}$$

$$\frac{(\Theta \vdash \psi)\,[x := M]}{(\Theta \vdash \psi)\,[x := N]}\,\beta \quad \text{when } M =_\beta N$$

Reductions

$$\frac{\dfrac{\overset{\vdots\,\pi}{\Theta, \phi \vdash \psi}}{\Theta \vdash \phi \to \psi}\,{\to}\text{-I} \qquad \overset{\vdots\,\rho}{\Theta \vdash \phi}}{\Theta \vdash \psi}\,{\to}\text{-E} \quad \Rightarrow \quad \overset{\vdots\,\pi[\phi := \rho]}{\Theta \vdash \psi}$$

$$\frac{\dfrac{\overset{\vdots\,\pi}{\Theta \vdash \psi}}{\Theta \vdash \forall x.\, \psi}\,\forall\text{-I}}{\Theta \vdash \psi[x := M]}\,\forall\text{-E} \quad \Rightarrow \quad \overset{\vdots\,\pi[x := M]}{\Theta \vdash \psi[x := M]}$$

$$\frac{\dfrac{\overset{\vdots\,\pi}{\Theta \vdash \psi}}{\Theta \vdash \forall X.\, \psi}\,\forall^2\text{-I}}{\Theta \vdash \psi[X := \{\, x \mid \phi \,\}]}\,\forall^2\text{-E} \quad \Rightarrow \quad \overset{\vdots\,\pi[X := \{\, x \mid \phi \,\}]}{\Theta \vdash \psi[X := \{\, x \mid \phi \,\}]}$$

Fig. 2. Second-order propositional logic (P2)

$$\dfrac{\dfrac{\Theta \vdash (\phi \to \psi)[x := M]}{\Theta \vdash (\phi \to \psi)[x := N]}\,\beta \qquad \Theta \vdash \phi[x := N]}{\Theta \vdash \psi[x := N]}\,\to\text{-E}$$

$$\Rightarrow \quad \dfrac{\dfrac{\Theta \vdash (\phi \to \psi)[x := M] \qquad \dfrac{\Theta \vdash \phi[x := N]}{\Theta \vdash \phi[x := M]}\,\beta}{\Theta \vdash \psi[x := M]}\,\to\text{-E}}{\Theta \vdash \psi[x := N]}\,\beta$$

There are similar conversions for each elimination rule. If an instance of β intervenes between an introduction rule and the corresponding elimination rule, preventing a reduction, then the commuting conversion can be used to push the rule beneath the elimination rule, allowing the reduction.

True, false, conjunction, and disjunction can be defined in terms of the connectives already given.

$$\begin{array}{lcl} \top & \equiv & \forall Z.\, () \in Z \to () \in Z \\ \bot & \equiv & \forall Z.\, () \in Z \\ \phi \wedge \psi & \equiv & \forall Z.\, (\phi \to \psi \to () \in Z) \to () \in Z \\ \phi \vee \psi & \equiv & \forall Z.\, (\phi \to () \in Z) \to (\psi \to () \in Z) \to () \in Z \end{array}$$

Here we assume Z does not appear free in ϕ or ψ, and write $()$ as shorthand for $\lambda x.\, x$. (It doesn't matter which term is chosen, any closed term works as well.)

As a further example of the power of P2, observe that it is powerful enough to express equality between terms. Following Leibniz, two terms are equal if one may be substituted for the other. Hence we define,

$$M = N \;\equiv\; \forall Z.\, M \in Z \to N \in Z.$$

That is, terms M and N are equal if any property Z that holds of M also holds of N. It is easy to see that equality is reflexive.

$$\begin{array}{ll} & M = M \\ \equiv & \quad \text{(definition)} \\ & \forall Z.\, M \in Z \to M \in Z \end{array}$$

It is more subtle to see that it is symmetric.

$$\begin{array}{ll} & M = N \\ \equiv & \quad \text{(definition)} \\ & \forall Z.\, M \in Z \to N \in Z \\ \Rightarrow & \quad \text{(instantiate } Z := \{\, x \mid x = M \,\}) \\ & M = M \to N = M \\ \Rightarrow & \quad \text{(equality is reflexive)} \\ & N = M \end{array}$$

One may similarly show transitivity, and that $M =_\beta N$ implies $M = N$.

A logic is *extensional* if whenever two terms are applied to equal arguments they return equal results. We define

$$(\forall x.\, M\, x = N\, x) \to M = N \qquad \text{(ext)}$$

where x does not appear free in M and N. We write P2 + ext for P2 with (ext) as an axiom. Extensionality for untyped terms is a stronger assumption than extensionality for typed terms. Arguably, it is stronger than one might wish, but several of our key proofs depend upon it.

3 The Reynolds Embedding and the Girard Projection

The Reynolds embedding takes a proof δ of a judgement

$$x_1 : A_1, \ldots, x_n : A_n \vdash u : B$$

in F2 into a proof δ^* of a judgement

$$x_1 \in A_1^*, \ldots, x_n \in A_n^* \vdash |u| \in B^*$$

in P2. Each type A maps into a predicate A^*, each typed lambda term t maps via type erasure into an untyped lambda term $|t|$, and each typing $t : A$ maps into the formula $|t| \in A^*$. The Reynolds embedding is defined in Figure 3.

The Girard projection takes a proof π of a judgement

$$\phi_1, \ldots, \phi_n \vdash \psi$$

in P2 into a proof π° of a judgement

$$z_1 : \phi_1^\circ, \ldots, z_n : \phi_n^\circ \vdash u : \psi^\circ$$

in F2. Here u is a typed term with free variables $z_1, \ldots, z_n$, which is uniquely determined by the proof π. The variables are assumed to be taken from a fixed list $z_1, z_2, \ldots$ of variables. Each formula ϕ maps into a type ϕ°. The Girard projection is defined in Figure 4.

We extend the Girard projection to predicates in the obvious way, taking $(\{\, x \mid \phi \,\})^\circ \equiv \phi^\circ$. Both the Reynolds embedding and the Girard projection preserve substitution, so that $(A[X := B])^* \equiv A^*[X{:=}B^*]$ and $\phi[X{:=}\{\, x \mid \psi \,\}]^\circ \equiv \phi^\circ[X := \psi^\circ]$.

The Reynolds embedding and the Girard projection are homomorphisms, in that each preserves the reduction structure of derivations.

Proposition 1. *(Preservation of reductions) If* $\delta_0 \Rightarrow \delta_1$ *in* F2 *then* $\delta_0^* \Rightarrow \delta_1^*$ *in* P2; *and if* $\pi_0 \Rightarrow \pi_1$ *in* P2, *then* $\pi_0^\circ \Rightarrow \pi_1^\circ$ *in* F2.

Proof. It is easy to confirm that the Girard projection takes the $\to$ and $\forall^2$ reductions in P2 into the corresponding reductions of F2, and the $\forall^1$ reduction

Terms

$$
\begin{array}{lcl}
|x| & \equiv & x \\
|\lambda x{:}A.\, u| & \equiv & \lambda x.\, |u| \\
|s\, t| & \equiv & |s|\, |t| \\
|\Lambda X.\, u| & \equiv & |u| \\
|s\, A| & \equiv & |s|
\end{array}
$$

Types

$$
\begin{array}{lcl}
X^* & \equiv & \{\, z \mid z \in X \,\} \\
(A \to B)^* & \equiv & \{\, z \mid \forall x.\, x \in A^* \to z\, x \in B^* \,\} \\
(\forall X.\, B)^* & \equiv & \{\, z \mid \forall X.\, z \in B^* \,\}
\end{array}
$$

Contexts

$$(x_1 : A_1, \ldots, x_n : A_n)^* \equiv x_1 \in A_1^*, \ldots, x_n \in A_n^*$$

Judgements

$$(\Gamma \vdash t : A)^* \equiv \Gamma^* \vdash |t| \in A^*$$

Proofs

$$\left(\frac{}{x_1 : A_1, \ldots, x_n : A_n \vdash x_i : A_i}\,\mathrm{Id} \right)^* \equiv \frac{}{x_1 \in A_1^*, \ldots, x_n \in A_n^* \vdash x_i \in A_i^*}\,\mathrm{Id}$$

$$\left(\frac{\begin{array}{c}\vdots\,\delta \\ \Gamma, x : A \vdash u : B\end{array}}{\Gamma \vdash \lambda x.\, u : A \to B}\,{\to}\text{-I} \right)^* \equiv \frac{\dfrac{\dfrac{\begin{array}{c}\vdots\,\delta^* \\ \Gamma^*, x \in A^* \vdash |u| \in B^*\end{array}}{\Gamma^*, x \in A^* \vdash (\lambda x.\, |u|)\, x \in B^*}\,\beta}{\Gamma^* \vdash x \in A^* \to (\lambda x.\, |u|)\, x \in B^*}\,{\to}\text{-I}}{\Gamma^* \vdash \forall x.\, x \in A^* \to (\lambda x.\, |u|)\, x \in B^*}\,\forall^1\text{-I}$$

$$\left(\frac{\begin{array}{c}\vdots\,\delta \\ \Gamma \vdash s : A \to B\end{array} \qquad \begin{array}{c}\vdots\,\epsilon \\ \Gamma \vdash t : A\end{array}}{\Gamma \vdash s\, t : B}\,{\to}\text{-E} \right)^* \equiv$$

$$\frac{\dfrac{\begin{array}{c}\vdots\,\delta^* \\ \Gamma^* \vdash \forall x.\, x \in A^* \to |s|\, x \in B^*\end{array}}{\Gamma^* \vdash |t| \in A^* \to |s|\, |t| \in B^*}\,\forall^1\text{-E} \qquad \begin{array}{c}\vdots\,\epsilon^* \\ \Gamma^* \vdash |t| \in A^*\end{array}}{\Gamma^* \vdash |s|\, |t| \in B^*}\,{\to}\text{-E}$$

$$\left(\frac{\begin{array}{c}\vdots\,\delta \\ \Gamma \vdash u : B\end{array}}{\Gamma \vdash \Lambda X.\, u : \forall X.\, B}\,\forall^2\text{-I} \right)^* \equiv \frac{\begin{array}{c}\vdots\,\delta^* \\ \Gamma^* \vdash |u| \in B^*\end{array}}{\Gamma^* \vdash \forall X.\, |u| \in B^*}\,\forall^2\text{-I}$$

$$\left(\frac{\begin{array}{c}\vdots\,\delta \\ \Gamma \vdash s : \forall X.\, B\end{array}}{\Gamma \vdash s\, A : B[X := A]}\,\forall^2\text{-E} \right)^* \equiv \frac{\begin{array}{c}\vdots\,\delta^* \\ \Gamma^* \vdash \forall X.\, |s| \in B^*\end{array}}{\Gamma^* \vdash |s| \in B^*[X := A^*]}\,\forall^2\text{-E}$$

Fig. 3. The Reynolds embedding

Formulas

$$
\begin{aligned}
(M \in X)^\circ &\equiv X \\
(\phi \to \psi)^\circ &\equiv \phi^\circ \to \psi^\circ \\
(\forall x.\, \psi)^\circ &\equiv \psi^\circ \\
(\forall X.\, \psi)^\circ &\equiv \forall X.\, \psi^\circ
\end{aligned}
$$

Contexts

$$(\phi_1, \ldots, \phi_n)^\circ \equiv z_1 \in \phi_1^\circ, \ldots, z_n \in \phi_n^\circ$$

Judgements

$$(\Theta \vdash \phi)^\circ \equiv \Theta^\circ \vdash t : \phi^\circ$$

Proofs

$$\left(\frac{}{\phi_1, \ldots, \phi_n \vdash \phi_i}\,\mathrm{Id}\right)^\circ \equiv \frac{}{z_1 : \phi_1^\circ, \ldots, z_n : \phi_n^\circ \vdash z_i : \phi_i^\circ}\,\mathrm{Id}$$

$$\left(\frac{\overset{\vdots\,\pi}{\Theta, \phi \vdash \psi}}{\Theta \vdash \phi \to \psi}\,{\to}\text{-I}\right)^\circ \equiv \frac{\overset{\vdots\,\pi^\circ}{\Theta^\circ, z : \phi^\circ \vdash u : \psi^\circ}}{\Theta^\circ \vdash \lambda z{:}\phi^\circ.\, u : \phi^\circ \to \psi^\circ}\,{\to}\text{-I}$$

$$\left(\frac{\overset{\vdots\,\pi}{\Theta \vdash \phi \to \psi} \qquad \overset{\vdots\,\rho}{\Theta \vdash \phi}}{\Theta \vdash \psi}\,{\to}\text{-E}\right)^\circ \equiv \frac{\overset{\vdots\,\pi^\circ}{\Theta^\circ \vdash s : \phi^\circ \to \psi^\circ} \qquad \overset{\vdots\,\rho^\circ}{\Theta^\circ \vdash t : \phi^\circ}}{\Theta^\circ \vdash s\, t : \psi^\circ}\,{\to}\text{-E}$$

$$\left(\frac{\overset{\vdots\,\pi}{\Theta \vdash \psi}}{\Theta \vdash \forall x.\, \psi}\,\forall^1\text{-I}\right)^\circ \equiv \overset{\vdots\,\pi^\circ}{\Theta^\circ \vdash u : \psi^\circ}$$

$$\left(\frac{\overset{\vdots\,\pi}{\Theta \vdash \forall x.\, \psi}}{\Theta \vdash \psi[x := M]}\,\forall^1\text{-E}\right)^\circ \equiv \overset{\vdots\,\pi^\circ}{\Theta^\circ \vdash s : \psi^\circ}$$

$$\left(\frac{\overset{\vdots\,\pi}{\Theta \vdash \psi}}{\Theta \vdash \forall X.\, \psi}\,\forall^2\text{-I}\right)^\circ \equiv \frac{\overset{\vdots\,\pi^\circ}{\Theta^\circ \vdash u : \psi^\circ}}{\Theta^\circ \vdash \Lambda X.\, u : \forall X.\, \psi^\circ}\,\forall^2\text{-I}$$

$$\left(\frac{\overset{\vdots\,\pi}{\Theta \vdash \forall X.\, \psi}}{\Theta \vdash \psi[X := \{\, x \mid \phi \,\}]}\,\forall^2\text{-E}\right)^\circ \equiv \frac{\overset{\vdots\,\pi^\circ}{\Theta^\circ \vdash s : \forall X.\, \psi^\circ}}{\Theta^\circ \vdash s\, \phi^\circ : \psi^\circ[X := \phi^\circ]}\,\forall^2\text{-E}$$

$$\left(\frac{\overset{\vdots\,\pi}{\Theta \vdash \psi[x := M]}}{\Theta \vdash \psi[x := N]}\,\beta\right)^\circ \equiv \overset{\vdots\,\pi^\circ}{\Theta^\circ \vdash \psi^\circ}$$

Fig. 4. The Girard projection

and commuting conversions of P2 into the identity. Similarly, the Reynolds embedding takes the $\to$ and $\forall^2$ reductions in F2 into the corresponding reductions of P2. A more subtle point is that the Reynolds embedding may introduce (β) rules that interfere with reductions, but these may always be pushed out of the way using commuting conversions. (Leivant's otherwise excellent tutorial [Lei90] appears to ignore role of commuting conversions.) □

We consider judgements and derivations in F2 as equivalent up to renaming of variables. That is, the judgements $x_1 : A_1, \ldots, x_n : A_n \vdash t : B$ and $y_1 : A_1, \ldots, y_n : A_n \vdash u : B$ are equivalent if $t = u[y_1 := x_1, \ldots, y_n := x_n]$.

The Reynolds embedding followed by the Girard projection is the identity.

Proposition 2. *(Girard inverts Reynolds) If δ is a derivation in* F2, *then $\delta^{*\circ} \equiv \delta$, up to renaming.*

Proof. Straightforward induction over the structure of derivations. □

As an example, here is the type of the Church numerals in F2.

$$\mathbf{Nat} \equiv \forall Z.\,(Z \to Z) \to Z \to Z$$

Applying the Reynolds embedding yields the following predicate in P2.

$$\mathbf{Nat}^* \;\equiv\; \{n \,|\, \forall Z.\, \forall s.\, (\forall m.\, m \in Z \to s\, m \in Z) \to \forall z.\, z \in Z \to n\, s\, z \in Z\}$$

It is easy to check that $\mathbf{Nat} = \mathbf{Nat}^{*\circ}$.

Let **two** be the second Church numeral in F2, and let two be its erasure, $\mathsf{two} \equiv |\mathbf{two}|$.

$$\begin{aligned} \mathbf{two} &\equiv \Lambda Z.\, \lambda s : Z \to Z.\, \lambda z : Z.\, s\,(s\,z) \\ \mathsf{two} &\equiv \lambda s.\, \lambda z.\, s\,(s\,z) \end{aligned}$$

If δ_t is the derivation of $\vdash \mathbf{two} : \mathbf{Nat}$ in F2, then δ_t^* is the proof of $\vdash \mathsf{two} \in \mathbf{Nat}^*$ in P2. It is easy to check that $\delta_t \equiv \delta_t^{*\circ}$.

Note that the Girard projection takes equality $M = N$ into the unit type $\forall X.\, X \to X$. In the term model, or in any parametric model, the only value of this type is the identity function [Wad89]. Hence, the Girard projection erases any information content in the proof of an equality judgement.

Also observe that the erasure of the extensionality axiom (ext) has the type $(\forall X.\, X \to X) \to (\forall X.\, X \to X)$. One may extend the Girard projection so that it maps axiom (ext) into the derivation of the term $\lambda i : \forall X.\, X \to X.\, i$.

4 Doubling and Parametricity

The Reynolds embedding corresponds to a unary version of Reynolds's abstraction theorem. We can recover the binary version by means of a *doubling* mapping from P2 to P2.

We represent binary relations as predicates over pairs. We use the usual encoding of pairs in lambda calculus.

$$
\begin{array}{lll}
(M, N) & \equiv & \lambda k.\, kMN \\
\mathsf{fst} & \equiv & \lambda z.\, z(\lambda x.\, \lambda y.\, x) \\
\mathsf{snd} & \equiv & \lambda z.\, z(\lambda x.\, \lambda y.\, y) \\
\{\, (x, y) \mid \phi \,\} & \equiv & \{\, z \mid \phi[x := \mathsf{fst}\ z,\ y := \mathsf{snd}\ z] \,\}
\end{array}
$$

Observe that $(M, N) \in \{\, (x, y) \mid \phi \,\}$ simplifies to $\phi[x := M,\ y := N]$ as required.

Doubling is defined with the aid of operations that rename variables. For each individual variable x there exists a renaming x'; and for each propositional variable X there exists a renaming $X^{\ddagger}$. We write M' for the term that results by renaming each free variable x in M to x'.

Doubling takes a proof δ of a judgement

$$\Theta \vdash \phi$$

in P2 into a proof $\delta^{\ddagger}$ of a judgement

$$\Theta^{\ddagger} \vdash \phi^{\ddagger}$$

in P2. Each formula ϕ maps into a formula $\phi^{\ddagger}$. Doubling is defined in Figure 5.

We extend doubling to predicates in the obvious way, taking $(\{\, x \mid \phi \,\})^{\ddagger} \equiv \{\, (M, M') \mid \phi^{\ddagger} \,\}$. Doubling preserves substitution, so that $\phi[Z := \psi]^{\ddagger} \equiv \phi^{\ddagger}[Z^{\ddagger} := \psi^{\ddagger}]$.

Again, doubling is a homomorphism.

Proposition 3. *(Doubling) If* $\pi_0 \Rightarrow \pi_1$ *in* P2 *then* $\pi_0^{\ddagger} \Rightarrow \pi_1^{\ddagger}$ *in* P2.

Proof. By examination of the reduction rules. □

What Reynolds calls the Abstraction Theorem [Rey83] and what Plotkin and Abadi call the Logical Relations Lemma [PA93] arises as the composition of the Reynolds embedding with doubling.

Proposition 4. *(Abstraction Theorem) If*

$$x_1 : A_1, \ldots, x_n : A_n \vdash t : B$$

is derivable in F2, *then*

$$(x_1, x_1') \in A_1^{*\ddagger}, \ldots, (x_n, x_n') \in A_n^{*\ddagger} \vdash (|t|, |t|') \in B^{*\ddagger}$$

is derivable in P2.

Proof. Immediate, since the Reynolds embedding followed by doubling takes a derivation of the antecedent into a derivation of the consequent. □

Formulas

$$\begin{aligned}
(M \in X)^\ddagger &\equiv (M, M') \in X^\ddagger \\
(\phi \to \psi)^\ddagger &\equiv \phi^\ddagger \to \psi^\ddagger \\
(\forall x.\, \psi)^\ddagger &\equiv \forall x.\, \forall x'.\, \psi^\ddagger \\
(\forall X.\, \psi)^\ddagger &\equiv \forall X^\ddagger.\, \psi^\ddagger
\end{aligned}$$

Contexts

$$(\phi_1, \ldots, \phi_n)^\ddagger \equiv \phi_1^\ddagger, \ldots, \phi_n^\ddagger$$

Judgements

$$(\Theta \vdash \phi)^\ddagger \equiv \Theta^\ddagger \vdash \phi^\ddagger$$

Proofs

$$\left(\frac{}{\phi_1, \ldots, \phi_n \vdash \phi_i}\,\mathrm{Id}\right)^\ddagger \equiv \frac{}{\phi_1^\ddagger, \ldots, \phi_n^\ddagger \vdash \phi_i^\ddagger}\,\mathrm{Id}$$

$$\left(\frac{\begin{matrix}\vdots\,\pi\\ \Theta, \phi \vdash \psi\end{matrix}}{\Theta \vdash \phi \to \psi}\,\to\text{-I}\right)^\ddagger \equiv \frac{\begin{matrix}\vdots\,\pi^\ddagger\\ \Theta^\ddagger, \phi^\ddagger \vdash \psi^\ddagger\end{matrix}}{\Theta^\ddagger \vdash \phi^\ddagger \to \psi^\ddagger}\,\to\text{-I}$$

$$\left(\frac{\begin{matrix}\vdots\,\pi\\ \Theta \vdash \phi \to \psi\end{matrix} \qquad \begin{matrix}\vdots\,\rho\\ \Theta \vdash \phi\end{matrix}}{\Theta \vdash \psi}\,\to\text{-E}\right)^\ddagger \equiv \frac{\begin{matrix}\vdots\,\pi^\ddagger\\ \Theta^\ddagger \vdash \phi^\ddagger \to \psi^\ddagger\end{matrix} \qquad \begin{matrix}\vdots\,\rho^\ddagger\\ \Theta^\ddagger \vdash \phi^\ddagger\end{matrix}}{\Theta^\ddagger \vdash \psi^\ddagger}\,\to\text{-E}$$

$$\left(\frac{\begin{matrix}\vdots\,\pi\\ \Theta \vdash \psi\end{matrix}}{\Theta \vdash \forall x.\, \psi}\,\forall^1\text{-I}\right)^\ddagger \equiv \frac{\begin{matrix}\vdots\,\pi^\ddagger\\ \Theta^\ddagger \vdash \psi^\ddagger\end{matrix}}{\Theta^\ddagger \vdash \forall x.\, \forall x'.\, \psi^\ddagger}\,\forall^1\text{-I (twice)}$$

$$\left(\frac{\begin{matrix}\vdots\,\pi\\ \Theta \vdash \forall x.\, \psi\end{matrix}}{\Theta \vdash \psi[x := M]}\,\forall^1\text{-E}\right)^\ddagger \equiv \frac{\begin{matrix}\vdots\,\pi^\ddagger\\ \Theta^\ddagger \vdash \forall x.\, \forall x'.\, \psi^\ddagger\end{matrix}}{\Theta^\ddagger \vdash \psi^\ddagger[x := M, x' := M']}\,\forall^1\text{-E (twice)}$$

$$\left(\frac{\begin{matrix}\vdots\,\pi\\ \Theta \vdash \psi\end{matrix}}{\Theta \vdash \forall X.\, \psi}\,\forall^2\text{-I}\right)^\ddagger \equiv \frac{\begin{matrix}\vdots\,\pi^\ddagger\\ \Theta^\ddagger \vdash \psi^\ddagger\end{matrix}}{\Theta^\ddagger \vdash \forall X^\ddagger.\, \psi^\ddagger}\,\forall^2\text{-I}$$

$$\left(\frac{\begin{matrix}\vdots\,\pi\\ \Theta \vdash \forall X.\, \psi\end{matrix}}{\Theta \vdash \psi[X := \{\, x \mid \phi \,\}]}\,\forall^2\text{-E}\right)^\ddagger \equiv \frac{\begin{matrix}\vdots\,\pi^\ddagger\\ \Theta^\ddagger \vdash \forall X^\ddagger.\, \psi^\ddagger\end{matrix}}{\Theta^\ddagger \vdash \psi^\ddagger[X^\ddagger := \{\, (x, x') \mid \phi^\ddagger \,\}]}\,\forall^2\text{-E}$$

$$\left(\frac{\begin{matrix}\vdots\,\pi\\ \Theta \vdash \psi[x := M]\end{matrix}}{\Theta \vdash \psi[x := N]}\,\beta\right)^\ddagger \equiv \frac{\begin{matrix}\vdots\,\pi^\ddagger\\ \Theta^\ddagger \vdash \psi^\ddagger[x := M,\, x' := M']\end{matrix}}{\Theta^\ddagger \vdash \psi^\ddagger[x := N,\, x' := N']}\,\beta\text{ (twice)}$$

Fig. 5. The doubling embedding

As an example, here is the type of the Church numerals in F2.

$$\mathbf{Nat} \equiv \forall Z.\,(Z \to Z) \to Z \to Z$$

Applying the Reynolds embedding followed by doubling yields the following predicate in P2.

$$\begin{aligned}
&\mathbf{Nat}^{*\ddagger} \equiv \\
&\quad \{\, (n, n') \mid \forall Z^{\ddagger}. \\
&\qquad \forall s.\,\forall s'.\,(\forall m.\,\forall m'.\,(m, m') \in Z^{\ddagger} \to (s\,m, s'\,m') \in Z^{\ddagger}) \\
&\qquad\quad \to \forall z.\,\forall z'.\,(z, z') \in Z^{\ddagger} \to (n\,s\,z, n'\,s'\,z') \in Z^{\ddagger} \,\}
\end{aligned}$$

Similarly, starting with the derivation δ_t of the second Church numeral **two** in F2 and applying the Reynolds embedding followed by doubling yields the derivation $\delta_t^{*\ddagger}$ in P2 of the judgement

$$\vdash (\mathsf{two}, \mathsf{two}) \in \mathbf{Nat}^{*\ddagger}$$

Here renaming has no effect on the two terms, which contain only bound variables.

The identity relation on a type is equality restricted to that type.

Definition 5. *The* identity relation *on type A is written $A^{=}$.*

$$A^{=} \;\equiv\; \{\, (z, z') \mid z = z' \wedge z \in A^{*} \,\}$$

It is easy to verify that $A^{=}$ is reflexive, symmetric, and transitive, and that $(z, z') \in A^{=}$ implies $z \in A^{*}$ and $z' \in A^{*}$.

The parametric closure of a type is the doubling of the Reynolds embedding of that type, with the relation corresponding to each free type variable taken to be the identity relation.

Definition 6. *The* parametric closure *of type A is written $A^{\approx}$.*

$$A^{\approx} \;\equiv\; A^{*\ddagger}[X_1^{\ddagger} := X_1^{=}, \ldots, X_1^{\ddagger} := X_1^{=}]$$

Here $X_1, \ldots, X_n$ are the free type variables in A.

It is easy to verify that $A^{\approx}$ is symmetric and transitive, so it is a partial equivalence relation, and that $(z, z') \in A^{\approx}$ implies that $z \in A^{*}$ and $z' \in A^{*}$.

It is interesting to consider those cases where the identity relation implies the parametric closure, or conversely.

Definition 7. *We say that type A is* parametric *when $A^{=} \subseteq A^{\approx}$, and* extensive *when $A^{\approx} \subseteq A^{=}$.*

An assertion that every type is parametric corresponds to Reynolds's parametricity condition, and an assertion that every type is parametric and extensive might correspond to Reynolds's Identity Extension Lemma [Rey83].

In Section 5, we will see that all algebraic types are parametric and extensive, in any model for which algebraic types have the usual inductive properties.

Is it consistent to assume that every type is parametric? This conjecture is plausible, since for any closed term M and closed type A, if $M \in A^*$ is provable, then by doubling $(M, M) \in A^{\approx}$ is also provable. But as of this writing neither a proof nor a counterexample has been found. We do not pursue the point further in this paper.

However, it would not be consistent to assume that every type is both parametric and extensive. Assume that types A and B are parametric and extensive and that $f, g \in (A \to B)^*$. If $A \to B$ is extensive, it follows that $f\,x = g\,x$ for all $x \in A^*$ implies $f = g$. But this is not appropriate, since in the untyped world we may apply f and g to arguments that are not of type A.

It is easy to construct a counter-example demonstrating this problem. (Easy, but not obvious; I'm grateful to an anonymous referee for the following.) As usual, let $\mathsf{zero} \equiv \lambda s.\,\lambda z.\,z$, $\mathsf{I} \equiv \lambda x.\,x$, $\mathsf{K} \equiv \lambda x.\,\lambda y.\,x$, and take $f \equiv \lambda n.\,\mathsf{zero}$ and $g \equiv \lambda n.\,n\,\mathsf{I}\,\mathsf{zero}$. We have $f\,n = \mathsf{zero} = g\,n$ for every $n \in \mathbf{Nat}^*$. (The second equality is easily proved by induction, which is justified by the results in Section 5 on the assumption that Nat is parametric.) Clearly, $f, g \in \mathrm{Nat} \to \mathrm{Nat}$, so if $\mathrm{Nat} \to \mathrm{Nat}$ is extensive we would conclude $f = g$. But this is false, since $f\,\mathsf{K} = \mathsf{zero} \neq \mathsf{I} = g\,\mathsf{K}$.

These considerations suggest that $A^{=}$ is not, in general, an appropriate definition of equality at type A in this framework. Indeed, it may be appropriate to simply take $A^{\approx}$ as the definition of equality at type A, in which case the Identity Extension Lemma holds by definition.

5 Algebraic Types and Parametricity

The grammar of algebraic types is shown in Figure 6. An algebraic type is either a type variable Z, the natural number type Nat, the empty type 0, the sum type $T + U$, the unit type 1, the product type $T \times U$, or the fixpoint type $\mu Z.\,T$. The natural number type is included only for illustration, since it is equivalent to the type $\mu Z.\,Z + 1$. The subtypes of a type are defined as usual, so for instance the subtypes of $\mu Z.\,Z + 1$ are Z, 1, $Z + 1$, and $\mu Z.\,Z + 1$ itself.

Each algebraic type has two interpretations, an *inductive* interpretation as a predicate in P2, and a *deductive* interpretation as a type in F2.

The inductive interpretation defines each type by its corresponding induction principle. For instance, $\mathsf{Nat} = \lceil \mathrm{Nat} \rceil$ is the induction principle for natural numbers.

$$\mathsf{Nat} \equiv \{n \,|\, \forall Z.\,(\forall m.\,m \in Z \to \mathsf{succ}\,m \in Z) \to \mathsf{zero} \in Z \to n \in Z\}$$

To prove a property of natural numbers by induction, one must show that for all m if m has the property then $\mathsf{succ}\,m$ has the property, and one must show that zero has the property. The above definition states that a value is a natural number if one can prove a property of it by induction. The idea of classifying induction principles using second-order propositional variables, and of defining a type via its induction principle, goes back to Frege [Fre79].

Syntax

Type variables	X, Y, Z	
Algebraic types	T, U	$::= Z \mid \mathsf{Nat} \mid 0 \mid T + U \mid 1 \mid T \times U \mid \mu Z.T$

Inductive interpretation

$$\begin{array}{lcl}
\lceil \mathrm{Nat} \rceil & \equiv & \{ n \mid \forall Z.\, (\forall m.\, m \in Z \rightarrow \mathsf{succ}\, m \in Z) \rightarrow \mathsf{zero} \in Z \rightarrow n \in Z \} \\
\lceil 0 \rceil & \equiv & \{ z \mid \forall Z.\, z \in Z \} \\
\lceil T + U \rceil & \equiv & \{ z \mid \forall Z.\, (\forall x.\, x \in \lceil T \rceil \rightarrow \mathsf{inl}\, x \in Z) \rightarrow (\forall y.\, y \in \lceil U \rceil \rightarrow \mathsf{inr}\, y \in Z) \rightarrow z \in Z \} \\
\lceil 1 \rceil & \equiv & \{ z \mid \forall Z.\, \mathsf{unit} \in Z \rightarrow z \in Z \} \\
\lceil T \times U \rceil & \equiv & \{ z \mid \forall Z.\, (\forall x.\, x \in \lceil T \rceil \rightarrow \forall y.\, y \in \lceil U \rceil \rightarrow \mathsf{pair}\, x\, y \in Z) \rightarrow z \in Z \} \\
\lceil \mu Z.T \rceil & \equiv & \{ z \mid \forall Z.\, (\forall x.\, x \in \lceil T[Z := \mu Z.T] \rceil \rightarrow \mathsf{in}\, x \in Z) \rightarrow z \in Z \}
\end{array}$$

Deductive interpretation

$$\begin{array}{lcl}
\lfloor \mathrm{Nat} \rfloor & \equiv & \forall Z.\, (Z \rightarrow Z) \rightarrow Z \rightarrow Z \\
\lfloor 0 \rfloor & \equiv & \forall Z.\, Z \\
\lfloor T + U \rfloor & \equiv & \forall Z.\, (T \rightarrow Z) \rightarrow (U \rightarrow Z) \rightarrow Z \\
\lfloor 1 \rfloor & \equiv & \forall Z.\, Z \rightarrow Z \\
\lfloor T \times U \rfloor & \equiv & \forall Z.\, (T \rightarrow U \rightarrow Z) \rightarrow Z \\
\lfloor \mu Z.T \rfloor & \equiv & \forall Z.\, (T \rightarrow Z) \rightarrow Z
\end{array}$$

Constructors

$$\begin{array}{lcl}
\mathbf{zero} & : & \lfloor \mathrm{Nat} \rfloor \\
\mathbf{zero} & = & \Lambda Z.\, \lambda s : Z \rightarrow Z.\, \lambda z : Z.\, z \\
\mathbf{succ} & : & \lfloor \mathrm{Nat} \rfloor \rightarrow \lfloor \mathrm{Nat} \rfloor \\
\mathbf{succ} & = & \lambda n : \lfloor \mathrm{Nat} \rfloor .\, \Lambda Z.\, \lambda s : Z \rightarrow Z.\, \lambda z : Z.\, s\, (n\, Z\, s\, z) \\
\mathbf{inl} & : & \lfloor T \rfloor \rightarrow \lfloor T + U \rfloor \\
\mathbf{inl} & = & \lambda x : \lfloor T \rfloor .\, \Lambda Z.\, \lambda k : \lfloor T \rfloor \rightarrow Z.\, \lambda l : \lfloor U \rfloor \rightarrow Z.\, k\, x \\
\mathbf{inr} & : & \lfloor U \rfloor \rightarrow \lfloor T + U \rfloor \\
\mathbf{inr} & = & \lambda y : \lfloor U \rfloor .\, \Lambda Z.\, \lambda k : \lfloor T \rfloor \rightarrow Z.\, \lambda l : \lfloor U \rfloor \rightarrow Z.\, l\, y \\
\mathbf{unit} & : & \lfloor 1 \rfloor \\
\mathbf{unit} & = & \Lambda Z.\, \lambda z : Z.\, z \\
\mathbf{pair} & : & \lfloor T \rfloor \rightarrow \lfloor U \rfloor \rightarrow \lfloor T \times U \rfloor \\
\mathbf{pair} & = & \lambda x : \lfloor T \rfloor .\, \lambda y : \lfloor U \rfloor .\, \Lambda Z.\, \lambda k : \lfloor T \rfloor \rightarrow \lfloor U \rfloor \rightarrow Z.\, k\, x\, y \\
\mathbf{in} & : & \lfloor T[Z := \mu Z.T] \rfloor \rightarrow \lfloor \mu Z.T \rfloor \\
\mathbf{in} & = & \lambda x : \lfloor T[Z := \mu Z.T] \rfloor .\, \lambda Z.\, \lambda k : \lfloor T \rfloor \rightarrow Z.\, k\, (\lfloor T \rfloor\, [\lambda x : \lfloor \mu Z.T \rfloor .\, x\, Z\, k]\, x)
\end{array}$$

Fig. 6. Algebraic types

One immediate consequence of the definition is that succ and zero do indeed construct natural numbers. Similar properties follow for all the algebraic types.

Proposition 8. *(Constructor Lemma) The following are provable in* P2.

$$\begin{array}{lll} n \in \mathsf{Nat} & \rightarrow \mathsf{succ}\, n & \in \mathsf{Nat} \\ & \mathsf{zero} & \in \mathsf{Nat} \\ x \in \lceil T \rceil & \rightarrow \mathsf{inl}\, x & \in \lceil T + U \rceil \\ y \in \lceil U \rceil & \rightarrow \mathsf{inr}\, y & \in \lceil T + U \rceil \\ & \mathsf{unit} & \in \lceil 1 \rceil \\ x \in \lceil T \rceil \wedge y \in \lceil U \rceil & \rightarrow \mathsf{pair}\, x\, y & \in \lceil T \times U \rceil \\ x \in \lceil T[Z := \mu Z.T] \rceil & \rightarrow \mathsf{in}\, x & \in \lceil \mu Z.T \rceil \end{array}$$

Proof. Straightforward. □

The inductive definitions, and the above proposition, do not depend on the particular value of the terms chosen for the constructors succ and zero and so on. They might, for example, be chosen to be uninterpreted constants. However it turns out there is a good reason to choose them to be particular untyped lambda terms, namely the erasures of the typed lambda terms that are the corresponding constructors in the deductive interpretation.

The deductive interpretation maps each type to the usual definition in second order lambda calculus. For example, the deductive interpretation $\mathbf{Nat} \equiv \lfloor \mathrm{Nat} \rfloor$ is the usual Church type of the naturals. Corresponding to this definiton are the usual constructors for the natural numbers in second order lambda calculus, namely $\mathbf{succ} : \mathbf{Nat} \rightarrow \mathbf{Nat}$ and $\mathbf{zero} : \mathbf{Nat}$.

The other definitions for each type and each constructor are entirely standard. To define the constructor for fixpoints, one makes use of the fact that if T is an algebraic type in which Z is free, then Z appears positively in the deductive translation $\lfloor T \rfloor$, and that if A is a polymorphic type in which Z appears positively, then for each $f : B \rightarrow C$ there is a canonically defined function $A[f] : A[Z{:=}B] \rightarrow A[Z{:=}C]$. (For details of the construction, see, e.g., Reynolds and Plotkin [RP90].)

Both interpretations preserve substitution, so that $\lceil T[Z := U] \rceil = \lceil T \rceil [Z := \lceil U \rceil]$ and $\lfloor T[Z := U] \rfloor = \lfloor T \rfloor [Z := \lfloor U \rfloor]$.

The deductive interpretation is so named because it can be deduced by applying the Girard projection to the inductive interpretation.

Proposition 9. *(Girard projection takes inductive to deductive) For every algebraic type T, we have $\lfloor T \rfloor \equiv \lceil T \rceil^{\circ}$.*

Proof. Obvious by inspection. □

Furthermore, the constructors in the deductive interpretation can be deduced from the constructors of the inductive interpretation. For instance, if succ and zero are uninterpreted constants, then there are canonical proofs in P2 of the following propositions; call these π_s and π_z.

$$\vdash n \in \mathsf{Nat} \rightarrow \mathsf{succ}\, n \in \mathsf{Nat} \quad \text{and} \quad \vdash \mathsf{zero} \in \mathsf{Nat}.$$

Applying the Girard projection to these proofs yields derivations in F2 of the following typings; call these $\delta_s \equiv \pi_s^{\circ}$ and $\delta_z \equiv \pi_z^{\circ}$.

$$\vdash \mathbf{succ} : \mathbf{Nat} \rightarrow \mathbf{Nat} \quad \text{and} \quad \vdash \mathbf{zero} : \mathbf{Nat}$$

In what follows, we assume that each of the inductive constructors is the erasure of the corresponding deductive constructor. That is, succ $= |\mathbf{succ}|$ and zero $= |\mathbf{zero}|$, and so on for the constructors of the other algebraic types. With this assumption, we will be able to show not only that the Girard projection takes the inductive interpretation into the deductive one, but also that, in the presence of parametricity, the Reynolds embedding takes the deductive interpretation into the inductive one.

Definition 10. *We say that algebraic type T is* deductive *when* $\lceil T \rceil \subseteq \lfloor T \rfloor^*$ *and* inductive *when* $\lfloor T \rfloor^* \subseteq \lceil T \rceil$.

We will show that all algebraic types are deductive. Further, for algebraic types, parametricity and inductiveness are equivalent: if all subtypes of a given algebraic type are parametric then that type is inductive, and if all subtypes of a given type are inductive then that type is parametric.

Thus, for algebraic types in the presence of parametricity, the inductive and deductive definitions are equivalent. That is, one has not only $\lfloor T \rfloor \equiv \lceil T \rceil^\circ$ but also $\lceil T \rceil = \lfloor T \rfloor^*$, and hence not only $\lfloor T \rfloor \equiv \lfloor T \rfloor^{*\circ}$ but also $\lceil T \rceil = \lceil T \rceil^{\circ *}$. In particular, we have $\mathbf{Nat} \equiv \mathsf{Nat}^\circ$ and $\mathsf{Nat} = \mathbf{Nat}^*$. Thus, there is a sense in which the Reynolds and Girard translations are not merely an embedding-projection pair, but truly inverses.

5.1 Every Algebraic Type is Extensive

As promised in Section 4, we show that every algebraic type is extensive, which corresponds, in a rough sense, to one half of Reynolds's Identity Extension Lemma [Rey83]. We require extensionality.

Proposition 11. *(Every algebraic type is extensive) If T is an algebraic type, then* P2 + ext *proves* $\lfloor T \rfloor^{\approx} \subseteq \lfloor T \rfloor^{=}$.

Proof. The case for a free type variable X is immediate, since $X^{\approx} = X^{=}$ by definition. Below is the proof for $T \times U$. The other cases are similar.

$$
\begin{array}{ll}
 & (z, z') \in \lfloor T \times U \rfloor^{\approx} \\
= & \quad \text{(definition parametric closure)} \\
 & \forall Z^{\ddagger}.\, \forall k, k'. \\
 & \quad (\forall x, x'.\, (x, x') \in \lfloor T \rfloor^{\approx} \to \forall y, y'.\, (y, y') \in \lfloor U \rfloor^{\approx} \to (k\, x\, y, k'\, x'\, y') \in Z^{\ddagger}) \\
 & \quad \to (z\, k, z'\, k') \in Z^{\ddagger} \\
\Rightarrow & \quad \text{(instantiate } Z^{\ddagger} := \{ (z, z') \mid z = z' \}) \\
 & \forall k, k'. \\
 & \quad (\forall x, x'.\, (x, x') \in \lfloor T \rfloor^{\approx} \to \forall y, y'.\, (y, y') \in \lfloor U \rfloor^{\approx} \to k\, x\, y = k'\, x'\, y') \\
 & \quad \to z\, k = z'\, k' \\
\Rightarrow & \quad \text{(induction hypothesis)} \\
 & \forall k, k'.\, (\forall x, x'.\, x = x' \to \forall y, y'.\, y = y' \to k\, x\, y = k'\, x'\, y') \to z\, k = z'\, k' \\
\Rightarrow & \quad \text{(extensionality on } k \text{ and } k') \\
 & \forall k, k'.\, k = k' \to z\, k = z'\, k' \\
\Rightarrow & \quad \text{(extensionality on } z \text{ and } z') \\
 & z = z'
\end{array}
$$

□

5.2 Every Algebraic Type is Deductive

We show that every algebraic type is deductive. We do not require extensionality.

Proposition 12. *(Every algebraic type is deductive) If T is an algebraic type, then* P2 *proves* $\lceil T \rceil \subseteq \lfloor T \rfloor^*$.

Proof. Below is the proof for $T \times U$. The other cases are similar.

$$
\begin{array}{ll}
& z \in \lceil T \times U \rceil \\
\equiv & \text{(definition inductive interpretation)} \\
& \forall Z.\, (\forall x.\, x \in \lceil T \rceil \to \forall y.\, y \in \lceil U \rceil \to \mathsf{pair}\, x\, y \in Z) \to z \in Z \\
\Rightarrow & \text{(take } Z = \lfloor T \times U \rfloor^*\text{)} \\
& (\forall x.\, x \in \lceil T \rceil \to \forall y.\, y \in \lceil U \rceil \to \mathsf{pair}\, x\, y \in \lfloor T \times U \rfloor^*) \to z \in \lfloor T \times U \rfloor^* \\
\Rightarrow & \text{(induction hypothesis)} \\
& (\forall x.\, x \in \lfloor T \rfloor^* \to \forall y.\, y \in \lfloor U \rfloor^* \to \mathsf{pair}\, x\, y \in \lfloor T \times U \rfloor^*) \to z \in \lfloor T \times U \rfloor^* \\
\Rightarrow & \text{(Reynolds embedding applied to } \mathbf{pair}\text{)} \\
& z \in \lfloor T \times U \rfloor^*
\end{array}
$$

□

5.3 Inductive Implies Parametric

If all algebraic types are inductive then they are also parametric. Extensionality is not required. Inductiveness is required not only of a type but also of all its subtypes, so that the induction hypothesis will apply.

Proposition 13. *(Inductive implies parametric) Let T be an algebraic type. If* P2 *proves* $\lfloor S \rfloor^* \subseteq \lceil S \rceil$ *for every subtype S of T, then* P2 *proves* $\lfloor T \rfloor^= \subseteq \lfloor T \rfloor^\approx$.

Proof. Below is the proof for $T \times U$. The other cases are similar.

$$
\begin{array}{ll}
& z \in \lfloor T \times U \rfloor^* \\
\Rightarrow & \text{(by assumption } T \times U \text{ is inductive)} \\
& z \in \lceil T \times U \rceil \\
\equiv & \text{(definition inductive interpretation)} \\
& \forall Z.\, (\forall x.\, x \in \lceil T \rceil \to \forall y.\, y \in \lceil U \rceil \to \mathsf{pair}\, x\, y \in Z) \to z \in Z \\
\Rightarrow & \text{(instantiate } Z := \{\, z \mid (z, z) \in \lfloor T \times U \rfloor^\approx \,\}\text{)}
\end{array}
$$

$$
\begin{array}{ll}
& (\forall x.\, x \in \lceil T \rceil \to \forall y.\, y \in \lceil U \rceil \to (\mathsf{pair}\, x\, y, \mathsf{pair}\, x\, y) \in \lfloor T \times U \rfloor^\approx) \\
& \to (z, z) \in \lfloor T \times U \rfloor^\approx \\
\Rightarrow & \text{(Proposition 12 and induction hypothesis)} \\
& (\forall x.\, (x, x) \in \lfloor T \rfloor^\approx \to \forall y.\, (y, y) \in \lfloor U \rfloor^\approx \to (\mathsf{pair}\, x\, y, \mathsf{pair}\, x\, y) \in \lfloor T \times U \rfloor^\approx) \\
& \to (z, z) \in \lfloor T \times U \rfloor^\approx \\
\Rightarrow & \text{(Abstraction Theorem applied to } \mathbf{pair}\text{)} \\
& (z, z) \in \lfloor T \times U \rfloor^\approx
\end{array}
$$

□

Reynolds and Plotkin [RP90] were the first to suggest that parametricity implies inductivity, and so far as I know, Hasegawa [Has94] was the first to suggest the converse. (Hasegawa asserts that a type is inductive if it is parametric, while here we assert that a type is inductive if all its subtypes are parametric. Analysis of Hasegawa's proof shows that he seems to have inadvertently omitted the condition on subtypes, since he relies on the Identity Extension Lemma at the subtypes and this depends on parametricity.)

5.4 Parametric Implies Inductive

Every algebraic type that is parametric is also inductive. We require extensionality. Parametricity is required not only of a type but also of all its subtypes, so that the induction hypothesis will apply.

Proposition 14. *(Parametric implies inductive) Let T be an algebraic type. If* P2 + ext *proves $\lfloor S\rfloor^{=} \subseteq \lfloor S\rfloor^{\approx}$ for every subtype S of T, then* P2 + ext *proves $\lfloor T\rfloor^{*} \subseteq \lceil T\rceil$.*

The proof depends on the following lemma. Böhm and Berarducci [BB85, Theorem 7.3] prove a similar result, though in a different framework and with a different technique.

Proposition 15. *(Böhm's Lemma) The following are provable in* P2 + ext.

$$\begin{array}{lll}
(z,z) \in \lfloor \mathsf{Nat}\rfloor^{\approx} & \to z\ \mathsf{succ}\ \mathsf{zero} & = z \\
(z,z) \in \lfloor 0\rfloor^{\approx} & \to z & = z \\
(z,z) \in \lfloor T+U\rfloor^{\approx} & \to z\ \mathsf{inl}\ \mathsf{inr} & = z \\
(z,z) \in \lfloor 1\rfloor^{\approx} & \to z\ \mathsf{unit} & = z \\
(z,z) \in \lfloor T\times U\rfloor^{\approx} & \to z\ \mathsf{pair} & = z \\
(z,z) \in \lfloor \mu Z.T\rfloor^{\approx} & \to z\ \mathsf{in} & = z
\end{array}$$

Proof. Below is the proof for $T \times U$. The other cases are similar.

$$\begin{array}{l}
\quad z \in \lfloor T\times U\rfloor^{\approx} \\
\Rightarrow \quad \text{(definition deductive interpretation, doubling)} \\
\quad \forall Z^{\ddagger}.\, \forall k,k'. \\
\qquad (\forall x,x'.\, (x,x') \in \lfloor T\rfloor^{\approx} \to \forall y,y'.\, (y,y') \in \lfloor U\rfloor^{\approx} \to (k\,x\,y, k'\,x'\,y') \in Z^{\ddagger}) \\
\qquad \to (z\,k, z\,k') \in Z^{\ddagger} \\
\Rightarrow \quad \text{(instantiate } Z^{\ddagger} := \{\,(z,z') \mid z\,k'' = z'\,\} \text{ and } k := \mathsf{pair}) \\
\quad \forall k',k''. \\
\qquad (\forall x,x'.\, (x,x') \in \lfloor T\rfloor^{\approx} \to \forall y,y'.\, (y,y') \in \lfloor U\rfloor^{\approx} \to \mathsf{pair}\,x\,y\,k'' = k'\,x'\,y') \\
\qquad \to z\ \mathsf{pair}\ k'' = z\,k') \\
\Rightarrow \quad (T \text{ and } U \text{ are extensive, } \beta \text{ reduction on } \mathsf{pair}) \\
\quad \forall k',k''. \\
\qquad (\forall x,x'.\, x = x' \to \forall y,y'.\, y = y' \to k''\,x\,y = k'\,x'\,y') \\
\qquad \to z\ \mathsf{pair}\ k'' = z\,k') \\
\Rightarrow \quad \text{(extensionality on } k'' \text{ and } k') \\
\quad \forall k',k''.\, k'' = k' \to z\ \mathsf{pair}\ k'' = z\,k') \\
\Rightarrow \quad \text{(extensionality on } z\ \mathsf{pair} \text{ and } z) \\
\quad z\ \mathsf{pair} = z
\end{array}$$

□

We can now prove Proposition 14.

Proof. Below is the proof for $T \times U$. The other cases are similar.

$$
\begin{array}{ll}
 & z \in \lfloor T \times U \rfloor^* \\
\Rightarrow & \text{(definition deductive interpretation, Reynolds embedding)} \\
 & \forall Z. \forall k. (\forall x. x \in \lfloor T \rfloor^* \rightarrow \forall y. y \in \lfloor U \rfloor^* \rightarrow k\, x\, y \in Z) \rightarrow z\, k \in Z \\
\Rightarrow & \text{(instantiate } Z := \lceil T \times U \rceil \text{ and } k := \mathsf{pair}) \\
 & (\forall x. x \in \lfloor T \rfloor^* \rightarrow \forall y. y \in \lfloor U \rfloor^* \rightarrow \mathsf{pair}\, x\, y \in \lceil T \times U \rceil) \rightarrow z\, \mathsf{pair} \in \lceil T \times U \rceil \\
\Rightarrow & \text{(induction hypothesis)} \\
 & (\forall x. x \in \lceil T \rceil \rightarrow \forall y. y \in \lceil U \rceil \rightarrow \mathsf{pair}\, x\, y \in \lceil T \times U \rceil) \rightarrow z\, \mathsf{pair} \in \lceil T \times U \rceil \\
\Rightarrow & \text{(Constructor Lemma)} \\
 & z\, \mathsf{pair} \in \lceil T \times U \rceil \\
= & \text{(parametricity } (z \in \lfloor T \times U \rfloor^* \rightarrow (z, z) \in \lfloor T \times U \rfloor^{\approx}) \text{, Böhm's Lemma)} \\
 & z \in \lceil T \times U \rceil
\end{array}
$$

□

An immediate corollary is the following.

Proposition 16. *(Girard-Reynolds isomorphism) If T is an algebraic type then $\lfloor T \rfloor \equiv \lfloor T \rfloor^{*\circ}$, and furthermore if T and its subtypes are parametric then* P2 + ext *proves $\lceil T \rceil = \lceil T \rceil^{\circ *}$.*

Proof. Immediate from Propositions 9, 12 and 14. □

Acknowledgements

Thanks to Andrew Pitts, Jon Riecke, and referees of POPL 1999, LICS 2000, and TACS 2001 for comments on this work; with special thanks to an anonymous referee and to Andrew Pitts for spotting errors.

References

[ACC93] M. Abadi, L. Cardelli, and P.-L. Curien, Formal Parametric Polymorphism, *Theoretical Computer Science* 121(1–2):9–58, December 1993. (Part of A Collection of Contributions in Honour of Corrado Boehm on the Occasion of his 70th Birthday.) Also appeared as SRC Research Report 109.

[Bar91] H. Barendregt, Introduction to generalized types systems, *Journal of Functional Programming*, 1(2):125–154, April 1991.

[BFSS90] E. S. Bainbridge, P. J. Freyd, A. Scedrov, and P. J. Scott, Functorial polymorphism, in G. Huet, editor, *Logical Foundations of Functional Programming*, pp. 315–330, Addison-Wesley, 1990.

[BB85] C. Böhm and A. Berarducci, Automatic synthesis of typed Λ-programs on term algebras, *Theoretical Computer Science* 39(2–3):135–154, August 1985.

[BC88] V. Breazu-Tannen and T. Coquand, Extensional models for polymorphism, *Theoretical Computer Science*, 59:85–114, 1988.

[CF58] H. B. Curry and R. Feys, *Combinatory Logic*, North Holland, 1958.

[CH88] T. Coquand and G. Huet, The calculus of constructions, *Information and Computation*, 76:95–120, 1988.

[Con86] R. Constable, *et al.*, *Implementing mathematics with the Nuprl proof development system*, Prentice-Hall, 1986.

[deB70] N. G. de Bruijn, The mathematical language of AUTOMATH, its usage and some of its extensions, *Proceedings of the Symposium on Automatic Demonstration*, LNCS 125, Springer-Verlag, 1970.

[DM82] L. Damas and R. Milner, Principal type schemes for functional programs, *9'th Annual Symposium on Principles of Programming Languages*, Albuquerque, N.M., January 1982.

[Fre79] Gottlob Frege. Begriffsschrift, a formula language, modeled upon that of arithmetic, for pure thought (1879). In Jan van Heijenoort, editor, *From Frege to Gödel: A Source Book in Mathematical Logic, 1879-1931.* Harvard University Press, 1967.

[Gir72] J.-Y. Girard, *Interprétation functionelle et élimination des coupures dans l'arithmétique d'ordre supérieure*, Ph.D. thesis, Université Paris VII, 1972.

[GLT89] J.-Y. Girard, Y. Lafont, and P. Taylor, *Proofs and Types*, Cambridge University Press, 1989.

[Has94] R. Hasegawa, Categorical data types in parametric polymorphism, *Mathematical Structures in Computer Science*, 4:71-109, (1994).

[Hin69] R. Hindley, The principal type scheme of an object in combinatory logic, *Trans. Am. Math. Soc.*, 146:29–60, December 1969.

[How80] W. A. Howard, The formulae-as-types notion of construction, in J. P. Seldin and J. R. Hindley, editors, *To H. B. Curry: Essays on Combinatory Logic, Lambda Calculus, and Formalism*, Academic Press, 1980. (The original version was circulated privately in 1969.)

[KP90] J.-L. Krivine and M. Parigot, Programming with proofs, *J. Inf. Process. Cybern. (EIK)*, 26(3): 149–167, 1990. (Revised version of a lecture presented at the 6'th International Symposium on Computation Theory, (SCT '87), Wednisch-Rietz, GDR, 30 November–4 December 1987.

[Lei83] D. Leivant, Reasoning about functional programs and complexity classes associated with type disciplines, *24'th Symposium on Foundations of Computer Science*, Washington D.C., IEEE, 460–469.

[Lei90] D. Leivant, Contracting proofs to programs, in P. Odifreddi, editor, *Logic and Computer Science*, Academic Press, 1990.

[Mai91] H. Mairson, Outline of a proof theory of parametricity, in J. Hughes, editor, *5'th International Conference on Functional Programming Languages and Computer Architecture*, Springer-Verlag LNCS 523, Cambridge, Massachusetts, August 1991.

[Mar82] P. Martin-Löf, Constructive mathematics and computer programming, *6'th International Congress for Logic, Methodology, and Philosophy of Science*, North Holland, pp. 153–175, 1982.

[Mil78] R. Milner, A theory of type polymorphism in programming, *Journal of Computers and Systems Science*, 17:348–375, 1978.

[Mog86] E. Moggi, Communication to the Types electronic forum, 10 February 1986.

[MR91] Q. Ma and J. C. Reynolds, Types, abstraction, and parametric polymorphism, part 2, in S. Brookes *et al.* editors, *Mathematical Foundations of Programming Semantics*, Springer Verlag LNCS, 1991.

[Pit87] A. M. Pitts, Polymorphism Is Set Theoretic, Constructively, in D. H. Pitt and A. Poigné and D. E. Rydeheard, editors, *Category Theory and Computer Science*, pages 12–39, Edinburgh 1987.

[Pit89] A. M. Pitts, Non-trivial power types can't be subtypes of polymorphic types, in *4th Annual Symposium on Logic in Computer Science*, pages 6–13, IEEE Computer Society Press, Washington 1989.

[Pit98] A. M. Pitts, Parametric polymorphism and operational equivalence, technical report 453, Cambridge University Computer Laboratory, 1998.

[PA93] G. Plotkin and M. Abadi, A logic for parametric polymorphism, in M. Bezem and J. F. Groote, editors, *Typed Lambda Calculi and Applications*, LNCS 664, Springer-Verlag, pp. 361–375, March 1993.

[PAC94] G. Plotkin, M. Abadi, and L. Cardelli, Subtyping and parametricity, *9'th Annual Symposium on Logic in Computer Science*, pp. 310–319, July 1994.

[Rey74] J. C. Reynolds, Towards a theory of type structure, in B. Robinet, editor, *Colloque sur la Programmation*, LNCS 19, Springer-Verlag.

[Rey83] J. C. Reynolds, Types, abstraction, and parametric polymorphism, in R. E. A. Mason, editor, *Information Processing 83*, pp. 513–523, North-Holland, Amsterdam, 1983.

[Rey84] J. C. Reynolds, Polymorphism is not set theoretic, in Kahn, MacQueen, and Plotkin, editors, *Semantics of Data Types*, Sophia-Antipolis, France, pp. 145–156, LNCS 173, Springer-Verlag, 1984.

[Rey90] J. C. Reynolds, Introduction to Part II: Polymorphic Lambda Calculus, in G. Huet, editor, *Logical Foundations of Functional Programming*, Addison-Wesley, 1990.

[RP90] J. C. Reynolds and G. D. Plotkin, On Functors Expressible in the polymorphic typed lambda calculus, in G. Huet, editor, *Logical Foundations of Functional Programming*, pp. 127–152, Addison-Wesley, 1990.

[Str67] C. Strachey, Fundamental concepts in programming languages, Lecture notes, International Summer School in Computer Programming, Copenhagen, August 1967. Reprinted in *Higher-Order and Symbolic Computation* 13(1/2):11-49, May 2000.

[Tak98] Izumi Takeuiti, An axiomatic system of parametricity, *Fundamenta Informaticae*, 33:397-432, IOS Press, 1998.

[Wad89] P. Wadler, Theorems for free!, *4'th International Conference on Functional Programming Languages and Computer Architecture*, ACM Press, London, September 1989.

[Wad91] P. Wadler, Recursive types for free!, manuscript, 1991.

Lightweight Analysis of Object Interactions

Daniel Jackson[1] and Alan Fekete[2]

[1] Laboratory for Computer Science,
Massachusetts Institute of Technology,
Cambridge, Massachusetts, USA,
dnj@mit.edu

[2] Basser Dept. of Computer Science,
University of Sydney,
Sydney, Australia,
fekete@cs.usyd.edu.au

Abstract. The state of the practice in object-oriented software development has moved beyond reuse of code to reuse of conceptual structures such as design patterns. This paper draws attention to some difficulties that need to be solved if this style of development is to be supported by formal methods. In particular, the centrality of object interactions in many designs makes traditional reasoning less useful, since classes cannot be treated fruitfully in isolation from one another. We propose some ideas towards dealing with these issues: a relational model of heap structure capable of expressing sharing and mutual influence between objects; a declarative specification style that works in the presence of collaboration; and a tool-supported constraint analysis to expose problems in a diagram that captures, at a design level, a pattern of interaction. We illustrate these ideas with an example taken from a program used in the formatting of this paper.

1 Motivations

The last decade has seen significant changes in the way high-quality software is developed. One important trend has been the wide adoption of practices that guide designers in the reuse not only of code but also of larger conceptual structures. The 'design patterns' movement has identified a range of problems that arise repeatedly in object-oriented design, and has named and articulated standard solutions to these problems. The movement has spawned a book [2] that is widely acknowledged as one of the most important contributions to software development practice in the last decade; on-going conferences extend this work. Some common structures (less general than patterns, but still applicable to a diversity of specific situations) have been expressed in 'frameworks' [1] whose classes express common aspects of a domain, while leaving 'template methods' with no behavior or only a default behavior; the details are then filled in by subclasses for each particular application.

Despite advances in formal methods, such practices still lack good support for reasoning at the design level. Does a design correctly express a pattern? When

N. Kobayashi and B.C. Pierce (Eds.): TACS 2001, LNCS 2215, pp. 492–513, 2001.

two patterns overlap, does one pattern undermine key properties supposedly ensured by the other? What obligations must be placed on a programmer who fills in a template method so that the framework properties are maintained? These kinds of questions might benefit from the ability to describe designs precisely, and analyze them automatically. Unfortunately, much of the theoretical work inspired by object-oriented programming has focused on providing tools to help language designers or compiler writers, leaving the software developer out in the cold.

To help developers reason about modern object-oriented software designs involving patterns and frameworks, several difficult issues must be addressed. One is collaboration: the interaction of two or more objects designed to work in tandem. Almost all patterns achieve flexibility and decoupling by having several objects (of different classes) continually interacting with one another, delegating operations back and forth. This means that reasoning cannot treat each class in isolation as in classical abstract-data-type reasoning [4]; there are global invariants that need to be maintained. For example, the Observer pattern is central to systems built with a Model-View-Controller approach: a 'subject' class maintains some state, and notifies a range of different 'observers' whenever its state changes: each observer in turn queries the subject to obtain an up-to-date value for the aspect of the state it cares about.

Another difficulty arises from the fact that patterns and frameworks express only partial information about the final system. A class that plays Subject in an Observer pattern may also be a Component in a Composite pattern, all in addition to its application-specific roles. We need to reason about some aspect of the behavior of a class, while still capturing frame conditions so that our reasoning is not invalidated by other behaviors not currently of interest. Similarly, a template method in a framework is not known completely when we reason about the framework's contribution to an overall design, but some aspects of the method's properties must be expressed in order to establish properties of the framework as a whole.

2 Example

Java's iterators illustrate some of the complexities of object interaction. To traverse a collection sequentially, one obtains an iterator object (by calling a method on the collection), and then makes calls on the iterator itself to yield the objects of the collection one by one. To avoid copying, the iterator is usually implemented as a cursor that references the internal data structure of the collection. If the collection is mutated in the lifetime of the iterator, subsequent calls on the iterator can fail. In the standard Java collection framework, iterators are 'fail-fast', and if such a mutation occurs, the iterator will throw an exception rather than fail unpredictably at a later point. Avoiding such a failure has been dubbed the *comodification problem.*

To make sense of Java iterators, an iterator and its underlying collection must be considered together, as a single interacting unit. The objects are not aliased in the traditional sense – they have different types – but a mutation of one can affect the other. In fact, because one often wants to delete objects during iteration, a Java iterator provides a method that safely removes the object last yielded from the underlying collection. So the interaction goes both ways: calls on the iterator can affect the collection, and vice versa. It is also possible to create several iterators simultaneously active on the same collection; in this case, there is a worry that a removal via one iterator will cause another iterator to fail.

Object-oriented programs are rife with these kinds of interactions, and they account for much of their complexity (and perhaps many of their bugs). Mutations to a hash key can invalidate the invariant of a hash table, so that a lookup on the key will fail even though it is present. Streams attached to network sockets are interdependent in Java; closing an input stream can cause an output stream on the same socket to be closed too. And the relationships between listeners, events and user interface components can be a major source of frustration even for experienced programmers.

For the rest of our paper, we will study the comodification problem in the context of a small text-processing program written recently by the first author (and used in the production of this paper). The program takes source text marked up with some simple tags that associate style names with paragraphs, name special characters symbolically, indicate regions of the text to be treated as mathematical formulas, and so on. It produces text marked up with more elaborate tags, in the import language of a typographic layout program such as Quark Xpress or Adobe InDesign. These import languages require more intrusive and low-level tagging than the source language; a special character (eg, †) is specified by font name and index, for example, rather than symbolically (\dagger). They are also application-specific.

The program works as follows. The source text is broken into tokens corresponding to commands, sequences of alphabetic characters, punctuation marks, etc. Tokens are classified into types, and a list of actions is associated in a registry with each type. When a token is read, the actions associated with its type are performed. For example, when the token for a special character command is read, the symbolic name is looked up in a table giving the font name and index, and the appropriate tagged output is generated. One possible effect of an action is to change the registry itself, by creating or deleting associations of actions with types. A command to enter mathematical mode, for example, produces a token whose action attaches an italicizing action to the token type corresponding to sequences of alphabetic characters, so that only letters (and not numbers or symbols) are affected.

The object model of Figure 1 expresses some of the heap invariants of the program. For readers unfamiliar with object models, here is brief explanation of the diagram's meaning; a full and more formal discussion of object models may be found elsewhere [7]. Each box corresponds to the set of objects belonging to the class (or interface) whose name is the label of the box. An arrow with a closed head from A to B says that the set of objects A is a subset of the set of objects B, usual ly because A is declared as a subclass of B. An arrow with an open head

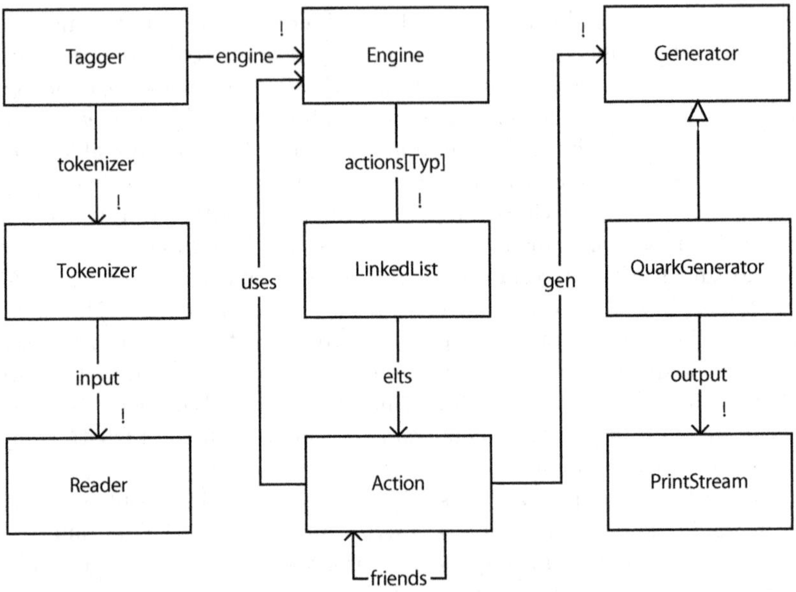

Fig. 1. Object Model for Tagging Program

labelled f from A to B says that each object in A references objects in B with a variable f, where f is usually a field name, but may also be a local variable available only transiently (eg, during a particular method call), or a reference bound by the formation of an inner class. An exclamation mark at the end of a reference arrow says that there is exactly one object obtained by navigating the reference; if absent, there may be any number of objects, usually due to the elision of a collection object such as an array. Finally, an arrow labelled $f[\mathrm{I}]$ from A to B indicates a set of indexed references: for each object i in the index set I, there is a reference $f[\mathrm{i}]$ from A to B.

The main class is *Tagger*. Its objects hold references to a *Tokenizer*, which provides tokens by reading from a file through Java's *Reader* interface, and an *Engine*, which consumes tokens. An *Engine* is a registry; for each token type, it references a *LinkedList* whose elements are *Actions*. An *Action* may hold references to one or more *Engines*, to other *Actions*, and to a *Generator*. The interface *Generator* hides differences between the tagging conventions of different layout programs. The class *QuarkGenerator* provides Quark-specific tagging, and holds a reference to a *PrintStream* for its output.

An object model does not have to be uniform in its level of abstraction. We have chosen to make explicit the presence of linked lists that hold actions in the engine, but to treat them abstractly as containers with a reference *elts* to their elements. The hash map that maps token types to lists is not shown, although its mapping is represented in the indexed relation from *Engine* to *LinkedList*. There are a number of subtleties that we shall ignore since their elaboration would add little to our discussion. The actions, for example, are in fact constructed from a variety of inner classes, which differ in what references they hold. A more accurate model would show these inner classes as subsets of *Action*, each with its own distinct references.

The events that occur when a token is consumed by the engine are shown in the interaction diagram of Figure 2. In short, the diagram is read as follows: time runs top to bottom; vertical boxes represent the activations of method calls; solid horizontal arrows represent method invocations; method returns are usually implicit, but when shown are drawn dashed. This diagram shows a particular trace. Invoking the *consume_token* method causes the engine to obtain the action list for the token's type by a lookup on its hash map. It then calls the *iterator* method of the list to create an iterator object. It then loops over the elements of the list: it checks that further elements are available, by calling *hasNext*; obtains the next element; calls the *perform* method on the action; and then repeats until the second call to *next*. The *perform* method registers an action with the engine; in response, the engine, obtains the appropriate action list and adds the action to it.

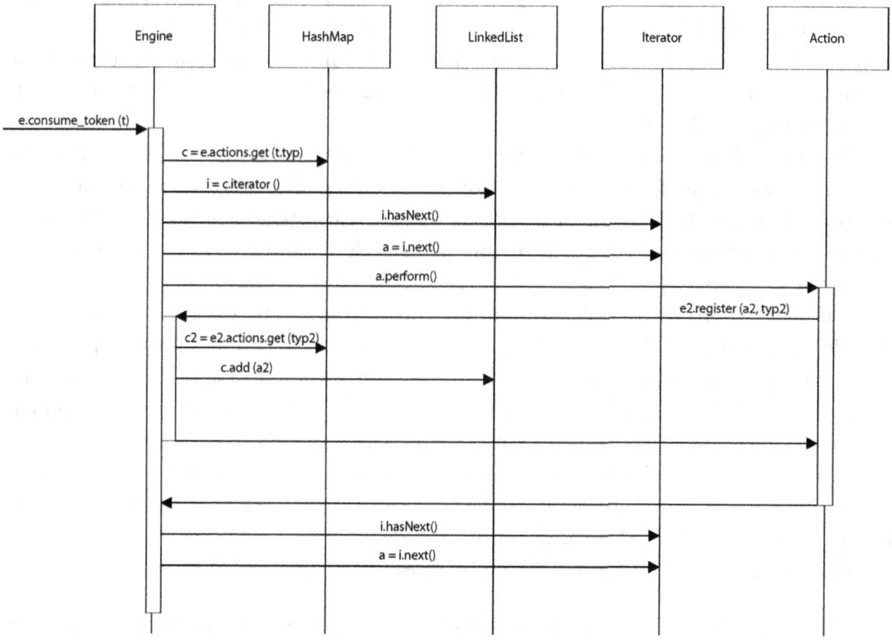

Fig. 2. Interaction Diagram for Tagging Program

This trace demonstrates a potential flaw of the design: a possibility of co-modification. If the list to which the action is added is the same list on which the iterator is based, the second call to *next* will fail.

3 An Approach

No comprehensive method for describing and reasoning about realistic object-oriented designs has been developed that can handle the kinds of object interaction due to collaboration, sharing, and overlapping patterns. Below we offer some fragmentary ideas we hope may contribute towards such a method. Before introducing them, let us summarize the main requirements a method will need to satisfy to be workable in practice.

Formal description must be lightweight [11]; this means that a software developer should not have to express everything about the system being developed, but can instead target formal reasoning at those aspects of the system that are especially difficult or risky. Furthermore, it must be possible to vary the level of detail applied to each part of the program or each aspect of its behaviour in a non-uniform manner. The developer will want to have some part of the design represented with attention to all the objects and the exact sequence of operations, while other parts are summarized by a declarative pre- and postcondition for each method, and still others are simply expressed in frame conditions saying that nothing significant happens.

Automated tool support is essential. Relying solely on the mathematical insight of software developers has not been successful. At the simplest level, a tool can check the syntax of a formal representation; at the other extreme, a tool can extract formal representations from code without user involvement and check them against predefined properties. We believe that developers will get most assistance from a tool that allows the developer to explore the behavior of a design, and that determines automatically whether some specified property holds. Some tools have concentrated on certifying that a property does hold by generating (or checking) a logical proof; our experience has led to an emphasis on tools that generate counterexamples when the property does not hold. This is based on the value of formal methods in finding mistakes in designs early in the life-cycle, and it also reflects our belief that a developer passes through many wrong designs before converging on a good one.

The elements of the approach we propose are:

- *A relational model of the heap.* We show how a simple model of the heap can account for the fundamental notions of object identity and sharing. Unlike previous models we have proposed [5], and the models used in shape analyses (such as [23, 19], this model represents dereferencing in two steps: with a relation that maps an object reference to an abstract mathematical value, and then a relation that projects the value to one or more object references. This allows frame conditions to be expressed more systematically and succinctly, and leads to a more natural specification style.

- *A declarative notation for specifying methods.* We show how, using this model, it is easy to construct succinct specifications of methods. Specifications are not only the yardstick against which code is measured, but are also proxies for missing code. Our notation, being a slight extension of first-order logic, is *declarative*, and expresses the behaviour of a method as a formula relating the pre- and post-states. Declarativeness is the lynchpin of partiality; it allows details of behaviour to be omitted, because they are not relevant to the analysis in hand, or because a program depends only on an interface of a component and not its particular implementation.
- *An extraction strategy.* To analyze some aspect of the program's behaviour, an abstract skeleton of the program is extracted from its code. This skeleton includes only those parts of the program relevant to the analysis, and represents methods by their specifications when possible. Aspects of behaviour that are not fully determined by the analysis may be left open using the declarative facilities of the specification notation. We have yet to investigate how this extraction might be done; a later section gives some initial thoughts about what kind of analysis might be required. For the purpose of this paper, we assume that an interaction diagram has been extracted, and we explain how such a diagram might be analyzed.
- *A constraint solving technique.* We use a technology developed previously [6] to analyze the skeleton extracted from the code. The idea, in short, is to reduce the analysis to finding models of a logical formula, so that any model found is a counterexample to the property being checked. A sequence of actions is represented as a conjunction of formulas for individual actions, with different variables explicitly representing the states between the actions. The formula is solved by translation to a propositional boolean formula, and then by application of an off-the-shelf SAT solver.

In presenting our example, we use the new version of our Alloy notation [8], whose tool is under construction. To check the example, we translated the description to an older version of the notation [7] so that we could use our existing tool [9]. The key difference between the new and old versions is that the new one has no built-in notion of state machines, and is thus more flexible in its application. Indeed, our example here is precisely the kind that motivated the design of the new language.

3.1 A Relational Heap Model

In Section 1, we identified the importance of knowing how objects collaborate, and being able to reason about cases in which changes to one object affect the state of another. In the case of our tagging program, any reasoning about the system requires a representation that captures which iterators may be invalidated by comodification; this means we must know which lists exist, and how different actions may belong to different lists.

To accomplish this, we propose an explicit representation of the heap structure of the system (or rather, of the heap structure of relevant parts of the system). In traditional abstract-data-type reasoning, each object instance is represented in the formal model by an abstract value from a mathematical domain: for example, a list might be represented as a mathematical sequence (that is a function from a prefix of the natural numbers). The only change we make to this view is that the primitive values from which an abstract value is constructed become object references, and a global relation that maps references to their abstract values is included in the program state. Thus a set of sets of integers, which would be represented traditionally as a mathematical set of sets, becomes a set whose elements are object references, each being a reference to a set object, which itself contains references to integers. For immutable types, it may be desirable to remove the indirection, but the loss of uniformity seems undesirable (and not compatible with Java, whose equality operator distinguishes, for example, two string objects containing the same character sequence).

The Alloy notation [8] gives a direct and reasonably succinct expression to these notions, and is amenable to automated analysis [6]. We hope that the notation is simple enough that an informal explanation of the example will suffice. There is one essential, and unconventional, idea underlying Alloy: the reduction of all data structures to sets and relations. Every expression denotes a set or a relation (and in fact a set can be viewed as a degenerate relation). There are no constructors for tuples, sequences, or records. Instead, every structure is objectified, so that a tuple, for example, is represented as an atomic individual, along with some relations that act as projections so that the elements of the tuple can be obtained (much like Java itself). Likewise, the states of a program are regarded as atomic individuals. There is no scalar type; a single individual is represented as the singleton set containing it.

3.1.1 Generic Heap Structure. The generic structure of the heap is expressed by the following declarations:

```
sig Ref {}
sig Object {}
sig State {
    refs: set Ref,
    obj: refs ->? Object
    }
static disj sig NullRef extends Ref {}
fact {
    all s: State, r: Ref | r = NullRef <=> no r.s::obj
}
```

Each *signature* introduced by the keyword *sig* declares a set of atomic individuals. *Ref* is a set of references to objects; *Object* is a set of abstract object values; and *State* is a set of program states. These sets have global scope, and should be regarded as constants. The declaration of the signature *NullRef* indicates that it extends *Ref*; this means little more than that its elements are a subset of the elements of *Ref*. Signatures with no extends clause represent basic types, and are disjoint from one another; so no individual can be at once a reference and an object, for example. The keyword *static* indicates that the set *NullRef* is a singleton: there is only one null reference.

The *fields* of the *State* signature are relations with global scope. Thus *refs*, for example, is a relation from *State* to *Ref*, and is intended to associate with each state the references that are live in that state. Given an expression *s* denoting a state (that is, a singleton set containing one element of the set *State*), the expression *s.refs* (in which the dot is relational image) denotes this set of references. The relation *obj* is ternary; *s.obj* will denote a relation from references in *s.refs* to objects. The question mark is a 'multiplicity symbol' that makes each such relation a partial function. Thus *r.(s.obj)* will denote a set containing one or no objects when *r* denotes one reference. For convenience, we allow this expression to be written equivalently as *r.s::obj*, in which the double colon has the same meaning as the dot, but binds more tightly.

The *fact* is a formula constraining the sets (corresponding to the signatures) and the relations (corresponding to their fields). It states that for every state *s* and reference *r*, the expression *r.s::obj* denotes a set of no elements exactly when *r* is the null reference. In other words, we associate an object with every reference unless null.

It will be convenient to have a name for the empty set of references:

```
sig NoRef extends Ref {}
fact {no NoRef}
```

3.1.2 Abstract Specifications of Classes. Particular Java classes or interfaces are represented in a similar way, with one signature for references and one for objects. For example, we might represent collections like this:

```
disj sig CollectionRef extends Ref {}
disj sig Collection extends Object {
    elts: set Ref
    }
```

where the field *elts* associates a set of references with each collection, abstracting away any ordering, and we might represent iterators over such collections like this:

```
disj sig IteratorRef extends Ref {}
disj sig Iterator extends Object {
    on: CollectionRef,
    left: set Ref,
    last: Ref
    }
```

The fields of *Iterator* map an iterator object to, respectively: a reference to the collection object on which the iterator is based (*on*); the set of references that have yet to be yielded (*left*); and the last reference yielded (*last*).

Subsignatures of a common signature, unlike Java subclasses, are not implicitly disjoint. The keyword *disj* on several subsignatures of a common signature makes them mutually disjoint. Thus *Collection* and *Iterator* are disjoint, and so are *CollectionRef*, *IteratorRef* and *NullRef*. We are therefore assuming that no object is both a *Collection* and an *Iterator*, and that the *on* field of an iterator is non-null, although the elements of a *Collection* and the *last* element of an *Iterator* may be null references.

We record the type constraints of references, so that an *IteratorRef* is indeed a reference to an *Iterator*, and a *CollectionRef* is a reference to a *Collection*:

```
fact {
    all s: State | IteratorRef.obj in Iterator
    all s: State | CollectionRef.obj in Collection
    }
```

A specification may be introduced for any class in this manner, and used in the analysis in the place of its code. This allows the analysis to be conducted in terms that are familiar to the user, without cluttering the analysis with irrelevant implementation details. In our example, we would likely provide a specification for *HashMap*, with a signature such as

```
sig HashMap extends Object {
    val: (Ref - NullRef) ->! Ref
    }
```

where the field *val* is a total function that maps (non-null) references to (possibly null) references. We will treat the *LinkedList* class as a *Collection*, since our analysis does not rely on any special properties of lists over other collections.

3.1.3 Extracted Specifications of Classes. For classes whose code is to be reasoned about, it will be appropriate to use a signature obtained directly from the code. From the *Engine* class, for example, we might obtain:

```
sig Engine extends Object {
    val: (Ref - NullRef) ->! Ref
    }
```

For some classes, we may want to apply some rudimentary abstraction manually to the extracted signature. For example, as the object model of Figure 1 suggests, we might collapse all references an *Action* has to other *Action* objects into a field *friends*, and all references to *Engine* objects into a field *uses*.

3.2 Declarative Specification

Methods are specified as parameterized formulas. For each method, we give a precondition, a postcondition and frame condition. The *add* method of *Collection*, for example, might be specified as follows:

```
fun add-pre (s: State, this: CollectionRef, e: Ref) {
    this != NullRef
    }
```

```
fun add-post (pre, post: State, this: CollectionRef, e: Ref) {
    this.post::obj.elts = this.pre::obj.elts + e
    }
fun add-modifies (pre, post: State, this: CollectionRef, e: Ref) {
    modifies (pre, post, this)
    }
```

The precondition requires that the reference to the receiver object (*this*) be non-null. The postcondition says that the set of elements of the collection object in the post-state is the set in the pre-state with the addition of the reference *e*. (The plus denotes set union). The frame condition says that the receiver object is the only object modified; it uses a generic formula

```
fun modifies (pre, post: State, rs: set Ref) {
    all r: pre.refs - rs | r.pre::obj = r.post::obj
    }
```

that constrains a pre-state, post-state and a set of references *rs* so that the values of all references live in the pre-state except those in *rs* are unchanged. (The minus denotes set difference.)

We have separated the method specification into these parts anticipating that in practice a syntactic sugar would be used. Traditionally, the state and receiver arguments are not declared explicitly, and each of the three parts is written as a clause of a single paragraph. A convenient shorthand would allow *e.pre::obj* to be written *e*∧, and *e.post::obj* to be written *e'*. For a language such as Java, it would be appropriate to regard a declaration of type *Object* as if it were actually a de claration of type *Ref*. Our specification might then be written:

```
class Collection {
    ...
    void add (Object e)
        pre: this != NullRef
        modifies: this
        post: this'.elts = this∧.elts + e
    ...
    }
```

The specification of the method as a whole is interpreted as an implication, stating that the post-condition and modifies clause are only required to hold when the precondition is satisfied:

```
fun add (pre, post: State, this: CollectionRef, e: Ref) {
    add-pre (pre, this, e) =>
        add-post (pre, post, this, e) && add-modifies (pre, post, this, e)
    }
```

We shall assume that all method specifications are assembled from their parts in this manner, and subsequently show only the formulas for the individual clauses.

3.2.1 Linking Objects. The *iterator* method of the collection returns an iterator object that is based on the collection, and its specification illustrates how a link between objects is established:

```
fun iterator-pre (s: State, this: CollectionRef) {
    this != NullRef
    } fun iterator-post (pre, post: State, this: CollectionRef, result: IteratorRef) {
    result.post::obj.on = this
    result.post::obj.left = this.pre::obj.elts
    no result.post::obj.last
    fresh (pre, result)
    }
fun iterator-modifies (pre, post: State, this: CollectionRef) {
    modifies (pre, post, NoRef)
    }
```

The *fresh* formula, used in the postcondition, states that a set of references *rs* has no intersection with the references of the pre-state *s*:

```
fun fresh (s: State, rs: set Ref) {
    no rs & s.refs
    }
```

3.2.2 Non-determinism. The specification of the *next* method of the iterator illustrates the use of non-determinism to hide details – in this case the order in which elements are stored and yielded. Its precondition says that there are some elements left to yield; its postcondition says that some arbitrary element is yielded; and the frame condition says that only the iterator is modified:

```
fun next-pre (s: State, this: IteratorRef) {
    this != NullRef
    some this.pre::obj.left
    }
fun next-post (pre, post: State, this: IteratorRef, result: Ref) {
    this.post::obj.on = this.pre::obj.on
    this.post::obj.left = this.pre::obj.left - result
    this.post::obj.last = result
    }
fun next-modifies (pre, post: State, this: IteratorRef) {
    modifies (pre, post, this)
    }
```

3.2.3 Mutation at a Distance. The specification of the *remove* method of the iterator illustrates an interaction between objects, encapsulated by specification in a single method. Its precondition says that there is a last element; its postcondition says that the last element yielded is deleted from the underlying collection, and the *last* field is made null; and its frame condition allows only the iterator and the underlying collection to change:

```
fun remove-pre (s: State, this: IteratorRef) {
    this != NullRef
    this.pre::obj.last != NullRef
    }
fun remove-post (pre, post: State, this: IteratorRef) {
    this.post::obj.on = this.pre::obj.on
    this.post::obj.left = this.pre::obj.left
    this.pre::obj.on.post::obj.elts =this.pre::obj.on.pre::obj.elts - this.pre::obj.last
    this.post::obj.last = NullRef
    }
fun remove-modifies (pre, post: State, this: IteratorRef) {
    modifies (pre, post, this + this.pre::obj.on)
    }
```

The key constraint of the postcondition is a little daunting written out in full, but using the shorthand it would become

```
(this∧.on)'.elts = (this∧.on)∧.elts - this∧.last
```

Note how our notation allows us to mix dereferencing in the pre- and post-states; expressions as a whole are not interpreted in one state or the other. Thus *(this∧.on)'.elts* denotes the value of the *elts* field in the post-state of the object obtained by dereferencing the *on* field of *this* in the pre-state.

3.2.4 Comodification. Finally, we consider how to say that comodifications should not occur by extending our specifications. Using a trick taken from [19], we associate with each collection and iterator object an abstract version:

```
sig Version extends Object {}
sig VersionRef extends Ref {}
sig Collection extends Object {
    ...
    cver: VersionRef
    }
sig Iterator extends Object {
    ...
    iver: VersionRef
    }
```

The *iterator* method gets a new constraint saying that the iterator's version matches the collection's (which the frame condition assures cannot have changed):

```
fun iterator-post (pre, post: State, this: CollectionRef, result: IteratorRef) {
    ...
    result.post::obj.iver = this.post::obj.cver
}
```

No alterations are made to mutators of the collection, such as *add*. The omission of a constraint will allow the collection's version to take on any value in the post-state.

The *remove* method includes a similar constraint as that of the *iterator* method:

```
fun remove-post (pre, post: State, this: IteratorRef) {
    ...
    this.post::obj.iver = this.pre::obj.on.post::obj.cver
    }
```

but since both objects may be modified, this allows new versions to be obtained, so that after a *remove*, although this iterator will be consistent with its underlying collection, another iterator on the same collection will not be.

Finally, the precondition of the *next* method says that versions should match:

```
fun next-pre (s: State, this: IteratorRef) {
    ...
    this.pre::obj.iver = this.pre::obj.on.pre::obj.cver
}
```

We have chosen to specify a behaviour slightly different from that of Java iterators. While our iterators are *allowed* to fail when a comodification occurs, Java iterators are *required* to. Our specification models exactly what happens when a key of a hashmap is mutated in such a way that the hashmap's invariant is undermined. In this case, it is impractical to demand that an exception be raised.

3.2.5 Subtypes and Subclasses. We have modelled Java's type hierarchy by associating a set of objects with each class or interface, and treating subclassing or extension simply as subset. This approach fails when objects of a subclass do not behave according to the superclass specification. The notion of equality is also problematic. In specifying the *get* method of *HashMap*, for example, we might write:

```
fun get-post (pre, post: State, this: HashMap, k: Ref, result: Ref) {
    result = k.(this.pre::obj.val)
    }
```

in which keys are matched by reference equality, but sometimes a more elaborate treatment of equality will be needed.

3.3 Extraction and Constraint Solving

Suppose we have extracted from the code the interaction diagram of Figure 2, representing the behaviour of the method *consume_token* as far as the second call to *next*. Although widely used, interaction diagrams have no standard meaning, and most attempts to provide semantics have focused on concurrency and not accounted for dynamic allocation and linking of objects. We are not able to give a formal semantics here, although our translation into Alloy is a starting point.

We shall treat the boxes that run along the top not as individual objects, but as sets of objects; thus *Engine* denotes the set of objects belonging to the *Engine* class. Each label on a method call explicitly identifies its receiver, and we shall assume a single global scope for the variables in the diagram. Method calls whose constituent steps are not shown – call these *basic calls* – will be modelled by their specifications; the remaining calls are merely transfers of control and can be ignored.

We now associate distinct states with each point on the vertical scale at which a horizontal arrow representing a basic call is present. We then construct a formula that constrains these states with the specifications of the calls, whose models will be the possible execution traces associated with the interaction diagram:

```
{   get (s0, s1, e.s0::obj.actions, t.s0::obj.typ, c)
    iterator (s1, s2, c, i)
    hasNext (s2, s3, i, True)
    next (s3, s4, i, a)
    get (s4, s5, e2.s4::obj.actions, typ2, c2)
    add (s5, s6, c2, a2)
    hasNext (s6, s7, i, True)
    next (s7, s8, i, a)
}
```

The *hasNext* method – the only one not specified above – has arguments for the pre- and post-states, the iterator, and a boolean result. Because the *hasNext* tests are assumed both to have succeeded in this trace, the result argument is instantiated as *True*. A sequence of formulas enclosed in braces is a conjunction in Alloy; this formula represents an execution in which *get* is called in state *s0*, resulting in state *s1*, then iterator is called in state *s1* resulting in state *s2*, and so on. The arguments to the parameterized formulas are Alloy expressions using variables whose declarations will be given below.

3.3.1 Checking Comodification. To check the comodification constraint, we assert that in any such sequence, the precondition of the final call to *next* is met:

```
assert {
    all s0, s1, s2, s3, s4, s5, s6, s7, s8: State,
        e, e2: EngineRef, actions: HashMapRef,
        t: TokenRef, c, c2: CollectionRef,
        i: IteratorRef, a, a2: ActionRef, typ2: TypRef |
            {get (s0, s1, e.s0::obj.actions, t.s0::obj.typ, c)
            iterator (s1, s2, c, i)
            hasNext (s2, s3, i, True)
```

```
        next (s3, s4, i, a)
        get (s4, s5, e2.s4::obj.actions, typ2, c2)
        add (s5, s6, c2, a2)
        hasNext (s6, s7, i, True)
        next (s7, s8, i, a)
        } => next-pre (s7, i, a)
}
```

An assertion in Alloy is checked by searching for a counterexample – that is, a model of the negation. In this case, the analyzer finds (in a few seconds) the expected scenario in which *c* and *c2* refer to the same collection. This can be displayed textually or graphically, with a snapshot for each state showing its heap structure. The textual output includes, for example:

```
c = Ref0
i = Ref1
c2 = Ref0
e = Ref5
e2 = Ref5
s5 = Sta5
s6 = Sta6
s7 = Sta6
...
State = {Sta1, ..., Sta5, Sta6}
...
CollectionRef = {Ref0}
Collection = {Obj0, Obj1}
...
Sta5 = {obj: Ref0 -> Obj0, Ref1 -> Obj2, ...}
Sta6 = {obj: Ref0 -> Obj1, Ref1 -> Obj2, ...}
...
Obj0 = {cver: Ref3}
Obj1 = {cver: Ref4}
Obj2 = {iver: Ref3}
...
```

which shows first the bindings of values to variable names, then the contents of sets, then the values of fields. Both *Collection* variables *c* and *c2* have the same reference value *Ref0* – that is, they are aliased – as do both *Engine* objects. The value of the state variable *s5*, called *Sta5*, maps *Ref0* to a collection object *Obj0* whose version field has the value *Ref3*. But the state after the *add* method, *Sta6*, maps it to the object *Obj1* with a different version. The version of the iterator object *Obj2* associated with *Ref1* remains unchanged. The pre-state of the final call to *next*, *s7*, has the same value as the state just after the *add*, *Sta6*, and because of the mismatch of versions, violates the precondition. (We performed the analyses discussed here using a tool that handles a previous version of the

Alloy language. The form of the output is different but the content is essentially the same.)

Alloy's analysis is incomplete. A formula may have a model (or counterexample) that the tool fails to find, since it only considers assignments in a 'scope' set by the user that bounds the size of the basic sets. Our hypothesis is that a high proportion of bugs can be found in a small scope.

3.3.2 Extending the Correctness Argument. We anticipate using the tool interactively. Having found a counterexample, we consider whether some invariant is needed to establish the property. In this case, it's clear that there may be a comodification unless we make some attempt to ensure that actions do not affect the collection to which they belong.

A reasonable discipline, which we followed in the construction of our tagging program, is to define for each action the types against which it is ever registered in any engine – call these its *registration types* – and then to require that no action share a registration type with a friend (that is, an action it registers or deregisters). This is easily checked statically, and seems to be liberal enough. We can express this discipline as a fact:

```
fact {
    all a: Action | no a.regtypes & a.friends.regtypes
    }
```

having previously added *regtypes* as a field of *Action*

```
sig Action {
    ...
    regtypes: set TypRef
}
```

along with a fact defining it:

```
fact {
    all a: Action | a.regtypes =
        {t: TypRef | some e: Engine, s, s': State, c: Collection |
            get (s, s', e.actions, t, c) && a in c.elts.s::obj}
}
```

Running the assertion again (with the new facts now implicitly conjoined to the negated assertion), a counterexample is still found. Studying the output shows a single collection of actions registered against two distinct types. This suggests that *Engine* needs an invariant requiring that the mapping be injective:

```
fact {
    all s, s': State, e: Engine, t1, t2: TypRef, c: CollectionRef |
        get (s, s', e.actions, t1, c) && get (s, s', e.actions, t2, c) => t1 = t2
}
```

This invariant can be established locally by checking the code of *Engine*, with each method checked by an analysis similar to our analysis of consume_token.

It is a strength of our approach that it can accommodate a programming discipline in the correctness argument. This decouples code and design analysis, so that it may not be necessary always to repeat the design analysis when the code is changed, so long as it still conforms to the discipline. The discipline embodies the essence of the design, and its articulation alone is likely to be valuable. A different discipline that suffices to establish the required property might be liberal enough for the program at hand, but not for anticipated extensions, or for other programs in a family using the same framework. We might, for example, have insisted that an action only register actions in a different engine, but that would be too restrictive.

3.3.3 Issues. The construction and analysis of the interaction diagram that we have sketched in outline presents a number of research challenges that will need to be addressed:

- *Extraction.* Given a property of interest – in this case the absence of comodification within *Engine* – an interaction diagram, or a similar kind of behavioural skeleton, is extracted from the code by static analysis. Statements not relevant to the property at hand are eliminated, and possible statement sequences across method calls are collected. The analysis should be simpler than slicing, since it will be acceptable to insert non-deterministic statements (eg, an assignment of an unknown value to a variable): the skeleton that is extracted should include all possible behaviours, but may admit some infeasible ones. How approximate the analysis may be will be determined not by the incidence of spurious counterexamples, but by their quality. It may be reasonable, for example, to ignore control dependences from extraneous data types. We expect that lightweight techniques that have been developed for object model extraction [22] will come in handy, as well as more generic and power ful type-based techniques [18].
- *Namespace.* It may be convenient to flatten the namespace as we did above, using something like SSA form, so that there is no need to express or analyze argument passing.
- *Loops and conditionals.* We considered only a single sequence of statements. Conditional statements might be represented explicitly in the interaction diagram, and then encoded using disjunction for analysis, or it may be better to generate separate diagrams for each path. Loops might also be represented explicitly, so that a loop invariant can be asserted. Alternatively, a loop can be unwound, and an analysis performed up to some finite number of iterations [10]. This will of course entail a further loss of soundness in the analysis.
- Simplification. The formula obtained from the diagram may be simplified before analysis. Post-state arguments may be eliminated, for example, from calls to methods that leave the state unchanged. But it is not clear how effective such simplifications would be.

4 Related Work

This paper builds on ideas the first author and his students have been developing in the last few years, most notably:

- A simple and flexible notation capable of expressing key properties of software designs in a declarative manner [?];
- An analysis whose automation makes it like a model checker, but whose ability to handle relational structure, and to handle arbitrary formulas, makes it more like a theorem prover [6];
- An encoding of program statements as logical formulas, allowing the analysis to be used to find bugs in code [10]; and
- A simple relational view of object-oriented programs [5].

The new ideas in this paper are:

- An improved relational model of the heap, which simplifies the interpretation of frame conditions, and corresponds closely to a style of specification that has been widely taught [16];
- Performing analysis over a design representation such as an interaction diagram that corresponds to code but deals at the level of abstraction at which a designer views a program;
- A simple treatment of sequential composition, in which intermediate states are made explicit and objectified; and
- Making explicit a discipline that decouples code and design analysis, whose accommodation depends on the ability of the analysis to handle declarative specifications.

4.1 Object Interaction

'Object-oriented programming' has increasingly come to refer to a style of programming in which interactions between abstract objects is fundamental, and a major focus of the design. Most design patterns [2] involve object interactions, and many popular frameworks, especially for graphical user interfaces, rely on them heavily. Overuse of object interaction is likely, of course, to make a program incomprehensible, but used carefully, it offers flexibility and a cleaner separation of concerns. In our tagging program, for example, the design allows all the code associated with mathematical mode to be localized. In a more traditional design, it would have been necessary to distribute flags throughout the program to achieve the different behaviour required when within that mode.

The paper that first identified the need for linguistic support for describing object interactions [3] used a largely operational notation, and focused on describing method call sequences. Its focus was primarily on documenting the calls an object is expected to make in order to partipate correctly in an interaction, rather than on analyzing its global effects. Several of the notations of UML [20] are intended for describing object interaction, but they treat objects as processes communicating in a fixed topology, and do not account for allocation or reconfiguration.

4.2 Interface Specification Languages

Recently, Leavens and his colleagues have developed a specification language for Java called JML [13]. Like Eiffel [17], it uses expressions of the programming language as terms in specification formulas. This allows pre- and postconditions to be interpreted as runtime assertions; the form *old(e)* is used in a postcondition to refer to the value of *e* in the prestate. The underlying model of the heap does not involve a notion of object values, but, like [5], treats fields as direct mappings from objects to objects.

The heap model of this paper uses explicit 'state functions' to map object references to object values, as in Larch-C++ [12]. We have chosen this approach for three reasons. First, it gives a simpler semantics to modifies clauses; with fields as relations between objects, the clause *modifies f* for a field *f* is an assertion about all fields except *f*, but a quantification over field names is not expressible in first-order logic. Second, the explicitness of state functions makes it easy to express and give meaning to sequences of method calls (and is also more expressive and more uniform than *old*). Third, the resulting specifications are compatible with a widely taught viewpoint and specification style [16] in which objects rather than locations are viewed as mutable.

ESC/Java [15] is a tool that checks code for basic properties such as lack of null dereferences and array bounds overflow. Its annotation language is a subset of JML. Unlike our approach, it aims at a uniform level of analysis across a large program, rather than an analysis focused on some aspect of object interaction. Modularity of reasoning has therefore been a central concern, and the approach takes advantage of a technique developed by Leino [14] for interpreting modifies clauses correctly in the presence of hidden components.

4.3 Model Extraction

A number of projects are focusing on verifying code by applying an analysis to an abstract model extracted from the code. The Bandera project [24] aims to extract finite-state machines that can be presented to off-the-shelf model checkers. The SLAM project [25] translates code into 'boolean programs' that are amenable to analysis with a specialized model checker. Both projects are more concerned with event sequencing issues than object configurations and interactions.

4.4 Static Analysis

A recent paper [19] shows the application of Sagiv et al's shape analysis framework [21] to the comodification problem. Our use of abstract version objects was taken from that paper. Unlike ours, the analysis is conservative, although, being operational rather than declarative, it requires consideration of the entire program. Our approach allows us to omit details of the behaviour of *Action* objects, for example, and admit any kind of registration behaviour satisfying some discipline. In their approach, however, heap shapes are only considered when code is present to construct them. This work is part of the Canvas Project at IBM

Research and Tel-Aviv University, whose aim is to provide a conformance check of client code against criteria specified by a component designer, and which has also investigated protocol analyses based on state machines.

Our work is also part of a larger project to find ways to check conformance of code to a high-level design. As part of this effort, Martin Rinard and his students have recently developed a static analysis that distinguishes objects according to their relationships with other objects. We hope to exploit this analysis in our model extraction.

Acknowledgments

This work benefited from discussions early on with Michael Ernst, Nancy Lynch and Butler Lampson on how to model sharing in the heap. It was funded in part by ITR grant #0086154 from the National Science Foundation, by a grant from NASA, and by an endowment from Doug and Pat Ross.

The first author dedicates this rather imperfect paper to the fond memory of his father-in-law, Professor Joseph Marbach z"l, a prolific researcher, paper-writer and perfectionist, who died during its preparation, many years before his time.

References

[1] M. Fayad and D. Schmid, Object-Oriented Application Frameworks, Special Issue, *Communications of the ACM*, 40(10), October 1997.

[2] E. Gamma, R. Helm, R. Johnson, and J. Vlissides, *Design Patterns*, Addison Wesley, 1995

[3] R. Helm, I. M. Holland, and D. Gangopadhyay. Contracts: Specifying Behavioral Compositions in Object Oriented Systems. *European Conference on Object-Oriented Programming / ACM SIGPLAN Conference on Object-Oriented Programming Systems, Languages, and Applications*, Ottawa, Canada, Vol. 1, June 1990, 169–180.

[4] C. A. R. Hoare. Proof of correctness of data representations. *Acta Informatica*, 1(4):271–81, 1972.

[5] Daniel Jackson. Object Models as Heap Invariants. In: Carroll Morgan and Annabelle McIver (eds.), *Essays on Programming Methodology*, Springer Verlag, 2000.

[6] Daniel Jackson. Automating first-order relational logic. *ACM SIGSOFT Conference on Foundations of Software Engineering*, San Diego, California, November 2000.

[7] Daniel Jackson. Alloy: A Lightweight Object Modelling Notation. To appear, *ACM Transactions on Software Engineering and Methodology*, October 2001.

[8] Daniel Jackson, Ilya Shlyakhter and Manu Sridharan. A Micromodularity Mechanism. *ACM SIGSOFT Conference on Foundations of Software Engineering / European Software Engineering Conference*, Vienna, Austria, September 2001.

[9] Daniel Jackson, Ian Schechter and Ilya Shlyakhter. Alcoa: the Alloy Constraint Analyzer. *International Conference on Software Engineering*, Limerick, Ireland, June 2000.

[10] Daniel Jackson & Mandana Vaziri. Finding Bugs with a Constraint Solver. *International Symposium on Software Testing and Analysis*, Portland, Oregon, August 2000.

[11] Daniel Jackson and Jeannette Wing. Lightweight Formal Methods. In: H. Saiedian (ed.), *An Invitation to Formal Methods*, IEEE Computer, 29(4):16–30, April 1996.

[12] Gary T. Leavens. An overview of Larch/C++: Behavioral specifications for C++ modules. In: H. Kilov and W. Harvey (eds.), *Specification of Behavioral Semantics in ObjectOriented Information Modeling*, Amsterdam, Holland, 1996, Kluwer, pp.121–142.

[13] Gary T. Leavens, Albert L. Baker, and Clyde Ruby. JML: A Notation for Detailed Design. In: Haim Kilov, Bernhard Rumpe, and Ian Simmonds (eds.), Behavioral Specifications of Businesses and Systems, Kluwer, 1999, Chapter 12, pp. 175–188.

[14] K. Rustan M. Leino. *Toward Reliable Modular Programs*. Ph.D. thesis, California Institute of Technology, January 1995.

[15] K. Rustan M. Leino, Greg Nelson, and James B. Saxe. *ESC/Java User's Manual*. Technical Note 2000-002, Compaq Systems Research Center, October 2000.

[16] Barbara Liskov with John Guttag. *Program Development in Java: Abstraction, Specification, and Object-Oriented Design*. Addison-Wesley, 2001.

[17] Bertrand Meyer. *Object-Oriented Software Construction* (2nd ed.). Prentice Hall, 1997.

[18] Robert O'Callahan. *Generalized Aliasing as a Basis for Program Analysis Tools*. PhD thesis. Technical Report CMU-CS-01-124, School of Computer Science, Carnegie mellon University, Pittsburgh, PA, May 2001.

[19] G.Ramalingam, Alex Warshavsky, John Field and Mooly Sagiv. *Toward Effective Component Verification: Deriving an Efficient Program Analysis from a High-level Specification*. Unpublished manuscript.

[20] James Rumbaugh, Ivar Jacobson and Grady Booch. *The Unified Modeling Language Reference Manual*. Addison-Wesley, 1999.

[21] M. Sagiv, T. Reps, and R. Wilhelm. Parametric Shape Analysis via 3-Valued Logic. *ACM Symposium on Principles of Programming Languages*, San Antonio, Texas, Jan. 20–22, 1999, ACM, New York, NY, 1999.

[22] Allison Waingold. *Lightweight Extraction of Object Models from Bytecode*. Masters thesis, Department of Electrical Engineering and Computer Science, MIT, May 2001.

[23] John Whaley and Martin Rinard. Compositional Pointer and Escape Analysis for Java Programs. *ACM SIGPLAN Conference on Object-Oriented Programming Systems, Languages, and Applications*, Denver, Colorado, November 1999.

[24] The Bandera Project. Kansas State University. http://www.cis.ksu.edu/santos/bandera/.

[25] The SLAM Project. Microsoft Research. http://www.research.microsoft.com/projects/slam/.

Typing Assembly Programs with Explicit Forwarding

Lennart Beringer*

Laboratory for Foundations of Computer Science,
Division of Informatics, The University of Edinburgh,
King's Buildings, Mayfield Road, Edinburgh EH9 3JZ, UK,
lenb@dcs.ed.ac.uk

Abstract. We consider processor architectures where communication of values is achieved through operand queues instead of registers. Explicit forwarding tags in an instruction's code denote the source of its operands and the destination of its result. We give operational models for sequential and distributed execution, where no assumptions are made about the relative speed of functional units. We introduce type systems which ensure that programs use the forwarding mechanism in a coordinated way, ruling out various run time hazards. Deadlocks due to operand starvation, operand queue mismatches, non-determinism due to race conditions and deadlock due to the finite length of operand queues are eliminated. Types are based on the shape of operand queue configurations, abstracting from the value of an operand and from the order of items in operand queues. Extending ideas from the literature relating program fragments adjacent in the control flow graph, the type system is generalised to forwarding across basic blocks.

1 Introduction

Modern processor architectures employ multiple execution pipelines and communicate operands not only through registers but also by *forwarding* them between functional units [11] [17]. Both mechanisms are usually shielded from the programmer by the instruction set architecture (ISA). In most cases the ISA defines a sequential model of execution where instructions are processed in program order and operands are communicated through registers. Verifying that an implementation with parallel out-of-order execution and operand forwarding respects the ISA semantics has been an active area of research in the processor design community since the introduction of Tomasulo's algorithm [30] [8] [19] [3].

We introduce computational models where the forwarding behaviour is explicit in the assembly code. We consider sequential processor models corresponding to ISA execution and parallel operation using multiple pipelines. Having both the

* Partially supported by the German academic exchange service DAAD under the HSP III program, reference no D/98/04840, and the Division of Informatics, University of Edinburgh.

N. Kobayashi and B.C. Pierce (Eds.): TACS 2001, LNCS 2215, pp. 514–534, 2001.

parallelism and the forwarding behaviour visible at the assembly level enables a type-based verification approach. We use structured operational models [27] [24] for describing program execution and introduce type systems based on notation from linear logic [16] for reasoning about the legality of programs.
Our approach separates the generation of forwarding tags (usually done in the control unit) from the issue of the legality of the resulting program. We expect this separation to be useful for a modular verification of processors (control unit, network of functional units). Furthermore, our computational model is particularly relevant for *asynchronous* processor architectures where progress in pipelines is decoupled and instructions execute locally in an operand-driven manner. In fact, our model is closely related to the programming model considered in [9], where forwarding is explicit in the opcode and an asynchronous circuit design style eliminates the system clock.
The forwarding tags in our case denote operand queues which an instruction accesses for reading its operands and writing its result. The type systems eliminate static and dynamic program errors where ill usage of operand queue names leads to non-determinism or deadlock. Types are based on the shape of operand queue configurations, abstracting from the value of an operand and from the order of items in operand queues.
We present our approach using an assembly language executing on four functional units. Conditional and unconditional jumps are included and forwarding across basic block boundaries is possible.
The language consisting of arithmetic and memory-accessing instructions is introduced in Section 2, and a sequential model of execution is presented for the sub-language not containing jump instructions. A type system based on linear logic is given, ruling out instructions which access operand queues unrelated to their functional unit and ensuring that enough operands are available to execute a program. Section 3 considers distributed execution, where instructions enter waiting stations (instruction queues). Head instructions are dispatched to functional units as soon as their operands become available. The computational model is inspired by asynchronous super-scalar processors and no assumptions about the relative speed of pipelines are made. The earlier type system guarantees executability of programs with respect to the distributed model, but it does not eliminate non-deterministic behaviour. In fact race hazards between instructions executing on different functional units can develop. We consequently extend the type system to eliminate race hazards before run-time. We then consider a restricted model where operand queues are of finite length. The program analysis for ensuring deterministic execution also eliminates deadlocks for this restricted model. Section 4 considers the full language including jump instructions. Based on earlier work in the literature [29], we give a type system for reasoning about the interaction between basic blocks. We require that all control flow successors of an instruction agree on the required shape of configurations. The approach is first presented for the sequential model and subsequently applied to distributed execution. A discussion, also motivating future research, concludes in Section 5.

1.1 Related Work

Explicit forwarding as main mechanism for communicating operands has been explored in the SCALP architecture [9] from a processor implementation point of view. Using an asynchronous circuit design style, this work aimed at high code density and low power consumption and did not focus on exploring the resulting programming model. Our work can be seen as an investigation into the legality of programs for SCALP-like architectures. In fact our type system rejects programs which were classified as having *programmer mistakes* and were not considered any further in [9]. Instruction *compounding* was presented in [4] in order to reduce the number of register accesses in an asynchronous super-scalar architecture. Compounds consist of groups of data-dependent instructions identified by the compiler which result in forwarding at run-time. Since our language includes instructions which read both operands from operand queues or forward their result to several operand queues, our approach generalises the *linear* compounds considered in [4]. Forwarding has also been employed in other asynchronous architectures [15] [22] [14] and is a well-known technique in synchronous architectures [17]. However, in these cases the responsibility to identify forwarding opportunities lies with the hardware. For these architectures, our type-based approach separates the generation of forwarding tags from their legality and thus enables a modular verification of forwarding schemes. In *transport-triggered architectures* [6], instructions *only* specify the movement of operands whereas the operations are triggered by the availability of operands at input ports of functional units. While a SOS-based description of the computational model was given in [25], legality of programs remained unexplored. We expect type calculi to be relevant for reasoning about operand transfer in TTA architectures, in particular in asynchronous settings such as [5].

The usage of types for reasoning about low-level behaviour of programs has been explored in the TAL project [7] [23], and linearity analysis in functional [31] [21] and imperative [18] programs aims at efficient usage of stack and heap. Typing the shape of the *operand* stack in the Java Virtual Machine (JVM) was introduced by Stata and Abadi in [29] for reasoning about subroutines in Java bytecode programs. The approach has been extended to object initialisation and other features of the JVM in [12] and [13]. [26] explored the relationship between [29]'s types and sequent calculi, resulting in a de-compilation approach based on proof translation in [20]. Our work differs from [29] in several respects. First, we consider sequential as well as distributed execution, in contrast to fixed JVM execution. Second, our types abstract from the order of items in queues whereas the JVM types are lists of element types. Third, the storage place for operands is distributed in our case and central in the case of JVM and a different storage policy is used (queue vs. stack). On the other hand, our treatment of basic blocks in Section 4 follows the approach taken in [29]. Control flow dependencies between program fragments require the input- and output types to match. Given the similarities between the the JVM typing and our approach, we can envision queue-based asynchronously distributed implementations of the JVM and are currently working on a type-preserving translation between the two models.

2 Assembly Language and Sequential Execution

This section introduces a small assembly language with explicit forwarding and an operational model for sequential execution of programs without jump instructions. Subsequently, we present a type system based on the $\otimes$-fragment of linear logic which is sound and complete with respect to the operational model: well-typed programs are guaranteed to execute without running into operand queue mismatches or deadlock due to starvation. We show that the type system has principal types, i.e. for each well-typed program t there is a type τ such that all other types for t are generalisations of τ.

2.1 Syntax and Operational Model

The syntax of the language is given by the following grammar. Instructions are pairs $[n]code$ of a unique label $n \in \mathbf{N}$ and an opcode with arguments from a set of operand queue names. We consider a model with four functional units. Operand values $v \in Val$ and memory locations both range over integers.

$$\begin{aligned}
v \in Val &::= \ldots\ -1 \mid 0 \mid 1\ \ldots \\
n \in \mathbf{N} &::= 1 \mid 2 \mid \ldots \\
op \in OP &::= p(n) \mid q(n) \mid r(n) \mid s(n) \\
fu \in FU &::= ALU \mid MEM \mid MUL \mid BU \\
code \in Opcode &::= dec\ op_1\ op_2 \mid add\ op_1\ op_2\ op_3 \mid mul\ op_1\ op_2\ op_3 \\
&\quad \mid ldc\ v\ op \mid ld\ op_1\ op_2 \mid st\ op_1\ op_2 \\
&\quad \mid id^{fu}\ op_1\ op_2 \mid dupl^{fu}\ op_1\ op_2\ op_3 \mid skip^{fu}\ op \mid \\
&\quad \mid if\ op\ n_1\ n_2 \mid jmp\ n \\
ins \in Instr &::= [n]code
\end{aligned}$$

Code sequences $s, t, \ldots$ are ;-separated lists of instructions with ε denoting the empty sequence. We omit labels whenever possible. It can be proven that ; behaves associatively and ε neutrally for all notions in this paper.

The first three instructions are arithmetic instructions for decrementing, adding and multiplying values. For example, an instruction $add\ p(1)\ p(2)\ s(2)$ removes the head values from operand queues $p(1)$ and $p(2)$ and sends their sum to queue $s(2)$. The next three instructions are memory instructions. $ld\ op_1\ op_2$ interprets the head value of op_1 as memory location and inserts the value found in that location into queue op_2. $st\ op_1\ op_2$ stores the head value of op_2 at the location given by the head of op_1 and $ldc\ v\ op$ inserts the value v into op. The next three instruction forms are parametric in the functional unit. For each parameter fu, id^{fu} transfers the head value of op_1 to op_2 while $dupl^{fu}$ in addition sends a copy of it to op_3 and $skip^{fu}$ simply consumes the value read from op. The last two instructions are conditional and unconditional jumps and will be dealt with in Section 4.

Non-parametric instructions execute on one functional unit only, and a parametric instruction executes on the functional unit indicated in its parameter.

Motivated by the structure of forwarding paths in realistic architectures [11], operand queues have an asymmetric access policy. While instructions can send their result to any operand queue, they can obtain their operands only from queues which are associated to their functional unit. (In SCALP [9], instructions in fact don't specify the source queues of operands at all but implicitly consume values from the queues associated to their functional unit.) No reduction is possible if an instruction attempts to read from a foreign operand queue. We use the notation $\gamma(op)$ for the FU to which op is associated. In example programs we set $\gamma(op) = ALU$ for all op of the form $p(n)$ and similarly map q-queues to MEM, s-queues to MUL and r-queues to BU.

The sequential model of execution corresponds to the instruction set architecture (ISA) of a processor and executes one instruction at a time. It is given by the relation $\mathcal{C} \xrightarrow{t} \mathcal{D}$ where configurations $\mathcal{C}$ and $\mathcal{D}$ are pairs (Q, M) consisting of total maps representing queue configurations and memory states. A queue configuration Q maps operand queue names to lists of values and a memory state M maps values (interpreted as locations) to values. We write $Q.op$ to represent the entry at op in Q and $Q[op \mapsto Vl]$ for the configuration which agrees with Q everywhere except op and maps op to Vl. A similar notation is used for memory operations. Queue configurations P and Q can be composed to $P; Q$ which is given pointwise by $(P; Q).op = P.op@Q.op$.

Figure 1 gives the definition of $\mathcal{C} \xrightarrow{t} \mathcal{D}$. Auxiliary operations $\xrightarrow{write}$ and $\xrightarrow{read}$ manage operand queue access and :: and @ denote the list operations *cons* and *append*.

Instruction execution according to the ISA model is deterministic.

Proposition 1. *If* $\mathcal{C} \xrightarrow{t} \mathcal{D}$ *and* $\mathcal{C} \xrightarrow{t} \mathcal{E}$ *then* $\mathcal{D} = \mathcal{E}$.

Programs fail to execute whenever a side condition of rule RD is not fulfilled. Failure of the condition $\gamma(op) = fu$ represents a (static) operand queue mismatch where an instruction tries to access an operand queue which is not connected to its FU. Failure of the second condition is a dynamic error which occurs if previous instructions (or the initial configuration) did not provide enough operands for an instruction.

2.2 Type System

Both types of error can be ruled out statically by associating types to instructions characterising the net-effect on the number of items in queues. Judgements have the form $t : A \multimap B$ where t is a code sequence and A and B are formal products over the set of operand queue names.

$$A, B \ldots \in \mathit{Product} ::= \mathbf{1} \mid op \otimes A$$
$$\tau \in \mathit{Type} ::= A \multimap A$$

Linear operators $\otimes$ and $\multimap$ are motivated by the fact that the *multiplicity* of items in an operand queue matters. We treat $\otimes$ associatively and commutatively with $\mathbf{1}$ as neutral element, and for $i \geq 0$ we write op^i for $\underbrace{op \otimes \ldots \otimes op}_{i}$.

$$\frac{\gamma(op) = fu \quad Q.op = v :: tl}{(Q, M) \xrightarrow{read(fu,op,v)} (Q[op \mapsto tl], M)}\ \text{RD} \qquad \frac{P = Q[op \mapsto Q.op\,@\,[v]]}{(Q, M) \xrightarrow{write(v,op)} (P, M)}\ \text{WR}$$

$$\frac{\mathcal{C} \xrightarrow{read(MEM,op_1,v_1)} \mathcal{E} \quad \mathcal{E} \xrightarrow{read(MEM,op_2,v_2)} (Q, M)}{\mathcal{C} \xrightarrow{st\ op_1\ op_2} (Q, M[v_1 \mapsto v_2])}\ \text{ST} \qquad \frac{\mathcal{C} \xrightarrow{read(fu,op,v)} \mathcal{D}}{\mathcal{C} \xrightarrow{skip^{fu}\ op} \mathcal{D}}\ \text{SKIP}$$

$$\frac{\mathcal{C} \xrightarrow{read(MEM,op_1,v_1)} (Q, M) \quad (Q, M) \xrightarrow{write(M.v_1,op_2)} \mathcal{D}}{\mathcal{C} \xrightarrow{ld\ op_1\ op_2} \mathcal{D}}\ \text{LD} \qquad \frac{\mathcal{C} \xrightarrow{read(fu,op_1,v)} \mathcal{E} \quad \mathcal{E} \xrightarrow{write(v,op_2)} \mathcal{D}}{\mathcal{C} \xrightarrow{id^{fu}\ op_1\ op_2} \mathcal{D}}\ \text{ID}$$

$$\frac{\mathcal{C} \xrightarrow{read(ALU,op_1,v)} \mathcal{E} \quad \mathcal{E} \xrightarrow{write(v-1,op_2)} \mathcal{D}}{\mathcal{C} \xrightarrow{dec\ op_1\ op_2} \mathcal{D}}\ \text{DEC} \qquad \frac{\mathcal{C} \xrightarrow{read(ALU,op_1,v_1)} \mathcal{E} \quad \mathcal{E} \xrightarrow{read(ALU,op_2,v_2)} \mathcal{F} \quad \mathcal{F} \xrightarrow{write(v_1+v_2,op_3)} \mathcal{D}}{\mathcal{C} \xrightarrow{add\ op_1\ op_2\ op_3} \mathcal{D}}\ \text{ADD}$$

$$\frac{\mathcal{C} \xrightarrow{read(fu,op_1,v)} \mathcal{E} \quad \mathcal{E} \xrightarrow{write(v,op_2)} \mathcal{F} \quad \mathcal{F} \xrightarrow{write(v,op_3)} \mathcal{D}}{\mathcal{C} \xrightarrow{dupl^{fu}\ op_1\ op_2\ op_3} \mathcal{D}}\ \text{DUPL} \qquad \frac{\mathcal{C} \xrightarrow{read(MUL,op_1,v_1)} \mathcal{E} \quad \mathcal{E} \xrightarrow{read(MUL,op_2,v_2)} \mathcal{F} \quad \mathcal{F} \xrightarrow{write(v_1*v_2,op_3)} \mathcal{D}}{\mathcal{C} \xrightarrow{mul\ op_1\ op_2\ op_3} \mathcal{D}}\ \text{MUL}$$

$$\frac{\mathcal{C} \xrightarrow{write(v,op)} \mathcal{D}}{\mathcal{C} \xrightarrow{ldc\ v\ op} \mathcal{D}}\ \text{LDC} \qquad \frac{\mathcal{C} \xrightarrow{s} \mathcal{E} \quad \mathcal{E} \xrightarrow{t} \mathcal{D}}{\mathcal{C} \xrightarrow{s;t} \mathcal{D}}\ \text{COMP}$$

Fig. 1. Sequential model of execution

For each instruction form *ins*, the type system contains an axiom

$$\frac{SC(ins)}{ins : X \otimes A_{ins} \multimap X \otimes B_{ins}} \qquad \frac{s : A \multimap B \quad t : B \multimap C}{s;t : A \multimap C}\ \text{CUT}$$

where side condition $SC(ins)$ and products A_{ins} and B_{ins} are given by Table 1 and product X is arbitrary. Typed program fragments are combined using the cut rule CUT.

Products representing the shape of configurations link the type system with the operational model.

Table 1. Type system

Instruction *ins*	$FU(ins)$	Side condition $SC(ins)$	A_{ins}	B_{ins}
$dec\ op_1\ op_2$	ALU	$\gamma(op_1) = FU(ins)$	op_1	op_2
$add\ op_1\ op_2\ op_3$	ALU	$\gamma(op_1) = \gamma(op_2) = FU(ins)$	$op_1 \otimes op_2$	op_3
$mul\ op_1\ op_2\ op_3$	MUL	$\gamma(op_1) = \gamma(op_2) = FU(ins)$	$op_1 \otimes op_2$	op_3
$ldc\ v\ op$	MEM	$--$	$\mathbf{1}$	op
$ld\ op_1\ op_2$	MEM	$\gamma(op_1) = FU(ins)$	op_1	op_2
$st\ op_1\ op_2$	MEM	$\gamma(op_1) = \gamma(op_2) = FU(ins)$	$op_1 \otimes op_2$	$\mathbf{1}$
$id^{fu}\ op_1\ op_2$	fu	$\gamma(op_1) = FU(ins)$	op_1	op_2
$dupl^{fu}\ op_1\ op_2\ op_3$	fu	$\gamma(op_1) = FU(ins)$	op_1	$op_2 \otimes op_3$
$skip^{fu}\ op$	fu	$\gamma(op) = FU(ins)$	op	$\mathbf{1}$

Definition 1. *The* shape *of a configuration* $\mathcal{C} = (Q, M)$ *with* $Q = [op_i \mapsto Vl_i]$ *is*

$$shape(\mathcal{C}) = op_1^{|Vl_1|} \otimes \ldots \otimes op_n^{|Vl_n|}$$

where $|Vl|$ *denotes the length of the list* Vl *of values.*

The type system eliminates both sources of deadlock and guarantees executability of a program. Moreover, it relates the shapes of initial and final configurations and is sound and complete for sequential execution.

Theorem 1. *Let* t *be a code sequence.*

1. *If* $t : A \multimap B$ *and* $shape(\mathcal{C}) = A$ *then there is a unique* $\mathcal{D}$ *such that* $\mathcal{C} \xrightarrow{t} \mathcal{D}$. *It is* $shape(\mathcal{D}) = B$.
2. *If* $\mathcal{C} \xrightarrow{t} \mathcal{D}$ *then* $t : shape(\mathcal{C}) \multimap shape(\mathcal{D})$.

The type system admits a derived rule $\dfrac{t : A \multimap B}{t : A \otimes X \multimap B \otimes X}$ for any X. However, different typings have different effects on the function a program calculates. For the *legality* of a program with respect to sequential execution this issue is irrelevant and we expect that the following notion of *principal* type will in most cases coincide with the programmer's intention.

Definition 2. *A typing* $t : A \multimap B$ *is* principal *if for every typing* $t : C \multimap D$ *there is an* X *such that* $C = A \otimes X$ *and* $D = B \otimes X$.

Every well-typed program has a unique principal type which can be obtained by type inference using a slight modification of the rules for $t : A \multimap B$. We use judgements of the form $t :: A \multimap B$ for this system. Axioms are of the minimal form

$$\frac{SC(ins)}{ins :: A_{ins} \multimap B_{ins}}$$

and composition performs the minimal generalisation necessary for a cut.

$$\frac{s :: A \multimap B \qquad t :: C \multimap D}{s; t :: A \otimes U \multimap V \otimes D}\ B/C = V/U$$

Here (V, U) is the cancellation of (B, C).

Definition 3. *Products A and B are* relatively prime, *written $prime(A, B)$, if the factors of A and B are disjoint.*
Types V and U are called the cancellation *of A and B, written $A/B = V/U$, if V and U are relatively prime and $U \otimes A = V \otimes B$.*

Proposition 2. *$t :: A \multimap B$ iff $t : A \multimap B$ is the principal typing for t.*

3 Distributed Execution

In this section we consider a distributed model motivated by execution in superscalar processors. Instructions are inserted into pipelines and enter functional units as soon as their operands are available. Distributed execution can interleave arbitrarily, depending on execution latency inside functional units. The observed out-of-order execution may exhibit race conditions between instructions which execute on different functional units but forward to the same operand queue. The type system of Section 2.2 is extended to detect race hazards and eliminate the resulting functional non-determinism. Finally, we consider execution models where the length of operand queues is limited. Programs deadlock if all possible reductions lead to configurations which violate the length restrictions. The type system from Section 2.2 is extended with information about the minimal length requirements necessary for deadlock-free execution.

3.1 Operational Model

Distributed programs are composed of three sequential programs by

$$\pi \in P ::= t_1 \parallel t_2 \parallel t_3$$

where $\parallel$ is non-commutative. For $\pi_1 = t_1 \parallel t_2 \parallel t_3$ and $\pi_2 = s_1 \parallel s_2 \parallel s_3$ we define $\pi_1; \pi_2 = t_1; s_1 \parallel t_2; s_2 \parallel t_3; s_3$. Each component of π represents an instruction queue in front of one functional unit and all members of a pipeline must execute on this functional unit. We define $\mathcal{C} \xrightarrow{t}_{fu} \mathcal{D}$ to hold if $\mathcal{C} \xrightarrow{t} \mathcal{D}$ is derivable in the sequential model in Figure 1 and all instructions t_i in t fulfil $FU(t_i) = fu$. Parallel interleaved execution $\mathcal{C} \xrightarrow{\pi} \mathcal{D}$ is given by the rules

$$\frac{\mathcal{C} \xrightarrow{t}_{fu} \mathcal{E} \quad \mathcal{E} \xrightarrow{\pi} \mathcal{D}}{\mathcal{C} \xrightarrow{\pi_t; \pi} \mathcal{D}} \quad \text{where } \pi_t = \begin{cases} t \parallel \varepsilon \parallel \varepsilon \text{ if } fu = ALU \\ \varepsilon \parallel t \parallel \varepsilon \text{ if } fu = MUL \\ \varepsilon \parallel \varepsilon \parallel t \text{ if } fu = MEM \end{cases}$$

For executing a sequential program distributedly, instructions are inserted into the instruction queues according to the program order.

Definition 4. *The parallel program $\delta(t)$ resulting from distributing a sequential program t among instruction queues is given by $\delta(\varepsilon) = \varepsilon \parallel \varepsilon \parallel \varepsilon$ and $\delta(ins; t) = \pi_{ins}; \delta(t)$ where π_{ins} is as above.*

The relationship between sequential and distributed execution is as follows.

Proposition 3. *1. If $\mathcal{C} \xrightarrow{t} \mathcal{D}$ then $\mathcal{C} \xrightarrow{\delta(t)} \mathcal{D}$.*
2. If $\mathcal{C} \xrightarrow{\pi} \mathcal{D}$ then there is a u such that $\delta(u) = \pi$ and $\mathcal{C} \xrightarrow{u} \mathcal{D}$.

Consequently, the type system presented in Section 2.2 is sound for distributed execution in the sense that typability entails executability.

Proposition 4. *If $t : A \multimap B$ and $shape(\mathcal{C}) = A$ then there is a $\mathcal{D}$ such that $\mathcal{C} \xrightarrow{\delta(t)} \mathcal{D}$ and $shape(\mathcal{D}) = B$.*

It is no longer complete.
Example. *Consider $t = add\ p(1)\ p(2)\ q(1);\ ldc\ 2\ p(2)$ and $\mathcal{C} = ([p(1) \mapsto [3]], M)$ for arbitrary M. Then $shape(\mathcal{C}) = p(1)$ and $\mathcal{C} \xrightarrow{\delta(t)} ([q(1) \mapsto [5]], M)$ but $t : p(1) \otimes p(2) \multimap q(1) \otimes p(2)$. A sequential execution of t starting in $\mathcal{C}$ deadlocks.*

The type system's adequacy for parallel execution is limited more drastically by the fact that the configuration $\mathcal{D}$ in Proposition 4 is not unique. While the *shapes* of all final configurations agree the *values* might differ due to race hazards between instructions executing on different functional units and forwarding to the same operand queue.
Example. *Let $t = add\ p(1)\ p(2)\ s(1);\ ldc\ 1\ s(1)$ and $\mathcal{C} = ([p(1) \mapsto [2],\ p(2) \mapsto [3]], M)$. Then there are $\mathcal{D} \neq \mathcal{E}$ with $\mathcal{C} \xrightarrow{\delta(t)} \mathcal{D}$ and $\mathcal{C} \xrightarrow{\delta(t)} \mathcal{E}$.*

One can deal with non-determinism by imposing side-conditions on the operational model which block the progress in one pipeline until other pipelines have reached a certain state. In an asynchronous setting such a solution is undesirable since the side-conditions correspond to central control and inhibit the operand-driven mode of operation. An alternative with no run-time overhead consists of characterising programs which might show a race condition and eliminating them prior to execution.

Definition 5. *Program t is* deterministic *for A if for all $\mathcal{C}$ with $shape(\mathcal{C}) = A$, $\mathcal{C} \xrightarrow{\delta(t)} \mathcal{D}$ implies $\mathcal{C} \xrightarrow{t} \mathcal{D}$.*

Since the type system from Section 2.2 is not sound for deterministic parallel execution, more program analysis is needed in order to eliminate race hazards.

3.2 A Type System for Deterministic Execution

Race hazards leading to non-determinism can be detected at compile-time by analysing the forwarding behaviour. In this section, we extend the type system from Section 2.2 such that it derives sequentiality constraints which guarantee deterministic execution: whenever two instructions forward their results to the same operand queue their execution order must agree in all interleavings. We then use instruction dependencies inherent in the executional model or program structure to ensure that the sequentiality constraints are met.

Extended judgements are of the form $(\Gamma, <) \vdash t : A \multimap B$. The set Γ contains declarations $\{op_1 : (l_1, k_1), \ldots, op_n : (l_n, k_n)\}$ such that the op_i are distinct and the $l_i, k_i \in \mathbf{N}$ are labels of instructions in t. An entry $op : (l, k)$ represents the fact that instructions l and k forward their result to op, and l is the first such instruction in t and k the last one. The sequentiality constraints consist of a partial order $<$ over $\mathbf{N} \times \mathbf{N}$ which is compatible with the order of instructions in t.
Figure 2 shows the rules for deriving $(\Gamma, <) \vdash t : A \multimap B$, embedding the earlier rules for $t : A \multimap B$. For $B_{ins} = op_1^{k_1} \otimes \ldots \otimes op_m^{k_m}$ we set $\Gamma_{[n]ins} = \{op_i : (n, n) \mid 1 \leq i \leq m\}$ and in the cut rule we use the notation

$$\begin{aligned} \Gamma \# \Delta = \{op : (l, h) \mid op : (l, k) \in \Gamma \text{ and } op : (g, h) \in \Delta\} \\ \cup \{op : (l, k) \mid op : (l, k) \in \Gamma \text{ and } op \notin dom\, \Delta\} \\ \cup \{op : (g, h) \mid op : (g, h) \in \Delta \text{ and } op \notin dom\, \Gamma\} \end{aligned}$$

and take $<$ to be $\sqsubset \cup \prec \cup \{(k, g) \mid op : (l, k) \in \Gamma \text{ and } op : (g, h) \in \Delta\}$.

$$\frac{SC(ins)}{(\Gamma_{[n]ins}, \emptyset) \vdash [n]ins : X \otimes A_{ins} \multimap X \otimes B_{ins}} \qquad \frac{(\Gamma, \sqsubset) \vdash s : A \multimap B \quad (\Delta, \prec) \vdash t : B \multimap C}{(\Gamma \# \Delta, <) \vdash s; t : A \multimap C}$$

Fig. 2. Type system for deterministic execution

As a consequence, instructions are serialised by $<$ whenever they forward to the same operand queue. The order of such instructions for each *op* agrees with the order in which they appear in the program.
Any distributed execution which meets (at least) the constraints $<$ forces the sequential execution to lead to the same final configuration. In the remainder of this section, $\sqsubset$ denotes a partial order over $\mathbf{N}$ which is compatible with the order of instructions in t.

Definition 6. *Program t is* sequential *for $\sqsubset$ and A if all interleavings of $\delta(t)$ starting in a configuration of shape A respect $\sqsubset$.*

Proposition 5. *Let $(\Gamma, <) \vdash t : A \multimap B$ and $<$ be contained in $\sqsubset$. If t is sequential for $\sqsubset$ and A then t is deterministic for A.*

Some constraints $\sqsubset$ arise naturally from the operational model. For example, a simple means of serialisation is given by the queuing order in front of functional units. Members of the same pipeline can never show a race hazard because no two instructions can be in operation concurrently.

Definition 7. *Given a code sequence t, an instruction m is* pipeline-dependent *on instruction n, written $n \lessdot m$, if $FU(m) = FU(n)$ and n occurs before m in t.*

Often serialisation by pipeline-dependencies suffices to ensure determinism. In particular, consider an architecture with one operand queue for each pair of functional units. Then any program can be transformed into an equivalent program such that the pipeline-dependencies contain the constraints $<$ necessary for deterministic execution. As an example, consider Program (1)

$$\begin{array}{lll} [1]\,ldc\ 1\ p(1) & [3]\,ldc\ 3\ s(1) & [5]\,mul\ s(1)\ s(1)\ p(1) \\ [2]\,ldc\ 2\ s(1) & [4]\,ldc\ 4\ q(1) & [6]\,add\ p(1)\ p(1)\ q(1) \end{array} \tag{1}$$

of type $\mathbf{1} \multimap q(1) \otimes q(1)$. Then $\delta(t) = [6] \parallel [5] \parallel [1];[2];[3];[4]$ and there are constraints $[2] < [3]$, $[4] < [6]$ and $[1] < [5]$ for writing access to $s(1)$, $q(1)$ and $p(1)$ respectively. The first constraint is easily fulfilled since [2] and [3] are pipeline-dependent. The second hazard can be eliminated by using an extra queue $q(2)$ for all forwardings $MEM \rightarrow MEM$ and dedicating $q(1)$ to forwardings $ALU \rightarrow MEM$. Similarly, the third hazard can be eliminated if a queue $p(2)$: $MUL \rightarrow ALU$ is available and $p(1)$ can be dedicated to $MEM \rightarrow ALU$. The resulting program is Program (2) of type $\mathbf{1} \multimap q(1) \otimes q(2)$ where all race hazards have been eliminated.

$$\begin{array}{lll} [1]\,ldc\ 1\ p(1) & [3]\,ldc\ 3\ s(1) & [5]\,mul\ s(1)\ s(1)\ p(2) \\ [2]\,ldc\ 2\ s(1) & [4]\,ldc\ 4\ q(2) & [6]\,add\ p(1)\ p(2)\ q(1) \end{array} \tag{2}$$

Having n^2 operand queues for n functional units might become intolerable as n grows. In such cases serialisation resulting from *data-dependencies* may be used. If, for example, only the additional queue $q(2)$ is available but $p(2)$ is not, determinism can still be achieved for Program (1). The first and second constraints are resolved as above and the third constraint holds because [5] consumes the values produced by [2] and [3] which in turn are pipeline-dependent on [1]. Consequently, [1] will precede [5] in any interleaving and no race can develop. Serialisation by data-dependencies is more complex than serialisation by pipeline-dependencies because it is influenced by contextual instructions. In particular, data-dependencies are not preserved by the generalisation rule. For example, suppose Program (1) is prefixed with code of type $A \multimap X$ where $X = s(1) \otimes s(1)$ and is itself given the type $X \multimap X \otimes q(1) \otimes q(1)$. Then the data-dependencies $[2] \rightarrow [5]$ and $[3] \rightarrow [5]$ are destroyed and a race hazard occurs.

Definition 8. *Let $t : A \multimap B$, $A = op^k \otimes X$ and $prime(op, X)$. Instruction m is* data-dependent *on n if there is an i such that n is the i-th writer to op in t and m is the $(k+i)$-th reader. In this case we write $n <_A m$.*

Instructions such as *add* $op_1\ op_2\ op_3$ may be the i-th as well as the $(i+1)$-th reader from *op* if $op = op_1 = op_2$. Similarly, a *dupl* instruction may be a multiple writer.

For satisfying the constraints, serialisation resulting from pipeline dependencies as well as data-dependencies can be used. For $t : A \multimap B$, let the partial order $\sqsubset_A$ be given by the transitive closure of $\lessdot$ and $<_A$ via $\sqsubset_A = (\lessdot \cup <_A)^+$.

Theorem 2. *If $(\Gamma, <) \vdash t : A \multimap B$ and $\sqsubset_A$ contains $<$ then t is deterministic for A.*

More sophisticated program analysis might result in larger sets $\sqsubset$ of naturally fulfilled constraints.

3.3 Finite Operand Queues

Both executional models considered so far contain operand queues of arbitrary length. In this section, the shapes of configurations are restricted such that for each operand queue a maximal number of elements is specified. If all successor configurations of a state violate the restrictions the execution deadlocks. We examine what effect the relaxation of restrictions has on sequential and distributed execution and modify the earlier type systems to determine length restrictions which allow deadlock-free execution.
The operational models are obtained by replacing the rule WR by the rule WR-LIM(C) where C is a type.

$$\frac{P = Q[op \mapsto Q.op\,@\,[v]] \quad \exists X.\ shape(P, M) \otimes X = C}{(Q, M) \xrightarrow{write(v,op)}_C (P, M)}\ \text{WR-LIM}(C)$$

We write $\mathcal{C} \xrightarrow{t}_C \mathcal{D}$ and $\mathcal{C} \xrightarrow{\delta(t)}_C \mathcal{D}$ if $shape(\mathcal{C}) \otimes X = C$ holds for some X and $\mathcal{C} \xrightarrow{t} \mathcal{D}$ and $\mathcal{C} \xrightarrow{\delta(t)} \mathcal{D}$ can be derived using WR-LIM(C) instead of WR.
Sequential execution admits the relaxation of length limitations and entails distributed execution under identical limitations.

Proposition 6. *If $\mathcal{C} \xrightarrow{t}_C \mathcal{D}$ then $\mathcal{C} \xrightarrow{\delta(t)}_C \mathcal{D}$ and $\mathcal{C} \xrightarrow{t}_{C\otimes X} \mathcal{D}$ for arbitrary X.*

Figure 3 shows a modified principal type system. Judgements $\vdash_C t : A \multimap B$ capture operand queue lengths necessary for executing t in an initial configuration of shape A. In fact $\vdash_C t : A \multimap B$ gives the *tightest* length limitations.

$$\frac{SC(ins) \quad B_{ins}/A_{ins} = V/U}{\vdash_{X\otimes A_{ins}\otimes V} ins : X \otimes A_{ins} \multimap X \otimes B_{ins}} \qquad \frac{\vdash_{C_1} s : A \multimap B \quad \vdash_{C_2} t : B \multimap D}{\vdash_{C_1\otimes V} s; t : A \multimap D}\ C_2/C_1 = V/U$$

Fig. 3. Type system for finite operand queue lengths

Proposition 7. *Let $\vdash_C t : A \multimap B$ and $shape(\mathcal{C}) = A$. Then*

1. *$\mathcal{C} \xrightarrow{t}_C \mathcal{D}$ for some $\mathcal{D}$.*
2. *$\mathcal{C} \xrightarrow{t}_D \mathcal{E}$ implies $D = C \otimes X$ for some X.*

For distributed execution the crucial property is absence of deadlock: whenever an arbitrary interleaving of t enters a configuration $\mathcal{E}$ under length limitations C it should be possible to reach a final configuration from $\mathcal{E}$ under the same restrictions C.

Definition 9. *A program t is* deadlock-free *for the pair (A, C) if $A \otimes X = C$ for some X and for all $\mathcal{C}$, $\mathcal{E}$, π_1 and π_2 with shape$(\mathcal{C}) = A$, $\pi_1; \pi_2 = \delta(t)$ and $\mathcal{C} \xrightarrow{\pi_1}_C \mathcal{E}$ there is a $\mathcal{D}$ such that $\mathcal{E} \xrightarrow{\pi_2}_C \mathcal{D}$.*

Absence of deadlock is a priori not preserved when operand queues are extended.
Example. *Consider Program (3)*

$$t = \begin{array}{lll} [1]\,dec\ p(1)\ s(1); & [3]\,ldc\ 2\ p(1); & [5]\,ldc\ 4\ s(1); \\ [2]\,mul\ s(1)\ s(2)\ p(1); & [4]\,ldc\ 3\ s(1); & [6]\,dec\ p(1)\ r(1) \end{array} \quad (3)$$

and $A = p(1) \otimes s(2)$, $B = p(1) \otimes s(1) \otimes s(1) \otimes r(1)$ and $C = A \otimes s(1) \otimes s(1) \otimes r(1)$. Then $t : A \multimap B$ and t is deadlock-free for (A, C). For the relaxed length restrictions $C \otimes X$ where $X = p(1)$, Program (3) deadlocks for an initial configuration $\mathcal{C}$ with shape$(\mathcal{C}) = A$. For $\pi_1 = \delta([3]; [4]; [5])$ we have $\mathcal{C} \xrightarrow{\pi_1}_{C \otimes X} \mathcal{E}$ for some $\mathcal{E}$, but no reduction $\mathcal{E} \xrightarrow{\delta([1];[2];[6])}_{C \otimes X} \mathcal{D}$ is possible.

Failure of this monotonicity property is practically relevant. Extending operand queues might be necessary for exploiting the instruction-level parallelism inherent in a program. The performance gain should not be paid for by new deadlocks in programs which were previously deadlock-free. For programs without race hazards extending operand queues is safe:

Proposition 8. *Let $(\Gamma, <) \vdash t : A \multimap B$, $<$ be contained in $\sqsubset$ and t sequential for $\sqsubset$ and A. If t is deadlock-free for (A, C) then t is deadlock-free for $(A, C \otimes X)$.*

Combining $\vdash_C t : A \multimap B$ and $(\Gamma, <) \vdash t : A \multimap B$ to a calculus for $(\Gamma, <) \vdash_C t : A \multimap B$ yields type information for sequential and deterministic distributed execution with restricted queues.

Theorem 3. *Let $(\Gamma, <) \vdash_C t : A \multimap B$ and t sequential for $\sqsubset$ and A where $<$ is contained in $\sqsubset$. Let shape$(\mathcal{C}) = A$. Then*

1. *$\mathcal{C} \xrightarrow{t}_{C \otimes X} \mathcal{D}$ for some unique $\mathcal{D}$ and any X.*
2. *t is deterministic for A and deadlock-free with respect to $(A, C \otimes X)$ for any X.*
3. *$\mathcal{C} \xrightarrow{\delta(t)}_{C \otimes X} \mathcal{D}$ for any X.*

4 Program Execution

In this section we consider the full language including the conditional and unconditional jumps *if op* n_1 n_2 and *jmp* n. A *basic block* is a pair (n, t) such that n is the label of the first instruction in t and t is a code sequence where at most the last instruction is a jump. A *program* $\mathcal{G} = (\mathcal{N}, \mathcal{A})$ is a directed graph with basic blocks $\mathcal{N} = \{N_1, \ldots, N_k\}$, $N_n = (n, t_n)$ as nodes and arrows $N_m \to N_n$ whenever the last instruction of t_m is of the form *jmp* n or *ifzero op* n_1 n_2 and $n \in \{n_1, n_2\}$. Both jump instructions are mapped to the functional unit *BU* (*branch unit*).

4.1 Sequential Execution

Configurations $\mathcal{C}$ are extended by a third component $\mathcal{C} = (Q, M, \tilde{n})$ where $\tilde{n} \in \mathbf{N} \cup \{nil\}$ represents the index of the basic block to be executed next. The operational model is given by the following rules where INJ injects the model from Section 2.1. Composition is achieved by the earlier rule COMP which now relates ternary configurations.

$$\frac{(Q,M) \xrightarrow{read(BU,op,0)} (P,N)}{(Q,M,nil) \xrightarrow{ifzero\ op\ n_1\ n_2} (P,N,n_1)}\ \text{IF-T} \qquad \frac{(Q,M) \xrightarrow{ins}_{fu} (P,N) \quad fu{\neq}BU}{(Q,M,\tilde{n}) \xrightarrow{ins} (P,N,\tilde{n})}\ \text{INJ}$$

$$\frac{(Q,M) \xrightarrow{read(BU,op,v)} (P,N) \quad v{\neq}0}{(Q,M,nil) \xrightarrow{ifzero\ op\ n_1\ n_2} (P,N,n_2)}\ \text{IF-F} \qquad \frac{}{(Q,M,nil) \xrightarrow{jmp\ n} (Q,M,n)}\ \text{JMP}$$

Basic blocks are issued according to the outcome of branches by the relation $\mathcal{C} \xrightarrow{L} \mathcal{D}$ where $L = [n_1, \ldots, n_l]$ is a list of labels $n_i \in \mathbf{N}$.

$$\frac{(Q,M,nil) \xrightarrow{t} \mathcal{C} \quad (n,t) \in \mathcal{N}}{(Q,M,n) \xrightarrow{[n]} \mathcal{C}}\ \text{EXECUTE} \qquad \frac{\mathcal{C} \xrightarrow{K} \mathcal{E} \quad \mathcal{E} \xrightarrow{L} \mathcal{D}}{\mathcal{C} \xrightarrow{K@L} \mathcal{D}}\ \text{COMPOSE}$$

Instructions *if* and *jmp* are typed according to the rules

$$\frac{\gamma(op) = BU}{if\ op\ n_1\ n_2 : X \otimes op \multimap X} \quad \text{and} \quad \frac{}{jmp\ n : X \multimap X}$$

with $X = \mathbf{1}$ for the calculus of principal types. Theorem 1 (soundness and completeness for sequential execution) can be generalised to the bodies of basic blocks where $shape(\mathcal{C}) = shape(Q, M)$ for $\mathcal{C} = (Q, M, \tilde{n})$ generalises Definition 1.

For programs $\mathcal{G}$ to be executable, the interfaces of basic blocks must be compatible in order to avoid operand starvation: all operands expected by a basic block must be provided by earlier basic blocks. We follow the approach taken in [29] where the shapes of basic blocks linked by a control flow dependency must match. In our setting, this means that $B_n = A_m$ should hold whenever $t_n : A_n \multimap B_n$, $t_m : A_m \multimap B_m$ and $(N_n, N_m) \in \mathcal{A}$. Formally, we introduce a judgement of the form $\Sigma \vdash \mathcal{G} : \circ$ where Σ is a *type environment* mapping basic blocks to types. For each basic block $N = (n, t_n)$, Σ has exactly one entry $N : A \multimap B$ where $t_n : A \multimap B$ must hold. The rule for $\Sigma \vdash \mathcal{G} : \circ$ then requires the above equality to hold for all arcs.

$$\frac{\Sigma = \cup_{N_i \in \mathcal{N}} \{N_i : A_i \multimap B_i\} \qquad (N_i, N_j) \in \mathcal{A} \text{ implies } B_i = A_j}{\Sigma \vdash (\mathcal{N}, \mathcal{A}) : \circ}$$

Consequently, basic blocks can be composed as required by the outcome of branches.

Proposition 9. *Let $\mathcal{G} = (\mathcal{N}, \mathcal{A})$, $\Sigma = \cup_{N_i \in \mathcal{N}}\{N_i : A_i \multimap B_i\}$ and $\Sigma \vdash \mathcal{G} : \circ$. For $(n,t) : A_n \multimap B_n \in \Sigma$ let $\mathcal{C} = (Q, M, n)$, $shape(\mathcal{C}) = A_n$ and $\mathcal{C} \xrightarrow{[n_1;\ldots,n_k]} \mathcal{D}$. Then $shape(\mathcal{D}) = B_k$ where $(n_k, s) : A_k \multimap B_k \in \Sigma$. If $\mathcal{D} = (P, M', \widetilde{m})$ and $\widetilde{m} \neq nil$ then a unique $\mathcal{E}$ exists such that $\mathcal{C} \xrightarrow{[n_1,\ldots,n_k,m]} \mathcal{E}$.*

The type system is restrictive in that only one entry for each block is allowed in Σ. This is motivated by the desire to control the shape of final configurations. Likewise, a more generous type system where constraints $B_n = A_m$ are replaced by constraints $B_n = A_m \otimes X$ for arbitrary X would still guarantee the executability of programs. However, loops would be admitted which increase the size of a configuration in each iteration. Since the number of iterations can in general not be determined statically, the restriction $X = \mathbf{1}$ is necessary for controlling the size of configurations.

Type Inference. Starting from typings $t_n : A_n \multimap B_n$ for the bodies of basic blocks we require that the types of neighbouring basic blocks be *unifiable*. This means that factors X_i and X_j should exist such that for the generalisations $A_i \otimes X_i \multimap B_i \otimes X_i$ and $A_j \otimes X_j \multimap B_j \otimes X_j$ the equation $B_i \otimes X_i = A_j \otimes X_j$ holds whenever $(N_i, N_j) \in \mathcal{A}$. Type inference has to (dis)prove the existence of factors X_i. The following approach calculates the *minimal* solution.

Definition 10. *Let $\mathcal{N} = \{N_1, \ldots, N_k\}$, $\mathcal{A} \subset \mathcal{N} \times \mathcal{N}$ and for $i \leq k$ let $N_i = (n_i, t_i)$ and $t_i : A_i \multimap B_i$. A tuple $\mathbf{X} = (X_1, \ldots, X_k)$* unifies $\mathcal{N}$ for $\mathcal{A}$ *if $(N_i, N_j) \in \mathcal{A}$ implies $B_i \otimes X_i = A_j \otimes X_j$.*
For k-tuples $\mathbf{Y}$ and $\mathbf{Z}$ let $\mathbf{Y} \otimes \mathbf{Z} = (Y_1 \otimes Z_1, \ldots, Y_k \otimes Z_k)$.
If $\mathbf{X}$ unifies $\mathcal{N}$ for $\mathcal{A}$, it is minimal *if for every $\mathbf{Y}$ which unifies $\mathcal{N}$ for $\mathcal{A}$ there is a $\mathbf{Z}$ such that $\mathbf{X} \otimes \mathbf{Z} = \mathbf{Y}$.*
Finally, we denote the symmetric and transitive closure of $\mathcal{A}$ by $\mathcal{A}^*$ and the transitive closure by $\mathcal{A}^+$.

For given $\mathcal{N}$ and $\mathcal{A}$ there is at most one minimal unifier. The following theorem shows how to obtain a minimal unifier for $\mathcal{A} \cup \{a\}$ from one for $\mathcal{A}$ provided that it exists.

Theorem 4. *Suppose $\mathbf{X}$ is the minimal unifier for $\mathcal{N} = \{N_1, \ldots, N_k\}$ and $\mathcal{A}$ and $a = (N_m, N_n) \notin \mathcal{A}$. Let $S = \{l \mid (N_l, N_m) \in \mathcal{A}^*\}$, $T = \{l \mid (N_l, N_n) \in \mathcal{A}^*\}$ and $(B_m \otimes X_m)/(A_n \otimes X_n) = V/U$. Then*

1. *$\mathbf{X}$ is the minimal unifier for $\mathcal{A} \cup \{a\}$ if $a \in \mathcal{A}^*$ and $V \otimes U = \mathbf{1}$.*
2. *$\mathcal{A} \cup \{a\}$ has no unifier if $a \in \mathcal{A}^*$ and $V \otimes U \neq \mathbf{1}$.*
3. *if $a \notin \mathcal{A}^*$, then $S \cap T = \emptyset$ and $\mathbf{Y}$ is the minimal unifier for $\mathcal{A} \cup \{a\}$ where*

$$Y_l = \begin{cases} X_l \otimes U & \text{if } l \in S \\ X_l \otimes V & \text{if } l \in T \\ X_l & \text{otherwise} \end{cases}$$

Consequently, type inference for $\mathcal{G} = (\mathcal{N}, \mathcal{A})$ can proceed by typing the bodies of all basic blocks separately and then visiting the arcs $\mathcal{A}$ in any order. An algorithm based on Theorem 4 either successively calculates minimal unifiers for arcs $\emptyset \subset \mathcal{A}_1 \subset \ldots \subset \mathcal{A}_n = \mathcal{A}$ or rejects the program as being ill-formed.

4.2 Distributed Execution

As in Section 3, a distributed model of execution can be defined on top of sequential execution. In this section, a model is presented where the loading of instructions from memory into the issue unit can interleave arbitrarily with program execution.
The model is based on a generalisation of ternary parallel programs to programs with four components $t_1 \parallel t_2 \parallel t_3 \parallel t_4$ where the rightmost component represents the BU pipeline. Composition $\pi_1; \pi_2$ and distribution δ are modified accordingly, where δ inserts instructions *if* and *jmp* into the BU pipeline. Parallel interleaved execution of instructions is achieved in a similar way as in Section 3 by the rule

$$\frac{\mathcal{C} \xrightarrow{t}_{fu} \mathcal{E} \quad \mathcal{E} \xrightarrow{\pi} \mathcal{D}}{\mathcal{C} \xrightarrow{\pi_t;\pi} \mathcal{D}} \quad \text{where } \pi_t = \begin{cases} t \parallel \varepsilon \parallel \varepsilon \parallel \varepsilon \text{ if } fu = ALU \\ \varepsilon \parallel t \parallel \varepsilon \parallel \varepsilon \text{ if } fu = MUL \\ \varepsilon \parallel \varepsilon \parallel t \parallel \varepsilon \text{ if } fu = MEM \\ \varepsilon \parallel \varepsilon \parallel \varepsilon \parallel t \text{ if } fu = BU \end{cases}$$

where $\mathcal{C}$ and $\mathcal{D}$ are ternary configurations of the form $(Q, M, \widetilde{n})$. The issue unit holds instructions which have been loaded from memory but have not yet been inserted into pipelines. It is represented by a new component of a configuration. The corresponding rules are given below. EXEC embeds distributed execution while the body of a basic block is loaded by LOAD and composition is achieved by the earlier rule COMPOSE which now relates configurations with four components.

$$\frac{(Q, M, \widetilde{n}) \xrightarrow{\pi_1} (P, N, \widetilde{m})}{(Q, M, \widetilde{n}, \pi_1; \pi_2) \xrightarrow{[]} (P, N, \widetilde{m}, \pi_2)}\,\text{EXEC} \qquad \frac{(n,t) \in \mathcal{N} \qquad \delta(t) = \pi_2}{(Q, M, n,\ \pi_1) \xrightarrow{[n]} (Q, M, nil,\ \pi_1; \pi_2)}\,\text{LOAD}$$

The type system of Section 3 is extended by the following rules for *if* and *jmp*.

$$\frac{\gamma(op) = BU}{(\emptyset, \emptyset) \vdash [n]\mathit{if}\ op\ l\ m : X \otimes op \multimap X} \quad \text{and} \quad \frac{}{(\emptyset, \emptyset) \vdash [n]\mathit{jmp}\ l : X \multimap X}$$

For typing programs, not only should the shapes of basic blocks be unifiable, but each basic block should be deterministic for the generalisation needed for composing it with its neighbours. We consequently insert a judgement $(\Gamma, <) \vdash N : A \multimap B$ into Σ provided that $N = (n, t)$ and $(\Gamma, <) \vdash t : A \multimap B$ holds such that t is deterministic for A. Given that pipelines might include instructions of several basic blocks we also have to consider race hazards between instructions of different basic blocks. We require that additional constraints $n < m$ hold if there is an *op* such that n is the last writer to *op* in its block N, m is the first writer to *op* in block M and there is a path from N to M in $\mathcal{A}$. Since different copies of a basic block execute identical sets of instructions, it suffices to consider simple paths $N, \ldots, M$ where at most the two outermost nodes N and M are equal and no intermediate blocks write to *op*. We denote such a path by $SP(N_i, op, N_j)$. In the typing rule

$$\frac{\begin{array}{c}\Sigma = \cup_{N_i \in \mathcal{N}} \{(\Gamma_i, <_i) \vdash N_i : A_i \multimap B_i\} \\ (N_i, N_j) \in \mathcal{A} \text{ implies } B_i = A_j \\ SP(N_i, op, N_j), op : (k,l) \in \Gamma_i, op : (g,h) \in \Gamma_j \text{ implies } l < g\end{array}}{(\Sigma, <) \vdash (\mathcal{N}, \mathcal{A}) : \Box}$$

the constraints $\{<_i \mid (\Gamma_i, <_i) \vdash N_i : A_i \multimap B_i \in \Sigma\} \cup <$ are to be interpreted modulo instantiations due to loops: in a constraint $n < n$ the right n will refer to the instance of n in the next iteration.

Proposition 10. *Let $(\Sigma, <) \vdash \mathcal{G} : \Box$ and $(N_1, \ldots, N_k)$ be a path in $\mathcal{A}$. Then there are Γ and $\prec$ such that $(\Gamma, \prec) \vdash t_1; \ldots; t_k : A_1 \multimap B_k$ holds and $\prec$ is contained in $\{<_i \mid (\Gamma_i, <_i) \vdash N_i : A_i \multimap B_i \in \Sigma\} \cup <$.*

Consequently, distributed executions are deterministic if we can fulfill the constraints in $<$. For entering the N_i into Σ we had to prove them deterministic, too, but we don't have to spend work on them again.

Proposition 11. *Let $(\Sigma,<) \vdash \mathcal{G} : \Box$, $(n,t) \in \mathcal{N}$ and $(\Gamma_n,<_n) \vdash N_n : A_n \multimap B_n \in \Sigma$.*

1. *If $(Q, M, n) \xrightarrow{L} (P, N, \tilde{m})$ then $(Q, M, n, \delta(\varepsilon)) \xrightarrow{L} (P, N, \tilde{m}, \delta(\varepsilon))$.*
2. *Let $\mathcal{C} = (Q, M, n, \delta(\varepsilon))$, $shape(\mathcal{C}) = A_n$ and $\mathcal{C} \xrightarrow{L} (P, N, \tilde{m}, \delta(\varepsilon))$. Let $\sqsubset$ be a partial order such that $<$ is contained in $\sqsubset$ and for all simple paths $SP(N_i, op, N_j)$, $t_i; \ldots; t_j : A_i \multimap B_j$ is sequential for $\sqsubset$ and A_i. Then $(Q, M, n) \xrightarrow{L} (P, N, \tilde{m})$.*

Again, for satisfying $l < g$ several natural serialisations can be used. The analysis of data-dependencies along paths might be too costly, but pipeline dependencies can be analysed more efficiently. In the special case where the number n of functional units is sufficiently small and the architecture has n^2 operand queues pipeline-dependencies suffice. Under these circumstances, the path condition can be replaced by requiring that $FU(l) = FU(g)$ holds whenever $op : (k,l) \in \Gamma_i$ and $op : (g,h) \in \Gamma_j$ and $(N_i, N_j) \in \mathcal{A}^+$. In other cases, *control-dependencies* can be used: a single conditional jump between l and g which is dependent on l guarantees that l will have retired when g is issued.
Consequently, typing $\Sigma \vdash \mathcal{G} : \Box$ is sound for distributed execution. Provided that the constraints are met, an execution is either infinite or terminates in the same configuration as sequential execution (see Proposition 9). We expect that in most cases the (minimal) unification used for sequential execution will be the one used for distributed execution as well. It is with respect to these A_i that the determinism of the bodies of the basic blocks should be evaluated.

5 Discussion

We presented SOS-based operational models for processor architectures with operand queues for forwarded values. An assembly language with explicit forwarding tags was considered and type calculi based on linear logic eliminated static or dynamic hazards. For well-typed programs, operand queue mismatches, deadlocks due to operand starvation or finite queue length and non-determinism could not occur. The language contained conditional and unconditional jumps and the operational models were extended correspondingly. Type inference was achieved by unifying the shapes of basic blocks. To our knowledge this is the first systematic investigation into explicit forwarding, and is relevant for hardware-based forwarding and transport-triggered and asynchronous architectures. This work motivates the application of programming language notions such as operational models of execution and typing for reasoning about operand communication during processor design.

The analysis regarding race conditions in Section 3 calculated constraints necessary for eliminating race conditions and subsequently gave serialisation orders which are naturally fulfilled. Further work is needed to evaluate the practicality of the proposed program analysis and its limitations. We considered the important case of finite operand queues and observed that deadlock-free execution requires similar sequentiality constraints as determinism.

We used a linear-logic-based notation to capture the multiplicity of items in operand queues. This usage of linear logic resembles applications to Petri nets [10]. In fact the unification for type inference in Section 4 corresponds to the (minimal) solution of a set of linear equations in the style of characteristic matrices for place-transition nets [28]. This motivates to study the algebraic and logical behaviour of forwarding further. For the language we considered, similar verification results could have been obtained using multisets. More complicated forwarding behaviour might need additional structure and thus favour a type-based approach.

The expressiveness of the computational model depends on the chosen instruction set. We treated a pure model in which all operands are communicated through queues, but a realistic architecture will employ a mixture between registers and forwarding. Consequently, a compiler will need to analyse the usage of values and replace some registers by forwarding. According to a study in [9], up to 65% of all values written to registers are read by only one successive instruction. With the duplication instruction *dupl* our language allows forwarding to be used even more widely. Analysing the *dynamic number of uses* of a value might be achieved using type-based approaches from the area of functional programming languages [31], complementing the analysis of *static assignments* (SSA, [1] [2]). On the other hand, the above figure includes cases where the destination of a value varies at run-time and is thus not known statically. Hardware-based approaches can set the destination of a forwarded value dynamically. For matching this flexibility at compile-time, language extensions are needed where the destination of a forwarded value depends on an additional input operand or the outcome of a branch. For dealing with such dependent forwarding, extensions of our typing systems need to be developed.

Acknowledgements

We would like to thank Colin Stirling for his continuous support and guidance regarding both the content and the presentation of this work. D.K. Arvind introduced us to forwarding in asynchronous architectures. The referee's comments and suggestions have been very helpful in improving the material. Paul Taylor's prooftree package was used during the preparation of this paper.

References

1. Bowen Alpern, Mark N. Wegman, and F. Kenneth Zadeck. Detecting equality of variables in programs. In ACM, editor, *POPL '88. Proceedings of the conference on Principles of programming languages, January 13–15, 1988, San Diego, CA*, pages 1–11, New York, NY, USA, 1988. ACM Press.
2. Andrew W. Appel. *Modern Compiler Implementation in ML*. Cambridge University Press, Cambridge, UK, 1998.
3. Arvind and Xiaowei W. Shen. Using term rewriting systems to design and verify processors. *IEEE Micro*, 19(3):36–46, May/June 1999.
4. D.K. Arvind and Robert D. Mullins. A Fully Asynchronous Superscalar Processor. In *Proceedings of the International Conference on Parallel Architectures and Compilation Techniques (PACT)*, 1999.
5. William Coates, Jon Lexau, Ian Jones, Scott Fairbanks, and Ivan Sutherland. FLEETzero: An Asynchronous Switching Experiment. In *Proceedings of the Seventh International Symposium on Advanced Research in Asynchronous Circuits and Systems*, Salt Lake City, March 2001.
6. Henk Corporaal and Hans Mulder. MOVE: A framework for high-performance processor design. In Anne Copeland MacCallum, editor, *Proceedings of the 4th Annual Conference on Supercomputing*, pages 692–701, Alburquerque, NM, USA, November 1991. IEEE Computer Society Press.
7. Karl Crary and Greg Morrisett. Type structure for low-level programming languages. *Lecture Notes in Computer Science*, 1644:40–??, 1999.
8. Werner Damm and Amir Pnueli. Verifying out-of-order executions. In Hon F. Li and David K. Probst, editors, *Advances in Hardware Design and Verification: IFIP WG10.5 International Conference on Correct Hardware Design and Verification Methods (CHARME)*, pages 23–47, Montreal, Canada, October 1997. Chapman & Hall.
9. Philip B. Endecott. *SCALP: A Superscalar Asynchronous Low-Power Processor*. PhD thesis, Department of Computer Science, University of Manchester, February 1996.
10. Uffe H. Engberg and Glynn Winskel. Linear logic on Petri nets. Technical Report RS-94-3, BRICS, Aarhus, Denmark, 1994.
11. Michael J. Flynn. *Computer Architecture: Pipelined and Parallel Processor Design*. Jones & Bartlett Publishing, 1995.
12. Stephen N. Freund and John C. Mitchell. A type system for object initialization in the java^{tm} bytecode language. In *Proceedings of the 13th Conference on*

Object-Oriented Programming, Systems, Languages, and Applications (OOPSLA-98), volume 33, 10 of *ACM SIGPLAN Notices*, New York, 1998. ACM Press.

13. Stephen N. Freund and John C. Mitchell. A formal framework for the Java byte-code language and verifier. In *Proceedings of the Conference on Object-Oriented Programming, Systems, Languages, and Applications*, pages 147–166, 1999.
14. J. D. Garside, S. B. Furber, and S.-H. Chung. AMULET3 revealed. In *Proc. International Symposium on Advanced Research in Asynchronous Circuits and Systems*, pages 51–59, April 1999.
15. D. A. Gilbert and J. D. Garside. A result forwarding mechanism for asynchronous pipelined systems. In *Proc. International Symposium on Advanced Research in Asynchronous Circuits and Systems*, pages 2–11. IEEE Computer Society Press, April 1997.
16. Jean-Yves Girard. Linear logic. *Theoretical Computer Science*, 46:1–102, 1986.
17. John L. Hennessy and David A. Patterson. *Computer Architecture: A Quantitative Approach.* Morgan Kaufmann, San Mateo, CA, second edition, 1996.
18. Martin Hofmann. A type system for bounded space and functional in-place update. In *Proceedings of the European Symposium on Programming (ESOP)*, Berlin, 2000.
19. Ravi Hosabettu, Mandayam Srivas, and Ganesh Gopalakrishnan. Proof of correctness of a processor with reorder buffer using the completion functions approach. In Nicolas Halbwachs and Doron Peled, editors, *Computer-Aided Verification, CAV '99*, volume 1633 of *Lecture Notes in Computer Science*, pages 47–59, Trento, Italy, July 1999. Springer-Verlag.
20. Shin-ya Katsumata and Atsushi Ohori. Proof-Directed De-compilation of Low-Level Code. In *Proceedings of the European Symposium on Programming (ESOP)*, Genova, 2001.
21. Naoki Kobayashi. Quasi-linear types. In *Proceedings of the 26th Symposium on Principles of Programming Languages POPL'99*, ACM SIGPLAN Notices, New York, NY, USA, 1999. ACM Press.
22. Alain J. Martin, Andrew Lines, Rajit Manohar, Mika Nystroem, Paul Penzes, Robert Southworth, and Uri Cummings. The design of an asynchronous MIPS R3000 microprocessor. In *Advanced Research in VLSI*, pages 164–181, September 1997.
23. Greg Morrisett, Karl Crary, Neal Glew, and David Walker. Stack-based typed assembly language. *Lecture Notes in Computer Science*, 1473:28–??, 1998.
24. Peter D. Mosses. Semantics, Modularity, and Rewriting Logic. *Electronic Notes in Theoretical Computer Science*, 15, 1998.
25. Jon Mountjoy, Pieter Hartel, and Henk Corporaal. Modular Operational Semantic Specification of Transport Triggered Architectures. In *Proc. 13th IFIP WG 10.5 Conf. on Computer Hardware Description Languages and Their Applications*, pages 260 – 279, Toledo, Spain, April 1997. Chapman and Hall, London.
26. Atsushi Ohori. The logical abstract machine: A curry-howard isomorphism for machine code. In *Proceedings of the 4th Fuji International Symposium on Functional and Logic Programming (FLOPS'99)*, Lecture Notes in Computer Science, LNCS 1722, pages 300–318. Springer, 1999.
27. Gordon Plotkin. A structural approach to operational semantics. Technical Report DAIMI FN-19, Computer Science Department, University of Aarhus, September 1981.
28. Wolfgang Reisig and Grzegorz Rozenberg. *Lectures on Petri Nets I: Basic Models.* Lecture Notes in Computer Science 1491. Springer, 1998.

29. Raymie Stata and Martín Abadi. A type system for Java bytecode subroutines. In *Proceedings of the 25th Symposium on Principles of Programming Languages POPL'98*, pages 149–160. ACM Press, 1998.
30. R. M. Tomasulo. An efficient algorithm for exploiting multiple arithmitic units. *IBM Journal of research and development*, 11:25–33, January 1967.
31. David N. Turner, Philip Wadler, and Christian Mossin. Once upon a type. In *7'th International Conference on Functional Programming and Computer Architecture*, pages 1–11, La Jolla, California, June 1995. ACM Press.

The UDP Calculus: Rigorous Semantics for Real Networking

Andrei Serjantov, Peter Sewell, and Keith Wansbrough

University of Cambridge
{Andrei.Serjantov,Peter.Sewell,Keith.Wansbrough}@cl.cam.ac.uk
http://www.cl.cam.ac.uk/users/pes20/Netsem

Abstract. Network programming is notoriously hard to understand: one has to deal with a variety of protocols (IP, ICMP, UDP, TCP etc.), concurrency, packet loss, host failure, timeouts, the complex *sockets* interface to the protocols, and subtle portability issues. Moreover, the behavioural properties of operating systems and the network are not well documented.

A few of these issues have been addressed in the process calculus and distributed algorithm communities, but there remains a wide gulf between what has been captured in semantic models and what is required for a precise understanding of the behaviour of practical distributed programs that use these protocols.

In this paper we demonstrate (in a preliminary way) that the gulf can be bridged. We give an operational model for socket programming with a substantial fraction of UDP and ICMP, including loss and failure. The model has been validated by experiment against actual systems. It is not tied to a particular programming language, but can be used with any language equipped with an operational semantics for system calls – here we give such a language binding for an OCaml fragment. We illustrate the model with a few small network programs.

1 Introduction

1.1 Background and Problem Distributed applications consist of many concurrently-executing systems, interacting by network communication. They are now ubiquitous, but writing reliable code remains challenging. Most fundamentally, concurrency introduces the classic (but still problematic) difficulties of nondeterminism: large state spaces, deadlocks, races *etc.*. Additional difficulties arise from intrinsic properties of networks: communication is asynchronous and lossy, and hosts are subject to failure. The communication abstractions provided by standard protocols (IP, ICMP, UDP, TCP *etc.*) are therefore necessarily more complex than simple message-passing or streams. Further, the programmer must understand not only the protocols – the inter-machine communication disciplines

N. Kobayashi and B.C. Pierce (Eds.): TACS 2001, LNCS 2215, pp. 535–559, 2001.

– but also the library interface to them. There is a 'standard' networking library, the *sockets* interface [CSR83,IEE00], lying between applications and the protocol endpoint code on a machine; the programmer must deal with what is visible through this interface, which has a subtle relationship to the underlying protocols. This relationship, and the behaviour of the sockets interface, has not been precisely described, and varies between implementations.

To provide a rigorous understanding of these issues requires precise mathematical models of the behaviour of distributed systems. Such models can (1) improve our informal understanding and system-building, (2) underpin proofs of robustness and security properties of particular programs, and (3) support the design, proof and implementation of higher-level distributed abstractions.

Previous work on the theories of distributed algorithms and of process calculi has developed models and reasoning techniques for concurrency and failure, but these models are generally rather abstract and/or idealised: to our knowledge, none address the sockets interface and the behaviour it makes visible, most ignore interesting aspects of the core protocols, and most do not support reasoning about executable code. The protocols and sockets interface are worth detailed attention – they are implemented on almost all machines, and underlie higher-level services, including those providing resilience against failure and attack.

1.2 Contribution We give a model that provides a rigorous understanding of the sockets interface and UDP, in realistic networks. To this we add an operational semantics for a programming language (an ML fragment), allowing reasoning about executable distributed programs. We have:

- carefully chosen a useful fragment of the sockets interface and built a thin layer of abstraction above it, focussing on UDP as a starting-point;
- constructed an experimentally-validated operational semantics that covers concurrency, asynchrony, failure and loss;
- developed language-independent semantic idioms for interaction between an application thread, its host OS, and the network;
- instantiated the model with a semantics for an executable fragment of OCaml, *MiniCaml*; and
- exercised our semantics by proving properties of some small example distributed programs.

Taken together, the above also provide a theorists' introduction to sockets/UDP programming.

1.3 Experimental Semantics A key goal of our work is to provide a clear and close correspondence between our semantics and the behaviour of actual systems. To achieve this, we cannot alter the extant widely-deployed OS networking code; the most we can do is choose which fragment to model, and add a thin regularising layer above it. Even then, the systems are too complex to analyse and hence *derive* an accurate semantics: consider the body of machine code and hardware logic embedded in their operating systems, machines, network cards and routers. We are forced therefore both to invent an appropriate level of abstraction at which to *express* our semantics, and to experimentally *determine* and *validate* that semantics. We call this activity *experimental semantics.*

In our case, the semantics is expressed at the level of the system calls used to communicate between the application language and the operating system sockets code. It was initially based on the relevant natural-language documentation (`man` pages, RFCs [Pos80,Pos81,Bra89], the Posix standard [IEE00], and standard references [Ste98,Ste94]), and on inspection of the sources of the Linux implementation. We validated the semantics by a combination of *ad hoc* and automated testing: writing code that interacted with the C sockets interface in the described ways, and confirming that the resulting behaviour corresponded with our model.

To date, the semantics has only been validated against the Linux implementation (in fact, against the Red Hat 7.0 distribution, kernel version 2.2.16-22, `glibc` 2.1.92). We intend also to use our automated test scripts to identify differences with BSD and with Windows operating systems, if possible picking out a useful common core.

1.4 Overview In the remainder of this section, we give a very brief informal introduction to networks, the protocols IP, UDP, and ICMP, and the sockets interface to them. We then discuss our choice of what to include in the model, and its structure, and highlight some subtleties that must be understood for reliable programming.

In Section 2 we describe the model, making these subtleties precise. Unfortunately the complete definition is too large to include – inevitably so, as the behaviour of even our small (but useful) fragment of the sockets interface is large and irregular by the standards of process calculi and toy languages. Most details are therefore omitted; they appear in the technical report [SSW01]. Section 3 outlines the MiniCaml programming language we adopt for expressing distributed programs, a fragment of OCaml 3.00 [L$^+$00]. Again most details are omitted – these are routine.

Section 4 discusses our experimental setup and validation. The semantics is illustrated with a few small examples in Section 5. Finally, we discuss related work and conclude in Sections 6 and 7.

1.5 Background: Networks and Protocols, Informally At the level of abstraction of our model, a network consists of a number of machines connected by a combination of LANs (*eg.* ethernets) and routers.[1] Each machine has one or more *IP addresses* i, which are 32-bit values such as 192.168.0.11. The *Internet Protocol* (IP) allows one machine to send messages (*IP datagrams*) to another, specifying the destination by one of its IP addresses. IP datagrams have the form

$$\mathrm{IP}(i_1, i_2, \mathit{body})$$

[1] We discuss in §1.7 and §4 how the model relates to actual systems.

where i_1 and i_2 are the source and destination addresses. The implementation of IP (consisting of the routers within the network and the protocol endpoint code in machines) is responsible for delivering the datagram to the correct machine. We can therefore abstract from routing and network topology, and depict a network as below (in fact this is our test network).

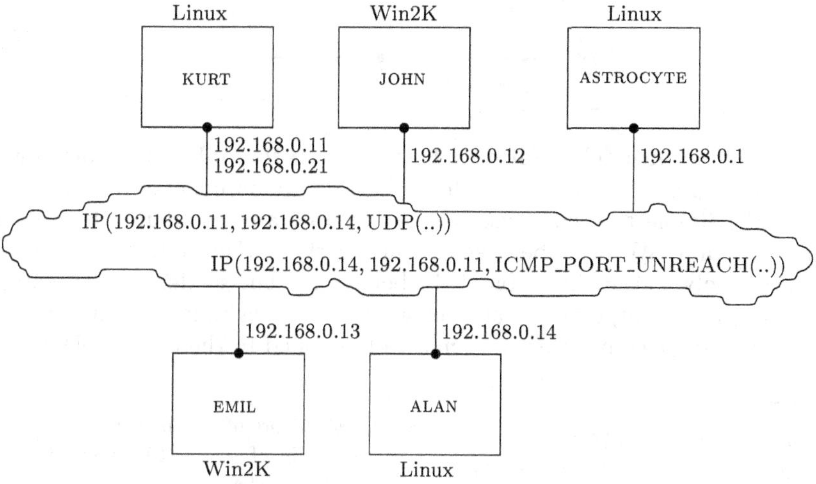

Delivery is asynchronous and unreliable – IP does not provide acknowledgments that datagrams are received, or retransmit lost messages.

UDP (the *User Datagram Protocol*) is a thin layer above IP that provides multiplexing. It associates a set $\{1, .., 65535\}$ of *ports* to each machine; a UDP datagram

$$\mathrm{IP}(i_1, i_2, \mathrm{UDP}(ps_1, ps_2, data))$$

is an IP datagram with a body of the form $\mathrm{UDP}(ps_1, ps_2, data)$, containing a source and destination port and a short sequence of bytes of *data*.

ICMP (the *Internet Control Message Protocol*) is another thin layer above IP dealing with some control and error messages. Here we are concerned only with two, relating to UDP:

$$\mathrm{IP}(i_1, i_2, \mathrm{ICMP\_PORT\_UNREACH}(i_3, ps_3, i_4, ps_4)), \text{ and}$$
$$\mathrm{IP}(i_1, i_2, \mathrm{ICMP\_HOST\_UNREACH}(i_3, ps_3, i_4, ps_4)).$$

The first may be generated by a machine receiving a UDP datagram for an unexpected port; the second is sometimes generated by routers on receiving unroutable datagrams.

TCP (the *Transmission Control Protocol*) is a rather thicker layer above IP that provides bidirectional stream communication, with flow control and retransmission of lost data. Most networked applications are built above TCP, with some use of UDP, but we do not yet consider it.

The protocol endpoint code on a machine, implementing the above, is depicted below (together with LIB, which we define in §2.1.3).

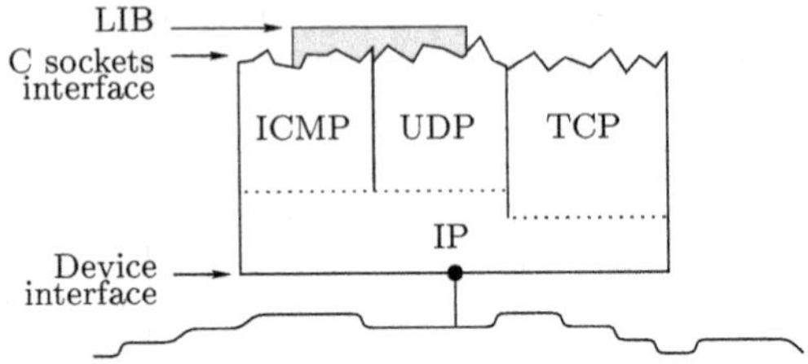

1.6 Background: The Sockets Interface, Informally To show how application programs can interact with the UDP endpoint code on their machines, we give the simplest possible example of two programs communicating a single UDP datagram. We describe a small part of the sockets interface informally, presenting only a crude intuition of the behaviour. The sender and receiver programs, e_s and e_r respectively, are below. They are written in MiniCaml (with some typographic conventions automatically applied to the executable code).

$e_s =$

```
let p = port_of_int 7654 in
let i = ip_of_string "192.168.0.11" in
let fd = socket() in
let _ = connect(fd, i, ↑p) in
let _ = print_endline_flush "sending" in
sendto(fd, *, "hello", FALSE)
```

$e_r =$

```
let p' = port_of_int 7654 in
let i' = ip_of_string "192.168.0.11" in
let fd' = socket() in
let _ = bind(fd', ↑i', ↑p') in
let _ = print_endline_flush "ready" in
let (_, _, v) = recvfrom(fd', FALSE) in
print_endline_flush v
```

Here the $*$ and $\uparrow$ are the constructors of option types $T\uparrow$. The types of the library calls are as in Figure 3, but without the 'err', as in MiniCaml an error return raises an exception. The example involves types fd of file descriptors, ip of IP addresses, and port of ports 1..65535.

The sender program e_s, which should be run on ALAN, defines a port p and an IP address i (in fact one of machine KURT) and creates a new *socket*. A socket consists of assorted data maintained by the OS, including an identifier (a file descriptor, which here will be bound to *fd*) and a pair of 'local' and 'remote' pairs of an IP address and a port. These are used for matching incoming datagrams and addressing outgoing datagrams. Program e_s then sets the remote pair of the socket to i and p using connect, and sends a UDP datagram via *fd* with body "hello".

The receiver e_r, which should be run on KURT, defines i' and p' to be the same IP address and port, creates a new socket fd', sets the local pair of fd' to permit reception of datagrams sent to (i', p'), and prints "ready". It then blocks, waiting for a datagram to be received by the socket, after which it prints the datagram body.

If e_s and e_r are run on ALAN and KURT respectively (but e_r is started first), and there is no failure in either machine or the network, a single UDP datagram will be sent from one machine to the other.

1.7 Choices: What to Model? To address the issues of §1.1, and support the desired rigorous understanding, the model must satisfy several criteria.

1. It must have a clear relationship (albeit necessarily informal) to what goes on in actual systems; it must be sufficiently accurate for reasoning in the model to provide assurances about the behaviour of those systems. For this, it is essential to include the various failures that can occur.
2. It must cover a large enough fragment of the network protocols and sockets interface to allow interesting distributed algorithms to be expressed. In particular, we want to provide as much information about failure as possible to the programmer, to support failure-aware algorithms.
3. In tension with both of these, the model must be as simple as possible, for reasoning to be tractable.

The full range of network protocols and OS interactions is very large by the standards of semantic definitions. As a starting point, in this paper we choose to address (unicast) UDP and the associated part of ICMP, with a single thread of control per machine, in a flat network. We choose the fragment of the sockets interface that is most useful for programming in these circumstances, and deal with the sockets interface view of message loss, host failure and various local errors. For simplicity, we do not as yet deal with any of the following, despite their importance.

- TCP, and associated ICMP messages
- broadcast and multicast UDP communication
- multithreaded machines and inter-thread communication
- other IO primitives (in this paper we choose, minimally, 'print' and 'exit')
- persistent storage
- network partition (especially for machines with intermittent connections)
- DNS
- IPv6 protocols
- machine reconfiguration and other privileged operations

We are not modelling the implementation of IP (routing, fragmentation *etc.*) or lower levels (Ethernet, ARP, *etc.*), as we aim to support reasoning about distributed applications and algorithms above IP, rather than implementations of low-level network protocols.

The standard sockets interface is a C language library. To avoid dealing with irrelevant complexities of a C interface (weak typing and explicit memory management) we introduce a thin abstraction layer, providing a clean strongly-typed view (we also clean up the interface by omitting redundancy). This LIB interface is defined in Figure 3; it was shown in the diagram at the end of §1.5.

In this paper we describe only an *interleaving* semantics. We anticipate that it will be straightforward to add fairness constraints, which are required for reasoning about non-trivial examples, and intend to investigate lightweight timing annotations, for more precise properties about examples involving time-outs. The model is not intended for quantitative probabilistic reasoning, *eg.* for quality of service issues. It may, however, provide a useful model for reasoning about some forms of malicious attack – *eg.* for networks with some malicious hosts, though with our flat network topology we do not deal with firewalls.

Blocking system calls are a key aspect of sockets programming, so it is natural to deal with sequential threads, rather than a concurrent programming language with language-level parallelism (for which blocking system calls would block the entire runtime).

1.8 Structuring the Model (and Language Independence) We want to reason about executable implementations of distributed algorithms, expressed in some programming language(s), not in a modelling language. We do not wish to fix on a single language, however, as the behaviour of the sockets interface and network is orthogonal to the programming language used to express the computation on each machine. We therefore factor the model, allowing threads to be arbitrary labelled transition systems (LTSs) of a certain form. One can extend the operational semantics of a variety of languages with labelled transitions, for library calls and returns, so that programs denote these LTSs (values used by the sockets interface are all of rather simple types, not involving callbacks, so this is straightforward). In this paper we do so for a fragment of OCaml, with functions, references and exceptions. This allows our example programs to be executed without change, by linking them with a module providing our thin layer of abstraction, LIB, above the OCaml sockets library (in turn implemented above the C library).

It will be convenient to be able to describe partial systems, for example to consider the interactions between the collection of all threads and the rest of the system, so we allow hosts and their threads to be syntactically separated. Networks therefore consist of a parallel composition of IP datagrams, hosts (each with a state v, giving the host's IP addresses, states of sockets *etc.*), and threads (each with a state e of an LTS). The precise definition is in §2.1.4, which uses the grammar below.

$N ::=$	0	empty
	$N \mid N$	parallel composition
	$\mathrm{IP}\ v$	IP datagram in transit
	$n \cdot \textsc{Host}\ v$	host n, with state v
	$n \cdot e$	thread of host n, with state e

The host semantics – the heart of the model – is outlined in §2.3. The behaviour of networks is defined in §2.2.2 by a structural operational semantics (SOS), combining the LTSs of hosts and threads, using process-calculus techniques (we give a direct operational semantics, rather than a complex encoding into an existing calculus).

1.9 It's Not Really So Easy The informal introductions to the protocols and sockets interface in §§1.5,1.6 above give a deceptively simple view. Real network programming must take into account the following, all of which are captured in our model:

1. IP addresses and ports with zero values have special meanings, being treated roughly as wildcards, both in the arguments to bind, connect, *etc.* and in the socket states. Our ip and port are types of non-zero IP addresses and ports; we use option types ip↑ and port↑ where the zero values ($*$) may occur.
2. The system-call interactions between a thread and its host are weakly coupled to the interactions between a host and the network. Messages may arrive at a machine, and be processed (and buffered) by the network hardware and OS, at almost any time. The sendto and recvfrom calls can block, until there is queue space to send a message or until a message arrives, respectively. Further, select allows blocking until one of a number of file descriptors is ready for reading or writing, or a specified time has elapsed. Communication between hosts is asynchronous, due both to buffering and the physical media.
3. Machines can fail; messages can be lost, reordered, or duplicated. There is buffering (and potential loss) at many points: in the operating system, in the network cards, and in the network routers. UDP provides very little error detection and no recovery. UDP datagrams typically contain a checksum (here we idealise, assuming that the checksum is perfect and hence that all corrupted datagrams are discarded). More interestingly, remote failure can sometimes be detected: a machine receiving a UDP datagram addressed to a port that does not have an associated socket may send back an ICMP message. These can asynchronously set an error flag in the originating socket, giving rise to an error from a blocked or future library call.
4. Many local errors are possible, for example (just considering bind): a port may be already in use or in a privileged range; an IP address may not belong to the machine; the OS may run out of resources; the file descriptor may not identify a socket. In MiniCaml, these are reported via exceptions, which may be caught and handled.
5. Machines can have more than one IP address – in fact, a machine may have several *interfaces*, each of which has a primary IP address and possibly also other alias IP addresses. Typically each interface will correspond to a hardware device, but a machine will also have a *loopback* interface which echoes messages back.
6. The sockets interface includes assorted other functionality – further library calls, socket options *etc.*

2 UDP – The Model

We now present the *UDP Calculus*, our model of the network and of the sockets interface to UDP. As the definition is far too large to include here, we give only the basic structure and selected highlights, leaving the full details to the technical report [SSW01]. Section 2.1 presents the static structure of the model, Section 2.2 explains the interactions between parts of the model, Section 2.3 illustrates the

T ::=	int		TL
	bool		TL
	string		TL
	()	unit type	TL
	$T_1 * .. * T_n$	tuple $(n \geq 2)$	TL
	T list	list	TL
	$T\uparrow$	optional type	TL
	T err	T or error	TL
	void	empty type	TL
	fd	file descriptor	TL
	ip	IP address	TL
	port	port	TL
	error	OS error	TL
	netmask	netmask	TL
	ifid	interface descriptor	TL
	sockopt	socket options	TL
	T set	finite set	
	ipBody	body of IP datagram	
	msg	IP datagram	
	ifd	interface descriptor table entry	
	flags	flags from socket descriptor table entry	
	socket	socket descriptor table entry	
	hostid	unique identifier of a host	
	hostThreadState	the OS view of a thread	
	host	a single host	

The clauses annotated by TL form a subgrammar of T, the *language types*. All values passed between a thread and its host OS are of a language type.

Fig. 1. Types

host semantics by means of some key rules, and Section 2.4 discusses some sanity results.

2.1 Statics: Types, Values, and Judgements

The model is largely built from the *types* T shown in Figure 1, which have *values* v composed of the *constructors* $\mathrm{C} \in$ Con given in Figure 2; constructors can be polymorphic. Each constructor has a natural number arity and a non-empty set of sequences (of length one plus that arity) of types; the sequences are written with arrows $\rightarrow$. The obvious typing judgement for values is written $\vdash v : T$. A number of invariants are captured by additional judgements, omitted here. *Notation:* We typically let i, p, e range over values of types ip, port, error, and is, ps, es over values of types ip$\uparrow$, port$\uparrow$, error$\uparrow$.

2.1.1 Hosts and Threads We separate a running machine into two parts: the *host*, representing the machine itself and its operating system; and the *thread*,

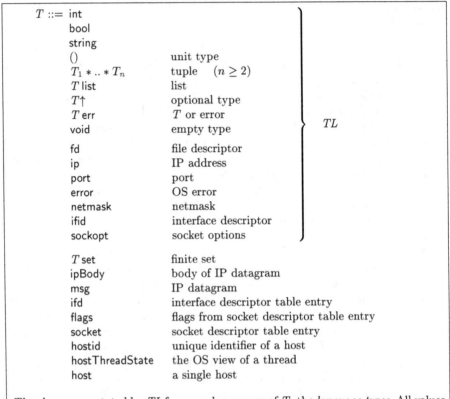

Partition Con into the language constructors:

.., −1, 0, 1, 2, ..	: int
TRUE, FALSE	: bool
octet-sequence	: string
()	: ()
(, .. ,) (mixfix)	: $T_1 \rightarrow .. \rightarrow T_n \rightarrow T_1 * .. * T_n \quad n \geq 2$
NIL	: T list
:: (infix)	: $T \rightarrow T$ list $\rightarrow T$ list
*	: $T\uparrow$
↑	: $T \rightarrow T\uparrow$
OK	: $T \rightarrow T$ err
FAIL	: error $\rightarrow T$ err
$1..2^{32}-1$	: ip
1..65535	: port
$\text{FD}_3, \text{FD}_4, \ldots$	: fd
LO, ETH0, ETH1, ...	: ifid
$\sum_{i \in j..31} 2^i$	: netmask for $0 \leq j \leq 31$
SO_BSDCOMPAT, SO_REUSEADDR	: sockopt
EACCES, EADDRINUSE, EADDRNOTAVAIL, EAGAIN, EBADF, ECONNREFUSED, EHOSTUNREACH, EINTR, EINVAL, EMFILE, EMSGSIZE, ENFILE, ENOBUFS, ENOMEM, ENOTCONN, ENOTSOCK	: error

and the non-language constructors:

IP	: ip * ip * ipBody	→ msg
UDP	: port↑ * port↑ * string	→ ipBody
ICMP_HOST_UNREACH	: ip * port↑ * ip * port↑	→ ipBody
ICMP_PORT_UNREACH	: ip * port↑ * ip * port↑	→ ipBody
HOST	: ifd set * hostThreadState * socket list * msg list * bool	→ host
SOCK	: fd * ip↑ * port↑ * ip↑ * port↑ * error↑ * flags * (msg * ifid) list	→ socket
IF	: ifid * ip set * ip * netmask	→ ifd
RUN	: hostThreadState	
TERM	: hostThreadState	
RET_{TL}	: TL	→ hostThreadState
SENDTO2	: fd * (ip * port)↑ * string	→ hostThreadState
RECVFROM2	: fd	→ hostThreadState
SELECT2	: fd list * fd list * int↑	→ hostThreadState
PRINT2	: string	→ hostThreadState
FLAGS	: bool * bool	→ flags
ALAN, KURT, ASTROCYTE, ...	: hostid	

Elements of T set are written $\{v_1, \ .. \ , v_n\}$. The TL subscript of RET_{TL} will usually be elided.

Fig. 2. Constructors

representing the application program controlling it. Threads are explained in §2.2.1. A host is of the form:

$\textsc{Host}(\mathit{ifds}, t, s, oq, oqf)$

A host has a set $\mathit{ifds} : \mathsf{ifd\ set}$ of interfaces, each with a set of IP addresses and other data. We assume all hosts have at least a loopback interface and one other. We sometimes write $i \in \mathit{ifds}$ to mean 'i is an IP address of one of the interfaces in *ifds*'. The operating system's view of the thread state is stored in $t : \mathsf{hostThreadState}$: the thread may be running (RUN), terminated (TERM), or waiting for the OS to return from a call. In the last case, the OS may be about to return a value from a fast system call (RET v) or the thread may be blocked waiting for a slow system call to complete (SENDTO2 v, RECVFROM2 v, SELECT2 v, PRINT2 v). The host's current list of sockets is given by $s : \mathsf{socket\ list}$. The *outqueue*, a queue of outbound IP messages, is given by $oq : \mathsf{msg\ list}$ and $oqf : \mathsf{bool}$, where oq is the list of messages and oqf is set when the queue is full.

2.1.2 Sockets The central abstraction of the sockets interface is the *socket*. It represents a communication endpoint, specifying a local and a remote pair of an IP address and UDP port, along with other parts of the protocol implementation state. It is of the form

$\textsc{Sock}(fd, is_1, ps_1, is_2, ps_2, es, f, mq)$

A socket is uniquely identified within the host by its file descriptor $fd : \mathsf{fd}$. The local and remote address/port pairs are $is_1 : \mathsf{ip}\uparrow, ps_1 : \mathsf{port}\uparrow$ and $is_2 : \mathsf{ip}\uparrow, ps_2 : \mathsf{port}\uparrow$ respectively; wildcards may occur. Asynchronous error conditions store the pending error in the error flag $es : \mathsf{error}\uparrow$. An assortment of socket parameters are stored in $f : \mathsf{flags}$. Finally, $mq : (\mathsf{msg} * \mathsf{ifid})\ \mathsf{list}$ is a queue of incoming messages that have been delivered to this socket but not yet received by the application.

2.1.3 The Sockets Interface A *library interface* defines the form of the interactions between a thread and a host, specifying the system calls that the thread can make. A library interface consists of a set of calls, each with a pair of language types. We take a library interface LIB, shown in Figure 3, consisting of the sockets interface together with some basic OS operations.

All of the sockets interface calls return a value of some type $T\,\mathsf{err}$ to the thread, which can be either OK v for $v : T$ or FAIL e for a Unix error $e : \mathsf{error}$. A language binding may map these error returns into exceptions, as the MiniCaml binding of §3 does.

2.1.4 Networks A network N (a term of the grammar in §1.8) is a parallel composition of IP datagrams IP v, hosts $n{\cdot}\textsc{Host}\,v$, and their threads $n{\cdot}e$. To describe partial systems, we allow hosts and their threads to be split apart. The association between them is expressed by shared names $n : \mathsf{hostid}$, which are purely semantic devices, not to be confused with IP addresses or DNS names. A well-formed network must contain at most one host and at most one thread

The sockets interface:		
socket	: ()	→ fd err
bind	: fd ∗ ip↑ ∗ port↑	→ () err
connect	: fd ∗ ip ∗ port↑	→ () err
disconnect	: fd	→ () err
getsockname	: fd	→ (ip↑ ∗ port↑) err
getpeername	: fd	→ (ip↑ ∗ port↑) err
sendto	: fd ∗ (ip ∗ port)↑ ∗ string ∗ bool	→ () err
recvfrom	: fd ∗ bool	→ (ip ∗ port↑ ∗ string) err
geterr	: fd	→ error↑ err
getsockopt	: fd ∗ sockopt	→ bool err
setsockopt	: fd ∗ sockopt ∗ bool	→ () err
close	: fd	→ () err
select	: fd list ∗ fd list ∗ int↑	→ (fd list ∗ fd list) err
port_of_int	: int	→ port err
ip_of_string	: string	→ ip err
getifaddrs	: ()	→ (ifid ∗ ip ∗ ip list ∗ netmask) list err
Basic operating system operations:		
print_endline_flush	: string	→ () err
exit	: ()	→ void

Fig. 3. The library interface LIB

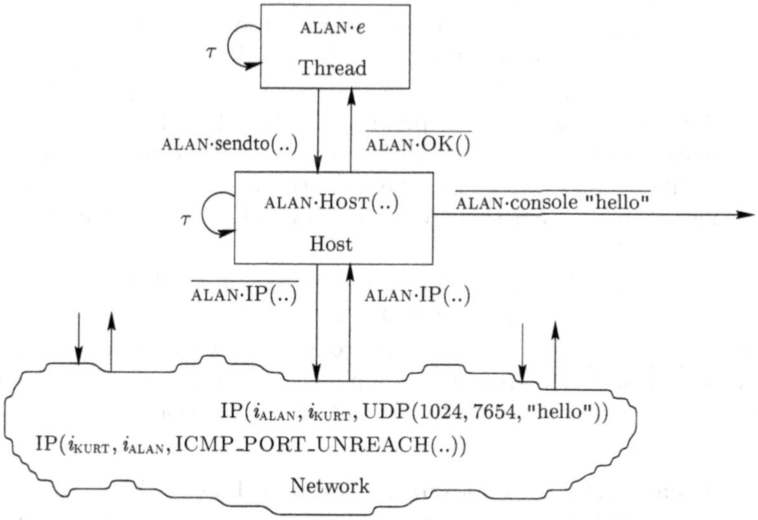

Fig. 4. Thread, Host and Network

LTS for each name. Hosts and messages must be well-formed, and no two hosts may share an IP address.

2.2 Dynamics: Interaction

The threads, hosts, and the network itself are all labelled transition systems; they interact by means of CCS-style synchronisations. Figure 4 shows the network

$$\begin{aligned} N = {} & \text{ALAN}\cdot e \mid \text{ALAN}\cdot\text{HOST}(..) \\ & \mid \text{IP}(i_{\text{ALAN}}, i_{\text{KURT}}, \text{UDP}(1024, 7654, \text{"hello"})) \\ & \mid \text{IP}(i_{\text{KURT}}, i_{\text{ALAN}}, \text{ICMP\_PORT\_UNREACH}(..)) \mid \ldots \end{aligned}$$

along with some of its possible interactions (showing the host LTS labels). Host and thread are linked by the hostid prefix on their transitions, but messages on the network are bare – messages are not tied to any particular host, other than by the IP addresses contained in their source and destination fields. As we shall see, the host and thread LTSs are defined without these prefixes, which are added when they are lifted to the network SOS.

The only interaction between a thread and its associated host is via system calls – a call and its return are both modelled by CCS-style synchronisations. A thread can make a system call $f\ v$ for any $f : TL \to TL'$ in LIB and argument $v : TL$, for example sendto(..). The operating system may then return a value $r : TL'$, for example OK(). In the above diagram, the host's ALAN·sendto(..) and $\overline{\text{ALAN}\cdot\text{OK}()}$ are part of call and return synchronisations respectively.

Invocations of system calls may be *fast* or *slow* [Ste98, p124]. Fast calls return quickly, whereas slow calls block, perhaps indefinitely – for example, until a message arrives. The labelled transitions have the same form for both, but the host states differ (as in §2.1.1). (In the absence of slow calls, one could model system calls as single transitions, carrying both argument and return values, rather than pairs.)

A host interacts with the network by sending and receiving IP datagrams: $\overline{\text{ALAN}\cdot\text{IP}(..)}$ and ALAN·IP(..) in the figure, respectively.

A host may also emit strings to its console with transitions of the form $\overline{\text{ALAN}\cdot\text{console "hello"}}$. This provides a minimal way to observe the behaviour of a network, namely by examining the output on each console.

2.2.1 Thread LTSs and Language Independence The interactions between a thread and the OS are essentially independent of the programming language the thread is written in – they exchange only values of simple types, the language types of Figure 1. Instead of taking a thread to be a syntactic program in some particular language, we can therefore take an arbitrary labelled transition system, with labels $\overline{f}\ v$, r and τ. It is then straightforward to extend an operational semantics for a variety of languages to define such an LTS, as we do for MiniCaml in §3.

Take a *thread LTS* e to be (Lthread, S, $\rightarrow$, s_0) where S is a set of states, $s_0 \in S$ is the initial state, $\rightarrow \subseteq S \times \text{Lthread} \times S$ is the transition relation, and the labels are

$$\text{Lthread} = \{\, \overline{f\, v} \mid f : TL \rightarrow TL' \in \text{LIB} \wedge \vdash v : TL \,\} \cup \{\, r \mid \exists TL\, .\, \vdash r : TL \,\} \cup \{\tau\}$$

Some axioms must be imposed to give an accurate model, as in [Sew97]. System calls are deterministic – a thread cannot offer to invoke multiple system calls simultaneously. Moreover, after making a system call, the thread must be prepared to input any of the possible return values, and its subsequent behaviour will be a function of the value. Threads may however have internal nondeterminism. A thread can always make progress, unless it has been terminated by invoking exit (the only system call with return type void). The precise statements of these properties are given in [SSW01].

2.2.2 Network Operational Semantics The transitions of a network are defined by the rules below, together with a structural congruence defined by associativity, commutativity and identity axioms for | and 0. Here we let x be either a host (with $\vdash x$ host-ok) or a thread LTS, $\vdash n :$ hostid, and $\vdash N_i$ network.

$$\frac{x \xrightarrow{l} x' \quad l \neq \tau}{n{\cdot}x \xrightarrow{n \cdot l} n{\cdot}x'} \qquad \frac{x \xrightarrow{\tau} x'}{n{\cdot}x \xrightarrow{\tau} n{\cdot}x'} \qquad \frac{}{0 \xrightarrow{n\cdot\text{IP}\, v} \text{IP}\, v} \qquad \frac{}{\text{IP}\, v \xrightarrow{n\cdot\overline{\text{IP}\, v}} 0}$$

$$\frac{N_1 \xrightarrow{n\cdot l} N_1' \quad N_2 \xrightarrow{n\cdot \bar{l}} N_2'}{N_1 \mid N_2 \xrightarrow{\tau} N_1' \mid N_2'}\ \textit{par.1} \qquad \frac{\begin{array}{l} N_1 \xrightarrow{n\cdot l} N_1' \\ l \in \text{Lthread} \cup \text{Crash} \implies n{\cdot}\textsc{Host}\, v \notin N_2 \\ l \in \overline{\text{Lthread}} \cup \overline{\text{Crash}} \implies n{\cdot}e \notin N_2 \end{array}}{N_1 \mid N_2 \xrightarrow{n\cdot l} N_1' \mid N_2}\ \textit{par.2}$$

$$\frac{}{0 \xrightarrow{n\cdot\text{IP}\, v} 0}\ \textit{drop.1} \qquad \frac{k \geq 2}{0 \xrightarrow{n\cdot\text{IP}\, v} \prod_{j \in 1..k} \text{IP}\, v}\ \textit{dup.1}$$

$$\frac{}{n{\cdot}\textsc{Host}\, v \xrightarrow{n\cdot\overline{\text{crash}}} 0}\ \textit{host.crash.1} \qquad \frac{}{n{\cdot}e \xrightarrow{n\cdot\text{crash}} 0}\ \textit{host.crash.2}$$

IP datagrams can arrive out of order, be lost or be (finitely) duplicated. Reordering is built into the rules above, but for the other kinds of failure we add the rules *drop.1* and *dup.1*. These are most interesting when constrained, *eg.* by fairness or timing assumptions. Hosts can also fail in a variety of ways. In this paper we consider only the simplest, 'crash' failure [Mul93, §2.4].

Our network has no interesting topological structure. It can always receive a new datagram, and can always deliver any datagram it has, with rules similar to those of Honda and Tokoro's asynchronous π-calculus [HT91].

2.3 Highlights of the Host Semantics

We now highlight a few of the most interesting parts of the host semantics, illustrating some (10 out of 72) of the host transition axioms. The definitions of several auxiliary functions are omitted. We aim to give some feeling for the intricacies of UDP sockets and to demonstrate that a rigorous treatment is feasible, without (for lack of space) fully explaining our semantics.

2.3.1 Ports: Privileged, Ephemeral, and Unused, and Autobinding The ports 1..65535 of a host are partitioned into the privileged = $\{1,..,1023\}$, the ephemeral = $\{1024,..,4999\}$, and the rest (these sets are implementation-dependent; we fix on the Linux defaults). The *unused* ports of a host are the subset of $\{1,..,65535\}$ that do not occur as the local port of any of its sockets. One can bind the local port of a socket either to an explicit non-privileged value, *eg.* the $p' = 7654$ of the e_r example in §1.6, or request the OS to choose a unused port from the set of ephemeral ports. The latter *autobinding* can be done by invoking bind with a $*$ in its port↑ argument, as in the *bind.2* rule:

bind.2 $(\uparrow i, *)$ **succeed, autobinding**

$$F(\mathit{ifds}, \mathrm{R{\scriptsize UN}}, \mathrm{S{\scriptsize OCK}}(\mathit{fd}, *, *, *, *, es, f, mq))$$
$$\xrightarrow{\mathsf{bind}(fd,\uparrow i,*)} F(\mathit{ifds}, \mathrm{R{\scriptsize ET}}\ (\mathrm{OK}()), \mathrm{S{\scriptsize OCK}}(\mathit{fd}, \uparrow i, \uparrow p'_1, *, *, es, f, mq))$$

$p'_1 \in \mathrm{unused}(F) \cap \mathrm{ephemeral}$ and $i \in \mathit{ifds}$

To reduce the syntactic clutter in rules, we define several classes of contexts that build a host. Here F ranges over contexts of the form $\mathrm{H{\scriptsize OST}}(\_{1}, \_{2}, S(\_{3}), oq, oqf)$, where S is a socket list context, of the form $s_1 @ [\_] @ s_2$. The rule also requires the IP address i to be one of those of this host. Autobinding can also occur in connect (if one connects a socket that does not have a local port bound), in disconnect, in sendto, and in recvfrom.

2.3.2 Message Delivery to the Net In the simplest case, sending a UDP datagram involves two host transitions: one that constructs the datagram and adds it to the host outqueue, and one that takes it from the outqueue and outputs it to the network. These are given by the host transition axioms below.

sendto.1 **succeed**

$$\mathrm{H{\scriptsize OST}}(\mathit{ifds}, \mathrm{R{\scriptsize UN}}, S(\mathrm{S{\scriptsize OCK}}(\mathit{fd}, is_1, ps_1, is_2, ps_2, *, f, mq)), oq, oqf)$$
$$\xrightarrow{\mathsf{sendto}(fd,ips,data,nb)}$$
$$\mathrm{H{\scriptsize OST}}(\mathit{ifds}, \mathrm{R{\scriptsize ET}}\ (\mathrm{OK}()), S(\mathrm{S{\scriptsize OCK}}(\mathit{fd}, is_1, \uparrow p'_1, is_2, ps_2, *, f, mq)), oq', oqf')$$

$p'_1 \in \mathrm{autobind}(ps_1, S)$
and $(oq', oqf', \mathrm{TRUE}) \in \mathrm{dosend}(\mathit{ifds}, (ips, data), (is_1, \uparrow p'_1, is_2, ps_2), oq, oqf)$
and $\mathrm{size}(data) \leq \mathrm{UDPpayloadMax}$ and $(ips \neq *$ or $is_2 \neq *)$.

In *sendto.1*: S is a socket list context, allowing the *fd* socket to be picked out; the autobind function provides a nondeterministic choice of an unused ephemeral port, if the local port of this socket has not yet been bound; the dosend function constructs a datagram, using the *ips* argument to sendto and the IP addresses and ports from the socket, and adds it to the outqueue (or fails, if the queue is full); the length of *data* must be less than UDPpayloadMax; and at least one of the *ips* argument and the socket must specify a destination IP address.

delivery.out.1 **put UDP or ICMP to the network from** *oq*

$$\textsc{Host}(ifds, t, s, oq, oqf)$$
$$\xrightarrow{\overline{\mathrm{IP}(i_3, i_4, body)}} \textsc{Host}(ifds, t, s, oq', oqf')$$

$((\mathrm{IP}(i_3, i_4, body)), oq', oqf') \in \mathrm{dequeue}(oq, oqf)$
and $i_4 \notin \mathrm{LOOPBACK} \cup \mathrm{MARTIAN}$ and $i_3 \notin \mathrm{MARTIAN}$

In *delivery.out.1*: the dequeue function picks a datagram off the outqueue (nondeterministically resetting the *oqf* flag), and checks the datagram has non-martian source and destination addresses [Bak95, §5.3.7]. It outputs the datagram to the network.

2.3.3 Return From a Fast Call After the invocation of a fast call, *eg.* an instance of the *sendto.1* rule above, the host thread state is of the form $\textsc{Ret}\ v$, recording the value v to be returned to the thread by *ret.1* below.

ret.1 **return value** v **from fast system call to thread**

$$\textsc{Host}(ifds, \textsc{Ret}\ v, s, oq, oqf)$$
$$\xrightarrow{\overline{v}} \textsc{Host}(ifds, \textsc{Run}, s, oq, oqf)$$

2.3.4 Message Delivery from the Net If the thread invokes recvfrom on a socket *fd* that does not have any queued messages, with the 'non-blocking' flag argument FALSE, the thread will block until a message arrives (or until an error of some kind occurs).

recvfrom.2 **block, entering Recvfrom2 state**

$$F(ifds, \textsc{Run}, \textsc{Sock}(fd, is_1, ps_1, is_2, ps_2, *, f, \mathrm{NIL}))$$
$$\xrightarrow{\mathrm{recvfrom}(fd, \mathrm{FALSE})} F(ifds, \textsc{Recvfrom2}\ fd, \textsc{Sock}(fd, is_1, \uparrow p_1', is_2, ps_2, *, f, \mathrm{NIL}))$$

$p_1' \in \mathrm{autobind}(ps_1, \mathrm{socks}(F))$

As in *bind.2* and *sendto.1*, the local port of the socket will be automatically bound (to an unused ephemeral port) if it is not already bound.

When a UDP datagram, *eg.* $\mathrm{IP}(i_3, i_4, \mathrm{UDP}(ps_3, ps_4, data))$, arrives at a host, the 4-tuple (i_3, ps_3, i_4, ps_4) is matched against each of the host's sockets, to determine which (if any) the datagram should be delivered to. This matching compares the 4-tuple with each $\textsc{Sock}(.., is_1, ps_1, is_2, ps_2, ..)$, giving a score from 0 to 4 of how many elements match, treating a $*$ in the socket elements as a wildcard. The lookup function takes a list s of sockets and a datagram 4-tuple (i_3, ps_3, i_4, ps_4), returning the set of sockets with maximal non-zero scores. The datagram is delivered to one of these sockets, by adding it to the end of the socket's message queue *mq*. This is expressed in the basic *delivery.in.udp.1* rule below.

delivery.in.udp.1 **get UDP from network and deliver to a matching socket**

$$\begin{array}{l} \textsc{Host}(\mathit{ifds}, t, s, oq, \mathit{oqf}) \\ \xrightarrow{\mathrm{IP}(i_3, i_4, \mathrm{UDP}(ps_3, ps_4, data))} \textsc{Host}(\mathit{ifds}, t, S(\textsc{Sock}(fd, is_1, ps_1, is_2, ps_2, es, f, \\ \quad mq :: (\mathrm{IP}(i_3, i_4, \mathrm{UDP}(ps_3, ps_4, data)), \mathit{ifid}))), oq, \mathit{oqf}) \end{array}$$

$\textsc{Sock}(fd, is_1, ps_1, is_2, ps_2, es, f, mq) \in \text{lookup } s\ (i_3, ps_3, i_4, ps_4)$
and $S(\textsc{Sock}(fd, is_1, ps_1, is_2, ps_2, es, f, mq)) = s$
and $(\mathit{ifid}, \mathit{iset}, \_, \_) \in \mathit{ifds}$ and $i_4 \in \mathit{iset}$
and $i_4 \notin \mathrm{LOOPBACK}$ and $i_3 \notin \mathrm{MARTIAN} \cup \mathrm{LOOPBACK}$

After this, a blocked recvfrom will be able to complete, using the *recvfrom.6* rule.

recvfrom.6 **slow succeed**

$$\begin{array}{l} F(\mathit{ifds}, \textsc{Recvfrom2}\ fd, \textsc{Sock}(fd, is_1, \uparrow p_1, is_2, ps_2, *, f, \\ \quad (\mathrm{IP}(i_3, i_4, \mathrm{UDP}(ps_3, ps_4, data)), \mathit{ifid}) :: mq)) \\ \xrightarrow{\overline{\mathrm{OK}(i_3, ps_3, data)}} F(\mathit{ifds}, \textsc{Run}, \textsc{Sock}(fd, is_1, \uparrow p_1, is_2, ps_2, *, f, mq)) \end{array}$$

2.3.5 ICMP Generation If a UDP datagram arrives at a host (so its destination IP address is one of the host's) but no socket matches its 4-tuple (i_3, ps_3, i_4, ps_4) then the host may or may not send an ICMP_PORT_UNREACH message back to the sender. This is dealt with by the rule below (in the non-loopback case). Note that the ICMP message is added to the host's outqueue *oq*, not put directly on the network. This uses an auxiliary function enqueue which is also used by dosend.

delivery.in.udp.2 **get UDP from network but generate ICMP, as no matching socket**

$$\begin{array}{l} \textsc{Host}(\mathit{ifds}, t, s, oq, \mathit{oqf}) \\ \xrightarrow{\mathrm{IP}(i_3, i_4, \mathrm{UDP}(ps_3, ps_4, data))} \textsc{Host}(\mathit{ifds}, t, s, oq', \mathit{oqf}') \end{array}$$

$i_4 \in \mathit{ifds}$ and lookup $s\ (i_3, ps_3, i_4, ps_4) = \emptyset$
and $(oq', \mathit{oqf}', ok) \in \{(oq, \mathit{oqf}, \mathrm{TRUE})\} \cup$
$\mathrm{enqueue}(\mathrm{IP}(i_4, i_3, \mathrm{ICMP\_PORT\_UNREACH}(i_3, ps_3, i_4, ps_4)), oq, \mathit{oqf})$
and $i_4 \notin \mathrm{LOOPBACK}$ and $i_3 \notin \mathrm{MARTIAN} \cup \mathrm{LOOPBACK}$

2.3.6 Asynchronous Errors When an ICMP_PORT_UNREACH message arrives at a host, it is matched against the sockets, in roughly the same way that UDP datagrams are. If it matches a socket (which typically will be the one used to send the UDP datagram that generated this ICMP) then the error should be reported to the thread. The arrival and processing of the ICMP message is asynchronous w.r.t. the thread activity, though, so what happens is simply that the error flag es' of the socket is set, in this case to ↑ECONNREFUSED.

delivery.in.icmp.1 **get ICMP from the network, setting error in a matching socket**

$$\mathrm{H{\scriptsize OST}}(\mathit{ifds}, t, s, oq, oqf)$$
$$\xrightarrow{\mathrm{IP}(i_4', i_3', \mathrm{ICMP\_X\_UNREACH}(i_3, ps_3, i_4, ps_4))}$$
$$\mathrm{H{\scriptsize OST}}(\mathit{ifds}, t, S(\mathrm{S{\scriptsize OCK}}(fd, is_1, ps_1, is_2, ps_2, es', f, mq)), oq, oqf)$$

$S(\mathrm{S{\scriptsize OCK}}(fd, is_1, ps_1, is_2, ps_2, es, f, mq)) = s$
and $\mathrm{S{\scriptsize OCK}}(fd, is_1, ps_1, is_2, ps_2, es, f, mq) \in \text{lookup } s(i_3, ps_3, i_4, ps_4)$
and $m = \mathrm{IP}(i_4', i_3', \mathrm{ICMP\_X\_UNREACH}(i_3, ps_3, i_4, ps_4))$
and $i_3' \in \mathit{ifds}$ and $\neg(\text{loopback}(m) \vee \text{martian}(m))$
and $es' = \text{if } (is_2 \neq *) \text{ or } \neg(\text{bsdcompat } f) \text{ then } \uparrow\text{ECONNREFUSED else } es$

Here X is either HOST or PORT. There are sanity constraints on the IP addresses involved, and the behaviour differs according to whether the bsdcompat socket flag is set. Note also that unmatched ICMPs do not themselves generate new ICMPs – there is no analogue of *delivery.in.udp.2* for ICMPs.

The error flag may cause subsequent sendtos or recvfroms to fail, returning the error and clearing the flag, for example in the rule below.

sendto.5 **fail, as socket in an error state**

$$F(\mathit{ifds}, \mathrm{R{\scriptsize UN}}, \mathrm{S{\scriptsize OCK}}(fd, is_1, \uparrow p_1, is_2, ps_2, \uparrow e, f, mq))$$
$$\xrightarrow{\mathrm{sendto}(fd, ips, data, nb)} F(\mathit{ifds}, \mathrm{R{\scriptsize ET}}\ (\mathrm{F{\scriptsize AIL}}\ e), \mathrm{S{\scriptsize OCK}}(fd, is_1, \uparrow p_1, is_2, ps_2, *, f, mq))$$

2.3.7 Local Errors A number of other sources of error must be dealt with. Firstly, there are straightforward erroneous parameters. Any call that takes an fd can return ENOTSOCK or EBADF if given a file descriptor that is not a socket. For bind we also have errors for a privileged port, a port already in use (modulo the reuseaddr flags), an IP address that is not one of the host's, and a socket which already has a non-$*$ local port. For sendto we have errors if the destination is $*$ and the socket is unconnected, and if the *data* is bigger than UDPpayloadMax. Both sendto and recvfrom return EAGAIN if the non-blocking flag argument is set but the call would block.

Secondly, any of the slow calls (sendto, recvfrom, select) can return EINTR from the blocked state if the system call is interrupted. Our model does not contain the sources of such interrupts, so all we can do is include a nondeterministic rule allowing the error to occur.

Thirdly, there are pathological cases in which the OS has exhausted some resource. A call to socket can return EMFILE or ENFILE, if there are too many open files or the file table overflows, and all calls can return ENOMEM or ENOBUFS if the OS has run out of space or buffers. Again, these are modelled by purely nondeterministic rules. We must also deal with the possibility that all the ephemeral ports are exhausted.

2.3.8 Loopback A datagram sent to a loopback address, typically 127.0.0.1, will be echoed back – without reaching the network. To model loopback, we use a number of additional delivery rules which are essentially the compositions of *delivery.out.** and *delivery.in.** rules. For example, a rule *delivery.loopback.udp.1* removes a loopback UDP from a host's outqueue and delivers in to a matching socket, in a single step.

2.4 Sanity Properties

We have proved type preservation and progress theorems for the model, and a semideterminacy result. The latter states roughly that for a given system call and host state, either the call succeeds (and exactly one rule applies) or it fails (several error rules may be in competition). The combination of the progress result, the thread LTS axioms and the network SOS rules exclude pathological deadlocks.

3 MiniCaml

MiniCaml is designed to be a sublanguage of OCaml 3.00 [L+00]. Its *types* (with corresponding constructors) are given by the grammar marked *TL* in Figure 1 (except $T\,\mathsf{err}$), together with:

$$T ::= \cdots \mid T \to T' \mid T\ \mathsf{ref} \mid \mathsf{exn}$$

The *syntax*, *typing rules* and *reduction rules* are standard, with additions to define an LTS satisfying the axioms of §2.2.1. We also prove theorems stating type preservation and absence of runtime errors.

We have written an OCaml module `Udplang` which implements almost all of LIB (together with the required types and constructors). The example programs in this paper are automatically typeset from working code, omitting an `open Udplang;;` at the beginning of each program and using mathematized concrete syntax, writing $()$, $T\!\uparrow, \uparrow\! e, *, \to$ for `unit`, `T lift`, `Lift e`, `Star` and `->`.

4 Validation

To develop and validate our host semantics, we set up a test network: a non-routed subnet with four dedicated machines (two Linux and two Win2K), accessible via an additional interface on one of our Linux workstations. In a few cases we ran tests further afield. Tests were written in C, using the `glibc` sockets library. Initially we wrote a large number of *ad hoc* tests, C programs that display the results of short sequences of socket calls, and also observed the resulting network traffic with the `tcpdump` utility. Certain hard-to-test issues were resolved by inspecting the Linux kernel source code.

Later, to more thoroughly validate the semantics as a whole, we translated the host operational semantics into C; we wrote an automatic tool, `udpautotest`, that simulates the model in parallel with the real socket calls. This tests representatives of most cases of the semantic rules, giving us a high level of confidence in our model. It helped us greatly in correctly stating the more subtle corners of the semantics, and will hopefully make determining the semantics of other implementations (such as Win2K or BSD) relatively routine.

The closed-box testing has a number of limitations, however (which we discuss further in [SSW01]). We do not directly observe the internal socket state (of which our SOCK structures are an abstraction), some pathological cases are hard to set up, and it is clearly impossible to exhaust all cases. Loss is very rare on our single subnet, and as far as we are aware reordering and duplication never occur. We therefore cannot regard the semantics as definitive, and would be interested to hear of discrepancies between it and real system behaviour.

We have endeavoured to make the model as accurate as possible, for the fragment of socket programming and the level of abstraction chosen in §1.7, and as far as one can with an untimed interleaving semantics. Nonetheless, it is in some respects idealised. Some of these are resource issues – we do not bound the MiniCaml space usage, and have a purely nondeterministic semantics for OS allocation failures. We simplify the real full-outqueue behaviour, and use an approximation to the treatment of 'martian' datagrams. We also assume unbounded integers and perfect UDP checksums, and have atomic transitions that have a subtle relationship to the detailed OS process scheduling.

No attempt was made to validate either the language semantics for MiniCaml (other than to check the evaluation order, which differs between the native-code generator and the bytecode interpreter), or the `Udplang` OCaml binding we used to test our examples. In the latter case, we assume the OCaml `Unix` module is a trivial binding to the C sockets interface; our `Udplang` module does little more.

5 Examples

5.1 The Single Sender We first show the possible traces of the single sender and single receiver from §1.6. Consider

$$\begin{aligned} N = \;& \text{ALAN}\cdot e_s \mid \text{ALAN}\cdot\text{HOST}(\mathit{ifds}_{\text{ALAN}}, \text{RUN}, [\,], [\,], \text{FALSE}) \\ & \mid \text{KURT}\cdot e_r \mid \text{KURT}\cdot\text{HOST}(\mathit{ifds}_{\text{KURT}}, \text{RUN}, [\,], [\,], \text{FALSE}) \end{aligned}$$

and discount rules modelling interrupted system calls or the OS running out of file descriptors or kernel memory. Suppose loss (*drop.1*) may occur, but duplication (*dup.1*) and host failure (*host.crash.∗*) do not.

One behaviour involves message $m = \text{IP}(i_{\text{ALAN}}, i_{\text{KURT}}, \text{UDP}(\uparrow p_1, \uparrow 7654, \texttt{"hello"}))$ (for $p_1 \in$ ephemeral) being successfully sent, with observable trace

$$N \xrightarrow{\overline{\text{KURT}\cdot\text{console "ready"}}} \xrightarrow{\overline{\text{ALAN}\cdot\text{console "sending"}}} \xrightarrow{\overline{\text{KURT}\cdot\text{console "hello"}}} N'$$

and resulting state

$$\begin{aligned} N' = \;& \text{ALAN}\cdot\text{RET}_{\mathsf{void}} \mid \text{ALAN}\cdot\text{HOST}(\mathit{ifds}_{\text{ALAN}}, \text{TERM}, [\,], [\,], \text{FALSE}) \\ & \mid \text{KURT}\cdot\text{RET}_{\mathsf{void}} \mid \text{KURT}\cdot\text{HOST}(\mathit{ifds}_{\text{KURT}}, \text{TERM}, [\,], [\,], \text{FALSE}) \end{aligned}$$

It is also possible for the "hello" to be received and printed with the message m arriving at KURT after KURT's bind but before the output of "ready", giving trace

$$N \xrightarrow{\overline{\text{ALAN}\cdot\text{console "sending"}}} \xrightarrow{\overline{\text{KURT}\cdot\text{console "ready"}}} \xrightarrow{\overline{\text{KURT}\cdot\text{console "hello"}}} N'$$

ending in the same state. If message m arrives at KURT before KURT's bind, however, it will be discarded, giving a trace

$$N \xrightarrow{\overline{\text{ALAN}\cdot\text{console "sending"}}} \xrightarrow{\overline{\text{KURT}\cdot\text{console "ready"}}} N''$$

ending with ALAN's state terminated as before but KURT in a blocked RECVFROM2 state. Here KURT may or may not generate an ICMP, which may or may not be delivered to ALAN in time to set the socket error flag, but as the socket is not used again and is removed on exit this is not visible.

Finally, there are two observable traces if message m is lost: the trace above and its permutation. In both ALAN runs to completion and KURT remains blocked; no ICMPs are generated.

5.2 The Single Heartbeat As a more realistic example, we present code for a simple heartbeat algorithm, a program e_A that checks the status of another program e_B (which one might think of running as part of a large application):

```
eA =
 let p = port_of_int (7655) in
 let i = ip_of_string ("192.168.0.11") in
 let fd = socket() in
 let _ = bind(fd, *, ↑p) in
 let _ = connect(fd, i, ↑p) in
 let _ = print_endline_flush "pinging" in
 let _ = sendto(fd, *, "ping", FALSE) in
 let (fds, _) = select([fd], [], ↑5000000) in
 if fds = [] then
   print_endline_flush "dead"
  else
   try
    let (_, _, v) = recvfrom(fd, FALSE) in
    print_endline_flush v
   with
    UDP(ECONNREFUSED)
      → print_endline_flush "down"
```

```
eB =
 let p = port_of_int (7655) in
 let i = ip_of_string ("192.168.0.14") in
 let fd = socket() in
 let _ = bind(fd, *, ↑p) in
 let _ = connect(fd, i, ↑p) in
 let _ = print_endline_flush "ready" in
 let _ = recvfrom(fd, FALSE) in
 let _ = sendto(fd, *, "ack", FALSE) in
 print_endline_flush "done"
```

Program e_B, which should be run on KURT, displays "ready" on the console, waits for a message from ALAN on a known port, and responds with an "ack" message when the message arrives.

Program e_A, which should be run on ALAN, displays "pinging" and checks the status of the remote machine KURT by sending a message on the known port. It then waits up to five seconds for a response (either a UDP reply datagram or an ICMP_PORT_UNREACH error). If there is none, it displays "dead"; if the response is a UDP datagram it displays its contents to indicate KURT is alive; and if the response is an ICMP it displays "down" to indicate that KURT is running but the responder thread e_B is down. Note that e_A will print "dead" if KURT is really dead, but it may also do so if the initial datagram is lost, or if the reply datagram or ICMP is lost, or if the reply ICMP is not generated.

Again discount rules modelling interrupted system calls or the OS running out of resources, but now allow loss, duplication and failure. Assuming further that only e_A and e_B run, on an otherwise-quiet network, we can prove that *no uncaught exceptions arise* during the execution of e_A. No errors can arise from any line of e_A apart from the recvfrom call, and the only error this may return is ECONNREFUSED. This means we are justified in omitting all error handling from the code of e_A. Further, we can show that the sendto and recvfrom calls in e_A will never block. On the other hand, the message duplication rule *dup.1* means that e_B might block temporarily in the sendto call, if the output queue has been filled with ICMP_PORT_UNREACH messages generated by "ping" messages arriving before the bind call, but at least one "ping" arrives after the bind. It is still guaranteed that no system call in e_B will fail.

6 Related Work

Work on the mathematical underpinnings of distributed systems has been carried out in the fields of distributed algorithms, process calculi, and programming language semantics. Distributed algorithms research has developed sophisticated algorithms, often dealing with failure, and proofs of their properties, for example using the *IO automata* of Lynch *et al.* [Lyn96] and the *TLA* of Lamport [Lam94]. Work on process calculi has emphasised operational equivalences and compositional descriptions of processes, and recently systems with dynamic local name generation – with calculi based on the *π-calculus* of Milner, Parrow and Walker [MPW92]. A few calculi have dealt with failure, including [AP94,FGL+96,RH97,BH00]. Building on process calculi, a number of concurrent or distributed programming languages have been designed, with associated semantic work, including among others Occam, Facile, CML, Pict, JoCaml, and Nomadic Pict [INM87,TLK96,Rep91,PT00,FGL+96,WS00]. Little of this work, however, deals with the core network protocols, and as far as we are aware none addresses the level of abstraction of the sockets interface. Further, most does not support reasoning about executable code (or adopts a much higher level of abstraction). The most relevant work is discussed below.

The IOA Language [GLV00] is a language for expressing IO automata directly. Work on proof tools and compilation is ongoing. This will allow reasoning about executable sophisticated distributed algorithms that interact with the network using higher-level abstractions than the sockets library, modulo correctness of the compiler. Using IOA rather than conventional programming languages aids reasoning, but may reduce the applicability of the method.

The approach of Arts and Dam [AD99] is similar to ours: they aim to prove properties of real concurrent programs written in Erlang. They describe an operational semantics for a subset of Erlang, a logic for reasoning about this subset, and use an automated tool to verify that a program satisfies properties expressed in the logic.

Less closely related, Biagioni implemented TCP/IP in ML [Bia94] as part of the Fox project, and the Ensemble system of [Hay98] provides group communication facilities above UDP. The latter is implemented in OCaml; some verification of optimisations to the Ensemble protocol endpoint code has been carried out. Neither involve a semantics of the network (or, for Ensemble, the underlying sockets implementation), however. At a lower level, work on the semantics of active networks [Swi01] has developed proofs of routing algorithms. Related work on monitoring protocol implementations – TCP in particular – from *outside* the hosts is presented in [BCMG01].

7 Conclusion

We have described a model that gives a rigorous understanding of programming with sockets and UDP, validated against actual systems. This demonstrates that an operational treatment of this level of network programming – traditionally regarded as beyond the scope of formal semantics – is feasible.

The model provides a basis for two directions of future work. Firstly, we plan to investigate the verification of more interesting examples, developing proof techniques that build on those of both the distributed algorithm and process calculus communities. Secondly, we plan to extend the model to cover a larger fragment of network programming, in a number of ways; we are considering machine support for managing the large definitions that will certainly result. We intend to define other language bindings, *eg.* for a Java fragment. Incorporating fairness and time is required to capture interesting properties of algorithms. As discussed in §4, we plan to apply our validation tools to other operating systems, to identify a common semantic core. Finally, we would like to address more of the points listed in §1.7, especially aspects of TCP and multi-threaded hosts.

Acknowledgements Sewell is funded by a Royal Society University Research Fellowship. Serjantov and Wansbrough are funded by EPSRC research grant GRN24872 *Wide-area programming: Language, Semantics and Infrastructure Design.*

References

[AD99] T. Arts and M. Dam. Verifying a distributed database lookup manager written in Erlang. In *World Congress on Formal Methods (1)*, pages 682–700, 1999.

[AP94] R. Amadio and S. Prasad. Localities and failures. In *Foundations of Software Technology and Theoretical Computer Science, LNCS 880.* Springer, 1994.

[Bak95] F. Baker. Requirements for IP version 4 routers. Internet Engineering Task Force, June 1995. `http://www.ietf.org/rfc.html`.

[BCMG01] K. Bhargavan, S. Chandra, P. J. McCann, and C. A. Gunter. What packets may come: Automata for network monitoring. In *Proc. POPL 2001*, January 2001.

[BH00] M. Berger and K. Honda. The two-phase commit protocol in an extended π-calculus. In *Proceedings of the 7th International Workshop on Expressiveness in Concurrency, EXPRESS '00*, 2000.

[Bia94] E. Biagioni. A structured TCP in standard ML. In *Proc. SIGCOMM*, 1994.

[Bra89] R. Braden. Requirements for internet hosts – communication layers, STD 3, RFC 1122. IETF, October 1989. `http://www.ietf.org/rfc.html`.

[CSR83] University of California at Berkeley CSRG. 4.2BSD, 1983.

[FGL+96] C. Fournet, G. Gonthier, J.-J. Lévy, L. Maranget, and D. Rémy. A calculus of mobile agents. In *Proc. CONCUR '96, LNCS 1119*. Springer, August 1996.

[GLV00] S. J. Garland, N. Lynch, and M. Vaziri. IOA reference guide, December 2000. `http://nms.lcs.mit.edu/~garland/IOA/`.

[Hay98] M. Hayden. *The Ensemble System*. PhD thesis, Cornell University, January 1998. Technical Report TR98-1662.

[HT91] K. Honda and M. Tokoro. An object calculus for asynchronous communication. In *Proceedings of ECOOP '91, LNCS 512*, pages 133–147, July 1991.

[IEE00] IEEE. *Information Technology – Portable Operating System Interface (POSIX) – Part xx: Protocol Independent Interfaces (PII), P1003.1g*. 2000.

[INM87] INMOS. *Occam2 Reference Manual*. Prentice-Hall, 1987.

[L+00] X. Leroy et al. *The Objective-Caml System, Release 3.00*. INRIA, April 27 2000. `http://caml.inria.fr/ocaml/`.

[Lam94] L. Lamport. The temporal logic of actions. *ACM Transactions on Programming Languages and Systems*, 16(3):872–923, May 1994.

[Lyn96] N. A. Lynch. *Distributed algorithms*. Morgan Kaufmann, 1996.

[MPW92] R. Milner, J. Parrow, and D. Walker. A calculus of mobile processes, Parts I + II. *Information and Computation*, 100(1):1–77, 1992.

[Mul93] S. J. Mullender. *Distributed Systems*. ACM Press, 1993.

[Pos80] J. Postel. User Datagram Protocol, STD 6, RFC 768. Internet Engineering Task Force, August 1980. `http://www.ietf.org/rfc.html`.

[Pos81] J. Postel. Internet Protocol, STD 6, RFC 791. Internet Engineering Task Force, September 1981. `http://www.ietf.org/rfc.html`.

[PT00] B. C. Pierce and D. N. Turner. Pict: A programming language based on the pi-calculus. In *Proof, Language and Interaction: Essays in Honour of Robin Milner*. MIT Press, 2000.

[Rep91] J. Reppy. CML: A higher-order concurrent language. In *Proc. Programming Language Design and Implementation (PLDI)*, pages 293–259, June 1991.

[RH97] J. Riely and M. Hennessy. Distributed processes and location failures. In *Automata, Languages and Programming, LNCS 1256*. Springer, 1997.

[Sew97] P. Sewell. On implementations and semantics of a concurrent programming language. In *Proceedings of CONCUR '97, LNCS 1243*, pages 391–405, 1997.

[SSW01] A. Serjantov, P. Sewell, and K. Wansbrough. The UDP calculus: Rigorous semantics for real networking. Technical Report 515, Computer Laboratory, University of Cambridge, 2001. `http://www.cl.cam.ac.uk/users/pes20/Netsem`.

[Ste94] W. R. Stevens. *TCP/IP Illustrated: The Protocols*, volume 1 of *Addison–Wesley Professional Computing Series*. Addison–Wesley, 1994.

[Ste98] W. R. Stevens. *UNIX Network Programming, Networking APIs: Sockets and XTI*, volume 1. Prentice Hall, second edition, 1998.

[Swi01] The SwitchWare project. `http://www.cis.upenn.edu/~switchware`, 2001.

[TLK96] B. Thomsen, L. Leth, and T.-M. Kuo. A Facile tutorial. In *Proceedings of CONCUR '96, LNCS 1119*, pages 278–298. Springer-Verlag, August 1996.

[WS00] P. T. Wojciechowski and P. Sewell. Nomadic Pict: Language and infrastructure design for mobile agents. *IEEE Concurrency*, 8(2):42–52, April–June 2000.

Unison: A File Synchronizer and Its Specification

Benjamin C. Pierce and Jérôme Vouillon

University of Pennsylvania

Abstract. File synchronizers are tools that reconcile disconnected modifications to replicated directory structures. Like other replication and reconciliation facilities provided by modern operating systems and middleware layers, trustworthy synchronizers are notoriously difficult to build: they must deal correctly with both the semantic complexities of file systems and the unpredictable failure modes arising from distributed operation. On the other hand, synchronizers are simpler than most of their relatives in that they operate as stand-alone, user-level utilities, whose intended behavior is relatively easy to isolate from the other functions of the system. This combination of subtlety and isolation makes synchronizers attractive candidates for precise mathematical specification.

We describe the specification and implementation of *Unison* – a file synchronizer engineered for portability, speed, and robustness, with thousands of daily users. Unison's code base and its specification have evolved in parallel, over several years, and each has strongly influenced the other. We present a precise high-level specification of Unison's behavior, an idealized implementation, and the outline of a proof (which we have formalized using Coq) that the implementation satisfies the specification. We begin with a straightforward definition of the system's core behavior – propagation of changes and detection of conflicting changes – then refine it to take into account the possibility of failures during reconciliation, then refine it again to cover synchronization of "metadata" such as permissions and modification times.

In each part, we address two critical issues: first, the relation between the informal expectations of users and our mathematical specification, and, second, the relation between our idealized implementation and the actual code base (i.e., the abstractions needed to obtain a tractable mathematical object from a real-world systems program, and the extent to which studying this idealized implementation sheds useful light on the real one).

N. Kobayashi and B.C. Pierce (Eds.): TACS 2001, LNCS 2215, p. 560, 2001.

Author Index